A. J. LIEBLING

A. J. LIEBLING

WORLD WAR II WRITINGS
The Road Back to Paris
Mollie and Other War Pieces
Uncollected War Journalism
Normandy Revisited

THE LIBRARY OF AMERICA

The paper used in this publication meets the
minimum requirements of the American National Standard for
Information Sciences—Permanence of Paper for Printed
Library Materials, ANSI Z39.48—1984.

Distributed to the trade
in the United States by Penguin Putnam Inc.
and in Canada by Penguin Books Canada Ltd.

Library of Congress Control Number: 2007938791
ISBN 978–1–59853–018–6

———

First Printing
The Library of America—181

Manufactured in the United States of America

EPIC HAMILL

IS THE EDITOR OF THIS VOLUME

A. J. Liebling's
World War II Writings
is published with support from

THE FLORENCE GOULD FOUNDATION

and will be kept in print by its gift to
the Guardians of American Letters Fund,
established by The Library of America
to ensure that every volume in the series
will be permanently available.

Contents

THE ROAD BACK TO PARIS

To
H. S., HORSE WATKINS
and
PINKY JOHNSON

CONTENTS

BOOK III
THE WORLD GETS UP

Book I
The World Knocked Down

CHAPTER I

The Shape of War

Two Negro soldiers sat with their legs dangling into two deep parallel slit trenches in the dead-looking land between Gafsa and Sened Station one morning last winter. Each was eating a cold mixture of meat and beans out of a small shiny tin can capable of reflecting the sun's rays to a distance of several miles in that flat country, and each turned his face upward periodically, with mouth full, to stare into the hot aluminum-colored sky. When I walked up to the end of one trench its proprietor, a tan man, looked at me while the other soldier continued to regard the sky. Then the tan man looked up at the sky, and his companion looked at me. "We was dive-bummed yesterday," this second soldier, a very dark man, said to me. "Driving the infantry up to the line in two-and-a-half-ton trucks. Dive-bumming makes me sick to my stomach." I tried to sound hearty and casual as I asked, "What outfit you men out of?" "Rolling Umpty-seventh," the tan man said while the dark man took his turn looking at the sky. The Umpties are a motor-truck regiment whom I had first met under happier circumstances, in England. "How you doing?" I asked, for want of a better question. "Really, sir, I don't belong on this battlefield at all," the tan soldier answered. "I'm strictly a non-combat man." I thought to myself we were two of a kind.

It was the second day of an offensive that we had started in the direction of Maknassy, the first all-American venture of the Tunisian campaign. Sened Station was the first objective. The bulk of Rommel's army was still only a little west of Tripoli, and there was a long, tempting, thinly held corridor between him and Von Arnim. The men making the attack believed that they would go on from Sened to Maknassy and from Maknassy to the coast of the Gulf of Tunis, cutting Rommel's line of supply and retreat. The major general in command had told the war correspondents he was going on to Maknassy at least and "draw the pucker string tight." We had understood from his manner that he meant to go farther than that if he got the chance.

I asked the colored soldiers how far the front of the battle was from where we then were. I put into my voice an implication that I wanted to rush right into the middle of things. The men did not know exactly where the battle was. Soldiers seldom and war correspondents almost never do. I learned afterward that the Umpties' vehicles, returning after unloading the infantry, had frightened a couple of my most dashing colleagues completely out of the battle area. They had mistaken the approaching trucks for a German tank column.

I walked back from the twin slit trenches to the jeep that had carried me out from Gafsa. Another correspondent was at the wheel. "They don't know where the battle is," I said to this other fellow. "Maybe we had better go ahead further." He said all right, so we started out across the sand again. We kept off the one road between Gafsa and Sened because there were trucks on it and they sometimes attracted strafers. The line of telephone poles along the side of the road gave us our general direction. When we had gone a short way I saw a couple of jeeps coming toward us, and we stopped. There were a couple of officers and eight men in the jeeps, all belonging to a tank-destroyer battalion that had lost its equipment earlier in the campaign. They were serving as battlefield military police, guiding traffic and waiting for prisoners to take charge of. The officers didn't know exactly where the front was either, but they invited us to have a can of coffee by a mud house a couple of miles away where the M.P.'s had set up their headquarters. There were a few scraggly olive trees around this house and a low mud wall around the trees, presumably to prevent the sand from blowing away from their roots.

One of the soldiers put a mixture of sand and gasoline in a couple of the shiny ration cans and lighted them. He filled two more ration cans with water from his canteen and placed them on the burners, and then when the water came to a boil he divided a packet of soluble coffee between the two improvised coffeepots. "The Statler people would give a million dollars to get hold of this process," he said. When the coffee had been drunk he started another batch. While I was waiting for my coffee I stood on the mud wall with one of the M.P. officers and looked over the country around. The railroad paralleled the highway, and we could see a station building with some trees around it about five miles away. It was an intermediate stop between Gafsa and Sened, needed God knows why. "Our guns were out behind there early this morning, and Jerry dropped a few shells in among those trees," the officer said, "but then our guns moved forward, 'way up toward Sened. I think you can go ahead eight or ten miles at least before you have to start to look around. You missed a good show this morning though. About twenty Stukas came over, and a dozen P-40's bounced them and shot down about eight. Boy, they were falling all over the place. They'll be back, though!" he added cheerily. When we had had our coffee we climbed back into the jeep and started forward again. The mud-house grove seemed in retrospect a pretty nice place to spend the day. Sened Station lies in a gap between two bare east-west ridges. As we moved toward it we spotted a number of dispersed scout cars and wireless-equipped jeeps, the vehicles characteristic of a reconnaissance troop. "A recon outfit!" my companion said knowingly, then, "Aren't they usually pretty well out in front of everybody?"

We drove over within fifty yards of one of the scout cars and climbed out. There were a couple of soldiers sitting with their backs against wheels of the car, reading paper books. They had their slit trenches ready dug beside them. I walked up to them and said, "What outfit is this, soldier?" One of the men, a corporal, looked up and said, "Sorry, sir, but you got any identification?" He reminded me of a stage doorman. We showed our identification cards, and the corporal explained that the recon outfit had been all the way around the enemy's position on the previous day and night and had come back to report and await another assignment. "We could have took the place, I guess," he said, "but that would not have seemed important enough." He was wrong, but reconnaissance troops, like small terriers, must have their illusions or they would lose their dash.

My companion, Boots Norgaard, who worked for the

Associated Press, started taking down the names and home towns of recon soldiers. This is always a fruitful procedure for a press-association man, because he can load up his dispatches with the names and the member papers in the home towns are glad to use them. Every soldier, when he named his home town, said, "And I wish I was there now," or, "Boy, how I wish I was there this minute!" The corporal I had first spoken to asked me if it was true that Bing Crosby was dead. I said I did not know, and he asked me if Groucho Marx was dead. He said he had heard that they were and that Jack Benny was dead too. The army in Tunisia was always full of rumors about well-known people who were supposed to have died at home. Battlefields, for that matter, are always ranged by false rumors about people supposed to have died in the immediate vicinity. When my companion had written down the names of enough towns like Owensboro, Kentucky, and Central Falls, Rhode Island, we moved on again.

We had a clear view of the ridge north of Sened Station, and after we had driven a mile or so forward we saw a number of tanks coming around the end nearer us, just below the crest, and snaking down the southern slope of the ridge toward the station. There were occasional puffs of gray smoke on the slope above them, where the enemy was lobbing shells over. We could hear our own guns up ahead quite loudly now. Then we wandered in among the ammunition half-tracks of an artillery outfit. The soldiers told us that the reconnaissance troop we had just left in good health had been annihilated on the previous day. They also said that a tank-destroyer outfit had lost all its vehicles. This was a reference to the tank-destroyer battalion the military policemen belonged to. The vehicles had been lost in a quagmire in northern Tunisia a month ago, but an artillerist, garbling some conversation with an M.P., had come up with the more fascinating report that the tank busters had been ambushed during this present action. I never like the vicinity of ammo during a battle. The soldiers said two batteries out of their battalion were a mile or two ahead of us. The guns were armored 105's, six to a battery.

We came eventually to a place on the plain where a tall captain with a Red Cross brassard was standing between two jeeps both carrying Red Cross flags. We stopped to talk to him, too.

The guns were in sight now, about four hundred yards farther on. The captain, whose name I remember was Bradbury, said he was battalion surgeon. Each of the jeeps had two litters slung to its sides, and when dive bombers or German counter-battery caused a casualty among the gunners Bradbury would run up in one of the jeeps and get the wounded man. He stood there looking at the guns like a spaniel watching for a ball to retrieve. "Yesterday I had seventeen," he said, "including several from the infantry that happened to be hit near us. Only three so far today. None in this position so far—we've moved half a dozen times since daybreak." All the shots we heard were going out, "boom-scream," and none coming in, "scream-boom," so we were unworried. I got out a can of Spam, and we ate it cold before continuing our advance.

"Maybe they have pulled their stuff out of Sened already," Norgaard said optimistically. I had watched the sky all day while he drove, sometimes looking straight up for Stukas and at others into the sun for strafers, but nothing had happened, and I began to hope that the P-40's had polished the local Luftwaffe off for the day.

When we had finished the Spam and said so long to Bradbury, we went on up to the guns and stopped the jeep behind them. They were in the open, because there was no cover anywhere around. They had quit shooting for the moment, probably changing a range or target, and we walked up to one gun crew who were smoking cigarettes beside their piece. As soon as we reached them an officer shouted over to them from an armored half-track to their right rear to get our identifications. "I'm sorry, sir," one soldier said, "but after all, how do we know who you are? We got no time for Ayrabs or casual strollers." We showed our identification cards, and the soldier, looking at mine, which describes me as correspondent of the *New Yorker*, said, "Huh, a *paesano*, practically. I'm from New York, too. Fourteent' Street and Avenue A. I wish I was dere now. At a movie, wit' my shoes off." Then they had to start shooting again, and we walked back toward the half-track, which we recognized from its high radio antenna as a command vehicle.

The officer who had shouted to the gunners was a square-faced fair-haired major who told us his name was Burba, executive officer of the battalion. He was in command of the two batteries, since his C.O., a lieutenant colonel, had been wounded. Major Burba said he was from McAlester, Oklahoma. He was a cool, methodical officer who looked as if he would have definite information about everything, so I asked him what his battery was shooting at. "Enemy guns in the grove of trees back of Sened," he said. "We think their infantry has pulled out of the town already." I asked him what range he was firing at, and he said five thousand yards. "I have one battery here," he said, "and another over about a mile to the right and slightly forward—you can see them over there," and he pointed. "Every fifth shell we fire is a smoke shell so we can see where we are hitting, and the fire of the two batteries is converging on that grove of trees. When we get all our fire together and just right, we will come down on them, and that will be the end of the battle." "Where is our infantry?" I asked in a careless tone, because I could not see any troops out in front of us. "There are two battalions in echelon in those two olive groves to the right and forward of the other battery," Burba said, pointing again. "When we have knocked out all resistance they will go forward and occupy the town. Or maybe the tanks will get there first."

The tanks, as a matter of fact, were already trying to get to the town before the infantry. They were crawling down off the southern side of the ridge where my colleague and I had observed them earlier, moving out in front of the 105's, reminding me of a file of mechanical toys that a street peddler winds up and sets down on a sidewalk. When they had deployed in front of us they turned left and rolled on toward the town. They must have been a couple of thousand yards ahead of us when something began kicking up dust and smoke, sometimes in front of and sometimes behind them. "It's those Jerry eighty-eights," Burba said. "They've got the tanks under a crossfire. We'll fix that in a few minutes." The tanks were now rolling back toward us, except for one which remained motionless out on the plain. "That's the way the infantry was yesterday," one of Burba's junior officers said. "They went up toward the firing line in trucks, and three or four of the trucks got dive-bombed before the fellows could get away from them. It was a mess. After that they couldn't get anybody back into the trucks for a while. After we knock out the opposition they will all be heroes."

"That eighty-eight's a great gun," Burba said admiringly, looking at the motionless American tank through his binoculars. "Ripped that thing just like a G.I. knife does a tin can. Flat trajectory. High muzzle velocity." "Pretty long range, hasn't it?" I asked. "Thirteen thousand five hundred yards," Burba said heartily, as if he were a salesman pushing the German gun on a reluctant prospect. Our six guns loosed off as one and the other battery followed.

Just then there was a prolonged shrieking noise and something monstrous landed a hundred yards behind us and ricocheted off toward Gafsa. It kicked up a lot of dust. It must have been an armor-piercing solid shot, because there was no explosion. Burba said, "Let's get behind the half-track," in the same tone he might have said, "Let's get out of this wind," so we moved over behind the vehicle. Something else shrieked past, through the interval between the two guns on the right flank of the battery, I thought, and I had a bitter intuition that while Burba had been explaining to us what we intended to do to the Germans, some equally competent, equally stolid German artillery officer had been outlining his plans of what he intended to do to us. "He should have snapped into it and not wasted his time talking to war correspondents," I reflected severely. But my colleague and I had an embarrassing feeling that we were not helping the battery by our presence and that if we got hit we would cause them a lot of extra trouble. We were also embarrassed by the thought that if we left too abruptly, Burba and the others might think us fair-weather friends. My colleague reminded me that he really had to get back to headquarters at Gafsa by five so he could get a fill-in on the general picture for the dispatch which he must file to catch the six-o'clock courier car to Tebessa. From there a plane would take it to the cablehead at Algiers. I didn't work for a press association and so had no bulletin to file, but we had only one jeep, and I decided that I couldn't expect the other fellow to wait. So I said, "I guess we may as well go, Major. See you some other time." Norgaard said something to the same effect, and we walked away feeling as sheepish as we ever have in our lives. We got in our jeep and drove back past the patient, expectant Captain Bradbury. We paused for a moment to say good-by to him, and I looked back and saw a column of black smoke rising from one of the gun positions, where the enemy had evidently got a hit.

Each knot of soldiers that we had passed on the way going out had seemed a friendly island that invited a prolonged stay. We were not tempted to stop to talk to any of them on the way back. "Tomorrow we will get an early start and bring out blanket rolls," I said to my companion. "That way we will be able to see more of the battle and not have to go back to Gafsa at night." He agreed. As we entered the center of Gafsa and were about to park our jeep opposite the town's one European-style hotel, which was serving as American headquarters, we saw in the street the major general who commanded the whole operation and who forty-eight hours earlier may have been thinking his name would live with Stonewall Jackson's. We stopped to ask him if the infantry had as yet entered Sened—we had been two hours on the way home—and he said they had, and Sened Station was now in our hands. "The only damned trouble," he said, "is that First Army has called off the whole offensive because there has been some kind of threat in the north. I guess we're going to play it safe and wait for Montgomery." At that time American troops were still under direct control of the British First Army. The greater part of an armored division which had been held in reserve just outside Gafsa to exploit our initial gains was sent north that night without having fought, and the great offensive went into the record as a raid.

The feeling I had had when I left the guns was the sort of thing that demands a rationalization, and I arrived at one while I was sitting on a ridge overlooking Gafsa on St. Patrick's Day, watching our people recapture the place. We had evacuated it a fortnight after the aborted offensive. The region is full of prehistoric artifacts and pieces of them, and I was trying to put together some kind of a form out of bits of flint I found on the hill. I never finished the job, but I think the result would have been ugly if I had. I thought then that I had viewed this war so long that it would be a shame to be knocked in the head before I had patched all my glimpses of it together and tried to reconstruct the shape of the beast.

CHAPTER II

Reflections in a Cul-de-sac

THERE IS an old proverb that a girl may sleep with one man without being a trollop, but let a man cover one little war and he is a war correspondent. I belong to the one-war category. I have made no appearances for Mr. Colston Leigh, the lecture agent, either in a gas mask or out of one, and I have no fascinating reminiscences about Addis Ababa or the Cliveden set. Prior to October 1938 my only friends were prize fighters' seconds, Romance philologists, curators of tropical fish, kept women, promoters of spit-and-toilet-paper night clubs, bail bondsmen, press agents for wrestlers, horse clockers, newspaper reporters, and female psychiatrists. I was writing excellent pieces about sea-lion trainers and cigar-store proprietors for the *New Yorker*, and I was happy.

Hitler had seemed to me revolting but unimportant, like old Gómez, the dictator of Venezuela. I habitually compared him in conversation to a boor who tortured his own family because he could not cope with the outside world, a classic German type. It never occurred to me that he might destroy France, because it would have been as hard for me to prefigure a world without France as survival with one lobe of my brain gone. France represented for me the historical continuity of intelligence and reasonable living. When this continuity is broken, nothing anywhere can have meaning until it is re-established. After the Munich settlement I began to be anxious.

On Sunday, September 3, 1939, everybody with the price of a newspaper knew that Great Britain and France were about to declare war on Germany, which had already invaded Poland. I was living down on East Thirty-third Street then, but I drifted up toward the *New Yorker* office because I thought that even though it was a Sunday I might find someone there to talk to. It was a hot afternoon, I remember. Wolcott Gibbs had a radio going in his office. I went down the fire escape from the main editorial office on the nineteenth floor to the cell on the seventeenth where I did my writing and sat there for a while, at moments glad because France still had pride, at others feeling guilty because I would not share the fight or the risk. I was sorry that I had left daily newspaper work four years before then, because if I had stayed on a paper I might have a chance to go to the war. The *New Yorker* appeared a cul-de-sac.

As I sat there I thought of M. Lebourgeois, a traveling sales-man I had met in the billiard room of the Hôtel du Cheval Blanc at Vire in 1926, and also of M. Perrin, the *patron* of the hotel in the Rue de l'Ecole de Médecine at Paris, where I had lived for two years while pretending to study medieval litera-ture, and my good friend Henri, who was the French repre-sentative of an American silk firm. All three had shared the quality of having escaped from a great danger with honor in-tact. None of them had come through the war unwounded, and none had achieved any great position since the armistice of 1918. But each took immense pleasure in not having been killed and in not having to be ashamed of himself.

When M. Lebourgeois had patted his stomach, while telling me of the table d'hôte at a favorite hotel in his territory, he had clearly been glad that the stomach had survived—the bullet had broken his left leg, which bothered him hardly at all ex-cept in wet weather. The merchants of the United States, M. Lebourgeois had told me, had absolutely the right idea—*le big business.* Undoubtedly, in that country of large orders, he had said, it was a pleasure to be a salesman. The retailers had vision; they were not like these retrograded types of the De-partment of Calvados, who bought a few articles at a time and those only with the most apparent misgivings. He had had one period of relative affluence, he had said—almost *le big business*, it had been—directly after the war, when he had gone about selling to small communities those life-size cast-iron figures of poilus which served as war memorials in most of rural Nor-mandy. On the base of each statue was the inscription "*Morts à l'Ennemi*," and under it the twenty or thirty names of the late heroes. The figure of the poilu was always poised on the ball of the right foot, the bayonet stuck out before him, the iron face constricted in defiance. "These opportunities don't recur often in a man's lifetime," M. Lebourgeois used to say when he told about it. "Figure to yourself—it is necessary to have a war before you can sell something in this bugger of a department." If M. Lebourgeois was sufficiently fortunate to survive this new war, he might make more sales, I figured to myself.

M. Perrin, my landlord, had taken a Chinese pleasure in disingenuous self-abasement. It was a privilege he had earned in the war. If he had deprecated himself before that, nobody would have contradicted him, because, as he used to say, he was a small, insignificant man without capacity or cultivation. Then, in order to survive, it would have been necessary for him to assert himself. He would have disliked that. But he had won the Legion of Honor for bravery under fire, and although he always shrugged away references to his decoration, he never left the ribbon off his coat. Also, he had been a captain. Intelligence is not requisite for a captain of infantry, he used to assure me. An officer of artillery or engineers, *that* required culture, but a captain of infantry, and especially one who began the war as a private, might be very stupid. It was a matter of luck, of survival, one might say. We would sit at a table in front of the Soufflet—which was later to be replaced by a gigantic modernistic chain-store café called Dupont—watching the Danish and Rumanian students and their girls, and the little waiter with the reddish eyes and the carroty mustache would not be so brusque with M. Perrin as with the other clients. M. Perrin's suits had been shiny, but the ribbon had given him an air. Almost, one would say, an instructor at the Ecole des Chartes near by. The instructors' suits were shiny too. The possibility of such a mistake had flattered M. Perrin, and he had tried by his manner to convey to strangers the idea that his ribbon was an academic honor.

M. Perrin was a native of Lille. He had lived with his wife, a large, hot-tempered Orleánaise, his mother, who was very old, and his daughter, who was adolescent, on the street floor of the hotel. Without the red ribbon to enhance his dignity, without the head wound he had received at Douaumont to explain his flightiness, M. Perrin, it was easy to see, would have been familially submerged. "My wife is very bitter after gain," he had sometimes said over the *apero*. But he had never refused to accept payment of a bill which she had harried some student into meeting. His mother had been in Lille during the occupation of 1914–18. Her confidence had never wavered, she had once told me, since the day when she had seen some German

officers eating lettuce. "They put sugar on it," she said, an indication to her of cretinism on a national scale. The reason I
thought so long of M. Perrin was that he had lived in what he
and I and everybody else had thought was a comfortable
aftermath. Another decoration would bring him no satisfaction commensurate with the first. Neither would another head
wound.

Henri had been most pleased to survive the war of any of
them, because to him it had seemed especially horrible. He
was a sensitive man, extremely tall, with a long, doleful coun-
tenance, watery blue eyes, and a great, drooping Gallic mustache. In 1914 he had been in the United States—it was there I
had first known him—and he had returned to fight. Sometimes I used to have dinner with Henri's family in their apartment on the Avenue de la Motte-Picquet, a neighborhood
roughly equivalent to Central Park West, and after we had
eaten, Henri would tuck a violin under his chin and his daughter Suzette would go to the piano, and then he would play and
sing "J'Avais Perdu la Tête et Ma Perruque," from *Les Cloches
de Corneville.* His son Jean, who had spent most of his young
life in America, would sit silent, uninterested, and slightly embarrassed. Jean liked to talk about automobile engines, using a
good deal of American slang. "He should be a handy man
around a tank now," I thought, "he's just the right age." Henri
had preferred to talk about "before the war," a period, he
would say, when Paris really had been fit to live in. Eglée, his
wife, had sometimes pretended to be bored by his reminiscences. I reflected that Henri, with luck, would be able to talk
someday about "before the war before last." As a matter of
fact he was not to survive this second war. He was to die of
cold and malnutrition and chagrin, "but principally of chagrin,"
his daughter would later write to me, in Paris in February
of 1941.

I began to think of Vire, where I had met M. Lebourgeois.
It is a little city built of gray granite, and its principal street
passes under a great gray clock tower that was once a gate in a
wall, but all the rest of the wall is gone. The clock strikes every
quarter-hour all through the night. There are two little rivers
that join within the city limits, one the Vire and one the name

of which I could not recall, and there is the Street of the Dyers along the bank of one of them, with old granite houses that jut over the water and low granite porches on the water level. I had once told the mayor, an anticlerical old doctor, that this street was fine, and he had said it was "an infection, a nest of microbes," and that the sooner somebody blew it up with dynamite the better it would be. The vales, *vaux*, of the two little rivers, *les vaux de Vire*, lent their names to form the word vaudeville, according to a plausible but I am now convinced inaccurate theory I had once heard told in a course in Old French at Columbia. I had arrived in Vire for the first time in 1926 because of that odd bit of information. I had always loved vaudeville at the Palace in New York. Besides, Henri had told me that during the last war he and another sergeant had brought some German prisoners from the front to a camp on the west coast, and that on the return trip they had stopped off at Vire, which was the other sergeant's home town, and that they had descended at the Cheval Blanc and eaten and drunk wonderfully well. Since I was an amateur medievalist and a vaudeville fan *and* a glutton, I had gone to Vire. On the first Sunday after my arrival I had attended some mounted trotting races that local farmers were holding at a village four miles from the city. The great heavy men on their great heavy horses —bred for sale to the field artillery—went thundering in a rough semicircle about a great cow pasture. It was easy to lose count of the number of rounds. The crowd stood inside the semicircle, most of the men amiably drunk, the women scarlet-cheeked and out of their heads with excitement, cheering their favorites. One fellow in a plaid cap led for several rounds, then his horse, a brown with a long barrel and short legs, broke into a canter. The man sawed at the horse's mouth to get it back into a trot, he kicked violently, and the horse broke into a sidling gallop and then began trying to throw him. Meanwhile another farmer, on a bay, took the lead easily without pushing his horse. The farmer had thick legs and a great heavy belly that rode in front of him like a sack of grain. He had a red face and a long mustache that drooped like a ship's ensign in a dead calm. He and his bay stallion were unexcited. They trotted in by fifty lengths. A tall old peasant standing next to me hit me on the back of the neck with the heel of his hand, a cordial gesture in Vire. "Pichart wins again!" he shouted. "It never pays to abuse a horse or a woman!"

I remembered M. Hédouin, the municipal librarian of Vire. The combined library and museum was a sort of annex of the City Hall. It was officially closed during the summertime. So I had had to pay M. Hédouin twenty francs an hour to open it for me and find books. He was a small, bent, wispy man, old, but not at all doting. There had been an early-fifteenth-century poet named Olivier Basselin in Vire, according to the *vaux-de-vire* theory which dated from about 1825. His drinking songs had become known as *vaux-de-vire*, by a transference easy to understand. Then the *r* had become an *l*, and then vaudeville had come to be a term for any gay song. The main evidence for this theory was a whole volume of Olivier Basselin's drinking songs, printed in the seventeenth century. There was no surviving manuscript. In order to have survived for two centuries outside of manuscript, the argument ran, the songs must have been very popular indeed. M. Hédouin told me that a nineteenth-century critic named Armand Gasté, a native of Vire and a professor at the University of Caen—there was a street in Vire named after him—had already disposed of the question in two or three volumes. M. Hédouin fished them out of the stacks for me.

M. Gasté demonstrated by a study of the texts that the poems had been written in the seventeenth, not the fifteenth, century and by a lawyer named Jean Le Houx of Vire. Le Houx had been an outwardly serious chap who had not wanted to be known as a composer of drinking songs. He had therefore invented Basselin, as Chatterton invented Rowley and MacPherson invented Ossian, and had published his "discovery." Since the term *vaux-de-vire* had never been applied to songs before Le Houx's time, the etymology for vaudeville from *vaux-de-vire* was almost impossible, Gasté noted. The word vaudeville already occurred in the seventeenth century and was probably derived from *voix de ville*, the voice of the city. I remembered only one of his textual arguments: "Basselin" in one song compared his own nose to the red wattles of a turkey. Turkeys had not been introduced into France until well after the discovery of America, Gasté pointed out. "It was all a humbug,"

M. Hédouin had told me with a New England kind of malicious pleasure in destroying a pretty story. What I remembered most keenly was the play of intelligences across time, like a wireless chess game. The seventeenth-century attorney and the nineteenth-century professor had played, the old librarian in the twentieth century had marked the score.

I did not think about Germany. When I was a small child I had had a succession of German governesses all indistinguishably known to me as *Fräulein*. They had been servile to my parents and domineering to me, stupid, whining, loud, and forever trying to frighten me with stories of children who had been burned to a crisp or eaten by an ogre because they had disobeyed other Fräuleins. The fairy tales of anthropophagic stepmothers and princes turned into white mice gave me nightmares. Once when I was very small I was escorted by the current Fräulein through the torture tower in Nuremberg and made to look down a deep well into which, she told me, it was customary to throw bad little boys. It was really the place where the jolly Meistersingers had been accustomed to drop the mangled corpses of people who disagreed with them, like a slot for used razor blades. She had bought me a little miniature of the Iron Maiden as a souvenir of our promenade, complete in detail, she liked to point out. Only Germans could be so thorough, she said with pride—there were miniature spikes inside the hollow maiden's hollow eyes, just like the spikes in the big one, that pierced the victim's brain. I suppose German-lovers would have called it *gemütlich*. Banse and Goebbels and their war by fear are in the main line of German culture, not twentieth-century deviations. Only people with hollow hearts can so count on the fears of others. The Fräuleins had shared a national habit of digging their fingernails into the flesh of my arm. When I was five years old I would rather have died with my milk teeth in a governess' ankle than tie the kind of bow in my shoelaces that she had wanted to make me tie. Anybody who had had a German governess could understand Poland.

CHAPTER III

Toward Paris: 1939

THE NEW YORKER turned out to be the best possible place for a reporter who had to see the war. The magazine had always considered London and Paris, although not Newark or Chicago, within its sphere of inaction. It had run a weekly or fortnightly letter from each of these capitals for years, with an occasional Letter from Salzburg, or Megève or Berlin (during the 1936 Olympics) or Bayreuth as a seasonal variant. The editors, although annoyed by the war because it posed new problems in the selection of comic drawings, thought that the Paris-London aspect of it ought to be covered as thoroughly as a Schiaparelli opening. Harold Ross did not think we would need much on the front, because he had been on the staff of *Stars and Stripes* in Paris in 1918 and felt he knew all about the fighting end, so that it was unnecessary to send out a military expert to represent us. This was lucky for me. The trouble with the *New Yorker* from my point of view as of September 1, 1939, was that all our European coverage was already being done by Janet Flanner, who signed her dispatches "Genêt," and that I could not conceive of a reporter coming away from a story just as it broke. Unfortunately for everybody but me, Miss Flanner's mother in California got sick and Miss Flanner notified the office that she wanted to come home. I got the Paris assignment because I had spent several man-hours of barroom time impressing St. Clair McKelway, then managing editor, with my profound knowledge of France. At about the same time the *New Yorker*, through a London literary agent, acquired the services of Mollie Panter-Downes to do the London Letter. No one in the office at the time of the hiring had ever seen Mollie—the whole transaction was a great boost for the pin-through-the-program system of picking winners at horse races.

I knew very little about Lady Mendl, Elsa Maxwell, Mainbocher and Worth the dressmakers, Mr. and Mrs. Charles Bedeaux, or a number of other leading characters in Genêt's Paris dispatches, but since it seemed probable that they would lam anyway, Ross was willing to overlook this deficiency and even agreed in a halfhearted way with McKelway's idea that I write about the reactions to war of ordinary French people. "But for God's sake keep away from low-life," Ross said. Meyer Berger had once written a *New Yorker* profile of a man who fished for lost coins through subway gratings, and Ross had been trying for months to disinfect the magazine by running pieces about Supreme Court justices and the Persian Room of the Plaza. I promised to keep my end of the war reasonably clean and high-class, and the office booked me a passage on a Pan American Clipper to Lisbon. It was not hard to get an eastbound ticket that season; there were only eight passengers on my plane, including me.

After I had got what I wanted and was sure to go, I had a couple of misgivings. German planes had not yet bombarded French cities, but people here thought that they eventually would, and I shared the general Sunday-supplement idea of what bombing could accomplish. I remember a sequence in a newsreel that September that showed the panic of a London crowd when some crank started throwing rubber balls about. The people had got the idea that there was a raid on; I remember one woman throwing her children on the ground and covering them with her body. I was never to see people so frightened during a real bombing. Walking down Lexington Avenue with Joe Mitchell of the *New Yorker* one warm night shortly before I was scheduled to take off, I said, "I bet I'll wish I was back on Lex a lot of times before this thing is over." The more a man sees of war the more immediate danger has to be before he starts worrying about it. I was talking last spring to a major in Leclerc's Fighting French column who was taking a sun bath in a cup in the hills during the battle of Enfidaville. We were all temporarily trapped by mortar fire, but none of the shells had yet landed in the hollow. They were bursting on the other side of the hill, fifty yards away. I still trepidate at fifty yards, so I said to this major, "That makes me a droll of an effect." He said, "It is all a question of habit," and continued to take his sun bath. In 1939 a lot of us scared at four thousand miles.

A couple of weeks after I talked to the sun-bathing major I met a 59-year-old second lieutenant in the Corps Franc d'Afrique who was on his way to lead an infantry attack, and he said courage was a question of digestion. On the morning of October 9, 1939, when I took off for the war my digestion was excellent, but I was nervous as hell.

At that period—it sounds like talking about stagecoach days —the Clippers still left from a yacht-club setting at Port Washington, Long Island. A friend of mine named Fred Schwed, a romantic soul who had been reared on Richard Harding Davis, although in early manhood he had switched to Scott Fitzgerald, had asked to drive me out to my plane in the early morning. Passengers were supposed to be at the plane with their luggage at eight o'clock. Schwed picked me up at an hour I never had experienced while sober, at the door of the house where I was living, and headed in what I took to be the direction of Long Island because the sun was rising over it. He drove me over one bridge, which was all right, and then around a wild farming country, in which I distinctly saw a hen and on another occasion what I took to be a cow—in one jump more I figured he would have me among the coyotes and Republicans—and then over another bridge, which was all wrong because it landed us in Westchester County. By then I had only an hour or so to catch the plane, so I began to curse, which I do well. The secret of good cursing lies in cadence, emphasis, and antiphony. The basic themes are always the same. Conscious striving after variety is not to be encouraged, because it takes your mind off your cursing. By the time Schwed got me to the landing he felt what a proper swine he was for having gotten up early in the morning to take me to the plane, and if the experience had broken him of volunteering to do favors for people it would have been worth while. I rushed into the dinky frame ticket and customs office they had there, still drooling obscenity, and saw my mother, who had gotten up early in another part of Long Island and come out to see me off. Sucking back four bloody oaths that I could already feel pressing against the back of my teeth, I switched to a properly filial expression, embraced the dear woman, and got aboard the Clipper feeling like Donald Duck.

There was one woman among the passengers, a myopic young American married to a fifty-year-old Englishman who told me he raised vast quantities of broad-*a* tomatoes in the

Canary Islands. The tomatist boasted of having financed
Franco's airplane trip from the Canaries to Spain at the beginning of the Spanish counter-revolution. He evidently thought
it had been a brilliant idea. They had a stateroom, a fact I note
for its antiquarian interest: I have seldom traveled since in a
plane that wasn't crowded beyond seating capacity. We all
floated in luxury on that trip, with two stewards to take care of
the eight of us, soundproofing that has since been eliminated
even from Clippers to keep down non-essential weight, and
Pullman-style berths to sleep in. The most notable passenger
was a French stage and screen star going back to report for
military service because, he explained to me, a French movie
star who remained in Hollywood during the war would lose
his popularity at home. Since he was fifty years old there was
not much chance he would be taken into the army, but he had
a faithful public in France which thought he was a good deal
younger than that. It startled me to see him making up his face
in the morning when he climbed out of his berth, but he was a
nice civilized Joe. It was the first time he had ever been in an
airplane, and he was pleased and excited. "Poor, sick old Europe," he kept saying to the rest of us between slugs of scotch,
"poor, sick old Europe." He had just been married in America
and thought it was the only country in the world that had a
future. We also had on board a professional correspondent
named Bob Nixon, of International News Service, a rich Peruvian kid who was going back to Paris to finish a course at the
Sorbonne, a German Jew who was a naturalized Cuban citizen
and on his way to France to sell the Government a kind of blue
paint to put over headlights so they would give full light but
would not gleam in the blackout—there was a fortune in it, he
told us all, if he could make the right connections—and a brocade manufacturer from Zurich who was going home to take
up his reserve commission in the Swiss Army. The Peruvian
was quiet and apparently airsick all the way across. The Swiss
was a solid sort who told me that the German-speaking cantons were more anti-Nazi than the French cantons. He said he
thought Switzerland could maintain her neutrality indefinitely
because her army could make invasion expensive for anybody.
I found this hard to believe.

When I got tired of talking to the other passengers I

thought about women. I frequently do this for hours without becoming bored; they are much pleasanter than sheep to think of when you are trying to fall asleep. Thinking about women also makes you insensible to mild fright or minor discomforts. Once I was sleeping with another fellow under a pup tent in a rainstorm in Tunisia, and at about two o'clock in the morning he woke me up. I said, "What's up?" and he said, "The tent's just blown away." The rain had turned into a cloudburst, and my blankets were soaked through. I got into the front seat of a jeep and wrapped the wet blankets around me. The top and windshield afforded some help, but the water lashed in from both sides. I thought about women for four and a half hours and never even caught cold.

The Frenchman and Nixon and I took the train north from Lisbon the day after we landed. The German-Cuban had no French visa, the Peruvian had disappeared, the Swiss was to take an Italian plane to Rome and go on from there; the tomato twosome were staying on in Lisbon. There was no more feel of war—or rather, since I did not know what war felt like, of difference from peace—in Lisbon than there had been in Port Washington. As soon as the train crossed the Portuguese-Spanish frontier at Fuentes de Oñoro we recognized by the atmosphere that we were in a belligerent country. The train passed camps surrounded by barbed wire and populated either by Republican prisoners of war or Franco soldiers. The victors were so miserably dressed that it was impossible for a stranger to tell them from the vanquished. The station platforms were crowded with soldiers in cotton uniforms and canvas shoes and with officers in boots and Sam Browne belts. The officers, who paid no fare, made a practice of boarding the train and riding for a couple of stations in the wagon-restaurant, where they regaled themselves on black bread, green apples, and imitation coffee, evidently a cut above what they ordinarily got at mess. An obvious flatfoot in plain clothes stood at the end of the corridor of our first-class carriage and watched the door of our compartment, and the bare rocky country through which the railroad passed stank of poverty and ruin. At Irun all the passengers bound for France were marched through the streets to the villa of the fascist governor and kept waiting in the garden for a couple of hours until an assistant had gone through our passports. From the manner of these strutting sparrows of men you might have got the idea that they had defeated France, the United States, and Great Britain, which they had in a way, of course, but by default, and that we were captives. After the tomato fancier's protégés had finished with us, the French actor, Nixon, and I walked across the international bridge to La Hendaye. Since the Pan American people had limited us to fifty-five pounds of luggage we had no trouble carrying our stuff with us. Coming into France, where there was no strain in the faces of the lazy-looking customs guards and where there were few soldiers in evidence and plenty to eat, was like arriving in a neutral from a belligerent country.

After we had gone over to the French *gare* and gotten aboard the Sud-Express for Paris we stood looking out the carriage window at France before the train started. The actor called my attention to an erect, worthy-looking old man in a derby hat and pepper-and-salt topcoat who stood on the platform, waiting to get aboard the train. He had a clipped white mustache and a fine, honest face. The actor was much moved. "It's Pétain!" he said. "He's ambassador to Spain now. Madame lives at La Hendaye." The movie actor had been an ordinary soldier in the other war. "What a fine old boy!" he said with emotion. I had not recognized the marshal, because I had always thought of him with the long, down-sweeping mustaches of his World War I photographs. I felt constrained to agree with my companion. "A great old gent!" I said. He was the first marshal of France I had seen, and his presence seemed a link with Napoleon and a happy augury. "He is young for his age!" the actor said with admiration. I had to admit that he didn't look a day over seventy-five.

The Sud-Express, except for the blacked-out windows and the dim blue lights in the corridor after nightfall, was as fine and punctual a train as it had ever been. The only person aboard who appeared affected by the war was an attendant whom I asked for a couple of bottles of Vichy Célestin. He said, "We have only Vichy Saint-Louis on the train now. You can't get everything you want now, there's a war on!" He wore the same expression of desolation as a waiter at Lüchow's in New York last summer telling me that there was no more Gaspé salmon, only Nova Scotia salmon, on account of the war.

The train arriving at Paris stopped at the Gare d'Austerlitz, far from the center of the city, and it took me a couple of minutes to get a taxicab, but the city, a considerable portion of which we had to traverse to reach my hotel, looked much as it had in 1927 except for the strips of paper pasted across shop windows to keep the glass from flying in case of a bombardment. I don't know yet whether this dodge is of any use. I can't remember seeing any on London shops and don't know whether they gave it up before I got there or just never tried it. The taxis I had seen outside the station were all ridiculously old *tacots*, which is French for jalopies, because the newer cars had been requisitioned by the Government. They had the old-fashioned hand horns that figure in the orchestration of *The Last Time I Saw Paris.*

I had decided on the Hôtel Louvois, facing the Bibliothèque Nationale, across the little Square Louvois. The façade and the square had always attracted me when I was a student. The Louvois would have been no good for me then, being on the Right Bank, and besides the allowance that my father sent me in those days would never have permitted such an expenditure—the Louvois was marked at least *tout confort* and possibly even *deuxième catégorie* in the Hachette Guide Bleu. I figured that as a war correspondent, however, I would be able to afford it. Room and bath cost me eleven dollars a week. I took a room that fronted on the square, overlooking the fountain with heroic allegorical figures representing the rivers of France. There were four statues, all expansively female and symbolizing, I think, the Seine, Rhone, Loire, and Garonne. From my balcony on the second floor of the hotel I had a fine view of the Garonne's navel, which was nearly big enough to hold a baseball. There were twenty-one trees, an even greater number of flowers, in season, and a *pissoir* and a *chalet de necessité* in the little park. There were also benches where lovers and nursemaids came to sit. The Rue Richelieu runs along the Bibliothèque side of the square; the Rue Chabanais with its meretricious associations begins on the hotel side. On the other two sides there were six-story buildings, one of them a hotel, with people living in them whom I saw principally when some event of general interest like a wife-beating was going on

in the square, when they would all appear on the little balconies in front of their windows.

In a general way I felt that my quarter included everything
between the boulevards and the river, from the Place de la
Concorde around to the Place de la Bastille, but my home
province in this empire was roughly bounded by Rue Saint-
Augustin, Rue Sainte-Anne, Rue Richelieu (with Rue Mont-
pensier and the Palais Royale on the other side of it), and the
Place in front of the Comédie Française, with the Café de la
Régence on the other side. A province of two hundred acres
that included the national library, the national theater, and the
national lupanar, all a bit overlaid with dust and tradition, but
still sound. It was part of the Second Arrondissement, represented in the Chamber of Deputies by Paul Reynaud. He had
been elected by seventeen votes. I often reflected, after he became President of the Council in March, that any nine electors
from among the pharmacists' assistants, bistro proprietors, and
sporting girls I got to know in the quarter might have changed
the history of France and of the world by their votes.

After I had left my bag and typewriter at the hotel I went
around to the Paris branch of the Guaranty Trust to get some
money on a letter of credit, and met Theodore Rousseau, the
director, who had once been a New York newspaperman and
then secretary to Mayor John Purroy Mitchel and had since
married the Princesse de Broglie. Rousseau invited me to a
wartime lunch at Larue's—it turned out to be just Marennes,
Pouilly Fuissé, *caille vendangeuse*, and Grands Echézeaux—
and then said, "You may have got here too late, old fellow.
There's a strong tip on the Bourse this morning that the war's
going to be called off."

CHAPTER IV

My Generals, My Generalissimo

WHEN I first arrived in France I was told that there were two
institutions beyond suspicion, the Church and the professional

army. The Church did not interest me, but the generals did. The interest did not date back only to the beginning of the war. Even at college I had occasionally risked the contempt of my fellow liberals by reading a book about a soldier. Perhaps it was because in childhood I had owned a picture book illustrated with plates representing Napoleon's battles (the Pyramids, with the Little Corporal surrounded by Mamelukes, was my favorite, and the Retreat from Moscow broke my heart) and had later read Dunn-Pattison's *Napoleon's Marshals*. I could once name all twenty-six of them—Augereau, Bernadotte, Berthier, Bessières, Brune, and then I lose the alphabetic thread. The first French general I had ever seen was Joffre, in New York during the other war; I had felt very knowing every time I referred to him as "Popper." The first I had ever spoken to was old Gouraud, who was on some sort of a cultural lecturing tour in 1928 when I met him on his way to Woonsocket, Rhode Island, which has a large French population. I was then in exile as a reporter on the Providence *Journal* and *Bulletin*; I had been fired from the sports department of the New York *Times* for frivolity, but in Providence I got all assignments bearing on European affairs because they knew I had been in Paris.

The general's train had pulled in from New York during the night, and he was sleeping in a Pullman car on a siding. I wanted to get him in time for a first-edition story for the *Bulletin*, so I went into the car and woke him up. He was in a lower berth, and his whiskers were hanging over the edge of it. I shook him by the shoulder and said firmly, "*La presse!*" He got the idea and started to get up right away. I guess he had had a lot of arguments with out-of-town reporters already. "*Nous débutons, messieurs!*" he sang out. He had a half-dozen officers concealed in uppers and lowers all around the car, and they all got up. He gave me an exclusive interview, saying he liked Americans and France wanted to be friends with the United States. I took it that it would be all right with him to say he liked Woonsocket, although he had not yet been there, so I put that in the story too, although I worried about the journalistic ethics of the procedure. In those days I was as ethical as Westbrook Pegler, although poorer.

All this will explain why I was predisposed in favor of French generals when I got to Paris in 1939, and why I have been ever since. A fellow who wanted to keep abreast with French history during the following years could not have picked a better specialty. The first project I had brought from New York with me was to write a *New Yorker* profile of General Gamelin, and that necessitated an orientation in his milieu. I looked forward to it with pleasure, like doing a piece about prize fighters or sporting women. Some fellows like to write about the stage or screen, but I never understood why. Others can contemplate without repugnance doing a profile of a politician, a newspaper publisher, or even an advertising man or somebody in the radio business, but my tastes do not run that way. Like Edward Gibbon, a military buff although he never licked anybody himself, I like to hear talk about fighting. The most sensible talk I ever heard on the subject was from Sam Langford, the old Boston Tar Baby; but a French general has something genteel and old-worldly about him that Sam lacks. A good specimen combines the charm of Raymond Weeks, my old professor of philology, and Tex Grenet, the courtly old man who used to make the morning line for the bookmakers before the pari-mutuel came to the New York tracks. Maybe it's a father fixation.

Thucydides and Plutarch saved anecdotes about generals; why should I be proud? A general once told me one about General Mittelhauser, who will be remembered only because he succeeded Weygand in Syria and then declined to continue the war by General De Gaulle's side. Mittelhauser and an aide were returning to Paris by air when the plane developed engine trouble. It began to lose altitude. Mittelhauser looked at his aide, the aide was calm. Mittelhauser thought, "There can't be anything serious. I will not show this young man I am alarmed." The aide looked at Mittelhauser. Mittelhauser appeared calm. The aide thought, "I will not show the boss I am alarmed." The pilot made a crash landing in an orchard; the plane ran between two trees and lost both wings. "Then," said the general who told me the story, "Mittelhauser and the aide knew there had been something serious." The aide pulled Mittelhauser out of the wrecked plane. Mittelhauser said,

"When does the next train leave for Paris?" The aide said, "My general, I don't even know where we are." Mittelhauser shouted in a rage, "Imbecile! You never know anything!"

Another general told me another anecdote about Weygand in the First World War. The general who was telling me the story had then been a lieutenant colonel of artillery; Weygand had been Foch's chief of staff. The artillerist had participated in an unsuccessful attack on a little hill; Weygand asked him why his guns had not been able to knock out the enemy's machine-gun positions. "Because they could not be brought to bear at that angle, my general," the artillerist had said. "You are of those who believe that infantry unsupported by artillery cannot take such positions?" "I am of those, my general." "Then bugger off," Weygand had said indignantly and stalked away.

Another old general, a fine old specimen who had been of Gamelin's *promotion* at St. Cyr, was telling me about 1894, when the Dreyfus case had split the French Army wide open. This general, by exception, had been a *Dreyfusard* as a young officer. His best friend at St. Cyr had been an anti-Dreyfusard. They had quarreled, and from that day they had stopped speaking to each other. After the war, in which both had distinguished themselves, my general was riding in a railroad train when at a station the compartment door opened and in walked his former friend, who now had 110 per cent disability for war wounds. My general had 120 per cent. The other officer sat down on the bench opposite my general without saying a word, and they glared at each other for about fifty miles. At last the former anti-Dreyfusard extended his hand and said, "Will you at least shake hands with me?" My Dreyfusard general said, "If you have arrived at better sentiments, yes."

If these stories amuse you, you may understand my obsessional interest in French generals; if not you may consider it a hobby without apparent charm, like peridromophily, which is the collection and classification of street-railway tickets.

I knew that it would be hard to get an interview with the generalissimo of all the Allied Forces while he was running such a large war, so I bespoke the good offices of William C. Bullitt, the United States ambassador, in obtaining it. Gamelin, in all the fall of 1939, granted only one interview, and that a mass affair for all the American correspondents. Bullitt had himself been the subject of a flashy profile by Genêt. He did not know whether it had been flattering or not, and neither did I after having read it only once, but it was expedient for both of us to act as if it had been, he in order to maintain his standing as man of the world and I because I wanted him to do me a favor. He was at any rate a *New Yorker* reader; so, I afterward learned, was Paul Reynaud, and I have sometimes wondered whether Reynaud got his copies regularly in his prisons after the Armistice. I reminded Bullitt that the *New Yorker*, despite its relatively small circulation for a national magazine, went to some pretty literate people all over the country, and that our stuff was filtered down through word of mouth and reprint until it had an effect on public opinion disproportionate to the number of first readers. He said he thought the interview could be arranged, if I wasn't in too much of a hurry. He sent me to Colonel Horace A. Fuller, the military attaché, now a major general commanding a division somewhere in the Pacific, and Fuller promised to talk to Colonel Jean Petibon, Gamelin's *chef de cabinet*, for me. Before interviewing Gamelin I knew that I would have to document myself on his views, his past, and enough of his technical background and jargon to make him feel that I knew what he was talking about. The preparation is the same whether you are going to interview a diplomat, a jockey, or an ichthyologist. From the man's past you learn what questions are likely to stimulate a response; after he gets going you say just enough to let him know you appreciate what he is saying and to make him want to talk more. Everybody with any sense talks a kind of shorthand; if you make a man stop to explain everything he will soon quit on you, like a horse that you alternately spur and curb. It is all in one of Sam Langford's principles of prize fighting: "Make him lead." Only instead of countering to your subject's chin you keep him leading. Once I asked Sam what he did when the other man wouldn't lead, and he said, "I run him out of the ring." This is a recourse not open to the interviewer.

In the summer of 1940 I went up to the Hotel Carlton in Washington to talk to General John J. Pershing about the subject of a profile I was then working on. I did everything I could to get the old man to loosen up, including pretty obvious flattery. "When they started to cut down the Army after the Armistice in 1918, General," I said, "you were against it, weren't you, because you foresaw this new European crisis?" The old boy looked at me in an angry, disgusted manner and said, "Who the hell could have foreseen this?"

The worst thing an interviewer can do is talk a lot himself. Just listening to reporters in a barroom, you can tell the ones who go out and impress their powerful personalities on their subject and then come back and make up what they think he would have said if he had had a chance to say anything. One of the best preps I ever did was for a profile of Eddie Arcaro, the jockey. When I interviewed him the first question I asked was, "How many holes longer do you keep your left stirrup than your right?" Most jockeys on American tracks ride longer on their left side. That started him talking easily, and after an hour, during which I had put in about twelve words, he said, "I can see you've been around riders a lot." I had, but only during the week before I was to meet him.

A profile of course is more than a well-prepared interview. You try to get anecdotes and objective views of the subject from people who have known him at various stages of his life, and then you fit the whole business together. I figured correctly that I would have plenty of time to dig up background before I would be allowed to see the generalissimo. I began by asking M. André de Laboulaye, a former French ambassador to the United States who was now the titular head of the American section at the Hôtel Continental, to recommend a general as a guide to higher strategy and tactics. Old M. l'Ambassadeur, who had some of the charm but none of the decisiveness of a general himself, sent me to General Pujo, who had retired from the command of the Army of the Air only a year before the war began.

General Pujo was a fine average specimen of a general, with ice-blue eyes, a firm chin, a good handshake, and a vast, high-ceilinged apartment in the Rue de l'Arcade with rooms full of Sèvres vases and Empire furniture. All generals, naturally, have a tendency to furnish in Empire because that was a period when generals were appreciated. His conversation was full of nice homely phrases like "we will have them" and "we will not

let go the morsel." He said that General Gamelin, an old acquaintance of his, was a man of "tranquil luminosity of mind."
Finally he recommended that I buy the *Instruction for the
Handling of Large Units*, a publication of the French General
Staff which set forth for commanding officers the official tactical doctrine. It had been prepared while Weygand was still
commander in chief of the French Army and published in
1936, but the doctrine, Pujo said, had not changed under
Gamelin, Weygand's successor. He gave me a note of introduction to Berger-Levrault, the great military booksellers on
the Boulevard Saint-Germain.

Berger-Levrault was a fascinating shop, surprisingly like
Champion, the publisher of medieval texts on the Quai
Voltaire, where I had spent good hours in my earlier Paris
time. The clerks, male and female, in their gray linen dusters
reminded me of Champion's. They had the same complete
knowledge of stock and mental catalogue of regular customers.
They regarded newcomers with the same suspicious indifference, but an introduction "*de la part du Général Pujo*" had
the same effect as a *de la part* of Joseph Bédier's would have
had at Champion's in 1926. The French made the art of war so
intellectually fascinating that the study must have stolen any
reasonable general from the practice. I went in for documentation on a massive scale, putting my purchases on my expense
account. General Gamelin had commanded a campaign against
the Druses in the twenties; I bought and read a magnificent
history of the Druses, an interesting if repulsive people, by the
way, and then a detailed military history of the campaign.
When I at length met the generalissimo I asked him one question based on this mass of stimulating reading, and used about
one line of what he said about it.

Gamelin himself had done a bit of writing, like most French
generals, and I searched Berger-Levrault's stock for Gamelin
items. One phrase of his, from a textbook, particularly impressed me: "Experience should be a springboard under our
feet, and not a ball and chain at our ankles." There was also a
paragraph that seemed slightly stuffy in an intelligent way: "It
is natural that the immediate collaborators of higher officers be
allowed to express their opinions freely, it being understood

that each must bow in just intellectual discipline once the decision has been made. Initiative, within the frame of intellectual discipline, is the strength of armies."

There was some difference of opinion about the generalissimo among officers of the French Army even in the early days of the war, although all admitted he was bright. The discontent came chiefly from two sources—partisans of General Weygand, who had been retired for age in 1935, and those of General George, chief of the armies in the war zone and heir apparent to Gamelin's job. The generalissimo had in turn recently attained the retirement age of sixty-seven, both parties pointed out, but they based different arguments on this fact. The Weygandists said that if the Government was going to overlook technicalities about age their man should have been kept on, especially since he was so chipper that he had been recalled at the beginning of the war and placed in command of the Army of the Levant. The Georgists said that Gamelin should have retired gracefully and handed over to George.

The only man to whom I spoke who even then predicted disaster was Charles Sweeny, an American who had been at various times a colonel in the Foreign Legion, a correspondent for the New York *World*, and a promoter of ice hockey at the Palais de Glace. He had white hair which he wore cut in a Roman bang, and he aspersed his conversation with allusions to the campaigns of Lucullus and Sulla, which perhaps led me to minimize the importance of what he said. He said that the Army was rotten because the officers were afraid to work the men hard; energetic officers were curbed by their superiors, who lived in fear of politicians. Colonel Sweeny thought also that the ten francs a day which in this war was the pay of men under fire was excessive and would lead to drunkenness and mutiny. Having all this money to spend did not seem to affect the fighting quality of French troops in Tunisia later, however, while the English have been able to fight pretty decently under the triple handicap of three bob, or sixty cents a day. The Americans have not been stopped by still higher pay, and the Australians have done all right with the highest scale of all. I think that Sweeny's political was better than his economic reasoning. At any rate he said the Army was nothing like as sound as the Army of the last war and that it would collapse at the first push. It did. Colonel Sweeny affected me like the dilapidated stranger who appears at least once in most racegoers' lives and tries to tout them onto a twenty-to-one shot, which then wins. I paid no attention to him.

My interview came to pass about two months after I had opened negotiations for it. Colonel Petibon, a hard-looking, hard-driving officer whose arrival at a colonelcy at the age of forty-five was considered precocious in the French Army, had first interviewed me in an office like a monastic cell off a long corridor of the Hôtel des Invalides, early in November. The colonel told me that he was a *New Yorker* reader too. He evidently decided I was all right and said I must not leave town; he would call me when the generalissimo could see me. It was just about four weeks later that he telephoned to me at my hotel.

Gamelin's headquarters was at Vincennes, which was a semipublic secret, but he seldom received there. When he was in Paris he used as his office a paneled Louis XV room at the Ecole Militaire which for years had served as Joffre's study. Joffre, of course, had been Gamelin's *grand patron*. Gamelin had risen under his aegis in the other war, serving him in the same capacity that Petibon now served Gamelin. The square on which the Ecole stands was renamed the Place Maréchal-Joffre after the First World War, and an equestrian statue of the marshal, who rode regularly and grimly to keep his weight down, stands in the center of it, or at least did then. The ivory-tinted walls of the generalissimo's suite, still decorated with crowns and fleurs-de-lis in gold, displayed large paintings of the battles of Fontenoy and Lawfeldt, eighteenth-century victories of the French Army. It was a raw day, and the room was heated by a small gas fire. In the anterooms were steel engravings of difficult Alpine defiles captured by the French in 1800. The entire place was reminiscent of an ancient, successful business house.

Gamelin fitted perfectly into the vaguely Dickensian setting. He is five feet four inches tall, which is not conspicuously short for a Frenchman. He has a good round Flemish head, his hair was blond and parted in the middle, his cheeks were rosy pink, and he wore a sandy mustache which had recently taken an optimistic, upward curl. The generalissimo seemed to me to have the face of a skeptical but indulgent Dutch uncle in a Frans Hals painting, although in newspaper photographs he often had appeared grim and strained. I consider him one of the most intelligent and sensitive men I ever met.

Gamelin did not favor the defensive *per se*, any more than an experienced automobile driver favors always going in one sense of the compass. He believed that an attack upon Germany would have no chance of success until the Allies had accumulated a superiority of material, including airplanes, and that only the defensive was feasible in the interim. The strategic concept was not bad. It was that upon which Great Britain was to fight the war after the fall of France. But Gamelin's correct conclusion was based on a false premise; Great Britain and France together, with the factories they had working for them in the United States, were not outproducing Germany then. Great Britain was not training troops as fast as Germany. The discrepancy of men and materials in the Germans' favor was increasing. It is hard to believe that the generalissimo did not know this; harder to believe that, knowing it, he could have seemed so optimistic, like a somnambulist jauntily strolling off a roof. Old schoolmates of the generalissimo had told me that Gamelin from the moment of his first arrival at St. Cyr had made the same impression as an ambitious young seminarist who his colleagues at once feel is destined for a high place in the hierarchy. They had said, "He would rather be generalissimo than anything else in the world." But he could not have wanted to be remembered as the commander of a disaster.

"You can't get out of the concrete," he said to me regretfully. "There isn't enough heavy artillery in the world to get out of the concrete." This respect for fortification hardly jibed with his omission of it on the north of his line. His failure was not of concept but of execution. "Twenty-five per cent for the theoretical solution of the problem," Foch, his old professor at the War College, had told him often enough, "seventy-five per cent for the application in battle." Then, in the spring, the Allies were to abandon even the strategic defensive and move into the Low Countries.

It is not enough to say that the French paid too little attention to the use of tanks and bombers by the Germans in Poland. They believed in anti-tank defenses, in anti-tank guns, in a strong tactical air force which would control the sky over the battlefield at least, in such elementary conservative chores as keeping the men supplied with food and small-arms ammunition. Their deficiencies in all these matters had nothing to do with strategic doctrine. But in retrospect it is hard for me to associate the calm little man in the big old-fashioned room with omissions in the most elementary parts of war. It is as if I had had a long conversation with a novelist—perhaps M. Jules Romains—and a couple of years later somebody came to me and said, "You remember M. Romains? He was an illiterate."

CHAPTER V

Bajus Disappointed

THE WAR of course was not called off, but there were few indications that it was on. Paris was a city in which people were tentatively picking up the threads of ordinary existence— tentatively and a little sheepishly, as if ashamed of their initial agitation. Several million Frenchmen had been mobilized, thirty-eight Communist Deputies had been put in jail, and the newspapers carried a daily communiqué which sometimes chronicled "operations" as small as the shooting of an enemy messenger dog. People distrusted the calm, but there was nothing they could do about it except talk. During each fortnight the city lived through two or three periods of intense preoccupation with the war and as many of groping toward an approximation of peacetime life.

Only the women clung to the hope of a continuing miracle —a war without hard fighting. "Hitler will surely blow out his brains," they said, or "Just think how much money the English must be spending for the revolution in Germany." They circulated with grave optimism the story that a gipsy woman had got into an autobus and sat down next to a Parisienne who had moved her handbag out of the gipsy's reach. The gipsy had then said, "Why do you do that when you have only eighteen francs in your bag?" The woman had exactly that sum.

Then the gipsy told each of the other passengers how much he or she had, down to the last *sou*. "Since you know so much," one passenger had asked, "tell us when Hitler will die." "On December second," the gipsy had said, and had got out at the next stop. A story like that gained currency not because Frenchwomen were silly but because they refused to believe that their sons and husbands would be killed—those sons and husbands who until then had been so miraculously preserved, it seemed. Miracles are perhaps to be distrusted; the men were being preserved for the bitterest destiny an army ever had, but nobody then divined it. The book of Michel Nostradamus, the old astrologer, had become a best seller. According to the exegetes of the full-length thirty-franc version I acquired, he had predicted the destruction of Paris by "birds from the East," and its reconquest a year later by a French king after a great victory in the Valley of the Loire, but there was some confusion about the dates for which he had predicted these events. Maybe Hitler will die on a December second—the odds are only 364 to 1 against it; perhaps there will be a battle of the Loire on the way back to Paris. Then the gipsy woman and Nostradamus will get credit for having seen clear, like experts on European affairs.

I was told that in September there had been emotion manifest in Paris; air raids had been expected hourly, reservists went to the front expecting to be hurled into counterattacks against an invader; the Poles had been the darlings of the public. But now that was all over. When people thought of the war it was with cold exasperation; there was a self-conscious distrust of phrases like "heroic poilu," "sacred soil," and "accursed Boche," but it had become clear that as long as Germany was free to mess up Europe every twenty years life would be barely supportable. Not quite everybody realized that life would not be supportable at all. It was the psychology of a defensive war; none other is possible to a decent people until it has suffered much, when a retributive counteroffensive spirit can be aroused. If all the newspaper files and foreign correspondents' books and White and Gray and Mauve Papers of a dozen governments were to be destroyed forever, the fact that the French fought would remain as proof they must have been right. They hated it so, and in the beginning they had had so clear an idea of the odds against them.

André Chamson, in his journal of the war at the front, wrote, "Hitler thought he would have us as he had had the Social Democrats—without fighting. He awaits the disintegration of the last man. But here around me the world is full of men." The Poles and the French had ended the sequence of conquests by bluff, and in doing so made Hitler's end inevitable. His capacity for bluff had been infinite; his capacity for conquest by arms, although great, was insufficient.

In Paris it was the great age of the strategists of the Café du Commerce, the French term for the armchair kind. And the hot blood that had rushed toward the national head during the month of September receded in October toward the feet already chilled by the overtures of a winter of rationed fuel. Behind the blacked-out windows of the cafés in the evenings there was some of the promiscuous sociability of speakeasy days in prohibition-time New York and, I am told, of air-raid shelters during the London blitz. Anybody at all was willing to tell you how the war could be won, but a majority favored gradual methods like the starvation of German war industry.

General Robert-Georges Nivelle, little remembered outside France then or now, had left a deep trace upon the feeling and thinking of his country. It was Nivelle who had talked his countrymen into the great offensive in the Champagne in April of 1917, remembered as the "great bloodletting." When a café strategist complained of seeming inaction in 1939, a confrere had only to wave a finger and say, "Nivelle," to shut him up. In six days in Nivelle's battle in 1917 the French had lost 35,000 killed and 80,000 wounded. As a measure of comparison, we had less than 15,000 casualties, not counting prisoners of war, in the whole African campaign. There were no hospitals reasonably near the battlefield for so many wounded, so they had to be distributed all over France; the trains of mangled men spread despair through the country. Mutinies had followed; every Frenchman of an age to be in civilian clothes in 1939 remembered that awful time. Eventually the Germans would have to attack, the café strategists said, but then we would have them.

Sometimes there was visible a bit of the surface ebullience that my friends told me there had been in Paris in the other war. One Sunday I was walking in Montmartre with my old Henri, whose American silk firm had folded its Paris office during the depression and who had lost all his money, and on the Place Blanche we saw a great crowd of soldiers and strollers around a song plugger who was selling a new ballad. The plugger, a youth about fifteen, wore four hats one on top of another and howled into a megaphone with indelicate gaiety:

> *"Hitler n'en a pas,*
> *Du tout, du tout!*
> *Hitler n'en a pas,*
> *Pas même un tout p'tit bout!"*

The lyrics were about things like ammunition and beefsteaks and gaiety. The plugger's gestures weren't included in the lyrics.

There was an evening when I heard two pimps arguing about the war in the bar of a brothel. Each was in fact the protector of one of the two *sous-maîtresses* of the house, and each was waiting until his particular protégée accumulated enough capital and good will to start in business for herself. So they were men with an assured future. It must have been in early October, when the French still held a minuscular strip of German territory in the Saar. "Them, they're not here!" one pimp shouted. "Us, we're there! So we must be winning." A moment later, to emphasize some point or other, he started showing off his World War I wounds and yelled, "I bet I am the only pimp in France with three citations." The proprietor of the house in which they were arguing was a naturalized Italian who, his wife always said, was a perfect gentleman because he never drank anything but champagne. "Not even in the morning!" Madame Lucie would say, looking adoringly at the fat procurer—"not water, not coffee, not beer, not even *mousseux* have I ever seen him drink!" I sometimes used to watch a drop of sweat gleaming on his fat ear and wonder if it tasted of Irroy '28, his favorite. Madame Lucie never told me.

Nearly four years later I was to meet a colleague of the boys under a field ambulance tent on the way to Mateur and Bizerte. He was in the Corps Franc d'Afrique, a volunteer shock-troop outfit. When the nurses had cut his uniform jacket away they had found a tricolor wrapped around his chest. It sounds like the verse of a maudlin song, but it's true. A hunk of shrapnel had gone through the white part of the flag, which was now rust-red. The lower half of a tattooed female extended down toward his scrotum from the place where the flag stopped. When I asked him where he came from he didn't bother saying "Paris"—just "Nineteenth Arrondissement." That's Belleville—the stockyards. He had been wounded in the fighting around La Maison Forestière, in the high brush east of Cap Serrat. He had a mouthful of gold teeth and a tough chin. I asked him, foolishly, what he had done in civil life. He said, "I lived on my income."

I do not want to give the impression that I covered Paris for the *New Yorker* entirely from cafés and brothels. I took the responsibilities of my new career so seriously that I joined the Anglo-American Press Association of Paris and went at least once a week to the Hôtel Continental, where the French had set up their equivalent of the British Ministry of Information, although they did not give it the status of a full ministry until the following spring. My sponsors in the Press Association were H. R. Knickerbocker, then with International News Service, and Percy Philip of the New York *Times.* Knick was by way of being a popular hero in Paris because he had broken a big exclusive story about how Nazi leaders had opened bank accounts in a number of neutral countries, including several they were subsequently to take over. He was enthusiastic about the war, meeting me, his apartment on the Ile St.-Louis, the sound of the French language, which he could not speak, and the womanhood of Texas. On subsequent occasions I was to meet him being enthusiastic about Winston Churchill, the heroism of the English people, the inspirational gifts of Major General Terry Allen, and the sweetness and fortitude of American army nurses. He and a rear admiral named Clark Howell Woodward are the only two men I ever met in my life who admitted they liked making speeches.

I went up to Knick's apartment one evening with Robert de Saint-Jean of the American section of the Hôtel Continental. Nobody can say Knick wasn't catholic in his choice of guests; it included Edgar Ansel Mowrer on one end of the political scale

and on the other a pathological little Frenchman named Jean
Fontenoy who wore a turtle-neck sweater with a lounge suit
and moaned, whenever he could collect an audience, because
the Government refused to call him up for service in the Army.
He had been a notorious sucker-around-Abetz and pro-Nazi
before the war, a fellow who wrote books boasting of the misery of his peasant parents and preaching that misery was good
for working people. It kept them honest, according to him.
He, of course, considered he had had a quasi-divine call to the
masters' table. He kept on moaning in drugged tones now
because he could not get a commission, but he was destined to
make collaborationist speeches in theaters after the Armistice
and to be found in the Seine with his throat cut. He was the
first overt European-type fascist I had ever seen in the flesh,
and he had a horrid fascination for me, like the first man a kid
sees wearing lipstick and long black stockings. The tomato
man on the Clipper had been respectable by comparison.
There were not many like Fontenoy to be seen about Paris,
and those who did appear in public pretended, like him, that
everything had changed for them with the beginning of the
war and they were now great patriots. The uncostumed collaborationist types got along swimmingly. Only the turtle-neck
sweater boys got into a little trouble, and they not nearly
enough. The others had had sense enough to stop talking
when the war began, and newspapers friendly to them urged
the Government as a national duty to accept them in positions
of trust.

The Communists had been inept; they had publicly announced their position against the war, and they were being
hunted down as traitors, in many cases by Rightist policemen
who were more dangerous types than their quarry. The Maurrases and Lavals, the blackmailers and libelists of *L'Action
Française* and *Gringoire*, used the Communists skillfully to
divert suspicion from themselves. It was Henri de Kerillis, a
Rightist himself, who in a speech in the Chamber of Deputies
called attention to "the former apologists for the Nazis who
are now trying to turn the whole war into a crusade against
Stalin." The press almost unanimously reproved him for en-
dangering national unity.

You cannot keep your mind indefinitely on a war that does

not begin. Toward the end of the year many of the people who three months before had been ready to pop into their cellars like prairie dogs at the first purring of an airplane motor, expecting Paris to be expunged between dark and dawn, were complaining because restaurants did not serve beefsteak on Mondays, Tuesdays, and Fridays, and because the season had produced no new plays worth seeing. There was even a certain disappointment among the less reflective elements of the population; the appetite for disaster in some human beings is so strong that they feel let down when nothing terrible happens. Cartoonists had developed a number of war-time civilian characters in the genre of Caspar Milquetoast. One of them, a petit bourgeois called Bajus, was shown in a December comic strip listening to a radio address by Hitler. At each howl from the radio set ("I will destroy England before breakfast," "I will show the French what total war means") little Bajus' hair stood on end, and at the close of the speech he turned to his radio, saying, "Oh, please, Adolf, don't stop; frighten me again." Thousands of Bajuses felt deprived of the terror which had become the most interesting component of their daily lives.

There was, even during the fall and winter of 1939, one occasional feature of Paris life that provided a brief reminder of the war in progress. This was the firing of the anti-aircraft guns at German planes that came over on reconnaissance or to drop dirty pictures. The pictures showed British Tommies making love to naked French girls while a poilu died tangled in barbed wire. They fetched a good price from souvenir collectors. The planes never dropped any bombs, but the sound of guns fired in anger and the sight of searchlights combing the night sky is the beginning of a non-combatant's habituation to war. We were being broken in very gently.

The year slid to an end through a nearly normal Paris Christmas season, with carillons and lifesize mechanical figures in the windows of the Galeries Lafayette, postcard hucksters' stalls along the boulevards, and a special Christmas circus at the Medrano, with the three Fratellinis appearing as guest stars. The Medrano was the most delightful little circus in the world, with one ring that had a cushion around it like a billiard table. The liberty horses waved their hoofs in the faces of the spectators in front-row seats. The clowns, clown proper, *auguste* and *grotesque*, shared the hegemony of the ring with the equestrians, according to tradition. The great Fratellinis were not as limber as they had been in my student time, and they took fewer falls, but they had some good mechanical gags and their marvelous faces. The oldest brother got one of the big laughs of the evening when he made his entrance carrying a gas mask. In September every member of his audience had been carrying a similar affair.

The French like old favorites. They go to see them over and over again to observe how time is treating them, and if a performer appears to be in good health they are delighted. They have a weakness for old generals, too, old frock coats, old airplanes. They forget that even the best material wears out. Once Lieutenant Colonel Vincent Sheean and I were riding in an old French airplane in Algeria and the door blew off. There was no particular reason except that it was an old plane and an old door—the wind blew it away. The co-pilot laughed and grabbed my typewriter just as it was about to slide out of the hole the door had left. The conservative spirit is susceptible of exaggeration.

The Medrano was one of my favorite diversions that year. Another was walking along the quais, where the fishermen and book merchants of the Seine pursued the placid, even tenor of their lives. A third was passing one afternoon a week in the hushed interior of the Hamman, the old Turkish bath behind the opera. The Hamman had a dome of colored glass like a mosque and a plunge three strokes long. The icy water plashed into the plunge through the mouths of metal frogs. When you lay on your couch afterward, dozing, you could hear the soothing, nostalgic water-sound like a broken toilet in a New York rooming house. Old François, my favorite rubber, was a tall, stooped Parisian with a face like a rummy Vercingetorix. He was an urban fellow, like me. One day I told him that I was going to the country. He appeared worried, but finally said, "The country, yes. I have heard that it is simply swarming with oxygen."

CHAPTER VI

Vire Revisited

VIRE, like hundreds of other little French cities, showed little outward evidence of the war. About eight hundred of the 6,900 inhabitants Larousse credited the town with had been mobilized, but since Vire had become the home of 1,400 refugees from the war frontiers it had the largest population in its history. Its history goes back to Robert the Devil, who was William the Conqueror's father. Some of the refugees had money, and they had rented every available house in town; others, called "official refugees," got ten francs (less than twenty-five cents) a day from the Government. The mayor, a tall, desiccated doctor who looked like an old-fashioned New England practitioner, said, "It isn't much, of course, but they get along." He told me he didn't think much of the refugees. Soldiers' wives who were residents of Vire received only eight francs a day for themselves and four for each child. The wives, however, having roots in the district, usually had unmobilized relatives who gave them milk and butter and vegetables, for Vire lies in the best dairy country in France. It rains two days out of three from October until July, and nobody used to complain, because the rain made the pastures lush. Now that the Germans have taken away the cattle the rain may be resented.

The Paris newspapers had been paying a good deal of attention to events in the United States. The repeal of the Neutrality Act had got them started, and they had sent a number of reporters to the United States who promptly filed staggering stories of the vast American aircraft industry which was rolling fighter planes off assembly lines as fast as Fords. One plant a fellow described, I remember, was within a couple of miles of Hollywood, and all the most beautiful stars of the cinema used to come out in their automobiles of great luxury to watch the new planes taking the air like flocks of birds. I was astonished myself when I got back to New York after the debacle to find that we had been producing less than three hundred planes a month, of all categories, at the period of the *grands reportages*.

This sort of thing was to cause a disastrous reaction in the spring, when the ground troops discovered that the flocks of airplanes were a myth.

The press of Vire remained strictly cisatlantic. One of the two weeklies, *Le Bocage*, headed its column of criminal proceedings with the news that butter, jam, cake, and sugar had been stolen from one Madame Grandérie by an eleven-year-old boy from a village called Beauquay who had entered her house by climbing a pear tree and breaking three window-panes. The next item told of the arrest of Joseph Jegu for mendicancy. "Let us add," said *Le Bocage*, "that the individual had a pocketful of money."

When I got to Vire I went to my old hotel, the Cheval Blanc, but found it had changed proprietors. The new man was not nearly as good a cook as the old, who had gone to Angers and taken over a larger hotel also called the Cheval Blanc, but food was as plentiful as before. Outside the grocery stores hung rows of silvery herrings, each with a nail through its tail; the grocers' windows were full of the black smoked sausages called *andouilles de Vire*; the cabbages and onions grew with tropical eagerness in the kitchen gardens even in November. All the local sauces were based on cream and butter and apple brandy —it was a fat country. I wonder how the Virois eat now.

I asked a postman, whom I saw in the café of the hotel, whether old M. Hédouin, the librarian, was still alive, and he said he wasn't.

The economic pulse was steady, I soon found. The farmers were selling beef cattle and horses to the Army at a fixed price which was not a bad one, and there was a new, mysterious war factory among the *vaux*, a mile or two above the town. The countryside reminded me again of southern New England, with rolling hills, birch and holly, elm and oak, except that in the *Bocage* the people had used granite for building houses and barns instead of walls between fields; they marked their boundaries with bands of standing birch and poplar trees. The wet climate has made the Virois quieter than Frenchmen who live in the sun—and harder drinkers. Apple brandy is their regional tipple, and all apple brandy in France is called Calvados in honor of the department in which Vire lies. All over France men had called on the name of this department at marble-topped tables and zinc-topped bars, twenty-four hours a day almost, counting the Paris marketmen who work all night and are great drinkers. Affectionately they had contracted the name to *Calva*, a beautiful name for a drunkard's girl child if any reader wants a tip.

War was no new or strange word in Vire; the Normans had fought the French there, the French the English, and the Huguenots the Catholics; one wall of a transept of the twelfth-century church was covered with the names of Virois killed in War '14. The mayor, to annoy the curé, always told visitors to Vire that the church dated only from the thirteenth century. He was a Conservative Republican, the mayor, which put him in about the same category as a Republican in Vermont. There were few Marxians in Vire, where they still talked of the French Revolution as a fairly recent event. But they accepted the fact of the Republic as unquestioningly as Vermont farmers do.

Le Bocage had an opposition weekly, *Croix du Bocage*, dedicated to the Catholic point of view. Both papers printed letters from Virois with the Army who said that they were playing with their regimental soccer teams, or wanted sweaters. Both papers published the citation of a lieutenant, the son of a dentist in a neighboring town, who, in one of the skirmishes of outposts in which the armies sometimes indulged, had led a detachment in the capture of a German blockhouse and had operated a machine gun after the death of the gunner. That sort of thing then seemed to an American Homeric.

Headquarters for civilian strategists in Vire was the Café de Paris, where the proprietor, whom I found playing innumerable games of dominoes with all comers, was Maurice Brocco, a man who once enjoyed immense seasonal fame in New York as the little six-day bike rider the crowds at Madison Square Garden liked above all others. Something about him amused the bleary-eyed nocturnal public, and for a long time after he retired Garden fans continued to yell "Come on, Brocco!" when there was a jam.

Brocco is French; he was born near Reims, in the Champagne, which is a flat country favorable to the development of bicyclists. He found, however, that Italian riders were drawing the gate in New York, and since his name sounded Italian he usually rode on the Italian team. It always tickled

him when the Italians in the infield yelled, "*Avanti, Brocco!*"
In Vire, as might have been expected, Brocco in his cap and
sweater was the pattern of dashing cosmopolitanism. I thought
that even the mayor, who referred to Brocco as "that good
rooster," was a bit jealous of him. With me to bear him out
Brocco told the other customers terrible lies about prohibition
in America. The lies reconciled them to the wartime prices of
apéritifs.

On a hill near the town there still stood part of a castle built
by Henry Beauclerc, the youngest son of William the Conqueror; and at the foot of the hill the gipsies still camped as
they had done seasonally since the tribe came to Europe,
snaring rabbits for their food. I came back from the trip feeling
pretty good about France.

The through train from Granville to Paris stopped at Vire.
When I got aboard I found in the first-class compartment I entered a short, thick-necked, thick-bodied little captain of an
Algerian regiment, a fellow with badger-gray hair and clipped
mustache who was reading a worn clothbound American edition of *The Man That Corrupted Hadleyburg.* "I reread it
often," he said in French, noticing me looking at his book. "It
is a taste I took in the Cameroons, where I was in garrison for
three years. This volume I acquired on a ship where I was of
passage to there. Like so many, I read English but I am afraid
to speak it. The book has a theme truly French, and an exqui-
site 'humor.'"

The little captain's regiment was in the northeast, he said,
up beyond the end of the old Maginot Line. He was returning
from a visit to two married sisters in Granville. He himself had
spent most of his life between wars in the colonies—his regiment belonged to the standing army. "It is a splendid regiment," he said. "No *chichi*—just Normans and Kabyles. Most
of the native non-coms fought in the other war. They are hard,
like the old Roman legionaries." In the North the French were
building formidable field defenses, he said. The captain, like
scores of Frenchmen I used to talk to, said that he had been
ashamed of the abandonment of the Little Entente. Daladier,
on his way back from Munich to Paris, had correctly anticipated this feeling. The anecdote of how he drove from Le
Bourget to the Quai d'Orsay expecting catcalls and was aston-

ished by being cheered instead is by now familiar, like his comment, "*Les cons!*" But the "spontaneous" demonstrators in the streets were the same hirelings who led the February 1934 riots, working for precisely the same employers—the eternal Nazi-lovers of the industrial cartels. Men of the caliber of my little captain never went into the streets to yell their thoughts at passing limousines. Daladier, a good Frenchman though perhaps a weak man, was puzzled; within a short while he knew that his first intuition had been right. He could not have abandoned Poland without provoking the disintegration of France.

"From Czechoslovakia the Czechs and Russians, and we from the headwaters of the Rhine—the movement of the shovel, what could have been more simple!" the little captain said. "But it would have meant giving up the concept of a defensive war behind the Maginot Line," he added. "You do not know what the concept means to us. It means the high wall topped with broken bottles that the provincial bourgeois puts around his garden. Behind it he is secure with his cabbages. He can wear his slippers, live the good life without bothering to button all the buttons of his trousers. Because I have lived so long outside metropolitan France I can see this."

CHAPTER VII

Merry Christmas, Horrid New Year

IF YOU were a correspondent in France in 1939 and wanted to go up to the French front you addressed a letter to Mr. Maynard Barnes at the United States Embassy, telling your place of birth, your journalistic history, some reference, and your reason for wishing to go. Barnes forwarded your request to the Intelligence Section at General Headquarters, and in a week or so you were usually granted a pink paper called "A Special Mission Accorded by the General Staff for the Purpose of Journalism," which was good for a week or ten days. You picked up the paper at the Intelligence Section bureau in the

Hôtel Continental, where Madame Gros-Perrin, a stout imperious woman with a good laugh, gave you instructions for getting to the front. She told you to go to Nancy and to wait at
the Hôtel Thiers there for a press officer from the Intelligence
Section who would have further instructions for you. She told
you to carry a gas mask and a field helmet. I already owned a
gas mask the first time I went up, but I borrowed an American
helmet from Captain Bob Schow, one of the assistant military
attachés at our embassy. The American helmet then looked a
bit like the British job; our new helmets resemble the German.

I left Paris on my first "mission" on December 23. I took the
noon train to Nancy, which rolled at its peacetime express clip
until nightfall, when, because of the dimmed signal lights, it
dropped into a cautious crawl. Arriving at Nancy that night, I
found the town blacked out completely. Luckily the hotel was
directly across the street from the station, so I was able to
reach it without any trouble. A woman at the hotel desk told
me that the press officer had not arrived yet, but if I cared to
step into the *brasserie* of the hotel I would find a number of
other American and English correspondents awaiting him. I
could immediately distinguish the correspondents in the
brasserie because their uniforms were much more magnificent
than those of the French military at the other tables. A particularly tailored-looking uniform on Pashkoff, a photographer
for *Life*, had the French officers gnawing their mustaches with
envy. The most lavishly accoutered man I have seen in France
turned out to be an employee of the Columbia Broadcasting
System. Since I was trying to get by in riding pants and a
vaguely brownish topcoat, I felt like the only ship passenger in
a lounge suit at the captain's dinner. I was cheered by the costume of a Mr. Browne of the *Christian Science Monitor*, who
had come to the war in tweeds. After one look at each other,
Browne and I decided to stick together so that we wouldn't
feel inferior.

Most of the correspondents, it developed, were planning to
go to a great Christmas Eve midnight Mass in a fortress of the
Maginot Line. Columbia and N.B.C. were to broadcast the
Mass, and a number of the newsreel companies were to film it.
Before the press officer appeared, I was afraid that I would be
packed off to the broadcast with all the others, since the Intel-

ligence Section, I figured, probably thought that all Americans were hysterically fond of *radiodiffusion*. But the officer gave Browne and me permission to take a train to Alsace the next afternoon and visit the front there. An officer would call for us when we arrived at a station the captain named, and in due time we would be allowed to see the front.

When, early the next afternoon, we got to our station, we could see we had arrived at the war, because there were no women in sight. Here, against a background of brown, frozen earth and sleety roads, of trees covered with rime, and of the ugly, amorphous buildings of a railway-junction town, there were only soldiers. Most of the men on our train were *permissionnaires* returning from furlough. They lingered around the railroad station unhappily, like students returning from a holiday, then moved off in the direction of their cantonments. Browne and I didn't bother to look for our officer; we were so incongruous in that crowd that he couldn't possibly miss us. After we had waited awhile, an officer stopped in front of us. He had a square jaw and high Celtic cheekbones, and was about as big as a Brooklyn baseball pitcher. "Lieutenant Sauvageon," he announced as he saluted, "aviation officer of the Divisional Staff." Sauvageon stepped aside, and we could see another officer behind him, a slight, smiling man who carried a bamboo cane and maintained a monocle in his right eye. Introducing him to us, Sauvageon said, "Captain de Cholet is one of the few cavalrymen in our sector. He is on the staff also." "I have a horse," the captain said, "but he is in Paris."

A soldier came up, took the one valise in which Browne and I had concentrated our possessions, and carried it to a 1936 Citroën that had a red-and-white-striped pennon on the forward end of the left mudguard. "*Fanion du général*," the soldier volunteered pleasantly, pointing to the pennon. The soldier's name, we learned, was Siegfried. It was a standing joke with the captain and the lieutenant that Siegfried, who was an Alsatian, had constructed the Siegfried Line. Browne and I rode in the rear with the captain between us, and the lieutenant sat in front with Siegfried, who drove. It was about three o'clock in the afternoon. The road was glassy and the mist was very heavy. "Evidently it is not a good day for observation," said the captain. "Moreover, we are sufficiently distant from anything to observe. Therefore, Lieutenant, where can we buy a drink?" "Siegfried," said the lieutenant, "can you discover the mess of the balloonists?" Siegfried did not answer, but after ten minutes of blind navigation he landed us in front of a shuttered tavern.

We all walked into the taproom, which was decorated with a green tile stove, a Christmas tree, and enough antlers to fit out a small museum. At a heavy, bare table a half-dozen soldiers of the Balloon Corps sat with anilin-dyed apéritifs, wrangling over a card game. A young lieutenant got up from among them to greet us. The officers' mess was upstairs, he explained, but he was the only officer in the house, so he had come down to the bar for company. We invited the lieutenant to join us, and Siegfried took his hand at the card table. We all ordered hot grog, and the drink stimulated Browne to ask the balloonist if he had seen anything of a war which, according to the people in the United States, was at that moment in progress between France and Germany. The lieutenant, it seemed, had actually been under fire. The company had an observation balloon at a near-by field, and twice, when it was up, Messerschmitts had come after it. Both times the ground crew had pulled the bag down safely. Lieutenant Sauvageon said that several German machines had come down in the sector. "Curiously," he added, "three of them were undamaged. The pilots said they were airsick. We reported them as shot down because we did not want their families to have any trouble in Germany."

After talking awhile, we said good-by to the balloonist, wished him a merry Christmas, and went out to the Citroën. By now we might as well have been in somebody's pocket for all we could see, but Siegfried, who knew the terrain, was able to feel his way. "It is now evidently quite impracticable even to try to observe," the captain said, "so we will take you to the fort where you are to lodge tonight. It is an old German fort, one they built after they took Alsace from us. It is not a very good fort, but is comfortable, and when we get there the colonel will buy us a drink." Sauvageon, still seated in front, turned around and said, "We picked this colonel specially for you because he is having a big Christmas party and he will have the best oysters and *foie gras* in the sector, better even than the general's. He is a Parisian and he likes to talk to visitors because he has been in the fort now for four months."

It took a long time to reach the fort, and when we arrived we had to cross a drawbridge spanning a moat to get to it. The forts the Germans built after '71 have the pseudomedieval quality of the National Guard armories in New York City. We entered by a wide, high portal and found ourselves in a thoroughly non-functional place of echoing corridors and vaulted ceilings. It seemed to have been built by people who enjoyed playing soldier. I couldn't help asking the first man to introduce himself to us, an artillery lieutenant, whether the fort had any defensive value against modern ordnance, since Siegfried had informed me we were only about five kilometers from the Rhine. "It would stand up to machine guns and field artillery," he said, "but a heavy shell hitting squarely would go right through the roof to the powder vaults, where there isn't any powder now anyhow. But we wouldn't use the fort to fight from. The regiment is scattered all over this part of the sector by batteries. All we have here is a headquarters company, a medical unit, a telephone central, and a guardhouse."

We all went into the mess hall to wait for the colonel, which, we were told, was the warmest place in the fort. There were two clusters of German lances on the wall, left behind by the Imperial Army when the French occupied Alsace. Captain de Cholet looked at them tenderly and said, "I left for the last war carrying a lance. I even managed once to stick a German with one, but later war ceased to be fresh and joyful." Sauvageon nodded sympathetically. Before long the colonel walked in. He was tall, straight, and consciously picturesque. He wore a brown beret which was barely balanced on the side of his head, like Rodolfo's in *La Bohème*. His cheeks were old rose and his eyes cobalt blue, and his long white mustaches did not droop, but descended in a powerful, rhythmic sweep, like the horns of a musk ox. He was an excellent colonel, we had been informed; he had commanded a large part of the heavy artillery in the campaign around Salonika twenty years ago. Between wars he was a banker in Paris.

"Gentlemen," the colonel said, after we were introduced, "I welcome you to the humble barrack of a sick old man. It is not the Meurice. It is not the Plaza Athénée. The fare is not that of Au Cabaret or the Berkeley." We assured him that his fort would do us very well. A soldier then wheeled over a tea wagon holding about twenty bottles—scotch, port, sherry, and various apéritifs. The colonel took an obvious pride in his gamut of alcohols; it proved he could "defend himself." The verb "*se défendre*" had acquired a very broad meaning in the French Army; it signified "getting along." An officer pulled a pair of old socks over his shoes so that he would not slip on the ice; a private met a stray hen and wrung her neck because otherwise she might fly into Germany; soldiers going on patrol in wooded parts of no man's land set rabbit snares so that on their way back they might pick up a tasty breakfast—all these expedients were part of the French concept of self-defense. It followed logically that a colonel defended himself on a grander scale than a subordinate.

De Cholet and Sauvageon took their leave. The staff, they said, had to accompany the general to midnight Mass. It would not be precisely gay; the general was a great friend of the bishop's. They promised to call for Browne and me early in the morning. As we talked to the colonel, most of the officers of his mess joined us around the tea wagon.

Shortly afterward the officers took their places around a large mess table for dinner. Browne and I were invited to sit flanking the colonel. I had on my right a fair-haired, blue-eyed captain, a Jew from Strasbourg. He said that two uncles and an elder brother of his had deserted from the German Army at the beginning of the war in 1914 and had fought with the French. Being only thirteen years old at the time, he had remained at home. In 1918 he had been conscripted into the German Army and had been stationed in that very fort. In civil life he was an industrial engineer. Most of the officers, he said, were, like himself, reservists, but a number of men from "the active" had been inducted into the regiment at the beginning of the war to set the pace for them. The soldiers were young reservists in the later twenties, and three quarters of them were Alsatians or Lorrainers. "This is a regiment that must be mobilized on the spot at the beginning of a war, because Germany is just across the river," he explained.

Before the dinner could begin, the *popotier*, or mess officer, had to make what I was told was a traditional address. In this particular mess, the popotier was a round, embarrassed little man with bulging eyes. He was an *adjudant* and the only member of the mess who wasn't a fully commissioned officer. "My colonel and gentlemen," he began, standing before his plate at the foot of the table, "I have the pleasure to announce——" He was interrupted by shouts of indignation and, correcting himself, said, "The *honor* and the pleasure to announce to you that the menu tonight, the twenty-fourth of December, will consist of soup of leeks and potatoes (a few scattered shouts of "That's what we had the day before yesterday!"), cauliflower au gratin ("O miserable popotier, without imagination!"), salad, cheese, fruits, and, as wine, Châteauneuf-du-Pape." "Thank you, popotier," the colonel said solemnly, "provided only that the Châteauneuf is tolerable."

The dinner was polished off with businesslike haste because there was a full evening ahead of us. After coffee and armagnac, a Christmas mood began to seem more attainable. We all walked along a corridor and down a flight of stairs to an unused powder vault which the soldiers had turned into a *salle de théâtre*. The walls of the vault had been painted to give a three-dimensional illusion of draperies, and at one end of the room there was a real curtain of the same color as the painted ones.

To one side of the curtain stood a great Christmas tree decorated with lighted candles. An orchestra, made up of a violin, saxophone, and piano, played what most Europeans think is the American anthem, "The Stars and Stripes Forever." There were about two hundred soldiers in the vault, wearing ugly, solid shoes and long khaki overcoats that looked like horse blankets. The men were in a state of juvenile excitement. An evening of amateur entertainment was a great event. The leader of the orchestra was a tall, flat-chested fellow with shiny hair and a receding chin. The surgeon major told me that the man was a Berliner who had acquired French citizenship by serving in the Foreign Legion.

After a long overture, a master of ceremonies appeared before the curtain wearing a Prince Albert coat. "Our first number," he announced, "will be a song by our Alsatian chorus —*Rose des Landes*." The chorus was made up of eleven artillerymen, each standing with feet wide apart and thumbs in his belt. "*Röslein, Röslein, Röslein rot, Röslein auf der Heide*," they sang. The non-Alsatian officers and men applauded mightily. As an encore, the chorus sang a marching song which began, "*O Strassburg, O Strassburg, du wunderschöne Stadt*." Then the choirmaster sang a long folk song about the character of the Alsatian people. I remember only one line: "A donkey is no hummingbird." The blond Jewish captain from Strasbourg said to me, "That is the Alsatian situation in one line. We refuse to be what we are not." Soldiers from Brittany and the Midi sang next, and a Parisian corporal delighted all the provincials by losing his nerve completely and breaking down in the middle of a line, belying the metropolitan reputation for nonchalance.

After the last turn there was a rough-and-tumble drawing of Christmas presents. Then the colonel made a speech. The merriest soldier was the best soldier, he said, but the poor, forlorn fellow on outpost duty on the bluffs rising from the Rhine must not be forgotten. He said he was sure every man there would gladly be killed rather than let the Boches pass. "It is very necessary for us to win this war," he added. I think everybody there agreed with him. "There will be a midnight Mass in our new chapel," he announced, "for those who care to attend. This is a free country." I noticed that almost everyone did go to chapel, including those who didn't cross themselves.

After Mass the officers went back to the mess hall for supper. They were in high spirits because they felt that their men had enjoyed the evening's entertainment. In that phase of the war one of the officers' hardest tasks was to keep their men from getting bored. Now the officers had a chance to enjoy themselves, and they were in such good humor that the popotier got through his ritual speech unheckled. There was a slight commotion among the diners, however, when the mess attendants served the consommé in soup plates. "There is a curse upon the mess!" grumbled the surgeon major. "There are no cups for the consommé!" After oysters and some *foie gras de Strasbourg au Porto*, we all began to drink champagne.

We had been sitting at the table for some time when suddenly the colonel shouted, "The battery departs! At a walk!" Immediately the officers began rapping their knuckles on the table, to produce the effect of horses walking. "At a trot!" the colonel ordered. The tempo of the rapping increased. "At a gallop!" The rapping grew faster. "Halt!" There was a second of silence, and the colonel shouted, "First gun—fire!" All the men brought their right fists crashing down on the table. "Second gun—fire!" "Third gun—fire!" "Fourth gun—fire!" After each "Fire!" the table took a sterner thump. After the fourth gun, the officers began to grin shyly, like small boys anticipating the point of a familiar joke. "Fifth gun!" ordered the colonel. That was the cue for the senior captain to speak up, with considerable gravity. "There isn't any, my colonel." (There are only four guns in a French battery.) The colonel appeared dumfounded. Then he recovered. "That doesn't matter!" he shouted. "Fire!" The officers hit the table with both fists. A glass broke, a bottle rolled onto the floor, one dignified-looking captain, overcome with laughter, fell on the neck of the surgeon major.

The party broke up at five o'clock in the morning. The only officer who seemed mildly unhappy was a gangling, thin-lipped captain, a transfer from the regular army, who said to the colonel doubtfully, "This is all very well, my colonel, but it isn't really war." The colonel, whose chest was covered with campaign ribbons and decorations from 1914–18, stopped chuckling and looked at the captain steadily. "Sometime you may look back on this evening," he said, "and you will say, 'The days at the fort were the good ones.' What the devil! A fellow has to defend himself."

I suppose they have looked back upon that evening infinitely often since the Armistice, when practically all of them became prisoners of war. As far as I could ever learn, the regiment was pulled back from the Rhine in early June of 1940, when the Germans had gotten behind the eastern defenses at both the northern and southern ends. Some of them got back into the Vosges, because Sauvageon the aviator, who was himself transferred from that area before the debacle and so did not become a prisoner, wrote to me that one officer I knew had been killed at Hohwald, a summer resort in the mountains fifty miles from Strasbourg. Long before the war I had stayed at Hohwald and walked over the hills to the monastery of St. Odile to drink the white wine called Lacrimae Sanctae Odiliae.

CHAPTER VIII

Colonel Albatross

BROWNE and I slept briefly, in a kind of dungeon where the stone walls sweated icicles, after the Christmas Eve celebration. Then Sauvageon and De Cholet arrived to take us to see the Germans.

The bridge across the Rhine between Kehl and Strasbourg remained intact, although for reasons easy to understand traffic over it had been light since the first of September. The mist on the river Christmas morning was so heavy that the French soldiers in the little redoubt on the Strasbourg side were hampered in their game of trying to see Germans through their machine-gun sights. They were not often allowed to shoot, mist or no mist, but at any rate they could look, and the Germans played the same game and sometimes talked to the French in French with a public-address system. The bridge was perhaps eight hundred feet long, and between the French and German redoubts at either end were elaborate festoons of barbed wire, which, when coated with white frost, produced a fine decorative effect.

It was cold on Christmas, and fog had covered the hard earth with a thin glaze of ice. The French soldiers holding the bridgehead were well pleased with themselves, for a young corporal from Lunéville had made his way across the bridge during the night and had stolen a Christmas tree which the Germans had set up in their barbed wire. He had also collected a few German newspapers he found lying about in front of the enemy redoubt, and the tree, decorated with strips of the newspapers, now surmounted the French post. All the company officers, from the captain to the tall, red-bearded second lieutenant who *dans la civile* had been a Protestant pastor, had formally scolded the corporal and then shaken his hand. The corporal, a nineteen-year-old volunteer, said, "What tickles me is that now they'll court-martial the sentinel over there. Those sentinels think they're wise guys, bawling us out with their loud-speaker." The troops did not shoot except when they lost their tempers badly, for they realized that shooting would only increase their common discomfort, but the lull had if anything increased the antipathy between the two forces. When I heard how seldom anybody fired I said I wanted to look over the parapet at the Germans, but the captain at the bridgehead made me take off my American helmet first. "If they think you are an Englishman they may fire," he said. "They have never seen any Englishmen down here, so we cannot say what the result would be." I looked over bareheaded and cannot truthfully say that I observed anybody.

A couple of months later when Sauvageon was in Paris on a ten-day leave he told me of a curious incident in this sector. There were two casemates that faced each other like these, but across an even narrower unbridged stretch of the Rhine. A German colonel, a nasty-looking fellow, used to come out of the German redoubt every evening to smoke a cigar by the water's edge and cock a snook at the French. One evening he started to *pipi* in the river, the better to mark his contempt. A French lieutenant on the left bank stepped to the loud-speaker and said, "You exaggerate. Get away from there or I shoot." The colonel cocked another snook and the lieutenant cut loose on him with a machine gun. The colonel fell on his back, Sauvageon said, his cigar flew out of his mouth, he was dead. Then the German loud-speaker was heard. The Germans said they were coming out to get the colonel's body; they had no hard feelings against anybody but the lieutenant, they said, but if the French fired on the men coming out for the body they would make it a general feud. The French in the casemate were angry at the lieutenant; they considered him in the light of the man who had shot the albatross that shielded them from harm. They did not fire on the Germans again, and they made life so miserable for the lieutenant during the succeeding weeks that he had to ask to be transferred to another casemate. Sauvageon said that he considered this an unhealthy *état d'esprit*. So did I.

The holiday season afforded a precious chance to break the monotony of the long pause, and the army in Alsace was taking full advantage of it. Hunting, for some ridiculous reason, was against the law in wartime even for soldiers, but that did not affect the supply of venison at the front. As one commandant blandly put it, "If deer insist on strangling themselves on the barbed wire, what can one do?" His explanation of the pheasant served at his mess was equally ingenuous. "The battalion medical officer runs over a dozen whenever he goes cycling," he said. "As he is not a veterinary he is unable to save their lives. So we eat them."

General Pichon, the *divisionnaire* at whose mess we stopped for Christmas supper, told us how he had visited a dugout in a forest and found a soldier skinning three rabbits he had illegally snared. "Sir," said the startled soldier, "I had just withdrawn my rifle from the loophole when in jumped these poor rabbits, one after another, and died of fear." "The poor unfortunates," the general had replied, turning to go out and continue his rounds. "Nature is cruel."

In some regiments in the sector eighty per cent of the men were Alsatians. Some had all their possessions locked away in apartments in Strasbourg, whence their families had been removed to Périgord. Strasbourg, through which our guides had Siegfried drive us, was incredibly sad. Ruins are something anyone can understand; but Strasbourg had simply been emptied of life; the stage and all the properties remained. Hats remained in modistes' windows, and beer glasses still stood on café tables where the drinkers had left them the day the war started. In the Place Kleber, where in other years one of the world's finest municipal Christmas trees had always stood, there was a tiny balsam surrounded by bread crumbs; it was a Christmas tree put up by the military police for the abandoned pigeons of the cathedral. With the Corps Franc in Tunisia long afterward I met a towheaded, blue-eyed sixteen-year-old volunteer. "What are you?" I asked him, because the Corps Franc has many German and Austrian and Dutch refugees in it. "French," the boy said. "What city in France?" "Strasbourg," he said, "the most beautiful." It was more than two years since Goebbels had announced the "incorporation" of Alsace-Lorraine in the Reich—like a louse on a man announcing he had now "incorporated" his host.

After Strasbourg, Nancy seemed feverishly gay. The cafés closed at eight-thirty, the blackouts were much blacker than the Paris kind, but there were still women to see and there was even an English correspondent's mess in the Hôtel Thiers, where, by special dispensation of the police, a visitor might stay up and drink as late as twelve o'clock if the lone, crusty old waiter didn't take it into his head to go home before that.

I spent the next couple of days on a conducted tour of a couple of Maginot Line fortifications near St. Avold in Lorraine. They seemed to me excellently contrived, like all the Maginot forts shown to correspondents. They contained mortars and anti-tank cannon but no heavy artillery. The heavy artillery, my conducting officer explained, was several miles back of the Maginot forts proper. This was so that the big guns might be shifted about on the "interior lines" beloved of military writers. Unfortunately interior lines by definition have to be inside something, and the exterior line of fortifications did not exist from Montmédy to the sea. The Germans were to push through unfortified space until they had got behind the left shoulder of the permanent Maginot Line and take it in reverse. As they approached each fort from the left rear, the heavy artillery would have to be pulled out from behind it. That would have left the men in the fort exposed to continual heavy artillery fire without hope of counter-battery. The fort on the extreme left end of the line was taken in this way. It held out through one hundred hours of continuous shelling. No troops came out alive. I heard about it on June 6 from Meyer Handler of the United Press, who had just returned from that sector. Most of the rest of the line was abandoned without fighting.

I returned to Paris on an express train that still had fine, crowded *wagons-restaurants*. These express trains were reserved for officers and civilians. Across the table from me I had a tall, earnest young lieutenant of an infantry regiment that had distinguished itself in the early fall fighting around Forbach. "There are only two armies in the world," he told me with assurance. "Us and them."

CHAPTER IX

Sample Supermen

A FEW WEEKS after I came back from the Maginot Line I went into Lorraine again to see some Germans in a prison camp.

The staff officer who accompanied me seemed embarrassed because there were no large groups of prisoners to see, as there would have been in the last war. "Unfortunately," he said as we set out from Paris, "we have taken few prisoners—perhaps a couple of hundred since the beginning of the war. It's the same with the Germans, of course. We have only the fellows that we bag on patrols between the lines, and the aviators who are shot down in our territory. You can't get many aviators at a time, though."

My guide had served as an artilleryman at the front from 1914 to 1918; now he had an office in the Ministry of War and spent much of his time journeying about to inspect his customers, as he called the prisoners, and to prepare for the reception of more. The camp we were going to was situated in a small city some fifty miles on the French side of the Maginot Line. In our railroad compartment, as we journeyed, the staff officer told me a good deal about prisoners of war. They are supposed to be treated, he said, in accordance with an international agreement signed at Geneva ten years ago, and since prisoners are, in a way, hostages, the three belligerents on the western front respected its terms. Germany did not show the same consideration for Polish prisoners, of whom there were thousands, he said, her official reason being that she did not recognize the Polish Government-in-exile. The real reason, naturally, was that no Germans were being held prisoner by the Poles. German prisoners who felt they were being abused might appeal to the Reich's "protecting power," which, in the case of France, was Sweden. France's protecting power in Germany was, at the time of my trip, the United States. Moreover, the International Red Cross inspected the camps of both sides, so all in all a reasonably close check was kept on the prison officials of the belligerents, he thought.

According to the Geneva agreement, prisoners of war are entitled to living conditions as good as those enjoyed by the garrison troops of the army that has captured them. The troops guarding the prison camps provide a practical measuring stick in this matter: prisoners have a right to the same rations and the same amount of space per man in their dormitories as their guards, and their beds must be as comfortable. They even receive from their captors the same pay as soldiers of equivalent rank in the army that has made prisoners of them. At the end of the war each side will be expected to reimburse the other for this pay. The scheme had worked out well enough so far between France and Germany, although there had been occasional grumbling among the prisoners themselves. The French at home are normally better fed than the Germans, and the Germans are better housed than the French. The men were sensitive to these differences, and to others which similarly upset their habits. The German prisoners, for example, got a ration of wine they couldn't appreciate, French prisoners got beer they didn't like, and neither French nor German can tolerate the other's smoking tobacco.

What I thought of most, going up on the train, was that I was at last to see some Nazis. I had not been in Germany since 1927, and it had been hard for me to understand how the uncertain-looking people I remembered from that trip had become so formidable. I wondered if I would see anybody resembling the thick-legged, bull-necked Storm Troopers in the cartoons left-wing magazines used to publish before the Reich-Soviet pact, or if there would be any of those German idealists you heard about who would say that Nazism was hollow and false. I asked the staff officer if he had heard of such a case of regeneration in any of the camps, and he looked at me as if he thought me remarkably silly. "No," he said. "Even if a prisoner were against Hitler he wouldn't say so, because he is still under the orders of whatever German noncommissioned officers are also at the camp." Commissioned officers were not quartered with the noncommissioned officers and the rank-and-file prisoners. "Anyway," my guide went on, "most prisoners have families in Germany. None of them argue about politics among themselves, except for some Austrians we have in another camp. They seem to think they would not be in this trouble if it were not for the other Germans, and a while back there was a bit of a row about that. Those Austrians are quite a problem. On the other hand, you will find this lot of prisoners we are going to see a very well-disciplined troop. There is an unusually high ratio of noncommissioned officers to men in this camp—about two to five. That is because many of them are aviation prisoners, and only officers and noncommissioned officers fly." I asked what would happen to a German soldier if, regarding the war as over so far as he was concerned, he told one of his German superiors in prison where to get off. The staff officer looked shocked. "We'd put the soldier in the guardhouse," he said. "It would be insubordination."

An army automobile was waiting when we arrived. It was only a five-minute drive out to the prison, a group of buildings which, I was told, had once been a factory. They were arranged in a rectangle, with a yard in the center and a gate at one end. Most of them had slanting glass roofs and were at least thirty feet high, with concrete floors and no upper stories. Halfway up on their walls were rows of enormous windows. The administration offices were near the gate, in what had been the offices of the firm which occupied the factory. We found the commanding officer waiting for us; he had not yet had enough visitors to be bored by them, and he seemed glad of a break in routine. He was a paternal, red-faced captain who appeared capable of taking a sympathetic view of the plight of a prisoner. Beside him was a tall, kind-looking old major, with a pink, bald head and gold-rimmed spectacles, who was introduced to me as an interpreter. The major said he had lived in Germany a long time and thought he understood the German mentality, although he did not approve of it.

The prisoners, it turned out, were in the section of the factory farthest from the gate, and on our way to see them we— the captain, the staff officer, the major, and I—had a chance to look over much of the plant. As we went from one unit to another we passed guards—men of forty or older, selected from a regiment of reserves. The Quartermaster Corps had fitted them out with antique uniforms of horizon blue, and for hats they had old Tank Corps helmets. Almost all looked like peasants, with long arms and hard muscles, and since all had fought in the last war, they handled their rifles with assurance.

The guards saluted dutifully as we passed, and that reminded the captain of something. "Wait till you see the Germans," he said, a trifle apologetically. "They *like* to salute." He showed me the guards' bunkhouse so that I could compare their quarters with those of the prisoners later on. The guards had two tiers of fairly wide bunks with metal frames and straw-filled mattresses; the only other furniture was a row of lockers. We walked on through a series of rooms which had been prepared for the reception of prisoners not yet captured. Barbed-wire fences had been rigged up inside all along the walls to keep prisoners away from the windows.

As we approached the occupied unit I heard a man shouting, and by the time we got inside, the prisoners there had quickly formed a double rank in the center of the room. A young German at the head of the platoon was bawling happily the Teutonic equivalents of "Eyes left! Eyes right! Right dress! Attention!" Spines snapped back convulsively, chins jerked up as if each of the Germans in line had received an invisible uppercut. They seemed to enjoy this rigmarole. Their leader turned to the captain with a magnificent salute, as if he had just performed a difficult trick and expected the captain to throw him a bouquet. The captain said hurriedly, "At ease," and looked flustered by so much attention. The German noncom turned on his men. "At ease," he said in a disappointed voice. The men relaxed, appearing depressed at not being asked to do more tricks. The captain said to me, in the tone of a curator explaining an unusual exhibit, "You see? It is their particular mentality."

I walked around the room, an immense one with a concrete floor and brick walls. There was no barbed wire in this unit; the windows were smaller and placed higher than in most parts of the plant. The Germans evidently spent most of their time in the part of the room nearest the door, to be close to the coal stoves which heated the place. The men's cots were arranged head to head in two long rows; they were not double-deckers, like the bunks of the guards, but had the same sort of frames and mattresses. Beyond the cots were a row of rough tables and several long benches. There were books on some of the beds, on which the Germans had evidently been reclining before we came in, and there were chess sets and playing cards on the tables. These little luxuries, I was told, had been sent to the men by their families, who are allowed to send letters and packages, but not newspapers, to the prison. A narrow shelf, with things on it like tooth powder and combs, ran along part of one wall. Each prisoner had a section of the shelf for his possessions and had written his name under it—Hoffmann, Betz, Keil, Muller E., Muller J. were some I noticed. I also noticed a portrait of Goering, torn out of a German magazine; above the portrait was a chunk of wood with a swastika burned into it. There was another picture, also from a magazine, showing tugboats and ice floes in the harbor of Bremen. Near it was a pencil drawing labeled "*Morgenstund*," which showed a snub-nosed prisoner, stripped to the waist, brushing his teeth in front of a troughlike sink, with a mustachioed sentry, helmeted and carrying a rifle with fixed bayonet, standing vigilantly in the background.

The Germans, eighty or ninety of them, remained standing at ease. With few exceptions they appeared to be between twenty and thirty years old. Most of them still wore the uniforms in which they had been captured, with the addition, in some cases, of a sweater. A couple of men whose clothes, I suppose, had been in particularly bad condition when they arrived were togged out in French tunics and trousers formerly of horizon blue and now dyed a sickly green. Many of the Germans wore smart-looking knee boots, and their forage caps resembled those of the British Royal Air Force. Their uniforms, those that had survived, were decently tailored and made of good cloth; apparently the ersatz fabrics of which one heard so much in France were for civilians.

I noted a variety of coloration and facial types among the men—more dark hair than blond, about as many round heads as long ones, sometimes slant Mongoloid eyes above a red Celtic beard. Regarded as crusaders for race purity, they seemed a mongrel lot. They were not big. The staff officer noticed this, too. "It's a curious thing," he said. "In the last war the prisoners we took at the beginning were almost all huskies." I suspected that the underfeeding of German children during the last war and in the postwar years might have had something to do with it.

The major was chatting with the noncommissioned officer

who had been giving orders, and I joined them. This German, a sergeant pilot, was of medium size but athletic-looking and well fed. He was a classic Saxon type—wavy blond hair, blue eyes, and a complexion like boiled ham. He had been piloting a single-seater Messerschmitt pursuit plane when it was shot down with eight other machines in an air battle in November, and upon arriving at camp he had taken command because he was the senior noncommissioned officer. The pilot said he was twenty-eight years old, came from Leipzig, where he had been graduated from the gymnasium, and had served in Spain and Poland. The Air Force obviously was his career, so there was no reason to ask how he felt about Hitler, who created the Air Force. It was a bore being a prisoner, he said; he found the lack of exercise hardest to bear and complained that there was no sports field for the prisoners. Unlike most of his comrades, he enjoyed wine, having acquired a taste for it in Spain; the food, he said, was all right, but there wasn't enough of it. He certainly did not look thin after five months of prison rations. The major said he thought the pilot only imagined he was hungry because the food was strange; Germans, he explained, are used to dark bread, boiled potatoes, cabbage, and fat, over-cooked meats, but in French prisons they get white bread, fried potatoes, leeks, and lean red beef. The pilot did not seem convinced by the explanation.

We started back to the office, where, the captain said, I would find it easier to talk at some length to a couple of the prisoners.

A few minutes after we got there the first prisoner chosen for an interview was brought in. "The pilot was a good example of a reliable Nazi," the major said. "Now take a look at this fellow." The prisoner, who came from Berlin, was one of the bloodless industrial-worker type which the postwar years produced in Central Europe. He was an ugly man with a rueful, conciliatory grin, and he looked middle-aged, although he said he was only thirty. He had worked in a hat factory until he was mobilized on the twenty-eighth of August 1939. He had previously served eight weeks in the army back in 1935, when compulsory service was revived in Germany, and that was all the military training he had had before the war. He had been undramatically captured in the Saarland early in September, when he and some other soldiers were sent out on bicycles to lay small mines. He had had more to carry than the others and, on the return trip, had fallen behind. Taking a wrong turn, he had run smack into a French patrol. That was all. Looking at him, I felt sure he had had just such luck all his life.

The major asked the man what he thought the war was about, and he immediately became voluble. As long as there was capitalism, he said, there would be wars. Capitalistic states had to make ammunition to cure unemployment, and then they had to use the ammunition. It was inevitable. I asked him what he thought of Hitler's Germany, and he said emphatically that he considered it a capitalistic state the same as all the others. Russia, he said, was only another dictatorship; she had made the alliance with Germany so that Germany would feel she could safely fight England; Russia hoped that both England and Germany would become exhausted, and then she would rule the world.

The major asked the prisoner what he thought of the showing the Finnish Army had made against the Russian troops. The man said he didn't believe the Finns had won any battles at all. "In Berlin we used to hear also about the big Red victories in Spain," he said, "but it wasn't true. It wasn't true about Finland, either." We asked him whether he knew that British planes had flown over Berlin, and he grinned incredulously, telling us that the German Air Force was the strongest in the world. "One thing I must say," he went on, as if he believed it. "The English have too many colonies. If they would give some to Germany, maybe even with Hitler I could make a living for my family." After he had left, the major said, "He is a Communist." I wondered what he really was.

The next prisoner to enter was another Berliner, who, like so many of his townsmen, had a Polish name. He was a well-set-up youth, thin but with good shoulders, and he still looked smart in his cap and uniform. He had high cheekbones, an aquiline nose, a thin mouth, which he kept drawn tight in an effort at self-control, and baffled green eyes. He was twenty-seven. Once, he said, he had been a tanner's apprentice, more recently he had become a white-collar worker, and just before the mobilization he had been working as an adding-machine operator. He had been captured while doing patrol duty between the lines. I was astonished to hear that he, too, had

had only eight weeks of military training—in 1935. "It's nothing unusual," the major said. "At the beginning of this war the Germans had four eight-week classes in their army—all the men from twenty-seven to thirty—and they had no trained reserves at all between the ages of thirty and forty. It is apparently a very spotty army, with all its strength concentrated in certain *corps d'élite* like the motorized divisions and the aviation. They have worked hard in the last seven months, of course, but so have we."

While we talked in French, the prisoner, tense and frightened, stood watching. He was not a Nazi party member, he told us when we asked him; he had never bothered with politics. He had once belonged to Workman's Sport, an affiliate of the old Socialist party, but that was just for the swimming and water-polo privileges of the organization; he had never been a Marxist. The pact between Germany and Russia didn't bother him. He said it was just for business, and anyway the Russians were all right. He had been in Moscow for four weeks in 1938 with a workmen's swimming team. The major asked him why Germany had gone to war. "Because of poverty," the former adding-machine operator almost shouted. "Germany has been poor all my life because we lost the last war." The major looked at him over his gold-rimmed glasses, like a blasé probation officer questioning an incorrigible. "You think war will cure poverty?" he asked. "What else?" said the puzzled soldier. "If we lose this war, it is the end of Germany. We will be Bolsheviks unless the English give us colonies. Colonies we must have or we will be Bolsheviks." The major interrupted him. "Don't you think," he asked, "that wars always bring poverty, even when you win?" Either this was beyond the prisoner's understanding or he was afraid to consider the question; at any rate, he just shrugged. Perhaps he didn't want to have his last hope destroyed until the slogan-makers had time to offer him another.

I would have liked to listen to more political thought from these men, but the staff officer, who had organized our trip as carefully as an offensive, told me that we had forty-two minutes before the next train back to Paris and that consequently we had thirty-seven minutes left in which to visit the German commissioned officers. I wasn't as interested in them, because aviation lieutenants and infantry subalterns at the beginning of a war are almost certain to be enthusiastic, no matter what army they belong to. If the officer comes from a rich family, he considers the war a lark; if from a poor one, he thinks being an officer is a fine job. The German officers I saw lived up to this rule. They were lodged in what, before the war, had been the city jail. The cell doors were solid, not made of bars like those in an American jail, and the cells were about as large as bedrooms in an average modern apartment house. I don't know what kind of prisoners they had been designed for, but they even had wallpaper.

The pleasantest of the officers I met was a Rhinelander, a tall, blond subaltern who reminded me of the young Germans who used to play deck sports on liners, laughing too loudly and trying with a grim will to win. This man was an artillerist who had had the unfortunate inspiration of going on patrol with the infantry. He was reading a book about golf when we came in. He received a salary of seven hundred francs a month from the French Government, which was the pay of a French second lieutenant "absent from duty." This was not as much as the same French officer would get in active service. The officers were charged three hundred francs a month for their food, so, even if they managed to buy a few incidentals from their guards, they probably saved more than half their pay. The notion of getting rich in prison amused the Rhinelander. "I can't get out to spend it, you know," he said in English.

I next met four aviators who shared a common living room during the day. All had shaved their skulls and grown long, brown beards. When I asked one where he came from he said, "Germany. There are no more Prussians or Bavarians or Saxons. We are all Germans." He said he was a German who happened to live in Berlin, and that was all I could get out of him. Of the others, one said he had been shot down by six Spitfires, another by seven Hurricanes, and a third by a dozen Curtisses. I had never heard such a concerted tribute to Allied superiority in the air; listening to them, I marveled that a Messerschmitt could find its way through the traffic. They were lying, of course.

"You remarked the fellow who said there were no Prussians, no Bavarians, et cetera, the most Nazi of them all, to hear him speak?" the captain said after we had left them. "He came down in an open field behind our lines because of engine trouble, he said, but none of our mechanics could find anything the matter with the plane. Naturally he has to put up a big bluff here or he would be under suspicion. If he sounded lukewarm the other prisoners might suspect the truth and send him to Coventry, or conceivably smuggle into their letters somehow a hint of his treachery and then his family in Germany would lose its pay allotment. But there are also fellows like the sergeant pilot who are really Nazi *cent pour cent*; two classes of cocky prisoners, *les vrais durs* and *les faux durs*, the true hard ones and the fake hard ones."

The proportion of *vrais durs* to *faux durs* among German prisoners in successive phases of the war, I have thought since, is the only significant index to the morale of the German Army. The circumstances of a man's capture are more significant than his tone of voice in replying to the interrogating officer. It is to a prisoner's interest to be cocky, after capture, for he is under the surveillance of his fellows and the governance of superiors whose Naziness is likely to be in proportion with their rank. The Geneva Convention was never drawn up to cover an ideological war; there is no inducement for the German prisoner who is democratic or just anti-war to let anybody know what is on his mind. Vanity also counts in the prisoner's attitude. He likes to think of himself as a Teutonic hero even when he knows he has quit cold.

A friend of mine, a lieutenant colonel with the Eighth Army, once interrogated three German prisoners after the Battle of Akarit in the African campaign, and when he had finished, one of the Germans, drawing himself up to their cataleptic version of attention, asked, "But do you not think we are fine soldiers?" The lieutenant colonel said, "Not especially." He said the Germans looked as if he had hit them with an elephant-hide whip. By this time they have probably complained against him for violation of the Geneva Convention against torture.

CHAPTER X

The Knockdown: Paris Postscript

THE new phase of the Second World War began for Paris at daybreak on Friday, May 10, 1940. People had gone to bed Thursday night in their habitual state of uncertainty; the governmental crisis in London which was bringing Winston Churchill to power was still the chief subject of preoccupation. With dawn came the air-raid sirens, startling a city that had heard no *alerte* during the daytime since the first weeks of the war. At once the little Square Louvois in front of my window took on the aspect of an Elizabethan theater, with tiers of spectators framed in the opened windows of every building. Instead of looking down at a stage, however, they all looked up. All wore nightshirts, which, since the prosperity of tenants in a walk-up is in inverse ratio to their altitude, appeared considerably dingier on the sixth and seventh floors than on the second and third.

The anti-aircraft guns were intoning such an impressive overture that startled birds flew out of the trees in at least one of the squares and circled nervously in squadrons over the roofs. As they did so, a large, formless woman in a gray nightshirt, making her *entrée* at a top-floor window, waved her right arm toward them and shouted "*Confiance!*"—putting all her neighbors in hilarious good humor.

The guns kept up their racket, and a number of tracer shells lit up the early morning sky. The noise of the airplane motors was distinctly audible, but in those pre-blitz days we could not distinguish between the sound made by bombers and that of French pursuit planes looking for Germans. At last one airplane appeared, flying so high that it looked like a charm-bracelet toy, and as it passed overhead there seemed to be a deliberate lull in the firing. People stared uneasily at the plane, as they would at a stinging insect near a ceiling, but it went away harmlessly enough, and then the guns opened up again.

The morning air was chilly, so most of the spectators soon closed their windows and went back to bed. In the Square

Louvois the neighborhood milkman, with his wagon drawn by two enormous old gray stallions, came along a few minutes after the plane, and the crash of his cans on the cobbles brought a few nervous folk back to their windows under the impression that bombing had begun.

The episode differed so from previous alarms, in which no planes were seen, that nobody seemed astonished to learn from newspapers consisting mostly of headlines that the real war—the war on the western front—had begun. "*Finie la drôle de guerre*," people said to each other with a kind of relief. Even the *guerre* in Norway had seemed *drôle*, because it was so remote. The rush to news kiosks was such that policemen had to shepherd would-be purchasers into queues, which in some cases were half a block long.

I had a letter from Jean, Henri's son, a corporal in one of the two French armored divisions which were created after the Polish campaign. They were good divisions, and Jean had no way of knowing that the Germans had six times as many. "The real roughhouse is about to begin," he wrote. "So much the better! It will be like bursting an abscess." Jean, whose parents were my oldest friends in France, was a strong, quiet boy who in civil life had been a draftsman in an automobile factory. He liked to play ice hockey and collect marine algae. He had not wanted a soft job in a factory during the war because he did not want to be considered a coward.

On the same morning I had a telephone conversation with another friend of mine, Captain de Cholet, who had just arrived from Alsace on furlough. Upon reaching the Gare de l'Est, he had learned that all furloughs were canceled, so he was going back by the next train. He called me up to say that he wouldn't be able to go to the races at Auteuil with me, as he had planned. "It's good that it's starting at last," he said. "We can beat the Boches and have it over with by autumn."

In the afternoon I went to Auteuil alone. I watched a horse belonging to Senator Hennessy, the cognac man, win the Prix Wild Monarch for three-year-old hurdlers. The track was crowded with people whose main preoccupations seemed to be the new three-year-olds and the new fashions being worn by the women. That day the Germans were taking Arnhem and Maastricht in Holland and attacking Rotterdam with parachutists. Nobody worried much. Everyone was eager principally to know whether French troops had yet made contact with the enemy. "The Boches have business with somebody their own size now!" they said pugnaciously. "They will see we are not Poles or Norwegians!" It was conceivable, of course, that the Germans would win a few victories, but it would be a long war, like the last one. All France, hypnotized by 1918, still thought in terms of concentrated artillery preparations, followed by short advances and then, probably, by counterattacks. Even if the Allied troops should fail to save Holland, they would join the Belgians in holding the supposedly magnificent fortified line of the Albert Canal. At worst, the armies could fall back to the Franco-Belgian frontier, where, the newspapers had been proclaiming since September, there was a defensive system practically as strong as the Maginot Line. Confidence was a duty. The advertising department of the *Magasins du Louvre* had discovered another duty for France. The store's slogan was "Madame, it is your duty to be elegant!" "They shall not pass" was considered *vieux jeu* and hysterical. The optimistic do-nothingism of the Chamberlain and Daladier regimes was, for millions of people, the new patriotism. Ten days before the war began in May, Alfred Duff Cooper told the Paris American Club, "We have found a new way to make war—without sacrificing human lives."

The news of the break-through at Sedan, which reached Paris on the fifth day of the offensive, was, for a few Parisians who were both pessimistic and analytical, the beginning of fear. But it happened so quickly, so casually, as presented in the communiqués, that the unreflective didn't take it seriously. The Belgian refugees began to arrive in Paris a few days after the fighting started. The great, sleek cars of the de-luxe refugees came first. The bicycle refugees arrived soon after. Slick-haired, sullen young men wearing pull-over sweaters shot out of the darkness with terrifying, silent speed. They had the air of conquerors rather than of fugitives. Many of them must have been German spies. Ordinary destitute refugees arrived later by train and as extra riders on trucks. Nothing else happened at first to change the daily life of the town.

Tuesday evening, May 14, I climbed the hill of Montmartre to the Rue Gabrielle to visit Jean's parents. Henri, Jean's father, had long limbs and sad eyes; he combined the frame of a high jumper and the mustaches of a Napoleonic grenadier. He was a good Catholic, and by birth and training he belonged to the wealthier bourgeoisie. By temperament, which he had never been allowed to indulge, he was a bohemian. A long struggle to succeed in business, which he secretly detested, had ended in a defeat just short of total. When war was declared, he was working for a firm of textile stylists whose customers were chiefly foreign mills. Since September, business had fallen off drastically and Henri had had nothing to do except drop in once in a while to keep up the firm's desultory correspondence. Henri spoke English, German, and Dutch in addition to French, and sometimes sang in a deep voice which sounded like a good but slightly flawed 'cello. He often said that he was happy to be living, at last, high on Montmartre, just under Sacré-Coeur. His wife, Eglée, would never have permitted him to live there for any reason less compelling than poverty. Eglée, before her marriage to Henri, had been a buyer in a department store. Recently she had devised a muslin money belt for soldiers to wear under their shirts. She worked an average of sixteen hours a day, making the belts with a frantic dexterity, but about once a fortnight she got so exhausted that she had to stay in bed for two or three days. She had placed the belts in several of the department stores, but her profit was small. Eglée and Henri were both about sixty years old. For thirty-five years Henri had pretended to like trade in order to hold his wife's respect, and Eglée had pretended to loathe trade in order to hold Henri's affection. Neither had succeeded in deceiving the other. He brooded, she scolded, he drank a little, they quarreled incessantly, and they loved each other more than any two people I have ever known.

As I came into their apartment Tuesday night, Eglée was saying she felt sure Jean was dead. Henri said that was nonsense. She said he was an unfeeling parent. Henri became angry and silent. Then he said that often, when he was at Verdun, Eglée had not heard from him for a week at a time. She said that Henri was always talking about Verdun and belittling "Jean's war." "To think that after these years of preparing to avoid the old mistakes," Henri said, "the Germans are now eighty miles from us. If they get to Paris, it's all over." Eglée said he was a defeatist to mention such an eventuality. He said, "I am not a defeatist. I am an old soldier and also an old traveling man, and I know how near they are to Paris." I tried to console him by saying that the Dutch, at any rate, were fighting better than anyone had expected. Henri had cousins in Holland. Eglée said the Dutch were Boches and would before long prove it.

The next morning there was a radio announcement that the Dutch had surrendered in Europe but were going to continue the war in the East Indies. In the afternoon some of the American correspondents, including myself, went to the Netherlands Legation to meet Mynheer Van Kleffens, the Netherlands Minister for Foreign Affairs, who had arrived from London to explain the Dutch decision. Van Kleffens, accompanied by the Netherlands minister to France and the Netherlands Minister for National Defense, received us and the journalists of other neutral countries in the Legation garden. While we were talking, sadly and quietly, among the trees, the French were losing the war. On that Wednesday, May 15, the Germans made the deep incision which a few days later was to split the Allied armies.

The Foreign Minister, a blond, long-faced man, had a pet phrase which he repeated many times, as a man does when he is too tired to think of new forms for his thought. "The Germans tried this," he would say, recounting some particular method of the German attack, and then he would add, "It failed." "It failed," he would say, and again, "It failed"—until you thought he was talking of a long, victorious Dutch resistance —and then finally, "But to fight longer was hopeless." "We will fight on" was another recurrent phrase. When we asked him whether the Dutch had any planes left to fight with, he said, "No. We had fifty bombers. The last one flew off and dropped its last bomb and never returned."

Holland, with one tenth the population of Germany but with several times the wealth per capita, had presented fifty bombers against five thousand. It had been comfortable to believe in neutrality, and cheap. Norway, with the fourth largest merchant marine in the world, had not built the few good light cruisers and destroyers which might have barred the weak German Navy from its ports. France herself had economized on the Maginot Line, had decided it was too expensive to extend the fortifications from Luxembourg to the sea. The democracies had all been comfortable and fond of money. Thinking of the United States, I was uneasy. I suspected that in proportion to our wealth we were the nakedest of them all.

The first panic of the war hit Paris Thursday, May 16. It affected, however, only the most highly sensitized layers of the population: the correspondents, the American and British war-charity workers, and the French politicians. In Paris, because of censorship, news of disaster always arrived unofficially and twenty-four hours late. On the evening of the catastrophic May 15, even the neurotic clientele of the Ritz and Crillon bars had been calm. But on Thursday people began telling you about Germans at Meaux and south of Soissons, points the Germans didn't actually reach until more than three weeks later. There was a run on the Paris branch of the Guaranty Trust Company by American depositors. I lunched in a little restaurant I frequently went to on the Rue Sainte-Anne, and after the meal, M. Bisque, the proprietor, suggested that we go to the Gare du Nord to see the refugees. M. Bisque cried easily. Like most fine cooks, he was emotional and a heavy drinker. He had a long nose like a woodcock and a mustache which had been steamed over cookpots until it hung lifeless from his lip. Since my arrival in France in October he had taken me periodically on his buying trips to the markets so that I could see the Germans weren't starving Paris. On these trips we would carry a number of baskets and, as we filled one after another with oysters, artichokes, or pheasants, we would leave them at a series of bars where we stopped for a drink of apple brandy. The theory was that when we had completed our round of the markets we would circle back on our course, picking up the baskets, and thus avoid a lot of useless carrying. It worked all right when we could remember the bars where we had left the various things, but sometimes we couldn't, and on such occasions M. Bisque would cry that *restauration* was a cursed *métier*, and that if the Government would permit he would take up his old rifle and leave for the front. But they would have to let him wear horizon blue; he could not stand the sight of khaki because it reminded him of the English.

"They say the English are very brave at sea," he would say, winking slowly, "but who knows? We don't see them, eh?"

The trip to the Gare du Nord was solemn. M. Bisque dragged me to see various mothers sitting on rolls of bedding and surrounded by miauling children; his eyes would water, and he would offer a child a two-franc piece and then haul me to the buffet, where he would fortify himself with a glass of Beaujolais. At the buffet I remember meeting a red-bearded gnome of a colonial soldier who kept referring to himself as "a real porpoise." "Porpoise" was the traditional army term for a colonial infantryman. "A real porpoise," the soldier repeated dreamily, "an old porpoise, and believe me, monsieur, the Germans need somebody to bust their snouts for them." He had two complete sets of decorations, one from the old war and one from the new. He was going north to rejoin his regiment, and he was full of fight and red wine.

Saturday morning I had another note from Jean. He enclosed a bit of steel from a Dornier shot down near him. "How I am still alive I have not time to write to you," he said, "but chance sometimes manages things well." The letter produced the same effect on me as news of a great victory. I called up Henri. He and Eglée had had a letter too.

On Saturday, May 18, I went to a press conference held by the Ministry of Information, which had just organized an Anglo-American press section, with quarters in a vast, rococo ballroom at the Hôtel Continental called the Salle des Fêtes. Pierre Comert, chief of the section, held conferences for the correspondents at six every evening, when he would discuss the day's developments from the Government's point of view. This evening he announced that Paul Reynaud had taken over the Ministry of National Defense. He also announced that Reynaud had recalled Marshal Pétain from Spain to advise him. General Weygand had already arrived from Syria, and it was understood that he would take over the high command in a few days. The two great names, in conjunction, were expected to raise national morale. The two old men, however, were military opposites. Pétain, cautious at sixty, when he had defended Verdun, was at eighty-four incapable of conceiving any operation bolder than an orderly retreat. Weygand believed in unremitting attack. One staff officer later told me, "Weygand's ideas are so old-fashioned that they have become modern again. He is just what we need." Strategically, the two men canceled each other, but politically they were a perfect team. Both were clericals, royalists, and anti-parliamentarians. There is something about very old soldiers like Hindenburg and Pétain that makes democrats trust them. But Pétain was to serve Laval's purpose as Hindenburg had served Hitler's. However, we were cheerful on the evening we heard about the appointments. The German advance was apparently slowing down, and all of us thought that Weygand might arrange a counterattack soon. A week earlier we had been expecting victories. Now we were cheered by a slightly slower tempo of disaster.

There was a hot, heavy pause the next few days. I took long walks on the boulevards and up and down dull, deserted business streets. The wartime population of Paris had slowly increased from late November until April, as evacuated families returned from the provinces, but since the beginning of the offensive the population had again decreased. All the people who had remained in town seemed to concentrate on the boulevards. It gave them comfort to look at one another. They were not yet consciously afraid, however. There were long queues in front of the movie houses, especially those that showed double features. You could get a table at a sidewalk café only with difficulty, and the ones that had girl orchestras did particularly well. One girl orchestra, at the Grande Maxeville, was called the Joyous Wings, and its bandstand and instruments had been decorated with blue airplanes. There were no young soldiers in the streets, because no furloughs were being issued.

It is simple now to say, "The war on the Continent was lost on May 15." But as the days in May passed, people in Paris only gradually came to suspect how disastrous that day had been. There was a time lag between every blow and the effect on public morale. I can't remember exactly when I first became frightened, or when I first began to notice that the shapes of people's faces were changing. There was plenty of food in Paris. People got thin worrying. I think I noticed first the thinning faces of the sporting girls in the cafés. Since the same girls came to the same cafés every night, it was easy to keep track. Then I became aware that the cheekbones, the noses, and the jaws of all Paris were becoming more prominent.

There was no immediate danger in Paris unless the Germans bombed it, and when the news was in any degree encouraging I did not think of bombing at all. When the news was bad I thought of bombing with apprehension. It helped me understand why troops in a winning army are frequently brave and on the losing side aren't. We heard anti-aircraft fire every night now, but there were no air-raid alarms, because the planes the guns were firing at were reconnaissance planes. The heaviest shooting would begin in the gray period just before dawn. You wouldn't really settle down to sleep until the morning shooting was over, and you wouldn't wake up until noon.

On the night of May 21, after Paul Reynaud announced to the Senate that the Germans were at Arras and that France was in danger, I had a *frousse*—a scare—of such extreme character that it amounted to *le trac*, which means a complete funk. It was an oppressively hot night, with thunder as well as anti-aircraft fire, interspersed with noises which sounded like the detonations of bombs in the suburbs. When I lay on my bed face down, I couldn't help thinking of a slave turning his back to the lash, and when I lay on my back I was afraid of seeing the ceiling fall on me. Afterward I talked to dozens of other people about that night, and they all said they'd suffered from the same funk. The next morning's papers carried Weygand's opinion that the situation was not hopeless. This cheered everybody. It has since been revealed that May 21, the day of the great *frousse*, was the day set for the counter-attack which might have cracked the Germans. It never came, and by May 22, when we were all beginning to feel encouraged, the opportunity had been missed.

Later that day word got around among the correspondents that negotiations were already on for a separate peace and that if the French didn't sign it the Germans might arrive in Paris in a few days. This counteracted the effect of the Weygand message. Still later I felt encouraged again as I watched a city gardener weed a bed of petunias in the Square Louvois, the tiny park under my hotel window. Surely, I thought, if the old man believed the Germans were coming in he would not be bothering with the petunias.

The greatest encouragement I got during those sad weeks came from Jean. Shortly after the Reynaud speech I went up the hill to Montmartre to take some flowers to Jean's mother. For once, Henri and Eglée were smiling at the same time. "You should have been here early this morning for a good surprise!" Henri shouted. "At five there was a knock at our door." "And who do you suppose it was?" his wife cried, taking over the narrative. "Suzette?" I demanded, naming their married daughter, who lived in Grenoble. I was sure that it had been Jean, but I wanted to prolong Eglée's pleasure. "No," Eglée announced happily. "It was Jean. He was magnificent. He looked like a cowboy." "He came with his *adjudant*," Henri broke in, "to get engine parts they needed for tanks. The boy has no rest, you know," he said proudly. "When the division goes into action he fights. When they are in reserve and the other fellows rest, he is head of a repair section. He is a magician with engines. And his morale is good! He says that the first days were hard, but that now they know they can beat the Boche." "On the first day of the battle, Jean's general was arrested," Eglée said, with a sort of pride. "What *canaille!* Jean said it was fantastic what a traitor the general turned out to be. And there were German spies in French officers' uniforms!" "They met a regiment of artillery without officers," Henri said, "but completely! 'So much the better,' the artillerists said. 'They were traitors anyway. But where in the name of God are we supposed to go?' Fifteen German bombers appeared over Jean's unit. 'We're in for it,' he said to himself. But the boy was lucky. The Germans had dropped their bombs elsewhere. Then Jean's unit met German tanks. He says our fellows rode right over them. 'There may be a great many of them,' he said, 'but we are better than they are. Our guns penetrate them, but they do not penetrate us. As for the spy problem, we have solved that. We simply shoot all officers we do not know.' Jean and the *adjudant* stayed for breakfast. Then they had to go away."

Although I knew that an individual soldier had no chance to understand a military situation as a whole, Jean's optimism raised my spirits considerably. I believed fully the details of the encounter with the German tanks. Jean was of that peculiar race of engine-lovers who cannot lie about the performance of a mechanical thing.

When I returned to my hotel I passed along Jean's confident report to Toutou, the hotel's cashier, with whom I often discussed the war. She was a patriot but a congenital pessimist. All the employees slept on the top floor of the hotel, and as soon as Toutou had read of the German parachutists in Holland she had bought a revolver and cartridges. "If one lands on the roof, I'll pop him!" she had said. "Or perhaps as he descends past my window!"

In each week of disaster there was an Indian summer of optimism. On the third Sunday after the offensive started, I had dinner with Henri and Eglée. We teased one another about our forebodings a fortnight earlier. "Do you remember how sure you were that the Germans would be here momentarily?" Eglée said to me. "And how you were certain that Jean was no longer alive?" Henri asked Eglée. "It seems a year ago," I said sincerely. "I must admit that the French had their heart well hooked on. Any other people would have caved in after such a blow. I wonder where Weygand will make the counterattack." "In Luxembourg, in my opinion," Henri said. "If he made the counterattack too far to the west he would not catch enough Boches. A good wide turning movement, and you will see— the whole band of them will have to scramble off. They will be on the other side of the Albert Canal again in a week."

We talked and listened to the radio, and, as usual, I stayed for tea, then for supper, and then for the final news-bulletin broadcast at eleven-thirty. The bulletins earlier in the day had been dull. But something in the speaker's voice this time warned us, as soon as he commenced, that the news was bad. We began to get sad before he had said anything important. Then he said, "Whatever the result of the battle in Flanders, the high command has made provision that the enemy will not profit strategically by its result." "What can he mean?" Eglée asked. "He means that they are preparing to embark that army for England," Henri said. "Unless the enemy captures the army, his victory is tactical but not strategical." "But why must they embark?" Eglée asked. "I do not know," Henri said almost

savagely. That was the day—though none of us knew it—that
King Leopold told his ministers he was going to give up. Eglée
began to cry. "Now they are coming to Paris," she said, "now
they are coming to Paris."

As late as Monday, May 27, people in Paris still believed that
the Allies stood a chance of closing the gap between their
southern and northern armies. That evening, Pierre Comert,
chief of the Anglo-American section of the Ministry of Information, announced at a press conference I went to that operations in the north were "proceeding normally" and that the
high command expected the Battle of Flanders to last at least
another two weeks. I slept well that night, awakened only
a few times by moderate anti-aircraft fire. In the morning
Toutou, the cashier at my hotel, stopped me as I was going
out and said, "Did you hear Reynaud on the radio? The King
of the Belgians has surrendered his army." She had been crying.

I walked about the streets stupidly the rest of the morning. I
had the map well in mind. The Belgians, by their surrender,
had laid bare the left flank of the Franco-British armies in Flanders, and I thought the armies would soon be surrounded.
Perhaps the French and British in the north would become demoralized and surrender. If they had been seeking an excuse to
quit, they had a good one now. People on the streets were
saying to each other, "And that isn't the worst of it. All the
refugees probably are spies." They did not seem depressed. A
fellow wheeling a pushcart loaded with wood stopped and
shouted to a colleague on the other side of the street, "Say, old
fellow, did you hear the news? Ain't we just taking it on the
potato!" In his voice was a note of pride.

I walked around the Place Vendôme a couple of times; the
luxury-shop windows had for me a reassuring association of
tourists and normal times. Charvet was showing summer ties. I
bought a couple from an elegant and hollow-chested salesman.
I didn't want to talk to him about the war, because he looked
sad enough already, but he began to talk about it himself. "We
are an indolent people, monsieur," he said pleasantly. "We need
occurrences like this to wake us up." Paris reminded me of that
conversational commonplace you hear when someone has
died: "Why, I saw him a couple of days ago and he looked perfectly well." Paris looked perfectly well, but I wondered if it

might not be better for a city in such danger to show some agitation. Perhaps Paris was dying.

That night, when the shock of the Belgian surrender had begun to wear off, I had a late dinner with two American friends in a little Marseillais restaurant on the Rue Montmartre. We were the only customers. We had Mediterranean rouget burned in brandy over twigs of fennel. Although all three of us knew that the war was lost, we could not believe it. The rouget tasted too much as good rouget always had; the black-browed proprietor was too normally solicitous; even in the full bosom and strong legs of the waitress there was the assurance that this life in Paris would never end. Faith in France was now purely a *mystique*; a good dinner was our profane form of communion.

Incredibly, beginning the day after the Belgian surrender, there was a great wave of exhilaration, based on the heroic action of the British and French armies fighting their way out of Flanders. People with relatives in the northern armies had, when they heard of the capitulation, resigned themselves to the capture or death of the trapped men. The German Government, in radio broadcasts, had threatened that even if the Allies were able to make a stand at Dunkirk the Germans would sink every boat that tried to embark troops. It was one German threat that didn't come off. People in Paris began to receive telegrams from relatives who had safely arrived in England. Several of my acquaintances received such messages, so we assumed that the number of troops saved was very large.

My old friends Henri and Eglée had not worried about their son Jean, because, having seen him on leave since the Germans drove the wedge between the Allied armies, they knew he was south of the Somme. But Henri's brother Paul, who at fifty had been called back into service as a lieutenant of artillery, was with the army in Flanders. One evening shortly after the Belgian surrender I climbed up to the Rue Gabrielle, just under the crest of Montmartre, to visit Henri and Eglée, and found them in a happy mood, because Paul had reached England. I tried to talk to Eglée about what she and her husband would do if the Germans turned toward Paris after they finished the Dunkirk job. Her answer was simply that she had an order from the Galeries Lafayette for five dozen of the soldiers' muslin money belts she manufactured at home and that after she completed the order she would have to wait eight days for payment, so how could she think of leaving Paris? As for Henri, he said he now constituted the whole office force of the textile-design company he worked for and couldn't leave without giving a month's notice. Peacetime thought patterns were mercifully persistent.

Everyone now was doing his best to forget that the Allied forces had had too few tanks and guns to begin with, and that now the evacuated armies had lost what little they had. We consoled ourselves with stories of individual heroism and with the thought that the Allies, after all, controlled the sea. Only when the evacuation was completed did the enthusiastic French suddenly take cognizance of the fact that there were no more British troops on their side of the Channel. As if spontaneously, the German gibe, "England will fight to the last Frenchman," swam into the popular consciousness and began to seem a portent.

Two kinds of person are consoling in a dangerous time: those who are completely courageous, and those who are more frightened than you are. Fernand, the night porter at my hotel, was completely courageous. "Well, what do you know?" he would ask me when I came home at night. Before I answered, he would say, "We will have them yet, the camels. It takes a few defeats to get our blood up. They poison our lives by provoking the anti-aircraft into making a noise at night. A surprise is preparing itself for those cocos!" It was a pleasure to see him during the frequent early-morning *alertes.* Hearing the sirens, he would go out into the small park in front of the hotel and, shielding his eyes with his hands, search the sky for airplanes. Seeing none, he would shake his head disgustedly and shout up to the female guests at the windows of the hotel, "Do not derange yourselves, mesdames, it is for nothing again!"

The most frightened man I saw in France was a certain well-known French journalist who wrote under various names in a dozen Parisian newspapers of varying political color. He had a broad, paraffin-textured face which, when he was alarmed, appeared to be on the point of melting. Long before the offensive began in May, he had tried to explain to me why Laval, the appeaser, and Paul Faure, the left-of-Blum Socialist, together

with Georges Bonnet, representative of the great banking
house of Lazard Frères, were all planning a move to get rid of
Paul Reynaud in order to liquidate the war as quickly as possible. They wanted to put Daladier back in Reynaud's place
because they knew that as long as Daladier headed the Government there would be no effectual war—that eventually the
war would die of dry rot, which was what ninety per cent of
the French politicians and all the French Communists, along
with the Germans, wanted. I had asked naïvely why Laval
didn't try to become premier himself. "Because, of course,"
my journalist friend had said impatiently, "then everybody
would *know* he was going to make peace. Then there would be
mutiny in the Army." Personally, he used to say, he was a decided partisan of both Reynaud, who wanted to fight, and of
Laval, who wanted to make peace. You were always running
up against things like that in French politics.

When I met my journalist at lunch one day the first week of
June, he was in as spectacular a funk as I have ever observed.
"What a terrible mistake to have provoked those people, my
dear!" he shrieked. "What madness to concern ourselves with
Poland! Laval was so right to have wished to conciliate
Mussolini. I am going to give my dog a lethal injection. He
could never stand the nervous shock of those bombs that
whistle. Working people are so insouciant. They know they
have us in their power. I cannot get a man to dig a trench in
my garden for me until tomorrow afternoon, and the bombers
may be here any minute!" As he stuffed asparagus into his
mouth, large tears welled out of his eyes. "Peace, quickly,
quickly!" he shouted, after swallowing the asparagus.

Sunday, June 2, I visited the country home of a French
newspaper publisher who lived with his large, intelligent family
near the town of Melun, thirty miles south of Paris. The countryside, hot and rich and somnolent, and the family, sitting on
the lawn after a chicken dinner, made me think of Sundays on
Long Island. It was as if no war had ever been. We sat around
in lawn chairs, fighting against drowsiness, talking unintently,
resisting the efforts of one woman to get up a game like charades. We spoke with no originality whatever of all the mistakes all the appeasers in the world had made, beginning with
Ethiopia. We repeated to one another how Italy could have

been squelched in 1935, how a friendly Spanish government could have been maintained in power in 1936, how the Germans could have been prevented from fortifying the Rhineland in the same year. We talked of the Skoda tanks, built according to French designs in Czechoslovakia, that were now ripping the French Army apart. The Germans had never known how to build good tanks until Chamberlain and Daladier presented them with the Skoda plant. These matters had become for every European capable of thought a sort of litany, to be recited almost automatically over and over again.

Women in the train which took me back to town that evening were talking about the leaflets German planes had dropped, promising to bombard Paris the next day. The word "bombardment" had a terrible sound, evoking pictures of Warsaw and Rotterdam. In the dimly lighted, carefully curtained compartments of the local train, the women looked tired and anxious rather than refreshed. Boarding the train at a tiny station, they would exchange the usual flippancies with the people they had been staying with. "Thanks for the peonies. I'll put them right in water when I get home," one of them might say, but her voice would be strained. Some of them must have been going back to jobs at the great Citroën plant on the Quai de Javel, where hundreds of women punched out parts of machines and sprayed paint. The train arrived at the Gare de Lyon after eleven. There were no taxis. In the last month they had become increasingly scarce even in the daytime; the drivers simply refused to risk their necks in the pitch-black streets at night. I could not distinguish one street from another. There was a cluster of dim, moving lights at a distance, like a luminous jellyfish seen by another fish at the bottom of the sea. I started toward the lights and tripped over a plank, skinning my knee. When I reached them I found that they came from the electric lanterns of a group of policemen who were stopping pedestrians and examining their papers. They were polite and quiet. One of them told me how to get to my hotel, which took me almost an hour.

Monday was hot, lovely, and until one o'clock, tranquil. People going out to lunch were just beginning to smile knowingly and to say to each other, "See, it was just another bluff," when the air-raid sirens sounded. At that hour I was of course in a bar, that of the Hôtel Lotti near the Continental, for the *apéritif*. It was a "day without hard liquor," so the apéritif was champagne. The waiters lowered the metal shutters. The bombardment was preceded by a tremendous noise of motors in airplanes too high to be seen, and by the angry hammering of anti-aircraft guns. It was as always hard to distinguish the sound of the bombs from these enfolding noises. After forty-five minutes, the roar of the planes stopped, but the shooting continued awhile, and then the sirens gave the all-clear signal. Everybody I met in the street afterward seemed to know exactly where the bombs had fallen. A taxi driver took me straight to the neighborhood bombed. Some six-story apartment houses in Passy had been shaved down to the first floor, as if by the diagonal sweep of a giant razor. The streets there were covered with broken glass, since every window for nearly a mile around was out, and housewives, not hurt but angry, were already out on the sidewalks sweeping up the glass with brooms. Of two large cafés at an intersection, one had been pretty well outed by a bomb, but the terrace of the other, twenty minutes after the all-clear, was doing a record business with clients who wanted to "*discuter le coup.*"

Technically, I was later given to understand, it had been, from the German standpoint, a very good bombardment. Two hundred and fifty planes participated, the largest number that had been assembled for a single operation in the war until then. The bombing, considering the height at which the planes flew—twenty thousand feet—was commendably accurate. However, the results looked nothing like the photographs of Warsaw and Rotterdam, because Paris was reasonably well defended. "The anti-aircraft fire was well nourished," the French said, "so the bombers stayed high." The pursuit squadrons, although they failed to intercept the bombers on their way to Paris, were on their tails so closely that the Germans dropped their bombs quickly and left. If there had been no defending batteries or planes, as at Rotterdam, the bombers would have loafed along a few hundred feet above the main thoroughfares and dropped their high explosives like roach powder. The bombs hit the huge Citroën factory on the Quai de Javel and knocked down a few scattered apartment houses, but the total effect on public morale was tonic. Forty-eight hours after the bombardment, M. Dautry, the Minister of War Industry, took a group of correspondents through the Citroën plant, which had been the chief German objective. There we found a smell of burnt paint, and a great deal of broken glass on the floor, but no serious damage to the great automobile-assembly lines or the part of the plant where shells were made. The women making shells worked on as calmly as girls in an American candy factory.

The day we visited the factory, June 5, was also the day the Germans began their second attack, the push southward across the Somme that was to carry them to the Spanish frontier. "It is the beginning of the second round," Pierre Comert announced at the press conference that evening. None of us could admit to ourselves that the war in France might be a two-round knockout. The French would surely be dislodged from the Somme-Aisne line, we conceded, but it would take weeks to do it. Then they would defend Paris and the line of the Seine, then the line of the Loire. By that time, perhaps, the British would be able to do something. Even the United States might begin to understand what was at stake and give a pledge which would put new heart in the defenders. But this fight was not to have even a decent second round. The rest after the first round had not been long enough; the French were still out on their feet. Unarmed and outnumbered, they were led by two old men who were at loggerheads. As for Reynaud, he had called into his government Ybarnegaray and Marin, two reactionaries whose only surface virtue was a blustering show of war spirit. Raised to power by Socialist votes, Reynaud had turned toward men whom he trusted because they were of his own Rightist background—Pétain, Mandel, Ybarnegaray, Marin. All his Rightist friends except Mandel joined in smothering him. They felt that by making war against Hitler he was betraying his own class.

After the bombardment the Government began an intensive, almost convulsive effort to get the United States Government to send over some fighter planes and, Reynaud may even have hoped, some pilots under the same sort of arrangement by which German pilots had gone to Franco or the American Volunteer group to China. Perhaps the French Government itself may have been deceived about the number of fighter planes finished or in construction in the United States. A red-haired Jewish captain in the Armée de l'Air, an ace in the other war but now a staff man, took me out to see a pursuit group in the field and show me how badly planes were needed.

CHAPTER XI

Who Do Not Fight, but Run Away

"THE situation is very bad," said the captain, as we drove into the country, "but it is not hopeless, because it could still be corrected so easily. We don't need anything like magic."

The captain did not appear to be much interested in the fumbling remarks I made about the machinery of Congress and the mysteries of public opinion in the United States. Every Frenchman with an American acquaintance had heard all that before. Over and over again, Americans tried to explain such things, but their voices lacked conviction, and they wondered as they talked whether their words had any real meaning and whether the Danish politicians talked any differently before they rolled over and died.

My companion said he thought we'd be able to get a good lunch in a town along the way. The day was hot and beautiful, and the land seemed very peaceful as our Renault limousine raced smoothly along over some of the world's best roads. "It is a very comfortable automobile," the captain said wryly. "It used to be employed to take deputies on tours of observation at the front. They invariably found everything perfect."

Driving across the plains of Brie and Champagne, we saw peasants working with their chunky horses in the rich, un-fenced fields; from time to time we passed canals in which boys were taking bellywhoppers, and occasionally we came upon a young woman pedaling along on a bicycle and smiling good-naturedly at the shouts of the soldiers in the camions. We had a magnificent lunch consisting of cheese tartlets, brook trout *amandine*, gigot, asparagus, cheese, cherries, and coffee, with a good bottle of still champagne, the local wine—all for slightly less than a dollar apiece. Our chauffeur ate with us. Most of the other lunchers were medical officers from a near-by hospital, who succeeded no better than such officers usually do in looking really martial, despite their fiercely scarlet kepis. After our meal we drove on a few miles and came to a town on which the Germans had dropped incendiary bombs early in their offensive. The bombs had ruined the stores and little houses and churches in about four blocks some distance from the town's main thoroughfare; driving straight through the center of the community, you would never know anything had happened.

We drove well on beyond the town and finally turned off the highway onto a dirt road where another Air Force car, a small, camouflaged Citroën, was waiting for us. It led the way for our shiny black limousine. We went down the side road for a mile or so until we came to a small house on the edge of a meadow. This, it turned out, was our destination—the post of command of a group of pursuit fliers. There were no runways or hangars or wind socks anywhere in sight, pursuit groups went about their business incognito. In back of the house was an automobile trailer equipped as a radio station, and stretched out on poles in the meadow were a number of brown canvas awnings, each of them concealing a pursuit plane, and, I was told, practically impossible to spot from the sky. "They bombed this field once," the captain said, "but they didn't hit anything. Sometimes they fly down with machine guns, hoping to shoot our planes on the ground, but our machine gunners drive them off before they are able to find what they are looking for."

An officer came back from the Citroën, presented himself, and then took us into the post of command. The commandant's office and his bedroom occupied the ground floor. On the wall of the office I noticed a bulletin board divided into five columns marked "Ready for Instant Departure," "Quick Departure," "Reserve," "On Mission," and "Out of Service," and hanging on nails under each heading were some tin markers shaped like airplanes. It was the sort of thing you might expect to find in the office of an up-to-date taxi company. To me, the number of markers, even including those under "Out of Service," seemed terrifyingly small. The commandant, a man in his late thirties, I should say, was a dark, good-looking fellow —a bit underweight and obviously tired, but there was something about him that suggested the taut ruggedness of an airplane strut. He was polite enough, but appeared skeptical about American journalists, of whom he had seen several since May 10, when, as he put it, the war began. His name was Murtin; I've since met him in Algiers under circumstances considerably happier.

The two escadrilles in the group and practically every pilot belonging to it, I was told, had been cited and decorated since the beginning of the offensive; for the haggard fellows who had lived around that meadow during the past four weeks, the war had been an alternation of death and felicitations. "In four weeks the group has shot down eighty-eight enemy planes," the commandant said, "but to be honest, we have lost thirty-five. Our losses include machines grounded in our own territory— technically not defeats, you know, but what's the difference, once they're out of commission? Well, you may say, eighty-eight planes shot down is very good. Unfortunately, it's not good enough. The way the Germans keep sending out new ones is unbelievable. To cut down their margin of superiority in numbers appreciably, we would have to shoot down six for one. To hold our own, we must down five for one."

He said that the pursuit force, to hold its own until production picked up, should have just double its present number of planes, a matter of several hundred. "But why talk of Utopia?" he said. "At the beginning of the offensive, we were lucky. A big shipment must have arrived from America just in time; at any rate, I got eight new Curtisses in a batch. Imagine! Eight Curtisses! I have never before or since seen so many new machines all at once. It was the riches of Peru!"

I shook hands with the commandant and went out to the field with the captain and a tall, pleasant second lieutenant who couldn't have been more than twenty and had shot down eight planes. "You mustn't mind the boss," the lieutenant said apologetically. "He just lost a good man for a couple of months. An explosive bullet drove isinglass splinters from the windbreak into the man's face, and he can't see. The boss takes things like that to heart." We walked out across that meadow dotted with canopies, and the boy said, "It is peaceful here in the country. The local people like us very much because they are sure that, with the pursuit group here, they are safe from bombing planes. They say, 'Now we can sleep on both ears.' They don't know that we may attract more bombers, and what's the good of telling them? Might as well let them be happy."

It was about a five-minute walk over to a frame pavilion where the pilots on duty await orders to take the planes up. The building was on a ridge, surrounded by tall beech trees, and its unpainted boards smelled good in the heat. There were several fliers on hand, among them a Czech who was playing the "New World Symphony" on a phonograph. He looked sheepish when he was introduced to me. He felt ashamed, his friends explained, because on his first patrol with their group he had got into a fight with a Messerschmitt and had had to bail out in a parachute. The other aviators had tried to tell him that that didn't matter, that it happened to everybody at one time or another, but the Czech still felt bad. There were a number of Czechs in the group, the lieutenant said, and a couple of them were among the best combat pilots he'd seen.

The senior officer on duty was a first lieutenant, who introduced himself as "Marin." He was Marin de la Meslée, destined to finish that phase of the war as the leading French fighter pilot, with twenty victories, and later resume in North Africa. He wore his flying suit, and his plane was on the field; in an emergency he could be in the air in less than two minutes. He was long-limbed, with an aquiline Yankee face, and he had a stoop which he had probably acquired from squeezing into cockpits. Several of us walked together over to a great, shallow gravel pit where most of the Curtisses were cached, concealed only by the awnings which, in addition to camouflaging them, served as a protection against stones that might be kicked up by a bomb falling in the middle of the pit. "This gravel is ideal as a cushion for bombs," Marin said, "and there is water not far below the surface, which doesn't help the incendiary ones any. They just drop in here, churn up a little gravel, and expire."

We looked at the Curtisses—small, unimpressive things. The total equipment of an escadrille, including thirty planes, probably cost less than two million dollars. One of the fliers pointed out the difference between the Curtisses available when the war started, which had four machine guns, and the improved ones, which had six—two in each wing and two over the propeller. "The new ones are a little faster, too," he said, "but essentially they're the same. We need a model with eight or ten machine guns, because it takes an average of three thousand bullets to bring down a bomber. Most of all, though, we need more speed. These are good old girls, but they drag their feet—three hundred and twenty-five miles an hour doesn't amount to much any more. You see, you used to be able to come at a Heinkel from the tail end and shoot it down. That was all there was to it. Easy. But now they have put machine guns in the tails of the Heinkels, and these make it very disagreeable. The best way to catch a Heinkel now is to go around it and attack it head on, and for that you need a fast plane. Ah, if I only had one of those English planes with fifty miles more an hour and plenty of machine guns!" He spoke as though he were wishing for a fourteen-room suite on top of the Ritz or a date with his favorite cinema actress.

"Some of the German pilots are good, but most not so good," the flier continued. "Nearly all the planes are good, though, and since the man in the plane you're after may by chance be one of the good pilots, you cannot afford to take anything for granted. The German pilots are very wrought up, too, and when we shoot them down, if they land alive, they continue to yell 'Heil Hitler!' One parachuted into the top of a tree, and when our fellows climbed up to help him descend, he shot at them with a revolver." Marin came over then and said, "The situation until the end of July will be very difficult because the Germans are so reckless and have so many airplanes. It is like a parachute jump. If we come out of it, all right."

When I got back to my hotel that night, tired and discouraged, Fernand the porter, looking radiant, said to me, "What they must be digesting now, the Boches!" He showed me a copy of *Le Temps*, which said the German losses were stupefying. All the attacks had been "contained," but the French Army had executed a slight retreat in good order.

By now there were perceptible changes in the daily life of Paris. There was no telephone service in the hotels, so you had to make a special trip afoot every time you wanted to tell somebody something. Taxis were harder than ever to find. My hotel, which was typical, had six floors. At the beginning of the war in September the proprietor had closed the fourth, fifth, and sixth floors. Now I was the only guest on the second floor, and there were perhaps a half-dozen on the first. The staff, naturally, dwindled like the clientele. Every day somebody said good-by to me. One by one the waiters left, and then it was the headwaiter, who had been kept on after all of his subordinates had been dismissed. The next day it was Toutou, who left the bookkeeping to the housekeeper. A couple of days later, the housekeeper herself left. Finally there were only a porter and one chambermaid in the daytime, and Fernand at night. "Perhaps, if the line holds, there will be an upturn in business," the proprietor said.

It was at about this time that my restaurateur friend, M. Bisque, with whom I used to make the rounds of the markets, decided to close his restaurant. It was not that the Germans worried him, he explained to me, but there were no more customers, and also his wine dealer was pressing him to pay his bill. M. Bisque and his wife, who kept the books, and his daughter Yvette, who possessed the *tour de main* for making a soufflé stand up on a flat plate, and his son, who had been an apprentice in the kitchen of the Café de Paris, and Marie-Louise, the waitress, were all leaving the city to run the canteen in a munitions factory south of Fontainebleau. I wished them Godspeed.

For a few days I had lacked the heart to visit Henri and Eglée. Then Henri had come to my hotel to tell me joyfully they had had another letter from Jean, who said he had been working twenty-one hours a day repairing tanks for his division. On Sunday, June 9, which was a warm and drowsy day, I returned Henri's call. On the way I stopped at a florist's shop and bought some fine pink roses. The woman in the shop said that shipments from the provinces were irregular, but that fortunately the crisis came at a season when the Paris suburbs were producing plenty of flowers. "We have more goods than purchasers," she said, laughing. When I arrived at the apartment I found Eglée busy making her muslin money belts. Henri was amusing himself by reading a 1906 edition of the Encyclopaedia Britannica, one of his favorite possessions, and drinking a *vin ordinaire* in which he professed to find a slight resemblance to Ermitage. "This time I think the line will hold," Henri said. "I served under Pétain at Verdun. He will know how to stop them. Only I don't like the talk of infiltration near Forges-les-Eaux."

"Infiltration" was a grim word in this war. The communiqué never admitted that the Germans had pierced the French line, but invariably announced, "Motorized elements have made an infiltration. They have been surrounded and will be destroyed." Two days later the "infiltration" became a salient, from which new infiltrations radiated. When I left the apartment Henri walked down as far as the Place des Abbesses with me. He wanted to buy a newspaper. As we stood saying good-by we heard a series of reports, too loud and too widely spaced for anti-aircraft. "Those sound like naval guns mounted on railroad cars," Henri said. "The Boches can't be so far away, then." That was the last time I saw Henri. I had a letter from Suzette a year later, telling me he had died in February 1941.

At six o'clock that evening I went to another Anglo-American press conference at the Hôtel Continental. We were told that the Ministry of Information was planning to provide us with safe-conduct passes to use in case we left Paris. That made us suspect that the Government would move very soon. Then M. Comert told us that Jean Provoust, who had just been appointed Minister of Information, wanted to talk to all the American correspondents. M. Provoust, the dynamic publisher of *Paris-Soir*, received us in his office with the factitious cordiality of a newspaper owner about to ask his staff to take a pay cut. He said that he didn't want the United States to think the situation was hopeless. "From a military standpoint," he said, "it is improving steadily. Disregard reports of the Government quitting Paris. We will have many more chats in this room." John Lloyd, of the Associated Press, who was president of the Anglo-American Press Association, waited to see Provoust after the talk and invited him to be guest of honor at a luncheon the correspondents were having the next Wednesday. The Minister said he would be charmed, and then hurried away.

On my way home I saw a number of garbage trucks parked in the middle of the streets to balk airplane landings. Evidently

Paris would be defended. I didn't think, after Provoust's talk, that I would have to leave Paris immediately, but the situation looked so bad that I decided to begin getting my passport in order.

Early the next morning, Monday, June 10, I set out in a taxi —which the porter had taken two hours to find for me—to go to the Spanish Consulate General to obtain a transit visa. This was easy to get if you already had the Portuguese visa, and luckily I had one which was good for a year. My taxi driver came from Lorraine, where, he said, people knew what patriotism meant. He had fought the other war, four years of it. The country needed men like Poincaré, a Lorrainer, now. "The politicians have sold us out," he said. "And that Leopold," he shouted, "there is a fellow they should have got onto long ago!" Now, he expected, the Germans would come to Paris. But it would be defended, like Madrid. "They will come here, the dirty birds," he said, "but they will leave plenty of feathers! Imagine a tank trying to upset the building of the Crédit Lyonnais! Big buildings are the best defense against those machines." He did not know that the real-estate men would never encourage such an unprofitable use of their property. "Even ten centimes on the franc is something," the rich men were already telling one another, "when one has a great many francs."

From the Spanish Consulate I went to the Préfecture of Police, where I asked for a visa which would permit me to leave France. A woman police official, a sort of chief clerk, said, "Leave your passport and come back for it in not less than four days." "But by that time, madame," I said, "the Germans may be here and the Préfecture may not exist." Naturally, I didn't leave the passport, but I was foolish to question the permanency of the Préfecture. The French civil servants are the one class unaffected by revolution or conquest. The Germans were to come, as it turned out, but the Préfecture was to stay open, its personnel and routine unchanged. Its great accumulation of information about individual Frenchmen, so useful for the apprehension of patriots and the blackmailing of politicians, was to be at the disposal of the Germans as it had been at Philippe-Egalité's and Napoleon the Little's and Stavisky's. The well-fed young *agents* were to continue on the same beats, unaffected by the end of the war they had never had to fight in. Yesterday the Préfecture had obeyed the orders of M. Mandel, who hated Germans. Now it would obey Herr Abetz, who hated Jews. Change of administration. *Tant pis.*

Afterward I stopped at the Crillon bar, where I met a Canadian general I knew. "The French still have a fine chance," he said. "I am leaving for Tours as soon as I finish this sandwich." I walked over to the Continental to see if M. Comert had any fresh news. As I arrived at the foot of the staircase leading to Comert's office, I met another correspondent on his way out. "If you're going up to the Ministry," he said, "don't bother. The Government left Paris this morning." Then he began to chuckle. "You remember when John Lloyd stopped Provoust last night and invited him to the Wednesday luncheon?" he asked. Yes, I remembered. "Well," he said, "Provoust was in a hurry because he was leaving for Tours in a few minutes." I said maybe we had better leave too, and we did.

CHAPTER XII

A Man Falling Downstairs

A PROVINCIAL CITY which becomes overnight the capital of a great nation is not like a boom town, because it has no ebullience. People arrive dead tired after a night spent in an automobile or by the side of a road and pass their first hours in town looking for a bed. Finding one is a brief triumph. After a few hours of heavy sleep the new arrival goes out, depressed, to look for other equally sad people whom he has known in the abandoned capital city. With Waverley Root, the correspondent whom I had encountered on the Ministry of Information steps, I entered and left two temporary capitals of France within five days after quitting Paris. Tours was the first.

Root had an old Citroën with a motor that made a noise like anti-aircraft fire and was responsible for a few minor panics during our journey, but it stood up through the constant starting and stopping on the one vehicle-choked road the military authorities permitted civilians to travel south on. John Elliott of the *Herald Tribune* rode with us. He had one of his ankles in a plaster cast; it had been broken when an automobile in which he was returning to Paris from the front had hit a truck in a blackout.

The last impression of Paris we carried with us was of deserted streets everywhere except around the railroad stations, where the crowds were so big that they overflowed all the surrounding sidewalks and partly blocked automobile traffic. About everybody who had any means of transportation, except certain special groups like munitions workers and hospital staffs, whose last-minute evacuation had been guaranteed by the Government, left the city on Monday evening, the tenth of June, or Tuesday, the eleventh. It was exactly a month after the beginning of the attack on the Low Countries. Those who left on Tuesday and re-encountered us at Tours reported a great cloud of black smoke over the city, caused, they thought, by burning villages and farms that had been used one after another as points of support in the retreating battle against the Germans. It seems more probable now that the smoke was a smudge the Germans used to conceal their crossing of the Seine below the city and that was carried on into town by the wind.

The roads leading south from Paris were gorged with what was possibly the strangest assortment of vehicles in history. No smaller city could have produced such a gamut of conveyances, from fiacres of the Second Empire to a farm tractor hitched to a vast trailer displaying the American flag and a sign saying "This trailer is the property of an American citizen." A few men rode horses along the grassy edge of the road, making better progress than the automobiles. During the first few kilometers cars stood still for from five minutes to an hour at a time, moving forward only a few yards to stop again with grinding brakes, a procedure which eventually proved fatal to hundreds of old and overburdened vehicles. The Paris autobuses, requisitioned for the occasion, carried the personnel of government offices and major industrial establishments, and on each bus was a sign saying "*Complet.*" Some of the girl stenographers and clerks appeared to be enjoying the excursion.

Although the road originally had been set aside for civilian

traffic, we soon met soldiers moving north to Paris as everybody else moved south. They seemed content with what they
were doing. There were infantrymen in camions and motorcyclists on their machines, and their faces were strong and
untroubled.

Once you have started to leave a place, you become apprehensive. When we were held up in suburban traffic jams we
noticed everybody around us looking up at the sky, probably
remembering the machine-gunning of civilians on Belgian and
Polish roads. But the only planes overhead were French. Not
even a German reconnaissance plane appeared.

About twenty-five miles out of Paris the crowds thinned,
and the surviving automobiles made pretty good time the rest
of the way. Inhabitants of the towns through which the unending caravan passed lined the sidewalks of the long main
streets, curious and quiet, probably wondering if they too
would have to be on their way soon. In the cities south of Paris
where the migrants began to stop at dark, restaurants and
hotels were overwhelmed by a rush of business that brought
no joy to proprietors who, while they sold much of what they
had on hand, thought that in a few days they might have to
abandon their establishments. On the first evening we had a
late dinner at the Jeanne d'Arc restaurant in Orléans, where an
R.A.F. mess was established. The British ate placidly and without apparent pleasure, preparing to quit France with about as
much emotion as if it had been Burma. We three Americans
were leaving without even having fought. France still hoped
for an effectual gesture from our country, so we benefited by a
last shred of popularity. Knowing how little the United States
was likely to do, however, I wondered whether we should ever
to be able to go back to Paris with our heads up.

There wasn't even a vacant sleeping space on the benches of
a *brasserie* at Orléans. Remembering old traveling-salesman
stories, we thought of going to local bordelloes for the night.
But all the bordelloes were full of earlier arrivals from Paris.
"They are so tired," the *sous-maîtresse* of one place, who came
to the door, said to me compassionately, "that some of them are
actually sleeping." So we had to pass the night in the Citroën.

The selection of Tours appeared to have been a mistake. It
was too small and too near Paris. The Government had just

begun to arrive there when it became evident that it would have to move again in a couple of days. A direct move to Bordeaux or even better to Biarritz, where there were great hotels that could have been requisitioned for the Government, would have been better psychologically and every other way. The hunted, pillar-to-post feeling that legislators get when they are evacuated twice in one week is an invitation to panic. From an administrative point of view Tours had such limited facilities that the offices of government had to be scattered over twenty square miles of villages, occupying town halls and school-houses. Publishing the addresses of government bureaus in the local newspapers was not permitted, on the theory that German agents might get hold of the papers and tip off the Luft-waffe. So much of the time in the new capital was spent in a sort of furious hide-and-seek, trying to find the functionaries with whom one had business. The ministers themselves, arriving from Paris with their flustered and indignant mistresses who put the blame for the whole inconvenience upon them, were unable to find their ministries in some cases. The mistresses occasioned a great deal of trouble; there were not enough suites at the Hôtel de l'Univers to go around. Some of the women had to choose between putting up with a room and bath or going to a second-rate hotel. Naturally they made things unpleasant for the protectors who had subjected them to such a humiliation.

Most of the minor officials of the Government and the inhabitants of Tours as well as all the civilian refugees expected Paris to be defended. When it became plain that it would not be, a great wave of defeatism swept the stop-off capital. The people of the city, unused to air raids and anti-aircraft fire, were hospitable but uneasy. They were also overworked, doing their best to take care of their unprecedentedly numerous friends and customers. Garage proprietors, for example, had to listen to scores of appeals every day from refugees whose automobiles had broken down anywhere within a radius of fifteen miles of Tours, and who begged the garagemen to haul in the cars and repair them. I heard a *garagiste* try to turn down a man from Boulogne-sur-Seine who said he had a wife, an old mother, and a couple of children in his car, with all their possessions. The garagiste, whose best employees had been called up for the army months before this great rush of work, finally agreed to take on one more job. He was already working day and night, like a surgeon in a field hospital during a battle. I talked to an old bookseller, a myopic man who wore a straw boater in his shop. I wanted a book about the period in '70–'71 when the Government had been temporarily at Tours. The old man said he might be able to find such a book for me in a month. "The Germans will not succeed," he said, "because they exaggerate. They lack a sense of measure. All the peoples that lacked a sense of measure perished, monsieur. Look at the Babylonians, the Romans of the late Empire." I left him carefully dusting the backs of an early collected edition of Diderot. The Government remained in Tours for four days, and we followed them out. "*Nous suivons le Gouvernement*," we always said to the military police who stopped us along the roads. They seldom made us show our papers. It became a refrain. "We follow the Government."

Anthony J. Drexel Biddle, Jr., who had been appointed envoy extraordinary to the Government of France, was following the Government too. Bullitt had remained in Paris, and Biddle, who as ambassador to Poland had followed the Polish Government to France, seemed to be making a career of pursuit diplomacy. Biddle was keeping Washington informed of the progress of the collapse. His dispatches must have read like a play-by-play account of a man falling downstairs. Paul Reynaud himself, who saw clearly what was happening, was beginning to succumb to self-pity. Hélène de Portes, his since-famous mistress, wept continually and urged him to ask terms from the Germans, with whom she had dubious relations. Reynaud, the small man with a big head, had interested me ever since the day I had first seen him at the American Club of Paris. Speaking in English, he had reminded me of an eager terrier struggling against a strange and heavy leash. Shortly after he had become President of the Council, in March, he had sent for General Giraud, commander of one of the armies in the north, and after their conference a rumor spread through Paris that Giraud was to replace Gamelin as army chief. It would have meant Daladier's resignation as Minister of Defense, and that in turn would have brought a vote in the Chamber which Renaud was afraid to dare. Giraud had gone back to his post and was now a German prisoner.

One man only showed any hope in Tours—the long-nosed, stork-legged Brigadier General Charles de Gaulle, Under-Secretary for War, who was there chiefly because the field commanders had refused to have him with them. He had offended both Weygand and Pétain in 1934 by advocating a mechanized army with a core of armored divisions. He had until then been considered in the Army as one of Pétain's personal *protégés.* Conventional army officers considered his stubbornness in this dispute proof of lightness and ingratitude. He had not remained within what poor Gamelin called "the just bounds of intellectual discipline." Weygand during the 1940 campaign had once ordered De Gaulle put under arrest unless he left the front.

The armored-division idea had not, as a matter of probability, offered much hope for France. If two nations go in for mobile armor and one nation has only half the industrial capacity of the other, the larger industrial nation will inevitably produce twice as great an armored force as its rival. Tanks cannot defend against tanks, and on the "tankable" terrain over which any Franco-German war must be fought the larger tank force, the German, would win by a quick knockout every time.

Biddle, who saw De Gaulle often in those days, remembers him as a gaunt watchdog in Reynaud's anteroom, sitting with his long legs stretched out before him and his nose and the visor of his kepi, nearly parallel, pointed at a spot on the floor just in advance of his right big toe. Whenever the advocates of surrender left Reynaud for a minute, De Gaulle would squeeze in and insist that now was the moment to begin a massed assault with the remaining French tanks. Reynaud cried at one point, "De Gaulle has the character of a stubborn pig, but he *has* character." It was more than he could say for the others around him. De Gaulle, in London a year later, told me that he still thought of Reynaud with respect. "He was like a man who knows he must swim a river," De Gaulle said, "and who sees the other bank clear. But he was not strong enough to reach it."

The day came when the Government abandoned Tours,

leaving a thin line of impassive Moroccans squatting by their machine guns along the Loire and pretending to ignore their rulers' desertion. The Moroccans stayed and were killed. But we followed the Government.

Bordeaux was the next capital. Reynaud had sent for Biddle when the move from Tours was decided upon, and asked him as a last favor to take Madame de Portes into the ambassadorial automobile and see that she got safely to the second provisional capital. He feared that if she rode in a French car she might be recognized and attacked. "Without her he couldn't have carried on at all, old boy," Biddle, a friendly and decorative diplomat, says now, "so we took her." All the way to Bordeaux she railed against De Gaulle.

Root and Elliott and I had been living in an idyllic little roadhouse on the left bank of the Loire between Amboise and Tours. It had rose bowers and a garden by the riverside, and the bedrooms were what the French call *coquette*. It must have been a pleasant place of assignation in time of peace, but when the Moroccans set up a machine gun in the rose bower we decided it was time to move. The ride down to Bordeaux was not as bad as the one from Paris to Tours. So many cars had fallen by the way; it was like a grim Grand National. Italy was in the war now, not that it made much difference. There was a persistent rumor that somebody had heard a radio speaker announce that Russia and Turkey had declared war on Germany and Italy, but nobody could confirm it, because it wasn't so.

We drove as far as a town called Barbezieux the first day, where we got a good supper but couldn't find any lodging until I began a conversation with the owner of a garage and automobile-parts store who was standing in front of his shop watching the refugees go by. Elliott had his ankle in a pretty spectacular cast. "It wouldn't matter for one of my colleagues and myself," I told the garageman, "but my other colleague there gravely wounded his leg at the front, and if he is compelled to remain in the automobile overnight in a cramped position the limb may be permanently deformed." The *garagiste* said that his wife would put a mattress on the dining-room floor for John. "And in effect, as long as we deprive you of your dining room, my other colleague and I may as well sleep on the floor alongside him," I said. "Do not derange yourself to find us mattresses." "But why not?" the garagiste said. "There are plenty of mattresses." So we all got into the house on John's bad leg. The people wouldn't take any money.

We had our *café au lait* with a professor of the local lycée in the garden of a restaurant the next morning. None of the little people one met, like the garagiste and the professor, considered that France might drop out of the war altogether or that Germany might win it. They took it for granted the Government would retain the fleet, go on to North Africa and fight from there. We weren't so sure. The little people hadn't seen the ministers and their mistresses. Poor Comert, whom I had seen only briefly in Tours, had said, resentfully, "The leaders are not worthy of their people."

Bordeaux was the worst of all. Day after day the exhausted piano player from Harry's New York bar in Paris slept at a table on the terrace of a café, his head cradled in his arms. He typified all uprooted Paris packed into this city of indecision. While there was still a chance that Reynaud would be able to take the Government to Africa to continue the war, Biddle tried his best to support the Premier's prestige by extraofficial means. France had been our dike as well as England's, and poor Biddle was cast in the role of the State Department's thumb, thrust in to stop a breach that was too big for a fist.

The American managed to be seen often in Reynaud's company, or on the way to the Premier's quarters, or returning from them, as if he were conveying some tangible offer from Washington. He was, however, under the handicap common to all American diplomats then of not being able to offer anything more satisfying than good wishes. When admitted to the Premier's presence, Biddle says, he could say only, "*Bon jour, mon pauvre vieux.*" Reynaud would say, "*Bon jour.*" Then they would sit in the office together for ten minutes so that people in the anteroom would think they were discussing something, and after that Biddle would return to the United States Consulate, which he was using as temporary embassy.

There was a climate of death in Bordeaux, heavy and unhealthy like the smell of tuberoses. The famous restaurants like the Chapon Fin had never known such business. Men of wealth, heavy-jowled, waxy-faced, wearing an odd expression of relief from fear, waited for a couple of hours for tables and then spent all afternoon over their meals, ordering sequences of famous claret vintages as if they were on a *tour gastronomique* instead of being parties to a catastrophe. I remember particularly the gay hissing dinner party of the Japanese Embassy at the Chapon Fin. They were having a jolly time. I said to Root and Elliott, "The people here look as if they had been let in on a fixed race. France is out of the war now."

It was on the night of June 16 that Reynaud was finally argued into relinquishing his place and putting the country in the hands of its betrayers, the representatives of the great industrialists. He did not give up, however, without one more long wrangle in which he found few supporters of continued resistance among the men he had invited to be his colleagues in the Government. Reynaud sent for Biddle early on the evening of the sixteenth and said to him, "I know you can't do anything tangible for us, but for my sake say you will return at midnight. That will gain six hours for me, during which I may still be able to persuade them to go to Africa." He then appealed to his colleagues to delay their final decision until Biddle had received a message the ambassador expected from Washington. Biddle returned at midnight. The report had got all about the city that he was awaiting word from his Government. Nights, the streets of Bordeaux were full of people; only the wealthiest or luckiest of the refugees could find a bed to sleep in. The rest walked about or sat on the curbstones and talked. As the ambassador's car made its way through the Place de la Comédie on its way to the rendezvous, the crowd packed so closely about it that the chauffeur had to stop for a moment. The people began to cheer. Somebody had started a rumor that the United States had entered the war on the side of the Allies and that that was why Monsieur Biddle was on his way to see Reynaud in the middle of the night. "Old boy, I sat there in that car and I had a lump in my throat," Biddle says now. "Because I knew that we weren't going to do a damn thing."

The men served by Laval, Chautemps, and their team of interchangeable shills and blinds at Bordeaux were the chiefs of heavy industry who since late in 1934 had been working for France's subjection to Germany. They preferred that she be brought into the German orbit as a satellite rather than annexed. They wanted to distribute the patronage, subject to confirmation by Germany, rather than have administrators imposed on them direct. They thought that Hitler would leave them their share of Europe and Africa to run, just as their colleagues the German members of the steel and coal cartels, which long antedated Hitler, had left them their share of the business. Theirs was the really dangerous International.

Those German colleagues had been the best missionaries for the Nazi state, which guaranteed profits—consider the Goering works, *mon cher!*—eliminated labor unions, and prevented the people from getting any foolish ideas in their heads by simply forbidding them to think. The French are peculiarly susceptible to ideas of justice. The steel masters thought the great stupid mass of Germany was just the anchor the French intelligence needed to keep it below the surface forever. This was the doctrine of the men who paid Laval's bills—heavy ones, but then it pays to patronize the best assassin, like the best dentist, when one has *le fric*.

The army chiefs had provided the defeat; Laval capitalized it for his clients. Laval had been lurking on the fringe of the battle like one of those naked peasants armed with a knife who waited on medieval battlefields until an armored knight was unhorsed and helpless, when they cut his throat. When France was down, Laval's knife flashed.

On Sunday, June 16, while Reynaud was entering his last fight at Bordeaux, Root and I were at St.-Jean-de-Luz, within a few miles of the Spanish frontier, relaxing. His wife and their baby daughter had been living at St. Jean all spring. There wasn't much war feeling there; the hotels were full of Parisians who had come to get as far from the fighting as they could without a passport. It is the kind of place that people who like Provincetown would like, to me vaguely annoying. Early the next morning the radio in my hotel announced that Reynaud had resigned and that a new government had been formed with Laval and Paul Faure, the Socialist collaborationist, in leading places. Shortly afterward, news got around that the Laval-Faure thing had not come off, that there was a Pétain-Weygand government, and that Pétain had appealed to the Germans for honorable terms. It meant that effective resistance was over. If the German authorities had publicly requested terms on November 4, 1918, the German Army would have dissolved before November 11 of that year. Whatever potentialities of resistance remained to the beaten French Army on June 16, there were none on June 23, when the Armistice was actually signed.

The primary reason for the French military defeat as of June 16 is not obscure; it was the disparity of population and industrial capacity between Germany and France. A great part of the reason for the speed and completeness of the defeat lay in the superior use the Germans made of their already superior potentialities.

But there are other reasons not completely apparent even now. It must have been a little like one of those football games in which one team seems certain in advance to beat the other by two or three touchdowns, but in which the inferior team plays far below its form. The worse the poor devils muck things up the more confidently the destined victors play, and the result is an unwarranted score. The French have an excellent word for this kind of losers' dementia. They call it *la pagaille*. After such a game the spectators always think the winning team much stronger than it really is and the losers weaker than they possibly could have been.

The French strategy had been amorphous, the tactics bad, and the material woefully and unexpectedly deficient, for the men had been assured repeatedly that there was enough of everything. This was worse than telling them from the beginning that they would have to fight barehanded. After a football calamity the professional coach, to save his reputation, sometimes implies his players lacked courage. It would not suit Laval's book to have too much of a scandal about war material, because his clients had supplied it. Nor could Pétain, Huntziger, and Weygand afford to disparage generalship, because they had supplied that. And so Pétain started out to spread the libel of decadence against his own countrymen.

The betrayed people were responsible for everything, he implied. Their morals were bad (this attracted to the new regime the support of the Catholic hierarchy). They had been in love with soft living (translate decent wages, hours, and housing). "Look at the Germans," the old marshal cackled—"weren't they wonderful?" (Material and generalship had had nothing to do with it.) "And see how many Germans there were! Be like them, breed!" he adjured his compatriots. People must have some pleasure to keep them from thinking, and that is undoubtedly the cheapest.

I wrote a letter of farewell to Sauvageon, who I knew was now with a fighter group at Marseille, and another to Suzette, Henri's daughter, at Grenoble, since I thought it more likely that she had stayed there than that the old people had remained at Paris. Both letters were full of more optimism than I felt. America would avenge France, I said. Damned if I haven't already seen part of it come true.

Then I took a taxi down to the international bridge at La Hendaye that I had crossed so briskly nine months before, went over to Irun, and bought a ticket and a sleeping compartment to Lisbon on an express train.

CHAPTER XIII

Once Down Is No Battle

I HAD a few hours to spare at Irun because the train left in the early evening, so I took a walk about the town, in which the damage done by the Franco people's shells in July 1936 was still unrepaired, and out to Fuenterrabia, an old Gothic town on a hill. A learner was playing a piano inside one of the steep Fuenterrabian houses. The weather, so beautiful all that ghastly spring, was like a false unchanging smile. I walked for the first time in nine months without thinking of France. I became conscious of this and felt guilty, as you do when you walk out of a hospital where your wife is and in a couple of blocks catch yourself whistling.

I had had a fairly adequate lunch, soup and veal, at the hotel in the railroad terminus; the fact that it was possible to get such a meal even at a price far beyond people who lived on Spanish wages appeared to me to mark some kind of advance. In the previous fall it had been impossible to get a satisfying meal at all. When I came back from Fuenterrabia I went into a wine bar on an Irun street for a glass of sherry and got to talking, in English, to a dark and a fair man. The dark man was a Spaniard who had lived in New York; he was rather pleased at what had happened to the French. He made bitter fun of the Italians, though. "The Germans will give them nothing at all," he predicted. The blond fellow was a German who said he had been a merchant seaman for a long time but now had some kind of business in Irun. He said he had been a prisoner in England in the last war. He asked me what I thought would happen next, and I said I didn't know, but that the United States had better get going before the Germans got around to us.

He said, "My dear sir, Hitler has absolutely no designs on Canada or the United States. He is a fair man who wants only his rights." It recalled what the Germans had said before each of their gobbles. I looked at this undistinguished specimen of a people so mean and stupid that they repeated their lies in unison like a marching song, and I thought of the weak bands of wolfish dolts who had drifted across the boundaries of the Roman Empire with protestations of friendship. Once in, they had looked about them like German servants in a Jewish household picking out objects to steal when the Storm Troopers came. The Germans had never been warriors, properly speaking; they had been the scavengers who plucked the eyes out of sick nations. This was their cultural heritage.

Returned to the railroad station, I found two oldish men who were also bound for Lisbon. One, who was indignant because all the first-class sleeping compartments had already been sold, kept waving a card under the nose of the woman Wagons-Lits agent and shouting in French, "I am the Baron Rothschild." The other, who had his accommodations already, was a Sir Charles Something-or-Other from the British Embassy in France, but no stock-company actor would have dared play the role so obviously. I think that his company on the journey down colored all my thinking about Great Britain with pessimism that was to prove unwarranted.

Lisbon was, for the moment, one of the few remaining comfortable cities left in Europe, but it was not easy in its mind. The events in France had placed a certain restraint on the preparations for the dual celebration of the eighth centennial of Portuguese independence and the third centennial of the "liberation from the Spanish yoke" which terminated a temporary union with Portugal's neighbor. The Portuguese, placid as they are, could not avoid the reflection that now there was nothing much to stop the reimposition of a Spanish yoke whenever Franco felt like it, and they hoped he would not take the festivities in ill part.

The regime of Senhor Salazar, the university professor of political economy turned plain-clothes dictator, had kept Portugal solvent, with one of the lowest living standards and highest venereal-disease rates in Europe, but virtually without armament. Fascist Spain, whose financial position was impossible, as any political economist could explain to you in ten minutes, was bristling with expensive ordnance. Senhor Salazar must have hoped that Franco was grateful for favors received during the Spanish Civil War. He was aware that, for the first time since the Peninsular War, the traditional Portuguese alliance with England had become more of a liability than an asset. But it was not the sort of association that even a dictator could end on short notice, for English was the second language of Lisbon, English banks controlled the country's finances, the English for centuries had been the best customers for port, and Portugal knew that if Great Britain was defeated in the war, the victors would confiscate the Portuguese colonies. Italians were not popular in Lisbon, and neither were Germans, of whom there were a good many. Some weeks before my arrival the police had raided the German club and school and uncovered a lot of arms—almost enough for a Portuguese army.

Few residents of Lisbon could forget this political background for long at a time, but outwardly the life of the town and of the crescent-shaped Portuguese Riviera, which begins just north of the capital and follows the shore for thirty miles, went on exactly as it always had. Windows were not darkened at night, some moving-picture shows started at one in the morning, and the Casino in Estoril, the beach resort, began to be gay at about three. British social life in Lisbon had always had the atmosphere of a colonial governor's garden party, and it continued in the same tenor of dropping cards on fellow residents, amateur theatricals (Sir James Barrie and Ian Hay continued to be the favorite playwrights), and mild gambling at the Casino. The Duke of Kent was expected to help open the centennial show, and a special committee of the Royal British Club was proceeding gravely with preparations for his reception, wondering the while whether Germans or Spaniards would arrive before him. The visit was subsequently canceled.

The Pan American Clippers to New York and the boats to South America were then about the only reliable means of leaving the country, and since the demand for passage to South America was not precisely lively, the hotels were full of Americans from France waiting for a place on a Clipper. The total number, perhaps a thousand, was not impressive, but in proportion to the number of passengers a Clipper could carry —twenty-five was about the maximum for the westbound trip —and to the number of good hotel rooms in Lisbon and nearby Estoril, it seemed large. The *New Yorker* had booked my passage already, and I found a good room in the Grand Hotel at Mont-Estoril, so I had no trouble of any kind. I had five or six days to wait for the Clipper, and I employed them in swimming from the beach at Estoril and playing roulette for small sums at the Casino in the evenings. I also visited a British oil company official I knew, an atypical chap because he had had a Spanish mother, spoke Portuguese well, and spent a great deal of time with the Portuguese, a practice disapproved by his peers. They thought it smacked of going native. He was the "number two" in his firm in Lisbon. His chief was a more conventional Briton; he hardly seemed to think that there was anything to worry about. This irritated but in a way reassured me. All of the Lisbon British were packed to move out on twenty-four hours' notice and go aboard British warships, but at the same time the women of the colony were busy taking care of British refugees from France. And, as I have already said, they went on with their amateur theatricals.

The British went about gravely wagging their heads and saying that it was sporting of Churchill to forego recriminations and that, really, what was left of the French Army should have been evacuated to defend the British Isles. The disappearance of that army had altered the position of every nation on the Continent so drastically that people as yet couldn't get used to the idea; it reminded me of the death of the uninsured breadwinner of a large and helpless family.

On the day after I checked into my hotel I went down to the beach to swim. After swimming I sat on the terrace of the bathing pavilion, drinking vermouth and eating remarkably good olives. The vermouth was called the Vermouth of the Good Jesus. (There is a bank in Lisbon called the Bank of the Holy Ghost and of Commerce.) The pavilion people gave you a whole tumblerful of olives with each drink. There were a few German refugee families about, sitting at little tables under beach umbrellas and tremulous with masochistic fear as usual, happily certain that everything was going to turn out for the worst. An Englishman whom I had met at the bar of my hotel sat down next to me, already tight as a tick although it was just midmorning, and began telling me how he personally had piloted the plane that brought Franco from the Canaries to Spain. This broomstick journey must have been a mass enterprise. "Within three years all Democrats will be shot or in prison!" this lovable character told me. There was a public-address system at the bathing pavilion, and the management played phonograph records over it, usually Carmen Miranda. But just as I was sipping the Vermouth of the Good Jesus and wondering whether I ought to knock out the Englishman's brain with an olive pit, adapting the size of the missile to the importance of the target, the phonograph soloist put on a record of Charles Trenet singing "Boum!" The salt water and the sun and the vermouth had put me in a good frame of mind; the happy Parisian tune and the crazy lyric had an exaggerated effect upon me. I looked at the sadist and the masochists and said to myself, "They will both be disappointed." And I remembered something said to me by an old man who had been the last bare-knuckle lightweight champion of the world and had retired undefeated. This old boy was named Jack McAuliffe, and he had told me, "In Cork, where I was born, there was an old saying:

"Once down is no battle."

Book II
The World on One Knee

No Place Like It

WHEN I was getting aboard the Clipper at the mouth of the Tagus to come home I told the radio operator, who was checking off the names on the passenger list, that I had been in France. "Yeah," he said offhandedly, "it looks like we'll have to beat the hell out of those Germans." I began to understand that Hitler would not have us as he had had the Social Democrats, without fighting. It made me feel better. At that time I may have had an exaggerated idea of the boldness of German strategy. I was sure that we had no ground or air forces that could meet a series of quick landings at widely separated parts of our or the Mexican coast. That was a good guess, because when I talked to General Marshall in Washington several weeks later he told me that we had "the possible equivalent of three divisions" of troops ready to fight, and that included the garrisons of the Canal Zone and Hawaii. I was not at all sure that Germany would not offer, and Great Britain accept, terms for a peace that would leave the British Empire temporarily intact and the Reich free to move against the richest, softest, and most inviting target: us. My estimate of Great Britain had been conditioned by ten months in France; like the French, I thought that the British showing had been halfhearted and ineffectual. The British newspapers flown over to Paris even in the last days we were there had been full of racing and cricket. If they were the expression of a nation, England wasn't even interested. It is unnecessary to state that I was wrong about what Great Britain would do, but I had logical reasons for being so, like poor Gamelin. The real wonder of the world, though, is that Japan didn't hop in then. If she had, the nearly disarmed British would have been simply outclassed, no matter how great their determination. Certainly no reasons of conscience deterred the Japanese. The dictatorships were too timid. They had the world on the point of a knockout, but they "lost" it, the way a novice boxer fails to finish another novice after having him groggy.

Getting off the plane and meeting people who had stayed in America was a strange experience, because they hardly seemed to know that anything was wrong. When you started to tell them they said soothingly that probably you had had a lot of painful experiences, and if you just took a few grains of nembutol so you would get one good night's sleep, and then go out to the horse races twice, you would be your old sweet self again. It was like the dream in which you yell at people and they don't hear you. I went down to Washington to do a profile of General Marshall. The War Department took the situation seriously enough, God knows, but when you had got out of the Munitions Building you were in an unconcerned world again. It reminded me of leaving a feverish last rehearsal in a theater and coming out on a sidewalk where few of the passers-by even know there's a show about to open.

After you had been here awhile you began to get stupid too, and more recent arrivals from Europe began to bore you slightly. Dick Boyer came back from Berlin, where he had been as a correspondent for *PM*, and visited me at the *New Yorker* office in October.

It was only the second day after Boyer's return, and he still looked at people with astonishment, because they did not seem worried enough. I, who knew the symptoms, understood the way Boyer felt as soon as I saw him come into the office. We were to have lunch together and talk about Europe and Boyer's experiences as a war correspondent. Boyer was bigger and blonder than ever; he walked with chin and nose pointed upward and talked with wide gestures. He would have a noble and stupid face if it were not for his malicious and intelligent little eyes, which redeem it. Boyer still talked a little too loud, as people do in a foreign country where they assume nobody around understands them. He had arrived by Clipper and so had not had time to change back from his foreign to his domestic personality. When we got into the elevator to go down to lunch, Boyer began talking about the bombings he had been in. "The first time they bombed Berlin," he said, "they didn't do enough damage." The office girls who were jammed into the elevator all about him, some with their shoulder blades against his belly and others with their chins against his shoulder blades, looked up with interest. "The second time they bombed it, they were really getting somewhere," he said. "It made me feel good down in my air-raid shelter. Those bastards in Berlin don't like it." When he said "bastards" the girls looked confused, because he had no right to say that to them, but they had no right to be listening, either.

I said in a perfunctory way, "The only bombardment I was in was at Paris." I had said it so often that it didn't even interest me any longer, and June 3, 1940, seemed as long ago as the Battle of Hastings. All the girls continued looking at Boyer as if I had not said anything at all.

The elevator reached the street floor, and Boyer said, "What I want is a really good meal. With wine. I am used to drinking wine with my meals." We headed toward Fifth Avenue. Boyer suddenly stopped and said, "What are we doing about our defenses? I mean, have we really started or are we still futzing around?" His voice sounded very anxious.

I remembered when I had felt the same way, coming back from Lisbon, but just before meeting Boyer for lunch I had been thinking principally about the heavy overlay against a race horse named Hash, on which I had failed to bet. Understanding Boyer's anxiety, I tried to formulate in my mind what I truly believed about defense, canceling out wishful thinking. "Yeah," I said, "I think we've started."

Boyer began walking again, looking over the heads of the people in the street, who were so unworried and foolish. "Well, maybe we'll be all right then," he said.

We walked uptown without any precise destination, until we came to the sunken roller-skating rink at Rockefeller Plaza. As usual, there were a good many people hanging over the railings, watching the skaters. We joined them. Two professional skaters were putting on an exhibition. The man wore a blue uniform like a moving-picture usher's, and the girl short skirts which showed chunky, chapped legs. They were going through a complicated sort of waltz to music relayed by a loud-speaker. The trouble was, however, that while they skated well, they would have danced badly under any circumstances. Several times the girl threw herself sideways through the air, the man holding onto her wrists, and when she landed on her skates with a clacking, mechanical noise, she looked around for approval. There were restaurant tables at either end of the rink and on a level with it.

"This is a pretty good place to eat," I said. "It's nice out-doors today." Boyer thought the place looked all right, too, so we walked down the steps and a maître d'hôtel showed us to a table.

After we had ordered oysters, lobster Thermidor, and a bot-tle of Pouilly, I asked whether the Germans seemed much bucked up by their victories. Boyer said the army Germans did but the civilians didn't. "But the civilians have nothing to say anyway," he said. "It's just the Army and the Party. The coun-try will never crack until somebody cracks the Army."

"Who?" said I.

We both knew the only possible answer.

Boyer looked gloomily at the people hanging over the railing above the rink and at the skaters. They didn't seem potentially formidable. "It's a wonderful country," he said, "but I think everybody is crazy."

I tried to be funny. "That's just a European frame of mind," I said, imitating the voice of a normal, unfrightened American, like Harold Ross. "You forget about the three thousand miles of ocean and the time Hitler will need to digest all the coun-tries he has already taken."

"People who talk like that give me a pain in the butt," Boyer said.

"I used to be like you myself, old man," I continued, "but now, after a couple of months in a sane atmosphere com-pounded of Lindbergh's speeches and editorials in the *New Masses*, I see how things really are."

Boyer said, "When you begin to think that sort of stupidity is even funny, you are beginning to go crazy yourself. The first batch of French prisoners I saw, I cried."

I was not listening very intently, because I had said the same things until I had noticed people didn't like to listen to me. Boyer was right, and nobody cared, I thought, and after a while Boyer would understand that without anybody telling him. A waiter served the oysters and poured two glasses of wine, and we began to eat. The beginning of a meal demands concentration, and while we were appraising the oysters and ranking the wine in the scale of all oysters and wine that had gone down our gullets, a tall girl came out of the little skate room under the stairs and began to move about the rink. There is nothing finer to watch than a graceful animal on legs a bit too long for symmetry—a two-year-old thoroughbred, a kudu, or a heron. The girl was leggy, and I thought she was brave to put on skates at all, because her little scut was such a long way from the ground in case she fell. There didn't seem much risk of that, though, the way she moved around. She seldom lifted her skates far off the surface, and she didn't jump up or squat on her haunches and revolve with one foot in the air like the instructress. She just moved well, and her hands made slight, disarticulated motions from the wrist, as if to call attention to the lovely, slow turns she was making.

Boyer had finished his oysters—he always ate with the speed of a small dog consuming meat in the presence of larger dogs of whose forbearance it is not sure—and was beginning to talk of the gray, tasteless fish in Germany and the gray, tasteless people who endured it when he noticed the girl. He said, "It's funny, but when you're terribly worried you're not interested in food. I didn't mind the taste of the stuff. But I wouldn't eat a piece of it now for a buck." The girl was wearing a black skirt and a thin shirtwaist through which the men could see the white, clean straps of her underwear. Boyer's nostrils flared, as if he could smell the faint aroma of laundry soap and ironing board that such underwear should have. If the girl had spoiled this bouquet with a perfume, as she probably had, nobody at that distance could know it.

"I know," I said. "Then, when you're a little less worried, you take an interest in food again, but not in women. When you take an interest in women, you're not worried."

Boyer said, "I don't feel like a man from Mars but like a man from earth who has landed on another planet. Don't the damn fools know what is happening on earth?" But his voice was milder than before, and he watched the girl's thin hips.

The girl summoned a male instructor with one of her small

motions, and the two of them skated hand in hand. She was very blonde, with fine, threadlike hair that wouldn't stay up, and she had dark eyebrows and a small, turned-up nose that gave her a silly, friendly look. Boyer and I followed her with our eyes, and both felt angry when she placed the instructor's arm around her, under her right armpit. We were glad she held his hand firmly in hers, so it did not touch her breast.

"That girl skates as if thousands of other girls weren't cold and hungry, or cowering from bombs," Boyer said with a last, feeble effort to appear outraged. But he was obviously more interested in her than in his talk.

"He's beginning to be comfortable," I thought, "and he's ashamed of it." Just then the waiter arrived with the lobster Thermidor. I said, tactfully, "Oh, what the hell! Why don't you tell me all about Europe some other time?"

Boyer looked relieved. "Sure," he said. "That girl looks like somebody I used to know."

CHAPTER II

Rape Is Impossible

THAT kind of feeling was involuntary. It was due to the mental climate. Even actions directly connected with war had an unreal quality when they took place here; I remember the curious feeling I had when I went to register for compulsory service on October 16, 1940, in a schoolhouse where I had to squeeze 215 pounds of me into a child's seat, behind a child's desk, to fill out a blank. The associations evoked were of learning long division and looking forward to recess, rather than of bombed cities. Yet I had seen bombed cities, which none of the other men registering had. After sitting in the small seat for a couple of minutes I began to be overawed by the schoolteacher who was issuing the registration cards. I hoped she wouldn't ask me anything I did not know. I just got into the draft by two days; on October 18 I was going to be thirty-six years old and officially middle-aged. The psychological benefit was not slight; I have thought of myself ever since as a mere kid. I never was destined to fight, though—just get shot at.

Remoteness from the war affected everybody, but there were at least two groups in the country that tried consciously to minimize our danger. They were precisely these that had worked to the same end in France—a strong faction of men of wealth and the Communist party. The money people wanted to prove fascism more efficient than democracy, the Communists that democracy offered no protection against fascism. A military victory for the democracies would shatter the pretensions of both.

Pierre-Etienne Flandin, a former premier who has never been rated a revolutionary, gave me last winter a concise account of the way in which the French industrialists arrived at their policy of collaboration. Retrospectively it clarifies for me a great deal of what went on here in 1940–41.

"The great industrialists had never contributed so largely to a national campaign as they did to André Tardieu's group in the general elections of 1932," Flandin said. "Tardieu was badly beaten. So they said, 'What has the Republic come to when you can't even buy an election? Evidently it is time to change the system of government.' Being French, they felt particularly bad because they had wasted so much money. So they began to back the French fascist movements—De la Rocque, Doriot, all that, with Chiappe of course running the show. They mounted the riots of February 1934, expecting to take power by a *coup d'état*. The coup didn't come off. Then they gave up on accomplishing anything from inside France and decided to wait for the arrival of the Germans. The Front Populaire Government, elected in 1936" (of which Flandin had been an active parliamentary opponent), "had nothing to do with their decision. They had made up their minds two years earlier."

The American opposite numbers of the men of the *grands cartels* had been too badly panicked in 1932 to get together then. It was not until after the Roosevelt-Landon campaign of 1936 that they began to despair of democracy and to get vocal about it. The little men in Statler Hotel bars and golf-club locker rooms echoed the official line. What good was a system

under which the majority of people voted to protect their own
interests? It was damn selfish of working people to vote that
way. "As a matter of fact this country was never meant to be a
democracy anyway," they would say with the same knowing air
with which they knocked a competing line of scrapple when
they were out peddling pork products, "it was meant to be a
republic. Get it?" And suffrage in a republic could be as limited as it was in a stockholder's meeting of Republic Steel.
Money had never articulated its dislike of democracy during
the years when it had been possible to elect McKinleys and
Hardings and Coolidges and Hoovers.

I do not think that the money men who were to turn isolationists ever backed an American fascist movement on a large
scale as the cartels had in France in 1934; they were not so conscious of what they wanted or perhaps so cynical as their European counterparts, and besides they had not completely given
up on the ballot box. In 1940 they applied not only money but
advertising techniques. When the advertising men failed to
elect a President, they had to regretfully inform their clientele
that the jig was up. There was no time to mount a nationalist
authoritarian movement. The money by-passed that step and
went in for isolationism, which was a form of passive aid for
the Axis.

I stayed in the United States from July 1940 until July 1941.
An important phase of the war was being waged all around
me. It went well for the ultimate good of the country, but a
trifle slowly. The election in the United States was a defeat for
Germany; newspapers there and in Great Britain treated it as
such. I had never been worried about it; the confidence expressed up to the last minute by my little friends who were
identified with big business showed they lacked all sense of reality. The advertising manager of the *Herald Tribune* took five
to four from me on the eve of the election. The beating did
Willkie good too; it served as a disinfectant bath to rid him of
parasites. He came out of the race minus the most antisocial
elements of his support. When I met him for the first time, in
the following January, he was still astonished by their desertion. I had imagined him a knave. I found him a naïf.

My most nightmarish memory of the year is of a trip I made
to Chicago to interview the leaders of America First for an

article I had been engaged to write for *McCall's Magazine* on propaganda in the United States. I was to cover all varieties of propaganda in two thousand words and make the subject as clear as a dress pattern. I hit Chicago during the debate on the Lease-Lend Bill. The Chicago *Tribune* carried on its editorial page the day I arrived a cartoon showing Liberty loaded with chains and being beaten with a spiked club by a sort of ape-man. The ape-man was labeled not "Nazism" or "Fascism" but "New Deal." The president of America First, an ecclesiastical-looking white-haired man rather like Warren Harding or Samuel Seabury, told me in a paternal, authoritative tone that Great Britain was in no danger but that it was no use trying to help her because she was doomed. It would be dangerous to help her while she was still in the war, he continued, but if we permitted her to get knocked out of the war we would be well able to take care of ourselves against any combination of powers that could have whipped her and us combined. I detected a certain confusion, but I was there to report and not to argue, and besides a reedy young man who was publicity-directing for the committee told me that the president knew all about modern war because he had been a Quartermaster General in 1917 and sold several million dollars' worth of sundries by mail catalogue every week. I am not sure yet whether all these people desired an Axis victory consciously, but the irrational stubbornness with which they denied its possibility made you think of certain women who continually and compulsively talk about the impossibility of rape. The subject fascinates them. It was a successful article, the editors of *McCall's* said, except that I had mentioned one America Firster's business connection with the Quaker Oats Company, which was an advertiser. They fixed it to read he was "an official of a cereal company."

Although I believed that in the United States, as in France, the para-Fascists were more dangerous than the Communists, the latter caused me considerably more personal annoyance, because a number of my friends had listened to them. I never expect to see eye to eye with a Ford personnel manager or the vice-president of an advertising agency, and it causes me no anguish at all to find myself in disagreement with a newspaper publisher. But I did hate to drop in on a perfectly good reporter or physician and find myself howling and banging the table because he thought that there was no choice between Churchill and Hitler and demanded who were we to object to the slaughter of a couple of million Jews in Poland when there were resort hotels right here that wouldn't take Jewish guests? Unpeculiarly enough, the two propaganda groups had taken the same line on perfecting the United States before we opposed the Nazis—Robert Maynard Hutchins of the University of Chicago, who was the accredited intellect of the money people, hit exactly the same note on that as *New Masses.*

I think I must say here what I believe myself, because if you are going to see a war through a man's eyes you ought to know what there is behind them. I think democracy a most precious thing, not because any democratic state is perfect, but because it is perfectible. It sounds heartbreakingly banal, but I believe that you cannot even fool most of the people most of the time. They are quite likely to vote in their own interest. I also believe that since a democracy is made up of individual electors, the electors will protect the rights of the individual. A democracy may sometimes grant too little power to its government and at others allow government to infringe on the rights of the individual—Prohibition is example enough—but the vote always offers the means of correcting imbalance, and the repeal of Prohibition is an example of that. Any system that is run by a few, whether they sit in a Fascist Grand Council or at the pinnacle of a pyramid of holding companies, is a damned bad system, and Italy is a fine example of that, but unfortunately we didn't have its finish to point to in 1940–41. And so much for my ideology.

I had thought all along that the Germans would invade Great Britain in the spring or summer of 1941 and that that was the place to be for a *New Yorker* man who wanted to see the war, but I had gotten to fiddle-fluting around with the State Department Passport Bureau about giving me permission to travel on a belligerent ship. I also fiddle-fluted with the British Ministry of Information about getting me a passage either on a freighter in convoy or a bomber, and before I got under way Germany had invaded Russia. That slimmed the prospects of an invasion of England, but I choked back my disappointment and decided to go anyway. June 22, when the news of the invasion of Russia got around in New York, was a hot Sunday. I walked up through Union Square, where the free-style catch-as-catch-can Marxist arguers hang out, and all the boys who two days earlier had been howling for Churchill's blood were now screaming for us to get right into the war. "Well," I thought, "we are on the same side of a question for once, anyway." Somehow, I remembered my old French general who had said to his estranged friend, "I will shake hands, if you have arrived at better sentiments." The reason I had thought all year that we should declare war on the Axis immediately was that I didn't think either the training of our Army or war production could attain even half-speed until the Government had war powers.

CHAPTER III

Destination: United Kingdom

ALONG in July I got my passport and my means of transportation straightened out. I was to go by bomber.

Since fairly early in the war the British had been flying American-built bombers from Canada for immediate incorporation into the R.A.F. The bombers which made these one-way trips were the light types, like Lockheed Hudsons, and after they had been fitted with extra fuel tanks for the long hop, they had little space for freight or passengers. However, during the past few weeks the British Air Ministry had been using a number of the big, long-range, four-engined Consolidated bombers, which had been christened Liberators, in a regular two-way service. On westward trips they brought over groups of small-bomber pilots and occasional voyagers like the Duke of Kent and Prince Bernhard of Lippe. Going east, they carried not only passengers, mostly British subjects on official business, but also light freight, such as engine parts.

The division of the Air Ministry which managed this transatlantic service then was known as Atfero, which stood for Atlantic Ferry. An Atfero man at a Montreal airport put a tag on my suitcase which read "Destination: United Kingdom," and in approximately sixteen hours, which included four hours of loafing at an air base in Newfoundland, I reached my destination. The actual flying time was less than half that of the Pan American Clippers between New York and Lisbon. A loaded Liberator is only about half as heavy as a Clipper, but it has four fifths as much power in its engines. Its published top speed is three hundred miles an hour and a Clipper's is a hundred and ninety, but the published top speed of a military airplane is likely to be an underestimate. A secondary advantage of travel by Atfero was that it spared you from the bleak scorn of the Lisbon hotelkeepers, all of whose rooms, I heard, had been full since the fall of France. The principal reason more Americans did not go by Atfero is that passengers had to wangle both an invitation from the British authorities and permission from our own State Department.

On the morning before my plane was scheduled to leave Montreal, I reported to the Atfero office in a large office building in the city. The manager, a Mr. Jackson, received me with all the excitement a Long Island Railroad conductor displays at the sight of a commuter. After looking at my credentials, he turned me over to a Mr. Hart, who gave me a slip of pink paper which said, in effect, that I had been accorded a trip to the United Kingdom in a bomber but if I broke my neck it was my own fault. Hart assured me that this was just a matter of form. He gave me, in addition to my ticket, two pages of mimeographed instructions to passengers. One instruction read, "The following subjects should not be referred to within the hearing of any unauthorized persons: airports of departure and arrival; departure and arrival times of aircraft; details of armament, supply, storage, and the performance of aircraft, engines, and other war material. Particular discretion should be exercised in speaking with representatives of the press, whose object it is to extract the maximum amount of information and who often collaborate and piece together the scraps of information they collect individually." There were also instructions for the use of oxygen equipment. For example: "On the flight it may be necessary to use oxygen owing to the height at which the aircraft may have to fly. Oxygen masks are provided for each person on board. They will be found already connected to the oxygen supply. Please use great care in the handling of the masks, as they are quite fragile and will break easily if mishandled."

"It gets pretty cold above twenty thousand feet," Hart told me, "and I advise you to buy one of the flying suits that Atfero sells for seventeen dollars. I'll bring the suit to the field for you." I gave him seventeen dollars and then went out to stroll around the grounds of McGill University, where I had once taken a summer course shortly after the other great war, when Canadians and Americans were still slapping each other on the back because Those People had been put in their places forever. The grounds were full of Royal Canadian Air Force cadets, marching smartly and self-consciously between classrooms, where they were studying the theory of flight. I then went into the quiet tavern of the Prince of Wales Hotel, on McGill Street, the place where I had first tasted ale, and polished off a couple of reminiscent pints. Then I walked back to the Mount Royal, where I was stopping. A car was to pick me up in front of the hotel early the next morning and take me to the airport.

As I stepped into the elevator with my bag the next morning, I met Jackson, the Atfero man. He said he usually stayed at the hotel when he had a batch of planes to send off. Four more men with bags, a couple of them carrying flying suits, were already standing outside the hotel when we got to the sidewalk, and I judged, correctly, that they were to be my shipmates. Jackson introduced me to two of the men, a brisk, sandy-haired Lancashireman named Steadman, evidently in his forties, who had been in the United States on some business for the British Government, and a tall, sallow young Hollander named Van Der Schrieck, who carried a small canvas sack in his left hand. It was a diplomatic pouch, he explained. He had been out in the East Indies for the Dutch Government. The other two fellows stood a little apart. They were both very young, perhaps eighteen or nineteen, and they wore Texas-style sombreros and fancy, high-heeled cowboy boots. "They are a couple of kids who are going out as transport pilots to fly planes from factories to flying fields in England," Jackson said. "They haven't had enough experience to take bombers across, so they are going over as passengers."

Steadman, Van Der Schrieck, and I got into an automobile with Jackson, and the two kids got into another car, along with most of the baggage. When they climbed out at the airport, they looked more at home than they had at the hotel. They began walking about the nearest plane and talking like a couple of horse fanciers around a nag. I guess they liked the plane all right. It was the four-engined one in which we were to make the journey, and it was a mottled tan and green. The silvery Pan American Clippers have always looked to me like something a giant built with a Meccano set. This thing looked like a big, ill-tempered insect. I went over and introduced myself to the two kids in the cowboy hats. They shook my hand with fervor. "It certainly is mighty good to meet someone from the States," one of them said. "We been up here nearly a week." "You from Texas?" I asked, looking right at the hats. "How did you guess?" the other kid asked with obvious admiration. "Yes, sir, and it's far away now."

While we waited beside our plane, one of its sister ships came in from England. The kids were frankly critical of the pilot's landing. "Landed with his brakes on," one of them said. Jackson came over with two men wearing blue uniforms and visored caps. Each wore three rings of gold braid on his sleeve, indicating that he was a captain of a British air line. Jackson introduced the older of the two men as the captain of our plane and the other as Jimmy, a colleague who was going to cross as co-pilot with us because he felt a bit under the weather and didn't want the full responsibility of a ship this trip. Our captain was a round-faced, pink-fleshed man of about forty with a voice something like Charles Laughton's. Jimmy, who might have been about thirty-five, was tall, broad-shouldered, and apologetic. "Tonsillitis, you know," he whispered. "Going up to London and have my tonsils out. Do you suppose it's frightfully painful?"

Hart, Jackson's assistant, delivered my flying suit. It was a big brown affair, like a sleeping suit, and had a hood. "You won't need it until you leave Newfoundland," Hart told me. "He won't really go up until then." By this time somebody had let down a flap in the Liberator's belly. There were a couple of steps on the upper surface of this flap, and one by one we boosted ourselves inside. Our captain and Jimmy went up into the insect's head, where they could look out, but the rest of us remained, undigested, in its windowless thorax. The forward end of this thorax, the deepest part of the ship, was divided into two decks. A radio man, facing his instruments, had the upper deck all to himself. A big, red-haired chap, munching an apple, he sat there like a professor on a dais. The aft end of the thorax was not decked, but had two fairly wide shelves along the sides, and a passageway about the width of one of the shelves between them.

The engines began to turn over, and a man who we had been told was our flight engineer appeared from up forward. He was a tow-haired, wild-eyed young man who galloped about the ship as if he had passed his boyhood running on the tops of picket fences. He motioned us to get down into the bomb bay, under the radio man's feet; the captain, it turned out, wanted our weight in that part of the ship. We scuttled obediently into the bomb bay, a dark and miniature hold, where packing cases were stowed. The cargo was heavy rather than bulky, so we had plenty of room, and the Atfero people had spread mattresses over the crates. The engine noise increased, and we could feel the plane start to move in a series of quick, gentle lifts, as if somebody were pushing against our diaphragms with the heel of his hand. Then she steadied and we knew we were up. One of the kids from Texas waved both hands, palms upward, and grinned.

The flight engineer, who had disappeared forward, came tearing back again and made signs that we could come out from under, so we moved into the space aft of the radio man. A glorious and welcome light was coming through eight little windows and a sort of skylight known as an astrodome. We could move still farther aft into the tail of the ship, clear back to the glass-enclosed perch that the rear gunner occupies when the plane is on a bombing mission. In a short while we distributed ourselves about the ship according to our various temperaments. The two kids scrambled all over like monkeys. Steadman went back to the rear gunner's seat and looked out, perhaps trying to identify landmarks. Van Der Schrieck stretched out on one of the shelves under the astrodome and started to read *Berlin Diary.* I lay down on the other shelf and did nothing at all. It was possible to talk above the noise of the four 1,200-horsepower engines, but sustained conversation would have been difficult. If you yield to the noise, the way a fighter rolls with a punch, it is soothing. The plane rode more smoothly than any other I had ever been in. Once I made motions with my lips at the radio man: "How high?" He understood and held up ten fingers, then waved his hands and held up two fingers more—twelve thousand feet. The sky, through the astrodome, was blue, and the sun was brilliant.

We had a couple of dozen thermos bottles of hot tea, coffee, and cocoa aboard, stowed in the forward part of the tail, and a stack of lunchboxes from the Mount Royal, but as we were going to make a stop in Newfoundland for lunch there was not much reason to eat now. Jackson had told us that we would arrive at the base there in four hours; it was approximately nine hundred miles from Montreal. My reflections, as I lay on my shelf, were not entirely happy, despite the ideal flying conditions. I began to worry about my oxygen mask and how I should use it. I noticed several petcocks marked "Oxygen" at intervals along the side walls. Still, I felt like a city fellow who sees a cow but doesn't know how to get milk from it. Besides, I had read somewhere that at thirty-five thousand feet there is a constant temperature of sixty-seven degrees below zero, and I hoped that the captain would not go *too* high even though I had a flying suit. These thoughts were interrupted when the plane began to descend toward the Newfoundland airport. Looking out through the windows, we could see what appeared to be an enormous bare spot in the middle of an infinite green forest. As we circled lower we could make out a great airfield, its runways dotted with planes and protected by machine-gun pillboxes. The captain put the big Liberator on the ground as lightly as a dragon fly alighting on a leaf. I looked at the two boys from Texas. Their faces were ecstatic. When the plane came to a stop, the boys opened the hole in her belly and we all crawled out.

A slender, grinning young officer in some sort of khaki uniform was waiting beside the plane to greet us. We couldn't hear what he said, but when he turned and marched off across the runways we followed him. We learned afterward that he was a member of the Newfoundland Ranger Force, which polices the airport. He led us to a big, square frame building which bore a sign saying "Eastbound Inn." It was like a very large and unpretentious summer resort hotel. It houses the airport personnel and aviators and passengers who for one reason or another are lying over at this way station. We had lunch there: steak-and-kidney pie, stewed pears, and tea. As our deafness wore off, we began to talk a bit. Presently the radio man came in and sat down at our table. He was a Lowland Scot named Mitchell, and he said that this was his eleventh ferry crossing. Nothing serious had ever happened to him, he told us. "This is one of the largest military airfields in the world," he added, "and it's all been hacked out of the scrub since the beginning of the war. It's many hours' travel by land to a railroad or a town." He said he had been grounded there by a blizzard last March and had not been able to get away for three weeks. "It was very quiet," he remarked.

Our captain and Jimmy had stayed inside the plane. Now they came in to lunch, and the captain stopped by our table to say that we would have a four-hour wait. "I don't want to get in before dawn," he said. "Nothing to be gained by it." I went for a long walk in the sun with Steadman. Then I came back to the inn and sat around with Van Der Schrieck. We talked about the ninth-century Middle Kingdom of Lothaire, which had included the Low Countries, Alsace-Lorraine, and what is now Switzerland. Finally I went into the recreation room and watched the Texas boys play table tennis. By the time a Ranger came to summon us to our plane, we were bored with Newfoundland.

When we got aboard the Liberator again we put on our flying suits and ate a large number of sandwiches, although it was only a few hours after lunchtime. The two shelves along the sides of the part of the ship we passengers chose had hinged longitudinal leaves, which, when raised and fastened together, formed a continuous deck on which to spread our sleeping things. We decided we would be better off there than down in the bomb bay, which was very drafty and where there were no windows from which to watch the sunset or dawn, so we dragged three mattresses up from the bay and spread them athwartship on our newly created deck. Our deck was slightly lower than the radio man's. We had a few light blankets, and we hung one over the aperture between us and the bay to shut off any draft. The radio man stayed at his instruments, wearing his headphones and munching another of what appeared to be an endless series of apples. He would be up all night, of course. We closed the door that led into the tail of the ship, and then the five of us lay down on the mattresses across-ship, forming an intricate mosaic of legs and arms. My feet were at the right of the Hollander's head, and his were next to my right ear. The arrangement proved fairly comfortable, but whenever some-body had to go out to make use of the toilet facilities, which were aft, it meant untying the human knot, opening the door, banging it several times to close it, and then reversing the whole operation on the return trip. The larder was also in the tail of the ship, and it seemed that as the air grew colder we thought more of food, so there were constant trips for ther-mos bottles and sandwiches. I realized after a few minutes that the plane had been badly tailored for me. It was about three inches too narrow. In order to lie down I had to bend either my neck or my knees just enough to develop a kink. Van Der Schrieck was a couple of inches taller, and the taller of the Texan boys was in as bad a plight. Steadman and the smaller Texan fitted all right. It was cold, but not as cold as I had ex-pected, and to my great satisfaction I was breathing easily at the altitude, whatever it was. I dozed, for exactly how long I did not know, and saw a raspberry-pink glow through the windows when I awoke. I wondered whether it was the late American sunset or the early European dawn, but soon the sky grew dark and I knew.

I awoke again in the night, chilled and stiff. All of us seemed to awake at about the same time. Maybe one of us, in turning, had joggled the others. Mitchell sat there unblinking, the dimmed bulb on his table the only illumination in the place. The small Texan stumbled out to the larder and came back with three lunchboxes and a thermos of hot tea. We all shared the tea and grabbed things out of the lunchboxes. I got a ham sandwich as stiff and chilly as a slab of ice cream. I took a cold, rigid piece of ham out of the sandwich and held it in my palm, inside my flying suit, until it got at least as warm as I was. Then I ate it and went to sleep again. The next time I opened my eyes it was to a new quality of twilight. I knew it must be daybreak. We all got up and began to stretch, stamp, and look out of the windows, but we could as yet see only clouds. After a short while we sighted land far under us—Scotland or Ireland, I guessed. We grew restless. It's like getting into Grand Central on a train; the minutes after 125th Street seem the longest. We packed our mattresses back into the bomb bay, climbed out of our flying suits, and began to exchange our English addresses. The captain made another good landing, and we crawled out of the plane for the second time. We saw, rather than heard, a brisk R.A.F. officer, waiting outside, say, "Good morning." A friendly bull terrier with one pink eye thrust his muzzle against my hand. Then we got into a couple of ancient Rolls-Royces and were trundled over to the officers' club at the edge of the flying field for a wash and breakfast. There was an immigration man with a couple of perfunctory questions to ask the aliens on the plane, who of course included me. By the time I got to the dining room for breakfast, our captain and Jimmy had established themselves at a table with Van Der Schrieck. I sat down with them, and we all had bacon, tomato, and sausage. The bacon was excellent, but the sausage contained, I was told, sixty-five per cent bread, which made it taste like a hot dog with the roll inside the frankfurter casing.

I complimented the captain on our fine crossing and then said, because I was a little curious, "We didn't have to use oxygen at all. Don't you usually fly higher than that?"

"Oh yes," the captain replied brightly, as he poured milk in his tea. "But I just kept her at thirteen thousand last night. Didn't want to aggravate Jimmy's tonsillitis."

CHAPTER IV

Non Angeli Sed Angli

I SPENT the night of my arrival in Britain at the Central Hotel in Glasgow. The Central has an indefinite number of rooms, alcoves, and lounges, all meant to drink in, spread along the sides of a corridor on the first floor. At that date it was still easy to get whisky in any of them early in the evening (by 1942

there was very little of it). At eleven o'clock service ceased except in a lounge marked "For use of residents only." This was
in deference to the eleven-o'clock closing law in public drinking places. If you are living in a hotel it counts as your home.
Everybody from the other rooms moved into this lounge and
continued to drink, but at midnight a lame waiter whom any
ex-Walter Scott fan could identify instantly as a crusty old
servitor, announced that drinks would be sold only to *actual*
residents of the hotel. After he had weeded out small tippers
and Englishmen whose faces he did not like he waved the survivors, mostly Scotsmen, Norwegians, Americans, and trulls,
into another, more exclusive lounge. He applied the fine comb
again at one o'clock and again we moved, to a lounge for *bona-
fide* residents of the hotel. At four in the morning I found myself in what I thought was my eleventh drinking nook of the
night, together with a major in kilts, a lieutenant in kilts, and a
merchant-navy skipper. The major spoke a trifle brusquely to
the waiter, and the waiter said, "Major, you've had enough.
Go to bed now." The major sulked for a couple of minutes and
then went, for he knew the waiter was the only man in Glasgow who could give him a drink. The merchant-navy man had
been glaring at the lieutenant disapprovingly, and now he said,
"It amuses me to see you wearing the kilt when I have better
Highland blood than you." This sounded like a quotation
from a Waverly novel, but I could not identify it.

The lieutenant said, "I have just come from a place called
Crrete. Have you heard of it? I am a MacInnes of Skye." The
merchant-navy man said, "I never cared for Skye." The lieutenant said, "That is no' imporrtant." The seafarer said, "I am
a MacNeill of Barra." The lieutenant said, "You lie. You have
not the faceel appearrance of a MacNeill of Barra." The crusty
old servitor got between them and said, "Gentlemen, you've a
wee thingie on both. There'll be no more drink tonight." I
went to bed still trying to figure whether they had framed me
with some amateur theatricals. But it had all been on the level.
The first fact one must accept about Britain is that all British literature, no matter how improbably it reads, is realistic. You
meet its most outrageous models everywhere you turn, because
Britain is full of improbable people, behaving in what an American or a Frenchman wrongly suspects is a fictitious manner.

Before coming to Britain I had intended to write about it from an American point of view, but the project reminded me of one Sam Langford once described. "It would be like a man who only understand Italian trying to teach French to a man who do not understand Italian either." The essential point in writing about Britain is never to try to explain it, and, in talking to Britons, never to try to make them explain themselves.

When I went down to my train the next day I was pleasurably impressed to find nearly all the seats in the first-class carriages occupied by private soldiers and aircraftsmen. The head porter of the hotel had sent a lad along half an hour ahead of time to get a place for me. I decided that the British social revolution, of which we had heard a good deal in America, had at last arrived. One minute before train time all the "other ranks" yielded their seats to officers and got out. They were batmen who had been sent to hold the places. "Obviously," I thought to myself, "in this country it is unwise to jump to conclusions."

The young man who had taken the seat opposite me in my compartment was a subaltern in a regiment identified for initiates but not for me by a pair of bronze pretzels on his lapels. They were, I was to learn later, representations of Staffordshire knots, and his regiment was the South Staffords. He was about six feet tall and rugged, but apparently suffering from concussion of the brain or an extraordinary hangover. I had a Penguin book that I had bought at a station newsstand in a hurry; it was the second volume of Robert Graves's *I, Claudius*. I had meant to buy the first volume. The subaltern slept for a while with mouth open; after we had ridden for half an hour he began to stir. In another half-hour he said, "Intrsting?" I said, "Yes, but I got the second volume by mistake and I haven't read the first volume." Half an hour later he said, "I think it's preferable to begin reading early on in a book. Don't you agree?" I asked him if he cared to read a newspaper, and he declined on the grounds of ill-health. "Just finished a physical-training course, you know," he said, "and I felt so nauseously fit I went on a frightful beano." I suggested that we might get a drink in the restaurant car, and a little color came back into his face, elevating the tint to a dead white. "Would've never have had the courage to go of my own accord," he said. "Thanks immensely for moral support." We got the drink—that was the golden

age when there were still restaurant cars and they still had a bit
of drink to sell on British railways—and then we got another.
Peter, the name the subaltern answered to when he had drunk
himself back to semi-consciousness, said the waitress looked
enfilable; a part of his boyhood had been spent at a school in
France. He had been tossed out of Oxford during his first year,
he said—not the intellectual type. He regretted it, because he
had hoped for a boxing blue if he had remained. What really
"intrsted" him was driving racing automobiles. He had enlisted as a private in the Brigade of Guards at the beginning of
the war and had worked his way up to a commission in the less
exalted South Staffords. "I attribute my success to working
jolly hard," he said. He was such a congenial type that I consulted him about setting up my London life. I said I didn't
want to go to the Savoy, which had from reports become a
transatlantic *succursale* of the Stork Club, and which was the
only London hotel I had ever heard of. Peter said he knew three
really British hotels, one in St. James's Place, one on Dover
Street—"that's where my parents always put up when they
come up to town," he said—and a third on Half Moon Street.
The parents put me off the Dover Street place. When we got
to Euston Station, Peter led me out into London to find a
lodging. We got in a taxi and had the cabbie drive us to St.
James's Place, but that hotel had been blitzed. "Awfully
sorry," Peter said, "I haven't been up to London in a couple of
months, you know." We tried the one on Half Moon Street
next. By that time our drunk was beginning to run down on us
and we were in desperate need of drinks to keep it going, so I
hardly looked around me before I registered. As I rushed out
into the London blackout with Peter, I retained only a vague
impression of a room with heavy yellow damask draperies. We
got into a place called the Lansdowne soon after that and had
some drinks with a boxer named Jackie Kid Berg whom Ray
Arcel in New York used to train, and then into the Hungaria,
where we were told we had to order dinner with our drinks
because it was after eleven o'clock. "We have an extension
until half-past twelve," they said, "but only for diners." So we
ordered up a couple of redundant meals, which would have
seemed to me curious in a country where food was rationed if
I had not quite resigned myself to being Through the Looking

Glass. After the Hungaria closed we went to a thing Peter knew called a bottle club, which was exactly like a 1924 New York clip joint with a cockney accent. For all I could tell they had imported it stone by stone, as Hearst used to buy himself knocked-down monasteries. This place had a dance floor as big as a copy desk, four colored musicians, a social secretary who was under indictment for crimes against nature, and the most terrible liquor in the world. It also had hostesses to help you drink this stuff. Everything was on a membership basis, cards and all; I wept joyous tears of recognition.

A couple of girls came over and sat with us; one was not making too much sense. "They laid the bodies on the dance floor," she would say. She'd had a lot. I gathered at last that a bomb had dropped next door during a blitz and the rescue people had really brought the dead and nearly-dead into the club and laid them out there. "Why don't you get out of this bloody awful London?" she said encouragingly. "Every time the blitz came I'd get blind drunk," she said, "and then I wouldn't mind it so, but next afternoon when I got up I'd have an awful hangover. Then the blitz would begin again and I'd get blind again. I thought I'd go mad." There hadn't been a blitz for nearly two months, but people were still edgy. I paid for one bottle of whisky—the legal theory was that it was your whisky and you just came there to drink it and bought chasers, so you couldn't ever order less than a bottle at a time. Peter paid for another and then, when I began to think of going home, I looked around and he wasn't there. I ran out into Denman Street, which was as black as deep mourning, and shouted "Peter! Peter!" but I never saw him again. Pamela, the blitz-batty hostess, got a cab and saw me home.

I put up at the hotel in Half Moon Street for six months following that and came back to it when I returned to England in 1942.

The hotel when I came there was governed by a board of directors largely composed of marquises, viscounts, and bart.'s —their names were printed on the stationery, which left so little room for correspondence that it was necessary to use two sheets of notepaper where one would ordinarily serve. None of these notables came in to operate the lift or the telephone switchboard, however, and the hotel, which has about forty

rooms, was as short of help as it was long on directors. The
rooms, even those that are technically on the same floors, are
all on slightly different levels, as in the country houses most
prized by Englishmen, and are always entered by falling down
one step, tripping over three steps, or marching up a hall with
a floor at a twenty-five-degree angle. The concierge by day was
a magnificently pink, pompous, and sly Devon man known as
Roberts either because that was his name or because he used
to refer to the days when he had been Lord Roberts' batman.
He wore a beautiful red-and-green-striped waistcoat that made
his belly look like a beetle's back, with wide gold buttons and
a watch chain over his paunch that you could have hung an anchor on, and he used to have a fairly good thing of pressing my
trousers on an ironing board that he had rigged behind the
desk. There was no valet *en titre*, but I always felt that a crease
good enough for Lord Roberts was good enough for me. The
concierge was respectful, pleasant-spoken, a man who had obviously understood how to limit his ambitions and adjust to his
world.

The night porter, whom I knew only as Mac, was gaunt,
yellow-toothed, limber, and rebellious. He was part Irish, part
Canadian, and all cockney; he played the races, horse and dog,
every day and usually came on duty tight but conscious and
self-controlled. He had been a noncom in India and had a cigarette case that the Duke of Windsor, then Prince of Wales,
had sent him for being one of a guard of honor at New Delhi,
of which he took an un-Kiplingesque view. The clientele of the
hotel alternately irritated and amused him, but he could put on
as soldierly a show of respect to an arriving leftenant-colonel as
would merit a half-crown from any decent lush. Once he had
graded the tipping proclivities of the colonel he would cool
off. Mac played darts on the team representing the Rule Britannia pub, Allen Street, Kensington, in the "News of the
World" tournament. The team had got to the finals one year,
but the cup had been dashed from the lip, as in most of Mac's
enterprises. He swam in the Serpentine every morning before
going home from work. Mac's domestic affairs, from the frag-
mentary references that he made to them in our conversations,
which usually occurred in the early morning before I went to
bed, must have been fairly involved. He was finally sacked for

threatening to bash the French chef in the nose; he said he could never stomach bloody foreigners.

The clientele of the hotel in the summer of 1941, when London was just beginning to fill up again after the blitz, consisted partly of people, mostly old, whom Roberts liked to refer to as "county." The typical dinner party in the restaurant —where the hors d'oeuvre invariably consisted of vegetable marrow, beetroot, celery, and one sardine—was made up of an old deaf gentleman, three deaf old ladies (presumably his wife and two of her or his sisters), four girls with buck teeth and large feet, and one elegant subaltern or sublieutenant, the heir and pride of the family. The dowdy girls would look adoringly at the young man, who had come to London on leave; the family had come up to meet him. His problem was to be sufficiently agreeable to the old people to borrow money, without spending so much time in their company that the leave and the borrowed money would do him no good. After he had left, the old people would converse in well-bred howls, because of their deafness, their comments on their acquaintances resounding to the furthest corner of what they always called the "restaraw." I remember one old Galsworthy type shouting that "Lady Viola must be eighty." "EIGHTY!" his *commère* shrieked back to him, "Why, she's older than I am!"

The cellar then was one of the best that survived in London, because young people never came to the place unless they could help it, and the old people's doctors did not allow them to drink much. Cerutti, the old Italian wine waiter, one of Thackeray's own illustrations, was a shabby but a proud man then. A year later, when the restaurant had become one of the gayest and most constantly crowded-out in London, I was to see him resplendent in a new long-tailed coat and a sommelier's glittering chain, but cringing because he knew that there was nothing left in the house fit to drink.

Outside the window drapes that veiled this inner nodule of British propriety there resounded pretty continually the cheerful click of the Piccadilly tarts' high heels. Half Moon and Clarges streets, which are traverses between Piccadilly and Curzon Street, are important trade routes of summer evenings. The Piccadilly packets, having picked up cargoes, convey them back to their Curzon Street and Shepherds' Market home ports. They come back up Clarges Street light, chattering happily. The police, except for enforcing certain trade agreements, deal with the girls in the same spirit of comradely venality as cops in any other country. The fine aroma of larceny in the air makes a New Yorker feel at home. If the British were half as stuffy as they like to think they are, nobody could live with them.

They are, for example, the only nation in the world that habitually boasts of its own modesty. It is commonplace to read in a London leader or letter to the editor, "It is perhaps our fault as a nation that we do not speak sufficiently often of our own achievements." Really, it is one fault of which not even the Irish would accuse them. The Noel Coward kind of underemphasis is as glaring an affectation as a Von Stroheim strut, but happily no Briton can maintain it beyond the second drink. Drink, by the way, may have represented the difference in the resistant qualities of British and French statesmen. Hitler, whenever he denounces the British Prime Minister as "that drunkard," betrays his puzzlement at something Sam Langford understood. "You can sweat oat beer," Sam used to say, "and you can sweat oat whisky. But you can't sweat oat women."

On my second evening in London, just at the official blackout time, I saw a light showing through the interstice between a window shade and sash in a basement window. A man in front of a house diagonally across the street from it shouted, "Put out that bloody light!" and then walked over and kicked in the windowpane. There were still a good many people sleeping in bunks in the tube stations, and blitz reminiscences were not entirely out of fashion. In the early morning hours of July 27 there was a raid, which I waited out in my hotel bedroom. I thought that when it got really bad I would go downstairs, but it never got as bad as I expected, and then the all-clear sounded. When the guns first awoke me I thought for a minute that I was a fool for not having stayed home, but the feeling soon wore off. A couple of days later I was at the great plant of the London Gas, Light and Coke Company, talking to some workmen, because I had brought from America the idea of writing a profile of a typical British workingman. I never found one who was typical of all; it was presumptuous of me to have supposed I would. But at the gas works that day I met a mechanic from Poplar, a district in the East End of London, who told me that in his immediate neighborhood the July raid had been one of the worst ever. A heavy bomb had fallen in a court in the center of three or four old riverside warehouses belonging to a dog-biscuit manufacturer that served the people as shelters. The warehouses had caved in, and about seventy persons had been killed and a couple of hundred injured. "Lucky as 'ow less and less is sleepin' in the shelters every night," the Poplar man said. "A month ago a big one in the sime spot would 'ave killed five 'undred. But they cawn't beat Poplar. One old woman about itey-one years of ige, when they dug 'er out of the debbris, she let out a cry, 'Bloody 'itler cawn't kill me!' Why, when the moanin' Lizzies started up that night it was like old times, and the barridges and all. But what was unfortunate, the pubs, what we could a done with that time of night, was closed, so we couldn't get the old darlin' a bottle of Guinness."

The mechanic, a "welder and burner," who earned between seven and eight pounds a week—twenty-eight to thirty-two dollars, and excellent pay by English standards—was not much like an American workman of the same grade. He was dressed like a caricature of a coster, with cap and neckerchief—again that disquieting resemblance to a "literary" concept—and he was apparently quite willing to live in a slum, because he had long possessed enough money to move out of it if he had wished. But he had a heart as big as a melon. "In Poplar we're cool, calm, and collective," he said. "And we're determined to defeat this bloody 'itler and 'e *will* be defeated and all, there's no doubt about that, because we're not 'aving any."

"Any what?" I asked.

"Any dictytor," he said, and with a sudden burst of eloquence, as if to make it all clear:

"Once a Britisher 'as put 'is back to the wall and 'e says, 'I am not going to 'ave it'—then 'e's not going to 'ave it. Because 'e's *determined* not to 'ave it. And consequently—'E WILL NOT 'AVE IT."

Poplar and a thousand places like it, I understood, formed the wall against which Churchill had put *his* back. They also, quite without enthusiasm on their own part, form a protective wall around Mayfair.

CHAPTER V

It Showed Nice Instincts

THE war, in the summer of 1941, had hit a dead level. All through 1940 and the first half of 1941 the Germans had knocked the world about. They had occupied France and western Europe and then bombed England and after that taken over the Balkans, but now to a fellow in London it looked like anybody's fight, or a deadlock. The Germans had gone into Russia and taken their bombers with them; Britain was getting stronger by the minute, with the German grip off her collar. It already began to be plain that the German victories in Russia had less significance than victories in western Europe. No way was apparent for Great Britain and Russia to win the war unless the United States came in, but it began to seem improbable they could lose it. And since American entry into the war was a good possibility, while Germany had no equal good fortune to anticipate, a betting man would have had to lay slight odds against the Axis. I tried to fight off undue optimism, but I couldn't help thinking that any side which had come so near winning and failed was not going to win at all. It was so irresistibly reminiscent of the first time Germany had tried. The Punic Wars were not decided by a rubber, best two out of three. The same side won the First, Second, *and* Third, and I had a hunch that the German Wars would be the same, except that no Third might be necessary. Cannae, of which the Germans had always talked so much, had been the winning battle of a losing army. In their souls they identified themselves with Carthage that had been beaten and Siegfried that had been murdered. Behind their arrogance they were full of self-pity. Poplar had a better ticker than Potsdam, but I didn't see how you could make a man quit by putting your own back to a wall. It was better to push him up to a wall and then knock his head against it. The power for the push would have to come from the United States, as it had the last time. In the meantime the only active warfare based on Britain was being carried on by the R.A.F., which had gained a distinct edge on the Luftwaffe. So I asked permission to visit a fighter field.

I could not help thinking that morning of the trip I had made to St. Dizier in June 1940, when the French pilots were outnumbered twenty to one by the enemy. Now, a year and a bit later, I was riding in an English train to an English flying field, and the offensive in the air war in the West had passed to the British. As in 1940, belligerent pilots were flying over France, but now it was the Germans, operating from French airports, who had to maintain the unending patrol against an enemy who could strike at the point and moment he chose.

The road to St. Dizier that June day had been filled with troop-carrying lorries and French tanks and anti-tank guns going up to reinforce the hinge in the new line that Weygand had set himself to defend without any faith in his chances. Moroccan troops stood along the village streets, watching the tanks go by. The Moroccans had been scattered through the countryside to deal with the parachutists, whom, it turned out later, the Germans were not to use in that phase of the war. The weather was beautiful, and there was a feel of death in the air. You wanted to get off the road and lie down under a big oak tree by a canal and forget what was going to happen, but you couldn't. To console yourself, you said, "There are only ninety-nine chances out of a hundred it will happen." That had been optimism.

There was nothing beautiful about the English weather on the morning of the second journey; just a sun the color of lard trying to burn a mist away. During the invasion scare railroad-station signs giving the names of places had been taken down, but not advertising signs, and from the car window I could view a succession of mildly pretty semisuburban towns, all apparently called Mazawattee Tea or Bovril. The names of towns in 1941 were usually marked in small letters on the backs of station benches, and a stranger traveled in a constant state of fear that he had passed his destination.

I had picked this particular field for my visit because there were Polish fighter squadrons there. Poles are not only good fighter pilots but hyperdemonstrative. Underemphasis is probably a sterling virtue, but I sometimes think the English overdo it. An officer I knew who commanded the ground defenses at another English airport had told me, "The Poles knock the Germans out of the air by the dozens, and when they come in from a good fight they land like a swarm of wasps, upwind, downwind, acrosswind, and all over the place. They jump out of their cockpits and kiss one another and they hold up their fingers to show how many Germans they have shot down." It had seemed to me that that would be a cheerful thing to see.

I succeeded in getting off at the right town and walked about half a mile through the streets of a neat, quiet community to the airport. An infantryman and an airman on sentry duty together at the gate inspected my pass from the Air Ministry and waved me on to the station adjutant's office. Soldiers are posted at all British flying fields to guard them against ground-strafing and parachutists, so that the airmen can concentrate on keeping the planes flying. The troops at this field belonged to the Irish Guards. The atmosphere of the place was relaxed. Men were raking and burning leaves along the tree-lined road that led to the administration building, and I suppose it was the smell and the season and the comfortable red-brick architecture which combined to remind me of the opening of a semester at an American university—a co-ed university at that, because there were plenty of girls about. These were Waafs, wearing the gray uniform of the Women's Auxiliary Air Force, with flat, visored caps and commendably short skirts. Naturally enough, few girls with unshapely legs volunteered for this branch of the service, although conscription of women has since brought the standard down, and I never saw more than two together without half expecting them to put their arms on one another's shoulders and dance off into the wings, but what the Waafs really did at the field was the clerical work and a good deal of just plain scrubbing-up around the place.

The station adjutant had been expecting me and had assigned a flying officer, an Irishman with a wide acquaintance among the Poles, to show me around. My guide's regular duty was to work with the Polish intelligence officers, piecing together their accounts of each day's operations. He and I got into a small car and started off toward what he called a squadron dispersal hut. There were three squadrons at the field, and their dispersal huts were widely separated, as were the hangars, workshops, and fuel tanks. Because of this, the flying officer said, the field had made a disappointing target for the Germans, who had never been able to do more than flatten one or two buildings and put a few holes in the runways.

Since a fighter plane has a limited fuel capacity, a sweep seldom lasts more than two hours, including getting out and back. Fliers taking part in the day's operations change into their battle clothes in the dispersal huts and wait there until they go off on their jobs. When they return, they report results at the huts, change to slacks, go over to the mess for tea, and are quite likely to show up for cocktails and dinner in the nearest big town.

As we drove along a road winding among the hangars, the flying officer waved toward a group of Hurricanes whose mottled camouflage was being painted solid black. "The good old Hurricanes are a little slow for day fighting now," he said, "but with some changes in equipment and a new coat of paint they make very useful night fighters." I could not help remembering how a French pilot had said to me in the previous summer, "Ah, if I only had a Hurricane!" We drove a couple of hundred yards farther and then stopped beside a field where half a dozen Spitfires were drawn up in front of a hangar. A man was tinkering under the cowl of one of them. We got out of the car and walked over toward him, and as we did so he straightened up to greet us. He was a blond chap, with a complete set of gold front teeth, and my guide introduced him to me as a Polish officer, an engineer charged with the maintenance of planes. I noticed that the fuselage of the Spitfire he had been working on bore not only the usual emblems but a drawing of the hind end of a kitten with a coquettish red heart on it, and I asked the Pole what that stood for. "Is design peculiar to pilot," he replied. "Without official significance. He is very original *esprit*." I asked if the original *esprit* was also a successful pilot, and the engineer said, "Moderately, yes. Here he has shot down two, three, *quatre*—yes, I think five *avions*. In Poland, two, I think, or three." The engineer flashed a golden grin. "We move so very much between countries," he said, "I have my Polish forgot, my French forgot, and English I have not yet ever arrived to learn, so sometimes I mix all together."

The engineer said that he, like ninety per cent of the Poles in the R.A.F., had been in the Polish Air Force, in which they all had flown crude Polish-built fighters with French engines. They had started the war with only a couple of hundred such planes and had managed to fly a few to Rumania when it was all over, but most of the pilots had crossed the border on foot. It took some of them months to reach France. There they had been incorporated in the Armée de l'Air and assigned to planes that were inferior even by French standards. "Squadron leader, who is our high man here, flew Caudron 406 in France," the engineer said, with his usual aureate display. "Took half an hour to climb ten thousand feet." He insisted on showing me over the Spitfire, one of the newest types, with two machine guns and a cannon in each wing. "Guns fire individually or all together," he said. "Just press button." He sounded like a very persuasive Manhattan radio salesman. Since arriving at this air-field early last summer, he told me, the three squadrons had shot down forty-five German planes and lost eighteen pilots. "Now, when a pilot is descended," he said, "is usually over France, so is captured. Last year we had many pilots shot down over Britain. They make forced landing or bail out, and next morning they report back to station for another plane."

We took our leave of the engineer and drove on down to the dispersal hut we had set out for, a one-story frame building, with a red-and-white Polish flag drooping from a staff in front of it. The mist had begun to clear, and the flying officer said to me, "I was afraid you had picked a bad day, but it looks as if they'll go up all right. It'll probably be just a sweep over the Channel, maybe over Cherbourg or Le Havre. I don't think they'll find much opposition." When the pilots on a sweep can't get a fight, he said, they sometimes drop low and "beat up" gun positions, airdromes, and anything that looks as if it might be a military objective. "Those two cannons can do real damage," he said, "but the most important thing about ground-strafing is that it keeps our fellows happy. Makes them think they're doing something, you know. The risk isn't great. I've known of only one plane from this station to be lost that way."

The hut was furnished with a double row of cots for the men to rest on and a set of metal lockers for their flying gear. The most prominent decoration was a very large poster of a

slinky and altogether attractive female—obviously a spy, if you
know your poster types. It bore the legend, "Keep mum. She's
not dumb." There was also a chart showing how to inflate and
make use of the pneumatic doughnut-shaped dinghies which
airmen carry on flights over the Channel. It was like a cartoon
strip, with drawings of an airman descending by parachute,
landing on the water, climbing into his dinghy, and finally
comfortably sitting in it, smiling happily. Someone had cut a
cheesecake picture of a Hollywood girl out of a magazine and
fitted her into the dinghy beside the airman. "Happy landing!"
a young Pole said when he saw me looking at it. There were
half a dozen pilots in the place, wearing their battle dress,
smoking cigarettes, and chattering in Polish. They illustrated
their words with great, full-arm gestures, imitating swoops and
sudden banks and climbs; you could follow three or four dogfights at once by watching them. Occasionally some flier would
make a clucking noise suggestive of a machine gun, and laugh
as if he had told a good joke. Their battle dress had a distinctly
Slavic look, consisting of a sort of Russian blouse pulled tight
at the waist and baggy, gray woolen trousers stuffed into black
boots.

They were all boys in their early twenties, except one tall,
hawk-nosed man, who, I was told, used to be a great land-
owner in Poland. He had been in the Polish Air Force Reserve
long before the war began and had returned to the service as a
fighter pilot. "He could have a ground job if he wanted it,"
the flying officer said, "but he prefers to go on sweeps. He's
very old for a fighter pilot—thirty-eight."

The hawk-nosed man offered to explain one of the hut's
most important features—a large-scale map of the southeast
coast of England, the Channel, and the French shore. He
pointed to a number of pins stuck into the map here and there
within the limits of the Channel and said, "Boats to pick us up
if we fall in. If a pilot knows he can't reach the coast—maybe
petrol tank punctured—he makes for nearest boat. We carry
this map in our heads. Very useful." Next he showed me his
Mae West—one of those partially inflated jackets airmen wear,
which look like an umpire's chest protector except that there is
a rear as well as a front panel. Each Mae West has a pocket with
a small container of compressed air in it, so arranged that the

pilot can release the air as he bails out, thus fully inflating the
contrivance in a few seconds. Another accessory in each jacket
is a phial of yellow fluid. The phial breaks as the jacket hits the
water, and the yellow stuff forms a large floating patch around
the flier, making his whereabouts easy to spot from the air. Still
another part of the equipment is a powerful flashlight, with
which to attract the attention of passing planes if the flier is un-
lucky enough to be still in the water after sundown. The Mae
West is practically unsinkable, but it will not, of course, protect
a man from the Channel's cold waters. That's where the pneumatic dinghy helps; it is attached to the pilot's parachute, and
if he can swim to it and get aboard, he probably has a much
longer lease on life. One Polish pilot lasted seventy-two hours
in a dinghy in mid-Channel, then was picked up, and returned
to duty within a week.

The flying officer suggested that we start for the mess, since
the pilots would be going out to their planes in a few minutes.
"We can have a sherry and then stand on the terrace in front of
the mess and see all three squadrons take off," he said. "After
that we'll have a spot of lunch, and by the time we're through
coffee they'll be back. Then we can stop by here again and see
what they did. I don't expect there'll be much, though. A
number of bombers from other fields will be going over, and
our fellows are supposed to get to the coast just as the bombers
reach it on their way back. If there are any Messerschmitts following the bombers, our crowd will tackle them. But I don't
expect there'll be any Messerschmitts to get; they seldom
come across any more. If the bombers aren't being followed,
our fellows will continue on and make a sweep over the Channel, with maybe a look over a corner of France."

We got into the car again and drove to the mess, which was
in a large Georgian brick building with a portico. The social
room, where we went for our sherry, was full of faded black
leather armchairs and settees that reminded me of the lobby of
a Y.M.C.A. There were portrait photographs of the royal family scattered about the vaguely green walls, and there were files
of half a dozen London newspapers, including the Polish daily
and the Polish weekly now published here and *France*, the
French-language daily. Most of the men in the place wore either
the R.A.F. gray or the khaki battle dress of the Irish Guards,

with its neat green-and-white shoulder badge. Irish and Poles were mingling as convivially as if they were all attending Notre Dame. "It is wonderful to have a Pole in our party when we're drinking," my companion observed. "Then, if we have any trouble with a policeman, we all pretend to be Poles. The real Pole says to the constable, 'I am sorry, officer, my friends don't understand good English. Perhaps you speak also Polish, no?' The copper just waves helplessly and says, 'Oh, go away!'"

When we had finished our sherry we went out onto the terrace. From there we could look down on a wide field where a row of Spitfires was lined up at either end, facing the center, as if for a quadrille. "This station was only built to accommodate two squadrons, or twenty-four planes," the flying officer explained, "and there isn't room for our three squadrons to taxi to the same side of the field and take off; there would be a lag of ten minutes or so. The first two squadrons would be out of sight before the third got into the air, or else they would be circling about, wasting petrol. So we divide the three squadrons into two sets and send them off in opposite directions. First set takes off over the second set's heads, second set takes off almost as the first gets into the air."

A good many of the officers in the mess hall had straggled outside to watch the take-off. I gathered that it was a fixture in their day, like the arrival of the noon train at a rural railroad station. A short, bull-necked pilot wearing flying clothes spoke to my companion. "I was going," he said, "but at eleven o'clock squadron leader changed plan. Where they go today?" "Le Havre, probably," the Irishman said. The Pole looked relieved. "Oh boy, I miss a beautiful useless trip!" he said. "They won't find anything. I was over there the other day—not one little Messerschmitt for shooting down."

A big officer with the chest, the shoulders, and the cheerful pink face of a New York police captain stopped directly in front of me and asked how I liked the place. His sleeves were ringed with the four stripes of a group captain, which is the R.A.F. equivalent of a colonel. "I heard you were coming," he said with a slow wink. "I have my sources of information." The enunciation was old-school-tie, but the tone and the manner were unmistakably Irish. "I am the group captain," he said, "and I have the misfortune to command this odd collection of mad people."

By now the noise of the Spitfires' motors was urgent and impatient, and the line of planes at our left began to move toward the center of the field. They picked up speed and soared like racing pigeons simultaneously released, and they were hardly in the air before the planes on the other side of the field began to advance. By the time the first set was a few hundred feet from the ground, the second had taken off. For a moment there seemed to be a single spiral of planes in the air; then the machines split up neatly into three groups and were off.

The planes disappeared in the direction of the Channel, and the group captain and I were turning to go back into the mess when a lone Spitfire started to tear across the field. "And who may that be?" the group captain demanded as the plane left the ground. He sounded startled. "It is the wing commander, sir," said a Pole at his side. "He decided to go too." The group captain kept a straight face until his informant moved away, and then he turned to me with a grin. "You see," he said, "the discipline is not what one would expect of a purely British wing. Only yesterday I was telling that wing commander that he must impress on his men the necessity of sticking to their formations. They leave formation and go out looking for individual fights. Well, if he goes off on his own, what is one to expect of the others?" I could tell by the group captain's tone that he thought the Poles were all right. "Last year, during the battle, we ran a little short of Spitfires at this base," he went on. "That wing commander was a squadron leader then, and his squadron lacked one Spitfire. He was certainly entitled to a fast plane for himself, but he chose to lead that squadron in a Hurricane and let his juniors have the Spitfires. He used to take off a quarter of an hour before the others and tell them to catch up to him over Brest or St. Omer or some such place. When they got there, they would find him in the middle of a dogfight. It was horribly irregular, but it showed nice instincts."

My flying-officer friend having faded discreetly away, the group captain and I lunched together in rather impressive solitude at the head table in the dining hall. The food was depressingly British—thick soup, joint and two veg, and suet pudding—but the group captain's spirits were immune to it. He told me that Poles from this field had brought down a hundred and thirty German planes during the Battle of Britain. At the start there had been some linguistic difficulties. "The most terrifying moment of my life came right out on that terrace last summer," the group captain said. "The first Polish squadron we ever had in the R.A.F. was making its first operational take-off. We had a New Zealand and a Canadian squadron at the field at the same time, and the whole lot were to take off just as you saw it done today. The New Zealanders and Canadians were on one side of the field and the Poles on the other. The officer at the control-room radio said to the Canadian flight leader, 'Lead and go first.' He said to the Pole, 'Lead and go last.' The Pole only understood 'lead,' and the two lines of planes started at the same second. There they were, rushing across the field at each other head on. I couldn't bear to look. Do you know, sir, those planes took off simultaneously, all thirty-six of them, without a single collision. It was just like putting the fingers of one hand between the fingers of the other. The Poles must have thought it was a particularly flashy maneuver."

By the time we had finished lunch and had coffee in the social hall, the group captain said he thought I had better be getting back to the dispersal hut to see the pilots come in, and sent for the flying officer, who again drove me to it. There we found only the squadron intelligence officer, a self-effacing man who had been in the old Polish Air Force since its formation. The three of us talked for a bit, and then we heard the planes and went out in front of the hut to watch them come in. Again they reminded me of pigeons, but this time of pigeons circling and swooping down to their loft as the owner signals with a white cloth on a pole. In a moment they were on the ground, and those from our squadron were jogging along toward the hut, their idly turning propellers high in the air and their noses hiding the pilots in the cockpits. As each plane neared the hut, a dozen Polish aircraftsmen rushed to greet it. Even before the pilots spoke, the men on the field knew there had been no fighting, because the rubber nipples on the muzzles of the planes' guns were unbroken. These nipples are put on to keep dust out of the gun barrels, and when the guns have been fired the rubber hangs in shreds about their mouths.

The Poles climbed out of their planes and walked toward the hut, lighting cigarettes. They were cheerful but not exuberant, because nothing much had happened. They crowded into the hut and gathered around the intelligence officer, who had spread a large map on a table. The squadron leader, a stocky, pugnacious little Slav with light gray eyes and a dented nose, pointed out the course his men had taken, and the intelligence officer marked it on the map with a pencil. The line crossed the English coast southeast of the airfield, zigzagged northeast over the Channel, crossed a corner of France, and came back to England again. One of the pilots said to me, "Nothing. No good. We saw three Messerschmitts, but too high, too far away. They beat it."

As the flying officer and I were taking our leave of the squadron, the tall, hawk-nosed pilot—the "old" one—said to me, "Is funny, no? In two summers, in two countries, we have only couple old planes. Then there come thousands Germans to hunt us from the sky. Now we have very many beautiful planes and we cannot find any Germans to fight with us."

CHAPTER VI

The Long Name for the Lifeboat

LONDON, during that summer of 1941 when the tide of war stood still at lowest ebb, just before it started to flow in, was the official capital of eight countries and the unofficial one of France; there were besides the governments of Great Britain, Norway, Poland, Holland, Belgium, Czechoslovakia, Yugoslavia, and Greece, and the Free French, a half-dozen semi-recognized national movements, free Danish, free Rumanian, free Bulgarian, and free Austrian. His Royal Highness Prince Hassan, legitimate heir to the throne of Persia—he was a brother of the last shah of the old line and had been acting as regent when Reza Khan took over the power—lived in the room next to mine at the hotel on Half Moon Street and would have been popped back onto a throne when the British and Russians ran Reza Khan out that summer, I think, if Reza's son, the present shah, had not been married to the sister of King Fuad of Egypt. His Highness was a cheerful ovoid little man who touched his heart and brow when he talked and was rather better in French than English. The town was full of intrigue over postwar Europe that began to assume some relation to reality as it became plain that the Reich would not win decisively. As yet, however, the cabals resembled deals in Imperial Russian bonds; even Balkan statesmen felt it silly to become really heated about remote possibilities. The acerbity among the exiled governments increased in proportion to their chances of getting home. In 1941 they resembled cabin passengers on a raft. They got on fairly well together, but as soon as they were rescued they would start jockeying for a stateroom with a bath, and by the time the rescuing ship reached land they would all be scrambling for the same taxicab.

All the governments had their own intelligence services. The prime ministers received exhaustive reports not only on what was happening in their German-occupied countries, where their sources supplemented and sometimes scooped the British Intelligence Service, but on what was happening in London. Ministers got reports on their opposite numbers in half a dozen other governments, and operatives shadowed each other, until lunch at Claridge's or the Ritz Grill resembled a traffic jam of characters out of an Alfred Hitchcock film. Operatives of lower categories and corresponding expense accounts shadowed *their* opposite numbers at the White Tower, the Greek restaurant on Percy Street. Every twenty-four hours there was a general pooling and interchange of information, probably held in Albert Hall or Piccadilly tube station, and then everybody heard the secret information that everybody else had been compiling. London, since Pepys's day and before, has been a gossiping city. The coffeehouses of the eighteenth century flourished with talk as the main attraction; the Englishman in his club is sometimes a marvel of malicious veiled curiosity. There is a fair argument for the thesis that all the careful barriers the Briton builds around privacy—the blackball, the no-trespass, the truth-increases, the libel principle in newspaper law, the mannered reserve, and the choked voice—began simply as precautions against the national weakness for talking too much. The flood of refugee gossip adding to the normally high stream of British indiscretions, the torrent of confidential conversation overflowed its banks and London became the gabbiest city in the world.

My favorites in Babel were the Norwegians and the Poles, I suppose because I am a sucker for extremes. The Norwegians listened and never talked. The Poles talked and never listened.

"Why did Mr. Murrow" (Ed Murrow, the Columbia Broadcasting System announcer) "talk for two hours with Dr. Beneš yesterday?" a member of the Polish Government once asked me at lunch, after receiving a report from one of his agents. The Poles are always worried about the Czechs. "Why he don't talk to me?" my Polish friend insisted. "Why nobody take us seriously? Because we laugh, my God?" The Czechs seem to the Poles solid heavy people like liver dumplings. They used to go about in 1941 impressing visiting members of the Foreign Policy Association and the like. I tried to reassure my Pole by telling him the bravura of the Polish pilots had a greater effect on public opinion than any amount of ponderous talk, but he remained unhappy. "After the war all the Poles so brave will be dead and the Czechs will own Europe," he said. A moment later he began to laugh. "The Ministry of Shipping is giving to Polish Government new merchant ship to replace one we lost," he said. "We are thinking of name for it. I would like to call *Alma Mater Cracoviensis*, Holy Virgin of Cracow. But this name is too long to paint on one lifeboat." He emptied his wine-glass, swallowed a mouthful of vegetable marrow, grimaced, and then said, in a discouraged tone, "Nobody take us seriously."

I suppose that on a strictly ideological basis I should not have favored the Poles. A Polish diplomat whom we all called Prince Tommy once said to me, with a delightful smile, "Poland was a democracy before the war, but without popular representation." That sounds like a National Association of Manufacturers' program for America, but whereas I might have bellowed with rage and started throwing beer glasses if a Republican had said it in the Artists' and Writers' Saloon, when Prince Tommy said the same thing it just sounded amiably ridiculous. Since I didn't work for the Chicago *Tribune* I wasn't bound to an ideological line anyway.

There was an extravagance about the gestures of the Poles I knew that would have repelled me if I had encountered it in a work of fiction, where I can always recognize an implausibility. What could be more trite than the story of the impoverished nobleman who borrows his arrears of room rent to save himself from being dispossessed and who stops on his way home and buys a bottle of champagne with the money? It sounds like the theme of an inferior *Lettre de Mon Moulin*. Except that I knew the protagonist. He was the Pole who once told me that he had been faithful all his life to one woman: "Any fragile blonde with a morbid expression."

There was also the story of Radomski. Radomski was a fighter pilot. On a sweep over France he broke formation, yielding to the bad Polish habit, and pursued three Messerschmitts, which when they had got him away from his comrades turned on him, according to the sensible German custom. "Radomski dive to get away," one of his colleagues told me, recounting the adventure, "and then he reach for the clutch to pull out. 'Funny,' he say to himself, 'cannot find clutch.' He reach again. Still cannot find clutch. He say, '*Curieux*,' and he look. Clutch was there, all right, but Radomski's left arm was shot away. He brought plane back across Channel and landed."

One Pole I knew in the Ministry of Finance had remained in Warsaw, where he had been a factory owner, until December of 1940 before he had been able to escape. "Four Schutzstaffel men came to my house a few weeks before Christmas," he said. "They came to pick out presents for their wives. They went through the house, opening closets, dressers, cabinets, to find nice things to steal. I understand German well, naturally, and I could hear what they said to each other. There was one man, the tallest of the four, who was ashamed of himself, but he did not dare say so. Everything that the others proposed to him to steal for his wife, he made an excuse for not accepting. 'These sheets would not fit our bed,' he would say, or, 'Trude does not like that color.' The others got angry with him. One, who was as a corporal, said at last, 'Take these handkerchiefs anyway. I command you.' The tall man took the handkerchiefs. I saw his face when he went out. He looked very crushed, very guilty. Now he was one of the gang. He had shared in the loot. This is the policy all through Germany. The furnishings, the clothes from Polish homes are transported there and distributed among the German civilians. Not to accept marks a family as anti-Nazi, so all accept. Then they are *participes criminis.* 'Stand fast,' the Government tells them, 'because if the Allies come and find the loot, the noose will be about your necks. Stand fast, now we are all gangsters together.' It will not matter, really," he said, smiling, "because we will kill them all." As a British friend once remarked to me, the Poles are great cards.

The points of view that the Allies brought to London were not easy to reconcile, although a number of nice old retired naval officers and brewers' widows were always trying to do it by promoting Allied circles and forums. I remember one gathering at the Hyde Park Hotel where a member of the Polish Government who had resigned because of the 1941 treaty of friendship with Soviets spoke, not on Russia, which would have been too controversial, but on what should be done with Germany after the war. As might be expected, his project resembled a blueprint for an ax murder. Then a Dutch economist got up and said that the future prosperity of Europe depended on the survival of an economically sound Germany. The Pole shouted, "That is the way your countrymen always were at Geneva—on the German side. Traitors!" There is nothing like free discussion for promoting good will. My friend who likes fragile blondes said to me after the row:

"It was so disgusting, so human, so deplorable."

CHAPTER VII

Rosie, You Be'ave Yourself

Wₕᵢₗₑ still hopeful of finding the typical British workingman I walked one summer day down to Bermondsey, where there is at least a homogeneous type known as the Bermondsey man. Bermondsey, across the Thames from the proper East End, is

the oldest transpontine borough of London. It is the only district on that side of the river named among the twenty-six
wards of London in Thomas Stow's "Survey," where it is
called Bridge Ward Without. It is named, according to Stow
again, for the monks of the Abbey of St. Bermond's Eye, a re-
doubtable relic. Despite these Elizabethan and medieval associations, and the street names like Tooley Street and the Old
Kent Road that suggest a pleasant antiquity, Bermondsey
doesn't look any older than a grim part of Pittsburgh. The architecture is divided between early-nineteenth-century slum
residential and late-nineteenth-century ghastly industrial. It
was not apparent to me why anybody should love the place,
and I don't think that any American workingman could.

But I knew from friends that Bermondsey people bred
Bermondsey people who in turn lived and died in Bermondsey. They worked on the Bermondsey docks or in the great jam
and pickle factories within the borough—the factories, of
course, got all the women—and they had their fun in the Bermondsey pubs and cinemas. "Over the water" in Bermondsey
means, not America, but Stepney, the East End Borough
across the river that you can nearly spit across. For Bermondsey it is a foreign land. "Stepney's full of Irish and Chinks and
Jews," one of the first Bermondsey men I met said to me.
"Here we've only our own people." A moment later he was
telling me how Sir Oswald Mosley and his blackshirts had once
tried to march through Bermondsey before the war. "We gave
them a proper bloody 'iding," he said with pleasure. Bermondsey's thinking is Left Labor, its feeling dominated by
xenophobia. In its emotional quality it sometimes reminds me
of a compact Brooklyn. Bermondsey constantly sends up to
Parliament a local physician who is an avowed pacifist and a
prohibitionist, being in direct disagreement with all his con-
stituents on both counts. But he is a Bermondsey man. If the
Government should send Anthony Eden down into the borough to contest the seat, I am convinced Eden would get
licked. The only non-Bermondsey men with whom Bermondsey people have anything essential to do are owners of housing
estates, owners of factories, and German airmen, and they
don't like any of them.

Walking down to the Bermondsey Town Hall, I passed the

blitz ruins of a great jam, pickle, chutney, and vinegar factory.
A rescue worker of the Bermondsey civil defense told me how
that had gone. "It was at night," he said, "so fortunately there
was nobody in it but the watchmen and nine people in a shelter in the bisement. You should've seen the flimes—and the
streets knee-deep in strawberry jam. We went in to dig the
people out of the shelter, we could 'ear 'em shouting. We
broke through a wall, but we couldn't put in the props to keep
it open while we went on. The place was all over jam, sir. The
props slipped away in the jam, and one of our chaps was
crushed. It was bloody awful to think of, sir, and the smell of
vinegar. We 'ad better luck some other times, o' course. Once
we got a girl and 'er mother that was buried under twenty feet
of debbris. It took sixteen hours. The girl was on top of her
mother, and after we'd worked a few hours I got to where I
could reach the girl's 'and. I 'eld it for hours to give 'er 'eart,
and the old lady underneath was cheerful as a lark. ''Old on,
Rosie,' I'd say to the girl. Most of us knows one another in
Bermondsey. When we got 'em out the old woman, that 'ad
been so plucky, went out like that. Dead. And the girl became
quite 'ighsterical. 'You be'ave yourself, Rosie,' I said. 'It won't
do, my girl.' It's criminal to lose one after you've dug for 'er so
long, sir."

There was another, rougher type of rescue worker there
who had more cheerful memories. "It would surprise you 'ow
much people can stand, sir," he said. "Once we dug all night
and got out a couple of old women weighing sixteen stone
apiece. Then there was the old cove a warden found sitting on
the kerbstone in front of where a lodging'ouse 'ad been a little
before that, only now there was nothing left except a lonely
criter. 'Come along with me,' the warden says. 'No,' says the
old bloke, 'I've paid my tanner and I want my kip.' 'E meant
to say," the rescue worker translated at my request, "that 'e 'ad
paid sixpence for 'is bed and 'e was going to stay there until 'e
got one or the other. It was like the chap who was in the
Dundee Arms when it was 'it and they brought 'im into a first-
aid stition with 'is chin split open. 'What 'appened to you?' the
doctor says, just to mike conver180sation, and the chap says,
'What 'appened to me? I was standing at the bar and I 'ad just
put down a florin and the guvnor 'ad just put a pint of bitter in

front o' me and wallop! I found myself in the cellar without the beer, and I've lost the chinge o' me florin.'"

A mild man, an ambulance driver, told me how he and his mates went into ruins to collect the injured that the rescue men had dug out. "When there's nobody to 'elp sometimes, we go about collectin' the pieces what's left," he said shyly. "I once scriped most of an old lydy off a wall. It does sound a bit ghouly, doesn't it, now? But it 'as to be done."

A still milder man, the chief of the borough mortuary service, said, "We wash every bit with soap, no matter 'ow small, and it would please you to see them, sir. Not a speck of dust on 'em. And they 'ave a coffin and all the rites. Only we can't save their clothes for the relatives. You'll agree with me that when a person gets bombed their clothes is not much good afterward."

I went into the garage that served as headquarters for the civil-defense men and talked to a lot of them, after that. There were twenty-five or thirty about, and they had nothing much to do until the next raid, which, incidentally, was not to come until the spring of 1943, although none of us would have been sufficiently optimistic to suppose so. I had been talking to Joe Blake, the town clerk, who is an intellectual. Joe had been bitter about the lack of free secondary education, or at least the great difficulty of obtaining it. That automatically prevented working-class boys from getting any higher degrees, he said. "Bermondsey has just short of a hundred thousand people in normal times," Joe had said. "Do you know how many Bermondsey boys have gone up to the universities in the last twenty years? Three." But none of the defense workers were indignant about that. In civil life they had been dockers, mechanics' mates, shop assistants, and the like. "I once knew a chap 'oo 'ad been to Oxford," one fellow said. "'E was a 'surance igent." That evidently settled the question for him.

I asked them what they expected to get out of the war, and most of them said with a puzzled air that they didn't expect to get anything except their old jobs, a vague something that they referred to as "better working conditions," and perhaps better housing, all in Bermondsey. "Of course we *should* get something out of it, shouldn't we?" one fellow said. "If we'd lost, we'd have lost something, wouldn't we? It's like putting

up a bet." This seemed to strike most of the others as a het-
erodox and perhaps dangerous thought. Of the whole group
only one had ever considered going to the colonies or America, having as a boy even obtained some free literature put out
by a Canadian government bureau in London. But he had
given up the thought. Curiously, for me, not one in the lot,
although they were all under thirty-five, expected that he as an
individual would ever earn twice as much as his best previous
salary. Since none of them had ever earned better than six
pounds, or $24, before, that meant that out of the thirty men
none ever expected to make $48 a week. It seemed to me that
of thirty New Yorkers in the same age range at least fifteen
would have had sure-fire private schemes to get up in the
world and make a lot of money, and most of the rest would
have trusted to luck to bring them money too. At least twenty-
five of the thirty New Yorkers would have been fooling themselves, I imagined.

CHAPTER VIII

Dev's Double

THE French in London had their full share of humanity.
    I had first heard the voice of Charles de Gaulle in the lounge
of the Grand Hotel do Mont Estoril in Portugal in June 1940.
It came over the radio from London: "I, the General de
Gaulle" . . . "France has lost a battle, not a war" . . . "I invite to join me" . . . "*Vive la France*." The voice spoke of resistance and hope; it was strong and manly. The half-dozen
weeping Frenchwomen huddled about the radio cabinet
where they had been listening to the bulletins of defeat and
surrender ceased for a moment in their sobbing. Someone had
spoken for France; Pétain always seemed to speak *against* her,
reproachful with the cruelty of the impotent. When I arrived
in London in the following summer I wanted to see General
de Gaulle as soon as possible and write a whacking profile
about a modern Bertrand du Guesclin. Du Guesclin was the

great fourteenth-century guerrilla knight who, anxious only to rid France of the invader (in that war the English), fought tirelessly until he had righted what appeared a hopeless military situation. Like most of my preconceptions, this one was on the romantic side. General de Gaulle, when I met him, was to remind me rather of another tall man whom I had encountered in Redmen's Hall over a cigar store in a shabby quarter of Providence, R.I., in about 1928. That man had been named Eamon de Valera, and at the time I had met him his party had been out of power in Eire and Dev had been barnstorming the United States to get Irish-Americans to sign away their claims to money from Irish Republican bonds. De Gaulle and De Valera both are tall and long-legged and long-nosed and narrow-boned, with long upper lips and the faces of a pair of hidalgos that El Greco might have painted on either side of the crucified Christ. They share the quality of being so long and narrow they appear out of drawing. They share also an Iberian pride, stubbornness, and suspicion of the people around them; there may be actual consanguinity, since De Valera's father was Spanish and De Gaulle comes from the part of France that Spaniards occupied repeatedly during the wars of the sixteenth and seventeenth centuries. Both are great patriots and have had to maintain their faith in causes of which more practical men would have despaired. But neither is easy to live with.

I learned from friends when I first got to London that I could not interview General de Gaulle at once. He was walking about in the streets contiguous to Carlton Gardens, his headquarters, but he was by official decree out of town. De Gaulle had displeased Winston Churchill by something he had said in Brazzaville, where the General had recently been, so neither the French nor British press was allowed to allude to his return to London. Naturally American correspondents couldn't allude to it either. "As soon as he makes it up with the P.M. it will be all right," my British friends told me, "but he has been a very naughty boy."

General de Gaulle's naughtiness in that instance had consisted of giving an interview to George Weller of the Chicago *Daily News* syndicate, in which he had put out a feeler for direct American support. Weller had quoted De Gaulle as offering to the United States bases in the African territories

and Pacific islands under Free French control "without demanding destroyers in return." The Free French were keen to
get Lend-Lease materials directly, instead of through the
British Government. His Majesty's Gov. construed the talk
about destroyers as a reflection on His Majesty's Gov. General
de Gaulle repudiated the interview, although Weller is a reliable reporter. And shortly after this public expiation the British
press acknowledged the General's return from Africa, sometimes spelled Coventry.

This sort of thing contributed to what one of my best-
informed and most British friends called De Gaulle's "justified
anglophobia," but it did nothing to encourage him in further
gestures toward America. De Gaulle is intolerant of restraint,
as he proved in the famous armored-division row in the
French Army, and his London irritation was increased by the
knowledge that Vichy propaganda in France accused him of
being under Churchill's thumb. It was natural that he should
try to bite a piece out of the thumb occasionally. But Churchill
was stuck with De Gaulle almost as firmly as De Gaulle was
stuck with Churchill.

If the Prime Minister had forced De Gaulle's permanent retirement to private life he would have confirmed the charge
that Great Britain controlled the Free French. He would also
have wasted a whole year of advertising De Gaulle's name. De
Gaulle had to stay on.

Among the thirty or forty thousand Frenchmen and
Frenchwomen in England, the General had no great personal
support. They consisted of French citizens who had been in
England before the fall of France, of refugees who had crossed
on the last boats from French ports primarily to get away from
the Germans, and only in small minority of young men who
had escaped from occupied France with the specific purpose of
joining De Gaulle. Members of the first group, the "French of
England," found difficulty in comprehending the extent of the
French disaster even in 1941. For them France had never
ceased to be a great power, French law had never ceased to operate, and De Gaulle was a fantastic, unauthorized intruder on
their schizoid dream. Many of the June 1940 refugees, hard
fighters themselves, resented De Gaulle's claim to one-man
leadership. They said that he had no right to claim a copyright

on France, that nobody had elected him, and that even in accordance with military rank he was junior to several other
officers who had escaped the debacle, like Catroux, a five-star
general, and Vice-Admiral Muselier. These critics included the
men of the Left, who doubted De Gaulle's republicanism, and
some others whose Gallic irreverence was outraged by the
man's mere aspect. "He looks as if he had swallowed his
saber," these latter said. There were very few white men in the
Free French "Empire" of Equatorial Africa. André Labarthe,
the founder of the revue, *La France Libre*, once referred to De
Gaulle as "*le roi des nègres.*" The *mot* made its instant round of
the limited French world in London; De Gaulle, who is as serious as a saint, never forgave Labarthe. Labarthe, a scientist,
military critic, and editor, whose republicanism, unlike De
Gaulle's, dated from long before the war, had demonstrated
his practical patriotism by kidnaping a ship loaded with copper
from Bordeaux and forcing the skipper to take it to England in
the last days before the Armistice of Compiègne. He had also
made *La France Libre* the best of anti-collaborationist publications outside France. Labarthe came down to Algiers in the
spring of 1943 and was made Minister of Information for the
Government of North Africa. But De Gaulle refused to enter
into the new combination government later that year until
Labarthe had been dismissed. He preferred as Minister of Information a Frenchman of restrained bellicosity, Bonnet, whose
name has unfortunate associations, and who had passed his
time since the Armistice lecturing in America. It was a similar
story with Vice-Admiral Muselier, whom General de Gaulle
eliminated first from the Free or Fighting French Committee
in London and then from any role in Algiers. Muselier had
seized St. Pierre and Miquelon to permit a plebiscite by which
the Free French gained those islands; he was perhaps the one
man most hated by Vichy admirals like Darlan. Collabora-
tionism was scarcely the basis of De Gaulle's trouble with him.

De Gaulle, however, protected with great obstinacy all
through 1941, and may still be protecting, for all I know, a
Colonel P——, who was considered a Fascist by every Frenchman and Englishman at all acquainted with the Free French
setup whom I ever met. P—— carried stories against other
Free Frenchmen; any attack upon him therefore aroused De

Gaulle's suspicion—"the others" were trying to deprive him of his faithful watchdog! I was to see General Giraud go through a similar routine in defense of General Bergeret, in Algiers more than a year later. Most reactions of French generals are interchangeable. Again, in the summer of 1942 when I was in London a putty-colored little man of archetypical Mussolini-Mosley mien, one Charles Vallin, who for years had been second in command of the Croix de Feu organization in France, appeared mysteriously in London. This little man, composed entirely of stomach and eyebrows, announced that although he had not changed any of his anti-democratic views he had seen the light (i.e., decided Hitler would lose) and was promptly accepted by De Gaulle as a great anti-German. The General did not proclaim that Vichyites were irredeemable, but that only he had the right to give absolution. A hint of papal infallibility was implicit in his pretension.

De Gaulle's enthusiasm for democracy required considerable prodding during his first year of exile. I can remember the struggle of the British Political Warfare people to induce him to say, "*Liberté, Egalité, Fraternité,*" during the course of a broadcast to France; he balked like a zebra and finally yielded with the air of Henri IV saying "Paris is worth a Mass." His imposition of the Cross of Lorraine on the Free French version of the tricolor never went down well with the anti-clericals among his compatriots. It left an opening for criticism which not even General Giraud in 1942 was to miss, although Giraud is no adept at controversy.

The politics of "the movement" furnished the subject for endless arguments over the wine-stained tablecloths of the "French pub," the York Minster in Dean Street, where the commonalty crowded in, as over the elegant napery of L'Ecu de France and Prunier's in the West End, where the immediate entourage of the General and the wealthy refugees made *langouste* and partridge serve in place of rationed meat and kept unquivering chins in spite of having to drink minor vintages. It was at the Ecu that the truly chic Free French of London gave a public farewell party for the young bloods leaving on the "secret" expedition to surprise Dakar in September 1940. Madame Prunier has carried on the London restaurant of the firm throughout the war, while Monsieur has continued to conduct the business in Paris. There were Frenchmen in London who were willing to be called "Free French" but not "De Gaullistes," and others who said that just "French" was enough, that a Frenchman was by definition free. One of the great weaknesses of the French community in Britain, considered as a microcosm of France, was that few representatives of labor and none of the peasantry had escaped the debacle. The two largest classes of French society were without expression in the plans for the future of their country. I had a good many friends among the soldiers and intellectuals who had come on to London after the fall of France, and I had, moreover, in a manner that it would be perhaps indiscreet to detail, rediscovered a number of old acquaintances in the British services concerned with work in occupied Europe, so that I found myself in the thick of the arguments. I always maintained the thesis, against Frenchmen who deprecated De Gaulle and Britons who complained of his crankiness, that since he was the only horse they had entered in the race they had better try hard with him. I thought him valuable as a trade-mark and as a person. For stubbornness and a lack of objectivity, in the leader of a forlorn hope, are rather qualities than defects. And I would quote Reynaud, with the addition of a softening *peut-être*, "He has perhaps the character of a stubborn pig—but he *has* character." It is, believe it or not, a great asset.

The consequence of this overelaborate discussion of every facet of De Gaulle's character was that by the time I interviewed him I was completely insulated against fresh impressions. I was in the frame of mind of a soldier entering a house that he has reason to believe booby-trapped. The General, suspicious by nature, had been made more so by numerous and probably conflicting reports on me, and my first innocent question, designed to stimulate conversation, was a disaster. "When are you coming to America, my general?" I asked him. He immediately had to decide whether I was a scout for the Foreign Office or whether Anthony J. Drexel Biddle, Jr., whom he knew I knew, had sent me over to feel him out with a view to a later official bid from the State Department. "I have not yet been invited," he said after a pause of a couple of minutes, and settled back in his chair as I have seen witnesses in a murder trial momentarily relax after turning a tough question from a cross-examiner.

De Gaulle is decidedly less imposing sitting down than standing up, because the part of him showing above a desk does not suggest a man of extraordinary stature. He is small-boned, with fine, slender hands and no great depth of chest or breadth of shoulder. His height folds up under his desk with his legs. He is consistently pale rather than sallow. It is as difficult to carry on a sequential conversation with De Gaulle as with De Valera. He reacts, but does not respond, to a question by delivering a speech on a tangential subject.

The General said that he was convinced the little people of France, the sailors, the peasants, the factory hands, the barbers, were for him and the rich were for Vichy and against him. I noticed, perhaps frivolously, that he did not say the little were against the rich or the rich against the little, but that he made of the breach between classes a question of reaction to De Gaulle. After the war, he said, a government with "bold ideas," "*des idées hardies*," would be necessary in France. He said that the people of France must determine their own future form of government, under a plebiscite to be called after the reconquest.

I left him without any idea that in the spring of 1942 he was to be canonized alive by the stay-at-home seers of the American press. It is nice to learn, however late, that one has talked with an angel.

CHAPTER IX

They Are Not Gone

THE workman and sailors of Great Britain made great war in 1941. Opportunities for fighting were limited by circumstance, but the need for war material was limitless, especially after Germany attacked Russia. Not only the great forges and shipyards turned out the stuff; there were hundreds of peacetime plants converted to war industry along the network of roads that radiate from Manchester to the scores of smaller factory towns around, places with names we never hear in America, like Blackburn and Bury and Ramsbottom and Rawtenstall and Eccleston and Rochdale and Warrington. The bare hills north of the city were full of them; the flatlands that stretch westward to Liverpool and south into Cheshire bristled with smoking chimneys. That was where the war was. A Lancashireman working for the Ministry of Labour said to me, "Lancashire people have co-operation in their blood. It's here the trade unions, as well as the factories, started. And the Co-operative Stores, which are the largest medium of distribution in all England now, began at Rochdale, a bit north of Manchester. Why, even the troupes of girls who dance in unison—precision dancers, I think you call them—originated here. The original Tiller Girls were recruited from Manchester."

The engineers were as good as the workpeople they directed, and they used every bit of equipment they had. I remember coming into one Lancashire village and seeing two meticulously beautiful new Bofors gun barrels on a wagon drawn by an aged white horse on the high street, en route from a machinery plant to the railway station. The animal looked as if it might have pulled a field piece at Waterloo. The plant was a hundred and ten years old, with flagstone paving. Most of the lathes dated from the last century. The strong, beefy old man who ran it was boring gun barrels with a tolerance of two ten thousandths of an inch of error with an arrangement of machinery he had improvised himself. Before the war he had made textile printing presses for coloring calicoes. The power for his pet ordnance machine came from a dismounted motorcycle engine; the Archimedes lever with which he met all engineering problems was a bicycle chain. "Anything for war," he told me. "Ah'm 'eart and soul in it." He said, with a juvenile pride, "Ah'm number one wi' Admiralty. They tell me send goon tubes to London by passenger coach, not goods train." Men like him had held the breach while Britain modernized its industrial plant with machine tools from America, but now production had already reached the turn.

The Lancashire lads and the Lancashire ladies were, in their northern phrase, "champion." My favorite town in all England, however, was and is Grimsby, Lincs., which rhymes with "drinks."

In the men's bar of the Ship Hotel at Grimsby, Englishmen speak to other Englishmen after less than five drinks. This is a tribute to Grimsby's genius, which is bacchic and maritime in equal parts. Grimsby sent ships to the fleet of King John and still sends its ships to the wars with Grimsby skippers and Grimsby crews, eked out, it is true, by a supplement of fellows from other parts of England, whom Grimsby men refer to impartially as "they dommed farmers." The farmers drown like the Grimsby men, but they cause them a lot of vexation in the interim. In the Ship bar one may meet fifty-year-old sub-lieutenants of the Royal Navy (Reserve, naturally) who have tattooed fists and unbutton their uniform jackets to allow room for beer. They are not quite gentlemen, of course, any more than middle-aged Lieutenant James Cook was a gentleman when he sailed to find a continent. The gentlemen lose the continents. The sublieutenants come ashore from the mine sweepers and patrol boats that used to be trawlers. Only the very old boats with maimed or ancient skippers fish now. As for the convivial part of the Grimsby tradition, Sir Fretcheville Hollis, a Parliament man for Grimsby, told Samuel Pepys in 1667 that to win an election there he had to spend £352 for beer. Pepys set this down as a "develish lie," but Pepys was no Grimsby man. Under the combined influence of Grimsby beer and Grimsby informality, even pink-cheeked and well-turned-out young officers off destroyers become relatively effusive. They say "Beastly weathah we ah having" to men to whom they have never been introduced. Since ships bigger than destroyers seldom come to Grimsby, the town is relaxingly free of officers of senior grade.

The highest-ranking officer in the bar as I entered one evening was a lieutenant commander named Armstrong, whom I had met at the naval base, where I had been getting material for a story. He was a big man who looked to be about forty but must have been a good deal older than that, because he had once told me that he had been in sail in 1904. He had fought in the other war and then been a captain in the merchant marine and then retired, and now he was in service again. Armstrong was a kind of patrol-boat admiral. He had under his command at least a dozen converted fishing boats, of about two hundred tons each, carrying crews of thirty men.

Most of the patrons of the Ship get their drinks at the bar and then carry them to the long wooden tables. Armstrong was at a table with a pint of the local brew in front of him, and he motioned me to come and sit beside him. I got my beer and joined him. "One of my fellows had a do with a German plane," he said, by way of beginning. "Plane was attacking some fishing boats, and my fellow went to help. Between all of them they shot the plane down, but they're rowing about who did it. Fishermen say they did; my chaps say they did, naturally. One fishing boat sank. A bomb dropped close to her and she just came apart. My fellow said that the bomb hit the water, and the next thing he thought he heard was a burst of machine-gun fire. 'But it wasn't machine-gun fire,' he said. 'It was her rivets popping out so fast it just sounded like machine-gun fire.' All of her crew were saved. I thought you'd like that description. Same chap once told me he'd seen a trawler bombed, and she went so high he could see the top of a near-by lighthouse under her keel. And two sea gulls over the lighthouse, he said." I said something about wishing the fellow would write a book. Armstrong said, "I once had one chap who did. Well, it wasn't a book exactly, but a diary, anyway." I got up and brought another round of beer.

"You know how it is in our boats," Armstrong said when I had sat down again. "The chap in command gets lonely. When the ship is fishing, most of the space in her hull is used for a fish hold. The men all muck in together, eating and sleeping in the smallest possible space, and the skipper mucks in with everyone else. They don't mind that, because they're on shares, and the more fish they carry the more money they get. But when we take the boat over for the Navy we convert the fish hold into quarters for the crew. The skipper has a cabin forward, and since he's the only commissioned officer aboard, he can't eat with the rest. He has to take his meals alone, and the others say 'Sir' to him. That makes him moody and some-times inclines him to drink. Spirits are tax-free in the Navy, as you probably know, and that is a temptation. Then he begins to brood about the new chaps in the crew. It would be splendid if we could man our boats a hundred per cent with fisher-men, but it's impossible. A fishing boat carries a crew of thir-teen, but when she goes to the Navy she needs thirty—gunners and fellows to handle mines and all that. And some of the new men have never been to sea. This chap who wrote the diary didn't drink heavily. The writing was his outlet. I came across it when I was going through his effects, poor chap. He copped it in a fight with some motor torpedo boats. A one-pound shell took half of his head off. I sent the diary, along with the rest of his things, to the widow, but I couldn't help copying a few entries."

Armstrong reached inside his jacket and brought out a type-written page, which he passed to me. These were the entries:

Dec. 11. Coventry, London. Manchester. Ow I wish I could come up with a Jerry plane. I would show them. Today my stew-ard put my knife spoon and fork in bucket of water to wash then forgot they were there chooked water overboard with them in it. I could of chooked im overboard too.

Dec. 16. I of a fine crew. One chap that worked in sweetshop. One bus conductor. One building workman. Two married men that of never been to sea.

What a bloody sample.

Dec. 21. I told cook to make rice pud. Late in day rice floating on galley floor he put about ½ a stone of rice in boiling water nice pud.

January 6. Today men grappled German mine were bringing it over side but not fast enough. I leaned over side and seized ca-ble to help. Opened my mouth to give order and upper and lower plates fell out.

They are not gone. I know where they are.

"Do you know," Armstrong said, "something about that last entry makes me rather sad. So many Grimsby lads, you know."

"Yes," I said. "I get it. We know where they are."

In November I began to feel more curious about the front in the United States than anxious about Britain. In the United States there was still a great decision to be taken; Britain could do nothing but wait. It seemed to me that the old British offi-cial propaganda line, "Give us the tools and we will finish the job," had begun to boomerang. I was certain that the British alone could not do all the fighting that would be required away from the Russian front, and I knew that we would never produce weapons in quantity commensurate with our industrial strength until we were in the war. I was afraid that people at home might be taken in by the official British optimism as they had been by the French. I went home by sea because I wanted to experience what the British press liked to call the Battle of the Atlantic.

CHAPTER X

Westbound Tanker

A TANKER is a kind of ship that inspires small affection. It is an oilcan with a Diesel motor to push it through the water, and it looks painfully functional. Its silhouette suggests a monster submarine with two conning towers. A destroyer's clipper-ship ancestry is patent in the lines of its hull, but neither tankers nor submarines betray any origin. They seem to have been improvised simultaneously by some rudely practical person and then put in the water to fight each other. A tanker scores a point when it completes a voyage. When the oil reservoirs of the Allied bases are full, the tankers are beating the submarines. They have been doing that since the beginning of this war, but few people think of a tanker as a fighting ship. When a tanker gets sunk you read about it in the paper, but when it docks safely nobody hangs any flags in the streets.

The *Regnbue*, on which I came home from England to the United States, is a Norwegian tanker. It is not remarkable in any way. Norway had a tanker fleet second only to that of the United States, and Norwegian tankers in 1941 carried fifty per cent of the oil that had gone to Britain since the war began. The *Regnbue*—the name means "Rainbow," as you may have surmised—was built at Gothenburg, Sweden, in 1930. She displaces nine thousand tons, a good, middling tanker size, and can do eleven knots loaded, a fair, medium speed. Her lead-gray hull was streaked with rust, and her masts and funnel and deckhouses showed only a trace of paint the first time I saw her. A grimy Norwegian flag, ragged at the edges, flapped from her mizzenmast, and there was a cowled four-inch gun on a platform raised above her poop. I was joining her as a passenger, but I didn't learn her name until I got close enough to read it on a small sign on the side of her bridge. This was because the Norwegian Trade Mission in London, through which I had booked my passage, believes in secrecy about ship movements. Since the German invasion of Norway, the Norwegian Government-in-exile has chartered most of the Norwegian ships in the world to the British Ministry of War Transport. The ships still fly Norway's flag, have predominantly Norwegian crews, and are, for the duration, in the custody of the Trade Mission.

An official at the Trade Mission, knowing I was ready to leave on short notice, had called me up at my hotel in London one Saturday morning and said that if I didn't mind sailing from London instead of a west-coast port, they had a ship for me. I said I didn't mind, although this would add several days to the voyage. Next morning I took a taxi to the Mission offices on Leadenhall Street and there handed over my passage money. The man who had telephoned me said that the ship was bound for New York in water ballast to take on cargo there. He gave me a sealed envelope addressed to one Captain W. Petersen and a slip of paper bearing written instructions for getting to the ship. I was to take a certain train at Fenchurch Street Station early Monday morning and travel to a small station near the Essex shore, a ride of an hour and a half. A taxi-man would meet me at the station and drive me to a pier, where I would find a boatman named Mace. Mace would put me aboard Captain Petersen's ship.

Shortly after eleven o'clock on Monday, December 1, I found myself in Mace's launch, moving through the water of the Thames Estuary toward the tanker, which lay about a mile offshore. The only other passenger in the launch was a Norwegian port engineer who was going out to examine the ship's motors. "Look at that paintwork!" the engineer said as we neared the *Regnbue*. "Tankers make such quick turn-arounds the crews have no chance to paint. Discharge in twenty-four hours or less, take bunker and water, and out to sea again. Oil docks are always in some place like *this*, too—miles from the center of the city. The men don't get a chance to see the town. I know. I was in tankers in the last war." Before he had time to tell me more about them, we were under the rope ladder leading to the *Regnbue*'s main deck. It was an extremely uninviting ladder, but the engineer went up it as if it were an escalator. A seaman dropped a line to Mace, who made a loop through the handles of my suitcase and portable typewriter, which then rose through the air like Little Eva going to heaven. I went up the ladder in my turn with neither grace nor relish. My style must have amused one of the several men who were leaning over the rail, because he looked down at me, then turned to the man next to him and said, "Commando."

This fellow, who was wearing a white jacket, was obviously a steward. He was of medium size but had long arms, so the jacket sleeves ended midway between elbow and wrist, baring the tattooing on his wide forearms. On the right arm he had a sailor and his lass above the legend, in English, "True Love." The design on the left arm was a full-rigged ship with the inscription "Hilse fra Yokohama," which means "Greetings from Yokohama." His head was large and bald except for two tufts of red hair at the temples, looking like a circus clown's wig. He had a bulging forehead and a flat face with small eyes, a turned-up nose, and a wide mouth. As soon as I got my breath, I said, "Passenger," and he took me in charge with a professional steward's manner, which, I afterward learned, he had acquired while working for a fleet of bauxite freighters that often carried tourists. The bauxite freighters had operated out of a port the steward called Noolians, and most of the tourists had been vacationing schoolteachers from the Middle West. Fearing emotional involvement with a schoolteacher, he had switched to tankers. "Tankers is safe," he said. "No schoolteachers." His name was Harry Larsen.

The steward led me along the rust-stained steel deck to the ship's forward deckhouse. The main deck of a tanker is simply the steel carapace over the tanks. In rough weather the seas break over this deck. The human activities of the ship are concentrated in two deckhouses, fore and aft. The forward one is like a four-story house rising from the main deck and contains the bridge and the captain's and deck officers' quarters. A long catwalk ten feet above the main deck serves as the highroad between the deckhouses, and even on the catwalk you are likely to get doused when there is a sea running. The engine room and the galley, the ship's one funnel, the cannon, the refrigerator, the crew's quarters, and the cat's sandbox are all jammed in and around the stern deckhouse. The steward showed me to my cabin, which was the one called the owner's, although the owner had never used it. It was next to the captain's office. His bedroom was on the other side of the office, and we were to share a bathroom. It was a fairly good cabin, with two portholes, a bed, a divan, and a desk. The steward said that the captain was still ashore but I should make myself at home.

I went out on deck to look around and was pleased to see one of the British Navy's barrage-balloon boats alongside. A balloon boat is a lighter with a half-dozen or so bright, silvery balloons floating above it, each attached to a slender wire. The *Regnbue* dropped a wire cable aboard the lighter, and a couple of naval ratings rove the end of a balloon cable to ours. They let go the cable and the balloon rose above our foremast, securely attached, as we thought, to the *Regnbue*. It wasn't, though. It blew away two nights later, but it was a pretty embellishment as long as we had it. While I was watching the transfer, a little man in a blue uniform came over and stood next to me. I asked him when he thought we would get under way. He said that he was the pilot and was going to take the ship a short distance farther down the river that afternoon. The captain was coming aboard after we got down river. The pilot was a black-haired, red-faced Londoner with a habit of laughing nervously after practically everything he said. "Good thing about a tanker in water ballast," he said. "She's just a box of air, what? Tanks half full of sea water, all the rest air—wants a long time to sink if she's torpedoed. Much as forty minutes, perhaps, eh?" He laughed. I said that I thought this was very nice, and he said that now you take a loaded tanker, it was just the opposite—the very worst sort of ship to be torpedoed aboard. "Flaming oil all about. Rather depressing, what?" he said. I agreed.

The steward came along and told us that dinner was on the table in the saloon, so the pilot and I followed him down a flight of stairs into a large, rectangular room with paneled walls and a dark green carpet. The most impressive feature of the saloon was a portrait, nearly life-size, of an old gentleman with a face the color of a Killarney rose and a bifurcated beard that looked like two blobs of whipped cream. The artist had used plenty of paint of the best quality. I could imagine a jury of boatswains giving the picture grand prize at a *salon*. "The founder of the line that owned this ship," the pilot said.

"Capitalist!" the steward said, simply and with distaste.

"Rum thing on Norwegian ships," the pilot said, "the captain doesn't eat with the other officers. As a passenger you'll mess down here in the saloon with the captain, and there'll be just the two of you at every meal. But in every other respect they're more democratic than our ships. Odd, what?"

The pilot had been at Dunkirk, he told me a bit later on. "I was in command of seven motorboats," he said, with his laugh, "transferring troops from the beach to destroyers. I lost the boats one by one. A motorboat doesn't take much smashing, does it? When the last one foundered, my two ratings and I swam to a destroyer's boat. What I shan't forget," he said, after a pause, "is the motor-bike races on Dunkirk beach. Chaps waiting to be taken off, you know. Never saw better sport. There were soldiers making book on the races. Couldn't leave the beach until all bets were settled or they'd be known as welshers."

The dinner of pea soup, corned beef, and baked beans, ending with a double-size can of California peaches for the pilot and me, was big by London standards. The portions were on a scale I had almost forgotten, and there was a lot of butter. The steward said the food had been loaded at Corpus Christi, Texas, in October. "We don't take any food in England," he said. "I hope we get to New York for Christmas. I got nothing to make Christmas at sea—no newts, no frewts, no yin for drinking."

"We ought to make it," I said, with the confidence of inexperience.

"It depends what kind commodore we get," the steward said. "If we get slow commodore, old man retire from Navy fifty year and only come back for the war, we lucky to get New

York for New Year's. I don't care much for New York anyhow," he added loftily. "Too much noise, too many Nor-
weeyans in Brooklyn, argue, argue, argue! I like better
Camden, New Yersey, go with the Polish girls."

The ship moved slowly down the estuary during the
afternoon. We dropped anchor again before dark at a point
where the Thames had definitely ceased to seem like a river
and where half a dozen other ships already rode at anchor. Our
men looked at them curiously, as one surveys the other occupants of the lounge car at the beginning of a long railroad
journey. There were a couple of British tankers with fancy
Spanish names, a gray, medium-sized Dutch freighter, and a
big, boxlike Elder Dempster boat that had once been in the
West African service. I have seen the Dutch freighter's name in
a newspaper since. She had shot down a German plane. There
was also a stubby, soot-black Norwegian steamer of not more
than three thousand tons, which had a single funnel so narrow
and long that it reminded me of an American river boat. The
third officer, a husky blond chap who wore an orange turtle-
neck sweater, pointed to the stubby ship and said to me, "That
is the slowest ship in the world. Once she made one trip from
Cape Town in four convooeys. They started two weeks apart,
and she kept on losing one convooey and getting into the
next. She was going full speed the whole time." All the ships
were, like ourselves, light and bound for America to get a cargo.

The pilot came down from the bridge and joined me when
the ship was at anchor. I asked him when he thought we should
get to New York, and he said that with luck we ought to make
it in about twenty days. It depended a lot on what connections
we made at the assembly ports, he said. The *Regnbue* was
going all the way around Scotland to get to the west coast of
Britain. We would spend the first few days of our voyage in a
small convoy sailing up the east coast of England to our first
assembly port. From there, we would go to the west coast in a
larger convoy, but we might have to wait a couple of days
while this larger convoy was being assembled. Then we would
proceed to the second assembly port and go through the same
business there. We might be just in time to leave with a
transatlantic convoy or we might have to wait a week. There

was no way of telling. "The most ticklish bit in the trip begins about twelve hours above here," the pilot added consolingly. "If we get off tomorrow morning, you'll be in it by night."

Captain Petersen came aboard shortly before nightfall. He was a small, stoop-shouldered man. His brown shoregoing suit was carefully pressed. He had a long, curved nose and lank, sandy hair, and he spoke English slowly but accurately, using American idioms. He had lived in Philadelphia, where he worked in an oil refinery, during part of the last war, he told me, and then had moved to Hoboken, where he had roomed in the house of an Irish policeman. After the war he had gone back to Norway to enter navigation school with the money he had earned in America. All the reminiscences of the United States that he politely introduced into our conversation dated from before 1919. He gave detailed accounts of several Chaplin comedies, like *The Count* and *The Cure*, which he had seen then. We went down to supper with the pilot, and Captain Petersen, pointing to the whiskered portrait, said to me, "That is a man who once owned eighty sailing ships. Even when he was ninety-two he combed his beard for one hour every morning. I remember seeing him in my home town when I was a boy. The company owns only a couple of ships now. It belongs to an old lady, who lives in my town also."

His town is a sleepy little city in southern Norway which in the nineteenth century was a great port for sailing ships. The *Regnbue*, the captain explained to me, is emphatically a ship from his town. Not only is she owned there—although, as he explained, owners captive in Norway had no control over their ships for the duration of the war—but skipper, chief officer, and second officer all came from there and had known each other as schoolboys. Both the captain and the chief officer, a man named Gjertsen, had even been married aboard the *Regnbue*. Their brides had joined them on the ship at Antwerp and Constanta, Rumania, respectively. Petersen had been second officer and Gjertsen third officer then, and they had honeymooned in turn in the captain's suite. The wives were at home now. "The second and third officers have wives in Norway, too," he said, "and so has the chief engineer. I was lucky enough to have a vacation in December 1939, so I saw my wife and boy only a little while before the Germans came."

Petersen told me that when the Germans invaded Norway the Norwegian Government had commandeered Norwegian ships all over the world, ordering those at sea to put into neutral or Allied ports. A radio message had been sufficient to accomplish this. Only a small part of the merchant marine had been caught at home. Now the exiled government's income from ship hire not only supported it but provided a surplus, which is to be used for the nation's reconstruction after the Germans are driven out. He didn't show any doubt that they would be driven out, nor did anyone I talked to on the *Regnbue*. The boatswain, a weathered gnome of a man, once said to me, "I couldn't sleep at night if I didn't believe on it." The owners of the ships were nearly all caught in the invasion. The Government had promised that after the war they would receive compensation for the use of their ships, provided they paid allotments to the sailors' families in the meanwhile. So the captive families had been receiving small amounts of money, but even with money there isn't much food.

There was a door at each side of the saloon. One led to the pantry and the steward's cabin, the other to the deck officers' quarters. The officers had their mess aft, in the other deckhouse. After supper on a normal evening aboard the *Regnbue*, I was to learn, the captain and the steward visited the deck officers. Then, at about eight o'clock, everybody visited the steward and drank coffee, made in a big electric percolator which the steward brought in from the pantry. I suppose a torpedo would have disrupted this routine, but nothing less could have. This evening marked my initiation into the ship's social life. Since we were still in port, it was a *soirée de gala*; none of the officers had to stand watch, and it was all right to use the short-wave radio in Gjertsen's cabin. Such sets are sealed at sea because they cause a radiation which can betray a ship's position. For news of the outside world you depend on what the wireless operator picks up on long-wave.

Around seven o'clock the captain, the pilot, the steward, and I marched into Gjertsen's cabin, where the other officers already were gathered. Gjertsen, a tall, dark man who looked something like Lincoln, was stretched out on his berth halfway between floor and ceiling. His wedding picture hung just above the berth. Gjertsen had not been home since 1937. Haraldsen, the second officer, who was small and jolly, turned the dials of the radio, with occasional professional counsel from Grung, the wireless operator, a serious young fellow whom the others considered something of a dandy. He came from Bergen, which is almost a big city. Bull, the third officer, the big fellow in the orange sweater, sat on the divan looking at a picture of the backsides of thirty-two bathing girls in *Life*. He didn't turn the page all evening. Nilsen, the gunner, sat on the floor and said nothing. He hardly ever said anything to anybody. The captain explained to me later that it was because Nilsen was a whaler. Whalers talk themselves out on their first voyage, the captain said. They exhaust all possible topics of conversation, then fall silent for life. "It isn't like a lighthouse-keeper," Petersen said. "He hasn't had a chance to talk in months, so he is bursting with it. But a whaling man is talked out." Gjertsen hated the radio, but he insisted on keeping the set in his cabin because he liked company. No matter what kind of music Haraldsen got, Gjertsen said it was rotten and Haraldsen should turn to something else. Whenever they got a news program he just fell asleep. He said there was enough trouble on the ocean without dialing for it. They were all low that evening because of a broadcast by the Norwegian radio of the news that the Germans were planning to cut off the money for their families. "I wonder how long people in the old country will be able to keep from starving," Haraldsen said helplessly. "Why don't the British start the invasion?" Grung demanded, looking sternly at the English pilot. "All the fellows who escape from Norway say there are only a few thousand Germans there."

"Full moon tomorrow night," the pilot said pleasantly, by way of changing the subject.

"Yes, fine moon for dive bombers," the radioman said resentfully. "We'll be right in the middle of E-boat Alley then."

"Maybe there'll be fog," the pilot suggested helpfully. "Fog is no good for bombers."

"Fog is fine for E-boats," Grung said. "Can't see them coming." Grung, I was to learn, liked to have something to complain about; actually, he worried little about enemy action. Danger at sea is like having a jumpy appendix: men can live with it for years, knowing in an academic way that it may cause trouble but forgetting about it most of the time. Haraldsen said that the *Regnbue* had always been a lucky ship—fourteen crossings since the war began and never a conning tower sighted. Everybody banged on wood. "The *Meddelfjord* always was a lucky ship, too, before the last time," Grung said, insisting on his right to grumble. "I lost a good pal on her, the second engineer. Burned to death in the sea. The oil was blazing on top of the water, and the fellows had to swim in it. That was a nice joke!"

"We didn't miss that by much ourselves," the captain said to me. "We were together with the *Meddelfjord* at Newcastle, both bound for London. We stayed to discharge some of our oil. The *Meddelfjord* and eight other ships went on. Three of them were sunk by planes and motor torpedo boats."

Bull put down his magazine and said in a matter-of-fact tone, "I like to catch a Yerman. Bile him in ile."

Unexpectedly, Nilsen, the silent, spoke up. "I have no respect for them," he said.

Before coming aboard I had calculated roughly that the chances are at least ninety to one against being torpedoed on any one crossing. Incidentally, the American marine-insurance companies then charged a premium of one per cent to insure tanker cargo, which indicated that they thought the odds are considerably longer than a hundred to one. It is not a great risk to take, once. The men in the *Regnbue* lived continually with this risk, which is quite a different thing. They seldom talked of danger except when they were angry about something else, like no shore leave or the British failure to invade the Continent.

Bull started turning the dials of the radio set again and got a program of jazz music from Stockholm. A woman was singing something that sounded like "Klop, klop, klop! Sving, sving, sving!" Bull and Haraldsen laughed so hard they could barely stand it. "I can't explain it to you," Haraldsen said to me, "but to a Norwegian the Swedish language sounds always very funny." We had three or four cups of strong coffee apiece in the pantry and then went to our cabins. Norwegians use coffee as a sedative.

Long before I got up next morning I could hear the anchor chain coming in, and when I got out on deck we were moving along in a column of eight ships. The strings of signal flags looked like holiday bunting, and each ship had its own bright new balloon. Half a dozen sloops and corvettes in pink-and-green camouflage milled around our column. The convoy was probably not moving better than eight knots, so the corvettes looked lightning fast. Machine guns were being tested on all the ships, and the intermittent bursts of gunfire added to the gaiety. The tracer bullets from the machine guns are fun to watch as they skitter over the water; they seem a superior kind of flying fish, with electric light and central heating. We had a pair of Hotchkisses mounted, one on each side of the bridge. If we were attacked they would be manned by the two seamen on lookout. We also had two British machine gunners, who manned a small fort on the poop deck, where they had a couple of Lewis guns. There was not enough open space around for our gun crew to try out our four-inch gun, but an anti-aircraft battery on shore was practicing. Its guns went off at one-minute intervals, and the shells made a straight line of white smoke puffs across the sky, like pearls on a string. A couple of mine sweepers dragging magnetized floats went ahead of us, in case the Luftwaffe had planted any magnetics during the night.

We dropped the pilot at noon. Life on the ship picked up its sea rhythm. The crew consisted of the usual three watches, each of which was on duty four hours and then rested eight. Haraldsen, the second officer, was on the bridge from twelve to four, Gjertsen, the chief, from four to eight, and Bull, the third officer, from eight to twelve, when Haraldsen relieved him. I had a chance to get to know some of the sailors, because they came forward to stand their watches on the bridge. However, the engineer officers and the rest of the crew, down at the other end of the ship, remained relative strangers.

When the men came forward they wore life jackets. The officers, when they went up to the bridge, carried their life jackets with them and tied them to a stanchion. I had bought a kapok-lined reefer from Gieves, the naval outfitter in Piccadilly, a swank garment that purported to double as an overcoat and life jacket. It was supposed to close with a zipper, and each clash with the zipper presented a completely new tactical problem. The zipper changed its defensive arrangements to meet my attacks; I could never throw it twice with the same hold. Sometimes I could close it in a couple of minutes, but on other occasions it beat me. I was sure that if a torpedo ever struck us, I would go down in a death grapple with my zipper. I had an ordinary life jacket in my cabin, of course, but I had paid good money for the reefer. I was also given a huge, one-piece rubber suit, so stiff that it stood up in a corner of my cabin like a suit of armor. It was a Norwegian invention, Captain Petersen said, and everybody on the ship had one. The idea was to climb into its legs and tie yourself into the rest of it, so only your face showed. The air in the folds of the suit would both hold you up and insulate you from the cold of the water. This consoled me until Grung, the radioman, told me that a crew had once demonstrated the invention for the Norwegian Minister of Shipping and that while all of them had floated for hours, a couple of fellows who went in head first had floated upside down. Grung was a man of few enthusiasms. For example, we had a large escort for such a small convoy, and this made him unhappy. "There must be trouble expected or there wouldn't be so many," he said.

Late in the afternoon we reached the bad spot about which the pilot had told me. This is a lane along the East Anglian coast that London newspapers have named E-boat Alley. The commodore of the convoy was in the ship ahead of us, a British tanker. Commodores are usually commanders in His Majesty's Navy; they carry a pair of aides and a squad of signalmen with them and communicate their orders by flag signal or flash lamp. This commodore would go with us only as far as the first assembly port; he was an east-coast specialist.

I was in the saloon just before suppertime, reading Hakluyt's *Principall Navigations, Voiages and Discoveries of the English Nation*, when I heard a noise that sounded exactly like a very emphatic blast during the excavation of a building site. The ship quivered, as if she had taken a big sea. Larsen, the steward, was the only other man around; he was laying out a few plates of salami and ham and herring salad as table decorations. I took it for granted that the noise was a depth charge and said "My, my!" to show how calm I was. Larsen winked and said, "Mak raddy der bahding suit!" Both of us, I imagine, wanted to run out on deck and see what had happened, but since we had only recently met, we tried to impress each other. Captain Petersen came down to supper ten minutes later and said that a mine had gone off a hundred feet from the commodore's ship and almost knocked her out of the water. "Gjertsen was on the bridge and saw it," he said. "He says it threw a column of water higher than the ship's masts. She was hidden completely. Then, when the water settled, Gjertsen could see the ship was still there, but she had only a little way on. Then she hoisted two red lights to signal she was out of control. The blast must have damaged her rudder. So she has to go back to port."

"Good-by, Commodore," Larsen said unfeelingly.

"It must have been one of those acoustic mines," the captain said, "but it didn't work well. It went off too soon." There was a certain wonder in his tone, as if he felt that the Germans must be overrated.

The explosion of the mine was the only evidence of enemy action we were to encounter during the whole trip.

Larsen, the steward, had it figured out that in order to get to New York by Christmas we would have to leave the west coast of England by December 7. "We get off with lucky seven and in seventeen days we come to New York," he said. "Get there Christmas Eve, the immigration officers ain't working, and we stay on the ship until December 26." This was a sample of what I got to know as Scandinavian optimism. We didn't reach even the first of our two assembly ports until December 5, so it looked certain that we would spend Christmas at sea. We were seventy-two hours going up the east coast from London, anchoring each night because of heavy fog. The second time we anchored, Larsen began getting out and repairing the green-and-red paper Christmas decorations that formed part of the tanker's stores. He went about his work during the day muttering a sad little refrain that I sometimes caught myself repeating: "No newts, no frewts, no yin for drinking."

The crew looked forward to spending its shore leave in Brooklyn, even if we got to New York after Christmas. To a Norwegian the finest part of the United States is Brooklyn. For the duration of the war it is the Norwegian fatherland. When a Norwegian seaman meets an American, he usually begins the conversation with, "I got a cousin in Brooklyn." Haraldsen, the second officer, had two brothers there. Larsen pretended to be supercilious about Brooklyn, but he fooled nobody on the *Regnbue*. The *Regnbue* had been in the Thames for only a couple of days, and few of her men had gone into London. The ship had been anchored at such an awkward distance from the city that it had hardly seemed worth the journey. Some men had got drunk at a hotel not far from the oil dock. Others had not even set foot on land. Corpus Christi, Texas, the ship's last American port of call, had not been exactly a Brooklyn, either.

Olsen the carpenter, Grung the radioman, and I were visiting the steward and drinking coffee on one of the foggy nights, and Olsen said, "The last time I was in Brooklyn I didn't take my shoes off for three weeks. My feet was so swollen I had to cut my shoes off." Olsen was a man who liked to startle people. "It must have been good liquor you were drinking," I said. This was just the kind of opening Olsen wanted. He put his head on one side and looked at me fixedly for a full half-minute, as if I were a dangerous lunatic. "Good liquor!" he finally said, contemptuously. "A man is a fool to drink good liquor. I never drink liquor that tastes good." He stared at me again, as if expecting me to leap at his throat, and then said, "Because why? I get drinking it too fast. Then I get drunk too quick. The best thing is whisky that tastes bad. Then you stop between drinks about ten minutes, until you need another one. Then you can keep on drinking for a month." The carpenter was a solid, rectangular fellow of fifty, with blue eyes set wide apart in a boiled-ham face. He could with equal competence make a davit out of iron pipe or reseat a rattan chair. He was the ship's delegate of the Norwegian Seamen's Union, to which all the men belonged.

The steward lay in his berth at the summit of a stack of drawers. There was no other place for him, because the rest of us occupied all the chairs. He said, "In Brooklyn I live in Hotel St. Yorge. Yentlemen! I don't go on Court Street in Eyetalian saloons. I yust buy good old bottle aquavit and go to my room and drink like yentleman. Go to Norweeyan church Sunday and put five dollars in collection. Brooklyn women too smart. Better leave 'em alone."

The radioman said that once he and some shipmates had been in a taxi-dance hall near Borough Hall and had asked a couple of hostesses to sit down and have a drink. The hostesses had charged them four dollars apiece for their time. "You got more for your money in Constanta," he said. Constanta, in Rumania, used to be a great port for Norwegian tankers before the war. "We had a man on one ship going down to Constanta," the carpenter said, "and he wouldn't believe all we told him about it. He said he had been in every other port in the world, and he wouldn't lose his head in Constanta. So he went ashore one night, and two days later we seen a man walking down on the dock with nothing on but his socks, and it was him. Always lots of fun in Constanta."

The steward found this so amusing that he reared up on the back of his neck and kicked the ceiling. He had been a leading light of the gymnastic society in a small town in southern Norway, and he liked to use the edge of his berth as a gymnastic bar. He spent a good deal of time composing to English and American girls on a portable typewriter he had in his cabin, and when he was at a loss for an English phrase he would get up, face his berth, and jump high in the air, twisting in time to land in a sitting position. Usually three or four jumps would bring him the phrase he wanted, and he would return to his typewriter. The steward called his cabin Larsen's Club, and the atmosphere was congenially ribald except when Captain Petersen was there. The skipper came in every night for his three cups of coffee. Captain Petersen was a friendly man who did not stand on formality, but he was a Methodist and a teetotaler. He didn't try to deter anybody else from drinking or talking randy, but Larsen seldom kicked the ceiling when the skipper was around. All the men were cut off from their home country and lonely, and the captain was the loneliest of all. Once he said to me, "It isn't so bad for a man who drinks and——" He stopped suddenly, as if just understanding what he had said, and went off to his cabin looking miserable.

At meals with Captain Petersen I had plenty of time for eating, because there was not much conversation. Once he said, as he began on his first plate of cabbage soup, "I have an uncle in New York who has been fifty-two years with the Methodist Book Concern." Twenty minutes later, having finished his second helping of farina pudding, he said, "He came over in a windyammer." On another occasion he said, "We had a Chinaman on the ship once. When we came to Shanghai he couldn't talk to the other Chinamen." After an interlude during which he ate three plates of lobscouse, a stew made of left-over meats and vegetables, he explained, "He came from another part of China." And once, taking a long look at the shipowner's portrait, he said, "I went to see an art gallery near Bordeaux." After eating a large quantity of dried codfish cooked with raisins, cabbage, and onions, he added, "Some of the frames were that wide," indicating with his hands how impressively wide they were. Once, in an effort to make talk, I asked him, "How would you say, 'Please pass me the butter, Mr. Petersen,' in Norwegian?" He said, "We don't use 'please' or 'mister.' It sounds too polite. And you never have to say 'pass me' something in a Norwegian house, because the people *force* food on you, so if you said 'pass' they would think they forgot something and their feelings would be hurt. The word for butter is *smor*."

It was morning when we reached our first assembly port, and the captain went ashore to see the naval authorities. He returned with word that we would sail next evening. In the afternoon a boat came out from shore and a naval officer climbed aboard to tell the captain that our destination had been changed from New York to Port Arthur, Texas. Luckily, the *Regnbue* had enough fuel for the longer journey or we would have lost more time taking bunker. The captain told me of the change and said he was sorry I would be carried so far from New York, but things like that happened all the time. The changes weren't made for strategic reasons, because no one could tell three weeks or a month in advance how the U-boats would be distributed off the American coast. It was just that there probably weren't enough "dirty" tankers to handle all the heavy oils from the Gulf of Mexico. A "clean" tanker handles only gasoline. A "dirty" tanker has tanks equipped with heating coils to keep heavy oils liquid. The *Regnbue*, the captain said with pride, was a first-class dirty tanker.

News of the change of destination quickly got about among the crew. There isn't much point in secrecy aboard a ship if none of the men are allowed to go ashore. Port Arthur is a dismal place compared to Brooklyn, and the seamen were disappointed. There are no Norwegians in Port Arthur, and no taxi-dance halls. Mikkelsen, the electrician, said that you couldn't even buy whisky in a saloon in Port Arthur; you had to buy a bottle at a package store and take it into a soft-drink joint to get a setup. Perhaps the most disappointed men on the ship were the British machine gunners, Ramsay and Robinson. They had been out to India and Australia with other ships but never to America. "Where is Texas?" Robinson asked me. "Will I be able to get up to New York for a week end?" Ramsay, who was a lance bombardier, laughed derisively. "You haven't got money enough to get that far," he said. "It's all of two hundred miles." Robinson earned three shillings and three-pence a day, of which the War Office sent one and three to his mother in Salford, slap up against Manchester. Ramsay drew nine-pence more for his single chevron, and he was always boasting to Robinson about his opulence.

The Britishers belonged to the Maritime Anti-Aircraft Regiment, generally called the Sea Soldiers at home. The Sea Soldiers ride on merchant ships in the manner of old-time American stagecoach guards. They have had more training with automatic arms than the seamen who man machine guns and are supposed to steady the seamen in a fight. Robinson and Ramsay had been partners on other ships and had been in a long running battle with some Axis submarines off the west coast of Africa just before they joined the *Regnbue*. Convoys were nearly always attacked off the African coast, they said. There was a belief among seamen that the Germans had a submarine base at Dakar, no matter what Pétain said. Robinson was a quiet lad who said, "A odn't been sottisfied i' infantry, so thought A'd try summat else, and this was fair champion— nowt to do." Ramsay was a Glaswegian, a hyperenergetic type who was always shadow-boxing on deck and shouting "Pooh!" or "Coo!" for no apparent reason. He used to brag about how many German planes he had shot down, although it is hard to apportion credit for bringing down a plane when a whole convoy is blazing away at it. One day he said that if we captured a German submarine—not a likely prospect—he would personally kill all the prisoners. Gjertsen, the chief officer, said to him seriously, "You can't kill anybody on this ship without the captain say so." This made Ramsay sulk. There were three other Britishers on the ship—a man in the engine room, a seaman, and a messboy. English seamen like to get on Norwegian ships when there is an opportunity, because the pay is better than the British scale. Nearly all seafaring Norwegians speak English, so there is no trouble about understanding orders. The only fellows on the *Regnbue* who knew no English were five youths who recently, and separately, had escaped from Norway by crossing the North Sea in small boats. They were all studying a textbook on Basic English. They had received word that after they had escaped their parents had been put in prison. News from Norway reaches England quite regularly by boat. There are even motorboats that smuggle mail between the two coasts.

Most of the men grew thoughtful when we cleared the first assembly port. We were within three hundred miles of Norway now, and they could not help thinking about it. Otherwise the tension, which had never been great, seemed to have completely vanished. There was no further danger from motor torpedo boats and not much from dive bombers. The big Focke-Wulf Kuriers and the submarine packs generally operated farther to the west, where the large convoys form, so we felt relatively safe. We had parted company with a couple of ships at the assembly port and picked up a couple of others. What bothered me was the weather. Captain Petersen advised me to chew on dry crackers and drink no water. The steward said, "Don't use nothing yuicy. Yust dry stuff."

The prescription of "a brisk walk around the deck," classic on passenger liners, is not much good on a tanker, because deck space is so limited. You can take a few steps on the bridge or make a circuit of the forward deckhouse, picking your way among ropes, slings, boats, and the entrances to two companionways. If you go aft you have a slightly longer promenade around the after deckhouse, although you have to crawl under the gun platform once on each lap to complete the circuit. The main deck, between the two deckhouses and forward of the bridge, is low and lashed by spray. There is a catwalk, an elevated pathway between the two deckhouses, but men with work to do are constantly passing back and forth on it, so there is no room for a *flâneur*.

At the beginning of the voyage I had decided to let my beard grow until I got home again. The boatswain, who came from a port in the far north of Norway, counseled me to shave my beard, on the ground that it would bring fine weather and then the ship wouldn't rock. The boatswain was a small man who looked as dry and tough as jerked meat. He had ice-blue eyes and a long, drooping, ginger-colored mustache, and he repeated his joke about the beard every morning. Then, later in the day, he would manage to ask me the time and say, "I had two gold watches but they're on the bottom now." His last ship had been bombed and sunk at her dock in Liverpool, and he had lost all his gear on board. Fortunately, he had been spending the night on shore with a respectable lady friend— the widow of an old shipmate, he was always careful to explain when he told the story. He had a French wife in Caen, but he had not seen her in seven years, because big ships seldom went there. I once tried to talk French with him, but he said with a sigh, "*Ya goobliay toute.*" The boatswain was aware that he said the same things every day, but he said them to be friendly. After all, nobody can think of something new to say when he sees the same shipmates daily for weeks on end. The quip about the beard contented the boatswain, and he laughed every time he said it. His laugh sounded like cakes of ice knocking together.

On December 7 we were in a gale. I turned in early and put my watch and fountain pen in the desk drawer, where they rattled like dice in a nervous crapshooter's hand. There is a difference of thirteen and a half hours between the time in Hawaii and Great Britain, and I was asleep before Grung, the radioman, picked up the first bulletin about the attack on Pearl Harbor. I heard the news when I went up on the bridge next morning. Bull, the third officer, pumped my hand and said, "We both allies now!" It felt more natural to be a belligerent on a belligerent ship than that anomalous creature, a neutral among belligerent friends. I tried to visualize New York. People at home must be frightfully angry, I imagined. I kept telling the Norwegians, "Americans aren't like the English. They get mad much quicker, and they stay mad." (I was to feel pretty silly about that after I got back to New York.) We all wondered why the fleet had been in Pearl Harbor and how the Japs had got there. The B.B.C. bulletins received by the radioman were skimpy. We were actually near the base of the British Home Fleet, but suddenly we felt far from the war. The ship had sailed with two neutrals aboard, and now it had none. The other neutral had been an ordinary seaman named Sandor, who was a Rumanian. Great Britain had declared war on Rumania a few days after we cleared, so Sandor had become an enemy alien. He took the news calmly. "Can't send me back now," he said. He had stowed away on the *Regnbue* at Constanta in the early summer of 1939 and had stayed with her ever since. He had learned Norwegian and English on the ship.

We were glad to get to our second assembly port, where we were permitted to turn on the short-wave radio in the chief officer's cabin. We sat around it for hours, listening to the B.B.C., the Norwegian broadcasts from London and Boston, and even Radio Paris, the Quisling station in Oslo, and Lord Hawhaw. We got some of our best laughs from an Italian English-language announcer who used to sink Allied shipping in astronomical quantities twice a day. It was a Norwegian broadcast from Boston, I remember, that told us Lindbergh had endorsed the war and a Free French announcer in London who said Senator Wheeler had done the same thing. The steward was amused. "Next thing, Quisling against Yermans!" he shouted.

As soon as we arrived at the second assembly port, the captain went ashore. When he came back he said that we were starting for America early the next morning. The port was at the head of a deep and narrow bay. The *Regnbue* and nine other ships were to start just before dawn and go to sea to meet vessels that would simultaneously leave other assembly ports. There would be from fifty to a hundred in the combined convoy, which was to be a very slow one. It would make only eight knots, because it included a lot of ships like the Norwegian steamer that Bull, the third officer, had pointed out to me some days before as the slowest ship in the world. We had lost her in the gale on December 7, but she had steamed into the second assembly port twelve hours behind us. She was called the *Blaskjell*, which means "mussel." An eight-knot convoy takes a long time to get across the ocean, Captain Petersen said, but going that way was better than hanging about waiting for a ten-knotter. Fast ships go alone, on the theory that they can run away from any submarine they sight, but the *Regnbue* was not nearly that fast.

It was about seven o'clock when we hove anchor next morning, but the moon was still high in the sky. The other ships that were going out showed one light apiece, and a corvette was talking to us in Morse code squawked out on a whistle that sounded like Donald Duck. A westerly wind was howling, and I remembered that we had received a gale warning the evening before. The moon slipped into a cloud abruptly, like a watch going into a fat man's vest pocket, and didn't come out again. When it is as dark as it was that morning it is hard for a landsman to tell if a ship is moving, because he can't see her position in relation to anything else. But after a while I was sure. When it began to get light I went up on the bridge and looked at the ships in front of us and astern. They were already plunging about. When you look at other ships in a heavy sea the extravagance of their contortions surprises you. Your own ship is going through the same motions, but you wouldn't believe they were so extreme unless you saw the other ships. The farther we got down the bay, the worse the weather grew. The commodore's ship, about a mile ahead of us, sent up a string of flags; the ships between us repeated the signal. Bull, who was on the bridge, said, "Commodore wants us slow down, says he can't hold his position." He threw the engine-room telegraph to "Half Speed." In heavy weather the *Regn-bue* steered well only at full speed, and the men at the wheel had an unhappy time from then on. Now and then her bow came clear out of the water—from watching other tankers I could see exactly how it happened—and the sea gave her a ringing slap on the bottom. I felt that this was an impertinence, precisely the sort of thing a German would do if he were running the ocean.

By noon we were getting away from land. I went down to the saloon to have dinner with Captain Petersen and found him already ladling his third plate of milk soup out of the tureen. Milk soup is made of condensed milk and water, heavily sugared and full of rice, raisins, dried apricots, canned peaches, and anything else sweet the cook can find about the galley. It is served hot at the beginning of a meal, and only a

Norwegian can see any sense in it. It appeared on the table regularly twice a week, and at each appearance the steward said, "Fawny soup today, Liebling." At the beginning of every meal, without exception, he would say to me, "*Vaer so god*" ("Be so good"), and bow. I would say the same thing to him and bow, and we would both laugh. It was like the boatswain's joke about the beard.

On the bridge that afternoon the captain was preoccupied. He said that unless we could go at full speed, he didn't see how we could get to the rendezvous before dark, but only about one other ship in our lot could keep up with us at full speed. Our entire escort was one 800-ton corvette, and if we left the convoy, we left the escort. Sometimes you have a big escort and sometimes you have a small one. It's like going into a shop in England: you get what they have in stock. Haraldsen, the second officer, who was also on the bridge, was as jolly as usual. "By and by Florida!" he would shout when water whipped across the front of the wheelhouse and splashed in our faces. That was *his* standard joke. The corvette seemed to stand on its head every time it went into a wave, and Haraldsen got a lot of fun watching it. "The little feller is doing good," he would say. "I hope they got a good belly." By three o'clock we had lost the *Blaskjell* and two of the others, and a half-hour later we could see the commodore's ship turning. The commodore was signaling us to return to port. He had judged that there was no chance of reaching the rendezvous before nightfall, and he didn't want us to be out on the ocean alone when morning came. "We made about thirty miles in nine hours," Captain Petersen said. We turned, and on the way back to the assembly port we picked up the *Blaskjell* and passed her. At nine o'clock we were again at anchor in our old berth.

The boatswain was not the only one who looked suspiciously at my beard after the return. "This has always been a lucky ship," the carpenter said. "I think we got a Rasmus on board now." A Rasmus is the Norwegian equivalent of a Jonah. The next day the weather was fine. The carpenter said that this was just what you might expect now that we had missed the convoy. Captain Petersen put on his brown suit and went ashore. He came back with word that we were stuck for at least a week. We had already been at sea for a fortnight. It was not entirely bad news to the boatswain and the steward. The boatswain could now put the men to work painting the ship. When a ship's paint gets streaky, a boatswain becomes melancholy and embarrassed, like a housewife who has not had time to wash the curtains. Griffin, the English seaman on board, once said to me, "If the bos'n ain't a bastard, the ship's no good." He added that the *Regnbue* was quite a good ship. The steward saw a chance to get the supplies he needed for Christmas. About all that the captain and I had been hearing lately at our meals was a monologue by Larsen about the horrors of Christmas at sea without newts or frewts or yin. Once a ship has left the port of origin, navy people permit only the captain and the radioman to go ashore—the radioman for a single conference before a convoy leaves—so Larsen gave the captain a list to take to a ship chandler. The captain found no nuts or fruits, but in a couple of days a lighter brought out a case of gin and two cases of whisky, which the steward put away in the pantry closet. Ordinarily, I was told, no liquor was served on the ship except to pilots and immigration officers, but Christmas was always an exception.

The days at anchor were tranquil. Every morning the captain went ashore and the rest of us painted and theorized about our false start for America. The officers worked alongside the men, and I daubed a bit for company. Some of the men argued that we should have started for our rendezvous at midnight instead of just before dawn, and others said that with a wind like that against us we shouldn't have started at all. Haraldsen said why complain, maybe the convoy we had missed would be attacked anyway. (A couple of days later we heard that all but fourteen ships out of seventy had had to turn back because of the weather.) Evenings, we listened to the radio and talked about the war. The men talked a lot about what they were going to do with Quislings in Norway after the war. They used Quisling as a generic term, just as we do. Some of the men wanted to put them on Bear Island, up north of Norway. Others just wanted to kill them. Even the messboys were angry at Knut Hamsun and Johan Bojer for having betrayed Norwegian culture. The ship had a library of four hundred volumes. None of the seamen would read Hamsun or

Bojer now. Norwegians seem more interested in books than music, and the captain was the only one who mentioned Kirsten Flagstad to me. He said Wagner had gone to her head.

Often, when Captain Petersen sat down to a meal, he would look at the customary plates of cold meat on the table and say, "I wonder what they have to eat in the old country now," or "I wonder what my wife has to eat." When we had fish he would say, "My wife never liked fish. Her father was a butcher," or else "My father-in-law always said, 'Fish is fish, but meat is nourishment.'" Once he heard me humming that old barroom favorite, "M-O-T-H-E-R." He said, "I heard a fellow sing that in vaudeville in Philadelphia. He had his wife on the stage and their six children. When he sang it one kid held up a card with 'M' on it. The next kid held up 'O' and so on until the smallest one held up 'R.' It was the cleverest thing I ever saw on the stage." Often he showed me photographs of his wife and their little boy.

We put to sea again a few days before Christmas. Just before we left, a naval man came out to say that our destination was now Baton Rouge. Nobody even speculated about the reason for this second change. We took it for granted that there was some kind of a muddle. Despite my beard and the carpenter's forebodings, we had normal North Atlantic winter weather this time. Early in the afternoon we sighted a huge fleet of ships on the horizon. This was to be a ten-knot convoy, so we had left the *Blaskjell* and a couple of other tubs behind. "Now we'll have something to look at," Haraldsen, the second officer, said as the courses of the large group and our small one converged. Every ship in a convoy has a number. Number forty-four had been assigned to us at the assembly port, and as we joined the others we hoisted the four flag and the pennon that corresponds to a ditto mark. All we had to do was find the forty-three ship and fall in behind her.

The small convoys we had traveled in along the coasts had gone in either single file or a column of twos. This one was in a column of eights. We had ships to port and starboard as well as ahead but only an escorting corvette behind us, as we were a file-closer. This tickled Haraldsen, because we wouldn't have to repeat any of the commodore's signals. A signal is passed down a file of ships, each repeating it for the benefit of the one behind. All the file-closer has to do is run up the answering pennon to acknowledge the message. Grung, the radioman, came out of his shack to look at the escort. There were only four corvettes for fifty-six large ships. "It's a bad yoke," he said bitterly. "Those English lords are sitting with girls behind drawn curtains on large estates and we can go to hell." When we had had a large escort on the east coast, Grung had said that was a bad sign. Haraldsen said, "Oh boy, I wish I had one of them girls here! Some fun." He had worked as a carpenter in New York during the building boom from 1924 to 1929 and talked of this as the romantic period of his life. "I got fifteen dollars a day," he said. "Fellows would wait for you in front of your yob—Yews, you know—and say, 'Listen, come with me. I give you a dollar more.' I like Yews." He had been on sailing ships during the last war, but he did not recall them with the same affection as, for example, John Masefield or Lincoln Colcord. "A sailing ship is hell in cold weather," he once told me.

It takes a combination of keen eyes and accurate navigation to keep a ship in its proper position in a convoy during the night, and the fleet is usually rather jumbled in the morning. This situation helped to kill time aboard the *Regnbue*. In the morning everybody was eager to see how badly the convoy had broken ranks. Bull, the third officer, was always on watch at dawn, and every morning he would say, with a sort of pride, "Dis der vorst convooey I ever see. Every morning all over der Atlahntic." The *Regnbue* nearly always held its position in relation to the commodore; either we kept to our course accurately or there was a telepathy which made him and us commit the same errors. Some of the other ships, however, would be far off on the horizon. This would always amuse Bull and the lookouts. The forty-three ship, which was supposed to stay just ahead of us, was nearly always miles to starboard, and when she tried to get back into her place we would, for the fun of it, speed up so that she couldn't edge in. She was an old tanker and slower than the *Regnbue*. Her skipper must have been a rather fussy sort; she would break into an angry rash of signal flags, and her radioman would bring out his signal flash lamp and deliver a harangue in Morse. Finally we would let her ease into the column. It usually took an hour or so to get

everybody aligned. The ships always reminded me of numbered liberty horses forming sequences in a circus.

After the convoy was re-formed we could kill another half-
hour trying to count the ships. There were a few less every day.
Ships drop out with engine trouble or get so far off the course
during the night that they lose sight of the convoy. These run
a bigger risk than the ones that keep pace, but most of them
turn up in port eventually. Two ships carried catafighters; that
is, Hurricane fighters that could be shot into the air from catapults if a Focke-Wulf appeared. In profile, the catapults looked
like cocked pistols. We used to find comfort in looking at
them, even though Grung said that the pilots were probably
seasick and the planes would break away from their lashings in
a storm just before we were attacked by an air fleet. Sometimes
ships in convoy talk to each other out of boredom, like prisoners tapping on cell walls. One morning I found Bull, signal
lamp in hand, carrying on a parley with a British tanker in the
column to starboard. When at last he put the lamp down I
asked what it was all about, and he said, "Oh, they invite us to
come aboard for lunch."

"What did you tell them?" I asked.

"Oh," Bull replied, "I say, 'If you got a drop of yin, I
wouldn't say no.'"

When you are in convoy it is sometimes impossible to remember whether a thing happened yesterday or the day before
yesterday or the day before that. You watch the other ships and
you read whatever there is to read and you play jokes on the
ship's cat. You go to the pantry and slam the refrigerator door,
and the cat runs in, thinking you are going to give him something to eat. Then you pretend to ignore him. Finally, when
his whining becomes unbearable, you throw him a few bits of
crabmeat. I had brought three books along with me on the
Regnbue, but I had finished them in the three weeks we spent
idling off the British coast. After that I read several ninepenny
thrillers by Agatha Christie and Valentine Williams that happened to be aboard, and then a copy of *Pilgrim's Progress*, donated to the ship by the Glasgow Y.M.C.A. Eventually I was
reduced to looking at September numbers of *Life*. Once I
found an early 1939 issue of *Redbook*. I read every page of it

gratefully, though it contained six stories about husbands who strayed but found that they liked their wives best after all. There was a strict black-out every evening, but I didn't mind it as much as I had in London, because on the ship there was no place to go anyhow. One of the lifeboats had a fashion of working loose from its fastenings in heavy weather, and then the boatswain would summon a gang to heave on the ropes until he could make it fast again. I used to look forward to the chance of pulling on one of the ropes. Whenever the crew had to make the boat fast while I was napping in my cabin, I felt slighted.

Some of the men were always speculating about our destination, Baton Rouge. It didn't show on any of the maps on the ship. If it had, they figured, the size of the print might have given them an idea of how big the town was. My own guess was that it was a city of a hundred thousand. Actually, the population is thirty-four thousand. American cities weren't listed in *Hvem, Hvad, Hvor*, the Norwegian equivalent of the *World Almanac,* and the favorite reference work on board. *Hvem, Hvad, Hvor* means "Who, What, Where." The book contains street plans of every city in Norway, even places of as few as five thousand inhabitants. The men used to mark the locations of their houses and show them to each other and to me. Once, Gjertsen, the chief officer, showed me where he lived in his home town. The next day he came into my cabin looking for me, with *Hvem, Hvad, Hvor* in his hand. "I made a mistake," he said, pointing to the plan of the place. "*Here* is where I live," and he showed me a dot about a quarter of an inch from the one he had made before.

As Christmas drew near, Larsen, the steward, was often missing from his cabin during the evenings. He was aft in the galley with the cook, constructing great quantities of "fat things" and "poor men," the Norwegian terms for doughnuts and crullers, respectively. On his journeys aft he carried with him a thick, calf-bound Norwegian cookbook. Larsen had formerly been a cook; he sometimes regretted his change-over from creative to executive catering. The cook was a tall, thin young man who looked as if he were built of candle wax. Together they elaborated on the plans for the Christmas Eve dinner. Rumors were spread by one of the British machine gunners, who had talked to the third engineer, who had it straight from a messboy, that there would be turkey. While the convoy moved along at its steady ten knots, nobody aboard the *Regnbue* talked of anything but the coming dinner.

On the great night the table was laid for a dozen persons in the saloon, where ordinarily the captain and I dined alone. We were lucky; the sea was reasonably calm. The steward and the boy who helped him in the saloon, which was forward, would have had a hard time in a gale, for the galley was in the after deckhouse and they had to carry all the food over the long catwalk between. Promptly at six o'clock the engineer officers came forward to dine with us. Larsen, the chief engineer, who was not related to Larsen the steward, was a girthy, middle-aged man who resembled Hendrik Willem van Loon. If I looked aft on a fair day I could generally see him standing by a door of the engine room with his hands in his pockets. He was a fixture in the seascape, like Nilsen, the gunner and ex-whaler, who silently paced the deck near the four-inch gun. Equally immutable was the British machine gunner on duty, wearing a pointed hood and sitting inside a little concrete breastwork on the poop deck, looking like a jack-in-the-box. Chief Engineer Larsen and his officers seldom came forward to visit us. To mark the occasion on this night, they were wearing collars and neckties. They looked scrubbed and solemn, and so did Captain Petersen and the three deck officers and the gunner and the radioman, all of whom were at the table.

Steward Larsen had set three glasses at each place—one, he told me, for port, one for whisky, and a third for gin. He had no aquavit for the Christmas dinner, and gin was supposed to replace it. To get the meal started, the steward brought in some porridge called *jul grot*, which is traditional and practically tasteless. Engineer Larsen said "Skoal" and emptied a glass of gin. We all said "Skoal" and did likewise. Then Steward Larsen served a thick soup with canned shrimp and crabmeat and chicken in it. We all drank again. The steward next served fish pudding, and there was more drinking of skoals. Then he brought in the turkey with the pride of a Soviet explorer presenting a hunk of frozen mammoth excavated from a glacier. The turkey had been in the ship's cold room since the September equinox, and ship chandler's turkeys are presumed to have been dead for quite a while before they come aboard. We had plenty of canned vegetables and, above all, plenty of gin. The teetotaler Methodist captain, who stuck to his principles and didn't drink, brought out a couple of songbooks that he had got from a Norwegian church and suggested we sing some Christmas hymns. His guests sang them, without much pleasure, it seemed to me, and we ate a lot of jello covered with vanilla sauce and drank some more gin. All the men's faces remained rigid and solemn. Engineer Larsen said, in English, "Merry Christmas to our American friend." The captain whispered to me, "You can tell he's from Oslo. He talks too much." The steward then brought in mounds of doughnuts and crullers, and some fancy drinks in tall glasses. He called the tall drinks Larsen's Spezials. They were triple portions of gin with lump sugar and canned cherries. Everyone said, "Thank you, Steward. Very good." The whisky was served straight, as a dessert liqueur. We all began drinking it out of jiggers and saying "Skoal" some more. The singing got fairly continuous and the choice of numbers gradually grew more secular. Most Norwegian songs, I noticed, have many verses, and the men who are not singing pay no attention to the one who is. They look as if they are trying to recall the innumerable verses they are going to sing in their turn. We all got together on one patriotic number, though. The last line, translated into English, was "If Norway goes under, I want to go too." We clasped hands on that one.

The captain asked me to sing "My Old Kentucky Home," which I couldn't remember many words of, but fortunately three other fellows started to sing three other songs at the same time. The steward, considering his official duties over, drew up a chair to the table and received congratulations. The cook, looking taller and more solemn than ever, came in and was hailed as a great man. The drinkers still made intermittent efforts to remain grave. They yielded slowly, as if they were trying to protect their pleasure. Now the dignitaries of the crew, who had finished a dinner with exactly the same menu in their own quarters, began to appear in the saloon and take seats at the table—first the argumentative carpenter, then the boatswain with the cackle, and finally the pumpman, a tall fellow who looked like a Hapsburg and spent his life shooting compressed air into clogged oil tanks. The carpenter arose to sing a song. He had the same argumentative, deliberate delivery that he had in conversation, and he paused so long between verses that the chief officer, who had come down off the bridge and entered the saloon just after the carpenter had finished a verse, thought the all-clear had sounded and began a song of his own. The usually timid cook, buoyed up by one of Larsen's Spezials, thundered, "Shut up, Chief Officer! Let the carpenter sing!" As the chief officer and the fourth engineer joined the party, the third officer and another of the engineers left to stand their watches. The machine gunner from Glasgow arrived to wish the captain a merry Christmas and snitch a bottle of whisky. Two seamen, lads of about eighteen, came in to convey the respects of the crew. They had, I imagine, thought of this mission themselves. One, a small, neat boy with a straw-blond mustache, sang a long song with the refrain "*Farvel, farvel*" ("Farewell, farewell"). It appeared to make him very unhappy. Nearly all the seamen on the *Regnbue* were youngsters, which would have been true on a Norwegian ship even before the war. After three and a half years at sea they are eligible to take a course at a mates' school if they can save or borrow the price. Boys who don't like the sea quit before then.

Presently Steward Larsen pulled me by the arm and took me off with him to visit the rest of the crew. Before leaving the saloon, he had handed out a bottle of whisky to each four men, and on the whole they were doing all right with it. "I am a Commoonist," he kept saying to me on our way aft, "so I want you to love these fellers." Everybody on the ship had received as a Christmas greeting from the Norwegian Government a facsimile letter signed "Haakon, Rex." The letters, which had been put aboard at London for the captain to hand out, told Norwegian seamen that they were their country's mainstay. The "Commoonist" read this letter over and over again and cried every time. The Government had also sent the crew a set of phonograph records of patriotic songs. The favorite was called "*Du Gamle Mor*" ("Thou Old Mother"), which means Norway. The boys aft were all wearing blue stocking caps, which had come in a Christmas-gift bundle with a card saying they had been knitted by a Miss Georgie Gunn, of 1035 Park Avenue, New York City.

By the time Larsen and I staggered back over the catwalk to the saloon, everybody but Captain Petersen was unashamedly happy. It was very close in the blacked-out saloon with all the ports shut, and I went up to the bridge for air. Bull, the third officer, was on watch up there. He had been moderately dizzy when he had gone on watch at eight o'clock after eating his dinner, he told me, but now he felt only a sense of sober well-being. "I see ships all around," he said, "so ve must be in de meddel de convooey." Sandor, the Rumanian seaman who had stowed away on the ship in 1939 and remained aboard ever since, was on lookout duty. He said, "This makes three Christmas on ship since I left home. No good. On ship you see thirty, thirty-five peoples. On shore you see hoondreds peoples. I like to get one Christmas ashore." Sandor's chances were not bright. The British immigration officers at our second assembly port had told him that, since he was now an enemy alien, he would not be allowed on shore in Britain for the remainder of the war. They had added that the Americans would probably also refuse to let him land, so he might have to remain afloat indefinitely. Griffin, the English seaman, was at the wheel. When Sandor spelled him, Griffin came out of the wheelhouse and we wished each other Merry Christmas. I had heard so much talk about home towns and traditions that night that I asked Griffin where he was from. "Blowed if I know," he said cheerfully. "Sandor don't know where 'e's going and I don't know where I come from."

When I went down to my cabin, a row that would have done credit to an early convention of the American Legion was going on in the saloon. I looked in, but everybody was shouting in Norwegian and no one looked sufficiently detached to translate for me, so I didn't hear what it was all about until the next day, when I was told that someone had been trying to get subscriptions to the Norwegian Air Force Spitfire Fund and that Grung, the radioman, had protested that the Norwegian Government, even in exile, was giving $300,000 a year to missionaries in China and Africa. "Let them spend the missionary money for Spitfires before they bother workingmen," he had said. The steward had called Grung a bad name and Grung had pushed him over a case of empty whisky bottles. Later, when I happened to see Grung coming out of the radio shack, I asked him what Larsen had called him. "He called me a Commoonist," Grung said.

The party gave us something to talk about for a couple of days afterward. The carpenter went around repeating a line he had memorized from the label of an Old Angus whisky bottle: "Yentle as a lamb." He would say it and roll his eyes and then exclaim, "Yeezis!" On Christmas morning an English ship signaled to us, "Merry Christmas. Keep your chins and thumbs up." Grung and Bull had a consultation and then, not being able to think of anything witty, just ran up the answering flag meaning "Message noted."

One morning, when we were about halfway across the Atlantic, I found Bull in a particularly good humor. "Look around," he said, handing me a glass. "Vare is escort?" I had a good look around and there wasn't any. The corvettes had disappeared during the night. "Does that mean we've reached the safe part of the Atlantic?" I asked. "Safe yust so long ve see no submarine," Bull said. Captain Petersen, who came up a half-hour later to look around, said, "Maybe the escort from America was supposed to meet us here, and it didn't, and the British corvettes had a date to meet an eastbound convoy off Iceland. We don't count as much as eastbound ships, because they're loaded." We went on all day without an escort. Grung came out of his shack and stared at three hundred and fifty thousand tons of valuable shipping moving placidly on, unprotected and unattacked. "Admiral Raeder must be lousy," he said at last.

Next morning a force of Canadian destroyers met us. No harm had been done. It wasn't the only time the *Regnbue* had traveled in an unconvoyed convoy, Bull said. Once she had left Halifax in a convoy escorted by a battleship that was returning from an American dockyard. A couple of hundred miles out, the battleship had been summoned to help hunt the *Bismarck*, so she had moved off at thirty knots and left the merchantmen to push on by themselves to England. There were never enough vessels for convoy duty, Bull said, but luckily there never seemed to be enough submarines, either. The Battle of the Atlantic sounded imposing, but it was rather like a football game with five men on a side.

A few days after we met the Canadian, the ships bound for

Gulf ports split off from the convoy. We were one of them. Each ship was to proceed as an individual, the theory at that time being that waters within a few hundred miles of the American coast were fairly safe. We had always cherished a notion that we were one of the fastest ships in our convoy. When dispersal day came, however, most of the others bound for the south quickly left us behind. Twenty-four hours after the split we were alone in the ocean, without another ship in sight. We steered southwest within a couple of hundred miles of the coast for nearly two weeks and saw only two vessels, neither of them a warship. Nor did we sight a single patrol plane. We hoped that no hostile aircraft carrier would ever have the same luck. The *Regnbue*, now that she was alone, zigzagged in a constant series of tangents to her course. This lost a mile an hour, which still further delayed my home-coming.

The weather stayed seasonably rough. We never ran into the kind of storm that sends smashed ships to port to make pictures for the newspaper photographers, but for days on end we couldn't see the sun long enough to get a position, and on New Year's Eve, when we were thirty-one days out of London, we had a sixty-mile gale, which made a second holiday party impossible. The day before we left the convoy I had been standing at the wheelhouse window watching the extraordinary antics of the tankers around us. A tanker in water ballast is a good sea boat but not a comfortable one. It rides the waves like a canoe, but it has a tendency to twist from side to side as it comes down. As I have already noted, this is even more disconcerting to watch than to endure. I was thinking about this when Mikkelsen, the electrician, a big, snaggletoothed West Norwegian, came up and stood next to me. He looked at the ships for a while, then said quietly, "Fine weather." According to his lights it probably was.

After you leave your convoy you may have no other ships to watch and discuss, but you have a chance to fire your gun. That is an event to look forward to for days. Admiralty regulations require a ship to fire at least two shots on each trip. The captain gave Nilsen, the gunner, the order to prepare to fire these ritual shots. A day was set for the performance—not too soon, because, on account of scarcity of ammunition, we couldn't afford such pleasures more than once and we wanted to prolong the period of anticipation. The ordinarily silent Nilsen became the embodiment of the busy-executive type. The other members of the gun crew were the Hapsburg pumpman, two Diesel motormen, the fourth engineer, and the little sailor who had sung "*Farvel.*" They assumed new dignity among their fellows during the days before the gun practice. Everybody on the *Regnbue* told jokes about the last time the gun had been fired. Some said that Larsen, the chief engineer, had been asleep in his cabin when the gun went off and had been knocked off his divan. Others told the same story about the cook, the steward, or the second officer. All of this was invention, because nobody on a merchant ship sleeps when the gun is to be fired. One might as well expect a small boy to sleep late on Christmas morning.

On the big day the raised gun platform served as an excellent stage for the gun crew and the protagonist, the gun. The boatswain had distributed pounds of cotton batting, and we had stuffed our ears with wads of the stuff. The little sailor, a romantic chap, had carefully smudged his forehead with black grease so that he would look like one of Admiral Tordenskjold's powder monkeys. An empty oil drum would serve as target. A couple of sailors threw it off the stern. Nilsen's crew loaded the gun. Then, after the ship had gone an estimated two thousand meters, they fired. There was a great spat of flame from the gun's muzzle, a satisfactory roar, and something splashed in the water a long distance away. I could not see the oil drum, but Haraldsen, the second officer, who had once been an ensign in the Norwegian Navy, said that the shell had not missed by much. We all shouted "Hurrah!" It was better than the Fourth of July. The gun was reloaded and fired again. After the second shot we all felt much safer, because we knew that the gun would not burst until the next trip.

The days continued alike as we went on, but they had a different feeling. After we had passed Hatteras even the carpenter and the radioman, the ship's leading grousers, began to admit it was probable we would make port. And all through the ship men made plans for whatever shore leave they might get. Larsen, the steward, who had once worked out of the port of "Noolians," proposed to the cook and a couple of others that they hire a taxi at Baton Rouge and drive straight to the French quarter in New Orleans. "I always say I'm going to save money," he told me, "but when I get near land I can't keep my temper." Captain Petersen looked forward to renewing acquaintance with the pastor of the Norwegian church in New Orleans, where he planned to go by train. A few of the men owned electric flatirons, and these were in heavy demand by shipmates who wanted to press their pants. Grung, the radioman, was in charge of the pay list. All of the men had fairly large sums coming to them, and each signified to Grung the amount he wanted to draw at Baton Rouge. Usually a man changed his mind several times, raising the ante each time. The cook and the steward held long conferences about stores, occasionally asking me how to spell "bitterscots pewding" or "tomates cetseps." The steward said that he would send the list ashore to a ship chandler in "Noolians" when we went through customs and have the stuff trucked up to Baton Rouge.

The ship had not taken stores for more than three months now, and the eggs caused a daily argument between the steward and me. For several mornings he had served them hard-boiled, a sign he had no real confidence in them. Each morning I would open my first egg and say, "*Darlig*," which is Norwegian for "Bad."

The steward would protest, "*Naj, naj.*"

"But this one has green spots inside the shell," I would say.

"Ex like dot sometimes," he would maintain.

The captain always ate his eggs without any remark; his silence accused me of finicking. At last, one morning toward the end of the voyage, he opened an egg and looked at the steward. "*Darlig*," he said. The steward looked embarrassed. Then the captain ate the egg; a bad hard-boiled egg is probably as nourishing as a good one.

Next morning the steward brought me an amorphous yellow mass on a plate. It tasted mostly of sugar, but he offered me a jug of maple- and cane-sugar syrup to pour on it. I took a spoonful, fancying it some Norse confection, and said, "Not bad. What do you call it?" The steward said, "I call it ummelet. Same ex." Once the captain opened up a bit more than usual and talked about the Oxford Movement. The Movement had been strong in Norway, he said, and had frequently coincided with Quislingism. "A shipowner in my town," he once said to me, "got crazy about the Oxford Movement. He took his wife and children to a public meeting, and then he got up in the meeting and said that when he went to Antwerp on business he used to use bad women. His wife fainted. I don't call that a Christian." Several times the captain talked about his native town. "It has two fine hotels, and the harbor is full of beautiful little islands," he said once. "You can take your family in a boat fishing and then have a picnic on an island. In the winter we go skiing. My boy is three years old, and he has his second pair of skis. In the summer we used to have lobster parties, or dumpling-and-buttermilk parties. But it probably isn't like that now."

"By and by Florida" had been a gag line with Haraldsen, the second officer, throughout the voyage, but one day we really got there. It was the first land we had sighted since leaving Britain, and it looked exactly like the newsreels, with fine, white hotels and palm trees and scores of spick-and-span motorboats in the blue water off-shore, fishing for whatever people fish for in Florida. The weather was clear but cold. When we got close to shore we were permitted to use the radio receiving set in the chief officer's cabin again, and one of the first things I heard was an announcer saying, "There is no frost in Florida. This morning's temperature was thirty-seven." I tried to get some war news and heard another announcer saying, "The slant-eyed specialists in treachery continue their advance toward Singapore." One, two, three, four, five seconds. "You could not employ them better than by making a lather of creamy Sweetheart soap." We sailed along the shore. There were plenty of airplanes overhead now. They swooped almost to our masthead and looked us over every five minutes. It made all the men happy just to see the coast. From the bridge we kept looking through our glasses for bathing girls, but the weather was too cold for them. We wondered what the people in the Palm Beach and Miami hotels thought of our rusty ship, with its wheelhouse fortified with concrete slabs and its ragged red flag with the blue cross. Fellows kept making attempts at jokes, like "There's the dog track; let's go" or "Grung, get out the flash lamp and signal women that want a date yust wait on the beach. I going to swim in."

That afternoon the steward came into my cabin and said that the captain and the officers were giving me a farewell supper that evening. As on Christmas Eve, it was formal dress —collars and neckties. The occasion itself was solemn; Norwegians are not effusive. My companions just sat there, talking Norwegian among themselves and ignoring me. Nobody made a speech, but at the end of the meal the cook carried in a cake about the size and shape of an Aztec calendar stone. It was encrusted with slightly damp sugar. He held it out to me, and I stood up and reached for it. It nearly pulled me forward on my face, and as I looked down on the top, I saw, written in icing, "*Farvel.*"

A few nights later we were at the mouth of the Mississippi, waiting for a pilot. A northerly gale howled down at us straight from Lake Michigan. There were plenty of lights visible on the shore, more than I had seen at a comparable hour since leaving New York in the summer. Somehow I had expected our lights to go out when we entered the war. It seemed strange coming in our blacked-out ship to a country that was neither neutral *nor* dark. A boy in a rowboat brought out the pilot, a heavy-set, shivering man in a leatherette jacket who announced as soon as he came aboard that it was the coldest damn winter he had ever known in Louisiana. He brought aboard a copy of the New Orleans *Times-Picayune*, containing a lot of basketball scores and society notes and a few stories about a war that seemed to be on some remote sphere. A naval party came aboard and sealed the radio shack. The pilot took us seventeen miles up the river and then was relieved by a second pilot, who was going to take us the eighty remaining miles to New Orleans. I turned in.

We dropped anchor off quarantine in New Orleans at about ten o'clock on the morning of the forty-second day out of London. It was Sunday. We had to pass the immigration and public-health officers' inspections before the *Regnbue* could continue up the river. I had my suitcase packed before the government officers arrived, hoping that I would be able to go back to shore with them. It was the sort of day we had had off Florida, chilly but bright, and the city looked good in the sunlight. The *Regnbue*'s men, lining the rails, talked about how fine it would be to be going ashore again. I had been at sea for only six weeks, but few of them had set foot ashore in four months. The immigration-and-health boat came out soon after ten with a party including a doctor and a rat inspector. The immigration men brought five armed guards to post about the ship to see that none of our allies would try to land too soon. Soon a customs officer came aboard and asked the captain if any man on the ship had more than three hundred cigarettes. Seamen buy their cigarettes in America, and our men had started to run short a fortnight before. Captain Petersen did not seem astonished by the question. He sent Grung to take a census of the cigarettes on board. Grung came back after a half-hour with word that only the second engineer had more than three hundred cigarettes. He had three hundred and twenty-five. The customs man asked if the twenty-five were loose, and Grung said that five of them were. The customs man said he thought he could let the second engineer keep the other twenty, although, he pointed out, he was making an exception. I pictured a large convoy missing a tide while the United States Customs counted cigarettes. Then the customs man asked about liquor, because he would have to seal up what we had on board. Grung went on a search for liquor and reported back that we had had two bottles of whisky and one of gin but that one of the public-health men had drunk about half of one of the bottles of whisky.

Next the immigration men came to the consideration of me. They said that since I had a good passport and had apparently been born in New York, I probably had a right to land in the United States, but not until my baggage had been passed by a customs appraiser. Unfortunately, they said, no appraisers had come along. "The last thing I expected to find on this ship was a passenger," the head immigration man said, giving me a rat inspector's look. He said that unless I wanted to stay on the ship for twenty-four hours longer I would have to pay two days' wages for the appraiser myself. Double pay for Sunday work. I said that would be all right, and they sent for an appraiser. It cost me $13.33. While waiting for the appraiser, I went out on deck. Captain Petersen came out too, and we stood looking at the shore. He was quiet, as usual, but he seemed to be struggling with an unusual emotion. At last he said, "Say, is it true the Hippodrome has been torn down?"

I said, "Yes, and the Sixth Avenue El, too."

Again he looked troubled, and I thought he was going to say he would miss me, but he said, "*The Big Show* were a wonderful play." That was an extravaganza that had played at the Hipp in 1917, when the captain had lived in Hoboken.

I said, "Yes, with Joe Jackson."

"A very funny man," Captain Petersen said.

A shabby motorboat came toward us from the left bank of the river. Captain Petersen said, "It must be a ship chandler after our business." There was a man on the forward deck with a megaphone, and as the boat came under our bow he called up inquiringly, "Captain, Captain?" Petersen pointed to his peaked cap, his emblem of office. The fellow shouted, "We got orders to send you on to Curaçao! You got enough bunker?" Curaçao is nine days from New Orleans for a ten-knot boat. Petersen showed no sign of surprise or disappointment. "We need bunker," he shouted back, "but we can get out in twenty-four hours!"

An hour later, when I was in a boat going ashore, I could see most of the *Regnbue* fellows on deck, leaning over the rail. There was the carpenter, with his square head and his obstinate shoulders, and the tall pumpman, and the electrician, and the two British gunners in their khaki uniforms. I could make out the bearish form of Sandor, the Rumanian, who would not have to stay on board alone now, because the others would stay with him. And there was Larsen, the steward, in a belted, horizon-blue overcoat and a bright green hat, his shoregoing uniform. He wouldn't go ashore, after all.

Book III
The World Gets Up

Toward a Happy Ending

PEARL HARBOR had left slight trace on the public mind, it seemed to a man coming off a boat in mid-January of 1942, but it had closed the second phase of the war. The first had ended with the disaster of the Pétain armistice. The second had been a negative success because our side had avoided collapse. The third, however unpromisingly it might start, however long it might last, was bound to end in the defeat of the avowedly fascist powers, because the combination of peoples they had attacked was too big, too strong, and too game for them. Hitler's chance to own the world had depended on a successful bluff. If, with the aid of the French industrialists and their counterparts in Great Britain and the United States, he could have secured a dominance of the West without war, isolating Russia, he might have brought it off. He still had had a chance as long as he could keep Russia and the United States neutral. But with all the holders of high cards in the game he was in the position of a poker player who has tried to steal a pot with no pair. He could keep on raising until he ran out of chips in order to delay the showdown; that would be an insane card player's reaction. His situation made me, personally, extremely and perhaps unreasonably happy. Millions of men meriting better than I have lived and died in humiliating periods of history. Free men and free thinking always get a return match with the forces of sadism and anti-reason sometimes. But I had wanted to see a win, I had wanted my era to be one of those that read well in the books. Some people like to live in a good neighborhood; I like to live in a good age. I am a sucker for a happy ending—the villain kicked in the teeth, the stepchildren released from the dark basement, the hero in bed with the heroine. Maybe the curtain will go up on the same first act tomorrow night, but I won't be in the audience.

By 1942 I had my personal hurts as well. I had Suzette's letter, which had taken nearly a year to reach me, telling of her father's death, cold, undernourished and humiliated, in the Montmartre flat where we had so often broken bread. Jean, the son, had won a Croix de Guerre and had been demobilized, Suzette had written—I could imagine him dodging about France to avoid conscription for German factory labor. Sauvageon, living in the *zone interdite* between occupied and unoccupied France, had managed to get a letter out to me too, through Switzerland. He had written of the mass emigration of the Alsatians and Lorrainers who had chosen to retain their French nationality.

The third round would be the good one, I thought, and I didn't stay long at home waiting for it to begin. I made the return trip to England by another Norwegian ship, this time a fast one that traveled without escort. The chief excitement of this trip was a long series of after-dinner checker games between me and the chief engineer, Johansen, who referred to himself as "some of the oldest engineers afloat." I once beat him with a quadruple jump, in a game for three bottles of beer.

London had changed more than New York since our entry into the war. It was full of Americans now, and one more attracted about as much attention as an extra clam at a shore dinner. I felt like an until recently only child whose mother has just given birth to quintuplets. And I was more of a stranger to the American news sources with whom I now had to deal, the Army and Navy Public Relations offices, than correspondents who had been in London for only three months, because the organizations had been set up since the time I had left.

I had a high idea of what the American Army in the European theater of operations would eventually be, and my first clues to it did not disappoint me. There were few ground combat troops in Great Britain as yet and many less Air Corps people than I had expected to find, but the preparations of the Services of Supply indicated how great the fighting force would soon be. The S.O.S. was building, for example, a depot in the

South of England for the repair of American Army motor vehicles, and from its size one could get a fair idea of how many
vehicles would be in operation and how big an army they
would serve. It was like estimating an elephant's size from the
print of one foot. The dimensions of the A.E.F. would certainly be elephantine, which pleased me because it indicated
that the Government had not been impressed by the Sunday-
supplement strategists who talked about an exclusively air war.

I knew that the quality of American troops would be
good, once they had paid their entry fee with a couple of bob-
bles, because Americans are the best competitors on earth. A
basketball game between two high-school teams at home will
call forth enough hardness of soul and flexibility of ethic to
win a minor war; the will to win in Americans is so strong it is
painful, and it is unfettered by any of the polite flummery that
goes with cricket. This ruthlessness always in stock is one of
our great national resources. It is better than the synthetic fascist kind, because the American kid wears it naturally, like his
skin, and not self-consciously, like a Brown Shirt. Through
long habit he has gained control over it, so that he turns it on
for games, politics, and business and usually turns it off in inti-
macy. He doesn't have to be angry to compete well.

While I had been away from London, Manetta, the manager
of the Savoy Grille, had taken over the restaurant in my old
hotel in Half Moon Street, and it was now one of the busiest
and noisiest pubs in London, with a British version of a swing
band, no tables available on less than three days' notice, American colonels crowding the members of refugee governments
away from the ringside, and Jack, the cockney bartender who
during my first visit had drooped disconsolately in front of a
fine assortment of whiskies, now overworked and under-
stocked, like the wine waiter. The hotel portion of the establishment looked much as it always had, although because of
the Americans it was harder to get a room. Some of the old
county women, having booked weeks in advance, would arrive
there and in time descend from their rooms, leading either a
spaniel or a small grandniece wearing a blue hair ribbon. They
would march stiffly toward the once tranquil dining room,
hear the first blast of the swing band, enter the gabble of the

cocktail lounge where the new clientele waited for tables, and then turn and hobble desperately away, dragging dog or child after them.

London had the atmosphere of a town where people are gathering for a gold rush or an opera festival; everybody felt that something good was going to begin soon. Psychologically we had already passed to the attack. The correspondents, while they waited to be let in on the time and place, wrote stories about the growing American forces in Britain. After three years of going out to French, British, and Polish troops for stories, I enjoyed the novelty of being with Americans, although the uniform I now had to wear when I went out to troops made me feel that I was play-acting. I had passed through British railway stations so often and so unremarked in mufti that the salutes of British noncoms now took me by surprise and I was generally well past the saluter before I realized I had left him with a poor view of American military courtesy. It would have been hopeless to explain each time that a correspondent didn't rate a salute—I was bald enough and old enough to be a field officer and was wearing an officer's uniform.

The Air Corps, which was just beginning to take over a few British fields, reminded me of a football squad beginning its training for the season. It would win a lot of games if it was not rushed into heavy competition too soon. My favorite unit in the first weeks was a Flying Fortress bombardment group that resembled a football squad physically too. There is an official maximum size for fighter and medium bombardment pilots, but the really big boys in the Air Corps get into the big ships, where there is relatively a lot of head room. The commander of one squadron of the group had been All-Southern at Mississippi State; one of his pilots had played tackle for Alabama in the Rose Bowl, and another had understudied an All-American halfback at Duke; Tommy Lohr, a rugged little lightweight back from Brown, was another pilot in the group, and altogether they would have made a good squad for any coach in a normal season. But this time they had other business.

The original public-relations crew in London, being for the most part newspapermen who had recently acquired uniforms and lived in deadly fear of irritating real soldiers, were not of much help in getting out to see troops. According to them the

C.O. of any unit a correspondent wanted to see was sure to be busy, and anyway there were no living accommodations for newspapermen at the flying field. I arranged all that with my Fortress fellows by always occupying the bed of a man who had gone on forty-eight-hour leave to London. While the man was in London he would sleep in my room at the hotel. When the regular occupant of the bed at the field returned there was always somebody else going up to town and I would move into his bed while he took mine in London. I never really interviewed anybody, just lived around the place and learned by osmosis, until I sometimes thought of myself as a redundant member of the group, a goldbricker nobody had yet caught up with. We were living in hutments and sleeping on cots; there were toilets that flushed and showers; between meals and after dinner we would sit in the lounge of the officers' club, where there were deep chairs and a bar. In retrospect, after we all got to Africa, it seemed a most luxurious period.

The Fortresses made their first flights over France while I was living with this group. The accuracy of their bombing, even in their first raids, astonished officers of British Bomber Command and the Ministry of Economic Warfare, who had selected the targets. The British thought at first that these were selected crews of veterans and that the accuracy couldn't be retained in large-scale operations. But I knew that they were boys who had had at most a year and a half in the Air Corps, and that there were thousands more like them at home. The factories would furnish the planes, the American system of public education would furnish the crews; it couldn't be anything but a win. And the ground forces, I felt confident, would be up to the air people in efficiency. The factories and the schools would work for them, too. And the good American food that the boys had eaten had given them the bone and lungs and recuperative power that no Nazi state system of physical education could superimpose on rickety frames.

The boys themselves, I thought, were the best proof they had something to fight for. Four officers fly in each Fortress, and every one of them at that time had to be a college man. You could look around the lounge in the evening and see 250 officers, all giving a common impression of fitness and good humor. There wasn't a raddled, vicious face in the lot. They had come from state universities and technical schools and little denominational colleges all through the country, where tuition fees were nominal or nonexistent. This brazen public defiance of the profit system had resulted in the creation of our greatest national asset. They hadn't had to spend their elementary-school days getting up competitive examinations which would admit them to secondary school, or their secondary-school days preparing competitive examinations for college. They had had time to play. Some of them were sons of rich men, a few were sons of mechanics, and most were in between, but there was no trace of class accent to distinguish one from another. There were regional accents, of course. And the standard of training in all those schools that to me had for years been just names in columns of football scores must have been pretty good, because the kids could all do their stuff as well as the few members of the group who had been to Ivy colleges.

I hadn't been with so many Americans so young in twenty years, and I thought they had an edge on my own college generation, although maybe I was less than fair in retrospect because I had been an insecure, intolerant undergraduate myself. All the boys had to do, I thought, was to look around at each other and they would understand that democracy was worth defending. The noncoms they flew with, six sergeants to a Fortress, were just as different from products of other regimes as the officers. They were all high-school men, even though in civil life they had clerked in grocery stores or driven laundry trucks. They had no idea that they were bound down in any social class, and they thought for themselves about everything they saw and did. They were good stuff.

The officers of the different ships wore no insignia to show which Fortress they belonged to, but it was easy to pick out crewmates in the lounge of the club. They were the men who usually occupied adjacent chairs, engaged in long sessions of insulting one another, and lent one another money in crap games. One of my favorites, a boy named Jones from Memphis, used to sit next to the phonograph, changing the records. The songs they liked were full of sobs: "I'll Be Around When He Is Gone," or "Someone's Rocking My Dream Boat," or "This Is the Story of a Starry Night." A psychiatrist has since told me that he considers such fare extremely depressing for men about to go out on bombing missions, but there were no suicides. I never hear those songs now without seeing the faces of the kids in the lounge, and sometimes I forget which of them are dead.

There was one Fortress pilot whom his colleagues called the Baron, who once told me that his only ambition for after the war was to sit in the grandstand at the Yankee Stadium every afternoon and watch the ball game. He was known as the Baron because once when he had been doing some drinking in the club he had said, "When we get to Germany I will be a baron if I feel like it because my family has a castle on the Rhine and I can walk in and claim it any time." His father had been an officer in the German Army in the war previous to this one, but that did not prevent the Baron from being the kind of suburban boy who shoots a good game of pool, plays semipro baseball on Sunday while he is still in college and officially an amateur, and is perennially worried about a pending charge of driving while under the influence of alcohol. When the home-town papers began to arrive at the station after the first few Fortress raids the fellows from small cities had a lot of fun reading each other their clippings. One town had had a Joe Snodgrass Day in honor of a navigator from there who had been in a raid, and it had raised a fund of $62 to buy candy and chewing gum for him, but not cigarettes because some of the subscribers objected to smoking. The Baron said to me, "In the town I come from the people think I am a bum, and I guess they would be surprised I am here at all." He had played varsity baseball at three colleges, none of them tough academ-ically, and you could deduce that he had not been exactly a studying type from the fact that he had been thrown out of two of them. He was a good pilot, and he flew in a careless, easy-looking way. "Flying is the hardest thing in the world to learn," he once said to me, "and the easiest thing to do after you've learned it." He had met a co-ed at the third college where he had played ball, and married her. He was always showing new acquaintances a picture of his wife, tall and dark, and she was very pretty. The Baron had a hard time emotion-ally in England. He didn't like anything he had heard about Hitler, but it used to make him angry when Englishmen referred to Germans as Huns. "My old man is all right," he used to say.

Quite a while afterward I met a bomber crew from that group in Africa, and they told me they thought the Baron had been killed over Lorient. "At least, when we last saw that ship it was blazing and only five hundred feet off the ground, and nobody had bailed out," the bombardier said. "It wasn't the Baron's regular crew. There was something the matter with a supercharger in his own ship that morning, and the pilot of the ship he was lost in had a heavy cold and the co-pilot was green, so the Baron volunteered to fly them. That was a raid when we had to come down lower than usual to get through cloud over the target. We don't know whether flak or fighters got the Baron's ship, but just as it made the turn after bombing, smoke and flames began pouring out of it and it began losing altitude. They could have bailed out all right, but they were heading into a group of German fighters, so they kept the guns going and they blew two 109's to bits on the way down. They were too goddam busy to jump."

I used to sometimes try to get fliers talking about what they wanted after the war, but most of them had ambitions rather like the Baron's. One fellow wanted to stay on his honeymoon until all his bonus money ran out, another wanted to play golf all day and poker all night every night and drink whisky constantly, and a lot of them wanted to stay in the Air Corps or get jobs in commercial aviation. They didn't have very much to say about the future of the world, if they thought about it. They weren't vindictive, either. They liked to hear me talk about my Polish friends. "I guess those boys are really bloodthirsty," they would say with objective astonishment. "It's better for us not to get mad," one of them said to me. "The type of precision bombing we do you've got enough to do without being angry."

CHAPTER 11

Birds of My Country

I SAILED for Africa from England on the night of November 9, twenty-four hours after the first African landings had been announced in London. For nearly two weeks before I left I had been subject to call at my hotel on twelve-hour notice. I had known there must be colleagues waiting for the same call, but I had never admitted that I was one of the elect, and none of the others had said anything to me. The secret of our destination had been well kept until November 8, but after the news of the first landings we who were still in London knew where we were going. We also knew that we had been only second-grade elect, having been left out of the first wave. Personally I felt all right about that, since I had never wanted to see a fight between Americans and Frenchmen. Our party, the second echelon of prose masters, left London late in the evening from a spur railroad station used only for troop movements, in an atmosphere thick with fog and mystery. It included Ernie Pyle, of Scripps-Howard, Bill Lang of *Time*, *Life*, etc., Red Mueller of *Newsweek*, Gault MacGowan of the New York *Sun*, Ollie Stewart of the Baltimore *Afro-American*, and Sergeant, now First Lieutenant, Bob Neville, whom I had known when he was on the *Herald Tribune* and *PM* and who was now going to Africa as a correspondent for the army magazine, *Yank*. I recognized a kindred spirit in Ollie the moment I saw him. "Where do you hope we land at?" he asked me. "Someplace where resistance has ceased," I told him. That established a perfect rapport.

I had had an attack of the gout in my right foot two days before pulling out, and I went limping off to the war instead of coming limping back from it. I had always previously felt a bit of pride in the recurrences of this fine eighteenth-century disease, a tribute to the high standard of living I had attained at a relatively early age, but this time I was peeved with it. I figured that someone might think it was psychogenic. It made me feel worse to find the Roosevelt Hospital unit from New York on the transport we boarded for the voyage; there were fifty-two nurses who got a first impression of decrepitude that I never consequently had a chance to overcome, because each was immediately appropriated by three Air Corps officers. Lieutenant Colonel Gurney Taylor, who was, I think, second in command of the unit, then turned traitor to his class by telling me about a ten-cent specific for the malady, a breach of confidence which will cost the civilian medical profession several hundred dollars a year for the rest of my life expectancy. I had to go to war to get a gout remedy. Except for the gout and the nurses the trip was without event; we docked at Mers-el-Kebir on November 21 without having seen any more enemy action than I had experienced in my two other sea passages.

There was a light air raid at Oran on the night of our arrival. The reaction to it of the local population seemed to me exaggerated; then I realized that there were still French-speaking people to whom an air raid was a novelty. I spent the next four weeks in and around Oran, making one excursion into eastern Morocco with the reconnaissance troop of the First Infantry Division when it seemed that the frontier of Spanish Morocco might become a war front. The fighting in Tunisia, as we heard about it from officers and correspondents who passed through Oran after visits to the front, was on a small scale, and few American troops were engaged. I used my time getting the feel of North Africa and gaining a gradual and unforced familiarity with the First Infantry Division, which had captured Oran, and remained in the Department. The First had many enlisted men from the sidewalks of the Bronx and Brooklyn, and a rich New York accent had new charms for me in Africa. There is an analogical sentiment in a chanson of Gace Brule, the thirteenth-century Champenois poet:

> *"The little birds of my country*
> *Have sung to me in Brittany,"*

where he was in exile, I think.

"Give da passwoy," I once heard a First Division sentinel challenge.

"Nobody told me nuttin," the challenged soldier replied.

"What outfitchas outuv?"

"Foy Signals."

"Whynchas get on da ball? Da passwoy is 'tatched roof.' "

"What is it mean?"

"How do I know? Whaddaya tink I yam, da Quiz Kids?"

It looked and acted and talked like a good division even then, making you know it could do the fine things it has since done. I got the same feeling from it that I had had the first time I had seen my Fortress group in England, before the Fortresses had been on a single operation.

CHAPTER III

What Do You Think That Bugle's Blowing For?

ORAN was the first part of metropolitan France I had been in since June 1940. I thought I might be able to gauge from it the effects of all the events since then upon the French. I knew how strong the anti-British sentiment had been at the armistice time, how guilty the French must have felt because of the Armistice nonetheless, and how greatly a sensation of guilt increases bitterness. A corresponding sense of guilt toward France underlies the most extreme instances of British francophobia. So I did not expect to find undiluted enthusiasm for the Allied cause. But Oran disappointed even me, and I was astonished by the American policy of coddling the most obviously disaffected Oranais. These were the high civil and military officials and the large landowners.

The Prefect, a M. Boujard, had come in during the Popular Front government of Léon Blum in 1936 and had performed a star turn in political contortionism by remaining at the head of the Department ever since. He had carried out economic collaboration with the resident German and Italian commissions, enforcing the Nuremberg-patterned anti-Jewish laws and exalting the rest of the Vichy program. No one had held a pistol at his head to compel him to stay. The General of Division, one Boisseau, a furtive gray fox of a man, had insisted on the determined defense of Oran that had lasted sixty hours and cost several hundred American and perhaps a thousand French lives. This resistance had been inspired by his belief that the Allies would be chased out of Africa and he would then lose his promotion and pension rights if he had not fought against them. I had the pleasure of hearing him address some of his officers on the firing range at near-by Arzeu when American soldiers were demonstrating material that was to be turned over to the French. An American mortar put in a couple of bad shots. "I had no illusions about the American Army!" the general announced with loud satisfaction. Officers suspected of having favored the Americans even in thought, like a Zouave major I met (who had, by the way, fought like a lion against us), were practically ostracized. Liaison officers assigned to American units were scolded for "fraternizing" with the Americans—nearly two months after we had officially become allies. Most of the officers above the grade of battalion commander were a sad lot; those not definitely hostile, because they owed their promotions to Vichy, were apathetic because in their hearts they had never expected to fight again and hated the prospect.

"They are selfish!" my friend the Zouave major said, "they are in love with their pensions. Let it pass! But the blasphemy is that they do not want to fight!" He was a Basque who had escaped from Occupied France and then asked for service in Africa in the spring of 1941 when he had become convinced that Great Britain would not be conquered. "I have been suspect here," he told me, "so that it was more necessary for me than for the others to fight well against the Americans. Else the higher officers would have said, 'His sentiments were dictated by cowardice.' I could not have remained in the army."

The higher civil servants were in the same category as the higher officers. The minor functionaries, like postmen and cops, were in the main decent enough, but had had to conform.

The great landed proprietors of the Department, grandsons of immigrant French peasants, had piled up huge fortunes in paper francs during the armistice period by exporting to Germany their grain, their fruit, and the alcohol made from their brandy. They were the most implacable enemies we had. The poor Oranais noticed a slight improvement in nutrition soon after we landed, because dates and oranges could no longer be exported and were sold for home consumption. But this was of no benefit to the big farmers. They had never suffered personally and would have preferred to continue exporting their fruit. The money that they had been piling up would have been eventually worthless, for the Reichsbank, turning out unbacked francs by the trillion, would have inevitably forced a howling inflation. We, by pegging their franc at seventy-five to the dollar, had turned their paper into real money, and a good many of them into real millionaires. But they were angry because we had not given them a better rate. When, a couple of months later, we hiked the franc up to fifty to the dollar, we pushed a lot more money their way, still without gaining their gratitude. The leading stevedoring firm, to which the American port authorities threw the army business, was Italian-Fascist. The harbor was wide open for sabotage. A few of the ships that the American naval salvage crew had raised with great difficulty after they had been sunk by the French naval authorities were "accidentally" rammed and resunk by towboats. The French naval people retained their posts. In the first days after our arrival, I learned, some of the business had been given to a smaller competing stevedore firm. The Prefect had made representations to the American command that the owner of this smaller firm was suspected of being a British sympathizer! So the business went to the Italian.

The great landowners of the Department are of a distinct species, French only in the sense that the pre-Revolutionary Carolina rice planters were English. They are African-born; they visit France only to make a splurge in Paris or to treat their obesity at Vichy, and they are reactionary to an extent only possible in a country where a few white men live by the exploitation of a large native population. The miserable Arabized Berbers who work their great estates get almost nothing. The planters say that if you give a native anything above the lowest subsistence level he will quit work; he would not really like adequate food or clothes. They talk exactly like Mississippians. Naturally they are not in favor of manhood suffrage, labor unions, or any talk about the equality of races. They had not really collaborated with the Nazis: the Nazis had come along belatedly and collaborated with them. While they had been included in one of the ninety-odd departments of a democratic nation they had been restrained from complete self-expression. The apparent German victory had started them saying, "I told you so, democracy couldn't last." Our arrival desolated them.

These landowners, and the Prefect and the general, were the solid people who entertained Major General Lloyd R. Fredendall, the local ranking American general officer, at their homes. He let them think they were translating public opinion for him and apparently accepted what they said. He was a soldierly man who may have felt that his position had been eased by the decision of the Vichy people and the local big shots to retain all their old perquisites and keep on running the Department. He received masses of alarming reports every day from his own counterintelligence service, the intelligence officer of the battalion of American infantry in the town, and the intelligence section of First Division, but these were filed away. One point the solid people were always careful to impress upon the general was the depth and fervor of anti-Semitic feeling in Oran. The solid people and their henchmen were administering Jewish real estate and cafés; their friends and relatives of the professional class were enjoying the practices Jewish doctors and lawyers had been forced to abandon. But they even got the American military administration to discharge French-English interpreters on the docks because the interpreters were Jewish (and of course pro-Ally). They said the Arab dockworkers would resent having Jews placed over them.

There was in truth a violent anti-Semitism in the city of Oran, but it was of the same kind as the anti-Semitism of Harlem, the result of deliberately inciting one exploited race against another. The Algerian-born French citizens of Spanish descent, colloquially called Néos, together with immigrants from Spain make up about a third of Oran's population. Another third is Moslem, and the two groups furnish practically all the manual labor of the city. About fifteen per cent of the population is composed of Algerian Jews. These Jews, Europeanized in varying degrees, had enjoyed French citizenship until Vichy adopted the German anti-racial laws. They had been neither great landlords nor important bankers, but shopkeepers, small moneylenders, renting agents or owners of a poor type of housing, craftsmen, chafferers, and professional people. The Oranais of French origin, a small minority, are mostly functionaries, skilled workmen or money people. A French physician, the official leader of the anti-Semitic movement in Oran, told me that there was a disproportionate number of Jewish doctors and lawyers, the classic complaint. The number of French physicians and lawyers in relation to the total Arab-Néo-Jew-French population was more disproportionate still, however. There were neither physicians, lawyers, nor men of property among the Arabs and Néos, the two most numerous groups of the population. But Arabs and Néos, as helpless against their major exploiters as a Harlem rioter against his, had been encouraged to hate the convenient Jew.

Oran is as odd as its ruling class. It has between 150,000 and 200,000 inhabitants and looks like a cross between Miami Beach and Washington Heights, although it is dirtier than either. The harbor lies in the shape of a crescent, with a continuous ridge of hills rising behind it, and the city is built on their slopes and crests.

Along the boulevards that offer good sea views there are *style-moderne* apartment houses with rounded corners, lots of glass, and balconies in the European manner of 1929. The older buildings are dingy but equally un-Oriental, and the climate is so cold in winter that the scattered palm trees look like a real-estate man's importation. A third of the population is *indigène*, which is the French term for the commingled Arabized Berbers and Berberized Arabs, but in weeks of walking about town I never saw a mosque. The only indigène who looked even faintly picturesque was an old fellow employed by a tintype photographer to pose with American soldiers in the Place du Maréchal Foch. The French say that Oran is the least French city in Africa, but it is at the same time the least African. Néos, Jews, native Oranais with French grandparents, and even the few indigènes who adopt European clothes and vocations seem to merge into the same vague Mediterranean type.

But since the Department of Oran, like the two other Algerian departments, was technically a part of metropolitan France, every action of the French and American authorities there might set a precedent for the reconquest, and I was shocked by the mess things were in. It was as if continental United States had extended statehood to Puerto Rico and Hawaii and had then itself been occupied by an enemy power, leaving the untypical new states to carry on pro tem as the United States of America, and the sugar companies had then been left free to run Puerto Rico and Hawaii.

Members of uniformed fascist organizations had left the city or at least hidden their *sturm* duds when the Americans marched in. They had sniped at our people all through the battle and might legitimately have expected to be backed against a wall and shot. But within a couple of weeks they reappeared in the cafés wearing their capes, monocles, and high boots and talking loudly about the day of revenge, not against the Germans, but us. The Légion des Anciens Combattants, the opposite number of the Sturm-Abteilung, paraded, the Service d'Ordre de la Légion, which corresponded to the Schutzstaffel, strutted; the Compagnons de France, facsimile of the Hitlerjugend, made early morning hideous with their marching song, "*Maréchal, Nous Voilà*." The civil servant who had been the local head of the Légion Tricolore, the battalion being recruited to fight against our Russian ally on the eastern front, was mobilized as a major in the French Army to fight by our side against the Germans. I had a faint suspicion he would not fight too hard. The Darlan government refused to mobilize Jews with their regiments. The Falange operated openly among the Néos, its leaders telling them that the Germans would soon appear in Oran and hand it over to Franco. Spain had held the city for two hundred and fifty years, until the Barbary Pirates had driven the Spanish garrison out in 1790. The French had moved in about forty years later.

The greed and violence of the ruling clique in Oran had provoked a more articulate reaction there than in any other African city. Long before 1939 Oran had been known as a city where political passions were strong. The Left Republicans, who drew their main strength from among the skilled workers and small functionaries born in France, had somehow managed to keep up a daily newspaper, *l'Oran Républicain*, even during the Pétain regime. It had had occasional issues suppressed and had appeared many times with large blank spaces created by the censor; its plant had been searched dozens of times for weapons or communist propaganda, but it had survived. Perhaps the Prefect, that pluperfect trimmer, had not wanted to neglect any possible hedge. The editors of *l'Oran Républicain* were by the time of my advent among the angriest and most disappointed people in North Africa. We had even left the old Vichy censorship undisturbed, so that when the *Républicain*'s leader writer prepared a pro-American editorial, the censors blue-penciled it. All through the Department Jews and Frenchmen who had publicly expressed satisfaction at our landing were now serving jail sentences for their bad taste. Post-office clerks and railway conductors who had been discharged for suspected pro-Ally sympathies were still out of jobs, and those who belonged to the uniformed fascist groups were being given more responsible jobs than ever. I asked a profound-appearing major in the British Political Warfare office at Oran about this, and he said, "People should not expect to profit from their patriotism." The slogan of the occupation was, "Keep the rascals in."

General Fredendall obviously did not formulate our policy for the North African theater. He got his directives from Algiers, where General Eisenhower and Robert Murphy of the State Department were running the show, and it was of course impossible to know whether they themselves were making policy or receiving it from Washington. But Fredendall's complacency in matters of detail jarred me. I spent part of one Sunday afternoon talking to him about the Service d'Ordre de la Légion, commonly spoken of as the S.O.L., the members of which had formed an elite guard of uniformed fascism, like the German SS after which they were patterned. The next time he saw me, in the lobby of the town's principal hotel, which had been requisitioned by the Army, he graciously approached me and said, "You don't have to worry about those S.O.L.'s anymore. Their secret intelligence section is working with us now." Within a few days they had probably turned in the name of every De Gaullist in Oran as a candidate for a concentration camp. There was a general understanding that the policy of leaving the Vichy people in power was in accord with the famous agreement with Admiral Darlan signed by Eisenhower or Murphy or both, but Fredendall said he had never seen a copy of the agreement. I would have liked to know its exact terms.

State Department special agents had done the undercover work of preparation for the Oran landing and had studied the local political situation for two years while they had the German and Italian commissions living in the same hotel with them. These agents were as surprised and nearly as angry as the Allied sympathizers in Oran at the turn political affairs had taken. Their attempt to organize a militant fifth column to aid the landing had not come off, but they had furnished the landing force with excellent intelligence, and the people who had risked their lives to secure this intelligence were now being openly threatened by the S.O.L. A very beautiful Scandinavian woman, married to a Frenchman, who had been one of our most effective agents, told me that she had received repeated menaces through the mail and that Fascists regularly scrawled insults on her door.

Toward the middle of December I began to think I had used up the material that interested me in Oran, but it was not until the day before Christmas that I actually got started toward Algiers. I went down to the airfield, about fifteen miles from the city, to get on a transport plane, but was stranded by a combination of low priority and bad weather. The field was deep in a quality of mud worse than Mississippi gumbo, or so Southern soldiers informed me. One plane got out loaded with lieutenant colonels and high-priority freight, which I subsequently discovered at Algiers was toilet tissue and laundry soap, both rated ahead of correspondents. Then the base operations officer announced that the weather had closed down and there would be nothing more that day. I was in the operations shack, madder than hell, when Lieutenant Colonel Joe Crawford, commander of the second battalion of the Sixteenth Infantry, wandered in and invited me home with him for a quiet infantry Christmas. His battalion was stationed about three miles from the airport, and he said he could bring me in again next day if the weather improved and get me on a plane. I liked the battalion, and I was so tired of Oran that I didn't want to go back to it even for one night, so I thanked Crawford and came along.

Headquarters company was billeted in the buildings and courtyard of a wealthy colonist's farm; the other companies were in tents on the slopes of a couple of hills. I had just pulled off one gumboot and broken a thumbnail doing it when the bugle began to blow assembly in the farmyard. The first note had hardly sounded, it seemed, when the top sergeant began to yell. The top sergeant of headquarters company was a New Yorker with a frozen movie-gangster smile and a hard mind, and he yelled, "C'mon, get goin'! Whaddaya tink dat bugle's blowin' for?" I looked out of a window and he was handing out bandoliers of rifle ammunition, spieling all the while like a peddler pitching popcorn at Coney Island, "C'mon, get your ammunition. Da mora dis we use da shorter it'll be!" He turned his head toward me and added, "We hope!" I didn't know what the bugle was blowing for, until Don Kellett, the battalion intelligence officer, came in and said that the radio had announced a state of alert ordered for American forces all over North Africa. The battalion was to get ready to move and fight on five minutes' notice, but the reason for the alert had not been stated. He surmised that the Spaniards had let the Germans through Spanish Morocco. Crawford thought there might be an outbreak of sabotage organized by the Fascists throughout North Africa, and Chuck Horner, the executive officer, bet on a plague of parachutists. Night was falling, and our Christmas carol was "What do you think that bugle's blowing for?"

It was a good battalion of a good regiment. In an unbelievably short time the company officers reported that their outfits were ready to go. No further orders came to the battalion, and the soldiers waited under arms, packs on backs. Then a rocket appeared over the airfield. It was a green one followed by half a dozen whites and some reds and blues. Kellett said he didn't know what the signal meant, but it looked like trouble. "Maybe parachutists have landed and those mugs are too excited to get off regular signals!" he said. The wind was toward us, and we could hear machine-gun fire. We tried to raise the airfield on the telephone and couldn't. "Get a couple of patrols over there," Crawford ordered.

The tough top sergeant went out himself with one patrol. They walked out into the dark, and Crawford and Horner and

Kellett and I awaited their return in the command post, the nerve center of the area. Every couple of minutes Kellett would walk to the door and come back, saying, "More rockets. Blue and green now," or "More shooting." Horner said, "It's a tough one to sweat." The sergeant returned after three quarters of an hour.

"We had to work our way onto the field to find out what all the shooting was for, sir," he said, "and their patrols fired at us. It was lucky it was the Air Corps that was shooting, because they can't hit nothing. When we got over on the field we found it was just a lot of drunks shooting off rockets and machine guns because it was Christmas Eve. They never heard of no alert." Crawford was pretty mad. He said, "That Air Corps mentality again!" He finally got the executive officer at the field on the telephone and said, "I have a lot of men with itchy trigger fingers here and your people are pretty lucky they didn't get brassed off." Crawford was so conscientious that he had even kept me sober, and we were all angrier about the Air Corps having such a good time than about anything else. The battalion slept in its clothes and on its weapons that night.

The first thing I heard in the morning was Kellett coming into the big sleeping room and saying to Crawford, "We got a flash that Darlan's been assassinated."

Crawford said, "Merry Christmas!"

CHAPTER IV

The Hat of M. Murphy

ALGIERS on Christmas Day, when a C-47 transport plane got me there from Oran, was calmer than any city had a right to be after having witnessed within the space of eight weeks a partially successful *coup d'état*, the landing of an army from another hemisphere and the assassination of an equivocal admiral. It was hard to determine whether the calm was due to apathy or to the Algerois' fear of expressing any anti-Axis sentiment when we might be looking for another Darlan to take

the defunct cheat's place. Certainly the average European or
Moslem inhabitant of the city seemed more preoccupied with
alimentation than with war.

The driver of the army car that brought me into town from
the airfield told me that good billets were scarce, but that I
might as well try my luck at the best hotel in the city first.
Allied Headquarters had set aside six double rooms for correspondents, he said, and since there were departures and arrivals every day I might find a bed. I recognized the hotel from
the motion picture *Pepe le Moko*. It was the one where Pepe's
mistress stayed with her rich protector while Pepe pined in the
Casbah.

My luck was in. As I started into the revolving door I met a
fellow named Dave Brown whom I had known in New York
for years. He said he had a room with one vacant bed in it.
Dave, an American, had worked in the financial department of
the New York bureau of Reuters, Ltd., the British news
agency, for twelve years without ever being sent out of the
office to cover a story. At last Reuters had sent him with the
American force that landed in Morocco, as a trial assignment,
I suppose, and he was doing a fine job of it. In New York Dave
had long lived above an Armenian restaurant near Radio City
and played the horses in partnership with the proprietor. I had
always suspected the Armenian of giving Dave good tips when
the rent was due and bad ones when it looked as if Dave were
getting prosperous enough to move. Living with a spot-news
man during a busy news period is a great luxury for a magazine
correspondent, because the spot-news fellow has to keep up
with the hour-to-hour situation and file frequent news bulletins. The magazine writer keeps posted without any exertion.
For a week after the Darlan assassination Dave would be summoned from his bed two or three times a night to go up to
General Eisenhower's headquarters for handouts, sometimes
during air raids. I could lie snug beneath my Berber blanket
and snore.

I found it difficult to distinguish at first, on walking through
the climbing streets of the city, whether I was in a friendly
place or an occupied enemy town. One could walk inter-
minably without seeing a single caricature of Hitler in a shop
window or an Allied newsreel advertised by a theater. The

windows of the bookstores near the University of Algiers were crammed with Germanophile apologetics—testimony, perhaps, to Anglo-Saxon belief in freedom of the press. There were no signs of patriotic street demonstrations, such as one occasionally saw even in the Paris of 1939–40. I gathered from café conversations that there had been a few immediately after the debarkation of the Allies, but that the local officials had discouraged them as examples of Jewish bad taste. The place had a restful, neutral surface quality like Dublin.

Perhaps the mysterious agreement with Darlan had included a clause barring pro-Ally propaganda; I could think of no other reason why up-to-date films presenting the best aspects of American life had not been rushed in almost with the first assault wave. As it was, the leading American film attraction in the city was a 1935 film featuring Victor Moore as a henpecked husband, a role peculiarly difficult for Moslems to sympathize with. Even Darlan's death had not cleared the air of the heavy smudge of ambiguity that had hung over Africa since the deal with him. On one of my first walks I went into a crowded restaurant for a change from army food. There was less nourishment but more flavor in civilian cooking, and you could afford the change once in a while if you had the solid army rations to fall back on when you got hungry. The only vacant chair was at a table, with a small blond man who soon told me that he was a Syrian-born Jew, owned the best jewelry shop in town, had been educated at the American University at Beirut, and knew Arabic so well he composed poems in it. He said that he didn't know what to make of the Allies' "desertion" of their pre-landing "friends," exactly the same turn of words I had heard many times in Oran. Here, however, the desertion seemed even more weird, because the friends had come out with arms in their hands and risked their lives for us on the night of our landing. The jeweler offered to introduce me to some of the men who had led the *coup* which had paralyzed the defense forces for several hours, and I accepted. We took a rendezvous for five o'clock that afternoon, at the apartment of Dr. Henri Aboulker, of the faculty of medicine of the university. It had been an uncommonly good lunch for a within-the-law restaurant in Algiers: some indistinguishable kind of stew meat cooked with a reddish sauce and olives.

You can hope for lucky encounters only if you walk around a lot. A distinguished blackface comic once told George Lyon, a former city editor of mine, that there are only three kinds of people in the world worth talking to, whores, newspapermen, and actors, and they all need sturdy legs in their business. After a roundabout stroll I got back to Dr. Aboulker's apartment on the Rue Michelet in time for my appointment.

Dr. Aboulker was seventy-eight years old. He was permitted to continue his practice and remain on the faculty of medicine, although a Jew, because citizens who had been wounded or received military decorations in the last World War were as yet exempt from the provisions of the racial laws. The stage in which they too would be barred would undoubtedly have been reached later, but even Vichy had hesitated to do it. It would have looked awkward for that professional war veteran, the Marshal.

The Pétainist African regime which had remained in under Darlan and had now apparently survived him had taken measures to avoid any future repetition of this awkward situation by excluding Jews from the new mobilization, however. No Jew would be able to say twenty-five years after *this* war that he had deserved well of his country, the Darlanois were determined. They had left one loophole, at the insistence of General Giraud, who was as stubborn in military affairs as he was politically indifferent. Jews, Moslems, foreigners held in concentration camps, former soldiers of the Foreign Legion, and anybody not formally enrolled with a regular class of the Army Reserve could volunteer in a new catch-all organization called the Corps Franc d'Afrique, which was promised immediate service in the front line. "If they want to fight, let them fight," Giraud said. "Nobody stops them." He was constitutionally impervious to the argument that segregation impaired their rights as Frenchmen. He meant it when he said that the only right that counted was the right to kill Germans. But the Pétainist civil officials considered the Corps Franc a beautiful invention for silencing obstreperous fellows of all creeds. "If you are such a patriot, join the Corps Franc," they said. Meanwhile they remained in their grandiose offices five hundred miles from the firing line, scheming to requisition all the most comfortable villas in Algiers and move into them before British or

American bigwigs did. The competition for palaces was keen and absorbed a deal of the war energy of all three allies.

Dr. Aboulker had both wounds and decorations in profusion. His right leg had been shattered by machine-gun bullets and then ingeniously patched together again, but he could walk only with the aid of a cane, a detail the humorous significance of which will become apparent shortly to the reader. His apartment, a collection of large high-ceilinged rooms on the second or third floor of a fine *immeuble* dating from about 1900, reminded me irresistibly of that of Dr. Perrot, the anti-Semitic physician I had visited in Oran. A man's taste is formed more by his culture, his profession, and the period in which he is young than by his race or politics. The two apartments contained the same mixture of pretentious nineteenth-century furniture, which looked archaic, and of painting which had been revolutionary in the two physicians' youth and still seemed fresh, from the late impressionists through *les fauves*. The doctor was a somber old man who kept his hat on in the house for fear of drafts. One of his sons, a straight, slender lad in his early twenties, was in the group that received me. The others, all, I think, Jews, included my jeweler friend, a philosopher, a couturier, and several others whose callings I do not remember, a paradoxical group of putschists. Two of the younger men there, they told me, had been at the by-now famous conference between General Mark Clark, Murphy, and the two French officers who had prepared the plan for our Algiers landing, when Clark had been brought by submarine to a beach villa owned by one of the group. One of the young men had waded into surf up to his chest to steady the kayak in which the general had made his way back to the submarine. They said that Murphy had used the Aboulker apartment as his headquarters during the months of preparation for the putsch and even on the night when the landing was expected. According to the original plans for that night, they said, the Americans were supposed to land in the harbor of the city at one o'clock. At eleven the putschists, 540 young men of whom 450 were Jews, went out with arms which the United States Government had furnished to them and seized the telegraph office, the municipal power plant, the Préfecture of Police, and other nerve centers, and arrested the ranking army officers

who were not in on the plot and Admiral Darlan himself.
Some of them said they were sorry they had not killed Darlan
then. He had temporized, saying he would join them, and
they had only held him prisoner. "It would have been easy to
finish him if killing had been part of our plan," one man said,
"but we lacked the habit of ruthlessness." The Americans had
not appeared on schedule, some of the officials whom the
putschists had missed at their first swoop had alerted the troops
stationed in the suburbs, and by two o'clock in the morning
the putschists themselves had been besieged in the various
buildings they had taken. The troops outnumbered them and
had artillery. After a resistance during which several of their
number had been killed, the pro-Allied civilians had surrendered. They had held Darlan for four hours, and it is easy to
understand how much their attack had served to distract attention from our landing. By eight o'clock the next morning
the Americans were in possession of the city. During the
course of the day they freed the men who, if our attack had
been a failure, would certainly have been tried and executed by
Darlan's gang. "It is now almost impossible for one of us to
see Mr. Murphy," the old doctor said. "He shuns us like a case
of an extremely contagious disease."

"The army brass hats and the people of the Préfecture
whom we arrested hate us," one of the younger men said.
"They hate us because we know what cowards they are. You
should have seen how miserably they acted when they saw the
tommy guns, the brave Jew-baiters. The chief of the secret
police, who has been of course restored to his position, kneeled
on the floor and wept, begging one of my friends to spare his
life. Imagine his feeling toward the man who spared him! An- ·
other friend, a doctor, is to be mobilized—in a labor camp, of
course—under the military jurisdiction of a general whom *he*
arrested." After a good deal more talk and the consumption of
a couple of glasses of white wine—too sweet, exactly like that
the anti-Semite had offered me—a couple of the younger men
drove me home to my hotel in an automobile. I was too late to
eat at the officers' mess, so I had dinner at a black-market
restaurant that had been recommended to me. I had mushroom soup, *rouget de la Méditerranée meunière*, a couple of
grilled thrushes, chicken en casserole, rum cake with cream,

oranges, coffee, and a bottle of Veuve Clicquot of a year I
hadn't heard of but which did well enough to wash down campaign fare. I was happy in the possession of a great deal of information which could do me no professional good because I
couldn't have got it through the censor. But useless possessions are always the ones we revel in. I was also happy that
night because I thought I knew that the pessimism of the
Aboulker circle was exaggerated. "Be patient," I had told
them, "the heart of the State Department is in the right place.
It has only been temporarily mislaid—perhaps under a lettuce
seed."

The telephone in our room summoned Dave Brown fairly
early next morning to the downtown office building where the
Allied Forces had set up their public-relations headquarters. I
fancied it had something to do with politics but didn't worry
much about it. At about eleven I had my breakfast of black imitation coffee, a dry piece of bread, and watery *confiture* and
my cold bath. I could have had a good breakfast at the mess up
until eight-fifteen, and there was hot water at the hotel until
nine, but I never got up that early. I dressed and walked down
to public relations myself to see if I had received any money.
When I entered the correspondents' room there Dave told me
that the French government of North Africa had announced
the arrests of fifteen persons for plotting to assassinate General
Giraud. Their names had not been announced, but anti-
collaborationists had already supplied half a dozen correspondents with tentative lists. "You hadn't been out of Dr.
Aboulker's apartment half an hour," Dave said, "when they
arrested everybody there. They picked up the fellows who
drove you home, too." It occurred to me immediately that the
secret police whom our sympathizers had arrested on the
landing night now were back in power, and that opportunities
for a frame-up were excellent. The boy who had killed Darlan
had been executed without any public hearing; the men of the
Préfecture could attribute any statement they wished to him.
Infallibly they would say he had implicated every prominent
De Gaullist in town in a double murder plot, of which he had
carried out the first half. That is what they did say.

A few days later—this incident is out of precise sequence,
but it seems to belong here—a small, dapper young man called

on me at the hotel and told me that the married daughter of
Dr. Aboulker wanted to see me to relate the circumstances of
his arrest, and that she and her husband would meet me in her
father's apartment that afternoon. I went up there with Dave,
whose superiors in London were continually bombarding him
with requests for information on the political story that he
couldn't send out. The daughter, whose married name I forget, was an extraordinarily pretty and spirited brunette. The
political police, armed with tommy guns, had arrived soon
after my departure, she said, when she was alone in the apartment with her father and her two children, aged three and
eight. Her father was in an electric cabinet, treating the leg
that had been shattered in the World War and that still
bothered him. She had answered the door and a plain-clothes
man had pushed a tommy gun into her stomach while another
had pointed his submachine gun at her eight-year-old boy and
ordered him to put his hands up. The brave Fascists were taking
no chances. Then a dozen detectives had searched the apartment for weapons. "There weren't any, luckily," she said,
"because we had got rid of those M. Murphy had furnished
to us." They had dragged her father from his cabinet, not
allowed him to dress, and hauled him off to jail without his
trousers. "They would not let him take his cane," she said,
"and without it he cannot stand upright, which amused them.
They dragged him down the stairs. I haven't been allowed to
see him in prison. By the way," she said, "I have something
here that will amuse *you*."

She walked off into another room and came back carrying a
black Homburg hat. She handed it to me. It was quite a good
hat, made by Christy's of London, the kind that anybody who
wanted to be mistaken for a Foreign Office man might be glad
to wear.

"The hat of M. Murphy!" she said. "He left it here that
evening of the landing. He said, 'I will be right back' and went
out. He hasn't been here since!"

CHAPTER V

Giraud Is Just a General

THE week that followed the arrest of our former agents in Algiers restored all the esteem I had had for newspapermen when I was twenty years old. After enough years newspapermen begin to pall on other newspapermen; they begin to take their good qualities for granted and wince at their shortcomings, of which the most common are a vanity that sometimes borders on the thespian and a sort of perpetual mental adolescence that I think stems from starting work on a fresh story every day or every week or month and never having time to get to the bottom of anything. They forget that newspapermen as a class have a yearning for truth as involuntary as a hophead's addiction to junk. The question of whether the junkie really loves hop is academic; he can't get along without it. A newspaperman may write a lie to hold his job, but he won't believe it, and the necessity outrages him so that he craves truth all the more thereafter. A few newspapermen lie to get on in the world, but it outrages them, too, and I have never known a dishonest journalist who wasn't patently an unhappy bastard.

There were about thirty journalists in Algiers at the time, including radio reporters, and not one of them accepted the official French version of the arrests—that the motive had really been the safety of General Giraud—or the far more disturbing official American efforts to play down the whole affair. The journalists, like my cockney in Poplar, weren't 'aving any. It made me all the happier that not only the professing liberals, but the representatives of conservative papers, and the plain routine second- and third-string representatives of press associations all got the idea. I think it even impressed the Army and State Department people running the North African show. They could stop us from sending our stuff out, and they did, but they saw in us an articulate, tangible cross section of the opinion they would have to face at home. There was no division on national lines; British and American correspondents were in complete accord.

Largely, I think, because of the row we raised, General Bergeret, who had come to Africa as Darlan's personal assistant and had remained with Giraud, virtually running the civil side of the administration, and Rigault, a character in charge of public relations, became aware that people of the Allied powers would not accept so crude a return to Gestapo government. The Anglo-American press of Algiers was therefore summoned to an interview with General Henri Honoré Giraud himself. The general thought our protest an unwarranted intrusion into a routine administrative affair. He had not checked on the affair personally because he was too busy with his army. Giraud believed, as a military principle, in standing by one's subordinates. All his principles are military. He was therefore going to put us in our places.

The office where he received us was in a secondary school for boys, and we were herded into his presence much as if we were going before the headmaster. After we had stumbled forward one by one to have our hands crushed in his psychologically steely grip, we stood back and waited, in our habitual civilian postures. The general's eye wandered over us moodily, and I imagined that he had expected us to hold "*Fixe!*" until he had said "*Repos!*" Brigadier General Robert McClure of the United States Army, who was in charge of Allied public relations and censorship in the theater of war, was to attend the mass interview, but his automobile had been delayed in the blackout. I could see Giraud getting angrier by the second at having to wait for a general four stars down to him. Giraud wears five. A few wispy hairs which stood apart from the main body of his moustache and got in the path of his breath quivered like shreds of paper in front of a powerful electric fan. He sat down at his desk, and his aide ordered us all out of the room until McClure arrived. We went into one of the classrooms and sat on some benches, hoping we would not be expelled from school.

Giraud is as straight and nearly as tall as De Gaulle, but he is better-proportioned, more in drawing. Also he has been a general for so much longer that he has settled into the role more comfortably. De Gaulle's expression is occasionally irascible, as if he anticipated that somebody might challenge his authority. The thought has not occurred to Giraud for years. The painter he suggests is not El Greco, but Meissonier. He is, as I had known ever since the Battle of France, a good general.

When General McClure arrived at the schoolhouse, we all filed into the Giraud presence again. McClure is happily ignorant of French; Giraud could not say anything to him except through the intermediary of an officer far junior to a brigadier general. One cannot say to a captain, "Ask the brigadier general, in English, where the hell he has been." According to military protocol the situation was impossible. All Giraud's actions are limited by military conceptions. He therefore said nothing to McClure.

He began his discourse to us by saying that he was happy to be making war by the side of an ally so rich in the most modern material. When his army had marched through Belgium and into Holland to engage the Germans in 1940 he had had only seven airplanes for a quarter of a million men. Now he had 50,000 men fighting in Tunisia, and fighting well, and he had hoped to have modern equipment for them. He had been promised modern equipment, but it was not here. He looked accusingly at us, as if some correspondent might be wearing a 2½-ton truck in a shoulder holster. He could not for the life of him, he said, see why there was so much fuss about a dozen civilians, who might or might not be guilty, when hundreds of his people were being killed every week because they were fighting with only rifle ammunition and little of that. A British captain named Hyphensmith translated for the benefit of those who could not understand French.

"I am not interested in politics," the general said, "I make war."

One of the correspondents said that since this was a war for democracy, a word which brought no change in the general's expression, it was important that the people of occupied countries should not get the idea that if they helped us we would after our arrival permit them to be put in jail. I said that many of the current North African officials who remained in power had been put in by Vichy as selected watchdogs who could be depended upon. The general said he did not know of one such official. Since he had been a prisoner of war through most of the Armistice and had arrived in Africa only after our landing, he may not have known much, but he had certainly heard a lot.

Frank Kluckhohn of the New York *Times*, through the intermediary of Captain Hyphensmith, passed up a list of the reported prisoners to the general and asked him to verify it. There were about a dozen names on the list, including those of a couple of men high in the political police who had known about the plot to aid the Allied landing and helped conceal it. There were Dr. Aboulker and two of his sons, a man named Brunel who was the son of a former mayor of Algiers, and some others. Giraud said, triumphantly, "See how accurate your information is!" and crossed off a couple of names, including that of Aboulker, who we all knew quite well was in jail. Giraud's manner recalled Napoleon calling a grenadier by name, after having just received the information from the grenadier's corporal. I was sure he had been misinformed by his Gestapo, even to the identity of the men arrested. When he came to the extremely Corsican names of the two police officials —one of whom he later appointed Prefect of Algiers—he said, "These men withheld information from their superiors. A good policeman does not withhold information from his superior!" He himself had been in a submarine on his way to Africa when the policemen had "withheld," and if these men had informed their superiors the landing would have been opposed and Giraud perhaps captured. But it was hard for him to pardon a breach of discipline, even in the enemy's camp. He said that no trials of the accused men were contemplated. He seemed genuinely puzzled by our exaggerated interest in the affair.

Giraud, although entitled to dozens of decorations, wore none. His un-ribboned, khaki chest would have been conspicuous even on a French captain. As we were about to leave, one of the British correspondents asked him why he wore no decorations.

"Because I have taken an oath not to wear any until I enter Metz at the head of a victorious army," Giraud said. I thought that his choice of an objective made the man clear. A politician would have said Paris, a sentimentalist would have named his own native province. But Metz is a garrison town, the most important strategically on the Franco-German frontier. The soldier wanted to get back to his barracks.

Giraud, I felt, would react to any attack on Bergeret and Rigault as De Gaulle had to reflections on his precious Colonel P—— in London a year or so earlier, by suspecting the detractors of his subordinates. But more than anything else he wanted to fight and beat the Germans, and he was as susceptible to a gift of matériel as a little child to candy. I had known civilian intellectuals incapable of visualizing the reality of war; Giraud was the reverse of the medal. He had no civilian imagination. Freudians would be astonished by a human 100 per cent masculine or 100 per cent feminine. Giraud is even more astonishing in his way. He is 100 per cent a general.

The dressing down of the correspondent corps by General Giraud having produced no carminative results, we were invited to the villa of M. Murphy for cocktails and a conference on New Year's Eve. This was a parallel to the hard and soft method employed by New York detectives in reducing a prisoner to reason. M. Murphy lived in a fine villa high on the fashionable hill. The cocktails were good, there was a fire on the great hearth, a dog wandered among the guests to soften their hearts toward its master, after the English manner. Everything was *très gentleman*. M. Murphy deprecated the importance of the arrests, regretted that the strict censorship of political despatches would have to stay on, implied that Darlan had not been such a bad fellow after all, and in general tried to pour gin on the troubled waters. He got so many arguments from correspondents that one of the headquarters colonels who was there for the free drinks became quite petulant about us. Military petulance is usually in proportion to the distance from the firing line and in inverse ratio to the probability of the officer who is being petulant ever getting there. "We have war to get on with!" this colonel said, fiercely biting the olive out of a martini. M. Murphy introduced the name of Marcel Peyrouton and asked us what we thought of him. Everybody who had been in France thought he was terrible, so Murphy decided to bring him on anyway. Personally, I think now that it was a good idea. Peyrouton had decided that we were going to win the war, and he made an excellent ferret for us, bringing numerous collaborationist rats out of the administrative sewers they were hiding in.

Within the next few months the political situation in Algeria got much better. The suspected "assassins" were released. Peyrouton replaced Chatel, the left-over governor general, and then got rid of the prefects of Algiers and Oran, who were replaced by anti-Axis men; Brunel, the former mayor, a De Gaullist, got an important place in the Government; the curious Rigault disappeared from the office of information and was replaced by General René Chambe, an aviator and man of letters who had recently escaped from France and a really top-notch sort; Bergeret lost his importance and was posted to an unimportant command in West Africa. The S.O.L. and the Légion were dissolved, although the Compagnons de France were not, De Gaullist publications from London were allowed into North Africa, the racial laws were abolished and General Giraud went on record in favor of a republican form of government for a redeemed France. I imagine that he did so after the same kind of an educational course that had preceded De Gaulle's "*Liberté, Egalité, Fraternité*" speech from London, but he said it. Critics of the regime complained of the slowness with which reforms were put into effect, but with the diminishing flagrancy of the things they objected to they began to seem merely querulous.

Along with this improvement in political matters, State Department officials in Africa tried to sell the idea that they had intended things thus all the time, and that the stand of the press at home and of the correspondents on the spot had had nothing to do with the change. If so they had certainly concealed their sentiments as expertly as their intentions. I do not think that anything would have changed if we had not got up on our hind legs and yelled. The thesis that the department goes serenely on its way, indifferent to the press, does not always accord with developments.

The trouble was that—

African political affairs had been in a frightful mess while Darlan lived and for about a month thereafter—what would have happened had he survived will always be a subject for unpleasant speculation. A bungling censorship had prevented the British and American publics from getting any exact information, and afterward the public would not believe reports of improvement even when they were true. Ken Crawford, of *PM* and the Chicago *Sun*, arrived in Algiers in February or March and found little to get indignant about. When he told his employers so they decided he had gone over to the enemy. But he hadn't been there in the bad time. Remembering the Darlan days, the liberal press refused to accept *anything* that Washington said about North Africa thereafter. I strongly suspect that the Free French publicity organization here—it sounds a bit absurd to call people on Fifth Avenue Fighting French, to distinguish them from Giraud's troops in Tunisia—took advantage of this opening in their smear-Giraud campaign last spring. They even invented a "Giraudist" movement which they said had been set up by the State Department against De Gaulle. The term *Giraudiste* simply doesn't exist in Africa, any more than "Eisenhoweriste" or "Pattoniste," or "Montgomeryiste." Giraud, by his own fervent wish, is just a general.

The time between January 1 and January 23, 1943, was from a military point of view the most ticklish of the whole North African campaign. In November and December the British force with American attached fragments in Tunisia had been small and the Americans along the Algerian coast few and extremely preoccupied with the possibilities in Spanish Morocco. But the German army at Tunis had been even more limited. It had been brought in by troop carrier, glider, and an occasional furtive steamer from Sicily, and it lacked heavy equipment, although it had a short line of supply to the land forces from numerous African ports. Rommel was too far to the east to help the Tunis force, and the supplies pouring into Tripoli went to him. When in January he fell back clear to Tripoli, however, he was in a position where he could shift troops up to Tunisia at will. A force that would not be important in the Libyan theater, where the armies were relatively large, might be strong enough to upset the whole balance of strength in Tunisia, where battalions were still considered important units. Then too there was always the chance that Rommel might pull all his troops out of Tripoli and race for Constantine and Algiers with his whole army.

The problem was eased when the British secured the port of

Tripoli on January 23 before Rommel had acquired too much
of a head start in the race north. With the short supply line
they now had they could keep on his heels all the way, which
they did, while the British First Army and the Americans were
steadily adding strength in the west. After that he was cooked.
Action, if it came at all during January, was bound to begin in
southern and central Tunisia, where the Rommel territory
overlapped that of Von Arnim, the northern commander.
Northern Tunisia was bogged down in mud. Early in January
I decided that I had stalled Ross long enough without contributing a story on the shooting war, so I started for the advanced area. I was fed up with the political atmosphere in
Algiers anyway.

The easiest way to get into the war was to ride a transport
plane out to an advanced airfield, where we had a fighter
group, and then if there was not enough to write about there
arrange to go by truck or jeep up to one of the two or three
detachments of American ground troops in the area. It turned
out that the transports were booked full for the morning I
had chosen for my departure. An Air Corps major whom I had
known in England and reencountered at Algiers said he could
fix that by reserving a place for me on the French courier plane
which made a circuit of British and American airports east of
Algiers every day, carrying mail and local passengers.

This plane, which was of a type that the French had been
allowed to use for courier service even after the Armistice,
because it used so little gasoline, did not look as if it could fly
into a strong wind. When I first saw it I was conscious of a lack
that I could not define. At last it came to me. It was like an illustration from a 1922 magazine and there should have been a
Coles Phillips girl in the foreground. A little man in a long
overcoat and a soft gray hat came up to me while I stood
gazing and asked me where I was going. I told him, thinking
he was some kind of a ticket collector, and he opened the door
of the plane, climbed in, and said, "Come along, you're the
only passenger." He was the pilot. Before he sat down at the
controls he pulled a Guide Michelin out of his pocket, looked
at it, put it back and said, "*Ça va.*" Then he took off.

We made our first landing at Telergma, south of Constantine, where we picked up a technical sergeant and a box of

dates addressed to a lieutenant in a fighter squadron. The man in the long overcoat said to me, "Up to here it's all right, but I've never been to your field, and it's said to be difficult to find, in between some mountains." We carried the tech sergeant to Canrobert and got two British aircraftsmen who said they were on pass and were going back to Algiers with the little man, clean around the circuit via Biskra.

When I had first asked my friend the major about means of flying into the advanced field he had said, "First you get a transport, and then you get about a dozen Spits to act as escort, and then you go in." The man in the long overcoat dropped into the field very nicely, begged me to be so good as to speed the box of dates on its way, tipped his soft hat and flew away, leaving me in the middle of the war.

CHAPTER VI

The Foamy Fields

IF there is any way you can get colder than you do when you sleep in a bedding roll on the ground in a tent in North Africa two hours before dawn, I don't know about it. The particular tent I remember was at an airfield in a valley. The surface of the terrain was mostly limestone. If you put all the blankets on top of you and just slept on the canvas cover of the roll, you ached all over, and if you divided the blankets and put some of them under you, you froze on top. The tent was a large, circular one with a French stencil on the outside saying it had been rented from a firm in Marseilles and not to fold it wet, but it belonged to the United States Army now. It had been set up over a pit four feet deep, so men sleeping in it were safe from flying bomb fragments. The tall tent pole, even if severed, would probably straddle the pit and not hit anybody. It was too wide a hole to be good during a strafing, but then strafings come in the daytime and in the daytime nobody lived in it. I had thrown my roll into the tent because I thought it was vacant and it seemed as good a spot as any other when I arrived at the field. I later discovered that I was sharing it with two enlisted men.

I never saw my tentmates clearly, because they were always in the tent by the time I turned in at night, when we were not allowed to have lights on, and they got up a few minutes before I did in the morning, when it was still dark. I used to hear them moving around, however, and sometimes talk to them. One was from Mississippi and the other from North Carolina, and both were airplane mechanics. The first night I stumbled through the darkness into the tent, they heard me and one of them said, "I hope you don't mind, but the tent we were sleeping in got all tore to pieces with shrapnel last night, so we just moved our stuff in here." I had been hearing about the events of the previous evening from everybody I met on the field. "You can thank God you wasn't here last night," the other man said earnestly. The field was so skillfully hidden in the mountains that it was hard to find by night, and usually the Germans just wandered around overhead, dropping their stuff on the wrong hillsides, but for once they had found the right place and some of the light anti-aircraft on the field had started shooting tracers. "It was these guns that gave away where we was," the first soldier said. "Only for that they would have gone away and never knowed the first bomb had hit the field. But after that they knowed they was on the beam and they come back and the next bomb set some gasoline on fire and then they really did go to town. Ruined a P-38 that tore herself up in a belly landing a week ago, and I had just got her about fixed up again, and now she's got shrapnel holes just about everywhere and she's hopeless. All that work wasted. Killed three fellows that was sleeping in a B-26 on the field and woke up and thought that was no safe place, so they started to run across the field to a slit trench and a bomb got them. Never got the B-26 at all. If they'd stayed there, they'd been alive today, but who the hell would have stayed there?"

"That thrapnel has a lot of force behind it," the other voice in the tent said. "There was a three-quarter-ton truck down on the field, and a jaggedy piece of thrapnel went right through one of the tires and spang through the chassix. You could see the holes both sides where she went in and come out. We was in our tent when the shooting started, but not for long. We run up into the hills so far in fifteen minutes it took us four hours to walk back next morning. When we got back we found we didn't have no tent." There was a pause, and then the first soldier said, "Good night, sir," and I fell asleep.

When the cold woke me up, I put my flashlight under the blankets so I could look at my watch. It was five o'clock. Some Arab dogs, or perhaps jackals, were barking in the hills, and I lay uncomfortably dozing until I heard one of the soldiers blowing his nose. He blew a few times and said, "It's funny that as cold as it gets up here nobody seems to get a real cold. My nose runs like a spring branch, but it don't never develop."

When the night turned gray in the entrance to the tent, I woke again, looked at my watch, and saw that it was seven. I got up and found that the soldiers had already gone. Like everyone else at the field, I had been sleeping in my clothes. The only water obtainable was so cold that I did not bother to wash my face. I got my mess kit and walked toward the place, next to the kitchen, where they were starting fires under two great caldrons to heat dish water. One contained soapy water and the other rinsing water. The fires shot up from a deep hole underneath them, and a group of soldiers had gathered around and were holding the palms of their hands toward the flames, trying to get warm. The men belonged to a maintenance detachment of mechanics picked from a number of service squadrons that had been sent to new advanced airdromes, where planes have to be repaired practically without equipment for the job. That morning most of the men seemed pretty cheerful because nothing had happened during the night, but one fellow with a lot of beard on his face was critical. "This location was all right as long as we had all the planes on one side of us, so we was sort of off the runway," he said, "but now that they moved in those planes on the other side of us, we're just like a piece of meat between two slices of bread. A fine ham sandwich for Jerry. If he misses either side, he hits us. I guess that is how you get to be an officer, thinking up a location for a camp like this. I never washed out of Yale so I could be an officer, but I got more sense than that."

"Cheer up, pal," another soldier said. "All you got to do is dig. I got my dugout down so deep already it reminds me of the Borough Hall station. Some night I'll give myself a shave and climb on board a Woodlawn express." Most of the men in camp, I had already noticed, were taking up excavation as a hobby, and some of them had worked up elaborate private trench systems. "You couldn't get any guy in camp to dig three days ago," the Brooklyn soldier said, "and now you can't lay down a shovel for a minute without somebody sucks it up."

Another soldier, who wore a white silk scarf loosely knotted around his extremely dirty neck, a style generally affected by fliers, said, "What kills me is my girl's brother is in the horse cavalry, probably deep in the heart of Texas, and he used to razz me because I wasn't a combat soldier."

The Brooklyn man said to him, "Ah, here's Mac with a parachute tied around his neck just like a dashing pilot. Mac, you look like a page out of *Esquire*."

When my hands began to feel warm, I joined the line which had formed in front of the mess tent. As we passed through, we got bacon, rice, apple butter, margarine, and hard biscuits in our mess tins and tea in our canteen cups. The outfit was on partly British rations, but it was a fairly good breakfast anyway, except for the tea, which came to the cooks with sugar and powdered milk already mixed in it. "I guess that's why they're rationing coffee at home, so we can have tea all the time," the soldier ahead of me said. I recognized the bacon as the fat kind the English get from America. By some miracle of lend-lease they had now succeeded in delivering it back to us; the background of bookkeeping staggered the imagination. After we had got our food, we collected a pile of empty gasoline cans to use for chairs and tables. The five-gallon can, known as a flimsy, is one of the two most protean articles in the Army. You can build houses out of it, use it as furniture, or, with slight structural alterations, make a stove or a locker out of it. Its only rival for versatility is the metal shell of the army helmet, which can be used as an entrenching tool, a shaving bowl, a washbasin, or a cooking utensil, at the discretion of the owner. The flimsy may also serve on occasion as a bathtub. The bather fills it with water, removes one article of clothing at a time, rubs the water hastily over the surface thus exposed, and replaces the garment before taking off another one. This is called taking a whore's bath.

There was no officers' mess. I had noticed Major George

Lehmann, the commanding officer of the base, and First Lieutenant McCreedy, the chaplain, in the line not far behind me.
Major Lehmann, a tall, fair, stolid man had told me that he
lived in Pittsfield, Massachusetts, where he had a job with the
General Electric Company. When I had reported, on my arrival at the field, at his dugout the day before, he had hospitably suggested that I stow my blanket roll wherever I could
find a hole in the ground, eat at the general mess shack, and
stay as long as I pleased. "There are fighter squadrons and some
bombers and some engineers and anti-aircraft here, and you
can wander around and talk to anybody that interests you," he
had said.

Father McCreedy is a short, chubby priest who came from
Bethlehem, Pennsylvania, and had been assigned to a parish in
Philadelphia. He always referred to the pastor of this parish, a
Father McGinley, as "my boss," and asked me several times if I
knew George Jean Nathan, who he said was a friend of Father
McGinley. Father McCreedy had been officiating at the interment of the fellows killed in the raid the evening before, and
that was all he would talk about during breakfast. He had induced a mechanic to engrave the men's names on metal plates
with an electric needle. These plates would serve as enduring
grave markers. It is part of a chaplain's duty to see that the
dead are buried and to dispose of their effects. Father
McCreedy was also special-services officer of the camp, in
charge of recreation and the issue of athletic equipment. "So
what with one thing and another, they keep me busy here," he
said. He told me he did not like New York. "Outside of Madison Square Garden and the Yankee Stadium, you can have it."
He wore an outsize tin hat all the time. "I know a chaplain is
not supposed to be a combatant," he said, "but if parachute
troops came to my tent by night, they'd shoot at me because
they wouldn't know I was a chaplain, and I want something
solid on my head." He had had a deep hole dug in front of his
tent and sometimes, toward dusk, when German planes were
expected, he would stand in it waiting and smoking a cigar,
with the glowing end of it just clearing the hole.

When I had finished breakfast and scrubbed up my mess kit,
I strolled around the post to see what it was like. As the sun
rose higher, the air grew warm and the great, reddish moun-

tains looked friendly. Some of them had table tops, and the
landscape reminded me of Western movies in Technicolor. I
got talking to a soldier named Bill Phelps, who came from the
town of Twenty-nine Palms, California. He was working on a
bomber that had something the matter with its insides. He
confirmed my notion that the country looked like the American West. "This is exactly the way it is around home," he said,
"only we got no Ayrabs." A French writer had described the
valley bottoms in southeastern Algeria and Tunisia as foamy
seas of white sand and green alfa grass. They are good, natural
airfields, wide and level and fast-drying, but there is always
plenty of dust in the air. I walked to a part of the field where
there were a lot of P-38's, those double-bodied planes that
look so very futuristic, and started to talk to a couple of sergeants who were working on one. "This is Lieutenant Hoelle's
plane," one of them said, "and we just finished putting a new
wing on it. That counts as just a little repair job out here. Holy
God, at home, if a plane was hurt like that, they would send it
back to the factory or take it apart for salvage. All we do here
is drive a two-and-a-half-ton truck up under the damaged
wing and lift it off, and then we put the new wing on the truck
and run it alongside the plane again and fix up that eighty-
thousand-dollar airplane like we was sticking together a radio
set. We think nothing of it. It's a great ship, the 38. Rugged.
You know how this one got hurt? Lieutenant Hoelle was
strafing some trucks, and he come in to attack so low he hit his
right wing against a telephone pole. Any other plane, that
wing would have come off right there. Hitting the pole that
way flipped him over on his back, and he was flying upside
down ten feet off the ground. He gripped that stick so hard
the inside of his hand was black and blue for a week afterward,
and she come right side up and he flew her home. Any one-
engine plane would have slipped and crashed into the ground,
but those two counter-rotating props eliminate torque." I
tried to look as though I understood. "Lieutenant Hoelle is a
real man," the sergeant said.

I asked him where Hoelle and the other P-38 pilots were,
and he directed me to the P-38 squadron's operations room, a
rectangular structure mostly below ground, with walls made
out of the sides of gasoline cans and a canvas roof camouflaged

with earth. A length of stovepipe stuck out through the roof, making it definitely the most ambitious structure on the field.

Hoelle was the nearest man to the door when I stepped down into the operations shack. He was a big, square-shouldered youngster with heavy eyebrows and a slightly aquiline nose. I explained who I was and asked him who was in charge, and he said, "I am. I'm the squadron C.O. My name's Hoelle." He pronounced it "Holly." There was a fire in a stove, and the shack was warm. Two tiny black puppies lay on a pilot's red scarf in a helmet in the middle of the dirt floor, and they seemed to be the center of attention. Six or eight lieutenants, in flying togs that ranged from overalls to British Army battle dress, were sitting on gasoline cans or sprawled on a couple of cots. They were all looking at the puppies and talking either to them or their mother, a small Irish setter over in one corner, whom they addressed as Red. "One of the boys brought Red along with him from England," Hoelle said. "We think that the dog that got her in trouble is a big, long-legged black one at the airport we were quartered at there."

"These are going to be real beautiful dogs, just like Irish setters, only with black hair," one of the pilots said in a defensive tone. He was obviously Red's master.

"This is a correspondent," Hoelle said to the group, and one of the boys on a cot moved over and made room for me. I sat down, and the fellow who had moved over said his name was Larry Adler but he wasn't the harmonica player and when he was home he lived on Ocean Parkway in Brooklyn. "I wouldn't mind being there right now," he added.

There was not much in the shack except the cots, the tin cans, a packing case, the stove, a phonograph, a portable typewriter, a telephone, and a sort of bulletin board that showed which pilots were on mission, which were due to go on patrol, and which were on alert call, but it was a cheerful place. It reminded me of one of those secret-society shacks that small boys are always building out of pickup materials in vacant lots. Adler got up and said he would have to go on patrol. "It's pretty monotonous," he said, "like driving a fast car thirty miles an hour along a big, smooth road where there's no traffic. We just stooge around near the field, and at this time of day nothing ever happens."

Another lieutenant came over and said he was the intelligence officer of the squadron. Intelligence and armament officers, who do not fly, take a more aggressive pride in their squadron's accomplishments than the pilots, who don't like to be suspected of bragging. "We've been out here for a month," the intelligence officer said, "and we have been doing everything—escorting bombers over places like Sfax and Sousse, shooting up vehicles and puncturing tanks, going on fighter sweeps to scare up a fight, and flying high, looking for a target and then plunging straight down on it and shooting hell out of it. We've got twenty-nine German planes, including bombers and transports with troops in them and fighters, and the boys have flown an average of forty combat missions apiece. That's more than one a day. Maybe you'd like to see some of the boys' own reports on what they have been doing."

I said that this sounded fine, and he handed me a sheaf of the simple statements pilots write out when they put in a claim for shooting down a German plane. I copied part of a report by a pilot named Earnhart, who I thought showed a sense of literary style. He had had, according to the intelligence officer, about the same kind of experience as everybody else in the squadron. Earnhart had shot down a Junkers 52, which is a troop carrier, in the episode he was describing, and then he had been attacked by several enemy fighters. "As I was climbing away from them," he wrote, "a 20-millimeter explosive shell hit the windshield and deflected through the top of the canopy and down on the instrument panel. Three pieces of shell hit me, in the left chest, left arm, and left knee. I dropped my belly tank and, having the ship under control, headed for my home base. On the way I applied a tourniquet to my leg, administered a hypodermic, and took sulfanilamide tablets. I landed the ship at my own base one hour after I had been hit by the shell. The plane was repaired. Claim, one Ju 52 destroyed." The intelligence officer introduced Earnhart to me. He was a calm, slender, dark-haired boy, and he persisted in addressing me as sir. He said he came from Lebanon, Ohio, and had gone to Ohio State.

Still another lieutenant I met was named Gustke. He came from Detroit. Gustke had been shot down behind the German lines and had made his way back to the field. He was a tall, gangling type, with a long nose and a prominent Adam's apple. "I crash-landed the plane and stepped out of it wearing my parachute," he told me, "and the first thing I met was some Arabs who looked hostile to me, and as luck would have it I had forgotten to bring along my .45, so I tripped my parachute and threw it to them, and you know how crazy Arabs are about cloth or anything like that. They all got fighting among themselves for the parachute, and while they were doing that I ran like the dickens and got away from them. I got to a place where there were some Frenchmen, and they hid me overnight and the next day put me on a horse and gave me a guide, who brought me back over some mountains to inside the French lines. I had a pretty sore tail from riding the horse."

A pilot from Texas named Ribb, who stood near by as Gustke and I talked, broke in to tell me that they had a fine bunch of fellows and that when they were in the air they took care of each other and did not leave anybody alone at the end of the formation to be picked off by the enemy. "In this gang we have no ass-end Charlies," he said feelingly.

I asked Lieutenant Hoelle what was in the cards for the afternoon, and he said that eight of the boys, including himself, were going out to strafe some German tanks that had been reported working up into French territory. "We carry a cannon, which the P-40's don't, so we can really puncture a tank the size they use around here," he said. "We expect to meet some P-40's over the target, and they will stay up high and give us cover against any German fighters while we do a job on the tanks. Maybe I had better call the boys together and talk it over."

A couple of pilots had begun a game of blackjack on the top of the packing case, and he told them to quit, so he could spread a map on it. At that moment an enlisted man came in with a lot of mail and some Christmas packages that had been deposited by a courier plane. It was long after Christmas, but that made the things even more welcome, and all the pilots made a rush for their packages and started tearing them open. Earnhart, one of the men who were going on the strafe job, got some National Biscuit crackers and some butterscotch candy and a couple of tubes of shaving cream that he said he couldn't use because he had an electric razor, and the operations officer, a lieutenant named Lusk, got some very rich homemade cookies that an aunt and uncle had sent him from Denver. We were all gobbling butterscotch and cookies as we gathered round the map Hoelle had spread. It was about as formal an affair as looking at a road map to find your way to Washington, Connecticut, from New Milford. "We used to make more fuss over briefings in England," the intelligence officer said, "but when you're flying two or three times a day, what the hell?" He pointed out the place on the map where the tanks were supposed to be, and all the fellows said they knew where it was, having been there before. Hoelle said they would take off at noon. After a while he and the seven other boys went out onto the field to get ready, and I went with them. On the way there was more talk about P-38's and how some Italian prisoners had told their captors that the Italian Army could win the war easy if it wasn't for those fork-tailed airplanes coming over and shooting them up, a notion that seemed particularly to amuse the pilots. Then I went to the P-38 squadron mess with Adler, who had just returned from patrol duty and wasn't going out on the strafe job, and Gustke, who was also remaining behind. This mess was relatively luxurious. They had tables with plates and knives and forks on them, so they had no mess tins to wash after every meal. "We live well here," Adler said. "Everything high-class."

"The place the planes are going is not very far away," Gustke said, "so they ought to be back around half past two."

When we had finished lunch, I took another stroll around the post. I was walking toward the P-38 squadron's operations shack when I saw the planes begin to return from the mission. The first one that came in had only the nose wheel of its landing gear down. There was evidently something the matter with the two other wheels. The plane slid in on its belly and stopped in a cloud of dust. Another plane was hovering over the field. I noticed, just after I spotted this one, that a little ambulance was tearing out onto the field. Only one of the two propellers of this plane was turning, but it landed all right, and then I counted one, two, three others, which landed in good shape. Five out of eight. I broke into a jog toward the operations shack. Gustke was standing before the door, looking across the field with binoculars. I asked him if he knew whose plane had belly-landed, and he said it was a Lieutenant Moffat's and that a big, rough Texas pilot whom the other fellows called Wolf had been in the plane that had come in with one engine out. "I see Earnhart and Keith and Carlton, too," he said, "but Hoelle and the other two are missing."

A jeep was coming from the field toward the operations shack, and when it got nearer we could see Wolf in it. He looked excited. He was holding his right forearm with his left hand, and when the jeep got up to the shack he jumped out, still holding his arm.

"Is it a bullet hole?" Gustke asked.

"You're a sonofabitch it's a bullet hole!" Wolf shouted. "The sonofabitching P-40's sonofabitching around! As we came in, we saw four fighters coming in the opposite direction, and Moffat and I went up to look at them and they were P-40's, coming away. The other fellows was on the deck, and we started to get down nearer them, to about five thousand, and these sonofabitching 190's came out of the sun and hit Moffat and me the first burst and then went down after the others. There was ground fire coming up at us, too, and the sonofabitches said we was going to be over friendly territory. I'm goddam lucky not to be killed."

"Did we get any of them?" Gustke asked.

"I know I didn't get any," Wolf said, "but I saw at least four planes burning on the ground. I don't know who the hell they were."

By that time another jeep had arrived with Earnhart, looking utterly calm, and one of the mechanics from the field. "My plane is all right," Earnhart told Gustke. "All gassed up and ready to go. They can use that for patrol."

The telephone inside the shack rang. It was the post first-aid station calling to say that Moffat was badly cut up by glass from his windshield but would be all right. The mechanic said that the cockpit of Moffat's plane was knee-deep in hydraulic fluid and oil and gas. "No wonder the hydraulic system wouldn't work when he tried to get the wheels down," the mechanic said. The phone rang again. This time it was group operations, calling for Earnhart, Keith, and Carlton, all three of them unwounded, to go over there and tell them what had happened. The three pilots went away, and a couple of the men got Wolf back into a jeep and took him off to the first-aid station. Hoelle and the two other pilots were still missing. That left only Gustke and me, and he said in a sad young voice, like a boy whose chum has moved to another city, "Now we have lost our buddies."

A couple of days later I learned that Hoelle had bailed out in disputed territory and made his way back to our lines, but the two other boys are either dead or prisoners.

A couple of days later I was standing in a chow line with my mess tins at another airfield, over the line in southern Tunisia, waiting to get into a dugout where some mess attendants were ladling out a breakfast of stew and coffee. The field is enormous, a naturally flat airdrome of white sand and alfa grass that doesn't hold rainwater long enough to spoil the runways. All around the field there are bulky, reddish mountains. The sun was just coming up over one of them, and the air was very cold. The mess shack was covered on top and three sides by a mound of earth. It served officers and men of a squadron of P-40 fighters, and on that particular Monday morning I stood between a corporal named Jake Goldstein, who in civilian life had been a Broadway song writer, and a private named John Smith, of New Hope, Pennsylvania, who used to help his father, a contractor, build houses. Goldstein told me about a lyric he had just written for a song to be called "Bombs." "The music that I think of when it goes through my head now," he said, "is kind of a little like the old tune called 'Smiles,' but maybe I can change it around later. The lyric goes:

> *There are bombs that sound so snappy,*
> *There are bombs that leave folks sad,*
> *There are bombs that fell on dear old Dover,*
> *But those bombs are not so bad.*

The idea is that the real bad bomb is when this girl quit me and blew up my heart."

"It sounds great," I told the corporal.

"It will be even bigger than a number I wrote called 'What Do You Hear from Your Heart?'" Goldstein said. "Probably you remember it. Bing Crosby sang it once on the Kraft Cheese Hour. If you happen to give me a little write-up, remember that my name in the song-writing business is Jack Gould." Private Smith started to tell me that he had once installed some plumbing for a friend of mine, Sam Spewack, the writer, in New Hope. "His wife, Bella, couldn't make up her mind where she wanted one of the bathroom fixtures," Smith said, "so I said——"

I never heard any more about Bella Spewack's plumbing, because Major Robert Christman, the commanding officer of the squadron, came up to me and said, "Well, it's a nice, quiet morning." He had his back to the east. I didn't get a chance to answer him, because I started to run like hell to get to the west side of the mound. A number of soldiers who had been scattered about eating their breakfasts off the tops of empty gasoline cans had already started running and dropping their mess things. They always faced eastward while they ate in the morning so that they could see the Messerschmitts come over the mountains in the sunrise. This morning there were nine Messerschmitts. By the time I hit the ground on the lee side of the mound, slender airplanes were twisting above us in a sky crisscrossed by tracer bullets—a whole planetarium of angry worlds and meteors. Behind our shelter we watched and sweated it out. It is nearly impossible to tell Messerschmitts from P-40's when they are maneuvering in a fight, except when one plane breaks off action and leaves its opponent hopelessly behind. Then you know that the one which is distanced is a P-40. You can't help yelling encouragement as you watch a fight, even though no one can hear you and you cannot tell the combatants apart. The Messerschmitts, which were there to strafe us, flew right over the mess shack and began giving the runways and the planes on the field a going over.

We had sent up four planes on patrol that morning, and they tried to engage the strafing planes, but other Germans, flying high to protect the strafers, engaged the patrol. Some "alert" planes that we had in readiness on the perimeter of the field took off in the middle of the scrap, and that was a pretty thing to watch. I saw one of our patrol planes come in and belly-land on the field, smoking. Then I saw another plane twisting out of the sky in a spin that had the soldiers yelling. We all felt that the spinning plane was a Messerschmitt, and it looked like a sure thing to crash into one of the mountains north of us. When the plane pulled out and disappeared over the summit, the yell died like the howl at Ebbets Field when the ball looks as if it's going into the bleachers and then is snagged by a visiting outfielder. It was a Messerschmitt, all right. A couple of minutes later every one of the German planes had disappeared, with our ships after them like a squad of heavy-footed comedy cops chasing small boys.

The fellows who had ducked for cover hoisted themselves off the ground and looked around for the mess things they had dropped. They were excited and sheepish, as they always are after a strafe party. It is humiliating to have someone run you away, so you make a joke about it. One soldier yelled to another, "When you said 'Flop!' I was there already!" Another, who spoke with a Brooklyn accent, shouted, "Jeez, those tracers looked just like Luna Park!"

We formed the chow line again, and one fellow yelled to a friend, "What would you recommend as a good, safe place to eat?"

"Lindy's, at Fifty-first Street," the other soldier answered.

"The way the guys ran, it was like a Christmas rush at Macy's," somebody else said.

Everybody tried hard to be casual. Our appetites were even better than they had been before, the excitement having joggled up our internal secretions. There were arguments about whether the plane that had escaped over the mountain would crash before reaching the German lines. I was scraping the last bits of stew from my mess tin with a sliver of hard biscuit when a soldier came up and told me that Major Rudenburg, whom I had never met, had been killed on the field, that five men had been wounded, and that one A-20 bomber had been ruined on the ground.

After I had washed up my tins, I walked over to the P-40 squadron operations shack, because I wanted to talk to a pilot familiarly known as Horse about the fight he had been in two days before, when I had seen eight P-38's go out from another field to attack some German tanks and only five come back, two of them badly damaged. A lot of Focke-Wulf 190's had attacked the P-38's over the target, and Horse and three other P-40 pilots, who were protecting the 38's, had been up above the 190's. Horse was a big fellow with a square, tan face and a blond beard. He came from a town called Quanah, in Texas, and he was always showing his friends a tinted picture of his girl, who was in the Waves. Horse was twenty-five, which made him practically a patriarch in that squadron, and everybody knew that he was being groomed to command a squadron of his own when he got his captaincy. He was something of a wit. Once I heard one of the other boys say that now that the field had been in operation for six weeks, he thought it was time the men should build a sit-down toilet. "The next thing we know," Horse said, "you'll be wanting to send home for your wife."

I found Horse and asked him about the fight. He said he was sorry that the 38's had had such a bad knock. "I guess maybe it was partly our fault," he said. "Four of our ships had been sent out to be high cover for the 38's. They didn't see any 38's or Jerries either, so when their gas was beginning to run low they started for home. Myself and three other fellows had started out to relieve them, and we passed them as they came back. The 38's must have arrived over the tanks just then, and the 190's must have been hiding at the base of a cloud bank above the 38's but far below us. When we got directly over the area, we could see tracers flying 'way down on the deck. The 190's had dived from the cloud and bounced the 38's, who never had a chance, and the 38's were streaking for home. We started down toward the 190's, but it takes a P-40 a long time to get anywhere, and we couldn't help. Then four more 190's dived from 'way up top and bounced us. I looped up behind one of them as he dived. My two wing men were right with me. I put a good burst into the sonofabitch and he started to burn, and I followed him down. I must have fired a hundred and twenty-five rounds from each gun. It was more fun than a county fair. Gray, my fourth man, put a lot of lead into another 190, and I doubt if it ever got home. The other two Jerries just kept on going."

The P-40 operations shack was set deep in the ground and had a double tier of bunks along three of its walls. Sand and grass were heaped over the top of the shack, and the pilots said that even when they flew right over it, it was hard to see, which cheered them considerably. The pilots were flying at least two missions a day and spent most of the rest of the time lying in the bunks in their flying clothes, under as many coats and blankets as they could find. The atmosphere in the shack was a thick porridge of dust diluted by thin trickles of cold air. Major Christman, the squadron leader, once said in a pleased tone, "This joint always reminds me of a scene in *Journey's End*." The pilots, most of whom were in their earliest twenties, took a certain perverse satisfaction in their surroundings. "Here we know we're at war," one of them said to me. "Not that I wouldn't change for a room and bath at a good hotel."

During most of my stay at the field I lived not in the *Journey's End* shack but in one known as the Hotel Léon because technically it belonged to a French lieutenant named Léon, a liaison officer between the French forces and our fliers. It was the newest and finest dugout on the field, with wooden walls and a wooden floor and a partition dividing it down the middle, and the floor was sunk about five feet below ground level. When I arrived at the field, there were plans to cover the part of the shack that projected above ground with sand, in which Léon intended to plant alfa. I had joined up with an Associated Press correspondent named Norgaard, whom I had met at the first field, and soon after our arrival Léon, a slender man with a thin, intelligent face and round, brown eyes, welcomed us to his palace. We put our stuff into the shack and emerged to find Léon throwing a modest shovelful of sand against one of the walls. Norgaard offered to help him. "There is only one shovel," Léon said with relief, pressing it into Norgaard's hands. "It is highly interesting for our comfort and safety that the house be covered entirely with sand. I am very occupied." Then he walked rapidly away, and Norgaard and I took turns piling sand around the Hotel Léon for endless hours afterward. Léon always referred to a telephone switchboard as a switching board, oil paper as oily paper, a pup tent as a puppy tent, and a bedding roll as a rolling bed.

After my talk with Horse, I walked over to the Hotel Léon and found it crowded, as it usually was. Only Léon and Norgaard and I, together with Major Philip Cochran and Captain Robert Wylie, lived in the hotel, but during the day Cochran and Léon used it as an office, and that was why it was crowded. When I had first come to the field, it had been operating for six weeks practically as an outpost, for there was just a unit of

American infantry, fifty miles to the southeast, between it and the region occupied by Rommel's army. Cochran, though only a major, had run the field for almost the entire period, but by the time I arrived he had reverted to the status of operations officer. The shack had telephone lines to detachments of French troops scattered thinly through the hills to our east, and they called up at all hours to tell Léon where German tanks were moving or to ask our people to do some air reconnaissance or drop bags of food to a platoon somewhere on a mountain. The French had no trucks to transport food. Sometimes Cochran flew with American transport planes to tell them where to drop parachute troops, and sometimes he flew with bombers to tell them where to drop bombs. Because of Cochran's and Léon's range of activities, they always had a lot of visitors.

Attached to the partition in the shack were two field telephones, one of which answered you in French and the other in English. Two soldier clerks, who were usually pounding typewriters, sat on a bench in front of a shelf along one wall. One of them was Corporal Goldstein, the song writer. The other was a private first class named Otto, who wore metal-rimmed spectacles with round lenses and belonged to the Pentecostal brethren, an evangelical sect which is against fighting and profanity. Otto owned some barber tools, and he cut officers' hair during office hours and enlisted men's at night. That morning he was cutting the hair of Kostia Rozanoff, the commandant of the Lafayette Escadrille, a French P-40 outfit that was stationed at the field. Rozanoff was a blond, round-headed Parisian whose great-grandfather had been Russian. Otto, perhaps taking a cue from the shape of Rozanoff's skull, had clipped him until he looked like Erich von Stroheim, but there was no mirror, so Rozanoff was happy anyway. Cochran, dressed in a dirty old leather flying jacket, had just come back from a mission in the course of which he thought he had destroyed a 190, and was trying to tell about that while nearly everybody else in the shack was trying to tell him about the morning's strafing. Also in the shack was Colonel Edson D. Raff, the well-known parachutist, who had once unexpectedly found himself in command of all the American ground forces in southern Tunisia and for weeks had successfully bluffed enemy forces many times larger. He had flown in from his post in Gafsa in a small plane which he used as his personal transport. He was crowded in behind Otto's barbering elbow and was trying to talk to Cochran over Rozanoff's head. Raff is short and always wore a short carbine slung over his left shoulder, even indoors. He invariably flies very low in his plane to minimize the risk of being potted by a Messerschmitt. "I have one foot trailing on the ground," he says.

Lieutenant Colonel William Momyer, the commanding officer of the field, was sitting between Rozanoff and Corporal Goldstein, telling about a mission he had been on himself that morning, escorting a lot of A-20's over Kebili, a town where the Italians had begun to repair a dynamited causeway across the Chott Djerid. "I bet the wops will never get any workmen to go back to that place," Momyer said. "We scared hell out of them." Momyer had shot down a Junkers 88 and a Messerschmitt within a week. He was hot.

Among the others in the shack that morning were Norgaard, the Associated Press man, and a tall P-40 pilot named Harris, who kept asking Léon whether any French unit had telephoned to report finding the Messerschmitt he had been shooting at during the strafing episode, because he was sure it must have crashed. It was the Messerschmitt we had seen pull out of the spin over the mountain. The English-speaking telephone rang, and Captain Wylie answered it. He has the kind of telephone voice that goes with a large, expensive office, which he probably had in civilian life. It was somebody up the line asking for Major Rudenburg, the officer who had just been machine-gunned in the strafing. "Major Rudenburg has been killed," Wylie said. "Is there anything I can do for you?"

There was a variety of stuff on the field when I was there. In addition to Christman's P-40 squadron and the Lafayette Escadrille, there was a second American P-40 squadron, commanded by a Major Hubbard, which had a full set of pilots but only five ships. This was because the powers that be had taken away the other ships and given them to the Lafayettes in the interest of international good will. Hubbard's pilots were not sore at the Lafayettes, but they didn't think much of the powers that be. There was also a bomber squadron. The people on our field were not by any means sitting targets. They constantly annoyed the Germans, and that is why the Germans were so keen on "neutralizing" the field. But they didn't come back that day, and neither lunch nor dinner was disturbed.

The guests of the Hotel Léon often didn't go to the mess shack for dinner, because Léon would prepare dinner for them on the premises. He was a talented cook, who needed the stimulation of a public, which was, that Monday evening, us. He also needed Wylie to keep the fire in the stove going, Cochran to wash dishes, and me and Norgaard to perform assorted chores. He got eggs from the Arabs and wine from a near-by French engineer unit, and he had gathered a choice assortment of canned goods from the quartermaster's stores. He also bought sheep and pigs from farmers. Léon's idea of a campaign supper was a *soufflé de poisson*, a *gigot*, and an *omelette brûlée à l'armagnac*. He made the soufflé out of canned salmon. The only trouble with dining at Léon's was that dinner was seldom ready before half past eight and it took until nearly midnight to clean up afterward.

During that Monday dinner we speculated on what the enemy would do next day. Norgaard said it was hell to have to get up early to catch the Germans' morning performance, but Cochran, the airfield's official prophet, said, "They'll want to make this one a big one tomorrow, so you can sleep late. They won't be over until two-thirty in the afternoon." Momyer, who was having dinner at the "hotel" that night, agreed that there would be something doing, but he didn't predict the time of day. Léon said, "I think also that there is something cooking in." Momyer decided to maintain a patrol of eight planes over the field all day. "Of course, maybe that's just what they want us to do, use our planes defensively, so we will fly less missions," he said, "but I think this time we ought to do it."

I had such faith in Cochran that it never occurred to me that the Germans would attack us before the hour he had named, and they didn't. The only enemy over the field the following morning was Photo Freddie, a German reconnaissance pilot who had become a local character. He came every morning at about forty thousand feet, flying a special Junkers 86 job so lightened that it could outclimb any fighter. The anti-aircraft guns would fire, putting a row of neat, white smoke puffs a couple of miles below the seat of Freddie's pants, the patrol planes would lift languidly in his direction, like the hand of a fat man waving away a fly, and Photo Freddie would scoot off toward Sicily, or wherever he came from, to develop his pictures, thus discovering where all the planes on the field were placed. The planes were always moved around after he left, and we used to wonder what the general of the Luftwaffe said to poor Freddie when the bombers failed to find the planes where he had photographed them. Now and then some pilot tried to catch Photo Freddie by getting an early start, climbing high above the field, and then stooging around until he appeared. Freddie, however, varied the hour of his matutinal visits, and since a P-40 cannot fly indefinitely, the pilot would get disgusted and come down. I do not think anybody really wanted to hurt Freddie anyway. He was part of the local fauna, like the pet hens that wandered about the field and popped into slit trenches when bombs began to fall.

At about twenty minutes past two that afternoon Norgaard and I returned to the Hotel Léon to do some writing. An Alsatian corporal in the French Army was working in front of the shack, making a door for the entrance. The corporal had been assigned by the French command to build Léon's house, and he was a hard worker. He always kept his rifle by him while he was working. He had a long brown beard, which he said he was going to let grow until the Germans were driven out of Tunisia, so I wouldn't recognize him if I saw him now. Only Goldstein and Otto were inside the hut this time. I said to Goldstein, "Why don't you write a new number called 'One-Ninety, I Love You'?" Otto, who had been reading the *Pentecostal Herald*, said, "I do not think that would be a good title. It would not be popular." At that precise moment all of us heard the deep *woomp* of heavy ack-ack. It came from one of the British batteries in the mountains around the field. We grabbed our tin hats and started for the doorway. By the time we got there, the usual anti-aircraft show was on. In the din we could easily distinguish the sound of our Bofors guns, which were making their peculiar seasick noises—not so much a succession of reports as one continuous retch. The floor of the shack, as I have said, was five feet below ground level, and the Alsatian had not yet got around to building steps down to the entrance, so we had a nice rectangular hole just outside from which to watch developments. The Germans were bombing now, and every time a bomb exploded, some of the sand heaped against the wooden walls was driven into the shack through the knotholes. The only trouble was that whenever a bomb went off we pulled in our heads and stopped observing. Then we looked out again until the next thump. After several of these thumps there was a straight row of columns of black smoke a couple of hundred yards to our right. I poked my head above ground level and discovered the Alsatian corporal kneeling and firing his rifle, presumably at an airplane which I could not see. The smoke began to clear, and we hoisted ourselves out of the hole to try to find out what had happened. "I do not think I touched," the Alsatian said. A number of dogfights were still going on over the mountains. Scattered about the field, men, dragging themselves out of slit trenches, were pointing to the side of a mountain to the north, where there was smoke above a downed plane.

Léon had a little old Citroën car, which he said had become, through constant association with the United States Army, "one naturalized small jeeps." He had left it parked behind the shack, and as Norgaard and I stood gawping about, Léon came running and shouted that he was going out to the fallen plane. We climbed into the "naturalized jeeps" and started across the field toward the mountainside. At one of the runways we met a group of P-40 pilots, including Horse, and I yelled to them, "Was it theirs or ours?" "Ours, I think," Horse said. We kept on going. When we reached the other side of the field, we cut across country, and Léon could not make much speed. A couple of soldiers with rifles thumbed a ride and jumped on the running boards. As we went out across plowed fields and up the mountain toward the plane, we passed dozens of soldiers hurrying in the same direction.

When we arrived where the plane had fallen, we found three trucks and at least fifty men already there. The plane had been a Messerschmitt 109 belonging to the bombers' fighter escort. Flames were roaring above the portion deepest in the earth, which I judged was the engine. Screws, bolts, rings, and unidentifiable bits of metal were scattered over an area at least seventy-five yards square. Intermingled with all this were widely scattered red threads, like the bits left in a butcher's grinder when he has finished preparing an order of chopped steak. "He never even tried to pull out," a soldier said. "He must have been shot through the brain. I seen the whole thing. The plane fell five thousand feet like a hunk of lead." There was a sour smell over everything—not intolerable, just sour. "Where is the pilot?" Norgaard asked. The soldier waved his hand with a gesture that included the whole area. Norgaard, apparently for the first time, noticed the red threads. Most of the soldiers were rummaging amid the wreckage, searching for souvenirs. Somebody said that the pilot's automatic pistol, always the keepsake most eagerly sought, had already been found and appropriated. Another soldier had picked up some French and Italian money. While the soldiers walked about, turning over bits of the plane with their feet, looking for some object which could serve as a memento, an American plane came over, and everybody began to run before someone recognized it for what it was. Just as we came back, a soldier started kicking at something on the ground and screaming. He was one of the fellows who had ridden out on our running boards. He yelled, "There's the sonofabitch's goddam guts! He wanted my guts! He nearly had my guts, God damn him!" Another soldier went up to him and bellowed, "Shut up! It ain't nice to talk that way!" A lot of other men began to gather around. For a minute or so the soldier who had screamed stood there silently, his shoulders pumping up and down, and then he began to blubber.

Léon picked up a large swatch of the Messerschmitt's tail fabric as a trophy, and as the soldiers walked away from the wreck most of them carried either similar fragments or pieces of metal. After a while Norgaard and I climbed into Léon's car, and the three of us started back toward the field. When we arrived we learned that a lieutenant named Walter Scholl, who had never been in a fight before, had shot down the Messerschmitt. He was the fellow who, in the Cornell-Dartmouth football game of 1940, threw the famous fifth-down touchdown pass for Cornell, the one that was completed for what was considered a Cornell victory until movies of the game showed that it shouldn't have been Cornell's ball at all and the decision had to be reversed. Two other pilots had shot down two Junkers 88 bombers. One of our planes on the ground had been destroyed, and a slit trench had caved in on two fellows, nearly frightening them to death before they could be dug out.

Norgaard often said that southern Tunisia reminded him of New Mexico, and with plenty of reason. Both are desert countries of mountains and mesas, and in both there are sunsets that owe their beauty to the dust in the air. The white, rectangular Arab houses, with their blue doors, are like the houses certain Indians build in New Mexico, and the Arabs' saddle blankets and pottery and even the women's silver bracelets are like Navajo things. The horses, which look like famished mustangs, have the same lope and are similarly bridlewise; burros are all over the place, and so is cactus. These resemblances are something less than a coincidence, because the Moors carried their ways of house-building and their handicraft patterns and even their breed of horses and method of breaking them to Spain, and the Spaniards carried them to New Mexico eight hundred years later. All these things go to make up a culture that belongs to a high plateau country where there are sheep to furnish wool for blankets and where people have too little cash to buy dishes in a store, where the soil is so poor that people have no use for heavy plow horses but want a breed that they can ride for long distances and that will live on nearly nothing.

"This horse is young," an Arab once said to Norgaard and me as he showed us a runty bay colt tied in front of a combined general store and barbershop in a village about a mile from the airfield. "If I had had a little barley to feed him, he would be bigger, but what barley we had we have ourselves eaten. It is a poor country."

We used to go down to this village to get eggs when we were too lazy to make the chow line for breakfast or when we felt hungry at any time of day. We'd take them back to the shack a bunch of us were living in and cook them. Solitary Arabs squat along the roadsides all over North Africa, waiting for military vehicles. When one comes into sight, the Arab pulls an egg out from under his rags and holds it up between thumb and forefinger like a magician at a night club. The price of eggs—always high, of course—varies in inverse ratio to the distance from a military post. Near big towns that are a long way from any post the Arabs get only five francs (ten cents at the new rate of exchange) for an egg, but in villages close to garrisons eggs are sometimes hard to find at any price. Norgaard and I followed a standard protocol to get them. First we went into the general store and barbershop, which was just a couple of almost empty rooms that were part of a mud house, and shook hands with all the male members of the establishment. Naturally, we never saw any of the females. Then we presented a box of matches to the head of the house, an ex-soldier who spoke French, and he invited us to drink coffee. The Arabs have better coffee and more sugar than the Europeans in North Africa. While we drank the coffee, we sat with the patriarch of the family on a white iron bed of European manufacture. The patriarch had a white beard and was always knitting socks; he stopped only to scratch himself. Once, as we were drinking coffee, we watched our French-speaking friend shave a customer's head. He started each stroke at the top of the cranium and scraped downward. He used no lather; the customer moistened his own poll with spittle after each stroke of the razor. Once, when the customer made a particularly awful face, all the other Arabs sitting around the room laughed. During the coffee-drinking stage of the negotiations we presented the Arabs with a can of fifty English cigarettes. After that they presented us with ten to fifteen eggs. Soldiers who were not such good friends of theirs usually got twenty eggs for fifty cigarettes, but it always costs something to maintain one's social life. One day I asked the barber why the old man scratched himself, and he said, laughing, "Because of the black spots. We all have them, and they itch." With much hilarity the Arabs showed us the hard, black spots, apparently under their skins, from which they were suffering. I judged the trouble to be a degenerate form of the Black Death, tamed during the centuries by the rugged constitutions of our hosts. Norgaard thought that the spots were just chiggers.

The Germans had come over our airfield on a Monday morning and strafed it, and they had come back on Tuesday afternoon and bombed the place. They were going to start an offensive in southern Tunisia, we later learned, so they wanted to knock out this, the most advanced American field. On Wednesday morning the Germans made no attack. That afternoon Norgaard and I decided that we needed some eggs, so we walked down to the Arab village. I carried the eggs home in my field hat, a visored cap which has long flaps to cover your neck and ears when it is cold and which makes a good egg bag. We got back to the Hotel Léon between five and six o'clock. Cochran was out flying, and Léon was out foraging. Jake and Otto, the two soldier clerks who worked there during the day, had gone to chow. There was less than an hour of daylight left.

Cochran, who had a fine instinct for divining what the Germans were likely to do, had been sure that they would come over for the third day in succession, and Lieutenant Colonel William Momyer, the commanding officer of the field, had maintained a patrol of P-40's over the field all day. Cochran was among those taking their turns on patrol duty now. In forty minutes more all the planes would have to come down, because the field had no landing lights. And nothing had happened yet.

The walk had made Norgaard and me hungry, and we decided to have our eggs immediately. We threw some kindling wood in the stove to stir the fire up, and I put some olive oil in the mess tin in which I was going to scramble the eggs. The olive oil belonged to Léon. I took the lid off the hole in the top of the stove, put the mess tin over the hole, and broke all the eggs into the oil. I think there were eleven of them. They floated around, half submerged, and although I stirred them with a fork, they didn't scramble. We decided that I had used too much oil, so we added some cheese to act as a cement. Before the cheese had had time to take effect, we heard a loud explosion outside—plainly a bomb—and felt the shack rock. Norgaard grabbed his tin hat and ran out the door to look, and I was just going to follow him when I reflected that if I left this horrible brew on the stove hole a spark might ignite the oil and thus set fire to the shack. I carefully put the mess on a bench and replaced the lid on the stove. I put on my helmet and followed Norgaard out into a kind of foxhole outside our door. More bombs exploded, and then all we could hear was the racket of the Bofors cannon and .50-caliber machine guns defending the field. I went back inside, removed the stove lid, and put the eggs on again. Just as some warmth began to return to the chilled mess, another stick of bombs went off. In the course of the next minute or so, I repeated my entire routine. Before I finished cooking dinner, I had to repeat it three times more. Finally the eggs and the cheese stuck together after a fashion and I drained the oil off. Then, since no bombs had dropped for a couple of minutes, I poured half the concoction into Norgaard's canteen cup, I put what was left in my mess tin, and we ate.

After we had eaten, we left the shack and started toward the large, round pit, some fifty yards away, which served as a control room for the field. Night had closed in. There had been no firing now for ten minutes, but as we approached the pit, our anti-aircraft opened up again, firing from all around the field simultaneously. The Bofors tracer shells, which look like roseate Roman candles, reminded me of the fireworks on the lagoon at the World's Fair in Flushing. The burst ended as abruptly as it had begun, except that one battery of .50's kept on for an extra second or two and then stopped in an embarrassed manner.

We saw a lot of our pilots clustered around the pit. A corporal named Dick usually stood in the pit talking to our planes in the air by radio telephone, but Major Robert Christman was in Dick's place this time. I recognized Christman's voice as he spoke into the telephone, asking, "Did you see the gunfire? Did you see the gunfire?" You wouldn't ask a Jerry that if you were shooting at him, so I knew they were firing the anti-aircraft guns to light one or more of our planes home. Christman asked again, "Did you see the gunfire? Did you see the gunfire?" Then he said to somebody else in the pit, probably Dick, "Hold this a minute." He stuck his head up over the side of the pit and shouted in the direction of a near-by dugout, "They say they saw the fire! Cochran's going to lead in and land to show the other ship the way! Lord, how that Cochran swears when he's excited! Tell the ack-ack to hold everything!" The switchboard through which the control room communicated with all the ack-ack batteries was in the dugout. Nothing was convenient on that field. It sometimes seemed that one of the pilots had scratched the whole thing out of the ground with a broken propeller blade after a forced landing.

We could see a plane showing red and green lights slowly circling over the field, descending gradually in long, deliberate spirals, as if the pilot wanted somebody to follow him. Then there was a blast of machine-gun fire, and a fountain of tracers sprayed up from a distant edge of the field. "God damn them!" Christman yelled. "Tell them to hold that fire! What do they want to do—shoot Phil down?" The plane coasted slowly, imperturbably lower. It was Cochran's firm belief, I knew, that the ack-ack on the field had never hit anything, so he probably wasn't worried. The plane skimmed over the surface of the field. There was one pitiful red light on the field for it to land by, like the lantern a peddler would hang on the tail of a hobbled donkey to keep him from being hit by a motorcar. "He'll never make it that way," a pilot near me said. "What the hell is he doing? He'll overshoot. No, there he goes up again."

In a minute Christman, back at the phone once more, said, "Cochran went up because the other fellow couldn't see him. The other ship says he saw the gunfire, though. Now he wants a burst on the southern edge of the field only." Somebody in the switchboard dugout yelled, "Come on now! Battery C only, Battery C only! Everybody else *hold* it!" All the guns on the field immediately fired together. I could hear Momyer's voice yelling in the dugout, "God damn it, I'll have them all court-martialed!" Christman shouted, "He says he saw it and now he can see Cochran! He's coming in!" Cochran was again circling in the blackness above the field. The pilot next to me said, "This is sure sweating it out." I recognized him, partly by his voice and partly by the height of his shoulders, as Horse.

"Did we get any of theirs?" I asked Horse.

"Yes, sir," Horse said. "Bent got one for sure. He's in already. And a French post has telephoned that another one is down near there in flames and that pilot out there with Cochran had one smoking. He must have chased it so far he couldn't get back before dark. Must have forgot himself. I don't rightly know who he is."

The ack-ack batteries fired again. They apparently did what was wanted this time, because nobody cursed. Christman called up from the pit, "They want one more burst, all together, and then they're coming in!" The message was relayed, and the ack-ack fired another salvo. Now there were two planes, both showing lights, moving in the sky above the field, one high and one low. "Cochran's coming in," Horse said. "Look at him. Just like it was day and he could see everything." The lower pair of lights drifted downward, straightened out and ran forward along the field, and stopped. The other lights slowly followed them down, seemed to hesitate a moment, then slanted toward the ground and coasted into a horizontal. "Good landing," Horse said. "We sure sweated that one." The second pilot to land turned out to be a lieutenant named Thomas, who had become too absorbed in the pursuit of a Junkers 88 to turn back until he had shot it down. That made three Junkers for us, each carrying a crew of four men. I learned that the German bombs had spoiled, to use the airmen's term, two of our planes on the field. A couple of minutes later a jeep that had gone out to meet Cochran's plane brought him to where the rest of us were standing. He is a short, box-chested man, and the two or three flying jackets he was wearing made him look shorter and stockier than he really is. He was feeling good. "I'm sorry I cursed you out, Bob! I was excited!" he yelled down into the control pit to Christman. Momyer, who had come out of the dugout, made as if to grab Cochran and hug him, but stopped in astonishment when he heard Cochran being so polite. It seemed to remind him of something. Looking rather thoughtful, he went back into the dugout and called up the lieutenant colonel in command of the ack-ack, which he had been abusing. "Thank you very much, Colonel," I heard him say. "Your boys certainly saved the day."

That evening was a happy one. Léon's shack was crowded with pilots talking about the successful fight and scrambling eggs and eating them out of mess tins. Cochran felt so good that he decided to have his first haircut since he had left New York, three months before, so he sent over to the enlisted men's quarters for Otto to do the job. Otto is a young man with reddish hair and white eyebrows and a long nose, and he had a habit of getting interested in a conversation between two senior officers and breaking into it. Once, hearing Colonel Edson D. Raff, the parachute-troop commander, telling Lieutenant Colonel Momyer that he could take Tunis with no more than four hundred and fifty men, Otto blurted out, "How can you be so sure?" Aside from this failing he is a good soldier, and when he gives a haircut he really cuts off hair, so nobody can say he is looking for a return engagement in the near future. "I never cut human hair back home on the farm, but I used to clip all our horses," Otto once said.

It was well after dark when Léon came in from his foraging, which had been a success too. "I have bought three small peegs," he announced triumphantly, "and when they are theek enough we shall eat them." He had left them in the care of a *hôtelier* in a town a few miles away. They were subsequently taken, and presumably eaten, by the Germans. At the time, however, Léon thought it a safe *logement* for the pigs. "I have also talked with the aide of General Koeltz," Léon said to Cochran and Momyer, "and he says that in the case any pilot sees any trucks moving on the road of which we have spoken yesterday, he is allowed to shoot without permission." While Otto cut Cochran's hair, we added up the box score of the three-day German attack on the field. The home team felt that it had done pretty well. During the Monday strafing the Germans had spoiled one of our planes on the field and another in the air and had killed one officer, a major, with machine-gun bullets. We had merely damaged one of their fighters. On Tuesday, while they had spoiled two more of our planes on the ground with bombs, we had shot down a Messerschmitt 109 and two Junkers 88's. That meant that we had lost a total of three planes but only one life while they had lost three planes and nine lives. One of our missions had also destroyed a Focke-Wulf 190 on Monday morning and a Messerschmitt had been badly damaged in the dogfight that had accompanied the strafing of our field. Wednesday evening we had destroyed three more planes and twelve men, and the Germans had succeeded only in damaging two planes on the ground, which gave us an imposing lead. "They won't be over tomorrow morning," Cochran said. "Maybe not all day. They'll want to think things over and try something big to make up for their losses and get the lead back. They'll be like a guy doubling his bet in a crap game."

That field had been fought over many times before in the course of history, and a corner of it had been the site of a

Carthaginian city. Bent, a pilot who talked with a British accent and had once done some digging among old ruins in England, said that every time he flew over that corner he could plainly see the gridiron pattern of the ancient streets on the ground. Horse was irreverent about Bent's archaeological claims. "Maybe a couple of thousand years from now," he said, "people will dig around this same field and find a lot of C-ration cans that we've left and attribute them to archaeology. They'll say, 'Those Americans must surely have been a pygmy race to wear such small helmets. It scarcely seems possible they had much brains. No wonder they rode around in such funny airplanes as the P-40.'"

Another officer who turned up in Léon's shack that evening was Major (afterward Lieutenant Colonel) Vincent Sheean, who always points out these days that he was once a correspondent himself. He said he had been driving in a jeep on a road near the field when the bombing started, so he had stopped and jumped into a ditch. Sheean had come down from the second highest headquarters of the African Air Forces to see that the French pilots of the Lafayette Escadrille, which had recently arrived at our field, received understanding and kind treatment from their American comrades. A couple of the Lafayette pilots happened to be in the shack when he arrived; they had imbibed so much kind treatment that they could hardly remember the words of "*Auprès de Ma Blonde*," which they were trying to teach to Momyer on a purely phonetic basis.

The next day, Thursday, was as quiet as Cochran had said it would be. The Germans left us completely alone. In the morning the Lafayette Escadrille fellows went on their first mission, covering a French local offensive in a mountain pass, and returned without meeting any enemy aircraft.

The exposed position of our mess shack had begun to worry Major Christman's men after the strafing we had received the Monday before, and he had ordered the chow line transferred to a place called the Ravine, a deep, winding gulch on the other side of the high road along one end of the field. Most of the men lived in the Ravine and felt safe there. They had scooped out caves in its sides and used their shelter halves to make doors. One stretch of the gully was marked by a sign that said "Park Avenue." Sheean and I stood in the chow line for lunch and then took an afternoon stroll along Park Avenue. Afterward I went back to Léon's shack to write a letter and found it crowded, as usual. An engineer officer who had been at the field a couple of days was asking Cochran how he could be expected to get on with the construction job he had been sent there to do if new bomb holes appeared on the field every day and his detachment had to fill them up. "We've been filling up bomb holes ever since we been here, and it looks like we won't get a chance to do anything else," the engineer said. "My colonel sent me down here to build revetments for airplanes, and he's going to expect me back soon." Another visitor, a captain in the Royal Engineers, asked him if there were any unexploded bombs on the runways. Men on the field always referred to this British captain as the booby-trap man, the planting of fiendish traps for the enemy being his specialty, and added with respect, "Even the parachute troops say he's crazy." He had made several jumps with Colonel Raff's parachutists to install his humorous devices in places where he thought German soldiers would later get involved with them. The American officer told him that there were several unexploded bombs on the runways and that he had marked off their positions with empty oil drums.

"But haven't you removed the fuses?" the booby-trap man asked with obvious astonishment.

"To hell with that!" his American colleague said with feeling. "They won't do any harm if they do go off. It's a big field."

"Oh, but they'll make quite a lot of noise," the booby-trap man said, still vaguely unhappy.

The American officer looked at the booby-trap man and Cochran as if they were both lunatics and went out of the hut without saying anything more. "How *extraordinary!*" the booby-trap man said. "He didn't even seem interested." He sounded hurt, like a young mother who has just learned that a visitor does not care for babies.

The booby-trap man looked like a conventional sort of Englishman, with a fair, boyish face and a shy smile. He spoke with the careful accent of the north countryman who has been to a university and he did not himself use the term "booby trap." He preferred to call his darlings, variously, trip mechanisms, push mechanisms, pull mechanisms, and anti-personnel switches. Trip mechanisms, for instance, are the ones soldiers inadvertently set off by stumbling over a concealed wire, and pull mechanisms are those they explode by picking up some innocent-seeming object like a corned-beef tin. The captain was an amateur botanist and seldom went out without a couple of pocketfuls of small devices to set about the countryside in likely spots as he ambled along, collecting specimens of Tunisian grasses. I asked him that afternoon how he had started on what was to become his military career, and he said with his shy smile, "I expect it was at public school, when I used to put hedgehogs in the other boys' beds. After a while the hedgehogs began to pall, and I invented a system for de-tuning the school piano, so that when the music master sat down to play 'God Save the King' it sounded god-awful."

"I sometimes try to imagine what your married life will be like, Captain," Cochran said. "Someday the baby will be in the crib and your wife will go to pick it up and the whole house will blow up because you've wired the baby to a booby trap."

"I trust I shall be able to restrain my professional instincts to fit the circumstances of domestic life," the booby-trap man said rather stiffly. He was a man who really took his branch of warfare seriously.

About a month later he blew himself up with a very special mine he was laying to protect our retreat from Kasserine. He simply disintegrated.

Sleep in the Hotel Léon was usually interrupted in the gray hour before dawn by the jangle of a field telephone that spoke French. Then Léon, whom the rest of us residents called *Monsieur le patron*, would sit up and pull the telephone from the holster in which it hung at the foot of his bed. He slept wearing all the clothes he possessed, which included several sweaters, a long military overcoat, and a muffler. When he grabbed the phone, he would say, "*Allo! Oui?*" (The rest of us sometimes would sing "Sweet Allo, Oui" to the tune of "Sweet Eloise.") The French voice at the other end of the phone was almost always audible, and, so that the half-awake American officers in the shack would get the idea of what was going on,

Léon would reply in a hybrid jargon. He would say, for example, "One *ennemi appareil* flying sousewest over point 106?
Merci, mon capitaine." Then he would hang up and fall back
into bed, muttering, "*Imbécile*, why he don't fly west? He will
be losted."

A partition divided Léon's shack into a bedroom, in which
four of us slept side by side, and an office, in which only two
slept. In the bedroom were Léon, Major Philip Cochran,
Norgaard, and myself. Captain Robert Wylie and Major Vincent Sheean slept in the office. We would ignore Léon's first
morning call, but before long there would be another;
Cochran would be asking what was going on, and we would
hear the roar of motors warming up for the dawn patrol and
the morning missions. Then we would hear Wylie clattering
around our stove in his G.I. shoes, and there would be a glow
in the shack when he put the match to the paper with which he
started the fire. Wylie, who wasn't a flying officer, always tried
to have the shack warm by the time Cochran got up, and he
wanted the major to stay in bed until the last minute. He was
as solicitous as a trainer with a favorite colt, and the rest of us
benefited from the care he took of Cochran, because we didn't
get up early, either. Wylie is a wiry man with a high forehead
and a pepper-and-salt mustache. He wears glasses and looks
like an advertising artist's conception of an executive who is
in good humor because he has had an excellent night's sleep
owing to Sanka. He is a highly adaptable man. After Wylie had
puttered around for a while, we would sit up one by one and
stretch and complain about being disturbed or about the cold
and then go outside to wash. Mornings on which the anti-
aircraft opened up against early visitors, the tempo was accelerated. Cochran undressed at night by loosening the knot in his
tie and drew it tight again in the morning as a sign that he was
dressed. These were symbolic gestures he never omitted.

On the morning of the fifth and last day of the small private
war during which the Germans had been trying hard to knock
out our field, it was the anti-aircraft that brought us out of
bed. We scrambled for the door, lugging our tin hats, our
toothbrushes, and our canteens. The Germans were already
almost over our field, but they were quite high, since our patrol planes had engaged them on the way in and they could

not break off the fight to strafe us. The German planes were single-engined fighters, which sometimes carry wing or belly bombs, but this time they were not bombing. Some of the defending planes were marked with the tricolor *cocarde* of the French Army. It was, I suppose, a historic combat, because the pilots of the Lafayette Escadrille were making the first French air fight against the Germans since the armistice of 1940. The Escadrille, which had been equipped with a number of our Curtiss P-40's in Morocco, had been with us only a few days.

As we watched, a plane fell, apparently far on the other side of a ridge of mountains near the field, and we yelled happily, thinking it was a Messerschmitt. After the fight we were to learn that it had been a P-40 with a French sergeant pilot. Cochran kept up an expert running commentary on what all the pilots were trying to do, but he frequently didn't know which were French and which Germans. During the battle we simultaneously watched and brushed our teeth. A couple of the French planes landed on the field while the others were still fighting, so we knew that they must have been shot up. Finally, one group of planes above the field started away and the others chased them, but the first planes simply outclimbed their pursuers and left them behind; then there was no longer any doubt about which were Messerschmitts and which were Curtisses. One German plane remained over the field, at perhaps thirty thousand feet, even after the rest of the invaders had disappeared. "That's what kills me," Cochran said, pointing to the lone plane. "There's that sucker stooging around and casing the joint for a strafe job, and he's so high nobody can bother him." Finally the stooge, evidently having found out all he wanted to know, took his leisurely departure.

A group of P-40's from one of the two American P-40 squadrons at the field rose to relieve the Lafayettes, and the French planes came buzzing in like bees settling on a sugared stick. In a few minutes Kostia Rozanoff, commandant of the Escadrille, and his pilots had gathered in Léon's shack to discuss the fight. All of them had had combat experience in 1939 and 1940, but the engagement this morning had been the *rentrée*, and they were as excited as if they had never seen a Messerschmitt before. Despite the fact that they were old hands, Cochran said, they had fought recklessly, climbing up to meet the Messerschmitts instead of waiting until the Germans dived. "If they don't dive," Cochran had frequently warned his own pilots, "you just don't fight." The French pilots' ardor had got them a beating, for besides the pilot whom we had seen fall and who, Rozanoff said, had not bailed out and was quite certainly killed, the two planes that had landed during the combat were riddled and would be of no use except for salvage, and one of their pilots had been wounded. The Germans apparently had suffered no damage at all. Rozanoff is thirty-seven and has a deep voice like Chaliapin's. He said that the pilot who had been killed was his wing man, and he could not understand how he had failed to see the Messerschmitt that had attacked him from the rear. "I cry him turn," Rozanoff kept saying. "I turn. He turns not. Poor little one."

It was extremely sad that the first Escadrille combat had not been a victory; it would have been such a fine story to bolster French morale all over the world. I remembered the sergeant pilot, who had been a likable fellow. An officer of the district gendarmerie brought the sergeant's wedding ring back to the field later in the morning.

My friend Norgaard and I had chosen that Friday for our departure from the field. We were going in to the big city, where the censors and the cable officers were, to write some stuff and get it off. There was air transportation between our field and the more settled places to the west, where staff officers and diplomats lived, but the service did not run on a formal schedule. Big Douglas transports skimmed in over the mountains once and sometimes twice a day, carrying mail and supplies, and they usually had room for passengers going back. They came at a different hour each day to make it as hard as possible for the Germans to waylay them. When they came, they stayed merely as long as was necessary, and the only way to be sure of a ride was to have your bedding roll made up and to stay near the landing field, waiting for the transports to appear. When they did, an officer would drive you and your luggage out to them in a jeep and you would get your stuff aboard. Norgaard and I hung around in front of our shack that morning, waiting. As the day wore on, a strong wind came up and blew great clouds of sand. At about eleven o'clock two transports arrived, escorted by some Spitfires. Cochran had planned to drive us down to the transports, but he was called to the telephone, and Major Robert Christman said that he would drive us instead.

When we arrived where the transports were standing on the runway, the transport captain, whose name, I noted from the leather strip on the breast of his flying jacket, was Lively, came over to the jeep and asked where his Spits could get gas. The name painted on his ship was Scarlett O'Hara. He and Christman started discussing what was the quickest way to get the gas. Christman and Norgaard and I stayed in the jeep. Dust was blowing over the field a mile a minute. Suddenly Christman looked over his shoulder, called on God, and vanished. Simultaneously Lively was also gone. I turned around to speak to Norgaard and discovered that he too had evaporated. I hate to sit in an empty jeep when I don't know why the other passengers have jumped. I do not remember actually getting out myself, but I know that I was already running when I heard somebody yell, "Hit the dirt!" Under the circumstances, this sounded so sensible that I bellyflopped to the ground, and I landed so hard that I skinned my knees and elbows. No surface in the world offers less cover than a runway. I regretted that my body, which is thick, was not thinner. I could guess what had happened: German strafers had ridden in on the dust storm, and nobody had seen them until they opened fire. I knew that the very nasty noises above me were being made by airplane cannon and that the even nastier ones close to me came from the detonation of the small explosive shells they fire. The strafers, I figured, were heading for the transports—large, expensive, unarmored jobs that you could punch holes in with a beer-can opener. I was therefore in line with the target and was very sorry to be where I was. I thought, illogically, "I am sorry to leave Liebling before I know how his life turns out."

As soon as there was a lull in the noises overhead, I got up and ran toward the edge of the runway to get away from the transports, but more noises came before I made it, so I flopped again. After they had passed, I got up and ran off the runway. I saw a soldier in a fine, large hole nearly six feet deep. He shouted, "Come right in, sir!" You can have Oscar of the Waldorf any time; I will always remember that soldier as my favorite host. I jumped in and squeezed up against him. Almost immediately the noises came a third time, and two transport pilots jumped down on my back. I was astonished that I had been able to outrun such relatively young men.

By this time all of our machine guns along the edges of the field were firing away, and there was a fourth pass, as the fliers say, and a loud crash, as if one of the Germans had dropped a bomb. A minute or two later the noise began to die down. Looking up from the bottom of the hole, we could see a man descending in a parachute. The big, white chute was swaying this way and that in the wind. The man had an awful time landing. We could see that even from a distance. The chute dragged him and bounced hell out of him after he landed. Afterward, word got around the field that he was an American. I didn't find out until a couple of days later, though, that the man with the chute had been Horse, the big, square-bearded, twenty-five-year-old Texan pilot I had come to know well. In landing, he hit his head against the ground and suffered a concussion of the brain. They put him in an ambulance and started for the nearest hospital, which was forty miles by road, but he had bad luck. The Germans had been strafing that road, too, that morning, and when the ambulance got within five miles of the hospital, it was blocked by two burning ammunition trucks. The shells on the trucks were exploding. The squadron surgeon and the ambulance driver put Horse on a stretcher and carried him around the trucks to a safe point on the other side, and an ambulance from the hospital came out to pick him up, but by the time it got there he was dead.

When the shooting at the field was over, the pilots and the soldier and I got out of the hole and walked back toward the transports, which were still there. Norgaard climbed out of another hole not far away. He said that when he had jumped out of the jeep he had crawled under it, and there he had found a transport lieutenant who had had the same idea. They had given up the jeep after the first pass and run for it, just as I had already done. We stared at the parallel furrows the Messerschmitt cannon had plowed down the runway, as if they had been the teeth of a rake and ourselves the field mice between them. The transport boys borrowed our jeep to get gas for the Spits, which had been immobilized during the raid because their tanks were empty. When the boys came back, we climbed into one of the transports. The big planes took off almost immediately. "Leave them laughing," Norgaard said to me when he recovered sufficient breath to say anything.

We learned later that the strafing had been done by eight Messerschmitts flying in four loose pairs, and that was why there had been four passes. Another Messerschmitt, making a run by itself, had dropped one bomb, ineffectually. There had also been a high cover of Messerschmitts; one of them had accounted for Horse. We were told that Cochran had said, with a hint of admiration in his voice, "It is getting so that the Germans patrol our field for us." A lot of Air Forces generals who were on a tour of inspection visited the field shortly after we left, said that the situation was very grave, and left, too. This point in the war over the field may be compared to the one in a Western movie at which the villain has kicked hell out of the heroine and just about wrestled her to the brink of ruin in a locked room.

At about two-thirty that same afternoon the Lafayette Escadrille was patrolling the field, in the company of two pilots from the American P-40 squadron that was commanded by Major Hubbard. This squadron had its full complement of pilots but only five planes. The pilots took turns flying the five ships, so they were not getting a great deal of practice. Nevertheless, Hubbard's squadron had already scored two victories that week. The two American pilots in the air were Hubbard and a man named Beggs. Two of their mates, Boone and Smith, were on the ground on alert call, sitting in their planes ready to reinforce the patrol if they were called.

This field didn't have one of those elaborate radio airplane-detectors that warn swank airdromes of the approach of enemy aircraft. It had to rely on its patrol system and on tips that watchers telephoned in. The tipsters were not infallible, as Norgaard and I had noticed that morning, and in the afternoon they slipped up again. Ten Junkers 88 bombers unexpectedly appeared, flying toward the field at three thousand feet. There was an escort of four fighters, unusually small for so many bombers, flying high above them and, as someone described it to me, acting oddly uninterested. The Frenchmen on patrol, also flying high, made one swipe at the escort and it disappeared, not to be seen again. Nine of the bombers were flying in three loose V's, and one ship was trailing the third V. Hubbard took the bomber on the right of the first V and shot it down. Beggs got the middle one, and a Frenchman knocked down the one on the left. The other Junkers had begun to drop their bombs. Boone and Smith came up off the field through the falling bombs to join the battle. Hubbard shot down another plane, and Boone, who had never fired a shot at a man or a plane before, came up behind one Junkers and blasted it out of the sky; it caromed against another Junkers on the way down, which gave Boone two planes with one burst of fire. He went on to destroy two more. Smith, opening fire at extreme range for fear that he would be shut out, blew the rudder off another Junkers, which also crashed. The tenth Junkers headed for home, but it never got there; the French picked off that one. It was the jack pot, ten out of ten. It was also the end of the five-day war over our airfield. No producer of Westerns ever wound up a film more satisfactorily. The Germans stayed away, in fact, for nineteen days and then came back only once, for a quick sneak raid.

Of the ten German bomber crews, only four men came out of the fight alive, and two of these died in the hospital. The two others said that the ten bombers had been escorted by four Italian Macchi C. 202 fighters, which had deserted them. Why the Luftwaffe should have entrusted four Macchis with the protection of ten Junkers 88's is harder to explain than the result. The Germans, fortunately for our side, sometimes vary their extreme guile with extreme stupidity.

I didn't have a chance to return to the airfield for about ten days, and then I stopped in on my way down to Gafsa, where the Americans were supposed to be launching a ground offensive. Captain Wylie, who told me about the big day at the field, said that Boone had come into the operations shack looking rather incredulous himself. "Probably I'm crazy," he had said to Wylie, "but I think I just shot down four planes." The Frenchmen said it was a victory for three nations: "The Americans shot down seven planes, we shot down two, and the Italians shot down the tenth so the crew couldn't tell on them."

The Americans left the field undefeated, for the two P-40 squadrons were relieved not long afterward by other outfits and sent back from the fighting zone to rest. Christman's squadron had been fighting there steadily for two months. I met the fellows from Christman's bunch again while I was trying to get a ride into civilization from another airfield, a bit west of the one where they had been stationed. A lot of trucks drove up and deposited the officers and men of the squadron on the field, with their weapons, their barracks bags, and their bedding rolls. Christman was there, and Private Otto, the squadron barber, and Corporal Jake Goldstein, the reformed song writer. I renewed my acquaintance with a pilot named Fackler, whom I remembered especially because he had once, finding himself in flying formation with two Messerschmitts who thought he was another Messerschmitt, shot one of them down, and I again met Thomas, the Oklahoma boy who had been lost in the air and had been lighted home by the fire of the field's anti-aircraft guns, and a non-flying lieutenant named Lamb, who used to practice law in New York, and a dozen others. I felt as if I had known them all for a long time.

Eleven transports came in to take the squadron west, and I arranged to travel in one of them. I was in the lead ship of the flight, and the transport major who commanded it told me that his orders were to drop the squadron at a field only about an hour's flight away. Then the transports would go on to their base, taking me along with them. It was pleasant to see the faces of the P-40 boys aboard my transport when it took off. They didn't know anything about the field they were going to, but they knew that they were going for a rest, so they expected that there would at least be huts and showers there. They looked somewhat astonished when the transports settled down in a vast field of stubble without a sign of a building anywhere around it. There were a few B-25 bombers on the field, and in the distance some tents. A transport sergeant came out of the pilot's compartment forward in our plane and worked his way toward the tail of our ship, climbing over the barracks bags heaped in the space between the seats. "I guess this is where you get out," he told the P-40 fellows.

A couple of soldiers jumped out, and the rest began passing out bags and rifles to them. Pretty soon all the stuff was piled outside the plane and the soldiers were standing on the field, turning their backs to a sharp wind and audibly wondering where the hell the barracks were. A jeep with an officer in it drove out from among the tents and made its way among the transports until it arrived at our ship. The transport major talked to the officer in the jeep, and then they both drove over to the transport Christman was traveling in and picked him up, and the three of them drove back to the tents. Some soldiers who had been near the jeep had heard the field's officer say that nobody there had been notified that they were coming. The transport major had replied that all he knew was that he had orders to leave them there. The soldiers who had heard the conversation communicated the news to the others by army telegraphy. "Situation normal!" one soldier called out, and everybody laughed. Soldiers are fatalistic about such situations.

Some time before, a report had circulated among the men that the squadron was to go back to the United States. Now I heard one soldier say, "This don't look like no United States to me."

Another one said, "When we get back there, Freddie Bartholomew will be running for President." He didn't seem sore.

Somebody said, "I hear they're going to start us here and let us hack our way through to South Africa."

Somebody else began a descant on a favorite army fantasy: what civilian life will be like after the war. "I bet if my wife gives me a piece of steak," he said, "I'll say to her, 'What the hell is this? Give me stew.'"

Another one said, "I bet she'll be surprised when you jump into bed with all your clothes on."

The delicacy of their speculations diminished from there on.

After a while the jeep came back. The transport major got out and said, "There seems to be some mistake. You'd better put your stuff back in the ship." We all got back into the planes, and the major told me that this obviously wasn't the place to leave the men but that he would have to wait until base operations could get headquarters on the telephone and find out their destination. We sat in the planes for an hour; then another officer came out in a jeep and said that nobody at headquarters knew anything about the squadron, so the major had better not take it any place else. The major told his sergeant to instruct the men to take their luggage off the planes.

"We enjoy doing this. It's no trouble at all," one of the soldiers in my plane said. The transports took off and left them standing there. I learned later that they eventually got straightened out. After two or three days someone remembered them; the pilots were sent to western Morocco, and the ground echelon was moved to another field.

All this happened what seems now to be long ago, in the pioneer days of the American Army in Tunisia. The old field, from which I had watched the five-day war, was never knocked out from the air, but it was taken by German ground troops with tanks, and then the Americans took it back and went on. The Hotel Léon, if the Germans hadn't burned it, was certainly full of booby traps for the Americans when they got there. I shouldn't have liked to sleep in it. Léon went back to Algiers, but he didn't like it and got back to the front for the last big push in April as liaison officer with a British tank outfit. Cochran has been promoted, and decorated several times and posted to a training command in the United States. He always said that he liked hatcheck chicks, but when he got back to New York, he says, he found that most of his favorites had become welders. I met the Alsatian corporal again in early May, on the Rue Bab-al-Zoun in Algiers. He was a sergeant by then and limping, because he had walked into an antipersonnel mine near Pichon. Happily it had not been set by an expert like our poor booby-trap man, because it had not killed him.

CHAPTER VII

First Act at Gafsa

GAFSA, the Capsa of the Numidians, is a very ancient town on a very slight hill. Warm springs gush from the foot of the hill under a fifteenth-century Arab citadel, which was wrecked by our engineers last February. The citadel was still intact when I first saw the place. There is an oasis around the town, which used to be an important knot in the cord of caravan routes between the Sahara and the Mediterranean. Gafsa had last winter, and by now probably has again, about ten thousand inhabitants, of whom five or six hundred are Europeans, eight hundred are native Jews, and the rest Arabs. The male Europeans, some of whom have their families with them, are government functionaries or employees of the railroad; the Jews, whose ancestors came there not a great while after the Destruction of the Temple, are traders and traditionally middlemen between the Christians and Moslems.

The climate there even at the end of January, when Norgaard and I reached the place, was warm and dry. A battalion of the Twenty-sixth Infantry was stationed in the town, with some batteries of French 75's, a battalion of Senegalese, and some Algerians, Zouaves, or Tirailleurs. The Americans, who were out of the First Division, were the only ground troops we had south of Sbeitla, which was about fifty miles away. They had been there for a month and were quite at home in the place, which, as almost every enlisted man you talked to was sure to say, looked like a set in a *Beau Geste* movie of the Foreign Legion. Old Jews sold surprisingly good native pastries, and Arabs peddled dates in the square in front of the American barracks. The soldiers had adopted Arab kids as mascots and clothed them in G.I. shirts and shoes. There was a great outdoor Roman swimming pool, filled by running warm water from the spring, which had a good deal of sulphur in it but was still pleasant to bathe in, and the Americans spent a lot of time swimming in it. The French soldiers preferred to dangle fishlines into the stream near its source and catch small blue fish, extremely voracious, which apparently were used to living in hot water. There was also a clean Arab bath, in a narrow *Arabian Nights* alley, where the attendants would stretch you on the floor and twist your arms and legs out of joint and then pound you with a hot brick before allowing you to steam yourself in peace. I remember seeing the English booby-trap man, pink and jolly from the steam, in the Arab bath, wearing a towel around his loins. People leave you with curious last pictures of them, in a war.

The men of the Twenty-sixth had carried out numerous raids against Italian detachments that occasionally appeared in the no man's land to the east, between Gafsa and Maknassy.

Neither adversary had any fixed garrison in this flat, desolate stretch of about seventy miles. Once the fellows from Gafsa had bagged eighty-four prisoners—that was reckoned a big haul for southern Tunisia in January. But during the entire night that followed the arrival of Norgaard and myself the sound of armored vehicles moving into and through the town never ceased; morning found most of the First Armored Division in readiness for the big thrust to the sea we had heard about.

Here, in the words of the old Yorkshire song, is where we get our own again. Earlier in the book I have described the fight that Norgaard and I saw between Gafsa and Sened, and I can continue here from the end of it. After we returned from the battlefield and heard that the offensive had been countermanded and our 200-odd casualties would apparently have to be written off to training, we went over to the mess of a French battery to have dinner. The battery was commanded by a captain named O'Neill, whose family had emigrated to France from Ireland in the seventeenth century. He looked like a conventional O'Neill, blue-eyed and florid and saddlenosed, but he spoke English to Norgaard with a heavy French accent. Captain O'Neill had a battery of three guns, one of the original four having been found useless, and he had as prime mover for the three guns one old motor truck that burned alcohol, so the battery moved in installments, one gun at a time. Their shooting, he said, was very good, but they never arrived at any place in time to shoot. We showed up at the mess before O'Neill and his officers, who were accustomed to dining late, whereas American Army chow is usually dished up early. A young native Jew who wore a blue beret and a European business suit invited us into his house for an *apéritif* while we waited. He had delicate Arab features and eyes as blue as O'Neill's, and he spoke excellent French.

The Jew's one-story house was large and square, with thick mud walls to insulate it from the summer sun. It was built around a small circular court that let in air and daylight. The house looked ageless, like most of the others in town; the Numidians had probably built in exactly the same fashion—but the rooms leading off the court were wired for electric light and filled with heavy gaudy contemporary furniture from some factory in Europe. The Jew's ancient bearded father, who spoke no French, and his small, comely brunette wife and gray-eyed daughter kissed our hands. He poured sweet wine for us and gave us olives and sliced turnips pickled in lemon. His name was Chemouni. When a servant who had been left on watch outside came in and told us that O'Neill had arrived, we left the Chemounis, feeling faintly embarrassed by their fervor. I remembered them a few weeks later, when I heard that we had abandoned Gafsa to the advancing Germans and Italians.

At Gafsa, Norgaard and I slept without blankets on the concrete floor of a former French barracks. A captain in a regiment of armored infantry had spread his bedding roll in a corner of the same building. His regiment was not in the fighting; he had been sent up by his colonel as some sort of observer. The captain was a Virginian; he and Norgaard got to talking about a book by Douglas Freeman, called *Lee's Lieutenants*, that they had both read. The captain, like us, had been out on the battlefield, observing. He seemed pretty tired. He said that he knew old Freeman well; the author was a friend of the captain's family, and as a boy the captain had accompanied the already adult writer on long rambles over the Virginia battlefields. The captain told us he had a house at Yellow Tavern, where Jeb Stuart had been killed. There were Yankee musketballs imbedded in the stair rails, he said. "People down in my part of the country talk about battles as if they were some kind of fine antique, like old lace," he said. "I always used to daydream about them as a kid. But, my God, if I'd known a battle was like this——"

It reminded me of Stendhal writing in his diary: "All my life I have longed to be loved by a woman who was melancholy, thin, and an actress. Now I have been, and I am not happy."

Next morning every soldier in town knew that the offensive had been called off. A part of the armor had already pulled out during the night, roaring north on the road to Feriana and Sbeitla. But the troops who had taken Sened Station held it firmly. We heard that there were captured enemy guns and tanks there, and since captured matériel, like prisoners in quantity, was still a novelty at that stage of the campaign, Norgaard wanted to drive out to have a look. As soon as we had got out on the naked road between Gafsa and Sened both of us, I think, were again sorry we had quit the shade of the palm trees and anti-aircraft guns. The hot metallic sky that it hurt your eyes to look into hung over the road and weighed down on your brain with its implicit Messerschmitts; every group of tanks or guns you met parked off the road seemed an invitation to air attack, and you hurried to get away from it. Then, until you reached the next collection of armor, you felt lonely. Signs along the road warned drivers to keep a 300-yard interval and look out for strafers. Sometimes as we passed an outfit we would see a man off by himself squatting on his hunkers and looking up into the sun, his right hand shielding his eyes, afraid to concentrate entirely on his most personal functions.

There was no temptation to drive across fields as we got close to Sened, for the fields had almost certainly been mined by the retreating enemy. Sened Station was sinister—a wooden *gare* full of wasps' nests, a *buffet*, in a separate building, which two of our booby-trap captain's noncoms were busily rigging with their trip wires, as happy as parents decorating a Christmas tree, three or four buildings, a water tower, and a church, all shattered by shell-fire. The booby-trap men at work meant that we in our turn were going to abandon the place almost immediately. You don't booby-trap where you are going to stay. We talked to the trappers, both Royal Engineers, one of whom was carrying so many one-pound cakes of dynamite under one arm that they seemed always on the point of wriggling loose. It looked like coarse white laundry soap. "Lord love you, sir, it wouldn't explode if it did fall, not without a deetonyter, it wouldn't," he said. They wore a fixed, slightly fatuous smile which seemed a mark of their curious vocation. "We 'ad some nasty ones to tike up before we put ours in," the man with the dynamite said. "We've rearrynged them so Jerry will 'ave a time with them, when 'e comes back. 'E won't be surprised, not 'alf."

There were three American medium tanks in a triangle where the main road went by the station, looking as if they had been punched clean through and then ripped with a giant can opener. Armor-piercing shot from German 88's had gone into them, bounced around inside like a buckshot in a rattle, and then gone out the other side, leaving something to be grilled

by the flames as the fuel burned. The broken bits had been extracted that morning and buried; a soldier's web belt, stiff with
blood, remained outside the hole through which they had
drawn the crew of one tank. A couple other soldiers were
looking at this tank and the belt. One of them seemed to feel
the same blood excitement as the fellow we had seen go wild
at the fallen German plane by the airfield. He was saying, over
and over again, "I'll never take no more prisoners, the bastards, I'll never take no more prisoners!" A couple of 88's had
laid doggo and caught the tanks with crossfire as they entered
the town.

The artillery was still firing in the hill ridge about five miles
away.

We asked a bearded, wild-looking soldier who was sitting in
a parked jeep what the guns were pounding at. "We got a lot
of Germans trapped up there on the mountain," he said.
"How many?" Norgaard wanted to know. "About a division, I
guess," the soldier said. "I don't see how you could hide a
whole division on that hill," Norgaard said calmly, and the soldier answered, "They got the mountain all hollowed out, and
that's where they're hiding." A couple of days later, when we
had got back to Second Corps headquarters, we asked the G-2
what had happened to the Germans trapped on the hill, and he
said, "Oh, you mean those last nine Heinies? They surrendered." We got back to town fast. There was an uncomfortable feeling about Sened, a tacit menace that made me feel
worse than actually being bombed or shot at. Norgaard said he
had exactly the same reaction.

The reason why none of our early operations in this area
could amount to anything was that we had no infantry available to occupy the tactically important hills and stay on them.
A war conducted almost exclusively with planes and armor is in
its essence a medieval conception. The armored knights ride
out, the armored knights ride back again, but they would
become helpless if they dismounted, so war is resolved into a
series of raids. And the strategic air-force scheme of destroying
the enemy's factories is strangely like the medieval one of
burning his crops.

I did not get back to Gafsa for six weeks after the affair at
Sened Station. In the meanwhile we had executed in rather

ragged fashion a previously determined withdrawal from Gafsa, Feriana, Sbeitla, and the old airfield on which Norgaard and I had lived during the private war. We had lost almost all of two battalions of armor and two battalions of infantry, and for the moment at least all our prestige with the French and Arabs. The Germans, pushing on our heels, had tried to get through to Tebessa, but they had failed. I had missed all this unpleasantness by going off on a frivolous trip in another direction, which has nothing to do with the story of the war, and I was rather glad I had missed it. I had had my bellyful of retreat in France.

When we prepared to go back to Gafsa it was in a substantial, intelligent manner, with plenty of infantry. It was more than just infantry, it was the First Division. I didn't have to file a daily dispatch, like the newspaper correspondents, so I decided to travel into action with the division and live with it. Major General Terry Allen, the division commander, whom I had met at Oran and again in Algiers, said it was all right with him as long as I kept out of his way, so I brought my bedroll down to division headquarters at Bou-Chebka, on the Algerian-Tunisian frontier, on the night of March 16. The division was moving to Gafsa that night, fifty miles across territory occupied neither by us nor the enemy, where we might bump into anything or nothing. It turned out to be nothing.

CHAPTER VIII

Gafsa Revisited

THE tents of Division Headquarters at Bou-Chebka stood on a hill covered with cedar trees. They were still standing when I arrived, but by the time I had had supper at the headquarters mess almost all the tents had been struck and loaded on trucks for the advance, and it was raining. The G-2, chief of the intelligence section of the divisional staff, a 34-year-old West Pointer with a high forehead and an almost prim manner, was worried during supper because he said a reconnaissance party had reported seven Italian tanks moving around on the very site which he had chosen in advance for the divisional command post, and whither the headquarters vehicles would be heading. The colonel commanding the tank-destroyer battalion had wanted to go down and get the Italian tanks while there was still light, the G-2 said, but the appearance of the tank destroyers down there might have given the show away. So General Allen had decided that the tanks should be left alone. "They'll probably go away anyway," he had said. The divisional chief of staff, who takes life seriously, let off a bit of steam by "eating out" the headquarters mess officer for serving C-rations at the last meal before the jump-off. "You know we have a limited quantity of C-rations, and it's the only form of ration the men can carry with them when they're fighting," he said. He did not say that we would have preferred a tastier meal ourselves because we did not know when we would get another. Brigadier General Teddy Roosevelt, the assistant division commander, was as restless and wriggly as a little boy whose family is taking him to a circus and who wants to get started early. Allen was in good enough humor but preoccupied. He had the responsibility.

I was to travel with a lieutenant named Ted Liese, who had once been in the display-advertising business in New York. He was now in charge of the liaison officers attached to division. A division is divided into three combat teams, each made up of a regiment of infantry and a battalion of artillery. Each team has a liaison officer, generally a young lieutenant, at headquarters. He travels back and forth between the CT command post and division, maintaining direct connection between the two. The division reconnaissance, or "recon" troop, the tank-destroyer battalion, the French, the British, and division artillery also maintain liaison men at division. Liese was a kind of housekeeper for the entire group. I permitted myself to be separated from my bedroll and typewriter, which were loaded on a truck that would follow us into Gafsa after the division had captured it, and retained only my musette bag with my mess kit in it and my rifle belt and canteen. I had no rifle, but I preferred a rifleman's belt to the usual pistol belt officers wear, because the cartridge pockets are ideal receptacles for ration chocolate and chewing gum.

The first echelons of the division started moving at dark, but we were not to get off until one o'clock in the morning. We waited in the rain. The jeeps assigned to us were being used on various errands in the early evening, but they got back in plenty of time. We climbed in and, after waiting around awhile, moved into the procession of vehicles of all kinds that now filled the Gafsa road. I had been over the main road a dozen times; it would have been of no interest to me even if I could have seen. The sensation of being in a great caravan of vehicles moving forward through the night is soporific; I had the comfortable certainty for once that if shooting started it would be well up ahead of me in the early echelons, and not from a plane diving out of the sky directly over my head. I slept. I woke up when we turned off the road somewhere south of Feriana. The tracks through the semidesert had been marked out with white tape, and there were M.P.'s everywhere to guide us. The parking spaces for the various units were marked with signs illuminated by blackout lights; I had the feeling I was being driven into the parking area around the Yankee Stadium on the night of a prize fight. We reached divisional-headquarters area at a little after four o'clock. I got out of Liese's jeep and then could not find it again in the dark, so I threw my mackinaw coat on the ground and flopped on it and went to sleep. The rain had stopped.

When I awoke it was daylight and the divisional artillery was making a loud, comforting noise. I find nothing objectionable in the sound of artillery fire when I know it is going out. I got up and looked around for my jeep, but somebody said Liese had already been sent on a mission to one of the combat teams. Our jeeps and trucks were widely dispersed on the plain, and as soon as the men awoke they picked themselves off the ground and started digging themselves foxholes. I would like to say someplace that foxhole is a widely misused term, being applied freely to deep, carefully constructed slit trenches as well as hasty burrows. The kind men make when they are out in the open in fear of imminent attack really are foxholes. But the German planes which had dived-bombed or strafed even single vehicles in the small-scale Sened thing six weeks earlier never put in an appearance to bother this divisional attack. It was a tipoff that the enemy had not awaited us in Gafsa but had already pulled out. We could not see the town from our first CP of the day, but at about eight o'clock we heard an explosion heavier than any of the artillery and saw a mighty column of gray-black smoke on the horizon toward Gafsa. The last elements of the enemy had blown a great munition dump.

I strolled over by Allen's tent and heard him successively telephoning his combat-team commanders, asking, "How you doing, kid?" The infantry were closing in on Gafsa through the hills. "It's all going like a maneuver," Allen would say at the conclusion of each call, "too good to be true."

Sergeant Jimmy Mimms, the general's driver, and an M.P. named Cawthorne who acts as bodyguard, were frying Deerfoot sausage and making coffee by the gasoline-burner process, and every time Mimms got an especially fine color on a sausage he would send it over to the general, to tempt him to eat. "He's just got to eat, Cawthorne," he would say. Allen paid no attention to the first six or seven burnt offerings. Finally he accepted one and sent Cawthorne back for more. "The battle must be going all right," Mimms said. "I guess we're in now."

We were. That afternoon the First Division moved into Gafsa, which had been deserted by the Arabs during the bombardment. The Arabs came back very slowly, as if they had bad consciences. Rain had begun again at noon. A waddy between division headquarters and the town appeared so swollen that headquarters decided to stay where it was for the night.

General Allen's aide, Major Kenneth Downs, had been a war correspondent for International News Service when I first knew him, and he now invited me to share his jeep and tag around with him for the rest of the offensive. Downs and his jeep driver and I charred some Spam and heated some soluble coffee in the shelter of a tarpaulin held against the side of a hill, and after the meal Downs and I pitched a pup tent. The driver decided to sleep under the tarp in what he thought was a sheltered nook in the hillside. We crawled under cover at seven o'clock. I never slept sooner or harder in my life. It must have been about two in the morning when Downs banged me on the head to awaken me, which he did. I said, "What's the matter?" and he said, "The tent has blown away." By that time my blankets were soaked through, but I was not concerned about that, because I had borrowed them anyway. I sat up in the jeep for the rest of the night. The driver, who had been rained out of his burrow, was in the jeep already. Downs, I think, managed to scrouge into the general's tent. Next morning we moved into Gafsa.

The French inhabitants of Gafsa had been evacuated in American Army trucks before the arrival of the Germans, so there were more good billets available in town than when I had been there before. Division headquarters moved into the Gendarmerie Nationale, a fine modern place. Gafsa was the capital of an administrative area with a population of about 150,000 natives, so the government buildings were out of proportion to the size of the town alone. It was the first town I had ever been in that our side had recaptured from the enemy, and was in its small way a symbol that this particular breed of bug could be dislodged like any other. But the science of booby-trapping has taken a good deal of fun out of following hot on an enemy's heels. Our engineers had been through the lower floors of the gendarmerie already, looking for booby traps, but they hadn't had time to do the living quarters in which Downs and I were billeted. It caused me acute distress to turn a doorknob or draw a shutter. In the end the division engineers decided that the Italians who had last been in Gafsa had lacked the time or possibly the skill to put any booby traps in the buildings. They had mined the roads and shoulders of the roads leading into and out of town, however, and protected most of their heavy mines with things the engineers called "bouncing babies." The babies were metal containers that were blown into the air by a charge of black powder when a soldier stepped on a hidden trip wire. They were packed with high explosives and steel ball bearings, and were timed to explode when about chest high in the air. The steel balls did the killing. Knowledge that there are bouncing babies about is disconcerting when you are in a jeep during a road strafing. You hesitate to dive for a roadside ditch.

Soon after we pulled into Gafsa I went for a walk about town to see how it had been affected by the occupation. The old Moorish citadel had been partially wrecked by an explosion. The engineers had used it as a storehouse for explosives and had blown it to save the stuff from the enemy. The destructions had not been well carried out; it had been planned, for example, to run a number of locomotives north over the railroad and then blow a railroad bridge north of town so that the use of the road would be barred to the enemy, but somebody had blown the bridge first, so that the locomotives were trapped in Gafsa. Then, since no preparations had been made to destroy them, they were abandoned and fell into German hands.

I met an Arab in the market place in front of the old citadel who said he had been some sort of a government employee, a police-court interpreter, I think, and had remained through the occupation. He was frightened, because the French notion of justice for Arabs is summary. The houses of all the Frenchmen had been thoroughly pillaged. So he was eager to talk and to convince me that his heart at least had been with the Allies. Most of the Moslems of Gafsa had fled to join their kin in the hills during the occupation, he said, because they wanted to escape the exactions of the Italians and because a great force of American bombers had come over shortly after the evacuation and flattened a lot of Arab houses. The bombers had killed about four hundred Arabs who were in a bread-line on the market place, he said. "The people were much impressed, and those who had gone about talking of the victory of the Germans as certain were discredited," he said, indicating that there are several kinds of propaganda. "They realized that the Americans must have mistaken them for Italian troops.

"When the Germans and Italians first came here they encouraged the people to rob the houses of the French and Jews," he said, "and some of the more ignorant elements of the population complied with their wishes. The Germans did not stay here long, but went on, leaving an Italian garrison. The Italians were revoltingly poor. They pulled up even the young onions out of the gardens in the oasis and ate them as if famished. They broke into Arab houses and stole carpets off the floors and sold them to other Arabs living in the surrounding country, to get a few *sous*. They are a people without shame." The German words, *Araber Laden*, or *Araber Geschäft* had been scrawled in chalk on the doors of a great number of shops, and the Arab said this had been done immediately after the evacuation, according to instructions from the Axis

Arabic-language radio in Tunis, to protect Arab-owned busi-
nesses from pillage by invading troops. "I never listened to
that radio, of course," he said, "but so I have heard it related."
I had never imagined that so many Arabs knew even a couple
of German words, but he said that a number in Gafsa had been
prisoners of war in Germany in 1914–18 and had learned the
language there. It was easy to guess that the place had been
full of Arab Axis agents during our previous stay there; some
of them were probably still wearing the G.I. shirts compassionate doughboys had given them.

I walked out to the house of the Chemounis, near the road-
block where the Feriana road entered town. It was still
standing, but when I looked inside it seemed that nobody had
lived there for years. There was nothing in the place but a few
pages of Hebrew printing on the hard earth floor and a chandelier that swung crazily from the roof of the room where
Norgaard and I had drunk wine. I wondered whether the family had escaped from Gafsa or been destroyed. I asked a lad I
met on the road near by what had happened to them, and he
said that they were in town, living in the old Jewish quarter, a
couple of fetid alleys where only the poorest and least Europeanized Jews had lived in January. The boy was Jewish himself. He guided me to the house where the Chemounis lived.
A scarecrow of a man, wearing a beret and a long blue robe,
precipitated himself upon me, blubbering and trying to kiss
me. "They have stolen even my trousers," Chemouni sobbed,
pressing his face against the front of my field jacket. Other
Jews, those who had recently been outwardly European now
like my friend indistinguishable from the most Oriental,
flocked about with their stories of the occupation. The Germans had come to the houses of the leading Jews on the first
night, but had taken worth-while things like money, jewelry,
and stocks of raw wool, leaving furniture and minor personal
possessions alone. Then they had gone on, but not before
inviting the Arabs to help themselves to the leavings. There
had been a wild competition between Arabs and Italians to gut
the Jewish houses. The Italian commandant of the place had
ordered all the Jews into a few houses in the old quarter and
had put them on a ration even smaller than that accorded to
the Arabs, which had been minuscular. No Jews had been

killed, although two young men had almost gone before a firing squad because an Arab accused them of having betrayed an Axis parachutist to the Americans in December. The two young men had escaped to the desert. The caïd of Gafsa, the chief Moslem official, had remained on the job through the occupation, and so had the spahis, the French-trained native police. The caïd had fled with the Italians, fearing the returning French would shoot him, but the spahis were still on the job, again under the orders of their original French superiors. They were recovering stolen Jewish and French property from Arab houses, but what they found was ruined or of slight original value.

Israel had been spoiled again, but naked as they had been the members of the community had apparently hoarded a few hens and roosters against the day of their deliverance. The *shochet*, the ritual slaughterer with his matted beard, was killing these chickens for the family feasts of celebration, holding the blade in his lips between strokes while he smoothed back the neck feathers of the chicken he was going to slit next. A couple of big Jewish soldiers from the Bronx, with tremendous hands that could palm a basketball and great feet that could kick a football sixty yards, had their arms comfortingly on the shoulders of ancient, tiny matriarchs with whom they had no means of communication except signs, because the Tunisian Jews speak no Yiddish. The Bronx Jews and the Tunisian Jews looked as different as a Percheron and an Eohippus.

"The Arabs are very bad," Chemouni said to me. "They have always been bad." "How long has your family lived in Gafsa?" I asked him. "I think for two thousand years," he said. His little girl, who spoke French as easily as any child in the Parc Monceau, looked at me with large frightened gray eyes. I asked him if she would go to live in France after we had won the war. He said no, of course not, she would marry and live in Gafsa. "Not a single bomb touched a Jewish house," he said. "God protects his people."

The *controleur civile*, the chief French administrative official for the district, had returned, and I went to talk to him. The Axis radio, he agreed, had had an important effect on the *indigènes*. Also the attitude of the Bey of Tunis had had an important effect. The Bey, Moncef Pasha, of the old Beylical

Hoceinite family, had allowed the Germans to put him at the head of an "autonomous" Tunisian government in Tunis. It would be necessary to install another bey as soon as the Allies got to Tunis. Since the beylicate was not hereditary from father to son as long as it remained within the Hoceinite clan, that would be easy. Moncef Pasha had dozens of cousins. The *controleur* was much concerned with the problem of bringing the wives of himself and the half-dozen other leading French officials back to Gafsa. "There are so many soldiers in the streets," he said, "I am afraid it will be very embarrassing for them." We moved out a couple of days later, to spare their blushes.

CHAPTER IX

Under the Acacias

GENERAL ALLEN had been pleased with the smoothness of the Gafsa operation, but he was uneasy, too, because he could not believe that the enemy would relinquish the region without a fight. The First Division had been ordered to capture and hold Gafsa as a railhead for the supplies of the British Eighth Army when the Eighth made its junction with the forces in our part of Tunisia, but you cannot hold a town unless you hold its approaches. There are two or three ranges of hills around the oasis of El Guettar, which is twelve miles southeast of Gafsa, and Allen thought of them as a dentist thinks about the possibly infected roots of a tooth. So the division slipped out of Gafsa with the same noiseless ease it had achieved in the other night move and attacked two of the ridges south of El Guettar.

Downs and his jeep moved with the division headquarters, and naturally so did I. This night ride was a short one. The headquarters vehicles turned off the main road at a point where hundreds of palm trees were silhouetted against the night sky, the oasis proper. I had recovered my bedroll after the first advance and had it in the jeep with me. After the driver had stowed the jeep under a tree, Downs and I dragged out our rolls and spread them near the side of the road, on the highest ground we could find. The oasis was on low ground, and we knew there must be a lot of mosquitoes in the grass. The Numidian frogs, which make a noise like parrots, sang from the shallow irrigation ditches that intersected the fertile land. When I awoke, to the accustomed thunder of the guns, I found myself in a Josef Urban stage set, appropriate to the last act of a musical comedy but not a war play. There were hundreds of acacia and almond trees in blossom under the palms. The white acacia blossoms and the pink ones of almond dripped down on us all through the battle.

A Ranger battalion attached to the division had attacked at four in the morning at one spot, and at six the infantry attacked at another. They found the enemy forces in strong positions, but these troops were sleepy, half-starved Italians who surrendered in droves and wept for joy when presented with C-rations, to our men the most despised form of army nourishment. First Lieutenant, now Captain, Ralph Ingersoll, the former editor of *PM*, was with the Ranger battalion which executed the first attack, and made of it the central episode of his book, *The Battle Is the Pay-off.* Our men made more than a thousand prisoners, but there was not one German in the lot.

Allen, who at first meeting appears to be a slapdash, reckless sort of fellow, perhaps because of his old-line cavalry personality and mannerisms, is in fact a worrier. He felt that things had been going too well to be on the level. He ordered an advance on Djebel Berda, the only ridge left unexplored, for the next morning.

Brigadier General Teddy Roosevelt, the assistant division commander, likes to circulate among the units in action during a battle. He invited me to make the circuit with him in his jeep on the day when the Djebel Berda attack was scheduled. Just as we were leaving the oasis a couple of the division engineer officers came up with Ingersoll in tow. One of them said, "General Roosevelt, I would like to have you meet Lieutenant Ingersoll." Roosevelt, who hadn't been thinking of the *PM* Ingersoll, said, "How do you do, Lieutenant?" and we walked away. I said, "That was Ralph Ingersoll, the *PM* editor." The general likes to descant on the thesis that all the prominent interventionists stayed safe at home while he, a hard-shell America Firster, went to war. He stopped sharply. "Hell," he said, "I always thought that man was a sonofabitch."

I had got to know Roosevelt pretty well at Sainte Barbe, near Oran, where the First Division headquarters had been when I first arrived in Africa. As assistant division commander he spends much of his time between battles visiting battalions and reporting back to division on their needs. His staccato, gamecock walk serves to identify him as long as he is within field-glass range. He always carries a short cane, head down, in the pocket of his field jacket, and he always makes a point of speaking to the mess sergeant of each outfit he visits. He asks the sergeant, for instance, if the company has enough baking powder. The sergeant invariably says no, and Roosevelt leaves him with the impression that if he, Roosevelt, were Secretary of War, there would be enough baking powder. Simple as this device is, it makes men feel that the divisional command is on their side. Roosevelt has a special way of saluting across his face, a little like Dave Chasen's celebrated gesture, and when he is on one of his tours of the division he goes out of his way to get saluted by as many soldiers as possible. He says that saluting is a criterion of division morale. He was in the First Division in the last war, in which he earned several wound stripes and decorations. After holding a reserve commission in the tranquil years between wars, he came back to the Army and his division in April 1941. He speaks of himself as an old First Division soldier, and when he visits regimental headquarters in back areas, bands play "Old Soldiers Never Die, They Simply Fade Away" for him. He has a memory for the first names of the veteran First Division noncoms he encounters. He is at his best, however, in battle; his gamecock strut and his slightly corny humor take on a new and attractive quality when they are being exhibited under fire. The men consider Roosevelt an intellectual because he carries a considerable stock of books in his blanket roll. His library includes anthologies of verse, which he memorizes in vast chunks; works on anthropology, a subject which he discusses on any provocation; and a large number of detective stories, with which he reads himself to sleep.

Roosevelt's aide, Lieutenant Mike Stevenson, drove the jeep

for us on the Djebel Berda morning. The German ground troops had not appeared on the previous day, but their planes had put in some energetic dive-bombings of American gun positions in the late afternoon. The Stukas had destroyed two field pieces and killed their crews, by far the heaviest loss of the day. The skies were full of German planes on the Djebel Berda morning, too, and the general, the lieutenant, and I spent considerable time clambering out of and into our jeep. I wedged myself so hard into the interstice between a parked truck and a bank of earth on one occasion, I remember, that when the planes disappeared I could hardly get out. I seemed to have contracted with fear, and when I expanded to normal size again I was stuck. I went in so hard that both pockets of my field jacket were completely filled with pebbles, as if I had been a human steam shovel. The general didn't seem to mind. The command post of the Eighteenth Infantry Combat Team was at the foot of a high hill which had an observation post on top of it. When we had got that far Roosevelt, who changes his mind as quickly as another man, decided that he wanted to stay at the observation post and watch the attack, which the Eighteenth was going to make. This was all right with me, and we all climbed up to the O.P.

This action took place on two ridges of hills which form an amphitheater that is open at both ends. The Americans, who already held the ridge which forms the northern side of the amphitheater, moved infantry by truck to both ends of the arc opposite them. The infantry detachments at the two ends then worked inward toward each other, for the enemy was supposed to be, if he was in the neighborhood at all, on the southern ridge at the center of the arc, at the point where the amphitheater was widest. If the battlefield had been a football stadium, the enemy would have had a seat on the fifty-yard line. The O.P. was in a correspondingly advantageous position on the American ridge. American artillery fired over our heads, blasting a spot on the hills across the way, where the enemy was supposed to be. G-2, the intelligence section of the divisional staff, had reported that two thousand Italian troops with three batteries of artillery were on Djebel Berda, but some skeptics still insisted that they must have pulled out. A force that size could not hope to hold out against a division, they argued, so it had probably vanished toward the coast.

Our infantry detachments, using ground cover and visible from the observation post only occasionally, and then just for a moment or two at a time, carried out their slow advance for four hours without a sign of enemy activity, as our guns continued to pound his ridge. The situation was beginning to get slightly embarrassing for General Allen, who had ordered the attack, and adherents of the no-enemy theory were starting to speak up when puffs of white smoke broke out on the opposite ridge at points in front of the advancing infantry. The enemy was firing on our men with mortars, and our infantry was temporarily pinned down. Our artillery searched for the mortar positions and evidently found them, for the mortar fire ceased and our infantry moved on again. Allen, in the O.P. with us, looked pleased with himself, like a dentist whose probe has at last hit the sensitive spot. He had found trouble.

By nightfall our infantry reported that the enemy apparently was caught in our pincers, where he could be finished off by a night or dawn attack. The Americans were now on both ridges, and our artillery was comfortably tucked in behind our infantry—like a fighter's chin behind his left shoulder.

We drove back to the oasis well pleased with the day's results, but I still sensed a lack, and I think in their hearts the others did too. American troops had not yet beaten German troops in battle in this war. The forces in Tunisia had won a few skirmishes against Germans and had a few hard knocks, but hadn't won an action on a large scale. The First Division had been broken into its component units and fed into the fighting a battalion at a time during the winter, and the individual battalions had fought well. As a division it had a success against the French at Oran, and now it had a victory over Italians. It is safe to say that all its officers felt it could hold its own against a German division, but it had never had a chance to try. Until American troops had beaten German troops in a fair fight, there would always remain a doubt in the back of the minds of the people at home. It was all right to demonstrate mathematically that we had enough men and enough factory capacity to make victory sure, but the Germans had done such a job of self-advertising that even Americans wondered whether they weren't a bit superhuman. The First Division was scheduled to furnish the answer, and other American divisions as they gained experience would amplify it.

At five o'clock next morning, as I slept in the oasis, a peremptory voice broke into my dream, which I have now forgotten. Half awake, I realized that it was no dream voice; then as I became fully conscious I knew that it came from inside a half-track equipped with radio which was parked about ten yards from me. This half-track belonged to the liaison officer of a tank-destroyer battalion. The battalion communicated with division headquarters through the radio set in the half-track. And now I could hear the voice on the radio saying, "Baker reports German tanks threatening to over-run —— Field Artillery." Lieutenant Colonel Herschel Baker was the commander of the tank destroyers. A moment later I heard, "Baker recommends infantry on lower slope ground fall back toward soft ground and resist tanks with rocket guns." I rubbed my eyes, spat, and walked over to G-2 to find out what was happening. It was the test match.

When I could find a G-2 man who had time to talk to me I learned that some tanks of the Tenth German Panzer Division had appeared on the plain between the two ridges that morning. They had entered the stadium through gullies in a part of the ridge still held by the Italian infantry, and they had begun the day by trying to climb a slope and overrun the batteries of American artillery which had been posted below our ridge. Our infantry and gunners stood firm, and our artillery had shot through several of the tanks. The T.D. outfit, coming to the rescue of the artillery, engaged the tanks, which moved off and started to make their way down the center of the field toward the western exit, which meant, incidentally, toward us at headquarters. The only combat troops in the oasis were the men of the headquarters defense platoon, which had four 37-millimeter cannon. The universal belief in the division was that these cannon would puncture nothing more heavily armored than a Kiddiekar.

Apparently the German intention was to come around the rear of the American position in the north stands and cut the main road back to Gafsa, then retake that town and thus leave the First Division stranded. If the maneuver succeeded, the entire disposition of Allied forces designated to contain the German Army in Tunisia while the Eighth Army smashed its way through the Mareth Line would be upset. We would have to retreat from them while they retreated before the Eighth Army. The German commander also probably hoped to cause panic among the cut-off American troops and get a lot of equipment and prisoners. "They think they can push us over and laugh at us because Americans can't stand up to German armor," my G-2 man said in a hard tone. Since the tanks were coming in our direction I decided that the oasis was as good an observation post as any.

The oasis was cut up into the small holdings of individual Arabs by crumbling mud walls and irrigation ditches. The Arabs had used the earth from the ditches to make the walls. There were red earthen water jugs nested in the tops of some of the palm trees—I suppose the owners, who climb like gibbons, carry water from the ditches up to the tops of the trees in dry spells and sprinkle the choice dates. In some of the others there were whitened bovine skulls, to frighten the birds from the ripe fruit. Under the palms were the acacias and almonds with their blossoms, and at ground level there were the thin green blades of spring onions and the flowers of black-eyed peas. The sun filtered through the blossoms; the drone of bees was so strong that it was hard to distinguish at once an approaching airplane motor.

A young liaison officer named Troup Howard Matthews, who was on call to carry messages to the First Armored Division, but who had nothing to do for hours at a stretch, suggested that we move to the outer edge of the oasis and observe. We strolled over there and sat on a mud wall. Matthews was twenty-five years old and one of the few mildly intellectual young officers I had met, a low-voiced New Orleans boy. He had worked for the National Broadcasting Company in New York before entering the Army, and as we sat on the wall waiting we tried to enumerate the bars in Rockefeller Center. We had had about one drink apiece in the previous month. Italian troops had occupied the oasis before us, and I tried to piece together a couple of torn Italian letters to see what their folks at home had been writing to them about.

There was a low plain between the oasis and the ridges we had watched on the previous day, and I hoped our engineers had put out some mines beyond the oasis' edge. There was a small salt lake in the middle of the plain, but the tanks would not have to cross it to get to us.

Matthews looked through his binoculars and saw a couple of small dots creeping hesitantly toward us like lice across a panhandler's shirt front. He said they were tanks. They came nearer, very indirectly and with frequent halts, until they got as big as bedbugs on a wall, and then geysers of black smoke and dirt began to appear near them. There were about a dozen dots now. Matthews said he could see twenty. They would stop sometimes when the geysers spouted up, and then I would think they had been hit, but soon they would come crawling on again. The geysers were shell-bursts; our howitzers, firing from their position back of the ridge we held, were shooting at them. The foremost tanks got within two miles of us, which is close for motorized battle, but I do not think they knew that the palm trees concealed the C.P., or they would have made a more determined effort to overrun it. Then the howitzers got to them. Four tanks were shot through. Their clumsy black bodies, belching dark smoke, remained on the field right below the command post now. You could see them with the naked eye, and they had outgrown the bedbug stage. They were about as big as caramels. The American 105 and 155 howitzers are not ideal anti-tank weapons, because of their high arching trajectory. But they had served. Matthews and I went to breakfast.

All day long, that day of the stadium battle, the German tanks toddled about the field and in the first rows of our hill grandstand while the artillery potted at them and the tank destroyers, waddling into action like bull pups, drew their fire and returned it. Finally, all eighteen tank destroyers were knocked out, but only after they had wrecked thirty-one tanks. By the time this tank-destroyer battalion was finished, another had arrived from the rear, so our position was not weakened. Old Baker, the tank-destroyer commander, came rolling into the oasis late in the afternoon to say good-by to General Allen. He said he had had surprisingly few casualties and was loading his men into trucks and taking them back to Feriana to get some new guns. Baker, with white hair, apple-red cheeks, and bright blue eyes, looks like Father Christmas minus the whiskers and is always full of bounce. He had been riding around among the tanks in a jeep and had somehow captured a German who had a lot of pornographic postcards in his wallet. Baker was as happy as a lark.

During all the fighting our infantry held firmly to the hills. Without it, the artillery, which was in this battle the striking arm, would have been overrun. G-2 had somehow picked up the information that the Germans would make their big attack at 4:45 in the afternoon. I went out to the edge of the oasis with some other idlers to wait for it, repeating to myself idly,

> "*The Spartans on the sea-wet rock, sat down and combed their hair,*"

and understanding for the first time that they had sat down not because they were heroes but because there was nothing else to do. Promptly at 4:45 twenty Stukas flew over the oasis, paying us no heed, and dived on our gun positions. The only American plane in sight all day had been a Piper Cub used by the artillery spotters. The echo of the Stukas' bombs and of the whistling devices between their front wheels had hardly died down before the enemy began his attack, but it was out of our sight. We could hear the guns and see the German shell-bursts on our ridge. This time, as I learned a little later, the Germans sent forward some armored infantry, known as Panzer Grenadiers, whose mission apparently was to climb through our infantry lines and reach our guns. German tanks followed the grenadiers. The guns killed all but nine of the two hundred grenadiers of the leading platoons, and the rest of the attacking party stopped and went away. The American guns fired time shells, and the divisional artillery commander, a calm, professorial kind of brigadier general, told me afterward that he was highly pleased with their effect. As it turned out, that particular battle ended at that particular instant, because the Tenth Panzer Division never resumed the attack. It had lost forty or fifty tanks, most of which remained in our hands and were blown up by our engineers so that they would be beyond repair. What was more important, it was licked.

If one American division could beat one German division, I

thought then, a hundred American divisions could beat a hundred German divisions. Only the time was already past when Germany had a hundred divisions to spare from the Russian front, plus God knows how many more to fight the British, plus garrison troops for all the occupied countries. I knew deep down inside me after that that the road back to Paris was clear.

MOLLIE
AND OTHER WAR PIECES

To many men who would now be in their forties

CONTENTS

FOREWORD

All the pieces in this book are about things that happened between the beginning of 1943 and the end of 1944; most were written from the field, but some in 1945, when I was just home. The latest in date is the pseudo-short-story *Day of Victory*, which was written in the summer of 1946, in celebration of the second anniversary of the Liberation of Paris, of part of which it is an unofficial report. A pseudo-short-story is one in which fact is turned to fiction by changing the names of the actors and perhaps juggling a bit with details. I have no compunctions in including two such stories with the rest of the reports.

I covered bits of the war in 1939–40 in France, and in 1941 in Britain and on the high seas, but those seem in retrospect not merely previous but different wars, with a different feeling, and so I have not included them. Collectively, the wars were the central theme of my life from October, 1939, until the end of 1944, and I sometimes feel a deplorable nostalgia for them—as my friend the Count Rzewski once said about something else: "So disgusting, so deplorable, so human." The times were full of certainties: we could be certain we were right—and we were—and that certainty made us certain that anything we did was right, too. I have seldom been sure I was right since. It had attractive uncertainties, too; you never had to think about the future, because you didn't know if you would have one. Yet the risk was so disseminated over time that you seldom felt that *this* was the moment when the future might end.

I know that it is socially acceptable to write about war as an unmitigated horror, but subjectively at least, it was not true, and you can feel its pull on men's memories at the maudlin reunions of war divisions. They mourn for their dead, but also for war.

A. J. LIEBLING

I
Confusion Is Normal In Combat

First Servant—Let me have war, say I, it exceeds peace as far as day does night. . . . . .

Second Servant—'Tis so, and as wars in some sort may be said to be a ravisher, so it cannot be denied but peace is a great maker of cuckolds.

First Servant—Ay, and it makes men hate one another.

Third Servant—Reason, because they then less need one another.

—*Coriolanus*

(The Third Servant then says: "The war's for my money," but I feared some reader might mistake the appearance of this line unsoftened by parentheses for an indorsement of his declaration.)

For Hal Boyle

Quest for Mollie

MOLLIE is a part of the history of La Piste Forestière, and La Piste Forestière is perhaps the most important part of the history of Mollie. La Piste Forestière, or the Foresters' Track, is a dirt road that connects Cap Serrat, on the northern coast of western Tunisia, with Sedjenane, a town twenty miles inland. The country it runs through is covered with small hills, and almost all the hills are coated with a ten-foot growth of tall bushes and short trees, so close together that once you leave the road you can't see fifty feet in front of you. From the top of any hill you can see the top of another hill, but, because of the growth, you can't tell whether there are men on it. This made the country hard to fight in. The hillsides that have no trees are bright with wild flowers in the spring, and when some other war correspondents and I travelled back and forth along the Foresters' Track in jeeps, we sometimes used to measure our slow progress by reference to the almost geometrical patterns of color on such slopes. There was, for example, the hill with a rough yellow triangle of buttercups against a reddish-purple background of other blooms; it indicated that you were five miles from the road's junction with the main highway at

Sedjenane. With luck you might reach the junction in two hours, but this was extremely unlikely, for the road was just wide enough for one truck—not for a truck and a jeep or even for a truck and a motorcycle. Only a man on foot or on a horse could progress along the margin of the road when there was a vehicle on it, and the horse would often have to scramble by with two feet off the road, like the sidehill bear of eastern Tennessee. When a jeep met a convoy, it sometimes had to back up for hundreds of yards to where there was room to get off the road and wait. Then, when all the heavy vehicles had passed, the jeep would resume its journey, perhaps to meet another convoy before it had recovered the lost yardage. Even when you got in behind trucks going your way, they were packed so closely together that they advanced at a crawl, so you did too. Bits of the war were threaded along the Foresters' Track like beads on a string, and the opportunity to become familiar with them was forced upon you. Mollie, for me, was the gaudiest bead.

The reason the Foresters' Track is such a miserable excuse for a road is that in normal times there is little need for it. There is a lighthouse at Cap Serrat and a forest warden's house about halfway between that and Sedjenane. The few Berbers in the district, who live in brush shelters in the bush, have no vehicles or need of a road. But in late April and early May of 1943, La Piste Forestière was an important military thoroughfare. The Allied armies, here facing east, lay in a great arc with their right flank at Sousse, on the Gulf of Tunis, and this little road was the only supply line for twenty miles of front; that is, the extreme left flank of the Allied line. The actual front line ran parallel to the road and only a few hundred yards east of it during the first days of the offensive that was to end the Allies' North African campaign, but because of the hills and the brush, people on the road couldn't see the fighting. However, American artillery placed just west of the road—it would have been an engineering feat to get it any considerable distance into the brush—constantly fired over our heads as our jeeps piddled along. The gunners hoped that some of their shells were falling on the Germans and Italians who were trying to halt our infantry's advance with fire from hidden mortars and machine guns. The Luftwaffe in Africa had predeceased the enemy ground forces; the budget of planes allotted it for the African adventure was exhausted, I suppose, and the German High Command sent no more. This was lucky for us, because one good strafing, at any hour, would have jammed the road with burned-out vehicles and Allied dead. By repeating the strafing once a day, the Germans could have kept the road permanently out of commission. The potential danger from the air did not worry us for long, however. You soon become accustomed to immunity, even when you cannot understand the reason for it.

Trucks left ammunition along the side of the road to be carried up to the fighting lines on the backs of requisitioned mules and horses and little Arab donkeys, a strangely assorted herd conducted by an equally scratch lot of soldiers. The Washington army had decided years before that the war was now one-hundred-per-cent mechanized, so the field army, quite a different organization, had to improvise its animal transport as it went along. The wounded were carried down to the road by stretcher bearers. Ambulances, moving with the same disheartening slowness as everything else, picked up the casualties and took them out to a clearing station near the yellow-triangle hill I have mentioned, where some of the viable ones were patched up for the further slow haul out. Cruder surgical units, strung out along the road, took such cases as they were equipped to handle. These units were always right by the side of the road, since in that claustrophobe's nightmare of a country there was no other place for them to be. The advanced units were French and had women nurses with them. A French doctor I knew used to say that it helped the men bear pain if nurses were looking at them. "Since we have so little anesthesia," he said, "we rely upon vanity." Sometimes I would sit in my jeep and watch that doctor work. He had broken down a few saplings and bushes by the side of the road to clear a space for his ambulance, and next to the ambulance he had set up a camp stool and a folding table with some instruments on it. Once a traffic jam stopped my jeep near his post when he had a tanned giant perched on the camp stool, a second lieutenant in the Corps Franc d'Afrique. The man's breasts were hanging off his chest in a kind of bloody ruff. "A bit of courage now, my son, will save you a great deal of trouble later on," the doctor said as he prepared to do something or other. I assumed, perhaps pessimistically, that he was going to hack off the bits of flesh as you would trim the ragged edges of an ill-cut page. "Go easy, Doctor," the young man said. "I'm such a softie." Then the traffic started to move, so I don't know what the doctor did to him.

The Corps Franc d'Afrique was a unit that had a short and glorious history. Soon after the Allied landings in North Africa, in October, 1942, the Corps Franc organized itself, literally, out of the elements the Darlanists in control of the North African government distrusted too much to incorporate into the regular French Army—Jews, anti-Nazis from concentration camps, de Gaullists, and other Allied sympathizers. A French general named Joseph de Goislard de Montsabert, who had helped plan the landings, had been thrown out by his collaborationist superiors, who, even after Darlan's agreement to play ball with the forces of democracy, had remained his superiors. De Montsabert, because he had a red face and snowy hair, was known to his troops as Strawberry in Cream. There had been, among the French in North Africa, a number of other professional officers and many reservists who, like the General, were apparently left out of the war because they were suspected of favoring de Gaulle or merely of being hostile to Germany. The Darlan regime had refused to mobilize the Jews because it clung to the Vichy thesis that they were not full citizens, and it did not want them to establish a claim to future consideration, and it was holding thousands of Spanish and German refugees and French Communists in concentration camps.

De Montsabert and a few of his officer friends, talking on the street in Algiers one rainy November day of that year, decided to start a "Free Corps" of men who wanted to fight but whom the government would not allow to. They took over a room in a schoolhouse on the Rue Mogador as headquarters and advertised in the *Echo d'Alger* for volunteers. The ad appeared once and then the Darlanist censorship, which was still operating under the Americans, like every other element of Vichy rule, suppressed it. But scores of volunteers had already appeared at the schoolhouse and de Montsabert sent them out with pieces of schoolroom chalk to write "Join the Corps Franc" on walls all over the city. Hundreds of new volunteers came in. General Giraud, who had arrived in Africa to command all the French but had subsequently accepted a rôle secondary to Darlan's, heard of the movement and interceded for it. Giraud, whatever his limitations, considered it natural that anybody in his right mind should want to fight the Germans. Darlan and his Fascist friends began to think of the Corps Franc as a means of getting undesirables out of the way, so the government recognized it but at the same time refused it any equipment. The Corps began life with a miscellany of matériel begged from the British and Americans. Its men wore British battle dress and French insignia of rank, lived on American C rations, and carried any sort of weapons they could lay their hands on. The most characteristic feature of their appearance was a long beard, but even this was not universal, because some of the soldiers were too young to grow one. After the Corps Franc's arrival in Tunisia, it added to its heterogeneous equipment a great deal more stuff it captured from the enemy. The Corps went into the line in February of 1943, in the zone north of Sedjenane, and it remained there into the spring.

Late April in Tunisia is like late June in New York, and heat and dust were great nuisances to our men when they were attacking. In February and March, however, coastal Tunisia is drenched with a cold and constant downpour. The Foresters' Track was two feet deep in water when the Corps Franc began to fight along it. There were two battalions to start with—about twelve hundred men—to cover a sector twenty miles long. A third and fourth battalion had been added by the time the Americans began their offensive. The Corps, in the beginning, had only two ambulances, converted farm trucks owned by a Belgian colonist in Morocco. The Belgian and his son had driven the trucks across North Africa to join the Corps. But the trucks were unable to negotiate the flooded Track, so the men of the Corps carried their wounded out to Sedjenane on their shoulders. I once asked my doctor friend why they had not used mules. "The mules rolled over in the water and crushed the wounded men," he said. "We know. We tried it with wounded prisoners."

Now that the great attack was on, there were other troops along the Track with the Corps—the Sixtieth Infantry of the American Ninth Division, part of the American Ninth

Division's artillery, an American tank-destroyer battalion, some Moroccan units, and some American motor-truck and medical outfits. The medics and the artillery made the French feel pampered and their morale got very high. One hot morning, I passed a lean, elderly soldier of the Corps Franc who was burying two of his comrades. He looked about sixty—there was no age limit in the Corps—and had a long, drooping mustache of a faded biscuit color. He had finished one grave and was sitting down to rest and cool off before beginning the other. The two dead men lay with their feet to the road. Blueflies had settled on their faces. I told my jeep driver to stop and asked the gravedigger what men these were. "One stiff was an Arab from Biskra," the old soldier said, "and the other a Spaniard, a nihilist from Oran." I asked him how his work was going. He wiped the sweat from his forehead and said happily, "Monsieur, like on roller skates."

A quarter of the men in the Corps Franc were Jews. A Jewish lieutenant named Rosenberg was its posthumous hero by the time I arrived in the Foresters' Track country. He had commanded a detachment of twenty men covering the retreat of his battalion during a German counterattack in early March. This was a sequel to the counterattack against the Americans at Kasserine Pass in late February, and both assaults were prototypes, on a small scale, of the counter-offensive the Germans were to launch in Belgium at the end of 1944—the last flurry of the hooked and dying fish. Rosenberg, holding one of the innumerable little hills with his men, had decided that it was not fitting for a Jew to retire, even when the Germans looked as though they had surrounded his position. He and his men held on until the rest of the battalion had made its escape. Then he rose, and, intoning the "Marseillaise," led his men in an attack with hand grenades. He and most of his men were, of course, killed.

Besides the Jews, the Corps had hundreds of political prisoners from labor camps in southern Algeria—Spanish Republicans who had fled to Africa in 1939, anti-Nazi Germans who had come even before that, and French "Communists and de Gaullists," to employ the usual Vichy designation for dissidents. The political prisoners had been released upon agreeing to enter the Corps Franc, which they did not consider an onerous condition. There were also hundreds of Frenchmen who had joined because they distrusted the Vichy officers in the regular Army, or because they were "hard heads" who detested any species of regularity, or because they were too old or ill for more conventional fighting units. In the Corps Franc, they were at liberty to march and fight until they dropped. There were also a fair number of Mohammedans, good soldiers who had joined to earn the princely wage of twenty-three francs a day, ten times what they would have got if they had waited to be mobilized in their regular units. Whenever I had a chance, I asked Corps Franc soldiers who they had been in civilian life and why they had enlisted. I remember a former *carabiñero* who had fought in the Spanish Loyalist Army, and a baker of Italian parentage from Bône, in Algeria, who said, "I am a Communist. Rich people are poison to me."

Other members of the Corps who made a special impression on me were a former admiral in the Spanish Republican Navy, who was now a company commander and would not allow junior officers to shout at soldiers; a Hungarian poet who had been studying medicine at the University of Algiers; a sixteen-year-old Alsatian from Strasbourg who had run away from home to avoid having to become a German citizen; and a French captain, a shipping broker in civil life, who proclaimed himself a Royalist. The captain's sixteen-year-old son was also in the Corps; the boy was a motorcycle dispatch rider. I also remember two tough Parisians who had not seen each other since one had escaped from jail in Dakar, where they had both been imprisoned for trying to join the Free French in Brazzaville. The other had escaped later. "Say, it's you, old pimp!" one of the men shouted joyously. "And how did you get out of the jug, old rottenness?" the second man shouted back. Once I shared a luncheon of C-ration vegetable hash, scallions, and medlars with a little fifty-three-year-old second lieutenant, one of those Frenchmen with a face like a parakeet, who until 1942 had been vice-president of the Paris Municipal Council, in which he represented the *arrondissement* of the Opéra. He had got out a clandestine paper and had helped Jewish friends smuggle millions of francs out of France. Betrayed to the Gestapo, he had been arrested and put in Cherche-Midi Prison; he had escaped with the aid of a jailer and come to

Africa and the Corps Franc. The middle-aged soldier who waited on us spoke French with a farce-comedy Russian accent; he had been a waiter at the Scheherazade, a night club in Montmartre, and had often served the lieutenant when he was a civilian. A handsome young Viennese half-Jew, who had been on the Austrian track team in the last Olympic Games, once asked me for some sulfanilamide. He had been in a labor camp for six months without seeing a woman but had been allowed one night's leave in Oran before being sent on to the front. He wanted the sulfanilamide, he said, so that he could treat himself; he was afraid that a doctor might order him away from the firing line. And in a hospital tent at the clearing station I came across a man with a French flag wrapped around his waist; the medics discovered it when they cut his shirt away. He was a hard-looking, blondish chap with a mouthful of gold teeth and a face adorned by a cross-shaped knife scar—the *croix de vache* with which procurers sometimes mark business rivals. An interesting collection of obscene tattooing showed on the parts of him that the flag did not cover. Outwardly he was not a sentimental type.

"Where are you from?" I asked him.

"Belleville," he said. Belleville is a part of Paris not distinguished for its elegance.

"What did you do in civilian life?" I inquired.

That made him grin. "I lived on my income," he said.

"Why did you choose the Corps Franc?"

"Because I understood," he said.

The American soldiers interspersed with the men of the Corps Franc along the Foresters' Track found them a fantastic lot. Most of the men then in the Ninth Division came from New York, New Jersey, or New England, and their ideas of North Africa and Frenchmen had been acquired from films with Ronald Colman as Beau Geste or Charles Boyer as Charles Boyer. They thought the Frenchmen very reckless. The Ninth had had its first experience in battle on the road to Maknassy, in southern Tunisia, only a few weeks earlier, and it was not yet a polished division. The men of the Ninth in Germany later took risks as nonchalantly as any Corps Franc soldier used to, but at the time I am speaking of they would sometimes call the Frenchmen "those crazy headhunters." This term reflected a tendency to confuse the Corps Franc with the Moroccans in the same zone; the Moroccans are not headhunters, either, but there is a popular American belief that they are paid according to how many enemy ears they bring in.

There were two tabors, or battalions, of Moroccans in the zone; a tabor consists of several goums, or companies, and each soldier who is a member of a company is called a goumier. For the sake of simplicity and euphony, Americans called the Moroccan soldiers themselves goums. The goums used to ride along the side of the road on bay mules or gray horses—sure-footed, mountain-bred animals—until they got near the place where they were going to fight. Then they would dismount and go off into the brush on bare feet, and return with their booty when they had finished their business. The goum's sole outer garment is the *djellabah*, which looks like a long brown bathrobe with a hood. It is made of cotton, wool, linen, goats' hair, or camels' hair and usually has vertical black stripes. It sheds water, insulates against heat and cold, is a substitute for a pup tent at night, and serves as a repository for everything the goum gloms, like the capacious garment of a professional shoplifter. In their Moroccan homeland the goums live with their wives and children in their own villages and are supposed to pay themselves with the spoils of tribes that resist the French government. In Tunisia the spoils were pretty well confined to soldiers' gear. As a goum killed or captured more and more enemies, he would put on layer after layer of tunics and trousers, always wearing the *djellabah* over everything. The girth of the goums increased as the campaign wore on. This swollen effect gave a goum an air of prosperity and importance, in his opinion; his standing as a warrior, he thought, was in direct ratio to his circumference. A goum who was doing well often wore, between sorties, one German and one Italian boot and carried a string of extra boots over his saddlebow. The funny part of it was that a goum wearing six men's clothing could slip noiselessly through a thicket that was impassable to a skinny American. The French officers commanding the goums assured me that their men were not paid by the ear; if a goum occasionally had a few dried ears concealed in a fold of his *djellabah*, one officer explained, it was because goums had discovered that such souvenirs had a trade value in G.I. cigarettes and chewing gum. "Far from paying for ears," this officer said, "we have recently been offering a small reward for live prisoners for interrogation. It is evident that a prisoner without ears is not a good subject for interrogation, because he does not hear the questions plainly." To hold the goums' respect, the officers had to be able to march, climb, and fight with them, and a goum is as inexhaustible as a mountain sheep and about as fastidious as a hyena. Most goums come from the Atlas Mountains and few of them speak Arabic, much less French, so the officers have to be fluent in the southern Berber dialects, which are all that the men know. The goums are trying companions in minefields, because, as one officer remarked, "They say, 'If it is the will of God, we go up,' and then they just push forward." Neither they nor the Corps Franc had mine detectors. An American captain named Yankauer, who was the surgeon at the clearing station near the yellow-triangle hill, was once digging scraps of steel out of a goum who had stepped on a mine. The man let out one short squeal—there was no anesthetic—and then began a steady chant. Yankauer asked a goum officer, who was waiting his turn on the table, what the goum was saying. The officer translated, "He chants, 'God forgive me, I am a woman. God forgive me, I am a woman,' because, you see, he has cried aloud, so he is ashamed." The goums' chief weapons were curved knives and long rifles of the vintage of 1871, and one of the supply problems of the campaign for the American G-4 was finding ammunition for these antediluvian small arms. Colonel Pierre Magnan, who had succeeded de Montsabert in command of the Corps Franc, was the senior French officer in the zone. I was with him one day when the commander of a newly arrived tabor presented himself for orders. "How are you fixed for automatic weapons, Major?" Magnan asked. "We have two old machine guns," the goum officer said. Then, when he saw Magnan's glum look, he added cheerily, "But don't worry, my Colonel, we use them only on maneuvers."

Magnan was a trim, rather elegant officer who, before the Allied landings, had commanded a crack infantry regiment in Morocco. On the morning of the American landings, he had arrested General Noguès, the Governor General of

Morocco, and then asked him to prevent any fighting between the French and Americans by welcoming the invading forces. Noguès had telephoned to a tank regiment to come and arrest Magnan. Magnan, unwilling to shed French blood, had surrendered to the tankmen and become a prisoner in his turn. The liberated Noguès had then ordered a resistance which cost hundreds of French and American lives. Magnan was kept in prison for several days after Noguès, who was backed by our State Department, had consented to be agreeable to the Allies. Magnan had then been released, but he was deprived of his command and consigned to the Corps Franc. He now commands a division in France, and de Montsabert has a *corps d'armée*, so the scheme to keep them down has not been precisely a success.

The Axis forces north of Sedjenane must have been as hard put to it for supply routes as we were. I don't remember the roads the Intelligence maps showed behind the enemy's lines, but they could not have been numerous or elaborate. The Germans did not seem to have a great deal of artillery, but they occasionally landed shells on our road. Once, I remember, they shot up a couple of tank destroyers shortly after the jeep I was in had pulled out to let them pass. Throughout, it was a stubborn, nasty sort of fighting in the brush, and casualties arrived in a steady trickle rather than any great spurt, because large-scale attacks were impossible. Our men fought their way a few hundred yards further east each day, toward Ferryville and Bizerte. Eventually, when Rommel's forces crumpled, men of the Corps Franc, in trucks driven by American soldiers, got to Bizerte before any other Allied troops.

On Easter Sunday, which came late in April, I was out along the Track all day, riding in a jeep with Hal Boyle, a correspondent for the Associated Press. At the end of the afternoon we headed home, hoping to get back to the press camp before night so that we wouldn't have to buck a stream of two-and-a-half-ton trucks and armored vehicles in the blackout. Traffic seemed, if anything, heavier than usual along the Foresters' Track, as it always did when you were in a hurry. The jeep stopped for minutes at a time, which gave Boyle the opportunity to climb out and get the names and home addresses of

American soldiers for his stories. Sometimes he would stay behind, talking, and catch up with the jeep the next time it was snagged. We could have walked along the Track faster than we rode. Finally we came to a dip in the road. Fifty yards below and to our right there was a shallow stream, and there was almost no brush on the slope from the road down to the water. This, for the Foresters' Track country, was a considerable clearing, and it was being used for a number of activities. Some goums were watering their mounts in the stream, some French and American soldiers were heating rations over brush fires, a number of vehicles were parked there, and Colonel Magnan and some officers were holding a staff meeting. As we approached the clearing, we were stopped again for a moment by the traffic. A dismal American soldier came out of the brush on our left, tugging a gaunt, reluctant white horse. "Come along, Horrible," the soldier said in a tone of intensest loathing. "This goddam horse got me lost three times today," he said to us, looking over his shoulder at the sneering, wall-eyed beast. He evidently thought the horse was supposed to guide him.

We moved downhill a bit and stopped again, this time behind an ambulance that was loading wounded. There was a group of soldiers around the ambulance. Boyle and I got out to look. There were four wounded men, all badly hit. They were breathing hard and probably didn't know what was going on. Shock and heavy doses of morphia were making their move easy, or at least quiet. The four men were all from the Sixtieth Infantry of the Ninth Division. A soldier by the road said that they had been on a patrol and had exchanged shots with a couple of Germans; the Germans had popped up waving white handkerchiefs, the Americans had stood up to take them prisoners, and another German, lying concealed, had opened on them with a machine gun. It was the sort of thing that had happened dozens of times to other units, and that undoubtedly has happened hundreds of times since. Such casualties, a Polish officer once said to me, are an entry fee to battle. That doesn't make them easy to take, however. The soldiers had been told about this particular trick in their training courses, but they had probably thought it was a fable invented to make them hate the enemy. Now the men around the ambulance had really begun to hate the enemy.

While Boyle was getting the names and addresses of the men, I saw another American soldier by the side of the road. This one was dead. A soldier nearby said that the dead man had been a private known as Mollie. A blanket covered his face, so I surmised that it had been shattered, but there was no blood on the ground, so I judged that he had been killed in the brush and carried down to the road to await transport. A big, wild-looking sergeant was standing alongside him—a hawk-nosed, red-necked man with a couple of front teeth missing—and I asked him if the dead man had been in the patrol with the four wounded ones. "Jeez, no!" the sergeant said, looking at me as if I ought to know about the man with the blanket over his face. "That's Mollie. Comrade Molotov. The Mayor of Broadway. Didn't you ever hear of him? Jeez, Mac, he once captured six hundred Eyetalians by himself and brought them all back along with him. Sniper got him, I guess. I don't know, because he went out with the French, and he was found dead up there in the hills. He always liked to do crazy things—go off by himself with a pair of big field glasses he had and watch the enemy put in minefields, or take off and be an artillery spotter for a while, or drive a tank. From the minute he seen those frogs, he was bound to go off with them."

"Was his name really Molotov?" I asked.

"No," said the sergeant, "he just called himself that. The boys mostly shortened it to Mollie. I don't even know what his real name was—Warren, I think. Carl Warren. He used to say he was a Broadway big shot. 'Just ask anybody around Forty-fourth Street,' he used to say. 'They all know me.' Me, I'm from White Plains—I never heard of him before he joined up."

"I had him with me on a patrol that was to contact the French when the regiment was moving into this zone last Thursday," a stocky blond corporal said. "The first French patrol we met, Mollie says to me, 'This is too far back for me. I'm going up in the hills with these frogs and get me some Lugers.' He was always collecting things he captured off Germans and Italians, but the one thing he didn't have yet was a Luger. I knew if I didn't let him go he would take off anyway and get into more trouble with the C.O. He was always in trouble. So I said, 'All right, but the frogs got to give me a receipt for you, so I can prove you didn't go A.W.O.L.' One of the soldiers with me could speak French, so he explained it and the frog noncom give me a receipt on a piece of toilet paper and Mollie went off with them." The corporal fished in one of the pockets of his field jacket and brought out a sheet of tissue. On it, the French noncom had written, in pencil, "*Pris avec moi le soldat américain Molotov, 23 avril, '43, Namin, caporal chef.*"

"Mollie couldn't speak French," the American corporal went on, "but he always got on good with the frogs. It's funny where those big field glasses went, though. He used to always have them around his neck, but somebody must have figured they were no more good to him after he was dead, so they sucked them up. He used to always say that he was a big-shot gambler and that he used to watch the horse races with those glasses."

By now the four wounded men had been loaded into the ambulance. It moved off. Obviously, there was a good story in Mollie, but he was not available for an interview. The driver of the truck behind our jeep was giving us the horn, so I pulled Boyle toward the jeep. He got in, still looking back at Mollie, who said nothing to keep him, and we drove away. When we had gone a little way, at our customary slow pace, a tall lieutenant signalled to us from the roadside that he wanted a hitch and we stopped and indicated that he should hop aboard. He told us his name was Carl Ruff. He was from New York. Ruff was dog-tired from scrambling through the bush. I said something about Mollie, and Ruff said that he had not known him alive but had been the first American to see his body, on Good Friday morning. The French had led him to it. "He was on the slope of a hill," Ruff said, "and slugs from an automatic rifle had hit him in the right eye and chest. He must have been working his way up the hill, crouching, when the German opened on him and hit him in the chest, and then as he fell, the other bullet probably got him in the eye. He couldn't have lived a minute."

It was a month later, aboard the United States War Shipping Administration steamer Monterey, a luxury liner that had been converted to war service without any needless suppression of comfort, that I next heard of Molotov, the Mayor of Broadway. The Monterey was on her way from Casablanca to New York. On the passenger list were four correspondents besides myself, a thousand German prisoners, five hundred wounded Americans, all of whom would need long hospitalization, and a couple of hundred officers and men who were being transferred or were on various errands. It was one of the advantages of being a correspondent that one could go to America without being a German or wounded, or without being phenomenally lucky, which the unwounded soldiers on our boat considered that they were. The crossing had almost a holiday atmosphere. We were homeward bound after a great victory in the North African campaign, the first the Allies had scored over Germany in a war nearly four years old. The weather was perfect and the Monterey, which was not overcrowded and had wide decks and comfortable lounges, had the aspect and feeling of a cruise ship. The wounded were glad, in their sad way, to be going home. The prisoners were in good spirits, too; they seemed to regard the journey as a Nazi Strength through Joy excursion. They organized vaudeville shows, boxing matches, and art exhibitions, with the energetic coöperation of the ship's chaplain, who found much to admire in the Christian cheerfulness with which they endured their increased rations. A couple of anti-Nazi prisoners had announced themselves on the first day out, but the German noncoms had knocked them about and set them to cleaning latrines, so order had soon been restored. "That's an army where they really have some discipline!" one of the American officers on board told me enviously. The prisoners had to put up with some hardships, of course. They complained one evening when ice cream was served to the wounded but not to them, and another time they didn't think the transport surgeon, a Jew, was "sympathetic" enough to a German officer with a stomach ache.

The hospital orderlies would wheel the legless wounded out on the promenade deck in wheelchairs to see the German boxing bouts, and the other wounded would follow them, some swinging along on crutches or hopping on one foot, some with their arms in slings or casts, some with their broken necks held stiffly in casts and harnesses. They had mixed reactions to the bouts. An arm case named Sanderson, a private

who wore the Ninth Division shoulder patch, told me one day
that he wished he could be turned loose on the prisoners with
a tommygun, because he didn't like to see them jumping
about in front of his legless pals. Another arm case, named
Shapiro, from the same division, always got a lot of amusement out of the show. Shapiro was a rugged-looking boy from
the Brownsville part of Brooklyn. He explained how he felt
one day after two Afrika Korps heavyweights had gone through
a couple of rounds of grunting, posturing, and slapping.
"Every time I see them box, I know we can't lose the war," he
said. "The Master Race—phooey! Any kid off the street could
of took the both of them."

Shapiro and Sanderson, I learned during one ringside conversation with them, had both been in the Sixtieth Infantry,
Molotov's old regiment. They had been wounded in the
fighting around Maknassy, in southern Tunisia, early in April,
the first serious action the regiment had been in. Molotov had
been killed late in April, during the drive on Bizerte, and until
I told them, the boys hadn't heard he was dead. I asked them
if they had known him.

"How could you help it?" Shapiro said. "There will never be
anybody in the division as well known as him. In the first place,
you couldn't help noticing him on account of his clothes. He
looked like a soldier out of some other army, always wearing
them twenty-dollar green tailor-made officers' shirts and sometimes riding boots, with a French berrit with a long rooster
feather that he got off an Italian prisoner's hat, and a long
black-and-red cape that he got off another prisoner for a can of
C ration."

"And the officers let him get away with it?" I asked.

"Not in the rear areas, they didn't," Shapiro said. "But in
combat, Mollie was an asset. Major Kauffman, his battalion
commander, knew it, so he would kind of go along with him.
But he would never have him made even a pfc. Mollie couldn't
of stood the responsibility. He was the greatest natural-born
foul-up* in the Army," Shapiro added reverently. "He was
court-martialled twenty or thirty times, but the Major always
got him out of it. He had the biggest blanket roll in the Ninth

---

*A euphemism, of course.

Division, with a wall tent inside it and some Arabian carpets and bronze lamps and a folding washstand and about five changes of uniform, none of them regulation, and he would always manage to get it on a truck when we moved. When he pitched his tent, it looked like a concession at Coney Island. I was with him when he got his first issue of clothing at Camp Dix in 1941. 'I've threw better stuff than this away,' he said. He never liked to wear issue. He was up for court-martial for deserting his post when he was on guard duty at Fort Bragg, but the regiment sailed for Morocco before they could try him, and he did so good in the landing at Port Lyautey that they kind of forgave him. Then he went over the hill again when he was guarding a dock at Oran in the winter, but they moved us up into the combat zone before they could try him then, so he beat that rap, too. He was a very lucky fellow. I can hardly think of him being dead."

"Well, what was so good about him?" I asked.

Sanderson, who was a thin, sharp-faced boy from Michigan, answered me with the embarrassed frankness of a modern mother explaining the facts of life to her offspring. "Sir," he said, "it may not sound nice to say it, and I do not want to knock anyone, but in battle almost everybody is frightened, especially the first couple of times. Once in a while you find a fellow who isn't frightened at all. He goes forward and the other fellows go along with him. So he is very important. Probably he is a popoff, and he kids the other guys, and they all feel better. Mostly those quiet, determined fellows crack up before the popoffs. Mollie was the biggest popoff and the biggest screwball and the biggest foul-up I ever saw, and he wasn't afraid of nothing. Some fellows get brave with experience, I guess, but Mollie never had any fear to begin with. Like one time on the road to Maknassy, the battalion was trying to take some hills and we were getting no place. They were just Italians in front of us, but they had plenty of stuff and they were in cover and we were in the open. Mollie stands right up, wearing the cape and the berrit with the feather, and he says, 'I bet those Italians would surrender if somebody asked them to. What the hell do they want to fight for?' he says. So he walks across the minefield and up the hill to the Italians, waving his arms and making funny motions, and they shoot at him for a while and then stop, thinking he is crazy. He goes up there yelling *'Veni qua!,'* which he says afterward is New York Italian for 'Come here!,' and *'Feeneesh la guerre!,'* which is French, and when he gets to the Italians he finds a soldier who was a barber in Astoria but went home on a visit and got drafted in the Italian Army, so the barber translates for him and the Italians say sure, they would like to surrender, and Mollie comes back to the lines with five hundred and sixty-eight prisoners. He had about ten Italian automatics strapped to his belt and fifteen field glasses hung over his shoulders. So instead of being stopped, we took the position and cleaned up on the enemy. That was good for the morale of the battalion. The next time we got in a fight, we said to ourselves, 'Those guys are just looking for an easy out,' so we got up and chased them the hell away from there. A disciplined soldier would never have did what Mollie done. He was a very unusual guy. He gave the battalion confidence and the battalion gave the regiment confidence, because the other battalions said, 'If the Second can take all those prisoners, we can, too.' And the Thirty-ninth and the Forty-seventh Regiments probably said to themselves, 'If the Sixtieth is winning all them fights, we can also.' So you might say that Mollie made the whole division." I found out afterward that Sanderson had oversimplified the story, but it was essentially true and the tradition endures in the Ninth Division.

"What kind of a looking fellow was Mollie?" I asked.

"He was a good-looking kid," Shapiro said. "Medium-sized, around a hundred and sixty pounds, with long, curly blond hair. They could almost never get him to have his hair cut. Once, when it got too bad, Major Kauffman took him by the hand and said, 'Come along with me. We'll get a haircut together.' So he sat him down and held onto him while the G.I. barber cut both their hair. And everything he wore had to be sharp. I remember that after the French surrendered to us at Port Lyautey, a lot of French officers gave a party and invited a couple of officers from the battalion to it, and when the officers got there they found Mollie was there, and the Frenchmen were all bowing to him and saluting him. He was dressed so sharp they thought he was an officer, too—maybe a colonel."

Another boy, a badly wounded one in a wheelchair, heard us

talking about Mollie and rolled his chair over to us. "It was the field glasses I'll always remember," he said. "From the first day we landed on the beach in Morocco, Mollie had those glasses. He told some fellows once he captured them from a French general, but he told some others he brought them all the way from New York. He told them he used to watch horse races with the glasses; he was fit to be tied when he got to Morocco and found there was no scratch sheets. 'Ain't there no way to telegraph a bet on a race?' he said, and then he let out a howl. 'Vot a schvindle!' That was his favorite saying—'Vot a schvindle!' He was always bitching about something. He used to go out scouting with the glasses, all alone, and find the enemy and tip Major Kauffman off where they were. He had a lot of curiosity. He always had plenty of money, but he would never tell where he got it from. He just let people understand he was a big shot—maybe in some racket. When we was down at Fort Bragg, he and another fellow, a sergeant, had a big Buick that he kept outside the camp, and they used to go riding all around the country. They used to get some swell stuff."

"He never shot crap for less than fifty dollars a roll when he had the dice," Shapiro said, "and he never slept with any woman under an actress." The way Shapiro said it, it was as if he had said, "He never saluted anybody under the rank of brigadier general."

During the rest of the voyage, I heard more about Mollie. I found nobody who was sure of his real name, but the majority opinion was that it was something like Carl Warren. "But he wasn't American stock or Irish," Sanderson said one day in a group discussion. "He seemed to me more German-American." Another boy in the conversation said that Mollie had told him he was of Russian descent. Sanderson was sure that Molotov wasn't Russian. "Somebody just called him that because he was a radical, I guess," he said. "He was always hollering he was framed." "He used to have a big map of the eastern front in his tent in Morocco," another soldier said, "and every time the Russians advanced he would mark it with pins and holler, 'Hey, Comrade, howdya like that!'" One boy remembered that Mollie had won fifteen hundred dollars in a crap game at Fort Bragg. "He had it for about three days," he said, "and then lost it to a civilian. When he got cleaned in a game, he would never borrow a buck to play on with. He would just leave. Then the next time he played, he would have a new roll. Right after we landed in Morocco, he was awful flush, even for him, and he told at couple of guys he'd climbed over the wall of an old fort the French had just surrendered and there, in some office, he found a briefcase with fifty thousand francs in it. The next thing he done was hire twelve Arabs to cook and clean and wash dishes for him."

"I was inducted the same time with him, at Grand Central Palace," an armless youngster said, "and him and me and the bunch was marched down to Penn Station to take the train. That was way back in January, 1941," he added, as if referring to a prehistoric event. "He was wearing a blue double-breasted jacket and a dark-blue sport shirt open at the neck and gray flannel trousers and a camel's-hair overcoat. They took us into a restaurant on Thirty-fourth Street to buy us a feed and Mollie started buying beers for the whole crowd. 'Come on, Comrades,' he says. 'Plenty more where this comes from.' Then he led the singing on the train all the way down to Dix. But as soon as he got down there and they took all his fancy clothes away from him, he was licked. 'Vot a schvindle!' he says. He drew K.P. a lot at Dix, but he always paid some other guy to do it for him. The only thing he could ever do good outside of combat was D.R.O.—that's dining-room orderly at the officers' mess. I've seen him carry three stacks of dishes on each arm."

When I told them how Mollie had been killed, Shapiro said that that was just what you'd have expected of Mollie. "He never liked to stay with his own unit," he said. "You could hardly even tell what battalion he was in."

I was not to see the Army's official version of what Mollie had done in the fight against the six hundred Italians until the next summer, when I caught up with the Second Battalion of the Sixtieth infantry near Marigny, in Normandy. Mollie's protector, Major Michael S. Kauffman, by then a lieutenant colonel, was still commanding officer. "Mollie didn't capture the lot by himself," Kauffman said, "but he was instrumental in getting them, and there were about six hundred of them all right. The battalion S-2 got out a mimeographed training pamphlet about that fight, because there were some points in it that we thought instructive. I'll get you a copy." The pamphlet he gave me bears the slightly ambitious title "The Battle of Sened, 23 March, '43, G Co. 60th Infantry Dawn Attack on Sened, Tunisia." The Sened of the title was the village of Sened, in the high *djebel* a couple of miles south of the Sened railroad station. It was country I remembered well: a bare plain with occasional bunch grass, with naked red-rock hills rising above it. The Americans had fought there several times; I had seen the taking of the railroad station by another regiment at the beginning of February, 1943, and it had been lost and retaken between then and March 23rd.

On the first page of the pamphlet there was a map showing the Italian position, on two hills separated by a narrow gorge, and the jump-off position of the Americans, two much smaller hills a couple of miles to the north. Then there was a list of "combat lessons to be learned," some of which were: "A small aggressive force can knock out a large group by determined action," "Individuals, soldiers with initiative, aggressiveness, and courage, can influence a large battle," and "Confusion is normal in combat." I have often since thought that this last would make a fine title for a book on war. The pamphlet told how an Italian force estimated at from thirty men to three thousand, according to the various persons interviewed in advance of the fight by S-2 ("Question civilians," the pamphlet said. "Don't rely on one estimate of enemy strength. Weigh all information in the light of its source."), had taken refuge in the village of Sened. G Company, about a hundred and fifty men, had been ordered to clean out the Italians. It had artillery support from some guns of the First Armored Division; in fact, a Lieutenant Colonel MacPherson, an artillery battalion commander, was actually the senior American officer in the action. This colonel, acting as his own forward observer, had looked over the situation and at four in the afternoon of March 22nd had ordered the first platoon of the company to attack. It was soon apparent, judging by the defenders' fire, that the lowest estimate of the enemy's strength was very wrong and that there were at least several hundred Italians on the two hills. Then, in the words of the pamphlet, "Private

Molotov"—even his officers had long since forgotten his civilian name—"crawls to enemy position with Pfc. De Marco (both are volunteers) and arranges surrender conference. C. O. refuses to surrender and fire fight continues. Individual enemy riflemen begin to throw down their arms. First platoon returns to Sened Station at dark with 147 prisoners, including 3 officers."

"De Marco was a friend of Molotov's," Colonel Kauffman told me. "It was Mollie's idea to go up to the enemy position, and De Marco did the talking. It must have been pretty effective, because all those Italians came back with them."

"G Company," the pamphlet continued, "attacks again at dawn, first and third platoons attacking. Entrance to town is deep narrow gorge between two long ridges. Town lies in continuation of gorge, surrounded on all sides by 1,000–2,000 foot *djebels* as shown in sketch. (Possible enemy escape route was used by Ancient Romans as park for wild animals used in gladiatorial matches.) Approach to gorge entrance is terraced and well concealed by a large olive-tree grove; five (5) or six (6) field pieces in grove have been knocked out by previous day's artillery fire."

Although the pamphlet didn't say so, the olive groves had once covered all the plain. That plain is now given over to bunch grass, but it was carefully irrigated in the days of the Roman Empire. The "wild animals used in gladiatorial matches" were for the arena at the splendid stone city of Capsa, now the sprawling, dried-mud Arab town of Gafsa, fifteen miles from Sened.

"Company attacks as shown on sketch," the pamphlet continued, "third platoon making steep rocky climb around right, first platoon (Molotov's) around left. Light machine guns and mortars follow close behind by bounds, grenadiers move well to front with mission of flushing enemy out of numerous caves where he has taken up defensive positions. Left platoon, commanded by Sergeant Vernon Mugerditchian, moves slowly over ground devoid of concealment, and finally comes to rest. Molotov goes out alone, keeping abreast of faster moving platoon on right, and assists Lt. Col. MacPherson in artillery direction by shouting."

The combined artillery and infantry fire made the Italians

quit. The pamphlet says, in closing, "Italian captain leads column of prisoners out of hills, bringing total of 537 (including officers). Total booty includes 2 large trucks, 3 small trucks, several personnel carrier motorcycles, 200 pistols, machine guns, rifles, and ammunition."

"Mollie liked to go out ahead and feel he was running the show," Colonel Kauffman said. "We put him in for a D.S.C. for what he did, but it was turned down. Then we put in for a Silver Star, and that was granted, but he was killed before he ever heard about it. He was a terrible soldier. He and another fellow were to be tried by a general court-martial for quitting their guard posts on the docks at Oran, but we had to go into action before court could be held. The other fellow had his court after the end of the campaign and got five years."

The officers of the battalion, and those at division headquarters, knew that I was going to write a story about Mollie sometime. Whenever I would encounter one of them, in a country tavern or at a corps or Army headquarters, or on a dusty road behind the lines, during our final campaign before Germany's surrender, he would ask me when I was going to "do Mollie." I am doing him now.

Even after I had been back in the States for a while that summer of 1943, I had an intermittent interest in Mollie, although La Piste Forestière assumed a curious unreality after I had been living on lower Fifth Avenue a couple of weeks. I asked a fellow I knew at the *Times* to check back through the casualty lists and see if the death of a soldier with a name like "Carl Warren" had been reported, since I knew the lists gave the addresses of the next of kin and I thought I might be able to find out more about Mollie. The *Times* man found out that there hadn't been any such name but that there was often a long interval between casualties and publication. I took to turning mechanically to the new lists as they came out and looking through the "W"s. One day I saw listed, among the Army dead, "Karl C. Warner, sister Mrs. Ulidjak, 230 E. Eightieth Street, Manhattan." The juxtaposition of "a name like Warren" with one that I took to be Russian or Ukrainian made me suspect that Warner was Molotov, and it turned out that I was right.

A couple of days later, I went uptown to look for Mrs. Ulidjak. No. 230 is between Second and Third Avenues, in a block overshadowed by the great, brute mass of the Manhattan Storage & Warehouse Company's building at the corner of Eightieth. Along the block there were a crumbling, red-brick elementary school of the type Fusion administrations like to keep going so that they can hold the tax rate down, a yellowish, old-fashioned Baptist church, some boys playing ball in the street, and a banner, bearing a number of service stars, hung on a line stretched across the street. As yet, it had no gold stars. No. 230 is what is still called a "new-law tenement," although the law governing this type of construction is fifty years old: a six-story walkup with the apartments built around air shafts. Ulidjak was one of the names on the mailboxes in the vestibule. I pushed the button beside it, and in a minute there was an answering buzz and I walked upstairs. A thin, pale woman with a long, bony face and straight blond hair pulled back into a bun came to the apartment door. She looked under thirty and wore silver-rimmed spectacles. This was Mrs. Ulidjak, Private Warner's sister. Her husband is in the Merchant Marine. She didn't seem startled when I said I was a correspondent; every American expects to be interviewed by a reporter sometime. Mrs. Ulidjak had been notified of her brother's death by the War Department over a week before, but she had no idea how it had happened or where. She said he had been in the Sixtieth Infantry, all right, so I was sure Warner had been Mollie. "Was he fighting the Japs?" she asked me. When I told her no, she seemed slightly disappointed. "And you were there?" she asked. I said I had been. Then, apparently trying to visualize me in the context of war, she asked, "Did you wear a helmet, like Ernie Pyle? Gee, they must be heavy to wear. Did it hurt your head much?" When I had reassured her on this point, she led me into a small sitting room with a window opening on a dark air shaft. A young man and a young woman, who Mrs. Ulidjak said were neighbors, were in the room, but they went into the adjoining kitchen, apparently so that they would not feel obliged to look solemn.

"Was your name Warner, too, before you were married?" I asked Mrs. Ulidjak.

"No," she said, "Karl and I were named Petuskia—that's

Russian—but he changed to Warner when he came to New York because he thought it sounded sweller. We were from a little place called Cokesburg, in western Pennsylvania. He hardly ever came up here. He had his own friends."

"Did he go to high school in Cokesburg?" I asked.

The idea amused Mrs. Ulidjak. "No, just grammar school," she said. "He was a pit boy in the coal mines until we came to New York. But he always liked to dress nice. You can ask any of the cops around the Mall in Central Park about him. Curly, they used to call him, or Blondy. He was quite a lady's man."

Then I asked her the question that had puzzled Mollie's Army friends: "What did he do for a living before he went into the Army?"

"He was a bartender down to Jimmy Kelly's, the night club in the Village," Mrs. Ulidjak said.

She then told me that her brother's Christian name really was Karl and that he was twenty-six when he was killed, although he had looked several years younger. Both parents are dead. The parents had never told her, as far as she could re-member, what part of Russia they came from. When I said that Mollie had been a hero, she was pleased, and said he had always had an awful crust. She called the young neighbors, who seemed to be of Italian descent, back into the sitting room and made me repeat the story of how Mollie captured the six hundred Italians (I hadn't seen the official version of his exploit yet and naturally I gave him full credit in mine). "Six hundred wops!" Mrs. Ulidjak exclaimed gaily. She got a lot of fun out of Mollie's "big shot" stories, too. She showed me a large, expensive-looking photograph of him "addressing" a golf ball. He was wearing light-colored plus-fours, white stockings, and brogues with tassels, and there was a big, happy grin on his face that made it plain that he was not going to hit the ball but was just posing. He had a wide, plump face with high cheekbones and square white teeth, and the hair about which I had so often heard looked at least six inches long. "He had a room at 456 West Forty-fourth Street, and a little Jewish tailor down in that neighborhood made all those nice things for him special," she said admiringly. She had never heard him called Molotov.

*

I went over to West Forty-fourth Street a few days later. The 400 block, between Ninth and Tenth Avenues, looks more depressing than the one the Ulidjaks live on. It is mostly shops dealing in the cheap merchandise that is used as premiums, and stores that sell waiters' supplies, and lodging houses favored by waiters and cooks. It was evident from the look of the house at No. 456 that though Mollie had spent a disproportionate share of his income on clothes, he had wasted nothing on his living quarters. No one at No. 456 remembered Mollie. The tenants and the janitor had all come there since his time. I couldn't find the little tailor. But on the north side of Forty-fourth Street, near Ninth Avenue, there is a building occupied by the Warner Brothers' Eastern offices, and I was sure that this had given Mollie the idea of calling himself Warner.

That evening I went down to Jimmy Kelly's, on Sullivan Street. Kelly's is the kind of club that never changes much but that you seldom remember anything specific about unless you have had a fight there. I had been there a few times in the late thirties, but I couldn't remember the bartender's face. Kelly's has a dance floor a little bigger than two tablecloths, and there is always a show with young, sometimes pretty girls imitating the specialties that more famous and experienced performers are doing at clubs uptown, and a master of ceremonies making cracks so old that they have been used in Hollywood musicals. The man behind the bar the night I showed up said he had been there several years and had known his predecessor, whose name was not Molotov. He had never heard of a bartender named Molotov or Warner or Mollie or Karl at Kelly's. After I had had a couple of Scotches and had told him the story, he said he wondered if the fellow I meant hadn't been a busboy. The description seemed to fit one who had worked there. "We all used to call this kid Curly," he said, "but Ray, the waiter who is the union delegate, might remember his real name."

Ray was a scholarly-looking man with a high, narrow forehead and shell-rimmed spectacles. "Curly's name *was* Karl C. Warner," he said after he had been told what I wanted to know. "I remember it from his union card. He was a man who would always stand up for his fellow-worker. Waiters and Waitresses Local No. 1 sent him down here in the summer of 1940 and he worked until late the next fall. He was outspoken but a hard worker and strong—he could carry three stacks of dishes on each arm. A busboy has a lot to do in a place like this when there is a rush on—clearing away dishes, setting up for new parties, bringing the waiters their orders—and a stupid boy can spoil the waiters' lives for them. We had another boy here at the same time, an Irish boy, who kidded Curly about the fancy clothes he wore, so they went down in the basement and fought for a couple of hours one afternoon. Nobody won the fight. They just fought until they were tired and then stopped. Curly had wide interests for a busboy," Ray continued. "When there was no rush on, he would sometimes stop by a customer's table, particularly if it was some man who looked important, and talk to him for ten minutes or so. The customers didn't seem to mind. He had a nice way about him. He had a kind of curiosity."

The Army stories about Mollie's wealth made Ray and the bartender laugh. "He used to come back here now and then during the first year he was in the Army," Ray said, "and always he would borrow ten or twenty dollars from one of us waiters. We would lend it to him because we liked him, without expecting to get it back." A busboy at Kelly's is paid only nominal wages, Ray told me—just about enough to cover his laundry bill—but the waiters chip in a percentage of their tips for the boys. "I guess Curly averaged about forty a week here," he said. "If he was anxious to get extra money, he might have had a lunch job someplace else at the same time, but I never heard about it. A tailor like he had probably made those suits for about twenty-five per. What else did he have to spend money on? His night life was here. He used to tell us he had worked at El Morocco, but we used to say, 'What's the difference? Dirty dishes are the same all over.'"

At the union headquarters, which are on the twelfth floor of a loft building on West Fortieth Street, Mollie was also remembered. The serious, chunky young woman in the union secretary's office said, "Warner was always a dissident. He would speak up at every meeting and object to everything. But we all liked him. He stopped paying dues a few months before he went into the Army, but at Christmastime in 1941 he came back here and said he heard that union members in the services were getting a present from the local, so he wanted one, too. So we gave it to him, of course. The secretary will be interested to know he is dead."

The young woman called the secretary, a plump, olive-complexioned man, from his desk in an inner room and said to him, "You remember Karl Warner, the blond boy with curly hair? He has been killed in Africa. He was a hero."

"Is that so?" the secretary said. "Well, get a man to put up a gold paper star on the flag in the members' hall right away and draw up a notice to put on the bulletin board. He is the first member of Local No. 1 to die in this war."

I thought how pleased Mollie would have been to be restored to good standing in the union, without even having paid up his dues. Then I thought of how much fun he would have had on the Mall in Central Park, in the summertime, if he could only have gone up there with his Silver Star ribbon on, and a lot of enemy souvenirs. I also thought of how far La Piste Forestière was from the kitchen in Jimmy Kelly's.

When I walk through the West Side borderland between Times Square and the slums, where Mollie once lived, I often think of him and his big talk and his golf-suit grin. It cheers me to think there may be more like him all around me—a notion I would have dismissed as sheer romanticism before World War II. Cynicism is often the shamefaced product of inexperience.

He has become a posthumous pal, though I never knew him when he was alive. He was full of curiosity—he would have made a great explorer—and fond of high living, which is the only legitimate incentive for liking money. He had faith in the reason of his fellow-man, as when he sensed that the Italians at Sened were no more eager to fight than he was. The action that earned him his Silver Star cost no lives. It saved them. He bragged, but when challenged he would not back off. The brag was like the line a deckhand throws over a bollard—it pulled performance after it. I lived with him so long that I once half-convinced myself he was not dead. This was when I began to write a play about him, and was reminded by more experienced hands that it is customary for the protagonist of a work of that nature to remain alive until the last act.

"Suppose," I said, "that the corpse with the face shot away that I saw by La Piste was not Mollie at all, but that Mollie had put his uniform and dog-tags on a dead goumier and gone over the hill wearing a Moroccan *djellabah*, to wage a less restricted kind of war, accumulating swag as he went?" And suppose he was living in Morocco now, with a harem, a racing stable, and a couple of Saharan oil wells? And suppose he returned to New York as a member of the Moroccan, or the Mauretanian, Delegation to the United Nations, or, better yet, a Delegate from the Touareg state that is sure to be formed sooner or later? The last would afford him the advantage of a veil covering his face below the eyes, to conceal his grin.

Mollie would like the fancy togs, and if any old rival, perhaps the Irish busboy, recognized him in the last scene and twitted him with his defection, he could pull out from his flowing sleeves hundreds of dried Nazi ears to prove he had waged war effectually to the last. If Allah has so willed it, the thing is.

Or suppose he had switched uniforms with a dead German, and thereafter, as a secret agent, confounded all the Wehrmacht's plans? He liked to operate in disguise, as he proved when he fooled the French officers at Casablanca, and superior officers of foreign powers confided in him on sight. I like him better as a Touareg, and I think he would have liked Touaregs better as company. I dropped the play because that was all the plot I could think of.

Long after I abandoned thought of writing about Mollie again, I had a letter from a lady in Mechanicsburg, Pennsylvania, that cleared up the question of how Mollie transmuted his last name. It had nothing to do with Warner Brothers—a warning, this, against adopting mere plausibility in place of valid evidence. She wrote that her brother, a Mr. Karl Warner, had come to Cokesburg as boss of a construction job in about 1932, and had given the Petuskia boy a job as watchman, in defiance of all local counsel. Young Petuskia was considered a bad risk. The boy proved honest, and afterward wanted to pull up stakes and follow the construction gang when it left town. Warner told him he was too young. The Mechanicsburg lady was sure the boy had subsequently taken the Warner name in honor of her brother.

I am sure she is right, but it sounds like a detail out of an old-fashioned boys' book.

The air vendetta that is described in the next set of pieces took place in an earlier phase of the war in North Africa—all, in fact, during the month of January, 1943. I wrote the stories in my room at the Hotel Aletti, in Algiers, in early February. There were no facilities for sending despatches from the rudimentary air fields, several hundred miles away, where the fighting happened. This was one of the good points of being a correspondent—you could leave the discomfort of the scene of combat without being wounded.

Headquarters were so far from our war that the censor officers read our despatches like notes on an unknown world. For the staff it was rather like running a war in Ohio from a hotel in Washington, except that their hotel was better. It was the Saint George, up on the hill. But the Aletti was a fine place too—you could have a bath, though seldom a hot one, in a bathtub, and receive female visitors if they stood in well with the concierge. In town there was a great deal of Algerian wine, which is maligned in France by the very blenders who import it in vast quantities to give body to their thin vintages, and there was excellent food to be had if you knew where to look for it, in the Street of the Gate of Weeping, in the establishment of a Swiss who considered himself, as a neutral, immune from wartime food regulations. The fish and the small birds were almost literally beyond price, and there was a wine so kind that if I had a daughter, I would give her its name—Miliana.

In the twilight, as we walked to our dinners, German planes would come like swallows out of Sicily, far away, and jettison their bombs before reaching the center of our magnificent anti-aircraft display, like a beehive drawn in lines of orange tracer. If Headquarters hadn't been there, we wouldn't have had such a pretty beehive, and the pilots wouldn't have flinched so soon. My debts to the Supreme Command are therefore double—it stayed in a safe place and it kept it safer.

Then, in the dark after the third armagnac, we would steal away to a place of enchantment called the Sphinx, where girls

would act charades that graying members of the American
Legion still dream of with nostalgia in Terre Haute. It was a
schizoid existence: in Tunisia, with your belly pressed to the
ground, the Hotel Aletti seemed a mirage, but when you were
in Algiers, you wondered whether you had lived on the Foamy
Fields or imagined them.

2

For Boots Norgaard

The Foamy Fields

IF THERE is any way you can get colder than you do when you sleep in a bedding roll on the ground in a tent in southern Tunisia two hours before dawn, I don't know about it. The particular tent I remember was at an airfield in a Tunisian valley. The surface of the terrain was mostly limestone. If you put all the blankets on top of you and just slept on the canvas cover of the roll, you ached all over, and if you divided the blankets and put some of them under you, you froze on top. The tent was a large, circular one with a French stencil on the outside saying it had been rented from a firm in Marseilles and not to fold it wet, but it belonged to the United States Army now. It had been set up over a pit four feet deep, so men sleeping in it were safe from flying bomb fragments. The tall tent pole, even if severed, would probably straddle the pit and not hit anybody. It was too wide a hole to be good during a strafing, but then strafings come in the daytime and in the daytime nobody lived in it. I had thrown my roll into the tent because I thought it was vacant and it seemed as good a spot as any other when I arrived at the field as a war correspondent. I later discovered that I was sharing it with two enlisted men.

I never saw my tentmates clearly, because they were always in the tent by the time I turned in at night, when we were not allowed to have lights on, and they got up a few minutes before I did in the morning, when it was still dark. I used to hear them moving around, however, and sometimes talk to them. One was from Mississippi and the other from North Carolina, and both were airplane mechanics. The first night I stumbled through the darkness into the tent, they heard me and one of them said, "I hope you don't mind, but the tent we were sleeping in got all tore to pieces with shrapnel last night, so we just moved our stuff in here." I had been hearing about the events of the previous evening from everybody I met on the field. "You can thank God you wasn't here last night," the other man said earnestly. The field is so skillfully hidden in the mountains that it is hard to find by night, and usually the Germans just wander around overhead, dropping their stuff on the wrong hillsides, but for once they had found the right place and some of the light anti-aircraft on the field had started shooting tracers. "It was these guns that gave away where we was," the first soldier said. "Only for that they would have gone away and never knowed the first bomb had hit the field. But after that they knew they was on the beam and they come back and the next bomb set some gasoline on fire and then they really did go to town. Ruined a P-38 that tore herself up in a belly landing a week ago and I had just got her about fixed up again, and now she's got shrapnel holes just about everywhere and she's hopeless. All that work wasted. Killed three fellows that was sleeping in a B-26 on the field and woke up and thought that was no safe place, so they started to run across the field to a slit trench and a bomb got them. Never got the B-26 at all. If they'd stayed there, they'd been alive today, but who the hell would have stayed there?"*

"That shrapnel has a lot of force behind it," the other voice in the tent said. "There was a three-quarter-ton truck down on the field and a jaggedy piece of shrapnel went right through one of the tires and spang through the chassix. You could see the holes both sides where she went in and come out. We was in our tent when the shooting started, but not for long. We run up into the hills so far in fifteen minutes it took us four hours to walk back next morning. When we got back we found we didn't have no tent." There was a pause, and then the first soldier said, "Good night, sir," and I fell asleep.

When the cold woke me up, I put my flashlight under the blankets so I could look at my watch. It was five o'clock. Some Arab dogs, or perhaps jackals, were barking in the hills, and I lay uncomfortably dozing until I heard one of the soldiers blowing his nose. He blew a few times and said, "It's funny that as cold as it gets up here nobody seems to get a real cold. My nose runs like a spring branch, but it don't never develop."

*The B-26 was Lieutenant-General James Doolittle's personal plane. He was on a tour of inspection, and the three soldiers were members of his crew.

When the night turned gray in the entrance to the tent, I woke again, looked at my watch, and saw that it was seven. I got up and found that the soldiers had already gone. Like everyone else at the field, I had been sleeping in my clothes. The only water obtainable was so cold that I did not bother to wash my face. I got my mess kit and walked toward the place, next to the kitchen, where they were starting fires under two great caldrons to heat dish water. One contained soapy water and the other rinsing water. The fires shot up from a deep hole underneath them, and a group of soldiers had gathered around and were holding the palms of their hands toward the flames, trying to get warm. The men belonged to a maintenance detachment of mechanics picked from a number of service squadrons that had been sent to new advanced airdromes, where planes have to be repaired practically without equipment for the job. That morning most of the men seemed pretty cheerful because nothing had happened during the night, but one fellow with a lot of beard on his face was critical. "This location was all right as long as we had all the planes on one side of us, so we was sort of off the runway," he said, "but now that they moved in those planes on the other side of us, we're just like a piece of meat between two slices of bread. A fine ham sandwich for Jerry. If he misses either side, he hits us. I guess that is how you get to be an officer, thinking up a location for a camp like this. I never washed out of Yale so I could be an officer, but I got more sense than that."

"Cheer up, pal," another soldier said. "All you got to do is dig. I got my dugout down so deep already it reminds me of the Borough Hall station. Some night I'll give myself a shave and climb on board a Woodlawn express." Most of the men in camp, I had already noticed, were taking up excavation as a hobby and some of them had worked up elaborate private trench systems. "You couldn't get any guy in camp to dig three days ago," the Brooklyn soldier said, "and now you can't lay down a shovel for a minute without somebody sucks it up."

Another soldier, who wore a white silk scarf loosely knotted around his extremely dirty neck, a style generally affected by fliers, said, "What kills me is my girl's brother is in the horse cavalry, probably deep in the heart of Texas, and he used to razz me because I wasn't a combat soldier."

The Brooklyn man said to him, "Ah, here's Mac with a parachute tied around his neck just like a dashing pilot. Mac, you look like a page out of *Esquire*."

When my hands began to feel warm, I joined the line which had formed in front of the mess tent. As we passed through, we got bacon, rice, apple butter, margarine, and hard biscuits in our mess tins and tea in our canteen cups. The outfit was on partly British rations, but it was a fairly good breakfast anyway, except for the tea, which came to the cooks with sugar and powdered milk already mixed in it. "I guess that's why they're rationing coffee at home, so we can have tea all the time," the soldier ahead of me said. I recognized the bacon as the fat kind the English get from America. By some miracle of lend-lease they had now succeeded in delivering it back to us; the background of bookkeeping staggered the imagination. After we had got our food, we collected a pile of empty gasoline cans to use for chairs and tables. The five-gallon can, known as a flimsy, is one of the two most protean articles in the Army. You can build houses out of it, use it as furniture, or, with slight structural alterations, make a stove or a locker. Its only rival for versatility is the metal shell of the Army helmet, which can be used as an entrenching tool, a shaving bowl, a wash basin, or a cooking utensil, at the discretion of the owner. The helmet may also serve on occasion as a bathtub. The bather fills it with water, removes one article of clothing at a time, rubs the water hastily over the surface thus exposed, and replaces the garment before taking off another one.*

There was no officers' mess. I had noticed Major George Lehmann, the commanding officer of the base, and First Lieutenant McCreedy, the chaplain, in the line not far behind me. Major Lehmann is a tall, fair, stolid man who told me that he had lived in Pittsfield, Massachusetts, where he had a job with the General Electric Company. When I had reported, on my arrival at the field, at his dugout the evening before, he had hospitably suggested that I stow my blanket roll wherever I could find a hole in the ground, eat at the general mess shack, and stay as long as I pleased. "There are fighter squadrons and

---

*This is known as a whore's bath. The impelling reason for exposing only one surface at a time was cold, not modesty.

some bombers and some engineers and anti-aircraft here, and you can wander around and talk to anybody that interests you," he had said.

Father McCreedy is a short, chubby priest who came from Bethlehem, Pennsylvania, and had been assigned to a parish in Philadelphia. He always referred to the pastor of this parish, a Father McGinley, as "my boss," and asked me several times if I knew George Jean Nathan, who he said was a friend of Father McGinley. Father McCreedy had been officiating at the interment of the fellows killed in the raid the evening before, and that was all he would talk about during breakfast. He had induced a mechanic to engrave the men's names on metal plates with an electric needle. These plates would serve as enduring grave markers. It is part of a chaplain's duty to see that the dead are buried and to dispose of their effects. Father McCreedy was also special-services officer of the camp, in charge of recreation and the issue of athletic equipment. "So what with one thing and another, they keep me busy here," he said. He told me he did not like New York. "Outside of Madison Square Garden and the Yankee Stadium, you can have it." He wore an outsize tin hat all the time. "I know a chaplain is not supposed to be a combatant," he said, "but if parachute troops came to my tent by night, they'd shoot at me because they wouldn't know I was a chaplain, and I want something solid on my head." He had had a deep hole dug in front of his tent and sometimes, toward dusk, when German planes were expected, he would stand in it waiting and smoking a cigar, with the glowing end of it just clearing the hole.

When I had finished breakfast and scrubbed up my mess kit, I strolled around the post to see what it was like. As the sun rose higher, the air grew warm and the great, reddish mountains looked friendly. Some of them had table tops, and the landscape reminded me of Western movies in Technicolor.* I got talking to a soldier named Bill Phelps, who came from the town of Twenty-nine Palms, California. He was working on a

*This use of the familiar false as touchstone of the unfamiliar real recurred often both in writing and conversation during World War II. "Just like a movie!" was a standard reaction. It assured the speaker of the authenticity of what he had just experienced.

bomber that had something the matter with its insides. He confirmed my notion that the country looked like the American West. "This is exactly the way it is around home," he said, "only we got no Ayrabs." A French writer has described the valley bottoms in southern Tunisia as foamy seas of white sand and green alfa grass. They are good, natural airfields, wide and level and fast-drying, but there is always plenty of dust in the air. I walked to a part of the field where there were a lot of P-38's, those double-bodied planes that look so very futuristic, and started to talk to a couple of sergeants who were working on one. "This is Lieutenant Hoelle's plane," one of them said, "and we just finished putting a new wing on it. That counts as just a little repair job out here. Holy God, at home, if a plane was hurt like that, they would send it back to the factory or take it apart for salvage. All we do here is drive a two-and-a-half-ton truck up under the damaged wing and lift it off, and then we put the new wing on the truck and run it alongside the plane again and fix up that eighty-thousand-dollar airplane like we was sticking together a radio set. We think nothing of it. It's a great ship, the 38. Rugged. You know how this one got hurt? Lieutenant Hoelle was strafing some trucks and he come in to attack so low he hit his right wing against a telephone pole. Any other plane, that wing would have come off right there. Hitting the pole that way flipped him over on his back, and he was flying upside down ten feet off the ground. He gripped that stick so hard the inside of his hand was black and blue for a week afterward, and she come right side up and he flew her home. Any one-engine plane would have slipped and crashed into the ground, but those two counter-rotating props eliminate torque." I tried to look as though I understood. "Lieutenant Hoelle is a real man," the sergeant said.*

I asked him where Hoelle and the other P-38 pilots were, and he directed me to the P-38 squadron's operations room, a rectangular structure mostly below ground, with walls made out of the sides of gasoline cans and a canvas roof camouflaged

---

*These praises of the Lightning now look as old-fashioned as a cavalryman's praise of the Anglo-Arab charger, and the mechanic's talk about an eighty-thousand-dollar airplane, below, sounds like a reference to the good nickel cigar.

with earth. A length of stovepipe stuck out through the roof, making it definitely the most ambitious structure on the field.

Hoelle was the nearest man to the door when I stepped down into the operations shack. He was a big, square-shouldered youngster with heavy eyebrows and a slightly aquiline nose. I explained who I was and asked him who was in charge, and he said, "I am. I'm the squadron C.O. My name's Hoelle." He pronounced it "Holly." There was a fire in a stove, and the shack was warm. Two tiny black puppies lay on a pilot's red scarf in a helmet in the middle of the dirt floor, and they seemed to be the centre of attention. Six or eight lieutenants, in flying togs that ranged from overalls to British Army battle dress, were sitting on gasoline cans or sprawled on a couple of cots. They were all looking at the puppies and talking either to them or their mother, a small Irish setter over in one corner, whom they addressed as Red. "One of the boys brought Red along with him from England," Hoelle said. "We think that the dog that got her in trouble is a big, long-legged black one at the airport we were quartered at there."

"These are going to be real beautiful dogs, just like Irish setters, only with black hair," one of the pilots said in a defensive tone. He was obviously Red's master.

"This is a correspondent," Hoelle said to the group, and one of the boys on a cot moved over and made room for me. I sat down, and the fellow who had moved over said his name was Larry Adler but he wasn't the harmonica player and when he was home he lived on Ocean Parkway in Brooklyn. "I wouldn't mind being there right now," he added.

There was not much in the shack except the cots, the tin cans, a packing case, the stove, a phonograph, a portable typewriter, a telephone, and a sort of bulletin board that showed which pilots were on mission, which were due to go on patrol, and which were on alert call, but it was a cheerful place. It reminded me of one of those secret-society shacks that small boys are always building out of pickup materials in vacant lots. Adler got up and said he would have to go on patrol. "It's pretty monotonous," he said, "like driving a fast car thirty miles an hour along a big, smooth road where there's no traffic. We just stooge around near the field and at this time of day nothing ever happens."

Another lieutenant came over and said he was the intelligence officer of the squadron. Intelligence and armament officers, who do not fly, take a more aggressive pride in their squadron's accomplishments than the pilots, who don't like to be suspected of bragging. "We've been out here for a month," the intelligence officer said, "and we have been doing everything—escorting bombers over places like Sfax and Sousse, shooting up vehicles and puncturing tanks, going on fighter sweeps to scare up a fight, and flying high looking for a target and then plunging straight down on it and shooting hell out of it. We've got twenty-nine German planes, including bombers and transports with troops in them and fighters, and the boys have flown an average of forty combat missions apiece. That's more than one a day. Maybe you'd like to see some of the boys' own reports on what they have been doing."

I said that this sounded fine, and he handed me a sheaf of the simple statements pilots write out when they put in a claim for shooting down a German plane. I copied part of a report by a pilot named Earnhart, who I thought showed a sense of literary style. He had had, according to the intelligence officer, about the same kind of experience as everybody else in the squadron. Earnhart had shot down a Junkers 52, which is a troop-carrier, in the episode he was describing, and then he had been attacked by several enemy fighters. "As I was climbing away from them," he wrote, "a 20-millimetre explosive shell hit the windshield and deflected through the top of the canopy and down on the instrument panel. Three pieces of shell hit me, in the left chest, left arm, and left knee. I dropped my belly tank and, having the ship under control, headed for my home base. On the way I applied a tourniquet to my leg, administered a hypodermic, and took sulfanilamide tablets. I landed the ship at my own base one hour after I had been hit by the shell. The plane was repaired. Claim, one Ju 52 destroyed." The intelligence officer introduced Earnhart to me. He was a calm, slender, dark-haired boy and he persisted in addressing me as sir. He said he came from Lebanon, Ohio, and had gone to Ohio State.

Still another lieutenant I met was named Gustke. He came from Detroit. Gustke had been shot down behind the German lines and had made his way back to the field. He was a tall, gangling type, with a long nose and a prominent Adam's apple. "I crash-landed the plane and stepped out of it wearing my parachute," he told me, "and the first thing I met was some Arabs who looked hostile to me, and as luck would have it I had forgotten to bring along my .45, so I tripped my parachute and threw it to them, and you know how crazy Arabs are about cloth or anything like that. They all got fighting among themselves for the parachute, and while they were doing that I ran like hell and got away from them. I got to a place where there were some Frenchmen, and they hid me overnight and the next day put me on a horse and gave me a guide, who brought me back over some mountains to inside the French lines. I had a pretty sore ass from riding the horse."

A pilot from Texas named Ribb, who stood nearby as Gustke and I talked, broke in to tell me that they had a fine bunch of fellows and that when they were in the air they took care of each other and did not leave anybody alone at the end of the formation to be picked off by the enemy. "In this gang we have no ass-end Charlies," he said feelingly.

I asked Lieutenant Hoelle what was in the cards for the afternoon, and he said that eight of the boys, including himself, were going out to strafe some German tanks that had been reported working up into French territory. "We carry a cannon, which the P-40's don't, so we can really puncture a tank the size they use around here," he said. "We expect to meet some P-40's over the target, and they will stay up high and give us cover against any German fighters while we do a job on the tanks. Maybe I had better call the boys together and talk it over."

A couple of pilots had begun a game of blackjack on the top of the packing case, and he told them to quit, so he could spread a map on it. At that moment an enlisted man came in with a lot of mail and some Christmas packages that had been deposited by a courier plane. It was long after Christmas, but that made the things even more welcome, and all the pilots made a rush for their packages and started tearing them open.

Earnhart, who was going on the strafe job, got some National
Biscuit crackers and some butterscotch candy and a couple of
tubes of shaving cream that he said he couldn't use because he
had an electric razor, and the operations officer, a lieutenant
named Lusk, got some very rich home-made cookies that an
aunt and uncle had sent him from Denver. We were all gobbling butterscotch and cookies as we gathered round the map
Hoelle had spread. It was about as formal an affair as looking
at a road map to find your way to Washington, Connecticut,
from New Milford. "We used to make more fuss over briefings
in England," the intelligence officer said, "but when you're
flying two or three times a day, what the hell?" He pointed out
the place on the map where the tanks were supposed to be,
and all the fellows said they knew where it was, having been
there before. Hoelle said they would take off at noon. After a
while he and the seven other boys went out onto the field to
get ready, and I went with them. On the way there was more
talk about P-38's and how some Italian prisoners had told their
captors that the Italian army could win the war easy if it wasn't
for those fork-tailed airplanes coming over and shooting
them up, a notion that seemed particularly to amuse the pilots.
Then I went to the P-38 squadron mess with Adler, who had
just returned from patrol duty and wasn't going out on
the strafe job, and Gustke, who was also remaining behind.
This mess was relatively luxurious. They had tables with plates
and knives and forks on them, so they had no mess tins to wash
after every meal. "We live well here," Adler said. "Everything
high-class."

"The place the planes are going is not very far away,"
Gustke said, "so they ought to be back around half past two."

When we had finished lunch, I took another stroll around
the post. I was walking toward the P-38 squadron's operations
shack when I saw the planes begin to return from the mission.
The first that came in had only the nose wheel of its landing
gear down. There was evidently something the matter with the
two other wheels. The plane slid in on its belly and stopped in
a cloud of dust. Another plane was hovering over the field. I
noticed, just after I spotted this one, that a little ambulance

was tearing out onto the field. Only one of the two propellers of this plane was turning, but it landed all right, and then I counted one, two, three others, which landed in good shape. Five out of eight. I broke into a jog toward the operations shack. Gustke was standing before the door looking across the field with binoculars. I asked him if he knew whose plane had belly-landed, and he said it was a Lieutenant Moffat's and that a big, rough Texas pilot the other fellows called Wolf had been in the plane that had come in with one engine out. "I see Earnhart and Keith and Carlton, too," he said, "but Hoelle and the other two are missing."

A jeep was coming from the field toward the operations shack, and when it got nearer we could see Wolf in it. He looked excited. He was holding his right forearm with his left hand, and when the jeep got up to the shack he jumped out, still holding his arm.

"Is it a bullet hole?" Gustke asked.

"You're a sonofabitch it's a bullet hole!" Wolf shouted. "The sonofabitching P-40's sonofabitching around! As we came in, we saw four fighters coming in the opposite direction and Moffat and I went up to look at them and they were P-40's, coming away. The other fellows was on the deck and we started to get down nearer them, to about five thousand, and these sonofabitching 190's came out of the sun and hit Moffat and me the first burst and then went down after the others. There was ground fire coming up at us, too, and the sonofabitches said we was going to be over friendly territory. I'm goddam lucky not to be killed."*

"Did we get any of them?" Gustke asked.

"I know I didn't get any," Wolf said, "but I saw at least four planes burning on the ground. I don't know who the hell they were."

By that time another jeep had arrived with Earnhart, looking utterly calm, and one of the mechanics from the field. "My plane is all right," Earnhart told Gustke. "All gassed up and ready to go. They can use that for patrol."

The telephone inside the shack rang. It was the post first-aid station calling to say that Moffat was badly cut up by glass

*Normal confusion.

from his windshield but would be all right. The mechanic said that the cockpit of Moffat's plane was knee-deep in hydraulic fluid and oil and gas. "No wonder the hydraulic system wouldn't work when he tried to get the wheels down," the mechanic said. The phone rang again. This time it was group operations, calling for Earnhart, Keith, and Carlton, all three of them unwounded, to go over there and tell them what had happened. The three pilots went away, and a couple of the men got Wolf back into a jeep and took him off to the first-aid station. Hoelle and the two other pilots were still missing. That left only Gustke and me, and he said in a sad young voice, like a boy whose chum has moved to another city, "Now we have lost our buddies."

A couple of days later I learned that Hoelle had bailed out in disputed territory and made his way back to our lines, but the two other boys are either dead or prisoners.

II

Not many Mondays ago I was standing in a chow line with my mess tins at an airfield* in southern Tunisia, waiting to get into a dugout where some mess attendants were ladling out a breakfast of stew and coffee. The field is enormous, a naturally flat airdrome of white sand and alfa grass that doesn't hold rainwater long enough to spoil the runways—terrain of the kind a French writer once said looked like foamy seas. All around the field there are bulky, reddish mountains. To the east, the sun was just coming up over one of them, and the air was very cold. The mess shack was covered on top and three sides by a mound of earth. It served officers and men of a squadron of P-40 fighters, and on that particular Monday morning I stood between a corporal named Jake Goldstein, who in civilian life had been a Broadway songwriter, and a private named John Smith, of New Hope, Pennsylvania, who used to help his father, a contractor, build houses. Goldstein told me about a lyric he had just written for a song to be called "Bombs." "The music that I think of when it goes through my

*This time it was Thélepte, in Tunisia.

head now," he said, "is kind of a little like the old tune called 'Smiles,' but maybe I can change it around later. The lyric goes:

> There are bombs that sound so snappy,
> There are bombs that leave folks sad,
> There are bombs that fell on dear old Dover,
> But those bombs are not so bad.

The idea is that the real bad bomb is when this girl quit me and blew up my heart."

"It sounds great," I told the Corporal.

"It will be even bigger than a number I wrote called 'What Do You Hear from Your Heart?'" Goldstein said. "Probably you remember it. Bing Crosby sang it once on the Kraft Cheese Hour. If you happen to give me a little writeup, remember that my name in the songwriting business is Jack Gould." Private Smith started to tell me that he had once installed some plumbing for a friend of mine, Sam Spewack, the writer, in New Hope. "His wife, Bella, couldn't make up her mind where she wanted the can," Smith said, "so I said—"

I never heard any more about Bella Spewack's plumbing, because Major Robert Christman, the commanding officer of the squadron, came up to me and said, "Well, it's a nice, quiet morning." He had his back to the east. I didn't get a chance to answer him, because I started to run like hell to get to the west side of the mound. A number of soldiers who had been scattered about eating their breakfast off the tops of empty gasoline cans had already started running and dropping their mess things. They always faced eastward while they ate in the morning so that they could see the Messerschmitts come over the mountains in the sunrise. This morning there were nine Messerschmitts. By the time I hit the ground on the lee side of the mound, slender airplanes were twisting above us in a sky crisscrossed by tracer bullets—a whole planetarium of angry worlds and meteors. Behind our shelter we watched and sweated it out. It is nearly impossible to tell Messerschmitts from P-40's when they are maneuvering in a fight, except when one plane breaks off action and leaves its opponent hopelessly behind. Then you know that the one which is distanced is a P-40. You can't help yelling encouragement as you watch a fight, even though no one can hear you and you cannot tell the combatants apart. The Messerschmitts, which were there to strafe us, flew right over the mess shack and began giving the runways and the planes on the field a going-over.

We had sent up four planes on patrol that morning and they tried to engage the strafing planes, but other Germans, flying high to protect the strafers, engaged the patrol. Some "alert" planes that we had in readiness on the perimeter of the field took off in the middle of the scrap, and that was a pretty thing to watch. I saw one of our patrol planes come in and belly-land on the field, smoking. Then I saw another plane twisting out of the sky in a spin that had the soldiers yelling. We all felt that the spinning plane was a Messerschmitt, and it looked like a sure thing to crash into one of the mountains north of us. When the plane pulled out and disappeared over the summit, the yell died like the howl at Ebbets Field when the ball looks as if it's going into the bleachers and then is snagged by a visiting outfielder. It was a Messerschmitt, all right. A couple of minutes later every one of the German planes had disappeared, with our ships after them like a squad of heavy-footed comedy cops chasing small boys.

The fellows who had ducked for cover hoisted themselves off the ground and looked around for the mess things they had dropped. They were excited and sheepish, as they always are after a strafe party. It is humiliating to have someone run you away, so you make a joke about it. One soldier yelled to another, "When you said 'Flop!' I was there already!" Another, who spoke with a Brooklyn accent, shouted, "Jeez, those tracers looked just like Luna Park!"*

We formed the chow line again and one fellow yelled to a friend, "What would you recommend as a good, safe place to eat?"

"Lindy's, at Fifty-first Street," the other soldier answered.

"The way the guys ran, it was like a Christmas rush at Macy's," somebody else said.

Everybody tried hard to be casual. Our appetites were even better than they had been before, the excitement having

---

*See note on p. 350. Luna was an amusement park at Coney Island, so famous that it gave its name to imitations all over Europe. Fireworks were a nightly feature, but they were pretty pallid compared to any respectable anti-aircraft barrage. Luna is no more.

joggled up our internal secretions. There were arguments about whether the plane that had escaped over the mountain would crash before reaching the German lines. I was scraping the last bits of stew from my mess tin with a sliver of hard biscuit when a soldier came up and told me that Major ——,* whom I had never met, had been killed on the field, that five men had been wounded, and that one A-20 bomber had been ruined on the ground.

After I had washed up my tins, I walked over to the P-40 squadron operations shack, because I wanted to talk to a pilot familiarly known as Horse about a fight he had been in two days before. The day it had happened I had been visiting a P-38 squadron's headquarters on the field. I had seen eight P-38's go out to attack some German tanks and only five come back, two of them badly damaged. A lot of Focke-Wulf 190's had attacked the P-38's over the target, and Horse and three other P-40 pilots, who were protecting the 38's, had been up above the 190's. Horse was a big fellow with a square, tan face and a blond beard. He came from a town called Quanah, in Texas, and he was always showing his friends a tinted picture of his girl, who was in the Waves. Horse was twenty-five, which made him practically a patriarch in that squadron, and everybody knew that he was being groomed to command a squadron of his own when he got his captaincy. He was something of a wit. Once I heard one of the other boys say that now that the field had been in operation for six weeks, he thought it was time the men should build a sit-down latrine. "The next thing we know," Horse said, "you'll be wanting to send home for your wife."

I found Horse and asked him about the fight. He said he was sorry that the 38's had had such a bad knock. "I guess maybe it was partly our fault," he said. "Four of our ships had been sent out to be high cover for the 38's. They didn't see any 38's or Jerries either, so when their gas was beginning to run low they started for home.† Myself and three other fellows had started out to relieve them and we passed them as they came back. The

*We were not allowed by the censor to mention names of casualties until they had appeared in the lists published at home. Now I cannot fill in this blank, because I forget the poor gentleman's name.

†See note p. 356 on confusion.

38's must have arrived over the tanks just then, and the 190's must have been hiding at the base of a cloud bank above the 38's but far below us. When we got directly over the area, we could see tracers flying way down on the deck. The 190's had dived from the cloud and bounced the 38's, who never had a chance, and the 38's were streaking for home. We started down toward the 190's, but it takes a P-40 a long time to get anywhere and we couldn't help. Then four more 190's dived from way up top and bounced us. I looped up behind one of them as he dived. My two wing men were right with me. I put a good burst into the sonofabitch and he started to burn, and I followed him down. I must have fired a hundred and twenty-five rounds from each gun. It was more fun than a county fair. Gray, my fourth man, put a lot of lead into another 190, and I doubt if it ever got home. The other two Jerries just kept on going."

The P-40 operations shack was set deep in the ground and had a double tier of bunks along three of its walls. Sand and grass were heaped over the top of the shack, and the pilots said that even when they flew right over it, it was hard to see, which cheered them considerably. The pilots were flying at least two missions a day and spent most of the rest of the time lying in the bunks in their flying clothes, under as many coats and blankets as they could find. The atmosphere in the shack was a thick porridge of dust diluted by thin trickles of cold air. Major Christman, the squadron leader, once said in a pleased tone, "This joint always reminds me of a scene in 'Journey's End.' "* The pilots, most of whom were in their earliest twenties, took a certain perverse satisfaction in their surroundings. "Here we know we're at war," one of them said to me. "Not that I wouldn't change for a room and bath at a good hotel."

During most of my stay at the field I lived not in the Journey's End shack but in one known as the Hotel Léon because technically it belonged to a French lieutenant named Léon,† a

---

*See note p. 350 on citations of the fictitious as criteria of reality.

†I suppressed his last name, Caplan, because he might have had relatives in France, who, if my piece in the *New Yorker* had reached France (highly unlikely), might have been made to suffer. Léon, when I saw him long after the war, was the number two man in the French Shell Oil Company—a *potentat petrolier*.

liaison officer between the French forces and our fliers. It was
the newest and finest dugout on the field, with wooden walls
and a wooden floor and a partition dividing it down the middle,
and the floor was sunk about five feet below ground level.
When I arrived at the field, there were plans to cover the part
of the shack that projected above ground with sand, in which
Léon intended to plant alfa. I was travelling with an Associated
Press correspondent named Norgaard, and soon after our arrival Léon, a slender man with a thin, intelligent face and
round, brown eyes, welcomed us to his palace. We put our stuff
into the shack and emerged to find Léon throwing a modest
shovelful of sand against one of the walls. Norgaard offered to
help him. "There is only one shovel," Léon said with relief,
pressing it into Norgaard's hands. "It is highly interesting for
our comfort and safety that the house be covered entirely with
sand. I am very occupied." Then he walked rapidly away, and
Norgaard and I took turns piling sand around the Hotel Léon
for endless hours afterward. Léon always referred to a telephone switchboard as a switching board, oil paper as oily
paper, a pup tent as a puppy tent, and a bedding roll as a
rolling bed.

After my talk with Horse, I walked over to the Hotel Léon
and found it crowded, as it usually was. Only Léon and Norgaard and I, together with Major Philip Cochran and Captain
Robert Wylie, lived in the hotel, but during the day Cochran
and Léon used it as an office, and that was why it was crowded.
When I first came to the field, it had been operating for six
weeks practically as an outpost, for there was just a unit of
American infantry, fifty miles to the southeast, between it and
the region occupied by Rommel's army. Cochran, though only
a major, had run the field for almost the entire period, but by
the time I arrived he had reverted to the status of operations
officer. The shack had telephone lines to detachments of
French troops scattered thinly through the hills to our east,
and they called up at all hours to tell Léon where German
tanks were moving or to ask our people to do some air reconnaissance or drop bags of food to a platoon somewhere on a
mountain. The French had no trucks to transport food. Sometimes Cochran flew with American transport planes to tell
them where to drop parachute troops and sometimes he flew

with bombers to tell them where to drop bombs. Because of Cochran's and Léon's range of activities, they always had a lot of visitors.

Attached to the partition in the shack were two field telephones, one of which answered you in French and the other in English. Two soldier clerks, who were usually pounding typewriters, sat on a bench in front of a shelf along one wall. One of them was Corporal Goldstein, the songwriter. The other was a private first class named Otto, who wore metal-rimmed spectacles with round lenses and belonged to the Pentecostal brethren, an evangelical sect which is against fighting and profanity. Otto owned some barber tools, and he cut officers' hair during office hours and enlisted men's at night. That morning he was cutting the hair of Kostia Rozanoff,* the commandant of the Lafayette Escadrille, a French P-40 outfit that was stationed at the field. Rozanoff was a blond, round-headed Parisian whose great-grandfather was Russian. Otto, perhaps taking a cue from the shape of Rozanoff's skull, had clipped him until he looked like Erich Von Stroheim, but there was no mirror, so Rozanoff was happy anyway. Cochran, dressed in a dirty old leather flying jacket, had just come back from a mission in the course of which he thought he had destroyed a 190, and was trying to tell about that while nearly everybody else in the shack was trying to tell him about the morning's strafing. Also in the shack was Colonel Edson D. Raff, the well-known parachutist, who had once unexpectedly found himself in command of all the American ground forces in southern Tunisia and for weeks had successfully bluffed enemy forces many times larger. He had flown in from his post in Gafsa in a small plane which he used as his personal transport. He was crowded in behind Otto's barbering elbow and was trying to talk to Cochran over Rozanoff's head. Raff is short and always wears a short carbine slung over his left shoulder, even indoors. He invariably flies very low in his plane to minimize the risk of being potted by a Messerschmitt. "I have one foot trailing on the ground," he says.

Lieutenant Colonel William Momyer, the commanding officer of the field, was sitting between Rozanoff and Corporal

*Rozanoff survived to fly jets. He will recur.

Goldstein, telling about a mission he had been on himself that morning, escorting a lot of A-20's over Kebili, a town where the Italians had begun to repair a dynamited causeway across the Chott Djerid. "I bet the wops will never get any workmen to go back to that place," Momyer said. "We scared hell out of them." Momyer had shot down a Junkers 88 and a Messerschmitt within a week. He was hot.

Among the others in the shack that morning were Norgaard, the Associated Press man, and a tall P-40 pilot named Harris, who kept asking Léon whether any French unit had telephoned to report finding the Messerschmitt he had been shooting at during the strafing episode, because he was sure it must have crashed. It was the Messerschmitt we had seen pull out of the spin over the mountain. The English-speaking telephone rang and Captain Wylie answered it. He has the kind of telephone voice that goes with a large, expensive office, which he probably had in civilian life. It was somebody up the line asking for Major ——, the officer who had just been machine-gunned in the strafing. "Major —— has been killed," Wylie said. "Is there anything I can do for you?"

There was a variety of stuff on the field when I was there. In addition to Christman's P-40 squadron and the Lafayette Escadrille, there was a second American P-40 squadron commanded by a Major Hubbard, which had a full set of pilots but only five ships. This was because the powers that be had taken away the other ships and given them to the Lafayettes in the interest of international good will. Hubbard's pilots were not sore at the Lafayettes, but they didn't think much of the powers that be. There was also a bomber squadron. The people on our field were not by any means sitting targets. They constantly annoyed the Germans, and that is why the Germans were so keen on "neutralizing" the field. But they didn't come back that day, and neither lunch nor dinner was disturbed.

The guests of the Hotel Léon often didn't go to the mess shack for dinner, because Léon would prepare dinner for them on the premises. He was a talented cook who needed the stimulation of a public, which was, that Monday evening, us. He also needed Wylie to keep the fire in the stove going, Cochran to wash dishes, and me and Norgaard to perform assorted chores. He got eggs from the Arabs and wine from a nearby French engineer unit, and he had gathered a choice assortment of canned goods from the quartermaster's stores. He also bought sheep and pigs from farmers. Léon's idea of a campaign supper was a *soufflé de poisson*, a *gigot*, and an *omelette brûlée à l'armagnac*. He made the *soufflé* out of canned salmon. The only trouble with dining at Léon's was that dinner was seldom ready before half past eight and it took until nearly midnight to clean up afterward.

During that Monday dinner we speculated on what the enemy would do next day. Norgaard said it was hell to have to get up early to catch the Germans' morning performance, but Cochran, the airfield's official prophet, and a successful one, said, "They'll want to make this one a big one tomorrow, so you can sleep late. They won't be over until two-thirty in the afternoon." Momyer, who was having dinner at the hotel that night, agreed that there would be something doing, but he didn't predict the time of day. Léon said, "I think also that there is something cooking in." Momyer decided to maintain a patrol of eight planes over the field all day. "Of course, maybe that's just what they want us to do, use our planes defensively, so we will fly less missions," he said, "but I think this time we ought to do it."

I had such faith in Cochran that it never occurred to me that the Germans would attack us before the hour he had named, and they didn't. The only enemy over the field the following morning was Photo Freddie, a German reconnaissance pilot who had become a local character. He came every morning at about forty thousand feet, flying a special Junkers 86 job so lightened that it could outclimb any fighter. The anti-aircraft guns would fire, putting a row of neat, white smoke puffs a couple of miles below the seat of Freddie's pants, the patrol planes would lift languidly in his direction, like the hand of a fat man waving away a fly, and Photo Freddie would scoot off toward Sicily, or wherever he came from, to develop his pictures, thus discovering where all the planes on the field were placed. The planes were always moved around after he left, and we used to wonder what the general of the Luftwaffe said to poor Freddie when the bombers failed to find the planes

where he had photographed them. Now and then some pilot
tried to catch Photo Freddie by getting an early start, climbing
high above the field, and then stooging around until he appeared. Freddie, however, varied the hour of his matutinal
visits, and since a P-40 cannot fly indefinitely, the pilot would
get disgusted and come down. I do not think anybody really
wanted to hurt Freddie anyway. He was part of the local fauna,
like the pet hens that wandered about the field and popped
into slit trenches when bombs began to fall.

At about twenty minutes past two that afternoon Norgaard
and I returned to the Hotel Léon to do some writing. An
Alsatian corporal in the French army was working in front of
the shack, making a door for the entrance. The corporal had
been assigned by the French command to build Léon's house,
and he was a hard worker. He always kept his rifle by him while
he was working. He had a long brown beard, which he said he
was going to let grow until the Germans were driven out of
Tunisia. Only Goldstein and Otto were inside the hut this time.
I said to Goldstein, "Why don't you write a new number called
'One-Ninety, I Love You'?" Otto, who had been reading the
Pentecostal Herald, said, "I do not think that would be a good
title. It would not be popular." At that precise moment all of
us heard the deep woomp of heavy ack-ack. It came from one
of the British batteries in the mountains around the field. We
grabbed our tin hats and started for the doorway. By the time
we got there, the usual anti-aircraft show was on. In the din
we could easily distinguish the sound of our Bofors guns,
which were making their peculiar seasick noises—not so much
a succession of reports as one continuous retch. The floor of
the shack, as I have said, was five feet below ground level and
the Alsatian had not yet got around to building steps down to
the entrance, so we had a nice, rectangular hole just outside
from which to watch developments. The Germans were
bombing now, and every time a bomb exploded, some of
the sand heaped against the wooden walls was driven into the
shack through the knotholes. The only trouble was that whenever a bomb went off we pulled in our heads and stopped observing. Then we looked out again until the next thump. After
several of these thumps there was a straight row of columns of
black smoke a couple of hundred yards to our right. I poked

my head above ground level and discovered the Alsatian corporal kneeling and firing his rifle, presumably at an airplane which I could not see. The smoke began to clear and we hoisted ourselves out of the hole to try and find out what had happened. "I do not think I touched," the Alsatian said. A number of dog-fights were still going on over the mountains. Scattered about the field, men, dragging themselves out of slit trenches, were pointing to the side of a mountain to the north, where there was smoke above a downed plane.

Léon had a little and old Citroën car, which he said had become, through constant association with the United States Army, "one naturalized small jeeps." He had left it parked behind the shack, and as Norgaard and I stood gawping about, Léon came running and shouted that he was going out to the fallen plane. We climbed into the naturalized jeeps and started across the field toward the mountainside. At one of the runways, we met a group of P-40 pilots, including Horse, and I yelled to them, "Was it theirs or ours?" "Ours, I think," Horse said. We kept on going. When we reached the other side of the field, we cut across country, and Léon could not make much speed. A couple of soldiers with rifles thumbed a ride and jumped on the running boards. As we went out across plowed fields and up the mountain toward the plane, we passed dozens of soldiers hurrying in the same direction.

When we arrived where the plane had fallen, we found three trucks and at least fifty men already there. The plane had been a Messerschmitt 109 belonging to the bombers' fighter escort. Flames were roaring above the portion deepest in the earth, which I judged was the engine. Screws, bolts, rings, and unidentifiable bits of metal were scattered over an area at least seventy-five yards square. Intermingled with all this were widely scattered red threads, like the bits left in a butcher's grinder when he has finished preparing an order of chopped steak. "He never even tried to pull out," a soldier said. "He must have been shot through the brain. I seen the whole thing. The plane fell five thousand feet like a hunk of lead." There was a sour smell over everything—not intolerable, just sour. "Where is the pilot?" Norgaard asked. The soldier waved his hand with a gesture that included the whole area. Norgaard, apparently for the first time, noticed the red threads.

Most of the soldiers were rummaging amid the wreckage, searching for souvenirs. Somebody said that the pilot's automatic pistol, always the keepsake most eagerly sought, had already been found and appropriated. Another soldier had picked up some French and Italian money. How these things had survived the pilot's disintegration I do not know. While the soldiers walked about, turning over bits of the plane with their feet, looking for some object which could serve as a memento, an American plane came over and everybody began to run before someone recognized it for what it was. Just as we came back, a soldier started kicking at something on the ground and screaming. He was one of the fellows who had ridden out on our running boards. He yelled, "There's the sonofabitch's God-damn guts! He wanted my guts! He nearly had my guts, God damn him!" Another soldier went up to him and bellowed, "Shut up! It ain't nice to talk that way!" A lot of other men began to gather around. For a minute or so the soldier who had screamed stood there silently, his shoulders pumping up and down, and then he began to blubber.

Léon picked up a large swatch of the Messerschmitt's tail fabric as a trophy, and as the soldiers walked away from the wreck most of them carried either similar fragments or pieces of metal. After a while Norgaard and I climbed into Léon's car and the three of us started back toward the field. When we arrived, we learned that a lieutenant named Walter Scholl, who had never been in a fight before, had shot down the Messerschmitt. He was the fellow who, in the Cornell-Dartmouth football game of 1940, threw the famous fifth-down touchdown pass for Cornell, the one that was completed for what was considered a Cornell victory until movies of the game showed that it shouldn't have been Cornell's ball at all and the decision had to be reversed. But this was one win that they couldn't take away from him. Two other pilots had shot down two Junkers 88 bombers. One of our planes on the ground had been destroyed, and a slit trench had caved in on two fellows, nearly frightening them to death before they could be dug out.

III

Norgaard often said that the country reminded him of New Mexico, and with plenty of reason. Both are desert countries of mountains and mesas, and in both there are sunsets that owe their beauty to the dust in the air. The white, rectangular Arab houses, with their blue doors, are like the houses certain Indians build in New Mexico, and the Arabs' saddle blankets and pottery and even the women's silver bracelets are like Navajo things. The horses, which look like famished mustangs, have the same lope and are similarly bridlewise; burros are all over the place, and so is cactus. These resemblances are something less than a coincidence, because the Moors carried their ways of house-building and their handicraft patterns and even their breed of horses and method of breaking them to Spain, and the Spaniards carried them to New Mexico eight hundred years later.* All these things go to make up a culture that belongs to a high plateau country where there are sheep to furnish wool for blankets and where people have too little cash to buy dishes in a store, where the soil is so poor that people have no use for heavy plow horses but want a breed that they can ride for long distances and that will live on nearly nothing.

"This horse is young," an Arab once said to Norgaard and me as he showed us a runty bay colt tied in front of a combined general store and barbershop in a village about a mile from the airfield. "If I had had a little barley to feed him, he would be bigger, but what barley we had we have ourselves eaten. It is a poor country."

We used to go down to this village to get eggs when we were too lazy to make the chow line for breakfast or when we felt hungry at any time of day. We'd take them back to the shack and cook them. Solitary Arabs squat along the roadside all over North Africa, waiting for military vehicles. When one comes into sight, the Arab pulls an egg out from under his rags and holds it up between thumb and forefinger like a magician at a night club. The price of eggs—always high, of course— varies in inverse ratio to the distance from a military post. Near

* The cactus, though, was imported *from* Latin America into North Africa, where it is considered a prime fodder plant, particularly appreciated by camels.

big towns that are a long way from any post the Arabs get only five francs (ten cents at the new rate of exchange) for an egg, but in villages close to garrisons eggs are sometimes hard to find at any price. Norgaard and I followed a standard protocol to get them. First we went into the general store and barber-shop, which was just a couple of almost empty rooms that were part of a mud house, and shook hands with all the male members of the establishment. Naturally, we never saw any of the females. Then we presented a box of matches to the head of the house, an ex-soldier who spoke French, and he invited us to drink coffee. The Arabs have better coffee and more sugar than the Europeans in North Africa. While we drank the coffee, we sat with the patriarch of the family on a white iron bed of European manufacture. The patriarch had a white beard and was always knitting socks; he stopped only to scratch himself. Once, as we were drinking coffee, we watched our French-speaking friend shave a customer's head. He simply started each stroke at the top of the cranium and scraped downward. He used no lather; the customer moistened his own poll with spittle after each stroke of the razor. Once, when the customer made a particularly awful face, all the other Arabs sitting around the room laughed. During the coffee-drinking stage of the negotiations we presented the Arabs with a can of fifty English cigarettes. After that they presented us with ten to fifteen eggs. Soldiers who were not such good friends of theirs usually got twenty eggs for fifty cigarettes, but it always costs something to maintain one's social life. One day I asked the barber why the old man scratched himself, and he said, laughing, "Because of the black spots. We all have them, and they itch." With much hilarity the Arabs showed us the hard, black spots, apparently under their skins, from which they were suffering. I judged the trouble to be a degenerate form of the Black Death, tamed during the centuries by the rugged constitutions of our hosts. Norgaard thought that the spots were just chiggers.

The Germans had come over our airfield on a Monday morning and strafed it and they had come back on Tuesday afternoon and bombed the place. They were going to start an offensive in southern Tunisia, we later learned, so they wanted to knock out this, the most advanced American field. On Wednesday morning the Germans made no attack. That afternoon Norgaard and I decided that we needed some eggs, so we walked down to the Arab village. I carried the eggs home in my field hat, a visored cap which has long flaps to cover your neck and ears when it is cold and which makes a good egg bag. We got back to the Hotel Léon between five and six o'clock. Major Cochran was out flying, and Léon was out foraging. Jake and Otto had gone to chow. There was less than an hour of daylight left.

Cochran, with his fine instinct for divining what the Germans were likely to do, had been sure that they would come over for the third day in succession, and Lieutenant Colonel William Momyer, the commanding officer of the field, had maintained a patrol of P-40's over the field all day. Cochran was among those taking their turns on patrol duty now. In forty minutes more all the planes would have to come down, because the field had no landing lights. And nothing had happened yet.

The walk had made Norgaard and me hungry and we decided to have our eggs immediately. We threw some kindling wood in the stove to stir the fire up and I put some olive oil in the mess tin in which I was going to scramble the eggs. The olive oil belonged to Léon. I took the lid off the hole in the top of the stove, put the mess tin over the hole, and broke all the eggs into the oil. I think there were eleven of them. They floated around half submerged, and although I stirred them with a fork, they didn't scramble. We decided that I had used too much oil, so we added some cheese to act as a cement. Before the cheese had time to take effect, we heard a loud explosion outside—plainly a bomb—and felt the shack rock. Norgaard grabbed his tin hat and ran out the door to look, and I was just going to follow him when I reflected that if I left this horrible brew on the stove hole a spark might ignite the oil and thus set fire to the shack. I carefully put the mess on a bench and replaced the lid on the stove. I put on my helmet and followed Norgaard out into a kind of foxhole outside our door. More bombs exploded and then all we could hear was the racket of the Bofors cannon and .50 calibre machine guns defending the field. I went back inside, removed the stove lid, and put the eggs on again. Just as some warmth began to return to the chill mess, another stick of bombs went off. In the course of the next minute or so, I repeated my entire routine. Before I finished cooking dinner, I had to repeat it three times more. Finally the eggs and the cheese stuck together after a fashion and I drained the oil off. Then, since no bombs had dropped for a couple of minutes, I poured half the concoction into Norgaard's canteen cup, I put what was left in my mess tin, and we ate.

After we had eaten, we left the shack and started toward the large, round pit, some fifty yards away, which served as a control room for the field. Night had closed in. There had been no firing now for ten minutes, but as we approached the pit, our anti-aircraft opened up again, firing from all around the field simultaneously. The Bofors tracer shells, which look like roseate Roman candles, reminded me of the fireworks on the lagoon at the World's Fair in Flushing. The burst ended as abruptly as it had begun, except that one battery of .50's kept on for an extra second or two and then stopped in an embarrassed manner.

We saw a lot of our pilots clustered around the pit. A corporal named Dick usually stood in the pit talking to our planes in the air by radio telephone, but Major Robert Christman, the C.O. of one of the post's fighter squadrons, was in Dick's place. I recognized Christman's voice as he spoke into the telephone, asking, "Did you see the gunfire? Did you see the gunfire?" You wouldn't ask a Jerry that if you were shooting at him, so I knew they were firing the anti-aircraft guns to light one or more of our planes home. Christman asked again, "Did you see the gunfire? Did you see the gunfire?" Then he said to somebody else in the pit, probably Dick, "Hold this a minute." He stuck his head up over the side of the pit and shouted in the direction of a nearby dugout, "They say they saw the fire! Cochran's going to lead in and land to show the other ship the way! Lord, how that Cochran swears when he's excited! Tell the ack-ack to hold everything!" The switchboard through which the control room communicated with all the ack-ack batteries was in the dugout. Nothing was convenient on that field. It sometimes seemed that one of the pilots had scratched the whole thing out of the ground with a broken propeller blade after a forced landing.

We could see a plane showing red and green lights slowly circling over the field, descending gradually in long, deliberate spirals, as if the pilot wanted somebody to follow him. Then there was a blast of machine-gun fire and a fountain of tracers sprayed up from a distant edge of the field. "God damn them!" Christman yelled. "Tell them to hold that fire! What do they want to do—shoot Phil down?" The plane coasted slowly, imperturbably lower. It was Cochran's firm belief, I knew, that the ack-ack on the field had never hit anything, so he probably wasn't worried. The plane skimmed over the surface of the field. There was one pitiful red light on the field for it to land by. "He'll never make it that way," a pilot near me said. "What the hell is he doing? He'll overshoot. No, there he goes up again."

In a minute Christman, back at the phone once more, said, "Cochran went up because the other fellow couldn't see him. The other ship says he saw the gunfire, though. Now he wants a burst on the southern edge of the field only." Somebody in the switchboard dugout yelled, "Come on now! Battery C only, Battery C only! Everybody else *hold* it!" All the guns on the field immediately fired together. I could hear Momyer's voice yelling in the dugout, "God damn it, I'll have them all court-martialled!" Christman shouted, "He says he saw it and now he can see Cochran! He's coming in!" Cochran was again circling in the blackness above the field. The pilot next to me said, "This is sure sweating it out." I recognized him, partly by his voice and partly by the height of his shoulders, as Horse, the big Texan who wore a square beard.

"Did we get any of theirs?" I asked Horse.

"Yes, sir," Horse said. "Bent got one for sure. He's in already. And a French post has telephoned that another one is down near there in flames and that pilot out there with Cochran had one smoking. He must have chased it so far he couldn't get back before dark. Must have forgot himself. I don't rightly know who he is."

The ack-ack batteries fired again. They apparently did what was wanted this time, because nobody cursed. Christman

called up from the pit, "They want one more burst, all together, and then they're coming in!" The message was relayed
and the ack-ack fired another salvo. Now there were two
planes, both showing lights, moving in the sky above the field,
one high and one low. "Cochran's coming in," Horse said.
"Look at him. Just like it was day and he could see everything." The lower pair of lights drifted downward, straightened out and ran forward along the field, and stopped. The
other lights slowly followed them down, seemed to hesitate a
moment, then slanted toward the ground, and coasted into a
horizontal. "Good landing," Horse said. "We sure sweated
that one." The second pilot to land turned out to be a lieutenant named Thomas, who had become too absorbed in the
pursuit of a Junkers 88 to turn back until he had shot it down.
That made three Junkers for us, each carrying a crew of four
men. I learned that the German bombs had spoiled, to use the
airmen's term, two of our planes on the field. A couple of
minutes later a jeep that had gone out to meet Cochran's
plane brought him to where the rest of us were standing. He is
a short, box-chested man, and the two or three flying jackets
he was wearing made him look shorter and stockier than he
really is. He was feeling good. "I'm sorry I cursed you out,
Bob! I was excited!" he yelled down into the control pit to
Christman. Momyer, who had come out of the dugout, made
as if to grab Cochran and hug him, but stopped in astonishment when he heard Cochran being so polite. It seemed to remind him of something. Looking rather thoughtful, he went
back into the dugout and called up the lieutenant colonel in
command of the ack-ack, which he had been abusing. "Thank
you very much, Colonel," I heard him say. "Your boys certainly saved the day."

That evening was a happy one. Léon's shack was crowded
with pilots talking about the successful fight and scrambling
eggs and eating them out of mess tins. Cochran felt so good
that he decided to have his first haircut since he had left New
York three months before, so he sent over to the enlisted
men's quarters for Otto to do the job. Otto is a young man
with reddish hair and white eyebrows and a long nose, and he
had a habit of getting interested in a conversation between

two senior officers and breaking into it. Once, hearing Colonel Edson D. Raff, the parachute-troop commander, telling lieutenant Colonel Momyer that he could take Tunis with no more than four hundred and fifty men, Otto blurted out, "How can you be so sure?" Aside from this failing he is a good soldier and when he gives a haircut he really cuts off hair, so nobody can say he is looking for a return engagement in the near future.

It was well after dark when Léon came in from his foraging, which had been a success too. "I have bought three small peegs," he announced triumphantly, "and when they are theek enough we shall eat them." He had left them in the care of a *hôtelier* in a town a few miles away. They were subsequently taken, and presumably eaten, by the Germans. At the time, however, Léon thought it a safe *logement* for the pigs. "I have also talked with the aide of General Koeltz," Léon said to Cochran and Momyer, "and he says that in the case any pilot sees any trucks moving on the road of which we have spoken yesterday, he is allowed to shoot without permission." While Otto cut Cochran's hair, we added up the box score of the three-day German attack on the field. The home team felt that it had done pretty well. During the Monday strafing the Germans had spoiled one of our planes on the field and another in the air and had killed one officer, a major, with machine-gun bullets. We had merely damaged one of their fighters. On Tuesday, while they had spoiled two more of our planes on the ground with bombs, we had shot down a Messerschmitt 109 and two Junkers 88's. That meant that we had lost a total of three planes but only one life while they had lost three planes and nine lives. One of our missions had also destroyed a Focke-Wulf 190 on Monday morning and a Messerschmitt had been badly damaged in the dogfight that had accompanied the strafing of our field. Wednesday evening we had destroyed three more planes and twelve men, and the Germans had succeeded only in damaging two planes on the ground, which gave us an imposing lead. "They won't be over tomorrow morning," Cochran said. "Maybe not all day. They'll want to think things over and try something big to make up for their losses and get the lead back. They'll be like a guy doubling his bet in a crap game."

That field had been fought over many times before in the course of history and a corner of it had been the site of a Numidian city. Bent, a pilot who talked with a British accent and had once done some digging among old ruins in England, said that every time he flew over that corner he could plainly see the gridiron pattern of the ancient streets on the ground. Horse, the bearded pilot, was irreverent about Bent's claims. "Maybe a couple of thousand years from now," he said, "people will dig around this same field and find a lot of C-ration cans that we've left and attribute them to archeology. They'll say, 'Those Americans must surely have been a pygmy race to wear such small helmets. It scarcely seems possible they had much brains. No wonder they rode around in such funny airplanes as the P-40.'"*

Another officer who turned up in Léon's shack that evening was Major (afterward Lieutenant Colonel) Vincent Sheean, who always points out these days that he was once a correspondent himself. He said he had been driving in a jeep on a road near the field when the bombing started, so he had stopped and jumped into a ditch. Sheean had come down from the second highest headquarters of the African Air Forces to see that the French pilots of the Lafayette Escadrille, which had recently arrived at our field, received understanding and kind treatment from their American comrades. A couple of the Lafayette pilots happened to be in the shack when he arrived; they had received so much kind treatment that they could hardly remember the words of "Auprès de Ma Blonde," which they were trying to teach to Momyer on a purely phonetic basis.

The next day, Thursday, was as quiet as Cochran had said it would be. The Germans left us completely alone. In the morning the Lafayette Escadrille fellows went on their first mission, covering a French local offensive in a mountain pass, and returned without meeting any enemy aircraft.

The exposed position of our mess shack had begun to worry

---

*I was back in 1956, but even the C-ration cans are gone. The natives of those parts are extremely poor, and may have thought even tin cans worth salvaging.

Major Christman's men after the strafing we had received the Monday before, and he had ordered the chow line transferred to a place called the Ravine, a deep, winding gulch on the other side of the high road along one end of the field. Most of the men lived in the Ravine and felt safe there. They had scooped out caves in its sides and used their shelter halves to make doors. One stretch of the gully was marked by a sign that said "Park Avenue." Sheean and I stood in the chow line for lunch and then took an afternoon stroll along Park Avenue. Afterward I went back to Léon's shack to write a letter and found it crowded, as usual. An engineer officer who had been at the field a couple of days was asking Cochran how he could be expected to get on with the construction job he had been sent there to do if new bomb holes appeared on the field every day and his detachment had to fill them up. "We've been filling up bomb holes ever since we been here, and it looks like we won't get a chance to do anything else," the engineer said. "My colonel sent me down here to build revetments for airplanes and he's going to expect me back soon." Another visitor, a captain in the Royal Engineers, asked him if there were any unexploded bombs on the runways. Men on the field always referred to this British captain as the booby-trap man, the planting of fiendish traps for the enemy being his specialty, and added with respect, "Even the parachute troops say he's crazy." He had made several jumps with Colonel Raff's parachutists to install his humorous devices in places where he thought German soldiers would later get involved with them. The American officer told him that there were several unexploded bombs on the runways and that he had marked off their positions with empty oil drums.

"But haven't you removed the fuses?" the booby-trap man asked with obvious astonishment.

"To hell with that!" his American colleague said with feeling. "They won't do any harm if they do go off. It's a big field."

"Oh, but they'll make quite a lot of noise," the booby-trap man said, still vaguely unhappy.

The American officer looked at the booby-trap man and Cochran as if they were both lunatics and went out of the hut without saying anything more. "How *extraordinary!*" the booby-trap man said. "He didn't even seem interested." He sounded hurt, like a young mother who has just learned that a visitor does not care for babies.

The booby-trap man looked like a conventional sort of Englishman, with a fair, boyish face and a shy smile. He spoke with the careful accent of the north countryman who has been to a university and he did not himself use the term "booby trap." He preferred to call his darlings, variously, trip mechanisms, push mechanisms, pull mechanisms, and anti-personnel switches. Trip mechanisms, for instance, are the ones soldiers inadvertently set off by stumbling over a concealed wire, and pull mechanisms are those they explode by picking up some innocent-seeming object like a corned-beef tin. The captain was an amateur botanist and seldom went out without a couple of pocketfuls of small devices to set about the countryside in likely spots as he ambled along collecting specimens of Tunisian grasses. I asked him that afternoon how he had started on what was to become his military career, and he said with his shy smile, "I expect it was at public school, when I used to put hedgehogs in the other boys' beds. After a while the hedgehogs began to pall and I invented a system for de-tuning the school piano, so that when the music master sat down to play 'God Save the King' it sounded god-awful."

"I sometimes try to imagine what your married life will be like, Captain," Cochran said. "Someday the baby will be in the crib and your wife will go to pick it up and the whole house will blow up because you've wired the baby to a booby trap."

"I trust I shall be able to restrain my professional instincts to fit the circumstances of domestic life," the booby-trap man said rather stiffly. He was a man who really took his branch of warfare seriously.

IV

Sleep in the Hotel Léon was usually interrupted in the gray hour before dawn by the jangle of a field telephone that spoke French. Then Léon would sit up and pull the telephone from the holster in which it hung at the foot of his bed. He slept wearing all the clothes he possessed, which included several sweaters, a long military overcoat, and a muffler. When he grabbed the phone, he would say, "*Allo! Oui?*" (The rest of us sometimes would sing "Sweet Allo, Oui" to the tune of "Sweet Eloise.") The French voice at the other end of the phone was almost always audible, and, so that the half-awake American officers in the shack would get the idea of what was going on, Léon would reply in a hybrid jargon. He would say, for example, "One *ennemi appareil* flying sousewest over point 106? *Merci, mon capitaine.*" Then he would hang up and fall back into bed, muttering, "*Imbécile*, why he don't fly west? He will be losted."

A partition divided Léon's shack into a bedroom, in which four of us slept side by side, and an office, in which only two slept. In the bedroom were Léon, Major Cochran, Norgaard, and myself. Captain Robert Wylie and Vincent Sheean slept in the office. We would try to ignore Léon's first morning call, but before long there would be another; Cochran would be asking what was going on, and we would hear the roar of the motors down on the field being warmed up for the dawn patrol and the morning missions. Then we would hear Wylie clattering around our stove in his G.I. shoes and there would be a glow in the shack when he put the match to the paper with which he started the fire. Wylie, who wasn't a flying officer, always tried to have the shack warm by the time Cochran got up, and he wanted the Major to stay in bed until the last minute. He was as solicitous as a trainer with a favorite colt, and the rest of us benefited from the care he took of Cochran, because we didn't get up early, either. Wylie is a wiry man with a high forehead and a pepper-and-salt mustache. He wears glasses and looks like an advertising artist's conception of an executive who is in good humor because he has had an excellent night's sleep owing to Sanka. He is a highly adaptable man. After Wylie had puttered around for a while, we would sit up one by one and stretch and complain about being disturbed or about the cold and then go outside to wash. Mornings on which the anti-aircraft opened up against early visitors, the tempo was accelerated. Cochran undressed at night by loosening the knot in his tie and drew it tight again in the morning as a sign that he was dressed. These were symbolic gestures he never omitted.

On the morning of the fifth and last day of our small private war, it was the anti-aircraft that brought us out of bed. We scrambled for the door, lugging our tin hats, our tooth-brushes, and our canteens. The Germans were already almost over our field, but they were quite high, since our patrol planes had engaged them on the way in and they could not break off the fight to strafe us. The German planes were single-engined fighters, which sometimes carry wing or belly bombs, but this time they were not bombing. Some of the defending planes were marked with the tricolor *cocarde* of the French Army. It was, I suppose, a historic combat, because the pilots of the Lafayette Escadrille, which was stationed at the field, were making the first French air fight against the Germans since the armistice of 1940. The Escadrille, which had been equipped with a number of our Curtiss P-40's in Morocco, had been with us only a few days.

As we watched, a plane fell, apparently far on the other side of a ridge of mountains near the field, and we yelled happily, thinking it was a Messerschmitt. After the fight we were to learn that it had been a P-40 with a French sergeant pilot. Cochran kept up an expert running commentary on what all the pilots were trying to do, but he frequently didn't know which were French and which German. During the battle we simultaneously watched and brushed our teeth. A couple of the French planes landed on the field while the others were still fighting, so we knew that they must have been shot up. Finally, one group of planes above the field started away and the others chased them, but the first planes simply outclimbed their pursuers and left them behind; then there was no longer any doubt about which were Messerschmitts and which were Curtisses. One German plane remained over the field, at per-haps thirty thousand feet, even after the rest of the invaders had disappeared. "That's what kills me," Cochran said, pointing to the lone plane. "There's that sucker stooging around and casing the joint for a future job and he's so high nobody can bother him." Finally the stooge, evidently having found out all he wanted to know, took his leisurely departure.

A group of P-40's rose to relieve the Lafayettes, and the French planes came buzzing in like bees settling on a sugared stick. In a few minutes Kostia Rozanoff, commandant of the Escadrille, and his pilots had gathered in Léon's shack to dis-cuss the fight. All of them had had combat experience in 1939 and 1940, but the engagement this morning had been the *ren-trée*, and they were as excited as if they had never seen a Messerschmitt before. Despite the fact that they were old hands, Cochran said, they had fought recklessly, climbing up to meet the Messerschmitts instead of waiting until the Germans dived. "If they don't dive," Cochran had frequently warned his own pilots, "you just don't fight." The French pilots' ardor had got them a beating, for besides the pilot whom we had seen fall and who, Rozanoff said, had not bailed out and was quite certainly killed, the two planes that had landed during the combat were riddled and would be of no use except for salvage, and one of their pilots had been wounded. The Germans apparently had suffered no damage at all. Rozanoff, a chunky, blond man who gets his name, as well as his coloring and his high cheekbones, from his Russian ancestry, is thirty-seven and has a deep voice, like Chaliapin's. He said that the pilot who had been killed was his wing man and he could not understand how he had failed to see the Messerschmitt that had attacked him from the rear. "I cry him turn," Rozanoff kept saying. "I turn. He turns not. Poor little one."

It was extremely sad that the first Escadrille combat had not been a victory; it would have been such a fine story to bolster French morale all over the world. I remembered the sergeant pilot, who had been a likable fellow. An officer of the district gendarmerie brought the sergeant's wedding ring back to the field later in the morning.

My friend Norgaard and I had chosen that Friday for our departure from the field. We were going in to the big city, where the censors and the cable offices were, to write some stuff and get it off. There was air transportation between our field and the more settled places to the west, where staff officers and diplomats lived, but the service did not run on a formal schedule. Big Douglas transports skimmed in over the mountains once and sometimes twice a day, carrying mail and supplies, and they usually had room for passengers going back. They came at a different hour each day to make it as hard as possible for the Germans to waylay them. When they came, they stayed merely as long as was necessary, and the only way to be sure of a ride was to have your bedding roll made up and to stay near the landing field waiting for the transports to appear. When they did, an officer would drive you and your luggage out to them in a jeep and you would get your stuff aboard. Norgaard and I hung around in front of our shack that morning, waiting. As the day wore on, a strong wind came up and blew great clouds of sand. At about eleven o'clock two transports arrived, escorted by some Spitfires. Cochran had planned to drive us down to the transports, but he was called to the telephone, and Christman said that he would drive us instead.

When we arrived where the transports were standing on the runway, the transport captain, whose name, I noted from the leather strip on the breast of his flying jacket, was Lively, came over to the jeep and asked where his Spits could get gas. His ship was named the Scarlett O'Hara. He and Christman started discussing what was the quickest way to get the gas. Christman and Norgaard and I stayed in the jeep. Dust was blowing over the field a mile a minute. Suddenly Christman looked over his shoulder, called on God, and vanished. Within a moment Lively was also gone. I turned around to speak to Norgaard, and discovered that he too had evaporated. I hate to sit in an empty jeep when I don't know why the other passengers have jumped. I do not remember actually getting out myself, but I know that I was already running when I heard somebody yell, "Hit the dirt!" Under the circumstances, this sounded so sensible that I bellyflopped to the ground, and I landed so hard that I skinned my knees and elbows. No surface in the world offers less cover than a runway. I regretted that my body, which is thick, was not thinner. I could guess what had happened: German strafers had ridden in on the dust storm and nobody had seen them until they opened fire. I knew that the very nasty noises above me were being made by airplane cannon and that the even nastier ones close to me came from the detonation of the small explosive shells they fire. The strafers, I figured, were heading for the transports—large, expensive, unarmored jobs that you could punch holes in with a beer-can opener. I was therefore in line with the target and was very sorry to be where I was.

As soon as there was a lull in the noises overhead, I got up and ran toward the edge of the runway to get away from the transports, but more noises came before I made it, so I flopped again. After they had passed, I got up and ran off the runway. I saw a soldier in a fine, large hole nearly six feet deep. He shouted, "Come right in, sir!" You can have Oscar of the Waldorf any time; I will always remember that soldier as my favorite host. I jumped in and squeezed up against him. Almost immediately the noises came a third time and two transport pilots jumped down on my back. I was astonished that I had been able to outrun such relatively young men. I was 38.

By this time all of our machine guns along the edges of the field were firing away, and there was a fourth pass, as the fliers say, and a loud crash, as if one of the Germans had dropped a bomb. A minute or two later the noise began to die down. Looking up from the bottom of the hole, we could see a man descending in a parachute. The big, white chute was swaying this way and that in the wind. The man had an awful time landing. We could see that even from a distance. The chute dragged him and bounced hell out of him after he landed. Afterward, word got around the field that he was an American. I didn't find out until a couple of days later, though, that the man with the chute had been Horse. In landing, he hit his head against the ground and suffered a concussion of the brain. They put him in an ambulance and started for the nearest hospital, which was forty miles by road, but he had bad luck. The Germans had been strafing that road, too, that morning, and when the ambulance got within five miles of the hospital, it was blocked by two burning ammunition trucks. The shells on the trucks were exploding. The squadron surgeon and the ambulance-driver put Horse on a stretcher and carried him around the trucks to a safe point on the other side, and an ambulance from the hospital came out to pick him up, but by the time it got there he was dead.*

When the shooting at the field was over, the pilots and the soldier and I got out of the hole and walked back toward the transports, which were still there. Norgaard climbed out of another hole not far away. He said that when he had jumped out of the jeep he had crawled under it, and there he had found a

---

*Horse's square name was Alton B. Watkins, but hardly anybody at Thélepte knew. Father McCreedy buried him under a metal plate marked "Horace."

transport lieutenant who had had the same idea. They had given up the jeep after the first pass and run for it, just as I had already done. We stared at the parallel furrows the Messerschmitt cannon had plowed down the runway, as if they had been the teeth of a rake, and ourselves the field mice between them. The transport boys borrowed our jeep to get gas for the Spits, which had been immobilized during the raid because their tanks were empty. When the boys came back, we climbed into one of the transports. The big planes took off almost immediately. "Leave them laughing," Norgaard said to me when he recovered sufficient breath to say anything.

We learned later that the strafing had been done by eight Messerschmitts flying in four loose pairs, and that was why there had been four passes. Another Messerschmitt, making a run by itself, had dropped one bomb, ineffectually. There had also been a high cover of Messerschmitts; one of them had accounted for Horse. We were told that Cochran had said, with a hint of admiration in his voice, "It is getting so that the Germans patrol our field for us." A lot of Air Force generals who were on a tour of inspection visited the field shortly after we left, said that the situation was very grave, and left, too. This point in the war over the field may be compared to the one in a Western movie at which the villain has kicked hell out of the heroine and just about wrestled her to the brink of ruin in a locked room.*

At about two-thirty that same afternoon the Lafayette Escadrille was patrolling the field, in the company of two pilots from the American P-40 squadron commanded by Major Hubbard. This squadron had its full complement of pilots but only five planes. The pilots took turns flying the five ships, so they were not getting a great deal of practice. Nevertheless, Hubbard's squadron had already scored two victories that week. The two American pilots in the air were Hubbard and a man named Beggs. Two of their mates, Boone and Smith, were on the ground on alert call, sitting in their planes ready to reinforce the patrol if they were called.

This field didn't have one of those elaborate radio airplane-

*See note on p. 350.

detectors that warn swank airdromes of the approach of enemy aircraft. It had to rely on its patrol system and on tips that watchers telephoned in. The tipsters were not infallible, as Norgaard and I had noticed that morning, and in the afternoon they slipped up again. Ten Junkers 88 bombers unexpectedly appeared, flying toward the field at three thousand feet. There was an escort of four fighters, unusually small for so many bombers, flying high above them and, as someone described it to me, acting oddly uninterested. The Frenchmen on patrol, also flying high, made one swipe at the escort and it disappeared, not to be seen again. Nine of the bombers were flying in three loose V's and one ship was trailing the third V. Hubbard took the bomber on the right of the first V and shot it down. Beggs got the middle one and a Frenchman knocked down the one on the left. The other Junkers had begun to drop their bombs. Boone and Smith came up off the field through the falling bombs to join the battle. Hubbard shot down another plane, and Boone, who had never fired a shot at a man or a plane before, came up behind one Junkers and blasted it out of the sky; it caromed against another Junkers on the way down, which gave Boone two planes with one burst of fire. He went on to destroy two more. Smith, opening fire at extreme range for fear that he would be shut out, blew the rudder off another Junkers, which also crashed. The tenth Junkers headed for home, but it never got there; the French picked off that one. It was the jack pot, ten out of ten. It was also the end of the five-day war over our airfield. No producer of Westerns ever wound up a film more satisfactorily.* The Germans stayed away, in fact, for nineteen days and then came back only once, for a quick sneak raid.

Of the ten German bomber crews, only four men came out of the fight alive and two of these died in the hospital. The two others said that the ten bombers had been escorted by four Italian Macchi C. 202 fighters, which had deserted them. Why the Luftwaffe should have entrusted four Macchis with the protection of ten Junkers 88's is harder to explain than the

---

*See note on p. 350. From here on, I will cease to call attention to this phenomenon.

result. The Germans, fortunately for our side, sometimes vary their extreme guile with extreme stupidity.

I didn't have a chance to return to the airfield for about ten days, and then I stopped in on my way down to Gafsa, where the Americans were supposed to be launching a ground offensive. Captain Wylie, who told me about the big day at the field, said that Boone had come into the operations shack looking rather incredulous himself. "Probably I'm crazy," he had said to Wylie, "but I think I just shot down four planes."* The Frenchmen thought up a gag. They said it was a victory for three nations—"The Americans shot down seven planes, we shot down two, and the Italians shot down the tenth so the crew couldn't tell on them."

The Americans left the field undefeated, for the two P-40 squadrons were relieved not long afterward by other outfits and sent back from the fighting zone to rest. Christman's squadron had been fighting there steadily for two months. I met the fellows from Christman's bunch again while I was trying to get a ride into civilization from another airfield, a bit west of the one where they had been stationed. A lot of trucks drove up and deposited the officers and men of the squadron on the field, with their weapons, their barracks bags, and their bedding rolls. Christman was there, and Private Otto, the squadron barber, and Corporal Jake Goldstein, the reformed songwriter. I renewed my acquaintance with a pilot named Fackler, whom I remembered especially because he had once, finding himself flying formation with two Messerschmitts who thought he was another Messerschmitt, shot one of them down, and I again met Thomas, the Oklahoma boy who had been lost in the air one night and had been lighted home by the fire of the field's anti-aircraft guns, and a non-flying lieutenant named Lamb, who used to practice law in New York, and a dozen others. I felt as if I had known them all for a long time.

Eleven transports came in to take the squadron west, and I arranged to travel in one of them. I was in the lead ship of the flight, and the transport major who commanded it told me that his orders were to drop the squadron at a field only about

---

*His luck did not last. He was killed a couple of weeks later.

an hour's flight away. Then the transports would go on to their base, taking me along with them. It was pleasant to see the faces of the P-40 boys aboard my transport when it took off. They didn't know anything about the field they were going to, but they knew that they were going for a rest, so they expected that there would at least be huts and showers there. They looked somewhat astonished when the transports settled down in a vast field of stubble without a sign of a building anywhere around it. There were a few B-25 bombers on the field and in the distance some tents. A transport sergeant came out of the pilot's compartment forward in our plane and worked his way toward the tail of our ship, climbing over the barracks bags heaped in the space between the seats. "I guess this is where you get out," he told the P-40 fellows.

A couple of soldiers jumped out and the rest began passing out bags and rifles to them. Pretty soon all the stuff was piled outside the plane and the soldiers were standing on the field, turning their backs to a sharp wind and audibly wondering where the hell the barracks were. A jeep with an officer in it drove out from among the tents and made its way among the transports until it arrived at our ship. The transport major talked to the officer in the jeep, and then they both drove over to the transport Christman was travelling in and picked him up, and the three of them drove back to the tents. Some soldiers who had been near the jeep had heard the field's officer say that nobody there had been notified that they were coming. The transport major had replied that all he knew was that he had orders to leave them there. The soldiers who had heard the conversation communicated the news to the others by Army telegraphy. "Situation normal!"* one soldier called out, and everybody laughed. Soldiers are fatalistic about such situations.

Some time before a report had circulated among the men that the squadron was to go back to the United States. Now I heard one soldier say, "This don't look like no United States to me."

Another one said, "When we get back there, Freddie Bartholomew will be running for President." He didn't seem sore.

*See note on confusion p. 356.

Somebody said, "I hear they're going to start us here and let us hack our way through to South Africa."

Somebody else began a descant on a favorite Army fantasy: what civilian life will be like after the war. "I bet if my wife gives me a piece of steak," he said, "I'll say to her, 'What the hell is this? Give me stew.'"

Another one said, "I bet she'll be surprised when you jump into bed with all your clothes on."

The delicacy of their speculations diminished from there on.

After a while the jeep came back. The transport major got out and said, "There seems to be some mistake. You'd better put your stuff back in the ship." We all got back into the planes, and the major told me that this obviously wasn't the place to leave the men but that he would have to wait until base operations could get headquarters on the telephone and find out their destination. We sat in the planes for an hour; then another officer came out in a jeep and said that nobody at headquarters knew anything about the squadron, so the major had better not take it any place else. The major told his sergeant to instruct the men to take their luggage off the planes. "We enjoy doing this. It's no trouble at all," one of the soldiers in my plane said. The transports took off and left them standing there. I learned later that they eventually got straightened out. After two or three days someone at headquarters remembered them; the pilots were sent to western Morocco and the ground echelon was moved to another field.

All this happened what seems now to be long ago, in the pioneer days of the American Army in Tunisia. The old field, from which I had watched the five-day war, was never knocked out from the air, but it was taken by German ground troops with tanks, and then the Americans took it back and went on. The Hotel Léon, if the Germans hadn't burned it, was certainly full of booby traps for the Americans when they got there. I shouldn't like to have slept in it. Léon is now in a large Algerian city, where he has been assigned to a calmer liaison job. Cochran was promoted and decorated and posted to a new command.*

_____
*He is now back in Erie, Pa.

P. S. ON ROZANOFF IN 1954

There are lines you pick up from a particular person that become parts of your habitual repertory. They have associations that keep them bright for you, but they sound so flat you feel called upon to explain what once made them seem funny. For example, I sometimes say between drinks: "It is better as a kick in za pants, so say my grandmozaire."

This expression never tickles anybody else, but it evokes the image of a round, pink Slavic face with a roof of yellow hair like the down on an Easter chick—the face of Kostya, le Commandant Rozanoff—and a conversational voice precisely like the old basso Chaliapin's.

Rozanoff would knock off three ounces of straight whiskey in a gulp. He was what old bartenders call a lip drinker: When he had got the edge of the vessel against his lower lip, he would throw his head back and the drink over his tongue and down. Then he would intone his cherished line of what he believed to be American, and hold out his canteen cup for more whiskey. The rest of his English was negligible. I forget how the alternation began—with the jest or the gesture—but it usually continued until the pink face blurred before my eyes. He was invincible.

Rozanoff fondled the illusion that all Americans drank their whiskey straight and in the manner he practiced. Like the grandmozaire gag, it was part of the tradition of his squadron in the Armée de l'Air, les Sioux, pronounced, under another misapprehension, "Syukes." (They assumed, apparently, that Americans would sound the "x," and they wanted to say it the American way.) The original members of the squadron, in World War I, had been American volunteers, and after they went, the squadron had kept the name, the insigne, and its concepts of American customs. The insigne, an Indian head in full war bonnet, was painted on the American P-40 that Rozanoff got out of when I first met him—at Thélepte, in January, 1943. "Rozanoff," he said, shaking hands, and then, before even declaring himself conventionally enchanted: "These machines respond to the controls too slowly, and then react too violently." He had been a test pilot before the war, and the habit stuck. When I met Rozanoff, he commanded a group of nine French pilots who had been assigned new P-40s at Casablanca. From Casa, they had flown toward the front, with a stop at Algiers to refuel. But only seven arrived at Thélepte.

Rozanoff told me that evening that he was thirty-eight, and when I relayed the information to some of our young pilots, they were gloomy, because we were short of planes at that field and they thought it wasteful to let a man so old fly a new fighter. "His reflexes are just too slow for three hundred miles an hour," they said. (They were flattering the P-40 slightly.) Ten years later, I read in a French magazine that Rozanoff, the leading test pilot of France, had hit eight hundred and thirty-seven in a Mystère IV, the new French jet. He had pierced the sound barrier—horizontally, not diving—five times in a single flight. Most of the young pilots who had survived the war considered themselves middle-aged by that time. It cheered me no end, especially considering the training regime of the Commandant, who had in the intervening years become the Colonel.

A few weeks ago, I saw on page 6 of the Sunday New York Times a headline that puzzled me for a moment:

FRENCH JET CRASH
PERILS MINISTERS

I don't like "perils" as a verb, although as I have ascertained it is in Webster's Unabridged. What was more important, I couldn't understand at first glance how a jet crash could "peril" a passenger. It would kill him. This was a momentary obtuseness. The Ministers had not been in the plane. The bank of the head explained:

PLANE PARTS FALL NEAR PLEVEN
AND BRITISH SUPPLY CHIEF—
NOTED PILOT IS KILLED

The lead said parts of the plane had fallen "about fifty yards" from the statesmen, which didn't excite me unduly. But the second paragraph began, "Col. Constantin Rozanoff, 49 years old, who was at the controls of the Mystère IV, France's latest jet, met instant death." Kostya is the diminutive for Constantin. I remembered Kostya had told me his grandparents were Russian and he was French. The *Times* said he was a native of Poland; his birth may have occurred during the family's westward migration.

Kostya had been showing off the plane before the visiting officials, including a British air marshal. I imagine he had wanted the R.A.F. to be stunned with admiration. Skimming the ground, he would have allowed a clearance of about one centimetre, if I knew him. I was happy to see he had not been at fault personally. "The plane encountered a strong gust of wind, one wing touched the ground, and the craft crashed, exploded, and burst into flames. Parts were hurled in all directions." It would have pained Kostya to think he was losing his touch, but winds at an altitude of almost nothing are unpredictable. From an air-mail copy of *Le Monde* that I saw a couple of days later, I learned that the French had been showing the British their jets with a view to selling them some. Kostya had been doing eleven hundred kilometres—six hundred and eighty-four miles—an hour.

While I was still reading the *Times* story, however, I didn't know about Kostya's added incentive. There was a picture that showed him wearing one of the enormous helmets that make all jet pilots look like hydrocephalics. The Indian head, his old talisman, was clearly visible on its front. Kostya was sitting in a cockpit, reaching down over the side, and some joker was handing him up a building brick, to celebrate his first crash through the "wall" of sound.

The joke was in Rozanoff's own vein. I remembered the time in Africa when a French division commander, General Welvert, fifty miles away, learned of the presence of Kostya and his pilots at the American field, and decided this gave him a private air force. The General telephoned an order for le Commandant Rozanoff to wait on him immediately. Rozanoff was too busy, fighting two or three times a day; besides, he had no idea of putting himself under the orders of a ground-force general. When Rozanoff didn't show up, the General sent over a message, by hand, ordering him to consider himself under arrest. Kostya got down into his hole so that only his head showed above ground at the entrance. He held two sticks vertically in front of his face and made a horrendous grimace.

One of his pilots took photograph of him that way, and they sent it over to the *divisionnaire* with the message "The Commandant Rozanoff in prison, at the orders of General Welvert." Old Welvert had had no right to send for him, of course. It was a time when all French generals were trying to accumulate as much authority as possible against the day when Giraud's people and de Gaulle's people would have to share the marbles. That was a day Welvert never lived to see; he was killed by a mine in the spring offensive. (An Algerian infantryman in one of his battalions was named Ahmed Ben Bella.)

Nobody could say Kostya didn't have a sense of humor. During the winter of the war that turned out not to be phony, he once told me, the French shot down a Messerschmitt of a new mark in the area between the two armies in Lorraine. The pilot had bailed out before the plane hit. By a lucky chance, it was not a complete wreck. The Army of the Air had a curiosity to examine a Messerschmitt of this latest edition; Rozanoff therefore went out into the disputed land to repair the plane. He worked at night under a tarpaulin, to hide his light, and slept under the wings by day. After several nights, he had repaired the engine, and one dawn he took off for France. But as he prepared to land on the airfield at Toul, the French ack-ack opened up and shot the unannounced Messerschmitt full of holes. He had to bail out, like the German pilot before him, and the plane crashed "in much worse state than before"—an irretrievable mess. He thought it very funny. "It is better as a kick in za pants," he said, and we had a drink on his adventure.

Kostya lived through a difficult time at Thélepte, until the victory over the ten bombers made everybody happy. He and his brother pilots had been, as I've said, members of the old Armée de l'Air. They had flown their planes to Africa after the debacle of 1940 in the belief the French government would continue the war. But when Pétain surrendered the empire, they had not skipped out to join de Gaulle. So their will to fight the Germans was still in question when I first met them. The seven out of nine who arrived at the field with the P-40s must have suspected the reason for the nonappearance of the two others, but they dared not admit their suspicion, even to themselves. Consequently, Rozanoff made constant inquiries about the two men, unreported since Algiers. Was it possible, he would ask, that there had been an unobserved air action deep in Allied territory in which they had been shot down, or that they had made a forced landing in the mountains and nobody had found them? "They were experienced pilots," he would say. "They had plenty of fuel. It is inconceivable that they lost their way." In fact, as we learned later, the two men had flown their planes to Vichy France and delivered them to the Pétainists.

I gather my memories of Rozanoff as the infantrymen gathered up the pilot's ring and papers. He was a barrel-chested man, and even in 1943 the barrel had begun to slip. The piece in *La Monde* said that with the years he had developed "*une certaine corpulence.*" He wore a dirty leather flying jacket, like everybody else at Thélepte, but he topped it with a visored blue cap circled with gold braid. His movements were brusque, his forms of speech were vigorous rather than graceful. "*Il manqué d'élégance,*" the French liaison officer at the field complained, and I was constrained to agree.

In the early spring of 1944, I was coming out of a newsreel theatre in Piccadilly when I saw a French aviator in a bus queue. I was with a pretty girl in a becoming blue uniform, and this type in the bus queue made her the eye. I regarded him with resentment, and then I saw it was Kostya, in a blue uniform storm coat, blue trousers, black shoes—completely regulation. He was a lieutenant colonel. He told me that after the African campaign he had been promoted and attached to the staff of the new French Air Force, which incorporated both de Gaullist and Giraudist elements. De Gaulle had by that time solidly established his leadership. Kostya said that he was testing planes again, and was happy. We made a date to have lunch at the *popote* of the staff, which was in South Kensington.

The lunch was gay. We drank a fair amount of cognac, and then I invited Kostya and some other officers, one of whom was the novelist Joseph Kessel, to accompany me to a remarkable club of which I was a member. The club was called Frisco's; it was in Sackville Street, in a bomb-damaged retail shop whose glassless windows were masked with heavy cardboard. The secretary and proprietor was Frisco, an American Negro legally named Bingham. Like hundreds of other such clubs in London, it was licensed to sell to members and guests during the afternoon hours, when ordinary pubs were shut. Its remarkable feature was the amount of whiskey Frisco was able to lay hands on in a period when even the best hotel bars gave clients a grim choice between gin and sobriety. In 1944, Frisco's was usually full of colored American soldiers, who ran a continuous jam session on an old piano. The secretary took on all comers at darts, and since he had the advantage of thirty years' expatriate practice, he cleaned up.

Kostya, rendered ecstatic by the presence of so much whiskey, shouted, "It is better as a kick in za pants, so say my grandmozaire!" as soon as he got his hand around a glass. Then he emptied the glass. His war cry rang out again, above the notes of "Don't Get Around Much Any More" in intricate syncopation from the old piano. At first, his cries were intermittent but regular, like the call of the bobwhite. Then they became more rapid and, finally, just about continuous. Kessel and I tried to fly on his wings, but he lost us. After the fourth drink, Kessel was flying blind, and I, a mere groundling, was in a spin. "Better as a kick, better as a say, better as my grandmozaire's pants." It was all a blur.

There was a crash. I had preceded Kostya through the sound barrier by eight years.

I never saw him again, and now I never will.

The next pieces are about ground fighting, or what passed for it, in the first month of our maiden effort in Africa. The troops, pacific by nature, eased themselves into it like an old man with chilblains getting into a hot bath.

Gafsa, the center of these operations, is one of the oldest continuously inhabited places on earth, which is a reflection on human selectivity, because it is a desolation; it was the seat of a prehistoric culture called by archaeologists the Gafsan, which has left stone artifacts as evidence of the near-idiocy of the first inhabitants. Norman Douglas, who visited it in 1911, quoted an Arab song about it that begins:

"Gafsa is miserable; its water is blood . . ."

During all its long, ignoble history this has been so. Sallust tells how Marius, the Roman general, took it by night marches across the desertic steppe to the north, followed by a surprise attack. The steppe offered a formidable barrier to large bodies of troops, because camels had not been introduced into North Africa, and water supply was a problem. Marius solved it by having his soldiers drive cattle before them to the last spring. There he had them slaughter the beasts, skin them, fill the hides with water, and begin their march burdened only with these and meat, a concentrated ration, traveling across the high steppe in the cold nights and laying up in the heat of the day. There was no air observation and they cut the throats of the few travelers they met. He achieved complete surprise, and when the Gafsans came out to work their gardens in their oasis, the Romans rushed them so fast they had no chance to shut the city gates behind them.

Marius, following a colonialist tradition already old, denounced the Gafsans as treacherous and uncivilized, before putting the men to the sword and selling the women and children into slavery. But the city grew up again as a Roman garrison and colony, and was fought over by Moslem princelings all through the Middle Ages because by then the camels had come to North Africa, and it lay across a great caravan route. And in time Major-General Terry Allen of the First Division captured the city by the same maneuver—a night march across the desert, this time in trucks and jeeps, to avert annoyance by the *Luftwaffe*. He did this, however, before the third episode in the following narration, when the First Division, which was precocious compared to all others, had already found its stride. Gafsa is about 50 miles southeast of Cochran's old field at Thélepte.

Gafsa

I — THE EIGHTH ARMY FROM GABÈS — 1943

The Anglo-American North African campaign is sure to furnish a lot of historical controversy sooner or later, so there is no harm in correcting the record on one point immediately. The junction of the American Second Corps and the British Eighth Army, fighting its way north from Mareth, was copiously reported in newspapers in this country last April. Most of the reporters said that the meeting took place on the Gafsa-Gabès road. According to their stories, the historic moment came when an American motorized patrol met a British motorized patrol. Actually, the Eighth Army and the Second Corps joined up more than two months before the motorized incident, in the hall of the Hôtel de France, a two-story palace in Gafsa. I know, because I was there. In fact, I might say that I introduced them.

Gafsa, called Capsa by the Numidians, is a very ancient town on a very slight hill in south-central Tunisia. Warm springs gush from the foot of the hill, below a fifteenth-century Arab citadel, which was wrecked by our engineers during the fighting last February. The citadel was still intact when I first saw the place. The climate of Gafsa, even in late January, when Norgaard and I reached it, is warm and dry. There is an oasis around the town, which used to be an important knot in the web of caravan routes between the Sahara and the Mediterranean. Last winter Gafsa had, and by now probably has again, ten thousand inhabitants, of whom five or six hundred are Europeans, eight hundred are native Jews, and the rest Moslems who call themselves Arabs but are predominantly of Berber stock, like most North Africans. The Europeans are administrators or railroad workers. The Jews, whose ancestors came there not long after the Destruction of the Temple, are traders and traditionally middlemen between the Christians and the Moslems.

When Norgaard and I arrived in Gafsa, a battalion of American infantry was stationed there, together with several batteries of French seventy-fives, a battalion of Senegalese, and some Algerian *tirailleurs*. The Americans, who belonged to the First Division, were the only ground troops we had south of the town of Sbeitla, which was sixty miles away. They had been there for a month and were quite at home in the place, which, as almost every enlisted man you talked to was certain to say, looked like a set in a Beau Geste movie. Old Jews sold surprisingly good native pastries and Arabs peddled dates in the square in front of the American barracks. The soldiers had adopted Arab kids as mascots and clothed them in G.I. shirts and shoes. There was a great outdoor Roman swimming pool, filled by warm running water from the springs. The water contained a good deal of sulphur, but it was nevertheless pleasant to bathe in, and the Americans spent a lot of time swimming in it. The French soldiers preferred to dangle fishing lines in a nearby spring-fed stream and catch little, extremely voracious blue fish,* which apparently were used to living in hot, sulphurous water.

There was also a clean Arab bath, in a narrow Arabian Nights alley, where the attendants would stretch you on the floor and twist your arms and legs out of joint and then pound you with a hot brick before allowing you to steam yourself in peace. I remember seeing, at the bath, an English captain I knew, a booby-trap expert, pink and jolly in the steam, wearing a towel around his loins. A couple of weeks later he accidentally blew himself up with an extremely special mine he had just devised. He simply vanished. Somehow I always think of him flying toward heaven draped in a towel and deeply embarrassed.† Gafsa also had a bordello offering a dozen girls whom a friend of mine described as "sort of French" and a madam who was a de Gaulliste. When a British lieutenant general came to town for a look around, the much-junior American officer who was his host wanted to give him a touch of real luxury—sheets to sleep between. He borrowed a pair from the madam.

*

*Tilapia.

†This never happened, although when I wrote this piece, I fully believed it had. One more instance of confusion—I had the story from a "reliable source" who knew us both.

Norgaard and I had gone to Gafsa because it was the American-held point nearest to Montgomery's advancing army and it seemed a likely place to witness the joining of the two forces. We expected the Americans either to hold on to the town until Montgomery arrived or else to launch an offensive from it in order to join him. The latter course presupposed heavy reinforcements, and we thought that we sensed their coming.

The Americans in Gafsa had carried out numerous raids against the Italian detachments that occasionally appeared in the no man's land to the east, between Gafsa and Maknassy. Neither adversary had any fixed garrison in this flat, desolate stretch of about seventy miles between the two towns. Once the fellows from Gafsa had bagged eighty-four prisoners. That was reckoned a big haul for southern Tunisia in January. Captured Italian carbines and automatic pistols, if you had a chance to get them back to Algiers, attracted much attention. Even the stars which Italian soldiers wear on their lapels had a certain curiosity value. If you gave one to an Army nurse at an evacuation hospital, she would be quite happy, for which reason few stars ever got back as far as Algiers, and nurses at base hospitals to the west didn't get to see any until April or May. But by then there were so many Italian prisoners that the stars were no longer chic.

Norgaard and I had been told, by Léon Caplan, to look up a friend of his at Gafsa, a French captain named O'Neill. O'Neill, whose family had emigrated to France from Ireland in the seventeenth century, pronounced his name "Onay." He looked like a conventional O'Neill—blue-eyed, florid, and saddle-nosed—but he spoke English, which he had learned at a *lycée*, with a heavy French accent. Captain O'Neill commanded a battery of three guns which had been buried in a cache after the fall of France and thus concealed from the German Armistice Commission. All three guns had to be hauled by one old motor truck that burned alcohol, so the battery travelled in installments, one gun at a time. They could shoot well enough, O'Neill said, but they never arrived anywhere in time to shoot at an enemy. O'Neill invited us to dine at the battery mess with him, his two lieutenants, and a chaplain attached to the unit.

We showed up at the mess, which was in a shed built onto the side of a one-story house, ahead of O'Neill and his officers, who were accustomed to dining late. American Army chow is usually dished up early. The owner of the house, a young native Jew who wore a European business suit and a blue beret, invited us in for an apéritif while we waited. He had delicate Arabian features, and eyes as blue as O'Neill's, and he spoke excellent French. The Jew's house was large and square, with thick, mud walls to insulate it from the summer sun. It was built around a small circular court that let in air and daylight. The house looked ageless, like most of the others in town— the Numidians had probably built in exactly the same fashion —but the rooms leading off the court were wired for electric light and filled with heavy, gaudy contemporary furniture from some factory in Europe. The Jew's ancient, bearded father, who spoke no French, and the younger man's small, comely, brunette wife and their gray-eyed daughter kissed our hands. The French took over Tunisia in 1881, and in the old man's youth there had been no French-language schools in the country, but in the son's there had been. The younger man poured sweet wine for us and gave us olives and sliced turnips pickled in lemon juice. The family name, he told us, was Chemouni. When a servant who had been left on watch outside came in and told us that O'Neill had arrived, we left the Chemounis, feeling faintly embarrassed by their fervor. I remembered them a few weeks later, when I heard that we had abandoned Gafsa to the advancing Germans and Italians.

O'Neill's mess was the most exiguous I have encountered in the French Army. We had a thin soup and a few scraps of breast of lamb, finishing off with some black imitation coffee sweetened with gray Arab loaf sugar. There was a bottle of rough red wine, and Norgaard and I had brought over three cans of American fruit for dessert. One of O'Neill's lieutenants was a hawk-nosed, Assyrian-bearded man who walked with a pronounced limp, assisting himself with a spiked cane. He was a French colonist who had farmed an oasis on the edge of the Sahara. The other was a handsome, wavy-haired young Parisian, a Regular Army officer who had escaped from the Occupied Zone in France and made his way to Africa in 1941. He spoke most nostalgically of Fouquet's, a restaurant which I had never admired but which, I had to agree, would have looked good in Africa. The chaplain, a young man with scraggly whiskers, was merely shy and hungry.

After dinner, Norgaard and I walked to the office of the American signals officer, in the Hôtel de France, to get the dope on how to send messages out of Gafsa. (They would have to go first by Army courier to where the censors were.) The hotel was a rectangular, flat-topped, yellow stucco building two stories high. It was neater and more modern than, I think, most Americans would imagine a hotel in Gafsa to be. There was running water in all the rooms and there were at least two bathtubs in the house. The American commandant, Lieutenant Colonel (now Colonel) Bowen,* had taken it over as a headquarters and lived upstairs. The signals officer presided over his telephones on the street floor, in what had once been the hall and dining room. We were talking to him when a French officer appeared in the doorway leading from the street and asked for Colonel Bowen. Apparently the signals man couldn't understand French, so when the officer asked for Bowen again, I took it upon myself to say, "He is upstairs. What do you want him for?"

"It is the British officers from the Eighth Army at Gabès," the Frenchman said. "Those he requested to see."

"The Eighth Army at Gabès?" I said, startled, because two days before I had heard that the Eighth was still a hundred miles south of there. I took this to mean that Montgomery had moved north that hundred miles in forty-eight hours, breaking the Mareth Line en route. That would have been a record even for him.[†]

"They are officers, three of them, from the Eighth Army, and they come from Gabès," the Frenchman said, "but the Army itself is not there. They say they come from a patrol that got up there somehow. They came into our lines at Kriz, on the Chott Djerid." His voice was quite matter-of-fact. "If you will show them to Colonel Bowen, I will leave them with

---

*And now (1962) Major-General.

†Our image of Montgomery then was of a dashing fellow. That was before we had to work with him.

you," he said, and ducked out into the dark without waiting for an answer. That was how I came to introduce the Eighth Army to the Second Corps.

A moment after the Frenchman disappeared, the three British officers came through the doorway. They walked with mincing steps, lifting each foot quickly as if they were glad to get it off the floor and putting it back reluctantly. Their shoes were wrapped in rags, and I deduced that their feet must be masses of blisters. Two of the men wore long beards and one, whose head was wrapped in a blood-soaked bandage, looked as if he badly needed a shave. All three were wearing khaki battle-dress pants and shirts, from which great swatches of material were missing, evidently torn off to make bandages. One of the men with beards carried a goatskin water sack, with the long hair outside; it reminded me of Robinson Crusoe. Their faces were sunken and their eyes seemed preternaturally large, and in one case really protuberant. The eyes of this fellow were round and sky-blue and his hair and whiskers were very fair. His beard began well under his chin, giving him the air of an emaciated and slightly dotty Paul Verlaine. "We walked forty miles farther than we should have," he said to me apologetically, "because some Arabs told us the Germans had taken Gafsa and that two thousand Americans were prisoners. But we knew that the French were at Kriz and Tozeur, so we went around that way. We've been walking for five nights and five days." Some soldiers who had drifted into the room brought in chairs for them and they sat down, looking about them a trifle incredulously, as if they had not really expected to get out of whatever awful scrape they had been in. A sergeant went upstairs to inform Bowen of their arrival. The soldiers gave the British officers cigarettes and offered to bring them food and water. The officers said that the French at Kriz and Tozeur had already given them as much as they could handle for a while, and they were no longer thirsty or hungry. The least bearded man passed his hand over his head, and Norgaard asked him, "Grazed by a bullet?"

The man shook his head slowly—you could almost hear it ring—and said, "No. An Arab hit me with a stone. They tried to strip us of our clothes, and when we fought they tried to kill us. We ran. We had no weapons, you see."

"Have any others come in?" the fair man asked us. "Have you heard anything about Big Dave?"

The signals officer said, "No, you're the first British who've come into our lines."

The man with the bandaged head said, in a discouraged voice, "Big Dave must have been killed. There was all that shooting back in the wadi." He looked on the verge of falling asleep.

The fair man said, in a tone of sudden energy, as if he were trying to carry out a duty before he too caved in, "It's very important that we put out a radio warning to all our people behind the German lines that the enemy may have got our code. We must change the code."

"Are you *really* from the Eighth Army?" I asked the man with the goatskin sack.

He said they were.

"When did you leave the Eighth?" I asked.

"November seventeenth," he said. This was January twenty-eighth. "We've been living behind the enemy lines ever since. We were supposed to stay out four weeks longer, but we had a bit of hard luck."

A lieutenant came down the stairs and said that Colonel Bowen wanted to see the men, and they climbed up, holding on to the banister and resting as much weight on their hands as possible. I could hear the fair man saying, "We've got to put out that warning immediately." After a few minutes the lieutenant came down again and sent one of the men out to get the medics' ambulance. "The Colonel doesn't know quite what to make of them," he said. "They seem to be all right, but he says they might be spies. So he wants to send them up to G 2 at Corps tonight. They'll be comfortable in the ambulance."

Corps, as Norgaard and I knew, was near Tebessa, in Algeria, a hundred miles away. Driving over the narrow road, partly through rocky hills, without lights, an ambulance would be lucky to make it in six hours. Norgaard and I had one jeep, with an Army driver, between us. We decided that we ought to follow the ambulance to Tebessa. We hurried over to barracks to get our bedrolls and our driver, whose name was Eddie. He was a good-natured pfc from Queens who had been impressed by the tales of war he had heard in Algiers and was now being stuffed with horror stories by the infantrymen with whom he had taken up quarters in Gafsa. He looked relieved when we told him we were getting out of there, even though it meant a cold night drive. It didn't take long to roll our bedding and get it into the rear seat of the jeep. When three men carry three bedrolls in a jeep, it means that the men all ride in the front seat.

When we got back to the Hôtel de France, we learned that the ambulance had not yet arrived. We found the three officers from the Eighth Army in the kitchen, drinking hot coffee and surrounded by officers and men who were asking them about the desert. I spoke to the man with the bandaged head, and he told me that the fair-haired chap, Sadler, was the only commissioned officer of the three, a lieutenant. The two others were sergeants. They all belonged to an organization known as the SAS, which stood for Special Air Service. I asked him if it had anything to do with the RAF and he said no, it was an air service in a negative way. "You see, when we were first formed, we used to specialize in destroying German airplanes on the ground," he said. "Get back of their lines, get onto an airfield at night—do in a sentry, you know, or something of that sort; it's easy—and then attach pencil bombs to as many planes as we could get to. The bombs are timed to go off in a short time. We do a bunk, the bombs go off, and all the planes burn. Quite a good idea. Colonel Stirling, the one we call Big Dave, really thought of it first. Bright chap.

"They used to drop us by parachute behind the lines and let us find our way back," he continued, gravely sipping his coffee. "Worked well in places like Crete and Greece, but no future in it in Africa. Distances too great, you know. Easy to drop your men near an airport but impossible for them to walk back. So Colonel Stirling thought of using jeeps. Wonderful things, jeeps, absolutely fine. They go anywhere in desert country. Our fellows swing wide of the actual fighting area, come in behind the enemy lines, and then simply live in the desert for weeks, annoying them. One chap in SAS has got a hundred and twenty planes with his own hands. Big Dave must have got nearly a hundred. But Jerry got onto that airport dodge. Now there are too many guards and too many booby traps. So on this last trip out we stayed away from

airfields and did just mines, traffic disruption, and general confusion. Sometimes we made Jerry and the Eye-ties think that
they had been flanked in force and that a whole motorized column was operating in their rear. We made a whole Italian division pull out of one area, frightened stiff. Glorious fun, really."

I asked the sergeant where he was from and he said Not-
tingham. He told me that his name was Cooper and that he
was twenty years old. He said he had been at school when war
broke out and had enlisted in the Scots Guards. "I didn't like
that," he said, "drill and spit and polish, all that. Big Dave was
an officer in the Scots Guards himself, and he mustn't have
liked it either. Then I went into the Commandos when they
were started, and they were quite good at first, but they got
formalized. Became too smart, you know—show yourself in
London bars, Captain Lord Thisandthat, meet Leftenant the
Right Hon., Lady Ursula's brother. So I became a parachutist
and then I went into this thing. This is heaven," he said, absent-
mindedly touching his bandaged head and then looking at
his fingers to see if any blood had soaked through. "Extra pay
and no drill or any of that foolishness." Cooper said he was a
gunner and land navigator. He and his companions took their
bearings in the desert just as if they were aboard ship, he said.

The other sergeant, the one with the goatskin sack, was a
Free Frenchman who had been in the French Legation at
Cairo when France fell. He was a navigator and an expert in
Arabic. He told me his name was Taxis and that he was the old
man of the group—thirty-one. He said that the disposition of
the Tunisian Arabs was very bad. "You must never drive out in
the desert without a gun," he said, "and the pilots must never
forget to carry their pistols when they fly over the desert, in
case they are forced to land." The Arabs who had tried to rob
the men of their clothes had not acted like the Arabs in storybooks, who respect the laws of hospitality. They had invited
the three ragged men to eat and then had pointed out a place
in a wadi that they had said was safe to sleep in. When the men
were dozing off, they had attacked them with stones.

"Our particular SAS lot started out with thirty men and a
dozen jeeps," Cooper said. "It's wonderful what you can get
on a jeep. We mount a heavy and a light machine gun on each
one, besides radio equipment, and then we tie supplies and

tins of extra petrol onto them until the springs barely clear the ground. They're the finest combat vehicle developed in this war. When you come to a deep wadi, where you can't progress farther, you can lower them into the wadi by ropes and get them out the same way on the other side. When a jeep breaks down seriously, we take the best of its tires and motor parts and use them as replacements on other jeeps, and the petrol helps too. So you have fewer and fewer jeeps as you go along. When your own petrol begins to run out, you raid an enemy petrol dump or shoot up some enemy trucks and take what they have. You lose all sense of strangeness, really, after a while. It seems as normal to go to an Eye-tie dump for your petrol as to one of our own places.

"We went along for weeks without any trouble. Big Dave himself commanded the party. When we started, the Eighth was still near Alamein and we operated for a while in true desert. We would always hide out in the daytime and sleep, and then do all our moves by night. When we got up into this semi-hill country, we would find deep wadies or crevices to hide away in. We would come out onto the roads by night and shoot up the enemy convoys. We weren't the only party out, of course. There were dozens of others, mostly LRDP, but all doing the same sort of thing, approximately. LRDP means Long Range Desert Patrol. They're very similar to us, but there are more of them. Altogether, we made a shambles of the enemy's line of supply. Their convoys became afraid to move by night at all, and when they used the roads by day, our fighter planes shot them up, so they had trouble both ways. One of our best tricks was to come onto a road and move along it *toward* the front, so they would never suspect us of being intruders. A string of empty lorries would come back from the front, having unloaded, and we would flash our lights at them for the right of way. They would flash back and then we would open fire with our machine guns, right at the lights. We got thirty-seven lorries that way one evening, left them flaming on the road. Once we had a battle with some Italian armored cars. We chased them with our jeeps. I suppose they thought we were at least light tanks, in the dark. We never had a casualty in six weeks, until the thing in the wadi north of Gabès."

"One of the most amusing bits was the mines," Sadler said.

"Yes, I nearly forgot," Cooper said. "Naturally, Jerry was preparing his retreat, and as our people got nearer, the German sappers would lay mines along the shoulders of the roads and in fields that columns would be likely to take a cut through. Their own people could keep on using the roads until the last minute because the engineers had marked the lanes through the mines. We used to go out sometimes to places where they had been working and take up their mines and then replace them in a slightly altered pattern. It must have been disconcerting when their lorries hit their own stuff.

"But we got to feeling too safe. We had gone so long unobserved that we thought it would last forever. Our party split up a couple of times and toward the end there were just fifteen in our particular group, travelling with four jeeps. We were lying up in a deep wadi about ten miles north of Gabès, a place with cliff walls four hundred feet high. I was fast asleep under my blankets when I heard the first shots. Germans with tommy guns were coming up both ends of the wadi. Some Arabs must have spotted us going in there and told Jerry. There wasn't a chance to fight our way out of that position. I managed to climb up a cliff, but I had no chance to get a weapon or a heavy coat. Sadler and Taxis got away by the same method, and we joined after we got to the top of the cliff. We waited around to see if any of the others would get away, but nobody did. There was a lot of shooting in the wadi and then silence. After a time, we began to walk."

The ambulance had finally pulled up in front of the Hôtel de France. A captain who had been deputed to escort the three suspicious characters to Corps was waiting at the kitchen door, and the three men got up and hobbled out to their conveyance. Norgaard and I went out after them and climbed into our jeep with Eddie and followed them up to Tebessa. It was the coldest, and it seemed the longest, ride I have ever had. We rode with our windshield down, on the theory that this would make it a trifle easier to see through the blackness, and we had a wind in our faces all the way. Norgaard and Eddie alternated driving, and I was always in the middle, with my arms stretched out behind them. I felt like a figure-head on a ship, driving chest first into a gale. The fellows lying inside the ambulance were of course more comfortable. Occasionally, when one of them sat up to smoke a cigarette and used a cigarette lighter, we could see a bearded face gleam through a rear window. Otherwise the ambulance was just a patch of blackness slightly more solid than the dark around it.

We got to Corps, which was eight miles outside of Tebessa, at two o'clock in the morning. A G 2 officer came out of the staff tent and climbed into the ambulance to talk to the Eighth Army officers. He had a bottle of whiskey with him, which was an excellent idea, because they were pretty well done in by that time. After half an hour he climbed out and told us that he thought they were all right.

II — WITH DR. FREEMAN IN AFRICA

Norgaard and I went back to Gafsa within a week, and by the time we got there a big military action for that stage of the war was already going on. It was an offensive in the direction of Maknassy, the first all-American venture of the Tunisian campaign.

Sened, thirty miles east of Gafsa, was the first objective. The bulk of Rommel's army was only a little west of Tripoli, and there was nothing but a long, thinly held, tempting corridor between him and von Arnim. The Americans making the attack believed that they could go on from Sened to Maknassy and from Maknassy to the coast of the Gulf of Gabès, cutting Rommel's line of supply and retreat. The major general in command* told the war correspondents that he was going on to Maknassy, at least, and "draw the pucker string tight." We understood from his manner that he meant to go farther than that if he got the chance.

Norgaard and I had an Army jeep, and we drove out from Gafsa to see the battle. We had formerly had an Army driver, but on this trip Norgaard himself drove. The battle was in its second day. A battle, in the sort of open, desert warfare that was going on then, is not an easy thing to find, and we often had to stop to ask directions. We made our first stop beside

*Gen. Lloyd Fredendall.

two American Negro soldiers, sitting with their legs dangling
into two parallel slit trenches cut in the dead-looking terrain.
Each man was eating a mixture of cold meat and beans out of
a small, shiny tin can which reflected the sun's rays a distance
of several miles in that flat country* and each turned his face
upward periodically, with mouth full, to stare into the hot,
aluminum-colored sky. I got out of the jeep and walked up to
the end of one trench, and its proprietor, a tan man, looked
at me, but the other soldier continued to stare at the sky. Then
the tan man looked up at the sky and his companion looked at
me. "We was dive-bummed yesterday," this second soldier, a
very dark man, said to me. "Driving the infantry up to the line
in two-and-a-half-ton trucks. Dive-bumming makes me sick to
my stomach."

I tried to sound hearty and casual as I asked, "What outfit
you men out of?"

"The Rolling Umpty-seventh," the tan man said, while the
dark man took his turn looking at the sky. The Umpties are a
motor-truck regiment which I had already met under happier
circumstances, in England.

"How you doing?" I asked, for want of a better question.

"Really, sir, I don't belong on this battlefield at all," the tan
soldier answered. "I'm strictly a non-combat man."

I thought to myself that we were two of a kind.

I asked the men how far ahead the front was. I put into my
voice the implication that I wanted to rush right into the middle of things. The men didn't know exactly where the battle
was. Soldiers seldom do.

I walked back from the twin slit trenches to the jeep. "They
don't know where the battle is," I said to Norgaard. "Maybe
we had better go farther ahead." He said all right, so we
started off across the sand again. We took to the desert, keeping
away from the main road between Gafsa and Sened, because
there were trucks on it and trucks attract strafers. The line of
telephone poles beside the road gave us our direction. When
we had gone a short way, we saw a pair of jeeps coming toward

---

*A khaki C-ration can came in later. Nobody in the Source of Supplies, ap-
parently, had had the imagination to foresee the tactical disadvantages of the
bright ones.

us over the sand, and we stopped. There were a couple of American officers and eight men in the jeeps, all belonging to a tank-destroyer battalion that had lost its equipment earlier in the campaign. They were serving as battlefield military police, guiding traffic and waiting for prisoners to take charge of.

The officers didn't know exactly where the front was either. They invited us to have a can of coffee beside a mud house, a mile or so away, where the M.P.'s had set up headquarters, and we all drove there together. There were a few scraggly olive trees around the house and a low mud wall around the trees, presumably to prevent the sand's blowing away from their roots. One of the soldiers poured some gasoline into a couple of empty ration cans and lighted it. He laid two strips of metal across the top of each can, then filled two smaller ration cans with water from his canteen and placed them on the burners. When the water came to a boil, he divided a packet of soluble coffee between the two improvised coffee pots. "The Statler people would give a million dollars to get hold of this process," he said. When we had drunk the coffee, he started another batch.

While I was waiting for more coffee, I stood on the mud wall with one of the M.P. officers and looked over the country. A railroad paralleled the highway and we could see a station, with some trees around it, about five miles away. It was a stop between Gafsa and Sened, needed God knows why. "Our guns were out behind there early this morning and Jerry dropped a few shells in among those trees," the officer said. "Then our guns moved forward, way up toward Sened. I think you can go ahead eight or ten miles at least before you have to start to look around. You missed a good show this morning, though. About twenty Stukas came over and a dozen P-40's bounced them and shot down eight. Boy, they were falling all over the place! They'll be back, though," he added cheerily.*

*

---

* Later that day the Stukas did come back with a strong escort of fighters, thirty-one planes in all. Six P-40s from Thélepte attacked them and five of our planes were shot down. They attacked to protect an infantry advance that had been canceled, which is the way things go. I saw the planes still smoking on the hills next day; the pilots, now ashes, had been among the victors of Jan. 15.

After Norgaard and I had finished our coffee, we climbed back into the jeep and started forward again. Almost immediately the mud-house grove seemed in retrospect a pretty nice place to spend the day. Sened lies in a gap between two bare, east-west ridges. As we moved toward it, we spotted a number of dispersed scout cars and wireless-equipped jeeps, the vehicles characteristic of a reconnaissance troop. "A recon outfit," Norgaard said knowingly. "Aren't they usually fairly well out in front of everybody?" We drove to within fifty yards of one of the scout cars and climbed out. A couple of soldiers were sitting on the ground with their backs against the wheels of the car, reading books. They had their slit trenches already dug beside them. Norgaard and I walked up to them and asked them what outfit this was. One of the men, a corporal, looked up and said, "Sorry, sir, but you got any identification?" He reminded me of a stage-door man. We showed him our identification cards and he explained that the scout cars, which were, as Norgaard had surmised, a recon outfit, had been all the way around the enemy's position during the previous day and night and had come back to report and await another assignment. "We could have took the place, I guess," he said, probably without much justification.

My companion, like a good Associated Press man, started making the rounds of the scout cars and taking down the names and home towns of the recon soldiers. This is always a fruitful procedure for a press-association man, because he can load up his dispatches with the names, and the papers in the home towns are glad to use them. Every soldier, when he named his home town, said, "And I wish I was there now" or "Boy, how I wish I was there this minute!" The corporal I had spoken to asked me if it was true that Bing Crosby was dead. I said I didn't know. He asked me if Groucho Marx was dead. He said he had heard that they were and that Fred Allen was dead, too. The Army in Tunisia was always full of rumors about well-known people who were supposed to have died. When my companion had written down the names of enough towns like Owensboro, Kentucky, and Central Falls, Rhode Island, we moved on again.

As we drove along, we had a clear view of the ridge north of Sened, and after we had driven a mile or so we saw a number of tanks coming around the western end, just below the crest, and snaking down the southern side of the ridge toward the town. There were occasional puffs of gray smoke on the slope above them, where the enemy was dropping shells. We began to hear our own guns up ahead, quite loud. Then we came upon the ammunition half-tracks of an artillery outfit. The soldiers told us, confidently, that the reconnaissance troop we had just left had been annihilated on the day before and that a tank-destroyer outfit had just lost all its vehicles. This was the tank-destroyer battalion the M.P.'s belonged to. The fact was that the vehicles had been lost in a quagmire in northern Tunisia a month before, but an artilleryman, garbling a conversation with one of the M.P.'s, had brought back the more fascinating report that the tank-busters had been ambushed during the current action. The soldiers said that two batteries out of their battalion were a mile or two ahead of us. The guns were armored 105's, six to a battery.

We drove on across the plain and eventually came upon a tall captain with a Red Cross brassard, standing between two jeeps, both of which were flying Red Cross flags. We stopped to talk to him. The guns we had been told about were now in sight, four hundred yards further on. The captain, whose name was Bradbury, said he was battalion surgeon. Each of the jeeps had two litters slung to its sides, and when dive bombers or German artillery caused a casualty among the gunners, Bradbury would run forward in one of the jeeps and get the wounded man. He stood there looking at the guns like a spaniel watching for a ball to retrieve. "Yesterday I had seventeen," he said, "including several from the infantry that happened to be hit near us. Only three so far today. None in this position so far. We've moved half a dozen times since daybreak." All the shots we heard were going out (boom-scream) and none were coming in (scream-boom), so we weren't worried. I opened a can of Spam and we ate it cold. "Maybe they have pulled their stuff out of Sened already," Norgaard said optimistically. I had been watching the sky all day while he drove, sometimes looking straight up for Stukas and sometimes into the sun for strafers, but nothing had happened, and I began to hope that the P-40's had polished the local Luftwaffe off for the day.

*

After we had finished the Spam and said so long to Bradbury, Norgaard and I drove on up to the guns and stopped
behind them. They were in the open, because there was no
cover anywhere around. They had stopped shooting for the
moment, probably to change range or target, and we walked
up to one gun crew, who were smoking cigarettes beside their
piece. As soon as we reached them, an officer shouted over to
them from an armored half-track to their rear, telling them to
check on our identifications. "I'm sorry, sir," one soldier said,
"but after all, how do we know who you are? We got no time
for Ayrabs or casual strollers." We showed our identification
cards and the soldier, looking at mine, said, "Huh, a *Lands-
mann*! I'm from New York, too. Fourteent' Street and Avenue
A. I wish I was dere now. At a movie, wit' my shoes off."

Then they had to start shooting again. We walked back
toward the half-track, which we knew, because of its high radio
antenna, was a command vehicle. The officer who had shouted
to the gunners was a square-faced, fair-haired major named
Burba. He was executive officer of the battalion and had been
in command of the two batteries since his C.O., a lieutenant
colonel, had been wounded. He was from McAlester, Oklahoma. He was a cool, methodical officer who looked as if he
had definite information about everything, so I asked him
what his battery was shooting at.

"Enemy guns in a grove of trees back of Sened," he said.
"We think their infantry has pulled out of the town already."

I asked him what range he was firing at and he said five
thousand yards. "I have one battery here," he said, "and another over about a mile to the right and slightly forward—you
can see them over there," and he pointed. "Every fifth shell we
fire is a smoke shell, so we can see where we're hitting, and the
fire of the two batteries is converging on the grove of trees.
When we get all our fire together and just right, we'll come
down on them and that will be the end of the battle."

"Where's our infantry?" I asked in a careless tone. I could
not see any troops out in front of us.

"There are two battalions in echelon in those two olive
groves to the right and forward of the other battery," Burba
said, pointing again. "When we've knocked out all resistance,

they will go forward and occupy the town. Or maybe the tanks will get there first."

The tanks, as a matter of fact, were in the process of trying to get to the town before the infantry. They were crawling down from the southern side of the ridge, where my colleague and I had already seen them, and moving out in front of the 105's, looking like a file of mechanical toys that a street peddler winds up and sets down on a sidewalk. When they had deployed before us, they turned left and moved on toward the town. They must have been a couple of thousand yards ahead of us when something began kicking up dust and smoke, sometimes in front of them and sometimes behind. "It's those Jerry 88's," Burba said. "They've got the tanks under a crossfire. We'll fix that in a few minutes." The tanks were now coming back toward us, all except one, which remained motionless on the plain. "That's the way the infantry was yesterday," one of Burba's junior officers, who had joined us, said. "They went up toward the firing line in trucks and three or four of the trucks got dive-bombed before the fellows could get away from them. It was a mess. After that they couldn't get anybody back into the trucks for a while. After *we* knock out the opposition, they'll all be heroes."

"That 88 is a great gun," Burba said admiringly, looking at the motionless tank through his binoculars. "Ripped that thing just like a G.I. knife does a tin can. Flat trajectory. High muzzle velocity."

"Pretty long range, hasn't it?" I asked.

"Thirteen thousand five hundred yards," Burba said heartily, as if he were a salesman pushing the German gun to a reluctant prospect.

At this point the six guns in Burba's battery let off as one, and the other battery followed. Then there was a prolonged shrieking noise and something monstrous landed a hundred yards behind us and ricochetted off to our left. It kicked up a lot of dust. It must have been an armor-piercing solid shot, because there was no explosion. "Let's get behind the halftrack," Burba said, in the same tone in which he might have said, "Let's get out of this wind." We all moved over behind the vehicle. Something else shrieked past, through the interval between the two guns on the right flank of the battery, it

seemed to me, and I couldn't help thinking that while Burba
had been explaining to us what we intended to do to the Germans, some equally competent, equally stolid German artillery
officer had been outlining his plans of what he intended to do
to us.

Norgaard and I had the embarrassing feeling that we were
not helping the battery by our presence and that if we got hit
we would cause them a lot of extra trouble. We were also embarrassed by the thought that if we left too abruptly, Burba
and the others might think we were fair-weather friends. My
colleague reminded me that he really had to get back to headquarters at Gafsa by five in order to file a bulletin. I wasn't
working for a press association and so I had no bulletin to file,
but we had only one jeep between us and I decided that I
couldn't expect my companion to wait. I said, "I guess we may
as well go, Major. See you some other time." Norgaard said
something to the same effect, and we walked away, feeling as
sheepish as we ever have in our lives.

We got into our jeep and drove to the rear, past the patient
Captain Bradbury. We paused for a moment to say goodbye
again. I looked back and saw a column of black smoke rising
from one of our gun positions. The enemy had evidently
scored a hit.

Each knot of soldiers we passed on the way to the front had
seemed a friendly island inviting a prolonged stay. We were not
tempted to stop to talk to any of them on the way back. We
reached Gafsa, and were about to park our jeep opposite the
Hôtel de France, which was serving as American headquarters,
when we saw in the street the major general who was in command of the American operation based on Gafsa. We stopped
to ask him if the infantry had got to Sened—we had been two
hours on the way home—and he said they had and that Sened
was now in our hands. "The only damned trouble," he said,
"is that the British First Army has called off the whole offensive because there has been some kind of threat in the north. I
guess we're going to play it safe and wait for Montgomery."
The bigger part of an American armored division which had
been held in reserve just outside Gafsa to exploit our initial

gains was sent north that night without having fought, and the great projected offensive went into the record as only a raid.

The American forces in the field were under the direct control of Lieutenant General Kenneth Anderson, who was commanding the British First Army at that stage of the campaign. Anderson himself was officially under the command of General Eisenhower, in Algiers. This occasioned considerable confusion of viewpoint among the men in the field, but things got a lot better later when the British Eighth Army, the British First Army, and the American Second Corps were all placed directly, and with equal status, under the command of General Alexander. The aborted offensive cost us a couple of hundred casualties, but we took a hundred and fifty prisoners, which in that period of the campaign seemed a lot. The battle had never developed into a really big affair, but at moments it had seemed about as big as Norgaard or I or anybody we saw between Gafsa and Sened had wanted.

This impression was confirmed when Norgaard and I got ready to turn in after dinner. When we were at Gafsa, we slept on the concrete floor of a small French barracks, which was used as a catch-all hostel for transient officers. In one corner of the barracks, a captain from an American armored-infantry regiment had spread his bedding roll. His outfit had not been involved in the day's action and he had been out in the field in a jeep as an observer of fighting methods. He was a florid, pleasant-faced blond of twenty-seven, and he was reading by the light of a candle he had placed next to one elbow on the floor. We said hello and walked over to talk to him. He was reading Douglas Southall Freeman's "Lee's Lieutenants," which Norgaard had also read, and they got to talking about it. The captain told us that he came from the battlefield region of Virginia, where children save Minié balls instead of Indian arrowheads, and that he knew old Dr. Freeman well. "I own a house at Yellow Tavern, where Jeb Stuart was killed," he said, "and there are some Yankee musket balls in the stair rail. When I was a boy, I used to walk over the battlefields with Dr. Freeman, and he would tell me where the different regiments had stood and where they had charged or retreated and who had been killed and where. I often used to dream of battles when I was a boy. I thought of them like an illustration in a book, all blue and gray and orange and blood-red, and not very noisy." He closed his book and lay down, ready to go to sleep. "My God!" he said. "If I had known they were like this!" I thought of a line in Stendhal's diary: "All my life I have longed to be loved by a woman who was melancholy, thin, and an actress. Now I have been, and I am not happy."

III — THE CHEMOUNIS REVISITED

On the next day, the High Command decided to call off the offensive of which the Sened action was to have been merely the first stage. The Command's decision was supposed to be a secret, but when tank units which had not yet been committed to the fight began pulling out of Gafsa and heading north, the troops remaining there understood what had happened. There was a feeling among the men that as soon as enough tanks had been withdrawn from the region the enemy might come back and counterattack at Sened, but he didn't until a while later, and in the meantime the men who had taken Sened sat tight.

Norgaard and I heard that there were captured enemy guns and tanks at Sened. Since captured material, like prisoners in quantity, was still a novelty at that stage of the North African campaign, we thought we would get into the jeep the Army had lent us and drive out from Gafsa, where we were quartered, to have a look. As soon as we had got out on the naked main road to Sened, both of us were sorry we had left the shade of the palm trees and anti-aircraft guns. The hot, metallic sky, which it hurt your eyes to look into, hung over the road and weighed down on your brain with its implicit Messerschmitts. Every group of tanks or guns you met, parked off the road, seemed an invitation to air attack, and you hurried to get past it. Then, until you reached the next collection of armor, you felt lonely. Signs along the road warned drivers to keep at three-hundred-yard intervals and look out for strafers.

There was no temptation to get off the road and drive across the fields to avoid strafing as we got close to Sened, for the fields had almost certainly been mined by the retreating enemy. Sened was sinister—a wooden *gare* full of wasps' nests; a *buffet*, in a separate building, which two British booby-trap noncoms were busily rigging with their trip wires, as happy as parents decorating a Christmas tree; three or four dwellings, a water tower, and a church, all shattered by shellfire. The fact that the booby-trap men were at work meant that we in our turn were getting ready to abandon the place. You don't booby-trap a place you are going to stay in. We talked to the trappers, both Royal Engineers, one of whom was carrying so many one-pound cakes of TNT under his left arm that they seemed always on the point of wriggling loose. It looks like coarse white laundry soap. When I expressed concern, he said, "Lord love you, sir, it wouldn't explode if it did fall, not without a deetonyter, it wouldn't." The two men wore the fixed, slightly fatuous smile which seems to be a mark of their curious vocation. "We 'ad some nasty ones to tike up before we put ours in," the man with the TNT said. "We've rearranged them so Jerry will 'ave a time with them when 'e comes back. 'E won't be surprised, not 'alf."

There were three torn American medium tanks in a cluster where the main road went by the depot, looking as if they had been punched clean through. Armor-piercing shot from German 88's had gone into them, had bounced around inside like buckshot in a rattle, and then had gone out the other side, leaving the crew to be grilled by the flames as the fuel burned. The charred bodies had been extracted that morning and buried. A soldier's web belt, stiff with blood, lay on the ground outside the hole through which the bodies in one tank had been withdrawn. A couple of soldiers were looking at the belt. One of them was saying, over and over again, "I'll never take no more prisoners! The bastards! I'll never take no more prisoners!" A couple of 88's had lain doggo and caught the tanks with crossfire as they entered the town.

Our artillery was still firing at the ridge of a hill about five miles away. We asked a bearded, wild-looking soldier who was sitting in a parked jeep what the guns were pounding at.

"We got a lot of Germans trapped up there on the mountain," he said.

"How many?" Norgaard wanted to know.

"About a division, I guess," the soldier said.

"I don't see how you could hide a whole division on that hill," Norgaard said calmly.

"They got the mountain all hollowed out and that's where they're hiding," the soldier answered. (A couple of days later, at the American Second Corps headquarters, we asked a G 2 officer what had happened to the Germans trapped on the hill and he said, "Oh, you mean those last nine Heinies? They surrendered.")*

Norgaard and I got back to Gafsa fast. There was an uncomfortable feeling about Sened, a tacit menace that made us feel worse than actually being bombed or shot at.

That night I left the Gafsa region, and I didn't return for six weeks. Meanwhile, the American forces executed, in a rather ragged fashion, a withdrawal from Gafsa and several other towns. We lost almost all of two battalions of armor and two battalions of infantry, and, for the moment at least, all our prestige with the French and Arabs. When the Army recaptured Gafsa, in March, it was in a substantial, intelligent manner, with the entire First Division of infantry. During the operation, I was permitted to tag along with the headquarters of the division. Our troops got back into Gafsa almost without fighting, for the enemy had pulled out before our obviously superior force. The hard fight of the campaign came about a week later, at El Guettar, but that has nothing to do with my memories of Gafsa.

Gafsa was the first town I saw after our side had recaptured it from the enemy, and to me it was, in its small way, a symbol of the fact that this particular breed of bug could be dislodged, like any other. Gafsa is the capital of an administrative district with a population of a hundred and fifty thousand, so the government buildings are far larger than the size of the town itself warrants. Division headquarters, and I with it, moved into the building of the Gendarmerie Nationale, a fine, modern place with sleeping rooms on the upper floors. But the science of

---

* This was approximately the place where Mollie, seven weeks later, was to help persuade the Italians to surrender. At the moment of which I now write, he was in Oran, facing charges for leaving his post.

booby-trapping has taken a good deal of the fun out of following hot on an enemy's heels. Our engineers had already been through the lower floors of the Gendarmerie looking for booby traps, but they hadn't had time to do the living quarters, in a corner of which I was billeted. It acutely distressed me to turn a doorknob or draw a shutter. Eventually the division engineers decided that the Italians, the last of the enemy to withdraw from Gafsa, had lacked the time, or possibly the skill, to put any booby traps in the buildings. On that first day of my third visit to Gafsa, though, I didn't know what they were going to decide.

Soon after we pulled into town, I went for a walk to see how it had been affected by the occupation, which had lasted four weeks. The sixteenth-century Arab citadel had been partly wrecked by an explosion. Our engineers had used it as a storehouse for explosives during our occupancy and, before our withdrawal, had blown it up to keep the enemy from getting the stuff. Our destruction in Gafsa had not, on the whole, been well done. It bad been planned, for example, to move a number of locomotives north over the railroad that ran through the town and, after they had gone by, to blow up a railroad bridge to the north, so that we would have the locomotives and the enemy couldn't use the line, but somebody had blown up the bridge first, so the locomotives had to be left in Gafsa. Then, since no preparations had been made to destroy them, they fell into German hands. There was another oversight: the French civilian population of about five hundred had been evacuated by truck, but the native Jews had been left behind.

I met a French-speaking Arab in the market place in front of the old citadel who said he had been some sort of government employee—a police-court interpreter, I think—and had remained through the German occupation. He was frightened, because the houses of all the Frenchmen had been thoroughly pillaged by Arabs and the French notion of justice for Arabs is summary. He was consequently eager to talk and to convince me that his heart, at least, had been with the Allies. Most of the Gafsa Moslems had fled to join their kin in the hills during the German occupation, he said, because they wanted to escape the levies of the Italians and also because a great force of

American bombers had come over shortly after the evacuation and flattened a lot of Arab houses. The bombers had killed four hundred Arabs on a breadline in the market place, he said. "The people were much impressed, and those who had gone about talking of the victory of the Germans as certain were discredited," he said, indicating that there are several kinds of propaganda. "They realized that the Americans must have mistaken them for Italian troops," he added adroitly.

I asked him to tell me more about the occupation. "When the Germans and Italians first came here," he said, "they encouraged the people to rob the houses of the French and Jews and some of the more ignorant elements of the population complied with their wishes. The Germans did not stay here long, but went on, leaving an Italian garrison. The Italians were very poor. They pulled up even the young onions out of the gardens in the oasis and ate them as if famished. They broke into Arab houses and stole carpets off the floors and sold them to other Arabs living in the surrounding country, to get a few *sous*. They are a people without shame." The German words "*Araber Geschäft*" had been scrawled in chalk by the Arabs on the doors of a great number of shops, and the Arab told me that this had been done immediately after our evacuation, under instructions given over the Axis Arabic-language radio in Tunis, to protect these Arab establishments from pillage by the incoming Axis troops. "I never listened to that radio, of course," he said, "but so I have heard it related." I said I was surprised that so many Arabs knew even a couple of German words, and he explained that a number of them in Gafsa had been prisoners in Germany during the last war and had learned the language. It was easy to guess that the town had been full of Arab Axis agents during our first stay there. Some of them had probably been wearing the G.I. shirts compassionate Yanks had given them.

Presently I walked to the house of the Chemounis, the Tunisian Jewish family which, on my first visit to Gafsa in January, had entertained Norgaard and me. There had been young Chemouni himself, dressed in a European business suit, and his old, bearded father, and his attractive wife, and little, gray-eyed daughter. The house was still standing, but when I peered in through the open door, it looked as if nobody had lived there for years. There was nothing left in the place but a few pages of some Hebrew book scattered on the hard earth floor and a chandelier that hung crookedly from the roof of the once comfortable room in which Norgaard and I had drunk sweet wine and eaten olives and sliced pickled turnips. I wondered whether the family had escaped from Gafsa or been murdered. I asked a lad who came along the road what had happened to them and he said that they were all alive and had moved to the old Jewish quarter of the town, a couple of fetid alleys in which only the poorest and least Europeanized Jews had lived. The boy, who was Jewish himself, guided me to the house where the Chemounis were now. A scarecrow of a young man, wearing a beret and a long blue robe, precipitated himself upon me, sobbing and trying to kiss me. I knew it was Chemouni, though I could hardly recognize him. "They have stolen even my trousers," he said, pressing his face against the front of my field jacket.

Other Jews—many who, like my friend, had a few weeks before been outwardly European and were now indistinguishable from the most Oriental of Jews—flocked about me with their stories of the occupation. The Germans had come to the houses of the leading Jews on the first night and had taken worth-while things like money, jewelry, and stocks of raw wool, but had not touched their furniture and clothing. They then had left town, but not before they had invited the Arabs to help themselves to the leavings. As it turned out, there had been a wild competition between Arabs and Italians to gut the Jewish houses. The Italian commandant of the place had ordered all the Jews into a few houses in the old quarter and had put them on a ration even smaller than that accorded the Arabs, which had been minuscule. No Jews had been killed, but two young ones had come close to going before a firing squad because an Arab accused them of having betrayed an Axis parachutist to the Americans in December. The two had saved their lives by escaping to the desert. The Caïd of Gafsa, the town's chief Moslem official, had remained on the job through the occupation, and so had the spahis, the French-trained native police. The Caïd had fled with the Italians, fearing that the returning French would shoot him, but the spahis were still at their posts, once more under the orders of their French superiors. They were recovering stolen Jewish and French property from Arab houses, but what they found was now either completely ruined or almost valueless. The Caïd had left a large house containing, as part of the harem, a private movie theatre supplied with an extensive assortment of pornographic films.

Israel had been despoiled again, but it had apparently managed to hoard a few hens and roosters against the day of its deliverance. Near where I was standing, the *shochet*, the ritual slaughterer, an old man with a matted beard, was killing these chickens for family feasts of celebration, holding the blade in his lips between strokes while he smoothed back the neck feathers of the chicken whose throat he was going to slit next. A couple of big Jewish soldiers from the Bronx, with hands huge enough to palm a basketball and great feet that could kick a football sixty yards, placed their arms comfortingly on the shoulders of ancient, tiny matriarchs with whom, because the Tunisian Jews speak neither English nor Yiddish, they had no means of communication except signs. The Bronx Jews and the Tunisian Jews looked as different as a Percheron and an Eohippus.

"The Arabs are very bad," Chemouni said to me. "They have always been bad."

"How long has your family lived in Gafsa?" I asked him.

"I think for two thousand years," he said.

Chemouni's little girl, who spoke French as easily as any child in the Parc Monceau, looked at me with large, frightened, gray eyes. I asked Chemouni if his daughter would go to live in France after we had won the war. He said no, of course not; she would marry and live in Gafsa.

IV — GAFSA REVISITED

The girl did not stay in Gafsa, nor did my Monsieur Chemouni. When I returned there in the spring of 1956, I learned that both were in Israel, but Chemouni's brother remained—a military tailor for the French garrison.

The "dissidence" in Algeria had brought new trade to Gafsa, this Chemouni explained. There was the biggest French garrison ever, both of ground and air troops, to stop the traffic in munitions across technically neutral Tunisia, which had just regained its independence, to technically French Algeria, which was in full rebellion.

The French still maintained troops in Tunisia—they were withdrawn in subsequent months, except from the naval base of Bizerte. While they were not officially allowed to attack the gun-runners on Tunisian soil, they could follow them and break up their operations as soon as they crossed the line. Airplanes and helicopters were particularly useful for this job. Meanwhile guerillas, all for official purposes Algerians, operated on both sides of the border against the French, while Tunisian troops supposedly operated against the guerillas to preserve Tunisian neutrality.

The French military said that some of the guerillas were themselves Tunisians, and that the army of the new neutral state merely cooperated with them. The situation was somewhat clarified when the French pulled out and moved across the line into Algeria, where they set up electric barriers along the frontier to keep the gun-runners out. When that happened the military-tailoring business must have fallen off drastically.

The tailor Chemouni told me that much of his work consisted in removing badges of rank from uniforms, because the military believed that the snipers, whether in fact Tunisian or Algerian, picked targets according to grade. Since the snipers had presumably served in the French Army themselves, they presumably recognized the insignia.

There had been a great change since 1943. Tunisians had taken over the civil administration, and French civilians no longer lived among the Moslems in the old town, around the fort and baths. They had removed to the military quarter, around the railroad station on the other side of the oasis, where they felt safer at night. There had been an incident on the road near town a week or two before, when guerillas of some sort had burned a truck and a bus, and cut the throats of the truck-driver, an Italian, and of a European couple traveling in the bus. The husband was a White Russian, employed at a phosphate mine.

Because of this I had had to pay a taxi driver in Tunis extra fare to drive me down to Gafsa, a hundred and fifty miles or so, but we had had a tranquil journey. We had paused only briefly, however, at the old airfield in Thélepte. It felt lonely there; we got the wind up.

The Hôtel de France was out of business in Gafsa; its only successors were two very dirty *pensions* near the depot. A young French fighter pilot who talked to me after dinner at one of them thought I was a spy for an American oil company. After I reassured him, he told me that we had been mad to come by road—the country was in a state of anarchy. This was, of course, normal.

At Tunis, the Armée de l'Air had offered to send me in a military plane because they could not guarantee the safety of the roads. The young man at Gafsa seemed overwrought—the dissidents, he said, had taken to shooting at planes with rifles when the planes strafed them. This made him nervous. I did not think he compared well with Rozanoff.

My taxi-driver, a naturalized French citizen of Sicilian birth, spent the night with a friend down the road, a Frenchman who continued to run the municipal electric plant, and whose throat nobody had cut, perhaps because that would have cut the current along with it.

The remaining Jews continued to live in the old town, as they had for a great many centuries before Mohammed was born. I visited another Chemouni there, chief, I was told, of the name. He was a swollen old man with dropsical legs, a merchant who kept a general store, and who lived in a second-floor flat with an electric refrigerator, an index of great wealth. He treated me to sweet liqueur, and said business could be better, but he wasn't thinking of moving, just yet.

There was an old Tunisian proverb, he said: "The worst of those we know is better than the best of those we don't know." So he was going to stay on a while.

Next day my driver, who was named Daniel Portanova, and I drove over to the coast of the Gulf of Gabès, and returned to Tunis by the shore road, uneventfully. I haven't been back to Gafsa since.

Those first few months of intimate, warm, confused war in northwest Africa were made for ad lib fighters like Mollie and Major Cochran. But the campaign reached the age of reason with a lecture which I attended without great expectations.

*

The first meeting of General Omar Nelson Bradley with the international public, as represented by British and American newspaper and radio correspondents, occurred on the crest of a brush-covered hill at a place called Béja, in northern Tunisia, on April 22, 1943. The American phase of the Allied offensive against the Axis forces in Africa was about to begin. Bradley, who was fifty years old, held the temporary wartime rank of major general, and had no combat record in the First World War and no idiosyncrasies that could be expanded into a legend, had been named to succeed Lieutenant General George S. Patton as commander of the American II Corps, which was the whole American ground force engaged in the African fighting. Since even Patton, for all his pistol-slapping and advance publicity, had failed to make the II Corps work as an offensive unit, correspondents took his replacement by an unknown to mean that the Americans would have a minor role in the final battle against the Axis on the African continent. Press briefings at Patton's headquarters, conducted by an intelligence officer, had been like formal audiences, with all present required to buckle the chin straps of their tin hats, in token of instant readiness to face the moderately distant foe. Before the offensive began, the press-relations officer at Béja had announced with some little embarrassment (the P.R.O. had been commissioned straight out of the publicity department of a movie company, so he was naturally mindful of military dignity) that the new man had decided that he would brief the correspondents in person, and, as there were at least thirty of them and only one of him, he would come to the press camp for this purpose. The new man arrived in a jeep, carrying a map under his arm and attended by his aide, a captain of almost juvenile appearance, who carried an easel and a pointer. The General wore a tin hat—not buckled under the chin, probably because his reconnaissances sometimes took him into shelling and he didn't want his head jerked off. He also wore a canvas field jacket, G.I. pants, and canvas leggings, thus qualifying as the least dressed-up commander of an American army in the field since Zachary Taylor, who wore a straw hat. He had a long jaw and a high, notably convex forehead, and he was wearing spectacles. After the Green Hornet, with his ruddy, truculent face and his beefy, leather-sheathed calves, the new general, lanky and diffidently amiable, seemed a man of milk.

The aide set up the easel in press headquarters; then the General hung the map, took the pointer, and, in a high, not loud voice, as Missourian as the Truman voice that later became familiar to radio listeners, began to demonstrate how the II Corps intended to progress in an eleven-day drive to Mateur, the key to Bizerte, through enemy positions that had stopped the best troops of the British First Army for five months. Some people think a general should have a voice like a recorded bugle call played over a loudspeaker. But the Bradley delivery is really an asset—hesitant, slightly rustic, compelling the hearer to listen hard for the next phrase and at the same time convincing him of the General's candor. At Béja, he laid down his schedule with no more panache than a teacher outlining the curriculum for the new semester. The Americans, he said, had been moved from the south-central to the extreme northwest arc of the Allied semicircle facing the Axis redoubt—because, the correspondents had suspected up to this point, they were to make merely a holding attack, in country so rugged that they could switch quickly to the defensive if the Germans came at them. Meanwhile, the British First and Eighth Armies were to crash through at more promising points on the Axis perimeter. When a correspondent who had been with the British in this zone through the bitter months of frustration asked how the inexperienced 9th Division was going to get Green and Bald Hills, two notoriously nasty positions that had stopped the Guards, General Bradley said that that was up to General Manton Eddy, the division commander, but that he didn't expect any undue delay. All parts of the inquiring correspondent visible above his battle dress turned purple.

Only two American infantry divisions, the 1st and the 9th, appeared on the General's map. The absence of the corps's other infantry outfit, the 34th Division, was interpreted by some to mean that it was being held in defensive reserve and by others that it had been sent home as useless. Either supposition, if confirmed, would bear out the notion that the American attack was not too banefully intended. There was, however, a gap half as wide as a divisional front between the 9th and the 1st. "What are you going to have in there, sir?" a knowing fellow asked. The new general looked at him with a gratified, pedagogical smile, as at a pupil who had asked a bright question. "I'm going to patrol that with a troop of motorized cavalry," he said. (A couple of days later, when General Eddy expressed his own disquiet about the gap, Bradley told him reassuringly, "If they come through there, Bill Kean and I will go in with a couple of BARs." BARs are Browning automatic rifles. Kean, who later commanded the 25th Division in Korea, was then the II Corps's chief of staff.) The new general didn't have much more to say. It was a historic début, although nobody knew it at the time. Had any programs been printed, they would sell at a big premium today.

Bradley had been in Tunisia two months without a command when he took over the II Corps. General George Catlett Marshall, then Chief of Staff of the Army, had, General Marshall later said, sent Bradley there "to be Eisenhower's legs and wisdom." He spent most of his time at the front, returning to Algiers to tell the Commander-in-Chief what was going on. General Eisenhower was not only several hundred miles away; he was—nominally, at least—in command of the British First and Eighth Armies and the French XIX Corps, in addition to the Americans, and was also supreme political arbiter of North Africa, which left him only limited time for tactical details. This had been Bradley's first experience in a real war, and he had been looking at it closely—going up into forward observation posts, and talking to company and platoon leaders and to riflemen to check on what he had learned and taught in the previous thirty-two years. So he was bringing to his first recital what a music critic unafraid of clichés would call a ripened technique and a mature understanding of the content of the music. Into the gap in his offensive alignment, when the time came, he slipped the fresh 34th Division, and, pushing it forward in depth on a rather narrow front, he sent it against Hill 609, the highest eminence of the first range he had to fight across. The 1st had already reached the flanks of 609 and could put artillery fire on it to help the attackers. So employed, the 34th, which so far in this campaign had known only defeat and was considered a liability, took 609 and came out believing itself a division *d'élite*, which was most of what it needed to be one. This made the new general's military gifts manifest to his first audience, and they have never had cause to change their opinion of him. Many generals, in the course of history, have taken a hill at the cost of a division, and as many have lost a division without taking a hill. Bradley took a key hill and gained a division. His troops reached each of their objectives almost exactly in accordance with the schedule he had laid down. "There was one time when Matt Eddy was a few hours behind, up on the left flank," General Bradley said a couple of years later, during the campaign in western France, "but I told him to step on it."

Bradley explained that small bit of virtuosity seven years later, over a drink.

"All hills, with narrow draws between them—a country just laid out for defense," he said of northern Tunisia. "They'd get up in the hills, and when you went down in the draws to get around them, they'd put fire on you." He had thought he knew what to do about the hills, he said—go straight up them, as you would when hunting wild goats in the mountains of Hawaii. It had also occurred to him that the German 88, though its flat trajectory made it wonderful for shooting across valleys at vehicles in the open, would not be much good at firing over hills at close range to hit hidden soldiers on the reverse slopes. "I remember that gap between the Ninth and the First," he said. "What I was thinking was that if the suckers did come in over those hills, they wouldn't have any good road they could get far on, and we could round 'em up before they got far into our rear. It was about nine miles from where they were over to the Djebel Abiod road, and by the time they had climbed down there we could have armor to meet them."

The Chairman sipped at his drink and looked across at the staircase as if he could see the Djebel Abiod road, in the shadow of hills covered with purple wild flowers and separated by narrow black gorges in which dwarf cows found water. Then he smiled. "I wanted that gap for the Thirty-fourth," he said. "Alexander [General, now Viscount, Alexander, the field commander of the joint Allied forces in Africa] and Bedell Smith [Eisenhower's Chief of Staff] had wanted to send the Thirty-fourth home for retraining, they thought it was so bad.

It had its tail down between its legs. I said, 'Leave it to me and I'll guarantee that it carries its first important objective, if I have to give it every gun in the Corps.' It's good for troops to feel they have an important objective. You may have to move them up and move them back once or twice when they're green, just to give them the habit of fighting, but if you do it too often they get the feeling they're being thrown away. That treatment had spoiled the Thirty-fourth. So I didn't want it in at the start, when they might think they were getting more of the same. Then I put them at 609. You remember it. It was almost a cliff. But the Thirty-fourth went up it. The suckers got down in the crevices when we put fire on it, and then after our fellows had passed over they came out and took them in the rear. But our fellows cleaned them up. After that, the Thirty-fourth had its tail over the dashboard. You couldn't hold it."

The Thirty-fourth was the division components of which had been so messed around with in the fighting between Sened and Maknassy, while other components had subsequently been set out on hills near Kasserine like goats set out to lure a tiger. Then, when the tiger, in the form of German armor, came, the American armored division that had been cast in the role of big-game hunter lost its nerve and let the Germans scoop up the infantry goats, along with about 100 of our tanks. The residue of the Thirty-fourth was left with a goat mentality, which it imparted to the replacements. Old Dr. Bradley's psychotherapy fixed it up. Confusion, though normal, is not inevitable.

3
Entr'acte

I WAS lucky enough to get back to New York at the end of the African campaign, as I have told in the first piece in the book, and had five months at home before I came to the wars again, this time as a passenger on a Norwegian fruit ship that was considered fast enough to run without escort—seventeen knots. She certainly was that time, although I heard she copped it later. You were always hearing that ships you had just been on were sunk, and sometimes it was true. This reefer was of 3,000 tons, very clean and yacht-like, and she landed me in the Adelphi Hotel at Liverpool on November 6, 1943, my fourth and last eastward crossing during the war. My notion was to get to England early in order to be sure of a good spot in the invasion. I did not want to get caught up in some ancillary theatre and then not be able to transfer out in time for the main event, and as the lone correspondent of *The New Yorker* I had to fight my own campaign against red tape and the stuffy lay bureaucrats of the large press organizations, who wanted to make the battle an exclusive feature for their employers, like *Gasoline Alley* or Arthur Krock. When not engaged in this sordid guerilla, I tried various activities to kill time. "Run, Run, Run, Run," arose out of one of them, or out of two of them if you like. It was such an unsettling experience that I didn't write about it at the time; it was hardly a news story, being about something that happened when I wasn't there and then didn't happen when I was. I wrote it in the fall of 1945, at home, but it is all true, except that I made the chief character a more obvious fraud than I am, by lending him some of the characteristics of correspondents I disliked.

Run, Run, Run, Run

When Allardyce Meecham heard that the boys were dead, he felt that he should have flown with them. Meecham was a war correspondent, but he had not yet had a chance to see much of the war. He had come to England in February, 1944, straight from the Hotel Algonquin, where he had had only four or five days to wear his uniform in the lobby, and he did not feel natural wearing it even after a fortnight in London. His nearest approach to action so far had been a visit to an American bomber station in Essex, where he had arranged to go on a bombing mission with a Marauder crew. Now he felt guilty because he had not gone. If he had he would have been dead, too, and that had not been part of his plan, but he felt somehow that this was an ignoble consideration. At the field, a squadron intelligence officer named Kobold had told him the mediums had been having very small losses, an average of one in two hundred sorties. "I wanted to fly one mission and write a story about it, and pretend to myself that I was a big man," Meecham thought self-accusingly, "but if I had expected they would be killed I wouldn't have gone with them." This may or may not have been true. There was no way now of proving it. But Meecham never gave himself the benefit of the doubt because he was afraid that if he did it once he would take advantage of the precedent. "What could you have done, anyway," he asked himself, "if you had known they were going to be killed? Would you have made some excuse and left? Or would you have tried to get them not to go? They would have wanted to know how you could be sure. They would have said you were crazy. They would have gone anyway." But he continued to feel as if he had done something wrong. Meecham had left the airfield because he had tired of hanging about waiting for flying weather. Three days' missions had been washed out and there was no sign it would open up, and he had a date with a British woman officer in London for Friday evening.

This was Sunday. Meecham was standing at the bar of his hotel in Piccadilly, and next to him was Kobold, the intelligence officer he had met at the bomber base. Kobold had come into London on a weekend pass, and he had just told Meecham the bad news. "I wasn't frightened," Meecham thought. "I really wasn't. I told them I was coming back to fly with them next week. They expected to be there. They had flown forty missions. They didn't think the weather would clear off during the weekend. They said I would be a sucker to stay." The weather had cleared on Friday afternoon, after he had left. Saturday morning the bomber crew had been killed. At what precise minute, Meecham wondered, but he felt almost sure he knew. It was March, and dawn came medium late. They would not have been fairly on their way before eight. Over Beauvais, in the north of France, at nine, nine-thirty, maybe. Perhaps at the moment he had picked up the telephone by his bed to order breakfast. "Two teas, sausage and tomato. Darling, do you want sausage and tomato or sausage and mushroom? There's bacon, but it's usually like eating a candle." That must have been the minute. "Two sausage and tomato, then. And lots of toast. Thank you."

"They had all their bombs aboard," Kobold was saying. He was an oldish lieutenant who felt that he should have been a captain months ago. "One big hell of a cloud of smoke, and then parts of the plane falling out of it. No chutes—no time for them. The other boys brought back wonderful pictures of it. Poor bastards." The intelligence officer talked loudly, a little truculently, because he wanted a couple of B-17 pilots at the other end of the bar to hear him. The heavy-bomber people sometimes talked as if they had all the losses; the lieutenant wanted to impress this pair. He never flew on operations himself.

Meecham stood just six feet in shoes, but because of his thin, long legs and short, beanlike torso he seemed longer than that when he stood up and shorter than that when he sat down. He had a white face, wide at the cheekbones and covered with faint, rusty blotches, and carroty hair that for the last five years had just failed to cover the top of his head. People seeing him at a bar thought of him as tall and red-headed, but others, who had looked at him seated at a restaurant table, remembered him as bald and middle-sized. His eyelashes were almost white. In New York he was a dramatic critic, but as the war entered its fifth year and all his acquaintances—book reviewers, editorial writers, political columnists, racing handicappers, and publishers' assistants—became war correspondents and went overseas, he had felt lonely. There must be something in the war that none of these people were fine enough to perceive, he had told his wife, who had a responsible job in the promotion department of a woman's magazine and always referred to herself as a "gal." She had agreed with him. She was a good gal. "Besides," she had said, "I think it would be a professional disadvantage for a dramatic critic after the war not to have been a war correspondent. No one would want to hear you lecture." She was having an affair with a Rumanian fashion photographer, who worked her for assignments. Meecham had been disappointed that even his own wife misread his motives. But, fighting down this disappointment, he had gone to his managing editor and asked to be sent to Europe. The editor had sent him because he rather thought there would be a lull before the invasion of the Continent. Meecham would spell one of the paper's regular correspondents accredited to the Army, who would come home for a short vacation before the big show began. "But, of course, if it should start suddenly, you'll be there," the editor had said. "Yes, sir," Meecham had said in a voice from which he had tried to exclude excitement. He had felt exalted as he walked over to Abercrombie & Fitch to be measured for his uniform. But, as he now reflected, he had not thought that he really might be killed. "I wanted something for nothing," he thought unmercifully. He was on the point of admiring how hard on himself he could be, and then he remembered that that would constitute self-approval, so he stopped.

Meecham remembered the interior of the Nissen hut he had slept in at the Marauder field. There had been cots and a table and a stove, hooks on the walls to hang clothes on, and even coat hangers, but to him it had been a Spartan place, where he had been more conscious of the war than in his room in London, which contained a good deal of inlaid furniture and a double bed with a yellow damask cover. There were electric-light bulbs in the hut, but they were not shaded, and you had to go outdoors to get to the latrine. There were six cots in the hut. A Marauder carries a complement of three officers and three enlisted men; the hut accommodated the officers of two planes. One set of three had gone to town on pass; men who flew together took their passes at the same time. This gave Meecham his choice of three cots. The boys of the other Marauder crew had just come back from forty-eight hours in London. Meecham found them in the hut when Kobold brought him there in the evening. He had stayed at the officers' club drinking gin and Italian with the C.O. and a couple of non-flying intelligence officers until the bar closed, at ten o'clock. Then Kobold had guided him to the hut. It would have been hard to find in the blackout if he had been alone. Kobold had introduced Meecham to the three crewmates. One of them, a large, hairy, blond young man, was in bed already. He was Captain Barry, the pilot. Barry was smoking a last cigarette before going to sleep. One bare, powerful arm lay outside the blankets as he puffed. A B-26, romantically known as a Marauder, is not an easy plane to fly, and old pilots get big forearms and biceps. Barry reached out a big hand to shake Meecham's. "Make yourself at home," he said. Brownlea, the co-pilot, a wiry young man with a crew haircut, sat at the table with his back to the stove, reading what Meecham observed wonderingly was a book by Robert Briffault, an author Meecham associated vaguely with Granville Hicks and Ouida. "I hope you don't mind loud noises," Brownlea said. "Barry is about to go to sleep. Luckily they have radar here or somebody would have shot him down before this. When he snores he sounds exactly like a four-motor job. He has the Air Force sack medal with so many clusters it looks like a bunch of grapes." "Brownlea is an intellectual," Barry said. "He is a wizard intellectual, they would say in the R.A.F. He is very cheesed with life. He thinks life is a ruddy pantomime. Someday when he is at the controls he will be thinking of an ideology and he will prang the crate. A wizard prang." Elkan, the bombardier-navigator, was sitting on a cot, looking over a set of shiny photographer's prints; he had interrupted the examination only long enough to nod at Meecham when Kobold introduced them. He was a thin young man who in civilian clothes could have been mistaken for a high-school junior. He could not weigh more than a hundred and fifteen pounds and he had a long, pointed nose and large ears. He was still wearing the Class A uniform blouse and pinks in which he had come back from London, and the garrison cap was still on his head. The left breast of his blouse was pretty well loaded with ribbons—even Meecham could recognize the Silver Star, the Distinguished Flying Cross, the Air Medal nutmegged with oak-leaf clusters, the E.T.O. ribbon dotted with stars, and a couple of the innocuous red-and-yellow ones that make good background even though they don't mean anything much.

Kobold went away and Meecham settled down on a cot. "I'm glad to have you here, sir," Brownlea said to Meecham. "Barry and Elkan are good joes, but Elkan is emotional and Barry is inclined to pure escapism. I have been wanting a chance to talk to someone who has really been around a lot."

Meecham was ashamed to tell him that his travels, until this trip, had been limited to a tourist-class vacation in France when he was in college and four trips to the Central City, Colorado, annual dramatic festivals, so he said nothing.

"Don't give Brownlea any encouragement, sir," Elkan said, "or he will read you the first ten chapters of his book."

"I wouldn't think of it," Brownlea said. "Anyway, they're only in a kind of outline form. I really don't know anything about writing. What I want to know is what you think of the Russians."

Meecham considered himself an untrammelled liberal—during the Spanish Civil War he had attended several cocktail parties for the benefit of the Loyalists—but he had heard talk at home about the Fascist mind of the Air Corps, so he was careful in answering. He liked these boys so much already that he didn't want to alarm or antagonize them. He said merely, "I know the Russians are our Allies. I mean, I believe they're sincere, and they're certainly fighting hard."

"Is that all?" Brownlea said. "Why, they're absolutely wonderful. They're the only hope I see for civilization. Surely, sir, you don't think capitalist society can survive all this? Say, have you ever read this man Briffault?"

"Brownie got a brushoff from a society dame at a bottle club in London," Barry said. "She said she was going to spend a penny and she never came back. He's been a militant proletarian ever since."

Meecham said that, of course, the rôle Russia would be called upon to play in the future should not be underestimated.

"Well, I don't worry much about that," Barry said, "although I still have a card in the typographical union, so it burns my ass when I read in the *Reader's Digest* that organized labor is to blame for about everything that gets screwed up. I worked my way through the University of California that way, setting type at night on a paper in Oakland. Where the hell does the *Reader's Digest* think I am, and where is the bird who is writing that stuff? Sitting on his can, I bet. But being from the Coast, I mean, I don't think very much about this war. I'd like to be out smacking those Japs around. I haven't got anything too much against the Germans, except Hitler is a son of a bitch."

"I have," Elkan said. "I'm a Jew, and they've been killing millions of Jews who didn't do a goddam thing to them. I hate the bastards. I like to think of what the bombs will do to them when we make our run."

"You see?" Brownlea said. "Pure emotion. Barry and Elkan don't know anything about the economic bases of imperialism. They reduce everything to personal relationships."

"She said she had to spend a penny," Barry said to nobody in particular. "Brownie offered to lend her a shilling. She gave him a look that said, 'Anybody that dumb . . .' And the brush."

Elkan said, "To change the subject, which of these pictures do you like the best?"

"Are they of a broad?" Barry asked.

"No, you wolf—me," Elkan answered severely. "I went down to see the Tower of London yesterday, and then I walked around and had some pictures taken at a photographer's. I want to pick out the best one and have some copies made from it to send home. I want to send them to my mother and my girl and people like that." Meecham had already learned that Elkan's parents lived in Bayonne, New Jersey, where his father had a dry-cleaning store. He had gone two years to Rutgers but hadn't had enough money to continue, and for a year or so before he enlisted he had helped in the store. He hadn't as much assurance as some of the bigger, louder boys, who gave the impression that the whole Air Force came from Texas, but the fellows in his squadron had a lot of respect for him. Barry, Brownlea, and Meecham began passing the photographer's proofs from one to another. Meecham could see that the two pilots were considering them very seriously. In all but one of the proofs, Elkan had the visor of his cap pulled well down and was scowling and puffing out his chest. The photographer had got a good, clear picture of the ribbons. But the thin, triangular face and the frail, bony neck still looked like a little boy's. Only one of the proofs showed Elkan smiling. The wide smile made him look younger and more ingenuous than ever, but the picture was the only one of the lot that wasn't absurd. All three of the consultants agreed it was the best.

"That's the only one that looks like the real Ernie," Barry said.

"That's the one your mother would like to have," said Brownlea.

And Meecham said, "That's the best." He could sense that Ernie was disappointed and that if he had not been there the little bombardier-navigator might have tried to argue with the others.

But Elkan accepted the reinforced verdict. "Christ," he said sadly, "I guess I'll never look like a hero." Meecham could see that he was worrying about his girl back home.

They had talked a while longer and then turned in. Meecham had felt unexpectedly ashamed because his body looked so white and old compared to theirs. He was forty-three and the last exercise he could remember had been a fight with the juvenile of a show he had panned in 1937, but the bartender and the home-and-garden editor had stopped it after the first swing, when the juvenile's pince-nez fell on the floor.

There had been no mission the next morning, on account of the weather. Meecham had got up at seven and gone dutifully to mess, but the boys had chosen to sleep until nearly noon.

"It must be awfully slow for you here, sir," Barry had said the next time Meecham saw him. "I suppose you wanted to go over with us and see some fun."

"It isn't dull at all," Meecham had said, and meant it. "It's very interesting." He had not added, "It's all new to me," because he felt a childish reluctance to let the boys know he was so green. He hadn't really thought of flying a mission on his first visit to the field, either. But Barry looked so competent and unworried that Meecham had found himself saying, "I sure would like to go with you. Do you think the C.O. would let me?"

Barry had grinned and said, "Sure. We've flew lots of correspondents in our ship. It breaks the monotony." And they had shaken hands on it.*

Meecham had slept in the hut a second and third night and each had been followed by a day of bad weather. Even in this brief time he had begun to think of himself as a member of the crew of the Typographical Error, the name Barry had given his B-26. He had gone through the preliminary processes of a Marauder mission, which at that time he had thought piquant rather than grim. The squadron intelligence officer had told him what to do if he had to bail out over France. He was to hide his parachute and then take cover and lie still until somebody found him. The French underground people would be pretty sure to find him, the intelligence officer said, and they would smuggle him across France and into a neutral country, although it might take months. The prospect had sounded alluring as the intelligence officer described it, and Meecham had been unable to stop daydreaming about adventures with admiring and sympathetic Frenchwomen. The one thing the officer had not said anything about was what to do if you were dead. So Meecham had not thought about it.

On the third bad morning he had begun to feel bored and had remembered the date with the woman officer in London. There was a train at noon and he had decided to leave by it. When he began packing his bag the boys were still in bed, and when he finished he went around to each cot and shook hands before he started for the jeep that was to take him to the railway station. Meecham could remember Barry's strong grip

*Harold Ross, the great editor of *The New Yorker*, said when he read this in manuscript that Barry, a college man and a linotyper, would not have said, "flew." My only answer was that the prototype of Barry in real life *had* said "flew." Since I was pretending to write fiction, this was not a valid argument, but I had my way. I can see now that "we've flew" looks unconvincing. But I hear the pseudonymous Barry's voice in my head sometimes, and he still says it.

* A RACIST, A MISOGYNIST, AND A PHILISTINE.

and Elkan's slender hand and Brownlea grinning and waving his clenched left fist. Brownlea's father, Meecham had learned, was president of a savings bank in Boston.

Remembering, Meecham felt that the date with them was more binding than if they had survived and that he could never be pleased with himself if he did not fly a mission now. But there was no exhilaration in the thought. He returned to Essex three days later. He found it easy to arrange, at Ninth Air Force Headquarters, for permission to go along on a bombardment. "The story has been done a lot of times before," a public-relations officer warned him. "There's nothing much to it." Meecham explained that he just wanted to see what it was like. He didn't say anything about the crew of the Typographical Error. It seemed to him for a moment, after they had said he could go, that he was doing a causeless thing. It isn't being brave, he told himself, because the mathematical chance of getting hurt is no greater now than it was last week, and then it was very small. Barry and his ship just had bad luck. And there won't be any story in it either. But he was afraid, and that was precisely what he could not afford to admit to himself. Nobody at the field seemed astonished that he wanted to do it. The boys at the officers' club made him welcome with gin and Italian vermouth, and he was introduced to the officers he was now assigned to fly with. Their ship was named the Roll Me Over,* and they were nice boys enough, Meecham thought, but it was like a widower's marriage; he could not get as interested in them as in the dead crew. Schifferdecker, the pilot, was a squat, broad-shouldered boy who had played football at Cornell, where he had taken a course in hotel management. He kept telling Meecham that after the war the British would have to build modern hotels all over England if they expected any Americans ever to come back there.

---

*From that great song:
   "Roll me over, in the clover,
    Roll me over, lay me down, and do it again—"
which was the pre-invasion "Battle Hymn of the Republic." It was frequently asserted, during World War II, that "this is not a singing war." It was—people always sing when they are frightened—but the songs did not lend themselves to community performance.

Thurman, the co-pilot, a tall, handsome young man from someplace in Wisconsin, did not have much to say for himself. He had a girl in a show in London, his crewmates said, and he considered every hour he had to spend at the field time wasted. "Missions are the only chance he has to catch up on his sleep," Schifferdecker said. Muldowney, the bombardier-navigator, was a pale, gray-eyed young man who looked like a very youthful Franchot Tone and knew it, and who had played in a dance band in St. Paul before enlisting in the Air Corps. "It's a good deal, having a correspondent along," he told Meecham. "We'll be in a soft spot, right in the center of one of the middle elements, where nothing ever happens. Those flak gunners loose off at the first ships, and then, when the first elements drop their bombs, the gunners run like hell. We'll have a breeze. Same thing for fighters. We haven't been getting much fighter opposition. The Heinies keep most of that in Germany to use against the heavy bombers. But what we have been getting usually lays for the rear element, on the way home, hoping to knock off stragglers. We lost a ship that way yesterday. The boys in the middle have a soft touch." Muldowney had a wide, white grin. "An easy one is always all right with me," he went on. "I've had twenty-eight missions so far, and every easy one means that much better a chance to finish the fifty."

There was no cot for Meecham in the hutment where the Roll Me Overs slept, so he spent the night in a hut in another part of the field, about half a mile from the mess hall. The men in the hut with him were armament and engineering officers. Only two were in bed when Meecham got there. The rest were up most of the night preparing planes for the takeoff. They got in so late that they had just begun to snore when an orderly turned on the lights before dawn next morning. They stayed in bed, the blankets over their heads, while Meecham and the two men who had been in bed early began to dress. Meecham hated to get up early in the morning for any reason at all, and on this particular day he felt worse than usual. He dressed fast, for him, but he was not yet familiar with lace boots, and he had to fumble around in his musette bag to find toothpaste and a towel. Then he felt colicky and went out to look for a latrine. By the time he returned the two other men had gone to the mess hall, and he began to fear that he would lose his way in the dark. The buildings were, of course, blacked out, so he would have no lighted windows to guide him. It would sound like an implausible excuse for missing the raid. He went out of the hut and saw the silhouette of a jeep moving up the road past the hut. There were at least a dozen men on it, some sitting on the hood. He yelled, "Going up to mess?" Someone shouted to him to jump on. Awkwardly he ran along beside the slowly moving jeep, not knowing quite how to get aboard without knocking some other rider off his perch. The jeep stopped and somebody said, "Come along, Pop. You can sit in the back." One of the youngsters in the back seat scrambled out and found a few inches of space on a mudguard, and half a dozen hands grabbed Meecham and hoisted him into the place just vacated. He rode along to the mess hall oblivious of everything except his humiliation. At table he found Schifferdecker and Thurman. Muldowney came along a couple of minutes later, carrying a shiny brown quilted flying suit which he had drawn for Meecham. The breakfast was poor—an omelet badly made of powdered egg and bacon that was all rind and grease. The fruit juice was all gone and the coffee tasted metallic. He wondered if the breakfast was really that bad or if he was frightened. "This is pisspoor chow," Thurman said, and Meecham was reassured. The men in the mess hall straggled out in little groups, crewmates and fellows who knew each other, and climbed into weapons carriers for the ride out to the dispersal building for the briefing. Meecham, of course, rode with the Roll Me Overs.

The briefing reminded him of a lecture in a compulsory course at college. The hall was filled with fellows in flying gear who talked to each other and did not seem too attentive. The intelligence officer stood on a dais at one end of the hall and waved a pointer at various spots on a large map that was projected on a screen behind him. Meecham learned later that all the fliers had been to these particular targets several times and that the lecture had about the same interest for them as an explanation of how to reach New Rochelle. "Our primary target today will be the Montdidier airfield," the officer said. "There is a battery of six mediums on the approach to the Montdidier field. Six mediums." Somebody whistled. "All of you can go now except the bombardiers. Bombardiers stay a minute after the others leave."

Meecham went out with Schifferdecker and Thurman and three sergeants who had joined them in the briefing hall. The sergeants were the rest of the Roll Me Over's crew—radio-gunner, flight engineer, and tail gunner. They were named Mickiewicz, Klopstock, and Leopardi. Muldowney had to stay to get his detailed bombing map. When he came out they all got into a weapons carrier with perhaps twenty other fliers. The carrier rolled along on the cinder path that circled the field, stopping at each plane to let off the men who were going to fly in it. So Meecham found himself eventually standing under the shadow of the Roll Me Over. It was daylight now, but the sky was still pink with the embers of dawn. In the truck the boys had been singing a song of which Meecham had been able to distinguish only the first line, "How's your love life?"* He put on the flying suit over his G.I. pants, his sweater, and his combat jacket. Muldowney was brisk and happy, although cold. He rubbed his gloved hands together furiously and stamped about in his flying boots. Schifferdecker was serious and conscientious, conferring with the sergeants. Thurman leaned against the fuselage and Meecham noticed that he looked sleepy. He wondered if Thurman could have got down to London on a late train and back in time to fly. Meecham nodded toward the ship and asked Muldowney if it was all right to get aboard. Muldowney said sure, and went ahead to show the way. This was a moment Meecham had anticipated with distaste, because he didn't know how to get into a B-26 and had a feeling it might call for some display of acrobacy. It was not so hard as he had feared. There were two metal stir-rups, no higher than those on an English saddle, and when you got one foot up you reached up with your hands and caught two metal handles in the interior of the plane. Then you swung yourself up and in. He could see that it would be easy to get out when they returned—he would only have to swing himself out by the handles and drop. Somehow this was

---

*This was not a classic, like "Roll Me Over," and I never heard it again. It sounded like something they would get off the other side of a hit record in the officers' lounge.

a major satisfaction. Muldowney motioned him into a compartment behind the nose of the plane. There was no need to
kneel or crawl. "There's a hell of a lot of room in these
things," Muldowney said. "More than in a Fort. You just sit
over there at the side on that pile of chutes." The others came
aboard one by one. Schifferdecker and Thurman went past
Meecham and into the pilots' compartment, in the nose. The
sergeants joined Meecham and Muldowney in the compartment behind the pilots' because Schifferdecker would want
their weight up forward for the takeoff. "This is a place for the
navigator to work," Muldowney told Meecham, "but there
isn't any real navigating to do when we follow the leader in a
big formation like today. Of course, if we got crippled or had
to beat it off by ourselves for any reason, it would be different.
I just wander around the ship when we get going, sometimes
here and sometimes in the bomb bay. We're carrying frag
bombs today, by the way. Thirty one-hundred-pound frag
bombs. We drop them on the runway and dispersal area to
take care of planes and personnel. Sometimes we carry a couple of big ones, but today frags." The motors were turning
over. Other planes taxied by them on their way to the runway.
Then the Roll Me Over began to roll, too. The motors made
such a noise that conversation became impractical, although it
was still possible to understand a shouted monosyllable. The
compartment in which Meecham rode was comfortable, but
there was only a view straight out to either side. There was
nothing to see in either direction except other B-26s. The
plane was swaying and slipping about and he could see Thurman turn and swear. Schifferdecker was running the ship. The
pilots sat next to each other. The backs of their seats were
armor-plated, as a protection against pieces of flak. Meecham
could see there was room for a man to crouch behind them,
and he looked forward enviously because there was more to
see from the nose of the plane. Thurman, as if reading his
thoughts, waved to him to come forward, and he did,
scrunching his torso and hams down behind Thurman's seat,
while his legs extended over behind Schifferdecker's.

Now the sky was as blue as the Bay of Naples on the wall of
a spaghetti joint, and it was full of B-26s. They flew in "loose
fives," their favorite formation. Meecham started to count all

those in sight; he made it sixty-seven, including the planes on the Roll Me Over's wings, but more appeared constantly and he stopped counting. He deduced that the B-26s were just circling while the groups assembled and that the serious part of the expedition had not begun yet. Then the course began to seem to him more purposeful. Almost before he was sure of this, Thurman was plucking at his elbow, waving an arm downward. They were over the coast, heading out over the Channel, which looked not blue but had, at its English edge, the color of a puddle of rain water glistening in sunlight. Then it became lead color. Meecham noticed for the first time that the motors were saying words. They were saying words, groaning, rather, "No, no, no, no." He had ridden in planes before but he had never recognized the words. When they got over the French coast, he thought, "I should be curious. I haven't seen France in twenty years." He looked and it seemed quite like England. He leaned close to Thurman's ear and shouted, "How long to over target?" Thurman howled back, "Twenty minutes." Meecham went back to the pile of parachutes in the navigator's cabin and Muldowney appeared, probably from the bomb bay, and seemed to be saying something about "fighters." Meecham returned to his place behind the pilots and looked down. He saw a midget plane far below them. It was a Spitfire, but he did not know it; he could not tell Allied fighters from Germans. All the attention began to embarrass Meecham. He felt that Muldowney was treating him like a grandfather on a Sunday auto ride. Muldowney reached through the doorway to the pilots' compartment and tapped Meecham on the shoulder. He wanted to show him something dead ahead, a series of specks in the sky. Then Muldowney grinned and started back to the bomb bay. The specks were not fighters, Meecham saw as the plane drew up on them, but puffs of black smoke. They multiplied, as he watched, and hung in the air, little black balls of grime. He knew what they were from his sporadic attendance at newsreel theatres. The planes of the forward elements were flying through them now. The flak was at very nearly the right altitude, and Meecham began to hear a new sound over the motors—a sharp "Pak!" like a champagne cork popping and then "S-s-s" like half the wine in the bottle fizzing out. The "Pak!" was the shell bursting, and the fizz was the flight of the fragments. Once Thurman threw up a hand in front of his face and flattened himself against the back of his seat, but nothing happened. Meecham wondered if it had been a close one or if Thurman was just jumpy from too much tomcatting. The co-pilot was waving his hand now and Meecham, following his gesture, could see the bombs falling away from the planes up ahead of them, like chewing-gum nuggets out of a vending machine. Then there were no more puffs in the sky. He felt Muldowney's hand on his shoulder again. The boy had been away only an instant, it seemed. Muldowney was laughing and waving his hands palms upward. Thurman took off his earphones and put them on Meecham, so Meecham could listen to the intercom. Schifferdecker said to Meecham through the intercom, "How'd you like it?" Meecham tried to smile, and for all he knew succeeded. Then Schifferdecker made Thurman take the ship. Meecham understood from that that they were on the way home. He gave Thurman the earphones again. The motors said now, "Run, run, run, run." He said to himself, "I am not making this up, that is what they are saying." He listened again and they were indeed saying, "Run, run," instead of "No, no." Meecham looked at the air-speed indicator and it said "330," which pleased him. Then he went back to Muldowney's compartment and relaxed on the parachutes. Muldowney was grinning and waving his hands and shouting into Meecham's ear, and finally Meecham could understand what he was saying: "I told you that flak would stop as soon as the first planes got their bombs away!" Meecham succeeded in asking whether *he* had got his bombs away and Muldowney joined a thumb and forefinger in a circle to show he had put his bombs right on the bull's-eye. Sergeant Mickiewicz, a bulky blond with a red face, appeared in the compartment and grinned at Meecham. Nothing happened on the way back, but it seemed five times as long as it had going out.

When they got out of the plane, Schifferdecker started swearing. "The goddam wash nearly made me airsick," he said. "Those goddam cowboys in the ships on our wings must think they're driving taxicabs. Whoever checked them out in a bomber ought to have his head examined. What a ratfuck!" He explained that a ratfuck was "a rat race, but all bollixed up."

Thurman said, "If they don't keep us too long at the god-dam interrogation I can catch the twelve-o'clock train to London."

Muldowney said, "Twenty-nine down and twenty-one to go. I hope they send us a correspondent on every trip! I wonder if any of those leading planes got flak in them."

Meecham felt unreasonably exalted. After all, he told himself reprovingly, he had only escaped from a danger that he had got himself into. And not a great danger, either, he thought. I didn't see one plane shot down. Still, he couldn't help thinking, pretty good for a dramatic critic. He had forgotten Barry and Elkan and Brownlea.

Meecham was still in the midst of his euphoria when he boarded the London train at Chelmsford in midafternoon. He had not been in as much haste to get away as Thurman, and had remained to eat a pretty good lunch of pork chops and canned pineapple at the field. The train was crowded, and although he had a first-class ticket, he had to stand in the corridor outside a compartment filled with American enlisted men who had got on further up the line. When they saw his war-correspondent shoulder flash they tapped on the glass and asked him in. They were all Fortress men who, it appeared, had been on dozens of twelve-hour missions over Germany, from almost all of which they had returned with their ships aflame and three engines out. Meecham was ashamed to tell them he had been only as far as France that morning. By the time the train arrived at Liverpool Street station his exuberance was waning. Coming out into Broad Street, he felt hungry again. He had had what for him was a phenomenally long day. He stopped in at a place called Gow's, a combination fishmonger's and restaurant, and ordered a dozen oysters at the counter. He ordered a second dozen, but the man behind the counter said that the Ministry of Food did not allow them to sell more than eight bob worth to a customer and he had had it. Meecham felt a certain resentment; he had half a mind to tell the man where he had been that morning. That would show him. But perhaps the man had a son in the R.A.F., so he would not be impressed. Or three R.A.F. sons, all killed in the Battle of Britain, so he would be pained by any reference to flying. The thought recalled

Barry and Brownlea and Elkan for the first time that day. Meecham wondered why it had seemed essential that, because of them, he go on a mission after they were dead. He paid for his oysters and went out into the street to look for a taxi. He hoped his girl was in town and had no date for the evening. After all, this ought to impress her.

Another time-killing expedient of mine was to try to construct from information what life in occupied France must be, and in this I had great assistance from friends in the British Political Warfare Board and with the Free French Government in London, who supplied me with hundreds of clandestine newspapers published in France and smuggled out by their agents. The next piece is one of a series I wrote that winter under the same generic title—the newspapers reminded me that another kind of war was going on across the Channel while we waited for spring. Looking at this sample now, I think it should help the people who have grown up since to understand a lot about current French attitudes.

Notes from the Kidnap House—1944

The secret newspapers of France do not give French people much news of the outside world. That is left to the British radio and the Algiers radio, which do not have the paper and distribution problems of the journals in enemy-occupied territory. Since most of the resistance newspapers are no larger than a sheet of typewriter paper and have only four pages, they concentrate on local news and editorial comment. The three largest groups of publications—those in each group are loosely affiliated—are Communist, Socialist, and Mur, this last name being short for Mouvements Unis de Résistance. Mur is an organization of "new men," men who are not connected with the old political parties, and is strongly de Gaullist. The masthead of all Mur papers carries the slogan "One chief, de Gaulle; one struggle, for our liberties." Mur is for "social as well as political democracy," by which it means the nationalization of banks and probably of heavy industry, ruthless punishment of the rich men and Vichy politicians who collaborated openly or tacitly, and the guidance of France by a "new élite" of men who have made their way up through the resistance movements. The editorials in its papers maintain that "the shame of Vichy does not excuse the shortcomings of preceding governments." Some editorials in the Mur papers oppose the presence in Algiers of men like Pierre Cot, Vincent Auriol, and other pre-Vichy government figures, although conceding that in the interest of unity they must be tolerated for a brief while. Mur is nationalistic, occasionally to the point of xenophobia, whereas the Socialist and the Communist newspaper groups place more emphasis on the class struggle and less on the personal leadership of de Gaulle and new élites. Yet these, too, endorse de Gaulle and the Algiers government, and Mur endorses in some degree the class struggle. The difference lies in the importance each faction gives the different aspects of the fight. The Socialists, the largest single party in France before the armistice, defend most of their party's record, and the heroic attitude of Léon Blum since his arrest, especially at the Riom trial, has added weight to this defense. Blum, like Edouard Herriot, has become a martyr in his own lifetime. *Populaire*, Blum's old newspaper, has seven regional editions, all clandestine, and reaches at least a million readers. Its preoccupation with the party's record sometimes makes it seem to look backward too much. Recently it published a noble but nostalgic appeal to President Roosevelt to vindicate the New Deal by disregarding the demands of American capitalists. The editorialist, in his hideout, apparently had not heard that the term "New Deal" is now in the same limbo as "Popular Front." In almost every issue, *Populaire* runs, under the heading of "Our Martyrs," a list of Socialist resistants shot by the Gestapo or murdered by the Vichy militia, as if to emphasize the fact that the Socialists have at last become a party of action. The Communist press, headed by the several editions of *L'Humanité* and comprising a number of newspapers for various vocational groups of intellectuals and workers, benefits not only from the present prestige of Russia but from the name that Communist resistants have won for courage and austerity.

There are dozens of other resistance papers, of political shades more difficult to classify, ranging from *L'Aurore*, the organ of conservative Republican resistance, to a little sheet called *Le Soviet*, which carries at its masthead the line "Long live Trotsky and Lenin! Down with Stalin, grave-digger of the Third International!" All, however, agree on at least two points. *The first of these is the French refusal to be patronized or treated as a decadent nation, especially by the English-speaking nations, whom the French blame for rebuilding Germany between the two great wars, before leaving France to fend for herself in 1939. The resistants look forward to liberation not as a favor but as the first small installment due them on a debt of blood.* Smuts'* speech last November served to intensify this feeling, which crystalized in the streamer headline of one clandestine paper, *Libération*: "Pétain, Badoglio, Smuts Examples of Intelligence of Marshals." "Great Britain three years ago carried all the hopes of our people; these are things one does not forget, in spite of the Smutses," an editorialist, in hiding from the Gestapo, wrote in *Libération*. "*France decadent? Really? Well, if all France were in ruins, if there survived of all her decimated people only a few women and old men, the representative of France, whoever he might be, would have the right to sit with Churchill, Roosevelt, and Stalin and be treated with the most profound respect,* because, if there hadn't been a certain nation called France and a certain battle called Verdun, Monsieur Smuts might now, with a little luck, be a junior native customs official in South Africa. . . . *With or without Smuts, the European resistance movement is going to remake the Continent into a free Europe of free citizens.* Taught by our common experience of slavery, we have more in common with the men of Free Belgium, of Tito or Ribar, than with most Francophile diplomats. Who knows if the greatest service Smuts could render us is not to awaken our compatriots to the true mission of France: to remake Europe and open Africa?" Another clandestine paper, *Franc-Tireur*, says, "*The countries that hoped to save themselves the horrors of war by neutrality and those who could organize for victory out of the reach of the enemy while for nine*

---

*I forget what Smuts said, but they didn't like it. I almost forget who Smuts was. That was before South Africa made the headlines.

months we held the line—haven't they also their responsibilities? Didn't they count too much on France and her Army, on the military qualities of her people, to conquer a force they had allowed to develop? This war, in which we were the sacrificed advance guard, has been waged against a racial dictatorship which intended to hold the world underfoot. It is unthinkable that it should end in another dictatorship, nationalistic or plutocratic. France, even defeated, remains great enough and has enough claims to gratitude not to merit the treatment of a vassal or a servant." This feeling was also revealed in a statement Daladier made to the German police who a year ago came to the prison of Bourrassol to remove him to the Reich. "I congratulate myself," he said, "for having declared war in 1939. A year later you would have won the war. Today I have the pleasure of telling you that you are irretrievably lost."

The second point of universal agreement is that France remains intrinsically great. These two basic sentiments make the resistance press hypersensitive to any hint of infringement on French sovereignty. A recent report from Washington that General Eisenhower would choose the Frenchmen with whom the Allies would treat meant to many resistants that the Americans would attempt to choose the rulers of France. Since, in the minds of French workingmen, America has always stood for big business and since the de Gaullists feel that the State Department has always worked against them, there is an almost universal fear that the English-speaking powers will try to impose a Kolchak government in striped pants, headed by a shifty *type* like Georges Bonnet. Bonnet was not allowed to participate officially in the Vichy regime because of his association with the Jewish bank of Lazard Frères, and therefore he could now be presented as being free of the Vichy taint. Camile Chautemps, who has been in Washington long enough to be able to disclaim any connection with the "later excesses" of the Vichy regime, is another bogey of the resistance men. The recollection of the high favor Bonnet and his friends enjoyed, back in the Munich days, with men still prominent in the British government, such as Halifax, Hoare, and Simon, does not dispose resistants to look forward to receiving British support against the tendency they think they see in American policy. An extreme statement of the frame of mind that has resulted from the refusal of the Allied governments to commit themselves is the following, in *Combat*: "*We think it would be criminal and absurd to have complete confidence in foreign military staffs, in foreign military representatives, or in officers of the French Army of the colonial type to set up a republic and let the citizens of France express themselves.* To say everything—if a choice has to be made one day between 'terrorism' and AMG, our choice is made. Of ourselves we are sure, of 'practical men' we are not."

More interesting to me than the editorial opinion of these journalists—who, since they live in constant danger of being captured, tortured to make them give information about their colleagues (usually by having their fingernails torn out), and then shot, lack the calm detachment of, say, Arthur Krock— are the pictures of French life presented, at least by implication, in such publications as *Bulletin des Chemins de Fer*, the clandestine organ of the railroad workers. Railroad men have perhaps the hardest rôle in the resistance movement. A factory saboteur faces the danger of detection and arrest, but when a railroad worker wrecks a train he may not survive to be arrested. Furthermore, trains and freight yards are constant targets of bombing attacks; a railroader takes the same risks as the German troops among whom he finds himself. There are no air-raid shelters in freight trains as there are in factories. Moreover, railroaders furnish much of the information about troop and ammunition movements that leads to air attacks, and thus they call down the lightning on themselves. These dangers are superimposed upon conditions which are difficult enough in themselves—"overwork, long hours, pathetic remnants of rolling stock left by the Boche, coal dust that hardly burns in place of the good fuel of other days"—and upon the psychological strain of having to work for the Germans. "I know your suffering at feeling yourselves unarmed executioners of your countrymen when you drive trains toward Germany heavy with conscripted French workmen," one writer in *Bulletin* tells his comrades. (Many times, it may be noted, train crews have managed to stop somewhere and give the deportees a chance to escape through the windows of the cars.) "I know how you feel when you drive toward Germany freight trains loaded with all the substance that the Boche has drained from our rich land," the writer continues, "but you must endure, because you alone can on the great day, you eight hundred thousand rail workers, prevent the German from applying his strategy, paralyze his troop movements, isolate his units, immobilize his supplies, break his power, and precipitate his defeat."

The remainder of the same issue of *Bulletin* is more matter-of-fact. There is a prescription for getting rid of a fellow-employee who appears to be spying on resistance activities (accidentally drop a packing case on his toes), a list of the past month's railroad wrecks, and a note on a low *type*, an assistant stationmaster at the Perrache station, in Lyons, who curries favor with the German police. This *type* was present when political prisoners in a train passing through were throwing notes to friends on the platform. He saw a man on the platform cover a note with his foot. "The swine pointed the man out to a cop," *Bulletin* records. "He will not be overlooked." There is also the story of the wrecking of three civilian express passenger trains, with a heavy loss of life. These wrecks were the work not of any resistance group, readers are informed, but of *agents provocateurs* trying to twist public opinion against patriots. Patriot saboteurs do not molest trains of no military importance, especially passenger trains.

Another publication I always like to find in a packet that a friend in the underground movement now and then brings to my flat in London is *La Terre*, which calls itself "the organ of peasant resistance." Farmers, as a group, have always had the temperament and the facilities for resisting official pressure. Readers of *La Terre* are continually enjoined to delay threshing, to hide their harvests until they can be turned over to the *Maquis*, or at least to sell their crops privately to other Frenchmen, since any food delivered to Vichy authorities will be siphoned off to the Germans and sent out of the country. The government has inspectors to check up on agricultural production and delivery. Some of the inspectors, of course, are "reasonable," shutting their eyes to all discrepancies, since they are at heart as anti-Boche as anybody else. Others, not "reasonable," are mobbed or ambushed and beaten up with farm implements. In a Breton village, my latest *La Terre* informs me, three hundred people gathered around an inspector who had complained of the light weight of some pigs delivered by a farmer, and chased him into the mayor's office, from which the gendarmes had to rescue him. In another village, also in Brittany, an officious gendarme tried to make the farm wives stop baking, because the farmers are supposed to deliver all their flour to the government. Enraged women dumped him into a horse trough. In the Yonne department, farmers hide requisitioned horses and cows; in Loir-et-Cher, the farmers deliver no eggs, insisting that the hens stopped laying in 1940. In Seine-et-Oise, the peasants have formed committees to demand high grain prices. Everywhere the peasants unite to hunt informers, just as farmers in Iowa, not long ago, used to chase process servers. *La Terre* holds up the example of the scorched earth set by the Russian peasants. Incidentally, "Le Père Milon," de Maupassant's story of a Norman peasant who spent his nights killing German soldiers during the 1871 occupation, has been republished, according to *La Terre*, as a resistance pamphlet.

There are labor papers of all political shades. One, *Les Informations Sociales*, analyzes for French workers, in the tone of the *New Republic*, the Beveridge Plan and the differences between the C.I.O. and the A.F.L. *Les Informations* describes itself as "the bulletin of information for militant unionists." In addition to publishing informative articles, it has reprinted, without comment, Stalin's decree dissolving the Third International. It reports feelingly the arrest and deportation to Germany of Léon Jouhaux, president of the Confédération Général du Travail, for a time a fellow-prisoner of Herriot in the fortress of Bourrassol, and it denounces several prewar labor leaders who had accepted posts in fake labor unions set up by Vichy and are now trying to hedge against the defeat of Germany. It gives a long list of leaders of miners' unions sentenced for starting a strike against the Germans and it praises miners for bearing so much of labor's struggle against the enemy.

C.G.T., clandestine journal of the now submerged but still powerful Confédération, argues the necessity of beginning at once to rebuild a world labor movement and cites an index of prices which have made life almost impossible for French workmen in the last few years. In October, 1942, bread was up, over prewar prices, a hundred and forty per cent, potatoes two hundred per cent, wine two hundred and thirty per cent, and shoes three hundred and twenty-five per cent. *Mouvement Ouvrier Français*, another labor publication, says that the working class is the main object of German attack: the employers continue to eat well, even though they must pay high prices, but workers have the choice of producing goods for the conqueror at starvation wages in France or of being deported to Germany, where, on rations almost as scanty, they will be killed by Allied bombers. *Combat*, the most widely circulated Mur paper, notes, apropos of the deaths of French workmen in air raids in the Reich, that the French censor forbids the phrase "Died in Germany" in the death notices that relatives insert in French papers, although the German papers, with their usual maudlin bad taste, carry long accounts of ceremonies held over the graves of French workers killed in the Reich. Germans put pansies on the graves of Frenchmen they have brought to Germany for forced labor, a proof, *Combat* says, of the well-known Boche sensibility.

One of the leading publications in the resistance press is *Cahiers du Témoignage Chrétien*, an excellently printed monthly which sets forth the Catholic arguments in favor of resistance. One issue, discussing whether collaboration is permissible for a Christian, decides that "collaboration with Nazism, perverse in itself, is against the interests and soul of France. Conclusion: *non possumus.*" *Cahiers*, which reaches a large portion of the clergy and Catholic intellectuals, presents religious arguments against racism and anti-Semitism. It is interesting to observe the parallel reactions to Nazism in publications of sections of the clandestine press representing widely divergent groups. *Lettres Françaises*, the underground organ of French writers, charges that "a high proportion of pederasts among the collaborationists is to be expected, for to be against one's own country is against nature." The same sort of thought on the depravity of collaboration occurs in one of the regional clandestine publications, *Combat du Languedoc*. "That the Boche tortures and massacres accords with his business of being a Boche, but that a Frenchman sells other Frenchmen to the enemy, that is the ultimate depth of abjection. On the day of liberation, patriots . . . will sweep away the obscure rabble of informers for the Gestapo. Not even the memory of their crimes must survive in free France."

The regional publications have the strongest and most acrid odor of conflict. One issue of *Combat du Languedoc*, for example, contains a long blacklist of the traitors in surrounding towns and departments. There is in one town an ex-Republican priest who now informs against other clergymen who harbor Jews and *Maquis*; in another there is a Negro doctor, "forgetful of Nazi doctrines," who spies, and "a woman who sent her husband to forced labor and remained with a German soldier." There is a man who took money to betray the place where patriots had hidden the Strasbourg Cathedral's bells, removed to southwest France in 1939. Another man listed was a gunrunner for the Spanish Republicans in the civil war who has now turned coat and informs against refugees escaping across the Pyrenees. There is the president of a chamber of commerce who toasted a German victory, the Germanophile prefect kept by the widow of a former president of the Republic, the French colonel who sent his son to a Schutzstaffel cadet camp. Collaborators are named in print, even down to a man who was seen to tear a Lorraine cross from the neck of a young girl. From another regional publication I cite this excerpt: "Clermont-Ferrand—Our comrade —— was arrested at sixteen-thirty, October 26th. He was brought to the morgue at two o'clock the next afternoon. His face was swollen almost beyond recognition; his neck bore marks of strangulation. All his fingernails had been torn out. One foot was swollen, enormous. He had two bullet holes in his temple. The executioners are known. They will not be tortured. They will be shot like dogs."

"*La Voix du Nord*," the oldest and most powerful regional underground publication in the north of France, which has been occupied by the Germans since 1940, begins the latest issue I have received with a eulogy of Cardinal Lienart, Archbishop of Lille, who in a sermon defended the refusal of labor to work for Germans. This, in strongly Catholic Flanders, is news of the greatest importance. *Le Patriote de l'Oise*, another regional paper, thanks the Bishop of Beauvais for his steadfastness, and *La France Unie*, published in Brittany, praises the leading Catholic preacher of Rennes for his sermons on resistance; he has, the paper says, proved that deportation contradicts the doctrines of Christ. The first two of these publications have a strong Communist tinge, which indicates that the Germans and Laval have brought the French church and the French Communist Party into agreement for the first time in history. *La Voix du Nord* cites as a less appetizing example the local Catholic official of Secours National, a Pétain version of *Winterhilfe*, who takes, for his nephews and nieces, the best shoes and clothes donated to this charity. His sister, *La Voix* declares, then distributes the remainder to the needy, but only to the needy who attend mass regularly. Another local petty grafter it names is a police adjutant who stops people carrying small parcels of food in the streets and confiscates them unless the people can prove that they have been bought legally but who himself levies an illegal tribute of a pound of butter every week from each farm wife. It notifies people living on the coast that Germans billeted in coastal villages have been provided with civilian clothing in which to escape if a surprise landing is made by the Allies. *La Voix* urges its readers to memorize the faces of these Germans, so that they will be able to point them out to Allied troops.

Le Patriote de l'Oise, which appears to be Communist, tells of police raids on "our de Gaullist friends" in the district in which it is published. It warns of the presence of Vichy state police in the town of Creil and advises readers to "leave cafés when these *types* enter." *La Voix* tells how gendarmes surrounded a house in which they knew a Communist was hiding, in a village in Flanders; it was his own house, in the town of his birth, and it was a public secret that he had returned there. The man tried to escape by an attic window and the gendarmes shot him off the roof. "We know them," *La Voix* concludes simply. Until some assurance to the contrary is received, many writers in the resistance papers seem to fear that the Allies are coming to rescue the gendarmes.

4
And So To Victory

WE DID get to France, as you must know if you have seen the Cinemepic called *The Longest Day*, in which with swash-buckling magnificence tricked out with little homely touches a glittering team Eisenhowered by Darryl Zanuck storms the Hun-infested shores, and with John Wayne and Robert Mitchum alternately carrying the ball sweeps on, over the hills, to the unforgettable refrain of a theme song that I keep get-ting mixed up with

> "Ballocks, and the same to you,"

which has been bowdlerized into the "River Kwai March." The original words fit in perfectly with the Wayne-Zanuck-Mitchum version.

Everybody, of course, had his own D-Day.

For Bunny Rigg

Cross-Channel Trip

Three days after the first Allied landing in France, I was in the wardroom of an LCIL (Landing Craft, Infantry, Large) that was bobbing in the lee of the French cruiser Montcalm off the Normandy coast. The word "large" in landing-craft designa-tion is purely relative; the wardroom of the one I was on is seven by seven feet and contains two officers' bunks and a table with four places at it. She carries a complement of four officers, but since one of them must always be on watch there is room for a guest at the wardroom table, which is how I fitted in. The Montcalm was loosing salvos, each of which rocked our ship; she was firing at a German pocket of resis-tance a couple of miles from the shoreline. The suave voice of

457

a B.B.C. announcer came over the wardroom radio: "Next in our series of impressions from the front will be a recording of an artillery barrage." The French ship loosed off again, drowning out the recording. It was this same announcer, I think—I'm not sure, because all B.B.C. announcers sound alike —who said, a little while later, "We are now in a position to say the landings came off with surprising ease. The Air Force and the big guns of the Navy smashed coastal defenses, and the Army occupied them." Lieutenant Henry Rigg, United States Coast Guard Reserve, the skipper of our landing craft, looked at Long, her engineering officer, and they both began to laugh. Kavanaugh, the ship's communications officer, said, "Now what do you think of that?" I called briefly upon God. Aboard the LCIL, D Day hadn't seemed like that to us. There is nothing like a broadcasting studio in London to give a chap perspective.

I went aboard our LCIL on Thursday evening, June 1st. The little ship was one of a long double file that lay along the dock in a certain British port.* She was fast to the dock, with another LCIL lashed to her on the other side. An LCIL is a hundred and fifty-five feet long and about three hundred deadweight tons. A destroyer is a big ship indeed by comparison; an LST (Landing Ship, Tanks) looms over an LCIL like a monster. The LCIL has a flat bottom and draws only five feet of water, so she can go right up on a beach. Her hull is a box for carrying men; she can sleep two hundred soldiers below-decks or can carry five hundred on a short ferrying trip, when men stand both below and topside. An LCIL has a stern anchor which she drops just before she goes aground and two forward ramps which she runs out as she touches bottom. As troops go down the ramps, the ship naturally lightens, and she rises a few inches in the water; she then winches herself off by the stern anchor, in much the same way a monkey pulls himself back on a limb by his tail. Troop space is about all there is to an LCIL, except for a compact engine room and a few indispensable sundries like navigation instruments and anti-aircraft guns. LCILs are the smallest ocean-crossing landing craft, and

*Weymouth.

all those now in the European theatre arrived under their own power. The crews probably would have found it more comfortable sailing on the Santa María. Most LCILs are operated by the Navy, but several score of them have Coast Guard crews. Ours was one of the latter. The name "Coast Guard" has always reminded me of little cutters plying out to ocean liners from the barge office at the Battery in New York, and the association gave me a definite pleasure. Before boarding the landing craft, I had been briefed, along with twenty other correspondents, on the flagship of Rear Admiral John L. Hall, Jr., who commanded the task force of which our craft formed a minute part, so I knew where we were going and approximately when. Since that morning I had been sealed off from the civilian world, in the marshalling area, and when I went aboard our landing craft I knew that I would not be permitted even to set foot on the dock except in the company of a commissioned officer.

It was warm and the air felt soporific when I arrived. The scene somehow reminded me more of the Sheepshead Bay channel, with its fishing boats, than of the jumping-off place for an invasion. A young naval officer who had brought me ashore from the flagship took me over the gangplank of the landing craft and introduced me to Lieutenant Rigg. Rigg, familiarly known as Bunny, was a big man, thirty-three years old, with clear, light-blue eyes and a fleshy, good-tempered face. He was a yacht broker in civilian life and often wrote articles about boats. Rigg welcomed me aboard as if we were going for a cruise to Block Island, and invited me into the wardroom to have a cup of coffee. There was standing room only, because Rigg's three junior officers and a Navy commander were already drinking coffee at the table. The junior officers— Long, Kavanaugh, and Williams—were all lieutenants (j.g.). Long, a small, jolly man with an upturned nose, was a Coast Guard regular with twenty years' service, mostly as a chief petty officer. He came from Baltimore. Kavanaugh, tall and straight-featured, was from Crary, North Dakota, and Williams, a very polite, blond boy, came from White Deer, Texas. Kavanaugh and Williams were both in their extremely early twenties. The three-striper, a handsome, slender man with prematurely white hair and black eyebrows, was introduced to me by Rigg as the C.O. of a naval beach battalion which would go in to organize boat traffic on a stretch of beach as soon as the first waves of Infantry had taken it over.* He was going to travel to the invasion coast aboard our landing craft, and since he disliked life ashore in the marshalling area, he had come aboard ship early. The commander, who had a drawl hard to match north of Georgia, was in fact a Washingtonian. He was an Annapolis man, he soon told me, but had left the Navy for several years to practice law in the District of Columbia and then returned to it for the war. His battalion was divided for the crossing among six LCILs, which would go in in pairs on adjacent beaches, so naturally he had much more detailed dope on the coming operation than normally would come to, say, the skipper of a landing craft, and this was to make conversations in the tiny wardroom more interesting than they otherwise would have been.

Even before I had finished my second cup of coffee, I realized that I had been assigned to a prize LCIL; our ship was to beach at H Hour plus sixty-five, which means one hour and five minutes after the first assault soldier gets ashore. "This ship and No. X will be the first LCILs on the beach," Rigg said complacently. "The first men will go in in small boats, because of mines and underwater obstacles, and Navy demolition men with them will blow us a lane through element C—that's sunken concrete and iron obstacles. They will also sweep the lane of mines, we hope. We just have to stay in the lane."

"These things move pretty fast and they make a fairly small target bow on," Long added cheerfully.

The others had eaten, but I had not, so Williams went out to tell the cook to get me up some chow. While it was being prepared, I went out on deck to look around.

Our landing craft, built in 1942, is one of the first class of LCILs, which have a rectangular superstructure and a narrow strip of open deck on each side of it.† Painted on one side of

---

*This officer's name could not be used then, either because he commanded a unit in the invasion, or because he was wounded in the course of this operation. He was Eugene Carusi, again an attorney in Washington.

†It was the LCIL-88.

the superstructure I noted a neat Italian flag, with the legend "Italy" underneath so that there would be no mistake, and beside the flag a blue shield with white vertical stripes and the word "Sicily." There was also a swastika and the outline of an airplane, which could only mean that the ship had shot down a German plane in a landing either in Sicily or Italy. Under Britain's double summer time, it was still light, and there were several groups of sailors on deck, most of them rubbing "impregnating grease" into shoes to make them impervious to mustard gas. There had been a great last-minute furore about the possibility that the Germans might use gas against the invasion, and everybody had been fitted with impregnated gear and two kinds of protective ointment. Our ship's rails were topped with rows of drying shoes.

"This is the first time I ever tried to get a pair of shoes pregnant, sir," one of the sailors called out sociably as I was watching him.

"No doubt you tried it on about everything else, I guess," another sailor yelled as he, too, worked on his shoes.

I could see I would not be troubled by any of that formality which has occasionally oppressed me aboard flagships. Most of the sailors had their names stencilled in white on the backs of their jumpers, so there was no need for introductions. One sailor I encountered was in the middle of a complaint about a shore officer who had "eaten him out" because of the way he was dressed on the dock, and he continued after I arrived. "They treat us like children," he said. "You'd think we was the pea-jacket navy instead of the ambiguous farce." The first term is one that landing-craft sailors apply to those on big ships, who keep so dry that they can afford to dress the part. "The ambiguous farce" is their pet name for the amphibious forces. A chief petty officer, who wore a khaki cap with his blue coveralls, said, "You don't want to mind them, sir. This isn't a regular ship and doesn't ever pretend to be. But it's a good working ship. You ought to see our engine room."

A little sailor with a Levantine face asked me where I came from. When I told him New York, he said, "Me too—Hundred twenty-second and First." The name stencilled on his back was Landini. "I made up a song about this deal," he said, breaking into a kind of Off to Buffalo. "I'm going over to France and I'm making in my pants."

Through the open door of the galley I could watch the cook, a fattish man with wavy hair and a narrow mustache, getting my supper ready. His name was Fassy, and he was the commissary steward. He appeared to have a prejudice against utensils; he slapped frankfurters and beans down on the hot stove top, rolled them around, and flipped them onto the plate with a spatula. I thought the routine looked familiar and I found out later that in his civilian days Fassy had worked in Shanty restaurants in New York.

While I was standing there, a young seaman stencilled Sitnitsky popped his head into the galley to ask for some soap powder so he could wash his clothes. Fassy poured some out of a vast carton into a pail of hot water the boy held. "'Not recommended for delicate fabrics,'" the steward read from the carton, then roared, "So don't use it on your dainty lingerie!"

Since the frankfurters and beans were ready, I returned to the wardroom. There the board of strategy was again in session. The beach we were headed for was near the American line, only a mile or two from Port-en-Bessin, where the British area began. Eighteen years before I had walked along the tops of the same cliffs the Americans would be fighting under. In those days I had thought of it as holiday country, not sufficiently spectacular to attract *le grand tourisme* but beautiful in a reasonable, Norman way. This illogically made the whole operation seem less sinister to me. Two pillboxes showed plainly on photographs we had, and, in addition, there were two houses that looked suspiciously like shells built around other pillboxes. Our intelligence people had furnished us with extraordinarily detailed charts of gradients in the beach and correlated tide tables. The charts later proved to be extraordinarily accurate, too.

"What worries me about landing is the bomb holes the Air Forces may leave in the beach before we hit," the commander was saying when I entered. "The chart may show three feet of water, but the men may step into a ten-foot hole anywhere. I'd rather the Air Forces left the beach alone and just let the naval guns knock out the beach defenses. They're accurate."

The general plan, I knew, was for planes and big guns of the fleet to put on an intensive bombardment before the landing. A couple of weeks earlier I had heard a Marine colonel on the planning staff tell how the guns would hammer the pillboxes, leaving only a few stunned defenders for the Infantry to gather up on their way through to positions inland.

"We're lucky," the commander said. "This beach looks like a soft one."

His opinion, in conjunction with frankfurters and beans, made me happy.

We didn't get our passengers aboard until Saturday. On Friday I spent my time in alternate stretches of talk with the men on deck and the officers in the wardroom. Back in Sicily, the ship had been unable to get off after grounding at Licata, a boatswain's mate named Pendleton told me. "She got hit so bad we had to leave her," he said, "and for three days we had to live in foxholes just like Infantrymen. Didn't feel safe a minute. We was sure glad to get back on the ship. Guess she had all her bad luck that trip."

Pendleton, a large, fair-haired fellow who was known to his shipmates as the Little Admiral, came from Neodesha, Kansas. "They never heard of the Coast Guard out there," he said. "Nobody but me. I knew I would have to go in some kind of service and I was reading in a Kansas City paper one day that the Coast Guard would send a station wagon to your house to get you if it was within a day's drive of their recruiting station. So I wrote 'em. Never did like to walk."

Sitnitsky was washing underclothes at a sink aft of the galley once when I came upon him. When he saw me, he said, "The fois' ting I'm gonna do when I get home is buy my mudder a washing machine. I never realize what the old lady was up against."

Our neighbor LCIL, tied alongside us, got her soldier passengers late Friday night. The tide was low and the plank leading down to our ship from the dock was at a steep angle as men came aboard grumbling and filed across our deck to the other LCIL. "Didjever see a goddam gangplank in the right place?" one man called over his shoulder as he eased himself down with his load. I could identify a part of a mortar on his back, in addition to a full pack. "All aboard for the second

Oran," another soldier yelled, and a third man, passing by the emblems painted on the bridge, as he crossed our ship, yelled, "Sicily! *They* been there, too." So I knew these men were part of the First Division, which landed at Oran in Africa in 1942 and later fought in Sicily. I think I would have known anyway by the beefing. The First Division is always beefing about something, which adds to its effectiveness as a fighting unit.

The next day the soldiers were spread all over the LCIL next door, most of them reading paper-cover, armed-services editions of books. They were just going on one more trip, and they didn't seem excited about it. I overheard a bit of technical conversation when I leaned over the rail to visit with a few of them. "Me, I like a bar [Browning automatic rifle]," a sergeant was saying to a private. "You can punch a lot of tickets with one of them."

The private, a rangy middleweight with a small, close-cropped head and a rectangular profile, said, "I'm going into this one with a pickaxe and a block of TNT. It's an interesting assignment. I'm going to work on each pillbox individually," he added, carefully pronouncing each syllable.

When I spoke to them, the sergeant said, "Huh! A correspondent! Why don't they give the First Division some credit?"

"I guess you don't read much if you say that, Sarge," a tall blond boy with a Southern accent said. "There's a whole book of funnies called 'Terry Allen and the First Division at El Guettar.'"

All three men were part of an Infantry regiment. The soldier who was going to work on pillboxes asked if I was from New York, and said that he was from the Bensonhurst section of Brooklyn. "I am only sorry my brother-in-law is not here," he said. "My brother-in-law is an M.P. He is six inches bigger than me. He gets an assignment in New York. I would like to see him here. He would be apprehensive." He went on to say that the company he was with had been captured near the end of the African campaign, when, after being cut off by the Germans, it had expended all its ammunition. He had been a prisoner in Tunis for a few hours, until the British arrived and set him free. "There are some nice broads in Tunis," he said. "I had a hell of a time." He nodded toward the book he was holding. "These little books are a great thing," he said. "They take you away. I remember when my battalion was cut off on top of a hill at El Guettar, I read a whole book in one day. It was called 'Knight Without Armor.' This one I am reading now is called 'Candide.' It is kind of unusual, but I like it. I think the fellow who wrote it, Voltaire, used the same gag too often, though. The characters are always getting killed and then turning out not to have been killed after all, and they tell their friends what happened to them in the meantime. I like the character in it called Pangloss."*

Fassy was lounging near the rail and I called him over to meet a brother Brooklynite. "Brooklyn is a beautiful place to live in," Fassy said. "I have bush Number Three at Prospect Park."

"I used to have bush Number Four," the soldier said.

"You remind me of a fellow named Sidney Wetzelbaum," Fassy said. "Are you by any chance related?"

I left them talking.

Our own passengers came aboard later in the day. There were two groups—a platoon of the commander's beach battalion and a platoon of amphibious engineers. The beach-battalion men were sailors dressed like soldiers, except that they wore black jerseys under their field jackets; among them were a medical unit and a hydrographic unit. The engineers included an M.P. detachment, a chemical-warfare unit, and some demolition men. A beach battalion is a part of the Navy that goes ashore; amphibious engineers are a part of the Army that seldom has its feet dry. Together they form a link between the land and sea forces. These two detachments had rehearsed together in landing exercises, during which they had travelled aboard our LCIL. Unlike the Coastguardsmen or the Infantry on the next boat, they had never been in the real thing before and were not so offhand about it. Among them were a fair number of men in their thirties. I noticed one chief petty officer with the Navy crowd who looked about fifty. It was hard to realize that these older men had important and potentially dangerous assignments which called for a good deal of

*He and I were having a Voltairean reunion right there. I had been at El Guettar too, and had never heard what happened to the battalion.

specialized skill; they seemed to me more out of place than the Infantry kids. Some sailors carried carbines and most of the engineers had rifles packed in oilskin cases. There were about a hundred and forty men in all. The old chief, Joe Smith, who was the first of the lot I got to know, said he had been on battleships in the last war and had been recalled from the fleet reserves at the beginning of this. He took considerable comfort from the fact that several aged battleships would lay down a barrage for us before we went in. You could see that he was glad to be aboard a ship again, even if it was a small one and he would be on it for only a couple of days. He was a stout, red-faced, merry man whose home town was Spring Lake, New Jersey. "I'm a tomato squeezer," he told me. "Just a country boy."

Cases of rations had been stacked against the superstructure for the passengers' use. The galley wasn't big enough to provide complete hot meals for them but it did provide coffee, and their own cook warmed up canned stew and corned beef for them for one meal. The rest of the time they seemed simply to rummage among the cans until they found something they liked and then ate it. They ate pretty steadily, because there wasn't much else for them to do.

Our landing craft had four sleeping compartments below-decks. The two forward ones, which were given over to passengers, contained about eighty bunks apiece. Most of the crew slept in the third compartment, amidships, and a number of petty officers and noncoms slept in the fourth, the smallest one, aft. I had been sleeping in this last one myself since coming aboard, because there was only one extra bunk for an officer and the commander had that. Four officers who came aboard with the troops joined me in this compartment. There were two sittings at the wardroom table for meals, but we managed to wedge eight men in there at one time for a poker game.

There was no sign of a move Saturday night, and on Sunday morning everybody aboard began asking when we were going to shove off. The morning sun was strong and the crew mingled with the beach-battalion men and the soldiers on deck. It was the same on board every other LCIL in the long double row. The port didn't look like Sheepshead Bay now, for every narrow boat was covered with men in drab-green field jackets, many of them wearing tin hats, because the easiest way not to lose a tin hat in a crowd is to wear it. The small ships and helmets pointed up the analogy to a crusade and made the term seem less threadbare than it usually does. We were waiting for weather, as many times the crusaders, too, had waited, but nobody thought of praying for it, not even the chaplain who came aboard in mid-morning to conduct services. He was a captain attached to the amphibious engineers, a husky man I had noticed throwing a football around on the dock the previous day. He took his text from Romans: "If God be for us, who can be against us?" He didn't seem to want the men to get the idea that we were depending entirely on faith, however. "Give us that dynamic, that drive, which, coupled with our matchless super-modern weapons, will ensure victory," he prayed. After that, he read aloud General Eisenhower's message to the Allied Expeditionary Force.

After the services, printed copies of Eisenhower's message were distributed to all hands on board. Members of our ship's crew went about getting autographs of their shipmates on their "Eisenhowers", which they apparently intended to keep as souvenirs of the invasion. Among the fellows who came to me for my signature was the ship's coxswain, a long-legged, serious-looking young man, from a little town in Mississippi, who had talked to me several times before because he wanted to be a newspaperman after the war. He had had one year at Tulane, in New Orleans, before joining up with the Coast Guard, and he hoped he could finish up later. The coxswain, I knew, would be the first man out of the ship when she grounded, even though he was a member of the crew. It was his task to run a guideline ashore in front of the disembarking soldiers. Then, when he had arrived in water only a foot or two deep, he would pull on the line and bring an anchor floating in after him, the anchor being a light one tied in a life jacket. He would then fix the anchor—without the life jacket, of course—and return to the ship. This procedure had been worked out after a number of soldiers had been drowned on landing exercises by stepping into unexpected depressions in the beach after they had left the landing craft. Soldiers, loaded down with gear, had simply disappeared. With a guideline to hold onto, they could have struggled past bad spots. I asked the boy what he was going to wear when he went into the water with the line and he said just swimming trunks and a tin hat. He said he was a fair swimmer.

The rumor got about that we would sail that evening, but late in the afternoon the skipper told me we weren't going to. I learned that the first elements of the invasion fleet, the slowest ones, had gone out but had met rough weather in the Channel and had returned, because they couldn't have arrived at their destination in time. Admiral Hall had told correspondents that there would be three successive days when tide conditions on the Norman beaches would be right and that if we missed them the expedition might have to be put off, so I knew that we now had one strike on us, with only two more chances.

That evening, in the wardroom, we had a long session of a wild, distant derivative of poker called "high low rollem." Some young officers who had come aboard with the troops introduced it. We used what they called "funny money" for chips—five-franc notes printed in America and issued to the troops for use after they got ashore. It was the first time I had seen these notes, which reminded me of old-time cigar-store coupons. There was nothing on them to indicate who authorized them or would pay off on them—just "*Emis en France*" on one side and on the other side the tricolor and "*Liberté, Egalité, Fraternité.*" In the game were three beach-battalion officers, a medical lieutenant (j.g.) named Davey, from Philadelphia, and two ensigns—a big, ham-handed college football player from Danbury, Connecticut, named Vaghi, and a blocky, placid youngster from Chicago named Reich. The commander of the engineer detachment, the only Army officer aboard, was a first lieutenant named Miller, a sallow, apparently nervous boy who had started to grow an ambitious black beard.

Next morning the first copy of the *Stars and Stripes* to arrive on board gave us something new to talk about. It carried the story of the premature invasion report by the Associated Press in America. In an atmosphere heavy with unavowed anxiety, the story hit a sour note. "Maybe they let out more than *Stars and Stripes* says," somebody in the wardroom said. "Maybe they not only announced the invasion but told where we had landed. I mean, where we *planned* to land. Maybe the whole deal will be called off now." The commander, who had spent so much time pondering element C, said, "Add obstacles— element A.P." A report got about among the more pessimistic crew members that the Germans had been tipped off and would be ready for us. The Allied high command evidently did not read the *Stars and Stripes*, however, for Rigg, after going ashore for a brief conference, returned with the information that we were shoving off at five o'clock. I said to myself, in the great cliché of the second World War, "This is it," and so, I suppose, did every other man in our fleet of little ships when he heard the news.

II

Peace or war, the boat trip across the English Channel always begins with the passengers in the same mood: everybody hopes he won't get seasick. On the whole, this is a favorable morale factor at the outset of an invasion. A soldier cannot fret about possible attacks by the Luftwaffe or E-boats while he is preoccupied with himself, and the vague fear of secret weapons on the far shore is balanced by the fervent desire to get the far shore under his feet. Few of the hundred and forty passengers on the LCIL I was on were actively sick the night before D Day, but they were all busy thinking about it. The four officers and twenty-nine men of the United States Coast Guard who made up her complement were not even queasy, but they had work to do, which was just as good. The rough weather, about which the papers have talked so much since D Day and which in fact interfered with the landing, was not the kind that tosses about transatlantic liners or even Channel packets; it was just a bit too rough for the smaller types of landing craft we employed. An LCIL, as its name implies, is not one of the smallest, but it's small enough, and aboard our flat-bottomed, three-hundred-ton job the Channel didn't seem especially bad that night. There was a ground swell for an hour after we left port, but then the going became better than I had anticipated. LCTs (Landing Craft, Tanks), built like open troughs a hundred feet long, to carry armored vehicles, had a much worse time, particularly since, being slow, they had had to start hours before us. Fifty-foot LCMs (Landing Craft, Mechanized) and fifty-foot and thirty-six-foot LCVPs (Landing Craft, Vehicles and Personnel), swarms of which crossed the Channel under their own power, had still more trouble. The setting out of our group of LCILs was unimpressive—just a double file of ships, each a hundred and fifty-five feet long, bound for a rendezvous with a great many other ships at three in the morning ten or fifteen miles off a spot on the coast of lower Normandy. Most of the troops travelled in large transports, from which the smaller craft transferred them to shore. The LCILs carried specially packaged units for early delivery on the Continent doorstep.

Rigg turned in early that evening because he wanted to be fresh for a hard day's work by the time we arrived at the rendezvous, which was to take place in what was known as the transport area. So did the commander of the naval beach battalion who was riding with us. I stood on deck for a while. As soon as I felt sleepy, I went down into the small compartment in which I had a bunk and went to sleep—with my clothes on, naturally. There didn't seem to be anything else to do. That was at about eight. I woke three hours later and saw a fellow next to me being sick in a paper bag and I went up to the galley and had a cup of coffee. Then I went back to my bunk and slept until a change in motion and in the noise of the motors woke me again.

The ship was wallowing slowly now, and I judged that we had arrived at the transport area and were loafing about. I looked at my wristwatch and saw that we were on time. It was about three. So we hadn't been torpedoed by an E-boat. A good thing. Drowsily, I wondered a little at the fact that the enemy had made no attempt to intercept the fleet and hoped there would be good air cover, because I felt sure that the Luftwaffe couldn't possibly pass up the biggest target of history. My opinion of the Luftwaffe was still strongly influenced by what I remembered from June, 1940, in France, and even from January and February, 1943, in Tunisia. I decided to stay in my bunk until daylight, dozed, woke again, and then decided I couldn't make it. I went up on deck in the gray pre-dawn light sometime before five. I drew myself a cup of coffee from an electric urn in the galley and stood by the door drinking it and looking at the big ships around us. They made me feel proletarian. They would stay out in the Channel and send in their troops in small craft, while working-class vessels like us went right up on the beach. I pictured them inhabited by officers in dress blues and shiny brass buttons, all scented like the World's Most Distinguished After-Shave Club.* The admiral's command ship lay nearby. I imagined it to be gaffed with ingenious gimmicks that would record the developments of the operation. I could imagine a terse report coming in of the annihilation of a flotilla of LCILs, including us, and hear some Annapolis man saying, "After all, that sort of thing is to be expected." Then I felt that everything was going to be all right, because it always had been. A boatswain's mate, second class, named Barrett, from Rich Square, North Carolina, stopped next to me to drink his coffee and said, "I bet Findley a pound that we'd be hit this time. We most always is. Even money."

We wouldn't start to move, I knew, until about six-thirty, the time when the very first man was scheduled to walk onto the beach. Then we would leave the transport area so that we could beach and perform our particular chore—landing one platoon of the naval beach battalion and a platoon of Army amphibious engineers—at seven-thirty-five. A preliminary bombardment of the beach defenses by the Navy was due to begin at dawn. "Ought to be hearing the guns soon," I said to Barrett, and climbed the ladder to the upper deck. Rigg was on the bridge drinking coffee, and with him was Long, the ship's engineering officer. It grew lighter and the guns began between us and the shore. The sound made us all cheerful and Long said, "I'd hate to be in under that." Before dawn the transports had begun putting men into small craft that headed for the line of departure, a line nearer shore from which the first assault wave would be launched.

Time didn't drag now. We got under way sooner than I had somehow expected. The first troops were on the beaches. The battleship Arkansas and the French cruisers Montcalm and Georges Leygues were pounding away on our starboard as we

---

*An allusion to an advertisement then widely familiar, but which I now forget.

moved in. They were firing over the heads of troops, at targets farther inland. Clouds of yellow cordite smoke billowed up. There was something leonine in their tint as well as in the roar that followed, after that lapse of time which never fails to disconcert me. We went on past the big ships, like a little boy with the paternal blessing. In this region the Germans evidently had no long-range coastal guns, like the ones near Calais, for the warships' fire was not returned. This made me feel good. The absence of resistance always increases my confidence. The commander of the naval beach battalion had now come on deck, accoutred like a soldier, in greenish coveralls and tin hat. I said to him cheerfully, "Well, it looks as though the biggest difficulty you're going to have is getting your feet in cold water."

He stood there for a minute and said, "What are you thinking of?"

I said, "I don't know why, but I'm thinking of the garden restaurant behind the Museum of Modern Art in New York."*
He laughed, and I gave him a pair of binoculars I had, because I knew he didn't have any and that he had important use for them.

Our passengers—the beach-battalion platoon and the amphibious engineers—were now forming two single lines on the main deck, each group facing the ramp by which it would leave the ship. Vaghi and Reich, beach-battalion ensigns, were lining up their men on the port side and Miller, an Army lieutenant with a new beard, was arranging his men on the starboard side. I wished the commander good luck and went up on the bridge, which was small and crowded but afforded the best view.

An LCIL has two ramps, one on each side of her bow, which she lowers and thrusts out ahead of her when she beaches. Each ramp is handled by means of a winch worked by two men; the two winches stand side by side deep in an open-well deck just aft of the bow. If the ramps don't work, the whole operation is fouled up, so an LCIL skipper always assigns reliable men to operate them. Two seamen named Findley and Lechich were on the port winch, and two whom I knew as

*I liked a woman who lived across the street from there.

Rocky and Bill were on the other. Williams, the ship's executive officer, was down in the well deck with the four of them.

We had been in sight of shore for a long while, and now I could recognize our strip of beach from our intelligence photographs. There was the house with the tower on top of the cliff on our starboard as we went in. We had been warned that preliminary bombardment might remove it, so we should not count too much upon it as a landmark; however, there it was and it gave me the pleasure of recognition. A path was to have been blasted and swept for us through element C (underwater concrete and iron obstacles) and mines, and the entrance to it was to have been marked with colored buoys. The buoys were there, so evidently the operation was going all right. Our LCIL made a turn and headed for the opening like a halfback going into a hole in the line. I don't know whether Rigg suddenly became solicitous for my safety or whether he simply didn't want me underfoot on the bridge, where two officers and two signalmen had trouble getting around even without me. He said, "Mr. Liebling will take his station on the upper deck during action." This was formal language from the young man I had learned to call Bunny, especially since the action did not seem violent as yet, but I climbed down the short ladder from the bridge to the deck, a move which put the wheel-house between me and the bow. The upper deck was also the station for a pharmacist's mate named Kallam, who was our reserve first-aid man. A landing craft carries no doctor, the theory being that a pharmacist's mate will make temporary repairs until the patient can be transferred to a larger ship. We had two men with this rating aboard. The other, a fellow named Barry, was up in the bow. Kallam was a sallow, long-faced North Carolinian who once told me he had gone into the peacetime Navy as a youth and had never been good for anything else since. This was his first action, except for a couple of landings in Nicaragua around 1930.

The shore curved out toward us on the port side of the ship and when I looked out in that direction I could see a lot of smoke from what appeared to be shells bursting on the beach. There was also an LCT, grounded and burning. "Looks as if there's opposition," I said to Kallam, without much originality.

At about the same time something splashed in the water off our starboard quarter, sending up a high spray. We were moving in fast now. I could visualize, from the plan I had seen so often in the last few days, the straight, narrow lane in which we had to stay. "On a straight line—like a rope ferry," I thought. The view on both sides changed rapidly. The LCT which had been on our port bow was now on our port quarter, and another LCT, also grounded, was now visible. A number of men, who had evidently just left her, were in the water, some up to their necks and others up to their armpits, and they didn't look as if they were trying to get ashore. Tracer bullets were skipping around them and they seemed perplexed. What I hate most about tracers is that every time you see one, you know there are four more bullets that you don't see, because only one tracer to five bullets is loaded in a machine-gun belt. Just about then, it seems in retrospect, I felt the ship ground.

I looked down at the main deck, and the beach-battalion men were already moving ahead, so I knew that the ramps must be down. I could hear Long shouting, "Move along now! Move along!," as if he were unloading an excursion boat at Coney Island. But the men needed no urging; they were moving without a sign of flinching. You didn't have to look far for tracers now, and Kallam and I flattened our backs against the pilot house and pulled in our stomachs, as if to give a possible bullet an extra couple of inches clearance. Something tickled the back of my neck. I slapped at it and discovered that I had most of the ship's rigging draped around my neck and shoulders, like a character in an old slapstick movie about a spaghetti factory. The rigging had been cut away by bullets. As Kallam and I looked toward the stern, we could see a tableau that was like a recruiting poster. There was a twenty-millimetre rapid-firing gun on the upper deck. Since it couldn't bear forward because of the pilot house and since there was nothing to shoot at on either side, it was pointed straight up at the sky in readiness for a possible dive-bombing attack. It had a crew of three men, and they were kneeling about it, one on each side and one behind the gun barrel, all looking up at the sky in an extremely earnest manner, and getting all the protection they could out of the gunshield. As a background to the men's heads, an American flag at the ship's stern streamed across the field of vision. It was a new flag, which Rigg had ordered hoisted for the first time for the invasion, and its colors were brilliant in the sun. To make the poster motif perfect, one of the three men was a Negro, William Jackson, from New Orleans, a wardroom steward, who, like everybody else on the LCIL, had multiple duties.

The last passenger was off the ship now, and I could hear the stern anchor cable rattling on the drum as it came up. An LCIL drops a stern anchor just before it grounds, and pays out fifty to a hundred fathoms of chain cable as it slowly slides the last couple of ship's lengths toward shore. To get under way again, it takes up the cable, pulling itself afloat. I had not known until that minute how eager I was to hear the sound of the cable that follows the order "Take in on stern anchor." Almost as the cable began to come in, something hit the ship with the solid clunk of metal against metal—not as hard as a collision or a bomb blast; just "clink." Long yelled down, "Pharmacist's mate go forward. Somebody's hurt." Kallam scrambled down the ladder to the main deck with his kit. Then Long yelled to a man at the stern anchor winch, "Give it hell!" An LCIL has to pull itself out and get the anchor up before it can use its motors, because otherwise the propeller might foul in the cable. The little engine which supplies power for the winch is built by a farm-machinery company in Waukesha, Wisconsin, and every drop of gasoline that went into the one on our ship was filtered through chamois skin first. That engine is the ship's insurance policy. A sailor now came running up the stairway from the cabin. He grabbed me and shouted, "Two casualties in bow!" I passed this information on to the bridge for whatever good it might do; both pharmacist's mates were forward already and there was really nothing else to be done. Our craft had now swung clear, the anchor was up, and the engines went into play. She turned about and shot forward like a destroyer. The chief machinist's mate said afterward that the engines did seven hundred revolutions a minute instead of the six hundred that was normal top speed. Shells were kicking up waterspouts around us as we went; the water they raised looked black. Rigg said afterward, "Funny thing. When I was going in, I had my whole attention fixed on two mines attached to sunken concrete blocks on either side of the place where we went in. I knew they hadn't been cleared away—just a path between them. They were spider mines, those things with a lot of loose cables. Touch one cable and you detonate the mine. When I was going out, I was so excited that I forgot all about the damn mines and didn't think of them until I was two miles past them."

A sailor came by and Shorty, one of the men in the gun crew, said to him, "Who was it?" The sailor said, "Rocky and Bill. They're all tore up. A shell got the winch and ramps and all." I went forward to the well deck, which was sticky with a mixture of blood and condensed milk. Soldiers had left cases of rations lying all about the ship, and a fragment of the shell that hit the boys had torn into a carton of cans of milk. Rocky and Bill had been moved belowdecks into one of the large forward compartments. Rocky was dead beyond possible doubt, somebody told me, but the pharmacist's mates had given Bill blood plasma and thought he might still be alive. I remembered Bill, a big, baby-faced kid from the District of Columbia, built like a wrestler. He was about twenty, and the other boys used to kid him about a girl he was always writing letters to.* A third wounded man, a soldier dressed in khaki, lay on a stretcher on deck breathing hard through his mouth. His face looked like a dirty drum-head; his skin was white and drawn tight over his high cheekbones. He wasn't making much noise. There was a shooting-gallery smell over everything, and when we passed close under the Arkansas and she let off a salvo, a couple of our men who had their backs to her quivered and had to be reassured. Long and Kavanaugh, the communications officer, were already going about the ship trying to get things ticking again, but they had little success at first.

Halfway out to the transport area, another LCIL hailed us and asked us to take a wounded man aboard. They had got him from some smaller craft, but they had to complete a mission before they could go back to the big ships. We went alongside and took him over the rail. He was wrapped in khaki blankets and strapped into a wire basket litter. After we had sheered away, a man aboard the other LCIL yelled at us to

*Every letter began: "Well, Hazel, here I am again."

come back so that he could hand over a half-empty bottle of plasma with a long rubber tube attached. "This goes with him," he said. We went alongside again and he handed the bottle to one of our fellows. It was trouble for nothing, because the man by then had stopped breathing.

We made our way out to a transport called the Dorothea Dix that had a hospital ward fitted out. We went alongside and Rigg yelled that we had four casualties aboard. A young naval doctor climbed down the scramble net hanging on the Dix's side and came aboard. After he had looked at our soldier, he called for a breeches buoy and the soldier was hoisted up sitting in that. He had been hit in one shoulder and one leg, and the doctor said he had a good chance. The three others had to be sent up in wire baskets, vertically, like Indian papooses. A couple of Negroes on the upper deck of the Dix dropped a line which our men made fast to the top of one basket after another. Then the man would be jerked up in the air by the Negroes as if he were going to heaven. Now that we carried no passengers and were lighter, the sea seemed rough. We bobbed under the towering transport and the wounded men swung wildly on the end of the line, a few times almost striking against the ship. A Coastguardsman reached up for the bottom of one basket so that he could steady it on its way up. At least a quart of blood ran down on him, covering his tin hat, his upturned face, and his blue overalls. He stood motionless for an instant, as if he didn't know what had happened, seeing the world through a film of red, because he wore eyeglasses and blood had covered the lenses.* The basket, swaying eccentrically, went up the side. After a couple of seconds, the Coastguardsman turned and ran to a sink aft of the galley, where he turned on the water and began washing himself. A couple of minutes after the last litter had been hoisted aboard, an officer on the Dix leaned over her rail and shouted down, "Medical officer in charge says two of these men are dead! He says you should take them back to the beach and bury them." Out there, fifteen miles off shore, they evidently thought that this

---

*This was me. It seemed more reserved at the time to do it this way—a news story in which the writer said *he* was bathed in blood would have made me distrust it, if I had been a reader.

was just another landing exercise. A sailor on deck said, "The son of a bitch ought to see that beach."

Rigg explained to the officer that it would be impossible to return to the beach and ordered the men to cast off the lines, and we went away from the Dix. Now that the dead and wounded were gone, I saw Kallam sneak to the far rail and be sicker than I have ever seen a man at sea. We passed close by the command ship and signalled that we had completed our mission. We received a signal, "Wait for orders," and for the rest of the day we loafed, while we tried to reconstruct what had happened to us. Almost everybody on the ship had a headache.

"What hurts me worst," Lechich said, "is thinking what happened to those poor guys we landed. That beach was hot with Jerries. And they didn't have nothing to fight with—only carbines and rifles. They weren't even supposed to be combat troops."

"I don't think any of them could be alive now," another man said.

As the hours went by and we weren't ordered to do anything, it became evident that our bit of beach wasn't doing well, for we had expected, after delivering our first load on shore, to be employed in ferrying other troops from transports to the beach, which the beach-battalion boys and engineers would in the meantime have been helping to clear. Other LCILs of our flotilla were also lying idle. We saw one of them being towed, and then we saw her capsize. Three others, we heard, were lying up on one strip of beach, burned. Landing craft are reckoned expendable. Rigg came down from the bridge and, seeing me, said, "The beach is closed to LCILs now. Only small boats going in. Wish they'd thought of that earlier. We lost three good men."

"Which three?" I asked. "I know about Rocky and Bill."

"The coxswain is gone," Bunny said. I remembered the coxswain, the earnest young fellow who wanted to be a newspaperman, and who, dressed in swimming trunks, was going to go overboard ahead of everyone else and run a guideline into shore.

"Couldn't he get back?" I asked.

"He couldn't get anywhere," Rigg answered. "He had just

stepped off the ramp when he disintegrated. He must have stepped right into an H. E. shell. Cox was a good lad. We'd recommended him for officers' school." Rigg walked away for the inevitable cup of coffee, shaking his big tawny head. I knew he had a headache, too.

A while afterward, I asked Rigg what he had been thinking as we neared the coast and he said he had been angry because the men we were going to put ashore hadn't had any coffee. "The poor guys had stayed in the sack as late as they could instead," he said. "Going ashore without any coffee!"

Long was having a look at the damage the shell had done to our ship, and I joined him in tracing its course. It had entered the starboard bow well above the waterline, about the level of the ship's number, then had hit the forward anchor winch, had been deflected toward the stern of the boat, had torn through the bulkhead and up through the cover of the escape hatch, then had smashed the ramp winch and Rocky and Bill. It had been a seventy-five-millimetre anti-tank shell with a solid-armor-piercing head, which had broken into several pieces after it hit the ramp winch. The boys kept finding chunks of it around, but enough of it stayed in one piece to show what it had been. "They had us crisscrossed with guns in all those pill-boxes that were supposed to have been knocked off," Long said. "Something must have gone wrong. We gave them a perfect landing, though," he added with professional pride. "I promised the commander we would land him dry ass and we did." Long has been in the Coast Guard twenty years and nothing surprises him; he has survived prohibition, Miami and Fire Island hurricanes, and three landings. He is a cheerful soul who has an original theory about fear. "I always tell my boys that fear is a passion like any other passion," he had once told me. "Now, if you see a beautiful dame walking down the street, you feel passion but you control it, don't you? Well, if you begin to get frightened, which is natural, just control yourself also, I tell them." Long said that he had seen the commander start off from the ship at a good clip, run well until he got up near the first line of sand dunes, then stagger. "The commander was at the head of the line about to leave the ship when young Vaghi, that big ensign, came up and must have asked him for the honor of going first," Long said. "They went off that way, Vaghi out ahead, running as if he was running out on a field with a football under his arm. Miller led the soldiers off the other ramp, and he stepped out like a little gentleman, too." The space where the starboard ramp had once been gave the same effect as an empty sleeve or eye socket.

It was Frankel, a signalman who had been on the bridge, who told me sometime that afternoon about how the wounded soldier came to be on board. Frankel, whose family lives on East Eighteenth Street in Brooklyn, was a slender, restless fellow who used to be a cutter in the garment centre. He played in dance bands before he got his garment-union card, he once told me, and on the ship he occasionally played hot licks on the bugle slung on the bridge. "A shell hit just as we were beginning to pull out," Frankel said, "and we had begun to raise the ramps. It cut all but about one strand of the cable that was holding the starboard ramp and the ramp was wobbling in the air when I saw a guy holding on to the end of it. I guess a lot of us saw him at the same time. He was just clutching the ramp with his left arm, because he had been shot in the other shoulder. I'll never forget his eyes. They seemed to say, 'Don't leave me behind.' He must have been hit just as he stepped off the ramp leaving the ship. It was this soldier. So Ryan and Landini went out and got him. Ryan worked along the rail inside the ramp and Landini worked along the outside edge of the ramp and they got him and carried him back into the ship. There was plenty of stuff flying around, too, and the ramp came away almost as soon as they got back. That's one guy saved, anyway." Ryan was a seaman cook who helped Fassy, the commissary steward, in the galley, and Landini was the little First Avenue Italian who had made up a special song for himself—"I'm going over to France and I'm making in my pants."

Along about noon, an LCVP, a troughlike fifty-footer, hailed us and asked if we could take care of five soldiers. Rigg said we could. The craft came alongside and passed over five drenched and shivering tank soldiers who had been found floating on a rubber raft. They were the crew of a tank that had been going in on a very small craft and they had been swamped by a wave.* The tank had gone to the bottom and the soldiers had just managed to make it to the raft. The pharmacist's mates covered them with piles of blankets and put them to bed in one of our large compartments. By evening they were in the galley drinking coffee with the rest of us. They were to stay on the ship for nearly a week, as it turned out, because nobody would tell us what to do with them. They got to be pretty amphibious themselves. The sergeant in command was a fellow from Cleveland named Angelatti. He was especially happy about being saved, apparently because he liked his wife. He would keep repeating, "Gee, to think it's my second anniversary—I guess it's my lucky day!" But when he heard about what we thought had happened to the men we put ashore, he grew gloomy. The tanks had been headed for that beach and should have helped knock out the pillboxes. It hadn't been the tankmen's fault that the waves had swamped them, but the sergeant said disconsolately, "If we hadn't fucked up, maybe those other guys wouldn't have been killed." He had a soldier's heart.

III

On the morning of D Day-plus-one, the LCIL was like a ship with a hangover. Her deck was littered with cartons of tinned rations left behind by the land fighters she had carried to the Norman shore. There was a gap where the starboard ramp had been and there were various holes in the hull and hatches to mark the path of the anti-tank shell that had hit her while she had been on the beach. Everybody aboard was nursing a headache. The big fellows running the show had found nothing for us to do since our one run to the beach, which we had reached at 7:35 A.M. on D Day. The reason we hadn't been sent in again was that the German resistance was so strong that now the troops were being taken in only on smaller craft, which offered smaller targets. So we hung around in the

*These were amphibious tanks, with inflated canvas "jackets," and they were self-propelled. The censor allowed no reference to them, since they were a novelty. Of 32 headed for our beach, 28 flooded out. Only the weather was to blame.

Channel, waiting for orders and talking over the things that had happened to us. The men in the engine room, which was so clean that it looked like the model dairy exhibit at the World's Fair—all white paint and aluminum trim—had sweated it out at their posts during the excitement on deck and the engine-room log had been punctiliously kept. On the morning of D-plus-one, Cope, the chief machinist's mate, a tall, quiet chap from Philadelphia, told somebody that from the order "Drop stern anchor" to the order "Take in on stern anchor," which included all the time we had spent aground, exactly four minutes had elapsed. Most of us on deck would have put it at half an hour. During those four minutes all the hundred and forty passengers we carried had run off the ramps into three feet of water, three members of our Coast Guard complement of thirty-three had been killed, and two others had rescued a wounded soldier clinging to the end of the starboard ramp, which had been almost shot away and which fell away completely a few seconds later. The experience had left us without appetite. I remember, on the afternoon of D Day, sitting on a ration case on the pitching deck and being tempted by the rosy picture on the label of a roast-beef can. I opened it, but I could only pick at the jellied juice, which reminded me too much of the blood I had seen that morning, and I threw the tin over the rail.

By D-plus-one we were beginning to eat again. That morning I was on the upper deck talking to Barrett, a seaman from North Carolina, when we saw a German mine go off. It threw a column of water high into the air and sank a ship near it, a transport called the Susan B. Anthony. German planes had been fiddling around above our anchorage during the night, without bombing us; evidently they had been dropping mines. We had seen three of the planes shot down. Barrett looked at the water spout and said, "If we ever hit a mine like that, we'll go up in the air like a arrow."

Susan B. put her nose in the air and slipped backward calmly, like a lady lowering herself into an armchair. In twenty minutes she was gone. It looked as if all her crew got off. Barrett had bet a pound, even money, that we would be hit during the action. I asked him if he had collected the bet and he said,

"Sure. As long as we got hit whether I take the money or not, I might as well take it." In the wardroom, Kavanaugh, the communications officer, talked to me about Bill, one of the Coast Guard boys who had been hit. Long told me about a patch he had devised that would expand in water and would close up any underwater holes in the hull, and seemed rather to regret that he had had no chance to try it out. Lieutenant Rigg kept repeating a tag line he had picked up from Sid Fields, a comedian in a London revue: "What a performance! What a performance!" But the most frequent subject of conversation among both officers and men was the fate of the fellows we had put on the beach, usually referred to collectively as "those poor bastards." We had left them splashing through shallow water, with tracer bullets flying around them and only a nearly level, coverless beach immediately in front of them and with a beach pillbox and more of the enemy on a cliff inshore blazing away with everything they had. We had decided that hardly any of our men could have survived.

Late that afternoon our landing craft got an order to help unload soldiers from a big troopship several miles off the French shore. We were to carry the men almost as far as the beach and then transfer them to Higgins boats. One of our ramps was gone and the other one was not usable, and it would have been superfluous cruelty to drop a soldier with a full pack into five feet of water, our minimum draught. We gathered from the order that the Germans were no longer shooting on the beach; this, at least, represented progress.

The soldiers who lined the decks of the transport, all eager to get ashore at once, belonged to the Second Division; they wore a white star and an Indian head on their shoulder flashes. A scramble net hung down the port side of the vessel, and soldiers with full equipment strapped to their backs climbed down it one by one and stepped backward onto our landing craft. As each man made the step, two seamen grabbed him and helped him aboard. It often took as much time to unload the soldiers from a big ship as it did for the ship itself to get from Britain to the Norman coast, and it seemed to me that a small expenditure on gangplanks of various lengths and furnished with grapples, like the ones used in boarding operations

in ancient naval battles, would have sped these transfers more
than a comparable outlay for any other device could possibly
have done.

While we were loading the men, a thirty-six-foot craft
approached us on the other side. There were two other thirty-
six-footers there side by side already. The newest thirty-six-
footer got alongside the outer one of the pair of earlier arrivals
and the crew boosted up a man who had been standing in the
stern of the boat and helped him on to the other craft. The
man made his way unsteadily across both of the intervening
thirty-six-footers to us, and men on the boats passed his gear,
consisting of a typewriter and a gas mask, along after him. He
was in a field jacket and long khaki trousers without leggings.
The clothes were obviously fresh out of a quartermaster's
stores. He wore the war correspondent's green shoulder patch
on his field jacket. His face and form indicated that he had led
a long and comfortable life, and his eyes betrayed astonishment that he should be there at all, but he was smiling. Some
of our Coastguardsmen helped him over our rail. He said that
he was Richard Stokes of the St. Louis *Post-Dispatch*, that he
had been a Washington correspondent and a music critic for
many years, that he had wanted to go overseas when we got
into the war, and that he had finally induced his paper to send
him over. He had got airplane passage to Britain, where he had
arrived two weeks before, and had been sent to the invasion
coast on a Liberty ship that was to land men on D-plus-one.
"It seems just wonderful to be here," Stokes said. "I can hardly
believe it." He had been very much disappointed when he
found out that because of the violence of the German resistance, the Liberty ship was not going to land her passengers for
a couple of days. The ship's captain had said to him, "There's
another crowd going ashore. Why don't you go with them?"
Then the skipper had hailed a boat for him. "And here I am,"
said Stokes. "It's too good to be true." He was sixty-one years
old, and the world seemed marvellous to him. He said he had
never been in a battle and he wanted to see what it was like.

We got all our soldiers—about four hundred of them—
aboard and started in toward the same stretch of shore we had
left in such haste thirty-six hours before. The way in looked
familiar and yet devoid of the character it had once had for us,

like the scene of an old assignation revisited. The house with the tower on top of the cliff was now gone, I noticed. The naval bombardment, although tardy, had been thorough. Scattered along the shore were the wrecked and burned-out landing craft that had been less lucky than ours. Several of our men told me they had seen the LCT that had been burning off our port quarter on D Day pull out, still aflame, and extinguish the fire as she put to sea, but plenty of others remained. Small craft came out to us from the shore that had so recently been hostile, and soldiers started climbing into them, a less complicated process than the transfer from the troopship because the highest points of the small craft were nearly on a level with our main deck. I could see occasional puffs of smoke well up on the beach. They looked as if they might be the bursts of German shells coming from behind the cliff, and I felt protective toward Stokes. "Mr. Stokes," I said, "it seems to be pretty rough in there." He didn't even have a blanket to sleep on, and he didn't have the slightest idea whom he was going to look for when he got in; he was just going ahead like a good city reporter on an ordinary assignment. He watched two boats load up with soldiers and then, as a third came alongside—I remember that the name painted inside her ramp was "Impatient Virgin"—he said, "Mr. Liebling, I have made up my mind," and went down and scrambled aboard, assisted by everybody who could get a hand on him. He got ashore all right and did some fine stories. A couple of weeks afterward he told me, "I couldn't stand being within sight of the promised land and then coming back."

There was nothing for us to do during the daylight hours of D-plus-two, but toward eight o'clock in the evening we got an order to go out to another troopship and unload more Second Division soldiers, who were to be taken to a beach next to the one where we had landed on D Day. The ship was an American Export liner. Several other LCILs were also assigned to the job of emptying her. I was on our bridge with Rigg when we came under her towering side, and the smell of fresh bread, which her cooks had evidently been baking, drove all other thoughts from our minds. Rigg hailed a young deck officer who was looking down at us and asked him if he could spare some bread. The officer said sure, and a few minutes later a steward pushed six long loaves across to our bridge from a porthole at approximately our level. They were an inestimable treasure to us. Everything is relative in an amphibious operation; to the four-man crews who operate the thirty-six-foot LCVPs, which are open to the weather and have no cooking facilities, an LCIL seems a floating palace. They would often come alongside us and beg tinned fruit, which they would receive with the same doglike gratitude we felt toward the merchantman for our bread.

The soldiers came aboard us along a single narrow plank, which was put over from the port side of the troopship to our rail, sloping at an angle of forty-five degrees. We pitched continuously in the rough water, and the soldiers, burdened with rifles and about fifty pounds of equipment apiece, slid rather than ran down the plank. Our crew had arranged a pile of ration cases at the rail, right where the gangplank was fastened, and the soldiers stepped from the end of the plank to the top case and then jumped down. We made two trips between the merchantman and the small boats that night, and only one soldier fell, and was lost, between the ships during the whole operation. That, I suppose, was a good percentage, but it still seemed to me an unnecessary loss. On our first trip from ship to shore, while we were unloading soldiers into small boats a couple of hundred yards off the beach, there was an air raid. The soldiers standing on our narrow deck, with their backs to the deckhouse walls, had never been under real fire before, but they remained impassive amid the cascade of Bofors shells that rose from hundreds of ships. Much of the barrage had a low trajectory and almost scraped the paint off our bridge. On one ship some gunners who knew their business would hit a plane, and then, as it fell, less intelligent gun crews would start after it and follow it down, forgetting that when a plane hits the water it is at the waterline. An anti-aircraft shell travelling upward at an angle of not more than twenty degrees wounded Commander Carusi sleeping in a dugout on the side of a cliff ashore a couple of nights later.*

*Carusi says that he was lying outside the dugout awaiting evacuation next morning, when one medical corpsman said to another, "No use taking that

A beach-battalion sailor came out to us on one of the first small boats from the shore. He was a big, smiling fellow we had brought from England on our first trip to the invasion coast, one of "those poor bastards" we had all assumed were dead. The cooks hauled him into the galley for sandwiches and coffee, and within a couple of minutes officers as well as men were crowding about him. Nearly everybody we asked him about turned out to be alive—the commander of the beach battalion; Miller, the Army lieutenant; little Dr. Davey; Vaghi and Reich, the poker-playing ensigns; Smith, the beach battalion's veteran chief petty officer; and others whom we had got to know on the ship. They had had a rough time, the sailor said. They had lain for five hours in holes they had scooped in the sand when they went ashore, while one or two American tanks which had landed shot at pillboxes and the pillboxes shot back. Then some infantrymen who had landed in small boats at H Hour worked their way up the beach and took the German positions, releasing our friends from the position in which they were pinned down. They were living on the side of a hill now and getting on with their work of organizing traffic between ship and shore. It was very pleasant news for us aboard the landing craft. We worked all night unloading soldiers, but the Coastguard crew didn't mind; they were in a good mood.

Early the next day, D-plus-three, I thumbed a ride ashore to go visiting. I hailed a passing assault craft, a rocket-firing speedboat, which took me part of the way and then transferred me to an LCVP that was headed inshore. The LCVP ran up onto the beach, dropped her bow ramp, and I walked onto French soil without even wetting my feet. This was the moment I had looked forward to for four years minus nine days, since the day I had crossed the Spanish frontier at Irún after the fall of France. Then the words of de Gaulle—"France has lost a battle but not the war"—were ringing in my ears, for I had just heard his first radio speech from London, but I had not dared hope that the wheel would turn almost full circle so soon. There was

---

white-haired old sonofabitch. He won't make it." It made Gene so sore he *ordered* them to take him. They got him back to England and he survived.

the noise of cannonading a couple of miles or so beyond the cliffs, where the First Division was pushing on from the finger-hold it had made good on D Day, but on the beach everything was calm. Troops and sailors of the amphibious forces had cleared away much of the wreckage, so that landing craft coming in would not foul their hulls or anchor chains; metal road strips led up from the water's edge to the road parallel with the shore. Men were going about their work as if there were no enemy within a hundred miles, and this was under-standable, because no German planes ever arrived to molest them as they unloaded vehicles and munitions for the troops up ahead. To men who had been in other campaigns, when a solitary jeep couldn't pass down a road without three Messer-schmitts' having a pass at it, this lack of interference seemed eerie, but it was true all the same. During the first week after the invasion began, I didn't see one German plane by daylight. Almost in front of me, as I stepped off the boat, were the ruins of the concrete blockhouse that had fired at us as we ran in on D Day. The concrete had been masked by a simulated house, but the disguise had been shot away and the place gaped white and roofless. I had more a sense of coming home to the United States Army than to France, for the first M.P. of whom I inquired the way to the command post of the beach battalion said he didn't know. This is S.O.P., or standard operating pro-cedure, because a soldier figures that if he tells you he knows, he will, at best, have trouble directing you, and if the direc-tions turn out to be wrong you may come back and complain. He has nothing to lose by denying knowledge.

I walked along the beach and met a beach-battalion sailor. He was equally unknowledgeable until I convinced him that I was a friend of the commander. Then he led me two hundred yards up a cliff to the place I had asked about. The commander was not there, but a Lieutenant Commander Watts* and a Lieutenant Reardon, both New Yorkers, were. They had gone ashore on another landing craft, but I had met them both while we were in port in Britain awaiting sailing orders. They had landed five hundred yards up the beach from us and had,

---

*Henry B. Watts, Jr., now chairman of the Board of Governors of the New York Stock Exchange.

of course, got the same reception we got. The command post was installed in a row of burrows in the face of the cliff from which the Germans had fired down on the incoming boats and the beach on D Day; now it was we who overlooked the beach. In the side of another cliff, which was almost at a right angle to this one, the Germans had had two sunken concrete pillboxes enfilading the beach, and I realized that the cross-fire had centred on our landing craft and the others nearby. Meeting these men reminded me of what the First Division soldier had said to me a few days earlier about "Candide:" "Voltaire used the same gag too often. The characters are always getting killed and then turning out not to have been killed at all, and they tell their friends what happened to them in the meantime."

Watts said that after they had left their landing craft, they had run forward like hell and then had thrown themselves down on the beach because there was nothing else to do. The forepart of the beach was covered with large, round pebbles about the size, I imagine, of the one David used on Goliath, and when the German machine-gun bullets skittered among them the stones became a secondary form of ammunition themselves and went flying among the men. "We had infantry up ahead of us, but at first they were pinned down too," Watts said. "A couple of tanks had landed and one of them knocked out a seventy-five up on the side of the hill, but in a short while the Germans either replaced it or got it going again. Then, after a couple of hours, two destroyers came and worked close in to shore, although there were plenty of mines still in there, and really plastered the pillboxes. The infantry went up the hill in the face of machine-gun fire and drove the Germans out of the trench system they had on the crown of the hill. I'll show it to you in a couple of minutes. It's a regular young Maginot Line. By nightfall we felt fairly safe. We found out later from prisoners that the Three Hundred and Fifty-second German Field Division had been holding anti-invasion exercises here the day before we attacked. They had been scheduled to go back to their barracks D Day morning, but when scouts told them about the big fleet on the way in, they decided to stay and give us a good time. They did." It wasn't until a week later, in London, that I found out that because of this untoward circumstance our beach and those on either side of it had been the toughest spots encountered in the landings, and that the losses there had not been at all typical of the operation.

I was delighted to discover Smith, the old chief petty officer, reclining in a nearby slit trench. He was looking very fit. He was forty-seven, and I had wondered how he would do in the scramble to the beach. He had not only made it but had gathered a large new repertory of anecdotes on the way. "A guy in front of me got it through the throat," Smitty said. "Another guy in front of me got it through the heart. I run on. I heard a shell coming and I threw myself face down. There was an Army colonel on one side of me, a Navy captain on the other. The shell hit. I was all right. I looked up and the captain and the colonel was gone, blown to pieces. I grabbed for my tommy gun, which I had dropped next to me. It had been twisted into a complete circle. I was disarmed, so I just laid there."

While I was listening to Smitty, Reardon, talking over a field telephone, had located the commander somewhere on top of the cliff, along the German trench system, which had been taken over by the amphibious engineers as billets. Watts and I decided to walk up and find him. We made our way along the face of the cliff, on a narrow path that led past clusters of slit trenches in which soldiers were sleeping, and got up to the crest at a point where some Negro soldiers had made their bivouac in a thicket. We followed another path through a tangled, scrubby wood. The Germans had left numbers of wooden skull-and-crossbones signs on the tree trunks. These signs said "*Achtung Minen*" and "*Attention aux Mines.*" Whether they indicated that we had taken the enemy by surprise and that he had not had time to remove the signs put up for the protection of his own and civilian personnel, or whether the signs were put there for psychological purposes, like dummy guns, was a question for the engineers to determine. Watts and I took care to stay in the path.

We found the commander, who was in good form. He said he had lost only a couple of the forty-five beach-battalion men who had been on the landing craft with us but that in the battalion as a whole the casualties had been fairly heavy. "Not nearly what I thought they would be when I left that boat, though," he said.

*

The trench system was a fine monument to the infantrymen of the First Division who had taken it. I couldn't help thinking, as I looked it over, that the German soldiers of 1939–41 would not have been driven from it in one day, even by heroes, and the thought encouraged me. Maybe they were beginning to understand that they were beaten. There were no indications that the position had been under artillery fire and I could see only one trace of the use of a flame-thrower. As I reconstructed the action, our fellows must have climbed the hill and outflanked the position, and the Germans, rather than fight it out in their holes, had cleared out to avoid being cut off. They had probably stayed in and continued firing just as long as they still had a chance to kill without taking losses. As the French say, they had not insisted. The trenches were deep, narrow, and so convoluted that an attacking force at any point could be fired on from several directions. Important knots in the system, like the command post and mortar emplacements, were of concrete. The command post was sunk at least twenty-five feet into the ground and was faced with brick on the inside. The garrison had slept in underground bombproofs, with timbered ceilings and wooden floors. In one of them, probably the officers' quarters, there was rustic furniture, a magnificent French radio, and flowers, still fresh, in vases. On the walls were cheap French prints of the innocuous sort one used to see in speakeasies: the little boy and the little girl, and the coyly equivocal captions.

An engineer sergeant who showed us through the place said that the Americans had found hairnets and hairpins in this bombproof. I could imagine an *Oberstleutnant* and his mistress, perhaps the daughter of a French collaborationist, living uneventfully here and waiting for something in which the *Oberstleutnant* had unconsciously ceased to believe, something that he wished so strongly would never happen that he had convinced himself it would happen, if anywhere, on some distant part of the coast. I thought of the Frenchmen I had known in 1939, waiting in a similar mood in the Maginot Line. The sergeant, a straight-featured Jewish fellow in his late thirties, said, "Those infantrymen were like angels. I tell you, I laid there on the beach and prayed for them while they went up that hill with nothing—with bayonets and hand grenades. They did it with nothing. It was a miracle." That made me feel good, because the infantry regiment involved had long been my favorite outfit.* The commander was sardonic about one thing. "You remember how I used to worry about how my men would fall into bomb holes and drown on the way in because the Air Forces had laid down such a terrific bombardment?" he asked. "Well, I defy you to find one bomb hole on this whole beach for a mile each way."

The commander and Watts accompanied me back to the shore. On the way, we stopped at a field hospital that had been set up under canvas. There I talked to some Italian prisoners who were digging shelter trenches. They were fine, rugged specimens, as they should have been, because since the Italian surrender they had undoubtedly had plenty of exercise swinging pickaxes for the Todt organization. Their regiment of bridge-building engineers had been disarmed by the Germans in Greece and the men had been given the choice of enrolling in Fascist combat units or in labor service, they told me. They had all chosen labor service. They seemed to expect to be commended for their choice. They had built many of the trenches in the district. "We wouldn't fight for Hitler," they assured me. I thought that the point had been pretty well proved. Now they were digging for us. They said that all Germans were cowards.

We went down to the shore, and the commander, who, being beachmaster, was in charge of all traffic alongshore, hailed a Duck for me. The Duck put me on an LCVP, which took me back to my ship. On the way out, I realized that I had not seen a single French civilian the entire time ashore.

When I came aboard our landing craft, Long, the engineering officer, grinned at me.

"Did you notice a slight list, sometimes on one side, sometimes on the other, the last two days?" he asked.

I said, "You mean the one you said must be on account of the crew's all turning over in their sleep at the same time?"

"Yes," he said. "Well, today we found an open seam down

*16th Regiment, First Division.

in the stern. She started to list that night the big bomb dropped next to us, but you were sleeping too sound to get up. So maybe we'll go back to port. She has no ramps, the forward anchor winch is sheered in half, and she may as well go into the yard for a couple of days."

The morning of D-plus-four, Rigg signalled the command ship for permission to put back to Britain. As soon as the signalman blinked out the message, every man on board knew there was a chance we would go back, and even fellows who had expressed a low opinion of Weymouth looked extremely happy. While we were waiting for an answer to our request, an LCIL that acted as a group leader, a kind of straw boss among the little ships, passed near us, and the lieutenant on her bridge ordered us over to help tow a barge of ammunition. We were to be paired with another LCIL on this job. The barge, a two-hundred-and-fifty-tonner, was loaded with TNT, and the idea was for one LCIL to make fast on each side of her and shove her in to shore. The Diesel motors of an LCIL, although they can move their craft along at a fair speed, haven't the towing power of a tug. The two LCILs bounced about in the choppy sea for quite a while as we tried to get towing lines aboard the big barge that would hold. Even after we finally got started, every now and then the lines would snap and we would bounce against the side of the barge, as we put more lines aboard her, with a crash that disquieted us, even though we had been told many times that the explosive was packed so carefully that no jouncing would possibly set it off. We were very happy when the barge grounded on the beach according to plan and we could cast off and leave her. Just before we had finished, the group leader came along again and an officer on her bridge shouted over to us through a megaphone, "Report to control-ship shuttle service!" This meant that we were going back to Britain; control ships organize cross-Channel convoys. We were not sorry to go.

By Sunday, D-plus-five, when we at last got started, the water had smoothed out so much that the Channel was like the Hyde Park Serpentine. The flat-bottomed LCIL will bounce about in the slightest sea, but today our craft moved along like a swanboat. The water was full of ration cartons, life jackets, and shell cases, and on the way over we picked up one corpse, of a soldier wearing a life jacket, which indicated that he had never got ashore. Since German planes were dropping mines every night, the lookout was instructed to keep a sharp watch for suspicious objects in the water, and this was almost the only thing it was necessary to think about as we loafed along. A seaman from Florida named Hurwitz was lookout on the bow in the early morning. "Suspicious object off port bow!" he would bawl, and then "Suspicious object off starboard quarter!" Most of the suspicious objects turned out to be shell cases. Finally, Hurwitz yelled "Bridge! The water is just full of suspicious objects!"

The main interest aboard now was whether we would get to port before the pubs closed, at ten o'clock in the evening. Long was getting unheard-of speed out of his motors and it seemed that we would make the pubs easily. Then we happened upon a British LCT that was all alone and was having engine trouble. She asked us to stand by in case her motors conked out altogether. We proceeded at four knots. When the British skipper signalled to us, "Doing my utmost, can make no more," which meant that our chance of beer had gone glimmering, Rigg made a gesture that for delicacy and regard for international relations must have few parallels in naval history. He ordered a signal that may someday be in schoolbooks along with Nelson's "England expects every man to do his duty." "Never mind," he signalled the crippled LCT. "We would have been too late for pub-closing time anyway."

I have left the story of *our* Longest Day—I did not stop to see Wayne and Mitchum lead their charge—in the form in which I wrote it and saw it through censorship and sent it on by wireless from London in parts, as fast as I could after getting ashore. The writing, naturally, took more than one day. While I was writing it the first of the doodlebugs, or V-1's, arrived in the London sky, and continued to pass overhead during the labor of composition.

They caused considerable confusion the first night because they came intermittently for hours, instead of in groups like normal bombers, and so the air raid sirens, controlled by radar, kept sounding alerts and all clears. The things though unmanned had motors. I had no right to pull aside my blackout curtain to see what was happening, and I did not want to interrupt my work to go down to the street—I had a twinge of gout, anyway—so I passed the night in a state of baffled curiosity and fell asleep toward morning. I was awakened by the waitress who brought my breakfast at the set hour, a big Irish girl, who had come to London to work for the good wartime wages. British girls of her age were subject to draft. She drew the curtains, and when I asked her what the Hell had been going on, she said, without heat:

"It's them pilotless airplanes. I do hope they won't be a success."

I have left it that way because it is on the whole more accurate than I could make it today. A situation later assumes meanings that it did not have at the time, and you write them into it in retrospect and fool yourself. I have, however, reinserted a few details barred by the censor, like the loss of the Susan B. Anthony, the nature of the flooded tanks and Gene Carusi's name and what happened to him. I have been inconsistent even in this. I find I have not named the men killed; the coxswain was Moran, the men at the winch Rocky Simone and Bill Frere. Bill was the man whose blood got on me, although I had seen shreds, too, of what I afterward learned had been Moran, and I was impressed, when I reflected on Frere's name, to think that I had been drenched in a "brother's" blood. Afterward I re-reflected and have settled for coincidence.

Also, the instant of that day that recurs to me most often has been that when I sat with roast-beef tin in my hand—the label said it had been packed in Uruguay—and couldn't eat, a most unusual difficulty for me. The meat in the opened tin had a jellied look, and the stuff sloshing on the forward deck, as the LCI-88 rolled, had a jellied look too—the shell had torn open dozens of the cans of rations the soldiers had left aboard, and the liquid on the deck was a mixture of blood and condensed milk, with Campbell's soup. It was an insult.

The rules of the censor also barred reporting that we had seen the LCI-85, another of our group, capsize and sink, riddled and abandoned, and there were other casualties we did not ourselves know at the time. Of the ten LCI's, including the 88, of LCI-flotilla 110, that went in at that hour, four were sunk, and all of the rest, I think, were hit. Those lost were, besides the 85, the 91, 92 and 93, all hit *before* they discharged their passengers, a high proportion of whom were killed. When it was all over, the planners decided that LCI's were too high and vulnerable for the work.

Altogether H plus 65 on Easy Red Beach, Omaha, was an even bloodier mess than we knew at the time, and I am glad we didn't. Anybody who thinks there was a theme song should have his head examined.

5
Direction: Paris

I CROSSED over into France again aboard a Landing Ship, Tanks, on June 24th. The Channel was criss-crossed by convoys, traveling without incident, and on Omaha there were new roads, and traffic M.P.'s to show you the way out. The five briefer stories that follow, all despatches, chronicle my advance on Paris, leaving out a few devious detours that I did not think would interest Harold Ross and Bill Shawn, my editors at *The New Yorker*. One was to Rennes, the first large French city we liberated after the breakout. I remembered Rennes from the pre-war past—1926—as a city whose warm ways belied its austere appearance, and early reports had the population, of both sexes, lavishing its gratitude on Americans. I had a particular memory of an establishment there called *La Feria* (the Fair) that had impressed me, in 1926, by its provincial elegance, as if a ring of the doorbell admitted you to the world of Maupassant's Maison Tellier. I remembered also that Rennes was the seat of an Archbishop, the primate of Brittany, who should be able to communicate a sharp insight into the relations between the devout Bretons and the Occupant during the invasion, a subject that suddenly interested me. I visited the Archbishop first, a splendid gentleman named Roques, who had been noble in the Resistance, and who was promoted to Cardinal within a short time, along with two or three other Resistance Archbishops, while a number of senior Pétainist Cardinals temporarily withdrew from public life. The Church never runs short of suitable spokesmen in a new situation. The Archbishop had taught, either French literature in Germany or German literature in France, I now forget which, for many years as a priest, and had a deep understanding of the German soul, which he found poorly cooked, like a runny *oeuf en gelée*, and so, likely to disintegrate at a slight shock, such as the vibration of a loud vulgar voice with an Austrian accent.

I proceeded later—not directly, for I have a sense of fitness —from the Archbishop's palace to La Feria, to which a cop was kind enough to direct me. It now stood alone, untouched, in a great expanse of bombing rubble around the railroad yards, which had received constant attention from our planes. I found only the Madame, who had been the *sous-maîtresse* in 1926, and two *pensionnaires* in residence, since the *Boche* had moved out, and La Feria's future under the new order was unclear. The decor had been modernized in a nasty way just before the war began. Madame was touched by my fidelity and long memory, but especially by my sense of what was proper in calling on the Archbishop first. She was, like all *Bretonnes*, pious, and told me she found it paid.

"Do you know," she said, "of all the buildings in the quarter of the railroad station, only the Cathedral and La Feria were spared by the bombardments."

Letters from France

JULY 14 (BY WIRELESS)

FOR a year before the Allied landings here, Germans occupied a large, moated, Norman farmhouse near which I now live. Sixty of them were billeted in it, sleeping in great, pine-panelled living rooms on mattresses they had stolen from a nearby summer hotel and in the fetid warmth which is a German soldier's ideal of comfort. This atmosphere is customarily maintained by keeping all windows and doors closed tight. The owners of the farmhouse, who moved into the kitchen wing when their guests took over, listened regularly to the B.B.C. broadcasts and always harbored from two to six young men who were evading forced labor in Germany. In the evening, Madame H.,* the matriarch who rules the family, clipped certain items bearing on the war from the German-controlled French newspapers, or, when there was nothing worth clipping, reread old items in the collection she was gathering. A couple of nights ago, while I was drinking warm milk in the kitchen, which, because Americans are billeted in

*Hamel was the name.

the house now, is still the family living room, Madame showed me her clippings. The first one was dated August 17, 1941. Each of them had to do either with a proclamation by a German *Kommandantur* or with a Vichy official threatening reprisal for some act of sabotage committed in northwestern France or with an announcement of the execution of hostages, invariably described as "Jews and Communists."

Madame H., who had no direct contact with the resistance movement and knew nothing first-hand about the victims named in the newspapers, felt certain from the first that they were on the only decent side. Collaborationist cant never deceived her for a moment, and yet she is of the type most susceptible to Pétainolatry—rich, intensely Catholic, and in considerable fear of "Reds." Her son, a blond, broad-headed chap with a decided limp, was a prisoner of war in Germany for three years. He had served in Alsace in a French engineering regiment and right after his capture was set to work with other prisoners digging up French mines. A mine exploded, killing six of his comrades and shattering one of his feet. Even after that, he was sent into forced labor, first in Alsace and then in Germany. Officials of the local *Kommandantur* approached Madame H. some time after the armistice with an offer to have her son sent home if she would persuade him to be an informer against farmers who were withholding cattle and fats from the Germans. She said she would prefer not to have her son home. Eventually the Germans released him anyway, along with a few thousand other crippled or tubercular prisoners, when, in 1943, Vichy put on a great drive to induce young Frenchmen to volunteer for labor in Germany to "relieve" prisoners of war who had been there since 1940. These incapacitated prisoners were supposed to be the advance guard of a great mass of returning Frenchmen; actually, they were the only ones ever released. Young H., as he will be known in the countryside as long as his mother lives, although he is now over forty, came home with a great admiration for the Alsatians, who, he says, are the most patriotic French he ever met, and with an almost patronizing view of Germans. "A German is either a bandit or a decent fellow," he says. "There are no in-between Germans. The bandits run the rest. I have seen the Germans in air raids, and individually they are shameless cowards, but fantastic discipline keeps them going." He says there was enough food, but it was all starchy, and that few German workmen, even at the time he left the country, seemed to believe that Germany could win the war, whereas most French prisoners were confident even in the worst days that Germany would lose.

When H. returned to Normandy and saw what the German Army had become by then, he grew optimistic, too, like most of the Normans who had stayed home. The athletes in uniform who had invaded western France in 1940 had given place to a mixed lot of Georgians, Russians, Poles, and adolescent and middle-aged Germans, and the motorized equipment that had amazed the French in the blitzkrieg days had been shipped away to active fronts and been supplanted in great part by horse-drawn vehicles. The soldiers of the polyglot regiments seemed resigned to defeat and stuffed themselves in quiet desperation, consuming Norman butter and milk as if they were trying to eat enough to last them through the black years they saw ahead of them. The arrogance of the invaders had given way to the alternate fits of meekness and ill manners of the garrison troops. The Germans were so short of motor vehicles that they commandeered farmers' carriages for their officers and sometimes drafted farmers to drive them. A substantial farmer, a neighbor of Madame H., tells about the time he drove a German major to a railroad station three miles from the officer's billet; he managed to take an hour getting to the station, pretending first that he didn't know the way and then that the horse had gone lame. The German missed his train and was furious about it, but the Norman pretended not to understand anything he said. This was the sort of thing that kept the Germans miserable; they had the feeling that they were constantly being tricked and laughed at. The German authorities knew that they were getting only a fraction of the cattle and dairy produce available, but they couldn't confiscate the herds without putting a stop to production, since they had no agricultural personnel of their own to put on the farms.

Few of the country people in Normandy expected a landing there. The majority, in fact, thought that there would be no landing at all but that the Allies would wear Germany down by bombing. They were perhaps persuaded to this way of thinking by a hope that their land would not be fought upon. But the landings, when they came, delighted them. The discomfiture of the Germans was particularly pleasing, and peasants, offering their best bottled cider to Americans, suddenly burst into laughter as they remember how the supermen scuttled off. During the first days of the invasion, there was a bit of foolish talk in British newspapers, and probably also in American papers, which I have not seen, about the Normans' lack of enthusiasm, stories evidently written by correspondents who acquired their ideas of Frenchmen from music-hall turns and comic drawings. One might as well expect public demonstrations of emotion in Contoocook, New Hampshire, or in Burrillville, Rhode Island, as in Normandy, where the people are more like New Englanders than they are like, for instance, Charles Boyer. Young men of the resistance groups did invaluable service both before and after the landing; they drew us plans of German fortifications before we landed and then went through the German lines repeatedly during the fighting in order to get information about enemy movements. Not one report of a French civilian's sniping at Allied troops has been authenticated, and relations between our soldiers and the country people are excellent everywhere, now that the inevitable misunderstandings of the early days have passed.

A common cause of misunderstanding was the farmers' habit of loitering about fields which had been requisitioned for Allied tank parks. One Armored Forces colonel was thinking of having the *maire* of a certain village shot as an obvious spy when a French-speaking American officer interrogated the *maire* and found that he was just waiting around for a chance to milk his cows. "There may perhaps be a war and you may perhaps be beating Boches," said the *maire*, with traditional Norman scepticism, raising his voice occasionally as the sound of guns threatened to drown his words, "but what I am sure of is that my horned beasts must be milked." Even the farmers who were happiest to see the Allied tanks arrive are now beginning to ask wistfully when they are going to get their pastures back again.

The French sometimes misinterpreted American actions, too. There was, for example, the *maire* of a small *commune* just

outside Cherbourg who came into Army Civil Affairs headquarters there five days after we took the city and complained
to a French liaison officer that American troops had put him
out of the *mairie* and that now he had no place in which to
carry on the affairs of the *commune*. The French liaison officer,
Captain Gérard Lambert, an energetic Gaulliste, replied emphatically, "But that is against all the policy set on high levels!
They have no right to commandeer a French Government
building unless for extreme military necessity," and he and the
maire immediately drove off to the *mairie*. There were no
American troops there, but a sign on the door said, "Keep Out
—U.S. Military Police." As Captain Lambert and the *maire*,
who must have been around seventy-five, climbed the stairs to
the first floor, the captain said, "This is curious. Why did they
order you out?"

The old man answered indignantly, "Because they said there
were mines in the cellar."

The captain said with dignity, "You are an idiot."

"However, my captain," the old man said, "it is not certain
there are mines in the cellar." So he did remain.

All sorts of difficulties were referred to our Civil Affairs
officers during the first few days following the liberation of any
city. The manager of the Cherbourg branch of the Banque de
France requested Lieutenant Colonel Frank Howley, Cherbourg Civil Affairs Chief, to have a guard posted over a certain
heap of rubble in Valognes, a town which had been almost
completely flattened by artillery fire. The bank manager explained that he had sent a hundred million francs to the Valognes branch for safekeeping, because he had expected the
bombardment of Cherbourg. A shell had demolished the Valognes branch and two adjoining buildings had collapsed on
top of it, so the hundred million francs were now buried under
all three. The manager seemed to fear that some casual looter
might shove the ruins out of the way and unearth the money,
a feat which, actually, a steam shovel will probably accomplish
in about two weeks.

Cherbourg, the nearest thing to a big city we have yet captured, was the first testing ground in France for the Allies'
Army Civil Affairs Branch. When the Americans took over, on

June 27th, the city had no water, electricity, gas, transportation, or government. The Vichy *sous-Préfet* had fled and so had twenty-five thousand of Cherbourg's civilian population of forty thousand. The Civil Affairs team, headed by Colonel Howley, an American, and including both British and American officers, moved in before the street sniping had ended, and immediately started in on the job of resuscitation. The Civil Affairs men's task, as Howley saw it, was to get the city government functioning normally again. The Civil Affairs Branch had no enlisted personnel it could put to work policing the streets or making repairs. Cherbourg had had a fairly modern water system; water was pumped from the little Divette River to a purifying plant, from which it was distributed through mains. Bombs had broken the pipeline from the river to the plant. Major John C. Diggs, a former sanitary engineer for the State of Indiana, is Public-Works Officer in the Howley team. He got together the staff of the Cherbourg water system, who told him that the Germans had taken away all the reserve pipe. He got piping from the Army Engineers, the French installed it with their own workmen, and on July 1st the city had water again. "All they needed was a little encouragement," Major Diggs told me. "I've seen several floods and hurricanes in Indiana and the effect on local governments is always the same— they're a bit stunned, like a man suffering from battle shock. A little shove gets them going again." When it was time to turn the water on, a new problem presented itself, one that it is safe to say nobody in Washington or London had foreseen. There were hundreds of empty buildings in Cherbourg, many of them partly wrecked. The hastily departing owners had left the taps open. When the water was turned on, thousands of gallons would not only be wasted but would do further damage to the structures. Men with loudspeakers borrowed from the local American Psychological Warfare Unit were sent through the streets to warn people to turn off their taps. This expedient did not, of course, take care of the empty houses, so the British Major Palfrey, Police Officer of the team, the American Lieutenant Colonel Hensel, who is its Civil Defense Expert, and the American Lieutenant Davis, who is a former battalion chief in the Columbus, Ohio, fire department, got in touch with the French police, the Défense Passive, and the local fire department, respectively, and members of all three services went, just to be sure, to every house in the city and turned off the open taps. Two other officers, Lieutenant Robertson and Captain Westervelt, who were utilities and telephone men in civilian life, got the electric-power and telephone system restored to service in much the same thorough-going fashion.

On June 29th, M. Coulet, General de Gaulle's Normandy delegate, installed in office, as the new *sous-préfet* of Cherbourg, M. Le Viander, who had been chief engineer of the municipality and active in the resistance movement. He had been absent from the city when the invasion came but had made his way to the Allied lines a couple of days after the landings. Police and civil servants fell into line and took orders from the new *sous-préfet*, who was, after all, a colleague who had been in civil service a long time, more readily, in most cases, than they had taken them from his Vichy predecessor. He knew precisely which of his subordinates had collaborated beyond absolute necessity, and he sacked them. They were not numerous. After that, the *sous-préfecture* and the Civil Affairs men worked smoothly together. The same thing had already happened in Bayeux, where M. Coulet had his headquarters and where he had installed another resistance *sous-préfet*. The Civil Affairs team in the much smaller but architecturally more interesting Bayeux is headed by a Britisher and includes both American and British officers.

Coulet, a tall, thin-lipped, smooth-shaven man of slightly sombre elegance, speaks English well. He has no army behind him, but he has the prestige, in a Norman's eyes, of representing the only French government the Normans recognize, the Gouvernement Provisoire, and he proceeds with complete assurance, making contact with the resistance group in each district as soon as the Allied forces enter it, and organizing the district with the assistance he receives from local resistance leaders. It is a program which up to now has worked smoothly and bloodlessly. So far, there have been neither legal nor unofficial executions.—

JULY 20 (BY WIRELESS)
The contrast which existed in the first World War between the front and behind the lines has returned with the present

Allied campaign in Normandy. Staff officers drive toward the front along roads upon which the shadow of a strafing plane never falls and, leaving it, return to an area in which traffic and sanitation are as well organized as in Westchester. Nobody worries about the possibility of a flanking movement or a breakthrough by the enemy because our flanks rest on the sea and the enemy has shown no signs of real striking power. Even within a couple of miles of the front there is only slight danger, because the Germans have disclosed little artillery. The arrival of a shell on a road near a command post is something to talk about for the next three days. The last few hundred yards make all the difference; the fighting is a nasty business in which hedgerows, drainage ditches, and apple trees have assumed the same lethal associations as Tunisian *djebels*. This struggle for orchards and pastures is disheartening because it is so repetitious. There is, as Army men say, no observation in this country, which means that you can't see an enemy position until you have taken the one in front of it. Even then you don't know that it really is an enemy position until a machine gun opens fire on you from a hedge or a mortar in the next field ahead starts dropping stuff in the one you have just taken. It is not safe to assume that any corner of any field you are attacking is undefended. The property sense of the Norman is so strong that no bit of useful land is without its surrounding hedge and ditch. The Germans dig in behind the hedges like moles—moles with excellent eyesight—and the pattern of the fields frequently gives them a fine opportunity for crossfire, which happens to be one of their specialties. The business of rooting them out of these fields is both dangerous and tedious, and it is one phase of war in which airpower is of almost no help, because foliage conceals the defenders from strafing planes and because bombing entire fields on speculation is likely to pay extremely small dividends in dead Germans. Our artillery is useful in inducing machine gunners to keep their heads down, but foot soldiers have to make the actual kills.

After each few days of this hedgerow fighting, one of our divisions comes to a small town, which it takes. The towns, except for their names, are as much alike as the orchards: always the main street that is merely a stretch of the motor highway; the austere gray stone church that had survived eight centuries and then been shattered the week before; the trepanned, amputated houses with glassless windows; and, if there is one café still ungutted, the sign upon is that says "Off limits to military personnel." A unit takes a mild pride in the catalogue of the towns it has captured—such as St. Jean de Daye, known to the troops as Saint John D Day, and La Haye de Puits, called Hooey da Pooey—but that's about all. There are usually several dead Germans in the buildings of these towns, snipers left behind by their retreating comrades and killed by incoming Americans. Our soldiers, preoccupied with the possibility of surviving snipers and with the mortar fire that the enemy is sure to drop back into any town he has abandoned, hurry past the bodies with only perfunctory interest. There is more affinity between a wax dummy and a corpse than between a corpse and a live man. Some of the corpses wear fairly good gray-green uniforms, and others wear nondescript rags. The most impressive corpses seldom come from the best regiments; the most effective German troops here are the starveling adolescents of the new Nazi formations. Older, more fully developed men give up sooner. The Russians, Georgians, and Poles who were starved into enlisting in German coastal regiments are naturally the easiest game of all. Unfortunately, we have liquidated most of these "static" troops and are now meeting a higher percentage of Germans. For all their stubbornness in defense, the Germans have not been making any counterattacks in force. This has led to a certain optimism, particularly in the zone beginning a thousand yards to the rear of the line. Some officers are saying that the situation reminds them of Tunisia late in April, 1943, when the Germans, though still hanging on to good defensive positions, were about to collapse rather suddenly.

Many peasants remain in their homes in the battle areas, despite the efforts of both Germans and Americans to move them out. The Germans have been trying to evacuate people and their livestock before them as they retreat, but the peasants hide themselves and their beasts. When American troops start fighting around their farmhouses, our Civil Affairs officers attempt to get the peasants to move back of our lines, for their own protection, but they usually say that they won't go unless they can take their cattle with them, and since they can't take their pasture along with the cattle this is not practical. A crop farmer can leave his land for a time and find it there when he comes back, but herds will stray or starve or sicken or wander into machine-gun fire if left to themselves, and the Normans stick to their cows. Near St. Lô, a refugee camp has been established for people whose homes have been destroyed. It is an unusual refugee camp, because it does not receive any supplies from the Army; the French authorities provide the food and the farmers of the district donate clothing and furniture. The refugees have organized themselves into a self-governing community and have succeeded in making themselves more comfortable than the American soldiers of the local Civil Affairs detachment, who are now taking French lessons from the refugee children. Almost every family has deaths to mourn, but the tragic aspect of the situation is naturally not comprehended by the children, who consider the affair a sort of large-scale picnic and are not disturbed by the racket of the American medium artillery immediately behind their temporary home. The subway-train noise the shells make as they go over the children's heads merely provokes them to imitative whistles. Very old people are similarly unmoved by the war. A well-to-do farmer's widow, crippled with rheumatism, and her *bonne* were the only inhabitants left in the village of St. André de L'Epine after two days of heavy fighting. When our Civil Affairs detachment got there, it evacuated them in an ambulance. The mistress was seventy-seven and the maid seventy-two, and the thing that had made the greatest impression on them was the fact that they hadn't been able to get any milk or vegetables for several days and had had to eat their pet rabbit. Their house had been badly damaged and every other building in the village had been flattened.

The Fourteenth of July apparently found everybody in the liberated zone happy. Tricolors that had not seen the light since the Pétain armistice fluttered over houses and draped window sills everywhere, usually along with homemade American flags and often with signs saying "Vive l'Amérique" or "Merci à Nos Libérateurs." The understanding recently reached between de Gaulle and the United States Government seemed to have removed the last suspicion entertained by the

French, and the crowds that gathered for the ceremonies in front of the *mairies* were unaffectedly joyous. As one thick-waisted old farmer, an ex-cuirassier, said, "An armored formation has cut up my best pasture, a promising heifer has gone up with a mine, and a bomb has removed most of the tiles from the roof of my house, but, *Monsieur*, I assure you, I was never so happy in my life." And Mme. Hamel said, as she put on her red-white-and-blue rosette (an extra-large one), "Last year I wore a blue dress, my daughter a white one, and my daughter-in-law a red one, and we walked down the street arm in arm, because it was forbidden to wear the tricolor. Now it is different." However, it would be a mistake to assume, because things have gone so smoothly in the part of France liberated up to now, that there will be no serious problems, especially of relief, in *départements* which are either less self-sufficient or which the Germans have had more time to loot. It is also too soon to be able to say that in the big cities the change of regime will be effected with as little violence as it has in the essentially reasonable, rural Normandy. Still, there is every justification for being satisfied with the way things have gone so far.

There was one ceremony on Bastille Day that had not been foreseen—the burial of Brigadier General Theodore Roosevelt, who had died of a heart attack after surviving more front-line perils than any other general officer in this theatre of operations. Nearly all of Roosevelt's scrapes were of his own seeking; he was as nearly fearless as it is given to man to be. The name "Rough Rider," in white letters on his jeep, was a familiar sight just behind the lines in four campaigns of this war. It had been painted out by the time of the funeral and the vehicle had been returned to the motor pool and anonymity, and there was no other charger to lead behind the scout car that carried this flamboyant little man's body to the grave. Nothing else was missing from the solemnities. The man who used to tell his friends in New York how as a small boy he had put on the shoes of his father, the former President, and walked ecstatically about his bedroom at Sagamore Hill was never a sufficiently acute politician to fill them, but he found his métier in 1940, when he took up his reserve commission in the Army. Old Teddy was a dilettante soldier and a first-class politician; his son was a dilettante politician and a first-class soldier. After serving with the First Division in Africa and Sicily and with the French in Italy, he was assigned to a new unit, as assistant division commander, a couple of months before D Day. It was the Fourth Division, which had never fought before, and, by his own example, he gave it much of the lift that took it across the beaches and all the way to Cherbourg. It is no longer a run-of-the-mill division but one of the best in the Army, and his death has endowed it with a tradition. In the circumstances, it was easy to condone his indiscriminate passion for reciting poems, which he rolled out with the large facility of a juke box full of quarters. He was a man you had to see fight to believe in.*

The taking of St. Lô was the climax of the hedgerow phase of our campaign. St. Lô, at the juncture of several major highways, is a larger version of the rural crossroads that are the prizes of smaller operations. The correspondents, going out every day in jeeps to the St. Lô sector of the front, got to know every turning in the lanes, bordered by the omnipresent hedges, that led to the suburbs where the final attack was to be made. Troops fanned out from these lanes to fight their way through the fields. Each day it was possible for vehicles to get past one or two more turnings in the lanes; one remembered these new turnings by the burned-out halftracks or by groups of dead cows. The jeeps that carried the correspondents breasted a seemingly regular stream of other jeeps with litters, each bearing two seriously wounded men, strapped to their hoods. The stream was regular because the casualties in this sort of war, though they vary from field to field, don't vary from day to day. You lose a few more men in one hedge-fenced pasture and one or two less in another; there is never a spate of casualties, but the stream never dries up, either. There were about as many German as American wounded on the litters, but we seemed to see many more German than American dead on the ground, probably because we were advancing over terrain that had been hammered by American artillery, whereas

*Roosevelt and I had a date to meet at the Café de la Régence in Paris on the fourteenth. Instead, we kept it as described above.

the enemy had employed comparatively little artillery. We also got to know every sizable gap in the ragged seven-to-ten-foot-high hedges along the lanes, for the gaps enabled enemy snipers and mortar crews to see and to shoot accurately. A rapidly moving jeep raised a cloud of dust that might bring down mortar fire even where there was no gap; a jeep creeping at the ten miles an hour that is prescribed in the area seemed to the occupants to be minutes getting past each gap. When, by the evening of July 18th, the Americans had fought themselves out of the turnings and hedgerows, they rushed into the town of St. Lô with all the joy of a band of claustrophobes released from a maze.

The Germans, as expected, broke out what artillery they had and bombarded St. Lô as soon as our troops came in, and our tired infantrymen, lying face down in the streets at the foot of the buildings, realized that life is just a succession of frying pans and fires. The correspondents, flat on their faces like the rest, wondered whether the Pulitzer Prize was worth all this trouble. They were further depressed by the magnificent aplomb of the brigadier general* who walked erect down the centre of the street, directing troop movements with a cane. When a sniper's bullet went through his right arm, he transferred the cane to his left hand. That gesture will be hard for us to match in our autobiographies.

AUGUST 4 (BY WIRELESS)

Riding, last week, down the road that led to Coutances, Avranches, and beyond evoked memories of the tragic June of 1940, when refugees streamed down the one route left open for civilians between Paris and Tours. Last week, as four years ago, the road was choked with vehicles moving as slowly as a trickle of water through dust, but this time, instead of autobuses and pitiful automobiles loaded with civilians, the traffic was halftracks, empty ambulances, tank destroyers, two-and-a-half-ton trucks, the small, tracked carriers (called weasels) that take ammunition across country, and, scattered through all the

*Norman D. (Dutch) Cota, then of the 29th Division. He later got one of his own, the 28th. The victor of St. Lô was the C.O. of the 29th—Major-General Charles W. Gerhardt.

heavy stuff, jeeps. The procession was heading toward the Germans instead of away from them. One would never have believed, in peacetime, that the mere act of riding slowly down a road in an uncomfortably crowded vehicle on two separate occasions could produce such antithetical emotions. In 1940, the unfortunates on the road stared apprehensively at the sky every time the procession stopped because of a jam. In 1944, soldiers in trucks grinned every time they heard an airplane motor. The Luftwaffe had lost its terror; the Ninth Air Force was patrolling the skies of France with absolute authority. The men moving forward had a hunch that no serious battle awaited them. It turned out that they were mostly right. There were some sharp local actions, which were less counterattacks than group attempts to escape, but in general the parallel with the end of the Tunisian campaign held good: German resistance, disconcertingly stiff in the earlier phase of the Normandy fighting, crumbled suddenly and swiftly, and American units heading toward their objectives unexpectedly found themselves racing other units that had progressed farther and faster than anyone had anticipated. It was a disturbing experience for the artillery officers, who soon found that there was no place that their shells would not be likely to fall among Americans advancing from other points of the compass.

I watched the air bombardment that preceded the breakthrough from an upstairs window of a Normandy farmhouse. The dwelling looked south, toward the area, five miles away, which was to be bombed. There were three ridges, the first two crowned with poplars, the third with pines, between the farmhouse and the target area. One stream of bombers came in to the left of the farmhouse, turned behind the third ridge, dropped its bombs, and came away to my right; another stream came in over my right, turned, and went off to the left. For two hours the air was filled with the hum of motors, and the concussions of the bombs, even though they were falling five miles away, kept my sleeves fluttering. I was living with a headquarters battery of divisional artillery, and some of the men in it, watching the bombardment from the sloping ground under my window, rolled on the grass with unsportsmanlike glee. Their emotion was crude but understandable. "The more bombs we drop, the less fight there'll be left in them," a soldier said, and, remembering the first bombs on Paris in 1940 and all the bombings I have seen decent people undergo since then, I could not feel ashamed of the men's reaction.

The only residents of the farm who seemed uncomfortable were a great, long-barreled sow and her litter of six shoats, who walked about uneasily, shaking their ears as if the concussions hurt them. At brief intervals, they would lie down in a circle, all their snouts pointing toward centre. Then they would get up again, perhaps because the earth quivering against their bellies frightened them. Puffs of black flak smoke dotted the sky under the first two waves of bombers; one plane came swirling down, on fire and trailing smoke, and crashed behind the second ridge of poplars. White parachutes flashed in the sun as the plane fell. A great cloud of slate-gray smoke rose from behind the trees where it had gone down. Soon after that the flak puffs disappeared; the German gunners either had been killed or, as one artillerist suggested, had simply run out of ammunition. The succeeding waves of planes did their bombing unopposed. It was rather horrifying, at that.

After the bombardment, we waited all afternoon for the order to advance. We had heard that the divisional artillery headquarters and the division's battalion of medium howitzers, which throw their shells about seven miles, were to be moved up that night to positions beyond the line the Germans had held that morning. As it happened, the breakthrough wasn't quite as abrupt as all that. We didn't move until the evening, and then we moved only a couple of miles, to a hollow behind the first ridge of poplars, territory that infantry of another division had won from the enemy a couple of days before. When night fell, neither our own infantry division,* which the Germans have been good enough to refer to as a *corps d'élite*, nor our armor had even gone into battle. The infantry divisions ahead of us† had been expected to move forward hard on the tail of the air bombardment and make an opening through which we and the armor would pass, but they had not advanced appreciably. Discouraging rumors, such as frequently

*The First, of course.
†Fourth, Ninth and Thirtieth.

attend the opening of offensives, cropped up in the small, exclusive mess of the divisional artillery that night. One was that the Germans had not been shaken by the bombardment, another that they had been annihilated but that bomb craters had made all the roads impassable. The favorite explanation of the delay, I am afraid, was that the divisions ahead of us had snarled things up as usual.*

Next morning, at seven o'clock, a combat team of infantry from the division I was with went into action. By nine o'clock, the news came that the men had advanced thousands of yards in the first hour, and all day they kept on moving forward, against slight opposition. Parts of two armored divisions, engaged at other points, also made rapid advances. The early discouragement around our headquarters disappeared. The mess even made generous allowances for the shortcomings of other infantry divisions. (It turned out afterward that they had run into an abortive German offensive just beyond the bombed area and had not done badly at all.) The artillery prepared to move up behind the infantry, in order to shoot it out of trouble when it ran up against the inevitable tough going. But the tough going that had developed at some point in every other operation the division had participated in, whether in the Mediterranean campaign or in France, did not develop in this curious advance.

"The dough," as officers of divisional artillery call the infantry, flowed forward for five days; the artillery followed, but it was hardly ever called upon to shoot. Whenever the Germans looked as though they might make a stand, some other American unit got behind them. By the fifth evening, the gunners found themselves in the impasse I have already described. It was an artillerist's nightmare: there was no place they *could* shoot without fear of hitting some of our own people. Army Corps headquarters had marked on a map what are called "no fire" lines; these lines completely hemmed our guns in. On that fifth night, the division stretched out toward Coutances like a long finger. There were—theoretically, at least—Germans

*This was unjust. Many of those glorious bombs had fallen short *on* the Thirtieth, which suffered its top day of casualties.

in front of us and on both flanks, but there was part of an American armored division behind the Germans in front of us and there were other American troops behind the Germans on our right. Still other American troops were supposed to be getting around to the rear of the Germans on our left, too, and all the Germans in the area were trying to get out at once. The chief danger we faced was being trampled to death by escaping supermen while we slept.

Divarty, the familiar term for divisional artillery head-quarters, is under ordinary conditions an ideal place to follow the progress of a battle, or at least one division's part in it, because Divarty controls the small spotter planes, usually Piper Cubs, which serve as the division's eyes. The pilots and observers in these craft, known to "the dough" as Maytag Messerschmitts, are not Air Forces men but artillery officers. They report not only on targets and the effect of the division's artillery fire but on all enemy troop and vehicle movements they observe. This information is channelized through Divarty to Division, which is short for division headquarters. When ground observation is available, Divarty has the best of that, too, for the artillery has its observers at points of vantage up in the line with advanced elements of the infantry. These observers have telephone lines to their battalions, and the battalions in turn have direct lines to Divarty. The infantry is served by a parallel but separate telephone network. Communications between the infantry and the artillery go through a division switchboard. The infantry and artillery of a division live like a sensible married couple—in the same house but in separate beds.

There is a detached, academic atmosphere about Divarty that is lacking in the larger, more bustling Division, and artillerists in general view war with the objectivity of men who seldom see their victims. The headquarters battery of Divarty has no guns; it merely has a switchboard, a set of maps, and a lot of telephone wires. Divarty is a small, itinerant brain trust which moves quietly with the front-line troops and calls down upon distant Germans the thunder of the division's battalions of artillery. It sets up its command post in a farmhouse or barn within the division area, lays its wires to the battalions, and blacks out windows and chinks through which light might escape. Then, after nightfall, when the Cubs come down, its higher officers sit around a long row of tables—in an atmosphere that recalls a newspaper copy desk during the slack hours—drinking strong coffee and playing cribbage while they wait for telephone calls. A call comes in, and an executive officer engages in a brief conversation, rings off, then remarks, "Infantry patrols report some sort of Jerry movement at that road junction at 4124. Mediums can reach it." He picks up the telephone again, makes a call, and returns to his cribbage game, and outside, in the night, twelve hundred pounds of high explosive scream toward the dark crossroad twenty-five times, at short, irregular intervals. In this particular engagement, however, we simply ran out of crossroads to shoot at.

My Dear Little Louise

DURING our breaking-out offensive in Normandy, the division artillery headquarters occupied four command posts in five days. A French family was living in one wing of the first house we used, although most of the roof was gone and a couple of the bedrooms had only three walls, but the farmhouses in which we had our second and third command posts were deserted. The Germans had forced all the inhabitants to leave. In our fourth one, we found civilians again. The Germans, not expecting so quick an advance, had not evacuated people from what they still considered the rear area. In the barnyard of that place, we found a dead Panzer Grenadier of a Schutzstaffel division. His paybook said that he had been born in Essen, and on his body there was a typewritten form which he had filled out but obviously had not had time to hand in to his company commander, asking for what we would call an emergency leave to go home. His reason was "Bombing deaths in family—urgent telegram from wife." He had been hit by a fragment of shell, but it had not torn him up much. A detail of our fellows buried him in back of the barn.

The dead cows were more of a problem. Now that we have

moved on to Brittany, one of the things that make us happy is
that we are out of dead-cattle country. The war moves more
swiftly and it isn't necessary to drop artillery shells on every
field and crossroad. Besides, the cattle in Brittany are fewer
and more scattered than in Normandy, where every pasture
was full of them. You need a bulldozer to bury cows properly,
unless you are going to take all day about it, and nobody had
men to spare for a large-scale interment detail. They lay in the
fields with their four legs pointing stiffly in the air, like wooden
cows discarded from a child's Noah's Ark, and their smell
hung over the land as the dust hung over the roads. Men are
smaller than cattle and they are always buried first; we lived in
the stench of innocent death. At our fourth command post,
there were more dead cows than usual, because, the people
on the farm told us, eighteen extra cows had arrived with the
Germans a couple of weeks before. There had been two sets of
Germans in the farm buildings—ten paratroopers who had
showed up driving eight cows, and forty S.S. men who had appeared driving ten cows. The paratroopers, one of whom was a
captain, had got there first and taken up quarters in the farmhouse. The S.S. men, arriving later, had billeted themselves
in the outbuildings, but only after a noisy argument, in which
they had failed to get the paratroopers out of the big house.
The captain had too much rank for them. The paratroopers
had been fighting a long time and were very down in the
mouth, the people of the house said. A soldier who served as
interpreter had told the French family that the war was over,
that Germany was beaten. But the S.S. fellows, who had come
from soft berths in Warsaw and Brno, were still *gonflés en bloc*
(blown up hard) and talked as if they owned the earth. That
was less than two weeks ago, but even the S.S. men, to judge
by those taken prisoner, have changed now. The S.S. soldiers
had brought a refugee family with them, to milk the cows, the
people on the farm said. Every day the paratroopers drank the
cream from their eight cows and threw the milk away. Both
sets of Germans had departed abruptly, but the S.S. had left
one man to guard the cows, presumably in case the reports of
the Allied attack proved exaggerated. A shell had killed the
cowtender.

*

I am sure that I will remember our two deserted command posts longer and more vividly than the two that were inhabited. Perhaps that is because you think more about people when they aren't there, and because you can be your own Sherlock Holmes and reconstruct them in accordance with your own hypothesis. The first deserted farm was a solid rectangle of stone and stucco buildings with walls nearly a foot thick. The farmyard, on which all the buildings fronted, could be reached only by narrow lanes that pierced the solid row of buildings at the front and at the back. It would have been a tough defensive position to crack if there had been any tactical reason to defend it. The farmhouse was very old and must have belonged to an aged, rich, crippled, bigoted woman or to a crippled man who had a fat old woman for a housekeeper. There was a crutch in the farmyard, lying as if it had fallen off a departing wagon, and in two of the bedrooms there was a pair of old, mended crutches that must have been discarded for newer ones. In the kitchen, by the great open hearth, there was a reclining chair with an extension on which to rest your legs, and in one bedroom there were several old and dirty corsets, whose whalebones, despite the garments' immense girth, had all sprung because of the continual effort to encompass a bulging body. There was a tall Norman clock in every room. Clocks of this sort are made in little towns, like Périers and Colombières and Marigny, which nobody outside Normandy ever heard of before this summer. Every crossroads seems to have had its clockmaker as well as its baker and its harness maker. The wooden cases of these timepieces are generally rather austere, but the dials are framed by hammered gilt sculpture; sheaves, golden apples, plows, and peasants in donkey carts are favorite motifs. The pendulums are vast, and they too are encrusted with ornament. A bride, I imagine, although no one has told me so, brings a clock as part of her dowry, and a house where there are many clocks has been ruled in turn by many women. This house was full of hideous modern religious images and of wax fruits and flowers under glass bells. There were no books except devotional ones and those that gave quick ways of making the computations a farmer must make in doing business with wholesalers. There were many of each kind.

The farmsteaders had left the place in a great hurry, and

some soldiers, either German or American, had been there afterward and rummaged through the house, littering the floors with things, useless to them, that they had pulled from the cupboards—women's high-collared blouses, skirt hoops, dingy photographs of family outings and one of a man in a cuirassier's uniform, with breastplate and horse-tail helmet, and three or four parchment manuscripts. One, dated 1779, was the deed of sale of a farm, another was a marriage contract dated the Year 3 of the First Republic. The contract enumerated the items the bride was to bring in her dowry, which included six pillowcases, one canopy for a bed, and ten handkerchiefs; the whole thing was to come to a thousand and fifty-seven francs. If the husband died before the wife, she was to be allowed to withdraw that much from the estate in consideration of her dowry. If the wife died first, the widower was to keep the pillowcases, handkerchiefs, and all the rest, probably to bestow on his next choice. I wondered, naturally, which of them had survived the other. There were canopies over the beds in all the bedrooms; one must have been the canopy listed in the contract. The house had stone floors that did not shake even when some guns just across the road were being fired, which happened for one entire night we spent there.

The guns were only three thousand yards behind the front line, but they were firing at a target—a railroad station or road junction—eleven miles away. They belonged not to division artillery but to a remote, unfamiliar entity called Corps. The battery commander, a harrassed captain, called on our artillery general as soon as we moved in and said he hoped the general did not mind guns; there were a lot of generals who couldn't sleep on account of the noise and he had had to move twice already. He was like a man apologizing to his new neighbors for having noisy children; he was sensitive. Our general said that the guns were music to his ears, and we all smiled mechanically and obediently. The captain said, "I'm sure glad to hear that, because I feel I have an ideal setup here."

Across the yard from the house, in a small storeroom, lived a donkey so old that he had a gray beard. His hoofs were long and misshapen, like the nails of an old dog who gets no exercise, and he stayed in his gloomy cell, blinking out at the world, without enough energy to walk into the adjoining barn and eat the hay, although he would accept cabbages if they were brought to him.

From the crippled woman's, or man's, house we moved into a region that had been heavily bombed on the first day of the offensive and was completely deserted except for the surviving animals. An officer who had done some reconnoitering had found a hamlet, Chapelle en Litige* (Chapel in Litigation), which was intact. Bombs had fallen into all the adjoining fields and bomb craters had made the roads into it almost impassable, but its half-dozen houses and the dependent barns stood untouched. One officer, who considers the Air Forces a form of artillery totally lacking in professional direction, said, "If they had dropped hundred-pound bombs instead of five-hundred, they'd have killed just as many cows without spoiling the roads."† The façade of the granite house in which we set up shop was hidden by pear trees *en espalier*, laden with fruit and lush with leaves. An old hen had made a nest in a branch under the hayloft window and was rearing her chicks there; they were hard to find, buried among the pears, and produced a noise that was inexplicable to us until we discovered them. Some of the soldiers with us took up quarters in smaller houses, and once they had found niches for themselves, we all strolled about the village looking over the interiors of the houses. The owners had evacuated them in an orderly fashion, taking most of their belongings with them. There was not much left except furniture.

I found a pile of letters, most of them old, a few recent, lying on a dressing table in one of the houses. In a nearby cupboard was a long row of schoolboys' notebooks filled with exercises in drawing, arithmetic, and composition. All the books bore the inscription, written in a hand which became progressively less slack, "Cahier d'Albert Hédouin." A couple of recent business letters were addressed to Veuve Hédouin, and I assumed that Albert was the widow's son. There were also in the cupboard a number of the usual breviaries and cheap books of

*La Chapelle en Juger, which is an older synonym for the same thing, was the right name.
†Brigadier-General (then) Clift Andrus, the 1st Division artillery commander.

devotion, including a pamphlet of prayers for prisoners of war. Idly, because as a camp follower I had nothing else at the moment to do, I took some of the letters and, sitting down on the threshold of the plain little house I was in, started to read them.

One was dated September 25, 1914. It began, "My dear little Louise: I utilize a little moment to send you news of me. I am in good health and hope my letter finds you the same. I'd rather be at Chapelle en Litige than where I am, for it isn't nice to sleep outdoors. If this thing ends soon, I won't be sorry. I am with Anatole and Désiré, and they are in good health, too. Probably the buckwheat has been harvested, if the weather is as good there as it is here. I'd like to help thresh it and drink a big bowl of cider instead of being here, but it's useless to think about it. When you wean the little colt, leave him in the barn for two days, then turn him into the fields of broom, where the donkey is. Put some branches on top of the gate, so he won't try to jump over it. When you get this letter, send me some news of what goes on at home. Have you made a barrel of cider for Pannel yet and have the cows turned out well? Excuse me for being brief, my dear little Louise and cherished babies. I write this letter in the open air, sitting on my knapsack, and now I must go. Your husband, who loves you and kisses you again and again, Louis Hédouin, 336th Infantry. P.S. Put the donkey in Fernand's field."

The next letter was dated in November, 1914, and began, "My dear little Louise: It is with great pleasure I learn that you are in good health. I too am in good health. Dear little Louise, I think you should make at least three barrels of cider, although I know it will give you a lot of trouble. Considering the price of apples and the price of cider, it pays better to make cider than to sell apples. And make a good barrel for us, so that we can have the pleasure of drinking it together when I come home." ("Come home," I thought. "That war had four years to go then.") "My dear little Louise, you tell me that you have planted some wheat. Good. Prices are going up. I hope you have sowed oats, dear one. Dear little Louise, I hope you are well. Also the cows and calves. Butter is selling at a pretty good price, if it can only continue. I was glad to hear you had someone help you thresh the buckwheat. Dear little Louise, I wish I could have been there, but it's useless to think about it. Here one is and here one stays—until when, nobody knows. Your husband, who loves and will never cease to love you and the dear little children, Louis."

Looking up, I saw that four or five cows, probably wanting to be milked, were staring hopefully at me, and I wondered how Louis Hédouin would have felt if he had known that in thirty years not even a woman would be left to care for the cattle in Chapelle en Litige. There was another letter, also written in 1914, in which he said he had been to mass and then eaten some ham dear little Louise had sent him; he would rather have attended mass at home, but it was "useless to think of it."

"Dear little Louise," he went on, "you say you have had a card from Aimable and he is in good health. So much the better, for you can't imagine how unhealthy it is where he finds himself. I couldn't either, unless I had been there, but don't worry, I'm all right. Dear little Louise, you say that Marie has had a letter from Pierre and he is a prisoner. So much the better. That way he is sure to survive. I know that threshing must be a lot of trouble to you. I am sorry you are alone and have so much work to do. Do you remember, on that evening before I want away, Enée said that this business wouldn't be over before Easter? I am afraid he was right. It is sad when I think of it. Days are indeed long. Louis."

And on March 15, 1915, he wrote that he was sorry to hear that Louise was suffering but hoped she would soon be delivered—the first indication I had had that he knew she was pregnant. "My dear little Louise," he continued, "I had a letter from Papa the same time as yours. He says he has sold the old cow for three hundred and forty-five francs. It's not bad, when you think that she only had four teeth left. What about the black cow you thought was going to calve March 8th and what are you doing with the Jersey? Tell me in your next letter. Dear little Louise, you say you have threshed the oats. Good. There must have been some loss, but you did the best you could. The worst of it is we probably won't be home in time for the haying this season. Excuse me for not having written. We were taking ammunition up to the front lines. Lately things go badly. The regiment has refused to march to an attack. Everybody is sick of this business, and we lose courage and ask for an end of this terrible war. A sweet kiss from your husband, Louis."

Then, on the twenty-second of March, the latest date I found on any of his letters, Hédouin wrote, "My dear little Louise: I have received with great pleasure your letter of the eighteenth. Your mother writes to me that you have had a nine-pound boy and are doing well, and the boy, too. My dear little Louise, you did well to have a midwife from Remilly, and she didn't charge much, either—eight francs. My dear little Louise, I'd like to be with you, but it's useless to think of it. Distance keeps us apart. I hope God will help you in your troubles. My parents write me that at home people are saying this will end soon. So much the better. Dear little Louise, the boy will be called Albert. Before telling you, I waited to see whether you would have a boy or a girl. Your husband, who loves you, Louis. P.S. What about the black cow?"

Nineteen-fifteen. I did a bit of subtraction. Albert would have been twenty-four in 1939—just the right age. I thought of the graded notebooks and the pamphlet of prayers for prisoners of war.

Letter from Paris

SEPTEMBER 1 (BY WIRELESS)

For the first time in my life and probably the last, I have lived for a week in a great city where everybody is happy. Moreover, since this city is Paris, everybody makes this euphoria manifest. To drive along the boulevards in a jeep is like walking into some as yet unmade René Clair film, with hundreds of bicyclists coming toward you in a stream that divides before the jeep just when you feel sure that a collision is imminent. Among the bicyclists there are pretty girls, their hair dressed high on their heads in what seems to be the current mode here. These girls show legs of a length and slimness and firmness and brownness never associated with French womanhood. Food restrictions and the amount of bicycling that is necessary in getting around in a big city without any other means of transportation have endowed these girls with the best figures in the world, which they will doubtless be glad to trade in for three square meals, plentiful supplies of chocolate, and a seat in the family Citroën as soon as the situation becomes more normal. There are handsome young matrons with children mounted behind them on their bikes, and there are husky young workmen, stubby little *employés de bureau* in striped pants, and old professors in wing collars and chin whiskers, all of them smiling and all of them lifting their right hands from the handlebars to wave as they go past. The most frequently repeated phrase of the week is "*Enfin on respire,*" (At last, one breathes!)

Happiest of all, in the French film manner, are the police, who stand at street intersections with their thumbs in their belts and beam paternally at everybody instead of looking stern and important, as they used to. Cyclists wave to them appreciatively. When, occasionally, a truck passes through a street, taking policemen to their beats, people standing on the café *terrasses* applaud and shout "*Vive la police!*" For Paris, where the street cry has always been "*A bas les flics!*" (Down with the cops!), this is behavior so unprecedented that the cops sometimes look as though they think it is all a dream. There is good reason for the change of heart; for the first time since Etienne Marcel led a street mob against the royal court in about 1350, the police and the people have been on the same side of the barricades. It was the police who, on August 15th, gave the signal for a mass disregard of the Germans by going on strike. It was also the police who, four days later, began the street fighting by seizing the Prefecture of the Seine, their headquarters, across the square from Notre Dame on the Ile de la Cité. Three thousand of them, in plainclothes and armed with carbines, revolvers, and a few sub-machine guns, took the place over and defended it successfully for six days before being relieved by the arrival of the French armored division of General Leclerc. This was the largest centre of patriot resistance during the struggle. Because it is in the middle of the city, it was the knot that kept the network of patriot strongpoints together. The Germans held fortresses in the Place de la Concorde, the Place St. Michel, the Luxembourg Gardens, and along the Rue de Rivoli. Von Choltitz, the German military governor of the city, was finally captured by soldiers of the armored division in the Hôtel Meurice, and the Crillon was fought for as though it were a blockhouse. During the five days of fighting before the first elements of Allied troops began to penetrate the city, the Germans sallied from their strongpoints in tanks and systematically shot up the town. The Forces Françaises de l'Intérieur had erected barricades to stop the tanks, and boys fourteen or fifteen years old, with courage that was more than a riposte to the fanaticism of the Hitler Jugend, often destroyed tanks by throwing bottles of incendiary fluid through their ports. The bottles were usually filled with mixtures prepared by neighborhood druggists. The youngsters who did the fighting were not always of the type that is ordinarily on good terms with the police. They included the problem children of every neighborhood as well as students and factory workers. So the oldest of all Paris feuds has ended.

It has perhaps already been hinted in the New York press that our army had not expected to take Paris quite so soon. The city was to be bypassed and encircled to save it from street fighting, on the theory that the last elements of the German garrison would withdraw just before being cut off. Thus a certain amount of damage to the city's buildings would be prevented, unless, of course, the Germans mined them before departing. As it turned out, the Germans laid mines, all right, but they didn't set them off because they were caught sitting on them. There were ten tons of explosives in the vaults under the Senate alone. But none of this is so important for the future of the world as the fact that the French saved their self-respect forever by going into the streets and fighting. The F.F.I.s were already in control of the city when the regular troops arrived, they like to tell you when you talk with them in the cafés. And, with a fine bit of military courtesy, the Allied Command, when it was informed that conditions in Paris called for an immediate move, sent in Leclerc's division first. Frenchmen had begun the liberation of Paris; other Frenchmen completed it. As a result, the Parisians are happy not only because of the liberation but because they feel they earned it.

The gratitude toward Americans is immense and sometimes embarrassing in its manifestations. People are always stopping one in the street, pumping one's hand, and saying "Thank you." It is useless to protest. To the Parisians, and especially to the children, all Americans are now *héros du cinéma*. This is particularly disconcerting to sensitive war correspondents, if any, aware, as they are, that these innocent thanks belong to those American combat troops who won the beachhead and then made the breakthrough. There are few such men in Paris. Young women, the first day or two after the Allies arrived, were as enthusiastic as children; they covered the cheeks of French and American soldiers alike with lipstick. This stage of Franco-American relations is approaching an end. Children, however, still follow the American soldiers everywhere, singing the "Marseillaise" and hopefully eyeing pockets from which they think gum might emerge. And it is still hard for an American who speaks French to pay for a drink in a bar.

The city is resuming normal life with a speed I would never have believed possible. The noise of battle has receded and the only visible reminders of the recent fighting are some damaged buildings, holes in a few streets, and a considerable number of captured German automobiles dashing about loaded with F.F.I.s and their girls, all wearing tricolor brassards and festooned with German machine pistols, Lugers, and grenades. French adolescents have for years been deprived of the simple pleasure of riding about on four wheels, and if they seem to find an excessive number of military missions for themselves, all of which involve riding down the boulevards and cheering, nobody can blame them. Until very recently they seemed to have great difficulty in resisting the equally natural temptation to shoot off their new weapons, and every day sounded like the Fourth of July, but the F.F.I., whose officers are serious soldiers, is now being absorbed into the French Army and the promiscuous shooting has come to an end. On a shattered concrete pillbox in the Place de la Concorde some playful fellow has printed, in chalk, "Liquidation. To rent, forty thousand francs." And, as I write, a painter is relettering "Guaranty Trust of New York" on the building next to the Crillon that the bank occupied before we went to war.

The physical conditions of life here are not too bad. Paris was spared the most uncomfortable experience a big modern city can have, for the water system has continued to work, a very important factor not only in sanitation but morale. Only a limited quantity of electricity is available; the power plants and distributing system are in good shape, but the hydroelectric power from central France is no longer coming in and there is a very small supply of fuel. Consequently, lights are on for only about two hours every evening, except in government offices. There is as yet no gas for cooking, but it has been promised that there soon will be. For that matter, there is not very much to cook; the city had no more than a two weeks' supply of strictly necessary foods when the liberators entered it, and though the American and French authorities have been steadily pumping food into the town, there is not yet enough for the reëstablishment of good eating at home, let alone good restaurant life. Only a few small black-market restaurants still exist. The price of *petit salé* (a kind of New England boiled dinner), one pear, and a half bottle of Bordeaux is seven hundred francs. This is the best fare you can get, and seven hundred francs, just to remind you, is fourteen dollars. Butter is four hundred francs a pound. However, the day of the black-market people is ending, because there are great quantities of butter, meat, and vegetables in Normandy, Brittany, and Anjou at about an eighth of Paris prices, and bringing them here is now simply a matter of transportation. Considering that all this food is only fifty to a hundred and fifty miles away, there is little reason to doubt that the problem will soon be solved. A decent pair of leather shoes costs a hundred dollars, a man's suit three hundred, and a portable typewriter five hundred and sixty. My advice to the Frenchman who wants any of these things is to do without for a few weeks, because such a situation can last only under the rule of the Germans, who drain a country dry of everything except grace, beauty, and good sense. The German occupation gave the black market a sort of moral sanction here. In Britain the feeling has been, ever since the blitz days, that a man who bought in the black market deprived other Britons of their share. Here people said, truthfully enough, that if you had money and didn't buy in the black market, what you wanted to buy would simply go to Germany. The black-market operators themselves are an unprepossessing lot, however, and a visit to a black-market restaurant will quickly convince anyone that a fair proportion of the patrons are engaged in other branches of the same racket.

The question of what is to be done with all this group is receiving considerable attention in the new French press. There are already eleven dailies in Paris, all almost direct offshoots of the clandestine resistance papers. Only three bear names well known before the war—the conservative *Figaro*, the Communist *L'Humanité*, and the Socialist *Le Populaire*. These three had been suppressed by Vichy, but *Populaire* and *Humanité* became as powerful as ever in their clandestine editions. Others, like *Combat*, *Libération*, and *Franc-Tireur*, are resistance papers appearing for the first time above ground and in full size. The editorial offices and printing plants of the big collaborationist papers have been handed over to the newcomers. *Populaire*, for example, is now published in the plant of *Le Matin*, on the Boulevard Poissonnière. The new papers have from the beginning taken divergent political lines; in the cases of *Figaro*, *Humanité*, and *Populaire*, it would perhaps be better to say that they have resumed them. They are in complete accord, however, on the prestige and position of General de Gaulle and his provisional government. So is every man, woman, and child I have heard speak of de Gaulle or his government in Paris. The man's prestige is so vast that it is slightly nauseating now to think of the "opposition" to him that rich Frenchmen were still telling credulous friends about in London and Washington only a few months ago. He put the seal on a personal legend last Saturday, when, on foot and towering above a couple of million compatriots, he led a parade down the Champs-Elysées and as far as Notre Dame, where he listened to the Te Deum while snipers and F.F.I.s exchanged shots around him. Such overwhelming popularity may in time prove to be a handicap to him; he must eventually disappoint some of the people who now expect irreconcilable things of him. His hold on the public could not possibly be greater. A united France has crystallized around him.

While de Gaulle led the march, a few Americans were otherwise engaged.

Day of Victory

AUGUST 26, 1944, the day after the official Liberation of Paris, was a brilliant, sunny Saturday. Allardyce Meecham, a war correspondent who had once been a dramatic critic in New York, descended the fifth, and last, flight of steps between the floor on which he had been billeted and the lobby of the Hotel Scribe. Meecham, an awkward, red-haired man of forty-three, felt himself an unimpressive representative of a victorious army, and his futile wait for the lift, which was apparently out of order, had accented his sensation of inadequacy. He had arrived in Paris early that morning. All of his colleagues he had encountered since getting to the Scribe had, by their telling, acted as advance scouts for motorized-cavalry units and infiltrated into the city on Tuesday, Wednesday, or Thursday, before the surrender of the German garrison, which had taken place on Friday. Meecham had missed even that. He had gone off on a side trip into lower Brittany early in the week and had not known that Paris was going to be liberated until it was too late for him to precede even the Public Relations officers. On his way into the freed capital, with some officers from a corps in Brittany who had no real business in Paris but wanted to see the fun, he had felt guilty because, although he complained in a loud tone about having missed the big moment, he knew in his heart that he was content to have the combat troops go first. Not once, in two months of war, had he arrived in a town alone in time to receive the surrender of an S.S. Panzer division, an experience apparently banal for Hearst correspondents. When, on a single occasion, at St.-Lô, he had inadvertently got into a bad spot, he had been so shaken that he had been unable to write the story.

Meecham was dressed in a tanker's combat jacket and a pair of dress-pink trousers, an incongruity caused by the circumstance that he had left his Class A uniform blouse hanging in the closet of a hotel in Angers, while the G.I. pants he generally wore with the combat jacket were in his estimation too dirty to wear in Paris. He had been a bit muddled with drink on leaving Angers and had forgotten the blouse. On his head he wore a helmet liner. His only overseas cap was in the pocket of the blouse in Angers.

When Meecham reached the lobby which was crowded with victorious correspondents and Public Relations officers, he pretended to be preoccupied and in a hurry, since he didn't want to hear them make light of their thrilling experiences and had none of his own to depreciate. As he made for the revolving door to the street, however, he was blocked off by Wallaby Bates, an Australian correspondent for a London newspaper, who was wearing British battle dress fronted by a landing net of ribbons from the last war. Wallaby shouted, in a concerned voice, "I say, Meech, haven't seen Larry Boddlebaum, have you? Our jeeps were cracking along on the way in from Chartres last week. Heard there were only a couple of middle-drawer Hun divisions left in Paris, so we thought we'd disregard them, what? Larry's jeep was behind mine, and as I went past an intersection, I saw a lot of their chaps around a dinkum super Mark VI tank—p'raps a Mark VII or VIII. I didn't have a chance for a proper dinkum look-see, what? I heard a spot of machine-gun fire behind me, and I wonder if poor old Larry copped it."

Meecham mumbled apologetically that he hadn't seen Mr. Boddlebaum, and hurried on toward the door. Just outside, he stepped on the heels of an oldish man in a costume that included a floppy garrison cap, worn fighter-pilot style, parachutist's boots, the patches of two armored divisions, one on each shoulder, and a new bit of purple ribbon. This was Larry Boddlebaum, war correspondent for a magazine popularizing scientific research and for another devoted to homemaking, to each of which he contributed one article a month. He had worn the purple ribbon ever since, in a black-out in Normandy, he had fallen over a latrine made from a packing box.

Boddlebaum turned in some irritation, but on recognizing Allardyce Meecham, he put on an expression of hearty good humor. "Why, if it isn't old Meech!" he shouted. "Haven't seen old Wallaby Bates, by any chance, have you? Wallaby and I were hightailing along a road near Fountainblue a few days ago, meaning to get under a parachute drop that we heard the boys were going to make behind the kraut line, him in one jeep and me in another. Next thing I knew, I was looking into

the muzzle of an eighty-eight, but I ducked into the brush just
as the thing went off. Haven't heard of poor old Wallaby
since."

"He's just inside the door, looking for you," Meecham said.

Boddlebaum did not seem as pleased as one might have expected. He waved his hand, with a gesture which Meecham interpreted as a dismissal, and turned to a group of three woman
correspondents, whom he halted with outflung arms and
shouts of greeting. Meecham, as he walked away, heard him
shout, "Haven't any of you girls seen old Wallaby Bates, have
you?"

The sidewalk and street in front of the hotel were crowded
with cheering, chattering, happy people who enthusiastically
waved their hands with fingers spread in the V sign whenever
they thought they saw a correspondent or a jeep driver look at
them. They left no path for jeeps and command cars, barely
parting before each arriving vehicle. "*Vive l'Amérique!*" a man
wearing a tricolor brassard marked "F.F.I." shouted. "*Vive
Roosevelt!*" He rushed at Meecham and seized him by the right
hand, which he clasped fervently. From the strength of the
man's clutch, Meecham deduced that he must once have been
a weight-lifter. Meecham's wife, a woman of such strong character that he never audibly disagreed with her, detested Roosevelt, so now he answered simply, "*Vive la France!*" Then,
perhaps because he, too, had begun to feel liberated, he said
boldly, "*Vive Roosevelt pour moi aussi!*" The man, still crushing
his hand, said, "He speaks French admirably!"

A young woman with bare brown legs and green wooden
earrings threw her bare arms around Meecham and forcefully
kissed him on the left side of his face. A taller young woman,
on whose equally brown limbs blond hairs glinted delightfully,
closed on Meecham from the right and kissed him on that side
of his face, pressing so hard he could feel her teeth through her
lips and letting her mouth stay against his cheek for an extra
second. The F.F.I. man cried, "Honor to the liberators!"
Meecham started to say, "I have done nothing. I am only a
journalist," but he couldn't speak French fast enough. By the
time he had said "nothing," the first young woman cried, "He

is modest! He is adorable!.," and kissed him again, this time on
the left temple, knocking the helmet liner over his right eye.

"How tall they are!" exclaimed a third woman, throwing
her arms about Meecham's neck and pulling his head forward,
while the F.F.I. man and the barelegged girls still hung on.
The woman kissed him firmly on the forehead. "Look! He has
lipstick all over!" a female voice farther back in the crowd
squealed.

Meecham, feeling the man's grip ease, managed to break
away and straighten the helmet liner. He grabbed a handkerchief from his hip pocket and made a motion to wipe the lipstick from his face, but there was a chorus of protesting voices
—"No, no, don't do that." To humor his admirers, Meecham
dropped his hand and stumbled on, the handkerchief still in
his fist. He was exhilarated in a way new to him. He had never
before experienced a manifestation of public approval, except
after a lecture at a women's club in Greenwich. That, since he
had been paid for his services, had been relatively tepid. None
of the clubwomen had offered to kiss him, and he could not
recall having regretted this omission.

As he turned the corner into the Boulevard des Capucines,
his insufficiency as a newspaperman no longer weighed upon
him. The press services would have kept his paper covered on
the spot news of the liberation of Paris, he knew. What his editor wanted of him, he reflected with satisfaction, was something more subtle. This was the sequel to a Greek drama—this
was "Prometheus Unbound." Replacing the handkerchief in
his pocket, he stopped, took out a pencil and a Press Wireless
blank, and wrote down the phrase. A woman grabbed him and
kissed him before he had finished. Another, looking up at him,
could not find a free space to leave her mark—she had, he noticed, a rather large mouth with flaring lips—so she took a
handkerchief out of her handbag, spat on it, and scrubbed
away at his face until she had cleared a sufficient area. Then
she, too, kissed him.

Feeling pleased but silly, Meecham moved on to the front of
the Café de la Paix. It was not open for business officially, but
a number of American officers and several correspondents
were already seated at tables on the terrace, and when he went

to the door and talked to the manager standing there, he obtained the privilege of buying a glass of white wine for thirty
francs. A waiter brought it to him at a table, and he began to
think out a lead for his story—something about how it was the
beginning of a return to normal when an American could
again sit at a table at the Café de la Paix and wait for everybody he knew in the world to come walking by. He wrote it
down.

When he had finished the glass of wine, he had another. He
called over a news vendor and bought a paper, one of the new
Resistance ones he had never heard of. General de Gaulle, he
read, was to lead a great procession that afternoon down the
Champs-Elysées and through the center of Paris to Notre
Dame, where there would be a solemn Te Deum of victory.
His French was really not too bad, especially after this two-
month refresher course, which had begun in Normandy in
June. The Te Deum would be the symbolic highlight of the
liberation, Meecham decided, and he would build his color
story around it. He had a third glass of wine and thought the
story might turn out better than Will Irwin's account of the
San Francisco earthquake. "Will Irwin once wrote a great story
and called it 'The City That Was,'" he would begin. "This is
the story of a City That Once Again Is." He had always liked
newspaper stories that began "This is the story of" and then
went on to whatever they were stories of. Stark. The lead
about sitting at the Café de la Paix was less stark, but too good
to throw away, he decided, so he might just as well use it further down in the story. Two women war correspondents from
the Midwest walked up and looked at his lipsticked face disapprovingly. "Having a good time?" one of them said. He didn't
ask them to sit down because they reminded him of his wife, a
magazine executive who always referred to herself as a gal.

One of Meecham's chief talking points, in persuading his
editor to send him to Europe, had been his familiarity with
France, a theme on which he had expanded until even he had
begun to forget that it was based wholly on a summer-vacation
trip taken between his freshman and sophomore years at college. But he had now begun to feel quite honestly at home.
After one more glass of wine, he started into the complex of

streets that begins in back of the Grand Hotel and that he thought he remembered led off in the general direction of the Champs-Elysées, where he intended to arrive in time for the procession. On the way, he thought, he might be able to find a restaurant at which to eat. He could also stop in some *bistros* and collect some good quaint quotes.

All the shops and all the restaurants that he passed were closed. The proprietors had lowered the shutters during the sporadic street fighting, which had ended only on the previous day, and had not yet opened them again. But a number of the little bars were doing business. Meecham went into one near the Rue Caumartin. On the customers' side of the short metal counter at the front of the place he saw a small Chinese and a bulky Frenchman with a mouth that stuck out like a door-knob. The Frenchman wore a jersey and beret, and when Meecham entered, he was showing something to the proprietor, a little snipe-nosed man who, on his side of the bar, was wiping glasses. When Meecham came closer, he could see that the man held out on an upturned palm a very small automatic pistol. "It was tough on the Place de la République," the man was saying. "*Ça ratatinait.*" The word sounded so much like machine-gun fire that Meecham got the idea immediately. "*Ça ratatinait*, my boy," the man repeated, "but the boys of the République, huh, the little old kids of the neighborhood— well, *Ça ratatinait.* I got one *Schleuh* myself, species of a *Fridolin*, what! He was coming out of the subway station and he tried to run away, but I got him! Of course, there has been some criticism among the neighbors because he was so old and, according to what they say, inoffensive. Evil tongues— ambushed enemies of the Resistance. Nearly seventy years old he was, a sort of clerk. He had been billeted in a hotel in the neighborhood, it appears, for four years. But a Boche, what! How could I know he wasn't preparing something nasty? He could have turned on me, if he had been armed, huh?"

"You were right," the proprietor said. "You killed him with that gun?"

"And how!" the bulky man said. The Chinese giggled.

When Meecham ordered a glass of wine, the proprietor said it was on the house. The Chinese said, "Next one is on me. All Allies." The bulky man was cool for a moment, as if he feared the arrival of an American might divert attention from his recital. Soon, however, he sensed the new tactical opportunity and began to tell Meecham the story from the beginning. The proprietor and the Chinese looked as if they were trying to think of something else while he talked. Probably they had already heard him through several times. "*Ça ratatinait*," the man said. And again, "*Ça ratatinait.*" While he was talking, they drank the Chinaman's round, and when the story was finished, Meecham bought one. Then the big man and the Chinese went out.

"He wouldn't buy a round, that one," said the proprietor, looking after the big man. "A dirty type. I'll bet he was a police spy before the Germans surrendered. He probably killed the old man to create himself a character as a patriot."

Meecham and the proprietor had another drink together. Meecham was now feeling the heat. It was high noon.

"I say, you're well arranged," the proprietor said, making his first allusion to the marks on Meecham's face. "The girls have been kind to you, what? You look like a real Red Indian in war paint."

"Perhaps I'd better wash it off," Meecham said.

"Sure. Then they can begin again. There's a washbasin in the back there."

After Meecham had washed, he felt a bit fresher, and asked the proprietor if he knew where there was a good restaurant open.

"It would be difficult to say, today," the proprietor said judicially, "but there is a black-market joint not far from here that I think will not be closed. The prices are horrible, of course. Take your right to the next street and then your right again until the next street and then your left for a hundred metres, and there you are."

Meecham had no trouble finding the place. It was a small restaurant with threadbare vestiges of chic. The plush on the divans was worn and footpaths were frayed across the pile of the carpets. The maître d'hôtel showed a black bow tie and a yellowish dickey under his white summer jacket. One American had already found the place before Meecham got there. Seated on the divan at the rear of the room, which was rather wide than deep, was a colonel named Rushby, one of the officers who had driven up from Brittany with Meecham. He was with a very pretty girl, Meecham noticed at once. The restaurant was full, and the maître d'hôtel said, "I regret, but we are complete for the moment."

"I will wait," Meecham said. "I have not seen any other restaurant in the quarter." He hoped Rushby would see him standing, since he might then feel obliged to ask him over. He felt sure that the Colonel did not want to be interrupted.

Before Rushby did see Meecham, a sleek Frenchman sitting alone at a table near the door rose and approached him. "Perhaps the gentleman would not mind sitting with me," he said. "It is ironic that on the day of victory one of our liberators should not find a place in a restaurant." The well-fed man was the only customer who had paid any heed to Meecham's entrance; the others—women of expensive appearance and men who looked as if they spent much of their time in barbers' chairs—seemed to pretend not to see him. "Certainly, M. Philippe," the maître d'hôtel said to the well-fed man, and Meecham said he would be delighted. When the two sat down, M. Philippe asked Meecham to share a bottle of nonvintage champagne that had just been opened for him. "It's not what I would have had with my lunch before the war," he said with resignation, "but *à la guerre comme à la guerre.*" Meecham smiled politely, and his host said, "You understand French admirably." When M. Philippe had filled Meecham's glass, he said, as if he were enunciating something startling, "To tell the truth, I am very glad to see American uniforms here. At least, you will be able to defend us from the Communists. The French, you know, Monsieur, are a very undisciplined people. They need a firm hand over them. The Germans could have taught us some valuable lessons, if we had been willing to learn."

"But Hitler—" Meecham began.

"Oh, I do not say there were not some portions of the doctrine that were perhaps excessive," M. Philippe said, refilling the glass the correspondent had just emptied. "But it is necessary to be a civilized being. Have you observed the condition of the streets, Monsieur? Paving stones torn up for barricades, burned-out tanks, barbed wire? All totally unnecessary."

Just as Meecham began to feel uncomfortable, he heard his name called in a loud voice. It was Colonel Rushby, yelling, "Hi ya, Meech! Come over here and help me talk to Michèle. She don't savvy coochy avec mwah."

Meecham got up and said to M. Philippe, "I am sorry, but I must go and have lunch with my friends. I had not seen them before."

"It is a pity," M. Philippe said with a wave of his hand, and went on placing creamed mushrooms inside his face.

Meecham, who was not quite sober, recognized without difficulty that Rushby was quite drunk. Michèle was a brunette with a triangular Hispanic face and a Lupe Velez coiffure. Girls in Paris, like those in New York, often styled themselves after Hollywood stars, Meecham already had noticed, but since they had seen no American films for five years, they imitated stars of an older vintage. He ordered food for three. Rushby had wanted only drink, and the girl had been afraid to order food for fear that the Colonel might not pay for it. The luncheon— roast pork, creamed mushrooms, and chocolate éclairs—was not the sort of thing Meecham would have expected in a good French restaurant, but it seemed to fit the pomaded clientele.* Rushby did not refuse to eat, and the food seemed to sober him somewhat. "Suppose we both got a girl," he said to Meecham. "You got to stick to me. I can't talk to these frogs. Maybe this babe has a friend." Michèle said all the girls she knew had by this time probably gone to watch the parade. "But there will be plenty in the streets," she said. "All you have to do is ask. You must stay with us, else I am afraid. I do not understand what he says. I thought it would be amusing not to understand, but it is rather frightening." Meecham had by this time decided that it was not essential that he literally see the parade. The feel of the city is what counts for *my* story, he told himself. He took the check, since it turned out that Rushby had only a few hundred francs. It came to about three thousand francs, which was sixty dollars of his newspaper's

---

*Fats and sweets were the rarest and dearest forms of food in a rationed society and were accordingly the most chic among profiteers and racketeers of the Occupation.

money. "They are giving you a special discount," Michèle said, seriously. "They are very decent." After the bill had been paid, they had a round of brandies on the house and then went out into the street arm in arm, Michèle between the two men.

The sun streamed down, the streets were full of holiday-makers, and Meecham, for the first time since he had left the Place de l'Opéra, was certain where he was—he could see the Madeleine. However the customers in the restaurant may have felt about the Liberation, these crowds in the street—parents with their children, girls with arms intertwined, larking young men in their shirtsleeves marked with tri-color brassards— were unaffectedly happy. They flocked down the Rue Royale and all the transverse streets leading to de Gaulle's line of march. Meecham could have found plenty of color to write about if he had any longer been looking for it. But now he was looking for a girl. There were, of course, hundreds, but they all seemed to be escorted or to be travelling in groups. He hesitated to approach a band and try to cut out one individual. Ordinarily, he would have given up the idea, but the drink, the sun, and the feeling of being a hero in the eyes of these happy people made him a man his wife would have recognized with difficulty. Rushby urged him on. "Go on and get yourself a number," he kept saying. "I'm going nuts out here in the sun."

Meecham fixed his attention on two tall girls, a blonde and a redhead, who were staring at his little group and smiling. They looked, he thought, like two unusually nice stenographers just back from a holiday at the seashore, brown and summery. The redhead was being Joan Crawford; the blonde was being either just herself or an imitation of some star Meecham did not recognize. "Come here!" he said to the blonde abruptly, remembering to use the familiar form of the imperative verb. "Come with us. It is the day of victory." Unhesitantly, the girl came to them. The redhead walked away into the crowd.

The girl took Meecham's arm, and now the four proceeded two by two, with Michèle and Rushby in front. "I know a hotel near here," Michèle said. "Lead on," said Meecham, now authoritative. He translated Michèle's remark to Rushby, who said, "That's swell!" The blonde said nothing, but clasped Meecham's arm as if she wanted to convert herself into a tourniquet.

In the hotel, it was cool behind Venetian blinds that had been kept closed against the sun all day. Meecham and the blonde had a room that was draped and furnished in imitation of the interior of a sheik's tent, but had a modern bed. There was a silver-framed photograph of Rudolph Valentino on a wall. To Meecham, the place seemed unconventional.

"What do you do when there is no holiday?" Meecham asked the girl, when they had become a little used to each other. "Do you work in an office?"

"No," the girl said. "I work in a house on the Rue Pigalle, and my sister, the redhead, and I had looked forward to twenty-four hours without men. Besides, I very much wanted to see General de Gaulle. But on the day of victory, I cannot refuse anything to one of our liberators."

Meecham had already begun to think of seeing the girl often during his stay in Paris, but a mistress in a brothel did not sound practicable. Afterward, though, he began to think of what a fine anecdote this experience would make, and was pleased.

Meecham ordered a bottle of champagne. It was brought up to the room and served by the housekeeper, a stout woman who was dressed in a kind of operetta maid's costume. After they had drunk a couple of glasses, they were tranquil, almost as if the champagne had been a sleeping potion, until what seemed a great noise of small-arms fire broke out over in the direction of the line of march. The sound was repeated and unmistakable. Yet inside the factitious Arab tent, war seemed a dream of the night before last. It couldn't be the Germans coming back, Meecham thought, reasonably. Even if the military situation had not precluded such a return, there would have been much artillery fire before they could reach the heart of the city. "It's the Militia, the murderers," the girl said. "There are plenty of them disguised with Resistance brassards now. They are shooting at the crowd because it is happy. And the real F.F.I.s must be shooting back. Stay here." Meecham had made no move to go.

In a couple of moments there came a burst of knocks at the

door, and the housekeeper precipitated herself into the room without even asking pardon. "Come quick!" she cried. "Your friend the Colonel has gone mad. He will get us all killed!" She pulled Meecham by the leg. He reached for his trousers, but the woman said quickly, "There is no time for that. Have you gone mad, too? He has a revolver and he is trying to fire out of the window of his room at some F.F.I. guards on a roof who he thinks are snipers."

The blonde understood. Parisians appeared to react quickly to such situations, Meecham thought afterward. "He has no uniform on!" the blonde wailed. "They will see a man shooting and they will turn a machine gun on the house! Madame is right! We shall all be killed." The women ran out through the door, and Meecham followed them.

They entered another door, and he followed them again. The room in which he now found himself, he at once noted, was lined with mirrors. The ceiling and all the walls reflected a sculpturelike group of struggling figures, most of them nude. Rushby's was dominant. The Colonel, a tall man and an extraordinarily hairy one, was holding his Colt .45 at arm's length over his head to keep it away from the four women who surrounded him. Michèle had grabbed him around the knees and the housekeeper had tackled him waist-high—to prevent his progress to the window, Meecham supposed—while the proprietress of the establishment, a rather elegant female in an evening gown, had slipped her arms around his chest from the rear, and the blonde girl, who was tall for a woman, jumped again and again at the revolver hand. As Meecham watched, the whole mass swayed and went down, and there was an explosion comparable to that a howitzer might make in a less confined space. The pistol, describing a high arc, soared toward him and fell near his feet. There was broken glass around, some of it powdered so fine it looked like synthetic Christmas-tree snow. The bullet had hit one of the wall mirrors. Meecham stumbled toward the recumbent group and started to pull women to their feet like a football referee endeavoring to find who has the ball at the bottom of the pile. When he got down to Rushby, the Colonel was snoring peacefully.*

*His head had hit the bidet.

Meecham and the women picked him up and laid him out on the bed, and a couple of hours later he was able to walk out almost sober. That must have been at about five o'clock, which was eleven A.M., Eastern War Time.

At 10 P.M., Eastern War Time, a copy boy began to lay takes of Meecham's story on the desk of his cable editor in New York.

"Will Irwin once wrote story called citythatwas," the lead began. "This is story of city that is again period bullets militia disguised as efefeye failed mar this sequel greek drama which originally never had such happy ending period this was prometheus unbound period it was throbbing heart-warming day of victory period burnedout tanks lay scattered about streets in front cafe de la paix like bits broken glass."

6

Massacre

I REMAINED in Paris, to report on political things, while my young friend David Lardner, who had come over for the purpose, relieved me as correspondent of *The New Yorker* with the Armies. Dave, extremely nearsighted, had been rejected from service, but was desperately keen to risk his skin. He was killed at Aachen in Germany when the jeep in which he was riding ran on a mine. He was one of the best.

With a photographer of a newly set up French War Crimes Commission, I made a trip to the Côte-d'Or, a region that, like Rennes, I had known in happier days. After I returned to Paris and wrote the following despatch, I went home, and missed the Battle of the Bulge. I never came back to the war. Before I could feel sufficiently ashamed for that, it was over.

The Events at Comblanchien— November, 1944

THE commune of Comblanchien, in the Department of the Côte-d'Or, lies on the stretch of the National Highway that runs between Lyon, to the south, and Dijon, to the north. Comblanchien is six miles north of Beaune and three miles south of Nuits-St. Georges, in the Burgundy wine country. The commune has an area of a thousand acres; most of them are on the eastern side of the highway, falling away gently toward the railway that parallels the road at a distance of half a mile and forms Comblanchien's eastern boundary. A narrower strip of the village lies west of the highway, and in this direction the ground slopes up and more abruptly. A hundred feet above the road on this side there is a big, box-like, gray-and-white building which the people of the countryside call a château but which looks more like an old-fashioned American summer-resort hotel. From a small cupola on the roof of this building there is an excellent view of the surrounding country. The thousand acres are, except for a few fields of cabbages and sugar beets and the open mouths of four or five granite quarries, fairly well covered with grapevines, as one might expect in this region. The Comblanchien granite has more than a local reputation and when transportation was available it was sent as far away as Paris. The wines of Comblanchien are classed among the Côte de Nuits, but they are a secondary *cru* and have no such fame as those of Vosne-Romanée and Vougeot, both nearby communes. The wines bring good prices but not the extravagant sums that make the heir to a few acres in one of those more favored communities a rich man by birth. The village had five hundred and twenty inhabitants according to the last census, but it has rather fewer now. None of them are what the French call "rich rich," but a few are comfortably off. The proprietors of the Comblanchien vineyards work with their hands, like their hired help. The stone quarries are owned by outside companies and worked by employees who get modest wages. What distinguishes Comblanchien from other communities in the region is the burned-out shells of its houses.

There are perhaps a hundred houses in Comblanchien. About fifty of them are strung out along the highway; the rest are either scattered or grouped in clumps of two or three among the vineyards and fields that extend from the highway down to the railroad. Forty of the fifty on the highway are now in ruins. One of the town's three cafés and one of its three general stores have survived. Its one church is burned out, and so is the post office. The part of the community back among the vines and fields has suffered less; there are about a dozen charred ruins here and there. At one side of the road, as you come into town from the north, you see a rude sign that says, "Honor to all our liberators, who will avenge the martyrs of our dear village. Long live Comblanchien. Long live France. Long live de Gaulle."

"The events at Comblanchien" or the "things that happened at Comblanchien," as they are usually called by the people of the countryside, have some of the elements of a mystery story. Around nine-thirty on the night of August 21, 1944, about two weeks before the liberation of the region, some German soldiers disembarked from a troop train that had halted in the village and, together with the Germans from other detachments in the vicinity, set fire to many of the houses, after killing all the miserable people they caught in them. Most of the other inhabitants of Comblanchien had hidden in the vineyards, and toward morning the Germans went away. The German authorities never offered any explanation of the attack, and the Mayor of Comblanchien, a timid man, never asked for any. There was nothing to stop the Germans from coming back and completing the massacre by daylight, but they didn't. The people of Comblanchien continued to work in the vineyards by day and sleep there at night until the region was liberated. Then M. Jordan, a sergeant of the gendarmes in Corgoloin, a village near Comblanchien, started an investigation to establish what had happened. Comblanchien has no *gendarmerie* of its own, because it is not large enough; it has only a *garde-champêtre*, or constable. Jordan, who was in the Maquis, had been hiding in the vineyards on the night of the attack. He came out of his hiding place when he saw the fires and, slipping around among the Germans, he heard them crying, "*Hunde! Schweine! Schweine! Terroristen! Hunde!*" "I think it was because they were so frightened," he said afterward. "It is unimaginable how frightened they were." He has not been able to discover any other motive for the massacre.

Comblanchien, for four years after the Germans marched into Burgundy, in June, 1940, was without a history, but it was not happy. Like thousands of other communities in France, it had an unending premonition of outrage. All through the land, fear was the most nearly intolerable feature of the occupation. France was a kidnapped country; the kidnapper might let her live in a locked room, but when rescue seemed at hand the kidnapper might try to kill her. Everyone had the feeling that the Germans might arrest or kill anybody, at any time, for no reason that would make sense to a civilized man. Materially, life was difficult. In Comblanchien there was more food than in a big city, but only the farmers really had enough. The quarry workers earned seven francs an hour, but the purchasing power of the franc had almost vanished, so textiles and matches and tools and clothing and tea and coffee, which came from outside Comblanchien, cost incredible amounts. These workers, who had only little patches of ground in which to grow things, could raise just a few vegetables and rabbits and chickens. They ate the vegetables and bartered their chickens and eggs and rabbits for such treasures as spools of thread to repair their clothes, or bits of leather with which the Comblanchien cobbler could patch their shoes. They seldom got meat and, though they lived in a wine-growing district, they rarely could afford to drink wine. The vineyard workers were in much the same predicament. Many couples in Comblanchien serve both the regional industries; the husband works in a quarry and the wife works in the vineyards. The commune owns some woods, and on Sunday the laborers of Comblanchien would cut enough firewood to last them the week. The buses which ran along the highway were infrequent and overcrowded; the men and women who were employed in other villages of the region couldn't be sure that they could ride to work. Only the relatively well-off owned bicycles, so people often walked five or six miles to work every day and back again at night, hurrying to get home before the nine-thirty curfew the Germans had imposed. There was not much chance for the people of Comblanchien to do any poaching; the Germans had attempted to confiscate all the sporting guns in the region, and the peasants who had defied the order to disarm and had retained their weapons kept them carefully hidden against the day they would have something more important than partridges to shoot. Besides, the German soldiers, who were always underfed, killed most of the game in the country. They shot at anything edible and even dynamited streams and fish ponds.

There were, it is true, some residents of Comblanchien upon whom the German occupation imposed no material privations. These were the dozen or so well-to-do farmers who were getting such high prices in Dijon that they were accumulating great wads of banknotes, although in a currency that shrank in value every day. But even they felt the oppression of something worse than want. The mere presence of Germans made everyone feel subhuman. The sound of German voices filled the farmers with a *malaise*, like the sound of rats scurrying within the walls of a house. The Mayor, M. Moron, was the wealthiest man of the commune. He owned a large pink building on the west side of the road, where he made and stored wine, and a good solid stone house on the east side of the road, where he lived. He was a tall, rather good-looking man, but no hero. "*Pas d'histoires*" was his motto, which might be freely interpreted to mean "For God's sake, no trouble." Moron is a common surname in Burgundy and has no pejorative connotation. The next wealthiest citizen was the deputy mayor and president of the communal council, M. Chopin. Chopin is also a Burgundian name. Chopin is a good solid chunk of a man with a bull neck and a strong, big-barrelled body like that of one of his prize plow horses. Both men regarded the Germans with a mixture of apprehension and dislike, the first sentiment dominating in M. Moron and the second in the more choleric Chopin.

One person in Comblanchien who did not seem to mind the presence of the Germans overmuch was Robert Ravigneaux, a café proprietor, whose bar was often filled with German soldiers who travelled the National Highway in convoys by night and stopped at Comblanchien to drink. Ravigneaux overcharged them for their drinks, and he told the townspeople that this was his form of resistance. The convoys didn't travel by day, because they were afraid of an Allied air attack. But even with their limited hours, they always seemed to have time to stop for refreshments, and there were no German equivalents of the "Off Limits" sign posted on the roadside cafés. Ravigneaux was a noisy, quarrelsome fellow who was not a native of the region—he had come to Comblanchien from the northeast of France five years before the war. He had an artificial left leg which was painted a pale flesh pink and on which he wore a sock and garter, just as he did on his other leg. When he got drunk, he would pull up the trouser of his amputated leg, slap the painted wood, and tell people that he had lost his leg in the last war, although everybody in Comblanchien knew that in 1944 he was only thirty-nine. Ravigneaux was drunk much of the time; it was his handsome, full-bosomed wife who watched the cash.

From time to time after the surrender of France, German soldiers were stationed in Comblanchien, in the Occupied

Zone, and then withdrawn. In May, 1944, a new detachment arrived and moved into the château. This unit was known in Comblanchien as the Schoning Company, because it was commanded by Oberleutnant Schoning, a naval reservist who in civil life had been an architect in Kiel. The men under him were Marines. The Germans had found little for their Marine Corps to do aboard a portbound navy, so they had assigned detachments from it to various duties all over Europe. Schoning had about fifty men. Their job was to patrol the area, and chiefly the railroad, between Beaune and Nuits-St. Georges, to guard against sabotage. The Oberleutnant was not much of a warrior. He was forty—just too young to have fought in the other war and just too old to have received any concentrated military training in the Nazi regime. He lived in fear that "terrorists" would attack the château, although the region is not really adapted to serious guerrilla warfare; it is too well cultivated and thickly inhabited. The vineyards would make excellent cover for a few snipers, but men cannot lie flat on their bellies for long. Schoning had been taken in by the Reich's propaganda. He saw terrorists everywhere. Soon after he arrived, he issued an order that every one of his men must learn to operate a field telephone so he could call the *Feld-gendarmerie* at Beaune immediately if the château were attacked. "The lives of each and all of us may depend on his comrades' presence of mind," Schoning's order read. What he lacked as a fighting man he made up for by abnormal arrogance, a phenomenon not confined to the German Army. He snarled and shouted constantly. Also, he never appeared outside the château without a machine pistol under his arm. As a joke, he invariably poked this weapon in Madame Ravigneaux's face when he visited the café. He was there often; he was an alcoholic, like Ravigneaux, himself a snarling man. There was something congenial to Schoning in the other disagreeable presence, although Schoning spoke no French and neither Ravigneaux nor his wife knew any German. The Oberleutnant's ignorance of French increased his suspicion of the citizenry. If anybody in Comblanchien laughed within his hearing, he was sure a joke had been made about him, and he would order the interpreter in his company, an Alsatian named Paul Zenses, to translate what had been said. Zenses had been drafted into the German

Marines after the Nazis had "incorporated" Alsace and Lorraine into the Reich, in November, 1940. When Schoning was not with him, the Alsatian was on friendly terms with some of the local people. However, Schoning communicated his edginess to the rest of his men, and the groups that patrolled the railroad frequently fired at animals or shadows, thinking they were Maquis. People got used to hearing bursts of fire at night and thought nothing of them.

There had never been any special reason Schoning should fear an attack or the people of Comblanchien should have been subjected to any unusual repressive measures. There had been no acts of resistance in Comblanchien since the beginning of the occupation, although a number of the men there belonged to Maquis groups that operated elsewhere in the region. Some of these men had joined a group that had been established in a nearby district immediately after D Day, when General Koenig, in London, had called all the French Forces of the Interior to rise in active resistance, but after these orders had been countermanded, the Comblanchien men had returned to their homes, with the exception of two who had got themselves shot. Now the local Maquis affair had apparently blown over, and anyhow everybody was too busy in the vineyards and fields to worry about it. Protracted panic is a luxury beyond the means of working people. If the local Germans had wanted to make trouble, however, an opportunity lay at hand. All the men who had been in the Maquis could be distinguished by the new shoes that the resistance organization had distributed to them. The shoes were of Army issue and had been hidden from the Germans when the French military were officially disbanded, in 1942. The shoes were too good to give up, even if they did identify the wearers as men subject to the death penalty. Jordan used to go about telling the youths to stain their shoes and scuff them. But the Germans in the château were too stupid to notice such things, the men figured.

By late August the inhabitants of Comblanchien had almost forgotten the affair of the Maquis, except for the young blowhards, who sometimes drank and boasted about the feats they claimed they had brought off. The *garde-champêtre* of Comblanchien, who is not precisely Hercule Poirot, had been in

the Maquis too, and he was soon going about telling people
he had killed five Germans, which was, to put it mildly, inex-
act. Even M. Moron breathed easy. He had been summoned
to the château to talk to Schoning three times, and each time
he had gone in the fear that he would be held as a hostage. On
the first occasion, Schoning had merely wanted to tell him that
the water supply at the château was inadequate and that he
would have to send a hogshead of water up the hill to him
every day. The second time Schoning wanted to complain that
the water had not been delivered promptly one morning.
Schoning had been exceedingly nasty about it and had
shouted even louder than usual. The third time Schoning was
furious because a woman who had been doing housework for
the Germans refused to come any more. She said she was sick,
but the Mayor suspected that her husband, who worked in a
quarry, had told her to give up her job at the château. The
other workmen had probably threatened him. Schoning had
ordered the Mayor to find a substitute, but he had been unable to find one. However, M. Moron had not been bothered
again.

There was a great deal of work to do late in August. Most
families, taking advantage of the double daylight-saving time,
worked in their gardens right up to the nine-thirty curfew
before going indoors to begin their suppers. A minute or two
after curfew on the evening of Monday, August 21st, an hour
easy to fix in the memory because the soup had just been put
on everyone's table, a bell rang in the cottage of the watchman
at the more southerly of the two grade crossings in the commune to warn of the approach of an unexpected train from the
south. This crossing, No. 191 on the railway maps, is something less than a mile from the other, No. 190, and between
them the rails run through a shallow cut. The passing of an
unscheduled train was not unusual. The Germans had been
using the railroad to move troops and matériel up toward
Normandy. This sort of activity had increased since the Allied
landings in the Midi on August 15th, because the Germans
were systematically withdrawing from the south of France,
evacuating base units as well as fighting troops. The watchman
at No. 191 was, and is, Louis Maublanc, a youth of nineteen,
who lives in the cottage with his widowed mother and a swarm

of small brothers and sisters. A moment after the bell rang, Maublanc went out to close the swing gates of the crossing. He went over the track to close the farther gate and had just got back on his own side of the track when the train came along. It was a long train, he remembers—perhaps fifty cattle cars, filled with troops. French railroad cars are small, but even figuring only forty men in each, there were two thousand soldiers. They were carrying rifles, tommy-guns, and machine guns. The engine stopped on the crossing. Some officers got out of the cars, walked up to the locomotive, and spoke to the engineer. Maublanc says that he heard the man shout something about Comblanchien, so the officers had probably asked where they were.

There is a story in the countryside that the train was deliberately stopped at Comblanchien, but that is not true. The train stopped at Comblanchien because there was another train on the track at Nuits-St. Georges, three miles north. Many of the men in the cars were drunk and were singing and howling at each other. It is hard to tell when German soldiers are angry, the French say, because they are always howling anyway. The cars must have been well stocked with wine—the right of way where the train had stopped was littered with empty bottles next day—and the noncommissioned officers aboard were taking no notice of all the drunkenness. This did not seem unusual to Maublanc. German soldiers heading north were never happy; they undoubtedly sensed, despite their own propaganda, that things were going badly up there and that they might be killed. So they were generally drunk. Dusk was coming on, but there was still enough light, Maublanc noted regretfully, to work by in the gardens, if he hadn't had to go indoors because of the curfew. He was looking toward the west, where the sunset colors were fading in the sky. Suddenly he saw a burst of tracer bullets flying from the western slope. At once the Germans in the train started shouting much more loudly than they had done before. Some of them began firing machine guns in the general direction the bullets had come from. Others piled out of the cars and flung themselves flat along the tracks. Twenty of them poured into the Maublancs' cottage and pointed machine pistols at the widow Maublanc and her little children. Other soldiers grabbed Maublanc by his arms and throat. In all the things being shouted at him, he could distinguish one word again and again—"*Terroristen!*"— a word that even Frenchmen who speak no German understand. Meanwhile, somebody gave an order and the train moved past the crossing and into the cut, whose embankment offered some protection from the fire from the slope. The train was so long that when it stopped the locomotive was almost at grade crossing No. 190. From the new position the machine gunners on the train laid down a real barrage. There was a volley of answering machine-gun fire from the west. Many villagers believe that the Germans attacked Comblanchien with malice aforethought and that they invented the story of the shots directed at the train. It has been established, however, that there actually was firing from the west. A few hundred yards west of the railroad line there is a poplar tree. When Jordan went over the ground, weeks later, he found bullets in both the east and west sides of the trunk and that many branches had been cut away from it. Lambert, the crossing watchman at No. 190, says that he saw five German soldiers on the train hit, but this testimony was impossible to check, because the train, when it did leave, carried away all the soldiers it had arrived with. Young Maublanc, who, like every other inhabitant of the region, knew that there was not a force of resistants within a hundred miles capable of attacking two thousand soldiers, was as puzzled as the Germans. The soldiers who had seized him finally flung him to the ground and left him there. Why they didn't kill him he doesn't know. As for his mother, she was so confused that she can recall almost nothing of what happened.

Nobody knows, and possibly nobody ever will know, who fired those first shots. Most probably, Jordan thinks, one of Oberleutnant Schoning's timorous, trigger-happy patrols let off a few rounds at a shadow in the vineyards, as the patrols often had before. It is known that two patrols were out when the shooting began. There is nothing to indicate that the first shots were aimed at the train or even came near it. The source of the heavier west-to-east fire which, a few minutes later, answered the barrage from the train is not mysterious. By what seems clearly to have been a coincidence, a German motor convoy had stopped on the National Highway in Comblanchien at the same time the train halted at the first grade crossing. It consisted of a dozen vehicles, each manned by a driver and a helper. There may have been in the group a couple of *Volkswagen* carrying officers, and perhaps some trucks had aboard a few hitch-hiking soldiers, but in all there could not have been more than fifty men. However, some of the trucks had machine guns mounted for use against strafing airplanes. The men in the convoy were scattered among the cafés of Comblanchien when the soldiers on the train began firing toward the highway. The convoy men, in their turn, shouted "*Terroristen!*" and ran to their machine guns. The fire was by now coming from two directions, most of it far overhead. Some of the convoy soldiers, therefore, fired to the east, toward the gun-flashes they could see below them from the railroad; others fired west toward some flashes they saw.

Oberleutnant Schoning, who was finishing his dinner in the château when the firing from the train started, was immediately frightened. "Terrorists have begun their attack on the château!" he shouted to Zenses, who has since told Jordan what happened in the château that night. No one else had heard, or at any rate paid attention to, the first few shots from the slope. It was the shooting from the east that made the first impression. The machine guns at the château immediately began firing in the direction of the supposed attack. It is not known whether the fire from the château or from the trucks was responsible for the casualties—assuming there were any— on the train. The château was hit, but not many times. Jordan found a couple of bullet holes in it later, but it is not certain that Oberleutnant Schoning even knew the house had been struck. Zenses, who was sure that an attack on the château was beyond the means of the local resistance, felt that there was a horrible misunderstanding of some sort. The fire from the château, he feared, might hit the innocent people of Comblanchien, and he thought that perhaps Schoning could avert a massacre. After a couple of minutes of the firing, which did not seem to be directed at the château, Zenses suggested to the Oberleutnant that he be sent with a patrol down to the village to see what was happening. "I will take a patrol down there myself," Schoning said. "You will come with us." It was a heroic decision for the ex-architect; his pride had prevailed. The Oberleutnant and ten or fifteen of his men put on helmets, filled their belts with incendiary grenades, slung machine pistols over their shoulders, and went down to their usual destination, Ravigneaux's café.

Ravigneaux and his wife were in the café when the firing began. They heard the first burst and then the sustained fire. Some truck drivers from the convoy had been drinking there and they had run out without paying. That was all the Ravigneaux could tell Zenses. Schoning saw the convoy people firing from the trucks. There was still fire from the east, but it was going over their heads. Schoning said to Zenses, "There is some mistake, but I cannot do anything to stop it. You go back to the château. I have no more need for you." Zenses, before he went back to the château, paused in the village street and looked down toward the railroad, from which, he could readily see, many of the bullets were coming. It was now completely dark. As he looked across the vineyards, he saw a pillar of flame rise, halfway between the railroad and the highway, about where a peasant named Sergent lived. He realized even then that the Germans had begun to burn the village.

II

Max Henry was one of the most respected citizens of Comblanchien. However, he had a hard time bringing up his family after the German occupation began. He was not a farmer but a salaried man, one of the few white-collar workers in the village, and he owned only the bit of ground surrounding his house. All prices were high in occupied France, and a man on a fixed salary was in a bad position, especially if he had to maintain appearances. M. Henry had two grown children to educate—a twenty-year-old son, Claude, and a sixteen-year-old daughter, Denise. Both went to the college in Beaune, six miles south of Comblanchien, and they continued to go despite the occupation. By August last year, Claude had finished a course preparing him to be an officer in the merchant marine. He must have been an optimist to choose that career, as he did, shortly after the armistice with Germany, when the French merchant marine had almost ceased to exist. He was to go to

Paris on September 20th to take his final examinations for a commission.

M. Henry was a bookkeeper at the Comblanchien quarry of Civet, Pommier & Company of Paris, dealers in cut stone. He had worked for the company for twenty-five years, the last thirteen of them in Comblanchien. He was in his early forties. During the first year of the war he had been acting superintendent of the quarry, for a brief period, after the superintendent had been mobilized, in September, 1939. Then, in the spring of 1940, M. Henry himself was mobilized and a rigger in the quarry was made temporary superintendent. After the demobilization, the company took M. Henry back, but only as a bookkeeper, and kept the rigger on as nominal superintendent. The original superintendent, who had got a higher salary than M. Henry had, was not rehired. M. Henry had to take over all the correspondence, because the ex-rigger was uneducated. So M. Henry was something more than bookkeeper, and his chief was something less than superintendent, and neither of them got a full superintendent's salary, which was probably the company's idea in the first place. M. Henry was paid twenty-eight hundred francs a month. This would not have been lavish for a man with two children in school even if the franc had had its prewar value, but the franc had lost almost all its purchasing power. Fortunately, the Henrys had their house and chicken yard and vegetable garden and enough vines to provide them with family table wine, and Mme. Henry was an excellent manager. She was a thin, worn-looking woman with high color in her cheeks and black hair drawn tight in a bun behind her head. She came from the Department of the Meuse, and her husband from Reims. Madame was decidedly better educated than the farm women of the community, but she worked as hard as any of them, and Claude and Denise worked too, when they were home. M. Henry was very tall and thin, so thin in proportion to his height that when he was a young man he had been excused from military service; in 1940 the Army was less particular and he was mobilized as a private.

Monday, August 21, 1944, was a hot day, and Claude and Denise, who were home from college, went swimming in a stream with friends. One of the friends took a picture of

Claude posed on a diving board. Mme. Henry still has it. It shows a tall, long-legged boy with heavy eyebrows, a straight nose, and the French variant of the crew haircut. On the evening of August 21st, until nine-thirty, when the curfew imposed by the Germans compelled everybody in Comblanchien to go indoors, the whole Henry family picked string beans in the garden. Because of double daylight-saving time, it was still light at curfew, but they had to go into the house just the same. They washed up (there was a bathroom in the Henry house, which was one of the most modern in the village) and sat down to supper. Like many of the buildings in the commune, the house fronted on the National Highway, which ran through the village; it was on the east side of that thoroughfare. M. Henry had built it himself in 1931. The exterior was of simulated gray-stone, an unconvincing concretish substance, and the house had six rooms, four on the ground floor and two in a kind of turret above. The front door was in the middle of the house and opened into a hall. M. and Mme. Henry's bedroom was at the right on the ground floor as you went in. Denise's bedroom was behind theirs. The dining room was on the left side as you entered, and the kitchen and the bathroom were behind that. The staircase leading to the turret was in the hall, and a shorter flight of stairs in the back led down to the basement. Claude's bedroom was on the second floor, in back; at the front of the turret was a spare bedroom.

The family had begun supper in the dining room when, Mme. Henry told me several weeks ago, while I was in Comblanchien, they heard two shots which, she said, sounded "like a signal." The sounds did not alarm them, because the patrols from the company of German Marines, frequently fired shots for trivial reasons; the idea that these shots were a "signal" is undoubtedly purely retrospective. Then there was a real outbreak of shooting. It seemed to come from the southeast and it was so loud that all the Henrys dropped to the floor. Mme. Henry remembers that as the family lay on the floor her husband pulled her away from the window. After a while there was a pause in the firing. M. Henry, perhaps to reassure the others, said that there was no accounting for Germans; he was going to bed. He went into his bedroom and began to undress. Mme. Henry followed him and sat down on the bed, but she was afraid to take her clothes off.

It happened that Claude Henry was a member of the Forces Françaises de l'Intérieur, and an effective one, but he had kept his activities so secret that not even his parents knew of them. He lived at home only during the college vacations and on weekends. He had helped in *coups de main* and acts of sabotage in parts of central France less accessible to the Germans than the Côte-d'Or, in which Comblanchien is situated, and had organized resistance groups in several villages. He had also tended a parachute strip on which Allied planes dropped arms for the Maquis. Claude, driving an old truck, would pick up the weapons and distribute them to comrades.

When, on the night of August 1st, his parents went to their bedroom, Claude went upstairs to his room, which faced east and south. Denise followed him after a couple of minutes. Looking out a window, they saw, through the gathering darkness, gun flashes down along the railroad, which was half a mile away, and then Claude pointed out to her what he said were groups of Germans moving up along the two roads that wound through the Comblanchien vineyards toward the village. Some of the men had flashlights, which they swung about as if they were looking for something. They stuck pretty well to the roads; the Germans were always timid about going into the vineyards, where, they fancied, the broad leaves might conceal snipers. Then Claude and Denise saw a house, midway between the railroad and the highway, begin to burn. The flames rose very high in an instant; the Germans were undoubtedly using incendiary grenades, which are usually effective immediately. "They are coming this way!" Claude said, and he hurried Denise down into the basement, shouting to his parents to join them. Mme. Henry hastened downstairs, but M. Henry, the methodical, bookkeeping kind of man, stayed in his room to dress.

A moment later there was a great crash on the ground floor. Some of the Germans had hurled grenades through the window of the dining room, setting fire to the house, and others had fired machine pistols and automatic rifles through the front door, their favorite way of breaking a lock. The three in the cellar heard boots and gunstocks on the floor over their heads, and then they heard the soldiers shouting at Henry. Claude, who had had six years of German at school and college, knew that the intruders were questioning his father. Claude also knew that his father did not understand a word of the language, so he ran up from the basement. His sister went up the basement steps behind him, but ran out the back door into the garden, where she threw herself down among the vines. Mme. Henry remained in the basement, too frightened to move.

Before his son had appeared, Max Henry had come out into the hall from his bedroom, although he had not finished dressing. The Germans presumably pushed him back against the wall and poked the muzzles of their automatic weapons against his body. He must have waved his hands in protest; he must have heard again and again, without understanding, the German words for "concealed arms." Denise, lying in the garden, saw the window of her brother's room, on the second floor, light up and Claude appear, followed by three or four Germans. He was gesticulating, evidently trying to convince them that there were no weapons concealed there, and he was talking fast. "He was talking the entire time I could see him," Denise told me when I was in Comblanchien. "Then they all went out of the room."

The house was already burning, and a minute later the flames mounted high in the sky. A dozen Germans ran out the front door, shouting and laughing. The night should have been growing darker rapidly now, but there was still light in the village, because the Germans had set fire to a score of houses, and the highway was illuminated by the fires in the houses lining it. Neither Max nor Claude Henry came out of the house. Denise, cowering among the vines, heard her mother call her name. She called back, and Mme. Henry crawled through the garden to her daughter's side. She had come up from the basement and out the back door the moment the Germans left the house. Flames were roaring in both the dining room and the bedroom at the front of the house, but they had not got into the hall between them, Denise said. Mme. Henry, who earlier in the evening had been the most timid member of the family, now found a courage that still astonishes her. "Claude and Papa must be in there," she said to her daughter. "Let us go in and find them." The two women went into the house through the back door. Max Henry lay in front of the door to his bedroom. His head had been severed from his body, apparently by a burst of machine-gun bullets. His blood puddled the floor of the little house he had built for his family. Claude Henry was lying at the foot of the staircase, his feet resting on one of the lower steps. He lay with his once handsome face among his brains. The Germans had probably killed M. Henry while Claude was still frantically talking upstairs; Claude must still have hoped to save the elder Henry when Denise saw him in his room with the Germans. When Claude had reached a point on the stairs from which he could see his father's body, a German behind him had presumably shot him in the back of the neck with his revolver. Then another German, apparently, fired a redundant shot into the boy's head as he lay dead. "We must put the bodies in the basement, where they will be preserved from fire," the mother said. The slight woman and the strong girl picked up the butchered bodies of their men—first the father and then the son—and carried them down into the basement. One of them must have made a third trip for Max Henry's head. The bodies were not touched by the fire and later received a proper burial. The women went outside again, but Mme. Henry, acting as incomprehensibly as people often do in crises, said, "The fire hasn't caught upstairs yet; maybe we can save some bed coverings and a mattress. They will be almost impossible to replace." So they went in and got some blankets. The flames reached upstairs before they could make another trip for a mattress.

Mme. Henry and her daughter lay in the garden all night. Houses were burning everywhere and there were intermittent bursts of gunfire. German soldiers passed back and forth on the highway a few yards from the two women, carrying things they had stolen from wrecked houses—quilts and chandeliers and chamber pots. They loaded them onto the dozen or so trucks of the convoy that had halted in the village that night. The magpie compulsion of a German soldier is hard to believe

unless one has seen German trucks overflowing with a rag-
man's treasure of miserable household wares, wrecked along a
roadside after a strafing.

The Henry house was one of a row of four on the highway
that stood a little apart from the rest of the village. A woman
named Gabut was in the house next to the Henrys', with her
four children, when the enemy came. The Henry women
heard her shrieking to the Germans not to kill her after her
house had been set afire. She said afterward that she thought
she had been spared because she had a crippled, subnormal
child that could not stand up. A German pulled the child from
its crib, and when the child fell to the floor he became interested in it. The crisis of blood lust past, he ran out of the house
without killing the woman.

On the other side of Mme. Gabut's house was the house of
a man named Salomon, a Communist who had led an abortive
Maquis uprising near Comblanchien in June. Salomon had left
the village some time ago, but his wife and her sister had lived
in the house during most of the summer. This night, however,
they, too, were away. It is logical that if this outbreak of arson
and murder had been a premeditated punitive expedition
against Comblanchien the Germans would have gone immediately to Salomon's house, since he was a known "terrorist."
But they did not. The fourth house in the row was inhabited by
a sixty-three-year-old man named Joseph Blanc, a retired postal
employee living on a pension, and his wife and daughter. The
Blancs, like their neighbors, must have trembled when they
saw the Gabut and Henry dwellings burning. They ran to the
basement of their house, but the Germans left them alone, at
least for the moment. Two widows, mother and daughter,
who lived not far from the Henrys but on the other side of the
highway, were less fortunate. One of these women, Mme.
Chapuzot, the mother, was sixty-eight. She worked in the
vineyards when there was work for her and made mattresses at
home when there was none. Her daughter, Mme. Voye, was
forty-six, a cheerful, hardworking woman who hoed in the
vineyards, did housework, and washed bottles for the wine
merchants whenever she had a chance. The Henry women
heard these two widows shrieking and begging the Germans
to spare them, but the soldiers killed them both. It is hard to

imagine that the Germans thought the two women dangerous. They were killing now simply because they had had a taste of blood, like weasels loose in a chicken yard.

At a farm in the commune they killed a young farm laborer named Marcel Julien. He was a pleasant, uneducated boy of eighteen who, unlike many Frenchmen of his age, had never been in the Maquis or done anything untoward. The Germans spared the other men on the farm, however. Their choice of victims that night was entirely capricious. The men who saw Julien killed say that the German who shot him was wearing shorts and an undershirt, carried a carbine, and was "slobbering" with fury. This led the people who later tried to reconstruct the massacre to think that this particular murderer must have come from the German truck convoy and not the troop train. German Army truck drivers were known to discard their outer clothes in hot weather. After some of the soldiers from the train had reached the National Highway and encountered the men from the truck convoy, who numbered about fifty, both parties must have realized that they had been firing at each other and not at an attack of what they called *Terroristen*. At any rate, the exchange of shots between the two groups ceased. The killing and burning, however, went on uninterrupted. In fact, it was now on a partnership basis. Some of the inhabitants of Comblanchien say that they recognized, among the soldiers attacking the houses, several of the Marines in Oberleutnant Schoning's detachment, but identifications in such circumstances are undependable. It is certain, however, that at eleven-thirty, an hour and a half after the murder of the two Henrys and the two widows, a band of Germans went to the Salomon house and began shouting for the "terrorist women" to come out. They must have meant Salomon's wife and sister-in-law, and this indicates to the man who has made the most careful study of the massacre—M. Jordan, the sergeant of gendarmes from Corgoloin—that officers from the troop train must have made contact with Schoning sometime between ten and eleven-thirty and asked him to point out the houses of people he suspected of "terrorism." In the absence of the Salomon women, the Germans set fire to the house and then went on to Blanc's, next door. They demanded that Blanc hand over the women, whom they said he was sheltering. The old man shook his head helplessly, and they shot him to death. They also fired at and wounded his wife and daughter, but the women escaped and managed to hide in the vineyards.

M. and Mme. Blaise Lieutard were a couple of retired railroad employees who had built themselves a house not far from the Henrys', fifty yards back from the road. They had lived in Comblanchien nine years. They had both worked in the Gare de Lyon, in Paris, for thirty years, he as an electrician and she as a messenger in the railway offices, and they had a joint pension of a thousand francs a month. The Lieutards had come to Comblanchien after their retirement because Mme. Lieutard's sister, Mme. Gauthron, lived there and Mme. Lieutard wanted to be near her. Mme. Gauthron was the village dressmaker and was married to a stonecutter in one of the quarries. M. Lieutard was a wiry little southern Frenchman of sixty, but, as his wife says when recounting her story of the dreadful night, "he looked older because he had had so much trouble." In Comblanchien the Lieutards had practiced severe economies, like all French couples of their type, who save throughout their working lives for the house they will build when they reach the pension age. Their pink stucco house—four rooms and a kitchen—might have seemed exiguous and jerry-built even to a promoter of Long Island building developments, but to Mme. Lieutard it was the fulfillment of a lifetime's hopes. She is a short woman with a broad, flat face and straggly, faded blond hair. Her eyes are blue-white and she has stubby little hands and feet; she could not have been pretty even when she was young, but her face, when she talks of the past glories of the little house, is radiant. On the ground floor there were two rooms and a storage "cellar." There was no inside staircase; to get to the second floor you walked up stone stairs on the outside of the house. The Lieutards had what Mme. Lieutard called a Louis Quinze bedroom, on which they had spent twenty thousand francs. In a corner of this room, and in a corner of the living room, which adjoined it, there were green-enamelled fireplaces. In the kitchen was a magnificent green metal salamander for heating water and a sink into which water ran from a long, convoluted pipe about as thick as a strand of macaroni. They had fine curtains on all the windows, and two overstuffed chairs which would have attracted attention in the window of any furniture store on the outer boulevards of Paris. Madame is in despair when she thinks of it. They were very comfortably off before the war, when the franc still had some value. Besides their pension, they had the usual chicken yard and garden and cages of fat rabbits, which were a joy as well as an auxiliary source of nourishment. Like all rustic French workers who have had to live in the city for a long time, they took immense pleasure in their return to the country. They had but one cause for anxiety: their only daughter, a Mme. Pascal, was a widow, her husband having died shortly after the Lieutards retired. She had two children, a boy and a girl. Her husband had left her no money and she had had to go back to her old job in the material office in the Gare de Lyon. Her parents, however, were able to help her out now and then with a few hundred francs or a fine hamper of country *charcuterie*.

Living conditions did not become difficult for the Lieutards until after the armistice. Under the Germans, it was impossible for them to live on their pension and send anything to their daughter and her children, so M. Lieutard went back to work, as chief electrician at the railroad station in Beaune. His salary was seventeen hundred francs a month, but his pension stopped, since he was now working again, so his income was only seven hundred francs a month more than it had been. M. Lieutard had no bicycle and could not afford to buy one, so he walked the six miles to Beaune and back every day. "And he had slightly flat feet," Mme. Lieutard recalls. Walking made him very hungry, but food was even more expensive in Beaune than in Comblanchien, so he had to eat in the workmen's restaurant there. It served nothing but vegetables and noodles, and all the cooking was *à l'eau*, which is repugnant to most Frenchmen, who believe that boiling takes all the nourishment out of food. When he got home at night, he was sometimes so hungry that there were tears in his eyes. He often ate bread with mustard on it, for lack of meat. When the chickens laid, the Lieutards had to barter the eggs for thread or salt or other necessities they could not afford to buy, and when they killed a chicken it went into the package they sent to Paris every week for their grandchildren. Sometimes M. Lieutard did not dare look at the rabbits, for fear he would be impelled to kill one and stew it, and thus enrage his wife. Cigarettes were of course beyond his means, so he planted a little tobacco in the garden. He had heard that it should be dried in the sun, but he never had the patience to wait; he would put the green leaves on the stove and try to toast them dry, so that he could smoke them immediately. Early in 1944, the Lieutards' daughter, who had saved up some money, decided that it would be easier to feed and lodge the children in the country than in Paris, even without her job, so she came to join her parents and brought the children with her. The girl was fifteen, the boy thirteen. She confided her savings—twenty-five thousand francs—to her mother for safekeeping. Mme. Lieutard hid the money in one of her overstuffed chairs, one that had cost three thousand francs. The Lieutards were happy to have their daughter and her children with them. Mme. Pascal helped her aunt, Mme. Gauthron, with the dressmaking, and the children went to school. It was no longer necessary to send packages to Paris, so M. Lieutard got a taste of meat once in a while now. During the summer the old electrician watched the German troop trains that passed through the station in Beaune and drew his own conclusions about how the war was going for "*ces messieurs.*" He talked to the train crews, who told him about air bombardments and sabotage along the line. He became optimistic, and used to say to his wife, "When this is over, we will offer ourselves a nice faceful of food and then we will repaint the house."

When Lieutard heard the firing begin on the night of August 21st, he summoned his family into the storage "cellar," a windowless part of the ground floor. The women were in their slips—they slept together upstairs—while Lieutard, exiled from his Louis Quinze room, shared a room on the ground floor with his grandson. "It was a genteel little room with green walls and folding beds," Mme. Lieutard says with infinite regret. The Germans ran up to the house and entered it. The Lieutards and Pascals slipped unnoticed out the back door of the "cellar" and into the garden, but there they were trapped, for they were fenced in by chicken wire except at the front of the house, and if they went out that way, they would run into the Germans. M. Lieutard tried to tear his way through the wire at the side of the house. A German soldier, coming from Mme. Lieutard does not know where, turned a flashlight on him. Mme. Lieutard, Mme. Pascal, and the two children took refuge behind a hen coop and lay flat on their bellies. Mme. Pascal's legs are long and her feet extended beyond the shelter. It was mere chance that the German didn't see them. M. Lieutard turned toward the light and said, in a faint voice, "*Qu'est ce que c'est?*" "He sounded as if his throat was stopped up, my little man," Mme. Lieutard says. The German fired—an explosive bullet that went in at Lieutard's right collarbone and came out the middle of his back, leaving an opening as big as a saucer. The inoffensive little man crumpled on the bit of garden earth he had spaded up so many times in the past nine years. "He bled! he bled!" Mme. Lieutard says. "He had planted celery on that spot, but he bled so much the celery never came up. They killed him like a wild boar." Mme. Lieutard's comparison seemed to accentuate the difference rather than the similarity between poor Blaise Lieutard and a savage beast. The German leaned over the stricken man and put his weapon to the victim's head and blew it to bits. Then he went away, shouting for his companions, probably to show them what he had done.

The women, clawing at the fence behind the chicken coop with a strength they had never suspected they had, were able to make a small opening between the wire and a fence post, and through this the children and then the mother and grandmother succeeded in wriggling. They crawled on all fours through a field of wheat stubble, lacerating their hands and knees and tearing their light garments to shreds, before they reached the nearest vineyard, where they hid under the leaves like vermin. And from between the vines Mme. Lieutard saw her small house, her treasure, burn. The overstuffed chair with Mme. Pascal's twenty-five thousand francs in it burned, too. Some of the chickens and rabbits survived, and Mme. Lieutard, who now lives with her sister, visits the ruined house morning and evening to feed them. I discovered her there when I visited Comblanchien. "I found a fork among the ashes today," she said, "but it was all black and twisted. We had such pretty tableware! Oh, Monsieur, if they had not burned the house, I would have had a roof to shelter my head and I would have had all our things to remind me of my poor husband! Or if they had not killed him, we could have got along without the house; we would have had each other! But this way they have left me nothing."

The Germans also killed a seventy-two-year-old man named Simonot, a stonecutter, but no witness to the crime remains in Comblanchien. Simonot lived with a spinster sister even older than himself, and she has moved away from Comblanchien.

Not even the bar of the irascible Robert Ravigneaux escaped. When Schoning and his interpreter, Paul Zenses, visited the café early that evening, as the trouble was just beginning, Schoning advised Ravigneaux and his wife to close their shutters and stay indoors. But at midnight the couple, in their bedroom, heard someone shouting, "Robert! Robert!" Whoever was calling sounded the final "t," which is silent in French but is pronounced in German. With that they heard a crashing in of shutters and windows, as if gun butts were being used on them, and then grenades exploded on the first floor. The house caught fire immediately and Ravigneaux and his wife barely had time to save themselves. "It must have been the *salauds* from the château," the surly innkeeper says, "because the others wouldn't have known my name. That's what you get for treating the Germans decently. Not that I was ever friendly with them!" he adds hastily when other villagers are listening. He is not a popular man.

The Mayor of Comblanchien, M. Moron, was more fortunate. The Germans came to his house, said they were going to burn it, and ordered him and his wife to get out. Mme. Moron told them that her little girl was ill and had a high fever, and Moron's son, a classmate of the unfortunate Claude Henry at the college in Beaune, talked to them in German. They finally left the house without setting fire to it, but they carried away a small barrel of wine. The survival of the Mayor's residence and his wine warehouse, across the road, did nothing to increase his popularity with his less fortunate fellow-citizens, but it seems to have been sheer chance. Of a hundred-odd buildings in the village, the Germans burned fifty-two, and their decision to spare some was apparently as haphazard as their decision to destroy the others. In addition to killing eight people, the Germans arrested twenty-four men and boys. They put these prisoners aboard the troop train, announcing that they would carry them away as hostages. The selection of the hostages was as inexplicable as everything else about the affair. One of them was a boy of fourteen, and none of them were important citizens—not, for example, the Mayor, the deputy mayor, or the town clerk. Next day, at Dijon, the Germans released twelve of the hostages. All had expected to be shot. The Germans put the twelve others aboard a train for Germany, but when the train was bombed by American planes, two more of the prisoners escaped. They eventually made their way back to Comblanchien. The remaining ten have not been heard from.

The shooting, burning, and looting continued until dawn. In the middle of the night, a truck rolled up from the *Feldgendarmerie* at Beaune, hauling a field gun. By that time it must have been obvious to all the Germans that they had not been attacked, as they may have thought at first, by the resistance forces, but the gunners fired a dozen rounds at the town hall and church. They hit the belfry of the town hall, knocking off a piece of stone bearing the letters "R.F." (République Française), but did no other damage. Shell cases found on the highway show that the gun was a thirty-seven-millimetre piece. This shelling was probably done for "moral effect." At dawn the truck convoy went on its way, the soldiers in it singing happily. The Germans from the troop train marched back to their cars in cadenced step, singing manly songs about morning in the forest and village maidens with dewy eyes. Oberleutnant Schoning had already gone to the château. In the vineyards, haggard women peered through the leaves at the smoking sockets of their houses.

Toward eight in the morning, it was discovered that the church was burning. The iron grille at the entrance had been locked, and the Germans, after firing a few ineffective shots at the lock in an attempt to break it, had gone off on some other drunken inspiration. But probably an incendiary bullet or grenade, going through a window, had started a smoldering fire that burst into flames hours later. M. Gilles, chief of the commune's volunteer fire company, and M. Chopin, the deputy mayor, went to the Mayor and asked for the key to the engine house, so that they could get out the fire engine. The Mayor said that the Germans had started the fire and might renew the massacre if an attempt were made to save the church. He refused permission to take out the engine, and the church burned to the ground.

Later in the day some of the Germans from the château appeared on the highway. They pointed to the ruins of the town and shouted, "*Boom boom kaput! Terroristen kaput!*" They seemed to find the scene amusing and laughed a great deal, but they made no move to attack any of the people they saw rummaging in the ruins of their houses. Schoning communicated with nobody in the village from then on. During the first week in September he and his Marine detachment evacuated the château and left town. French and American troops arrived in Comblanchien on September 7th.

While the fires were still at their height on the night of the massacre, M. Jordan, the gendarme from Corgoloin, came secretly to Comblanchien to see what was happening there. M. Jordan is a sallow, long-faced man with a hawk nose and a grizzled mustache. He is intelligent and logical and has a professional fondness for phrases like "reconstitution of the crime," since for the past sixteen years he has been a police officer. Until he fled to join the Maquis a couple of weeks before the massacre, M. Jordan had been a *maréchal des logis*, or sergeant, of the national gendarmerie. For the sixteen years of his service he had been stationed at the *gendarmerie* nearest Comblanchien, in the neighboring commune of Corgoloin, so he was intimately acquainted with the district and all its people. During the occupation he had pretended to help the Germans, but he had consistently forewarned everybody he was instructed to arrest. He had salvaged a few weapons so damaged that the Germans had thrown them away, and he had painfully and ingeniously repaired them, so he and the three gendarmes under him were armed with carbines and a submachine gun in addition to the gimcrack revolver and nine rounds per man the Germans allowed French gendarmes to retain. The four gendarmes had gone into the Maquis after they had been warned of an impending raid upon their cache of arms. On the night of the massacre, M. Jordan remained in

Comblanchien for an hour watching the Germans. He realized by then that he could do nothing to amend matters, so he crawled off through the vineyards until he got well away, because, even though there was no moon, the flames cast a brilliant light. After the liberation, he returned to the *gendarmerie* at Corgoloin. As soon as he had cleared up a few routine matters, like the arrest of a couple of Germans in civilian clothes who remained in the region, he began a careful investigation of the slaughter of his fellow-citizens at Comblanchien. His findings have not pleased all his neighbors, for people everywhere like to believe in diabolical plots, and M. Jordan has not been able to establish that there was one.

When he began his inquiry, there was already a story in the countryside that the arrival of the train and of the truck convoy at Comblanchien had been coördinated that night for the purpose of making an attack on the village. It had become an article of faith that the few shots before the massacre were a prearranged signal. "The few shots, of course, might have been a signal," Jordan says, "but there had been shots like them in the night on dozens of previous occasions, always proceeding from those nervous Marine patrols. As to the thesis that there really was an attack on the train by men of the resistance and that the Germans fired in defense, I am in a position to say that it cannot be sustained. There were no F.F.I. patrols in Comblanchien that night. Moreover, if the handful of men of Comblanchien had meditated anything so mad as an attack on a two-thousand-man troop train, would Claude Henry, an F.F.I. officer, have been picking string beans in the garden when the train arrived?"

M. Jordan also heard in the countryside a story that people had seen rockets fired from the château before the attack began, but he could never actually find these people. There was also a story that Schoning's Marines had appeared, completely equipped for battle, at the Ravigneaux café an hour before the first shots, but M. and Mme. Ravigneaux and Paul Zenses, the Alsatian interpreter, who subsequently deserted from the German Army and joined up with the French, agreed that Schoning had appeared in the café *after* the firing started. There was also a very persistent report that the German commander of the troop train had insisted, at Corgoloin, the station below Comblanchien, that "the train must go through because we have to get to Comblanchien this evening." The Corgoloin stationmaster told Jordan that the officer had wanted to get as far as Dijon, not Comblanchien, and that the train had stopped there only because another one was ahead of it. "The strongest argument against the thesis of a deliberate punitive attack on Comblanchien," Jordan says, "is the fact that if they had wanted to kill all the people, the Germans could have remained on the scene the next day and killed them at their leisure. But they didn't. Well, then, there was no premeditation. Well, then, what happened?

"This is what happened. Two detachments of Germans, arriving here simultaneously from two directions, with their customary brutality exacerbated by fear and chagrin, frightened each other into an exchange of shots. The precipitating influence was probably one of the patrols from the château, which were always frightened. The patrol fired two or three shots and soldiers on the train replied with a massive fusillade. Those of the truck convoy replied to this fusillade with a nourished fire. The château joined in. Train and convoy fired on the château. This I know because I have found imbedded in the château two machine-gun bullets that came into it through open windows. No glass is broken, but remember that it was a hot night. One bullet had entered at such an acute upward angle that it was lodged in a ceiling. It must therefore have been fired from the road directly below the château. The other had lodged in a wall almost on a level with the window sill and therefore must have been fired on an only slightly rising trajectory—from the train on the other side of the village. The evidence of a poplar tree, standing between train and convoy, and blasted by fire from the two directions, proves that the Germans fired on each other.

"Now, however, please remark that I do not exonerate these brutes for what they did. Mistakes sometimes occur, even in armies which, like the German, propagate a legend of their own perfect discipline and skill at warfare. If some innocent inhabitants of the village had been caught in the crossfire and wounded, that would have been regrettable but not a crime of war. But notice—the Germans descended from the train and killed eight persons in their houses, firing point blank. These persons were not only unarmed; of the eight, three were men more than sixty years old and two were women, persons unlikely to be dangerous. They did not kill only in the first access of fury, because it was an hour and a half after the first attack that they killed old man Blanc. Long after they discovered their mistake, they continued to burn houses. What was their crime? In my opinion, any court would convict them of murder."

I have been advised to write an epilogue to this book to "give it unity" and "put it in perspective," but I find this difficult, because war, unlike drama, has no unities, classical or otherwise. It is discursive, centrifugal, both repetitive and disparate. Also, I have never got it into perspective myself— It is sometimes as much part of now as then, particularly the moment when I saw the blood mixed with milk. ("The symbolism was too obvious," a literary friend said to me afterward, mistaking me for a creative writer.) Also, although I am a rationalist without belief in the hereafter, some of the pieces are irrationally filled with spooks, like the dead airplane crew in "Run," that wanted me to fly with them, and this makes it hard for me to write about these stories—they must speak for themselves.

A.J.L.

UNCOLLECTED
WAR JOURNALISM

Letter from Paris

OCTOBER 22 (BY CABLE)

PARIS at this writing is a city in which people are tentatively picking up the threads of ordinary existence—tentatively, and a little sheepishly, as if ashamed of their initial agitation. Theoretically, there is as much danger from the air this week as on the first day of War '39, as Frenchmen call this one to distinguish it from the other, but habit is stronger than reason. Wives who were rushed to the country at the outbreak now want to come back to rejoin their husbands in Paris, and in most cases the women are having their way. People buy newspapers as mechanically as they light cigarettes and, after looking at the headlines, leave them on café tables virtually unread because there is no news. The public at first blamed censorship but has now begun to sense that simply nothing has happened, and in the French fashion it has begun to make fun of the baffled journalists. One of the favorite butts is Mlle. Geneviève Tabouis, of *L'Œuvre*, who writes circumstantially every day of events in Germany, where, of course, she isn't. She has many less eminent imitators.

Paris newspapers have never carried so much German news as now, when the sources of this news are inaccessible. One reported Monday that Hitler had confided his testament of thirty pages to Göring, who presumably was decent enough to count them for the Allied press. Havas announced later that the Führer was practicing revolver shooting at moving targets, a sign he feared assassination. Another journalistic genre, already hackneyed, is the conducted visit of illustrious correspondents to the front. The correspondents, often members of the Académie Française or Goncourt, are invariably taken to Strasbourg, which was cleared of inhabitants when the war began. Each Academician compares Strasbourg to a dead city or a sleeping beauty, according to his taste, and professes to have been startled by the sound of his own footsteps in the empty streets. One columnist wrote, after reading a series of these *rapportages*, "Monsieur X was not frightened by his own footsteps, but by the fourteen correspondents behind him."

Serious editorialists, like Gallus, of *Paris-Soir*, have felt impelled to reprove such public levity and to warn their readers that the situation remains potentially grave.

The French have an enormous confidence in their army, especially now that the Germans have let slip the opportunity for a surprise attack. They suspect that the German High Command will not attempt a great offensive unless its hand is forced by *ce fou d'Hitler*, and discussions of strategy in the cafés invariably hinge on just how *fou* Hitler is. As for air raids on great cities, the public senses now that the Germans are loath to begin; while waiting, people say, it is no use torturing oneself.

A few theatres have reopened. The Comédie-Française gives several performances a week, the evening ones beginning at six-fifteen, and the companies of the Opéra and Opéra-Comique share the latter's home on the Rue Favart, each on a one-show-a-week basis. Several music halls have begun their season, and night clubs are struggling against the handicap of an eleven-o'clock closing. Les Halles, where restaurateurs used to go to market long before dawn, now operate in daylight from noon to three in the afternoon, but there is all the old profusion of *primeurs* and game, rock lobsters and oysters. Nothing reassures Parisians more than this gastronomic normality. As they eat, lovingly and with discrimination, they like to talk about the short rations *chez l'ennemi*; it is that, they are convinced, which will provoke a German revolution.

To the visitor returning to Paris for the first time since the beginning of War '39, no major change is apparent in the city by day. There are the air-raid-shelter signs, the strips of paper pasted over shop windows to stop glass from flying in case of an air raid, and sandbags around some public buildings; one soon becomes accustomed to these. The streets are well filled and those favorite subjects for water-colorists, the fishermen and book merchants of the Seine, pursue the placid, meagre tenor of their lives. There are a great many uniforms everywhere, but uniforms never were rare in Paris, and a French soldier seems a normal enough feature of civilian life.

At night, of course, all this changes; windows and street

lights cast only the dimmest of rays. Behind the café fronts, however, shrouded by blue paper, one finds groups of people made sociable by the war, consuming their beer and coffee and demonstrating with matches on the tables the strategies that could quickly win War '39. This willingness to talk to almost anybody resembles the fraternization of speakeasy days in New York.

Parisians, always grumblers, are beginning to complain about the air-raid restrictions now that they realize the first alarms were only for practice. "Let's have the lights again," one owner of a *bistro* said to a group of customers a day or so ago. "Light is like the butterflies and the verdure that lifts the spirits." "And if the light attracts the bombers of Monsieur Hitler?" a customer asked. "Then turn off the lights," the *bistro* man said. "All you have to do is press a button."

The New Yorker, October 28, 1939

Letter from Paris

JANUARY 12 (BY CABLE)

ONE of the things that couldn't happen anywhere but here is Charles Trenet, who sings morbid songs in a circus with such hilarious enthusiasm that children scream with laughter when he shouts that he is a ghost making love to the wife of the man who shot him. Trenet is a very young man who has the honest pink face of an athletic shipping clerk from Astoria; he has been on a ten-day leave from an aviation field where he is a non-flying noncom. Like most French soldiers who have ways of earning money while they're back from the front, Trenet went to work as soon as his furlough began. Instead of choosing an intimate Dwight Fiske setting, he picked a circus ring, where he walks on his heels, jumps on a grand piano, and acts out the seduction of a waxwork marquise with such gaiety that nobody cares if his couplets happen to be bitter. Trenet is about twenty years younger than Maurice Chevalier and should outlast him if the Germans don't start bombing aviation fields.

Not all soldiers on leave are lucky enough to be musical stars, and a good many of the extra waiters whom restaurants put on during the holidays were fellows back from the front and trying to build up a reserve of spending money. A French soldier gets fifty centimes a day unless he is under fire, when he draws ten francs. It's a sizable raise, but a soldier-waiter at one of the big cafés recently told a customer that he had been through ten-franc days when he'd have been glad to settle for fifty centimes and relief from the firing.

Paris is really accepting the war as a part of its daily life now. A war play has arrived at last; it is called "The Black Folder" and stars Victor Francen and Gaby Morlay, the King Edward VII and Queen Victoria of the film "Entente Cordiale." Mlle. Morlay impersonates the Swiss mistress of a French industrialist in the first act, seems to be a German spy in the second, and reveals herself in the third as a very wonderful French counter-spy, which makes everything perfect. When Morlay, trying to keep her incognito and her lover at the same time, says, "I am

576

a German, but I am not a Nazi," Francen replies, "That's what they all say"—a line that brings down the house.

One of the most arresting surface phenomena here is the amount of German spoken; in a number of Czech and Viennese restaurants it is the predominant language. German-speaking aliens are being continually checked up on, but, although Parisians like to think that any German at large has been investigated by the police and found to be harmless, they keep on worrying.

The Académie Française, which always has a long waiting list of aspirants, filled a lone vacancy yesterday by the election of Paul Hazard, a professor at the College of France who once lectured at Columbia and is therefore known to at least some Americans, which distinguishes him from seventy-five per cent of his immortal colleagues. M. Hazard is a lieutenant colonel at present, with a suite of offices in the Hôtel Continental, where he directs the more intellectual phases of French propaganda abroad; his academic specialty is comparative literature, and his greatest worry before the war began was the indifference of Anglo-Saxons to Racine. The reception given a new member of the Académie is always a bigger show than an election, so right now the principal interest among *aficionados* of the institution is the coming induction of Jérôme Tharaud, who was elected several months before M. Hazard. Members will wear green breeches and swords supposedly symbolizing the continuity of civilization, and the function is expected to have a reassuring effect on conservative readers of the *Journal des Débats*.

The race meeting at Vincennes is having a similarly reassuring effect on the great, solid public of *petits bourgeois* who like to have a bet down and enjoy taking apart the characters of trainers and jockeys after an afternoon which they think should have turned out more profitably. Vincennes has never been a fashionable track. Ten francs will get you there in a taxi; the cabs cruise the boulevards during the lunch hour picking up passengers, as they do on Broadway in Saratoga. This is a trotting meeting, but half the races are mounted trots—something the United States doesn't have. The trot jockeys are apt to be stocky middle-aged men who train horses and also race in sulkies. The average riding weight is 154 pounds, and a jockey's efforts seem to be mainly devoted to preventing his horse from being disqualified for breaking into a gallop; a nose-and-nose finish inevitably looks like a pulling match. When the race is over, all the holders of losing tickets laugh bitterly and hasten to buy tickets on the next one.

The Association for the Amelioration of the Half-Thoroughbred Horse, which controls trotting here, has gone in for a system of classification by initial letters: the names of all horses which are four years old this season begin with "O;" all five-year-olds have names starting with "N." Owners are driven to extreme lengths to find names—one colt who ran here the other day was called Ni Oui Ni Non II.

People continue to be delighted by the events in Finland; the victories of the Finns sometimes seem almost too good to be real, and in the general jubilation it is hard to remember that the Russians are dying horribly.

Naturally, everybody would like to know what the Italians and the Hungarians are up to, but neither group has taken even Mme. Tabouis into its confidence. If the Balkan nations would only choose sides like boys before a baseball game, there might be a real war in the Near East this spring; if they don't choose sides, they may possibly be able to stay out of war altogether. Perhaps that is exactly what the Balkan politicians are thinking about.

In the meanwhile, the most pressing question in Paris is that of coffee. The government insists that there is coffee to be had; the grocers deny it. You can't even buy the tinned American brands which used to stay on grocers' shelves for years because they were so expensive, to say nothing of the fact that Parisians detested them. Large hotels and restaurants still have stocks, but some of the smaller places are beginning to run out. When a patron phones in advance to order a dinner of, say, frogs' legs and woodcock, both of which are plentiful, the proprietor is likely to ask him to bring the coffee for his party.

The New Yorker, January 20, 1940

Letter from France

UNTIL last November, when the French government decided upon Angers as the place where the Poles could set up a new capital, most Frenchmen thought of this quiet old city in the valley of the Loire only as the home of Cointreau and of a certain sweet white wine. The people of Angers, in their way, were equally provincial, for although the Cointreau factory is the largest local industry, before the arrival of the diplomatic corps practically none of the 90,000 inhabitants of the community had ever heard of a cocktail called the Side Car. Now all that has changed; the Angevins have a broader point of view and the rest of France knows the city as the headquarters, until further notice, of a nation's President and Premier as well as of a group of diplomats which includes United States Ambassador Biddle, a Papal Nuncio, and, most remarkable of all, a French Ambassador.

When the Angevins, a friendly and unadventurous people, learned that their city was to become the capital of a distant nation, they were flattered but not altogether happy, for it occurred to many of them that the new distinction might attract bombers when and if the bombing started. However, once the Poles began to arrive and the bombers did not, civic pride overcame apprehension, and now the natives seem pleased that things turned out as they did. The townsfolk have rented any number of furnished rooms to white-collar workers employed in the offices of the various dignitaries, and the owners of several large, drafty buildings have been able to lease their properties as chancelleries. Every local notable, from the Prefect to the president of the Angers Rotary Club, has had a chance to welcome at least one batch of newly arrived diplomats.

The winter climate of Angers is wet and fairly chilly, but palm trees grow here and people go about their business in the rain just as they do in Dublin. When the Poles arrived in this atmosphere of humid calm, many of them succumbed to a kind of inverted shell shock; Angers was so quiet that it frightened them, and they ran up to Paris, a hundred and seventy miles away, every chance they could get. These days, however, bureau chiefs have difficulty finding men to go on out-of-town missions, because the Poles have come to love a calm they had forgotten existed. They are by no means happy, though, even in this retreat. Among the young Polish diplomats in Angers are some who once contributed largely to the gaiety of several world capitals, including Washington; they have become a grim bunch, living in cheap hotel rooms and, when they are not at work, discussing the unbelievable brutality of the Nazis in Poland. The older men, who once worked for a free Poland, achieved it, and have seen it sink beneath the surface again, are an even sadder crowd. They try to cheer themselves by reminding one another that the Belgian government carried on at Le Havre for four years during the last war.

Like the Belgians then, the Poles now have their own army in France. When fully organized, it probably won't amount to more than one army corps, but it already includes Polish volunteers from nearly every country in the world. The Poles have their own hoard of gold in France, too, and their government borrows against it for running expenses, which are cut to the bone. The gold amounts to about $30,000,000—Poland's national reserve, which was taken out of the country in trucks, some of it through the Baltic countries and some of it through the Balkans, just before the converging German and Russian armies closed in.

The Biddles occupy a small château (small, that is, as châteaux go hereabouts) at Seiches, a village a few kilometres from Angers. It is owned by a retired cavalry officer and has a moat around it which creates a mist even when the sun is shining, however weakly, on the rest of the countryside. The American Chancellery is a small house on the Rue de la Préfecture; it looks just about like any other house in Angers and would be hard to find if it were not directly across the street from the office of the city's most prosperous midwife, whose large swinging sign is something of a landmark. Most of the attachés and secretaries who formerly served under Mr. Biddle have been transferred to busier diplomatic posts on the Continent, and the personnel here at present consists only of the Ambassador; a third secretary, Mr. C. B. Elbrick; an interpreter; and a stenographer named Miss McWhorter.

If titles meant what they used to in Warsaw, one of the busiest men in the United States Foreign Service at the moment would be Mr. Elbrick, who, since the staff has been thinned out, has become acting first and second secretary as well as military and naval attaché at the Embassy. Mr. Elbrick, however, does not find his duties in Angers too burdensome; in fact, he considers his life here restful after what he has recently been through in Central Europe. He and his wife dodged bombs from Warsaw to the Rumanian border and got to Bucharest on the day King Carol had nine Iron Guards shot and left in the street to show the others how he felt about them. Continuing on their way, the Elbricks reached Munich on the evening of the beer-hall explosion. The rest of their journey was comparatively uneventful.

The diplomats visit to some extent among themselves. Besides Mr. Biddle and the French Ambassador, there are the British and Turkish Ambassadors, and Brazil, Chile, Egypt, and a couple of other countries have legations here. The receptions are invariably informal, however, because almost all members of the corps lost their dress clothes and decorations when they fled from Poland.

The New Yorker, February 17, 1940

Letter from Paris

MARCH 9 (BY WIRELESS)

SUMNER WELLES arrived in Paris on the fourth anniversary of the German reoccupation of the Rhineland. If the French in 1936 had squelched the Nazis without worrying about possible repercussions on public opinion abroad, the visit of an American Assistant Secretary of State now would be important news only for the Paris edition of the *Herald Tribune*. As it is, the French expect little good and no harm from his visit; Paris newspapers bade him welcome in their editorials, M. Daladier invited him to dinner, and everybody went right on thinking about a long war.

There are already at least fourteen versions in Paris of what Hitler said to Mr. Welles in Berlin; everyone agrees that the German Chancellor talked a tremendous fight, and most say that it was all a bluff. Next week people will be trying to reconstruct what M. Daladier and Mr. Chamberlain said to Mr. Welles; then the American will take an Italian boat and be forgotten—or so Paris thinks.

Mr. Welles' presence in Europe has had one mildly reassuring effect: people are confident the Germans won't start their great offensive while he is here. Not many of them think that there will be an offensive after he leaves, either; a couple of military critics and several dozen astrologers are the only really confident prophets of Armageddon. The astrologers say that Hitler has always made decisive moves in March, a month he considers lucky. The generals argue, more soundly, that great offensives usually start in the spring or not at all. The constant discussion of a German offensive completely muffles any general talk about an Allied attack, although the French and British are certainly in as good a position for an aggressive move as the army on the other side of the line. For one thing, a drawn battle probably would be a disaster for the Germans but of advantage to the Allies, because it would exhaust the German supply of gasoline. This sort of talk has largely displaced other kinds of table conversation in Paris; it has been going on so long that it seems as impersonal as what people used to say about the Davis Cup prospects or women's hats. It is only in the army zone that you recover a feeling of the war's relevance to the flesh and blood of your friends.

Paris had its first *alerte* of 1940 a few nights ago. The excitement, but not the sirens, started at about eight-thirty in the evening, when an anti-aircraft battery began banging away at a German reconnaissance plane, wounding half a dozen Frenchmen with its spent shells. Later that night, a druggist returning home from his shop found a shell standing on his slippers by the foot of his bed. It was a dud which had fallen through the roof and the garret floor. There was no *alerte*, because of a sensible rule that the traffic in the streets is not to be interrupted just for one or two stray airplanes. At about four o'clock that morning, however, the sirens began, but this time there was no anti-aircraft activity. When Parisians could hear no gunfire, they decided the danger was not serious and went back to sleep. As it turned out, they were right.

That same night, when the British flew over Berlin dropping tracts, the German batteries didn't fire, either. This is a war in which the refined instruments of destruction are restrained by even more refined instruments of detection; there are whole regiments of artillery at the front which have never fired a shot in earnest, because when a battery opens up nowadays, even for a few rounds, it has to move elsewhere immediately. Both sides have a virtually foolproof system of detecting a gun's position by sound measurements and simple mathematics. Occasionally a regiment is withdrawn from the front for practice.

Americans who came to Paris to escape prohibition in the good old days would be shocked by the most recent sumptuary decree here. Bars and restaurants can't sell hard liquor on Tuesdays, Thursdays, or Saturdays; after July 1st, retail stores will not be permitted to sell less than two litres of it at a time— a strange bit of legislation, since, as Paul Reynaud, the law's sponsor, will soon find out, it is almost certain to increase the consumption of alcohol in homes. M. Reynaud has never lived in a package-law state. Small bistros are less hard hit on the taboo days than the flashier places with a foreign patronage, for they have always done a good business in wine by the glass, and scarcely any of their customers mind switching to wine. Elsewhere, things are different; for example, the Crillon Bar was a stricken place at cocktail time on the Tuesday the new law went into effect. The diplomats and the newspapermen were home mixing their own drinks, and the only customers were several British aviators who were on furlough and had no flats to go to. The government maintains that the decree will help build a reserve of industrial alcohol, although it is hard to imagine the French mixing cognac with their aviation gasoline. Meanwhile the winegrowers, who have the most powerful legislative lobby in France, are not complaining.

There has been racing at Auteuil on the last two Sundays. All the events, which are over jumps, drew fields of from twenty to twenty-five horses; small stables and public trainers have won most of the purses. Steeplechasing here has the same picaresque attraction that flat racing has in America—an identical atmosphere of engaging skulduggery motivated by avarice which nobody is ashamed to display on a race course. The most striking feature of the Auteuil reopening, aside from the spring costumes, was the way the big shots of racing were outshone by many of the common spectators. The owners who appeared in uniform were almost all sergeants or second lieutenants, while scores of less affluent chaps, who in other years were inconspicuous fifty-franc bettors, showed up as majors or colonels of cavalry, wearing long red spahi capes and so many spurs and buckles that they sounded like Swiss bell-ringers.

The New Yorker, March 16, 1940

Letter from Paris

APRIL 21 (BY CABLE)

THE low point of French morale in this war was reached in the middle of March, after what many people thought of as the abandonment of Finland; the high point came about a month later, with the news of the defeat of the German squadron at Narvik. The change is graphically expressed in the two votes of the Chamber of Deputies on the Reynaud government. In March, the government survived by one vote on the question of confidence; last week, on the same question, no votes were cast against the government and 515 were recorded in its favor. The news from Norway that has given most satisfaction here was yesterday's report: "French troops have landed." Frenchmen's admiration for the British Navy is unlimited, but they regard the British on land in something of the spirit of a husband watching his wife drive an automobile.

People who have advocated an "energetic war" are pleased with the impression which the Allied stand in Norway has made upon the constantly less numerous neutrals. After the defeat of Finland, Rumania and the Scandinavian countries became extremely conciliatory toward the Nazis, but since Narvik, all the neutrals have been clapping German agents into jail and announcing their determination to fight if invaded. Even Italy, while its official press continues to deny Allied successes, is giving a pretty good impersonation of a man who has taken a mouthful of unexpectedly hot *minestrone* and would like to get rid of it without prejudice to his dignity.

The great question here is Führer Hitler: after his Norwegian adventure is settled, one way or another, will he turn toward the Balkans or France? If Hitler becomes engaged in the Balkans, the French say, the war may last longer than it would otherwise, but the shock of an eventual attack on France will be less violent, since, like a hooked fish, he will lose strength with every lunge. Most Parisians, however, would prefer the "big knock" as soon as possible, in order, as they are likely to put it, "to finish with a *sale type* who has ceased to interest us."

Le Français moyen—that average Frenchman who is the national hero—has always had a low opinion of the average German; it was only in the upper economic and social groups, here as in England, that Germanism made inroads during the late thirties. Now that the attempt to take Europe by surprise has failed, the common man's cockiness is an inestimable asset. The French will not be shaken by initial defeats, if such there are to be, because they remember the early years of the 1914 war, and are convinced that the Germans always quit, if one holds on long enough. The Nazis, for all their bluster, can have no such confidence; even a Göring must remember sometimes that in 1917 the Central Powers held Bucharest and Brussels and Lille—advanced posts considerably more impressive than Copenhagen.

The lightheartedness with which people here face things to come was illustrated beautifully at a gala held at the Opéra for the benefit of soldiers' recreation centres. The striking thing about it was not the enormous turnout or the presence of MM. Lebrun and Reynaud, but the joyous inconsequentiality of the entertainment. Two clowns from the Cirque Médrano played a serenade on a bicycle pump which was much appreciated by the President of the Republic, and an Englishman, introduced as "Stinker" Murdoch, performed on something that sounded like a peanut whistle. The official stars of the occasion were Maurice Chevalier, who has become a truly national figure, and Gracie Fields, who, like Yorkshire pudding, arouses enthusiasm among the British and to other people seems merely inoffensive. The setting represented an improvised theatre behind the lines, and Paul Goube, one of the Opéra's best dancers, who is now in the Army, came back from the front to lead a ballet. The audience was almost as much British as French and those who weren't bilingual caught only half of the show, but French and British alike enthusiastically applauded the parts they didn't understand in a touching demonstration of mutual faith.

Paris is having its first major Salon since the war began—a joint showing of the Salon d'Automne, the Salon des Tuileries, and the Artistes Décorateurs, all at the Palais Chaillot on the Place du Trocadéro. There are seven hundred paintings. None of them, perhaps, will ever be listed in guidebooks, but neither are any of them representative of those slicked-up, colored-photograph sort of thing which used to get into the Salon shows of twenty years ago, and which has been restored to the position of high art on the other side of the Westwall.

Soldiers on leave are as numerous, in proportion to the other visitors, at the Salon as in the music halls. They study every landscape gravely to see whether the painter has done justice to the French stones and the French grass and the French waves, in all of which, as Frenchmen, they take a highly personal interest. What use is there in defending three chestnut trees or an old church in Poitou if some dauber is permitted to malign them behind one's back?

The great joke of the past fortnight has been the publication in a newspaper here of a speech by Herr Goebbels, in which he is supposed to have said that Hitler would be in Paris by June 15th. "What pretension!" exclaimed a girl in a crowd surrounding a news kiosk. She sounded as indignant as if Herr Goebbels *in propria persona* had pinched her where no gentleman would. Most of the readers, though, seemed merely amused. That night at the Petit Casino, the great proletarian music hall on the Boulevards, a comic stepped down to the footlights and asked the orchestra leader, "Have you been to the Ecole Berlitz?" The leader asked why. "To learn German," the comic said, "so you can talk to Adolf when he gets here." The answering howl of laughter was a more impressive vote of confidence than M. Reynaud got from the Chamber of Deputies.

The New Yorker, April 27, 1940

Eight White Ships of Denmark

THERE are sixteen Danish ships dawdling in New York Harbor. Half of them are tied up at the Bayonne Port Terminal, a peninsula of made land which juts about two miles into upper New York Bay opposite Staten Island and is as quiet as any place you'd find within view of the Statue of Liberty. The Terminal was opened a couple of years ago in anticipation of increasing ocean-borne traffic in the harbor, but since the increase never came, the old wharves of Manhattan and Brooklyn and Hoboken and Jersey City have been able to take care of all the ships. Lack of demand makes wharfage at the Terminal cheap, and the inexpensive wharfage in turn makes the Terminal an ideal berth for Danish ships, which must stay in port because they would either be seized by the British if they ventured outside or would fall into the hands of the Germans if, by some miracle, they succeeded in getting home to Denmark. The British say that Denmark has been a sort of vassal of Germany ever since the invasion on April 9th, and that ships flying the Danish flag may therefore be made prizes of war. By minding their own business, the Danes have thus attained the status on the high seas of Chinese pirates, accorded no rights by anyone.

Eight ships belonging to the J. Lauritzen Line of Copenhagen were tied up at Bayonne on the raw, gray afternoon last week when I journeyed over there by the Liberty Street ferry and the Central Railroad of New Jersey. The eight other Danish ships in the harbor, which are of varied ownership, are scattered about by ones and twos. The Lauritzen Line, until last April, was one of those profitable but unspectacular family enterprises that typified Danish industry. Its small, neat ships, as standardized and dependable as Danish eggs, enjoyed Lloyd's highest classification as insurance risks because they were so new, so well constructed, and so ably navigated. They got back to Denmark only at long intervals, for they were assigned runs between North and South America, between the fruit-growing countries and Antwerp, or on any other route where money was to be earned by carrying cargo.

I brought a letter of introduction to the Lauritzen ship-masters at Bayonne from Mr. Tage Nielsen, agent for the company in America. Mr. Nielsen, a blond, round-faced, correct young man, has a small office at 67 Broad Street. He was quite willing, when I called upon him, to have me visit his ships, but he said he did not like to discuss what he called "the political aspects of the question;" the United Press had recently sent out a report that the Danish vessels in American ports might be requisitioned by the United States government and turned over to Great Britain.

"It is a very delicate situation," Mr. Nielsen said while we waited for his blonde, round-faced, correct stenographer to type out my letter of introduction. "The British want to put our ships through their prize court at Halifax and allocate them to English firms for operation under their flag. Then, they say, when the war is over, they will return the ships if they haven't been sunk, or they will pay for them if they have any money, perhaps. But the ships in neutral ports will be one of Denmark's few assets when the war ends. If we keep them under the Danish flag, they can go out and earn money and send it home while we reconstruct our agriculture and our industry." I felt that for Mr. Nielsen assets, freight charters, well-regulated agriculture, and profitable industry were among the immutable truths of life, like personal cleanliness and setting-up exercises, and that he considered the war a mere pause in the orderly processes of commerce. When the letter was ready, we shook hands and I started for New Jersey.

The eight Lauritzen ships at Bayonne reminded me of a family of nice Danish girls, fair and almost excessively scrubbed, drawn up in pairs, arm in arm. The eight lay in a double file along the pier, the inshore and outshore vessels of each pair connected by a plank walk. On their white sides were painted Danish flags and the word "Danmark" in lofty letters, the markings prescribed for their rôle as neutrals during the first part of the war. Like girls, the ships were named Sessa, Paula, Nora, Maria, Marna, and so on. The taximan who drove me out to the ships from the railroad station at Bayonne asked me which ship I wanted. I said it didn't matter particularly, and as we were abreast of the Marna when he asked, I thought I might as well begin with her. There was no one on deck when

I marched up the gangplank, but on the ship tied beside the Marna I could see a short, plump man wearing a sweater and a beret, busily chipping rust and making a tremendous racket at it. I walked forward on the Marna to the captain's cabin, which was indicated by a sign on the door, and knocked. A big, sleepy voice said "*Kom*," so I pushed the door open and found myself in a little sitting room that had a divan on one side of it, a settee on the opposite side, and in the centre a table covered by a green baize cloth. A vase containing some wilted ferns stood on the table, and the steel walls, painted to simulate mahogany, were decorated with a few Finnish knives in leather sheaths. A vast, merry-looking man in a leather jacket was sitting on the divan. "Captain—" I began, gropingly. "Jensen," the big man said, pronouncing the "j" in the Danish fashion, like our "y." "Usually on a Danish ship you would be safe to call the captain Jensen. On the Nora also the captain is Jensen." He was a red-faced man with narrow eyes which had many wrinkles at the corners, and his arms were as thick as a wrestler's neck. When I showed him Nielsen's letter and said I would like to know how Danes on ships tied up in an alien port felt about their curious position, he seemed puzzled. He said, "I feel all right. I feel at home. I don't know how to explain this to you." He thought a while and then said, "An American uses a ship just like a car. He rides in it and he comes home and puts it away, just like it was in a garage. But a Dane uses a ship like a house. So how could you feel not at home in your house? The street that the house is on makes no difference. And, anyway, this would be a dirty day at sea—fog."

Captain Jensen told me that the Marna had been built in 1936 and that he had commanded her since 1938, running between New York and the port of Talcahuano in southern Chile. The round trip consumed seventy days and included intermediate stops at twenty-nine ports. He had not expected to go home to Denmark for a long while, so he was not homesick—just anxious about his wife and children. But he got letters from them pretty regularly by air mail, he said. "All the letters are read by the German censor, but at least I know my family are all well," he said. The Captain told me he lived aboard the Marna with his chief engineer, two deck officers, two engineering officers, one cook, and one steward. The rest of the crew had shipped out again, on Swedish, Norwegian, and even British vessels. "Naturally, they like the Scandinavian ships better," Captain Jensen said, "but better than wait, some go British." Swedish vessels are classed by the British as neutral, while Norwegian vessels, because their government is carrying on the war from a temporary capital in England, are belligerents. Great Britain allows Danish seamen to sail the Atlantic, even though Danish ships may not without risking seizure. Sailors on Danish ships sign not for a single round-trip voyage, as Americans usually do, Captain Jensen said, but for a term of eighteen months. The Danish companies have not asked any of the men here to quit, but since the invasion they have been able to pay them direct only a small part of their wages. The shipowners pay the rest of the money to the men's nearest relatives in Denmark. Since wages are payable in Danish kroner, which have depreciated from a peacetime value of about twenty cents to about eight, the men would not be exactly flush even if they received full payment. Most of the seamen prefer the hazards of navigation to the monotony of a long stay in port with little money to spend.

"It's the same as this on all the Lauritzen ships at Bayonne," the Captain told me. "Just officers, cooks, and stewards left. The captain of the Paula has his wife and two kids living aboard, and the second officer of the Sessa has his wife and a baby, too."

"Then who is working so hard on the ship alongside?" I asked. Captain Jensen said, "That's my neighbor, Captain Nielsen. On Danish ships the captain works too." There was less life than usual in the squadron, he explained, because the men were moving a Danish ship belonging to some friends across the bay to a drydock in Brooklyn, and she had steamed out of Bayonne that morning with about half the available manpower of the eight other ships as her crew. "Oh, she has a good crew, all right," Captain Jensen said. "Chief officers for deckhands and first engineers for firemen." Ordinarily, all the officers would be busy at maintenance work on their own ships. "Any vessel here could get under way in two hours," he told me. "Everything shipshape. Would you like to have a look around?" I said I would, and he put on a cap and led the way to the wheelhouse and the chartroom. As we inspected them, he told me that the Marna was of 2,900 registered tons; burned coal as she progressed at a steady, dreamily smooth ten knots; had five hatches and plenty of gear for handling all kinds of cargo, except refrigerated; and was in every way an amiable and successful creature. He said it took only about twenty-five men, including officers, to handle her. "When you hear of a shipping man going broke," he said as we ascended to the bridge, "it is always with big ships. Nobody goes broke with good, small ships, and they don't need any subsidies, either." The Nora, the largest of the Lauritzen vessels at Bayonne, is of 4,500 tons, and the ships there include every type in the company's fleet of forty-eight scattered throughout the world.

We went to look at the compact, powerful wireless set, which, according to New York Harbor regulations, must be kept sealed in port. "We used to get messages every day from the home offices in Denmark over that set," Captain Jensen said. "Off the Pacific coast of South America and everywhere. The last message was April eighth. Just routine stuff, you know. And then, after that, nothing. They didn't have a chance to say goodbye." He looked at the set uncertainly, as if it might begin again, spontaneously, and tell him the nightmare was over. "We were two days out from the last Chilean port on our northbound trip. We picked up the news broadcast, naturally, so we knew what had happened, and there was a broadcast from Copenhagen that we should get into the nearest neutral port. So I got into Paita, a little harbor on the coast of Peru, and we lay there two months. Then the British government agreed that Danish ships that had been en route between two neutral ports could complete their voyages. A lot of the Danish boats had cargo on board that was intended to be transshipped to Great Britain. So they let me come up to New York." During the summer, he said, the Lauritzen ships were anchored in the Hudson above the George Washington Bridge, so they had no wharfage to pay. It is not convenient to spend a winter in midstream, beset by fog and snowstorms, and unable to communicate with the shore except by motor launch, so in November the ships moved down to Bayonne.

We left the wireless room to visit the crew's quarters amidships. These consisted of outside cabins, each accommodating two men. The cabins were somewhat better than tourist accommodations on most passenger liners. There was one comfortable messroom for the seven seamen of the deck department and another for the six firemen. For the thirteen men there were two washrooms, each with three washbasins and showers. Two cabins for apprentices were further forward, near the officers' quarters. Most officers in the Danish merchant marine start as apprentices and work their way up as firemen or seamen, Captain Jensen said. Sailoring in Denmark is a skilled trade. Living conditions are good aboard, he said, because of the high standards set by the Danish labor laws, and the employers gained by the high standards, because a small crew of skilled seamen could work a ship better than a larger crew of inferior men. The empty cabins were clean and tidy, just as the sailors had left them. The Captain didn't urge me to go down into the engine room. "I have been thirty-five years at sea," he said, "and all I know about a fireman is that he is necessary to have on board. I went to sea as a cook." He said that he had been seventeen then.

The noise of work on the Maria, the ship tied beside the Marna, had ceased, and I suggested that we call on the captain who had been chipping rust. We walked across the plank between the two ships. Captain Nielsen's dog, a brown, smooth-coated bitch which looked like a dachshund on terrier's legs, came bounding to greet us. Jensen stopped to fondle her. "Her name is Nula," he said. "She was born in Barcelona, but she has spent all her life at sea, so now she is afraid of the land. When we take her ashore, she runs back on board. She is a nice girl." Captain Nielsen, a peppery, jocular little man, was in his cabin, shaving. He bowed and winked and protested with exaggerated solemnity that if he had known we were coming, he would have put on a frock coat. He lived in an even lonelier state than Captain Jensen, he explained, with only his first officer and a steward, who doubled as cook. The Maria had been on a fruit run between South American ports and Europe, and in April, after the invasion of Denmark, he had taken refuge in a Brazilian port, as Jensen had in Paita. The British had later given him permission to sail to New York. On a dresser there were silver-framed photographs of

Captain Nielsen's wife, with plump cheeks and a pointed nose exactly like his own, and of three children, and of a low, tile-roofed house in a town called Odder.

"We are not badly off here," Captain Nielsen told me. "We can't complain. We have the English school and it is very good." A WPA English class, which meets in a junior-high-school building in Bayonne four evenings a week, provides the main distraction for the Danes at the Port Terminal, he said. Twenty Danes walk from the ships to the classroom every school night. The walk takes an hour. They spend two hours in class and then another hour walking home. By that time they are ready to turn in. Captain Jensen, perhaps because his English is already excellent, prefers to stay home and read. Nula sits with him during Nielsen's absence. "Everybody got A-perfect in attendance, except the Knudsens and the Carlsens, the two married couples," Captain Nielsen said. "When Captain Knudsen goes, Mrs. Knudsen got to stay with the kids, and when Mrs. Carlsen goes, Second Officer Carlsen got to mind the baby. But that Carlsen is a regular scholar. He must have gone to high school in Denmark."

"Young Carlsen is a very talented fellow," Captain Jensen agreed. "He built a toy motorboat with a real gasoline engine in it, and it runs twenty miles an hour. Also, while we were in the Hudson, the Sessa's motor launch burned right down to the water. Carlsen has rebuilt the whole boat better than new, and he never was apprenticed to a carpenter. On top of that, he has the biggest baby I ever saw for eight months old."

We took our leave of Captain Nielsen after having a drink of Scotch with him, and Captain Jensen asked me if I would like to see the Carlsens' baby on the Sessa. The Sessa, he said, was a replica of the Marna, and therefore perfect. We walked across from the Maria to the Marna and then down the gangplank to the shore. It was already dark as we descended the Marna's side. A light burned in the deckhouse of the Sessa. When we opened the door to the deckhouse, the baby, who was large and grave, and was sitting in a corner, looked out calmly at the night and the sea. Mrs. Carlsen, a slim girl who appeared to be in her late teens, was feeding the child some sort of ground meat with a spoon. The second officer, small, thin, and brown-haired, stood near her, admiring. He had brought his bride over from Denmark, he told me, when he was put on the run between New York and Chile. She had lived in Brooklyn during his absences. The baby was born the day before the Sessa returned to port the last time. "Not many sailors' babies can say they had their fathers with them all their lives," young Carlsen remarked with a grin. When his income had been reduced to almost nothing, mother and child came to live with him aboard ship. There was room to spare, since so many men had signed off, and there was plenty of food. No ship chandler hesitates to extend credit when he knows that he has a fine vessel as security. The family occupies Carlsen's cabin and also that of an officer who has taken a job ashore. Alien seamen are not supposed to do that, but during a war the United States Immigration officials are not strict about such violations. Mrs. Carlsen had hung the windows of the other officer's cabin with cretonne and turned it into a nursery, and Carlsen had built the baby a crib. "When we were lying in the Hudson, the baby used to be on deck all day in the sun," Carlsen said. "That's why it's so big and healthy." After we had admired the baby long enough to satisfy protocol, Captain Jensen and I started back to the Marna. The Captain urged me to stay for supper. Thinking of the dismal trip back to New York, I quickly accepted.

Supper was served at five-thirty. It was a good meal, including at least a dozen kinds of hors-d'œuvre, mostly salt fish and smoked sausages. The food was well laced with Danish akvavit and Jersey beer. We ate with Mr. Hansen, the chief engineer, a thoughtful, mild-mannered man. There was plenty of butter, but the officers spread their bread with lard which had been melted and mixed with fried onions and apples and then allowed to cool. I tried it and found it excellent. We talked of a time when Captain Jensen, then in command of another ship, had run the Franco blockade of the Straits of Gibraltar during the war in Spain. He had had a cargo of fruit from Cartagena, he said. The Nationalists had searchlights and batteries on the European and African sides of the Straits, at Algeciras and Ceuta. But it was a thick night and the searchlights were not able to pick up the Danish ship. An armed trawler came out of Ceuta to chase her, but the Danes soon left her astern. The line lost several ships during the Spanish war, Mr. Hansen said. They were sunk by Franco bombs. As if she had heard us speak of Spain, Nula, the Spanish dog, came in to join us. "Aha," said Captain Jensen, "Nielsen must have left for school." Mr. Hansen excused himself and went out. The Captain and I walked back to his cabin.

The ship's lone steward brought us two bottles of beer, and Captain Jensen said, while pouring some into my glass, "It isn't bad, for a change, to see a little of the land. My father was a landsman, a farmer, but my two brothers and I found our way to the water like ducks. So I am interested always in farming when I have a chance to go inland. A couple of weeks ago I went in as far as Connecticut. I have a friend there, a Swede, who runs a dairy farm. He runs it very clean, but it does not matter; the milk must be pasteurized anyway. At home we appreciate milk better when it is not pasteurized."

"There are people in New York City who like it better that way, too," I said, "but we can't risk any contaminated milk getting in with the city's supply. Some dairies aren't as careful as others."

"But why not?" Jensen asked. "Haven't they any coöperatives? It is to the interest of the dairies to be clean. Then they would get a premium for the milk. It is just like ships. If you have a good ship, with the proper number of watertight compartments and all new safety things, then you pay such a low insurance rate, you know. And if you treat the crew right, it is a good crew, and then you don't have to pay so many men. In Denmark it is all worked out so beautifully. In a coöperatve one bad one hurts all the others. As an illustration of what I mean, I will tell you how Denmark arranges eggs. All the farmers belong to coöperatives, and when a farmer takes an egg from the nest, he marks it with his personal stamp and the date. Then, after the egg is exported, if a woman even in Brazil, say, buys a Danish egg and it is bad, it can be traced back to the farmer, and maybe even to the hen. If it was the farmer's fault, he would have trouble with his coöperative. If it was the hen's fault, the farmer would know what to do. The woman in Brazil would get her money back. For that reason, people all over the world have confidence in Danish eggs." I have few ideas about eggs, so the conversation stopped.

We had two more bottles of beer, then Captain Jensen went

over to a wall cabinet and got out a large and decorative book, which he laid on the table between us, just as one boy might show another a favorite volume. "The book is called 'Konsul,'" he said, "and it is a kind of biography of *Konsul* Ditlev Lauritzen, the founder of our company. He died in 1935. In his life he owned a hundred ships." We looked together at the frontispiece, a portrait of an old gentleman with a long jaw and white chin whiskers. "I do not even know how he got the title," Captain Jensen said, "but everybody called him *Konsul*, anyway. And this little ship," he said, pointing to a drawing on one of the early pages, "was the first one he owned, in 1880. He was not a sailor himself, because he went to sea once when he was a boy and he was seasick. This is a drawing of a Danish cottage," he said, turning a page, "such as there are near the town where the *Konsul* was born. It has a thatched roof and the trees in the picture are bent toward the east because the west wind is always blowing there. Here, in this part of the house, live the people, and here they got stalls for two cows and a horse. No, let me see. I don't know about the horse," the huge man said, peering hard at the little drawing. He considered a while and then said firmly, "Yes, they got a horse. Here is the first chapter about the *Konsul*'s father, who was a timber merchant. Here it says the *Konsul*, when he was a boy, he started already in the potato business." Captain Jensen chuckled, as if he found it extraordinarily funny that a man destined to own a hundred ships should ever have bothered about a potato. Together we went through the book, the sort of illustrated success story that in other circumstances would have seemed a bore. That night, in the cabin of the exiled ship, it held me like a sad fairy story, because I couldn't help thinking that probably nobody in Denmark would ever write that kind of book again.

We saw the picture of the *Konsul*'s first office in Esbjerg, and of the office boy who rose to be senior captain of the line, and of the *Konsul*'s father, Jorgen, whose initials, J. L., the *Konsul* in filial respect caused to be painted on the funnels of his ships. We followed the chronicles of the *Konsul*'s real-estate dealings, his public benefactions, and his fish cannery, the Scandinavian Canning Company, Ltd., and then we came to a part about the ships, which gave the history and description of each one. I think that is the part Captain Jensen likes best. "For her time she was a beauty," he said of one, and, in a lower voice, of another, "In my opinion she was a failure. Top-heavy and not enough cargo hoists." We even went through several eulogies of the *Konsul* at the back of the book; here, though, I thought that Captain Jensen skipped quite a bit. "In Denmark everything is worked out very well," he said. Then he put away the book about that famous shipowner of whom I had never until that day heard. The kindly, wide-shouldered Captain Jensen, in his leather jerkin, appeared to me for a moment like an Inca priest who had been telling a foreigner what life was like before Pizarro came.

The New Yorker, January 11, 1941

Notes on Repatriation

A LETTER has just come to me from Sauvageon, an aviator I knew when I lived in Paris in the early days of this war. Ever since I returned from France last summer, I have expected to hear from him. I didn't think there was much chance Sauvageon had been killed or captured. I last saw him in Paris in April, when he told me that his escadrille was being transferred from Alsace to Marseilles to prepare for the war against the Italians. You seldom read of the Italians' hurting anybody. I recognized Sauvageon's handwriting on the envelope immediately. His script is almost microscopic, but the letters are so well formed that they are completely legible. The handwriting is incongruous to anyone who knows Sauvageon, because he is a very big man, with the shoulders, neck, and jaw of a plunging fullback. When I saw the envelope, I thought of a letter he wrote me from Alsace when I was still in Paris. He had written about the sun sparkling on the snow and the clouds of crows which blackened the highways in the wake of the horse-drawn baggage trains, so the roads looked like bands of crape across the white land. "It reminds me of old Breughel's painting of winter that we used to go to see in the good days in the museum at Vienna," he wrote then.

Now Sauvageon tells me he is living in Unoccupied France in a little town on the frontier between the Occupied and Unoccupied Zones, in the Jura region. He has been too depressed to write before, he says, "for we have fallen low indeed." I knew that Sauvageon in civil life had been an engineer employed by a syndicate which owned a dozen factories in different parts of France. He has been demobilized, he writes, and is stationed by the syndicate in the border town in order to receive the company's employees, who are being expelled from occupied Lorraine and have to find homes in what Sauvageon terms "the France called free." "The Germans are driving out of Lorraine about 350,000 persons," he writes, "having given them the choice between going to Poland or Unoccupied France. I am enclosing a copy of Gauleiter Burckel's proclamation to the people of Lorraine, brought to me by a refugee. It will serve as an indication of what is in store for all of us."

The typewritten sheet that he enclosed reads, in a bad German sort of French: "People of Lorraine! All of you know the task that the Führer has entrusted to me. This province must be German for eternally ever. It is why we must absolutely have a repatriation from the zone of mixed languages. For in the zone in question there are a number of places where the inhabitants have been in the course of time completely Francisized. This is especially true of the peasant population of the region." Sauvageon writes in the margin at this point, "Some of the peasant families have inhabited the same house in the same village for seventeen generations!"

"Now," the proclamation continues, "it is possible to pacify a frontier only by a repatriation, such as we have already executed in southern Tyrol, in Volhynia, and in Bessarabia. But we can repatriate you only to the east of the German Reich, because it is only there that we have the necessary space. It is why I ask of the population if it desires a repatriation to Unoccupied France or a repatriation to the Warthegau on the eastern frontier of Germany." Sauvageon writes marginally, "The animal speaks of repatriating people to places they have never seen in their lives."

The proclamation goes on: "The reply to this question must be a decision for France or for Germany. Your decision will entail grave consequences. I know that in spite of your love for France, repatriation is painful for many of you." Sauvageon writes, "They have to leave their houses, their fields, and their vineyards, and are allowed to take with them 110 pounds of baggage for each person and 1,350 francs in cash."

"Just as the Reich has repatriated its Germans from the Tyrol," Gauleiter Burckel continues, "France now must repatriate those Lorrainers who confess themselves French. We respect this decision. It is a decision of men of honor, of character, who draw the necessary consequences from their national convictions. I have got into touch with the French Government to assure:

"1. That the repatriation will be carried out in good order.

"2. That the repatriated families will suffer no material loss.

"For this reason the exact value of the personal and real

property of the repatriated families will be communicated to the French government." Here Sauvageon writes, "They order the French government to pay for what *they* are stealing from Frenchmen."

The proclamation concludes: "To those among the workmen and office workers who wish to contribute to the formation of a solid German district here at the frontier"—the Gauleiter had evidently despaired of the peasants—"I will be glad to give the chance to prove their loyalty. [Signed] Burckel, Gauleiter."

"Of course, all the people choose to come to France," Sauvageon writes. "The populations of whole villages depart, singing the 'Marseillaise.' At the head of each flock march the *curé* and the old people, who will perhaps never again see their houses or the villages where they were born. From one of our factories at Château N—— (renamed N——burg now!) the Germans expelled thirty-six out of thirty-seven workmen. The workers marched around the factory with a tricolor, singing the 'Marseillaise' and a refrain, 'No, you will never keep Alsace and Lorraine.' Then they left for the France called free. The German authorities think they can erase the past by effacing all inscriptions in French and by dynamiting all the monuments to the French war dead of 1870 and 1914–18. They are mistaken. Our country will rise from the mud in which we lie."

The rest of the letter is about officers we both knew—some are dead, many are prisoners, and a few are in Morocco, waiting. The letter ends with the words "We will awake from this nightmare." Those are good words to hear from big, grave, rough-looking Sauvageon, who went to war but could not help thinking about the crows and Breughel.

The New Yorker, February 22, 1941

Colonel Britton and the Rhythm

THE V campaign, which has raised the morale of an occupied continent and has kept the equivalent of several Axis divisions busy on the mainland of Europe erasing chalk marks and tracking down suspected listeners to the British radio, probably costs less than the advertising of the average American toothpaste manufacturer. It makes up only a small part of the programs of the European News Service of the British Broadcasting Corporation. The entire news service has a payroll of a few hundred employees, including English and Continental writers, announcers, technicians, and studio attendants. All the salaries are less than modest by New York standards. The spread of the V through the occupied countries has therefore given the men running the show some of the satisfaction that a boy feels when he shatters a large, impressive pane of glass with a five-cent slingshot. The success of the V as a fetish, an advertising symbol, and a parlor stunt all over Great Britain and the United States has not caused them similar pleasure. The campaign was never pointed at Great Britain or America, they say, and some of them endorse the sentiment of Low's recent cartoon contrasting the V's meaning in England and in occupied lands; in Britain, Low indicated, the display of the symbol meant V for Vulgarity. However that may be, the V has caught people's imagination in Britain; it gives them a feeling that luck is on their side, and that is not a bad feeling for a fighter to have. It is the first effective counterpart of the swastika.

The concept of the V, one of the catchiest advertising notions in history, did not first occur to a professional propagandist but to a gentle, slow-spoken Belgian lawyer named Victor de Lavelaye, who was a member of the Belgian Parliament until the Germans overran the Low Countries. De Lavelaye, who before the conquest of Belgium had never had anything to do with publicity or radio, found himself a refugee in London in the summer of 1940. The B.B.C. was setting up units to broadcast special programs to each of the occupied countries and placing natives of those countries in charge. De Lavelaye, who had nothing to do, was sleeping in a dormitory with some Polish soldiers and Breton sailors who were hoping to be employed in the units when a man in the British Foreign Office whom he had known in Brussels happened to ask him if he would like a job broadcasting. The Belgian naturally said that he would. He has an excellent speaking voice, with that slow, distinct Walloon accent that carries conviction to Belgian listeners, and he was a success from the first. Communication by water between Belgium and England has been good for a long time now; Belgians cross the North Sea almost at will, despite the German garrisons. Last winter, de Lavelaye learned from some of his countrymen who had just arrived in London that patriots all over Belgium were marking the letters "R.A.F." on walls and sidewalks. Reflecting on this, he got the idea that it would be easier, quicker, and more effective to draw a V, which stands for *Victoire* in French and, it also occurred to him, for *Vrijheid* ("Freedom") in Flemish as well. On last January 14th, during one of the daily broadcasts of the Belgian units of the B.B.C., he proposed that the V be substituted for "R.A.F." The studio audience at the historic event consisted of a B.B.C. sub-editor, a Flemish professor who broadcasts half of each Belgian program in his own language, and one of the pretty girls whom the B.B.C. calls studio manageresses. There was no room for others in the dismal little studio, about the size of a hotel bathroom, from which de Lavelaye was broadcasting. Within six days he knew that the V sign had spread all through his own country and into northern France, for German-controlled newspapers in Brussels and Antwerp, which reach London almost as quickly as the Glasgow *Herald*, were carrying editorial denunciations of "the fools who defaced walls with evidences of their treasonable wishful thinking."

Broadcasters of other B.B.C. language units elaborated on de Lavelaye's campaign for the V, urging that the letter be written in chalk or painted on walls and other surfaces, or scratched with a sharp point in the varnish of German Army cars. A corps of B.B.C. lexicographers, leafing through foreign-language dictionaries, found that for the people of Yugoslavia V could stand for *Vitestvo*, which means "Courage," and in the case of the Hungarians for *Vam*, meaning "Duty;" the Poles have the word *Wolny* ("Free"), and phonetically their "w" is a "v;" the Dutch, like the Flemish, have *Vrijheid*. The Greeks write the first letter of *Nike* ("Victory") like a Roman small "v." This was stretching a point, but the Greeks proved ingenious enough to get the idea.

De Lavelaye's only possible rival for the honor of originating the idea is the London Gas Light & Coke Co., which started painting large, glaring white V's on the curbings of the city streets a couple of days before the war began. These V's stand for "Valve," and they have the purpose of guiding the company's crews during blackouts in their work of shutting off mains broken by bombs. They are easier to spot than the inconspicuous valveheads of the mains, and the gasmen know that each valvehead is a certain number of feet directly in front of the base of a V. The Gas Company people admit that until de Lavelaye came along they hadn't thought of any further significance for their V's. "But," one of their foremen remarked to me, "'oo can say but this Delavaleer chap was walkin' along with 'is 'ead down, and the V so himpressed itself on 'is subconscence mind, one might say, that 'e couldn't shike it orf? It's a large subject."

The next great step in the V campaign came when an English-language broadcaster who calls himself "Colonel Britton" began playing it up in his Friday-night talks to English-speaking listeners in all the occupied countries. Britton, who is a mysterious, invisible presence in the B.B.C. European studios, of the genre of Conan Doyle's Professor Moriarty,* adds considerably to the juvenile charm which the British people find in the whole procedure. The public is told that his identity cannot be divulged. His broadcasts are made from records to protect the secret. When a visitor to broadcasting headquarters facetiously taps on a wall to find the concealed entrance to Colonel Britton's hiding place, a B.B.C. official will suggest courteously, "You may already have met Colonel Britton." There are, of course, dozens of men around the B.B.C. who might well make the Britton broadcasts. An American reporter talked to him once. The journalist made such a point of having an interview with him that one was finally granted, on the condition that a partition separate the two during their talk. The arrangements were carried out by

* NOT A "genre," AND NOT A CRIMINAL AS MORIARTY WAS.

the B.B.C. men in a spirit of high good humor; the reporter didn't learn anything he hadn't known before. In his broadcasts, the Colonel says "spyahhaid," "Norweh," and "clyah," for "spearhead," "Norway," and "clear," but this, among B.B.C. male voices, is not significant. His suggestions in his weekly talks for making even more of the V campaign are appropriated by the foreign units, translated and slanted for their homelands, and put on the air as the words of Colonel Britton. All the units make daily news broadcasts, most of them more than one a day, and they fill parts of these programs with V stuff.

The third great moment in V history came on the night of June 27th, when the V sign was translated into sound—the three dots and a dash that signify V in Morse code. Colonel Britton carefully tapped out the signal for the listeners to his program. "Do you get it?" he asked them. "Ah you suah?" That talk also marked the introduction of the first bar of Beethoven's Fifth, or Vth, Symphony—three short notes followed by a long one—as the radio signature of the V campaign. There was by this time nothing haphazard about the V broadcasts. Ivone Kirkpatrick, the Foreign Office Counsellor who is principally known in America as the man who went to Scotland to talk to Rudolf Hess after the capture of the German there, is the political chief of B.B.C.'s European service. Kirkpatrick is not as dull-witted as Foreign Office people are popularly supposed to be. He is, as a matter of fact, not dull-witted at all. By the time the Beethoven notes were being used for the signature—or "interval signal," as B.B.C. calls it— Kirkpatrick had fully realized the potentialities of the V. He, with Colonel Britton (who may be Kirkpatrick himself) and a number of B.B.C. men (any one of whom may, on the other hand, be Colonel Britton), had held numerous meetings with the B.B.C. musical staff and the heads of the various exile broadcasting units. This group makes up what Kirkpatrick calls Colonel Britton's Syndicate. They chose the Beethoven V in preference to the V produced by the first four notes in the grace-note version of the old "Chauve-Souris" "Parade of the Wooden Soldiers," a decision which would have caused infinite grief to the New York publisher who owns the "Soldiers" copyright had he known of it. It would have been a wonderful plug. The choice, however, put the campaign on a solemn and ominous basis. The quick-step interval signal of the wooden-soldier number might have reduced the V effort to an operetta level. The Syndicate even devoted several auditions to choosing the instruments with which the signal was to be recorded. A combination of two oboes and a trumpet gave the most dramatic effect, but tests proved the tone to be so penetrating that it would be likely to summon a Gestapo man anywhere near a radio listener's house. The interval signal finally recorded, and now used at the beginning and end of all V broadcasts, is played on a tom-tom. It is presumed to carry a suggestion of doom and at the same time to be reasonably confidential.

Colonel Britton, pushing the three-dots-and-a-dash idea for all it was worth, urged the friends of liberty on the Continent to rap the signal on tables to summon waiters, to knock it on doors, to sound it on automobile horns—all tricks which are by now familiar in a United States and a Britain where it is quite safe to perform them. The reaction was almost instantaneous. On July 1st, the German-controlled Dutch radio station at Hilversum came on the air with a doleful complaint about "the fools who go around whistling stolen German music." For B.B.C. purposes, the outcry from Hilversum was as good as a top Crossley rating would be to an N.B.C. feature. The V's and the V sounds in themselves are undoubtedly annoying to the Nazis, who see and hear in them the constant, ubiquitous evidence of German unpopularity, but they have an even greater value as a means of concentrating latent hostility and of giving anti-Germans in the occupied countries an intimation of their own numerical strength. During the past six weeks or so, Colonel Britton has also been guiding his army of V scratchers and tappers in a less markedly psychological offensive against the occupying forces. Schemes to obstruct German plans for economic warfare and to create unnecessary work for German manpower in the occupied territories are mapped out in the sessions of Colonel Britton's Syndicate. Sometimes they are suggested by the heads of the various foreign units, sometimes by the Foreign Office, and quite often they come in letters smuggled out of occupied Europe. Colonel Britton personally explains the stratagem on the air first and the radio units of exiles follow with *reprises* in all the languages of the races that hate the Nazis. Listening to a round of the broadcasts is like a day at a Berlitz School of Loathing.

I went down to the studios of the B.B.C. European News Service late one afternoon not long ago to watch the V broadcasters and listen to them. B.B.C. has grown so during the war that its personnel has overflowed from Broadcasting House on Portland Place, which in peacetime accommodated the entire local staff of the corporation, to studios scattered all over London. The European services are housed in the lower floors and basement of one of those great commercial buildings, looking like squat, flattened-out skyscrapers, that made their appearance in London between wars. The broadcasting to Europe goes on twenty-four hours a day from studios that are almost all tiny, with walls of bare brick and no accommodations for audiences comparable to those which attend the least important American broadcast. A B.B.C. man named Eldon Moore had been assigned to show me about. He has a thin face and an impressive, upcurling beard, equally reminiscent of Bernard Shaw and D. H. Lawrence, and we became firm friends at once because I made some allusion to an announcer's extreme Oxford accent. "*I* went to Cambridge," Moore said proudly, in what sounded as if it might have been a recording of the announcer's voice.

Moore first took me through the B.B.C. European news room, which is actually a series of compartments each arranged like a very rudimentary newspaper city room. At the entrance to this section there were three large tables shoved together, and at the head of the middle one sat the fellow in charge, like a *père de famille*, surrounded by his assistants. "All the dispatches of all the British news services come over this table," Moore said. "The copy-taster—that's the man in the middle—looks at them, sees what they're about, and distributes them to the splash-subs, as we call those chaps all around him. The splash-subs prepare a précis of each item, and the précis are distributed to the European editors, who take what they want for their own language broadcasts and, naturally, translate it." Nearly a score of tables were scattered through the rooms, each one surrounded by a group of half a dozen earnest men and women. "That table is Rumania," Moore said, waving his hand. "The next one is Albania and over in the corner are Denmark and Norway. France and Belgium are in the next room with Germany and Greece." We strolled through the fields of international journalism and then Moore led me to a closed door that suggested the entrance to a dungeon. "You're going to hear a Yugoslavian V broadcast," he said. "I can't go with you, because there isn't room for more than one extra chair. Here are the English and Yugoslavian texts of the broadcast, so you'll know what it's about." He handed me two sets of carbon copies. "There's a Slovene professor broadcasting in there now," he said, "but he'll finish in a minute, and then look sharp. We only allow twenty seconds between broadcasts."

By that time, a squat, brown-haired man with a determined air, whom I took to be the Yugoslavian broadcaster, had ranged up alongside us in front of the door. I learned afterward that he had been a concert violinist before the war. With him was a very pretty, exotic girl with high, Slavic cheekbones. Moore introduced us, and I shook hands silently with both of them. Then the door opened, there was an outward rush of Slovenes, and we popped into the studio they had just vacated. We sat around a little table, the girl at the head and the Yugoslavian and I facing each other, with a microphone between us. The girl gestured to the man that he was on the air, and he began reading his lines in a tense, heavy voice. The girl took notes as he spoke.

"This is Colonel Britton speaking to the V army," he began in Yugoslavian, and I noted that in that language "Colonel Britton" sounds like "Pukovnyik Britonia." "This week I'm again asking you to buy anything and everything and leave nothing for the Germans. Buy before your money becomes worthless. . . . Farmers, soon you'll be getting your harvests in. The Germans want to get their hands on your crops, but there are ways to hide them. You will need them to keep your families from starving during the winter, and if you can save a little more than you need for yourselves, it will be worth its weight in gold. . . . A lot of you city people have insurance polices. Nearly all the insurance companies have been bought up by the Germans, so every time you burn a hole in your carpet or break some china, don't forget to claim; bury the Germans in paperwork. And if you can't do any of these things, mark up the V where they'll see it. Beat out the V rhythm. . . ."

"V" in Yugoslavian is pronounced "Vuh," and as I listened to it being spoken by the heavy voice of the nameless man in the little studio (he has relatives in the Nazis' power and therefore goes under an incognito) I imagined that I could see thousands of people, alone or in groups of two or three, huddled over muffled radio sets in blacked-out rooms in the homes of a country where I have never been, listening with me. To them the V campaign was grim. Pukovnyik Britonia was the voice in the darkness.

And now the program ended with the V interval signal, which we couldn't hear in the studio because, being recorded, it was broadcast from elsewhere in the building. We dived out through a detachment of incoming Turkish broadcasters and I rejoined Moore. He and I went on to other studios, where I listened to a crisp young Norwegian who, Moore said afterward, had been the second-best-known broadcaster in Norway before the occupation; to a large, pink, placid Danish woman who, for variety, read a Danish translation of a speech by Dorothy Thompson; and to a Greek and a Czech, both of whom had been newspaper correspondents in London before the disasters to their countries. Moore told me that the number of broadcasts given by the various language units ranges from the one-a-day schedule of the Persians and Bulgarians to the fifteen broadcasts put on every twenty-four hours by the French. French reactions to the programs are easy to check, because B.B.C. gets hundreds of letters from France—some smuggled, but many simply by ordinary mail from the technically unoccupied territory. The latter are so frank, even when the envelopes are marked "Opened by Censor," that the B.B.C. people think the minor officials in Pétain's France must be anti-German and that letter-writers take their complicity for granted.

The Frenchmen who produce the fifteen daily programs have been recruited from almost every calling except radio and advertising. There are twelve in all, among them a painter, a cinema technician, a Parisian cartoonist, an actor of the

Comédie-Française, two newspapermen, and a comedienne who acts most of the feminine rôles in the many double-edged dramatic sketches which are produced. The director, who in London bears the name of Jacques Duchesne, although he was well-known on the French stage under another one, arrived in England by way of Dunkerque, wounded. Moore and I talked to Duchesne for a while after one of his broadcasts. He is a blondish, middle-aged man who suggests that stock figure of the French theatre, the lovable but slightly bewildered husband who wears a smoking jacket and a string tie and slaps the gigolo's face in the last act. He told us that he got into B.B.C. through the circumstance that just as he began to be able to walk about again after being wounded, the Pétain government signed the armistice and the Frenchman who had been in London all through the war as the broadcaster for the French State Radio departed for Vichy, where he became the mouthpiece for the defeatists. Duchesne, whose reputation as an actor extended to England, stepped into the job.

One of the French unit's masterpieces, popular response has indicated, was its first followup of Colonel Britton's introduction of the V sound. It was a compound of malice and poetry in which Duchesne presented, among other things, a sketch showing how the people in a French village might live to the accompaniment of the V signal—cock crowing, dog barking, *facteur* knocking on a door, bar patron rapping a coin against his glass—in such a way as to drive any German within earshot mad.

It was getting late, so Moore and I said goodbye to Duchesne and went out to dinner. "Well," Moore said, "I expect you have an idea how it works now. I'm sorry that we couldn't show you Colonel Britton." But I wasn't sorry; it is best for everyone, I suspect, that the Colonel should remain just a concept. Suppose the actual Colonel Britton should turn out to have a wart on his nose or to be a Foreign Office chap with striped trousers and a monocle? His picture would probably be filched by the Germans and published in the newspapers of the occupied countries. Observing it, the Serbs and Croats would exclaim incredulously, "Is *that* Pukovnyik Britonia?," and the spell would be broken.

The New Yorker, October 4, 1941

The Lancashire Way

GREAT BRITAIN just now is producing about seventy-five per cent as much war material as she is capable of producing, according to Lord Beaverbrook, who considers this a reproach to his countrymen. The United States is turning out around twenty per cent of its capacity, according to other Britons, who try not to sound reproachful when they mention it to an American. "That's about as well as we were doing in 1938 and 1939," a man I know in the Ministry of Supply told me resignedly the other day. It has become such a matter of course for each nation to repeat the mistakes of others that no one any longer becomes excited about it. In an effort to cheer him up, I said that when I left New York a few months ago our armament plants were working two or three shifts and we were building new plants as fast as we could, and he answered, "Yes, that's how we tried to do it at first. We stopped depending on the obvious soon after Dunkerque. Now, when we need more cartridges, we don't wait until we have built a new cartridge factory. We get some from a man who used to make fountain pens and some more from a chap who once manufactured lipsticks. We get shell fuses from a shop that once turned out prams—baby buggies, you know—and fuse components from costume-jewelry fellows. In the first year of the war those little fellows used to swarm into the Ministries looking for work and we would send them away. Now we hunt for them and think up things they can do with the sort of plants they have. It's poppycock to say that a country with a great peacetime industrial plant has to scrap it and start all over again in a war."

Before he got through he had me so interested in the possibilities of what Britain calls its "bits-and-pieces" system that I made a date to go to his office in the Ministry and discuss his pet subject at greater length. "And I'd like to see a couple of those embattled notions factories, too," I told him, thinking that here seemed to be the pith of the 1941 phase of the war in the British Isles. When I presented myself on the appointed day I found that he had prepared for me not only a dossier on bits-and-pieces but an itinerary. "Actually, there's an astonishing number of little factories turning out important war jobs even in the heart of London," he told me, "but the best place to see the system in operation is in Manchester. All of Britain is divided into twelve Production Areas, which incidentally coincide with the Civil Defense Areas. And each area is divided into districts. There are six districts in London alone, with what we call a clearing office for each one. You wouldn't think of Westminster, for example, as an industrial district, but our Westminster clearing office helps place about seventy-five thousand pounds' worth of war contracts in a month. They're mostly for small items, of course, things like screws and primer caps and strikers and tank-engine parts, but orders of big stuff running into the millions would be held up if they had to wait for those parts. In Westminster we have a candlemaker doing tank parts, for instance. Some of the candlemaker's lathes are a hundred years old. A fellow who used to make dental pumps—you know, those things the dentist puts under your tongue to draw away saliva—is now making an important part of the mechanism of the Bren gun. Then the fellows who used to make the metal tops of soda-water siphons are very useful, and so are beer-bottle-cap makers, who, with the aid of a little jiggery-pokery, change over to cartridge cases. A lot of those small fellows are damned good mechanics. A man whose shop has only a couple of machines which he has been using for several different operations often proves more adaptable than a big-factory boy who has been used to ordering a special machine tool for each new job.

"I'm afraid that you might get too limited an idea from enterprises as small as those, so I want you to go down to Lancashire to see the same thing done with big factories. Lancashire, you know, used to be at least seventy per cent textile before the war. There were, of course, the textile mills. Then there were the machine shops, which turned out textile machinery for the most part, and there was a good deal of miscellaneous light industry. However, there weren't any steel mills or locomotive plants or motor works. It's only twenty per cent textile now, and it's working full blast—harder than ever in its history. Some of the mills are still making textiles required for the war effort and for a minimum civilian consumption; the others have been closed down. But the machinery plants have been expanded and the textile labor has gone into them. Most of the people have been weavers and spinners for generations and never went near a lathe. There's a sort of sense, though, that people acquire from being around any kind of machinery. They get the swing of the new work much faster than, say, agricultural workers or white-collar fellows turned into a mill. The companies that are allowed to continue making textiles act as trustees for the whole industry. The owners of the closed plants get an indemnity out of the profits of those that stay open. The companies that stay open are pledged to protect the future interests of the closed ones—take care of the other fellows' customers as well as possible during the war, for example."

A couple of days later I arrived in Manchester equipped with letters of introduction to the Area Officer of the Ministry of Supply and the Regional Controller of the Ministry of Labour. My friend in the Ministry of Supply had even got me a reservation at one of Manchester's two big hotels, a cross between a balloon hangar and a Victorian boudoir, the kind of place, I'd been told, in which the harried chambermaids hardly have time to change sheets between the departure and arrival of travellers, the supply of soda but not of whiskey runs out punctually at half past nine in the evening, and the public bars close with the playing of "God Save the King" at ten, after which everybody in sight pretends to be a guest, because residents are privileged to drink all night, assuming they can keep a waiter awake to serve them.

The day I arrived I looked up the Area Officer, an energetic and astoundingly voluble Scot, who seemed delighted at a chance to show off Lancashire's versatile factories. He had prepared a huge catalogue of people who used to make one thing and were now turning out something different and lethal. We whittled down his list to a couple of typical plants, a large one and a small one, on which we would pay calls. "The only trouble, from your point of view, is that you can't write exactly what the large places did before the war, because that might put Jerry onto them," he said. I promised not to mention the real peacetime uses of the larger factory I would visit. The other, a fountain-pen factory, the Area Officer said, was too undistinguished to be identified. He said that an automobile would pick me up at my hotel the next morning. The driver would know the way and the Area Officer would telephone the company officials to expect me.

I spent the rest of the afternoon with the Ministry of Labour man, on the twelfth floor of the Sunlight Building, Manchester's nearest approach to a skyscraper. The Labour man had the evangelical manner of so many men in the British trade-union movement. Trade-unionism is in Britain a kind of dissenting church; if the foxhunting rector has his political equivalent in certain types of Conservative M.P.'s, the Wesleyan preacher has his among the Labour people. "In Manchester and its suburbs alone forty thousand men and women came over from textile work to the war factories," he told me. "The textile industry always employed a high proportion of women, and the proportion increased during the first year of the war, when a number of men went into the services, so a majority of the workers changing over were women. Some of our people have worked in the same mills for generations, and they always settle near the place they work. In the old days it was an adventure for a man or a girl to change to a mill a quarter of a mile away from the old one. This county, you know, is where the industrial revolution started, and families have been spinners or weavers ever since. Well, not long after Dunkerque, the governing body of the textile industry closed down three hundred and twenty-eight mills, and the people signed up for jobs in various war industries. When we could, we got them into factories near their homes, but some women had to travel as much as thirty miles a day, at least one way in the blackout. It was a great change in their habits, but they didn't complain. In most mills that shut down the workers got together and held a sort of ceremony on the last night, and all the women cried. Then the people went to work learning their new jobs. It takes only about a week to train a woman for the simplest work, filling shells. They train up to six or eight weeks for more skilled jobs, getting paid while they learn. After they were all sorted out you'd think they'd never worked with anything but metal. Lancashire people have coöperation in their blood. It's here the trade unions, as well as the factories, started.

And the Coöperative stores, which are the largest medium of distribution in all Britain now, began at Rochdale, a bit north of here. Why, even the troupes of girls who dance in unison—precison dancers, I think you call them—originated here. The original Tiller Girls were recruited from Lancashire. So when people understood what they were up against, they set themselves to win the war in the Lancashire way. The money is good, by our standards. A woman filling shells gets three guineas to three pounds seven a week, she gets the extra four shillings as a kind of bonus when she works with TNT, because it temporarily discolors her complexion."

"Three guineas a week doesn't seem an awful lot," I said. A guinea nowadays is about four dollars and a quarter.

"It's good money up here, though," the Labour man said. "More than most of them made on textiles. You must remember that our people lived comfortably on their textile wages when they were working. They only got into difficulties when they were unemployed. One great service the war has done is to destroy the fiction of the unemployable. We have two and a half million men and women registered as workers in this area, which includes three counties besides Lancashire. Recently we checked up and found we had just fifteen thousand unemployed. Five thousand were really industrial wrecks. Ten thousand were just workers changing from one job to another, the sort of thing you'd find on any given day. Yet a few years ago, when we had hundreds of thousands out of work, there were rich men who said that most of the fellows on the dole were either useless or shiftless, that if a man had no job it was his own fault."

The driver who called for me at the hotel next morning was a trim matron with steel-blue hair and a tailored uniform that would have done credit to a wealthy subaltern. It was khaki, with pale-blue piping, and a profusion of leather goods was arranged like a trellis on her coat. She was a member of the Mechanized Transport Corps, she explained, a voluntary organization of women who supply their own cars and buy their own uniforms. They drive officers and civil servants on official business, and the government reimburses them for the petrol they use. She turned out to be an excellent driver, and since she was Lancashire-born she knew her way around the network of roads that radiate from Manchester to the scores of smaller factory towns around, places with names we never hear in America, with populations of from twenty-five thousand to a hundred and fifty thousand. The bare hills and valleys north of the city are full of them; the flatlands that stretch westward to Liverpool and south into Cheshire bristle with smoking chimneys. As we drove along the roads, I could not help thinking of the perplexity of a German bomber pilot if he got over this region. Industry is not concentrated, but is almost anywhere, and between the clusters of factories there are stretches of pasture land into which his bombs would drop harmlessly if he missed. It is impossible to blanket such an area with bombs. More and more the British are decentralizing their production, thus taking the sting out of mass raids.

Our first stop was a factory twenty miles from Manchester that once made—or so I'll say—refrigerators and kitchen cabinets. We drove up in front of the old, grimy office, which reminded me of hundreds I have seen in southern New England. Inside the door I found Mr. Bradshaw, the works manager, a stubby, determined little badger of a man who, I soon found out, is proud of his plant's versatility. There were pictures of all sorts of iceboxes on the walls, but in the place of honor on the mantelpiece stood a magnificent twenty-five-pound shell, the leader of the firm's new line. The plant had begun changing over in June, 1940, *after* Dunkerque, Mr. Bradshaw said. The Chamberlain government, with its policy of business as usual, had encouraged the manufacture of kitchen cabinets for export. The factory had got its first new machines in July, 1940, actually a set of ancient German power lathes. In October, the Ministry of Supply had installed a battery of really new Canadian machine tools. "But we're using ninety-five per cent of our old equipment as well," Mr. Bradshaw said, "and we're using our engineering brains. The design of weapons is highly specialized, but there's nothing superhuman about making them, provided that you know how to use your machines. That's the engineer's job. Once the machines are set, the operator can't make a mistake. We work a little finer on armament jobs than on most peacetime products," he said as he steered me through the back of the office and into the shops. "On the coarser war jobs we work to a thou'. That's a thousandth-of-an-inch margin of error. On the better grade we work to one or two ten-thousandths. When you have a mechanism with dozens of moving parts a very small error will jam the whole works." He piloted me between rows of machines that looked like monster, power-driven pencil-sharpeners, each putting a point on a bar of steel. Women manipulated these planers by levers, nursed the steel, bathed it in a soapy-looking liquid, flicked away long streamers of steel shavings, and lifted the rough-turned shells from the machines. "Roughing shells from the blanks," Mr. Bradshaw said in passing. "Women are allowed a maximum of three minutes for the operation, but they average two minutes and a quarter after they've been here a while. All of them used to be in shops, mills, or paper-box factories. You're interested in what we do with our old stuff? I'll show you our annealing furnaces."

Mr. Bradshaw led me to a shed where, in one of the walls, there was a row of furnace doors. "We can get a temperature of nine hundred degrees in them," he said. "We used them for putting the vitreous finish on enamel. We did a lot of enamelling, naturally, making kitchen stuff. Now we use the same furnaces for hardening tank armor. We're using the same furnaces to harden solid-armor-piercing shot for antitank guns, too. It's an eighteen-pound shot of solid steel. The ordnance people take lots at random and test them. Out of six shots fired against two-and-a-half-inch armor, at least four have to go clean through without breaking up. Quite a change from kitchen enamel. Now I'll show you our tin shop. We used to do a lot of light cylindrical stuff—you know, home equipment, like sanitary cans. Well, now we make sea-markers for the Admiralty and the R.A.F. A sea-marker is a light metal cylinder with powdered aluminum inside. When it's dropped on the sea from an airplane, the impact drives the aluminum up through the top. It spreads over the water, forming a big, shiny disc, and that marks the position of the crippled German submarine that the pilot thinks is down below the surface. The pilot flies home, gets more bombs, comes back to finish the job. Ingenious, what?"

All the workers in the tin shop were girls, wearing green smocks. Most of them seemed to be of high-school age. "We had about twelve hundred workers before the war," Mr. Bradshaw said. "The number dropped off to seven hundred while we were changing over, but now we have two thousand. Naturally, there are very few peacetime plants that can simply go over to war work without alterations. They aren't balanced, as we say. That means that if you're making a product that requires a great deal of milling and not so much boring, or a lot of boring and not so much milling, you may not have the correct proportion of machines for a war job. But the fellow over the hill, making a different product, may have a surplus of the machine capacity you need for your war work, and you may have just what *he* needs. So you marry demands and capacity. Maybe out of a hundred assorted factories you get the equivalent of twenty modern, balanced armament plants. It would take years to build the new plants, whereas with a little jiggery-pokery you can begin getting stuff out of the old ones in a few weeks. With our furnaces, for example, we can do the hardening for several factories that aren't equipped for it. It's like one artisan borrowing a tool from another. We have a second plant about two miles away from here, a former textile mill that the government has fitted up with the best sort of new machinery, American stuff. They turned it over to us to run because by the time they had got it equipped we had built up a lot of experience in war production. That's another point. If we had waited for a new plant to be built, we wouldn't have had the experience."

We went out to the car, and my M.T.C. driver, following Mr. Bradshaw's directions, took us to the newly equipped plant. The machines there, I noticed as soon as I went in, were for the most part glossy gray and displayed in large letters the names of such familiar points of origin as Milwaukee and Cincinnati. There were also a couple from Plainfield, New Jersey, and one friendly steel beast from Nashua, New Hampshire. "The machines on this side of the room," Bradshaw said, "are turning out incendiary bullets for machine guns. An incendiary bullet is practically a miniature infernal machine. You can see for yourself how complex it is." As he said this, he picked up from the foreman's table a large-scale drawing of an incendiary bullet and showed it to me. "There are eight separate operations," he said, "and they are all down to a thou' or finer. The machines in this row do the eight simultaneously and turn out the finished bullet. It's like grinding out sausage. That's what you can do with the right kind of machine when you can get it." He looked slightly contemptuous of such easy success.

He took me to another part of the plant, where girls were making the components of fuses for twenty-five-pound shells. "There are thirty-four separate parts to a fuse," he said. "We make them all here and then assemble them. The government inspectors, those girls in the khaki smocks, test samples of each sort of component, and then they test samples of the finished fuses." He picked up a fuse and showed me how it worked. There was a minute chamber at the bottom, which was to hold the detonating charge. This chamber, Bradshaw explained, had a roof one five-thousandth of an inch thick. There was a steel pin perpendicular to this roof, and, as Bradshaw pointed out, when the shell hit, the impact would drive the pin against the roof of the detonator, through that delicately milled five-thousandth, and into the explosive. "It's very simple," he said, "so simple that you couldn't even handle the thing without blowing yourself to bits if we made it that way. So we have a steel disc with a shutter between the pin and the roof. When the gun is fired the shell begins to rotate, and when the rotation reaches a certain speed the shutter winks back. It's all based on centrifugal force. The pin drops through the hole and rests against the detonator chamber, and the shell explodes at the precise instant of contact. It's a watchmaker's job, and we turn them out by the hundreds of thousands."

My driver and I left Bradshaw at his new plant. Miles before we arrived at our next destination, the country ceased to look industrial. After two or three inquiries we arrived before a weathered red-brick building with a small brass doorplate that bore the legend "Robinson Pen Company" in script. I marched into a cubbyhole of an office where an old chap in worn striped trousers and office coat sat at a high desk. For the anteroom to an arms factory, the décor was perfect Hitchcock. To carry out the motif, the old chap insisted on seeing my identity card, my alien-registration certificate, and my passport. Finally, he pushed a button in the panelled rear wall and a concealed door opened before me, something I had never expected to see except from a seat in the Rialto Theatre.

Mr. Robinson, the head of the firm, who met me inside, was in his early forties. He favored the "American" style that became a fashion in England in Harold Lloyd's heyday, when "go-getter" was a new bit of slang. He was complete, from tortoise-shell glasses to soft white shirt and baggy flannel pants. Mr. Robinson said he was the son of the founder. The firm had existed in a modest way for forty years, making pens without trying to advertise them. "We use very rudimentary machinery," he said. "I expect you'll find it amusing. But it's so simple that it's adaptable. We employ girls almost exclusively—always have. Most of them work on a small, electrically driven hand lathe that can be quickly reset for a great variety of operations. But the girl has to pay constant attention to what she's doing; it's rather like work at a sewing machine. Then we have the machines on which we used to stamp out gold nibs for pens. We're still making some pens. As a matter of fact, they need a certain number in the war effort. Making pen nibs is rather fine work. I'll show you." I followed him down a steep flight of stairs into a basement which, again in the Hitchcock tradition, was unpredictably large and high. There must have been a hundred and fifty girls down there working at machines, and above the collective racket I could hear a radio loudspeaker blaring "Only Forever." "The girls like the radio on loud like that," Robinson said. He took me to one side of the room to watch a machine that he said was normally used on pen nibs. "This is what we do on it now," he said, shoving a box of tiny copper discs with raised edges toward me. "These are the primer caps for a sensitive incendiary shell, a one-pounder used in anti-aircraft guns. They are the last bit fitted to the loaded shell. The explosive is so sensitive that just a microscopic roughness on the edge of the disc will set off the charge. A few workers in arsenals are walking around without hands now because of those shells. The flat surface of the disc is four ten-thousandths thick and the edges two ten-thousandths. The whole thing is about an eighth of an inch in diameter. There's never been an accident with our discs. Only one other firm has been able to make them, and that happens to be a gramophone company. Now come over and look at what the girls are doing on their lathes."

As I was telling Mr. Robinson about the plants I had visited earlier that day, he picked up a small object that a girl had just taken from her lathe and placed in the box before her. I recognized it immediately. "Why, that's one of the incendiary bullets that they're turning out on those big American machines at Bradshaw's place," I said. "Yes," he said, "but *we* break the job down into four operations, and a battery of four girls with hand lathes turns out the same bullet that Bradshaw's machine does in one operation. It isn't quite as fast or as cheap, but the bullets meet the same tests. In fact, I think we have rather fewer rejections than they. Those big specialized machines are efficient, of course, but there aren't enough of them in the world. Also, they cost the government upward of a thousand pounds apiece. Actually, our production costs are about ten per cent higher. But the country needs all the production it can get, and it can only get production by using us all. I suppose you saw them make all the parts for the fuse up there and then assemble them. Well, we assemble the same fuse here from parts made in little shops in a dozen parts of England. The thirty-four parts are contributed by twenty-six different factories. Separately, the things look like small articles you'd pick up on the hardware counter of a Woolworth's."

I said goodbye and started back to Manchester with my M.T.C. driver. On the way I had plenty of time to think of the deadly trifles that might someday come out of zipper and razor-blade factories in the United States.

The New Yorker, November 22, 1941

Paddy of the R.A.F.

THE few British fighting men who have become popular legends during this war have done so without the connivance of His Majesty's Government. German and Russian communiqés are studded with the names of individual heroes, but even the R.A.F., although garrulous compared to the British Army and Navy, believes fliers should be almost anonymous. Whereas the Luftwaffe would announce that the late Werner Mölders had shot down his ninety-ninth plane—and, incidentally, British airmen would take no stock in his score— the Air Ministry says merely that a pilot attached to one of its squadrons scored his eleventh victory. Weeks later, perhaps when the pilot is due for a decoration, his name will appear in the London *Gazette*, a government newspaper few civilians read. For this reason, a high score is not enough in itself to make a fighter pilot a new personality. He has to have some particularity that the public can remember. Flight Lieutenant Brendan Finucane—Distinguished Service Order and Distinguished Flying Cross with two bars—has established himself in the public mind by being profoundly Irish, so Irish that strangers spontaneously address him as Paddy, which is also what his friends call him. He is neither Ulster Irish nor Anglo-Irish nor public-school-and-Oxford denatured Irish but middle-class Dublin Irish, and so proud of it that he has a big shamrock painted on his Spitfire. It is a shamrock designed by the adoring Yorkshire rigger and Canadian fitter who look after his plane. The shamrock has the initials "B.F." in the centre and is surrounded by thorns. The rigger says he knows that thorns belong on a rose, but he feels they are appropriate, and Paddy agrees with him. The same rigger once, after the pilot had shot down his twenty-first plane, thought he would please him by painting twenty-one little swastikas around the periphery of the shamrock. Paddy got angry at this, saying they were an affectation of elegance, and made the rigger remove them. Paddy is twenty-one years and a couple of weeks old, and has a boyish eagerness to avoid any implication of swank. The way he got his most serious war injury fits in almost miraculously with his public personality; he broke his right foot jumping over a wall at a wake.

Being Irish is not itself a rare distinction in the R.A.F. At least five hundred citizens of Eire wear pilots' wings on their tunics and about fifty have been decorated. What made Paddy identifiable even before the public knew his name was his being both Irish and attached to an Australian squadron. When the Londoner at his breakfast table reads, for example, about a Polish pilot in the R.A.F. shooting down a plane, he has no way of knowing whether or not it is the same Pole he read about last Thursday, but the designation "an Irish pilot officer attached to an Australian squadron," which began to thread its way through the communiqués last June, gave Paddy his public identity. Subsequently the Londoner could follow Paddy's promotions as well as his triumphs, because the communiqués, which early last summer mentioned him as an Irish pilot officer (a pilot officer being the equivalent of an American second lieutenant), later spoke of him as a flying officer and then as a flight lieutenant. The last rank is like our captaincy. Finucane's decorations piled up even faster. He began the summer with a Distinguished Flying Cross left over from 1940, when, as a comparative novice, he had shot down five "certains," as the unquestionably disposed-of planes are called, in the Battle of Britain. As the summer progressed, he added two bars to the cross, and then, just before his birthday, he received the Distinguished Service Order. A couple of days later he broke his foot. By that time he had accumulated twenty-three "certains" and about a dozen "probables." He doesn't try to remember the planes he damages but does not bring down.

There are a good many men in the R.A.F. who think Flight Lieutenant Finucane is the most accomplished fighter pilot of the war, although he has not actually downed the most planes. In support of their argument, they point out that he made almost all his kills last summer and that 1941 was a poorer season for German planes than 1940 had been. Firth, Paddy's Yorkshire rigger, holds this point of view. In 1940, he says, there were "oondreds of jerries—all you'd to do was fly oop in air and poosh booton. But this year, when Paddy wants one, he has to go to France for it." Also, the technique of air fighting has been much refined since 1940. As there has been no general melee this year, German and British veterans alike have had time to teach the new pilots their tricks. None of the other pilots in Paddy's outfit, Squadron 452, had fought before last June, though they were the pick of the first lot to enter training in Australia. They had continued their training in Canada and Scotland. Paddy, who had been in the R.A.F. since 1938, joined them last spring at their first fighter station, which was in England, with the assignment of teaching them by example. They were the high-scoring squadron in England in August and September. They were nosed out by the American Eagle Squadron in October, while Paddy was nursing his foot, as he still is.

The wake at which Paddy broke this foot was expressly an Australian fliers' variant of the rite. All squadron members leave a couple of extra shillings in a kitty each time they settle their mess bills; then, when a pilot goes missing, the survivors drink up what he has left. The day before this particular observance, a sergeant pilot had been shot down over France. He had left two pounds ten, which was enough to finance only a modest wake. That, Paddy says, is why it was emotion and not drink which was responsible for his accident. The sergeant had been a close pal of his, and when, at the party, Paddy came upon a wall, he decided to jump over it, as a gesture of respect. There was a blackout, he says, and the wall looked like any other wall in the same circumstances. However, there happened to be a twenty-foot drop into an areaway on the other side, so he broke his foot. He was consoled a couple of days later by the news that the sergeant was safe in a prison camp. "In a way, the whole party was a waste," he says, "but I don't bear him any hard feeling." The hospital ward to which he was immediately afterward assigned was devoted entirely to R.A.F. leg injuries, and every pilot present, except himself, had been hurt either in a motorbike accident or a Rugby match. This excess of animal spirits may result in the loss of some flying hours, but it is also a sign that the men are in prime condition.

Paddy Finucane is an unusually serious young fighting man except when he is actually in the midst of the Australians, which is perhaps why he likes them so much. One Australian flight lieutenant, called Blue because he has such red hair, says, "We had to teach Paddy to play the fool when he came to us. The poor man had been with an English squadron so long he was trying to act dignified." The Australians, though few of them are older than Paddy—one pilot officer with a magnificent drooping mustache is nineteen—are relatively worldly types. One, upon returning recently from what the fliers call a sweep, remarked that he had shot a German into the Channel and that after the plane had struck, a bright-green stain had appeared on the surface of the water, something he had never seen before. "Heavy crème-de-menthe drinker, no doubt," he concluded. Most of them, before joining the Force, were university undergraduates or students in Australian public schools, whereas Paddy, right before he enlisted in the R.A.F., was an assistant bookkeeper in an office in London. Yet today, on all questions pertaining to air fighting, the Australians defer to Paddy's advice and obey his instructions. When he is flying with them, he sometimes, by radio-telephone, directs four dogfights simultaneously. "Has one of those beautifully efficient minds that work along just one line," a disciple of his says. "He can remember the positions of a dozen planes at once, although they change by the split second. And he has phenomenal eyes. Some fellows say Paddy smells Messerschmitts, but what really happens is that he sees them before anybody else can."

This exceptional vision may be the one quality all great pilots have in common. Once Paddy's mates saw him going after two Messerschmitts 109 F's, of which he downed one. The second plane flew into a cloud and was lost to view. Finucane flew in after it, opened fire while in the cloud, and a moment later flew out of the other side as the German fell out of it, trailing flames. Another time, when the Australians and a New Zealand squadron were taking part in a sweep, Paddy, three miles away, saw some Messerschmitts flying near the New Zealanders and warned them before they were aware of their own danger. He isn't a "suicide fighter," his comrades say. He will sometimes maneuver his section for five or ten minutes before he sends it in to the kill, but when he does, every Spitfire is apt to be on a German plane's tail. "The idea isn't just to get a plane for yourself," Finucane himself says. "You want to see the other fellows get some shooting, too." He derives more pleasure from helping a new pilot to his first certain than out of increasing his own bag. Paddy thinks his squadron is perfect. "All the Australians are mad," he says in a tone of heartiest approbation. "Waggle your wings, and they'll follow you through hell and high."

Paddy is of almost exactly medium weight and height; he is probably an inch too short for the New York police force. He boxed as a welterweight on the R.A.F. team in a match against the combined Scottish universities just before the war began, which means he weighed a hundred and forty-seven pounds, or ten stone seven in the national jargon. He is a few pounds heavier when he isn't in boxing trim, and he has the strong neck, the wide cheekbones, and the broad jaw of a good Irish ring type. He has wavy dark-brown hair, blue eyes, and a pink-and-white complexion that looks like a soap ad; he reddens to his ears when flustered. He was wild about boxing until he turned to air fighting, which he thinks a more exhilarating form of competition, and constantly draws analogies between the two. "Some pilots roll better to their right than to their left," he may say, "the way some boxers move better to one side." Or he says, "You have to take the play from the other fellow, just like boxing. I don't let them dither around." It isn't that Paddy is frivolous or brutal; in his direct way, he has made a mental adjustment that he couldn't have bought from a psychoanalyst for under a million dollars. "The personality never enters my mind," he says. "I always think to myself, 'I'm just shooting down a machine.' Some things get you rather angry, though," he adds. "For instance, if they shoot at our chaps after they've bailed out. That's like hitting a man when he's down." He has never seen this happen, he explains, but he has talked to fellows who say they have. He used to like Rugby almost as well as boxing. When the Army beat the R.A.F. at Rugby this fall, 30–3, Paddy took it as hard as missing three Germans. He watched the game on crutches.

He has never been shot down or wounded or forced to bail out, although during the 1940 hurly-burly he got a number of bullets through various Spitfires he was piloting. All last summer his planes went unscathed, a proof of his skill at maneuvering. Pilots like to find a couple of bullet holes in their planes after they get safely back to the airdromes, because it gives them something to talk about at mess. Once this year Paddy landed with holes in the tail fin of his plane, but they proved to have been made by the branches of a tree he had scraped. His rigger and fitter say he was much disappointed. He has never fought in anything but Spitfires, and has had them in all their editions. During the summer he ran through five planes—three early Spits and two of the latest Spit fives. He cracked up two machines on his own airdromes, stunting near the ground. Stunting is an officially discouraged but universal custom among fighting pilots. He is very careful about selecting a plane; he not only puts it through all the tricks he knows but he fires several trial bursts with its cannon and machine guns. If a cannon jams, he gets out instantly and walks away from the machine. Once he has picked a Spit, he leaves it in the care of his rigger and fitter, who work with an armorer, an electrician, and a radio man. Aircraftsmen in the last three categories take care of three planes apiece, so they are not identified with one pilot as a rigger and a fitter are. Finucane does not fancy himself an engineering shark. When he comes in from a sweep, he may say to his retainers, "She's flying left wing down," or "right wing down," but he leaves the remedy to the ground crew. This delights them. Firth, the rigger, who is dark, solid, and snaggle-toothed, says, "When Spit's been in dogfight, she's oopsey." His tone implies that the ordeal is rather like a childbirth for a delicate woman. Moore, the fitter, who is small and blond, says, "Some officers get a big head when they down one or two planes, but not Paddy." They both carry decks of snapshots of Finucane in their pockets.

After Paddy has chosen a plane, his shamrock and the letter "W" are painted on it. Each plane in a squadron is identified by a letter, as moviegoers who saw "Target for Tonight" know. Senior pilots usually get low letters, but Finucane insists on his "W," for sentimental reasons. It stands for Wheezy Anna, a nickname he gave his first Spit because its engine made such strange sounds. In those days the R.A.F. was short of planes and young pilots took what they could get. "Wheezy was a good old girl," Paddy says. "I cracked her up so hard I had the mark of the stick on my chest for a month."

*

When Paddy is on leave, as he is now on account of his foot, he lives with his parents, a small brother named Joseph, and two sisters, Monica and Claire, aged eleven and seven, in Richmond, the London suburb south of Kew. He has another brother, Raymond Patrick, who is nineteen and a sergeant air gunner in the Bomber Command. The house looks like several thousand others in suburban London and America. It is Tudor of a recent vintage, complete with the path of irregular concrete flagstones from gate to front door. Paddy's father is a night office manager at an airplane-parts factory that works the clock around. He is black-haired, energetic, witty, and a firm teetotaller. He looks a good deal younger than his forty-nine years and used to be an amateur soccer star in Ireland. Mr. Finucane pronounces his surname "Finewcan," but Paddy says "Finoocan." Paddy, who admires his father, has never developed a taste for beer or whiskey. Recently, in an effort to keep up with the Australians, he has learned to order a bottled drink called Pimm's No. 1, which is like a sweet Tom Collins. Mrs. Finucane is good-natured and hospitable. When Joe, the small brother, gets home from school, his favorite reading is a monthly publication called *Rockfist Rogan of the R.A.F.*, the adventures of a British Superman with a war slant. Rockfist, typically, will jump from his flying plane into that of a wounded brother pilot, drag him from the cockpit, and make a double parachute jump to safety, perhaps lassoing the propeller of a Heinkel on the way down and hauling the crew into captivity. This serial greatly increases Joe's respect for his older brothers. Paddy himself prefers more realistic books about flying. There is a recently published one called "Fighter Pilot," which he describes as wizard, his favorite adjective of praise. He uses it, too, to describe the two Australian flight lieutenants who roomed with him at the airdrome up to the time of his jumping over the wall. One, the red-haired fellow called Blue, is addicted to mystery stories and the other reads poetry, forms of composition which Paddy runs down at every opportunity, out of a spirit of contradiction. The poetical Australian says he knows Paddy has a poetic soul, a suggestion that drives Paddy into a picturesque fury. The mystery-story Australian, who has downed ten German planes, wears the jacks of spades, hearts, clubs, and diamonds inked on his "Mae West," as the fliers call their bulbous yellow inflatable life-saving jackets, because these cards are the sign of a fictional detective he admires.

The mantelpiece in the Finucanes' dining-sitting room is decorated with cutouts of Snow White and the Seven Dwarfs made by Monica, a large square clock with an inscription saying it was presented to Flight Lieutenant Brendan Finucane by the night staff at the factory where his father works, and a bronze cigarette-lighter in the form of an aircraftsman spinning a propeller. This last is a gift to Paddy from his girl friend. He doesn't think it a good idea to get married during the war, he says, because "someday I might be going on a sweep and I would have it in the back of my head that I wanted to get back that night and that would distract me." Even now, he acknowledges, he sometimes has "a funny feeling in my tummy" just before he takes off, and he is afraid that marriage might make it funnier. He is a devout Catholic and attends Mass whenever he gets a chance. The Australians, he says regretfully, are "free and easy" about spiritual matters. He gives you a feeling that this worries him a little. He is always worrying about the fellows he flies with. Blue says that Paddy once woke him at four in the morning by shouting "Break, Blue! There's a Messerschmitt on your tail!" "I guess he dreams about air fighting all night," Blue says.

The Finucanes' move from Dublin to Richmond took place early in 1938. In Dublin, Paddy had attended a wonderful institution of learning called the O'Connell School, where the headmaster was a retired Army officer who had held a service boxing title. Like headmasters the world over, this one believed in his own favorite sport as a character-builder. Every morning at eight-thirty, according to Paddy, the boys were turned out under a large shed in the schoolyard and told to whack each other. Paddy developed such a taste for whacking that the future pattern of his life lay clear before him when he came to England; he was destined to be a fighter pilot. He was too young to enlist in the R.A.F. immediately, so he worked without pleasure at an office job until May, 1938. Then, on the precise day that he became seventeen years and six months old, the minimum age allowed, he enrolled for a course leading to a short-term commission. Richmond had seemed somewhat humdrum after the O'Connell School, and the Finucane brothers, during their first few months there, found the English rather "standoffish." After Paddy joined the R.A.F. things went much better. He is still, however, a vocally patriotic Dubliner. Being an R.A.F. officer, he does not go in for political arguments, he explains, but occasionally somebody says something about Eire which betrays a lack of understanding, and then Paddy puts him right.

Men accepted for the course Paddy took were supposed to put in four years of active service and then pass to the volunteer reserve for six more. That was considered the expedient way to raise a body of fliers for what some people thought might be an emergency. The British did not sufficiently hurry the training of their pilots even after the war began to give Paddy an opportunity to fly in France with the expeditionary squadrons. He did not get into action until June, 1940, a couple of weeks after Dunkerque. He was first posted to the East India Squadron at an airdrome in the south of England. The squadron got its name from the fact that people in India had contributed money for its Spitfires. Most of the pilots were British. That is a fine squadron, Paddy says; he had a good deal of fun there. "First the Germans started pushing over high-flying fighters, and then bombers with fighter escort," he reminisces happily. "There was something doing all the time." On his first flight with a formation in combat, he says, he was so preoccupied with keeping his place in the formation that he "could not see a sausage." The squadron broke up an incursion of eighty German fighters, but Paddy says he wasn't much help. Afterward formation flying became automatic, and then he began to enjoy himself.

In the East India Squadron days, the pilots slept with their flying suits on when the weather was clear, and their planes were kept warmed up constantly. One time, Paddy remembers, the squadron was just taking off when some Heinkels started bombing the field. A number of Spitfires bumped over fresh bomb craters as they got into the air. A bomb dropped directly in front of a pilot named Kenny Hart, and the blast stopped his propeller. He scrambled out and ran for a shelter trench, with bombs continuing to drop about him, while his mates, gaining height, took after the Heinkels. "We shot down a couple of them," Paddy says, "but seeing Kenny run was the cream of it." On another occasion the boys were gathered around a table in the middle of the field, having afternoon tea before taking off for a sweep. Unexpectedly, some Messerschmitts dived on the field and started plunking cannon shells into the tea service. The pilots, conspicuous targets in their yellow Mae Wests, dashed for shelter while the ground defenses had a go at the Germans, who got away intact. "Things like that amuse us when we think of them," Finucane says. He shot down five certains while he was with the East Indias and contributed to the destruction of other enemy planes, and the Fighter Command tabbed him a coming man.

There is nothing unorthodox about Finucane's methods. The secret seems to be that he does everthing exactly right, and a fraction of a second before his opponent. A fighter pilot aims at his adversary by means of a small, electrically operated arrangement called a reflector. When the enemy shows in the reflector he is in line with the guns, although, of course, he may be at a quite impractical range. There are two ideal shooting positions: one close behind the other plane, the other head on. Paddy prefers the first. The inconvenience of the second is that you are at the same time in line with the other fellow's guns. Polish pilots like this position. Even if you are hit, they say, you can ram the German before it is possible for him to pull out. You are therefore certain of your German. Paddy has a high regard for Polish pilots, but his mind does not run in the same channel.

The most difficult style of attack is called deflection shooting. This means firing as an enemy plane flies across your path. The angles of approach, rates of climb or descent, and speeds of the two planes all enter into the instantaneous guess the pilot must make as he pushes the button which operates the cannon and machine guns. Inexperienced pilots usually fire behind the other plane. Old hands have a tendency to fire in front of it. Paddy is a wizard shot, but he does not consider that deflection shooting pays. "Sometimes you take a long squirt at something that way and see bits fly off it, but you don't see it crash," he says. "What you want to do is get on their tail, close in. I give them a squirt in the tank and if they break up, I'm quite happy." A squirt is the burst of cannon and machine-gun fire that results from pressing the button and holding it down a couple of seconds. Paddy gets on the other fellow's tail in various ways: by pouncing, if he has an initial advantage in height; by waiting for the German to dive and then getting him as he pulls out; or by facing him at a safe distance and then circling him, as a mongoose goes around a cobra, finishing up at the back of his neck. A Spitfire can out-turn a Messerschmitt, although it cannot out-climb one. By practicing rigid economy in shooting, which is usual with him, Paddy once was able to down three German fighters in a single trip and arrive back at his airdrome with a quarter of his ammunition. It was his best afternoon's work. The squadron, collectively, got eight. The Australians had been "squatting on top of the bombers" that afternoon; that is, flying just above some Blenheims which were going to France for a daylight raid. A big formation of German fighters had dived from a great altitude, ignoring the Spitfires and going straight for the bombers. They dived right past the bombers without getting any. Then, as the Messerschmitts pulled out of their dives, Paddy, who was commanding the whole squadron that day, led the Spits above and at them.

Paddy has no personal feeling against Germans. His contacts with them have been limited. He remembers once seeing a couple at the Dublin Horse Show, and last August, after the East Indias shot down a Dornier near their airdrome, he and some other pilots went over to a hospital to visit the wounded German pilot and observer. "They had never flown together before," he says. Crews in the British Bomber Command rehearse their teamwork many times before they go out on a serious job.

Paddy's assignment to the Australian squadron was a masterpiece of psychology, as well as a good technical selection, because the Australians might have taken less kindly to a more formalized version of the British officer. At almost any time five or six of them are likely to he found around a table in one of the squadron's huts playing poker and saying, on any provocation, "Ectualleh." One boy will say "Two cards," and the dealer will say "Ectualleh?" The next will say "I'll have three," and the dealer will say "Ectualleh?" again. Then another will say "I'll stand" and the dealer will shout "Ectualleh!" and they will all roll on the floor with laughter because they believe that a certain type of Englishman never says anything but "ectualleh." Their own favorite interjection is "bloody oath," which they consider more spirited and democratic. They also say "very *crook*" when they mean put-out, and "fair dinkum" to indicate good faith. By this time Paddy is so steeped in their patois that it is sometimes hard to tell whether he is talking Irish or Australian. All the Australians are given to puns, and Paddy, who affects to be above them, used to run around punching the punsters on their biceps. One night some Australians went out and painted kangaroos all over his Spit's shamrock, an outrage which excited him for days. The Australians love to tell Finucane stories, and they think he is wonderful.

When Paddy is to go on a sweep, he usually sleeps late in the morning and then takes an extremely hot bath. Most athletic trainers say hot baths are enervating, but Paddy says they just make him feel relaxed. He then has tea and goes to receive the day's orders from the commanding officer. Last year R.A.F. fighter squadrons generally had the mission of intercepting German bombers. This year they escort British bombers to France and protect them from enemy fighters. In a sweep, which may involve a dozen squadrons, each has a special rôle. Sometimes the Australians fly closely above the bombers, sometimes they fly beneath or among them ("on the deck"), and sometimes they go very high, looking for Messerschmitts in ambush in the sub-stratosphere. The last is the assignment that Paddy likes best. The conventional order that goes with it is "Seek out and destroy." The only mission he really dislikes is a Balbo, which is an R.A.F. term for a reconnaissance in formation without any particular object. It is named after the late Italian aviator, who always flew high and never hurt anybody.

There are days when no large general operation is planned and the planes go off in pairs, flying very high, looking for some object of innocent merriment, like a little train on a *chemin de fer départemental* that may be carrying German Army supplies, or a lorry loaded with middle-aged Landsturm

men on a road. Coastal steamers are particularly agreeable
sights to them. When they fix on a target, they come plum-
meting down as straight as a stalk and squirt twenty-millimetre
cannon shells just to see what will happen. Paddy remembers
that one time he hit a steamer and it flew to pieces with a report which was heard on both sides of the Channel. "It must
have been full of ammo," he says. The best day's sport he ever
had resulted from another patrol. He and a pal were flying
high and got into a cloud bank. Suddenly the cloud dissolved
and they saw that they were sitting in among twenty Messerschmitts. "Twenty was a wee bit too many," Paddy says,
"because we had the height and the sun against us, so I said to
my mate, 'Come on along and beat up some gun positions,'
and we left. We got down to about ten thousand feet and ran
into another forty Messerschmitts, so we gave them a squirt to
help them on their way and continued. Then, way down below
us, just over the Channel, we could see two Messerschmitts attacking a lone Spitfire. We went along down and each shot one
of them into the water. That brought me pretty low, and I was
just above the surface when I saw cannon shells splashing into
the water in a steady stream, so I could figure that one of the
big bunch of jerries had followed me on down and was in back
of me. It is a very good position to be in in a fight, because you
can judge the angle of fire by the splashes, and then you know
where your man is. As the angle gets smaller, you can figure
he's getting in line with you. Just before that happens, you
give a quick turn. If he tries to follow, he goes in the drink,
because he won't he able to pull out quick enough. If he
doesn't follow, you whip up behind him, and there you are. I
got him and went home quite happy, with the other lad."

Paddy doesn't know what he will do after he goes back to active duty, or rather what the Fighter Command will tell him to
do. He may get a new outfit to whip into shape next spring, by
which time, other R.A.F. officers say, he is fairly sure to be a
squadron leader. What he would like most is to travel to the
Middle East, or anywhere else, even if it's only by bomber.
"My brother Raymond Patrick has all the luck," he says. "He
goes to Bremen and other fascinating places every week, but I
hardly get out of the country." His pet scheme, which the

Fighter Command probably won't endorse, is to get to the United States as the pilot of a Catafighter. A Catafighter is a land plane carried on a merchant ship and launched from a catapult whenever one of the big German flying boats appears. The pilot shoots down the flying boat and then tries to get to the nearest land on the petrol he has left. If he can't make it, he lands in the water and hopes for the best.

"That would be wizard," Paddy says. "Free passage and all. Besides, I have an aunt and uncle and three cousins in Detroit, all named O'Callahan."

The New Yorker, December 6, 1941

Guerrilla from Erie, Pa.

A MINOR accident knocked the artificial cap off one of Major Philip Cochran's upper front teeth last fall, putting a gap in his grin. This is perhaps the most striking feature of his appearance. Up to a month ago the thing about Cochran that you noticed second was his mop of hair, the color and apparent texture of steel wool, which he wore in a pompadour and long in back, like the late Buffalo Bill. The dust lodged in his hair made it look even grayer than it naturally is. Cochran, then, as now, living at an airfield in southern Tunisia, was flying two or three missions a day himself and was in charge of running a guerrilla air war above an area of twenty thousand square miles. "If we ever get a rainy day out here so I can't fly, I'll have time to get a haircut," Cochran used to say. On the evening of January 13th, while he sat astride a wooden bench in his hut at the field, eating a mess of scrambled eggs out of a canteen cup, he allowed Private First Class Ralph Otto of California to shear away part of his mane. "I never cut human hair back home on the farm, but I used to clip all our horses," Private Otto said. "Civilization is creeping up on us on this front, so why the hell struggle against it?" Cochran grumbled. He could see that the vast region which for a month had been his private battleground was turning into a major front of formalized warfare, and he felt depressed. On that very day he had received an oblique reproach for his unsoldierly appearance from the first brigadier general he had seen in several weeks. Cochran, ever since he landed in Africa last November, has worn the same leather jacket, pants, and British flying boots. He sleeps in them, too. The general had said, "Major, if you are captured in those clothes, you will have to wear them until the end of the war, and they look about ready to fall off now." "Can you tie that?" Cochran said later to one of his pals. "There is nothing the matter with these clothes except they are full of dust." Cochran's ideas of military dress have never been regulation. He remembers that while he was in the R.O.T.C. at Ohio State University, a general making an inspection found him wearing black-and-white shoes with his uniform. "I told him they were the only ones I had to my name," Cochran says. "I imagine I was lying."

The dust in Cochran's part of Tunisia is so heavy that a group of Messerschmitts once came in on the tail of a dust storm and started strafing his field before anybody knew they were there. This left him speechless, a rare state for him, because he can usually anticipate what the Germans are going to do. His own Curtiss P-40 fighter was on the field and got shot full of holes. "It was already just a lot of holes tied together with piano wire," Cochran says. "They even shot away the connections between the holes. I had seen one of those Messerschmitts at about twenty thousand feet that morning and I knew he was casing the joint for a strafe job, but I didn't think they'd pull it that way."

A few days later Cochran rolled out of bed and predicted that a combined force of German bombers and fighters would appear over the field at two-thirty in the afternoon. He was wrong. The bombers and fighters—seven Junkers 88's and eight Messerschmitts—appeared at two twenty-eight. Cochran had seven fighters in the air waiting for them and they shot down a Meserschmitt and two Junkers. "I felt they would come then because they had been over a couple of times at dawn and a couple of times just before dark and they would want to do something different." He says it is like sensing when to hop on or off a guy who is shooting craps.

"On the day after the two-twenty-eight raid," Cochran recalls, "I have a hunch that if they do not come over at ten-thirty A.M. they will come over at a quarter to six, with bombers." It was due to get dark at six. The Germans did not come at ten thirty. Consequently, Cochran put eight planes, including his own, in the air at a quarter to six, but nobody appeared. At five fifty-five he decided to come down and ordered the other planes down by radio. He was low over the field, and had his landing wheels half down when the man in the field's control room—a circular hole in the ground with a radio telephone in it—called, "Enemy planes reported." Cochran started to climb into the gathering dark, and by the time he got to seven thousand feet he saw some flak and, looking down to find out why, saw that three Junkers 88's were bombing his field. "I dived for the first one and hit him, but he gave it the blossom—gave it the gun, you know—and got away over a hill to the south," Cochran says when he tells the story. A lieutenant named Bent got on this plane after it had escaped Cochran and shot it down behind the hill. "Then I got on the second one and just flew formation with him," Cochran says. "I kept on shooting tracers into him, and the lights turned green and orange when they hit, like the Fourth of July. You never know how pretty tracers are until you see that effect. I went around him and saw the gunners die. The one on top stopped firing first, and then the side gunner. The one in the belly lived longest. The plane went down and down into the valley and me after him, and dark as hell, and I kept saying, 'Go down, you sucker. Go down.' Then I saw a big flare of light, and it wasn't gunfire, and it stayed in one place, and I left the plane burning in the valley and pulled up, not knowing where I was, but I found my friend the river—that *wadi*, which shows light tan in the dusk—and I started to follow it home. When I tell it, it sounds like a movie.

"Then I began to hear one of the kids over the radio saying he was lost, asking for directions." This was a lieutenant named Thomas, of Ada, Oklahoma, who had hopped the third Junkers and chased it out into the night fifty miles before bringing it down. It was when Thomas was pulling up from his kill that he found he was lost. He was not a veteran pilot like Cochran and lacked the older man's photographic memory of the region. "I tried to keep up his spirits by insulting him," Cochran says. "I thought he was somebody else, anyway—a fellow named Brown. I would say, 'I don't mind losing you, you stupid lug, but we can't afford to lose another P-40. Try and see the lights on my ship and steer a thirty course.' The kid would answer very politely, 'I don't see your lights, sir.' He never forgot to say 'sir.' But he was confused. Of course he couldn't see the lights we had out on the field, so I got an idea. I phoned down to the control room to tell the ack-ack to fire. I told him to tell the battery at the west edge of the field to fire, and then the one to the east, and so on, to outline the field. And then all together. I stayed up with my lights on. The kid saw the field all right and got his direction, and we both came down. When you tell about it, it sounds just like a movie." The German bombers didn't damage a single American plane.

*

Cochran is a barrel-chested one-hundred-and-fifty-pounder of medium height. He has high cheekbones, a jaw extremely broad at the base, and white teeth that are generally visible in a smile. He is a first lieutenant in the Regular Army, a captain in the Army of the United States, and a Major in the Air Forces. Cochran was at first the ranking officer at his post but is now out-ranked. There are at least four lieutenant colonels above him. However, because of his knowledge of the country, he is still the one who selects and directs the post's missions, as he did during his guerrilla days. He is thirty-two and has been in the Air Forces ever since he left Ohio State nearly eight years ago with a degree in business administration and advertising. He had never been in combat before last November, but he had enjoyed a certain fame in the Air Forces as a tactical pilot and instructor of other pilots, as well as a certain vicarious celebrity with several million young Americans who follow the syndicated cartoon strip called "Terry and the Pirates," in which he appears under the name of Flip Corkin. Milton Caniff, the creator of the strip, went to college with Cochran and used him as a model for Flip, who is an aviator.

The attention that the Germans pay to Cochran's field is not unsolicited. He thinks that the way to fight anybody is to keep pushing him off balance and he is constantly devising new ways of pushing. For instance, there was his one-man expedition to Kairouan, a Tunisian city within the German lines. Cochran had heard that a German divisional commander had his headquarters in a certain building near the town and he had earmarked a bomb to drop on him, but for a couple of weeks he couldn't find time to do it. He didn't want to send anybody else, because the idea of dropping a bomb on a general amused him and also because dropping a bomb from a P-40 with any degree of accuracy calls for considerable experience. He kept putting the venture off, like his haircut, until he had a day coming up with nothing important on his early-morning schedule. The evening before, he told his armorer to put a bomb on his plane. "I woke up a couple of times during the night, laughing at what I was going to do in the morning," Cochran says. "In the morning I got up and climbed into my plane and went over the joint once very high, just at dawn, and nobody spotted me. I had a good look at the target and then I went around and came in from the north, which was just where they wouldn't expect me, and I made my run so low that I had to pull up to get over the building." When he tells the story, he totters forward with bent knees, like a little man carrying a big load, to show how he toted the bomb up to the target. "When I was right over the target, I let the bomb go and gave her the blossom," he says. "Then I looked over my shoulder, and there were pieces of building flying all around me. I looked over my shoulder again at the Kairouan airfield and made sure that nobody had taken off after me—or so I thought. Then I decided to have a look over the French advanced positions to see if I could spot any German tank concentrations before I went home. About forty miles from Kairouan I noticed a lot of flak. I thought that this was a funny place for flak, so I looked around again, and a guy in a FW-190 was shooting at me with a cannon and by that time he had shot away my right aileron and most of my tail, so I headed for home. He came after me, and I decided I would have to make a crash landing, so I started down. It was just like a movie. He got so close to me that I figured I would have to turn or he would shoot hell out of me, but the only way she would turn was to the right, and that was into him. So I fired one burst, and he gave it the blossom and went back toward Kairouan. He must have figured I had been kidding him when I'd started down. Then I said to myself, 'If she can steer at all, maybe I can get her home after all,' so I did."

At his airfield Cochran has a small entourage of admirers who give him the anxious care a singing teacher and manager expend upon an opera star. He lives in a *gourbi*, a Tunisian hut sunk into the ground and banked with sand on all sides. Unlike most *gourbis*, his has a wooden floor and walls and a tin roof, but the roof has been covered with sand and alfa grass has been planted on top for camouflage. His *gourbi* was built by a French corporal out of material foraged by a French Jewish lieutenant named Léon, who is the liaison officer between the French forces and Cochran's fliers. Only Léon, a talented forager, could even have suspected the survival of such a quantity of building material in North Africa. Léon, who lives with Cochran in the *gourbi*, likes to talk American slang; when he hears that something seems to be stirring in a certain direction, for instance, he may tell Cochran, "Up by Fondouk there is something cooking in. It is really boiling. Hot intelligence." Cochran, though he can't speak a word of Arabic, knows the terrain so well that he needs only a casual reference to any *chott* (dried lake) or *oued* (river bed) or *djebel* (mountain) to get into his plane and go there. He doesn't need a map any more.

Another resident of Cochran's *gourbi* is Captain Robert Wylie, of 1060 Park Avenue, in peacetime an executive of the American Radiator & Standard Sanitary Corporation. Wylie, a leathery, middle-aged gentleman who won a Croix de Guerre while serving with a Yale ambulance unit in the last war, is always the first one up in the morning. He gets the stove going so that Cochran, who rises an hour before dawn, will not catch cold. Léon is a brilliant amateur cook. Whenever he thinks Cochran's appetite is failing, he prepares special dishes, which he and Wylie try to induce Cochran to eat. As a matter of fact, Cochran's appetite is good, but he neglects it because of his chronic preoccupation with flying. When he remembers that he is hungry, he wolfs quantities of scrambled eggs, accepting them gratefully from anybody who happens to be around and equipped with a mess tin to cook in. Cochran's list of chefs in Tunisia has included enlisted men, visiting Tank Corps officers, war correspondents, French pilots, and even a British booby-trap expert, who, out of consideration for Cochran, was careful not to put any high explosive in the eggs. The booby-trap man, a captain in the Royal Engineers, is continually inventing devices for blowing people up when they step on them and refers to these engines of destruction as rather amusing. He puzzles Cochran, who once said, "I can *tell* when an American is crazy."

Cochran was born in Erie, Pennsylvania, and his parents still live there. His father, Bernard Cochran, is a lawyer and a real-estate expert for the city government and is known to most of the population as Barney. Cochran's mother, a woman of strong character, never liked this public familiarity with her husband, so she long ago decided that she would give all her sons solid saints' names that would not lend themselves to conversion into chummy nicknames. "We got names like Paul and Philip," Cochran says. He has four brothers. "The only trouble was that my oldest brother, Paul, got the nickname of Shanty, which has been a handicap to him in his profession as a lawyer. Mother was very displeased." Shanty, who is thirty-six, is now an enlisted man in the Navy. One of Phil's younger brothers is an ensign and the youngest of the lot is an Army Air Forces cadet. "Paul used to have a beautiful contralto voice when he was a kid," Cochran recalls, "but it is bass now. Anyway, he was the means of getting me into singing as an altar boy and in a choir of fifty-two boys we had at our church. You know, 'Little Town of Bethlehem' and stuff like that. It came in handy later, when I sang with a band to work my way through college.

"Erie is not a bad joint," Cochran says loyally. "There are a lot of beer clubs that you can join for fifty cents a year, so you can drink on Sunday, and the clubs are always planning to do something ambitious, like run a clambake, but it always mucks up." Cochran went to Central High School and played football, even though he then weighed only a hundred and fourteen pounds. "I was substitute for the All-State Scholastic quarterback, and I used to sit on the bench and pray for him to break his leg so I could play," he says. "It would have been horrible if he had, because I stank. But he played every minute of every game. They only sent me in once, and as I ran out on the field the gun went off and ended the game. I was so nuts about football that I wouldn't go to college until I was big enough to play, so I stayed out for two years and carried ice, the way Red Grange used to. My muscles developed, but I only weighed one twenty-eight then and I figured it was no use waiting any longer or I would just be in the ice business for life."

At Ohio State, which Cochran calls "a good poor boy's school," he worked his way through, like at least half the student body. He waited on table at the Sigma Alpha Epsilon fraternity house for his meals and picked up some cash by singing with dance bands in dives around Columbus. "My longest engagement was at the Ritz," he says without pride. "That was an eatery across the street from the campus where dinner is fifty cents if you take pot roast and seventy-five cents for steak. My singing was like stealing money. Every now and then I catch myself singing 'Stormy Weather' or something else from that period of my life. I wonder I am not in prison. There was a roadhouse called Valleydale near Columbus where I used to get eight dollars a night three nights a week until the depression got terrible." Cochran's income fell off after he had finished three years of college, so he went back to Erie to regroup, as he says, and worked two years in the Hammermill paper factory. He returned to Columbus for his senior year and was graduated in 1935, when he was twenty-five. Shortly after that he decided to take an examination for the Air Forces cadets. He had never flown, but he thought he would like to. The examination was to he held in Detroit and to finance his trip from Erie he sold the gold case of a watch his maternal grandfather had left to him and played a game of semi-professional football, having by that time attained his full growth. "I never thought I'd pass the test, but I did," he says, "and so I got a blue uniform and seventy-five dollars a month for two years." He received a Reserve commission as second lieutenant in June, 1937, and remained on active service, drawing officer's pay. It wasn't until September, 1939, that Cochran got his Regular Army commission. "It took me three years and eight months to become a real second lieutenant," he remarks.

As the expansion of the Air Forces was speeded up, promotion became more rapid and he was soon a major and in command of a squadron. It was at about that time that Milton Caniff, the "Terry and the Pirates" artist, decided to document himself on aviation. "He remembered me from Ohio State," Cochran says, "so he looked me up. I had a squadron up at Groton, Connecticut, and he came up and lived with the boys and learned the lingo, and we put on dogfights for him, and he began drawing us into his strip. The Air Corps liked it because it was great stuff for recruiting. About half the people I know call me Flip now, after the comic-strip character. One thing that causes trouble, though, is that he has me—that is, Flip—all mixed up with a beautiful nurse named Taffy in this strip, and people get curious when they meet me and want to know who is Taffy. There is no Nurse Taffy, as far as I am concerned. I like hatcheck chicks and showgirls."

One of the things Cochran sometimes says when he feels lonely is "The hatcheck chicks are certainly going to catch hell when I get back to New York." He thinks the Copacabana is

the finest spot in America and sometimes says he is going to
spend all his time there after the war. "I had a squadron out at
Mitchel Field a year ago," he says. "We were big operators.
One of the fellows had a girl who was a hatcheck chick at the
Larue, and when we had a new kid that didn't know his way
around New York we would send him to the Larue, where
he would say, 'Hello, Sport, Major Cochran sent me,' and she
would say, 'Roger Wilco,' which means, in radio procedure,
'Message received. Will coöperate,' and she would see that he
got along all right."

During his stay in Connecticut Cochran got his only American decoration so far, the Soldier's Medal, for rescuing a student pilot from a burning plane. He received a Croix de
Guerre a couple of weeks ago for his work on the Tunisian
front.

Cochran entered Africa by way of Casablanca. Before that, in
the States, he had trained and lost a few squadrons, which
were taken out from under him and shipped abroad while he
was left behind to teach new batches of fliers. This made him
rather irritable. Finally he was ordered to take thirty-four
young fliers and thirty-five planes to Africa. The idea was that
the kids were to be replacements for pilots who might be
killed. Shortly after the kids arrived, they decided that since
few pilots were being killed, their only chance to see action was
to form their own squadron, which might get to the front by
mistake even though it had no official existence. Cochran took
them to Rabat, Morocco, for further training and christened
them the Joker Squadron, because they had no number. They
had no table of organization, no mechanics, no mess fund, and
no medical attendance, and they sponged on other outfits.
Sometimes they messed with an infantry regiment which, as
Cochran puts it, they found in the brush, and sometimes with
a unit of engineers. They slept in pup tents and went to a
French military hospital with their afflictions. They practiced
gunnery by towing canvas engine covers aloft and firing at
them. By the time the higher echelons of the Twelfth Air
Force staff, which had jurisdiction over them, discovered what
they were up to and ordered their dispersal, a number of the
boys had developed into pretty hot pilots. Cochran, who was

now a major without a command or function, was directed to take his seven brightest pupils and fly to Tunisia, where they were to be posted to some squadron or other. When they got to an airport called Oudjda, in eastern Morocco, another order came through grounding the seven Joker pilots and assigning their planes to more experienced men. Cochran was ordered to stop at Oudjda, too, but he flew on alone anyway, since by that time he was getting fed up with not fighting. He reversed the procedure of the celebrated soldier who made an advance to the rear, by telling airport officials at every stop in his journey that he was going back to Casablanca and then taking off and flying east.

When Cochran finally arrived at an airfield in southern Tunisia, he found a squadron of P-40 fighters on a bare plain without much idea of what they were doing or should do there. Southern Tunisia was sketchily defended by a few French battalions with about twenty-five rounds of rifle ammunition to a man, a few old seventy-fives, and a few score American parachutists. Luckily, the German and Italian forces in the region were small, but it was evident that this was a critical area, into which Rommel might move from the southeast to form a junction with the Axis forces in Tunisia. Or Axis troops in Tunisia, if dislodged by the Allies before Rommel moved, might attempt to join him in Tripolitania. The situation called for officers who were good at guessing, bluffing, and guerrilla tactics, and Cochran found himself in the spot he had dreamed of all his military life. He was not officially in command of the airfield, but he ranked any officer there and was moreover the only one of the lot with much idea of what to do in such an irregular situation. "So I called the boys together one day after they had mucked up something terrible on a raid by following the wrong line of railroad track and getting lost and finding the wrong target and having their rump shot off, and I told them I was going to run the field," Cochran says. "It was just like something you'd see in a movie. After that Léon came here, and the French began to call us up and tell us about tanks and trucks they saw on different roads, and we would go out and look for them, and quite often they were there. We were big operators. One day Captain Levi Chase, my operations officer, went out by himself and destroyed eighty-four trucks and a few guns. We must have destroyed about three hundred trucks altogether, and for the last three weeks, incidentally, the Germans and Italians haven't moved a truck over a road anywhere in Tunisia by daylight.

"After doing that for a while, we got to know the country pretty well ourselves and began to think of other things to do. We knew the enemy had only about a dozen locomotives on all the little lines down here, so we got to blasting them, and also went after oil dumps and munition dumps. Chase was the best man I ever saw at spotting those things from the air. One time he strafed a lot of haystacks and they all exploded, proving he was right. We used to hunt light tanks all over southern Tunisia. We would strafe them with our fifty-calibre machine guns and they would play dead, and then at night the crews would run them into Arab courtyards or dry gullies and camouflage them, and we would have to find them again and shoot some more holes in them before they could be repaired. We didn't have armament to blast them, but we kept them out of action. We would observe troop movements and report them to the French and then go back and strafe them, and the French would occupy one more town.

"Then the people back at headquarters saw we were doing so well that they sent us a squadron of bombers to fool around with, and we had fun thinking up bombing missions and then escorting the bombers. Escorting is nice, clean work for fighters. It is a thing they are supposed to do in textbooks. A lot of fighter pilots at home would think that wrecking transport and strafing tanks and giving ground cover was unconventional. A P-40 can't climb like a German fighter or dive like one, and they can pull away from us on the straight, but it has quite a wallop and it can take an awful beating and bring you home safe. If you know how to use a P-40, you can get a Messerschmitt or even a Focke-Wulf 190. You just have to wait for them to dive and then turn into them as they get down to your level. If you climb after them, they've got you. In our first month of operations we got thirteen planes for six and we only had one pilot killed."

Cochran has a high respect for German fliers. "They are big operators," he told two war correspondents not long ago.

"They are very methodical Joes. When they are going to start an offensive, they lay off you, conserving their forces. Then, when they think you are going to attack, they attack you to draw you and get you off balance. They expect you to play it the same way. I am in favor of attacking hell out of them all the time, and then they never know what to expect. Another thing they do is let you get away with something a couple of times and pretend they don't notice it and then come in and catch you right. For instance, the way our transport planes come up here and land on the field and stay right where they land until they take off again. I used to send out and tell them I wouldn't have my men service them until they dispersed, but it's no use. Someday those guys are going to get it." Cochran delivered himself of this particular speech while saying goodbye to the two correspondents, who were walking down to the runway to board a transport. Ten minutes later one correspondent was hiding under a jeep and the other was lying flat on his belly on the runway while sixteen-millimetre explosive shells from some Messerschmitts were digging furrows all around them and miraculously missing them and the transports. "If I keep on calling the turn like that," Cochran said afterward, "I will find myself up on Park Avenue after the war with a thing around my head, charging twenty-five dollars a reading."

The New Yorker, February 13, 1943

Letter from Tripoli

MAY 1 (BY RADIO)

THE city of Tripoli, now entering upon what British authorities call the second phase of occupation, is like a show window without goods in or behind it. It is a town with three first-class hotels, a flamboyant governor's palace, and other public buildings appropriate to the capital of a fair-sized country, but it has never had a population of more than a hundred and twenty thousand, of which forty thousand were Europeans, and has neither industries nor a productive hinterland. Now that artificial stimulation of its development by Italy has ceased, it looks something like the site of a defunct World's Fair, with overpretentious structures that are already beginning to show signs of decay, and the number of pedestrians one sees in its streets seems absurdly small in this grandiose architectural setting. The impression is accentuated by traces of bomb damage, which is especially prevalent near the waterfront, and by the fact that a quarter of the normal Italian population has fled. Various British agencies are installed in some of the public buildings, including one which contains a violently tinted mural of Mussolini's triumphal entry into the city in 1937. The troops stationed here feel like people visiting a summer resort between seasons. The soldiers who have been on the desert a long time have accumulated considerable back pay, and they wander among shops whose typically boardwalk stocks are limited to postcards and cheap colored handkerchiefs marked "Ricordo di Tripoli" or "Gruss aus Libia," looking for presentable souvenirs to send home. They look mostly in vain, since even before the war the shops' stocks were scaled to the requirements of Fascist and Nazi tourists, who had almost nothing to spend.

Tripoli presents a complicated job for the British Occupied Enemy Territories Administration, known familiarly as Oeta, which must recreate an approximation of peacetime life for the city as the battle front recedes. There is no evident intention of utilizing this captured show window of Fascism as a display advertisement for democracy; the brigadier general who is the cheerful, bouncing local chief of Oeta says frankly that the place is to remain merely on a "care-and-maintenance" basis until the peace conference. To advocates of dynamic forms of political warfare this may seem like knocking a man down and then merely holding his hat for him until he gets up, but the British are going about their task with an honesty and practical efficiency that constitute a quietly effective contrast to the regime of bribery that preceded them. At the beginning of the war the local Italian officials stopped all trading in merchandise under the pretext of military necessity and then issued permits to buy or sell only to businessmen who paid for them. Government by felony had become such an accepted practice here that when the British, on entering the city, set up a fire-fighting brigade of Italian prisoners, who were technically still soldiers in the Italian army, the Italian lieutenant placed in charge sold one of the fire engines under his command quite as a matter of course and appeared rather indignant when he was jailed for it. It was a spare engine, he said, and had been out of commission for some time. The firemen are not the only Italians who still held government jobs; practically all civil servants and functionaries who stayed when the British came have been kept on, including Dante di Paragna, prefect of Tripolitania. The Governor General of Libya, the chief official in this region, got out with the Axis armies.

British officials, who of course have the actual power, supervise the Italian personnel of all agencies. In only one instance have they made a deliberate attempt to find and employ anti-Fascists in the government. This was when the Oweta officials, all of whom need confidential Italian secretaries, consulted the records of Pai, more formally the Polizia Africa Italiana, the Tripoli equivalent of the Gestapo, and employed only persons described as being highly suspect of having Allied sympathies. Almost all of them were Jews. The imitation Nuremberg racial laws, never enforced by the Italians, remain on the statute books as an equally dead letter under the British. Oeta's judicial authorities say that the Army has no right, by international law, to change the civil law of occupied enemy territory but can suspend enforcement of it. In this case enforcement never even began. Italo Balbo, as governor of Libya, always fought to protect the Jews, and they were not molested even after his death, in 1940, until January 1st of this year, when the government gazette announced that the racial laws would be put in effect. The Eighth Army, however, arrived before they were.

The Italian authorities who left before the British came removed all the foodstuffs they could carry and then opened the city's warehouses to the remaining populace, which looted them. There were consequently no stocks of food when the Eighth Army showed up, and little was brought in for the civilians because the Army's urgent need for war supplies meant that almost no space on its incoming vessels could be devoted to non-military needs. For a while the Italian bread ration of approximately six ounces a day was cut to two; it has since been increased to five. What the people get is a roll which costs two lire. The lira is now worth approximately one cent.

Tripolitania, which is the western part of the former Italian colony of Libya, has six hundred thousand Mohammedans living in it, as against the million and a half who were there when the Italians came in 1912. The difference represents the number of those killed off or driven into Egypt and the Sudan by Marshal Graziani in the twenties. It is a sharp contrast to the situation in Algeria, where the Moslem population has tripled under French rule. The Tripolitanian Arabs are so dispirited that they have no articulate aspirations or opinions. The British, made cautious by their experiences with other Arabs after the last war, are not trying to arouse any latent nationalist ambitions. Arab expressions of resentment against the Italians are, if anything, discouraged by the British, but by allowing publication of an Arabic newspaper, permitting large public meetings of Arabs, admitting them to cinemas, and giving them the same bread rations as the Italians, they are establishing among the Arabs a sentiment in complete contrast to what they felt for their erstwhile Italian masters. The Italians left in Tripolitania seem to have no more political consciousness than the Arabs.

Tripolitania never has had industrial workers or peasants with regional sentiment. Most of the Italian settlers came out from the home country as farmers under a subsidized colonization scheme known as Ente Coloniale. The Ente colonists moved onto land prepared for them (and owned) by the government; houses, livestock, and supplies of food were waiting for them. They were supposed to work for several years more or less as government hired men for about thirty dollars a month. After that they were to go on a sharecropping basis, giving the Ente administration half of what their farms produced and keeping half for themselves, until they had paid off the government's lien on the property, at which point they would become the proprietors. As the scheme didn't really get under way until 1938, most of the colonists were still receiving wages when the British took over. Only a few were on half shares and none yet owned land, all of which technically remains the property of the Royal Italian Government. Oeta, following its care-and-maintenance policy, has assumed the Fascist government's rôle and is paying wages and subsidies against crops and taking first mortgages on the farms as security. By virtue of the record crops anticipated, the British may break even on the operation this year, which would be a stroke of luck the Italian administration never enjoyed. In any but an exceptional year, Tripolitanian farming is almost certainly a losing proposition, and Oeta has already introduced a group of South African agricultural experts who are trying to devise methods of cutting losses.

The Italian colonists remaining on the soil have been through hard times but are not consciously anti-Fascist. Until recently they believed that the Axis was certain to win the war and that protest against the regime was useless, and although they have begun to realize that the Fascist newspaper and radio station here deceived them, they are not at all sure that the news they now get is not just a new species of lying. Having been selected for robustness, they are almost all in their twenties and thirties and have never conceived of a life under any but an authoritarian regime. Most of them, like the Jews and the Arabs, work as civilian laborers for the British military authorities when they are asked to, because this is almost the only way to get cash, and prices of even the most trifling articles are high. The Italians read the *Corriere di Tripoli*, which is the Italian-language side of a one-page, two-language newspaper printed here by the Ministry of Information (the English side is called the *Tripoli Times*), because they have no other news source, but they do not try to fraternize with the occupying forces, who find the place pretty but rather a bore.

Poor Tripolitanians, whether Italians, Jews, or Arabs, live largely on beans and other vegetables, which are fairly plentiful at the moment, but they will have a more solid diet after June 1st, when the mills will begin turning the anticipated record crop of grain into flour for home consumption. This crop will be one result of the phenomenal spring rains, for which the Arabs give the British full credit. "The English have the blessing of God," the Arabs say. "They are people with wet feet." The Oeta officer in charge of Arab affairs is doing nothing to disclaim credit for the rain-bringing.

The New Yorker, May 8, 1943

Notes from the Kidnap House

I

THE only great nation with a completely uncensored press today is France. All valid French newspapers are illegal, printed at the risk of death, and circulated under penalty of long imprisonment, conditions which at least insure their freedom from official guidance. Physically, of course, much of the prewar press, now in collaborationist hands, still exists, as corrupt as, and perhaps more profitable than, before. It receives subsidies direct from Berlin and it makes unregulated profits on the Vichy Government job printing it does on the side, this, incidentally, being one of the main sources of Laval's income. Laval owns *Le Moniteur*, which is published in Clermont-Ferrand and gets a large share of the Vichy printing contracts. In using this method of tapping the public till, he has patterned himself closely after those other newspaper owners Hitler and Streicher. The collaborationist press publishes official bulletins about when and how ration cards are to be used, information without which life in France is literally impossible. It therefore retains its large circulation. But as *Paroles Françaises*, one of the resistance publications, said in a recent issue, "Let nobody be fooled. Apart from journals of resistance, there is no longer a French press. The official press is morally dead; the disgust of the people has killed it." In circulation, the clandestine newspapers have already nearly overtaken the collaborationist ones. *Combat*, a clandestine paper with a half-dozen regional editions, claims a total press run of three hundred thousand. Since every copy is passed around until it wears out, *Combat* may reach a couple of million readers. There are other secret newspapers with comparable circulations and there are hundreds of lesser journals.

These clandestine French publications are, in general, very small. Most of them are about the size of a sheet of typewriter paper and have only four pages. Some of them are printed, some are mimeographed. Small bales of them, transported over routes which I naturally cannot reveal, arrive in London, where I am living at present, with great regularity, and I have spent a good many odd hours over them, piecing together a picture of the country from which they come, a country which I left in June, 1940. It is as if one were to try to piece together a theory of what is going on behind the familiar façade of a house across the street where a friend is held prisoner by a kidnap gang. These tiny newspapers are like messages scrawled on bits of paper and dropped from a window by the prisoner.

The newspapers arrive from a hundred points of observation, intellectual as well as geographic. Their diversity results from the current fragmentation of French national life. It is impossible for resistance groups to print a few great papers in Paris and distribute them over the country, like the big French newspapers of peacetime. The resistance newspapers are products of small, self-sufficient regional or vocational groups, so they vary ideologically. The one tenet they all have in common is resistance. Each paper contains, in its small format, a mass of almost photographic local detail that was entirely lacking in the old days of a centralized press. They deal with the murders of local patriots and the executions of local stool pigeons, examples of successful sabotage, the names of sadistic French detectives marked for vengeance, the dope on local employers who blackmail workers by threatening them with deportation to Germany, and even information on local girls who walk out with Nazis. Among the papers that represent occupational groups, one of my favorites is *Le Palais Libre*, the secret organ of the Paris bar. "*Palais*" in this case stands for "palace of justice." Each number consists of eight pages, imperfectly mimeographed but written with style and taste. The French bar, from the days of Louis IX right up to 1940, had been a worldly, overly logical, formalistic corporation, too drastically separate from the rest of France. At the same time it was cultured and lucid. In a struggle to defend the integrity of a body of laws that go back to the Romans, it has for generations been independent and stubborn, and under the German occupation it has been valiant. The latest struggle has not been bloodless. One magistrate and five lawyers, for instance, were murdered in their cells by the Gestapo shortly before the publication date of the latest copy of *Le Palais Libre* I possess. The magistrate, René Parodi, had declined to hold "suspects" without evidence; the lawyers had defended patriot prisoners. *Le Palais* makes these men seem like characters in a realistic novel. The lawyers were Maître Nordmann, an Alsatian music lover; Maître Frank, a Jewish intellectual; Maître Pitard, who came from the Midi and was a hero of the last war, a noisy and expansive fellow who gave half of his time to the unpaid defense of destitute children; Maître Hajje, a grave Syrian Marxist; and the apparently timid, easily blushing young Maître Rolnikas, who in his heart believed that France would have "tomorrows that sing." The Gestapo called them all Communists. This is an example of Nazi and collaborationist propaganda that has boomeranged. Unwilling, in the years following the armistice, to admit that Frenchmen were being executed only because they were patriots, the Germans and their bought press labelled either Communist or Jew every man executed for sabotage or underground activity. One consequence was the indelible association of the words "Communist" and "patriot" in the French popular mind, and within the last two years they have become synonyms, which gives an increased impetus to the Leftward tendency caused by the treason committed by the great industrialists.

Le Palais cites a Vichy decree, dated last July, which was designed to end "obstructionism," such as that of Magistrate Parodi, who released prisoners arrested by the French police before the Gestapo could get at them. The decree orders magistrates to hold prisoners "even if the offense cannot be proved immediately, because more evidence may develop later." *Le Palais* comments, "This fixes the rank of magistrates in the Vichy hierarchy—below stool pigeons." *Le Palais* cites in each issue pronouncements of Nazi jurists, such as the one uttered by a man named Schmitt, who wrote in a German law journal, "Law is what is useful to German people. Law is what *der Führer* says," or by a colleague named Freisler, who wrote, "Only that which responds to needs of the National Socialist community is right. Everything else is bad and as a consequence punishable."

"Justice for us is not defined by the interest of some Nazi community or master race or caste of chiefs," *Le Palais* says. "It has as its object the protection of man in his dual aspect as an individual and a member of the community. We are custodians of an unfinished but infinitely precious achievement of civilization." The chief weapon of the bar in its long fight against the Germans has been the threat of a strike of the courts, which would make the pretense of civil administration impossible. Vichy, at German behest, installed as Minister of Justice a Frenchman named Gabolde, whom his colleagues call "Von Gabolde," a professed prewar Leftist who now fawns on Nazi officers and has said publicly that he wishes he had been born in the Reich. Gabolde has failed laughably as Minister. On one occasion, when he demanded the reinstatement of a disbarred attorney, who happened to be a collaborationist, the bar committee turned him down by a unanimous vote. When he brought some German officers into a courtroom as guests, no lawyer present would shake hands with him. It was the jurists' stubborn adherence to the spirit and forms of laws that forced the abandonment of the Riom trial and made it impossible for Vichy to murder patriots through the formal processes of law. Because of these hindrances, Vichy set up a special *Tribunal d'état*, under the control of the late Pierre Pucheu, then Minister of Interior, in September, 1941. Pucheu picked his judges, from among a handful of renegade jurists and retired generals, to deal retroactively with "deeds injurious to the French people." This court, for its début, retried three resistants—including a war hero, ex-Deputy Catelas—who on their first trial had received sentences which the Gestapo considered too light. Pucheu's court ordered their execution. The *Tribunal d'état* recently sentenced to death a midwife, the mother of three children, because she had helped a woman abort the consequence of her rape by a German soldier. The only person the court ever acquitted, *Le Palais* records without comment, was a colonel who had embezzled funds collected for prisoners of war in Germany.

Like all resistance publications, *Le Palais* is obsessed by the fear that the so-called *Malins*, the not quite too compromised collaborationists who have been slick enough to stay out of Vichy Ministries, will get into power by some "combine" with "Wall Street and the City of London," influences which resistants hold responsible for the Darlan and Badoglio deals. My latest issue of *Le Palais* carries a brief biographical sketch of Anatole de Monzie, whom it considers the prototype of a *Malin*. Monzie was a Minister in Daladier's Cabinet during the

...nd, according to *Le Palais*, gave information *to* first war even then. "His is the kind of intelligence that se- the community," *Le Palais* says. "He ate at all troughs, ac- ... envelopes from all corruptionists. He was for Munich and every conceivable capitulation, yet was in the government ...til ejected by Paul Reynaud. Since the armistice he has made a fortune defending big profiteers in the black market. Now, with the complicity of German censorship and the approval of [Marcel] Déat, he makes fake attacks on Pétain to dissociate himself from Vichy." The particular bogey of the patriot press is Georges Bonnet, Minister of Foreign Affairs at the time of Munich, whom *les Malins* advertise as a liberal because he took bribes from Jewish banks, which proves, of course, that he is not anti-Semitic. It proves also that he likes banks, which pa- triots, rendered perhaps unduly suspicious by the tortures of the past four years, think will have something to do with de- termining whom the Allies will recognize.

Le Médecin Français, in a format like that of *Le Palais*, records the French doctors' fight to protect the national health, which is unquestionably being deliberately attacked by the Nazis. One form the attack has taken was a German draft of five thousand young French doctors for service in the Reich. "The enemy pursues the physical destruction of our people— to take away its doctors is a means to this end," *Le Médecin* points out. Vichy, under German orders, withholds gasoline from rural doctors so that they cannot make their rounds in the country. Yet, *Le Médecin* notes, the collaborationist press is fond of reminding its readers that the Wehrmacht has plenty of fuel for its tanks and planes. Great pressure is being put upon French doctors to make them accessories to the deportation of their countrymen. Every man the Vichy authorities deliver into the hands of the German Labor Ministry must pass a medical examination to make sure that he will not die en route or carry a contagious disease into Germany. The doctors turn down almost every man presented to them. Whenever Vichy offi- cials, forced by the Germans, raise a row, the doctors certify a few legless and armless men. Some officials, secretly unsympa- thetic to the Germans, "inadvertently" call up young collabo- rationists for labor service. The doctors invariably certify these men immediately. Then the collaborationist le. the Germans for their release, which is always 'g' appeal to Germans do not need workmen in the Reich, whosted. The capacity is insufficient to absorb the slave labor alreads..., but they are trying to remove patriotic Frenchmen om the potential battle area. The motivation of the Germans glaringly clear. Just as, in accordance with the Nazi concept o. law, suspects are to be held without any evidence whatever, so, in accordance with the precepts of Nazi medicine, labor conscripts are to be certified fit without any real examination. One Grasset, Vichy Minister of Health, has issued instructions to doctors which are rather like Gabolde's to the bar. "Examination for labor service is not, of course, complete, like an examination for induction into the Army," Grasset says, in a decree cited by *Le Médecin*, "but a simple, superficial check without X-ray or laboratory procedure. That is to say, there ought to be no rejections except for those actually ill or crippled, since in the present circumstances men merely in poor health should not be exempted." "Nothing could be clearer," comments *Le Médecin*, "than that he wants us to send to certain death consumptives and chronic cases of all kinds."

Just as *Le Palais* cites excerpts from German legal journals on justice, *Le Médecin* quotes selections from contemporary Nazi medical thought. "The healthiest nation is not that with the lowest infant mortality, the fewest consumptives, the least syphilis or rheumatism or cancer," one such sample reads. "No! It is the nation which sees its racial heritage increased by the uninterrupted flow of births." Another specimen is a synopsis of a Nazi doctor's research on the effect of fear on the ovaries of women condemned to decapitation.

Along with the persistent efforts of the Germans, through its French-born tools, to hamper the work of physicians, there is a steady drive to lower the standard of French medical education. The Vichy Ministry of Education has lately abolished the pre-medical year of instruction in physics, chemistry, and biology at the great universities. The Ministry has also insulted the medical school of the University of Paris by founding a chair of Racial Anthropology, which is devoted to advancing the Nazi race myths. Students leave the "professor" in solitude for weeks at a time and then unexpectedly invade his lecture hall in hundreds to heckle him and smash his exhibits, departing before he can take any names.

The suppression of the pre-medical year also furnishes subject matter to *L'Université Libre*, the clandestine paper of the French universities. "The progress of medical science, which utilizes and often inspires the most recent discoveries in physics and chemistry, calls for exactly the opposite policy," *L'Université* editorializes. "The danger is great; a generation of doctors unequal to their task will result. It is a prelude to the debasement of the profession. There will soon be two classes of physicians: 'health officers,' provided with only a superficial, hasty education, and 'specialists' . . . dedicated to the protection of the Gauleiters' health and the collection of high fees." The attack on French higher education is general, *L'Université* says. "It is easy to see why champions of 'the new order' want to destroy scientific culture in France. France deindustrialized will have no need of engineers or chemists. But the Nazis also want to make impossible the appearance of Frenchmen who by study of geography or history might draw practical conclusions from past struggles. They do not want Frenchmen able to see through the lying myths of superior races and slave peoples. They are still far from their goal. Teachers and professors every day are repulsing their attacks on our culture. Little by little, however, the framework of education is being whittled away."

The principal tool of the Germans in this work is the poet Abel Bonnard, an Académie Française "Immortal," whom nobody had read for the past thirty years and whose very survival had been forgotten by the public until Pétain reasserted the rights of senility. The traditional Cartesian clarity of the French universities, with its scrupulous insistence on proof, whether in the laboratory or in literary research, is of course the antithesis of Nazi mysticism. Consequently, Bonnard and his coterie have had to repudiate every noteworthy intelligence in the history of French culture clear back to Voltaire and Diderot. The excuse Vichy most often invokes in its campaign against education is economy. The budget for higher education has been cut eighty per cent, and, to compensate in part for this, university fees have been doubled. Fees have always been modest by

American standards, but the increase of even a couple of hundred francs a year, as *L'Université*, notes, "will make it still harder for young people of modest means to study. It is another gain for the enemies of public education—partisans of an 'élite.' Students are undernourished already, and often harried by the difficulties of a family life in which the student must replace a father in a prison camp and earn a living for an overworked mother. The lack of books and paper has hindered education. We must not permit this further blow at the base of an edifice of higher education which the entire world envied us!" The university faculties, to their great honor, have stood up to this pressure, even though it means the continual risk of livelihood and occasionally the risk of life. The late Henri Bergson, who refused to be made an exception when the Nuremberg Laws were invoked against French Jews, has become the martyr of the University of Paris. Recently collaborators tried to get scholars to sign a protest against the Allied bombing of occupied territories. Of some two hundred members of the Institut de France and five hundred members of the University of Paris faculty, fifteen signed the petition. Among these fifteen, *L'Université* proudly notes, "there was not a great name, not a single authority, not a savant of reputation. There were only a few obscure bootlickers."

L'Université speaks to me perhaps more poignantly than any other clandestine paper because quite a few years ago I myself matriculated at the Sorbonne and lived for a while in the narrow Rue de l'Ecole-de-Médecine in a room from which I could look down on a statue of Ambroise Paré, the surgeon who said, "I treat, God cures." I remember the pale, intelligent youths and the frugal, courteous, colorless little coëds (the only frumpy girls in Paris), who sat beside me in my classes. In the library of the Sorbonne one could consult books but not take them away. Students put their names on a long list for a chance at a work like Achille Luchaire's "Manual of Capetian Institutions." They would come back every evening until they got their turn at the book they wanted, then sit in the library—generally on the floor, because the place was always overcrowded—to read and take notes. My classmates were as punctilious as they were poor. They would not allow me to treat them because they could not reciprocate. It was dismal to see them sit so long in brasseries with one drink. Now the Nazis are trying to round up these students' successors, some perhaps sons and daughters of my friends, to carry them off into slavery. But the university underground railway is operating against the project. When the French police and the Gestapo appear in the Latin Quarter, students of the age being sought disappear, some to join the *Maquis*. When the police withdraw, the remaining students demonstrate in the streets. "By thousands they make the Boul' Mich' and the Luxembourg echo to cries of 'Laval to the firing squad, Bonnard to the privy, down with deportations!'" *L'Université* says. It was Paris students who rioted after gathering on November 11, 1940, at the Tomb of the Unknown Soldier—the first great public manifestation against the new order. University of Lyons students staged a riot in that city in May, 1942, and prevented a concert by the Berlin Symphony Orchestra. The University of Strasbourg was evacuated to Clermont-Ferrand at the beginning of the war and has been there as the guest of the local university ever since. When the Germans marched into Vichy France in November, 1942, and the Germans declared that Alsatians were nationals of the Reich, the students from Strasbourg refused to go home and enjoy their new national status. The Germans, after their invasion of the former *Zone Libre*, rounded up faculties and student bodies to sort out any Alsatians. Gestapo men with tommy guns carried out the raids. They went through the now habitual routine of making old professors stand with their backs against walls and their arms over their heads for hours and of forbidding women to go to toilets—all the ritual of petty beastliness that they introduced, after the *Anschluss*, in Vienna and have carried with them everywhere else as a bedbug carries its smell. As usual, they made an example: one old man finally dropped his arms and was shot dead. Two phony students, Gestapo stools, betrayed the Alsatians and members of resistance groups. Hundreds of students were taken away. They were never heard from again.

In their attempt to destroy France, the Nazis have especially attacked workingmen and intellectuals. Pétain, acting for his masters, tried, unsuccessfully, to set the peasants against the workingmen and the clergy against the intellectuals. The result was merely to create a stronger bond between the workers and intellectuals than existed in prewar France, when most intellectuals, however poor, came from families that considered themselves bourgeois. A woman who escaped from France last spring told me a story that is symbolic. She had a friend in Paris who was a brilliant physicist and traditionally absent-minded. "Like everybody, he had a couple of false identity cards," she said. "One never knows when they'll be necessary. But, negligently, he carried his false cards and his true one at the same time and in the same pocket. He was caught in a police dragnet one day and sent to a concentration camp for a few months. There was nothing against him except the cards, however, and he was a distinguished man, with many friends. Nearly all the other people in the camp to which he was sent were Communist workingmen. The professor had not been allowed to send home for a change of clothes, so when he arrived, his trousers were torn and the shoes he had on were an old pair, which soon wore through. He went to a fellow-prisoner, who was a tailor, and to another, who was a cobbler, and asked them to help him.

" 'I am not an institution of charity, comrade,' the tailor said, 'but maybe we could barter services. What did you do outside?'

" 'I was a professor of physics at the Collège de France,' my friend replied, rather hopelessly.

"The tailor was enthusiastic. 'All my life I have entertained the most lively intellectual curiosity about physics,' he said. 'Lecture to me while I repair your trousers for you and I will consider myself obliged.'

"The cobbler, too, was pleased to swap services. Soon there were so many prisoners who wanted to hear about abstract physics that the professor organized classes. 'I had more success than the professor of accordion,' he told me proudly when he came out. 'Those people are charming.'"

The New Yorker, April 15, 1944

III

"No one knows the frightful sadness that comes up from the banks of the Seine unless he has heard an old street organ wheezing away in the afternoon in front of the Plaza-Athenée, where the German sailors laugh—unless, under the great trees of the boulevard, where formerly he would have heard all the sounds of a happy day drawing to its close, he has been oppressed by a silence so complete that he has heard even the rustling of the leaves. Paris is a city emptied of its wine—the phantom of a city. Walk of a Sunday along the streets leading to the Champs-Elysées. You will see Nazi flags drooping from the façades of luxury hotels. Nobody . . . Germans . . . nobody . . . more Germans . . . nobody . . . nobody but Nazis in white summer tunics walking as if they were in the park of a garrison town. A horse-drawn carriage passes. In it are two Junkers, who look around through field glasses, vapid. No distinct sound anywhere, except the sound of *their* boots and *their* motors." So a writer in *Le Père Duchesne*, one of the many French clandestine newspapers I have been receiving in London from a friend in the underground movement, describes the slumbering, waiting Paris.

Gaiety is gone from Paris, but wit, of the bitter, railing sort François Villon practiced in the same setting, remains. Laval is the main target. He attracts ten insults to Pétain's one; the remaining insults are shared about equally by such smaller fry as Joseph Darnand, Philippe Henriot, Anatole de Monzie, Georges Bonnet, Charles Maurras, and Marcel Déat. Laval and his family are the protagonists of a cycle of anecdotes in which greed, shamelessness, cynicism, and rapacity are made to seem almost comic. As a mild example, *Libération*, another clandestine journal, notes that the horse Pennsburg, which won the Grand Prix de Paris last summer for one Madame de Bonard, was really running for José de Chambrun, née Laval, who uses de Bonard as a *nom de course*. The horse was one of several confiscated from Ralph Beaver Strassburger, the American horseman, before he left France. *La Vie Ouvrière*, a secret trade-union newspaper, tells how workers in the perfume industry, feeling themselves exploited, appealed to the Vichy government for help. Vichy announced that it would set up, as it already had for other industries, a corporation of perfumers, like a medieval guild, for the protection of both the workers and the employers. The perfumer Guerlain went to René de Chambrun, Laval's son-in-law, and gave him a contract according to which he will represent Guerlain in America after the war, with a ten-per-cent commission on gross sales and a nice sum down as a binder. The government then appointed Guerlain czar of the perfume industry, free to dictate terms to the workers who had made the appeal. Another paper, after listing a stupendous menu that had been served at a love feast of collaborationist factions in a hotel in Dauphiné, adds, "Humanitarian Note: Madame de Chambrun fed to her dog the carcasses of two chickens," this in a country in which at least four-fifths of the population is undernourished.

Laval, who is usually referred to either as Kalmuk, because he looks Mongoloid, or as Bougnat, a contemptuous term for an Auvergnat coal-and-wood seller, divides his time between running errands for Hitler and devising schemes for making money which even he must now realize he has no chance of keeping. His avarice is pathological, a classical case of the kind described in fine, clinical detail by Molière and Balzac. Each of his new rackets is recorded in the clandestine press. Recently, for instance, he decreed that all mayors must subscribe to a certain new municipal-affairs magazine; the magazine, of course, was to be printed in the plant of *Le Moniteur de Clermont-Ferrand*, Laval's newspaper—"an affair of only 300,000 francs' profit yearly, but nothing is too small for him," *Libération* notes. François de La Rocque, the more or less comic leader of the Croix de Feu, the first French Nazi-model costume organization, induced some industrialists to stake him to a newspaper in Paris, *Le Petit Journal*, just before the war, but he got into the bad graces of the Germans and Laval because he couldn't help them enough. A more violent form of Fascism than his was needed. In the winter of 1942, Pétain appointed de La Rocque to his staff, an organization which has served as a refuge for collaborationists who are on their way out. However, the Gestapo, at Laval's request, arrested de La Rocque in Vichy and he has not been seen since. *Le Petit Journal* nevertheless continues to appear with the legend "Editor de La Rocque" at the masthead. This trademark still carries weight with some of the small bourgeoisie, who used to think the Croix de Feu was a good thing and have never quite reconciled themselves to the more brutal organizations, like Doriot's and Darnand's, that supplanted it. This paper, moreover, is printed on Laval's presses. It is perhaps his compulsion to amass money that keeps Bougnat alive in a world where he knows that he is unwanted.

René de Chambrun was in the United States at the time of the armistice, preparing a moral climate for the acceptance of treason by advertising papa-in-law as a nice safe man. He evidently believes that he himself will be received there again, either as a perfume salesman or, possibly, as a State Department adviser on French affairs.

Writers in the clandestine press take the same sardonic pleasure in contemplating the present terror of the collaborationists that Villon felt when he predicted that his oppressors would die and rot. Journalists and other writers who have worked for the Nazis naturally are attacked in the clandestine press, because writers are peculiarly sensitive to the treason of other writers. There are things which the French intellectual had learned to expect at the hands of the industrialist or the politician but which he was not prepared to expect from writers. "It was not enough to have delivered the capital of the world to the Nazis, to the Schutzstaffel, to the firing squads. It was not enough to see posted on walls handbills announcing the execution of hostages. It was not enough to have to see the Vélodrome crowded to the gates three nights with [doomed] Jewish women and children," *Le Père Duchesne* said. "There had to be men, Frenchmen, who every day with zeal, with joy, with ecstasy followed out and even exceeded the shameful orders, flattered the executioners, thanked the assassins." The clandestine writers have been gloating over the growing discomfiture of newspapermen like Charles Maurras of *L'Action Française*, Marcel Déat of *L'Œuvre*, and Stéphane Lausanne of *Le Matin*, but their gloating is perhaps occasionally interrupted by anguish and impatience as the liberation, of which Frenchmen felt sure soon after Tunis, is again and again postponed.

I can easily visualize the reactions of two collaborationists I once knew whose names recur in the resistance newspapers.

One, Alfred Mallet, who wrote in *L'Intransigeant* under the name of Gallus and in other papers under other names during the first nine months of the war, when I knew him, was then trying to make himself *persona grata* simultaneously with Reynaud and with Laval. He had a round, waxy face. It is probably as round as ever, because the black-market restaurants in Paris are good, if expensive, and Mallet could always get money. The disasters of May, 1940, decided his political reorientation; he took the Laval line, repeating everywhere that resistance was hopeless and capitulation was the only way out. For once he was not motivated only by the hope of profit; the thought of an air raid made him ill with terror. I remember him in a restaurant on the Rue Saint-Augustin in the spring of that year, eating asparagus and crying. The tears from the corners of his eyes were running down his cheeks to mingle with the drawn butter around the corners of his mouth as he sniffled and stuffed. Unable to repress either of his dominant passions, greed and fear, for an instant, he let them have a go together. Within an hour of the coup d'état that set up the Pétain government, Mallet was giving everyone the impression that he had never even known Reynaud. He soon became one of the ranking Germanophiles of the collaborationist press. He must have flattered himself on his adaptability, but now, facing the certainty of a German defeat, Mallet, who is a realist, must be close to tears of terror again.

The second man I knew was Louis Ferdinand Céline, author of "Voyage to the End of the Night" and "Death on the Installment Plan," which, whatever I think about the man who wrote them, I still consider to be two of the best books written between the wars. At least he can say that he was as hysterically pro-German during the last few years before this war as he has been since the armistice. Céline, who suffered from insomnia and hallucinations while he was writing his first novel, is by this time undoubtedly mad. Ten years ago he complained incessantly of the aftereffects of a head wound, suffered in the last war, which caused what he called a "buzzing" in his head. Recently he wrote in *Je Suis Partout*, a Nazi organ in France, "Are collaborators, then, so broken, so timid that they insist on dying . . . like fools and calves, assassinated, chained, without having spit back into the faces of our murderers, all their dirty hypocrisy, their rotten cant?" The clandestine *Lettres Françaises*, the organ of the patriot men of letters, comments, "Céline will die as he has lived, raving and foaming at the mouth." It is easy for a Céline reader to imagine the furibund and fear-stricken Céline; few other authors have so well described paroxysms of rage and terror. For myself, I shall always remember him as a big-shouldered man, unexpectedly rugged and tweedy for a Frenchman, sitting in the dining room of the Hotel Vanderbilt in New York in 1934, eating strawberry ice cream after rare roast beef and at intervals pausing between enormous mouthfuls and great, gasping swallows to shout obscene regret for the Middle Ages, when the Church assured the common people that they would go to hell after death and be miserable in the meantime. "Then, at least, there were no false hopes," he said. He will die, I think, like a character in a Céline novel, perhaps like the professor of medicine in "Death on the Installment Plan," who preached stoic dignity and then, stricken by angina, died in humiliating contortions at the feet of his students.

Perhaps the most revolting example of collaborationist prose is a maudlin paragraph by Clément Vautel, for years the author of tasteless best-sellers, who in Paris wrote in the collaborationist daily *Le Journal* of his pleasure at hearing the German military band play "La Madelon" on the Champs-Elysées. It showed that the Germans were good fellows after all, he said. "He is enraptured, the *canaille*, that the Germans are there," exclaims an underground paper called *Franc-Tireur*. Of the well-known writers who went over to what seemed the stronger party—the group includes Jean Cocteau, Paul Morand, Henri de Montherlant, Jean Giono, Jacques Chardonne, Henri Béraud, Abel Hermant, Abel Bonnard, and Henri Bordeaux, who make a strange gamut from surrealism to academic senility—none has a truly great name in the English-speaking countries. A number of the important writers, such as Maritain, Romains, Gide, and Malraux are now in exile or in North Africa, but several famous faces in the gallery of contemporary letters are completely missing. The high quality of both the prose and verse in the clandestine press leads one to suspect that some of the ranking writers have "disappeared" into the resistance movement. There exist not only clandestine newspapers and magazines but at least one clandestine book-publishing house, Editions de Minuit. But the writers do not claim credit for inspiring resistance. "Resistance started from the depths, from the people, without guidance," *Lettres Françaises* says. "The intellectuals merely contributed."

The treason of a writer is explicit, because he puts it in words; a painter's thoughts can be his own. *L'Art Français*, which is for the graphic arts the opposite number of *Lettres Françaises*, records a friendship tour of the Reich by twelve painters, including van Dongen, Dunoyer de Segonzac, Vlaminck, Derain, and Despiau. That was in the days, not long after the armistice, when Otto Abetz was still trying to flatter France, and these fashionable masters may have felt a patronizing sympathy for the amateur painter Hitler. One of the few painters invited who turned the junket down was Albert Marquet. In 1941, when a Paris art gallery proposed a retrospective show of Marquet's work, he refused to permit one until the Germans had cleared out. Naturally, he was not then in the occupied part of the country. *L'Art Français* reports that all the students of the Ecole des Beaux-Arts called up for compulsory labor service failed to report and are now fugitives from the Gestapo. Most of them presumably have joined the Maquis. Also according to *L'Art Français*, a painters' and sculptors' resistance committee, in which artists of all tendencies and schools work together, has been functioning since the fall of 1941 in Paris. This is very probably the first time such unity has ever been achieved in France. The committee helps young artists to obtain false identity papers, hiding places, ration coupons, and money. The same issue of *L'Art Français* which records these things tells of the confiscation by the Germans of all collections of art belonging to French Jews and of the delivery by the Laval government to the Reich of van Eyck's painting "The Mystic Lamb," a Belgian national treasure entrusted to the custody of the French State in 1940, after the invasion of the Low Countries. It also carries a report on the Autumn Salon of last year, which, it says, was refreshingly good, perhaps because the Nazis are now too busy to devote time to the persecution of modern art.

There is no resistance publication for the stage and screen, as far as I can find out. Clandestine newspapers of all types take Gallic digs at Sacha Guitry, who seems to have carried over into real life his rôle in "The Story of a Cheat." He, these publications say, enjoys such favor with the Germans that when another collaborationist movie producer not long ago made a film on the same subject as one of Guitry's, Guitry simply had the other fellow's film suppressed. The worst record, by percentage, of all seems to have been compiled by the lovely women we learned to know in French films just before the war. Collaboration is a euphemism for the behavior of several well-known actresses, according to the clandestine Winchells. The temptations of actors are, of course, great. One can conceive of a clandestine writer but not of a clandestine movie star.

Another character who frequently engages the attention of the clandestine paragraphers in their lighter moments is Sisley Huddleston, a veteran British foreign correspondent who recently became a naturalized Vichy French citizen, which is tantamount to his becoming a second-class German subject. There is at least one clandestine humorous publication, *Le Gaullois*. The spelling of the name is a play on the general's name and *esprit gaulois*. This paper recently reported that, following Huddleston's example, Hitler asked Laval to have him naturalized as a French citizen. Laval took him to Pétain's office. Hitler went in, got naturalized, came out, and walked past Laval without speaking. Laval asked, "What is the matter, my Führer?" Hitler said, "I don't speak to Boches."

Jokes are only one facet of the obsessive fear, more solemnly expressed by editorial writers, that all the people who have disgraced France will try to escape the consequences of their treason by uniting, after the inevitable defeat, to support a government of "demi-virgins" like Georges Bonnet, Anatole de Monzie, and Ludovic Frossard. Such men have lived on good terms with Vichy but have never entered the government, either because, like Bonnet, they were excluded from it, or, like de Monzie were too shrewd. This particular Kolchak government, the resistants fear, will appeal, in the name of law and order, to the English-speaking powers to prevent a massacre of collaborationists and especially to forestall the setting up of a Communist regime. One clandestine paper says, "These people are calling everybody a Communist who believes in universal suffrage. They would impose their own Fascism after the defeat of Hitler's." The same paper says, diplomatically, "The industrialists slander Americans by letting it be understood that they have an agreement with the United States." The fact is, nevertheless, that millions of Frenchmen in the resistance movement suspect that the "slander" has a basis in truth. The elaborate double-talk of our State Department does nothing to reassure them. The resistance press also reports uneasily that many collaborationist industrialists are beginning to hedge against the evil day of collapse by contributing to the support of certain Maquis groups. By donating a small part of the profits they have piled up in making war matériel for the Germans, they hope to prevent the seizure of their plants after the liberation. Clandestine papers detect in this maneuver a plan by the industrialists to set the politically conservative Maquis groups against the Leftist Maquis groups, just as the Germans split the Yugoslav and Greek resistance movements. This plan would be successful only if the Comité Français de la Libération Nationale were prevented from setting up a firm provisional government in France. The resulting anarchy would weaken France for years. I regret to report that a prominent member of the not sufficiently defunct Cliveden set is now saying in London that we should keep the Algiers government out of France and "let the Frenchmen fight it out among themselves." There are a number of people in London who share his views, either because they dislike de Gaulle's intransigence or because they feel that the French are an inferior nation, whose "politics," by which they mean sentiments, are beyond English understanding. They seem unconsciously to loathe the idea of a strong France. According to them and, I am afraid, some Americans, all Frenchmen are on the same ethical level and the attitude of the resistance movement toward Vichy is merely vindictive. When I hear one of these Londoners talk, I think of a document printed in *Lettres Françaises*—the last letter of Daniel Decourdemanche, the paper's founder, whose nom de plume was Jacques Decour. His name appears on each issue of *Lettres*, along with the notation "Shot by the Germans, Saturday, May 30, 1942."

"My dear parents," the letter begins. "For a long time now you have been waiting for a letter from me. You did not think you would get this one and I hoped I would never have to give you the pain of reading it. . . . Look, I might have been killed in the war or even in last night's air raid, so I am not sorry to have given meaning to my death. You know I have committed no crime; you don't have to blush for me. I don't think of my death as a catastrophe when I think that at this moment thousands of soldiers of all countries are dying. . . . You know I have been two months waiting for what will happen to me this morning. I have had time to prepare, but as I have no religion I have not foundered in meditation on death. I look upon myself as a leaf that falls from a tree to make new soil. The quality of the soil will depend on the quality of the leaves that fall. By soil I mean the youth of France, in which I place all my hope. . . . You must pardon me for causing you this pain. . . . And now here are a few things you can do for me. . . . If you see my beloved, take her to your heart. Give her the things that are in my apartment: the volumes of the Pléiade, La Fontaine's Fables, 'Tristan,' the two water colors, the old map of Paris. . . . I want you always to think not of the fine things that might have happened if I had lived but of the fine things that really did happen to us all together. During these two months of isolation, without reading matter, I have relived all my travels, all my experiences, all my good meals. I have even made a plot for a novel. . . . I am going to write a message for Brigitte at the end of this letter; you will copy it out for her. She has not seen her papa for two years. . . . It is eight o'clock, nearly time to go. I have eaten, smoked, drunk coffee. I can't think of anything more to do. My dear parents, I kiss you tenderly. I am near you and the thought of you remains with me. Your Daniel."

Under that, *Lettres* adds simply, "It was Pucheu who handed over Jacques Decour to the executioner."

The New Yorker, May 6, 1944

Letter from France

AUGUST 10 (BY CABLE, DELAYED)

EVERYWHERE the Allied troops go in Brittany, the French wear smiles of pure contentment. They walk like happy lovers, smiling without shame and a little foolishly, knowing that the whole world understands. Even the Archbishop of Rennes noticed it on the first Sunday of liberation. "People had walked around every Sunday," he said to me when I talked with him, "but this Sunday everybody smiled. It is a commentary on the quality of a race when its mere absence can make other people so happy." The Archbishop, Monseigneur Roques, was a professor of German in a seminary before he was advanced to his prelacy, and he spent many of his student years in Germany, so he has some qualifications as a judge. "A race of men without individuality," he says. In the mind of a Frenchman, this is the ultimate condemnation. For four years the Archbishop, who is not a Breton but a Gascon, had the delicate task of dissuading his people from flying at the invaders with knives and stones, and being massacred for it, and at the same time of trying to temper the Gestapo's fury against Bretons whom it knew to be intransigent. His problem was complicated by the German-supported and German-financed Breton separatist movement. Leaders of the small but loud separatist sect, who had been forced into discreet obscurity when France went to war, came into the open when German troops occupied Brittany, and they denounced the Archbishop as a Frenchman who was antagonistic to a Nazi world order. Now, like many other varieties of quislings, they are discredited. Some Breton priests were active in the Maquis, who made attacks against isolated groups of Germans all through the four years of occupation. "It was better not to know of these matters—officially," the Archbishop says. Certain Nazi officials told him that Germany was not anti-Catholic, that there were Catholics in the Nazi Party. "But the Catholics had no influence on the Party, of course," he said. He sometimes found officers of the army of occupation amenable to reason, but officials of the Gestapo were almost impossible to deal with. Whenever priests were arrested because of articles they had written for diocesan publications, the Archbishop succeeded in getting them released only by assuming the entire responsibility for their acts and by challenging the Germans to arrest him. They never did.

In milieus less exalted than the Archbishop's palace, I found similar sentiments. One evening, in a dark little café near the ancient house of Bertrand du Guesclin, I heard a sergeant in the resistance forces, which have now come out into the open under the name of the Forces Françaises de l'Intérieur, or F.F.I., telling how the Germans had "interrogated" his wife after he had gone off to join the Maquis. She had been seven months pregnant and they had beaten her until she had lost the child, but she had not told them anything. The sergeant, a lanky, good-natured man with a turned-up nose, didn't speak of this as if it were an exceptional event. Two middle-aged men at the next table told him that they had been imprisoned for six months for no stated reason. They presumed that an anonymous letter had denounced them as patriots. They had at last been released, still without being told why they had been arrested. They didn't seem excited; they were slightly apologetic about even mentioning it, like Londoners in a pub diffidently exchanging bomb stories. After they had finished their reminiscences, all three of them began to laugh. They slapped their knees, they bent double, they choked, they wiped their eyes, and finally one of them sputtered, "And to think, we are rid of the bastards for good!" Then they all had another glass of wine.

The proprietress, joining the group, said that the German military had imposed a curfew hour and that the German soldiers would come after hours and insist on being served. "They would break the lock on the door, throw chairs at the waitresses' legs, and threaten to have the place closed for good if we didn't violate their own rules," she said. One waitress at whose well-shaped legs some chairs had been thrown interrupted to say, "Once, when I said that the English who had been in Rennes in 1939 were not so bad, some German soldiers reported it and the place was closed for a month." A prostitute, sedately sipping an apéritif near the zinc bar, said, "Once I called a German soldier a Jew just to make him angry. He reported that I had called Hitler a Jew. The Gestapo arrested me, and I had thirty-three days in prison on bread and water. They were great talebearers." The day Rennes was liberated, crowds in the streets mobbed some women who had been mistresses of Germans, and shaved their heads, but full-time prostitutes were by common consent exempted from this treatment. "A prostitute is a prostitute and a German is a German, and each acts according to his nature," a resistance sergeant explained to me.

In Normandy, whose great agricultural output was badly needed by the Germans and whose rich farmers they thought they could win over by appealing to their greed, the Nazis made some efforts, during the early days of the occupation, to conciliate the people, but in Brittany they did not attempt to be "correct." They knew it was hopeless. The Bretons started to kill German soldiers eight days after the invaders arrived, in June of 1940, and the ambushes and reprisals, the attacks on German road convoys and executions of hostages, never ceased. Now Bretons of the F.F.I., armed in part with Sten guns dropped from Allied airplanes and in larger measure with captured German rifles and machine pistols, scour the woods and side roads, rounding up bands of German soldiers who have been outdistanced by the rapid American advance along the main roads. Small parties of Frenchmen are bringing in scores of prisoners. The fight has gone out of these Germans. They hide in the woods not because they have any hope of rejoining the German forces, by now many miles to the east, but because they are afraid that if the French capture them they will be killed. This fear is unfounded, because the F.F.I. detachments are now officially a part of the French Army and observe the Geneva conventions as carefully as the American and British troops.

In the fighting for such places as St. Malo and Lorient, the patriots have frequently been able to cut German communications before the Americans arrive. They also take a considerable part in any sort of fighting in which straight shooting and a knowledge of terrain can offset heavy weapons, which the patriots do not as yet possess. Sometimes the resistance soldiers capture a town before the Americans get there, and our armored column arrives to find the local garrison already under lock and key. In one such town, I talked to the only avowed collaborationist I have met. He was a pot-bellied little man of fifty-six, with a face that was puffed from a beating some women had given him. "They were widows of men he betrayed to the militia," a resistance man who had brought me to see the collaborationist in his prison informed me. The pot-bellied man was locked in a cell of the Gendarmerie. He lay on a concrete dais, which was the nearest thing to a bed the cell contained, his grotesque, almost feminine figure wearing a dressing gown and blood-stained pajamas. Some resistance men had gone to his house and dragged him from his bed at night. His head was swathed in a turban of bandages; he looked like the self-portrait of Hogarth wearing a nightcap. "No, no, I didn't betray them!" he cried to me. "I never betrayed them! It's a lie!" He added, surprisingly, "I'm willing to be shot as a collaborator, but not for having betrayed those men. Somebody told the women I had betrayed their husbands, but it isn't so." In the cell with me, the collaborator, and my guide, who was a small, nervous fellow with the three slanting gold chevrons of a sergeant on the lapel of his civilian jacket, were a young gendarme in a tan uniform and black leather leggings and a great, heavy-set farmer armed with a German rifle, who was serving as the prisoner's special guard. All three Frenchmen began to argue with the prisoner at once.

"You know that you talked to the militia the day before they jumped those fellows!" cried the sergeant. "And then, animal, the night after they murdered our men, you had the officers of the militia to dinner at your house!"

"Shut up, thing of filth!" the gendarme thundered, from professional habit, even though the prisoner wasn't speaking.

"It wasn't you who always had a good word to say for the Boche, *hein*?" the farmer rumbled.

"Yes," the man on the concrete dais said, "I was pro-German. I acknowledge it. I worked for them. I took money from them. It is finished for me. I want to be shot."

"Let me get this straight," I said. "You want to be shot?"

"Yes," he said.

"*Il n'est pas difficile, vous voyez*," the gendarme said to me. "A curious mentality."

The sergeant said, "He's an architect. He built barracks and blockhouses for the Germans. Aren't you ashamed of yourself, miserable object—you, an educated man?" he howled at the prisoner.

The pot-bellied man looked fixedly at the wall without replying.

"Why did you work for the Germans? Did you think they could win?" I asked.

"Not after the Allied landing," he said, "but then it would have been disgusting to change. I could have run away, but I stayed. I am willing to be shot."

We walked out into the courtyard of the Gendarmerie. Seven gendarmes and their families were living in the barracks. All of them had been active in the resistance movement and they were very happy now. The Germans had not trusted them; they had taken away all their ammunition except nine bullets apiece for their old-fashioned revolvers. "They were right, of course," one of the gendarmes said to me. "We were all against them. Any time the Gestapo told us they wanted a man, we warned him. They told us as little as possible after the first few months of the occupation. The militia did their dirty work. Once a band of militiamen even attacked the Gendarmerie and we had to beat them off with our nine rounds apiece. They have no guts." The militia, the Germans' only reliable auxiliary in the effort to keep France down, was recruited from French convicts, who were released from jail and given what amounted to a full license to pillage and torture in a society that had rejected them. They particularly hated the gendarmes because the gendarmes had their records. "We had a Maquis group of about eighty men here," the sergeant told me. "Here, in northern Brittany, there isn't cover for large groups of resistants, as there is in the wilder regions. But these were men of quality, most of them non-commissioned officers in the old Army. On the night of June seventh, one day after the American landing in Normandy, the men of the Maquis were going to attack a German road convoy moving north toward Normandy. The man you have just seen betrayed them. He knew that everybody in the countryside hated him. Children made fun of him. Women spat at him. He hated us all. That evening two hundred militiamen and Gestapo agents at-

tacked our fellows. They had machine guns, mortars, and grenades. We had a German machine pistol, perhaps twenty rifles,
and one revolver. We killed twenty-one of them. They took
only fifteen prisoners. The militiamen loaded them into two
trucks and started toward Rennes, where they intended to take
them to Gestapo headquarters. But one of the trucks turned
aside and drove to a quarry near here. It had eight prisoners in
it—seven Frenchmen and one American. The American was a
parachutist who had landed here on June sixth. The Maquis
had fitted him out with civilian clothes, so that he would not
be spotted. The militia refused to admit that he was a soldier,
although he had his identity discs. They were found on his
body later. They stripped him and the other fellows and tortured them—tore out their fingernails, crushed their most
sensitive parts, that sort of thing, so that they would give information about the Maquis. Then they took them to the edge
of the quarry and shot them, so that their bodies fell over the
cliff. Then some of the bastards climbed down and finished off
one or two survivors with pistols. They told nobody. A farmer
who saw the shootings informed the gendarmes, and they
climbed down next day and got the bodies. Now you understand why this man will not admit he gave them the information and why he wants to be shot. He does not want to be
released from jail, Monsieur. It would be the worst thing that
could happen to him."

This town had been able to muster a hundred and fifty
armed men the moment the American armor swept down
through Avranches and headed toward Brittany. The Maquis
proper were now being helped by all the other active resistants, men who had continued to live in their homes and work
at their trades under the eyes of the Germans. The local chief
of resistance was a sly, merry man with a double qualification
for his rôle. He was district tax collector, so he knew everybody's business and had a good excuse to circulate everywhere
and correspond with everybody, and he was the greatest
poacher in the countryside, so he knew all the trails through
the woods. He was also, as I subsequently found out, a dis-
criminating collector of old Calvados and Armagnac. His principal aides were the town's leading physician—an elegant,
youngish man, clean-shaven and wearing shell-rimmed glasses

to indicate his modernity, but retaining the black worsted jacket and striped trousers that symbolize the professional man —and a florid, smiling, thick-fingered man who owned a local bus line. They, like the tax collector, had perfect reasons for travelling a great deal and seeing many people. The couriers between the district organization and the regional head-quarters in the nearest city were several pretty young women of good families who rode their bicycles along the highways, as it has become normal for young women in France to do when they want to go anywhere. The leaders used to meet in the shop of the town milliner; they were constantly taking hats there for their wives—"God knows it's impossible to get any-thing new in France and the only way for women to freshen up a little is to have something done to an old hat." The Ger-mans, as soon as they took over the town, had ordered the sur-render of all firearms on penalty of death but the local F.F.I. had assembled a small stock, mostly by killing German soldiers and militiamen who were carrying particularly tempting items.

In the town there was a large hospital, which before the war had been a tuberculosis sanatorium. When the Americans began their advance, it had a couple of hundred German wounded, and the German field commander had sent a de-tachment of troops to protect their evacuation. The resistance men captured both the hospital and the protecting detach-ment, mostly by bluff. Other F.F.I. patrols lay in ambush on the side roads off the Avranches-Rennes highway because they surmised that small detachments might try to escape along these byways and make their way to a German port garrison. They captured three hundred and fifty men in all. It was a clean-up job that would have occupied a couple of infantry companies for a week. "We were very anxious the night before the Americans reached this town," the tax collector told me. "There we were, with all these prisoners, in the dark, only one guard to each twenty prisoners, and we were afraid that some fanatic among the Germans might talk the others into at-tacking us. But nothing happened." Then he showed me a re-ceipt an American M.P. officer had given him for a hundred and seventy-five unwounded or slightly damaged prisoners.

The seriously wounded Nazis and the German doctors were still in the hospital the day I went to see the place. I was taken to the office of the chief surgeon. He was a swarthy, square-shouldered Bavarian in his middle thirties, with a decent enough face. He had taken good care of several wounded resistance men, I was told. I asked him why the German soldiers had let themselves be disarmed by a handful of French with a few guns. He insisted that all the Germans had been seriously wounded and bedridden. I asked him if he thought the war was over, as far as Germany was concerned, and he said yes, the war was lost. "Three million Germans have been killed or wounded to save Europe from Bolshevism," he said, assuming that martyred look which the Germans always used to put on when, as "reasonable men," they discussed the last war with Americans they took for suckers. I could see a new myth—which would replace the "stab in the back" and the "English plot"—building up in the muddy, Teutonic mind, and I felt just like kicking the doctor in the seat of the pants.

The New Yorker, August 26, 1944

Letter from Paris

SEPTEMBER 15 (BY WIRELESS)

Tнe press of Paris, from a professional point of view, is now an experiment. The newspapers are owned neither by private individuals nor by the government but by nonprofit organizations. There are more of them than ever before and new ones appear almost every day. The supply of newsprint is so small that, with two exceptions, the newspapers are limited to a hundred and eighty thousand copies. The Communist *Humanité* and the Socialist *Populaire*, because they had huge circulations before they were suppressed in 1939 and 1940, respectively, are allowed to print about fifty thousand more copies than the others. The papers all have two eight-column pages and sell for two francs. Since the public, which has been starved for honest news for four years, is now apparently insatiable, the papers sell out every day, which gives them enough money to pay their way. Except for *L'Humanité* and *Le Populaire*, the only pre-armistice papers are *Le Figaro* and *L'Aube*, which voluntarily ceased publication rather than print German propaganda and so have been allowed to resume; all the other papers are continuations of the tiny clandestine sheets that played such an important part in the liberation of France. Every resistance group that ever published an illegal newspaper is now represented by a legal one, and the metropolitan press displays names that became familiar during the dark and bloody years: *Franc-Tireur*, *Libération*, *Résistance*, *France Libre*, *Combat*, *Le Front National*, *Défense de la France*, and the rest.

The trend in prewar Paris, as in New York, had been toward fewer papers and larger circulations. Parisian newspaper plants were big enough to print editions running into the millions. To make full use of this capacity, a group of three or four of the new newspapers has been assigned to each of the great collaborationist plants. For example, *Combat*, *Franc-Tireur*, and *Défense de la France* use the old *Intransigeant* building; *Libération*, *Le Front National*, *Ce Soir*, and the weekly *Lettres Françaises* amicably share the modern facilities of *Paris-Soir*.

The rent they pay for these premises goes to a trustee appointed by the government. After the trials of the newspaper owners accused of collaboration with the enemy, the newspaper plants of the convicted publishers will be confiscated by the government. So will the rentals paid for these properties. Most of these publishers have prudently disappeared. What will happen in case any of them are acquitted has not been decided yet, but it is difficult now to conceive of the acquittal of men who printed the chief evidence against themselves day after day for four years and distributed it by hundreds of thousands of copies. Yet even stranger instances of whitewashing daub the history of the Third Republic, and the possibility that not only these publishers but the great industrialists who collaborated will escape punishment is causing a certain disquiet. France, as General de Gaulle said in his speech at the Palais Chaillot last Tuesday, has returned to the laws of the Third Republic, "which are not perfect, but which are the law." And the laws of the Third Republic permitted an infinity of abuses. Happily, treason is high crime by any man's law, and no special legislation is needed to expropriate the *grands patrons* who have already sold a controlling interest in their plants to Germany.

The new newspapers, unlike most of the prewar ones, are honest, are not subsidized by antisocial groups, and are free even from the pressure of advertisers—who in France always demanded puffs—because there is now no space for advertisements. But they are far inferior to what they were in their clandestine state—little sheets that were edited in the white heat of hatred and in a peril that seemed to heighten the sensitivity of the writers. They have lost their unity of theme. For four years they had two interlocking motifs: a fierce criticism of Vichy and an appeal to throw the Germans out of France. Now, five-sixths of France has been liberated and Vichy is so discredited that attacking it seems like kicking a dead dog—although there are smirking suggestions among the clientele of the black-market restaurants that the spirit of Vichy is merely playing possum. The new press, therefore, having won freedom of expression, has relatively little to express. The great exception, apparently, is *Lettres Françaises*, the weekly organ of the National Committee of French Writers, headed by François

Mauriac, Georges Duhamel, and Paul Valéry. Mauriac, the great chronicler of tortured, introspective minds, took no apparent interest in politics before the war, but after the surrender he became a leader of the intellectual resistance, a part he played negatively by refusing to publish anything while the Germans occupied France and positively by writing for the clandestine press under the name of Forez. What he is writing now is the clearest expression of the need for continued unity and the most lucid exposition of the intellectual errors that were the basis of the debacle. These errors antedated Locarno, the Stavisky Affair riots, the muddle-headedness of the old generals, and the Front Populaire of 1936. They date back to the Dreyfus trial. Members of L'Action Française (a movement which has been dissolved as treasonable), anti-republicans who called themselves "integral nationalists" and are professional patriots like our own Ku Kluxers, after failing to reshape France according to their own desires, worked for forty years to undermine French faith in France. Their leaders, the pseudo-intellectuals Charles Maurras and Léon Daudet, provided the cavaliers of industry with a ready-made rationalization of their thievery—the Republic was sinful and absurd, therefore it was all right to plunder and betray the Republic. When what the Maurrassians called their "principles" triumphed in Italy and Germany, the "integral nationalists" turned anti-nationalist and became the executioners of their own countrymen. Mauriac makes clear the importance of this intellectual manuring of the field in which the poison mushrooms grew. His editorials may prove the most potent weapons against the return of the old mob to power, but politicians and industrialists may be too obtuse and slow to suspect that.

The falling off in the quality of the press is conceded, a little wryly, by the editors themselves, who did so much better when they hid in cold hotel rooms, listening as they worked for the knock of a Gestapo agent on the door. Roger Massip, the present editorial chief of *Libération*, one of the most promising new papers, got out its last twenty-seven clandestine issues, which appeared over a stretch of twenty months. "Maybe it was because it is easier to make it a good paper once every three weeks than once a day," he told me a couple of days ago, "or maybe because the format was so small that a piece had to be very good or very important before we could find space for it. It was not worth risking the lives of our carriers to disseminate an interview with a cinema star. Just the same, we are much happier now."

One of the aspects of the clandestine press that always amazed foreigners encountering it for the first time was the quantity of newsprint available to patriot editors. Even though these underground publications were small, it took a good deal of paper to print one like, say, *Libération*, which had an average circulation of a hundred and fifty thousand copies. It wasn't much of a trick to get the paper, Massip says. Wholesalers had laid in huge stocks of newsprint during the first year of the war. The Germans froze all of it and set a low official price on it, so wholesalers were glad to sell it at the higher black-market price. They never asked what the paper bought from them was used for. In many cases they must have known that it was being bought for the clandestine press, but since they were making money on it they never informed. Some of the money for paper and printing came from sympathizers in France; the rest came from the de Gaulle committee in London. It was brought by messengers parachuted into France. Printing was more of a problem than paper, and a problem that often had to be solved anew on short notice when the German Gestapo or the French militia put a printery out of action. *Libération*, like most clandestine papers, began its career in the unoccupied zone shortly after the armistice. The German police were not so numerous there and one could count on the complicity of many Vichy officials. After November, 1942, when the Germans moved across the line of demarcation and occupied all of France, these advantages no longer existed and most newspapers moved their headquarters to Paris, since the risks were now no greater there than elsewhere and since one could feel there the beat of the national pulse and prepare for the liberation everyone knew was coming.

Massip took over the direction of *Libération* in January, 1943, during this transitional period. The paper had decided to move, but because of the difficulty of finding a Paris printing plant, it remained temporarily in the south. The editorial "office" was an apartment in a Lyon working-class district.

Massip and two colleagues lived and worked there. They had a mailbox in another tenement where they received reports from regional correspondents. *Libération* had local offices in Lyon, Toulouse, Marseille, and Montpellier. These correspondents supplied news of the underground struggle in their territories. At another mailbox, *Libération* received communications from its political and diplomatic correspondent, an official in the Vichy Ministry of Foreign Affairs. (Most big resistance papers had correspondents in the government who furnished them with depressingly intimate details of Laval's and Pétain's *petite combine*.) *Libération*'s political correspondent was eventually arrested and interrogated by the Gestapo. He got out of it alive and without "giving" any of his colleagues. According to Massip, the correspondent's body is covered with a tattoo of cigarette burns and, although he is only thirty-eight years old, his hair has turned completely white.

Massip and his two sub-editors sifted the news and wrote editorials and articles. When they wanted something that called for special knowledge or a satirical touch, they called upon some journalist they knew to write the piece, even though the man might be outside the organized resistance movement. No newspaperman ever gave them away. When they had decided on the contents of a number, they made a dummy and a resistance railroad man or travelling salesman carried it to the town of Montélimar, in the Massif Central, where there was a sizable job printery that worked largely for the movement. The printery would set the type and print twenty or thirty thousand papers for distribution in the immediate region. But it was not judicious to print a whole number at one plant, since distribution over a large area was a difficult problem, and besides, there would always be the danger that the Gestapo might capture a whole printing if it should happen to make a raid. Montélimar would therefore send back to Lyon carefully printed proofs on good paper, and technicians would photograph them and make a half dozen sets of zinc printing plates from the photographs. In this work, the resistance papers had the wholehearted aid of the photo-engraving departments of the Lyon collaborationist newspapers. The plates were distributed to little printing plants here and there, from Toulouse to Marseille. These plants were operated by partisans. Each plant printed an edition of a few thousand. Some of the papers were loaded in packing cases deceptively labelled and shipped by train to stations where resistance railroad men were waiting for them; others were carried in suitcases by ostensible *voyageurs de commerce*, who risked their lives every time they travelled, for Vichy agents rode many trains searching for contraband— black-market food and Spanish cigarettes. If, in searching for these, they opened a suitcase full of newspapers, they turned the carrier over to the Gestapo. (If they found food, they jailed him, sold the stuff, and pocketed the proceeds.) They were always hard on a newspaper carrier, presumably because they were angry when they found nothing to steal. One of Massip's printers was a priest who had a press in his church. The occupation authorities allowed him to have electric power in church only on Sundays, when he held services, so between masses he would print. This priest was caught, arrested, and immersed repeatedly in a bathtub of water just above freezing to make him talk. He didn't talk. He was then given intravenous injections of ice water. He still didn't talk. The Germans next tried to see how long they could hold his head under water without drowning him. They miscalculated and drowned him, but he hadn't talked.

At last the Gestapo smuggled a German officer into the Montélimar plant. He was a linotyper provided with a union card and a complete set of resistance identification papers, and he spoke perfect French. The plant was raided and put out of business, but all the personnel escaped except the foreman of the photo-engraving department. He was tortured to death, but he didn't talk, either.

In the fall of 1943, *Libération* moved to Paris. The new editorial office was an unheated room on the fourth floor of a shabby hotel on the Boulevard Raspail. There was a Gestapo office next door. "Obviously a factor of security," Massip says. "They would never expect to find us so close." Once, however, a Gestapo agent with an original turn of mind stopped Massip outside the hotel and frisked him, but without avail, for Massip never carried compromising papers. The printing problem in Paris was solved in a new way. It was hard to find a plant that was not under surveillance, but Paris was full of big collaborationist papers and all the compositors were militant unionists and Boche-haters. The men set type for resistance newspapers on the machines of the collaborationist sheets. Every time there was a pause in the flow of the copy they had to set for their employers, they set a few sticks for the resistance papers and put them aside. Most of the foremen knew what their men were doing and covered up for them. In the black of early morning, when their shift was done, the printers would take the resistance type away in suitcases. They would stop off, on their way home, at a corner bistro and another resistance man would pick the type up. The average weight of a loaded suitcase was seventy pounds. One linotyper is happily telling his friends now how he set hundreds of columns of resistance copy on the machines of the *Pariser Zeitung*, the German daily of Paris. Finding presses to print on was more of a problem. *Libération* emerged painfully from a dozen foot-pedal presses and hand presses in tiny plants; only the plants of collaborationist papers had electric power.

The centralization in Paris brought certain advantages to the whole resistance press. These papers had a joint news agency, which furnished them all with political and foreign news; an *agence d'information* for documentation; and a bureau which provided their journalists with false identity papers and changed them whenever an identity seemed to be wearing a bit thin. Still more important, the resistance journalists could now meet and discuss common problems. One of these was preparation for the day of liberation. During the winter of 1943, resistance groups drew up the scheme now in use. Immediately after the landing in Normandy, they made detailed plans to take over the Paris newspaper plants. Each collaborationist plant was assigned to a group of resistance papers. Resistance men, lean and shabby, with their revolvers and their false identity papers in their pockets, must have grinned whenever they passed one of the collaborationist news palaces. Editors recruited the enlarged staffs they would need when they started putting out standard-size papers. Some were journalists who had been discharged for too openly expressed de Gaullism; others were men who had worked on collaborationist newspapers, but without doing any of the dirty jobs, and had contributed articles on the side to resistance publications. The recruits unfortunately included a number of male and female sob sisters who write as badly as their American opposite numbers, but they were at least people of good will. The printers' union, which of course had operated illegally since the armistice, assigned crews to the clandestine journals. Everybody knew for weeks beforehand just where he was going on "Le Jour."

On the night before the police took over the Préfecture and began the armed insurrection, word was passed around among the men of the press to stand by. The editorial and mechanical staffs of *Libération*, *Le Front National*, and *Ce Soir*, which were to occupy *Paris-Soir*, were told to meet at a café near the Louvre the next night. The siege of the Préfecture began on August 19th, and that night, while German tanks rumbled through the streets firing at anything that moved, reporters and copyreaders, proofreaders and linotypers, pressmen and copy-boys and apprentices, armed with whatever they could lay their hands on, marched into the *Paris-Soir* building and took possession. There was no resistance. None had been expected. The old watchmen were glad to see the resistance men move in. The men had brought arms, in case the Germans made an attempt to wreck the plant when they learned that resistance papers were using it. Of some three hundred printers, twenty had firearms, mostly revolvers. A lot of apprentices had Molotoff cocktails—in their version, champagne bottles full of an incendiary mixture of gasoline and phosphorus to throw at tanks. For further protection, there were forty-two members of Marshal Pétain's special guard, fine types in resplendent uniforms, whom the Germans, as a compliment to Pétain, had allowed to be armed like real soldiers. They had helmets and tommyguns and carbines. These guards had been sent to Paris from Vichy to escort some Vichy minister who wanted to go home and was afraid to show himself in the Paris streets without an armed guard. When the detachment arrived in Paris, however, the minister had already departed by airplane. The guards had decided to join the uprising. They occupied the ground floor of the buildings flanking *Paris-Soir* so that they could protect the main entrance with a crossfire. Inhabitants of the quarter pulled up stone paving blocks and built barricades on the street. Massip and his colleagues on the other papers sat down to write their first editorials for the liberated press. The papers began to appear on August 20th, and continued to appear every day, even though there was fighting on the Rue de Rivoli, just a few blocks away, until the evening of August 25th, when the German General von Choltitz surrendered. There was never a real attack on the *Paris-Soir* building; the Germans had too many other things to think about. Stray bullets snicked through windows occasionally, but the copyreaders never even looked up. The circulation department suffered the only casualties. When a boy or a woman bicyclist delivering resistance newspapers blundered into a German patrol, the Germans would throw away the newspapers, confiscate the bicycle, and shoot the carrier. Half a dozen of *Libération*'s and *Le Front National*'s vendors disappeared during those days. (Unidentified bodies are still being dragged out from behind the bushes of the Bois de Boulogne and the Bois de Vincennes every day.)

One of the first things I bought when I got into Paris on the twenty-fifth, several hours before the German surrender, when I was still afraid to turn a corner without the police's assurance that it was safe, was a Paris newspaper saying that the city had been liberated. It is sad to reflect that those days of combat may have marked the end of the golden age of French journalism.

The New Yorker, September 23, 1944

Letter from Paris

SEPTEMBER 22 (BY WIRELESS)

Paris has been liberated for only four weeks, but an American arriving now would find it hard to believe that the Germans had been here for any considerable time. The Germans build nothing. In Paris, because of the fortunes of war, they were also prevented from destroying anything. Culturally sterile, they have left no imprint on thought or on manners here, except that people still laugh when they recall how the Germans used to shout at each other in cafés and how the privates would twist themselves into knots and quiver in ecstatic terror at the approach of a corporal. They have left one other reminder—the memory of the hundred and twenty thousand Parisians they tortured and killed. But other Parisians will be born to replace the mutilated dead and the horror will be forgotten. The Beauty, in Ludwig Bemelmans' last book, said, "I will tell you how I feel about Germans. In time of war I detest them. In time of peace they don't exist for me." It is perhaps the most dangerous quality of Germans: they are so easy to forget and, after a few years, so hard to believe in. Perhaps the French government should preserve the torture chambers of the Gestapo as national museums; for example, that shooting gallery in Issy-les-Moulineaux, where prisoners were placed barefoot on metal plates, which were then charged with electricity. Each time a charge was shot into the plates, the victims leaped high into the air, galvanized into human bounce balls. They dug their fingernails into the walls at heights never achieved even by Olympic jumpers. The marks are still there. But if the government preserved this establishment, twenty years from now the intellectuals would be saying that the museum was a chauvinist fake.

The physical conditions of life in the city are slowly approaching normal. The subway is running about half its normal service, electric light has been restored for a few hours each evening, and the food supply has definitely improved, though belts are still fairly tight. The fighting front is now as far from the city as it was in May, 1940, but wheras the front was then moving toward Paris, it is now moving toward Berlin, which makes the war seem remote. As the war recedes, people think and talk more about the future of France. Many of them feel that General de Gaulle has an opportunity, never offered to any other man, to make sure that this future will be a bright one. France, these people say, has oscillated between revolution and excessive legalism for the past five hundred years. Written law is a fetish in France; the French worship it. It defines the political rights of the individual and the privileges of property, and most Frenchmen think of themselves as small property owners, or at least as potential ones. This passion for law alternates with a passion for social justice, and the two are sometimes in conflict. The revolutionary terror of the First Republic was a triumph of justice over law, and the suppression of the Commune in 1871 was a triumph of concrete code over abstract justice. Many resistance leaders feel that de Gaulle's opportunity is unique because he can, if he wishes, reconcile these two tendencies and seal the rift in the national psyche. They say that he could proclaim what they call an "economic revolution by due process of law."

The broad political problem is closely linked with the more specific problem of punishment for collaborators, a subject that obsesses the public. De Gaulle's popularity is possibly unequalled in French history, and therefore what many people call his slowness in approaching these problems is being blamed on everybody but himself. Editorial writers have been criticizing his ministers and suspect that there has been foreign interference in France's internal affairs, but none of them has yet presumed to attack the General himself. One popular theory is that he wants to get full recognition of the Gouvernement Provisoire and a good seat at the peace table before he sets up an internal program that will very probably antagonize certain British and American elements. The orthodox government line (in politics, orthodoxy is a quick-growing weed), as expressed in the newspaper *France Libre*, is that external affairs must take precedence over everything else at this stage and that internal disputes must be deferred until after the return of the prisoners of war, the general elections (which are not to be held until these men are home again), and the signing of the peace treaty. The detractors of this line say that by that time the traitors—those among the industrialists and bankers, at least—will again be protected, physically and financially, by phalanxes of lawyers and a labyrinth of interlocking directorates and Swiss holding companies, and that the inevitable whitewashing of these collaborators will be followed by an equally inevitable revolution. It is true that General de Gaulle, as a professional soldier, took no part in internal politics before 1940 and that in his incarnation as statesman, which began so dramatically on the twenty-third of June that year, he at first confined himself to foreign and colonial affairs because his government had no control over France itself, but only a year later he was saying that "bold ideas" were needed in shaping the social and economic structure of the France of the future. He spoke of his debt to the working people, who were at that time the chief support of the Free French cause in France. There is little reason to think that his fundamental conceptions have changed or that he has forgiven the men of Vichy; he seldom forgives anybody. In any case, instead of the blood bath confidently predicted by certain people in Washington and London "if that man de Gaulle gets control in France," Paris is now witnessing merely the desultory interrogation of a few hundred putative collaborators picked up here and there and the incarceration of some of them to await trial in calmer times.

The *roman feuilleton*, or continued novel, was always an important feature of the French press, and Parisian newspapers are fortunate now, when space is so limited that few of them can print a real *feuilleton*, in having the daily running story of the investigation of the Lafont and Bony gang. Lafont and Bony, former inspectors of the French Sûreté Générale, opposite number of the F.B.I., were broken before the war because their corruption exceeded anything ever known even in the Sûreté, the organization which blandly protected Stavisky while the Paris police were looking for him. This denoted a remarkably high level of dishonesty. When the Germans came in, this precious pair of cops were highly recommended to Laval's partner-conquerors. Both acquired German citizenship and received commissions in the Gestapo, and then, gathering a nucleus of administrators and stool pigeons, they organized the French section of the Gestapo. Their milieu, as reconstructed during the investigation, is reminiscent of both Chicago gangland and the milieu in which the Lonergan affair had its being. They had magnificent houses in the Etoile-Elysée district and mistresses who included a White Russian princess, a night-club marquise, and a German film star. There were fake Baltic barons, pastiche French vicomtes, and in general a café-society hoopla. In addition, on the fringe, there were characters like the little man who picked people's eyes out with a fork and another who specialized in cutting off noses and fingers, and the German art expert and fence known as Manuel Flatfoot.

The police who are conducting the investigation have the true *feuilleton* manner of developing a story; every day they introduce one or two new characters who make good reading. Yesterday it was a man called Jo La Terreur, whose relevancy seems to depend entirely on his being a friend of Violette Morris. Violette was an English-born auto racer who was supposed to have killed men for calling her a woman and who had a surgeon remove her breasts so that she would look mannish. Violette, being a sadist, was quite at home with the Gestapo. Three months ago, while she was stalking a man in the Maquis who was to be arrested and tortured, some Patriots shot her to death. The police freed Jo La Terreur, but not until his name had made a fine headline and the details of Violette's personality had given the newspapers a walloping good *Daily News* story. The Lafont and Bony gang specialized in fake raids and arrests. They would rob the apartments they raided and kidnap the occupants, and then torture the "arrested" people until a ransom was paid. Since the gangsters held cards in the Gestapo, they could not be prosecuted. Naturally, the victims of their raids were always carefully selected—a corps of finger men did this work—and the hauls were magnificent. They had to split the take with the German Gestapo men to hold their franchise, and Manuel Flatfoot saw to it that they didn't hold out the good items and pass along the shoddy ones. The French and German Gestapos maintained a joint marketing organization to dispose of the varied loot: securities, specie, jewelry, paintings, antiques, and vast quantities of more common-place but valuable objects like felt hats and groceries. They were businesslike. To keep in good with the more earnest elements in the German parent organization, Lafont and Bony sometimes had to forego big profits and arrest or liquidate real Patriots. For instance, Lafont kidnapped the head of the Belgian Intelligence in France and delivered him to the Germans, who tortured him to death. On another occasion, Bony pretended he was an R.A.F. pilot who had bailed out of a plane, and, when some Patriots took him in, informed on them to the German Gestapo. The gang also recruited North African thugs to fight against the Maquis. These chores they performed to prove their good faith. They didn't relish them, for there was little money in them.

The trouble with a story so full of horror and cynicism is that after a while the reader begins to follow it as if it were actually only a *roman feuilleton*. Lafont and Bony are becoming, in a perverse way, public heroes, like Landru—the Bluebeard of 1919—and Doctor Petiot, who, during the German occupation, killed and dissected a hundred and sixty people. Like Lafont and Bony, Petiot was welcomed to the bosom of the Gestapo. He is now somewhere in Germany. His game worked this way: he promised to get people out of France and into America. Naturally, a great many of them were de Gaullists and Jews. Petiot would impress them with the necessity of secrecy; they must tell nobody they were leaving or where they were going—just take all their money and come to his cottage in a suburb of Paris, where he would start them on the underground railway. When they arrived at the cottage, he would tell them that the American authorities insisted on inoculations and that, luckily, since he was a doctor, he could give them. Then he would shoot them full of morphine and start to dissect them before they came to. He kept their money and turned over their papers to the Gestapo, which was grateful for his aid in protecting Europe against the "Bolshevist peril." Men such as Lafont and Bony and Petiot are dangerous in the same way the Germans are—because nobody really believes in them. People read about them as they read about the Lublin massacres and say they're too bad to be true.

*

The exuberance of the first week of liberation has died down. The children in the little park under my window who sang the "Marseillaise" all day every day that week and walked about waving tiny flags are now playing the French equivalent of hopscotch, as they used to in 1940, when I lived in the same room I live in now, overlooking the same park. The small *gardien* in the green uniform who stood by the fountain in the park on the day I went away is there again, his hands locked behind his back. The fountain, with its four allegorical female figures (the rivers of France), plays on and I am once again tempted to throw peachstones into the navel of the fat stone woman who represents the Loire. A fat flesh-and-blood woman in a flowered wrapper comes out on a sixth-story balcony of a house fronting on the park and waters some geraniums. I recognize her; she is the woman who came out on the same balcony early in the morning of May 10, 1940, when German planes first appeared over Paris, and waved at some frightened pigeons and cried, "Confidence!" And I remember how people at other windows on the square laughed and waved, too. She was wearing a flannel nightgown then. The children have forgotten the Germans already, I am sure. The rest of us will forget too soon.

The New Yorker, September 30, 1944

Letter from Paris

WHEN I wrote in these columns, a month or so ago, that the Germans had left hardly a trace in Paris, I was being superficial or philosophical, or both. It is true that people here seldom speak of them, and it is possible that in a few hundred years the invasion of the Nazis will blur in with those of their kinsmen—the Cimbri, the Alamanni, the Burgundians, the Ostrogoths, the Bismarck Prussians, and the rest—until only specialists in history will remember whether the Nazis came before or after Ariovistus. But they have left one very definite trace, and that is on the health of this generation of Frenchmen. Fifty-four per cent of the children born in Paris since the armistice, for example, have rickets as a result of the insufficiency of vitamins in their diet, according to Professor Pasteur Vallery-Radot, a physician just elected to the Academie Française who has compiled a comprehensive set of statistics on French health today. The death rate in the Paris area is eighty per cent higher than it was in 1939, and cases of serious illness have increased by sixty-seven per cent. Fifty-seven per cent of the deaths among people in their twenties are now caused by tuberculosis, whereas forty-three per cent of the deaths in this group were caused by this disease before the war. Infant mortality has very nearly doubled. Deaths among nursing babies from gastroenteritis have risen fifty per cent. Delayed growth and anemia are general among French children; in Lyon, forty per cent of the public-school children, who are at the age when their rate of growth should be greatest, either lost weight or did not gain during the last school year. Among adults, bones break with sickening ease because of the deficiencies of calcium and phosphorus in the French diet. Somebody once said that the average height of Frenchmen declined by an inch because of the Napoleonic wars; French doctors are now reporting many cases of adults who have lost as much as four inches in height because of the effect of these deficiencies on their vertebrae. These doctors are also familiar with another phenomenon among their clients—a sudden torpor which, after a few hours, becomes a coma; it is due to the deficiency of sugar in the diet. Hundreds of boys who were heroes in the Paris street fighting had the humiliating experience of being turned away from recruiting depots when it was decided that they were to be incorporated into the regular army. Rejections ran as high as fifty per cent in some battalions of boys who had wrecked German tanks with bottles of gasoline and fought German infantry with revolvers.

These figures of Dr. Vallery-Radot's have nothing to do with the unforgettable picture of the thousands of pretty girls on bicycles who greeted us Americans in Paris on the day of its liberation, or with the fact that, for the equivalent of fifteen dollars, one can buy a really good dinner in Paris. Young women dying from tuberculosis do not ride bicycles, and workers suffering from malnutrition do not patronize fifteen-dollar restaurants. Some of the correspondents who spent the first week after the liberation sending dispatches to their papers about the luxuries of life in Paris are now flying across the Channel, whenever they can, to get a hot bath in a London hotel. There is practically no coal in Paris, and it is a measure of the bleak discomfort here that in retrospect even London hotel rooms seem delightfully warm and cozy. Bathing has become a serious problem with the arrival of colder weather, for there is hot water only in hotels like the Crillon and the Ritz, which are reserved for rear-area officers of extremely high rank. The more modest hotels, which have been requisitioned for transient officers, have no hot water, apparently on the theory that many of the guests have just come back from the front, where they were not used to such a luxury.

Dr. Vallery-Radot believes that the health of the children, at least, can be saved if they get large quantities of the proper foods in the near future. Now that the Germans have stopped draining France of anything edible, the food situation must improve, but it cannot improve greatly until the French railroads and trucking systems have been sufficiently restored to ensure distribution of what is available, which will not happen for some time. At best, this will be a critical winter for France's urban population. Some French doctors, who think that it will be impossible to heat city houses this winter, advocate importing large amounts of fats. An augmented ration of fats, they say, would enable the population of Paris to resist the cold. Besides, the amount of shipping and trucking needed to import butter and margarine would be small compared to that which would be needed to bring in coal.

It takes longer to destroy a nation's culture or even its industry than to wreck its health. The Germans worked systematically to destroy French culture, however. They withheld stocks of paper from publishers who wanted to reprint the classics or works of non-collaborationist authors, whereas no quantity of paper was too great, no quality too fine, for collaborationist books or Goebbels brochures. As a consequence, there is now a book famine in Paris. An ordinary one-volume edition of Verlaine, published in 1938, is a collectors item. Stendhal, except for deluxe illustrated editions of two of his novels, is not to be had. Strangest of all, the works of such popular contemporaries as Duhamel and Mauriac, which a few years ago were printed in paper-back editions of tens of thousands, are as hard to find as minor classics like Alfred Jarry's "Ubu Roi." Some booksellers are asking big prices for what were once run-of-the-mine books, when they have them. Others, especially combination bookseller-publishers like Henri Martineau, the Stendhal expert, honorably continue to sell their publications, as long as they are in stock, at the original price. The ban on reprints has now been lifted, but there is, naturally, a paper shortage, and this will delay the replenishment of stocks for a long time. Some booksellers say it will be ten years before it again becomes easy to buy a cheap edition of a classic. However, Mauriac, Duhamel, Aragon, Malraux, and other contemporary writers who have grown in stature during the resistance period will soon appear in fairly large reprintings. Translations of English and American books published since 1940 are awaited with feverish eagerness and will have a high priority in the publishers' plans for what to do with their paper stock. All in all, there is little doubt that Corneille, Racine et Cie. will have to wait.

General de Gaulle, in his first mass press interview since his return to France, spoke of the satisfactory condition of French agriculture compared to that of industry. The plight of French industry, too, is a result of systematic German effort during the four years of occupation. France, in the Nazi scheme, was to be reduced to the rank of dairy, delicatessen, wine cellar, and auxiliary breadbasket for the Reich, so agriculture was hardy interfered with at all. (The products of course, were siphoned off.) The nation was to be de-industrialized. Workmen and machine tools were carried off into the Reich. A certain portion of French industry had to be left in place for strategic reasons, mostly because Allied bombings made a complete centralization of manufacturing inadvisable, but it was made complementary to German industry and rendered incapable of independent existence. French automobile manufacturers were allowed to turn out only parts, not complete vehicles; airplane plants were neutralized in the same way. All assembling was done in the Reich. A great number of French industrialists acquiesced in the German plans; they even coöperated in the castration of their own enterprises. They accepted walloping profits and they paid no such income or excess-profits taxes as their American or British opposite numbers did. Many of them threatened their workmen with deportation for forced labor in Germany to prevent a revival of the old unions. It seems unlikely that the workmen will forgive them for that. The action taken by the provisional government at the end of September, when it requisitioned the Renault factory and arrested Louis Renault, the prototype of the ruthless French industrialist, did much to maintain the faith of the workers in the sincerity of de Gaulle's program of "social and economic renovation." Most of the resistance men prefer to call it "revolution," but that is a matter of taste. Renault, who was ill, was allowed to enter a private hospital, but was kept under surveillance. He died this week, at the age of sixty-three. A feature of his obituary in most papers was the statement that in a national newspaper poll conducted shortly before the war he was voted by an enormous majority of workmen the "worst boss in France."

Renault, like many men who prefer that other people think them self-made, was actually a rich man's son. He went into the automobile business early in his career and did well at it. During the occupation, he had thirty-five thousand people in his plant at Billancourt, making truck and tank parts for the Nazis. He owned ninety-seven per cent of the shares in his company and publicly stated his belief that an employer had no social responsibility of any kind. It is hard to say what will happen now to his properties. He died before he could be tried for treason, and the permanent confiscation of his factory depended upon his conviction, an event which appeared likely. The provisional government's gesture nevertheless remains; the precedent has been set. Other industrialists have been arrested since, but it was Renault's imprisonment that dramatized the industrial purge.

An event just as important, symbolically, was the condemnation to death, early this week, of Georges Suarez, the Paris journalist who edited for the Germans a collaborationist sheet called *Aujourd'hui*. His trial was held in a court that has been set up in the Palais de Justice expressly to try collaborationists. For weeks the no-longer-underground resistance press had been complaining of the delay in bringing accused traitors to trial. Editorials reflected, or were reflected in, the talk of thousands of men and women who had risked their necks in the resistance movement. The Communist *Humanité* spoke with increasing sharpness of the likelihood that, once popular feeling had cooled down, traitors would get off scot free. Finally, the new court got under way, and Suarez attained a certain place in history by being the first man condemned by it to die. Before the war, he was a journalist of the type familiar in Paris since Balzac's day—blackmailing, puffing, or attacking for hire, always in need of money for women and always in need of women to bolster his belief in himself. During the occupation, he sold himself to the Germans as automatically as he would have sold himself to any other highest bidder. Men like him had always found protection in France; it is unlikely that it ever occurred to Suarez that he was letting himself in for a rap he would be unable to beat. He had never heard of that sort of rap. The only evidence offered against him by the government was a collection of a hundred editorials he had signed, some calling for the extermination of "terrorists" (Maquis), others saying that a German victory was the only hope of Europe, still others calling on Frenchmen to join in a holy war against the Allies. The judge said that it hurt him to read them. Suarez seemed astonished. He called witnesses to prove that he had several times used his influence in favor of patriot prisoners of the Gestapo—he had once got a prisoner a twenty-four-hour leave from jail. Every collaborator in France, the resistance men claim, has done at least one favor for a Maquis or a Jew. "That is a traitor's insurance policy," they say. Suarez appeared to feel cheated when the judge ruled his benevolence irrelevant. The verdict had symbolic importance because it was a blow to the cult of *Débrouillardise*, the notion that if one is slick enough and knows enough people one can get away with anything. This was one of the doctrines—all the more dangerous because it never attained the dignity of explicit statement—that had most to do with the rotting of France. The Suarezes of France were not such imposing figures as the Renaults, but they were always there to do the Renaults' dirty work.

The New Yorker, November 4, 1944

Colonel Baranoff and
The Newspaper "PM"

Every now and then I read that Russian mistrustfulness is lacerating the sensibilities of some contemporary journalist. For example, the Russians approached the San Francisco Conference, it appears, like a small boy who would willingly pick a dime off the sidewalk if he weren't afraid that the coin had just been heated and left there by a practical joker. I feel guilty when I read such a lament, because I fear that I am in part responsible for this Russian attitude. The Russians have long had at least a couple of excuses for being leery of the capitalistic world, such as the press campaign against them that began at the time of the Revolution and has never stopped. However, I sometimes think that I poured into the ebullient brew of Russian feelings about America the last little drop of doubt that made the mixture overflow. It happened late in April, 1943, while I, then a correspondent on the American front in Tunisia, was sharing a tent with a Colonel Baranoff. Baranoff—that is not his name, but it will do—was a correspondent for Tass, the Soviet news agency. He was also a colonel of artillery on the active list of the Soviet Army, which gave him enough rank to impress the hell out of the American and British public-relations officers in the field, who seldom topped major. Not long ago he was put on one of those joint Allied commissions that run countries in the Mediterranean, and since many of his colleagues on the new beat are colonels, he has been upped to major general.

Baranoff had been with the British Eighth Army in Libya for several months before he came over to look at the Americans. I had heard a lot about him when I was in Tripoli earlier that month, but I had never chanced to meet him until he came with us. The British have a system of assigning what they call accompanying officers to correspondents, which in practice often means that the correspondents have to accompany the officers. The Eighth Army correspondents travelled in parties of three newspapermen to one accompanying officer, plus a couple of drivers who doubled as batmen. Each party was also provided by His Majesty's Gov with a couple of lorries equipped with cots and typewriter tables. Eighth Army Public Relations, operating with its customary felicity, had placed Baranoff under the protection of a particularly fluttery ex-member of the Duke of Windsor set. Baranoff, British newspapermen had told me, got a bit of innocent fun out of this situation. Every evening, when his party started to pitch camp, Baranoff would, if any artillery was at all audible, turn to the accompanying officer, who was a baronet, and say something like, "Sir Papa [a form of address of his own devising], that last salvo was not far from us. To the north a little only." Then he would listen again, and after the next salvo he would say, "*That* one was to the south. We are bracketed. On my honor as an artillery officer, Sir Papa, next one will land here. Perhaps on the table where you are about to have tea." So the little caravan would pack up and move elsewhere. If Baranoff and the other press men felt lively, he would do this two or three times in an evening, and it cheered everyone, except Sir Papa, immeasurably. On the whole, Baranoff held himself rather apart from his colleagues; only once, they said, had he seemed to feel himself really in rapport. That was during one of the engagements that punctuated the Eighth's long advance from El Alamein to northern Tunisia. A British brigadier had not only failed to get some guns across a wadi but, what was worse, he had reported to his divisional commander that the guns were across when they weren't. This had, of course, balled up ensuing operations. On the following morning some correspondents, including Baranoff, called at the brigade command post to investigate the incident and found that the brigadier was no longer there. "The brigadier!" Baranoff inquired. "Where is he?" "They bowler-hatted him," an officer said, meaning that the brigadier had been relieved of his command—in obsolescent American slang, "handed his hat." "Ah," said Baranoff, smiling with quick comprehension, "I understand. You have shot him." When he learned that they had not shot the brigadier, he looked puzzled, and could see that he felt he was up against the inscrutable Occident again.

*

Tripoli, early in April of that year, was already several hundred miles behind the front lines; the Eighth Army had pushed west across the desert and then north along the shores of the Gulf of Tunis until it was up around Gabès and Sfax, in Tunisia. Tripoli had supplanted Alexandria as chief supply port for the British forces and was rapidly acquiring the more obvious characteristics of a base: an Army newspaper, theatricals, and "flicks," tall, impractical-looking Sudanese sentries wearing green turbans, and swarms of rear-echelon officers competing for the de-luxe quarters. There was actually something to compete for in Tripoli, since the Italian government, fond of operatic magnificence, had built fine houses for even minor colonial officials. All the littlest vermicelli, as well as the biggest macaroni, of the Fascist hierarchy there had departed in a hurry, leaving their *palazzi* ready for the British. The Eighth Army public-relations officer at the base was a captain who wore the shoulder flash and cap insigne of the Grenadier Guards, because as a youth he had served with them for a year in London. He had sensibly preëmpted a villa in the suburbs, a mile or two from the port itself, which still drew occasional bombardments from enemy planes based in Sicily. The villa, although it had housed only a minor Italian official, a street-cleaning superintendent or the secretary of a Fascist club, was imposing—a long building of Italian-Arab architecture, with two wings of bedrooms separated by a suite of dining and living rooms. The Guardee reserved one wing for himself; he allowed the correspondents, of whom, it is true, there were seldom more than ten or fifteen, to use the other. There was a bathroom in each wing. The one in the captain's wing worked; the one in the correspondents' didn't. While I was there, a band of British correspondents came back from the battle of Wadi el Akarit. One of them had been conked by a piece of a shell and had just spent a few days in a field hospital. They couldn't get a bath. There was a deep artesian well that supplied the villa with water. Another well, nearby, supplied the native Jews and Arabs of the surrounding suburb. Both wells were pumped by stationary engines. The engine that worked the neighborhood well broke down, but the Guardee wouldn't let the Jews and Arabs draw water from the villa well because he didn't like to have them tramping across the lawn. He would lurk among the orange trees on the grounds at dusk, and when he saw little girls sneak up on the well, he would wait until they had filled the gasoline tins they had brought for water and would then rush out and hit them across the backside with his swagger stick. The girls would drop the tins and run away, howling. "If they really needed water, the beggars could draw it from their own well by hand," the captain would say.

In the mornings the captain would sit swilling tea, on the open terrace that ran the length of the villa, until the wasps trying to get at his marmalade became too numerous, which usually happened at about ten o'clock. He didn't try to hit the wasps with his stick, because he was afraid of them. When he had had enough of them, he would take his cap and his stick, blow hard through his nostrils until the ends of his long brown mustache fluffed out, and go off in his motor. It was only a Humber; he was pained that he had not succeeded in pinching an Isotta-Fraschini from a departed Italian. "The chaps who arrive in the first fortnight snaffle everything good," he used to complain. He always was secretive about his morning missions, implying that it would be a breach of censorship to tell us what they were about. One morning I was talking to Major Robb, a Scotch agronomist, at the Tripoli Agricultural Research station, when our captain arrived there on one of these missions, his chest pushing the front of his battle dress, mustaches floating on his breath, "hrrrumph"s rising in his throat, a gruff, manly condescension in his voice. He introduced himself and then tried to cadge an electric fan and a quart of cream. For lunch, a meal that he tried to make the best of the day, because fewer correspondents were at the villa than at breakfast or dinner, the captain would customarily eat a bit of fresh mutton bought at the public market, and then perhaps a treacle tart. The mutton was openly bought, not black-market. Only bread was rationed in Tripoli, since the British argued, reasonably, that the Arabs didn't have money enough to pay for meat and weren't used to it anyway. Replete, the captain would retire to his office, a room in which no correspondents were allowed, and compose letters to his superiors in Cairo asking for more enlisted men and vehicles. He already had

sixty-ur men when I was there, though he needed no more
sixty-ve, but he felt that having more men under his com-
tha i would add to his dignity. He put up the ones he had in
uple of villas across the road, to keep them from getting
derfoot.

The captain's solicitude for his dignity reacted disastrously
only once while I was in Tripoli. When I arrived, he had a soldier cook who, for the British Army, did quite a decent job.
However, the soldier was rated merely as a driver and he had
learned cooking by experimenting on correspondents in the
field. The captain thought that a man of his consequence
should have a graduate of an Army Catering Corps school.
Negotiations had been proceeding, I discovered, for months,
and a Catering Corps alumnus, a sergeant, arrived on the sixth
day of my stay. We expected the correspondents from Wadi el
Akarit to come in that evening, and knowing how hungry they
inevitably would be for fresh meat, I went to the market and
bought eight pounds of lamb chops for the equivalent of nine
dollars—not too bad a price, it seems in retrospect. (You
would pay that much for one portion in Paris now.) I turned
them over to the Catering Corps sergeant and he boiled them,
with the fat on, until the meat broke down into tiny shreds,
which floated about in the greasy water. We drank our lamb
chops out of cups—all but Willie Forrest, the fellow who had
been hit on the head. He got sick, in the full British sense of
the word. By the time I left Tripoli, the captain had started negotiations with Cairo to take the wretched sergeant away. It
was a delicate subject because the captain had already raised so
much hell with Cairo to get him. It was these boys from Akarit
who told me the first yarns I heard about Baranoff.

I went up to the Eighth Army front after my stay in Tripoli and
spent a few days with the Fourth Indian Division at the
beginning of the battle of Enfidaville. Then Lieutenant
Colonel Tealeaf Stevens, the public-relations officer of the di-
vision, lent me a lorry, with a driver named Whitaker, from
Hull, in Yorkshire, to take me back to the American Second
Corps. The front by that time was continuous from the Gulf of
Tunis to the Mediterranean shore west of Bizerte, and
Whitaker and I travelled along back of it, passing through the

zones of the Eighth Army and the French Nineteenth ~~rps~~
and the British First Army before we got up to where~~e~~
Americans were preparing to jump off. Whitaker was a b~~e~~
like, hairy man, and the Desert Army shorts and the shirt op~~e~~
at the neck made the hairiness conspicuous. He had high
cheekbones and narrow eyes. Both his parents, he told me,
were Polish, but he had been born and reared in Hull;
Whitaker was an Anglicized approximation of the Polish family
name. He had been out in Africa for three years and had attained the rank of corporal. He was also one of the most accomplished foragers I have ever met in any army. When he
wanted eggs, which we boiled hard and carried with us as a
supplement to our rations, he would stop the lorry, even in an
apparently uninhabited waste, and, standing on the running
board, hold out some tea leaves on the upraised palm of his
right hand. Then he would shout, "Eggis! Eggis!," a word
which he fondly believed was Arabic for eggs. (The tea leaves
were a special product. They had already been boiled out
when he was making tea for his own use—he liked his tea
strong—and then had been dried in the sun so that they could
be used for barter.) Instantly dozens of Arabs would appear
with eggs, and Whitaker always got as many as he wanted.

The only notable event that occurred on our journey was a
miracle. When we started out, there was hardly a drop of liquor
left in the entire Eighth Army area. British officers were entitled to buy a certain amount of spirits from the N.A.A.F.I.
(Navy, Army, and Air Force Institute), an organization maintaining stores like our Army Post Exchanges, and there were
N.A.A.F.I. shops, under canvas, scattered all the way from
Cairo to Enfidaville. But the stocks of liquor west of Tripoli
were exhausted. So Whitaker's chief had provided him with a
couple of thousand francs and ordered him to keep an eye
open for French farmers who might have brandy or, failing
that, wine, to sell, which he could take back to the chief.
Whitaker and I drove some three hundred miles without traversing any wine-growing country. Then, as we approached a
road intersection behind the extreme left flank of the British
First Army, only a couple of miles short of the American zone
(where we could be *sure* there would be nothing to drink), the
motor stopped. This it had done once before—on a road

under mortar fire, near Enfidaville—and Whitaker and I had had to get out and push. This second time, Whitaker fiddled with all the buttons and levers within reach, then muttered something about "bloody water in the bloody petrol line," and got out to have a look under the lorry, taking some tools with him. He stayed there for a couple of disgusted minutes, crawled out from under, probably to get more tools, looked at a low, mud-walled Arab granary by the side of the road, and stood transfixed, pointing at a paper placard over the granary door. The placard said, "N.A.A.F.I." Whitaker said, "Fate works in mysterious ways." Watching his face, I could see him size up the situation. "They be First Army," he said. "Happen they'll have liquor. They get it through those Algerian ports." Whitaker's desert shorts and the lorry, with its sand-colored camouflage, marked him as one of the Desert Heroes that people at home in England had been reading about. The First Army had not come out until 1942, and this part of the First Army was so far from the Eighth that it was possible the N.A.A.F.I. clerks had never seen a Desert Hero. Whitaker was from outside the territory that the First Army N.A.A.F.I. was supposed to supply, but the clerks might give him a break. "I'll have a try," he said, wiping some extra dirt across his face with the hand that he had had in the machinery while he was beneath the car. "I'll tell them that we're dying of thirst, *all* of us." He went into the granary and came out in a couple of minutes, grinning. "It worked," he said. "The sergeant told me to fill out a requisition for the total number of officers and men we've got in our unit. They don't give much for each one, of course." He took a well-chewed pencil stub from the breast pocket of his shirt, chewed on it some more, and said, "There's just four officers and eleven men, to be truthful. But we have sixteen other officers at Cairo, and about seventy-eight men." I could sense, when he got to the "about seventy-eight," that he was beginning to improvise. Then he said, "And we have hundreds more at Calcutta. Do you think it would be wrong to draw for them?" I reminded him that he had just one lorry, so he compromised by adding only the Cairo lot to his own group. He got seven bottles of Scotch, four of gin, and some beer. One of the pale, lately-from-England soldiers in the N.A.A.F.I. store carried it to the lorry for him. When Whitaker got back into the driver's seat, the motor started instantly. Neither of us was able to figure it out.

The American press camp, which we found after a bit of trouble, was on top of a narrow, pine-covered ridge near a town called Béja. It was all tents, ranged in single file along the crest of the ridge. The trees afforded pretty good cover, but, as we were soon to find out, there wasn't much need for it, because the German air force in Africa was by then almost nonexistent. There was a large cook tent and an even larger tent that served as a mess and newsroom. The correspondents lived in small wall tents so well provided with blackout flaps that you could burn an electric light inside them at night. A mobile generating plant supplied the power. Each tent was big enough for only two men. When I reached camp, there was just one vacancy, and that was in the tent occupied by Colonel Baranoff, who had arrived a few days before. He came home that evening after supper. He had eaten at the First Division headquarters, which he had been visiting. Our artillery particularly interested him; it is an arm well developed in both the American and Russian Armies. He had a set speech he used whenever he was presented to a divisional commander. He would say, "How do you do, sir? You have a magnificent army here. You are teaching your teachers. You should begin immediately a Second Front. You have nothing to fear."

Baranoff was a straight, slender man in his early thirties. He had fair hair, cut very short, a narrow, blond mustache, two gold teeth in the front of his mouth, and a precise, almost staccato manner, as if the first phrase he had learned in English was "Count off!" He was not undersized, as W. L. White says Russian officers are, or oversized, like Feodor Chaliapin or the late Grand Duke Nicholas or a wrestler I used to know named Matros Kyrilenko, all of whom grew up before reading Mr. White's book. I would say that Baranoff was a legitimate welterweight. Senior residents of the camp had cots, but there weren't enough to go around, so I slept on the floor that night. But I knew that a lieutenant in the camp was going to Algiers the next day, and that meant he would have to get up before dawn to drive out to the nearest airfield. I arose early, stumbled around to the lieutenant's tent, and came back to my tent with the cot before any of the other cotless correspondents were awake. When Baranoff opened his eyes and saw me, across the tent, in the cot, my head on the same level with his, he grinned. "Very good capture," he said. "Example of primary acquisition."

It was hard to think of things to talk to Baranoff about. When you asked him about anything Russian—the Soviet air force, for instance—he just said it was wonderful and stopped. You felt that you offended him a little by inquiring, as you would by asking a waiter at a good restaurant if the fish was fresh. The press camp had been in one place for ten days, which was unusual, and quite a lot of mail, including several bales of newspapers, had caught up with the fellows there. There were about twenty copies of The Newspaper *PM*, in sequence, dating, as I recall, from February. I thought Baranoff might like something to read, so one night, after the camp poker game broke up, I carried half a dozen copies of The Newspaper *PM* back to our tent with me. Baranoff was a light sleeper. He woke when I came in.

"Turn on the light!" he said. "It is O.K."

I said, "I have some copies of one of our more liberal New York newspapers here. I thought you might like to read them. It might help you to understand what people at home are thinking about Russia." I hoped he would never see a copy of the *News*.

"Oh yes," Baranoff said. "Thank you. How interesting! I will look." He took The Newspapers *PM* from my hand and looked at the top one. He glanced at it casually, and then turned over on his stomach, holding the newspaper close to his eyes. He was silent for several minutes. "It is a series of articles entitled 'Foes of the Soviet Union in America,'" he said after a while, in explanation of his silence. "It appears that your State Department is honeycombed with them. What a fine expression! How interesting! Also the universities and labor unions. The banks, of course—that was to be expected!"

And when I fell asleep he was still reading.

For a couple of nights after that, I got no conversation out of Baranoff at all, because he was always reading The Newspaper *PM*. "How interesting!" he would say now and then. "I had no idea we have so many enemies." I looked at a couple of the papers one afternoon when he wasn't in and found just one of the usual series about Fascists and reactionaries that named a fairly large percentage of people in the telephone book. But it was no use trying to tell Baranoff. "How interesting!" I would hear him say. "How interesting!" Then I would fall asleep. "These people they talk about," I once ventured, "of course, they may really be enemies of Russia, but they don't represent the Administration's views."

"No?" asked Baranoff. I decided that he was trying to figure out why, in that case, the Administration didn't shoot them. "How interesting!" he finally said, and I could see that he was not convinced.

Then came a day when I went jeep-riding over what seemed most of northern Tunisia, getting in and out of the machine a score of times to scramble up to observation posts. I had with me an old gold Waltham watch that had belonged to my father. This was foolish, because I had no pocket to put it in that it couldn't slide out of. When I got back to camp that evening, I became aware that the watch was missing. I had had it in the pocket of my field jacket. I searched the back of the jeep, where I had been sitting, but it was no good. I was annoyed, because my father's mother had given him the watch when he was twenty-one years old, and he had always bragged that he had never dropped it hard enough to break the glass, and he had been accustomed to say that I lost everything. Now, although he couldn't say "I told you so," because he had been dead six years, I *had* lost it, and it made me angry. When I returned to the tent, I said to Baranoff, "I had tough luck today. I lost my watch." I washed up and went to the mess. When I came back, he was lying on the dirt floor, looking under my cot. "What are you looking for?" I asked him.

"I look for your watch," he said.

"But I know I didn't leave it in the tent," I said. "I lost it getting in or out of the jeep, on the road."

"How can you be sure?" he said. "I do not like such things should happen when I am sharing the tent with you, you know. Have you looked in your bedding roll? Perhaps it is there. I will look."

It was then it occurred to me that he might think I suspected him of stealing my watch. You can't say to a man, "I know you didn't take my watch" or "I don't suspect you for even a minute," because that would be an admission that you had considered the possibility. And he couldn't conceivably have taken it, of course; I was frightened by the notion that he might consider me capable of suspecting him. "I know I had the watch with me at an O.P. this afternoon," I said. "I looked at it several times." Baranoff did not seem impressed, and I thought, "Maybe he believes I'm framing him. He has probably seen a movie in which an agent of a foreign power falsely accuses a Soviet officer of theft." Baranoff said nothing more then, but he looked unhappy. I thought he might visualize himself as an Inter-Allied Dreyfus. I could imagine a montage of headlines flashing past behind Baranoff's eyelids: "Soviet Officer Steals Watch," "Soviet Officer Falsely Accused of Stealing Watch," "Red Army Man Denounced by Propaganda Liar," "*PM* Unveils Another Anti-Soviet Plot." I tried to be especially cordial to him in order to show him that the watch was a bagatelle, already forgotten. As I fell asleep, he was again reading The Newspaper *PM*—probably an account of how evidence had been faked against some labor leader in a Southern state. I wished I had never seen the watch or that I had left it in a safe-deposit vault in New York.

When I went into the news tent for breakfast next morning, one of the soldiers who worked in the cook shack came to tell me about the second miracle figuring in this rather brief narrative. An Arab had found my watch in the dust where I had dismounted from the jeep the night before at the camp, right at the foot of the hill the camp was on. He was one of the Arabs who helped with K.P. in return for scraps of food, and he had been either honest (a fantastic hypothesis), or too unsophisticated to know how to dispose of a watch, or afraid that if the French gendarmerie found him with it they would shoot him. The odds against a Tunisian Arab's returning a gold watch are, I suppose, about equal to those against my now picking the winner of the 1955 Kentucky Derby. "We knew it was your watch," the soldier waiter said to me, "because you been hollering your head off, and besides it has your name inside the case. The Arab is out in the kitchen now." I went to the kitchen, got my watch, and gave the Arab two hundred francs, which was four dollars. That was as much as he could have earned in four weeks on a road gang, so he was pleased. I didn't bother about breakfast, although I was hungry. I jogged right back to my tent, with the watch in my hand. Baranoff was sitting on his cot, looking at the floor. "Hey, I found my watch!" I said. "An Arab found it. I was getting out of a jeep—" Baranoff sprang up. He was obviously a man discharged of a heavy load. The two gold teeth flashed like the headlights on a two-and-a-half-ton truck coming against you at night. He placed his hands on my shoulders and looked at me with emotion. "Colleague!" he cried. "How glad I am to hear this! How happy I am that you have found your watch!"

After Colonel Baranoff had left the camp for the day to make his speech about the second front to another general, I hurriedly gathered all the copies of The Newspaper *PM*, took them out in a field, and burned them. In the evening, I told Baranoff that their owner had insisted on having them back. I said that the owner had been one of two correspondents who had left camp that day to go over to the British zone.

"I am very sorry," Colonel Baranoff said, "but fortunately I have taken interesting notes. Documentation, I think is the correct word. Few people, even among the highest Soviet officials, have an *idea* what goes on in America. They should read The Newspaper *PM*."

The New Yorker, June 23, 1945

Colonel Grinker and Major Spiegel

I WAS moved a few weeks ago, in reviewing a publication of the War Department's Historical Division called "Omaha Beachhead," to say that it was one of the two best books about this war I had read. In response to a single inquiry from my readers, I am today revealing the name of the other book. It is "Men Under Stress" (Blakiston), by Lieutenant Colonel Roy R. Grinker and Major John R. Spiegel, two psychiatrists who, during the war, were attached to the Army Air Forces in Tunisia. This book, their major work, was preceded by a slim volume called "War Neuroses," in which the documentation is more concerned with Ground Forces problems. In Tunisia, Grinker and Spiegel had a good chance to observe the effect of combat on ground soldiers, too.

A great history of the war by a Thucydides would be a fine thing, and so would a great war novel. I could use a lot of space telling why I don't think they will ever be written. What modern could identify himself with both parties to World War II, as Thucydides could with the contending Greeks? The modes of thought of the Germans are impenetrable to us, and ours, it seems, to them. The plain, unrhetoricked story of a beach battle, in which photographs are an integral part of the book, may be our best substitute for a long time. There have been hundreds of recorded wars and only a dozen or so novels of any sort that have been generally esteemed great. Of these, only one, "War and Peace," touches upon war more than incidentally. Any odds layer can interpret these statistics for you. The Grinker-Spiegel books are not novels, but they contain material, dehydrated, like certain Army potatoes, for an indefinite number of them. There are sixty-five case histories in "Men Under Stress" and twenty-four in "War Neuroses." Add water and you could furnish a whole library with better war novels than we have seen thus far.

The prime mover of all these novels would be the participants' recognition of the immediate likelihood of death. In ordinary life, only the neurotic worries about dying. In battle, the neurotic suddenly finds himself "normal." Fear, for the infantry soldier, is centered on artillery and mortar fire. He can retaliate against enemies he can reach. As for the flier, "Men Under Stress" reports, "The enemy's fighter aircraft . . . are not as great a source of anxiety as flak. . . . Aerial combat attacks the ego with fine, chiselled blows. . . . The physical stress of aerial combat is severe but is not as prolonged or as debilitating as the physical strain to which ground combat troops, especially the infantry, are subjected. . . . One sees more seriously disintegrated and regressed anxiety states among ground-force personnel." But the end result is the same for all soldiers. "In no matter what arm or service, the combat men carry on, as a rule, and endure their anxiety until they are relieved from combat or until the ego is so stripped of resources that it cannot carry on any functions at all."

Psychiatrists believe that the capacity to endure anxiety is probably different in different individuals from birth. "No one," the authors say, "has been able to achieve maturity without some psychological scarring, some crack in the psychosomatic equipment with which he faces the world. Everyone has a limit to the amount of stress which he can withstand." Under stress the scar shows through, like the design on a coin when a piece of paper is pressed down on it and a pencil is rubbed over the paper. I remember a dugout in Tunisia, lined with gasoline tins, and a first lieutenant who was in command of his fighter squadron because the three men who outranked him had been shot down within two weeks. "The fellows in this squadron who were red-hot a month ago are getting edgy," the lieutenant said. "And those who weren't too keen on fighting then— well, now you have a hell of a time getting them near a plane."

But the problem is not simply a matter of men with unequal resistance submitted to a uniform stress. War distributes stress inequitably: one man may fly fifty combat missions without serious trouble; another, and stronger, man may have to bail out on his first mission and then experience a long series of near-disasters. The relatively tough man may crack before the other. "For the vast majority the only valid test for endurance of combat is combat itself," Grinker and Spiegel conclude. As anxiety develops, "the drawn and haggard faces give the young fliers the appearance of old men. . . . Little arguments rapidly lead to explosive rages far in excess of the demands of the disagreement. . . . Symptoms may have progressed to the point where the flier makes mistakes in flying and now has his own incapacity to fear as well as the other conscious and unconscious sources of anxiety." To revert to my own checking file: I remember a boy in a chow line at the field at Thélepte, in Africa, telling me how nearly he had missed being killed when he had been caught cold by a Messerschmitt he should have seen—a failure that terrified him. Next time he flew, he lost control of his P-40 for no apparent reason and was killed.

"Depressed states . . . among combat flying personnel . . . are always combined with varying amounts of anxiety. . . . In a few instances . . . a flier has quietly taken off in his plane without orders and never been seen again. . . . Depression is frequently precipitated by the loss of a close personal friend." I remember a tall, thin boy who used to tap his nose and make gloomy noises whenever he picked up a poker hand, *before* he looked at the cards. He took off from his field, quietly and without orders, a couple of days after his idol had been killed, and has not been heard of since.

Grinker and Spiegel have noted that in Tunisia there were "'hot' outfits with an impressive record . . . rewarded by public recognition" and "'snafued' units, badly organized, bogged down with bad morale and discontent, and exhibiting chronically bad combat efforts." They were additionally handicapped, in many cases, by an inferior plane like the P-39. "The type of aircraft flown by an organization has a pronounced effect upon the personality characteristics of the group." The authors have also touched on a lesser psychiatric problem, the schizoid fliers, who were too bold. Icarus, who disregarded Father Daedalus's orders and crashed, was a schizoid, Grinker and Spiegel think. They call him the "prototype of the 'hot' pilot."

Air Corps men were encouraged to talk out their troubles with the flight surgeons of their units. When their difficulties became more serious, the flight surgeons referred them back to psychiatrists like Grinker and Spiegel at base hospitals. When the flier couldn't talk it out, he was frequently aided by the administration of sodium pentothal, after which he could be induced to recount and act out his bad experiences.

There is a counterweight which nearly balances the load of

apprehension that breaks men down in war. Without this, battle would end instantly in universal panic. The soldier fights as long as he can because he will not let down his partners in combat. "The men seem to be fighting more *for* someone than *against* somebody," the authors note. "But the loyalty itself involves another risk." The loss of friends in combat is the second most important cause of emotional stress; survival, however accidental, carries with it a sense of guilt. In the Air Corps, the last mission of a tour was considered the jinx. The man flying it could never feel that he had merited his coming good fortune; his guilt made him jittery.

Case 26 of "Men Under Stress" is, I think, a classic example of this unwarranted feeling of guilt. A twenty-three-year-old Liberator pilot who had completed sixty-five missions, considerably more than a normal tour, during which flak had compelled him to make six crash landings, was grounded to await return to the United States. Several day later, because of a shortage of pilots, he was asked to take his crew out once more, but he refused, feeling that he had earned his reprieve. The operations officer went in his place. The plane was shot up and crashed in the sea with the loss of all but one crew member. "The patient then felt badly because his crew looked up to him. They had often written and told their folks they were in good hands as long as they were flying with him. . . . He felt that if he had gone on the fatal mission, he would have brought them back." Not unnaturally, he found his way to a hospital, "chronically ill and depressed," after his return to the United States. The rest of the concise, two-page case history goes deeply into the boy's background. He recovered, by the way.

Removal from combat environment was enough to bring about the recovery of certain victims of neuroses who probably would have had no emotional trouble at all in civil life. There were also, however, neurotics whose adjustment to life had always been tenuous, and they could not recover from the shock of combat. After the Tunisian campaign, Grinker and Spiegel returned to the United States and were assigned to the Don Cesar Hospital, in St. Petersburg, to apply their field experience to patients from all theatres of combat. The case histories they gathered there tell more about the United States of

America than about war. Twenty-seven-year-old virgin males and precociously depraved tough kids, rejects of broken homes and spoiled products of too much affection, looked much the same in uniform. But, as the two doctors have made very plain, that seeming homogeneity dissolved under the impact of machine-gun fire or flak, and the results were diverse and strange.

The New Yorker, May 18, 1946

The Conscience of Monsieur B

M Y friend Monsieur B is a carver of retables and altar chairs, and since many churches in his native Nancy and the surrounding countryside of Lorraine were damaged during the first World War and many during the second, he has seldom lacked employment. Indeed, in some instances he has had the privilege—he would scarcely call it a pleasure—of carving three successive sets of chairs for one parish, his first two creations and the churches they adorned having been destroyed by German shells. Monsieur B, never completely satisfied with any of his carvings, has relished the opportunity to improve upon them, but he wishes his earlier pieces had survived for purposes of comparison.

Despite his vocation, or perhaps because of it—since a large acquaintance among clerics is seldom conducive to awe—Monsieur B is not much of a churchgoer. He inherits his politics from Poincaré and Clemenceau, who were less than punctilious in their worship, and he is inclined to rate priests simply according to their stature as Frenchmen. His wife has sometimes reproached him for this, but he has never gone into the matter deeply with her, having an old-fashioned belief that to be happy a husband must keep many of his thoughts and experiences to himself. He is a tall, spare man, who was already thirty-seven in 1914 but who nevertheless served through the four years of that war. He won the Croix de Guerre with star, later acquired a second star, and in 1918 refused a third because, he says, by that time they were sending the decorations up to the front with the rations as morale builders. One of the citations he did accept was given to him for holding a section of trench alone for an hour and three-quarters against an attack, serving and firing his machine gun after all his companions had been killed.

At the end of that war, Monsieur B returned to Nancy. His family at the time consisted of his wife and their two daughters, whom Monsieur B, a man who cherishes his privacy, has asked me to call Odile and Céleste. He was kept busy at his trade for the next several years, and when, in the thirties, the number of churches to be restored had diminished, he even constructed a bit of secular furniture, mostly accurate copies of old pieces. At the beginning of the recent war, he was spending the summer in a two-room cottage he owned in the village of P——, which is in the Vosges, about fifty miles from Nancy. With him were his wife, their daughter Odile—an unmarried school-teacher getting on toward forty—and an orphaned grandniece ten years old. Knowing that Nancy, which was the headquarters of an army group, was almost sure to be bombed by the Germans and that it is always easier during a war to get food in the country than in a city, he thought he might as well stay in P——for the duration. It was there that I met him, in December, 1939. The encounter was not an accident. Monsieur B's other daughter, Céleste, is married to a friend of mine and lives in New York. I had gone to Paris shortly after the war broke out, and Céleste had sent me her parents' address, asking me to look them up if I had a chance. After the Germans occupied France, Céleste worried a good deal about her parents. She heard little from them until the winter of 1944, when letters began to arrive regularly and she learned that they had survived in good shape.

Last spring, Céleste was able to get over to France to see them. When she came back, she brought with her a document enclosed in an envelope addressed to her husband. It consisted of six double sheets of letter paper, each page marked off by faint lines and crosslines into seventeen columns and ninety-six horizontal rows. The paper was covered with the strong, precise, vertical handwriting of Monsieur B, who is now sixty-nine. Each letter was exactly two rows high and filled exactly one-third of a column, and below every line of writing two rows were left blank. The letters were as distinct as if Monsieur B had cut them out with a whittling knife. They seemed to have a third dimension.

Céleste said that her father had written this document in one afternoon, when, troubled by arthritis, he had been unable to walk around and had been so cross that it was a question of finding him something to do. During Céleste's visit, he had often told her anecdotes about the German occupation, and she had suggested that he write out a connected narrative of his most memorable experiences for her to take home to her

American husband, of whom the old man is fond. The son-in-law showed the manuscript to me because I know Monsieur B. I began to read out of politeness, and continued, I think, because I was hypnotized by the letters marching across the page like wooden legionaries on a carved Stations of the Cross. Also, the beginning of the narrative recalled a time that I can vividly remember but seldom think of nowadays, the time when our side was down and the others were up.

In the little Vosges town of P——, the Mayor's secretary had been mobilized early in 1939, and when I visited there that year, Monsieur B, who, since he fixed his own working hours, had a more flexible routine than most of the other residents, had temporarily taken over the secretary's duties. There is an allusion to this in the opening sentence of Monsieur B's narrative, which I have received his permission to publish:

"After the sixteenth of June, 1940, we at the *mairie* got no more orders from the local préfecture," the story begins. "The gendarmes had been ordered to be ready to evacuate their barracks at any time. We didn't know or understand anything of what went on outside our immediate region; we just heard rumors. On the evening of the sixteenth, the artillery headquarters of the Fifth Army arrived in P—— from the front with four or five trucks loaded with equipment and set up its telephones and tables in the reception room of the *mairie*—but not for long. It left next morning, abandoning most of the gear. So we knew that the retreat was really on and that the artillery general had no hope of an improvement. Until then, we old sweats of 1914–18 had been unable to believe that the French Army had retreated as quickly as people were saying—all the way from one big city to another in one day, sometimes. In the last war, we had so often held out in small groups, under the command of a corporal or with no command at all. The Germans never moved more than a few metres at a time through us.

"Next day, the gendarmes got their orders and left in the direction of Dijon, moving southwest along the only main road that was not already barred by the enemy. On the same morning, the tide of refugees, moving in the same direction, reached our village. We learned from some of them that a

German army, driving south from Champagne, had already reached the Haute-Marne Department, while another, which had broken through at the south end of the Maginot Line, was advancing to the northwest, with the object of encircling the French Army stationed in Alsace and the Vosges. If they succeeded, our town probably would be bypassed and there was a good chance that there would be no fighting in the immediate vicinity. Just the same, everybody who could leave began to prepare to join the refugees. People who owned any kind of vehicle got together the most valuable portable possessions they had. It is a sad sight, an exodus.

"Sitting on the bench in front of the *mairie*, examining the license plates of the vehicles as they passed, I could see practically the whole population of the Meurthe-et-Moselle Department moving along this one free road. Often I would hear my name called by somebody in an automobile, without being able to make out by whom, because the cars were packed so close together that I couldn't see everybody. Women, children, men—some on foot or riding bicycles, others crowded into vehicles of every kind—pressed against one another, hampered one another, were loaded down like donkeys with all they could carry. I went back into my house feeling very low.

"For a while I wondered if I should yield to the contagion and get out too. There was still a train in the railroad station, which would leave the next morning for some indefinite destination. I felt that at least it was my duty to urge my wife and daughter to take this last chance and leave with our little niece. After thinking it over, I decided that, as for myself, I would stay.

"That night, neither my wife nor my daughter nor I slept, but none of us said a word. The prospect of parting and the difficulty of ever getting together again kept us awake. Morning came, and with it the time to part. The hand luggage was packed. Everybody had something to carry and a parcel of food for the journey besides. My little niece was even carrying her straw hat with her. Odile begged me to come along with them. I still said no. Then she said, 'Well, if you won't go, we won't go either.' And they all put down their bags. 'If we are going to be killed,' she said, 'we'll all be killed together.' I was happy. I was glad that I would not have to be separated from them, and at the same time felt that I had done my duty as head of the family by suggesting that they leave. Odile's decision turned out to be lucky; it saved us a great deal of trouble and an unknown amount of suffering.

"The next day, the escape corridor was cut off by the Germans at a point about sixty miles south of our village. All the sad horde that had fled toward Dijon had to turn back, and since other thousands, not knowing what had happened, continued to push south, the road was soon choked. The Boches were reported within a day's march of P——. At about one-thirty that afternoon, while on my way to the *mairie*, I turned a corner and found myself nose to nose with an armored car which had stopped. Its machine gun was pointing straight at me. The front of the car was draped with a great red cloth ornamented with a white swastika. No mistake, the Boches had arrived. And ahead of schedule. I walked on, trying not to show any emotion, and once I had passed the car, restrained myself from looking back at it. There were two other armored cars in P——, an advance element of a motorized column. They took a turn through the town and stopped for a considerable time in front of the wine cellars of a wholesale liquor dealer, whom they made give them drinks. Then, after loading their vehicles with sufficient reserves for the road, they headed back toward Bourbonne.

"Next morning, the Germans arrived in force, and rolled through the principal street all day, heading northwest. It was an armored division, impressively disciplined, impeccably equipped, a formidable unit of picked men of uniform age, uniform height, uniform courtesy. Doubtless by command, they saluted the monument to the dead of 1914–18 in front of the *mairie* as they passed. Those who paused in P—— were polite, modest, and invited friendship, but nobody was taken in for a minute.

"Now I began to understand why our Army had had to retreat so quickly. I could see that our enemies had studied everything out and left nothing to chance, while we had napped, relying on our treaties. Every bit of mechanism was well oiled and every man at his post. I didn't despair altogether, but I doubted that we would ever be able to get rid of this terrible army, twice the size of ours and infinitely better armed.

"On the day after that, I learned that the Germans had passed Mirecourt and were pushing rapidly toward Nancy. I made up my mind to keep pace with them and get to the city at nearly the same time they did, so I could try to keep our house from being requisitioned or looted. I made ready my little motor bike, wrapped up some bread and meat to eat on the road, and got going. As far as Mirecourt, all went well, but between Poussay and Diarville, to judge by the look of the road, the abandoned military gear, and the dead or straying horses there must have been pretty heavy fighting on the previous day. Useless fighting, since the French Army was surrounded. Hundreds of horses encumbered the road. Most of the strays were wounded; one lay dying down-side up in the middle of the road, with an enormous, gaping wound in his chest, his glazed eyes indifferent to a pitched battle between two Arab stallions, now at liberty, who were fighting around the spot where he lay.

"I feared that I would not be able to go much further, for on the far side of Diarville, the cannon thundered and there seemed to be a big battle. I got through the village without being stopped, but the inhabitants advised me to go no further. I am stubborn, however, and I hoped to ride along side roads, so I pushed on. But after I had travelled a couple of miles, I was passed from behind by two Germans mounted on one motorcycle. They stopped soon after passing me, and when I caught up to them, halted me and by signs ordered me to dismount from my little motor bike. The loss of it would have stranded me at an equal distance from P—— and Nancy. I protested as energetically as I could and clung to the handle bars, pulling the bike my way while they pulled it theirs. To cut the argument short, one of them drew a grenade from his musette bag and made a motion as if to throw it at me, crying, '*Kaput!*' There was no good resisting further, so with a heavy heart I let go my grip. I saw them ride away, one on the motorcycle, the other on my bike, and I was sad. How could I reach Nancy on foot? I walked on, nevertheless, not giving up hope, and in a few seconds I saw that the two thieves had stopped again and were making motions at me that I didn't understand. I did understand, though, when I saw them abandon my machine by the roadside and both again mount the big motorcycle and depart at high speed. I concluded that they had found my bike too slow to keep up with the motorcycle and so of no use to them. Rejoicing, I hurried to take possession of my property again. After this scare I made a couple more attempts to get through to Nancy, but since the battle seemed to be moving in my direction, I gave up. I went back to P—— for the night, happy that I hadn't lost my bike.

"But I could not stay home. I filled her up with gas next morning and this time I swore I would get to Nancy, no matter what happened."

The picture of Monsieur B, his trousers held in at the ankles of his long legs by bicycle clips, trundling his mechanized Rosinante out onto the cobbled street to begin again his trip through the whole German Army made me pause at this point the first time I read his story. He must have known that even if he could reach his home in Nancy, he could do no more than protest against the seizure of his house and wood-carving shop, just as he had when the soldiers had taken his motor bike. He was sixty-three years old, and the journey, as he had discovered on the previous day, was not without its dangers. It reminded me of those Norman peasants who, in 1944, used to return to farms that were in the middle of battles to milk their cows—"because otherwise the beasts would fall ill." Monsieur B, in 1940, I suppose, could not accept the idea of a society in which a man had no rights, and he must also have believed, like many other Frenchmen, that a right unasserted lapses. He had to go to Nancy to make an assertion. The courtesy of the German soldiers in P—— had not fooled him; if their discipline and politeness had made a favorable impression on him, it had been erased when the motorcyclists had pinched his bike.

"I left early in the morning," the manuscript continues. "This time, I got as far as Tantonville without being stopped. I saw some German supply troops there, but went right by them and on through the town. Beyond it, though, I had to take a roundabout road because the German military police were now patrolling the main roads continually, watching over the rear elements of their steadily advancing column. I met some refugees who told me that the head of the German column must already be at Nancy. This news spurred me, but the difficulties were becoming serious, as I perceived when I came out on the main road again, at the top of the slope at Ceintrey. There I was stopped almost immediately, and in spite of my papers, which were in order, forced to go into a barbed-wire cattle pen. [Monsieur B's progress was halted, I assume, by German M.P.s.] There were already a couple of dozen other civilians there, guarded by a sentry who walked a post that ran the length of the pen. I left my bike leaning against a tree outside, thinking that I might soon have use for it again.

"I passed about an hour in that place. I went in dry, but emerged soaked, because a thunderstorm came up while I was there. It didn't last long, but the water came down hard for a while. My fellow-captives told me that we were to be let go after the passage of a big convoy of prisoners which was being sent on to Nancy. Without waiting any longer, and profiting by the sentry's being at the other end of his post, I lay down on the ground and, wrapping my arms about my chest, rolled under the barbed wire and bumped against the rear wheel of my faithful bike. It took only an instant to push it out on the road and mount it, shielded from the view of the sentinel by an embankment. I coasted down the slope without using the motor, and didn't start it up until two hundred yards further on, at the beginning of the almost impassable little side road that leads to Clérey."

At this point, I must confess, my old acquaintance Monsieur B began to astonish me. I had not thought of him as either so agile or so reckless. He was not bound upon a mission of great public importance, nor were his loved ones in danger. In his place, I should have stayed in the pen. I can ascribe the increasing vigor of his reactions only to his increasing sense of injustice. After all, his papers were in order.

"I took the little side road," the narrative goes on, "to avoid two German military policemen on a motorcycle with a sidecar who, my fellow-captives had told me, were patrolling a triangular beat from Ceintrey to Tantonville to Vézelise, coming around once every seven or eight minutes. The triangle had two long sides, of about two miles each, and a short base, of about a mile. The side road cut through the triangle near its tip, bypassing Ceintrey. On this bad road, fortunately not very long, but muddy after the downpour, I had to dismount and walk several times. This delay threw my timing off, and I expected to be overtaken when I emerged from the side road, for I knew that I would have to take the Ceintrey-Vézelise road as far as the village of Omelmont. But I pushed on as fast as I could, all soaked with rain and sweat. I got to the Ceintrey-Vézelise road and reached Omelmont safely. There I asked whether I could get over to the Vézelise-Pont St. Vincent highway without going all the way to Vézelise, where I feared there would be a past of military police. As I was receiving directions, I heard the sound of the motorcycle with the sidecar. I had just time enough to skip into a barn—a close call. I again had seven or eight minutes' grace.

"According to the directions given me, there was only one way to get to the highway I wanted without going through Vézelise. This was to go down a goat path as far as a little stream, carrying my bike on my back, cross over the stream on the trunk of a tree that had been left there to serve as a footbridge [but not for old gentlemen carrying motor bikes!], and so reach the little village of Houdreville, which is on the highway. I took the chance without hesitation and succeeded in crossing over the tree trunk without mishap. How I managed it, I hardly know. I marvel every time I have another look at the place. Happy at my exploit, but worn out, splashing through puddles, badly shod with rubber soles that had no grip on the clay soil of the vineyard slopes, I pushed my motor bike along with difficulty, falling to my knees many times. I tried to use the motor to get up the slope of the ravine on the Houdreville side of the stream, but the narrow path, slippery with rain, made it impossible. I still had a hundred yards to go when all at once I heard that blasted motorcycle behind me. It was passing on the road that I had left to cut across country, about three hundred yards away. I immediately tried to hide in some vines, but I had been seen. The motorcycle stopped, and the fellow in the sidecar took aim with his carbine and loosed a clip of bullets at me that hit all around but didn't wound me.

Instinctively, I let myself fall limp, abandoning my motor bike. I saw the butchers on the other side of the ravine looking toward me and wondering, probably, how they could get near me. I gathered that they thought it too much trouble, for presently they drove off, heading in the direction of Ceintrey.

"Some minutes later, believing them definitely gone, I resumed my Calvary and finally got onto the highway I had been trying to reach, but I had scarcely put foot on it when I saw my pursuers on the other side of the ravine again. They had turned and were travelling in the direction of Vézelise this time, doubtless meaning to get over on the Vézelise-Pont St. Vincent road, where I now was, and take me alive.

"I lost no time in getting under way, knowing that their heavy machine was a great deal faster than my poor little put-put. But in spite of my best efforts, after leaving Houdreville I heard the noise of their powerful motor once again and knew that they were getting closer and closer. The race being unequal, and I having no place to hide, I felt that I was lost. The road along which I was riding, like several I had already been on, was littered with the debris of an army in rout. Gear and arms of all sorts lay strewn along the ditches, scattered among dead men, and this abandoned road, on which, for the moment, I and my pursuers were the only living beings, seemed sinister in its loneliness. I fled, but, like a hard-pressed beast, I felt myself about to be taken. I expected the impact of a bullet against my spine at any second.

"Going down a slope, I saw that the road turned at its foot and that there, was a thicket in a ditch just by the turn. I heard the danger behind me, and I decided to jump into the thicket to hide. I hadn't looked about for a weapon, but at my feet, as I dismounted, were several rifles. I grabbed one of them, and automatically, without thinking what I was doing, I checked it to see whether there was a cartridge in the chamber. Then, jumping down it the ditch, I crouched behind a sapling, on one knee, awaiting my pursuers. A few seconds passed. They appeared, and raced into easy range—thirty or forty yards, perhaps—undoubtedly thinking I had gone on around the turn. Calm, aiming right at the torso, I fired at the man driving the motorcycle. The machine went on for ten or fifteen yards and then crashed into the ditch. It burst into flames instantly."

*

Here, when I first read the manuscript, I paused. Now, when I reread it, I still pause. To say that I was and am surprised by Monsieur B's action would be an understatement. But there was, on reflection, a quality of inevitability about it. You start pushing around people who aren't used to being pushed around and droll consequences are to be expected.

"I was half crazy, I believe," Monsieur B's account continues. "I jumped on my bike without worrying about the Boches, who lay still by their machine, and made off as fast as I could. I got to Xeuilley, the next village, completely exhausted and terribly thirsty. I couldn't refrain from stopping for a drink in the local inn. I was the sole customer, because the countryside was almost deserted. The young woman in charge of the place looked at me with an astonished air. She must have wondered where I came from. I was hatless and unshaven, and my hands, knees, and elbows were covered with mud. I must have looked like a poilu of 1914 who had been buried by a shell and dug out alive. I asked her for water and did a summary wash job on my face and hands. I then heard her say, 'Aren't you Monsieur B? I thought so when you came in, but I couldn't believe that you could be in such a state. My name is Poirot. I used to live with my parents in Nancy, near your house, but I was very young then, so probably you don't recognize me. But I recognize you very well.' I explained my appearance by telling her I had got caught up in the battle and had had all kinds of trouble getting out of it. She served me a Pernod, diluted with plenty of water, which helped quench my thirst, and I admit (I hope I'll be pardoned for it) that I immediately ordered another one, which I drank this time with no water at all. It was now late, and, still hoping to get to Nancy that day, I said good-bye, and a quarter of an hour later arrived at Pont St. Vincent, where I found part of the town in flames and the big bridge over the Moselle completely destroyed. One more difficulty for me, since I had to get over to the other side. I decided to cross by the bridge at Maron, a few miles downstream, and I was driving along the towpath by the bank when I saw the Boches building a temporary bridge to replace the destroyed one. A boat which they had commandeered had just unloaded some materials on my side of the river. One of the Frenchmen in it, seeing me with my motor bike, quite evidently looking for a way to cross over, called to me and offered me a place in the boat. It set me down on the other bank. [What the Boches thought of this arrangement, Monsieur B failed to mention.] My cup of joy now flowed over. I was sure to arrive, for from here on there was not a road or bypath where I would not be perfectly at home. I put my leg over the bike and struck off on the main highway. An hour later, at about eight in the evening, I arrived at my house — sore, crook-backed, hungry, but happy. I was not to begin to worry until the next day, for I went to sleep almost immediately and slept as if I had nothing on my conscience.

"Very early in the morning, I was awakened by the sound of marching troops. Looking out of my bedroom window, I had the pain of seeing a great convoy of French prisoners passing. I stood at an open ground-floor window and watched the prisoners march past all day and part of the next night. What a humiliation! Our Army of the East, betrayed and surrounded, had surrendered to the enemy. All the men I was able to speak to complained of having been sold out and abandoned by their generals.

"I began to think of the horrible consequences my hasty act might have had. I could have been apprehended, and in that case it would have been all up with me. The consequences for my family would have been something I was afraid to contemplate. It wasn't certain, for that matter, that I had not been observed. In my excitement I had seen nothing, noticed nobody; I had acted without the least precaution. And then, too, I began to feel a kind of remorse. Had I had the right to kill? And then to abandon my victims! I argued with myself, unsuccessfully, that this was war and that I ought to consider it a legitimate act of self-defense. But I had not been in uniform. I could not regain my calm. The night was restless and full of nightmares. I felt tired when I got up next morning.

"I decided I ought to go back to P—— to reassure my family, but my true reason was a desire to know what had happened to the two Germans. Like an assassin, I could not stop myself from returning to the scene of the crime. I decided I

would retrace the route I had followed forty-eight hours earlier. I hoped to learn the details of what had happened, either
by going over the terrain or by questioning people who lived
nearby. I had no trouble travelling this time. The war had
passed over us. There were few Germans left in the countryside, and in any event an armistice had been declared. When I
got back to the thicket at the bend in the road I stopped, and
pretended to putter with my motor. The first thing I noticed
was the burned-out wreckage of the motorcycle. There were
also a few shreds of burned clothing. That was all. Much
moved, I tried to reconstruct the scene. Nothing had been
changed and a rifle I saw lying in the ditch was probably the
very one I had used. My conscience was less and less easy. I
wished I knew what had happened to the two men. Were they
dead or alive? Had they suffered much? I left this silent place,
hoping to learn a little further on that my victims were not
dead.

"I went on as far as Houdreville, and as I entered the village
I saw a priest, with a cane in his hand, who seemed to be out
for a stroll. He was coming toward me, walking briskly, and he
didn't have the look of a village priest about him. As we approached each other, I saw that he was still relatively young
and a wearer of the Legion of Honor, and I felt sure that he
must be the chaplain of some Army unit. I stopped and asked
him if he had any news. We talked about the catastrophe and
exchanged a few ideas, and then I had an inspiration. Perhaps
this man would be able to tell me what I wanted to know. I
thought I could have confidence in him because of his rank,
his cloth, but above all because of his affable, honest air.

" 'Monsieur Chaplain,' I said, 'for that's what I'm sure you
are, I have something serious to communicate to you, and a
great service to beg of you.'

" 'Do you want to confess to me?' he asked.

" 'When you have heard me out, you may call it a confession
or a confidence, whichever you please.'

" 'Come with me,' he said. 'As you have guessed, I am not
the cure of the village. Only the turn of events has forced me
to remain here, in the house of an old lady, for a few days or
perhaps a few weeks. If, during that time, I can be of any use

to you, I will do my best. Now come with me and tell me what it's all about.'

"So, confidentially and without any third party present, I got rid of my load of care by telling this man, without omitting a single detail, all the events of that terrible day and the way I now felt about them.

"After listening to me with every indication of interest, he attempted to raise my spirits, endeavoring, with touching words, to demonstrate that my scruples were exaggerated, that war was a sad business, but that it was a duty to defend oneself when in danger. Finally, he assured me that he would do everything possible to find out what I wanted to know. He had already heard something about the affair, he said, but had not paid much attention to it because it hadn't seemed important. Now circumstances were changed and he would make inquiries. We agreed that I would come back that way in a few days, on my return from P—— to Nancy, and that if he had to go away before, then he would leave a letter for me with his landlady. He would mark the envelope with the numerals of his military class, '14, and of mine, '97. To obtain the letter from the landlady, I would have only to repeat these numerals.

"Having reached this agreement, we parted, and I continued toward P——, where I arrived during the afternoon. I stopped at the *mairie*, where Odile had been doing my work during my journey. I met the mayor there. Noticing my look of exhaustion and distress, he asked me what in the world had happened to me. I told him. He said I had done well, but emphasized the risks I had run. The mayor and the chaplain were the only ones I ever took into my confidence about the matter until today. Not even Odile and her mother know the whole story. Thirty-six hours after my arrival at P——, I set off for Nancy again, promising myself to see the chaplain at Houdreville and find out what he had learned. He had had to leave the village early that morning, I was told, but I found the letter waiting. I wasted no time opening it. It is no slight thing to think one has killed another human being, even in self-defense.

"To bring this narration to an end, I enclose a copy of the chaplain's letter."

*

Monsieur B's enclosure was written, in an altogether different, sprawling hand, on both sides of an old piece of foolscap, conscientiously marked "*copie*" in the upper left-hand corner. It follows:

BELOVED FRIEND:

Listening to your story and feeling the great distress of your conscience, I was unable to find the word of consolation equal to the circumstance. My priestly heart perhaps blamed you, but my old soldier's heart beat in unison with yours. I prayed God to inspire me, that I might bring comfort to a great soul in pain, and He has granted that—from today on, at least—you shall have the moral solace you so much need. Without delay, as we agreed, I write out the following information (not the fatal sort you feared).

I located the place of the accident you described without any trouble, especially as boys playing nearby gave me some useful information, without even knowing that I was especially interested. There remained on the spot only some twisted metal, a knapsack, and two charred waterproofs.

Mme. Petitier told me that the Thouvenin boy had brought the two injured Germans to her house at about six-forty-five on the evening you remember so well. He had been on the way home from the fields when he saw the motorcycle and sidecar in flames. One of the wounded men, the motorcyclist, had received a bullet in the shoulder, and his left arm was badly burned. The other, badly burned about the face and neck, seemed to have either a fracture or a bad sprain of the right leg; in addition, both had abrasions and cuts on their heads. An ambulance came at about eight o'clock to pick them up. By that time, they had already been bandaged by medical soldiers from the dressing station at Omelmont. According to the medics, neither was in danger of death.

As to the wounded, there is no doubt that somebody fired at them. The motorcyclist lost control and ran into a tree, the gas tank took fire, and the men had a hard time getting clear of the burning machine. There was no search for their assailant, because they hadn't seen anybody and, as many French soldiers were still scattered through the forest on that Saturday, the shooting was attributed to some straggler.

I think that your exaggerated regret will find a palliative in the reading of this message. Your scruples, which I respect, were due to a fine sensibility, but should now be dissipated. They will give place completely to the peace of mind that you must already have partially recovered if you have prayed to God, as I advised you.

Next time you come by, stop and see me; I have a number of things still to tell you. We will chat like comrades, soldiers of '14, over a bottle of excellent local wine; we will talk especially of the not so distant time when we were happy, when we hoped that the age of atrocities had passed forever, and that the sacrifices we had made would permit us to hope.

Your friend,
M. ALBERT

"But I have never seen the good man again," Monsieur B concluded. "He never returned to that region. The incident had no sequel, and I am writing it out for you now only because I have an attack of arthritis which prevents me from doing something more useful, and I thought it might interest you.

"Affectionately,
"Your father-in-law,
"B"

The New Yorker, September 21, 1946

The Republic of Silence

ARGUMENT OF THIS BOOK

O NE of the most dangerous stories in the French language is *La Chèvre de Monsieur Seguin*, by Alphonse Daudet. It is intrinsically dangerous because of its moral implications. It is dangerous to France because of its effect on world opinion. *La Chèvre* of the story is a young white nanny goat who refuses to stay tethered. She wishes to go up on a mountain which she can see from the yard of Monsieur Seguin's house, in order to fulfill her destiny. Monsieur Seguin adjures her to play it safe, which he calls being reasonable. "There is a bad wolf on the mountain who will eat you if you go up there," he says, talking as Marshal Pétain used to. "But if you will be a spineless unimaginative nanny goat and demonstrate a will to co-operate I will even lengthen your tether. There is plenty of grass here if you will just learn to adjust yourself to condi-tions." But the nanny goat slipped her tether and went up on the mountain, and the wolf ate her, which proved Monsieur Seguin had been right. The Messieurs Seguin-Pétain-Daudet and the counterparts they have in every country are always right, if you accept the stories they make up themselves.

In real life, the men of the French Resistance were like the white nanny goat. They refused to listen to Marshal Seguin-Pétain, even though in real life one story-book attribute had been transposed and the Marshal had the quavering voice of the goat. The Resistance men went up on the mountain and met the wolf. But there real life and the story diverged. Because the Resistance men beat the tar out of the wolf, who only has power over those who fear him. Walt Disney wrote a healthier wolf parable than Alphonse Daudet. The Daudet story is particularly dangerous because it ascribes benevolent characteristics to the counselor of caution. I once intended to call this book THE NANNY GOAT WAS RIGHT, or MONSIEUR SEGUIN WAS WRONG, but I gave up the idea because it embarrasses people to ask for a book with an odd title. *The Republic of Silence*, which is not my own invention, is much better. Nevertheless the book is the story of the refusal of the French to accept a lengthened tether in exchange for a destiny. It is told for the most part in their own words, which I think you will find admirable.

Looking back it has occurred to me that a good part of the American misconception of the nature of France, where it existed, may have been due to the kind of texts on which students formed their early notions of the language. *La Chèvre* is the archetype of these. In quest of texts that would be at the same time simple, not too colloquial, proper and without relevance to life, compilers went too often to writers remembered in France with the same amused indulgence reserved for a Second Empire bibelot, say a stuffed hummingbird suspended by a supposedly invisible wire over a bowl of wax fruit, the whole under a glass bell. The stories were too often sentimental and what the French call *niais*, which means corny. And since our opinion of a culture new to us is likely to be based upon our first contact with it, the American inducted into French via the *niaiseries* of Monsieur Daudet and comparable saps is likely to go through the rest of his life believing Frenchmen to be quaint imbeciles. Students who begin French in the first year of high school are less likely to suffer from this initiation than those who begin it in college. Daudet, François Coppée, Edmond About and the rest are on about the same aesthetic and intellectual level as a Greer Garson picture and the pre-adolescent may not notice anything wrong with them. But college men and women are likely to be put off by the disparity between the intellectual content of what they discuss in non-language courses and the dreadful corn syrup they are asked to ingurgitate in the course of learning simple French. I first got this book together for the use of college French teachers, keeping the French parts in French and me in English, or my own approximation thereof. Then I got to thinking that there were a lot of people who had been discouraged from learning French by their first classroom experiences, but who could be reached by a version with the French done into English.

The idea is succinctly expressed on the title page of my copy of *Le Moyen De Parvenir*: "A new edition corrected of many faults which were not there in the first place and augmented by several new ones."

The selections that I have tried to arrange in an approximation of a pattern in the following pages were all written by Frenchmen between May 10, 1940, when the German Army opened the campaign that ended with the Pétain armistice, and early September, 1944, a couple of weeks after the liberation of Paris. All the selections, with two or three exceptions, which will be duly noted, were written in France under the German occupation. Some, a number that surprised me when I totted up after making the selections, are by writers who had excellent and well-founded reputations before this war—for example Louis Aragon and François Mauriac. Others are by professional writers like Vercors and Claude Roy whose fame is a wartime development. But many, as you will see, are by complete novices, such as a corporal in an armored division recording his first sight of refugees, or a boy of seventeen setting down his last thoughts before facing a firing squad. "All the same, it's hard to die," the boy concludes. It was only by the fortune of secret war that the corporal too did not wind up before a firing squad. Two years after he saw the refugees he was in the Resistance, running parachuted arms to hidden arsenals.

Some items are anonymous, pieces culled from that great clandestine press which arose under the occupation and waged a war of ideas that turned public opinion completely against the conquerors—who had to aid them in their propaganda only limitless funds, powerful radio stations, all the printing establishments of France, and some thousands of miserable traitors. You will find a great many references to these last in this book. The fact of betrayal is an integral part of the story of France under the occupation, as it is of the New Testament. Incidentally, I wonder whether from a pedagogical standpoint Judas is not the most successful symbol in the Christ story. Not everybody has learned to love Christ, but virtually everybody succeeds in hating Judas.

Many of the writers represented here were such only in that they put words on paper, and not in the professional sense at all. Their writings are simply colloquial speech fixed in ink. The least experienced authors, as you will notice, were sometimes the most ornate. They felt that they had to "take things big." And yet their overblown verbiage fails to conceal the tragic import of what they had to express.

The approximation of a pattern that I have tried to follow in my selections and their arrangement is simple, but hard to classify. It might be called a case history of a sick nation, beginning with the crisis of the disease, and following through to convalescence and recovery. But there is something entirely too passive in the concept of France as a patient. Or it might be called *The Autobiography of a Nation, 1940–44*, except that that is too inclusive. The France Gertrude Stein wrote about in *Wars I Have Seen* also existed during those same years, I am sure. That was the France of the middle-aged and the old, who appear with relative infrequency in the chronicles of the Republic of Silence. And when, like Marc Bloch, they do appear, they are playing young men's roles.

This certainly isn't an anthology, if you think of an anthology as a selection of the "best" writing of a period, because as I have said some of the pieces have no literary quality at all. And I have omitted many fine things written during the four years that didn't seem to fit into the book, as well as many others that I have not happened to read. I am not a student of Resistance literature; candidates for the degree of doctor of philosophy will have their crack at it later. Then there will be bibliographies, and theses, and monographs of minor writers, and in time chairs of Resistance Literature endowed by the descendants of cartel millionaires and filled by professors exactly like Monsieur Seguin.

The book, the French writers' part of it, that is, begins with the catastrophe. But it is the catastrophe as seen by four or five men involved in it. It goes on through selections that tell how Frenchmen viewed their plight and what they thought about it, and what they thought were the chances of getting out of it. And what they did, and what life and death were like, at different periods of the occupation—for moral and material conditions were very different in 1940–1 from 1942–3, for example. The bits of language show how hope grew, and how the fear and cruelty of the occupant kept pace with it. Finally there are some accounts of how men felt during the liberation and immediately afterward.

In the spring of 1944, when I was in London waiting for
D-day, I had the opportunity to see some hundreds of Resistance newspapers of all sorts that were flown out of France to
the headquarters of the Provisional Government—which the
United States of course did not then recognize as even a provisional government—and from them I made up a kind of mosaic of what life must be in France under the occupation. I
compared the process to salvaging scraps of paper dropped
from a house where a friend was held prisoner by kidnappers.
Each paper might have a word or two written on it, and then
one would put the papers together and try to read a continuous message. I wrote three long pieces for *The New Yorker*,
following that scheme, and arrived at a result that I found
afterward had been pretty accurate—much more so than that
achieved by our own State Department, for example, which
had been getting its information from a man at the Brookings
Institution looking into a crystal ball. The Department had the
quaint notion that there was somewhere in France an anti-De
Gaulle, inactive, Monsieur Seguin kind of a collaborationist
Resistance movement that would come to light once danger
was past and gratefully receive France from the hands of a third
secretary. When they sought this alternative group with which
to do business they naturally looked not to groups left of De
Gaulle, but to his right, not understanding that he was already
as far right as any French leader could go without losing his
leadership. They talked of a large, inert, conservative mass in
France which would manifest itself if given a chance in a free
election. Two free elections have been held there since the liberation, at this writing, and the vote cast by elements to the
right of De Gaulle have been negligible. De Gaulle himself, in
fact, has proved too conservative to stay on top.* This book is
the same kind of a reconstruction as those articles, but one on
which I have had a chance to check before publication.

Men seldom write as ingenuously ten years after the event as
when they are in its grip. This is particularly true when it in-

*Harry Butcher's book, *My Three Years with Eisenhower*, proves, to my sor-
row, that Mr. Roosevelt, if not originally responsible for this error, was even
more stubbornly persistent in it than his subordinates. To paraphrase Mr. La
Guardia, the President made few mistakes, but when he did they were
beauts.—L.

volves national *amour-propre* or the apportionment of individual and party responsibilities. Samuel Pepys, writing at Clapham in his retirement in 1680 concerning the years covered in his diary, would have presented a much less veracious record of what had happened, as well as a duller one. He would have written about what, by that time, he thought must have happened, in the light of his own later opinion of himself. So I have a high esteem for history that may be picked out of accounts as contemporary as these, like the sweet meat from the claws of a lobster.

I once knew a school committeeman named Rowland Palmer in Exeter, Rhode Island, who held that it was foolish ever to buy new history-books of the Civil War, because, he said, it stood to reason that the sooner after the war a man wrote the more he would remember about it. The flaw in his argument against buying the books, I think, was that the old ones he had hadn't been written soon *enough* after the war. For history written a hundred years after the event is more accurate than the kind written ten years after it. After a hundred years the participants are dead and the historian doesn't have to justify his friends. To form his conclusions he goes back to the contemporary sources and ignores most of the stuff written in between.

In reading the first version of this book, therefore, college students learn not only French, but a better grade of European history than will be academically available for ninety-eight years, and should receive double credits toward graduation, although the volume is sold at a single price. It reminds me of a little Japanese picture-book I have, with text in Japanese, Chinese and English. "By this book," the English foreword says, "you may see all world-renowned sites of beautiful Japan, without making any travel, and spending only a trifle for it."

Perhaps it would be a good idea for me now to explain why I felt impelled to put this book together. A man should have some reason for anything he does. I love France, just as I love New York City or the smell of burning leaves on a Long Island lawn. This does not mean that I love all the French or everything French, but the things I do not like I can often find excuses for. This is a pretty sure sign of an emotional attachment.

In this book I am not an author but a go-between. I try to fill in gaps in continuity and to supply bits of background when it would be difficult otherwise to understand the motivation of certain pieces. I should call myself a master of ceremonies if that term were not reminiscent of night-club and music-hall brashness, and if this were not an extremely serious book. There is a French term, *compère*, for a chap who explains what is going to happen in a revue, and as he goes off-stage often pinches (Fr.: *peloter*) the showgirls' bottoms. But that also has too flippant a connotation. Then there is the narrator of documentary films—like the one who should say, "Time stands still, or so it seems while you are listening to this ominous croak." With him I care still less to be confused.

I am very conscious of the master-of-ceremonies analogy. It is a rôle difficult not to overplay, and I remember with misgiving some of the hams I have seen getting between show and audience instead of bringing them together. I will try not to get in the way of the performance. But it seems I should make some allusion here to what had happened before May 10, 1940, when the curtain rises.

————

IN LIEU OF EPILOGUE

The publishers of this book had the idea that I should round it off by an epilogue. But an epilogue is a speech at the end of a play, and history has no end. Artistically, the liberation might seem a good place to round off the story of France. There have been, in the course of that same story, a dozen other aesthetically satisfactory places to write Finis and Epilogue. One was the coronation of the Dauphin Charles VII at Reims in 1429 which marked the completion of Saint Joan's mission; another the coronation of Henry IV which marked the end of the Wars of Religion and in the opinion of the contemporary world the triumph of common sense. The fall of Robespierre, the battle of Waterloo, the triumph of 1918, all offered good opportunities for a narrator to draw his threads neatly together, tie a knot and then snip off the loose ends. Unfortunately, from the point of view of the amateur of certainties, history is not composed by playwrights. This is lucky, from mine, since I do not desire any ending to the story of France, even a happy ending. That is of course inconceivable in the case of a nation anyway. Not even Father Divine has ever promised a heaven for dead nations.

France was threatened with a death that besides being death was as squalid and humiliating as suffocation in the arms of a Yahoo. Her predicament puts me in mind of Gulliver's when, while he was bathing, the Yahoo, "which smelled very rank," embraced him "in the most fulsome manner." France resisted and escaped. And with her there escaped from the hairy and ill-smelling arms of the bleary beast all hope for the continuity of civilization. But people in France are not living happily ever after, any more than are people in the United States, or Norway, or the United Kingdom or Russia. I do not think this cause for disillusionment. Escape from extinction is a pretty good thing in itself. As a cross-grained Irish waiter in a grim restaurant once said to me: 'What do you expect for two dollars?—a gold watch?"

Jean-Paul, the Armored Division soldier who wrote to me from the front on May 10, 1940, when he saw the refugees from Luxemburg, was demobilized in the Vichy "free" zone after the Pétain armistice. He went back to Paris, found little to do, and after a while drifted to Orléans, where he started a small trucking business. With his unfailing gift for tinkering with motors, he repaired a couple of venerable vehicles and converted them to run on charcoal. He then got into the Resistance and used his trucks to retrieve and haul to safety Sten guns and other arms parachuted by the R.A.F. He found a fine, merry woman in a town near Orléans and married her.

When the Americans approached Orléans in August, 1944, Jean-Paul, who speaks American well, went out to meet them and formed the liaison between them and the F.F.I. His guidance was at least partially responsible for the capture of Orléans with a loss to us of only fourteen men. After the liberation he returned to Paris and got a place as manager of a big garage, an appointment which carried with it a fairly comfortable apartment above the garage and the right to raise chickens on the roof. But the government requisitioned the garage for military vehicles and Jean-Paul found himself doing the same chores he had performed with the Armored Division in 1940.

When I last heard from him he and his wife still had the apartment, however, and during the cold winter of 1944–5, when they could keep only one room heated, they were raising fifty small chicks in the living room. "*Des vraies poules de luxe*," he wrote. "*Poule de luxe*," literally a luxury chicken, means colloquially a luxuriously kept woman. So *le petit soldat Français* with his *debrouillardise caractéristique* continues to make himself a little life of his own.

My friend Louis Pavageau, of whom I haven't said anything before, a big square-jawed aviator I met in Alsace in 1939, went back after the Pétain armistice to Dombasle in Lorraine, his home, and there lived out the four-year agony of that eastern province. He was in the Resistance there, and his great day came in September, 1944, when, with the Americans approaching, the F.F.I. men could come out into the open and fight. "We had only one automatic rifle and one sporting rifle for a hundred and fifty men," he wrote to me, "but what a relief it was to fight." He sent me news of other men I had met in Alsace.

One of them, a Major Bourgon, I had remembered during the dark years with mixed feelings. He was a sanguine, thick-necked, middle-aged survivor of the first World War who looked like Henry VIII and had similar tastes. He had commanded a battalion in a forest near the Rhine and had set the best table in Europe, having managed to snare a roast-chef from one great Paris restaurant and a pastry cook from another. There had been a wartime order against hunting, but there was always plenty of venison on Major Bourgon's table. "Can we help it if the deer strangle themselves in the barbed wire?" he once asked me. "And the pheasants?" I said, with a rapturous glance at three fat, redundant birds that soldier waiters had just carried in. "The battalion surgeon runs over them on his bicycle," Major Bourgon replied. At the time I had thought this magnificent, but after the débâcle I had wondered if such concentration on the good life was compatible with relentless war.

Pavageau wrote me that Bourgon had been killed "*sur place*," in 1940, defending his deer forest.

Pavageau had had a Belgian brother-in-law, also a flier, Jean Demay, who had escaped to the United States in 1942. He returned to Europe as a soldier in the American Army, made first lieutenant, and was killed at Metz.

Pavageau thought that things were slowly, very slowly, getting better. Jean-Paul thinks so too. And Georges Adam, the man who used to carry the *Lettres Françaises* copy to the secret printer, and who was in the United States last winter, is sure France will "get out of the dough trough" eventually.

Personally, I believe that France has a great future, because France is full of great people. This is an old-fashioned, romantic point of view for which I have recently been taken to task by a young friend who has never been anywhere but who reads all the heaviest political, economic and literary magazines to be obtained in Brentano's basement. "It's interesting," he said to me the other day when I had been talking about the efforts of the individual men and women who had found each other to form the Resistance—"but in this atomic age it's dated already."

Courage, however, has no date.

It outlasts "Thousand-Year Empires."

It is a little white goat on the hills.

From The Republic of Silence, 1947

Letter to
The New York Times Book Review

To the editor:

Mr. J. Donald Adams, in objecting to my recent remarks on Alexander Baron's "From the City, From the Plough," has used them as an excuse for writing a series of capsule reviews of three other books, "The Naked and the Dead," "An Act of Love" and "The Young Lions," of whose merits, incidentally, I hold unequal opinions, but which I certainly hadn't mentioned in connection with "From." I do not happen to share Mr. Adams' reverence for "All Quiet on the Western Front," but that is equally irrelevant. The authors of war books whom I contrasted to Mr. Baron were those brash young Yanks, Richard Aldington and Siegfried Sassoon, who wrote outside the genre tradition of G. A. Henty ("True to the Old Flag," "St. George for Merry England"), in which, I am afraid, Mr. Baron belongs. I did not know, until I read Mr. Adams' piece, that fourteen American publishers had turned down "From." If true, it is the most encouraging thing I have heard about the publishing business in years.

Mr. Adams made a great case of the fact that Mr. Baron "served in the ranks for six long years." So did several million other men, who might write just as badly about their experience if they had a try at it, and possibly a few who will write the great books about World War II—if any are to be written.

I made no "wisecracks about British character," as Mr. Adams suggested, but several about the character of sentimental British military fiction, a historical outline of which I attempted to trace for the benefit of those who had wasted less of their youth than I in reading it.

The one portion of Mr. Adams' piece that I am tempted to take seriously is his query about the kind of troops I associated with during the war, in which I sensed an implied reflection on their quality. I was with very good troops indeed, among them the First, Ninth and Twenty-ninth Divisions, the Thirty-third fighter group, the Corps Franc d'Afrique, and the Fourth Indian Division. I have seen tank battalion soldiers dragged yammering back toward their own lines along the sunken road that led through St. André l'Epine on the way into St. Lo, and seen fine big stolid Midwestern infantrymen frozen to a wall in the fighting to take La Haye du Puits, unable to move, or be moved, forward *or* back, although the front had moved a thousand yards ahead of them. I have seen good pilots arrive at a point where nobody could make them get into a cockpit, and a man on a landing craft on D-Day make a most heroic rescue—and then blow completely several days later, when the pressure was off. This, as I don't expect Mr. Adams to understand, is because every man has a threshold of endurance, although no two thresholds are of identical height, and, when the flood of painful experience piles high enough, it comes over.

It is the highest honor of the civilized soldier that he goes into battle knowing he may crack, but it isn't his knowledge that makes him crack, if he does. I have seen Negroes from Tchad and hillbillies from the Ozarks blow when accompanying university men haven't, and I have seen it work the other way. In any case you don't know what the sum total of the other man's previous experience may have been, so you never have any reason for feeling superior. No troops are exempt from these laws—an opinion which may be supported by reading Aldington and Sassoon or the reports of the RAF and Royal Army psychiatrists and by consideration of the different characters of the two battles of Tobruk. For that reason I am willing to take oath that there never was an organization like Mr. Baron's Fifth Battalion of the Royal Butterscotch, or whatever it was, outside the fifty million pages of pipe-clayed poppycock that noncombatant Parson Sterne brought down on posterity's head by writing a fictionized tribute to his military father.

This is not an angry piece, but one written in pained amazement, from the point of view of one who is invited to tea and then jabbed with hatpins by his host's aunt.

A. J. LIEBLING.

New York.

The New York Times, March 13, 1949

France's Strange Defeat

MARC BLOCH was a historian who attempted no vast syntheses pieced out with mystic intuitions. It is possible that he would have called the preceding sentence a tautology, since he would not have conceded that a Toynbee or a Spengler, a de Gobineau or a Karl Marx, was in any serious sense a historian. Bloch was Professor of Medieval History at the University of Strasbourg and, later, Professor of Economic History at the Sorbonne. One of his early works traces the appearance and spread of the water mill in medieval Europe, as recorded in ancient deeds and leases. The ancients knew the principle of the water-powered mill, but slave labor was so cheap that the masters relied on human power. The spread of the water mill, then, Bloch reasoned, measured a rise in the price and dignity of labor. Another celebrated Bloch monograph deals with the attested power of kings during the Middle Ages to cure some cases of certain diseases by touch. The suggestibility of their subjects indicates the realness of the medieval belief in the literally sacred character of royalty. So Bloch balanced the material and irrational elements in the feudal world that was his field of study, and that he anatomized in his crowning work, "La Société Féodale," published, in two parts, in 1939 and 1940. In this, Bloch held that feudalism reached its greatest development between the Rhine and the Loire, where the admixture of German tribalism and the Latin landlord system also reached its peak.

This region was Bloch's France. Before 1940, it had never occurred to him that as a Jew he was not qualified to explain this France, because he had never imagined that he was less a Frenchman than, let us say, General de Gaulle or Georges Carpentier. His great-grandfather had borne arms for France in 1793, his father in 1870; he himself had been gravely wounded and four times decorated in the war of 1914–18. Like so many other graying French reservists, he was mobilized again in 1939, this time as a fifty-three-year-old captain. From a post of fuel-supply administrator at the headquarters of the French

First Army, he viewed the debacle of 1940 with an objectivity it had been impossible for him to attain as a young man in the trenches.

Returned from this disastrous war (and to a period that must have reminded him of the days following Crécy and Agincourt, when medieval France seemed as darkly lost), Bloch sat down to write a memoir of his observations during it. There was then no foreseeable date of publication. "How much easier it would be to plead weariness and discouragement as an excuse for doing nothing!" he wrote. "But if the kind of documentation that I plan is to have any value, it must be put into shape at once, while the subject is still fresh and living in my memory. Nor can I really persuade myself that the effort will be wholly useless. A day will come, of that I am convinced, after no matter how long a delay, when this old and sacred soil of France, from which, in the past, so many harvests have been lifted—harvests of free thought and of judgment unrestrained —will once more burgeon into ripeness. In that happier future many secret records will be made public. Gradually the mists of ignorance and malice, which now begin to gather about the most terrible collapse in all the long story of our national life, will thin. It may be that then those on whom the duty falls of seeing through them to the truth beyond will be helped in their task by glancing at the pages (should they come their way) in which an eyewitness has set down the events of the year 1940, just as he experienced them."

The manuscript was not published until 1946, when, under the title of "L'Etrange Défaite," it was issued in Paris by men who had been Bloch's comrades in the Resistance. The historian had by then fought in a third war for France, and the book bore on its cover the notation, under the author's name, "Shot by the Germans in June, 1944." The frontispiece of the French edition is a photograph of the author—a pleasant, slightly comic professorial type, with white hair and clipped, grizzled mustache. His myopic eyes stare kindly through round, shell-rimmed lenses. Beneath is a quotation from the text: "I say frankly: I hope, in any case, that we shall still have blood to shed. . . . I do not speak of mine, to which I attach little value."

In 1942, the Professor joined the F.-T.P. (Francs-Tireurs et Partisans), one of the most combative Resistance organizations. Under the pseudonym of Narbonne (that city glorious in the Middle Ages), he rose to become one of the triumvirate that directed the entire Resistance in the region of Lyons. Captured by the Germans early in 1944, he underwent torture without "giving" any of his comrades. And on June 16th he was executed by a firing squad.

Georges Altman, editor of the Parisian daily *Franc-Tireur* and, under the name of Chabot, one of Narbonne's comrades in the underground war, has contributed a memorable foreword to "L'Etrange Défaite." It is an account of the Professor in the underground, and of his death. A translation of this foreword appears in the English-language edition of "L'Etrange Défaite"—"Strange Defeat" (Oxford), recently published in this country. "They killed him alone with a few others who had found strength in his courage," it states. "For it is known in what manner he died. A boy of sixteen was standing next to him, trembling. 'Will it hurt?' Marc Bloch took him affectionately by the arm, and merely said, 'No, my boy: it won't hurt at all.' He was the first to fall, crying 'Vive la France!' "

This sublimely pedagogic exit, and Altman's moving foreword, rather overshadow Bloch's sober text. Altman is a literary man; Bloch was a historian, trying to put down some notes for historians to come. Of the professional soldiers, Bloch says, "Our war, up to the very end, was a war of old men, or of theorists who were bogged down in errors engendered by the faulty teaching of history." The professional soldiers not only succumbed to a "spirit of apathy" but, in Bloch's eyes, committed an even worse sin. They quit cold. "In their hearts," he goes on, "they were only too ready to despair of the country they had been called upon to defend, and of the people who furnished the soldiers they commanded." The sentence reminded me of a remark once made to me by a Major Iriart, a Basque I met in North Africa during the war. Speaking of the Vichy generals, Iriart told me, "The blasphemy is that they don't *want* to fight."

Almost three-quarters of Bloch's book is given over to the military failures he watched. Then comes his most interesting chapter, "A Frenchman Examines His Conscience," dealing extensively with what ailed France in the years immediately preceding the war. In it, one reads, "In no nation is any professional group ever entirely responsible for its own actions. The solidarity of society as a whole is too strong to permit the existence of the sort of moral autonomy, existing in isolation, which any such total responsibility would seem to imply."

Bloch raps the press: "Many newspapers, even those which openly wore the livery of party beliefs, were secretly enslaved to unavowed and, often, squalid interests." He has a go at the politicians; takes a full share of blame for his own group, the educators, as traditionalist as the Army; and then magnificently tells off the bourgeoisie, to which he belonged, in this fashion: "Let me say, then, that, when in speaking of Frenchmen I employ the term bourgeois, I mean someone who is not dependent for his livelihood on the work of his hands; whose income . . . permits him to live in easy circumstances, and gives him a sense of security such as no mere wage-earner can ever know in his own hazardous existence; whose education . . . is richer in texture, better in quality, and more pretentious in kind than the minimum cultural training enjoyed by the ordinary man in the street. . . . He [the bourgeois] grew indignant at the thought that the manual worker had now enough free time to enable him to go to the cinema like his boss. . . . Because they were unused to making the mental effort which social analysis demands, they preferred to condemn out of hand. . . . How many employers of my acquaintance have I ever found capable of understanding, for instance, what nobility may lie behind a 'sympathetic' strike, no matter how unreasonable? 'It isn't,' they say, 'as though the men were striking for their *own* wages.' . . . Turn and turn about, either they refused to take the masses seriously, or they trembled before their implied threat. What they did not realize was that, by so doing, they were separating themselves effectively from France." But the trade unions are not exonerated, either. Bloch finds that "their vision was limited to immediate issues of petty profit" and that their "vague lack of purpose . . . was made far worse by the incredible contradictions of French Communism."

In parading his own remorse, Bloch declared himself

"actuated by no sense of gloomy pleasure." To prove it, he took the opposite course from that of the old men of Vichy. He turned precept to example and died like a character in those *chansons de geste* in which he used to search for details of feudal society.

The New Yorker, September 10, 1949

Pyle Set the Style

LESS than three months ago, a four-hundred-and-twenty-eight-page biography of Ernie Pyle would have seemed as outdated as the word "foxhole." Yet the appearance now of "The Story of Ernie Pyle," by Lee G. Miller (428 pp., Viking), seems the result of a miracle of publishing prescience—a prescience our intelligence services unfortunately did not match. For there has been in the interim a revival of Pyle's subject matter.

This is an example of Pyle, from a 1943 column, quoted by Mr. Miller, who, as managing editor of the Scripps-Howard Newspaper Alliance, was the late correspondent's editor and one of his greatest admirers:

> The men are walking. They are fifty feet apart, for dispersal. Their walk is slow, for they are dead weary, as you can tell even when looking at them from behind. Every line and sag of their bodies speaks their inhuman exhaustion. On their shoulders and backs they carry heavy steel tripods, machine-gun barrels, leaden boxes of ammunition. Their feet seem to sink into the ground from the overload they are bearing. They don't slouch. It is the terrible deliberation of each step that spells out their appalling tiredness. Their faces are black and unshaven. They are young men, but the grime and whiskers and exhaustion make them look middle-aged. The line moves on, but it never ends. All afternoon men keep coming round the hill and vanishing eventually over the horizon. It is one long, tired line of ant-like men. There is an agony in your heart and you almost feel ashamed to look at them. They are just guys from Broadway and Main Street, but you wouldn't remember them. They are too far away now. They are too tired. Their world can never be known to you, but if you could see them just once, just for an instant, you would know that no matter how hard people work back home they are not keeping pace with these infantrymen in Tunisia.

The thin, old-looking reporter who was killed by a Japanese sniper on Ie Shima in April, 1945 (he was only forty-four, but to enlisted men he seemed as old as a senior admiral), contributed a stock figure to the waxworks gallery of American history as popularly remembered. To a list that includes the frontiersman, the Kentucky colonel, the cowboy, and Babe Ruth, Ernest Taylor Pyle, to give him the full name nobody ever called him by, added G.I. Joe, the suffering but triumphant American infantryman. The portrait was sentimentalized, but the soldier was pleased to recognize himself in it, and millions of newspaper readers recognized their sons and lovers in Pyle's soldiers and got some glimmer of the fact that war is a nasty business for the pedestrian combatant. Through millions of letters from home enclosing clippings, the soldiers learned that their folks read Ernie Pyle. He provided an emotional bridge. When he died, something like seven hundred papers were buying his column. I have no figures on Homer's syndication in Hellas, but he is reputed to have begged his bread, which Pyle, had he survived, would never have had to do. A substantial fraction of the readers of the seven hundred papers read nothing about the war but Pyle and the headlines. He was the only American war correspondent who made a large personal impress on the nation in the Second World War.

Ernie, whom I knew in Africa and France, had a profound capacity for self-pity—for which he had more reason than most —and a knack of projecting it. You could have been sleeping on the ground for a fortnight without thinking much about it, but when you read that he had slept on the ground, your bones ached. In 1940, before he had been to war, he wrote to a friend whose parents he had just visited, "Seeing my own folks—so old, so disappointed, so eager and helpless—and seeing your folks so exactly like my own—it kind of throws me. There is no sense to the struggle, and there is no choice but to struggle." He had intimations of goshawfulness.

Ernie took his writing seriously. I was about to say he sweated over every sentence when I remembered that he was never warm enough to sweat and complained almost continually of cold. He suffered acutely when he read clippings of his columns and noticed the editorial excision of a phrase. On such occasions, he damned the transatlantic Mr. Miller, who handled his copy personally. He had frequent doubts about the quality of his stuff and often demanded reassurance. After he was killed, near the end of the war, he became a fixed part of a historical period that appeared to have come to a close with the dropping of the first atomic bomb. The prototype of what was evidently to be the war correspondent of the future emerged in the person of William L. Laurence, the science expert of the New York *Times*, who rode in the plane that dropped the second atomic bomb, on Nagasaki. Mr. Laurence's erudition contrasted strongly with Ernie's highly emphasized simplicity, and it looked as if anybody who wanted to cover a future world conflict would need a degree from M.I.T. or Carnegie Tech. (Laurence is a Harvard man, but he has filled in the gaps in his education by extensive reading. Ernie, incidentally, was not so innocent of formal education as his folksiness implied; Miller says he got as far as the middle of his senior year at the University of Indiana, when he quit after he had been turned down by a coed. I would never have thought him so romantic.)

As of today, however, Pyle is the most imitated writer in America, just as he was in 1945. The newspapers are again full of G.I.s, front-line quotes, M-1s, and bazookas, and more than ever the individual combatant fights under the glaring light of publicity, since the ratio of correspondents to combatants in Korea is without parallel in the history of warfare. The Pyle influence was evident in the early dispatches of the men doing straight news stories of the Korean fighting; even while fleeing through rice paddies with invading tanks close behind, the correspondents found time to get the name, rank, and home town of every soldier they talked to. For example, a story by Tom Lambert, of the Associated Press, on July 12th quoted Lt. Edward James, of Columbus, Ga.; Pvt. Freddy Pickens, of Columbus, Miss.; Pvt. Robert Reed, of Michigan City, Ind. (who said he had had a carbine and then a rifle shot out of his hands); Pvt. Edward Rounds, of Thurman, N.Y.; Pvt. Tommy Bishop, of Quitman, Miss.; Pfc. Leon Wilson, of Sullivan, Ind.; Sgt. W. F. Wociechowski, of Chester, Pa.; and Pvt. Edwin L. Rowland, of Paducah, Ky. (who "nodded assent"). On July 5th, Marguerite Higgins, of the *Herald Tribune*, saw a "blond G.I." die and gave the occurrence intimate coverage. There was a general disposition to report war through the eyes or, more often, the spoken recollection of the soldiers themselves; this was, perhaps, inevitable at a time when there were only five hundred Americans in combat, according to our Korean headquarters. In such warfare, each soldier had the importance, in relation to the whole force engaged, of a war-strength regiment in the American Army of 1945, and the blond G.I.'s death was approximately equivalent to all the American casualties on the Norman D Day.

It was not until the last part of July that the more formal aspirants to the Pyle role began to arrive. Pyle's copy was aimed primarily at afternoon papers and was never spot news or "big picture." He wrote almost always about individual soldiers—including, sometimes, generals—and, most importantly, about himself. The afternoon-paper field in New York is limited and has been even more so this summer; if Pyle had been covering the Korean campaign, he would have had no New York outlet during the first nine weeks of the fighting, because he worked for the Scripps-Howard Newspaper Alliance, and the Scripps-Howard paper here, the *World-Telegram & Sun*, was closed down by the Newspaper Guild strike during all that time.

The two afternoon dailies to which this city was temporarily reduced—the *Post* and the *Journal-American*—have been represented by an average of one and a half Pyle-type war correspondents: the *Post* by Jimmy Cannon and the *Journal-American* by Frank Conniff and Bob Considine. Cannon, Conniff, and Considine, besides being alliterative, have a number of other qualities in common—they are Celtic, knowing, and representative of the Toots Shor, or man-about-town, school of journalism; Cannon is a sports columnist and Considine used to be. Their backgrounds place them at an initial disadvantage in the Pyle stint, for Ernie had spent six years before the war building up a reputation as an Average American. During that time, he produced a column that dealt mostly with subjects like the beauty of the Grand Canyon and the human qualities of human beings in all parts of Nebraska. But an even more serious handicap for his successors has been the repetitiousness of situations. This, for example, is Cannon, who got to Korea on July 18th, writing about soldiers coming around a bend there on August 2nd:

The farther forward you go, the younger the troops are, but the older they look. All men age with fatigue, but these combat soldiers seemed abruptly deprived of their youth and stricken with crippling maturity just before they turned the bend in the road and came, stooped and shriveled with weariness, toward trucks which would transport them to a more dangerous sector of the front. . . . The act of dragging themselves on trucks seemed unbearably difficult for them, as though the blood in their young bodies had been frozen by the years. They were round-shouldered under the burden of their arms. Dirt turned to mud as sweat clotted on eyelids. Their ears were foul caves. Some of them wore goatees which didn't seem incongruous on their trouble-pinched faces but gave them the wizened look of wise, sleepy, year-drugged old men. They were quiet—the very old are silent—transfixed by memories. . . . But they belong where you are. . . . Remember them not as dedicated men but as kids similar to the ones you know who are hurt by nothing more than the sickness of first love.

It is plain that Cannon is confronted with a problem. The last war ended only five years ago, and we are all in danger of becoming callous. But Cannon's soldier dialogue is more accurate than Pyle's, who was really good only on old draftees. (Cannon was an enlisted man, albeit a correspondent for soldier newspapers, for four years during the Second World War.) And on August 5th, he produced a column that shows he is not incapable of emotion.

Put this down as an hysterical piece written by a 41-year-old adolescent whose adult life has been concerned with games [he wrote]. Sports journalists are permanent residents of boyhood and we reject middle age to dwell as frightened aliens in a country of youth. . . . It is inconsequential now if a fight manager is a scoundrel, if Notre Dame will ever play Army, if Jake LaMotta will fight Ray Robinson for the middleweight championship. . . . What does it matter who got loaded in Shor's and what comedian they're knocking at Lindy's? . . . Remember this is not a USO war with actors telling their gags especially written for the occasion. It is a war in which generals use bazookas.

Conniff, as the campaign has worn on, has turned out some good columns, particularly one cowboy-and-Indian-style yarn about how tanks were menacing Pohang airfield, which the Air Force was soon to quit. But on August 7th, by which time he had arrived in the classic Pyle situation—"Conniff in a Fox Hole," the *Journal-American* labelled his story of that date— he was acknowledging the common difficulty. "Now that I have read this over I realize that it is just another shelling story," he wrote, "a story of something that happened again and again during the last war."

Considine, a late starter, had, as of last week, advanced only as far as a regimental headquarters, and had then returned to Tokyo for a breather. The fateful headline "Considine in a Fox Hole, Too," has, as I write this, not yet appeared.

But none of the current correspondents is likely to replace the subject of Mr. Miller's biography, who appears in its pages as a more complex man than I had supposed. When I first met Ernie, in the fall of 1942, he seemed jarringly like the character he had created for himself in his column, then only moderately successful. He had complained in a letter to his wife, quoted in the book, because his column, which he was then writing from England, had only forty-five newspaper clients. (Miller, measuring success by the number of clients, notes that by January, 1943, it had sixty.) Ernie in those days was abstinent and resolutely Philistine. He would have been the last to admit that he had ever read a book. Since he disliked wherever he found himself, I took it for granted he was homesick. I also assumed, without definite knowledge, that he was devout. He was quiet, friendly, and obliging in the small details of communal life in cramped quarters. We travelled to Africa together aboard a transport, and during the campaign there I used to run into him in places like Tébessa and Gafsa and Béja, and wherever it was he was always coming down with a cold or recovering from a mild attack of dysentery. He was invariably worried because he had not prepared a sufficient supply of columns in advance—at that time he was writing them three weeks ahead of publication date. It was not until rather late in the African campaign that he made his first prolonged stay in the front lines, going out from Béja to spend a week with a battalion of the First Division that was fighting its way toward Bizerte in what was to be the last, decisive battle of the war in Africa.

When I met up with Ernie again, in the press camp at Vouilly, in Normandy, in 1944, he was at the height of his vogue. He was drinking more than a bit, and his nerves were not too good. I evolved a theory to account for the change in him. The success of his front-line series from Africa, I deduced, had caused his home office to needle him into increasingly frequent trips into real danger, on the ground that readers of the column, once blooded, would never again be content with stories about poker-playing officers in quartermaster depots who missed their friends in Merchantville, N.J. Ernie, under this pressure, I figured, had abandoned his Hoosier abstinence in order to keep up his nerve, and the remedy was not a complete success.

This theory, I learn from Miller's book, was far too simple. Ernie's African phase had been atypical in that it marked about his longest stay on the wagon. He was a heavy drinker and in the twenties had been a conventional Menckenian rebel against stuffiness, mixing gin in the bathtub and living in fake sin with his legally wedded wife, Jerry. ("For years they made a fetish of insisting they weren't really married," Miller records.) He was an agnostic: Miller quotes a letter he wrote to his ailing wife in January, 1945, in which he told her, "You say you want to learn to pray. That has to be up to you, of course, but it is so different from anything you or I have ever felt. I want you to get well, but I wouldn't want you to get pious—for then you wouldn't be *you*. I don't think you can get well by any mystic device or even willing it so. . . ." The simple Hoosier shell had been an induced accretion of Pyle's column-writing years.

I also learn that most of the time Pyle was overseas he was in a terrible emotional tangle; his wife, whom he had married in 1925, when both were twenty-five years old, had gone mad in 1941. Pyle had written to Miller then, "For more than ten years Jerry has been a psychopathic case. In the past few months it has reached a stage in which you would have to turn your back to call it anything less than a form of insanity. She is a dual personality, you might say a triple personality—one side of utter charm and captivation for people she cares nothing about; one side of cruelty and dishonesty toward the few people she does care about; and another side of almost insane melancholy and futility and cynicism when she is alone, which is her true personality." In the years since 1941, she had shuttled between institutions and the outside world.

Far from being homesick, Ernie appears on Miller's showing to have been terrified at the prospect of going home. He must have felt guilty at his knowledge that he didn't want to go. While he was certainly afraid of being killed, he must often have wished he would be. The trips to the front were perhaps a kind of Russian roulette that he played with himself. (I must say that he never seemed to me a reckless man; he protracted the game.) His constant illness now appears to have been largely hypochondria. Miller says Ernie often had himself examined by doctors, and they never found anything much the matter. In short, his appearance of placid, pawky normality seems to have been as deceptive a dickey as ever covered a troubled breast, and I like him a lot better for it, and for keeping his troubles to himself.

Miller was under no obligation to make these troubles public now, but after all Ernie is dead and so is Mrs. Pyle (since November, 1945), and it is better for Ernie to be remembered as a man than as a hick character in a movie.

The New Yorker, September 2, 1950

The Eternally Kicked-in-the-Pants

IN 1944, at the formal surrender of von Choltitz, the German military commander of Paris, in the Gare de Montparnasse, a German officer complained to correspondents that while being led to an automobile at the conclusion of the *Kommandantur*'s token resistance he had been kicked in the pants by a person unknown. The fingerprints of the Gestapo's victims were still fresh on the walls of the shooting gallery in Issy-les-Moulineaux. The bodies of the women and children lay beneath the charred timbers of the church in Oradour. But it did not occur to the kicked-in-the-pants officer that he was lucky not to have had his brains blown out. I can follow his reasoning easily, having been subjected to several German servants when I was young. It is wrong to kick a prisoner of war in the pants, and thus the French were in the wrong. In a war, the party who is not in the wrong is in the right. The invaders, therefore, including the kicked-in-the-pants officer, were in the right. The defeat of the right is reason for self-pity. Among sub-Teutonic peoples this kind of thing would be considered mental buffoonery. Among multitudes of Germans it is normal intellection.

"Fragebogen," by Ernst von Salomon, now published here by Doubleday, was the first great postwar best-seller in the Western Zone of Germany and in Berlin, which is disquieting evidence that among these multitudes nothing has changed. "Fragebogen" is one of those glass-fronted cross-sections of an ant-hill in which even children can see the insects work, and the ants bumbling through the longitudinally bisected tunnels of von Salomon's mind are sprinkled with crumbs of *Lebkuchen* over which the reader is invited to cry.

The *Fragebogen* was a lengthy questionnaire issued in 1945 by the Allied Military Government of Germany to all political suspects. Von Salomon, writing his book in the form of a very full reply to that questionnaire, has turned it into an indictment of the persecution of an almost blameless people, the Germans, by practically everybody else in the world. The questionnaire form gives him a chance to refute at the start any suggestion that his name is Jewish. (Like the unlamented Dr. Rosenberg, Hitler's chief racial theorist, he is obsessed by a need to affirm endlessly that he isn't what some people might think he is.) Not much farther on, in answer to "List any crimes of which you have been convicted," he has an opportunity to establish that he is a true German nationalist, not a snivelling liberal framing a fake repentance. He recounts, with dignified pride, his participation in the murder of Walter Rathenau, Foreign Minister and strongman of the Weimar Republic, in 1922. It is an honor that, he modestly asserts, nobody can take away from him, since he served five years for it. This was his first martyrdom. (There were three hundred and fifty-four political murders in the first year or two of the Weimar Republic. Political murder seems to have amounted to a fad.) After proving that he is neither Jew nor liberal, von Salomon goes on to qualify as a completely unbiassed social observer by insisting he wasn't a Nazi, either. He helped kill Rathenau not, he says, in order to clear the way for Hitler—whom he had not yet met—but for an absurd Navy captain named Ehrhardt, who had it in mind to take over the government but waited too long to pick up the ball the murder of Rathenau offered him. Ehrhardt had to leave Germany after the Roehm purge. This miscarriage of honest effort convinced von Salomon of the futility of political action. He therefore turned to writing novels and moving-picture scenarios, by means of which he kept happy and waxed fat. Acquaintances of his got sent to concentration camps and waned thin, but, he remarks, with the candor that seems to have endeared him to millions of fellow-Germans, he didn't pine over them. He was so nonpolitical that he even turned down a proposition to help assassinate Hitler.

When war came, von Salomon informs his readers, he would have been delighted to face the foe. (He bristles with manliness like a lout's chin.) He was sound as a bell, by his own testimony, as virile and dashing a fellow as ever helped plan a gang killing. But the Nazis would not honor his commission as a second lieutenant in the reserves; they wanted him as an enlisted man. Naturally, he refused; serving on that basis, he implies, was the privilege of *any* German without political influence, and he was allowed to go on with what he had been doing—

writing nonpolitical movies. He considered trying one about the horrors of a concentration camp—a British concentration camp in South Africa during the Boer War. He decided against it, not because the idea appeared ironical—such a reflection would have been impossible for a von Salomon—but because he believed movies should not be used for propaganda.

Then came his second martyrdom, the big, tear-jerking sequence and sales punch of his book. When the war ended, he was living in quaint comfort in a mountain village in southern Bavaria, still peacefully writing scenarios. The pictures were made in Munich, which was frequently bombed, so he rarely went there. His life was a lilt of *Lederhosen* and lieder, but he did not forget the brave boys on the Russian front, with whom he would have been glad to serve as a second lieutenant. His mistress, a young Jewish actress whom he had "taken under his wing" when Hitler came in, often sent them packages of goodies, and each package was accompanied by his very best wishes. Then the American "invaders" arrived. (He says nothing about who began the invading business.) Von Salomon was picked up by the United States Army Counter Intelligence Corps, a "Gestapo-type of organization." This, he suggests, was a brutal blunder. The C.I.C. should have understood that his safe, comfortable position in life indicated that he had no drag with the party in power; it should have had an up-to-the-minute dossier on him. He was, after all, a person of prominence; he had once helped commit a murder. But there it was; the Americans, just like the Nazis, arrested the innocent as well as the guilty.

That the Nazis boiled the innocent down into soap, while the Americans let the guilty go free, cannot lessen a von Salomon's resentment, even though the footling upshot of the mass arrests of 1945 was quite apparent in 1951, when "Fragebogen" was published in Germany. The Americans, despite all the advance publicity about their efficiency, were bunglers, von Salomon says; they kept him in custody longer than they needed to—from May of 1945 to September of 1946. (Had he been arrested by their predecessors in power, I imagine he would have gone down the drain in soap bubbles in much less time than we took to wash our hands of him.) He adds that American soldiers beat him. This, of course, is deplorable. It is wrong, everyone will surely agree, to beat prisoners before, during, or after interrogation; it is wrong to beat prisoners at any time, even though you suspect them of having behaved more cruelly than weasels in a chicken pen. It does not justify even one slap to point out that von Salomon wasn't hung by his chin on a hook, or gassed to death when he expected a shower bath, or fatally immersed in icy water as a "scientific experiment"—all fates meted out to better Europeans by the million, according to two carefully documented recent books on German affairs that make excellent collateral reading. They are "The Scourge of the Swastika: A Short History of Nazi War Crimes," by Lord Russell of Liverpool (Philosophical Library), and "Tyranny on Trial: The Evidence at Nuremberg," by Whitney R. Harris (Southern Methodist University Press).

The principle, with a type like von Salomon (or the officer who got kicked), is what counts. For him, therefore, the Americans are as bad as the Germans. Worse, in fact, because they are hypocrites. Professing horror at what they found in Dachau and Buchenwald, the Americans made their own prisoners eat K rations. The British are also worse, because they, too, are hypocrites. The French are hypocrites of a different kind, because they repress their love of the Germans, an affection that is evident to von Salomon. To support his theory, he evokes the memory of a number of Vichy Frenchmen who were in the American stockade with him. They loved Germany so much they were reluctant to go home. In the women's section of the same camp was a French prostitute named Yvonne, who had followed the German Army in its retreat. She, too, he says, preferred to stay in Germany. The Russians, naturally, are the worst of all. Well, if everybody else in the world is worse than the Germans, who is better than anybody else in the world? The evidence is as plain as *Ja, das ist ein Schnitzelbank*.

I regret one possibly unavoidable omission from the American edition of the book; it would have been fun to see an appended copy of the *Fragebogen* von Salomon filled out for the A.M.G. in 1945.

A more frightening though infinitely less offensive book is "Kesselring—A Soldier's Record" (Morrow), the memoirs of the German field marshal who commanded first an air army and later two major ground fronts during the war, a record in military versatility. It is frightening because, while a von Salomon is merely an ass (though an indicative ass), an Albert Kesselring illustrates the anomaly of the German intelligence at its near-best—vast technical capacity and incredible industry combined with obedience as a substitute for morality. Kesselring is a man solid, conscientious, proud of his workmanship, and without suspicion of his own moral indignity. Beginning his career with the artillery before the First World War, he served through it, while undergoing a sound General Staff training, and then under von Seeckt during the latter's discreet rehabilitation of the Reichswehr under the Republic. Kesselring's prose is full of good old saws—the *vis inertiae* is the foe of new methods; a sound military education is a *sine qua non* for a staff officer—and studded with respectful pleasantries; the princely Army commanders of the Hohenzollern world war were, he ventures archly, "not exactly 'Fredericks.'" By contrast, in World War II "every important post was occupied by a thoroughly efficient soldier who had had the experience of an excellent preliminary training as a G.S.O. [General Staff Officer] in World War I." One of these, naturally, was Kesselring. He was transferred to Herr Göring's shiny new Luftwaffe in 1933, changing from an artillery colonel to an air commodore—the equivalent of a brigadier general—overnight. Promptly he began learning to fly, at the age of forty-eight, and loved it from the first.

By the time World War II began, he commanded Air Fleet I, which represented the Luftwaffe on the Eastern front. The order to attack shocked him; he did not think Germany was ready to win a war. The facility of the victory in Poland cheered him. The following summer, he commanded the Luftwaffe in the Battle of Britain, an action he says was doomed to failure because it was not combined with an invasion by ground and naval forces. "It was clear to every discerning person, including Hitler, that England could not be brought to her knees by the Luftwaffe alone," he remarks. "It is therefore no good talking of the failure of the German air force to reach an impossible goal." (That the Luftwaffe, having been designed for tactical cooperation with ground forces, was ill-fitted for this solo mission is made thoroughly clear by General Adolf Galland, wartime commander of the German fighter forces, in "The First and the Last," published by Holt, another notable recent contribution to our Germanic studies. "The old fighter pilots from World War I," such as Milch and Göring, who "were stuck on the idea that maneuverability in banking was primarily the determinating factor in air combat," had hindered quantity production of the Messerschmitt until too late, Galland says. That is, the Germans didn't get Messerschmitts in quantity until the British had Spitfires in comparable quantity. Meanwhile, old military types drafted into the air force —he does not mention Kesselring by name—had favored dive-bombers instead of longer-ranging ones, which could have delivered big bomb loads in the heart of Britain.)

After the abandonment of the Battle of Britain, Kesselring commanded air operations in the invasion of Russia. Here he became a back-seat driver who must have enraged his old Army confreres. "Von Bock [the commander of the ground forces on the central Russian front] knew that I was not trying to teach him his business," he protests, but von Bock nevertheless ignored his suggestions, a mistake to which Kesselring modestly attributes the escape from destruction of the Russian armies. He had plenty of time to spare for coaching, he explains, because for the Luftwaffe of 1941 the annihilation of the Russian bomber force had proved "sheer 'infanticide.'" Kesselring still believes that even after the failure to destroy the Russian ground forces (per his advice) in the encircling battle of Smolensk, Hitler could have changed the course of the war against Russia by throwing all his weight into the thrust at Moscow before winter set in. The secondary objectives could have been cleaned up later. The Marshal disapproved of the German severity toward prisoners and civilians because, with encouragement, "vast numbers of magnificent and willing Russians" could have been recruited to fight against their compatriots. "Thus in the military field, and not only in the guerrilla section, the price was exacted for the mistaken racial policy of Hitler and his associates." It is Kesselring's nearest approach to an ethical judgment.

At the conclusion of the Russian summer-autumn campaign of 1941, Kesselring was transferred to the job in which he had remained primarily interested even while trying to think like an airman. He was made commander of the Axis forces in the Mediterranean, and while they included aircraft and the Italian Navy, they consisted chiefly of ground troops, the *sine qua non* of gratification for an officer with a sound General Staff training. "However much I might welcome the prospect of a new assignment in sunnier climes I was sorry to leave von Bock's Army Group and some of my own formations in a situation that was still obscure," he writes dutifully, but without being very convincing.

In the Mediterranean, Kesselring inherited two handicaps— his Italian allies and his prima-donna subordinate, Erwin Rommel. The Italians, a weakness and an exasperation, eventually made Kesselring lose his temper, and his liberty along with it. Rommel, whom he makes out to be a manic-depressive, was as great a trial to him as Montgomery, Rommel's opposite number, must have been to Alexander, Kesselring's opposite number. Montgomery was cantankerously overcautious. Rommel was by turns oversanguine and too easily discouraged. Kesselring favored a bold solution in the Mediterranean, as he had in the campaigns against England and Russia. He wanted to make an airborne invasion of Malta, the capture of which would have given the Axis control of every Mediterranean supply route. Rommel wanted all available resources for a thrust into Egypt by his Afrika Korps. Hitler sided with Rommel. Kesselring says, "At that period Rommel exercised an almost hypnotic influence over Hitler, who was all but incapable of appreciating the situation objectively." But Rommel quit when the going grew rough. The "iron determination to persevere was lacking," says the Marshal. "That being so, and given our knowledge of the full risk of the gamble, the attack [at Alamein] ought never to have been begun." After the check, he notes, Montgomery advanced too slowly and Rommel retreated too fast. The delaying actions demanded by Kesselring were never fought, and by the time Rommel was invalided home to Germany, early in 1943 (with an illness Kesselring clearly considers psychosomatic), the opportunity for a prolonged resistance in North Africa had been squandered. Ironically, Kesselring, by his own account an offensive-minded commander whose pet offensive schemes had been turned

down, was to win his chief laurels as the conductor of a vigorous defense that began in November, 1942, in Tunisia, and
continued, until the end of the war. His two-year fighting retreat up the Italian peninsula proved that Italy, instead of
being the soft underbelly of Europe, was its bony elbow, and
in his delaying action the Allied troops he engaged outnumbered his own men two to one, while the disparity in matériel
committed was far greater.

Because of this remarkable demonstration of Fabian warfare, Kesselring was recalled to the Western front in March
of 1945 to preside over the slow liquidation of the Reich's
Western armies. His official mission, as Hitler explained it to
him, was to hold fast while the German armies in the East defeated the Russians. Kesselring soon perceived that his task was
actually to maintain some sort of cohesive force that could absorb the remnants of the armies retreating before the Russian
advance. The Remagen bridgehead fell. "The main feature of
the situation at the front [in the West] was the enemy's extraordinary superiority in men and material on the ground and
his absolute ascendancy in the air. . . . The supply situation
was bad; in some areas critical. . . . Furthermore, symptoms
of disintegration were perceptible behind the front which gave
cause for uneasiness. The number of 'missing' was a disquieting indication that a rot was setting in. The attitude of
the civilian population in several districts, particularly in the
Rhine Palatinate and the Saar, confirmed this tendency. Even
among military staffs political talk could be heard which under-
mined the solidarity of resistance and nourished defeatism at
lower levels. Yet my orders were categorical: 'Hang on!'"

What ensues is an account of a military nightmare. The
flanks of his disarticulated armies collapse like the wings of
shot birds. The Palatinate is lost, then the Ruhr. "The reasons
for the sudden collapse . . . I shall try to explain as follows,"
Kesselring says, and then lists "continuous action for months,"
"irreplaceable losses," "interfering instructions by Hitler," "advanced deterioration of the situation," "the American attack
came so early," "the enemy air force was overwhelming," "the
best general cannot make bricks without straw." His Army
Group B, three hundred thousand men, surrenders on April
17th, "the reason being the simple fact that officers and men

had ceased to see any sense in continuing the war. . . . Model, its commander, and a brave and dashing soldier, took his own life. Looking back today, who can blame him? He is in my thoughts now, and I shall always remember him." On the lower Rhine, "Army Group H accepted the inevitable with a certain fatalism which was obvious to me at every conference."

"After I had formed a picture of the general situation," the wretched Kesselring writes in April, 1945, "I felt like a concert pianist who is asked to play a Beethoven sonata before a large audience on an ancient, rickety, and out-of-tune instrument." Nevertheless, he intersperses technical data on the performance of his opponents: they had improved amazingly, he says, especially in armor, but they still failed to exploit advantages to the full; "the lion's share of the glory in the Palatinate falls to the Allied air force." As for Hitler: "The last time I saw him, on 12 April 1945, he was still optimistic. How far he was play-acting is hard to decide. Looking back, I am inclined to think that he was literally obsessed with the idea of some miraculous salvation, that he clung to it like a drowning man to a straw." (Among the possible instruments of this salvation were the new German jet fighters, twice as fast as American Mustangs, but Kesselring had no faith in them. They lacked maneuverability, he notes. Galland, on the contrary, thinks the Reich could have reversed the course of the war if swarms of these machines had been available early in 1944. Their production, like that of the Messerschmitts, had been first delayed, then messed about, by Hitler and his advisers.)

Kesselring had no illusions. "After Stalingrad and the capitulation of Tunis, 'victory' had become impossible," he says, "and now there wasn't a ghost of a chance to save anything. Round 20 April [1945] this whole question [of surrender] began to trouble me really urgently. The defensive battles in both East and West had disappointed our hopes. Berlin was in danger. Yet once again I made my decision for holding out. The orders which reached me from Hitler's headquarters were so emphatic that a soldier could not act 'independently.' "

So Kesselring ordered his soldiers to continue being butchered for three more weeks, after which he yielded to a truth he had recognized two years earlier. It is not up to a commander to make "political" decisions, he says. "I now had time on my hands and was able to contemplate my future," he writes after the surrender. "Should I do that which would absolve me from inevitable further burdens?" The temptation must have been great, but the Marshal resisted. "As my demise would only place them on someone else's shoulders, I decided not to." This paragraph would have provided a fitting ending to the wartime autobiography of an accomplished, boring, but not uncongenial man. Unfortunately, Kesselring had, when he found the Italians particularly annoying, committed what turned out to be a serious *gaffe*. On the twenty-fourth of March, 1944, he had authorized the execution of three hundred and thirty-five Italian hostages in the Ardeatine catacombs, near Rome, as a reprisal for an attack by Italian partisans on a company of M.P.s—"elderly, respectable Tyroleans." The hostages could not have attacked the elderly, respectable Tyroleans, because they were in jail when the attack took place. Kesselring was tried by a British military tribunal in 1947 and sentenced to be shot. Instead of being overjoyed by the court's decision to relieve him of his burdens, he reacted like the officer in the Gare de Montparnasse. It was not that the Marshal *minded* being shot, he makes clear. He resented the slur on his honor. "It can only be assumed that the sworn testimony of my officers was considered untrustworthy," he notes sorrowfully, "which was incomprehensible to all of us. . . . The court must have considered it proved that von Mackensen [his co-defendant] and I had not permitted any reprisals on *our own responsibility*, of which we had been relieved by Hitler's order. . . ." On July 4th, a date whose significance he fails to note, the death sentence passed on Kesselring was commuted to life imprisonment, but this was no solace. "Then and afterward I often said that this reprieve was an aggravation of punishment." In 1952, he was released from prison because he was supposed to have an incurable illness.

Lord Russell's "The Scourge of the Swastika" comes in handy in considering not only von Salomon's but Kesselring's book. When Hitler's headquarters ordered a ten-for-one "reprisal" for the attack on the elderly, respectable Tyroleans, Kesselring passed the order on to von Mackensen and Maelzer, both general officers serving under him. Among the victims, Lord

Russell reports, were two hundred and eighty prisoners who happened to be in the principal Roman jail. There were added, "for good measure, fifty-five Jews, none of whom had any connection with the partisans and some of whom were not even Italian nationals." The non-Jews included a man of seventy, a boy of fourteen, and a man who had been acquitted of something or other and was simply waiting to go home. The execution was carried out by the S.S.

"At the trial of Field-Marshal Kesselring in the Tribunale di Giustizia in Venice in February 1947," Lord Russell records (His Lordship was the legal adviser to the British Commander-in-Chief), "Kappler [the Nazi security chief in Rome] described the shooting of these unfortunate people. They were made to kneel down, five at a time, their hands were bound behind their backs, and they were then shot in the back of the head. There were sixty-seven batches of five and all afternoon the slaughter went on. There was no medical officer present to see that one batch were all dead before the next came along. When the last victim had been despatched the cave was blown in to conceal all trace of the crime. [This act hints that even the Nazis may have had misgivings about the legality of their reprisal.] The Germans never even pretended that most of these people had anything to do with the bomb incident. Some had already been held in custody for a long time; many of them did not live near the Via Rasella [the scene of the attack]; some did not even live in Rome at all and fifty-five of them had merely had the misfortune to be born Jews. The bombing of the German police detachment [the elderly, respectable, etc.] was of course an offense against the Occupying Power, and those responsible for it could have been tried by a German military court and doubtless sentenced to death. None of those put to death in the Ardeatine Caves had been even tried, let alone convicted. . . . The word 'reprisal' can be widely interpreted but it cannot be properly contended that the arbitrary killing of innocent inhabitants becomes justifiable merely by calling it a reprisal. The massacre in the Ardeatine Caves was only a precursor of what was to follow." Lord Russell here cites some general orders subsequently issued by Kesselring. "I will protect any commander who exceeds our usual restraint [sic] in the choice and severity of the methods he adopts against partisans. In this connection the old principle holds good, that a mistake in the choice of methods in executing one's orders is better than neglect or failure to act. . . . Whenever there is evidence of considerable numbers of partisan groups, a proportion of the male population of the area will be arrested, and in the event of any act of violence being committed these men will be shot. . . . Should troops be fired at from any village it must be burnt down and the ringleaders will be hanged in public." Lord Russell uncharitably calls this a "clear incitement to murder and arson." Ten days after the proclamations, the German town major of the little Italian city of Covolo announced that he would shoot *fifty* inhabitants for every German "injured."

I have been saving up items of Germaniana for some time, and I happened to mark my place in Lord Russell's book with a clipping from a 1954 issue of the *Times*. It says:

BONN, GERMANY, Aug. 29—The green-gray uniform and the jack-boot reappeared on the German scene last night at a meeting of leaders of the Stahlhelm, a war veterans organization.

The meeting took place in Recklinghausen, in the Ruhr. Albert Kesselring, former field marshal, presided. Eight hundred leaders of the Stahlhelm cheered the speakers. . . .

Kesselring, once sentenced to death by British court-martial for atrocities committed by his troops in Italy, proposed that West Germany should refuse any military contribution to a Western alliance as long as war criminals remained in Allied jails.

A considerably more recent item in the *Times*—January 10th—reports the return to West Germany of that younger eager beaver, former Lieutenant-General Adolf Galland. He had been serving for some years as adviser to the Perón Air Force in Argentina. More magnanimous than Kesselring, Herr Galland told reporters in Frankfurt that "he did not come to Germany with a count-me-out attitude."

The New Yorker, March 26, 1955

Monsieur Flandin's Domaine

READING the obituary page of the New York *Times* on a recent day, I came upon a face that was once briefly familiar to me, but at a time considerably later than the period when the photograph must have been taken. This experience is always puzzling. I felt that I knew the face, but I could not identify it until I read the caption underneath: "Pierre-Etienne Flandin, as he looked some years ago." In the *Times* picture, which probably dated back to 1934, when he became the youngest Premier of the Third Republic, Flandin had the look of a man about to tuck his napkin under his chin and attack a huge dish of grilled pigs' feet Sainte-Menehould, or a *plate-côte de bœuf* succulent with broth. The future smiled and he had appetite. His hair was dark and his jowls were fat. They had been gray and puffy, respectively, when I knew him—an elephantine, worried, and defensive man. But the features were the same—the forehead high, wide, and noble, the nose impressive, the mouth slack below the ragged mustache.

Looking up from the picture, I read the spidery two-column italic headline, the kind that the *Times* puts on obituaries that are important enough to go on the front page of the first edition on a dull news day if nothing better should turn up:

FLANDIN DEAD IN FRANCE AT 69;
EX-PREMIER AND VICHY OFFICIAL
Pétain's Foreign Minister in
'40 Decried Hitler Threat
on Rhineland Invasion

According to the *Times*' practice in dealing with obituaries, the headline is supposed to tell as much as possible of the story that follows, but in M. Flandin's case the restrictions of space had strangled the head-writer's effort to summarize his biography. This gave a confusing impression that the threat had occurred in 1940, while Flandin was Pétain's Foreign Minister. But by that time all Hitler's threats had been realized—half of France was occupied, the rest dominated. The episode that the head-writer had tried to telescope occurred in 1936, when

Flandin was Foreign Minister in the Cabinet of a forgotten politician named Albert Sarraut. Flandin was the star, or, in the misleading journalistic phrase, the "strong man," of that Cabinet. He had already had one turn as Premier, and in the normal course of Third Republican politics he could count on several more. Then Hitler, weak but temerarious, announced that he would remilitarize—not "invade"—the Rhineland. ("Invasion," though, will fit into a smaller space than "remilitarization." It is thus that the inelasticity of type shapes the writing of popular history.) The Germans owned the Rhineland, but they had renounced the right to have troops there. Once they had reëstablished their Rhineland defenses, they would be hard to deal with. Flandin called the attention of his colleagues in both the French and the British governments to the danger of inaction. He then joined them in doing nothing.

"Had his urgent advice been followed, many students of international affairs have said, Hitler's power and prestige would have been so diminished that World War II might have been averted," the obit written in the *Times* morgue remarked. But the copy of the Paris paper *Le Monde* that I received that same evening said that Sarraut had wanted to send the French Army into the Rhineland and that Flandin had deterred him. In any case, the French generals had said they would not take the responsibility of intervention without a full-scale mobilization; there was no striking force ready to conduct a limited war. The Ministers feared the effect of full-scale mobilization upon the electorate, and the British refrained from encouraging—or refused to support, or threatened to oppose, according to how you hear the story—unilateral French action. And so the Germans walked over, trembling inwardly because they knew they were not prepared to fight a war.

The Flandin I knew told me that he had flown to London at the moment of crisis, in the first week of March, 1936, to rally Stanley Baldwin, the British Prime Minister, to joint action, or at least to a pledge of support if France moved. "When I arrived," he said, "I was told I could not see Baldwin. He had gone down to Worcestershire for a week to see the cherry trees in bloom." It must have been an early season for cherries.

Flandin's later effort at Vichy was more creditable. In 1936, when he had a chance to stop Hitler, he had funked it. But in

1940, when he hadn't a chance, he at least tried to maintain an illusion of an independent foreign policy, and Otto Abetz, the German gauleiter in France, had him fired. His career does not lend itself easily to succinct explanation.

The way I became acquainted with M. Flandin needs a bit of recounting. On a day early in February of 1943, I was sitting at a sheet-metal table in front of the Hotel Aletti, in downtown Algiers, writing a letter. In those days, it was pleasant to sit at a table in the open in Algiers; there were no patrols of chaps with tommy guns walking about in single file, as they do now, rotating their heads as if a *fellagha* were lurking behind each potted palm, and looking over your shoulder to see what paper you are reading. There was a war on then, but between equals. In the evening, six or a dozen German planes would come over from Sicily and drop bombs in the harbor. Aside from that everything was quiet. The pilots' targets were the long piers sticking out into the sea, and as there was always a big anti-aircraft display, they usually dropped short and never overflew. Every Sunday, there was an inter-Allied parade—French, British, and American—and since Americans march so informally, our Army usually ran in a few tanks as its contribution. The Gaullistes, Jews, and other refugees from the mainland fraternized with the correspondents and the young officers; the rich *colons*—the European Algerians—who had collaborated with the Germans through Vichy, and were frightened, entertained the generals and the generals' political advisers. They had made a great deal of money exporting their oranges and wine to Germany, so they could afford to entertain in style. The soldiers fraternized as best they could. It was an era of good feeling.

The Aletti was a large, modern hotel, opened in 1930 to celebrate the centennial of the liberation of Algiers from its Turkish rulers by the French. (That is the official French version of what happened.) Every room had a bath, with hot water for one hour every morning, and you could have breakfast in bed if you felt like it. Breakfast consisted of a piece of gray bread, imitation coffee, and a saucer of thin, sugarless fruit jam. If you enjoyed hotel life, though, and had been deprived of it for a long time, this was better than getting up

early to eat scrambled reconstituted dried eggs in an officers'
mess a block away. The Aletti was under military control but
civilian management, which meant, in tangibles, that the room
was free but you paid for the breakfast. Correspondents and
transient officers who could find accommodations at the hotel
put up there. General Eisenhower and members of his headquarters lived aloof at the Saint George, an elegant hotel of
Anglo-Mauresque architecture atop the Hill of Mustapha. We
had a better time at the Aletti. Rooms were hard to come by if
you left town and then returned, as I continually did, but, by
luck, I had met an old friend when I first arrived in Algiers,
on Christmas Day—a Reuters correspondent named Dave
Brown, who was a permanent guest because he covered Allied
headquarters for his wire service in London. Brown's room,
facing the waterfront, had two beds in it. The waterfront side
of the Aletti had a minor drawback: it shook when the barrage
went up. As compensation, we had beauty. Every evening,
there were flowerpots of star shells and roman candles of
tracers—a hundred beehives suddenly profiled in intersecting
arcs. The racket stimulated the adrenals and gave the rear
echelons the happy illusion that they were in the war. Once, it
is true, a bomb landed on a pier right in front of the hotel—
without killing anybody—and the blast removed Brown's
window and blew him out of bed, but I was in Tunisia. There
is a Turkish proverb that goes, "The viper that doesn't sting
me, may he live a thousand years!"

    In the Algiers of 1943, there were swarms of Red Cross girls,
American psychological warriors, British political-warfare wal-
lahs, Foreign Office and Foreign Service chaps in military uniforms, generals trying to be diplomats, Quartermaster Corps
lieutenants in their late thirties keeping whole Algérois families, naval aides of generals, military aides of admirals, French
liaison officers with the Americans, American liaison officers
with the French, R.A.F. liaison officers with the Air Forces,
and enough newspapermen and newpaperwomen to write, simultaneously, full accounts of a royal wedding, the Olympic
games, the World Series, a Presidential internal obstruction,
and four headless-torso mysteries. There were Vichy statesmen
being squired about by Britons who touted them as alterna-
tives to General de Gaulle, who was then confined to England

by joint action of the Foreign Office and the State Department. There were also Gaullistes who insisted that all other nuances of French were Fascists. There were Zionists who said that the Jews were the Allies' only sincere friends, and anti-Semites who said that having the Jews on our side would alienate both Christians and Moslems. There were royalists, including an antic Belgian princess who fed diplomats, and, for a few days, the Count of Paris himself. (He said that he would return to the French throne if he were drafted, but he wasn't.) All these, and a lot more, constantly plucked at the correspondents' sleeves. There were also, of course, Moslems—commonly referred to as "Ay-rabs"—in town, most of them working at the humblest jobs, but I cannot remember that they ever had much to say. They affected the general character of the place as little as the Puerto Ricans affect Rockefeller Center. Also, in chic bars—the Hotel Oasis was their favorite —there were great two-hundred-pound-and-upward dignitaries in wraparound headdresses with side drapes; white burnouses, which resemble shower curtains; purple silk gandurahs, which are blouses; and baggy white duck séroual, which are trousers, with shiny European shoes showing underneath like the cloven hoof. They smoked cigars that must have cost black-market fortunes, and knocked back a comfortable quantity of champagne, and all of them looked like the character called the Sheik in the old comic strip "Barney Google." When Americans remarked, as every American was sure to, that they had thought Moslems didn't drink in public, a Frenchman who "knew the country" was sure to explain that the big fellows were *chorfa*—members of *cherifian*, or saintly, families, descended from particularly venerable relatives of the Prophet. "They do as they please on earth; they will be judged in Heaven," the expert always expounded. "It is not for mere man to judge a hereditary saint." He would add, "They have great power over political opinion. They are venerated. They hold the people in the hollow of their hand." (In Paris last year, though, I got a different report on these fellows. I asked an old Algérois acquaintance, a police inspector, why the saints with cigars didn't stop the insurrection. "Oh, them," he said, laughing. "We call them the Beni Oui-Oui—the Tribe of Yes-Men. They're the ones we have to protect from the others.")

At any rate, there I was, sitting in front of the Aletti. I had just come from a battle in southern Tunisia that had been aborted for reasons that are still unclear. The plan had been to move east from Gafsa to the shore of the Gulf of Gabès, cutting the communications between Rommel's army, which was retreating westward from Libya, and von Arnim's, in Tunis, which it was retreating toward. Most of three new American divisions—one armored and two infantry—were committed; they moved forward awkwardly, against little opposition except strafing airplanes. Then, just as they were getting the feel of their work, the whole deal was called off—a discouraging initiation, since they had lost men for nothing. One battalion in the 9th Division did learn something; its Intelligence officer got out a mimeographed "lesson" sheet that began, "Confusion is normal in combat." The action was not the kind that inspired writing about, and that was my temporary dilemma. I had gone to Gafsa by jeep with another correspondent, Noland Norgaard, of the Associated Press, breaking the journey at Thélepte, a fighter field where we had good friends in the 33rd Pursuit Group. The 33rd had had a rough time in early January, when the Germans were over so often that, according to the 33rd's C.O., it looked as if Messerschmitts were patrolling his field. This time when we dropped in, the 33rd, after a great victory (ten planes downed), was in high fettle again, patrolling its own field and everything between the Southern Salt Lake and the Gulf of Gabès. The pilots came out of their dugouts to talk to us. They lived in a sort of prairie-dog village on the rim of the field; the earth heaped up at the entrance to each hole was camouflaged with alfa grass, which grows wild on the steppe and in peacetime is the chief export of that poverty-stricken region. It is used in the making of paper for banknotes.

I returned to Algiers from Gafsa without calling in again at Thélepte, so I did not know that six boys from the field had flown a sortie to protect an infantry advance in the Gabès offensive from an attack of thirty enemy planes; to die in protecting an advance that will be called back anyway is as normal as confusion. Five whom I remembered laughing in the sun were dead. But, not knowing this, I was in good spirits, because I myself was back in a lively, friendly city, so much more comfortable than Gafsa or Thélepte. It did not occur to me that our presence in North Africa was an intrusion, or that the wine merchants could have delivered the country from the Germans by themselves. This was a part of the French Fascist mythology that developed later.

As I drank wine and wrote my letter, a British officer approached my table, verified my identity, of which he was certain, and announced his, with which I was familiar. It was Captain Randolph Churchill, dressed in a Commando coverall that fitted like a green-grocer's bag around a single onion. We made a plump pair of rumpled amateur military figures; Algiers was full of such. Churchill, having accepted an invitation to have a glass of wine, began by saying that, for an American, I showed an astonishing understanding of the French, and that I wrote very good English for a fellow who wasn't English. I immediately began to like him. Churchill also said that he had heard I was a *bon vivant*, citing as his authority an Englishman who wouldn't know a *grenouille au vin blanc* from a toad-in-the-hole.

"*Monsieur mon Père*," he said, "has a friend on the Riviera here who has a *cordon-bleu* cook. Pierre-Etienne Flandin. Charming fellow, charming wife."

"Flandin?" I said. "The fellow who was Premier? I didn't know he was in North Africa."

"He came here shortly before the Allied landings," said *le fils de Monsieur son Père*. "Bought a place on the coast near Philippeville to grow wine. Living the life of a squire. Elder statesman, you know. Pleasure to talk to him, full of wisdom. *Monsieur mon Père* would like you to meet him."

This flattered me, because I had never met *Monsieur son Père*. I wondered if Flandin could be the candidate that *Monsieur son Père* was readying to pull out of the hat when the Allies, executing the Churchillian strategy of the long way around, finally arrived in France. The Allied heads of government did not like de Gaulle; Giraud wouldn't do; and Darlan had been shot—by a Gaulliste agent, according to the Americans, or by an American agent, according to de Gaulle. Of Flandin I remembered little from my newspaper reading between wars except that he was tall and had in his day been considered an Anglophile. But political speculation was not my specialty. I said I had a lot of writing to do and then wanted to return to the front, to the units I knew. (It was a small, intimate war, compared to what it afterward became, and personal loyalties were engaged.) Therefore I would have no time to visit M. Flandin.

Fils was prepared for that. He said that I could take my typewriter with me; the *domaine* of M. Fiandin was an ideal scenic retreat for literary composition. Also, it was in the east—about three hundred miles away—and thus well on my way to the front. "I have a new vehicle at my disposition," he said. "A lorry just out from England that I have to take to a Commando training site on M. Flandin's domain. We could be off tomorrow. If you get bored, I'll lend you the lorry and a driver any time, and you can pop off to the nearest airfield—it's at Constantine, I believe—and get a transport plane to where you're going."

Recklessly, I said that I would go. Churchill *fils*, I knew, had spent several months in a hospital the previous spring after overturning a car in Egypt, and it didn't occur to me that the British Army would let him drive. I expected him to have a driver, but when I brought my gear to the front of the Aletti at the appointed hour the next day, I found him alone and triumphantly smiling in the high cab of a khaki Bedford lorry; his driver, Corporal Williams, he said, was out at the camp catching up on his Commando training. I, a non-driver myself, found no reason to take exception to *Fils*'s performance at the wheel, though it did seem a bit odd to me once when he tried to go around a two-and-a-half-ton General Motors truck on a *corniche* road and the driver, a Moslem soldier, crashed his truck into the cliffside in order to avoid putting us over the edge. The driver had been trying his best to stay ahead of us, apparently in the futile hope of getting to the next widening of the road, but his truck was heavy-laden with 105-howitzer shells, while our Bedford was racing-light. "Get on with it, get on!" I could hear *Fils* saying impatiently when we were within a foot of the G.M.'s tailboard, and I thought at first that his plan was to hurdle the truck, but he decided to pass with our starboard wheels over the abyss. We made it, thanks to the truck driver's choice of two evils, but there after the Bedford limped slightly on the near forewheel.

In the evening, we reached a place called Azazga, in the coastal region of Kabylia, where there was a comfortable hotel (*des Touristes*, thirteen rooms), as un-African in aspect as possible, being built of wood in a mountain-summer-resort style. Azazga was in a forest a couple of thousand feet above sea level. Here it was winter again, and cold. The proprietress, a French-woman, operated the hotel alone with her Kabyle servants; the only guests in residence when we arrived were another woman and her several small daughters—a family from Algiers who had retired into the country because of the superior nourishment available, the mother told me. Rationing, she said, was strict and black-market food dear in the city, swollen with a couple of hundred thousand refugees from the mainland. Kabylia was undernourished, too, but money went farther there than in the city, and there were no air raids. Both the British First Army and the American II Corps fronts were hundreds of miles away. Clearly, there was little sense of war and none of danger in a region that is now a center of the Algerian revolt, swarming with troops unable to control the country. It was idyllic. The Kabyle villages, of stone and mud, crowned the crests of high, sharp ridges that fell away into valleys seldom wide enough to run a road through. The Kabyles terraced and farmed the slopes, which were hard for a European to climb without using his hands. Their poverty was already intolerable, but armed dissidence in Kabylia did not exist.

Kabyles are Berbers, the descendants of the Numidians who were the opponents, the mercenaries, and, at times, the allies of Carthage—now exacting tribute from the Semitic city, now paying it, until the city disappeared, as intruders in Kabylia always have. When Islam was an expanding imperialism, the Arabs conquered the Berbers on the plains but never in the mountains. The Kabyles profess the faith, but in many regions they speak no Arabic. They are of the same aboriginal Mediterranean strain as the Sicilians and the Sardinians, the Calabrians and the Maltese, and Islam in Kabylia is like the Catholicism of the Calabrian mountains—a label and a banner covering old pagan place cults. On the north shore of the sea, the local deities have taken the names of Christian saints; in Kabylia, those of Mohammedan saints—the Marabouts.

Azazga is only about a hundred miles from the Aletti, but Churchill and I agreed that we might not find so comfortable a place to stay if we pushed on. "The feature of my military record of which I am proudest," Churchill said, "is that I have never, even in the most difficult circumstances, found myself compelled to sleep in a bed without two clean sheets." It was hard for me to control my admiration. I had always cherished the same objective, but in the part of Tunisia where I had lately campaigned I had been unable to find a bed, or even a cot. I had graded billets by the hardness or softness of the floors, and outdoor sleeping surfaces by the geological quality of the terrain. As for sheets, when Lieutenant-General Anderson, the commander of the British First Army, visited Gafsa, the American battalion there had to borrow a pair from the local bordello to tuck the General in. When the Germans and Italians launched a brief delaying offensive and we abandoned Gafsa temporarily, the madame and her *pensionnaires* departed in a truck to escape the embraces of the invaders, for whose currency they saw no future in Africa.

The hotel at Azazga was comfortable and *familial*, although we didn't get a meal worth remembering. Philippeville was about two hundred and twenty miles away by road, and we made it by twilight the next day. The *domaine* of M. Flandin, Churchill explained en route, was on the other side of a rather large mountain just beyond Philippeville, and was accessible only by a tricky unpaved road that twisted all the way. If the lorry went into a ditch, we would be benighted on the mountain. He suggested that we stay over with some friends he had made in Philippeville—the family of Senator Paul Cuttoli, a statesman who had once represented the Department of Constantine in the Upper House of the French legislature. In the Department of Constantine, as in Mississippi, only a small percentage of the population voted. A few great families of proprietors, with a firm grip on agricultural credit, could bring the small European farmers to heel as they wished, and the only political competition was among the big fellows, some of whom even gave themselves the luxury of being left-of-center in Paris—on all save Algerian issues. Cuttoli, a Corsican, had been one of these prewar liberals, I think, but he had voted at Vichy for the abolition of the Republic, and had then retired to Algeria to cultivate his oranges and vines. The great man was not at home—he had business interests all over Algeria—but his family made us welcome to the palace. There were daughters, daughters-in-law, and assorted children, besides the Moslem Servants, who, I did not need to be told, were devoted-because-they-were-understood. I had been over the same line of country in another hemisphere. "A question of race," one of the ladies said. "They are just like children." (St. Augustine was a Berber from Bône, the next port east along the coast.) Churchill and I dined with the family, and well. Later, in a redundant wing of the enormous house, we briefly visited the senior officers' mess of the Philippeville Base Section of the British First Army. Base Section messes in all armies are dull. By day, the officers composing them perform useful work, but, as nearly as can be arranged, it is what they have done in civilian life. Pier superintendents pier-superintend, railroaders railroad, bookkeepers bookkeep, and people in the amorphous category known simply as "executives" try desperately to conceal their inutility, exactly as they do in their offices at home. In the British Army, this last maneuver is executed behind a huge mustache. In the evening, all these uniformed but otherwise undisguised civilians meet and intermittently talk military slang, like schoolboys who have agreed to converse in pig Latin but lapse into normal speech when they get interested in what they are saying. Homesickness without the distraction of fear is the leitmotiv, and the perpetually imminent failure of the supply of strong liquor is the recurrent topic of conversation.

The mess at Philippeville was no exception. The city offered few diversions—not even subjects for photography. It was entirely modern—all built by the French during the past century—with checkerboard streets, and villas in the mainland suburban taste. There were sixty thousand inhabitants—Europeans transplanted for two or three generations, and the Kabyles who worked for them. Among the Europeans, those of Italian and Corsican descent were the most numerous. Corsica, like Kabylia, or Kerry, is a poor country. Its sons, like Kabyles and Kerrymen, migrate to find work. But whereas the Kabyle men, in peacetime, go to France as manual laborers and send their earnings home, the Corsican comes to North Africa as a *petit fonctionnaire*—a cop or a postman—and brings his family with him. In the nineteenth century, his scale of living was not inordinately superior to the Kabyle's before they changed places, but when he arrived in Africa he found himself with a tidy *situation*, as well as caste and authority. French government employees serving in Africa receive a supplement of one-third of their base pay—a combined inducement to leave home and compensation for the supposed additional expense of colonial life. (Actually, for a hundred years, living in Algeria or Tunisia has been cheaper than living in France, and the coastal climate is not greatly different from that of Ajaccio or Bastia.) The *fonctionnaires* developed a vested, hereditary interest in their jobs. A livelier, richer, and more important—and, in the end, even a more populous—Corsica grew up in North Africa, like the Magna Graecia that grew up in Italy. (When Corsica itself was taken over by the Algerian Committee of Public Safety this spring, it was a reannexation of Little Old Corsica to Big New Corsica.) The *fonctionnaires*, as they retired on pension, took to farming. Their descendants, too numerous for government jobs, exploited the soil and branched out into sardine fishing, business, the professions. The *fonctionnaire* caste does not consist of Corsicans exclusively, although they are its symbols; Marshal Juin's father, for example, was a French-French gendarme at Bône. The caste's proprietary feeling about its jobs is so strong that in 1956, when Robert Lacoste, the French Governor-General, suggested that half of all government jobs be reserved, in principle, for Moslems, who constitute eight-ninths of the population, there were student riots in Algiers. The demonstrations, naturally, were encouraged by the demonstrators' cousins, the police, who had the jobs. Even in the midst of a national revolt, they couldn't visualize a time when they might have to share them with "*les indigènes*." The Cuttolis were a glorious example of Corsicans who had it made; the Senator's bedchamber, which I was permitted to view, was a replica of one of Napoleon's.

The next day, Churchill and I went around the mountain. He put the lorry into the ditch only once, but we were fortunately within hailing distance of a road gang—a score or so of barefoot Kabyles. They got us onto the road again by taking hold of the wheels and heaving. Happily, we encountered no vehicle coming in our direction, and after an hour or less we descended into a pirate's cove, about a mile across, where a stream ran down into the sea between two mountains. There was a crescent beach cupped in the amphitheatre of curving mountain flanks. The valley, wide at the beach, where it was nearly level, narrowed as it climbed into the interior. It was the broadest expanse of terrain I had seen since leaving Algiers, and much of it, I noticed, was under neat vines. There was a low, wide-spreading white house on the west side of the cove, and out near the eastern headland there was a clump of tents— the Commando camp. "Splendid place for landing exercises," Churchill said. "Hidden. Pity the chaps haven't a boat." He had selected the site himself, he said, while visiting the Flandins, and then had had a bit of a time selling the idea to his superiors. I could see that the place offered advantages for small-scale amphibious maneuvers—not only concealment and a shelving beach but rocks to be scaled, which are a *sine qua non* of all Commando operations. ("If there are no cliffs to climb, move to another part of the coast and ruddy well find some" was, I believe, the first rule in the Commando tactical manual.)

We headed for the white house, and when we arrived, M. and Mme. Flandin were waiting for us on a trellised terrace in front of the door. The former Président du Conseil was extraordinarily tall—six feet five, according to one obit I read the other day, or six feet six, according to another. That would have made him an inch or two taller than General de Gaulle, whom the newspapers have agreed to call six feet four. Flandin didn't look as tall as de Gaulle, though, because he didn't hold himself—as de Gaulle's aides used to say of their boss—"as if he had swallowed his sabre." Nor was he exaggeratedly narrow, like the de Gaulle of those days; Flandin had already acquired the abdominal convexity that shows only in new photos of de Gaulle. His face was a mottled pink—amiable, slack, and reconciled to age, like that of a merchant of wines retired to the country. It was at once dignified, sly, and tired, though he could have been only in his mid-fifties. I found it hard to imagine him thrusting his way back onto the international stage, or even rolling in from the wings with both Churchills pushing from behind. He wore the loose garments, made of a material that approaches mattress ticking, that drape the old-fashioned Algerian planter at home. Mme. Flandin's head reached his shoulder; she was as tall for a woman as he was for a man. She was one of those massive, square-shouldered Frenchwomen who have style without chic, and charm without seduction. *Monsieur le Fils* had told me, en route, that she was of a ranking family of the office-holding bourgeoisie; her brother had been French Ambassador to Poland at the beginning of the war. M. Flandin was of the same caste; his father had been a lawyer, a deputy, a professor of law, a judge, and, as the climax of his career, Resident-General in Tunisia from 1918 to 1920.

The Flandins were delightful hosts. There was nothing to do but talk, except for a bit of drinking, and it was soon clear that M. Flandin had no political plans that he wanted to impart to me. He must have been completely puzzled by my intrusion into his oenological retreat. I decided within the first hour of my visit that Churchill *père* had never heard of me and that his son had brought me along merely because he wanted company. M. Flandin must have set my presence down simply as a whim of the unpredictable *fils* of the *père* upon whose good will his safety depended—for Flandin clearly saw then, as could anybody with a tithe of his shrewdness, that the Allies would win the war. He himself had neither adhered to the Germans, like Laval, nor resisted, like Reynaud—to name two other prominent members of his own Alliance Démocratique (conservative). His status was equivocal, depending on the victors' interpretation of the position he had not taken. If decent Frenchmen had unanimously refused to participate in the Pétain regime when France collapsed in 1940, he said to me at lunch, trying to explain his course, the country would have been left entirely at the mercy of crooks and gangsters; it had therefore been the duty of Frenchmen who were neither to continue serving the state. This was a civil servant's point of view. Throughout, Flandin's career had been of a piece with his conduct in 1936, when the precocious blossoming of the cherry trees prevented him from saving Europe. He had thought clearly, and in large terms. He had expressed himself lucidly and convincingly, and then had failed to act. He had physical courage; during the First World War he flew a fighter plane when it required nerve even to get in one. He had the principles of the caste of high civil servants—personal honor, service to the state—but he could not compete with types like Laval in the ignoble catch-as-catch-can of French politics between wars, and he lacked the political conviction that enabled a Léon Blum occasionally to dominate such types. I have since read, in Robert Aron's excellent "Histoire de Vichy," that at the joint session of the National Assembly convoked by Pétain and Laval in July, 1940, to abolish the Constitution of the Third Republic, Flandin's defense of republican institutions was superb. He annihilated the crafty, horse-trading arguments of Laval, who had preceded him on the rostrum. But he finished by voting for the abolition of the Republic, on the ground that the Nazis would abolish it if the delegates didn't.

A few months before the Allies came to Africa, M. Flandin told me, the idea had occurred to him to move there, so he had traded an estate he had in Burgundy for the one near Philippeville, where he cultivated five hundred acres of vines. He was not the only French statesman to experience such an intimation; Darlan had arrived three days before the landing. For Flandin, no role in the provisional government of North Africa had yet been announced—and, as things turned out, none ever was to be. It is possible that Churchill *père* and Roosevelt planned a whole series of mild ameliorations of the alternative-to-de Gaulle regime, but the General forced their hand the next summer, and the moment for Flandin's entrance never came. He remained in the wings awaiting a cue that had been cut from the script.

After a long midday meal—a *déjeuner dînatoire*, as the French used to say long ago—M. Flandin took a siesta, and I went walking on the hillside that overlooked the bay. It was covered with a scrub growth that was as yet merely lush; in April and May it would be a jungle, in July and August sere and brown. The goat paths were easy to follow. There were wild boar on the mountain, but I could not distinguish their trails from the others. Occasionally, I met men or women carrying bundles of brush for firewood; they were submerged peasant types, more like emaciated Calabrians than like the sometimes spectacular Bedouins I had met in the south, in Tunisia—the women in their red robes stalking along, distaff in hand and spinning as they walked, the hawk-visaged men riding their small, wiry horses up and down a line of burdened camels. Those spoke Arabic, and would sometimes fall upon a lone man on the steppe—a pilot who had bailed out, for instance. I felt no menace in these northern peasants, in a region settled by the French for nearly a hundred years. Yet there was no joy in them, either; they reminded me of Indians on small reservations in the Eastern states, who have lost their Indian qualities for a sub-Caucasian shabbiness.

I scrambled about for an hour and returned to the house, with a virtuous feeling of having exercised, to find the Flandins sitting down to tea—an English custom they had adopted early in life, Madame said. Churchill had gone off to report to his commanding officer in the Commando camp on the austerity side of the cove. This gave me an opportunity to listen to somebody else, and I asked M. Flandin if he would have time, after tea, to tell me what he thought were the causes of the French debacle—a subject that obsessed and puzzled me, because I had lived through it in Paris three years earlier, incredulously watching the collapse, without anything so dignified as a crash, of what I had thought was permanent. The debacle had descended suddenly and with a hint of fraud, as when a circus tent falls in on the audience because the management has used old, frayed guy ropes. At the time, overestimating the strength of the tent, I had overestimated the strength of the blast that blew it down—the Nazi attack. In the light of what I had learned in the intervening years, the collapse had become increasingly mysterious. I was more interested in that than I was in M. Flandin's future, if any; he had been close to the management. M. Flandin said graciously that he would be glad to explain, after we had had our tea, and when the Kabyle servant had removed the cups and Madame had excused herself, he said, "I can put it in the simplest terms this way: The great industrialists, the men of the cartels, made their last investment in democracy at the time of the general elections of 1932. André Tardieu was their man then—a brilliant fellow, but with a gift for making enemies. They did all they could for him—bought the press, bribed every deputy and every elector who could be bribed." (Flandin had served in the Tardieu government.) "When Tardieu was badly beaten in 1932, the big industrialists gave up on the electoral system. They said, 'What has the Republic come to when you can't even buy an election? Evidently, it is time to change the system of government.' Being French, they felt particularly bad because they had wasted so much money. So they began to back the French Fascist movements—Colonel Casimir de La Rocque, Doriot, all that, with Chiappe, of course, running the show." (Chiappe had been the arch-Corsican chief of the Paris police.) "They mounted the riots of February, 1934, expecting to take power by a coup d'état. The coup didn't come off. Then they gave up on accomplishing anything from inside France and decided to wait for the Germans. The French Hitlers were ersatz. But across the frontier they saw the real thing."

From Flandin, a conservative by birth and in politics, a statement so unqualified astonished me. I noted it down immediately; opinion has therefore had no opportunity to deform memory. I asked him if the accession of Léon Blum's Front Populaire government in 1936 (which Flandin had bitterly opposed) had decided the industrialists' course—"better Hitler than Blum"—but he said that that had nothing to do with it; they had made up their minds two years earlier.

"In the nineteenth century," M. Flandin continued, "France changed its form of government twice under the impulsion of national defeat. Defeat ended the First Empire, and defeat ended the Second Empire. The men of the cartels told themselves that defeat was essential to overthrow the Third Republic." (It was a thought that recurred to me in the nineteen-fifties, when the French Right insisted on the policies that made defeat inevitable in Indo-China, in Egypt, and in North Africa.) M. Flandin was perhaps correct in saying that Blum and his social reforms had not alienated the Right, which had made its mind up. The good, comfortable bourgeois in the middle of the road, like him, were the ones Blum had alienated, so that they withdrew from the struggle. I did not need to ask him why he had been counted among the appeasers in the years after 1936. I knew he would have said that he wished to avoid war, for which France was unprepared, and the inevitable defeat, and the consequent rule of the defeatists.

The colloquy could only have ended in a wrangle—and M. Flandin was a gracious host and down on his luck.

I turned the conversation to my stroll. M. Flandin said that though his scarecrow workmen looked miserable, they really weren't. It was an illusion. "The Arab wants nothing better," he said. He called all North Africans Arabs, although few in his region could understand a word of Arabic beyond the Koranic texts they had learned by rote. "If you give an Arab your old clothes, he will show up for work next day in his usual rags," he went on. "If you paid him better, he would work only one day a week. The rest of the week he would sit in a *café maure* talking." It would have occurred to M. Flandin, if he had been thinking with his French-French mind, that the "Arab" sold the clothes because he could not afford to retain anything salable, but in Africa the French of the mainland cease to reason; he was telling me what he had been told by chaps who "knew the country," like the ones in Algiers who were always ready to explain the power of the *chorfa*. In the region of Philippeville in August, 1955, there occurred a horrifying massacre of Europeans by these happy agricultural natives, and the mountains between Philippeville and the port of Collo, to the west, have never since been won back to French control. It was a striking example of Numidian ingratitude. In the fourth century, when Romans were the European landowners in this same province of Africa, the region was ravaged by a rebellion of the Kabyle workmen, who were called *circumcelliones* (dwellers in Hoovervilles)—a term that had the same significance for Rome that the term *dissidents*, of the current French communiqués, has for Paris.

That evening, when Churchill had returned from his military service, we had a dinner liberally moistened with the produce of the vineyard, which was, as I remember it, barely promising. Neither the wines nor the vines themselves were old, the Flandins apologized, but there was a plenitude of cognac after the meal. One of the subjects that Churchill and I got onto was Sir Oswald Mosley, the leader of the prewar British Black Shirts, who, with other British Fascists, was being held prisoner by *Monsieur son Père* under a war-time security act known as 18-B. *Fils* was for turning him loose, because he no longer represented a threat to security, and holding him longer actually constituted punishment for his beliefs. I was for keeping him in, to show that we weren't condoning Fascism now that we had it licked. *Fils* then acted out a charade in which he impersonated the spirit of habeas corpus. "*Je suis l'esprit de habeas corpus,*" he said, "*et cet homme-là est* in jail." He pointed to an imaginary presence in an empty chair. "*Moi, je* kick him bloody well out." And he kicked the chair. The Flandins maintained a polite fiction of interest and amusement.

Next morning, heavy with remorse for having imposed my presence on the Flandins, and also for having wasted four working days, I walked down to the Commando motor pool and looked up Corporal Williams, Churchill's driver. I told him that Captain Churchill had authorized him to drive me to Constantine in the Bedford, so that I could make a plane connection for our front. (I based this on what Churchill had said before we took off.) The Corporal was delighted. He said that he had to take the Bedford down to Constantine, where the Royal Army Service Corps had proper repair shops, in any case. "We can't put her right here," he said. "There's something gone vitally wrong. Bloody shame, too, when we need transport so. Might I inquire, sir, if anything out of the way occurred on your journey up here?"

"Nothing at all," I said. "I expect the inspection in the works is lax in wartime."

"I daresay, sir," the Corporal said, "but she do look as if she'd been knocked about frightful."

We had a pleasant and uneventful forty-five-mile drive to Constantine in second gear.

In the light of much that has happened since, the journey to the *domaine* of M. Flandin no longer seems wasted. I looked again at his newsprint face in the *Times* and recognized one of my instructors in contemporary history.

The New Yorker, September 13, 1958

The Beginning of the End

Booked about war fall into two classes—those about what it was like and those about what happened. The what-it-was-like books appear first, because they are subjective and require no digging; they record only the reactions of their authors to what they thought was happening. The military historians come along later to tell what did happen, which inevitably differs from what even the participants remember. It is like running off an old fight film slowly. The bets have long been paid off, but curiosity is at last gratified. How the result was at last obtained is at last apparent. Arguments twenty years old are resolved or protracted on the basis of new evidence. To the satisfaction of knowing what decided the event is then added the sport of speculation on what might have happened if something else hadn't. And while the military historian is generally the soberest of writers, trying not to transmit emotion but to eliminate it, his book must for many a reader play the role of the matter-of-fact entries in an old diary rediscovered.

A sentence like "Middleton's VIII Corps finally secured La Haye-du-Puits on July 8" evokes, for me, a Chinese-American pfc. in a company command post in an abandoned *estaminet*, drunk on a bottle of *eau-de-vie* he had salvaged intact from the broken majority behind the bar. The brandy and the fragile walls gave him the illusion of security while the town burned all around. A hundred yards away, a dead S.S. officer sat in a wicker garden chair on the terrace in front of a small château, his field glasses in his lap. He had been looking down the road for American tanks that were nearer than he thought. The men pronounced the place Hooey da Pooey.

Or, "Although St.-Lô was taken, it was by no means safe" brings back the sensation of lying on cobblestones, face down, and looking up to steal a glance at the man lying in front of you, noticing that his eyes were closed, like those of a girl waiting to be kissed. Yet he was a brave man, always pushing to get out in front. And a sequin of red-hot metal, too tiny to do harm, floating down before your eyes and lodging on the cloth

of his trouser leg, where it made a hole like a very small cigarette burn. Or the Army driver, frozen to the wheel of his jeep
by distaste for shellfire, who imperilled his passengers' lives
and his own more on the slippery road coming out of St.-Lô
than the German shells had done within it. He could not bring
himself to slow down in the face of the oncoming tanks, and
the passengers remembered Tom Treanor, the correspondent
who had been chewed up by tank treads in the same circumstances a few days earlier.

Or, "The 18th Infantry cleared Marigny on the morning of
27 July" recalls an ancient donkey, bearded and with hoofs,
overgrown because of inactivity, that were shaped like wooden
shoes, who was the sole occupant of the stone farmhouse
when Divisional Artillery headquarters moved in that night.

Still later than the what-happened books come the disdainful hindsight writers, to say what the uncultivated commanders
should have done, and what would have happened then. Unlike the generals, who, they say, are always fighting the last war,
these writers are usually writing the war before last, which
gives them an advantage.

Official Army histories are what-happened books. The
operations of the Office of the Chief of Military History, Department of the Army, are therefore as constantly deliberate as
those of General George Brinton McClellan, the old Civil War
slowpoke. In its advance across France from the beachheads of
1944, however, the Office has outdone itself in lack of haste.
Its narrative of the Second World War got to the base of the
Cotentin Peninsula in 1951 (seven years after the Army left
there) with "Cross-Channel Attack," the official history of
D Day and the campaign up to July 1, 1944, by Gordon A.
Harrison—an excellent piece of work. With "Breakout and
Pursuit," by Martin Blumenson, published more recently, it
reaches the line achieved by about September 1, 1944, having
thus consumed a dozen years (without enemy opposition, at
that) in covering ground that it took the Allies two months to
traverse. Mr. Blumenson—like Harrison, a civilian historian
under Army charter—has also brought out, hot on the heels of
"Breakout," a private venture called "The Duel for France,
1944" (Houghton Mifflin), which is a tighter and less cluttered
treatment of his official work, shortened from seven hundred

and forty-eight to four hundred and thirty-two pages. (This diminution is, for the war buff, a dead loss, since Blumenson has achieved the cut largely by omitting the footnotes, with their citations of sources.)

The British military historians of the campaign of France, even slower off the mark than ours (they have caught a bit of the old Montgomery spirit), landed *their* armies on French soil only last fall, eleven years after "Cross-Channel Attack," but caught up with the Americans in one sedate bound by doing June–September in a single piece—"Victory in the West, Volume I. The Battle of Normandy" (five hundred and ninety-five pages), in the History of the Second World War series, issuing from Her Majesty's Stationery Office. The new histories bring the Allies into line again as they were when the glorious summer ended—stretching from Antwerp down to the Swiss border. The British component is by Major L. F. Ellis, plus lieutenant Colonel A. E. Warhurst, Air Chief Marshal Sir James Robb, and Captain G. R. G. Allen, Royal Navy. The collective eighteen hundred and sixty-two pages of "Cross-Channel," "Breakout," and "Victory in the West I" include the German side of the story, too, since the Allied historians had full use of the losers' records, including even personal telephone conversations.

An unfortunate result of the long lapse between the appearances of "Cross-Channel" and "Breakout" is that during it popular history has dramatized D Day until even the veriest child knows that John Wayne and Robert Mitchum, double-handed but with the support of a notable cast including Richard Burton and Red Buttons, captured the beachhead in the noisiest battle ever recorded on tape, in the cinemepic epidrama "The Longest Day." Undeterred by the hideous sounds of war, Wayne and Mitchum planted Old Glory on the hills, where it shall rest in memory and press sheets until the sun shall no more gild them, and after the great moment in that great saga when the extras, strung out for several miles, file over the captured ridge in the wake of the explosion of Mitchum's bangalore torpedo—effective area five hundred square feet—it will come to millions as an anticlimax to learn that the scoundrel foe contiuued to resist. The best-seller "The Longest Day," on which the interminable movie was based, leaned heavily on "Cross-Channel" for facts, but by the time Harrison's sober soldiers got to the screen they had been transmogrified into ham and the battle into cowboys-and-Indians in tin hats, and the German defenders sat out along the skyline like ducks in a shooting gallery. The trouble on the off-screen D Day was that one couldn't see them.

Only a sequel with Wayne as General George S. Patton and Elvis Presley as his aide-de-camp can interest the public in the rest of the war in France. And to get the idea across, the sequel, which I have tentatively titled "Blood and Guts," must, like "Longest Day," have a theme song, this one to be sung by Presley. This lack is what Hanson W. Baldwin, the eminent military critic of the *Times*, must have had in mind when he wrote, in his review of "Breakout and Pursuit," "The battle does not sing."

Off-screen a battle lurches along until it comes to a series of grinding jerks, like a train entering a Long Island Rail Road station. Then, just as those involved think it will lurch again, it stops. This was the situation of the Allies in that September, when the British and American campaign histories end. "No one knew it yet," Mr. Blumenson writes on page 696 of "Breakout," "but the pursuit was over." By that time, the Allies had cleared all France and almost destroyed the German armies that fought there, but they had then "lost" their opponent, as the fight fans say when a boxer hasn't finished his man. *Generalleutnant* Hans Speidel, chief-of-staff of the German armies in the West, was to write in 1949 that the Allies, if they had pushed their pursuit hard enough, could have ended the war six months earlier, and many Allied officers agree with him. The campaign histories are therefore narratives of an unparalleled success coupled with a partial failure. The failure has had historical consequences far more important than they seemed then, and these, though unexpressed by either Mr. Blumenson or Major Ellis, lend a constant undertone to their disagreements.

Major Ellis, naturally, writes more fully of British operations than of American, and Mr. Blumenson more fully of American than of British. Each, however, pauses frequently to dress his line on the Ally as the armies make their joint advance. The difference in their styles reflects the one between the British and American Army zones in France; Ellis, disciplined and conventionally military, is likely to say things like "Not without difficulty, the division reached its objective," while Blumenson, a gabby sort of writer, is sure to tell you what the difficulty was and to relate the inevitable squabble about the blame. The personalities of British officers seldom enter into Ellis's narrative, while Blumenson likes to talk about American officers and to quote their comments on one another. Ellis, as a consequence, often seems to be writing about an army of digits, identifying corps and divisions moving by some inner mechanism, while Blumenson's army consists of people, most of them not used to being at war.

I once read a small mimeographed pamphlet put out by a battalion Intelligence officer whose unit had been engaged for the first time in Tunisia. Its title was "Lessons to be Learned from the combat at S——," and the first one was "Confusion in combat is normal." I therefore prefer Blumenson's discursive narrative to Ellis's neatly buttoned account; war is of its nature digressive, exasperating, and easy to conduct only in retrospect, when, all the hole cards having been turned up, it becomes clear what the generals betting against them should have done. Major General Robert C. Macon's words to the green 83rd Division, which he commanded, had no effect on the course of the campaign, since nobody obeyed, but I am glad Blumenson includes them:

In mid-afternoon a regimental commander reported infiltrating enemy. "They won't hurt you any," Macon promised. "They shoot us," the regimental commander explained. . . . By evening the General was shouting, "To hell with the [enemy] fire, to hell with what's on your flank, get down there and take the area. You don't need any recon. You have got to go ahead. You have got to take that objective if you have to go all night." . . . But telephonic exhortation, no matter how pertinent, could not blow down the defended hedgerows.

This was not a reflection on American troops in particular. Five weeks later, *Generalfeldmarschall* Guenther von Kluge, commander of the German Army of the West, was shouting to *Generaloberst* Alfred Jodl, Hitler's Chief of Staff, on a telephone line that stretched from France to East Prussia, "No matter how many orders are issued, the troops cannot, are not able to, are not strong enough to defeat the enemy. It would be a fateful error to succumb to a hope that cannot be fulfilled, and no power in this world [can accomplish its will simply] through an order it may give. That is the situation." A few days later, he killed himself with cyanide.

Determination will carry the soldier only as far as the place where he dies, and few soldiers care to go quite that far.

In the first week of July, when the 83rd and many another division floundered, the Allied line ran for roughly seventy miles across the Cotentin Peninsula, a minute part of France, from about Bayeux and the Channel on the east to about St.-Sauveur-le-Vicomte and the Gulf of St.-Malo on the west. It faced not east, toward Germany, but south. The British-Canadian Twenty-first Army Group was on the eastern side of the line, the American First Army on the west. The armies in the peninsula struggled, like the djinni in the fisherman's bottle, to push out the cork, and they were having small success.

The chain of command devised for the occasion was odd. General Eisenhower, still in England, was Supreme Commander, but General Bernard Montgomery, British, was commander of the Twenty-first Army Group. As such he was superior by a rung to General Omar Nelson Bradley, of the American First Army, which was, however, about equal to the Group in size. General Montgomery enthusiastically endorsed what he construed to be the American theory of command, which emphasized the autonomy of the field commander, whom he construed to be himself. This practically freed him of Eisenhower. (But he rather objected to leaving similar independence to Bradley.) He therefore claimed full credit for anything his Group accomplished, anything Bradley accomplished, and anything he himself *didn't* accomplish, on the ground that his unaccomplishment was meant to help Bradley. At the same time, as a British officer operating within two hundred miles of Whitehall and under the British theory of command which allowed less autonomy, he was under the thumb of Sir Alan Brooke, Chief of the Imperial General Staff, who didn't figure in the SHAEF table of organization at all.

The German generals opposite these forces were strategically handcuffed and limited to minor tactical decisions, because Hitler, even farther from the front than Eisenhower, ran their war by telephone, and they could do nothing of consequence while his receiver was off the hook. If the tolerant Eisenhower was General King Log, the interfering Hitler was General King Stork, which for an army at the end of a telephone line is far worse.

The first theme of disagreement between Blumenson and Ellis is Goodwood, the offensive that Montgomery's Army Group launched, behind a vast interallied bombardment, against the right wing of the German line on July 18th. His intention, Supreme Allied Headquarters back in Britain believed, was to shatter the Germans at the shoulder and then race on toward Falaise, Argentan, the Seine, and Paris. They believed this because Montgomery had induced them to by a series of letters to Eisenhower and his Deputy Commander, Air Chief Marshal Tedder, that are impossible of misconstruction. Montgomery later disclaimed any such aspiration, but if nomenclature can be adduced in evidence, Goodwood, named for a summer English race meeting, bespoke an ambition to go galloping on. The Twenty-first Army Group got away from the barrier well, with tanks in front—an unhappy innovation. But, met head-on by massed German armor, it ground to a stop after five blood-sodden miles, having lost thirty-six per cent of the British armored vehicles on the Continent—five hundred tanks knocked out—and six or seven thousand men. Montgomery had proposed the attack, and Eisenhower, in a letter quoted by Blumenson, had hoped it would be decisive. It was, in his expectation, to be coördinated "like a left hook—followed by a right cross" with Cobra, the American offensive planned by Bradley, which was intended to hit the left of the German line a day or two later.

Cobra was to prove, in Blumenson's words, "the key maneuvre from which a large part of the subsequent campaign in Europe developed." But if Goodwood had succeeded, the *double* rupture of the line, exploited by American *and* British armies, might have resulted in the encirclement and annihilation of the German armies in France by August 1st, instead of their near-encirclement and near-annihilation three weeks later, chiefly as a result of the singlehanded American success.

In the first case—the double rupture—the Allies, no matter how dilatory, could hardly have failed to get deep into the Reich that summer, and the Germans at home, no matter how quickly they reacted, could hardly have set up an effective defense in time to keep the Allies out of Berlin that fall. But the German *réplique* would in all likelihood have been a bit slow, because the attempt to assassinate Hitler, in the course of which he was wounded, occurred on July 20th. I have never seen it printed that Allied intelligence was connected directly enough with the German plotters to have synchronized the *attentat* with Goodwood and Cobra. I find it hard to believe, though, that the Allies did not sense that something was up.

Montgomery's failure may have been unavoidable, but he maddeningly insisted that his sanguinary misadventure had been intended not as a left hook but as a feint. This was as if the plotters had contended, after the event, that they had really wanted not to hurt Hitler but just to frighten him. Ellis offers in Montgomery's support a letter he sent on July 14th to Sir Alan Brooke, in Whitehall: "And so I have decided that the time has come to have a real 'showdown' on the Eastern flank, and to loose a corps of three armored divisions in the open country *about the Caen-Falaise road* [italics Ellis's]." This is an example of the difference between the British and American languages: to have a showdown, in American, surely means to go all the way.

On the same day, Ellis indicates, the British commander sent his aide, a Lieutenant Colonel Dawnay, to the War Office with this statement:

General Montgomery has to be very careful of what he does on his eastern flank because on that flank is the only *British* Army that is left in this part of the world [italics *mine*]. . . . Having broken out in the country southeast of Caen he has no intention of rushing madly eastwards and getting Second Army on the eastern flank so extended that that flank might cease to be secure. *All the activities on the eastern flank are designed to help the* [American] *forces in the west while ensuring that a firm bastion is kept in the east* [italics Ellis's]. At the same

time all is ready to take advantage of any situation which gives reason
to think that the enemy is disintegrating.

Blumenson's and Ellis's citations are not contradictory; they
may be mutually explanatory. Both the letter to Brooke and
Dawnay's message went to *exclusively British Army destinations* (italics mine), and the Imperial General Staff was still
haunted by the memory of Dunkerque, where Britain had
once before found herself "without an army in that part of the
world." If he were dealing with a strategos less firmly entangled in a friendly flag, no historian could fail to conclude that
the author of the two sets of letters wrote one thing to SHAEF,
a joint Allied command, from which he wanted "the whole
weight of air power," and another to Imperial General Staff,
from which he wanted permission to engage his army. He
therefore told each what it wanted to hear—SHAEF that he
would be Prince Rupert and IGS that he would be Fabius
Cunctator. If he achieved the breakthrough, he would be a
hero and Brooke would forgive him. If he failed, he had prepared a line of historic retreat with his letter to Brooke. In the
actual event, he disappointed both his bosses—Eisenhower by
failing and Brooke by incurring heavy losses. Yet he escaped
censure. This was his towering gift. Of his famous predecessors, the one of whom Monty most reminds me is McClellan,
a cautious fellow who always had a bold plan and a kind word
for himself when he flubbed it. A horseback statue of McClellan stands in a *carrefour* in Washington overlooked by the
windows of an apartment house largely occupied by retired
generals and their families. Major General Clift Andrus, one of
the tenants, once said to me, pointing to the statue, "There he
stands, just as he would have wanted, with five avenues of retreat open all around him."

Generalleutnant Speidel, writing five years later, in 1949,
was still, like Eisenhower, under the mistaken impression that
Montgomery had been trying to break through. "In the
course of a frightful four-day struggle in which he engaged five
infantry divisions, three of armor and three armored brigades
—more than 1,000 tanks on a very narrow front," the *Generalleutnant* wrote, "the Englishman progressed about five miles
in depth, but did not succeed in piercing, as he had hoped."

This is a picture of an offensive, not a feint, but lesser warriors never could fathom Montgomery's mind.

After the war, British journalistic historians, of whom Chester Wilmot is representative, popularized in Britain the thesis that Montgomery had won our battle by losing his, having "held the German armor off the Americans." But among those deceived, along with the foe and SHAEF, by Goodwood when it happened were all the British correspondents at the American First Army press camp at Vouilly, near Isigny, where I was then in residence. They took their quota of jeeps and drove up into the British zone on July 18th and 19th to see the Twenty-first Army Group make its attack, and when they came back they were extremely depressed. Montgomery had not told them, either, of his limited intentions. By choosing the British show, they had passed up the capture of St.-Lô, on July 18th—the culmination of a fight so long and an approach so slow that the press was bored with it—and the American correspondents attended the show out of a sense of duty. (The road up through St.-André de l'Epine became as familiar as the taxi ride to the office in the morning. The farthest bit ran between deep banks of earth topped by hedges that afforded concealment and protection if you didn't stand up in your jeep. Then there came a stretch where you walked until you reached a point at which you felt justified in protecting your publication's interests by returning to file a story. On the jeep trip back, you gave lifts to walking wounded and asked them what life was like beyond the hedges.)

There is nothing in the record of German troop movements —which was accessible to both Blumenson and Ellis—to support the notion that Goodwood drew Nazi armor or troops from the First Army front before Cobra started. The only Panzer divisions moved to the Goodwood area were the 116th, which came from across the Seine, and the 12th, which had been at Lisieux. Goodwood consequently brought them *nearer* to the site of the forthcoming Cobra. The other units of *General der Panzertruppen* Eberbach's *Panzerkorps* were held on Montgomery's front not by the attack but by the threat of it, which was far bigger before Monty lost the five hundred tanks. He could have achieved a greater effect simply by continuing to stand still. When von Kluge finally did move his armored divisions to counterattack the Americans after Cobra, he had no trouble in detaching them from the British front. At most it could be said that the Twenty-first Army Group, during Goodwood, had "written down" (in Montgomery's phrase) a good many German tanks and combatants, but it had lost many more of its own. In the what-would-have-happened-if-something-else-hadn't area, it is hard to overestimate what the British and Canadians could have accomplished immediately after the Cobra victory if they had retained their Goodwood forces intact.

After we correspondents had spent as short a time as possible in captured St.-Lô, which was under lively artillery fire, we raced back to the headquarters of the victorious 29th Division and asked its commander why Bradley had so insisted on capturing it. The *divisionnaire*, Major General Charles Gerhardt, said, "I guess because its name fitted so well in headlines." But a couple of nights later General Bradley unambiguously briefed the press corps. This was his scheme for Cobra: At a point midway between St.-Lô and the town of Périers, to the west, Allied heavy and medium bombers were to "saturate" an area four miles long and two miles wide with bombs of all calibres. Major General Lawton Collins, with a corps expanded to the size of a virtual army, was to attack, almost as the explosions ceased. He would put his lead infantry through this hole, and swing south and west-southwest toward the city of Coutances as his men enlarged the opening. Major General Troy Middleton's VIII Corps, now arrested on the coast of the Cotentin, would push due south toward Coutances, and between them they would cut off and destroy the extreme left of the German line of battle, replacing it with a vacancy that would release the djinni from the bottle. Bradley did not suggest that this might be a feint. The attacking forces would join at Coutances, whence some would pass south into Brittany and seize the Breton ports. Because St.-Lô was now in American hands, Eberbach's *Panzerkorps*, if it tried to seal the breach, would have to come a long way around. (Gerhardt had, of course, known all along what St.-Lô's value was.)

Cobra—like Overlord, the D Day plan—worked almost, if not quite, as plotted, although our Air Forces dropped a number of bombs on our forward infantry elements, which somewhat slowed the start. Middleton's armor got to Coutances before Collins. The bag of prisoners was disappointing, but by July 30th there was an irreparable hole in the cork. In the beginning, though, we came out of the bottle more in the manner of lunchroom tomato ketchup than like an angry djinni. First there was a long hesitation, then a trickle. Blumenson writes, "The word *breakthrough*, frequently used during the planning period, signified a penetration through the depth of the enemy defensive position. The word *breakout* was often employed later somewhat ambiguously . . . to describe the results of Cobra. . . . Reporters writing after the event and impressed with the results stressed the breakout that followed rather than the breakthrough that was planned." Blumenson, in both "Breakout" and "The Duel for France," is particularly good on this period of empiricism.

Once in a long while a set operation works out with a sufficiently recognizable likeness to its design to reduce confusion to, say, forty per cent. As soon as the set operation ends, confusion is again normal. Newspaper correspondents, restrained by limitations of space, have a habit of compressing the actions of a hundred units, stumbling in various directions at various speeds, and in some instances stopped dead, into the "thrust" or the "rush" of an army that "pours" or "races" or "smashes" as if it were a single creature. Headlines fix the patterns of memory; it is likely that at least half the people who read about General George S. Patton in those days thought of him as moving at the maximum speed permitted on state highways. And it is instructive now to read of the "push" to Brittany through Avranches (*Hôtel France et Londres, belle vue sur le Mont St.-Michel*), the town commanding the coastal highway that runs west from Normandy. (The hotel, when I came upon it in 1926, had a semitropical garden, with fig trees and palms. The armpit that the Cotentin forms in joining the mainland shelters the coast below and gives it an artificial warmth.)

The first tank company to creep into Avranches, on July 30th, found it "an undefended city for all its prize aspects," but Middleton, the VIII Corps commander (represented in the legend as "racing" toward the breakout), could not at first bring himself to believe that his foremost troops had got that far. The tank company, instead of "racing" on without instructions, sat there for a day, after which Middleton, "Breakout" says, "acted with dispatch" and ordered the 4th Armored Division, of which the tank company was the most advanced unit, to push on through. But in the meanwhile a German road convoy that had escaped the trap came bowling down the road at night *from* Normandy. (The only time that units of any army really move at headline speed is in flight.) The convoy's appearance from the wrong direction made the tankers, not unnaturally, think that *they* were cut off and had in some way got on the wrong side of the German Army. "But when Germans in several of the trucks opened fire with rifles the tankers returned the fire and destroyed a few vehicles, thus blocking the road." I quote "Breakout." The Germans, several hundred of them, then surrendered, but the first ones to be interviewed said that a bigger convoy of escapees was coming along behind them, heavily armed. "The men of the tank company became jittery," Blumenson sympathetically reports.

The second convoy appeared, a shell from it struck an ammunition truck, and the tank-company commander "reached a quick decision. . . . Without having lost a man or a tank, the company abandoned several hundred prisoners and the Granville road bridge" and got out. Granville was the last big town north of Avranches, so the tankers were now in retreat, too. Other Germans, also in retreat, rolled over the bridge and into Avranches, which their comrades had abandoned a day or so earlier to flee south. Suddenly transformed into the recaptors of a vital objective, some Germans began to fortify it. More sensibly, "others, in a column of trucks, horse-drawn vehicles, and tracked vehicles, turned eastward and disappeared in the darkness, headed toward Mortain," a town, twenty miles inland, that was to have its turn in the spotlight a few days later. "Still others moved toward the southern exits of Avranches." But additional troops of the 4th Armored had moved on through the tank company and were now farther south. These came back toward the racket, and, "surprised, both Germans and Americans opened fire."

All this was normal confusion, but here a more serious note enters the story of Avranches. "In the confused fight, the action of one machine gunner, Private William H. Whitson, was a deciding factor. Before he was killed, he destroyed nearly 50

Germans and more than 20 light vehicles with his .30 calibre gun," Blumenson says. This frequent recurrence of the serious character is, by the way, what spoils writing about war for still another kind of author—the satirist. There are Falstaffs, but there are also Hotspurs, and both varieties make their entrances at the wrong moments for the artist. Since the division had trained long in the United States and had not been in combat long enough to receive replacements, Whitson must have been with it for a coniderable period, and the fact that he was still a private indicates that he was a soldier of independent mind. He got a posthumous Distinguished Service Cross.

"Breakout" goes on to say:

The Germans turned back, but only to reorganize for a second attack that came after daylight. The CCB infantrymen were ready. Using white phosphorus mortar shells effectively and supported by the providential appearance of a flight of P-47's, they held their ground. When the attack collapsed, several hundred Germans surrendered. Meanwhile, General Dager had discovered the abandonment of the bridge on the Granville road and ordered the tank company commander to return. The company reached its former positions on 31 July, about the same time that advance units of CCA were arriving on the scene. When the German artillery pieces on the bluff opened fire on CCA, tankers engaged them while armored infantrymen crossed the river, mounted the bluff, and captured the pieces. [CCA and CCB, or Combat Commands A and B, were subdivisions of the 4th. Armored divisions were split into combat commands, as infantry were split into regimental combat teams.] By the afternoon of 31 July General Dager [of CCB, directing the "thrust"] was sure that the Germans at Avranches had actually been seeking an escape route and not attempting to recapture Avranches.

General Dager got a Distinguished Service Cross, too, but not posthumous.

After this action, the armor "poured" some more. Avranches, abandoned in turn by Germans and Americans, was the key to Brittany, the door to all France.

War is inevitably and perhaps essentially composed of such episodes. A "push" into the unknown is more like the hesitant progress of a child going to bed in a large, strange house. The only pushing involved comes from a headquarters that to the men out front seems parasangs to the rear and in a country safe as London, though it may in fact be only a couple of miles back.

Collins' VII Corps, reduced back to normal size, pushed south on the range of hills that parallels the coast at a distance of twenty miles, protecting the road into Brittany. The Germans made their counterattack there, with divisions withdrawn from Montgomery's front, in the first week in August. It was a *contre-attaque à contre-cœur*, against the wishes of the officers who led it. Hitler, hundreds of miles away, had noticed what a child could have spotted in an atlas: there was a corridor between Avranches and Mortain that looked narrow on a large-scale map. He could not see the hills between, and would not believe the generals in the field who told him that their divisions were reduced to regimental size. Any flinching appeared to him proof of treason. After the plot, he thought all professional officers were plotters against him anyway. The attack was to focus on Mortain, a delightful small town (*Hôtel de la Poste, alpes normandes, alt. 232 m.*). The brook trout there are remarkable.

Four Panzer divisions, all from Montgomery's front and considerably "written down," made the attack. The American 30th Division was in Mortain when the assault hit, but, having arrived six hours late to relieve the 1st, which had pushed on, it was not yet firmly in the saddle. The terrain was as strange to it as Mars. The Germans, however, were also hours late in making their attack, which gave the 30th a bit of a chance to settle in. The moral for civilians is: Never stop running because you are late for a train; the train may be late, too. The attack achieved surprise but little else, since, as its unhappy commanders had predicted, it lacked the power to penetrate.

General George Patton's Third Army was activated on August 1st, *after* the breakthrough, from components of the old First Army plus newly arrived divisions, and took over the development of the enemy defeat. Patton "pushed" armored divisions toward Brest and Lorient, the chief Breton ports, but their commanders hesitated just long enough, so they found the ports barred in their faces by garrisons that a couple of days earlier had been irresolute. If Patton had then moved against the ports with his full strength, he might have taken them at the expense of just a week or a fortnight, and the supply difficulties that the Allies, particularly the Americans, were to encounter in September might never have occurred. On the other hand, the German armies in Normandy, with the road to their rear clear, might have escaped by a retreat in good order instead of succumbing in a general *sauve-qui-peut*. Falling back on prepared positions, they might have prolonged the Battle of France into winter. There is a chance, though, that they would have stayed put, as Hitler stubbornly ordered, and, like a blue crab clinging to a bait without a hook in it, would have awaited Patton's delayed maneuver. In that case, the Americans could have bagged the ports *and* von Kluge's Army Group B, and pushed on with their supply problem licked. Having missed their first snap at the ports, the Americans chose to seal them off and to go first for the Army Group and the mainland of France, hooking back east and north. They thereby almost totally destroyed the first objective and gained the second; it is only in retrospect that the thought arises that they might have made another choice and scored a clean sweep. By the middle of August, the ports were forgotten, except by the two divisions that were besieging them. The German collapse in France was so nearly total that it seemed, by optimistic extrapolation, that it must extend all the way to Berlin.

There was another muffled interallied row on, about the closing of the gap between the British-Canadians and the American armies in the rear of the trapped Germans as Patton hooked around behind them—the "Falaise Pocket" of popular memory. Montgomery, again assuming precedence in a maneuver that directly involved the armies of both nations, had set the date for the closing of the gap as August 13th-14th, by which time the Americans were to be on a line just south of the town of Argentan, where the British, having moved through Falaise, would join them. By the appointed date, the Americans had reached their line, but Montgomery had not yet got Falaise; moreover, he forbade our people to move up into his zone. I cite General Bradley, in a press conference at Laval on August 20th.

The Twenty-first Army Group's progress from Caen to Falaise was of almost pre-Cobra deliberation—twenty-one miles in thirty-eight days. Between August 13th and August

21st, when the Polish Armored Division, which was attached
to the British forces, and the American 90th sealed the gap, an
estimated forty thousand Germans, without vehicles or armor,
managed to escape, but this number seemed so inconsiderable
at the time that nobody really worried about it. It was only
later, when these experienced soldiers reappeared, reëquipped,
in the German ranks at the Battle of the Bulge, that recriminations warmed up.

The British-Canadians, definitely uncorked after the Falaise
battle, began to move along the north coast as rapidly as the
Americans were moving toward the upper Seine; another
American Army, with French components, had landed in the
south of France and was moving north, almost without opposition, to join the chase. It was at this point that the revolt of
the civilian population of Paris, on August 18th, forced the hand
of the American command, which had intended to bypass the
city on both sides and pick it up later. It is also here that a
reader of "Breakout and Pursuit" has the sensation that something has gone wrong at the bindery, resulting in the inclusion
of a chapter of another book, and one considerably inferior.
This is Blumenson's chapter on the liberation of Paris, an excursion outside his military specialty for which he apparently
was coached by a member of a State Department sect—since
discredited by events—that for four years persuaded President
Roosevelt that General de Gaulle had no real support within
France. Like the stray Mormons who every now and then are
discovered practicing crypto-polygamy in the desert, the survivors of this odd fraternity still exist, perhaps in some cranny
of the Metropolitan or the Cosmos Club, from which they
sally forth to capture the ear of the innocent military historian.

"The political factor working against immediate liberation
[of Paris in August, 1944] stemmed from the aspirations of
General Charles de Gaulle, chief of the Free French movement," Blumenson writes. "Though Marshal Henri Pétain
headed the government in France, de Gaulle several days
before the invasion had proclaimed his own National Committee of Liberation the provisional government of the French
Republic. . . . The result [of freeing Paris too soon] might
be the imposition of a government on France that the French

people might not want." This was a reflection of the cult view, in 1944, that de Gaulle commanded the support of "less than fifteen per cent of the French." (I cite the veteran diplomat J. Rives Childs, who heartily disagreed.)

Pétain was at the time not the head of a government but a captive of the Prime Minister, Pierre Laval, and refused even to go through the forms of exercising power. The "government" in Vichy was the captive of the Germans, who had occupied all France in November, 1942, abrogating even the fiction of continued French sovereignty south of the Allier. The National Committee, which had functioned as a government since June, 1943, in North Africa and all the French colonies, provided the French troops operating with the Allies in Italy and France and frequently proved its independence by refusing to take orders from its English-speaking Allies—a reason for the strong Washington bias against it. Within France, de Gaulle had no rival in popularity, as the days following liberation would prove. To the old prejudices of the diplomats Blumenson adds the petty peeves of a couple of generals who apparently thought of the Free French as a kind of Pawnee scouts attached to the Army. The Free French thought of themselves as the equal army of an equal Ally.

The French 2nd Armored Division, which was under the command of General Philippe Leclerc, and which was equipped like an American division and had the same table of organization, had been selected by the Allied command even before the Division reached France as the instrument for the liberation of Paris when the appropriate day arrived. This was a wise decision, designed to bolster the pride of France, and it was a political decision, since any other division could have performed the same mission. But when the date of liberation was advanced, the 2nd found itself more than a hundred miles from Paris and had to be brought into position.

De Gaulle called the French 2nd Armored a French division that he, as provisional head of the French state, had lent to the American Army for the campaign. General Leonard Gerow, commander of the V Corps, and, as such, Leclerc's official superior, held that it had the same status as any other unit: "For his part, General Gerow saw no reason to employ the French Division any differently from the American units, for

Paris was no specific concern of his," Blumenson records. Gerow ordered it not to march in de Gaulle's victory parade on the day after the liberation, because it was "needed" to clean up possibly disorderly elements in the streets, which were as safe as those of Allentown, Pennsylvania. Gerow apparently failed to realize that for Frenchmen all over the world the day was the first assuagement of four years of defeat. He also entertained a notion that he should be hailed as the Liberator of Paris, for his superior, General Courtney H. Hodges, commander of the First Army, had decided that "it would be fair for General Gerow, the corps commander, to have the task of liberating Paris because he and Collins had been the two American D-Day commanders and Collins had had the honor of taking Cherbourg." But General Leclerc captured von Choltitz, the German commander of Paris, and made him surrender the city to the French alone, which Gerow apparently still thinks of as a personal affront.

Even more poignant was the case of General Raymond O. Barton, of the American 4th Infantry Division, which entered Paris on the same day:

Leclerc had installed his command post in the Montparnasse railway station, but he himself went to the Prefecture of Police. Barton, who was in Paris and wanted to coördinate the dispositions of the divisions with Leclerc, located him there having lunch. Holding his napkin and appearing annoyed at being disturbed, Leclerc came outside to talk with Barton. Without inviting him to lunch, Leclerc suggested that Barton go to the Montparnasse station. Barton, who was hungry as well as irritated by Leclerc's attitude, finally said, "I'm not in Paris because I wanted to be here but because I was ordered to be here." Leclerc shrugged his shoulders. "We're both soldiers," he said. Barton then drove to the Gare Montparnasse, where he found General Gerow already taking charge of the enormous responsibility of Paris.

That afternoon, at the Gare Montparnasse, I saw both the American generals, looking uncommonly gloomy for such an occasion, but then I didn't know they had lunched on K rations, like me. By courtesy of M. Robert Aron, author of "Histoire de la Libération de la France" (1959), I am now able to tell General Barton about the lunch at the Prefecture. It was a good one, but Leclerc had time to touch it only "with the tips of his lips;" he was, besides, distraught. M. Luizet, the Prefect of Police, had had a table "set with all the luxury with which, in times of peace, the City of Paris habitually entertains her guests of honor: white tablecloth, deluxe china, flowers from the municipal greenhouses. Leclerc sits down, but the street fighting continues and does not leave him the leisure to enjoy such a meal. He will remain seated only ten minutes, receiving meanwhile the reports of couriers." When Barton arrived, therefore, Leclerc probably had finished lunch. I feel it incumbent on me, as a brief and slight acquaintance, to make Leclerc's excuses for him, he having died sixteen years ago in the crash of a plane upon a hill in Africa.

Blumenson follows another cultist line in praising Raoul Nordling, the Swedish Consul-General in Paris, a half-Frenchman who all through the Occupation ran a factory that made ball bearings for the Luftwaffe. Nordling acted as intermediary between the Resistance and von Choltitz in arranging an imperfect truce that lasted from the twenty-first to the twenty-third of August, when the insurrectionists, who had never honored its terms anyway, repudiated it. It is significant, as an indication of Blumenson's sources of information, that he says the Resistance leaders were "fortunate" in securing Nordling as an intermediary, while Aron says that the demi-Swede "proposed himself" for the role. Nordling remains an equivocal figure, whose success would have left the Germans in possession of the city until the arrival of the Allied armies, not only depriving the Parisians of the consolation of thinking they had liberated themselves but opening the way for a deal with some anti-Gaullist faction of *attentistes* (chaps on the fence, and not too seriously compromised as open collaborators)—a deal that de Gaulle feared up to the last minute. Gaullists and Communists, united in the insurrection, were also united in this fear. Blumenson likewise repeats the canard about the French in Paris fighting among themselves, citing as authority von Choltitz! The traumata set up in this period of de Gaulle's dealings with his Western Allies have affected his feelings about them ever since, and American diplomacy is still paying for the mistakes of the Vichy cult in our State Department.

What Blumenson never describes in his brief excursion into a strange world is the chief reason de Gaulle had to distrust the

Americans, which was that an American administration group had consistently tried to short-circuit him and bring in a Giraud, a Darlan, a Peyrouton, a Flandin. The intrigues of factions that claimed American support continued, with increasing intensity, even as the armies neared Paris. De Gaulle, because of his unhappy experience, had no way of knowing how far the claims were justified. Aron says that the Resistance Intelligence service had reported a group within Paris that consisted in the main of *attentistes*, "who now believed that, in liaison with the Americans, their hour had arrived. Monzie, Frossard, Bonnet [Georges, an ex-Minister, not Henri, who was later Ambassador at Washington], Paul Faure, were supposed to be among the promoters of this movement; Chautemps and Monzie, in indirect contact with Admiral Leahy and Robert Murphy, were said to be extremely busy. It was said even that the group wanted to keep Marshal Pétain." (Leahy had been our Ambassador to Vichy after the Armistice of 1940, Murphy the *Grand Manitou* of our thinking about France.) "This new movement," the Intelligence bulletin concluded, "recruits its strength particularly among *attentiste* officers of the regular army. [These men had been from the beginning de Gaulle's bitterest enemies.] It seems, in any case, according to a report of Brinon's, that the Anglo-Americans have already given personal assurances to certain pro-Vichy elements."

It is doubtful that such assurances were being honored as late as August, 1944, although with a certain type of diplomatic mentality anything is possible. But it is definite that Pierre Laval, the archplotter of collaboration, who was assuredly not a fool, had come to Paris from Vichy early in the month to make a last stab at forming such a government and setting up such a deal with the Allies. Laval must have thought he had a chance. He left Paris only on the day the insurrection broke out. De Gaulle, still recalling his long experience of American intrigue with his enemies, could hardly be blamed for his suspicions, which he transmitted to his subordinates, among whom he counted the commander and officers of the French 2nd Armored Division as well as civilian officials in Paris.

By omitting from "Breakout" any of the four-year background of relations between the Roosevelt administration and de Gaulle, Blumenson endorses the picture, given by his military interviewees, of the French as petty, irritable, unduly suspicious, insubordinate, and frivolous. Once out in the open country again, though, he regains his, and the Allied forces', stride. The last week in August and the first days of September were a winner's dream of war—an enemy, apparently demoralized, intent only on escape or surrendering on sight. "The German situation was every bit as bad as the Allies thought." But the Allies were running into supply difficulties. An armored corps needed a quarter of a million gallons of gasoline to move fifty miles, and some of the American corps were grounded for days at a time, except when they captured German fuel with which to piece out their own. "The Third Army's eastward advance during the last week in August was a spectacularly fast movement against disorganized opposition—pursuit warfare at its best. . . . By its nature opportunistic and relatively uncontrolled . . . it was a motorized advance, everybody riding on tanks, trailers, and jeeps. It was a frantic search for bridges or fords. . . . It was a period of confusion when a jeepload of soldiers who had missed a turn in the road might capture a village, when an anti-aircraft battery or a few Quartermaster truck drivers might take a hundred Germans prisoner, when a single officer might go way ahead of his unit only to find that another outfit had already seized his assigned objective."

Major Ellis, for the British, writes, "It has been aptly said that a rapid advance is paradise for the tactician but hell for the quartermaster."

In this situation, another discussion now arose. Three great units—the British Twenty-first Army Group (Montgomery) and the American First Army (Hodges) and the Third (Patton)—were pushing the pursuit and advance from different directions. There was not enough gas and ammunition to keep them all moving and shooting, but there was, conceivably, enough to keep one moving full tilt if the others stopped dead. In the enemy's apparently difficult state (*v.* Speidel), this one might be able to smash on into the heart of Germany and perhaps end the war. There were, then, two chief subjects of debate. One was whether the circumstances justified such a gamble, for in the event that the Germans behind the border were in better shape than seemed possible, the thrust force might find itself in a perilous position. The second, in the event there was to be a gamble, was which of the three forces should receive the gas and the go-ahead while the others waited.

It was at this point that General Dwight D. Eisenhower moved Supreme Allied Headquarters to France and assumed personal control of all the armies. He had theretofore, as has been said, operated a chain of command through Montgomery over Bradley and through Bradley over Hodges and Patton. The Montgomery link was now eliminated, and the supreme chief was to operate through Montgomery and Bradley as equals. Eisenhower has never been a gambler, and he announced a "broad front" strategy, with all the armies advancing simultaneously at the best rate they could manage on the supplies made available to them, which he divided equally. Pursuit, in consequence, slackened everywhere, and the Germans' "miracle of the West" was accomplished. They got away and achieved an astonishing cohesion behind the West Wall, which a week earlier had appeared to all the Allies to be a paper barrier. (Officers of the 1st Division, in Paris on leave, said they actually had been through the West Wall once with exactly one casualty. Then they had been halted for lack of fuel and recalled to a less exposed position.)

"Perhaps strong leadership at this point in the campaign was not important," Blumenson writes charitably. "Eisenhower judged the hostile army 'no longer a cohesive force, but a number of fugitive battle groups, disorganized and even demoralized, short of equipment and arms.'" Nevertheless, they got away. The fantastic notion obtrudes, at this interval, that since the fleeing Germans mostly were on foot, or horse-drawn, the Americans and British, abandoning their stalled vehicles except for guns and ammunition trucks, might have improvised a pursuit on foot, with a minimum of fuel.

That military empiricist Major General Terry de la Mesa Allen, faced with a similar situation on a much smaller scale (one battalion) in North Africa, had once said, "Damn it, let the infantry walk!" General Allen, however, was now at home, training a new division, and the concept was too bold to occur to generals committed to the idea that a corps must move fifty miles a day or not at all. So the pursuit ceased, except for feverish bursts of movement when gas arrived. An army on foot escaped from an army on wheels. Major Ellis Writes:

With the end of the battle of Normandy in sight, General Montgomery meanwhile had first disclosed his view of future policy in a telegram to the C.I.G.S. on August the 18th:

"HAVE BEEN THINKING AHEAD ABOUT FUTURE PLANS BUT HAVE NOT (REPEAT NOT) DISCUSSED SUBJECT WITH IKE. MY VIEWS ARE AS FOLLOWS. AFTER CROSSING SEINE 12 AND 21 ARMY GROUPS SHOULD KEEP TOGETHER AS A SOLID MASS OF SOME 40 DIVISIONS WHICH WOULD BE SO STRONG THAT IT NEED FEAR NOTHING. THE FORCE SHOULD MOVE NORTHWARDS. 21st ARMY GROUP SHOULD BE ON WESTERN FLANK AND SHOULD CLEAR THE CHANNEL COAST AND THE PAS DE CALAIS AND WEST FLANDERS AND SECURE ANTWERP. [He would get Antwerp on September 4th, but would not free the port until November 9th.] THE AMERICAN ARMIES SHOULD MOVE WITH RIGHT FLANK ON ARDENNES DIRECTED ON BRUSSELS, AACHEN AND COLOGNE. THE MOVEMENT OF AMERICAN ARMIES WOULD CUT THE COMMUNICATIONS OF ENEMY FORCES ON CHANNEL COAST AND THUS FACILITATE THE TASK OF BRITISH ARMY GROUP. THE INITIAL OBJECTS OF MOVEMENT WOULD BE TO DESTROY GERMAN FORCES ON COAST AND TO ESTABLISH A POWERFUL AIR FORCE IN BELGIUM. A FURTHER OBJECT WOULD BE TO GET ENEMY OUT OF V-1 OR V-2 RANGE OF ENGLAND. BRADLEY AGREES ENTIRELY WITH ABOVE CONCEPTION. WOULD BE GLAD TO KNOW IF YOU AGREE GENERALLY. WHEN I HAVE GOT YOUR REPLY WILL DICUSS MATTER WITH IKE."

He had discussed future policy with General Bradley the day before he wrote this, but apparently he was mistaken in his belief that Bradley agreed entirely with him. For Bradley wrote afterwards that he and Patton had been thinking of a quite different plan for future action. "The first or predominantly American plan called for emphasis on a thrust to the Reich straight through the middle of France to the Saar and beyond the Saar to the Rhine in the vicinity of Frankfurt. . . . Both the First and Third American Armies . . . would be required for this major effort." [Ellis is here quoting Bradley.]

Montgomery saw Bradley again on the 19th and learned from him then that "Ike wants to split the force and send half of it eastwards towards Nancy." Knowing this when he issued his directive on the 20th he told the C.I.G.S.: "I have so worded my directive that *we shall retain the ability to act in any direction*" [italics again mine].

This had all the built-in marks of the Montgomery mind—the demand for an overwhelming force that "need fear nothing," the use of the Americans to "facilitate" the task of the self-chosen instrument, the misrepresentation of Bradley, and especially the reservation of the intention, withheld from the Ally, to do anything he pleased if he felt like it. But here he faced disappointment, as did Bradley and Patton:

General Eisenhower, however, was holding to the concept of policy for the advance into Germany on two axes which he had approved on May the 27th and the command arrangements foreshadowed in his directive of June the 1st. Reporting to the Combined Chiefs of Staff, he gave September the 1st as the target date on which the final system of command, as foreseen from the beginning of the campaign, would be put into operation and General Montgomery's responsibility "for coördinating actions between 21st and 12th Army Groups" would terminate.

For Eisenhower, who disliked the work of arriving at a decision, a policy once adopted was too valuable to be thrown away, and even though both of the policies cited had been arrived at in advance of the first landing, and although events since had not been foreseen, he stuck to them. Eisenhower could, at that, be excused for being slightly leery of Montgomery's projects after Goodwood. Ellis says:

Thus, General Eisenhower envisaged that two groups of armies, each with its separate Commander-in-Chief acting directly under orders of the Supreme Commander, might, if conditions allowed, advance north and south of the Ardennes, the Central group giving such assistance as might be needed to the Northern group in its advance through northern France and the Low Countries. General Montgomery, on the other hand, held that both groups of armies should advance together north of the Ardennes, and both remain under the control and direction of a single commander. It will be found, as the story of the campaign develops, that this difference of opinion persisted and had effect on the conduct of operations—and indeed on the final outcome of the Allied campaign in the West.

It did. The insufficiently fuelled Army groups broke down on both axes, the home-field spirit of the Germans asserted itself, and it was not until the following May that Breakout and Pursuit had their final effect.

But in the I hope immortal words of Major General Leland S. Hobbs, commander of the 30th Division, which led Breakout, and got bombed by the Air Forces: "I claim we may be the spearhead that broke the camel's back."

The New Yorker, October 19, 1963

NORMANDY REVISITED

To Moran, Frere, and Simone

CONTENTS

FOREWORD

In 1943 I wrote a book called *The Road Back to Paris*, but the title was merely predictive. It was, in fact, about the road I followed from Paris, via the French retreat of 1940, the neutral United States of 1941 in which Lend-Lease had just squeaked through, and England as the English began to get their second wind. The road led to the United States again in an uneventful 42-day convoy, during which the Norwegian tanker crew and I learned through the radio operator that the United States was in the war. Then it led back to Britain, and to North Africa, which was the visible turning. I did not get back to France until June 1944. We moved so fast on the true Road Back then that I had no time to write another book, although correspondents turned them out quickly in those days, throwing the manuscripts over their shoulders in the general direction of the United States while continuing to advance intrepidly for the glory of their employers.

I wrote despatches for *The New Yorker* on fighting, politics, and peasantry (none of the stories I wrote then are in this book) and arrived home three days before Christmas 1944, with a great many memories that it would have done me good to write, if I had been ready.

After my return to peaceable preoccupations, my best therapist was a man named Joe Braun, who, with a partner named Harry Kaplan, runs a place called the Palace Bar & Grill on West Forty-fifth Street, between Longacre Square and Sixth Avenue. On the night of June 6, 1946, the second anniversary of D Day, I was in his place but without good friends and maudlin. Joe, who works nights, is a sallow man, calm, a cigar-chewer, and a speaker of the side-street New York language, which is flattened, unemotional, and unpolluted by Iobraskan or Virgissippian, the *Volksprache* of the Executive Belt to the east of his saloon, or by Hollywood-Jambonian, which is the Swahili of Sardi's, to the west. He talks like my father.

"Have you ever seen a deck awash with blood and condensed milk?" I asked him, as he broke ice cubes apart with the handle of the pick. He put ice in highball glasses, poured the accompanying whisky, and went away to serve the drinks. When he returned he said, "No." Then he moved away to serve more drinks, leaving me embittered by his insensitivity.

But when he came back next time he proved he had been considering what I said. He took his cigar out of his mouth, put it on the bar, and said, "If you seen that, Joe, it will stay with you."

After that, I knew it would, and I might as well leave it alone.

"Leave them alone, and they'll come home, wagging their tails behind them" is particularly true of memories. In time they recur in forms so implausible that you must go back and make sure the events they represent were real.

When this desire grew strong, I returned to a part of France that has a peculiarly personal relation to me, as I hope I make clear in the following narrative.

A.J.L.

"If one American division could beat one German division, I thought then, a hundred American divisions could beat a hundred German divisions. Only the time was already past when Germany had a hundred divisions to spare from the Russian front, plus God knows how many more to fight the British, plus garrison troops for all the occupied countries. I knew . . . that the road back to Paris was clear."

—Last of The Road Back to Paris, *written in August 1943 and published in January 1944. The American Division that beat the German Division was the 1st Division, at El Guettar in Tunisia, in 1943.*

I

Weymouth Pier

THE London weather, ominously good in late April, then bad through May, came bright again in the first week of June, reminding me of the stretch of weather before the embarkation for the Allied invasion of France in 1944, when I was in what a girl I knew then called a nugly mood. For at least a month before D Day, I was continuously angry at the press-relations officers of FUSAG (for First United States Army Group), a pre-invasion echelon destined never to function on the Continent under that name. I was equally angry with the correspondents of the major American news agencies and dailies in pre-invasion London, a number of whom I had until then considered my friends. (I now reconsider some of them such, but others I have never forgiven.) This was because the Army Group P.R.O.s, few of whom had ever heard a shot fired in anger—the old taunts come back to mind with the old combinations of initials—refused to let me accompany the 1st Division across the Channel, even though Major General Clarence Huebner, its commanding officer, had invited me. It is painful to let friends go into danger without you; abandoning them later comes easier. It is like knowing that a friend is critically ill in hospital: having visited once or twice, you stay away with relative equanimity. I considered myself bound to the 1st by ties of friendship and honor that dated from the North African campaign. Historical curiosity also entered into my feelings, since, wherever the 1st was, the best story was sure to be. Because it was the most thoroughly tested American division, it had to go into the trickiest place. This saved a reporter the trouble of trying to divine official intentions; while my colleagues stared helplessly at maps depicting German-held Europe from Spitsbergen down to Hendaye, I had only to stick to the 1st and the Great Riddle would come clear in due course.

Some giant mind higher than Army Group, however, had imagined that the way to please the press was to let an association of permanent American correspondents in London decide

who might cover the invasion, and how. The members of the
association were not military correspondents but sitters at the
ends of cable lines. Since, in the nature of things, they worked
for the press services and dailies that maintained permanent
bureaus in London, they reserved all the good spots for their
fellow-employees. (None asked to make the landing personally.) This ridiculous association would do nothing to help
me, and I suspected its overcordial dignitaries of promoting a
monopoly.

In those pre-invasion days, I used to go for a run every
morning in Hyde Park—from Hyde Park Corner to Kensington Palace and back—and as I jogged along I would reflect on
the ignominy of being left out of an event to which I had
looked forward for four years, ever since the fall of France, a
country I had left in June 1940. I was not consoled by the
P.R.O.s' assurance that I would get over some time, days or
weeks after D Day, or even, perhaps—if I was good—be permitted to witness the event itself from a ship so big that there
were butter plates and celery on the officers' dinner table. The
running was sensible, because I knew from experience that infantry war takes a lot out of even a spectator's legs. If my permission came through, I wanted to be in shape to take
advantage of it. I was four months short of forty, and had been
waiting all winter in London, training in pubs and bottle clubs.
The greatest benefit of the running, however, was that it
helped me work off the surplus adrenal juices that accumulated whenever I thought of the P.R.O.s, for whom I invented
appropriate civilian pasts as I ran along. I decided they had
been moving-picture press agents, office boys in advertising
agencies, or newspaper legmen with metatarsal defects. I also
devoted sweaty miles of thought to the press-service bureau
chiefs—Sweet Alices trembling at the frown of fatheaded Ben
Bolts five thousand miles away. Whenever I invented an insult
that especially amused me, I would break my jog and walk a
furlong to savor it. One puffball had particularly infuriated me
by offering a confidential tip that the Army expected casualties
of ninety-five per cent in the first hours. This was not only
monstrously untrue but insulting, because it suggested that I
could be frightened. I could, of course. As for him, he had not
the faintest idea what he was talking about, having never, in

the phrase of the immortal Dan De Quille, "seen the elephant nor hearn the owl." This same *bête noire* (or, rather, *bête rose*; he had a pink, snouty face like a Walt Disney porker's) had made up a slogan: "Every typewriter in a landing craft takes up space needed for a machine gun." He was patriotically willing to waive his own claim to passage. "*Ça, ç'est un blasphème*," a Basque major of Zouaves in Tunisia had once said to me of the Vichy generals who didn't want to fight, and I repeated it as I pounded along, regarded without astonishment by old gentlemen feeding the ducks on the Serpentine. London is used to eccentrics.

I lived at a hotel on Half Moon Street, which is one block long and runs from Piccadilly to Curzon Street. My fever came to a head one noon as I walked home through Curzon Street after my run. I was drenched in sweat but still full of rage when I saw a very small English automobile draw up at the curb ahead of me, in front of a house bearing a doctor's doorplate. A woman got out of the driver's seat, opened the door on the sidewalk side, and extracted from the hind portion of the car first a pair of crutches, which she leaned against the hood, and then part of an old man, who was so wedged in that he could get out of his shell only about as far as a periwinkle. I was twenty yards past before it occurred to me that I ought to help —the gaffer didn't look like an AP man. I doubled back, grabbed the bony wrist extruding from the metal carapace, and jerked so violently that he came out flying. (He was an emaciated old gentleman and couldn't have weighed much more than a collie.) When I saw the mingled gratitude and alarm on the woman's face, I realized how mad I must have seemed. A few paces farther on, I began to laugh, and it was then I realized that, for a time, at any rate, I had beaten off paranoia.

I was rescued from my invasion frustration by a pair of Kentuckians in naval uniform—Barry Bingham, of the Louisville *Courier-Journal*, and John Mason Brown, both of them prewar friends of mine—who were running Navy public relations for the great day. When they first proposed that I go as a naval war correspondent I was scornful. But my 1st Division prospects got no better as I pulled successive strings. Instead, as they say in Dublin, they disimproved, because some of the

strings got crossed. Brown then artfully suggested that the
Navy had little ships as well as big ones. The little ships included LCIs (Landing Craft, Infantry) that would run smack
aground in a yard of water to land the troops they carried,
beginning within half an hour of the first small-boat landings.
Some of the LCIs, Bingham said insinuatingly, would be
loaded with 1st Division infantry. I could travel to the other
shore on one, and then make up my mind about getting off. If
I went ashore, though, he said with regret in his voice, I would
not be able to get any dispatches out; the Army P.R.O.s and
censors would stop that, he was afraid. If I came back with the
LCI—he realized that this was asking a lot, because he knew
how anxious I would be to stay on the beach—I *would* be able
to write a hell of a story, and the Navy would get it out for me.
And, of course, he said, holding up a hand to forestall my
protestations of insatiable pugnacity, the LCI, after discharging
its first package of soldiers, would go back to the transports
lying farther offshore and fetch another load.

"Coming in several times during the day that way, you'll get
a splendid idea of how things are going," Bingham said.
"You'll be able to judge the intensity of fire at the waterline."

"I could get you on a good early one," Brown said. "I
wouldn't want you to miss anything."

So when SHAEF (Supreme Headquarters Allied Expeditionary Forces) summoned us from our hotels for the last time
and then shipped us south by bus, my destination was Landing
Craft, Infantry, Large (157 feet), No. 88, berthed at Weymouth, in Dorset.

At Weymouth it was instantly plain that there would have
been room on LCIL 88 alone for a hundred more passengers.
An army does not load its invasion craft like excursion boats
but rather to deliver units capable of action to an appointed
spot at a useful time in the planned development of battle. It
would be murderous, as well as useless, to send in odd lots of
troops simply because there was room on the boats. Onshore,
they would simply have to stand around and be shot at. I was
as welcome as the flowers in May, once the crew knew that I
was going across with them. A man who thinks he may have to
be a hero is consoled by the thought that his friends may read
about it.

The Weymouth pier had landing craft lying alongside lashed together three abreast. The gangplank to the LCI closest inshore would slope down steeply except at extreme high tide; the grumbling soldiers, carrying their gear, plus part of a machine gun or mortar, would fight against slipping, or else, if they weren't too closely packed, come down at a reckless run. The passengers for the two outer boats passed over the inshore one. On the 88, which was next to the pier, it was like living on Route 1. I lived aboard her for four days before we sailed and got to know all her complement of thirty. Three were killed off Omaha Beach at seven thirty-five on the morning of D Day, June 6. Our first trip in was our last for the day; an armor-piercing shell that hit our bow reduced our effectiveness as a landing craft by removing our ramps. When we limped back to Weymouth on Sunday evening, June 11, after five days of shuttling about in the transport area off the beach, I was glad to see the place; but I didn't stay long. Early Monday morning, I took a train for London. I journeyed part of the way with an American soldier who said he had been fished out of the Channel off Omaha Beach and brought back to England by a returning LST. He lacked the guts to rejoin his outfit, he said frankly, and was headed over the hill to an English town where he had a girl. Going back to my own comfortable hotel in London to write my story, I was in no moral position to be censorious. I lent him a pound. He ducked off down the corridor to another compartment when a dazzling Red Cross girl got in at the first station up the line; he was afraid she might ask questions, I suppose. I rode the rest of the way to London with her, practicing the art of heroic understatement as I had studied it in British war films in the Noel Coward manner.

Thinking of all these things in the miraculous London warmth that recalled them, I walked around St. James's Square four times, sniffing the pollen of the mulberry trees, which made me sneeze, without benefit of snuffbox, in the true eighteenth-century style of the quarter. On the façade of Norfolk House, an office building on the east side of the Square, a plaque in polychrome stone relates that within the building, between January 16 and June 6, 1944, General Dwight D. Eisenhower, in conjunction with the heads of the Allied

governments planned and launched the excursion in which I
participated. With my sneeze, but without causal connection
between them that I can trace, came an impulse to go down to
Weymouth again and see what it looked like. It was Saturday,
June 4, 1955, and we had sailed from there on the evening of
Monday, June 5, 1944. I am fond of anniversaries, although I
do not believe in letting them get the better of me. I had never
before observed June 5, for example, but that was no reason I
shouldn't. A rail strike was on, so I asked Arthur, my hotel
porter, to find a man to drive me down to Weymouth next day.

I had often been in the southwest of England in that other
spring, when every sizable market town was the headquarters
of an American division. As the date set for the invasion
neared, the roads choked up with American trucks and tank
transporters; Red Cross clubs huddled in the shadows of
cathedrals; soldiers from prohibition states drank the pubs out
of beer. The gentle West Country girls yielded with increasing
facility to the pleas of men unlikely to trouble them again, and
a haze of last-minute love hung over the land with the heat. I
remembered the bus ride to the embarkation area, with military traffic ever heavier as we neared Weymouth and the adjacent coastal town of Portland. From Dorchester down, the
M.P.s worked like cops at a bridge approach fifteen miles long.

On the Sunday of the anniversary, the weather held fair. In
the morning, Mr. George Biggs, a staunch friend of Arthur's,
came to fetch me in a Vauxhall, a nippy little car manufactured
by a British subsidiary of General Motors, and at nine o'clock
we set out. The ways in and out of a great city, being so unin-
teresting in themselves, allow opportunity to get acquainted
with a hired driver. Mr. Biggs was a man of conservative aspect, with a gray mustache, glasses, an alpaca jacket, and a cap
with a visor. His features underlay a glaze of respectable impas-
sivity, and his opening remarks were not of a startling nature.
"Fat pillows of cloud against a blue sky," he said. "I always
think they are quite nice, don't you, sir?" And a moment
or two later, as he whirled with phlegmatic dash around a
mooning family vehicle: "Putterers and picnickers—that's
what we shall have to contend with from here to the other side
of the New Forest, sir."

After we stopped at Winchester for a nice cup of tea, he

loosened up a bit. I remembered when the headquarters of Major General Manton S. Eddy, commanding the 9th Division, had been there. I had known the 9th in Africa, where it depended on half-trained mules and untrained muleteers to bring up ammunition, and had found it again in green Hampshire during the pre-invasion entr'acte. It was a crack division by then, and probably the chief architect of its excellence, next to Eddy, had been a private named Warner and nicknamed Molotov, which was later shortened to Mollie. I had seen him dead by a wadi north of Sedjenane a year earlier. Once Mollie had walked up a *djebel* under fire and captured six hundred Italians by asking them if they weren't tired of acting so miserable. His death resulted from a subsequent similar hunch, which turned out less well. That earlier time in Winchester, I had talked about Mollie with fellows who had been in his company. Now the only strangers in town were weekend putterers like us, who had stopped for elevenses and a look at the cathedral. It was unlikely that they had ever heard of Sedjenane.

All the way from London we had been threading our way among barelegged, bicycling girls. They occur in clubs, as fish do in schools, and once you have sighted the rearmost rump, high off the seat as the owner pushes to keep up, you sometimes run among them for five minutes before you leave the leader's pink, determined face behind. There were also, as one might expect, automobiles of all descriptions, and motorbikes with a girl riding sidecar or pillion, or with two girls riding sidecar *and* pillion, or with mother and baby in the sidecar and dad and the boys on the bike. The motorbike, in all its forms, is to the British highways what the small donkey is to those of North Africa. Buried under a super-structure of humanity and tea things, it snarls along on two, three, or even four wheels. Many an apparent automobile reveals itself, as you come closer, to be a bubble built out from and over a basic motor bicycle, with the rider, his face inside a plastic windscreen, as grave as the front half of a comedy horse. The attractions of the road beckon: "Thirteenth Century Cottage—First Left —Car Park—Teas, Snacks, Fully Licensed"; "Four Hundred Yds. to Fresh-Picked Strawberries"; "Purebred Herefords and Cocker Spaniels." In the New Forest, which was set aside as a royal hunting ground by William the Conqueror when there may have been trees there (the forest visible from the road now looks like Long Island scrub), our progress was further complicated by the New Forest ponies, wild horses of an ancient breed that line the road on Sundays to mooch tea buns from picnickers. English nature lovers have told me that the New Forest pony, with that uncanny instinct for survival that savage creatures develop, has learned to count to seven and never misses a Sunday, frequently turning up at the roadside with a bunch of wild primroses between its teeth to swap for boiled sweets or Yarmouth bloaters. The pony mothers bring their foals along to pose for photographs, knowing that more tea buns are forthcoming from camera amateurs who want the ponies to stand steady than from putterers who have no cameras. They are reported to have followed cars with cameras in them for miles, but this is on the dubious authority of letter writers to the *Times*. In appearance, the ponies are uncommonly hard to tell from small, undistinguished horses that have been left out in the rain. They cross the highway in both directions as they see carloads of tea-bun prospects approaching. The motor vehicles stop when the drivers see the ponies, and, as the drivers of sequential vehicles do not always see them at the same time, this leads to rearend collisions, while squads of children, leaping down and skinning their knees, add further perils to William the Conqueror's old line of country. Mr. Biggs egg-danced among them without hitting a pony, or even a child.

At Wimborne, a few miles beyond the New Forest, Mr. Biggs and I turned with relief onto the byroad that leads to Blandford, a town that once sheltered the headquarters of the 1st Division. This is one of the prettiest bits of road I have seen in England, running in part through an avenue of ancient beeches, which Mr. Biggs, checking by his speedometer, said was two miles long. (A bar waiter in Blandford told me later there were three hundred and seventy-five beeches, and that a society of ladies in Blandford cut the ivy off them every two years; he had a Sam Weller look about him, however, and may well have been in the habit of writing letters to the *Times* himself.) In Blandford there were soldiers in the long street, because the British Army has a permanent camp there, but they wore British battle dress instead of our field jackets.

Blandford is built around the bend of a pleasant small river called the Stour, and the main street, after a few constricted turns, runs over a bridge. "The town contains numerous fine 18th-cent. buildings including . . . the Crown Hotel, most of which were designed by the Bastard brothers."—The Little Guide series; Dorset, page 49. It is an old town, but nothing like as big or historic as Winchester. I bade Mr. Biggs stop for lunch at the Crown, because I remembered it as the principal inn of the place. In its bar, elegant but no longer animated, three or four customers in good jackets were solemnly drinking sherry. I had something stronger and told the gentlewoman behind the bar that I had been there before, with the Americans, and she said that *did* seem a long time ago. I pursued the subject no further, but she must have quoted me to other members of the staff; as Mr. Biggs and I made our way to the dining room a few minutes later, I heard a much younger gentlewoman at the reception desk say over her shoulder, "It was a bit livelier then, I daresay."

The cold meat was quite good, and only the flavor of the brown soup recalled the war. As I tasted it, a tune came into my head (this association of two sensory memories is, I believe, called synesthesia), but I had to down the spoonful of soup and hum two experimental bars before I could identify the air. It was "There'll Always Be an England." Mr. Biggs looked astonished and remarked, "I've always said there's nothing like a dash of high spirits, sir." The gentlefolk at the other tables looked peculiarly depressed, as if they had all come down into the country to hear the wills of relatives who had left them nothing. Mr. Biggs, having finished the last mouthful of the two kinds of potatoes and one kind of cabbage that had accompanied his mutton, looked around him slowly and then back at me. With a flash of perception that surprised me, he said, "We *are* a sad people to look at, aren't we, sir?"

On the sunlit road again, barreling down to Dorchester and Weymouth, I found it hard to keep my mind on the anniversary. There was no weekend traffic here, a hundred miles from London. In those other days, the road had been full of men going to a war, and now it wasn't. King Arthur probably used the same road going up to Badbury Rings, by the avenue of

beeches, to whip the West Saxons. "Badbury is identified by
Dr. Guest with Mount Badon, or Mons Badonicus. . . . Dr.
Guest's case is a strong but by no means overwhelming one."
Op. cit., pp. 43–4. That was in circa 520, and there had been
operations in between. In the fields by the road, red Devon
cattle had replaced the Jerseys and Guernseys nearer London.
The country looked less carefully tended, less self-consciously
old, than the Home Counties. It has been there so long that
there is no need to call attention to a post-Arthurian horror
like a thirteenth-century cottage. I could smell the Channel,
and Europe across it. This was an illusion based on reality,
because for me the smell of the lower Norman coast—sea and
broom plant—is the smell of Europe, and Dorset has sea
and broom plant, too. For years, I did not know the second
ingredient of this smell; it was a botanically informed friend
who identified it for me. Last April, at Lanark, in western Scotland, where there is a lot of broom, I smelled Europe all about
me. Glasgow does not smell like Europe, but that is because
the broom gets no chance. (Broom has a light, pleasant, spicy
smell, like fresh-baked ginger cake but enough different so
you know it can't be.)

The gaunt boarding villas that lined the highway as it entered the town limits of Weymouth were as lugubrious as the
Blandford lunchers, and their looks contrasted pitiably with
the names the original proprietors had chosen for them—Bon
Repos, Miramar Chalet, and the like. Weymouth in peacetime
is more celebrated as a beach resort than as a port. The sea air
had already nibbled at the villas' high, late-Victorian façades
of brick and stucco, which advertised the dankness within.
Nothing ages faster than a jerry-built house by the sea. There
are desolations within New York City, by Jamaica Bay, where
trees grow out through the glassless windows of facsimile châteaux, and house fronts gape like crazed Faulknerian ladies from
behind hedges of privet grown twenty feet high—desolations
that I can remember raucous with silk shirts, white flannel
pants, buckskin shoes, straw skimmers, gypsy orchestras, and
women in pretty good diamonds, forty years ago. Skip painting
a house by the shore for one season and it starts to go; ten and
it's gone. The pollution of Jamaica Bay and the coming of the
automobile did to those shore resorts close to town what

Faulkner thinks the Civil War did to Chuggetybuggety County, which would have gone bust in the natural course of events anyway.

These Weymouth villas had missed a lot of paintings, but somebody had always come along in the nick of time to save them from falling to pieces altogether. I knew that in a shore resort the boardinghouses farthest from the sea are always the shabbiest. Making full allowance for that, I found the approach to the Weymouth harbor sad in the Biggsian sense. I had stopped at Weymouth for tea once on the way down to some landing exercises in Devonshire in early spring, before the genuine embarkation, and I had retained from this visit a memory of a prodigiously long row of gaunt lodginghouses and hotels with nobody in them, staring out to sea across a beach encumbered with barbed wire. Then there had been the second, anxious time, in the LCI, with the beach still deserted but the town rumbling with troops and vehicles headed for the pier, while I, with crew and fellow-passengers, was confined to the 88 from the moment I came aboard. Bon Repos and the rest confirmed those first gloomy impressions. What Mr. Biggs and I saw when we reached the sea front abashed me, and perhaps him, because it was so different.

Weymouth Beach is a semicircle rimmed by an esplanade a mile long. The pier stands out to sea at the south end of the arc, which is the end away from the normal landward approach. The conflicting music of competing roundabouts down on the sand supplied a background to the shouts of children, who yell more and louder when they are by the sea than anywhere else, keeping in touch with one another in the face of bravely imagined dangers. On the breeze blowing from the direction of the pier I could identify occasional strains of band music and the screams of a number of mad sea gulls, inspired to vocalism by the general clamor as they dived for the discarded butts of ice-cream cones. From flagpoles set at intervals of not more than fifty feet along the esplanade fluttered the banners of Uruguay, Norway, Mexico, Italy, and about every other nation with gay colors. The great red brick hotel, the Gloucester, once the summer residence of George III (*Op. cit.*, p. 174), was cheerfully rubicund; the *pensions* with the Pullman-car names—Nyanza Chalet, Windermere Cottage,

Tickety-Boo-sur-Mer—flirted discreetly with the day trippers, employing tablecloths instead of handkerchiefs. There were flowers and cones of napery on the tables by their windows, inviting the trippers to the seven-and-six *prix fixe*. I imagined subterranean cisterns of brown soup, h. and c., but for the most part nearly c., supplying taps in all their kitchens; the thought depressed me only momentarily. The tide was low, and not one of the bathers I could descry walking out into the water—some of them mere dots at a distance of a nautical mile—had yet got up to his armpits; but a pedestrian with perseverance and an early start might reach swimmable depths and get back in time for a late tea. Some jolly good sunburns were already on view among the returning footsloggers.

Mr. Biggs parked the Vauxhall at the end of the esplanade farthest from the pier, just by an Italian flag, and we set out on foot. By the time we had gone a sixteenth of a mile, I realized that about every third flag was Italian; the chap in charge of decorations was either an Italian himself or enamored of red, white, and green. Abandoning all thought of finding the car again—I was glad I didn't own it—I strode on happily with Mr. Biggs, who was smiling, too, in a reserved way, past queues for teas and queues for ices at stands on the beach below our path, past queues at bathing tents, which here take the place of bathhouses.

We paused to look down on a Punch-and-Judy show. There was no Judy in it, though; perhaps the Lord Chamberlain had turned thumbs down on the battle of the sexes as entertainment for children. Instead, there was a smarmy male character, who outwitted Punch with the active connivance of the children in the audience. "Not Angles but Angels," St. Gregory said when he saw the captive English children in the slave market; and the small, beautiful faces turned up to the puppet show on Weymouth Beach made it easy to understand him. The smarmy puppet said to Punch, "'Old out your 'and. I won't 'urt you." He held a sledge hammer behind his back. Punch shrieked apprehensively and waved his hands about his head. Smarmy appealed to the angels. "I won't 'urt 'im, will I, children?" he asked them. "*No!*" they all shouted in chorus, following with an explosion of knowing squeals. Poor Punch wavered. He appealed to his little friends in turn. "Will 'e 'urt me if I put my 'and out, children?" "*No!*" followed by more squeals. "All right, pal. 'Ere's my 'and." He extended his right hand, palm up. Smarmy hit it with the sledge hammer. Punch screamed realistically, and the angels howled so hard with laughter that mummies and nannies had to drag half of them away to public lavatories. Even Mr. Biggs had to laugh. "Children *are* cruel, don't you agree, sir?" he said, when he could control his voice. After that, the puppet man, a topical cove, put on two boxing puppets in the roles of Rocky Marciano (boos) and Don Cockell (excited cheers). Cockell had all the best of it, and the "three-round exhibition" ended with Marciano out on the ropes while Cockell alternately butted him in the stomach and pulled his nose, a historical inaccuracy that the children accepted with enthusiasm.

Farther along, a cathedral builder had finished one half of the façade of Westminster Abbey in wet sand; the model was seven-feet high. A placard on an easel said, "Sand and water only used in this construction," and the man was working with a trowel. There was a bit of old carpet on the sand between the Abbey and the esplanade, and passing lovers of the fine arts showered down coins. Like the others, I felt that it was important for the master mason to finish his dedicated labor before high tide reduced it to ruins; a finished work of art, once it has existed, exists forever. I threw the man a sixpence, which landed fair in the middle of the carpet, but when I passed that way again, the Abbey was in the same unfinished state; he knew from experience, I suppose, that if he completed the job, no further appropriations could be expected. His game was to play upon the public anxiety.

At the end of our demitour, we reached the pier. It was a double pier, perhaps a thousand yards long, with a sunken railroad track in the middle. I had not remembered it exactly that way. There was relatively deep water only on the side away from the beach, facing a dredged inlet I did remember, which led into Weymouth's little port, beyond the pier end of the esplanade. The pier was of concrete; I recalled one covered with planks. Tied alongside, where I thought I remembered the LCIs end to end and cheek by jowl, were two steamers. The first, spruce and fairly ambitious, was a passenger liner serving the Channel Islands. The one out beyond her, a low, almost square-bowed coaster, was a potato boat from Jersey, where vegetables are earlier than in England. The potato boat was unloading; Sunday is a working day when there is a question of getting the new stuff to Covent Garden in time for the opening of the Monday market. Farther inshore, at the quay-side of the port, a tomato boat from Guernsey was unloading. Mr. Biggs and I picked our way along the pier, among the cranes and lorries and potato sacks, while I tried to reconcile my memories with what I saw. Across from the very end of the pier, and forming the mouth of the inlet with it, was a round fortification dating from Napoleonic times. I remembered that LCIL 88, commanded by Lieutenant Henry Rigg, U.S. Coast Guard Reserve, had passed this fort on the evening of Sunday, June 11, 1944, coming into port with a hole forward and enough of a list to get her sent back from Normandy for repairs. Off the fort, an old fellow had rowed out to us in a boat, shouting greetings and asking after friends of his in the crew. He brought us eleven bottles of beer because the pubs were closed.

Mr. Biggs and I talked to some of the longshoremen. The younger men had themselves been away in service, but a ganger, or foreman, said he remembered the LCIs well; he had worked as a fitter in the engine-repair shops set up for them in Weymouth. As to the exact berth of the 88, which he didn't remember, he said that if I recalled planks she must have lain up the inlet, where the Guernsey boat was now unloading tomatoes. "That quay is concrete now, same as this pier," he said, "but in 1944 there was still planks across the top of it. It's been rebuilt since. This here pier was concrete already then, same as like it is now."

So Biggs and I walked back, I by this time beginning to feel silly about the whole business. If the quay had been rebuilt, as the ganger said, it wouldn't look the same anyway. And what was I going to do if I did find the berth? I asked myself. Put a plaque there like the one on Norfolk House? "At this point in space and history 177 (approx. fig.) men (among many thousands of others) sweated out the invasion of *Festung Europa*, telling what jokes they could think of and playing poker badly for small sums"; or "Sacred to the memories of Moran, Frere, and Simone, whose first names I have forgotten. Moran was going to write a book, and Frere had a girl named Hazel." They hoisted Frere and Simone, dead, aboard a hospital ship, and when I reached up to steady one of the wire baskets, blood poured down in my face. I was soaked in blood, and when I washed it off my glasses I looked down and saw the stuff on the deck. The soldiers, who messed on deck, had left a case of canned milk, and a piece of our shell had opened the cans. We walked down to the tomato boat just the same, and I said it looked like the place all right, but of course it didn't.

We were hot and a bit footsore by that time, so I said to Mr. Biggs that it might be nice to go out to the end of the shallow-water side of the double pier, where there was a band concert, and sit down in deck chairs and have an ice. This side of the pier is divided from the working side by the railroad track and an iron grille. It is an amusement pier, and admission costs eighteen pence. Posters at the entrance said that the concert was being rendered by the Yeovil Workmen's Silver Prize Band. Yeovil is a small city in Somerset, not very far away. The posters did not say who gave the band the prize, or why it was only silver. Mr. Biggs and I walked out to the end again and hired deck chairs for sixpence apiece and sat down. There was a breeze out there. I bought a large-size, sixpenny ice-cream cone filled with brilliantly white ice cream that tasted as American ice cream bought at the beach used to when I was a boy (before the trees grew through the windows). The ice cream tasted of honest mucilage and vanilla, not imitation-rum-chocolate-chip-pistachio-cherry dextrose, like the contemporary variety. The band, which should have had all the prizes going, played a bewitching medley, including "The Maple Leaf Forever," "Widdicombe Fair," "The Minstrel Boy to the War Has Gone," "Rule, Britannia" (which made me feel retrospectively heroic), and, by a special dispensation of chance, "The Ace in the Hole":

> Others have friends in the old Tenderloin,
> That is their Ace in the Hole.

How the Ace got into the Yeovil medley I will never know. I hummed as I licked the delicious white ice cream. Mr. Biggs, that perceptive man, was watching me, although I was not at that moment aware of it. He had declined an ice, preferring to save himself for a nice cup of tea on the road. "The grimmest things, afterward, in the course of time," he said, "are softened, aren't they, sir?"

2

The Men in the Water

EARLY geographers had a habit of studding their maps with representations of monsters supposed to exist in the regions they delineated, and my geographical memory works the same way. For eleven years after D Day, the five-mile stretch of beach under the cliffs between Port-en-Bessin and Pointe de la Percée, on the Channel coast of Normandy, was marked in my mind by a line of American soldiers waist-deep in water and immobilized by fear. Descending arcs of tracers were entering the water around them, an LCT (Landing Craft, Tank) was burning nearby, and they could not bring themselves to move. They seemed as permanently fixed in time and space as those Marines in the statue of the flag-raising on Iwo Jima, but the circumstances were different. While the men stood there, the LCIL 88, on which I was a deeply impressed observer, went in on their right and landed its passengers, and then pulled out. That image of the beach, for me, superseded pleasant earlier memories of the same strip of coast. Prior to 1944 I had visualized the water there as blue under a summer sun, as it had looked to me in 1926, when I strolled along the tops of the cliffs behind it. After 1944, I remembered it as gray, except for the lines of the tracers, and disquietingly narrow between the LCIL 88 and the beach.

In 1955, a few days after my run to Weymouth, I went down from Paris to Port-en-Bessin, which is a cinematogenic fishing port, to have another look. D Day had been stormy, but this time the weather was perfect, as it had been in June 1940, when the Germans were on the outskirts of Paris (the weather was seldom on the side of the side I was with). For the expedition, I had hired a Versailles, which is a small car developed in France by Ford but now built by Simca. A Versailles is a sparrow compared to an American Ford, which in France is now a *voiture de grand luxe*, but in relation to other French-built cars it is a giant of the road; when you park one in a provincial town, boys dash out of alleys crying, "*Regardez la Versailles!*" The very small French cars are undoubtedly well adapted to

French purchase taxes, French gasoline prices, French village streets, and French distances, but they often remind me of a famous French clown named Toto, who years ago did a standard turn in Keith vaudeville and at the Hippodrome. Toto made his entrance folded up inside what seemed to be a toy sedan, which operated under its own power. After he had extracted himself from it—a thin man, he was fairly tall, or at least he knew how to make himself look so—he would haul out a valise, a string of sausages, a dog, and a feather duster. He was an unrecognized pioneer of the contemporary French automotive industry. The Versailles towers above the Totomobiles one encounters on French highways.

With my elephant of the roads came a mahout—a White Russian named Michel, who took care of it as carefully as if it had been an atom-fueled jet airplane. He changed the oil every seven hundred miles, had the car greased nearly every time we stopped for a beer, and probably slept with it under his pillow. Michel was a polite man, fifty-four years old, with strands of black hair carefully plastered over the bald top of his head and soft brown eyes continually wide with wonder at his escape from the Ukraine in 1920, from Bulgaria in 1928, from the Germans during the occupation of Paris, and from various hotel concierges, who ordinarily clipped him twenty per cent of his fee every time they got him a driving job. (I had hired him through the carhire man, who, Michel said, did not clip him.) For thirty-five years he had lived with all the perils, real and imagined, that beset the life of a permanent foreigner. He still had a Nansen passport; since 1939, his wife, a Pole, had also been without a country. Her brother had been talked into going back to Poland, and the current Polish government wouldn't let him out. All this Michel conveyed to me in pidgin French during the first twenty minutes I knew him. There had been 22,000 White Russians in Paris when he arrived there, he told me—all chauffeurs, taxi drivers, or maîtres d'hôtel—and with 21,999 of his fellow-countrymen to talk to he had never felt the need to learn sequential French. In the summer, he drove American clients who knew no French at all. The concierge in whatever hotel they were staying at would tell him where they wanted to go, and he would take them there.

If they had further instructions for him, they could relay them through the concierge at the next hotel. Every time we stopped, Michel would get out, run around the back, open my door for me, and bow. Whenever I got out before he could reach me, I saw he felt snubbed. (It would have been impossible to explain to him that the mannerisms he had learned while driving a Hispano-Suiza were not appropriate to a Versailles, since he thought of the latter as a vast vehicle, pulsating with power.) He won me over our first afternoon out, and from then on I sat and waited for him to come around and open the door.

Michel was a good driver as long as he knew what road he would be on for the next fifty miles. But he expected Americans to travel in their regular orbits—Paris-Deauville, Paris-Biarritz, Paris-châteaux-of-the-Loire—and it disconcerted him to be instructed to leave these known trajectories. He was not much on maps and drove too fast to read the signs at *carrefours*, so he often took us several miles in a wrong direction. When this occurred, he would look at me reproachfully for not having wanted to go to Deauville, and then get out to search for a deaf and dumb old lady or, in her default, the next most unlikely source from whom to request directions. I was unaware of these idiosyncrasies until we reached Caen, a hundred and fifty miles from Paris. Up to that point, it had been main road all the way.

"Where now? Where?" Michel asked, and I said, "Bayeux," which is the nearest town of prominence to Port-en-Bessin. He leaped from the car, ran across a traffic circle to an Algerian rug peddler, and engaged in animated consultation. Then, waving his arms, he abandoned the Algerian and stepped in front of an old gentleman on a bicycle. There was wild pantomime, after which Michel returned, his eyes wider than ever with amazement, which was now mingled with pity. "*N'esista pas, Moosioo,*" he said. "*N'esista pas, Boolioo.*"

It was my turn to be astonished. "No *Boolioo*," I said, already falling into his gibberish. "*Bayeux!*"

"*Oui, Moosioo, Boolioo, mais n'esista pas,*" he said.

I got out a Michelin road map and pointed to Bayeux on it. Michel carried the map to a nearby café and came back looking

disappointed. "Ba-*yeux!*" he said, with an inflection that asked
why I couldn't pronounce it properly. "Ba-*yeux! Ba-yeux
esista.*"

Michel resigned himself to not going to Biarritz, and we
drove along the route his consultant in the café had indicated
until we saw the towers of the cathedral, indisputably tangible
and ferocious. Michel and I had not conversed much after he
recited the autobiography that he had succeeded, probably
through practice, in organizing into an almost intelligible
form. Other attempts at prolonged communication had fallen
down, and I was rather glad they had, since I wanted to think
about what lay ahead.

I pass as a Francophile, but there are only two parts of
France with which I have had more than a fleeting connection.
One is Paris. The other is a ragged triangle in Lower Normandy, two of whose sides are formed by the English Channel
and the third by an imaginary line drawn from Caen south and
west to Mont-Saint-Michel, with a slight deviation to take in
Vire and Mortain. All this lies within the departments of
Manche and Calvados. The reasons that persuaded me to go
there first were sensible but slight. I had two months to spare
before the opening of the Sorbonne in the fall of 1926, and I
wanted to travel in some part of France that wasn't Paris.
Lower Normandy was easy to get to, it had a historic cachet,
and I had heard that it was agreeable but not spectacular.
Because it was not spectacular, it was not tourist country, and
I was terribly afraid of being mistaken for a tourist. At that remote period of my life, I liked to walk fifteen or twenty miles a
day, but I wanted a good bed to sleep in at night, and I was a
great glutton. I had read Guy de Maupassant in English when
I was still in short pants—I was in them again in 1926, but I
called them plus fours—and this gave me a feeling of confidence about plunging into Normandy. I knew what to expect
of its peasants; they would be like New Englanders. The precipitating pretext for my choice was a mild curiosity about a
medieval poet who was supposed to have lived in Vire. When I
got there, I found that he was a hoax long since exploded, but
the story of the hoax was amiable.

This country, which I had chosen so lightly, gripped me—

partly, I suppose, because it was the first foreign land I had traveled in alone. Paris is foreign to no literate person, and the sensation of being abroad is the only pleasure I have never known there. Within my Norman triangle, I noticed differences from, as well as analogies with, home, the beauties of small landscapes, the taste of food prepared in ways new to me. Even the old wheezes of such a land are irresistibly funny, because you have never heard them before. Old jokes survive because they are good jokes; if our own old jokes seem flat to us, it is because we have heard them so often. Coming to a new old city, I would walk all through it, smell it, look at streets house by house, as if I were going to live there all my life. People I saw around me became important. I devoted more reflection, for example, to the possibilities of one waitress in the Hotel du Cheval Blanc in Vire—snub nose, pasty color, in spite of the incredible amount of hard physical work she got through, small eyes, but splendid forearms and legs—than to all the women, some of them dazzling, who passed me on the Champs-Elysées that same summer. I cannot remember now what any one of *them* looked like, though I thought they were all hot stuff at the time. In the mornings, the waitress would wash down the floors of the hotel, and for that she would wear wooden clogs. At lunchtime she would take off the clogs and put on stockings and high-heeled slippers, a gesture of coquetry I can still see her performing. After she had pulled on the slippers, she would wash her hands at the spigot over a painted metal basin that was placed at the entrance of the dining room for the use of fastidious clients. She left an enduring impress on my life, although our relations were always impersonal. At my first meal at the hotel, I asked for a salad plate. She brought it to me, saying, with a superior smile, "*Chacun son pays, chacun sa façon.*" I have taken my salad on my meat plate ever since, dabbling the lettuce in the leftover gravy.

The sojourn had a no less pronounced effect upon my tastes in food. I am still of the opinion that Lower Normandy has the best sea food, the best mutton (from the salt meadows of the Avranches region), the best beef, the best butter, the best cream, and the best cheese in Europe, and that the ideal light lunch is a dozen *huitres de Courseulles*, an *araignée de mer* (spider crab) with a half pint of mayonnaise on the side, a dish of *tripes à la mode de Caen*, a partridge Olivier Basselin, poached in cream and cider and singed in old Calvados, a *gigot de pré-salé*, a couple of *biftecks*, and a good Pont l'Evêque. I can no longer stand up to it in one sitting, as the Irishmen say in the storybooks, but that is not the fault of the menu. It is my metabolism that has collapsed.

The Norman takes his vegetables in the form of animals. "Herbivores eat grass," one hotel landlord told me. "Man, a carnivore, eats herbivores." The Norman takes his fruit in the form of cider and its distillate Calvados. "Those big, beautiful apples are good, perhaps, to look at," the same sage said, "but our little ones make better drinking." I have never wavered since in my belief that old Calvados has a more agreeable bouquet, a warmer touch on the heart, and a more outgoing personality than cognac. It is less precocious, but that is only a confirmation of its more profound character. The barrel of Calvados laid down at an infant's birth matures with him; he is unlikely to need it until he is at least eleven, and by that time it will be passable. If the boy is to drink Calvados at its best, however, it is better to lay down several barrels, so he will still have some when he is fifty.

Because of my feeling about the region, I sneaked back there for a week in the winter of 1939, the first year of the war, and I found that I thought no less of it. Consequently, when, on Friday, June 2, 1944, I learned that the destination of the cross-Channel expedition was my ragged triangle, I felt as if, on the eve of an expedition to free the North from a Confederate army of occupation, I had been told that we would land on the southern shore of Long Island and drive inland toward Belmont Park. It was a British naval officer who briefed my lot of correspondents at Whitehall that Friday morning before they shoved us off to the invasion ports. "If it's a good show, as we rather hope, all will be tickety-boo by D-plus-1," the naval bloke said cheerily. I forget whether he added "Good hunting!" or whether I merely heard that one in a motion picture. From the Whitehall briefing, which gave us the large, inter-Allied naval picture (a British admiral, Sir Bertram Ramsay, was in over-all command of the naval operation), we progressed, after a long bus ride, to another briefing, this one by an American admiral aboard the command ship *Ancon*, off Portland Bill, in Dorset. The Admiral told us about the American half of the project—everything from Port-en-Bessin west to Utah Beach, on the Cotentin peninsula. But it was not until I got to LCIL 88, at Weymouth, that I learned her precise destination—a zone of Omaha Beach known by the code name of Easy Red. The "tickety-boo" stuck; I quoted it numerous times in the following week, and it was taken up by our little social group on LCIL 88. "Tickety-boo on Easy Red" became our catch line, and after the shell hit it acquired piquancy.

Once aboard the 88 and restricted to her small hull, I received all the detailed information I could possibly want—in fact, a bit more about the enemy capabilities than I possibly wanted. The 88 was to land a mixed lot of special units that would be needed early—engineers to blow out obstructions, naval beach-battalion men to guide small-boat traffic, and the like—at a point about three miles west of Port-en-Bessin, where, I remembered at that moment, I had once eaten a magnificent sole *normande*, bedewed with shelled mussels, on the terrace of a restaurant looking out on a summer sea. I asked Lieutenant Henry K. Rigg, the 88's commander, whether I would be able to see Port-en-Bessin from where we were going in, and he said that if the day was clear, I might see the lighthouse and the long west jetty, but he thought I would have a lot of distractions.

The houses of Port-en-Bessin are folded into a draw between two rows of cliffs where a stream, the Dromme, comes down to the Channel. Two stone jetties, or moles, form an artificial outer port, which leads to two inner basins, one behind the other, where the fishing boats tie up. The weather on D Day—a Tuesday—wasn't clear, and Rigg's surmise proved correct; there were so many nearer objects calling for attention that I never looked in the direction of my gastronomic idyl. Before we went back to Weymouth on the following Sunday, I learned that Port-en-Bessin had been captured promptly and without serious damage.

Bayeux has been for many years one of my favorite cities, but as Michel and I neared the sea, my need to look at Easy

Red became imperative, so we paused in the town only long enough to drink a glass of beer at the Hôtel du Lion d'Or. When I had last seen the hotel, in 1944, it was Field Marshal Montgomery's headquarters; now there was no trace of the great man, not even a high-pitched echo. When we had finished our beer, I told Michel we would push on. By road, it is 9 k., or five miles and five furlongs, from Bayeux to Port-en-Bessin. The road, bordered sometimes by hedges and sometimes by rows of tall, scraggly poplars, led past a couple of gray stone country churches, nine hundred years old, fields full of white-and-liver-colored Norman cattle, a dappled Percheron mare with her bay foal, and a disconsolate man standing beside a stalled Totomobile (Citroën, two horsepower). We stopped and went back to the man; he was out of gas. "And just to think," he said as he got into our car, "I'm a salesman for a gasoline company."

"It is the son of the cobbler who wears shoes with holes in them," I said, coming up with a Lower Normandy chestnut I had not been able to utilize in the previous quarter of a century. At Port-en-Bessin, he told us, he would buy a flimsy of gas, and have the garageman drive him back to his car. A creature like a weasel ran across the road well ahead of us with something in its mouth—a field mouse or a bird's egg. A similar creature had run across my course on the same road twenty-nine years before, and I had always meant to ask a peasant what it might have been. I made the same resolve about this one and then forgot to ask. I was momentarily saddened by a sign I saw posted in a field. "MYXOMATOSE," it read, indicating the presence of the rabbit disease that had decimated the warrens of western Europe. I suppose the sign was to warn sportsmen of the unhealthy nature of the rabbits to be found there (although if the disease had caught on in the neighborhood, there wouldn't be many), but it reminded me of my baptism of fire, which I underwent in 1926 on the fields atop the cliffs between Arromanches and Port-en-Bessin.

For a week in that magic end of summer, I lived in a hotel at Bayeux and walked almost every day, blackthorn stick in hand, to one of the small shore resorts—Arromanches, Asnelles, or Port-en-Bessin. Turning at the sea, I would proceed along the tops of the cliffs to an adjacent village and then return to

different road. On a Sunday morning, I walked to
Bayeux, took a copious *apéritif* there, and then headed
Arr footpath that led to the sole *normande* I was to deal d remember. That Sunday was the opening day of
ing season. Nobody had told me. As I pushed along,
what French military communiqués call a "nourished"
ns fire from the direction in which I was advancing.
dden, but too late, I perceived its source—a rank of
nen moving forward in a skirmish line, pressed in from
ds, for want of space, until they were almost elbow to
oow. They were preceded by a stampede of terrified dogs—
briquets, griffons, and Brittany spaniels—over whose heads
they discharged their automatic shotguns as they advanced.
They were the sportsmen of Port-en-Bessin.

Had I been on the summit of some distant acclivity, like
Napoleon at Regensburg, I would have admired the spectacle.
It was magnificent, but it was not hunting; it was rather in the
tradition of Fontenoy—the cadenced step and the fire by companies. My position being what it was, however, I beat a retreat, effecting a *repli* sufficiently abrupt upon Arromanches.
(The idiom of the communiqué continues to impose itself.)
Then I heard, to what had been my rear, a fire equally well
nourished and the baying of another pack of dogs. The sportsmen of Arromanches were out, keen on getting their share of
rabbits. I ran to the edge of the cliff, but there was no escape
in that direction, for the tide was all the way in. I therefore
tried to make myself as conspicuous and as unmistakably human as possible. Waving my arms high over my head, with my
blackthorn stick clutched in my right hand, I walked deliberately toward the nearer danger—the ambulatory fusillade from
the direction of Port-en-Bessin. I did not tie a white handkerchief to the end of the stick; that is merely a detail I invented
the fourth time I told the story and have since decided to discard. My approach was observed just before I got within shot-
gun range. The fire died away; one or two final charges of
buckshot whistled high over my head as I reached the line of
dogs—merely shots fired at a sea gull somebody had mistaken
for an edible lark. I passed through the disgruntled ranks of
the *chasseurs*, who leaned upon their *fusils* and did not even say
"*Bonjour.*" Scarcely had I resumed my promenade when I

heard behind me the crash of a new volley. It terri
imagine what would happen when the two detachme
and I hurried on in order to avoid being called as a wito

I was thinking happily of my miraculous escape from
pothunters when Michel reached Port-en-Bessin. We dropp
our passenger at a garage on the outskirts and then continue
down the road, which soon changed to Port-en-Bessin's main
street, running along the west bank of the two boat basins.
Masts rose on one side of the street and on the other were
stores and a couple of cafés. "Fishing port," Michel said
knowingly, and then, waving his hand at some men on the
quay, added, "Fishermen." He pointed to the boats. "For the
fishing," he said. Little had changed that I could notice since
the day of the rabbit shoot and the sole *normande*. The quay
and the street made a right-angle turn where the outer harbor
began, and there, in front of the Hôtel de la Marine, I had a
view of the sea—blue again, and smiling. "Little place," said
Michel. "Peasants." He inhabits a walkup on a street just off
the Champs-Elysées. This has given him a sense of belonging
to *le monde chic*. When I was in Port-en-Bessin before, it had
1,334 inhabitants, according to the *Guide Bleu* of 1926; the
latest *Guide Bleu* says it now has 1,314. This seems odd, considering the apparently high proportion of children in the population, but it is probable that many of the males drown or
enter holy orders, while a good number of the females leave to
take jobs inland.

The ground floor of the Hôtel de la Marine is bar, café, and
kitchen. At mealtimes, paper tablecloths turn the café into a
restaurant. A movable screen partitions off one corner of this
room for the group social life of the proprietor and his wife
and their swarm of children. He reads a newspaper, she shells
peas, and the children make noises. The room above is a long
salle for wedding and Communion banquets. The kitchen of
the Hôtel de la Marine is the cause of innumerable detours
from the Route Nationale that joins Paris and Cherbourg. In
the *Guide Michelin*, which is the automobilist's vade mecum,
Port-en-Bessin is identified on a map of France as a place
where one may enjoy "a particularly well-prepared meal, preferably regional in character" at a moderate price. The *Guide* de-

fines a moderate price as seven hundred francs (the equivalent of two dollars, or fourteen shillings), including wine. There are less than a hundred restaurants on this map as compared with nearly seven hundred cited elsewhere in the *Guide* as having outstanding cuisine. Cherbourg, fifty-six miles up the road, is the nearest dot on the moderate-price map. The woman at the desk consented to harbor us for one night, on condition that we not try to stay longer, because all the rooms would be needed for the guests at a Communion banquet on the following day. "After what they will send themselves, it is better that they do not drive," she said.

The upper floors of the Hôtel de la Marine have the excessively bare look common to hotels whose management expects guests to track sand through the halls; they also have showers. It was six o'clock by then, and I was eager to get out on the west jetty, which is a third of a mile long; but it had been hot on the road, and I decided to have a cold shower first. The beach I wanted to see would be just like any other beach, I told myself, and at that distance I would not even be sure where Fox Green ended and Easy Red began. And the men could not have been standing in the water all this time. Somebody would have noticed them and invited them to come ashore and rest up.

I was drying myself with a towel six inches square—the largest available at the Hôtel de la Marine—when a hideous noise broke out, like the quacking of a monster mad duck against the background of the shriek of an air-raid siren. As I was on my way back to my room, a man I passed in the hall told me it was the foghorn of a small lighthouse that stands on the top of the cliffs west of town. I looked out the window, but not far, because a white fog was pressing against the glass. It had come up in a matter of minutes. There was no use going to the jetty now; visibility was about ten feet. The fog, the quacking, and the shrieking went on unabated, and the harmless quality of the place seemed to have vanished with the blue sky. I imagined boats in the fog steering toward the sound and slipping past the fingertips of the men in the water off the beach, who still waited for a lift.

I went down to the café and took a *pastis*. There were four young fishermen there, off a dragger named the *Notre-Dame de la Délivrance*, and they were glad they had made port before the fog set in. The siren, which was driving me mad, did not annoy them; they admired it as a beneficent mechanism. "*Quel potin!*" (What a row!), one of them said. "It makes itself heard eleven miles out at sea." They had brought in a fair catch of *raie* (skate), a fine cash fish in France, this sailor said, and a lot of oddments that also came up in the nets—*tourteaux* (like English or Cuban crabs), *araignées de mer, congres* (conger eels), *encornet* (squid), *carangue* (a small blue fish that the sailor described as "the female of the mackerel"), *limande* (plaice), and a number of species for which I could not recall any familiar counterparts. The price of fish was low, the sailor said, compared to that of the fuel oil needed to propel the boats. The fish "rarefied" themselves more every year, and the boats had to go farther all the time to get them. In winter, they often stayed out ten days. When bad weather caught them off the Cornish coast, the crews sometimes had to put into English ports, where they were *mal vus*—they got hard looks. Fishermen were suspected of smuggling not only in England but in their own *petit pays*. As the sailor was talking, a shadow passed in the fog, close to the window. "Look," he said. "It's the customs guard. Always nosing around for trouble. This is a quiet little place—never a row, no funny business. You never see the nose of a gendarme here from one year's end to the next. But the customs men, they show off. They claim storms drive us too often into Falmouth."

One of the other fishermen, a reserved and, until then, expressionless male-beauty-contest type, said with violence, "They know about storms, the customs men? They're sailors, them? *C'est des Parisiens!*"

"And is there no smuggling off this coast?" I asked, remembering to smile.

"Oh, Monsieur, one isn't living in the eighteenth century," the first sailor said. "There isn't much any more."

One of the sailors was a dark, heavy-set fellow who looked as if he might be from the Midi, but when I asked him, he told me that he had been born in Port-en-Bessin, like all the others. "There are almost no foreigners—that is to say, *sailors from other ports*—working on our boats," he said. "We are all a little more or less related. Fellows go away from the port, of course, but they come back after they finish their service in the Navy."

There were thirty-odd boats working out of the port, the sailors said, and about three hundred and fifty seamen. "Including engineers and fellows who work in boatyards," the handsome boy, a stickler for exactitude, added.

"But the engineers are marine engineers," the dark sailor said. "They go to sea, what?"

"They aren't sailors," the purist replied. "If you want to call them quasi-sailors, I agree."

I asked the men if they remembered D Day, when, as well as I could judge by looking at them, they must all have been between ten and thirteen years old. They remembered it as a super Fourteenth of July celebration. Not many shells had fallen on Port-en-Bessin, they said, because the Allies wanted to take the port intact. A number of summer villas on the slopes overlooking the town had been destroyed by artillery fire laid down to stop the Germans from moving up supporting units. But no one had been hurt, because it was early in the season and the summer people had not yet moved in. At dawn, the boys had heard the guns on the long beach to the west and had seen a cloud of artificial fog spread over the landing operations. I had forgotten the fog, but it must have added to the gloom of the rainy, windy day.

The scout plane of the *Georges Leygues*—a Free French cruiser in the fleet covering the landings with fire—had flown low over the town, dropping leaflets warning the people to take cover. The *Georges Leygues*, the sailors told me, had fired more shells than any other ship in the fleet. Two of the young men had subsequently done their military service aboard her, and she was a great favorite in Port-en-Bessin. I remember the *Georges Leygues* well—a self-assertive vessel.

Soon after the airplane with the leaflets, British Commandos had appeared on the east jetty and American infantry on the west, the sailors continued. Canadians had moved in on Port-en-Bessin from the land side, and the Germans had not insisted; some took off and others were "done like rats." There had never been many of them in the town—a couple of companies, perhaps.

The sailors went home to their suppers—we had sent

ourselves a few by then—and Michel and I now settled down to the selection of a particularly well-prepared meal, preferably regional in character, from the menu presented by Georgette, the waitress, whose name I had learned from my nautical acquaintances. She had red hair and a short upper lip, but the traveler in the Norman triangle must be several days out of Paris before he begins to pay waitresses the concentrated attention I gave the one at Vire. The fog cleared at sunset, as abruptly as it had come, and the foghorn ceased its infernal *potin*.

To insure the regional character of my meal, I ordered an *araignée*, to be followed by *raie au beurre noir*. The *araignée*, a beast of loathly aspect in a state of nature, is a warty, long-legged creature with a carapace resembling a slightly flattened baseball. It looks more like a land crab than a water crab. It is of a despicable khaki color, which gives it protective coloration on mud bottoms, and it has acquired a trick of tangling seaweed around its legs, possibly to make itself appear innocuous or inedible. Whatever its object, it has created the latter impression so successfully on the New England and Long Island coasts that I have never known anybody there to eat one. It is a great bait grabber, and when Americans fishing for blackfish or flounder haul one of these crabs aboard, they consider it a calamity instead of a stroke of luck and dash the crab to death, or stamp on it, before they throw it back into the sea—the men in the party swearing and the women, if there are any aboard, shuddering. What doesn't occur to those fishermen is that the *araignée*, placed in hot water, will turn red like any other crustacean, and so lose its repulsive color. It turns a peculiarly beautiful red, in fact—the color of those old-fashioned rambler roses that smell like raspberries. On the other hand, the *tourteau*, so popular in Britain, where "crab" means only *tourteau*, will blush no deeper than a yellowy pink, attractively set off by black claw tips, while our own blue crab assumes in hot water the angry color of a newborn baby.

Set down on the plate right side up, the cooked *araignée* has the appearance of an ambulant rosy-red apple. The Norman cook has already made a discreet incision around the periphery of the carapace, permitting the spider-eater, after he has sufficiently admired his specimen, to lift the top like a lid and attack the white interior from above. There is a good deal to eat in an *araignée*; while there are none of the large chunks of meat you find in a lobster or *langouste*, every part of it except the lid may be profitably scrunched between molars. The long legs, passed between the incisors, yield their sweet juice to a gentle pressure. Just as the nectarine combines peach and plum, the taste of the *araignée* suggests both lobster and crab, with the tantalizing added suggestion of *oursin*, or sea urchin.

Skate is a less peculiarly regional dish, but in support of my choice of this relative of the shark I appropriate a statement by a woman I once knew about Long Island fluke. "Once plucked from the water, they lose their flavor as quickly as corn on the cob," she said, and the observation is equally pertinent to the skate. The *raie au beurre noir* of West Forty-eighth Street or Soho is to the *raie au beurre noir* of Port-en-Bessin what the Joe Louis of 1951 was to the Joe Louis of 1938. The inland chef's sole recourse in preparing skate is to stoke the *beurre noir* with capers until the *raie* tastes no worse than deep-frozen Pacific Coast swordfish bought in cellophaned slats from a supermarket.

By the time I had finished the skate and a mound of strawberries, Port-en-Bessin seemed to have resumed its harmless quality, even though the foghorn was again raising its benevolent *potin*. I now found the noise agreeable. Michel retired for the night. "*Pas Deauville, Moosioo,*" he said sadly before going. "*Pas Place Etoile.*" He could hardly have complained that it was too quiet. I got to sampling the hotel's various Calvados. It was the first night I had spent in the triangle since July 1944, by which time, after six weeks of residence, the Allied forces had drunk up all the Calvados in the region. The new, ten-year-old stuff I was served in the Hôtel de la Marine was rough but showed promise. Presently my fishermen came back and told me what an absurdly puritanical country England was. The cafés close at eleven, they said, and they put you to the door. Georgette threw them out at ten-thirty and then stacked chairs on my table. I went to bed.

The night cleared, and the foghorn fell silent. I was sleeping when it opened up again. It was hard to disregard the quacking of the mad, asthmatic duck when there was neither conversation nor Calvados to cushion the impact on the eardrums. I lay wondering whether I would be able to have my look at the beach next day or whether the fog was going to keep me around long enough to develop an interest in Georgette. Toward dawn, the *potin* stopped, and I fell asleep, as I used to do after the all-clear in wartime London.

Despite my untranquil night, I was up early, and I took a turn by the boat basins, where I joined a knot of men and women around an auctioneer who was just beginning his *marché à la criée* of the fishermen's haul. The boats lay ranged along the main-street quay, their catches spilled out in open crates or baskets that were aligned on the quay in front of them. The auctioneer started with the boat lying nearest the entrance of the harbor and worked his way inland, calling for bids on every lot, even if each consisted of but three lobsters or a couple of kilos of undersized scallops. He was a Norman out of the storybooks—blond, blue-eyed, all his facial capillaries exploded by wet weather and good living and his neck bursting out of the top of his blue shirt like a tree trunk out of a hole in a sidewalk. His clothes appeared to conceal the torso of a Percheron. He was a ringer for a ship's carpenter named Andresen I once knew on a Norwegian tanker called the *C. T. Boe*. If you put the two men together, you would need no further documentation of the story of the Viking migration to Normandy under Rollo.

The auctioneer talked very fast, like his colleagues the world over. As he stopped at each lot, he would begin, "*Mesdames, Messieurs, regardez les belles limandes*," or "*les beaux turbots*" (there were, unfortunately, not many of these), or "*les belles lamproies*," or "*les beaux congres*," or "*les belles roussettes*" (these last three are hideous lampreys, conger eels, and spotted dogfish, with faces like Picasso women of the artist's most misogynistic period). All fish were beautiful to the auctioneer. He would then start at what he considered a reasonable minimum price per kilo. "Eighty francs the handsome Saint-Pierre," he might say, referring to a fish with the retreating forehead of a Chicago alderman. "Eighty-one, eighty-two, ninety," he would patter on mysteriously, as if he were doing the bidding, and then stop just as mysteriously by naming the purchaser, who hadn't said a word. An assistant would write the buyer's name on a chit and throw it in the crate, and the auctioneer would lead the way to the next lot. Most of the prospective buyers ate raw scallops as they walked along, nipping them out of the baskets on the quay. I noticed that one of the bidders, a fishwife, had brightly polished toenails. As the lots were sold, huskies loaded the crates into motor trucks parked on the quay, and after the last lot was knocked down, the trucks roared off for Caen and Paris, the latter less than four hours by road. Large skates, I observed, brought a hundred and eighty francs a kilo, which works out to about twenty-five cents a pound, on the dock. Skate is a poor man's fish the world over. The cost of living is high in France these days.

When the *marché* broke up, I introduced myself to the auctioneer, and he asked me if I had been able to follow him; he was obviously proud of how fast he could talk. So I said that I had not understood a word, and he looked happy. I asked him how he spotted the bids so fast. He said he knew his customers, since they were the same ones every day, and their ways of bidding—by wiggling their thumbs, rubbing their noses, or just winking. There was a *marché* every morning, and Thursday's was the biggest, because it came just before Friday. We were Thursday.

I told the auctioneer that I had been nearby on D Day, in 1944. On a point at the east side of the entrance to the boat basins there was a gaunt and decrepit structure that looked like an abandoned barracks, and I asked him whether it had been a partial casualty of the attack. He said no, that it was an old hotel that had belonged to a rich widow, who had willed it to the state to be used as a school for orphans, on condition that they be taught by Sisters of Charity. It had been assigned, somehow, to the police of Paris for the use of orphans of policemen, but the Prefect of Police had insisted on lay teachers. The lawyers for the widow's estate had sued the government to recapture the building for the residuary heirs, on the ground that the terms of the bequest had been violated. Neither party to the litigation had cared to risk any money on repairs pending the result of the *procès*, which dated back to the time of Tardieu. Consequently, the hotel was falling to pieces.

"The port was little damaged on D Day," the auctioneer

said. "It was really in much better shape than it had been six months earlier. The Germans had been working in an endeviled manner to dredge the entrances from the outer port into the inner basins, clear the mudbank from the west quay, and perfect the harbor in every way. They used it for flak barges [the Siebel ferries that were designed for the invasion of England and later converted into floating antiaircraft gun platforms]. It shows how little they expected an attack on this part of the coast. If they had known it was coming here, they would have done all they could to make the port unfit for use in case of capture. There was an English officer, disguised as a German, who needled them to push the work. He had the shoulder tabs of a German staff officer, and he would come here in a big car, as if direct from high headquarters. 'The Führer wants it ready by the end of May,' he would say. '*Allez, hop!* Big things in the wind! Don't mention it even to the Army commander.'"

"You knew he was English?" I asked.

"No, not personally," the auctioneer replied. "But I have a friend who talked to him one day, in English. My friend speaks English well, having been a deck steward on the *Paris* before he retired. The English chap was dressed as a colonel, a Fritz, and he spoke German perfectly, you understand. 'Ah, well,' he said to my friend, 'I am not a German at all. I am a spy, but don't say anything about it.' My friend, naturally, didn't say anything about it, even to me, until after the landings. On the day following D Day, my friend saw the chap again. He was still a colonel, all right, not a doubt. But an English one."

"They're shrewd, the English," I said.

"More than one would think, to look at them," the auctioneer said.

I have made no attempt to verify the story about the British colonel.

We walked across the cobbled street to a small place called the Café du Port, where the auctioneer ordered some kind of poison-green alcoholized "pippermint," because, he said, his doctor had told him coffee was bad for his kidneys. I risked the coffee, but added a jolt of Calvados as a kidney guard.

"Seeing the Germans work so hard to improve the port, we didn't expect the attack here, either," the auctioneer went on.

"Still, when we heard the guns at dawn, we said, '*Ça y est.*' But that's all in the past. It's the fish that annoy us now. They rarefy themselves. The total catch of the port is greater than during the between-wars, but that's because there are more boats. The catch per boat is less. And each boat represents such a placement of money! There is a new one in the basin— a seventy-three-footer—with every latest gadget for spotting fish. She must have cost thirty million francs [eighty-five thousand dollars] to build. The owner won't get his money back for twenty years. I used to own two boats, but I sold them."

"Doesn't the Bishop of Bayeux still bless the fleet every year?" I asked.

"Yes, Monsieur," the auctioneer replied. "But the fish have lost the Faith."

Leaving the Café du Port, I walked along the edge of the outer harbor to the beginning of the long west jetty that I might have seen from the LCIL 88 on D Day, had the weather and circumstances been otherwise. The outer harbor was described concisely in a monograph issued in 1944 by Admiral A. G. Kirk, commander of United States Naval Task Force 122. It is a "semicircular basin approximately 1,640 feet E-W and 1,260 feet N-S, encircled by two granite moles. The western mole is 1,490 feet long; the eastern 1,390 feet long. . . . A spur, called the Epi de la Poissonnerie, extending 312 feet from the shore, divides the basin into two parts, of which only the eastern part is usable. . . . The western portion . . . though larger, cannot be used to secure ships as it is encumbered by a mudbank drying out at 10 to 13 feet. . . . The entrance channel lies between the heads of two curving moles. . . . The width of the channel is 328 feet."

The western part of the basin—the one that dries out, or almost—is the *plage* of Port-en-Bessin, where at low tide children hunt shrimps or paddle in the inshore tidal pools and the braver adults venture out into the shallow swimming waters inside the elbow of the jetty, where it swings over toward its fellow. The jetty was built in 1860, out of great, carefully cut blocks of stone. A rampart, also of stone, runs around the outer, seaward edge. The inner side is a steep stone slope, with a few flights of steps cut into it at intervals. Sometimes the children use the steps, but for the most part they simply scramble up and down the seaweed-covered slope like flies on a wall. The tide was low when I began my walk, and the jetty acted as a sounding board to echo the voices of the swarms of juveniles within the amphitheater. Each tidal pool was the center of a band with its own pecking order—very small boys trying to drown very small girls, small girls trying to drown very small boys, and medium-small boys trying to frighten medium-small girls by pretending to drown them. Older, manlier types, from eight to eleven, had stationed themselves on the rampart with long fishing poles, dangling bait in the deeper water outside. They apparently banned girls from this serious activity. Girls of the same age group lay on the sand farther inshore, their skirts drawn up to their underpants, their eyes closed, and their faces toward the summer sun, trying as hard as they could to incubate themselves into women.

I walked out on the jetty to a point just before it turned and looked west toward the sweep of Omaha Beach, with the calm water in front of it and the green cliffs in back. The cliffs were not imposing at that distance. They were no more than a hundred to a hundred and thirty feet high where they flanked Easy Red. I had remembered them swollen with danger. There were a couple of small sails—draggets with auxiliary engines, probably—down toward Pointe de la Percée, but although I looked carefully, with racing glasses, I could see no soldiers standing in the water anywhere.

3
Tickety-Boo on Easy Red

WHEN I first came to the ancient, illustrious, minuscule city of Bayeux, as an American newly entitled to vote, the book I carried in my pocket was the 1926 edition of the Hachette *Guide Bleu* for Normandy. In it, the capsule description of the city began:

BAYEUX: 7,026 inhabitants (*les Bayeusains*), former capital of the Bessin [the low-lying area between Caen and Isigny], seat of a bishopric, is situated in the verdant plain watered by the little River Aure. Its cathedral is one of the most beautiful of France, and the "tapestry of Queen Matilda" constitutes a curiosity unique of its kind. Bayeux, which is as the bird flies but 7 k. 5 from the sea, is the point of access of the small shore resorts of the Bessin.

After a résumé of the city's two thousand years (it was the Roman city of Augustodurum), the *Guide* threw in a bit of interpretive reporting:

On the eve of the Revolution the old city was above all a city of the Church. . . . It was also a city of bourgeois and retired government officials. . . . The immense changes of the nineteenth century have hardly touched it; it remains a city of priests and *rentiers*, where the rich stockmen of the region meet on market days. It may be seen what interest Bayeux has for those enamored of the past.

Nearly all the next nine pages were devoted to the cathedral and to the "tapestry," which is, to be more precise, a narrative cartoon strip embroidered on linen, telling Matilda's husband's side of his conquest of England, along with the events leading up to it. At the time the cartoon appeared, her husband, William the Bastard, was just beginning to be known as William the Conqueror. (Lebatard is still a common surname in Bayeux, but those who bear it claim no royal descent.) The tapestry was a publicity release. Because it was in pictures, the vast illiterate majority got the general idea, and the running legend made its points in extremely easy Latin for the benefit of the small literate minority. The cartoon is simple and stylized, with plenty of violent action, like "Smilin' Jack." Matilda and her ladies added a border of uninhibited medieval female fantasies for the beef-cake, or reverse-cheesecake, trade. She had the tabloid formula cold. As a consequence, her version of that prototypical colonial war has prevailed in popular history. Harold, according to William's wife, was not only a crude fellow but a cad. He maintained a love nest in England while getting himself engaged to a fine, pure girl in Normandy. It was both as a jilted future father-in-law and as a bilked legatee that William launched his expedition, and any attendant territorial acquisitions were purely incidental to his civilizing mission. (In a lost sequel to the tapestry, of which we have only a description by a Norman monk, Matilda is thought to have shown how the Normans improved sanitary conditions in England and taught the natives to wear blazers.)

When I decided to go back to the part of Normandy that includes Bayeux, I bought the latest edition (1952) of the *Guide Bleu*, in order to be prepared for any striking changes. This time I read, under "Bayeux":

City of 10,246 inhabitants (*les Bayeusains*), former capital of the Bessin, seat of a bishopric, is situated in the verdant plain watered by the little River Aure. Its cathedral is one of the most beautiful of France, and the "tapestry of Queen Matilda" constitutes a curiosity unique of its kind. Bayeux, which is but 7 k. 5 from the sea, is the point of access of the small shore resorts of the Bessin. . . . On the eve of the Revolution, the old city was especially an ecclesiastical city, where the people of the Church supported numerous beggars; it was also a city of retired bourgeois and government officials. . . . The immense changes of the nineteenth century hardly touched it; it remains a city of priests and *rentiers*, where the rich stockmen of the region meet on market days. It may be seen what interest Bayeux has for those enamored of the past.

This reassured me. I had visited the former Augustodurum once between the 1926 and 1952 editions of the *Guide Bleu*, when it was the headquarters of the Allied Twenty-first Army Group, Field Marshal Sir Bernard Montgomery commanding. That was soon after the Allied landing in Normandy in June 1944—the Army Group included the British Second and American First Armies—and for a while it looked as if the Field Marshal might install himself there *en permanence*, like William in his English capital city of Winchester long ago. The

British occupied Bayeux on June 8, which was D-plus-2. The Germans pulled out of the verdant plain without defending the city, so it was freed without damage. They fell back on the stronger position in front of Caen, fifteen miles to the southeast, where they held for the next seven weeks, penning the British into the Bessin. (It has been contended since by one school of military historians that the Marshal was holding the Germans out of the Bessin, but if he was, it was in the manner of the Rhode Islander who stuck his hand into a hole after a weasel. "Have you got him?" the fellow's brother yelled. The weaseler yelled back, "The sonofabitch has got me!") During all this period—longer than the Austro-Prussian War of 1866—the enemy made no serious bombing attack on Bayeux. Pursuing some higher strategic aim, they forwent attack upon the military vehicles swarming up from the beachhead. As these vehicles arrived, the British military police channeled them into a series of traffic circles around the center of town, and from the air the place must have looked like a shooting-gallery target, with the cathedral in the middle to mark the bull's-eye and the Hôtel du Lion d'Or, which was the Army Group command post, in the next ring outside it. The circles were designed to let the lorries get around the town on their way to forward areas, and the military police maintained the circular pattern so staunchly that visiting jeeps bound for the Lion d'Or were sometimes forced to revolve around the city until their gas ran out or their occupants gave up and went away. A dream of the Bayeux shopkeepers had come true: There were tens of thousands of potential customers. But there was nothing to sell except Camembert cheese, which is produced in the region, and which was prevented by the battle line from taking its normal course toward Paris. A flood of Camembert had backed up on Bayeux. Shop-windows normally devoted to other kinds of merchandise were full of cheese. There is no mass market for Camembert in either the British or the American Army. Caught in an outer eddy of the traffic whirlpool one evening, a jeep driver and I made three two-and-a-half-mile circuits between walls of window-displayed Camembert. I at last got out and bought some, telling the driver to pick me up on his next time around. When we arrived back at the First Army press camp, at Vouilly, near Isigny, I offered to share the

cheese with colleagues, jeep drivers, and, finally, in desperation, Army press-relations officers, but none would have any. A
supply of Camembert is not the sort of thing you keep under
your cot indefinitely, even in a well-aired tent. I wouldn't
throw mine away, though, and I didn't have to, because while
I slept, the late Ernie Pyle stole it from under me and threw it
away himself.

Another of my memories of the city in its phase of atypical
animation is an occasion when I allowed myself to believe that
even in wartime a French-speaking American willing to pay adequately might find a French meal in Bayeux. I failed miserably, involving in my failure a jeep driver, whom I had kept
away from Vouilly and the mess tent. Determined to restore
the situation, I thought of M. François Coulet, the former *chef
de cabinet* of General de Gaulle, who had been placed at the
head of the civil government of liberated France—it consisted
entirely of the Sous-Préfecture of Bayeux at the time—by the
French Provisional Government, in London. It had been important to the Free French to take over smoothly in Bayeux, in
order to set a precedent. The Western Allies, it is painful to recall, had not recognized the Provisional Government as the
government of France, even provisionally, and the Free French
feared the same kind of *fait accompli* that had faced them after
the landings in North Africa. So before anybody in Washington had time to dredge up a Darlan, the Gaullists had popped
M. Coulet, a strong personality, into Bayeux. The *fonctionnaires* there had accepted him without any fuss, and the precedent would be hard to upset as the Armies liberated new
territory. Where M. Coulet was, I knew, there would be a
square meal, and he did not disappoint me.

Aided by the gathering darkness and a French cop, the
driver and I sneaked through the whirling circles and arrived at
M. Coulet's residence, a private house that sat behind a walled
garden near the cathedral. Coulet is very tall, like his *patron*,
and, like him, chilly-mannered for a Frenchman, but he relaxes
more easily than the General. Beneath the manner, which is
perhaps mimicry, he is a friendly man, lucid and amusing. He
had had his dinner, but an old woman servant, the first civilian
to cook for me in freed France, produced another—an omelet,

veal cutlets, and a salad. She then offered us some Camembert, but we declined it.

After dinner, we talked of politics. The conversation turned on de Gaulle, and I remember two details that may serve some future Plutarch. Coulet said that the General never sweats, even after the most violent exertion, and that he knows all the works of Racine by heart. In circumstances of stress, he said admiringly, the General was likely to break into *alexandrines* he considered apposite. Coulet, recognizing their source, would reply with the next couplet. Master and disciple would go along that way for nine or ten scenes and feel spiritually refreshed. Coulet himself was later French Ambassador in Belgrade, but it is unlikely that he talked to Marshal Tito in couplets.

After I had looked long at the whole sweep of sand that stretched away from the end of the Port-en-Bessin jetty without seeing a single ghost, I told Michel we would go back to Bayeux. I wanted to look at the cathedral, but I didn't tell him so. He already considered me mad for having hired a car and him to bring me down from Paris to look at an empty beach.

"*Après, Moosioo, Deauville?*" he asked insinuatingly. Michel liked destinations where he would be likely to meet hired-car chauffeurs of his acquaintance. Once they delivered their American charges to the concierges of Palace Hotels at the end of each day's driving, the chauffeurs were free for an evening of refreshment and trade talk, the latter in Russian. In this system of transportation, of which I got occasional glimpses during my difficult conversations with Michel, the concierges furnish the sole means of communication between the chauffeurs and their paying prisoners, and levy a heavy commission on both. Once committed to the chauffeurs selected for them by the concierges of their Paris hotels, the Americans, like runaway slaves on the Underground Railroad, are entirely dependent on their silent guides. It is a tribute to the devotion of the concierges of France that few such consignments are lost in transit, although, Michel allowed me to understand when we knew each other better, the human shipments sometimes arrive at a wrong destination—Saint-Jean-de-Luz, for example, instead of La Baule, or Ostend instead of Geneva. "*Pas importa beaucoup*," he said, with a merry Ukrainian laugh. "*Noo soo rend compta oo sont.*" (In *langue chauffeuroise*, which has affinities with both Provençal and Old Slavonic, this means, "It doesn't matter much. They never catch wise to where they are.") The concierge of the hotel where they arrive simply readdresses them and forwards them to where they were supposed to go. In the hotels of *grand tourisme*, chauffeurs get rooms and meals at a special rate. For Michel this was an important point, because he had asked me for a flat salary, out of which he paid his own expenses. In villages like Port-en-Bessin, where no one was used to chauffeurs, there was no price differential. This increased his antipathy for his surroundings. "*Paysans*," he said disparagingly of the Port-en-Bessin citizenry, as if the Ukraine of his youth had been a land of private eyes and taxi dancers. "*Chassa poisson.*"

"After Bayeux," I told him as we walked toward the car, not wishing to instill any false hopes, "we are going to a place called Vouilly, but on the way we are going to stop off at the beach of debarkation—*Plage* Easy Red." He opened the door at the right of the driver's seat, waited until I got in, closed it behind me, bowed, and then walked around behind the Versailles to take his seat at the wheel.

"*Après Boolioo*," he said with resignation, "*Voolioo.*"

There are only two cathedrals I have ever liked in my life. One is Notre-Dame de Paris, but only at a distance. The other is the cathedral at Bayeux, which is also called Notre-Dame but is about as ladylike as a Norman knight whacking off a thane's head. The knights who followed William the Bastard wore simple shirts of chain mail, like iron mackintoshes and about as ornamental; they rode short, strong horses they could jump down from easily when they saw a dead man with a ring finger worth chopping off and could jump onto again as nimbly when they saw his friends coming. They were all muscle and business, like Moon Mullins. You can see them in Matilda's comic strip. To understand the decline of Western chivalry as a military force, you need only compare Matilda's pirates on horseback with the gloriously illuminated fifteenth-century *Livre des Tournois* of King René, in which manicured Clydesdales swathed in *robes de chambre* transport knightly

Fancy Dans encased in patent burglarproof vaults—and at that the passengers used blunted lances, to be doubly sure of not hurting one another. Off their horses, they were as helpless as sea turtles turned on their backs, and out of their armor as vulnerable as hermit crabs drawn from their shells.

The cathedral offers corroborative reading matter for those enamored of the past. The front consists largely of two great, blocky stone towers, combinations of skyscraper and donjon, whose façades are broken only by slits of windows with outlines like armor-piercing shells. These towers remain from the Romanesque cathedral that William the Bastard ordered built after his great amphibious operation. Most of the other elements of the original cathedral were destroyed by fire in 1105—a great pity, because they were replaced with comparatively namby-pamby Gothic. In the two original towers, William built the kind of fortress for God that God would have liked had He been William. They constituted a defensive position a small detachment of angels could hold against all the Powers of Hell, pending the arrival of reinforcements. The Powers must have been easy for William to visualize, because his direct ancestors in the preceding century had been Norse pagans.

The later architecture is a clear record of the progressive enfeeblement of the Middle Ages, like the transition from mail shirts to couturier armor. Early in the thirteenth century, a bishop of Bayeux named Robert des Ableiges surmounted William's savage towers with spires, which was like putting New Year's Eve clown hats on busts of Sulla. In 1099, when William's towers still looked like fortresses, William's son Robert and other rough men stormed Jerusalem; by the late fifteenth century, when Louis XI was adding the last *style-flamboyant* jingle bells to the cathedral, the Turks had taken Constantinople, and Bayeux was a city of priests and *rentiers*.

I reflected on these things as we drove to Bayeux, and Michel, presumably disgruntled, said nothing. At the Hôtel du Lion d'Or, I abandoned Michel and the Versailles and set out on my own, wandering through the town, inspecting the cathedral, and having a glass of Calvados, which was the only new thing since 1926 that I could notice. Then I routed out Michel, and we set off for Easy Red Beach and Vouilly. Just outside Port-en-Bessin, we turned off to the left on a third- or fourth-class road, and presently passed through the village of Sainte-Honorine-des-Pertes, named for the many shipwrecks at the foot of its cliff. We breathed the sea, although we couldn't see it over the tops of the cliffs. On the seaward side of the road, there were wild roses in the pastures, the grass was coarse, and the cattle had a more enterprising, world-conscious look than the inland animals on the other side. At Colleville, five miles along the road, we turned right, onto a miserable downhill dirt track that had once been the subject of exhaustive Intelligence reports. One of the few exits from the beach, it marked the eastern limit of Easy Red, and it was given the name of Exit E-1. The planners depended on these widely spaced primitive exits to get all our vehicles over the cliffs and onto the existing road network. The spire of the Colleville church, seen over the cliffs from the sea, was the marker for E-1, and the Intelligence sheets expressed hope that the spire wouldn't disappear during the preliminary bombardment. When I first saw E-1, a couple of days after the landing, it was lined with signs that read, "*Achtung Minen!*"

Michel went down the hill as cautiously as though it were still mined, for the Versailles, as he reminded me every time we hit a root, was brand-new, and the hired-car man would give him no further jobs if he brought it back with a neurosis. This was its maiden cruise, and despite the fact that I had rented it as a medium of transportation, Michel tried to make me feel that I was merely the chosen instrument of its introduction to life, a Lord Melbourne to this thirteen-horsepower Victoria.

A government or a public-spirited magnate interested in the maintenance of French self-esteem would subsidize the production of a large, fast, beautiful automobile to replace in the world scale of elegance the vanished Hispano-Suizas, Delahayes, and Panhard-Levassors. Never before have the French been at the same time so susceptible and so automobile-conscious, and the fact that the Americans, the British, the Germans, and, latterly, even the Russians, have been building big, luxurious cars contributes to an unavowed feeling of lost status. France is a nation where, more than in any other, inner well-being depends upon outward appearance. The point was well understood by Louis XIV, both Bonapartes, and General de Gaulle. That the popular symbol of success the world over is now a big car may mark a regression from the more sensitive age of Stendhal, for whom it was a good carriage; in any case, it is out of the question for most Frenchmen to make the symbol of success a Cadillac, which in France costs as much as a Rolls-Royce does in America. The Cadillac symbol also adds subtly to the sum of anti-Americanism. The proletarian, unable to afford that good omelet that is not made nowadays without breaking six-cent eggs, sees a rich compatriot in a big American car and thinks of him as a *parasite américanisant*. If he saw him in a big French car, he would still think of him as a parasite but not as an *American*-type parasite. If, for reasons of economy, a French government must choose between subsidizing this car and holding Madagascar, it would do well to drop Madagascar.

By the time we reached the beach and turned onto the rudimentary road, hardly more than a pair of parallel ruts, that follows the high-water mark, Michel was showing symptoms of nervous collapse. Since I was depending on him to get me to Vouilly, I allowed him to stop the Versailles on the safe side of a tidal puddle in the road three-eighths of an inch deep. He sat murmuring "*Waterloo, Waterloo, n'avansa pas*," which I took to mean "*Voiture lourde*" (heavy car) "can't go farther." To show my displeasure, I got out before he could run around the Versailles to open the door for me.

I walked off along Easy Red, trying to remember how it had been on that rough morning eleven years ago, but it was no use. The tide was far out (at H Hour it had been high), and the sand, smooth and yellow, shimmered in the sun. I walked along a grassy bank, a foot or so high, just above the high-water mark. It had figured prominently in our advance intelligence, and hundreds of Americans, emerging from the water, had claimed its uncertain shelter. Now it was just a little ledge covered with bunch grass, daffodils, and a kind of yellow ranunculus. There was a single hull still on the beach—an LCT. It looked like an island between sea and grass, equidistant from me and from the blue water. I walked out toward it across the damp, firm sand, crosshatched with tidal rills. The tide was still going out. Offshore, a few concrete chunks of Mulberry, as the artificial port floated over from England was named, still showed above the water. Out on the horizon, where I had seen a big transport, the *Susan B. Anthony*, lift her nose out of the water and settle on her bustle, nothing moved. Swinging on her cable at the turn of the tide, she hit a mine dropped in the water by a German plane the night before, and sank, stern first, in less than fifteen minutes—a gracefully impressive casualty. The water around her boiled with landing craft; never was a crew better-situated to be rescued. That was a couple of days after D Day, when Mulberry was about the busiest port in the world. LCTs, barges, DUKWs, and assault craft ferried men and ammunition, and, farther out, the commandeered merchant ships and the LSTs lay at anchor. Now it was as if I had come back to the Upper Bay and found it empty.

As I started toward the abandoned LCT, I could see a family group—two couples and three or four children—scouting gingerly about her, as if they still feared an explosion. She lay deep in the sand, and in settling had made a shallow moat about her, which retained a few inches of water. A woman started to climb aboard, and one of the men grabbed her arm; I suppose he was telling her some nonsense about booby traps or live shells. The children squatted in the water under her bow. I thought I might join the group and get off a few instructive lines about the way things had gone on the great day—how they could not imagine the difference between that day and this. I was still preparing my little *discours*, which would present me and the heroic American nation in the best light—without pretension, of course, and even with a suspicion of humor—when I saw one of the men, who had been observing my approach, signal to the others in the group. The adult members of his band gathered around him like wild horses around an old stallion with his nose in the wind. All then started to move inshore, herding the children in front of them. They were upwind from me, and as they came abreast of me, I heard this chap say to his probable wife, "It was a near thing. If I hadn't spotted him, we would have been for it. He would have said hello and then told us for the next half hour how he and his pals came ashore on this very spot." They were not French but English. I wished William the Bastard were there to deal with them.

I was amused that the boor should have thought me capable

of forcing my company upon strangers. Ignoring him as ostentatiously as possible, I went on to the LCT and regarded it for a long time, as if I had never seen one before, until the trippers were so far away that it was perfectly plain I wanted nothing to do with them. Just as a small boy who knows himself to be safely awake tries to re-establish the mood of a nightmare, I looked back at the cliffs. A couple of nights after the landing, I recalled, Commander Gene Carusi, a Navy beach-battalion C.O. who had crossed with us on the LCIL 88, had been sleeping in a cave on the side of a hill, believing all his troubles were over, when an American antiaircraft shell, fired on a low trajectory from a ship, nearly killed him. Carusi had prematurely white hair, and an Army medic bending over him said to another medic, "It's no use moving that old bastard; he'll die anyway." This interservice irreverence made Carusi so mad that he survived. Looking at Easy Red in the sunlight, I found it impossible to believe that anything violent had occurred there. The great conical bird cage of tracer bullets over Mulberry at night, with the German planes flying between its bars, was hard to hang over the *petite plage du Bessin* in memory. There are places where you can believe in history and others where it is more difficult. We had no Queen Matilda to record our episodes—only millions of photographs, and nobody wants to look at them.

After a while, I headed back for Michel and the Versailles. He greeted me warmly. He had begun to think of me as his only link with the world of private eyes and taxi dancers. I was glad to see him, too. As a sign of reconciliation, I allowed him to get out and open the door for me, and we started back to the road at Colleville, away from Easy Red and bound for the place Michel called *Voolioo*.

4
Madame Hamel's Cows

O N JULY 18, 1944—a Tuesday, as I remember it—part of the 29th, or Blue-and-Gray, Division, which was formed originally from Maryland, Virginia, and Pennsylvania National Guard units, fought its way into the city of St. Lô, the seat of the prefecture of the Département de la Manche, in Lower Normandy. St. Lô, which had a prewar population of about twelve thousand, was deserted, except for unevacuated German dead. Correspondents—among them me—who entered shortly after the troops saw little, because they either hugged what they hoped would prove to be the lee of a wall or lay flat on their faces during their sojourn. The Germans, having been thrown out of the city, were reacting like a drunk who has been chucked out of a saloon and then throws a beer bottle through the window. Rising briefly to cross a street at an intersection, I saw the assistant division commander, Brigadier General Norman D. Cota, receive a wound in his cane-carrying arm. He shifted his stick to his other hand and stepped inside a gaping shop front while a medic put a dressing on the damaged member. Cota came out in time to see the correspondents departing as rapidly as possible, and my last memory of that victory is of the laughing general waving his stick and yelling, "Don't leave me now, boys! Don't leave me now!" The wound hurt worse later. When I next saw the General, he said, "I was standing out there to give the boys confidence, but it didn't work out right." A couple of days before the wounding, I had encountered him in the wooded country near St. André de l'Epine, a hamlet on the right flank of the German position. He was stopping soldiers who were drifting back from the firing line. "Where are you going, boys?" I heard him ask a pair of stragglers, and they pulled up sharp when they noticed the star on the helmet of the spindle-shanked, Roman-nosed old man alone in the road with his walking stick.

"The Lieutenant bugged out, sir, and we thought we might as well, too," one of them said.

"Harses! Harses!" the General said in a non-Harvard New England accent. "I haven't seen any lieutenant coming this way. Get up there before he notices you've been away." Cota was a Regular, born in Massachusetts. He waved the stick and they went back.

After leaving General Cota in St. Lô, some of the correspondents went to see Major General Charles Gerhardt, the division commander, a couple of kilometres farther back, to congratulate him on his capture of the city, for which the 29th had been fighting hard for a month. General Gerhardt was a sporting type, an old West Point third baseman who had acquired the habit of pepper talk. "Sir," one correspondent said, in a highly technical tone, "could you explain to us the strategic significance of St. Lô? Why has First Army made such a point of capturing it?"

"Well, Peanut," the General said, "it's a catchy name. It fitted well in headlines, and the newspapers took to using it every day. After that, it became a morale factor, so we had to capture it."

The General knew better, but his answer stirred up the sediment of *War and Peace*-cum-Siegfried Sassoon that lies at the bottom of every civilian's thinking about the Military Mind. St. Lô was the confluence of arterial roads from the south and east, through which the enemy might have been able to pour reserves to smother a breakthrough farther west. Its capture was like a tourniquet on an elbow, permitting an operation on the forearm. The General couldn't have said that without giving the next move away, but he might at least have said something Delphic and stuffy that the fellows could have put in their dispatches.

Gerhardt's reactions were snappy, as an infielder's have to be, but he didn't always stop to think of their effect. For example, there was the occasion, after the storming of Brest, when the Division buried a couple of thousand of its dead. The Division's Catholic chaplain told me afterward in Paris, in the bar of the Hôtel Scribe, that, marching the men away from the cemetery, the General had the band play "Roll Out the Barrel." He wanted to change their mood. The chaplain considered it an inappropriate choice. Furthermore, he objected to the prayer the General had offered at the funeral formation; the chaplain thought the General should have left that to the professionals. "He said, 'May the good God in Heaven, if there be one . . .' " the chaplain reported. "Who is he to voice a doubt of the existence of God?" I said it was just a reflex—the General wanted to be sure all bases were covered before he threw the ball. As a matter of fact, Gerhardt used to say grace before every meal in his mess.

When St. Lô fell, there was for the moment nothing for the correspondents to write about, and this was bad for their dispositions. Deprived of the progress-toward-St. Lô report that had been the essential element of their daily stories, my colleagues, especially the press-association men, began to bicker. All of them had used the St. Lô dateline on their stories of the capture (I had seen nobody carry a typewriter into town, much less stay long enough to write a story), but one man was charged by his colleagues with having used the dateline when he had not actually been in the town at all. The others considered this unethical. The press-association boys constantly competed among themselves on a strict time basis, like milers. The day after the capture, a United Press man wandered through my tent and his, carrying a copy of a cable he had received from his home office. " 'Beat nearest competitor one minute forty-five,' " he read aloud proudly. " 'Kudos, kudos, kudos.' " Then he looked up and asked, "What does 'kudos' mean?"

"It means they've decided not to give you a raise," another correspondent said.

The tents were in the First Army press camp, where there were censors and excellent mobile facilities for the transmission of our stuff by Press Wireless. The camp was at a place called Vouilly, which was near Isigny, an early capture, and about fifteen miles north of St. Lô. Vouilly was a crossroads, an old church, a harness-maker's shop, and a grocery-café. Down a wooded private road beyond the crossroads lay a big farm with an immense, moated farmhouse that was known as the Château. In that country of rich peasants and hard-drinking gentry, the line between large farmhouses and small châteaux is seldom clear; houses, like families, cross and recross social lines. Mme Hamel, the proprietress of the Château, made no claim to nobility, but she looked a proper chatelaine—tall and straight, with a high forehead, a long, straight nose, bright-blue eyes, and white hair. She was sixty-two. The living room of the Château, equipped with Army chairs and tables, was our pressroom. It was bigger than the city room of the Providence *Journal & Evening Bulletin* when I worked there a long time ago. The dining room, as long and almost as wide, was never used; Mme Hamel, her son and daughter-in-law, the farm servants, and the neighbors made their headquarters in the kitchen, which was a fine room in itself, with a wall spigot that ran hard cider. Our tents were in front of the house, along the edge of one of the great pastures, which we shared with fifty cows. Every morning during the fighting for St. Lô, we would have a large, hot breakfast in the mess tent and then climb into jeeps, two or three correspondents to a driver, and take off for the battlefield. The mess tent was our ace good-will builder with the farmers; it was run cafeteria style, and all of us generally left a lot on our plates. The swill was of a magnificence unparalleled in that thrifty countryside, and the farmers carted it away for their young pigs and the mothers of their still younger pigs.

By five o'clock in the afternoon, we would be back. It was a sensible way to work, but it created what the quarterly-review fellows call a dichotomy—we were in the war from nine to five and out of it from five to nine. The weakness of the Luftwaffe at that stage increased the discrepancy between the front and Vouilly. There was no danger on the roads, and although we maintained a blackout at night, we felt silly about it. The best route to the front was a sunken road that led up through St. André de l'Epine. For days, the progress of the 29th along it was slow, bloody, and sometimes nearly imperceptible. If you stuck to the road in the Division's wake and went slowly, in order not to raise dust, you could not be seen, except at gaps in the high hedges that lined both sides, and there was not much chance of your being hit. There was always fire going over the road, clipping leaves from trees and making you feel important, but you would have needed a stepladder to climb up to it. The Germans believed in firing their weapons often—as advocated by the distinguished American military critic, General S.L.A. Marshall, and numerous Chinese tacticians of the fifteenth century—in order to keep their spirits up. When we got to the point where vehicular traffic ended—there was

always an M.P. on the spot to say where it was—we would dismount and walk as far up front as the mood moved us. It was
on one of these forward excursions that I heard Cota talking
to the stragglers. The feature writers would try to cull thrilling
incidents from company commanders and walking wounded,
and the correspondents from places like Minneapolis would go
around trying to find soldiers from Minnesota to ask them
what R.F.D. route they lived on. During the last days of the
battle, I had been heartened by the number of abandoned
German bodies in the road; it showed that the survivors were
moving backward a lot faster than they wanted, or they would
have carried their dead with them. They were unlikable people
and they had no business in that part of France anyway.

The infantrymen and artillery spotters, who had to fan out
in the fields on both sides of the road, naturally were more
likely to be hit than we were. The wounded who could walk
had their hurts dressed at first-aid stations by the roadside and
then hiked, or hitched jeep rides, to the rear. When we turned
back at the end of each day's outing, we picked up as many of
them as we could. They would sit on the hood of the jeep, embarrassed because they had been hit. "Looks like we might
have some rain," they would say, or "Wonder how the Yankees
are doing." This embarrassment is the mark of a good competitor. He neither complains nor tries heroically to pretend it
was jolly good fun; he feels that he personally is responsible for
whatever happened to him. His prototype is General Joe Stil-
well, who said, after his eviction from Burma, "I claim we got
a hell of a beating"—not "I claim the cards were stacked
against us" or "I claim we won a hell of a moral victory."

Driving homeward, we would look into the faces of the infantrymen coming up to the line, in single file, well-spaced,
heavily burdened. They were preoccupied faces, neither aggressive nor self-pitying, from a region that was neither Big
City nor Wild West. They had been twenty months in Devon
before coming to France, and they had fitted in well with the
gentle Devon people. "The finest physical men I ever saw,"
General Cota had told me in England when he first went to
the Division. "But there's no meanness in them. I try everything I can think of to make them mean, but it's no use." The
General had come from the 1st Division, which was loaded

with Brooklyn boys, and they had convinced him that the best premilitary preparation was two brisk battles daily for a seat in the subway. "Those fellows in the First were little, but they didn't care who they stepped on," he said, explaining his theory.

When I got back from my exciting incursion into St. Lô, I rushed to the kitchen of the Château to inform Mme Hamel of our glorious feat of arms. The family still possessed a private stock of old Calvados, and these tidings were, I thought, of a sort to stimulate hospitality. I was in a great hurry to get there before André Rabache, the Agence Française correspondent, who also knew about the Calvados. I arrived to find the Hamels and a large collection of neighbors seated around the long kitchen table. I could sense that they had been engaged in a serious discussion.

"Madame," I said proudly, for I wanted her to think well of the American Army, "I come from St. Lô. The city is ours! Now we can advance!"

"I felicitate you, Monsieur," she said. "I am happy to hear it."

"I also, *mon Commandant*," said a neighboring farmer, whose name was Lesavoureux. "*Correspondant*," which is not a military rank, seldom registered with the Normans, who usually promoted us to *commandant*, or major. "But I ask myself what will happen to the pigs."

"The pigs?" I asked. My mind was still on Cota, directing traffic among the shells.

"Yes, *mon Commandant*—the young pigs who depend for their nourishment on the leftovers of the mess," he said.

The only ray of hope I could offer was that the enemy might make a tenacious defense of the environs.

Mme Hamel, who had the manners of a marquise, came to the rescue. "The pigs are already well launched," she said, turning a disdainful eye in M. Lesavoureux's direction. "They have had a good start in life and will make out for themselves perfectly. Perhaps Monsieur would like a glass of Calvados? The day must have made you some emotion."

The Normans are not a sheeplike people. Give them a lead and they start in the opposite direction. While M. Lesavoureux wanted the Army not to advance, a farmer down the road, whom I visited one night with Hamel *fils*, was irritated by our procrastination. He had part of an armored division in his pasture. "I was extremely pleased to see them arrive," he said, "but they are ruining my hay crop." I had been reliably informed that this farmer owned several barrels of old Calvados, and it was my object to obtain one of them for our mess. To do this, I was prepared to buy one of his pigs, also for the mess. (The correspondents made up a pool for these supplementary purchases and declared the Army personnel in.) The farmer's counterplan was to use a small amount of the Calvados to get me drunk, and then sell me the pig, but no barrel. After a long evening, I came away with neither the barrel, which he wouldn't sell, nor the pig, which I wouldn't buy without the barrel. But I had the makings of a frightful hangover free, and M. Hamel said that nobody else had ever got anything for nothing from the host of the armored division.

I was thinking of all these things as I rode west from Colleville to Isigny with Michel. We were on the road that runs along the top of the cliffs overlooking Omaha Beach, and at Isigny, where our road would end, we would look for a road that led south to Vouilly, where I hoped to find Mme Hamel as magnificent as before. I wondered, too, about the descendants of the pigs. When we got to Isigny, which is famous for producing the thick cream that comes to the table with strawberries in French restaurants ("Isigny: 2,787 inhabitants; specialties: butter, tripe, cream, mussels; sixty per cent destroyed by bombardment on June 8, 1944."—*Guide Bleu, Normandie*), Michel was favorably impressed by the white stone buildings, in the style of Robert Moses comfort stations, that have replaced the sixty per cent destroyed. "*Moderne!*" he said. "*Pas comme Boolioo.*" He had been unfavorably impressed by the fishnet of medieval alleys that entangles the cathedral. Isigny is dominated by the large, modern, double-winged plant of the Reunited Butteries & Creameries, a modern-Norman testimonial to God's bounty. At a quartermaster's dump in Isigny in 1944, I drew the best pair of shoes I have ever owned, free. I was sure that it was no use looking for the quartermaster's dump now, however.

Michel stopped in front of the Reunited Butteries & Creameries and went inside to ask the way to Vouilly. He came out visibly depressed, as always when he had to ask directions. "*N'esista pas, Moosioo,*" he said, in what I had learned to recognize as his notion of French. "*Voolioo, personne a entendoo.*" He stood with folded arms, his great brown eyes liquid with astonishment at his plight, like those of an abandoned straggler from Denikin's army who has heard the first howls of the advancing Bolsheviki. His eyes told me that I had been a fool to leave the caravan routes between Paris and Deauville or Paris and Cannes in order to lead him after a mirage. Nothing to do now but throw our burnooses over our heads and wait for the St. Bernard dogs.

"*Voolioo,* evidently, does not exist," I said to him, in an excessively reasonable tone. "But *Vouilly, Vouilly, Vouilly* exists!" I made a move as if to go myself to ask directions.

"Ah, Vooyee!" Michel said, starting back at a run, and adding, over his shoulder, "*Pooquoi Moosioo dit Voolioo?*" Michel had lived in France for twenty-seven years, and it was a point of professional honor that he, the resident, should translate for me, the foreigner. It was a little like traveling through the British Isles with a Gurkha dragoman who insists on carrying on all intercourse with the natives. Michel returned from the Reunited this time with the expression of a Scotland Yard inspector who has cracked a big case. "*Ça y est,*" he announced. "*Vooyee—ah!,*" and he looked at me indulgently before he headed the Versailles in the right direction.

Vouilly is less than a dozen miles inland, but when you get there the sea is forgotten. Bayeux, with its ten thousand inhabitants, seems an incredibly large city in retrospect, and its cathedral, embodying renovations right up through the fifteenth century, is Saarinen compared to the small, unornamented Romanesque church of Vouilly, with its front and rear elevations like equilateral triangles on squares and its tower no higher in proportion than a peaked helmet on a Norman swordsman. The Vouilly church hasn't been changed since the eleventh century. The tower is off to one side of the peaked roof, like a fighter's head tucked in behind his shoulder. It surveys a countryside where the fields are surrounded by ditches and banks of earth, with trees, all ensnarled with vines and bushes, growing out of the tops of the banks—the most ancient of cattle fences. The rain falls most days, the grass grows all through the year, and the cattle turn it into milk. During the fighting in Normandy, the Army Civil Affairs branch tried to evacuate peasants from farms that became battlefields, but they wouldn't go. They said the cows had to be milked. The cattle, in the open all year round, but never out of call of the milkmaid, develop a character that is neither wild, like that of range cattle, nor passive, like the milk factories that spend most of their lives in front of a manger. They are, like the Normans, independent, gluttonous, and indomitable. The Germans defended the hedged fields as fortresses, and the cattle remained in them as audience, chewing the rich grass as the shells burst among them and falling on their sides like vast milk cans. In the immediate vicinity of Vouilly, however, there had been no fighting.

Michel asked a woman at the café the way to the Château, and she said to turn left on the first "avenue" past the crossroads. She meant the first avenue of trees, but Michel was amused. "*Elle appelle 'avenoo' oona toota petita roo*," he said. "*Paysanne.*" For Michel, "avenue" was a term reserved for the Avenue des Champs-Elysées, the Avenue Foch, and thoroughfares of equivalent luminosity. He consented to turn down the bucolic version of an avenue, though, and after about a mile I saw the Château in front of me, sleeping among the trees. Its tower was higher than that of the church, but not high enough to rise above the oldest trees around it.

We drove between the hedged fields, over the bridge and into the farmyard. Mme Hamel and her son were sitting under an apple tree, shelling peas. They were surrounded by fat, sleepy hens, among whom walked peacefully a fat, sleepy tomcat. When Michel stopped the Versailles, Madame looked at us, shading her eyes with one strong hand, and called out to her son, "It's he!" She rose—a trifle heavier but even more impressive than I had remembered her—like a great, noble Percheron mare, white with age, getting up in a field, and walked over to the car as I got out. Her son came with her, and as they reached the car, she said to him, "I knew he would come back someday." To me she said, "Why didn't you come last year with the others?" In 1949 and 1954, I knew, airlines had organized two junkets to Omaha Beach for former war correspondents who had been there—and some who hadn't—

thus reaping a modest harvest of mentions in news stories. I had not been with either party, and Mme Hamel, in consequence, had felt slighted. She liked all her old guests to come back to her. For five weeks in 1944, the Château had been one of the news centers of the world. Scores of millions of people in America had hung on the stories of the ugly fighting among the dead cattle, and every word had gone out through the mysterious wireless trucks on Madame's farm. She had not been insensible to the honor, or to the excitement of feeling herself in the know, and she had not begrudged us the use of her pastures. All the old guests who made the junkets came back to visit, she said. She remembered me particularly, because I had hung around the kitchen so much, cadging refreshments.

Her son is a quiet man, short, wide-shouldered, and long-armed. He walks with a limp that dates from the time when, as a prisoner of war of the Wehrmacht, he was made to work at clearing French minefields in Alsace. (It was in 1940. Pétain had capitulated, and the Germans were paying only nominal heed to the Geneva Convention rules on the treatment of war prisoners.) Hamel had stepped on some kind of antipersonnel device, crippling himself so badly that the Germans had sent him home during a much-publicized "restoration to their families" of a number of French prisoners incapable of useful labor. The Vichy regime had touted this as a great concession. By 1944, when I first met him, he had got around to thinking of his accident as a stroke of luck. He could walk again—although with a limp—he could work as well as ever, and he was home, on the right side of the Allied line, while the fate of his former fellow-prisoners was dubious. They had already had to undergo four years of heavy Allied air bombardments, and it was still possible that the S.S. would massacre the survivors when Germany was invaded. (As it turned out, they didn't, but the omission was probably due to a loss of nerve.) Hamel *fils*, therefore, didn't hold the minefield incident too strongly against the Germans. Certain aspects of his captivity had even amused him—particularly the fright of the civilian population during the first great air raids.

Every evening, while the correspondents pounded at their typewriters, he would circulate among them with a cup and a jug of milk still warm from the cow, like a hospitable precursor of M. Mendès-France. He was married, but the dowager Mme Hamel remained the chatelaine, and I had only to see the Hamels together to know that nothing had changed since 1944. The pastures stretched green and profitable before us, with not a tent in sight. The cows roamed free over the site of the vanished latrine, a part of the pasture that for some bovine reason they always resented being dispossessed from. They upset the simple installation almost every night, I recalled.

I asked Mme Hamel about the health of some of the cows I remembered: L'Anglaise, so called because she came from the Channel Islands; La Nageuse, who leaped into the moat to cool off; La Nitouche, who pretended a maidenly aversion to the bull. None survived, Madame said, but they had left daughters and granddaughters to make assault upon their records of lactation. She kept a book listing the names, biographies, and milk records of her cows—usually about fifty. I remembered Madame and her lady in waiting, the milkmaid, leading La Nitouche to the bull, who was the terror of the soldiers, even though he was fastened to a stake by a chain and nose ring. "Do you remember the day the bull broke loose and charged the jeep?" she asked me, as if she had been following my unspoken recollections. I remembered, of course. He had knocked out one of his eyes, which occasioned rejoicing among the men.

In the pasture on the other side of the road, where the mess tent had stood, the grass had the look of never having been disturbed by man. I could not help asking the question that had been on my mind all the way from Omaha Beach.

"And the pigs, Madame?" I asked. "The pigs that were fed on the leavings of the *popote* and that we abandoned when the Army was compelled to advance?"

"Most of them died," Madame said. "But of indigestion. They had been *too* well fed. Figure to yourself, Monsieur. A pig fed on pancakes and sirup—God never intended it. It was Providence that the Army advanced when it did, because in three more days they would all have perished." I was happy to learn that, in effect, the interests of First Army and of the pigs of M. Lesavoureux had coincided, although M. Lesavoureux was too shortsighted to recognize it.

The day was hot, and Mme Hamel proposed that we go in-side the Château. In the long, cool hall that parallels the front of the house, I felt I had come back to one of my homes. (A mobile man has many. There is, for example, a cabin on a Norwegian tanker that I wake in often, although I haven't slept there for fourteen years.) On one of the great oak doors leading off the hall, a sign reading "Press Room" preserved the memory of the *grande époque*. Mme Hamel led me into the room next to it, the dining room—a symbol that the Château was on a peacetime footing. M. Hamel and Michel trailed along, Michel with his beret in his hand, and looking about him with a new appreciation of the Hamels' status. These were more than *paysans*; they were kulaks.

The dining room was full of furniture I could not remember from the war days; there was a long Norman table of old, scarred oak, surrounded by carved chairs, and a buffet and an armoire, equally old. All were in what I judged to be the style of the late sixteenth or early seventeenth century; the *fer-ronerie* of the buffet and the chest was of a chaste hammered crudity that proclaimed the age of all the work. "I made them myself, all but the armoire," said M. Hamel soberly. "The ar-moire is real, of the sixteenth century, and I copied it."

"And the hardware? The handles, locks, hinges?"

"All," he said. "Everything."

"How did you age the wood?"

He smiled. "It's my secret."

On one wall hung a portrait of a rough-coated chestnut foal with upstanding crest and ears. "The colt that was born while you were here," Mme Hamel said. "The foal of the mare the Cossacks abandoned." There had been Cossacks in the region before we came, part of the Vlasov Army of Russian prisoners of war, who had consented—under threat of death, they in-evitably said when captured by us—to fight for Hitler. They were an anomaly in the German Army, since the Germans never trusted them sufficiently to issue them any armament that dated from later than the First World War. They had therefore been used principally to garrison and overawe re-gions where nothing much was expected to happen, and they had a nasty reputation for pillaging. The German soldiers had as low an opinion of them as they had of their Italian allies in the Mediterranean, and when the Allies landed in Normandy, the Russians fought only until it was apparent that the debarkation was no mere raid. Then they quit. Prisoner-of-war pens were full of them well before we began to get genuine Germans in quantity. The Cossack horses wandered through the pastures and mixed in with the herds of cattle. I remembered the mare and her foal, a pair of tolerated free boarders among Mme Hamel's cows. She didn't have the foal any longer, she said, but the old mare was still around. Young Mme Hamel, the daughter-in-law, had painted the picture.

Mme Hamel brought out a bottle of muscat de Frontignan, a cloyingly sweet white wine from the south of France. Wine is a ceremonial drink in Normandy, where none is grown or made. It is not expected to taste good. M. Hamel came to my rescue by bringing out a carved wooden bottle of Calvados. "I remember you always preferred this," he said. "It's some of our own make, ten years old." I reflected bitterly on the greed of all the Americans, including me, and all the British who had passed through in the war years and accepted the one-or-two-drinks-at-a-time hospitality of the Hamels, drying up the pre-war stock. This 1945 Calvados was merely promising, but I got a couple of glasses down in order not to offend my hosts. While I was tasting the Calvados and Michel was sipping the horrid wine with the air of a connoisseur, Madame went to the armoire and returned with a great black scrapbook of clippings, like a grand old lady of the theater; she resembles one. These were her clippings of things that had been written about her, unfortunately all in English.

"This is by M. Beyle," she said, and I looked at the byline and saw that it was not by the M. Beyle who took the nom de plume of Stendhal but by M. Hal Boyle, the Associated Press columnist and an old tenter in the pasture, who wrote how glad he was that Madame was alive and well and nicer than ever. There were other clippings of the same tenor; the authors, or other Americans who saw them in print, had evidently sent them to her. On pages where no clippings had been pasted, former guests had written appropriate sentiments and their names and addresses. One of these entries was by Colonel Monk Dickson, the G-2, or head Intelligence officer,

of First Army, dated a couple of days after the fall of St. Lô. It
said, as nearly as I can remember now, "To the good family of
the Château de Vouilly, which was the repository for a week
of the secret of Cobra." Cobra was the code name of the
breakthrough, on the road that stretched west from St. Lô to
Périers, that stove in the left wing of the German Seventh
Army. It led to the great hooking movement that rolled the
Germans up like a window shade. Dickson's name reminded
me of an incident at the Château that I had forgotten. A bit
after the capture of St. Lô, General Omar Bradley came there
to see the correspondents and tell us about the next move, so
that we could prepare to cover it. The tall, long-jawed, gravely
humorous Missouri general who was so great a soldier that he
never felt compelled to bark to prove it, arrived by jeep with
his aide, Major Chet Hansen, and Dickson. Hansen carried a
map under his arm. The lecture room in which he chose to announce the impending doom of the German Seventh Army—
"I may be sticking my neck out in predicting it," he said, to
soften any hint of cockiness—was a shed that had been extended forward with canvas tent sides and roofing to serve as a
movie theater for the troops. General Bradley said that he
hadn't wanted to trouble us to come over to his headquarters
—there were so many of us. It had also been a far better idea,
from the point of view of security, for him to disappear from
headquarters for an hour than to convoke fifty correspondents
and their jeep drivers, which would have given an always possible enemy agent a decided notion that something was up. But
Bradley did not mention this second consideration; it was as if
he shrank from encouraging the idea that anything he did
could be important. General Collins' VII Corps, so reinforced
that it virtually constituted an army—four infantry and two armored divisions, I think—was to make the strike, amputating
the arm that Gerhardt had bound off. Then Patton's Third
Army was to come into official being—it already existed incognito, behind the First Army line—and race through the hole
south and west into Brittany. (The plan worked even better
than that, of course, but a fighter starting a combination of
blows can't know in advance the other fellow's capacity to absorb them.) I suppose that if I had heard Scipio, before the

Battle of Zama, describe how he was going to cancel out Hannibal's elephants, I would have thought it a historic occasion, but it took Monk Dickson's handwriting in Mme Hamel's book to remind me that I had heard Bradley call his shot.

"Do you remember when General Bradley came here and spoke in the shed?" I asked Madame.

"Yes," she said. "There were no movies that night."

The breakthrough, I remembered, was originally scheduled for July 21. It was aborted by soaking rain, which spoiled the ground for armor and made it impossible for the bombers in the preparatory air strike to see their targets. So Collins didn't jump off until July 25, when, aided by perfect visibility, the Air Corps inflicted heavy casualties on our 30th Division. I remembered that because I had watched the planes, not knowing where their bombs were falling. We had wondered why the 30th didn't get along and let us move.

I felt that it was time to go, because there was not much left to say. I answered all the usual biographical questions: How was my family? Did I continue to occupy myself with journalism? It was superfluous to ask Madame how she occupied herself: the fifty cows, the hay crop, the chickens answered that. Her son, I was sure, was an excellent farmer, but she would never dissociate herself from any of his farming. Seeking a question slightly less idiotic, I asked her how she amused herself.

"All, well, there is always fishing," she said brightly.

This was a side of Madame's personality I had never divined. She scarcely seemed the type to put on waders and dangle feathers at the end of a line.

"Where?" I asked.

"But here, in the dining room," she said. "Look."

She led me to a window, and we looked down at the moat, covered with lily pads, beneath which the water barely moved. It was originally formed by diverting a stream and leading it around the house, but the stream was no Mississippi to begin with.

"It is full of carp," Mme Hamel said. "Every day, I throw bread and bits of potato out the window. The carp accustom themselves to the snack. Then I put a hook in a potato and drop my line from the window. Instantaneously, I have a magnificent carp. You cannot make yourself an idea how good really fresh fish is."

I gazed at her with an admiration whose extent I could not express. No sunburn, no squint from looking at the shimmer on water, no bony shins sticking out of Bermuda shorts—she displayed none of the usual stigmata of the sports fisherwoman, yet her technique was of an intellectual refinement that my friend Colonel John R. Stingo would have appreciated. The Norman carp is a conservative investor, not to be taken in, like a trout, by the flash of an obviously spurious insect flourished under his nose like a prospectus for Montenegran carbuncle mines. The kind of chump who is really worth taking has to be encouraged by a series of unwarranted dividends. "When the habituation is achieved," Colonel Stingo once said to me, describing a parallel process, "the chump, ascribing his success to his own talents, demands a further opportunity to invest. He is then ready for the *coup de grâce.*"

I did not wish to take time to explain to Madame who Colonel Stingo is, so I did not call her attention to their affinity. Instead, I asked another question: "Are there pike?"

"Not here, but in the pond," Madame said. The pond is behind the house, at a distance of perhaps a hundred yards. It is a large pond, shadowed by great willows, and in 1944 we used to swim in it. "My son goes out there," Mme Hamel said. "I don't often have the time. He has also arranged a pair of shooting holes, with sliding shutters, in the back of the carriage house, which is turned toward the pond. When the wild fowl settle on the pond, he goes into the carriage house, slides back a shutter, and shoots them."

It sounded to me like the only shooting and fishing preserve I ever wanted to lease.

The Hamels, *mère et fils*, entreated us to stay for dinner, but I had it in my mind that I wanted to get back to Bayeux before dark.

"Come back soon," Madame enjoined me as we departed. "I am getting old, and who knows?" She looked imposingly durable.

As Michel and the Versailles and I headed back up the avenue of trees, I composed in my mind the text of an advertisement I meant to insert in the *Times* when I was next in

London: "Syndicate of keen guns being organized to fish Merovingian carp moat, hunt Gallo-Roman duck bath in attractive country surroundings."

A cow, perhaps a daughter of L'Anglaise or La Nitouche, stopped eating to watch us as we passed, then again put her head down in the grass.

5
The Communion Card

FOR eleven years, now, I have carried in my wallet, along with a slowly changing repertory of telephone numbers, Irish Sweepstakes tickets, and family snapshots, a fraying card, printed in France, that bears an engraving of a small boy dressed in a black suit of adult cut, with a white sash tied around his left arm, kneeling on a faded pink carpet before a lamentably insipid representation of Jesus, who, standing before an altar, is holding a chalice in His left hand and offering a wafer to the boy with His right. An elderly saint, clutching an Easter lily, stands to the right and rear of the boy, and all three figures are grouped against a background so lacking in the illusion of perspective that it resembles a photographer's prop. At the bottom of this St.-Sulpice buckeye—such cards are sent out by the hundreds of gross from Paris to churches in the provinces to be used as First Communion announcements—is printed this invocation, in French:

> Be, O Jesus, present in the Eucharist, the joy, the happiness of all my life. (Abbé Perreyve)

On the other side is written, in the small, Sunday-best hand of a French schoolboy:

> Souvenir of my solemn Communion, taken in the church of Barneville the 30 July, 1944. Raymond Legaillard.

Whenever, through the years, I chanced to come across this card, usually while shuffling through the contents of my wallet to find my social security number, a postage stamp, or a theater ticket, it reminded me of a blond boy—pug-nosed and slightly freckled, and dressed like the figure in the Communion scene but not minding it a bit—staring up woozily at me from his seat at a table between two Norman uncles, who had made him ecstatically drunk on Calvados in the dining room of the Hôtel de Paris, in the village of Barneville. The boy was the magnet of all attention for perhaps the first time in his life.

He was eleven. His relatives had gathered to do him honor. His uncles, red-faced men with downsweeping mustaches, looked like ancient Gauls, and their wide backs strained the black broadcloth coats they had long ago worn at their weddings and that they would be buried in, by which time their torsos might be sufficiently reduced to be again comfortably encompassed by the garments. They forced great wedges of creamcake and slugs of Calvados alternately upon their nephew. A great-aunt—a wiry, animated old woman who made her living catching lobsters trapped in rock pools when the tide went out—did not disapprove of the way the uncles plied the boy. She took drink for drink with him. The sun beat down on the kernel of Barneville, which consists of a huge old church, two elementary schools—one for boys, one for girls—a market place, and a single business street, a hundred yards long. The town, which by then had been out of the fighting for some weeks, is a shore resort, but the beach and its hotels are a mile away. The boy's sister, a tall girl of seventeen, handsome but already inclined to flesh, sweated candidly through the long-sleeved dress she had worn to church. She was not actively gay; rather, she was solemn, as if drink had made her reflective. Her downy upper lip quivered occasionally as her mood continued to droop. The *patronne* of the Hôtel de Paris, which was the center of the social life of the year-round inhabitants, flitted in and out of the dining room, keeping tabs on the waitress, Andrée, who was very pretty and whom the male guests pinched in the behind at every opportunity.

There were women of all ages in the party, and I asked M. Ribaud, the Barneville electrician, which of them was the boy's mother. It was M. Ribaud who had drawn me, and a jeep driver lent me by the Army, into the Communion party. His wife, who was the teacher at the girls' school, was one of the boy's numerous aunts. I had met M. Ribaud only that morning, in a less chic café, down the street. *Pastis*, patriotism, and then Calvados ripened our friendship quickly. He dragged me and the driver to his home, behind his shop, for the midday meal, explaining that he needed us as tangible excuses for being an hour late; Mme Ribaud had a *gigot* that might by now be overcooked. The *gigot* proved not at all too cooked, because Madame, who understood her husband, had popped it into the oven an hour later than she had told him she would. Afterward the Ribauds had brought the driver and me along to the Communion party—a true Norman *carrousse*, which had begun after the church ceremony with a dinner for all the relatives who didn't live in Barneville proper, and was apparently going to continue forever.

Answering my question, M. Ribaud told me that the boy's mother had died in a hospital in Cherbourg the week before, and that his father, driving a civilian ambulance on a road fairly near the front lines, had been killed only a few days earlier by a strafing airman, either a German or an overenthusiastic Ally. The boy knew of neither death; the sister knew of both.

The boy gave me the card, and I have carried it with me ever since.

While I was in Normandy, I thought I would like to go to Barneville and look up the Ribauds and see what had happened to the boy, Raymond Legaillard, who by that time should have been twenty-two and just what his surname signifies—a brisk strong fellow. Michel and I were at the Hôtel du Lion d'Or, in Bayeux, when I told him of our new destination. He had almost resigned himself to the criss-cross cat's-cradle pattern our path made over this part of Normandy. I am not a very imaginative person, and so I am constantly seeking out sequels, instead of taking it for granted that they have taken place and letting it go at that. If I leave a town in flames, for example—as I left La Haye-du-Puits, some twelve miles from Barneville, in 1944—it is likely still to be burning whenever I think of it. So I find it comforting to go back and make sure that somebody has put the fire out. I suppose that what drove Sinbad back to sea all those times was the same inability to let ill enough alone. He was not a creative artist, although posterity has chosen to think of him as a liar. He had the opposite, reportorial deformation—a compulsion to have another look.

Distances are not great in that corner of Normandy, in which the Germans contained the Allied armies between June 6 and the beginning of August 1944. A straight line from just west of Bayeux, in the northeast section of the Cotentin peninsula, to Lessay, in the southwest, is hardly forty miles long. It corresponds roughly to the American front in mid-July of

that year. The most direct route from Bayeux to Barneville is
by Isigny, but on the morning of this excursion I had Michel
make a slight southward loop by way of St. Lô, so that I could
again see the new city that has been built on the site of the one
I saw destroyed. There are some Norman towns, like Bayeux
and Port-en-Bessin and Vouilly, that the war passed over without changing anything essential about them; returning to
them, I had been reassured. In St. Lô, however, when the war
moved on, it took the scene with it. I recall the disappointment of the Army Civil Affairs team, which spent weeks, while
the infantry was fighting for St. Lô, formulating plans for re-
viving the municipal administration. By the time shells ceased
to burst in the streets, there was nothing left to administer.
Now I saw that in the years since the war something had been
built in the old city's place that was about as Norman and
time-hallowed as the Cross County shopping center in
Yonkers. Driving through the streets of the new St. Lô with
Michel, I felt like the man in Fitz-James O'Brien's story "The
Lost Room." This chap is ejected by a group of reveling evil
sprites from his furnished room in the New York of 1850 and
returns a moment later to discover that the room itself has
vanished. I could not find the convent wall against which I had
pressed for shelter or the street intersection where I had seen
General Cota wounded, because they no longer existed.

"*Beau, beau*," Michel said as we entered St. Lô. "*Moderne.*"
His urban ideal is the Avenue des Champs-Elysées between
the Rond-Point and the Etoile. St. Lô was modern enough,
but I didn't feel that I had ever been there before. "Don't
stop, Michel," I said. "To Lessay and then La Haye-du-Puits."
My 1944 jeep driver, an Iowan named Whitey White, used to
pronounce the latter town "Hooey da Pooey." Michel pronounced it in precisely the same way. What ancient links
between the Ukrainian and Iowan dialects this indicates I am
not prepared to discuss. Once I had Michel fairly launched
along the road leading from St. Lô to Lessay—the road, incidentally, across which our VII Corps made the first great
attack of the breakthrough—I again began to think of Barneville, where I ate every Sunday dinner of that remote July.

The lot of a spot-news war correspondent is trying when his
side neither advances nor retreats. There are often intervals of

more than a day between events—a truth that the daily paper, by its very nature, must deny, or it would have no excuse for coming out daily. The correspondent can exaggerate whatever is going on, but the official communiqué and the censor are there to cramp his style, and when several days pass without confirmation of his melodramatics, readers yawn and editors give the play to other fronts. The newsman can, alternatively, take the portentous tack, pretending he knows that a sensational development is imminent, but when nothing continues to happen, that peters out, too. The press-association men watch each other morosely, afraid to stray from Army Headquarters lest they miss a small lead. In a better position are the fellows from the dailies and the writers of syndicated features. The handout catchers of the press associations will cover the former on any actual new developments, while all the latter have to do is collect anecdotes—humorous or heroic, as the mood or editorial demand moves them. Most fortunate are the writers for magazines, who, when nothing happens, do not have to write about it.

The essential Allied activity in Normandy in early July of 1944 was building up a reserve of supplies and of troops to support an offensive. Nobody, naturally, was allowed to report how that was progressing. There was the ugly, constant, grinding struggle in the apple orchards as our 29th Division of XIX Corps, aided by the 2nd, on its flank, inched its way southward toward St. Lô, but the day-by-day results of the fighting were not spectacular. People reading of them must have thought it was a return to the positional warfare of the First World War, in which gains were measured in hundreds of meters. We correspondents accredited to the First Army, which at that stage was the only active American army in France, went curiously and dutifully into the St. Lô fight several times a week. We also made jeep trips to other parts of the line. It was in the course of one of these diversionary explorations—to VIII Corps, on the extreme right of the American line—that some of us discovered the Hôtel de Paris, in Barneville. As I remember, VIII Corps consisted of two or three inexperienced infantry divisions and one airborne division, and was pushing, but not rushing, southward— "maintaining pressure" is the cliché that comes back to me out of a disused vocabulary. Its right reached to the sea, and there were marshes in front of its left, so all the pressure was maintained in the direction of La Haye-du-Puits, which straddles the one highway south from Barneville.

A colonel who was the chief of VIII's Intelligence section showed us maps and told us that, as far as he could find out, the enemy had less power than VIII, but, having a rather favorable defensive position, was holding—stubbornly and irrationally, in line with Hitler's prescription. Thinking back, I can see that these odd lots of under-strength Wehrmacht divisions and exotic auxiliaries recruited from prisoner-of-war camps, with a stiffening of a few good parachute units, had no future in the region. They were like the blue crab, which stupidly hangs on to an unhooked bit of meat while the crabber slips a scoop net under him. I did not know that Bradley was preparing the net, the handle of which he poked through the German lines below St. Lô approximately four weeks later; the Germans, Balts, Russians, and Mongols comprising this makeshift Nazi left flank were the first crabs to land in the basket. In default of this knowledge my colleagues and I found nothing stimulating in the situation, and after politely excusing ourselves from the midday meal in the VIII Corps mess, which would probably have been no better than ours at Vouilly, we made for Barneville and the Hôtel de Paris, which I had noted from the road. (I once had a flair for making such finds, but it has been destroyed by the *Guide Michelin*. While I have no confidence in the *Michelin*'s stars for superior restaurants, I am touted off the places it doesn't star.)

The meals at the Hôtel de Paris were good indeed. In this corner of the Cotentin there were shellfish and inshore fish to complement the butter and beef that abound in the whole region. The proprietress, the owner of a café in Cherbourg who had taken refuge in Barneville, ran the kitchen with a touch of big-town sophistication. She was a scrawny, enameled ex-soprano, whose extravagant circumspection inspired doubts about her past. In order to get good wines from her (these, unlike the cream and butter, were irreplaceable), we had to pay her a bit of court. The *soi-disant* leading candidate for her favors was Bob Casey, of the Chicago *Daily News* syndicate, who spoke no French but looked like a major general. Casey would roll his eyes and emit terrifying groans, representing passion, and I would order up the last bottles of Nuits-St.-Georges '37.

The country around Vouilly had nothing like the Hôtel de Paris, so Sunday trips to check up on VIII Corps became part of the press-camp routine. They continued until the break-through, on July 25. The Communion day must have been my last Sunday visit to Barneville, for a week later the war of position was over. The front lines and the press camp alike shifted far forward, and we were Paris-bound. Yet I remember dashing back on a weekday to get some lobsters that the old rock-pool woman had caught and left for me at the Ribauds' electrical shop in a shoe box with holes punched in the lid. They were packed in seaweed. At the shop, M. Ribaud asked me to call on his brother, who was also an electrician, in Villedieu-les-Poêles, on the other side of what had been the front lines, to tell him the Barneville Ribauds were safe and sound. So by then we must have already broken through, and how I managed the trip back for the lobsters, I do not recall. A couple of days later, I got to Villedieu-les-Poêles and delivered the message.

I have written before of the dual character of the Normandy front during the period of buildup and containment—nasty going up front, and lovely, fat, tranquil farming country a couple of miles back, undisturbed by enemy aviation or artillery. I have noted, too, the oddly guilty feeling it gave us, who did not have to remain in the front lines but had the option of going there whenever we pleased. We seldom visited Barneville without also puttering around some spot that we could permit ourselves to consider hazardous. On the afternoon after our first dinner, I remember being in a division's command post—I think it was the 79th's—which was in an apple orchard infested with snipers, who, a colonel informed me, were harmless if you kept moving. Division commanders vied in getting their headquarters as far front as possible. This one, whose name I forget, used to sleep on the ground and make his staff do likewise.

The colonel who reassured me about the snipers was an Ozark type; he said they couldn't have done much shooting before they got into the Army, since they didn't know how to lead a moving target. "If you just keep walking, they almost always shoot behind you," he told me. I looked around, and it was the most perambulatory headquarters personnel I had ever seen. The G-3 and the assistant G-3 were walking arm in arm, discussing something, and the G-4 and the assistant G-4 were walking arm in arm in the opposite direction, discussing something else. Even the warrant officers had for once got up from behind their tables and were walking. "We got some old Missouri squirrel-hunters in this outfit, and we are hunting the snipers down pretty good," the colonel said. "But we could do better if we had dogs."

While these martial memories filled my mind, Michel guided the Versailles west to Lessay, where we turned north, toward La Haye-du-Puits, on the road that parallels the coast. Michel is a comforting companion when you don't want to talk. It is when you try to bring up some mutually comprehensible concept that your troubles begin. "Hooey da Pooey!" he said triumphantly upon spotting the road sign in Lessay, and beamed with the relief of a Captain Frémont whose Indian guide has led him aright. Michel never quite believed in any of the places we set out for until we got to them, but he accepted road signs as favorable omens. The country we now started to drive through is not so rich or so thickly wooded as the land from Bayeux down to St. Lô, but the road is straight and good, running all the way from Mont-St.-Michel to Barneville and beyond with hardly a fork at which a driver has to make a decision—a course that suited Michel's talents. We consequently arrived in La Haye-du-Puits before I'd had time to get myself into a properly somber mood for it.

On July 9—the second Sunday of the month—I had gone down to Barneville with Casey and Hal Boyle, both of whom wrote feature stories, mostly good ones. Stopping in at VIII Corps before dinner, we learned that its forward elements were engaged in cleaning out La Haye, which in the interval since our previous visit had developed into a minor St. Lô. It was smaller than St. Lô and at the extreme western end of our line, so it was hard to ascribe any pivotal importance to it. If its defenders were pushed out, they would simply be shoved straight south on Lessay, where they had another good position. Because of the sea, there was no way of getting around them. But taking La Haye meant as much to VIII Corps as taking St. Lô did to XIX. Casey and Boyle and I all felt it would be callous to tell the G-2 we were cutting his battle in order to eat *sole bonne femme* and *tournedos Choron*. We decided, therefore, to attend the battle, but not until after lunch, when we would be in a better frame of mind for it. The Spartans on the sea-wet rock sat down and combed their hair before Thermopylae, and Casey, Boyle, and I ate *sole bonne femme*.

It was odd, though, finishing the big meal and the wines that went with it (we had white and red Burgundies), and then climbing into our jeep and heading south, past the summer villas in the summer sun, on our way to the fighting. From Barneville down to La Haye is, as I've said, a distance of only twelve miles, and for the first seven of them the road was unencumbered except for a few ambulances we met coming back and a few trucks we passed going forward. We felt none of the apprehension of the North African campaign—that enemy tanks might appear in a place where they were not expected or that planes might come out of the sky and hover on our radiator cap while we scrambled for a ditch. This feeling of security was newly acquired. (I had seen no enemy planes since the night raiders over the ships at Omaha Beach, and saw none until, during the breakthrough, I witnessed one attack by rocket-carrying Messerschmitts. Behind the German lines, things were different, as we discovered by the number of shot-up German vehicles we found along the roads when we advanced.)

As we drove down the road to La Haye that Sunday it was like going to Jamaica in time to have a bet on the third race, when most of the crowd has already gone through. Near La Haye, however, traffic was slower; it is amazing how frequently, when approaching danger, drivers who can read a road map perfectly feel that they must stop and ask directions. We ourselves stopped at a Medical Corps clearing station in a large villa that had a walled garden, where jeeps and ambulances were parked. We wanted to know how far to take our vehicle, but mostly we just wanted to stop.

A couple of big, country-looking soldiers out of one of the new divisions were standing at the south end of the garden, grinding their heads against the wall like little boys having a tantrum. They had the palms of their hands against it, too, and were digging into the mortar with their nails, as if clinging for shelter against a hail of bullets, but there was no shooting going on around them. Some medics were trying to talk the pair into getting into an ambulance, so they could take them to the nice, quiet rear, but the men couldn't or wouldn't budge, or even talk. Instead they continued to grind themselves into the wall, sniffling, now, like little boys who have cried themselves out.

We left our jeep and driver in the garden, having been informed by the medics that "it" began just around the next bend in the road. Before long we were angry because they had not told us it was such a long walk.

I remember being in two places in La Haye-du-Puits that day, but I am not sure of the sequence. One was a very big modern house, with landscaped grounds around it (I took it to be a sanatorium or summer hotel), which the Germans had used as a barracks and then as a redoubt. It was foul with the smell that poured out of their abandoned blankets and mess utensils. (The German Army had two smells—one of sour cabbage, which permeated even its sweat-soaked blankets, and one resembling a blend of a camel house and raw ether, which attached even to fragments of shotdown aircraft. I don't know yet what that one was, but it was known from Norway to Cyrenaica as the Boche smell.) There were numerous bodies around the big house, but they hadn't begun to smell dead. I remember particularly a tall German, who had dragged a wicker chaise longue from the house and placed it on a hillock in the garden. There he had sprawled himself, binoculars in hand, to look about for likely places on which to call down fire. It was flat country, and even this slight elevation was serviceable. A fragment from an air burst had saved him the trouble of getting up. There was no fire on this house while we were there, although shellbursts were visible not far away, but I cannot remember whether I was there before or after we went into the town.

There was plenty of shellfire in the streets of the town, whenever it was we went into it, but street fighting, in my limited experience, is not particularly dangerous unless you want to fight personally. Observation for marksmen is limited, and there is defilade everywhere. You sprint from shelter to shelter. Even while I was running, I felt that it was a game that did not in any way affect survival. It is plausible that the basis of many gestures of self-preservation is simply superstition. The man involved feels that if he does not show solicitude for his own skin he will invite the retaliation of a dark power. This mechanism works heavily in favor of the companies that offer one-flight insurance to air travelers. Having taken out sixty-two thousand dollars' worth of insurance for two dollars and a half, the traveler feels sure he won't crash. Sprinting, nevertheless, through the burning town, we reached a company command post in a wrecked café. A Chinese pfc. from Elizabeth, New Jersey, had found an unbroken bottle of Calvados there, but he hadn't saved us any. The Company Commander was pleased to have visitors. We stayed around awhile, rather at a loss for conversation, and then left, feeling that we had atoned for our good lunch.

The 1955 town had been rebuilt more thoroughly, and also, I thought, more attractively, than St. Lô. We stopped at a café on the Grande Place that may well have been on the site of the one where the Chinese soldier found the Calvados; the new building stone had not had time to lose its first pallor, and the interior was late Third Avenue American, with a jukebox and a pinball game. Leaving Michel there, I walked on to where the road left the north side of town, trying to figure where the big house with the dead Germans around it had been; it was not a long walk. La Haye-du-Puits, like many other war objectives, is of such inconsiderable size that you wonder that it meant so much. There was no big house in sight when I reached the town limits, so I came back to the center of town. There I talked with a dashing man in a tweed jacket, *très anglais*, who was peering through a surveyor's transit, apparently to see if they had got the main street in straight, and he said that he was not familiar with the house I described, but that he was not of the region. He suggested that I inquire at the *mairie*, still housed in a temporary one-story plank building, which stood near the railroad station and was almost the last such structure in town. The municipal authorities must have feared criticism if they got their offices rebuilt before the taxpayers got theirs. At the *mairie*, I talked to the secretary to the *maire*, who corresponds to town clerk. *M. le Secrétaire*, who had a chewed gray mustache and wore spectacles on the end of his nose and a linen duster to protect his clothes, told me that the big house had burned to the ground on the night of the last capture of the town; La Haye had changed hands four times, he said. He himself had managed to avoid being evacuated by the Germans before the fighting began and had lived through it all in his house, a mile or two away. "They were times full of emotion, Monsieur, full of emotion," he added. "We are lucky to have survived them."

We shook hands on that, and I went back to the café, where Michel, neat and citified in his blue suit and white shirt, was keeping watch over the parked Versailles with the manner of a horse holder left alone in Indian country. He smiled gaily to show me how brave he had been, and after a bad beer we headed for Barneville. (You have to go far from the big centers in France now to get the bad old kind of sour French beer—all belch and no body, and served in a *canette* with a porcelain stopper attached to its neck by a wire.)

I was sure Barneville would not have changed outwardly, and I was right. There, on first view, was the surprisingly big eleventh-century church at the turnoff from the highway. The other buildings of the town are low and unimpressive, and I cannot think why Barneville should have rated such a commodious place of worship nine hundred years ago. Then the Hôtel de Paris, narrower and meaner than I remembered it, caught my eye, and the triangular market place, with the business street running out of its pointed end toward the sea. I told Michel to leave the car near the hotel and come with me, but it was a market day and he said he was afraid that boys or drunkards would break into the magnificent Versailles while he was away. Michel treated his mount as if he were Father Divine's chauffeur and the Versailles were Father's Rolls-Royce. So I left him standing guard over it, a neat and alien figure among the peasants who were hefting screaming pigs by an ear and the tail. It gave me a holiday feeling to be in one town that I had never visited except in quest of innocent pleasure—the only kind any of us ever succeeded in finding there, because *la patronne* kept such close tabs on Andrée.

The sun beat down as it had on all those successive Sundays in 1944, and the breeze off the sea came straight from the Channel Islands. I had no trouble locating the electrical shop of M. Ribaud, but the chap in charge informed me that M. Ribaud was on a three-week holiday. "You can find Mme Ribaud at the *école des filles*," he said. "Opposite the church." I turned back, sorry to miss the electrician but sure his wife could bring me up to date on the chronicles of Barneville. The town's two elementary schools stood side by side, each two stories high and narrow as a small private house. The doors were closed, and I supposed the summer holidays were on. Nevertheless, I rang the bell at the door of the girls' school, and a pretty girl opened it—a girl certainly far too young to be Mme Ribaud, but not young enough to be a pupil in elementary school. She, it turned out, was the Ribauds' daughter, who had been six when I last visited the family, and who now, at seventeen, had just passed her baccalaureate examination in Cherbourg and come home for the summer. I told her who I was, and she called her mother, who came to the door wiping her hands on her apron, as if she had miraculously prepared another *gigot* against my arrival. This time, she said, it would be only beefsteak and fried potatoes, which she had begun to cook for lunch for her son and daughter; during the summer the Ribauds lived at the school. The son, who was eighteen, had also passed his baccalaureate a few days before, and would go to the university in Caen in the fall. The girl was hesitating between the university and a teachers' college.

Mme Ribaud asked me to stay to lunch, but I said I couldn't. I would have liked to, but I didn't see how I could ring Michel in on the invitation, and I didn't want to abandon him. We went out to the kitchen, which was the school's domestic-science room, so Madame could watch the beefsteaks. She remembered the Sunday of the delayed dinner and the Communion party. Her daughter said she thought she could remember it, too. Madame also remembered the message to Monsieur's brother. She said the two brothers were taking their holiday together, driving. Presently her son came in from swimming, having bicycled up from the beach. He was a cheerful lad, wide between the shoulders, like the Norman uncles, but, quite unlike them, wearing shell-rimmed glasses and a crew cut. The mother and daughter—thin, quick, with clever, mobile faces—reminded me by their agility of the lobster lady I remembered so well. Mme Ribaud brought out a sweet white wine of the same genre that Mme Hamel had produced when I visited her in Vouilly. We talked of how I had met M. Ribaud that Sunday morning and of the *gigot*, which Madame insisted, in retrospect, *had* been overdone, and which I assured her hadn't. The children, amused but proud, said it was just like their father, making friends with strangers and inviting them home with him. I told them how much Whitey, whom Madame remembered as *le petit soldat*, had liked the family, although he hadn't been able to converse with them.

Then I asked Madame about her nephew, Raymond Legaillard, the principal figure of the Communion party. "He ought to be a grown man by now," I said.

"He was," Madame said. "He's dead."

"What a pity," I said. "How?"

"There was really nobody for him to live with as he grew up," Madame replied. "So he went up young to naval training school. He did well. He was a specialist and liked submarines. In 1952, he was on the *Sibylle* when she submerged in the Mediterranean and didn't come up. He was a very jolly boy, and very handsome. Wait!" She went upstairs and returned with a full-length portrait photograph of a smiling sailor in a striped *maillot*, white summer ducks, and the beret with the pompon—a wide-shouldered, narrow-waisted, long-legged, and impudent-looking young man. And, as Madame had said, very handsome. I thought of what had happened to his parents and then to him, and remarked, without originality, "He had no luck."

"Evidently," Mme Ribaud said. But when I asked her about Raymond's great-aunt, the old lobster lady, she told me she was doing fine—as spry as a plover.

I took my leave of the three Ribauds, all of whom I thought admirable, and walked back to the Hôtel de Paris. There I found Michel shaking his fist at a small, vague dog, which had been overcuriously inspecting the Versailles. I invited Michel to lunch with me, and he followed me over the threshold, looking back distrustfully at the dog. The enameled *patronne* no longer ran the hotel. Possibly she had gone back to her café in Cherbourg. The present proprietors, a pastry cook and his wife, had partitioned off half the front of the *grande salle* to make a pâtisserie, with a separate entrance from the street, which accounted for the narrowing I had noticed. The new *patronne*, who explained all this to me, was a blonde with a fig-ure like a *vol-au-vent* of generous diameter and a skin like smooth custard. Several dealers from the market were already busy with the regular lunch, and as they appeared to be doing themselves well, I told the *patronne* that we would have the same. It began with a *croûte de volaille*, which, as the Hôtel de Paris presented it, was a bit of crisp, hot pastry with chunks of chicken embedded in it. "*Pirozhki!*" Michel exclaimed. There followed skate, not with the familiar black butter, but with a *sauce matelote*, made with red wine, and, after that, a *contre-filet* of beef, rare and beautiful, and about the best thing of its kind I have had since Barney Gallant closed his restaurant on University Place in 1948—two glorious square slices of beef, each a quarter of an inch thick, with *frites* as crisp as larks' legs. Then came string beans engulfed in butter, a lettuce salad, a Pont l'Evêque, and one's choice of the proprietor's *éclaires* or his *mille-feuilles*, still warm with the breath of the oven. The complete lunch went for five hundred francs a head, and I treated Michel and myself to a bottle of not-bad *muscadet* to accompany it. These, I did not trouble to inform Michel, were the funeral baked meats.

I still have the Communion card in my wallet, although I am afraid it will rub the luck off the Sweepstakes tickets.

6

The Hounds with Sad Voices

I REMEMBERED another Norman house called a château, where the press lived for a week after the breakthrough, but the memory was like Le Grand Meaulnes' of the house he dreamed. I no longer knew precisely where it was, nor could I recall the surname of the proprietor, though I had one in my mind—de Fives. From Vouilly the press camp moved to a place called Canisy, of which I remember nothing except that the tents were in an apple orchard; and then in a few days to a house on the skirts of the Forest of St.-Sever. It was near a hamlet called Fontenermont, which is near the small ancient town of St.-Sever, which is not far from the small city of Vire.

This was a baroque house, although in rural Normandy, where the baroque lingered, it may have been of the late eighteenth century. It was tall in relation to its length, with a square tower that had a top like an *accent circonflexe* (∧). It was of gray granite, like most of the other buildings of the region of Vire, which is hilly and in many places wooded—the Bocage, or Bosky Land. Compared to the flat and rich Bessin, where Vouilly lay, the Bocage is romantic and energetic. The land is still good, but shading off toward the austerity of Brittany to the south. In the Bocage you begin to smell Brittany. It has a high incidence of small noblemen, of families that officered the Army, the Navy and the Church before the Revolution.

This house might have been built by a retired frigate's captain or a colonel, a younger son of such a family, returned from the wars against the English in the East or West Indies, and content in middle age to follow the staghounds in the Forest of St.-Sever. They hunted the stag with dignity and clamor, the slow, deep-voiced hounds driving him in wide, then narrowing circles, he running from the sound and not the sight of them, working into the center of the deep but not sufficiently entangled woods. At last he would stand exhausted in a clearing, or in a pond, up to his neck in water. Then the hired huntsman would advance and cut his throat, and the bandsmen would play their taradiddles for wind instruments. The horses, never out of a canter all day, would be turned toward home and the waiting holocausts of venison and game birds and the old Calvados, the dice boxes, and the canopied curtained beds closed like confessionals and full of secrets.

This family had enjoyed another period of prosperity in a more recent era, to judge from the vestiges of the chic of the early Third Republic that cluttered the house, like props for the production of a dramatic version of *Bel-Ami*. There were trophies of African spears and Arab scimitars on the walls, which were papered with an imitation of brocade, and faded green plush portieres drooped crazily from valances askew. Notably there was a stuffed leopard, its lips pulled back in a savage snarl from teeth that were no longer present. Age affects the grip even of plaster gums. The background of the leopard's rosettes had faded to the color of bad California white wine. Most of the furniture was crank and perilous to sit upon.

It all reminded me, sadly, of the illustrations in the thirty-volume-or-so set of Maupassant, bound in three-quarter green imitation morocco with gold ornaments on the spine, that had been the chief advertisement of sophistication behind the glass of my parents' Globe-Wernicke sectional bookcases. In those volumes I sought my first clues to sex, and to this day I retain a prejudice that gentlemen with curved jet-black mustaches and long-tailed coats are wickeder than others, and that ladies with big behinds and small feet are the most irresistible. I had arrived, at last, in my chosen décor, but sixty years too late. Maupassant was a Norman, and my long liaison with Normandy began in the Globe-Wernicke mahogany sectional bookcases, and probably in a bad translation.

I thought the proprietor, when young, might have shared the glories of the Normans-transplanted-to-Paris I remembered in the illustrations, slipping from behind portieres exactly like the ones that now hung in shreds, to put their arms about the hourglass waists of chambermaids in white lace caps. I was sure he had slain the leopard and had his photograph published, wearing *le casque tropical*, his feet and the stock of his rifle behind the prostrate victim's head: "*M. le Vicomte de*

Fives avec une belle pièce de gibier. Ce léopard faisait la terreur des noirs du Limpopo français avant que le sportsman normand l'arrêtait en pleine fureur avec une balle bien placée dans chaque narine." But by the time we arrived he had regressed into peasantism. A great, heavy figure of a man, he went about in shirt sleeves, with checked denim trousers held around his pendulous paunch by an old harness strap.

The only vestige of the old chic that I confidently attributed to him was a hard straw hat, a *canotier*, or boater, that he wore indoors and out. (He was probably bald.) The old man's face and wattles were suffused with blood, and his mustache, of the color and aspect of hempen rope, no longer curled upward, as I was sure it must have once, but hung limp under his forceful nose.

The house stood on a low ridge with a higher ridge behind it. Our tents were pitched out behind the house, and to get to it we had to walk across what had once been a garden with flower beds marked out with rocks, and gravel paths between them. These boundaries were wiped out now; the rose bushes had gone to briar, but there were still late-season blooms, falling to pieces on their stalks. Petunias ran as wild as morning glory on a beach, and there were dusty zinnias.

We spent our days upon the roads, now that the war was all of movement, but in the evening we returned, and after supper wrote our dispatches in the blacked-out house, using as typewriter tables Levantine taborets inlaid with mother-of-pearl stars like those that cluttered living rooms from Lodz to Laramie in 1900. They still manufacture them in Damascus, but they must export them to places like the Dominican Republic. The censors and the Press Wireless men were set up amid the shards of elegance as we were.

Between the edge of our camp and the beginning of the garden we had to walk along the outside of a run fenced in with chicken wire, which contained eight or ten gaunt, sad hounds, with long heads and short legs, whose sad voices had the quality, at first emission, of echoes that have bounced around a valley. They were bassets of some kind, I knew at once, but higher on the leg and of a less studiously abnormal appearance than the English sort. Their flanks, as corrugated with ribs as a hunger striker's, were white flecked with black, their long, wide, trailing ears solid black and their faces black flecked with white. They were *bassets de Gascogne*, the old man told some one of us, the only pack of that strain in the northwest of France. I never talked to him myself; he did not invite conversation.

They were so thin, the old man was reported to have said, because under the conditions of the Occupation and rationing, it was hard to get meat to feed them on—even the meat of old horses brought high prices as *filet Longchamp*. (And because of the same phenomenon, I thought uncharitably, he would be sure not to feed them any of his own livestock when he killed.) Because the Germans had allowed the Normans to possess no ammunition for hunting, much less use any, the dogs were unexercised and unhappy. The old man said his hounds were of such an ancient and glorious breed that he could have sold them in couples, or one by one, at whopping prices, particularly to the Germans, but he had not wanted to disperse his breeding stock. I think he fed them on snared rabbits and other oddments as available.

The jeep drivers and cooks, some of whom came from hound-dog country, used to spend a lot of time in front of the chicken wire talking to the dogs, but the bassets were distant and surly. They scorned K rations. They might be down, but they were not so flat as all that.

If the soldiers had been horse cavalry, they might have found an unpopular officer's mount for the hounds to eat, but they had only jeeps. One night somebody stole one of the bassets, but I was away on an overnight trip to the Falaise pocket and so escaped suspicion. The abduction made a great stir. The old man protested to the lieutenant colonel in command of the press camp that it was not a question of the theft of a vulgar dog. His pack was a national historical monument, and Haro XVIII's disappearance reflected the blackness of the error committed by Louis XVI when he temporized with the mob. It was a delayed effect of the Revolution.

The lieutenant colonel made a serious try to find the historic animal, but he failed, as I expected he would. I have seen soldiers carry large dogs aboard a transport slung across their shoulders in barracks bags, and setters abducted from England leap from the cockpits of fighter planes landed on Tunisian airfields. The First Army moved ahead toward the Seine, and the press camp followed to Bagnoles-de-l'Orne, but the fate of Haro XVIII remained a mystery.

My fear of Michel's scorn kept me from trying to rediscover this house unaided. I could foresee his reactions if I asked him to begin inquiring after a house whose owner, of whose name I was uncertain, had once kept dogs with sad voices, or if I even let him know that such was the object of my search. When we arrived at l'Hôtel du Cheval Blanc in the city of Vire, however, I dismissed Michel and the Versailles, lunched, and then went on foot in search of M. Marcel Le Cornec, the publisher and editor of *La Voix du Bocage*—The Voice of the Bosky Country—a newspaper that I have received in New York every week since the conclusion of the war by M. Le Cornec's courtesy.

M. Le Cornec is a man of sensibility as well as intelligence. He respects the capricious forms nostalgia often takes, and when I related to him my desire to see for inconsequential reasons this Chateau of the Mournful Hounds, he volunteered to help me find it. St.-Sever and Fontenermont are fifteen miles or so from Vire, but well within the zone of circulation and influence of *La Voix du Bocage*, which is the most powerful organ of public opinion between St. Lô and Avranches. But, to begin with, he said, my recollection of the family name as de Fives and of the old man as a Vicomte must be erroneous.

M. Le Cornec is a tall and very handsome man who looks like George Washington *en littérateur*, Roman nose, blue eyes, high complexion, and mane of white hair long in back, over a string tie and corduroy jacket. He is as his name shows, of Breton family origin, but began life in Paris. There he was a commercial artist during the twenties. He came to Vire to design packages and draw advertisements for a wholesale grocery firm.

Vire, like a number of other Norman towns at rail and road junctions, was destroyed by the Allied air bombardment of June 6 designed to stop the Germans from reinforcing their coastal troops. The city's printing plants disappeared in the ruins. When Vire was freed in August, M. Le Cornec founded its first postwar newspaper, printing at first in a less damaged

city, until he could re-establish printing in Vire. I do not remember now, although M. Le Cornec told me, whether the
publisher of the prewar paper was killed in the bombardment
or disqualified for collaboration. At any rate, M. Le Cornec
and his wife, a witty and spirited woman, made a paper with a
decided personality.

Since M. Le Cornec is not a native, he takes an objective
view of the remarkable world in which he lives. He keeps the
paper's face straight, but his amusement sometimes filters
through his long and circumstantial accounts of such affairs as
the suit for defamation, for endless billions of francs, that a
rich farmer brought against *La Voix du Bocage* ten years ago,
for printing a speech of the mayor of the farmer's community.
In the speech the mayor accused his *administré* of "moistening
his milk" before selling it. To moisten milk is, in Norman, to
add water to it.

When the farmer sued, *La Voix* recorded the news, along
with a restatement of the grounds on which he was suing. He
then sued them for a reiteration of libel. But the mayor's
speech was an official statement, since he had made it at a
meeting of the municipal council. *La Voix* contended that a
newspaper must publish official statements. What had loosed
the mayor's wrath against the rich farmer was that the rich
farmer opposed the use of municipal funds to provide free milk
for school children. Reading *La Voix* in New York, I was sure
that was why the paper reprinted the story so many times, but
they never said so.

Vire was the place where I stayed longest on my first exciting
prise de connaissance with lower Normandy in 1926. I saw it for
only a few minutes in 1944, so dreadfully demolished that I
could not bear it for longer. Now a Vire had risen on the old
site, solid, ugly, new without being modern. There was, in
1955, still a noise of drills and bulldozers. Construction was
going on, but it was already irremediable. Each property
owner had wrung as much money as he could from the State
for reconstruction of what he said he had had, and then built a
house containing the maximum number of cubic feet that
could be roofed over, leaving the upper floors to be finished at
his leisure in the years to come. One surviving monument was

the Tour de l'Horloge, the old Clock Tower, that had once been a gate in the medieval city wall. The rest of the wall had been leveled by Henri IV, after the Wars of Religion.

The tower, with the gateway under it, stood astride the main street of the Vire I knew. Traffic passed between its legs. The bombs had cleared a space around it but left it crazily erect at the hub of the city. The traffic now passed around instead of through, and, indeed, the vibration set up by trucks might have brought La Tour down on the drivers' heads if they had persisted in the old way.

The sixteenth-century clock that banged out the time every quarter of an hour, night and day, was silent, knocked out of time when the bombs fell. The old Hôtel du Cheval Blanc stood next the clock tower, and a guest unable to fall deeply asleep in fourteen minutes flat had a fat chance of getting to sleep at all. The new Cheval Blanc has been erected fifty yards from the old site, and when I slept there I was willing to forgive the Municipal Council for not having restored the historic chimes. There is a limit to my archaeological purism. But I found it harder to forgive that the surrounding proprietors had been allowed to mass high, bloated new buildings all around the new traffic circle, and that the bit of space remaining in the center was used for parking automobiles, instead of for a plaza or small park. So the Tower stands like a stag at bay in a pond, the ugliness ringing it and closing in, awaiting the inevitable hour when some municipal engineer will declare it a menace and workmen will come to cut its throat. Vire will then be indistinguishable from St. Lô or Isigny or any of the other rebuilt towns of the same size. I spent an unhappy afternoon walking about.

I had M. and Mme Le Cornec to dinner that evening at the new Cheval Blanc. Michel had found himself a cheaper lodging in town. The pre-June 6 Cheval Blanc was a posting inn several hundred years old, but as gradually accumulated as the rest of pre-bombardment Vire. It had an archway leading from the street to the courtyard behind the house, and at the back of the courtyard was the old stable, remodeled into a garage, with a café and a billiard table on the floor above.

You reached the café by a narrow stairway, and once there you drank horrid-tasting French drinks like St. Raphael, Gentiane Suze and Raspail, and talked to commercial travelers from Cherbourg and Le Havre, who voyaged by train and made a point of passing the night at Vire instead of Granville at the end of the line from Paris, because Granville was infested with large, expensive summer hotels. One ate better for less at Le Cheval Blanc or at its rival in Vire, the St. Pierre, they said, and then, one was more at home. On a drummer's earnings, one couldn't rivalize with the swells, "a?" they said, closing the sentence with a sound like the "a" in "at," which is customarily transcribed *hein*. (When I first read the green Maupassants, I thought this ever recurrent *hein* was pronounced like the first syllable in "Heinie." I was disillusioned because I never heard anybody say it.)

The commercial travelers sometimes talked about the miserable Norman character, which impelled their customers to demand goods in niggardly quantities at prices based on shipments in carloads, and even to demand rebates on single shoes because they had sold the other of the pair to a one-legged man who refused to pay for two. But mostly they spoke of hotels where the best and the most food was to be obtained at a fixed price: the Hôtel du Centre et de la Victoire at Caen is one I still remember. Others, widely traveled, would oppose to the best of these Norman bargains the meals, four times as marvelous and only half as dear, to be obtained in other provinces.

At l'Hôtel du Commerce in Vendôme, for example, a fellow told me, one had for lunch a magnificent *hors d'oeuvre—rillettes, pâté*, country ham, good things, what? and then *tripes à la mode de Caen* copiously served, a magnificent beefsteak with potatoes, and half a pheasant, followed by *fromage cendré*, the cheese of the country that is lightly coated with ashes, *pommes bonne femme*, and all you could drink of wine.

"It isn't great wine, but it's still better than the cider you get with the *prix fixe* in this region of misers."

"Don't you pay extra for the pheasant at Vendôme?" I asked.

"A small supplementary payment," he admitted.

In the following winter I lunched at the Hôtel du Commerce in Vendôme with a friend who was an instructor in a school for Armenian orphans in a château that a New York rug

merchant had bought from the Duc de Dodon Rochefou-
cauld. The rug man had not thought fit to hire the Duc's chef
for the orphans, and my *convive* brought a hearty appetite to
the meal, which was served at the head of a long table, with a
half dozen *commis-voyageurs* ranged around the other end of
the board.

Paniguian, my friend, was twenty-four and I was twenty-
three. We were both confirmed gluttons. We ate the precise
menu that the *commis-voyageur* at Vire had described, with
some amendment in the wine department. We had a bottle of
the landlord's best local wine to begin with and then a Corton
Clos du Roi with the pheasant. The gentlemen of commerce
were patronizing when we sat down and placed our napkins in
our laps. They tied theirs around their necks, so that they
could forget caution in grappling with their grub. But when
we cleaned the serving platters of *rillettes*, of *pâté de lièvre*, of
jambon cru du pays, of *andouilles* (inferior to those of Vire, but
acceptable), and even of salt herring and scraps of *gigot* left
over from yesterday's Sunday dinner and freshened with
onion, they were admirative. They still felt superior, though.
One was sportsman enough to warn us, "Attention, there's
more to come!"

It was presumption on his part to think we didn't know.

After we devastated the *tripes à la mode de Caen* a look of
speculation broke water in their faces, as in a pool shark's when
his intended victim runs 15 from the break.

Our performance on the beefsteaks and soufflé potatoes was
so apocalyptic that I saw one of them pause, his fork halfway to
his mouth, to watch us—a pause so unusual, for a Frenchman
eating, that I thought for a moment he had a stroke. When we
had eaten five or six beefsteaks apiece while each of them was
despatching a humdrum three, the waitress cleared the table,
and all of us regarded one another with satisfaction, like men
who have rowed a creditable race in the same boat. The drummers' fear that we would eat all the beefsteaks was assuaged.
They were full and could afford to be complimentary.

"Here you truly ring the bell!" one drummer said, and another corroborated, "What one sends oneself, it's something!"

The waitress placed a cheese tray and a couple of baskets of

Saint-Jeans, which we call seckel pears, before the drummers, and went away.

One called down to us, "Why aren't you having any cheese? Are you full already?"

Then his paternal bonhomie changed to an expression of compound hate, a mixture of xenophobia (the franc was falling) and the Spirit of the Barricades. He saw the waitress bringing in the pheasant, just for us.

It was a remarkable pheasant, served on a skinned and lightly toasted loaf of bread, in which a trough had been made and filled with a salmi of the bird's insides. I have never since believed the legend that all game must be hung, because I had seen the gunner bring in the pheasant early that morning. It remains the best bird in my memory.

Long before we had eaten all and crushed each bone in our teeth, the drummers had disappeared. They could not bear watching us and had elected to take their coffee and *eau de vie* in a café down the street. After we had done full justice to the goat cheese in ashes, the seckel pears and the puckered baked apples with cores of jelly, we called for the *patron* and congratulated him on an unforgettable meal. We offered him a glass of his own best Armagnac, taking a gamble that, since we were not in Normandy, he might respond by buying us the next round.

The *patron* said modestly that it was the regular Monday lunch, all except that little bird that he had been fortunate enough to come by that morning, and it was too bad we hadn't come later in the week, when he made an effort.

"You know how it is on Monday," he said. "After the substantial repasts of Sunday, nobody has any appetite."

This has developed from a merely culinary into a geographical digression, but I can never approach the memory of that meal without wanting to go into it. It has the same attraction for me as Costello's saloon. I seldom encounter a pheasant nearly so good nowadays, and when I do, an *hors d'oeuvre* and possibly the tripe is all I can manage at one meal besides the bird. (I am writing this on a lunch exclusively of turtle soup, as I am trying to take off weight.)

*

Monsieur Secher, the *patron* of the old Cheval Blanc, was not so lavish with his meals *en pension* as his colleague at Vendôme, although he set what I thought was a remarkable table. Even the travelers admitted it wasn't bad. He stood, in relation to the meals at fixed price, in the position of a great couturier who has consented to sponsor a line of ready-to-wear. He was not truly *engagé* in this mass aspect of his art.

Monsieur Secher lived in his chef's *toque* as the old man at Fontenermont lived in his straw hat. It is conceivable he wore this *toque* to bed, to stimulate dreams about food. He was a tall, slender man, who had performed his military service at the school of cavalry at Saumur in the epoch made familiar to movie-goers by *Les Grandes Manoeuvres*, with Gérard Philipe and Danielle Darrieux, and he wore a waxed mustache and imperial. His primary interest in the hotel was the creation of *spécialités sur commande* for clients with plenty of money, who were rare in those days of relatively limited *automobilisme*. Vire is 150 miles from Paris. What happened upstairs—if the water closets ceased to function or the one electric-light bulb in a bedroom was extinct—was of little moment to him. Sleep was to him a fashion of passing time between meals and love an activity for people without imagination.

From my arrival he cultivated me as a prospective client for one of the *plats* he had presented at a gastronomic exposition in Paris, where he had put on a Day Consecrated to the Classic Cuisine of Vire. He had won a magnificent specimen of calligraphy on parchment attesting his glory. An American, even a young one, must be in at least easy circumstances, he believed. I was not flush, though, and wanted to be sure, before I gave him his head, that I would be able to finish the month out and return by rail to Paris.

When, near the end of the month, I was sure that I had a safe margin of twenty-five dollars, about seven hundred and fifty francs at the rate then, I commissioned a repast *de gala*.

On that evening, when I came to the dining room I was placed at a table by myself, sequestered from the vulgarians of the long table. They had to make do with Cistercian fare such as *potage mongole*, *merlan en colère*, and *canard aux navets*, followed by a salad. What the meal began with, I am ashamed to say I do not remember, nor how it ended. But the main dish was a partridge Olivier Basselin, cooked in cream and old Calvados, a dish named in honor of a fifteenth-century poet and drunkard reputed to have lived in Vire. The poems formerly ascribed to Basselin are now known to be the work of a hoaxing Virois named Le Houx who lived two centuries later, but Le Houx made use of a name and a tradition already extant. The peculiar glory of the partridge Basselin was that the cream smoothed the Calvados and both impregnated the bird without turning it into a mess like Stroganoff. It tasted like a partridge that had been fed all its life from a bottle of Calvados fifty years old.

Thirteen years later, in the first winter of the Second World War, I returned to Vire and stopped at the Cheval Blanc again, but I learned that M. Secher had sold the hotel and gone to Angers. There he had bought another of the same name, l'Auberge du Cheval Blanc. Two much younger people, a Monsieur and Madame Delaunay, had taken over the Vire Cheval Blanc, but had not changed it. Vire, too, was the same.

Early in 1940 I went from Paris to Angers to prepare a story on the Polish Government-in-Exile, which had set up its capital there, and naturally I went to the Angevin Auberge du Cheval Blanc. Monsieur Secher was himself an Angevin.

Angers is a great city compared to Vire. It had then perhaps 100,000 inhabitants—Vire had 5,000. It had a great cathedral, that of St. Maurice, a Château-Fort that is one of the marvels of France, a municipal theater, a night life centering around the Place du Ralliement, a diplomatic corps accredited to the Polish Government, two or three restaurants renowned throughout France, and a history that once encompassed that of England. (It was the Angevin Henry II who became King of England, not an Englishman who became Count of Anjou.) All this, I thought, must have produced some effect on M. Secher, who was on his native soil again.

The Auberge du Cheval Blanc at Angers was even older and more intricately accumulatively constructed than the one at Vire. Part of it dated from the thirteenth century. It had a courtyard, and in a small glassed-in office adjoining it sat Monsieur Secher, still wearing a *toque*.

I went in and reintroduced myself. He professed to remember me, and we chatted awhile about Vire and the war. I asked him if he preferred Angers to Vire; I expected he would. He thought a moment and then said, "It is difficult to say. The chickens here are better, beyond discussion. They are more delicate and symmetrical. The vegetables are also better, and the fruit, there's no comparison. But the *charcuterie* of Vire is hard to beat. And the cream, the butter, the cheese! What a delight! Not a bad country for game, either, you know. Monsieur, your question is very hard to answer."

7
The Farmer's Boy

THE new Hôtel du Cheval Blanc has a round lobby with high walls, like a well, and in the center there is a smaller well with the reception desk in it. The walls are stuccoed glaring white, and off the lobby is the café, with a bar *améri-cain* all succedaneum chromium and *véritable* plastic. Over the back bar there is a striped tent, as in similar decorating jobs from Tel-Aviv to Wichita. The architect has tried to create the new Cheval Blanc in the mood of *Match*, the French picture-weekly equivalent of *Life*. To what degree he has succeeded I am incompetent to say, but I wish he hadn't tried.

Monsieur Delaunay, who was still the proprietor as of June 6, 1944, was killed in the bombardment, which knocked the old hotel to bits. It was beyond the power of his widow to re-constitute the old warren even if she had wished. I am sure she was advised that the day of the *commis-voyageur* was over, and that to prosper a *hotelier* must appeal to the taste of the mo-torized bar trade, which is the same everywhere. And still . . .

When I came downstairs to await the Le Cornecs in the café that evening, the chromium-fluorescent bait had brought in two couples who sat up at the bar. The women's tight, round little bottoms perched up on the bar stools like the tops of swizzle sticks. The V-backs of their motoring dresses started just above the caudal cleft, their hair was rose platinum, and their voices suggested they wore microphones in their garter belts. They and the men, who looked like *compères* in a mar-seillais road show, were drinking Scotch, as everybody does in France now who does not wish to be taken for a tourist. Their dialogue, aimed to impress the barmaid and me, was full of al-lusions sealed to any except the two million readers of the gos-sip columnists in *France-Soir*. They claimed all the columnists' subjects as close friends. Their main subject, though, was the rusticity of the surroundings. They gave the impression that they were in a goatherd's hut in the Cevennes.

Madame Le Cornec arrived alone, bringing her husband's

excuses because he was still writing the editorial for the paper that was going to press. She herself, she said, had just finished writing the court column headed "*Tribunal,* or *En Correctionelle,*" which is my favorite reading in *La Voix du Bocage*. She is a slender, resilient woman, with a thin, pretty face, and she said she enjoyed court reporting more than anything else she did.

"This afternoon, for example, we had two farmer's wives in court who charged each other and were charged by the court with reciprocal assault and damages to the person. I thought they would fight again in court. The husbands were there, great hulks of men, in their town clothes, each trying to avoid his woman's eye. They were intimidated by the law, the men, they wanted to keep the fines as low as possible. They testified that they had taken no part in the fight, and when they said that you should have seen the wives look at them!

"They had just stood there while the women fought, one man said—it must have interested them!—and then, when the hair began coming out in handfuls, and 'it looked like there might be breakage,' he had taken his wife up by the waist and his neighbor had taken his, and they had carried them away—'like two hens that are quarreling.' The intervention was understandable; a woman is a useful animal on a farm too. But you could see that the women thought their men should have stood up for them. Murders have grown from such disputes!"

"And what was the fight about?" I asked.

"It appears there is a rill of water that runs down through the farmyard of the neighbor higher up the slope and across the farmyard of the lower neighbor—very advantageous for the ducklings and the chickens. But there is bad blood between the two women—an old story of one having accused the other's brother of slander. So the higher-up woman dammed the rill with stones and turned it out of its course so the water would stay longer on her land. The other woman crossed the property line and took the stones away—trespass! Now they will have a long civil suit. That will please them."

"And what was the verdict today?"

"The judge fined them ten thousand francs apiece with suspended sentence and adjunction not to recommence. I think the husbands will make them keep the peace. Ten thousand francs, after all, it's ten thousand francs."

During Madame Le Cornec's *compte-rendu*, the sophistication at the bar continued to bray. When she finished, she regarded them for the first time.

"We have a saying here," she said. "Africa begins at Paris."

I told her that in her collected court columns of ten years she must have the makings of a hundred short stories as dry and as high in flavor as an *andouille de Vire*, the smoked sausage made of tripe cased in tripe that is the specialty of the city. Maupassant used just such anecdotes as the bases of some of his best stories.

"Some of the best ones I can't write in their entirety in the columns of *La Voix du Bocage*, which is, after all, a family journal," Madame Le Cornec said. "Although in this country, where everybody knows the principals, each reader fills in the details for himself. There was, for example, one that I wanted to send to you for publication in the journal *The New Yorker* of which you are the director."

(This is an illusion the Le Cornecs have had for years; my copy of their paper always arrives addressed to me as Director of *The New Yorker*, and I do not want to tell them that I am not because they might then send it to the real editor instead.)

I urged her to tell me the story now that she had the chance, and she said, "It concerned a rich farmer with a jealous wife. He wanted a divorce, but naturally on the best terms for himself. So he put the eighteen-year-old farm boy in her way as much as possible, gave them all opportunity, and naturally he caught them one day *en flagrant délit*.

"He frightened the boy into signing a long confession, and as further punishment made him agree to work two months without wages. But the woman denied everything, and the farmer was afraid that when the case came to trial the boy would repudiate his confession. So he took the boy on a tour of the neighboring farms one Sunday, ordering him to repeat the story of his adulteries at each farm, so that he could call the neighbors to testify that they had heard the boy tell all without duress.

"Well, the reaction was what you would expect. At the first

farmhouse, when he announced the purpose of his call, the peasant howled with laughter. He invited his wife and all his sons and sons-in-law and their wives to hear this wonderful *divertissement*. They plied the farmer and the boy with Calvados, with old hard cider for a chaser. The reception was the same at each house. It was an ovation, a triumphal progress!

"The boy, timid at first, saw that he was the leading man. He felt a hero. Pretty soon he began going into details, a bit boastful. He was drunk. He extolled the virtuosity of the farmer's wife; everybody clapped him on the back and asked for more information. The farmer, in rage, knocked the boy down and began to beat him. 'I brought you here as a witness,' he roared, 'not to make commentaries!'

"Then it was the boy who became the plaintiff. He brought the farmer into court for aggravated assault with outrage and withholding two months' wages. The wife was summoned as a witness for both sides. She sat there in the court, with a long curved feather in her hat, like a plumed serpent, fixing both with her hard, glittering eyes. She hated her husband for himself, and the boy as much for blabbing. The boy lost the case. The court acquitted the farmer and allowed him to keep the unpaid wages as balm for conjugal wrongs.

"The farmer obtained the divorce, but when he drives up to a farmhouse now, he risks to have the neighbor call out: 'Say, *Aimable*, have you brought the boy along to tell us some good ones?'"

The platinized Paris women and their *mecs* continued to gabble at the bar, but they were no longer the loudest element of sound in the café of the Hôtel du Cheval Blanc.

Between twenty and thirty male and female Germans of matched unattractiveness, alike monochromatic—hair, hides, and trenchcoats of the same tint, and all equally hard-jawed, bespectacled, thick in the middle, and hung about with cameras—had entered the café. They moved three or four tables end to end to form a long single *Stammtisch*, and seated themselves around it. They were a party, traveling by chartered motorbus, of veterans of the war of 1939–45 and their wives. The husbands were revisiting the scenes in which they had passed so many happy Occupation hours, and bringing the wives to share their sentimental journey—"There is some por-

tion of a foreign land *das immer und immer Deutschland ist,*"
I suppose they were snorting at each other across the beer. (I
had heard of one such group that swarmed all over the monument to the hostages executed by the Gestapo at Châteaubriant in Brittany, taking photographs.) The lot at Vire did
nothing particularly awful, beyond being there. They didn't
sing marching songs or yodel, but drank their beer and communicated in their sniffling, bitter howls. When they returned
to Germany, I imagined, they would say they had been well received, that the inhabitants looked fondly back on the days of
the beneficial Occupation, and that the time appeared ripe for
the resumption of their civilizing mission.

Happily Monsieur Le Cornec arrived, to rescue me from
further consideration of these *revenants,* carbon copies of remembered corpses. ("Why isn't it as natural for a German as
for an American to wish to revisit his old battlefields?" any one
of them would have said, if aware of my irritation. It would
have seemed to him a parallel.)

Monsieur Le Cornec said he had just written an editorial
about an agitation to drive from popular usage the term Basse-
Normandie—Low Normandy—for the departments of La
Manche and Calvados. Vire is the seat of one of the *arrondissements,* or administrative subdivisions, of Calvados.

"It has been Basse-Normandie forever," M. Le Cornec said,
"and its people have been Bas-Normands, and proud of it,
but now the Syndicates of Initiative and Tourism have decided
that 'low' has a connotation of inferiority. It is a movement
that began in other parts of France—for example the Department of Seine-Inférieure, in the other part of Normandy, has
changed its name officially to Seine-Maritime, to escape the
imputation that it is 'inferior' to the Department of Seine,
which includes Paris. Basse-Normandie, however, is not an official but a historic, a popular, appellation. What shall we call
ourselves, if not Low Normans? Surely we do not wish to be
confused with the inhabitants, mediocre in all respects, of the
three eastern departments, Orne, Eure and Seine *soi-disant*
Maritime? Bocains? Bretons Supérieurs?

"Our Mayor, Monsieur Halbout, the pharmacist, says the
solution is simple. 'Let us call ourselves simply Normans,' he
says. 'The other three departments aren't Norman at all. They

are by this time suburbs of Paris. Normandy begins at Caen.' But unfortunately, I told him, they will continue to call themselves Normans anyway. 'Get a court order,' he says, 'or a law of regional appellation.'"

"The boundaries of Africa are expanding," I said, "if Africa begins at Paris and Paris begins at Caen!"

"The boundaries of barbarism are indeed expanding," said M. Le Cornec, serious now. "It is an age of the Ram, violence, and upheavals are inescapable." He is the exponent of a Zodiacal system of historical inevitability, which does not interfere with his practical sense as a newspaper proprietor. "My wife is shrewd but not intelligent," he sometimes says. "She does not share my wider views."

We went in to dinner, which, if not up to the glories of Monsieur Secher's time, was at least honorable. The *charcuterie de Vire*, featuring the renowned *andouilles*, was as remarkable as always. We agreed that Michel and I, with the Versailles, should pick up M. Le Cornec at his printery the following mid-morning, and that we should set out together in quest of the château with the stuffed leopard and the sad baritone hounds.

"It would be well, I think, to consult the Colonel de Petiville," M. Le Cornec said. "He lives between Vire and St.-Sever, and his mind contains an Almanach of the nobility of the region. If there is a Vicomte de Fives at Fontenermont, he will know him. The Colonel de Petiville is a brother of the Marquis de Petiville, and is my most popular collaborator on *La Voix du Bocage*. He contributes long essays on the antiquities of Vire—'Trade Guilds in Vire in the Eleventh Century,' for example—but he takes a strong political slant. The decadence of France was determined, according to *M. le Colonel*, when the barons declined to follow Louis IX en masse to the Seventh Crusade in 1270. He says the Sieur de Joinville was an archetypical liberal. The Baron's refusal announced a national surrender to egoism, and everything that has happened since has but confirmed the deplorable symptomatology. It is a comfortable point of view, because it blames neither the Communists nor the parties of the Right Center, the Center-Right, and the Right-of-Center Left, which are, in that order, the strongest in the region, except when they group, in face of the

Communists, to form a Center-Center lightly to the left of Right."

When we arrived at the entrance to the Colonel de Petivile's estate next morning, however, a chain lay on the ground across the roadway, an indication, M. Le Cornec thought, that the Colonel was from home. We drove on up to his house, hoping to leave a message for him with the caretaker—Monsieur Le Cornec said the Colonel had a peasant farmer who worked the estate—but we found the place garrisoned exclusively by peacocks. It was a high, narrow stone house, smaller but more graceful than the one at Fontenermont, and I noticed that the stoop and balcony were ornamented with graceful wrought iron painted white, as on houses in New Orleans. Save for the cries of the peacocks, silence reigned under the great trees that shaded the house.

"The Colonel has perhaps gone to Vire, to carry me his weekly essay," M. Le Cornec said. "I think he was contemplating something on the disastrous amiability of Louis XVI when he omitted to have the Swiss Guard shoot all the delegates of the Third Estate as a prophylactic measure. But since he is not here, we will have to continue our quest alone." And he directed Michel toward Fontenermont. Michel, incredulous as always, pointed the Versailles along the obviously dead-end road M. Le Cornec indicated. Before we started off, however, he turned upon me a monumental, Champs-Elysian wink, to show he wasn't being fooled. It was a typical beginning of a day with me, he seemed to say—a visit to an empty house—and now we would go somewhere equally ridiculous.

I rode in front with Michel, and as we proceeded on this new wild-goose chase he told me about his evening in Vire. He had found lodging over a stationery and newspaper store and had attended a moving picture, about an American gangster trafficking in *stupéfiant* drugs, who disguised himself as an agent of the police of *stupéfiants* in order to drag down another gangster who had stolen from him his mistress and 500 kilos of *schnouf*. In so doing he enlisted the sympathies of a young female American, *très chic*, the daughter of a millionaire, but when he admitted that he had abused her confidence —he was in fact not an agent but a gangster—she said not to be put out, because she was in fact not a *jeune fille* but a feminine ace of the police. I said it sounded sufficiently complicated, and he agreed.

"She couldn't arrest him, of course," Michel said. "They were in bed together. Figure to yourself."

I don't know the answer yet, because M. Le Cornec advised that we stop at a roadside store where he thought the people might know of a man at Fontenermont who kept hounds. "The man here is a great hunter," he said, "President of the Circle of Hunters and Fishermen with the Pole of Saint-Sever." The shopkeeper, who also exercised the trade of blacksmith, told us there was no Vicomte, or Comte, or even simple Monsieur de Fives at Fontenermont, but in the matter of hounds practicing hunting by pursuit there was in effect a Monsieur de Carville! In effect, a great gray house! He had never been asked in, so he couldn't say whether there was a straw-filled leopard. He gave directions to M. Le Cornec—in effect, on the very edge of the Forest of Saint-Sever, the last house on the road before the forest began. We drove three miles or so along a road I now began to think I recognized and took a private road through a copse not yet continuous with the Forest. And there, beyond the trees, I saw the house I remembered. It stood, against the un-Norman background of hill and forest, as when I had left it for Bagnoles de l'Orne.

The house was silent, and I suggested we drive down to the barns, where we could see a couple of men fiddling about as farmers do.

"We will be able to ask them if the proprietor is about," I said. I could see the chicken wire not far from the barns, and as the Versailles approached, a baritone psalmody rose on the air, as if the dogs were rehearsing the "Pilgrims' Chorus" from *Tannhäuser* in the original language. We stopped the Versailles near the barn, and the men interrupted their agricultural routine—taking hay out of the barn or putting hay into the barn—which they may have pursued throughout the intervening eleven years, for all the sense my urban eye could make of it.

I asked for Monsieur de Carville, and they said he was off in the field on the other side of the house, harrowing. That indicated to me that it couldn't be the old man, and when I asked, they said, sure enough, that the old man was dead. The present proprietor was his son, who had also been here when the Americans were here. The working men themselves had not been on the farm then, they said—they had been prisoners in Germany. One of them came along back to the house with us. He left the car on the driveway and went off across the field to get M. de Carville, whom we could see in the distance, atop the two-wheeled, one-horse harrow. When the man got within shouting distance of the harrow, he stopped, and shortly thereafter we saw the driver head the horse toward us. It was a bay at least eighteen hands high, and a good ton on the hoof. When he got within fifty yards of the car M. Le Cornec and I walked out to meet him.

As we came even with the horse, the driver stopped, and M. Le Cornec introduced himself and me. It was the editor who made the impression. M. de Carville, who was wearing a straw boater—possibly inherited from his father—removed it with *empressement*. "I have never before had the pleasure of meeting you," he said, "but of course I have heard a great deal about you. I am a constant reader." I was well sponsored.

M. de Carville was a man in his early forties, lean, tanned, fair-haired and blue-eyed, with a hard New England look about him. He was in his shirt, with his sleeves rolled up and held by elastic bands, and his forearms and wrists showed that he had driven a lot of big horses in his time. But his profile was, as M. Le Cornec observed, *racé*, and his language was courteously old-fashioned.

M. Le Cornec explained who I was, and M. de Carville said that he remembered the Americans and added courteously that he thought he recalled me. (I had forgotten him entirely, remembering only the gross old man.) I said that I would like to see the stuffed leopard again, and he invited us inside, jumping down from the harrow and turning the horse over to the farm hand. We went around to the rear of the house, where the garden still agonized, and entered through the kitchen, a vast raftered room hung with hams and shotguns. There was a cot in one corner. "I live here now," M. de Carville said. "I'm alone, and it isn't worth the trouble to keep up the rest of the house." The old disorder was gone, though. The combination gun room, larder, kitchen, dining room and bedroom was of an ascetic neatness.

The sun was blazing in the field, as I remembered it eleven years before, but in the dark kitchen there was a welcome coolness, and M. de Carville said, "I'll show you into the rooms you remember, and then I'll go down cellar and get a bottle of old *cidre bouché*. It's an occasion." He opened a door and led us through the great living room to the dining room. The shutters were closed, and the rooms were semi-dark, but I could see the leopard. It was really a small specimen, a half-grown male or a young female, looking a bit like the ones you used to see in side-street furriers' windows.

Seeing me pause before it, Monsieur de Carville said, "Father Dupuy, a missionary, sent it to my father from Conakry in West Africa a long time ago." He thus shattered my fantasy that the old Vicomte, who, it now appeared, hadn't been a Vicomte either, had personally killed the leopard. Nor had I thought of the old rip as an associate of missionaries.

The room, like the kitchen, was clean now. There had been no attempt to restore the old fripperies, but they had been shoved decently aside and were evidently dusted sometimes. It was a rectangular room, and in each of the four corners was neatly wedged a great high-backed sofa, like a triangular segment of a pie, with a curved outer edge. The backs, of conforming shape, rose to the ceiling, where they had apparently been sawed off. I did not recall them specifically, and I now looked at them with such interest that M. de Carville said, "They are the four quarters of a round sofa, with a high upholstered pillar in the middle, that the Imperial Russian Ambassador in Paris had had made for the Embassy in the last century. When it was finished he found he couldn't get it into the Embassy, so he sold it at auction at the Salle Drouot. Naturally there were few bidders, but my grandfather, who was there, couldn't bear to pass up a bargain. He bought it and had it sawed into quarters, from top to bottom. Then all he had to do was trim off a metre or so at the tops, and the pieces fitted in very nicely. What my grandmother said I don't know."

He showed us into the dining room, and M. Le Cornec, Michel, and I took seats at the table, in the dark streaked with sun that came through cracks in the shutters.

"I saw you drive in," M. de Carville said, "but I didn't come to meet you because I suspected you were city people looking for antiquities. They bother me a lot in the summer, driving up and demanding to know what I have to sell. When I tell them, nothing, they insist on coming into the house anyway. 'You may have something of great value that you don't know about!' they say, as if I were a noodle. They can be quite rude."

He went in search of the cider, and M. Le Cornec said, "It is as you remember it?"

I said, "Essentially. But less remarkable."

Michel said, "He needs a wife. He must have to pay a servant quite a lot."

Monsieur de Carville returned with the litre of cider and four glasses. The cider was cool from the cellar, and the bubbles in it carried an overpoweringly intoxicating smell of decaying apples into the drinker's nostrils. *Cidre bouché* can be a mighty drink, as strong as a generous wine. We drank it gratefully, but when we finished, M. de Carville offered no second bottle. He had the rest of his harrowing to do.

"I remember the day the Americans came," he said. "We had a family of friends from Caen staying with us, and when the Germans fell back from their first line they took the house as a battalion headquarters. It was full of them. I got away and walked into Vire, where I heard the Americans had already arrived, to tell them how things were. I didn't want them blundering into the Germans and having a battle in my house; it would have been a ruin. Luckily I encountered a French liaison officer with the Americans who was an old friend. He assured them that I was not a spy, but they didn't look too convinced. M.P.s are all alike, be they of France or of Navarre. I didn't get back here for twenty-four hours, and then in a jeep with some hard-looking boys. But the Germans, fortunately, had decamped. It was after that the Americans decided to put the press camp here."

"Your pack of hounds has survived," I said. "Always the same strain, I see."

"Yes," M. de Carville said. "It is easier to find food for them now, but expensive. They are marvelous dogs."

"Do they track?" I asked.

"Infallibly," M. de Carville replied. "They drive out all sorts of game, foxes, pheasants, rabbits, boars—it remains only to shoot it. I have five couples."

"There was some *histoire* about a soldier who stole one of the dogs while I was here," I said.

"It was not a soldier," said M. de Carville with conviction. "It was a correspondent. An Englishman. He begged my father to sell him a dog. My father, naturally, refused. The morning this Englishman went away, the dog disappeared."

From the tone in which M. de Carville said "Englishman" I could tell there was no use arguing with him. The English had taken Canada from Normandy. Why not a *basset de Gascogne*?

I longed to ask M. de Carville the history of his family, down to, and especially, his father's generation. But he was too well bred, and too occupied with his farm. We said polite goodbyes, and half an hour later we were back in hot, white Vire, with its smells and noises of construction.

8
Michel's Mountain

THE Germans had gone, perhaps to Omaha Beach and Easy Red, to tell their feminine counterparts how they had repulsed the invasion, only to be betrayed by the Jewish General Rommel, who ordered them to advance in the wrong direction. After that they would have a picnic with cervelat and bierkase. The Parisians had also gone, perhaps to a seaport where the men would book the women as "entertainers" for a tour of South America. I felt small desire to stay in the new Vire, and so we said goodbye to M. Le Cornec and pushed on for Mont-Saint-Michel, where I had decided to pass the weekend and then return to Paris.

Michel was pleased when I told him where we were going. Mont-Saint-Michel is a standard attraction for American tourists, and he was sure to meet other White Russian tourist-wranglers there, freshly arrived from Paris with convoys of sightseers they had turned over to the concierge of La Mère Poularde Hôtel. He in turn would hand them over to licensed guides who would make them climb all the stairs and stumble down them again. In the meanwhile the chauffeurs, peaceably remaining at the base of the mount, would drink *pastis* together, eat at the chauffeurs' half-rate table d'hôte in the hotel, and exchange stories of the accidents of the route, like the crews of slavers after having discharged their cargoes at São Paulo or Belem in the reign of the good Dom Pedro. The inhabitants of the Rock are accommodating, particularly the chambermaids who come over from the mainland to work the summer season in the hotels.

Headed for such a haven, the Versailles sped along like a livery hack pointed in the direction of the stable. We reached the coast road at Granville and turned due south, with the Channel at our right hands, where it is more than 100 miles across to the invisible Devon shore. We came down through a row of small summer resorts, Carolles and St.-Jean de Thomas, favored by the English in pre-B.E.A. days, when it was less easy than now to reach more distant and exotic places. The sea was sometimes far below us and sometimes close. I remembered swimming at Carolles in that magic summer after the breakthrough. (The swims of wartime were memorable because so widely spaced: Tabarka in Tunisia in April 1943, Carteret and Carolles in 1944. I do not count the pond in back of Madame Hamel's, or a brook nine feet wide in Berkshire, because they were not salt water; nor the wadi at Gafsa where the jeeps washed away and we scrambled among the floating cadavers of camels.) The road led through Avranches, *chef-lieu* of an *arrondissement*, like Vire. Through Avranches Bradley had funneled Patton's new army into Brittany, a subcutaneous injection from which the Germans never recovered, and in Avranches I had slept in September 1926, in the hotel on top of the hill that has a view over Mont-Saint-Michel and a garden with fig trees. When the Germans put in their big counterattack against the road through Avranches in 1944, against the advice of all the surviving German generals who have written their memoirs, including General Speidel, the commander in chief of ground forces of NATO in Europe, Bradley stood it off with one division, the 30th, at Mortain, a town I walked to from Vire in 1926. The distance, which I have checked, is 27 kilometres—16⅞ miles. I had an excellent meal in the Hôtel de la Poste at Mortain; I remember the brook trout still. Then I hired the local taxi man to drive me home to the Cheval Blanc.

(I was getting into the lift at the Fifth Avenue Hotel in New York in the spring of 1945 when I saw a young fellow-guest who had obviously been badly shot up not long before. I asked him where he had been, and he said Mortain. This proves (a) that the world is a diminutive place, and (b) that a town does not have the same associations for everybody.)

From Avranches in 1926 I went to the village of Genêts (the Broomplants) and hired a carriage to take me across the sands at low tide to Mont-Saint-Michel. There were men in the village who made their living that way. There was, of course, already an automobile causeway to the Mont, but it seemed more authentic to cross the sands in the *calèche*, with its wide-rimmed sand wheels. There was no danger of being engulfed by the incoming tide or *enlisé* in the quicksands, but my world was so without peril in 1926 that I found it pleasant to conjure up small shudders.

In 1944 a couple of battered old correspondents I knew crossed the same sands in a jeep, and arrived at the Mont in time to liberate it—the only Germans there, a weather-observation unit, had left, and the official Army had not arrived. I believe they had a good welcome. Hemingway made the Hôtel de la Mère Poularde his headquarters after that. He had a good time and wrote and recruited his strength for his dash on Paris. I went there myself once or twice that August and had a pleasant time. Nothing was important to us then—to Hemingway and the rest who had lived in Paris—but getting back there. The war was winning itself; the Germans were on the run. When we encountered officers we knew from divisions we had been with in the hard days, the stories they had to tell were of scooping up prisoners at will, and their only complaints were of failures in supply that impeded their advance—some other sonofabitching Army, or Army Corps, was getting all the gas. The infantry thought the armor was hogging it all, but the armor thought it must be going to the British, who were sitting on their asses as usual, waiting for a lead.

It would have been difficult for me to communicate these varied memories to Michel, so I maintained what must have been a welcome silence, never breaking it to suggest he go down some side road in quest of a farmhouse I thought I remembered. We went to the Mont by the causeway this time, because the Versailles was no sand-wagon. Michel parked outside the walls of the great fortress and the porters came to lug my bag, as they had thirty years before. The Hôtel Poularde is just inside the gates, and built *en espalier* against the side of the rock, like everything else in the place. It is a good hotel, well modernized. It is now operated by a hotel chain, perhaps Swiss, which exploits skiing in one succursale, cave drawings in another—at the Mont, omelets and ecclesiastical architecture. The *patron* and *patronne* of 1944, great friends of Hemingway's, were gone, but the omelets were as good as ever.

The Abbey, built up artfully over a nub of rock like a resplendent porcelain dental cap over a spike of tooth, was again on the basis of 1926, pure honky-tonk, which I find soothing. I

went up on the ramparts, as I always do, skirting the ammo-
niac places under the arches, and at first resisting the solicita-
tions of the proprietors of the small hotels that have cafés
opening onto the ramparts. There they sell little Cancale oysters all summer through, with *palourdes* and *praires*, the
French cousins of the Rhode Island quahog, which is the cher-
rystone or little neck of New York and points south. You can
walk from the ramparts into the upper floors of these hotels
and so on down two or three flights of stairs to the narrow,
slithery, slanting, cobbled street. At the third or fourth café I
sit down and begin eating the sea-water-salt shellfish and
drinking muscadet. I look over the mud flats to Normandy, if
it is low tide, and think I smell Jamaica Bay, in New York City,
where as a small boy I used laboriously to dig my own clams, a
score or so at a time, and then with other boys roast them in a
fire to kill the germs, since our elders assured us that the waters
were polluted. There was an old drunk who lived along the
shore by crabbing and fishing, who used to chase us because
we called him Chewterbacker. "Chewterbacker, Chewterbacker, here he comes! Run!" The age of the cigarette had arrived, and it seemed to us grotesque that he spat tobacco juice.
We were snobs.

It was a Saturday evening. Mont-Saint-Michel, like Brigh-
ton, Rockaway Beach, Block Island and South Bend, is af-
flicted with rainy Sundays. The weather for a week or more
had been superb, but now it began to mist up, and soon to
rain. The merchants of *crustacés* and crucifixes and souvenirs
made of synthetic cockleshells, crouching in their recesses like
hermit crabs to dart their pincers at the Sunday visitors, began
their almost weekly moan. The season is so short, rents, taxes,
high, and all the *fric* must be extracted on the weekends. As
for the tourists who come to the hotels, the hotel-keepers en-
globe their last *sou*. When the weather is good, the Sunday
trippers, bound for the Abbaye on top of the island, linger
along the steep path, stopping frequently to get their wind,
and then they look in the fronts of the shops selling religious
goods and, for the English-language trade, the novels of
Henry Miller. They pause at the cafés and can be pulled in to
have *apéritifs* at double the mainland price, or even meals. But
when it rains, they pull their coats about their faces and push

along grimly, to get under cover at the top of the path, where the uniformed attendant with his diploma from the Service of Historic Monuments will take them over and hustle them through the cloisters, the refectory, the Merveille, stumbling up and down dark staircases, until he turns them out again after they have bought all the post cards and guide books they are ever likely to want. Once they have been through his mill, they are no market for the shopkeepers' similar wares.

They hurry down the hill, slipping and sliding and turning their ankles, for the main and only street of the Mont is, like the Lewes racecourse in Sussex, not only sloping but tilted to one side. They are by now wet through and eager to reach the charabancs parked on the causeway. The chartered charabancs will take them home. No good trying to get them into cafés to wait for the rain to abate; they've had it now. Perhaps, at the very bottom, they stop for a shot of calva, and that's all the hermit crabs' take for the day. A miserable life, Monsieur.

It isn't the aspect of Mont-Saint-Michel that excited Henry Adams; but he was, on the subject of the Middle Ages, what Monsieur de Carville calls a noodle. You may be sure that in the centuries when there were pilgrims there were hermit crabs, and that the monks shook visitors down for alms, for the noble purpose of adding another story to the skyscraper. And as for the skirmishes between French subjects of the French-speaking kings of England and French subjects of the French-speaking kings of France that enlivened the history of the rock, they decided nothing and were, you may depend on it, miserably contested, with a maximum of irresolution and confusion, like medieval warfare in general. It was a time when panic decided five battles out of six, the nadir of the military art in Christian countries until the Hussites and the Swiss revived it.

The Middle Ages were neither brave nor spiritual, but full of cunning, lechery, speculation unlimited by knowledge, and the passionate enjoyment of good things as available, because they so irregularly were. A gorge of salt fish or a whack at a girl under a bush were opportunities that might not come again in a lifetime. The stones of medieval cities, and of Mont-Saint-Michel, exude the sweat and smell of that time, which is why I love them.

In the evening, in the restaurant of the Hôtel Poularde, a

shrill American couple arrived with three specimen demons from a breeding farm run by Hieronymus Bosch. They had apparently crept in and out of the woman's womb and convinced her they were human children. All, the woman recited in a monotonous imitation of a train whistle, had been on the road all day, coming from Paris. They probably had tried to do the Château district on the way. It was nine o'clock, and she demanded that her children be fed instantly. The children saw a large *langouste*, whose fiery hue possibly reminded them of their last pre-earthly habitat. They screamed that they wanted for their supper "lobster," and the mother shouted that they never liked lobster, reminding them how they had spewed it out at Dinard, and how deathly sick it had made them at Plymouth. The father said what the hell was the use, let them have lobster, but not cold. They wanted it broiled. The *maître d'hôtel* had learned his English in England—he might have understood "grilled," but broiled stopped him—and the woman screamed that none of these stinkers could understand English, that "they" had sworn in Paris that this was a good hotel, and here were her little children starving to death. The director of the hotel came and understood that they wanted hot lobster—it would demand thirty minutes, he said. Nothing else would do.

The children, waiting, screamed continually, and one of them lay under the table, kicking his father's shins. The director of the hotel suggested the permissive pair remove the children from the dining room; he would serve the hot lobster, which he of course realized they would reject in some disgusting manner, in their living quarters. At that, the woman went off her chump completely. I left, and when I returned at midnight, after a discreet patrol of the hermit crabs' bars, I heard the woman howling still, in her bedroom, that she would not stay the night in a hotel where they insulted her li'l children. Her husband, I judged from the cadence of her howls, was slugging her by now, and I went to sleep hoping he would kill her, strangle the incubi and commit suicide.

On Monday morning Michel and I left for Paris in the Versailles. He said he had encountered a chauffeur friend since boyhood days in the Ukraine, who told Michel that he had arrived from Paris transporting a mad American couple and three children. But when Michel awoke Sunday morning, his friend and the friend's clients had disappeared. I suppose they decided they had seen enough of Mont-Saint-Michel.

Michel and I parted on excellent terms, and he said he hoped he would have the pleasure some day of driving me to St. Jean-de-Luz or Deauville.

9
Days with the Daydaybay

R EADING a French newspaper in a restaurant in Paris one winter, I came upon a heading of a kind that would not ordinarily interest me: "*Ventes de Charité.*" I had time to spare, however, having asked for my check while the waiter was skinning a *truite au bleu* for another customer, so I read the first item in the column. (After all, the waiter was quite right: the *truite*, if abandoned, would get cold, and the check wouldn't.) The item stated:

The sale for the benefit of the Veterans of the 2nd Armored Division will open today in the salons of the Sorbonne (entrance: Rue des Ecoles). Presiding will be Mme la Maréchale Leclerc de Hauteclocque, who will direct a booth devoted exclusively to souvenirs of the General. Numerous booths will be devoted to exotic products and artifacts. At the book booth authors such as André Maurois and Louise de Vilmorin will autograph their works.

I divined without trouble that Mme la Maréchale was the widow of General Leclerc, who had been made a Marshal of France after his death in an airplane accident in Algeria, in 1947. Leclerc's name in obscurity, before he escaped to England to join General de Gaulle in 1940, had been de Hauteclocque— Philippe-François-Marie de Hauteclocque, to give him his full due. De Hauteclocque was a name that had marked him from school days as an unreformed aristocrat. In England, taking a pseudonym to protect his family from reprisals, he had chosen a common French name, the exact equivalent of Clark. Changing from de Hauteclocque to Leclerc was like shucking tails for a sweatshirt. Once, in 1944, as a correspondent with the American First Army, I asked him what his real name was. It was an awkwardly worded question, because everybody knew by that time. All I really wanted was to verify the spelling; those two "c"s are tricky.

"What does my name matter as long as I fight?" he asked. He had been affable up to that point, or as affable as he knew how to be, but the question about the name nettled him. I thought that he was like the countless little boys who have wished, and have gone on wishing all their lives, that they hadn't been named Elwyn or Abbott.

We were in a field near Fleuré, in the Département de L'Orne in Normandy, and all around us were vehicles that the Americans had supplied to the Deuxième Division Blindée, or D.D.B.—pronounced by the French as a single word, "Daydaybay." The Daydaybay was known to the American forces as the French 2nd Armored Division; there was an American 2nd Armored Division in western France, too. Fleuré, which is so small that if you are driving fast you are likely to miss it entirely, is near Argentan, which was then the southern jaw of the pincers that Bradley and Montgomery were trying to close on the escaping Visigoths of the Seventh Army and the Fifth Panzer Army. The Daydaybay, pushing out into the middle of the receding Germans, joyfully managed to get itself surrounded, and killed a great many of the enemy before being called back to the American side of the gap. Leclerc, a red-haired little man with a long nose and a bristling red mustache, reminded me of an interrupted terrier that sniffs more rats under a barn door.

Like so many quests for simplicity, Leclerc's, I noted with regret while still awaiting the check for my meal, had ended only in further complication. As a surname, Leclerc de Hauteclocque is even more of a mouthful than de Hauteclocque. Moreover, I reflected, there is by now hardly a town in what became the Daydaybay's path across France—from the Cotentin to the Rhine—that is without its Avenue du Général Leclerc, a name that is perpetuated because "Avenue du Maréchal Posthume Leclerc de Hauteclocque" just won't fit on a street sign.

Then, remembering a journey I had once made in attendance upon the Daydaybay, it occurred to me that I might as well go over to the Sorbonne and spend a few francs with my old fellow-travelers. I had nothing else in the world to do except go back to my hotel room and work, and I hate that. When I was at last allowed to pay for my simple repast—a dozen oysters followed by a pair of thrushes roasted with juniper berries—I decided to walk to the Sorbonne in order to prolong my respite. I find it hard to deter myself from walking in Paris, with or without a pretext. There was a time when I thought I might never walk in Paris again, for it had fallen under a spell that was supposed to last a thousand years, and now, I suppose, I walk its streets for reassurance.

From the restaurant, which is at the Fontaine Gaillon, I walked up the Rue Saint-Augustin and turned down the Rue de Richelieu, a narrow gulch of one-way, hornless traffic these days, where, if you step off the meager sidewalk to let an old woman with a market basket pass, you risk silent obliteration by a motorized baby buggy magniloquently called an automobile. One of the unadvertised benefits of the law forbidding Parisians on wheels to sound their horns is the increased pleasure of the driver, who is now under mandate to sneak up without warning on his prey. This swells his *tableau de chasse*, or total bag. (The highest award of the Friendly League for the Ecrabouillement Piéton, or Squashing of Pedestrians, goes to the member who succeeds in killing a man with a motor scooter, which is considered comparable to getting an elephant with a bow and arrow.) I followed the street down past the discouraging baroque bulk of the Bibliothèque Nationale and the charming front of the Hôtel de Malte, which received its first guests in 1777. As I approached the Rue de Rivoli, I passed under the colonnade of the Comédie Française, with its wall medallions of Molière, Racine, and the rest, in a Hydrox Biscuit style of sculpture, and its yellow *affiches* announcing the casts of next week's *Cinna*s and *Athalie*s. Coming out from under the colonnade, I paused in front of a bust of Alfred de Musset to read again on its socle one of my favorite cheer-up bits of literature:

> *Les plus désespérés sont les chants les plus beaux*
> *Et j'en sais d'immortels, qui sont des purs sanglots—*

which might be freely translated as

The most utterly lachrymose lyrics are frequently good jobs,
And I could cite some deathless instances that are
    unadulterated sobs.

I repeat the couplet to myself when I am feeling low, and it works as well as three fingers of bourbon.

On reaching the Seine, I walked past the fishing-tackle shops and the bird stores to the Pont au Change, at the Châtelet, and then across the Ile de la Cité, past the Préfecture of Police, where the Paris police barricaded themselves against the German garrison and raised the tricolor on August 19, 1944, setting off the week of insurrection. When I got over on the Left Bank, I ascended the Boulevard Saint-Michel as far as the big, brassy Restaurant Dupont, at the corner of the Rue des Ecoles. The Dupont never fails to enrage me, because it occupies the disfigured former premises of the Taverne Soufflet, an establishment of majesty and tranquility, which in 1926, when I first stayed in the Latin Quarter as a casual student at the Sorbonne, was still the exact image of the French cafés Maupassant had taught me to expect.

In the Soufflet, the long banquettes were upholstered in garnet plush, with backs topped by a manger of brass rails, into which the customers tossed their overcoats after crumpling them up into the smallest possible bundles. The tables in front of the banquettes had white marble tops and were placed end to end, with no space between. There were vast mirrors, which permitted refracted flirtation. The waiters were individualists who improved on acquaintance; they had little use for a new-comer until he had been in the Quarter long enough to achieve their own cultural standing. The girls who frequented the Soufflet did not frequent the Café d'Harcourt or the Source, farther up the Boulevard, nor did the demoiselles of the d'Harcourt or the Source invade the Soufflet. Each habit-ual customer at the Soufflet had his table, and each girl had hers. There she would arrive in mid-afternoon and begin to write on stationery furnished by the house. The girls were as prolific as a pack of Mme de Sévignés, but none of them was ever seen to affix a postage stamp to an envelope. Perhaps they were diarists. Any one of them could nurse an infusion of pep-permint through a long afternoon; it was the *consommation* that she felt the least temptation to finish, and so the one that enabled her to hold the franchise longest. Male acquaintances would pause by the girls' tables to shake hands, to chat, and, rarely, to stand treat. The girls knew the limitations of the academic budget. They snubbed nobody because he bought seldom. They were young, averaging only a year or two older than the students, and not particularly pretty.

The students in the cafés were exclusively male. A number of coeds attended lectures, but they used no makeup, wore cotton stockings, took masses of notes, and disappeared as soon as class was over. They went straight home, I imagine, or else to a room in some dark and hideous *pension de famille*, with a window giving on a court into which boys threw lynched cats. I used to suspect that in order to win their parents' consent to such unwomanly careers the coeds had to make a show of being completely uninterested in sex, like nuns, and that in default of a habit they utilized steel barrettes and straight hair to advertise this indifference. Nowadays there are almost as many *étudiantes* as *étudiants* in the cafés of the Quarter—a lot of them married and living with their husbands, and others still single but living *en ménage*. The *petites femmes* of the kind I remember, a species peculiar to the environs of the university, have been eliminated, like the Soufflet. Many of the women students today are prettier than the Soufflet girls, but they are more intimidating.

"*Ce n'était pas vraiment du vice*," a very old friend of mine who still inhabits the Quarter said recently, reminiscing. "*C'était une espèce d'artisanat.*" From the point of view of the bashful foreigner, one advantage of the *petite* who could always be found in the same place was that he could observe her at leisure—for several evenings, if he chose. He might learn to like the way she looked up to greet fellows she knew, or the way her head sat on her neck or her neck on her shoulders. That would achieve what Stendhal baptized the "crystallization." By the time the young man approached, he felt that he knew her as well as the girls in his high-school class, whom he had first observed in the same manner. He would find her receptive but not precipitate, practical but not rapacious. The greatest treat he could offer, within what the boys on the quarterlies would now call the Soufflet's frame of reference, was the *prix-fixe* dinner on the wide balcony that overhung the *grande salle*. (It was not reasonable to assume that a customer who could afford better would be at the Soufflet at all.) The *prix fixe* more than nourished the girl; it raised her standing with the management and with her other male acquaintances. Best of all, it infuriated her colleagues who had not been invited anywhere and who bitterly watched her as they masticated the sandwiches that hunger had at length impelled them to order grudgingly for themselves. The *prix fixe*, at sixteen francs, comprised a choice of soup or a spectacular *hors d'oeuvre varié* and then fish, entrée, vegetable, salad, and cheese and fruit or dessert. Wine was included, but coffee wasn't. The franc was twenty-five to the dollar.

I cannot truthfully say that I think of all these details specifically whenever I see the Restaurant Dupont on the site of the Taverne Soufflet, but I have thought about one or another of them so often on reaching that corner that the memory of the whole scene hits me ready-blended, like a smell. As for the Dupont, it is one of a chain of restaurants, all flaunting the disputable slogan "*Chez Dupont, Tout Est Bon.*" It has fluorescent lighting overhead and electric lamps, with candy-striped shades, on wall brackets. The walls are further decorated with posters displaying offensive colored photographs of fried eggs and blobs of pink ice cream and conveying such inspirational messages from the management as "Eat Oysters—Good for Your Health" and "The Management insists upon impeccable courtesy and compliance on the part of its employees—Messieurs les Clients are urgently recommended to report with exactitude any infraction of servility." The Dupont waiters, naturally, pay no attention to the latter poster, but they tolerate it. Those of the old Soufflet would have ripped it from the wall and made Messieurs les Clients eat it.

In front of the Dupont I paused to look across the Boulevard Saint-Michel at the *pâtisserie* in the building that, shaped like a flatiron, stands where the Rue Racine and the Rue de l'Ecole de Médecine converge. The *pâtisserie*, which used to be open all night, closes early now, but it is still there, and that is something. Above the bargain bookstore in the acute angle of the Rue Racine and the Boulevard is the Hôtel de la Faculté, where, in the fall of 1927, I last saw Angèle, one of the pleasantest girls at the Soufflet. Angèle was twenty years old and chunky, and she had a snub nose. On this occasion she complained of having a fever and said she was going to die. Three or four of us from the Soufflet, sitting on her bed, assured her that she would be up and around in a few days. Shortly thereafter she died, and since then I have wondered sometimes what a girl with a snub nose has to do to be taken seriously. In the Rue de l'Ecole de Médecine, from which the Medical School has departed, is a plaque marking the birthplace of Sarah Bernhardt, who made hundreds of thousands of people cry by merely pretending to die. She had the profile for it.

When I had had my look, I turned, entered the Rue des Ecoles, and walked on, past the entrance to the narrow Rue Champollion and past the Brasserie Balzar, another surviving landmark. Outside the Sorbonne I saw posters bearing the emblem of the Daydaybay—a white silhouette map of France with the Cross of Lorraine on a blue field superimposed. A blue banner hung above the door, and on the wide steps in front of it there was a double stream of well-dressed people, some making for the entrance and the others leaving it. Those going in were empty-handed; those coming out carried amateurishly wrapped packages. Inside the door, I found myself in the high marble vestibule at the foot of the Grand Escalier of the Sorbonne, a place I hadn't been in for nearly thirty years. It looked just about the same.

In 1926, all an American needed in order to matriculate at the Sorbonne was a diploma from an American university. The old fellow who took your minuscule matriculation fee wouldn't even make you unroll the diploma. "Ahbay?" he would ask, signifying Bachelor of Arts, and if you said "Ahbay," he would nod knowingly and extend to you the privilege of listening to the big-league medievalists. (At least, that was the privilege I was interested in.) Ahbay was the only American degree the old boy had heard of, and it served no useful purpose to open your diploma and explain that it was Bay anything else.

M. Ferdinand Lot, the professor who in those days taught the Dawn of the Middle Ages, gave out a bibliography as long as my two arms. When I went to the library to get started on it, I saw a considerable number of my fellow students—who, unlike me, were working for degrees—standing in line and waiting for books that other students were reading, several of them sitting on the floor, for lack of seats. This made me feel guilty, so I bought some of the books from dealers and took them to my room to read, and soon I stopped going to Professor Lot's lectures. I was afraid of being found out as a dilettante. Another of my lecturers was Professor Antoine Thomas, who taught Old Provençal. I remember that he had a spade-shaped white beard and that he accused Professor Anglade, of the University of Toulouse, his rival in their common field, of approaching the origin of a verb I have forgotten "*avec sa légèreté coutumière*" ("with his habitual frivolity"). What an epithet can be derived from that—"Frivolous philologist!" For thirty years I have been waiting for a chance to use it, but every time I get into an argument with a savant, he turns out to be of some other persuasion—a psychologist, perhaps, or a podiatrist. The neck my knife would fit has never presented itself.

When I had whiffed all these matters, in the same manner that I had my memories of the Soufflet, I climbed a flight of white marble stairs that leads off to the left of the Grand Escalier and takes one to the salons where the charity sale for the benefit of the Daydaybay was being held. The salons of the Sorbonne are a set of high-ceilinged rooms, each about forty feet by sixty, arranged *en suite* for exhibitions and academic receptions. Outside the entrance to the sale, I perused a panel listing the maids and matrons who were serving at various booths and counters. A high proportion of the names were *en courants d'air*—spread out in bits, with drafts through them—like Leclerc de Hauteclocque. I could see that Mme la Maréchale had built up a social cachet for the Daydaybay in the years following the General's death. I observed none of the Corsican, Mussulman, and Jewish names that had been so common in the ranks. Nearly every counter—toys, comestibles, books, perfumes, yard goods, flowers—was garrisoned by women with horse-cavalry surnames, usually a promise of a high standard of good looks.

Inside, I made a clockwise tour of the counters and bought a book, entitled *Leclerc et Ses Hommes* and illustrated in color, from its tall and distinguished-looking author, identified by a card on the table in front of him as Pierre Nord. I told M. Nord that I had accompanied the Daydaybay into Paris on August 25, 1944, the day of the Liberation. M. Nord informed me that he was a colonel in the Regular Army, and that Nord

was a nom de plume. He is not the sort of author who dis-
misses customers with a mere signature, and after a moment of
thought he wrote in my book, "In homage to a sincere fraternity of arms, to the American friend and war correspondent of
our difficult years. Faithfully, Pierre Nord (Colonel Brouil-
lard)." It made me inflate my chest, and I went and bought a
flask of white pepper, a carton of matches, and a can of pineapple, each from a different pretty girl. The salons were
crowded, and the warm air, heavy with the evaporation of samples at the perfume counter, made me sweat; I took off my hat,
which happened to be what elegant Londoners call a titfer (tit
fer tat, bowler hat) and the French a *melon*. Try, sometime,
taking off a hard hat, holding it, and wiping your brow with a
handkerchief while grasping a book and a flask of white pepper
in one hand and a can of pineapple and a carton of matches in
the other. Of course, the dicer fell to the floor, where it rolled
between a woman's feet. In attempting to get to it, I bumped
into her. "*Polisson!*" she said firmly.

The situation was saved by a one-legged chap on crutches,
who swung down like a bird from a perch and retrieved my
hat for me. He was selling copies of a publication entitled
L'Amicale Sportive des Mutilés de France. I bought one and
asked if he had been with the division at the Liberation. "No,
Monsieur," he said apologetically. "I joined up after the division got here. I was wounded in front of Strasbourg." He was
embarrassed by not having lost his leg soon enough.

I had somehow had an idea that the benefit would be like
the reunion of an American division, with a lot of old noncoms
lined up at a bar to exchange lies, and, as a possible French
variant, a continuous raffle for ducks and geese. But the *vente*
for the Daydaybay was exactly like a *vente* for any other charity
with excellent social sponsorship. Except for a number of am-
putees selling *L'Amicale Sportive*, there was nobody present
who looked to me like a former noncom or enlisted man. That
is probably the way a charity sale should be in order to turn a
profit for good works, but it did not correspond with my recollections of hot roads, dead Germans, and cheering crowds. I
therefore descended the white marble stairs, carefully re-
enthroning my titfer when I got beyond jostling range, and
walked over to a place called L'Alsace à Paris, a few blocks

away, which has nothing in particular to recommend it except that the proprietor, Robert, used to be the *patron* of the Taverne Soufflet. The waiters, who are not Alsatians, wear red waistcoats, as in all Paris Alsaces; the prices are fairly stiff, and there are no little women. "This is a more serious affair than the old place," M. Robert says. He still has the same students among his clientele—students of the twenties, grown into bald dentists and sedate *avocats*. I ordered a *formidable*, which is a litre of beer in a stone mug, and, while rehydrating, reviewed the recollections that my late experience did not correspond with.

On Monday evening, August 21, 1944, I attended a press conference that was addressed by the then Lieutenant General Omar Nelson Bradley at Laval, a town in the Département de la Mayenne, in western France. Bradley, whose infrequent lectures I had been following with rapt attention ever since he took over II Corps in North Africa, in April 1943, had in sixteen months progressed from the command of a corps through that of an army (the First) to that of an army group (the Twelfth), but his manner—benevolent, pedagogical, and slightly apologetic—had not changed. A month before the Laval press conference, I had listened to him in a shed behind Mme Hamel's at Vouilly, as he outlined to correspondents the plan for the First Army's new offensive. Before that, I had heard him at Béja, in Tunisia, explaining how he was going to try to take Bizerte, and then in Bryanston Square, London, offering his opinion, take it for what it was worth, that we would get ashore in France. At Laval, everybody knew that the most recent effort, like the ones previously adumbrated by the General, had come off nicely. It had been set back a couple of days by rain and had then wheezed a bit when the most impressive assemblage of air power ever up to then on view outside a Howard Hughes production flew over from England and, getting mixed up, dropped a lot of its bombs on the American 30th Division instead of on the Germans, just beyond. But, once under way, the offensive had discombobulated all the German defensive arrangements in the West and had changed the war of position into one of pursuit, with the First, now confided to Hodges, sweeping north behind the

German Seventh Army and Fifth Panzer Army and joining the British, Canadians, and Poles in a grand *battue* of fugitives at the Argentan-Falaise escape gap while Patton's newly activated Third dashed southwest and then east.

As Group Commander, Bradley controlled both the First and the Third, and he had selected Laval as the headquarters of the moment because it was approximately behind the point where the zones of the two armies overlapped. Laval was a good long jeep ride from First Army Headquarters and press camp, at Bagnoles-de-l'Orne, in central Normandy. It was equally far, I suppose, from Third Army Headquarters, although I have no idea where the Third was. (To judge by the telling of it by Third Army correspondents, its advance elements were already on the outskirts of Vienna, but you couldn't believe everything those fellows said.) As the conference wouldn't be over until after dark and none of us First Army correspondents wanted to ride any farther than we had to on a road full of blacked-out trucks and tanks, my colleagues had entrusted me with the mission of reserving promising billets for them in hotels and inns along the way back to Bagnoles-de-l'Orne. I had done that, saving for an officer friend—Lieutenant Roy Chitterling—and myself accommodations in a small town called Ernée, whose hotel looked too comfortable to tell the others about.

It was the most cheerful briefing I had yet attended. Tall, bespectacled, and Missouri-speaking, Bradley had the pleased look of a Sunday-school superintendent announcing that the cake sale had brought in eleven dollars and fifty cents more than anticipated. The German Seventh Army was in a satisfactory state of disintegration, he said, although "annihilation" might be too rosy a term to use in describing it yet, since a number of its men, abandoning their equipment, had made their way out through the gap. A part of our First had crossed the Seine between Mantes and Vernon, northwest of Paris, and the Third was hooking around Melun, south of Paris. We all knew there had been an American landing in the south of France on August 15, and we assumed that up north Montgomery's Britons and Canadians were barreling along at last. They constituted the Twenty-first Army Group, and Bradley's briefing did not cover them.

The General said, with a smile, that he knew what we all wanted to find out was when did we get to Paris. Well, the important thing was to destroy the German armies, and the next after that was to secure Paris as nearly intact as possible. So we would just hook around Paris, north and south, he said, and the German garrison would probably pull out to avoid capture, since, with Americans across the Seine both above and below the city, it would have no military usefulness, as the Germans were sure to see. A Third Army correspondent said that General Patton had bet him five dollars the Third would be in Paris before the First, and General Bradley remarked that he might just take it into his head to tell General Patton to go someplace else. First Army people present regarded this as a good omen. One thing we could be sure of, Bradley said—we weren't going to make a rush for Paris.

Bradley has what psychiatrists call a therapeutic personality. We all shook hands with him after the briefing, like members of a congregation shaking hands with their minister, and one of the First Army correspondents said, "General, I'm always glad to see you, because you always make me feel good." Then Chitterling and I got on the road at the head of our motorcade, and started dropping jeeps off a couple at a time—each jeep containing three or four correspondents and a driver—as we came to the various *auberges* in which we had booked rooms. After we had dropped the last one, we pushed on to Ernée. Since General Bradley had assured us that there was no hurry about Paris, Chitterling and I played hooky the next day, pursuing some projects that failed to pan out, and did not get back to Bagnoles until Wednesday. There seemed to be no reason for haste; from a journalistic point of view, the war was marking time. You could drive in a jeep all day without finding any rational German resistance, although you might run into a band of vindictive fugitives and so get yourself shot. Or you might find isolated groups shooting away their stocks of ammunition because their commanding officers had listened to too much Wagner, like the drunken *Kommandant* of the fort at Saint-Malo who had made a senseless four-day stand against an all-out barrage and had then capitulated, contrary to the orders of the Führer. But such episodes were anodyne after the events of the breakthrough; the next big story coming up was the redemption of Paris, which the General had told us wouldn't occur immediately. It would be the biggest story of all for me, because I had left the city on June 10, 1940, when crowds of would-be refugees were overflowing into the streets around the railway stations. In my mind, the war would pretty well end with the road back to Paris. The rest would be epilogue.

I was bowled over, therefore, when, on returning to the press camp Wednesday afternoon, Chitterling and I found that it had been deserted by the other correspondents. Bagnoles-de-l'Orne is a summer resort of the most grisly vintage and variety, encumbered with great clapboard-and-stucco hotels of the early days of the Third Republic. The hotels are built around shallow lakes, which, while the press camp was there, at least, were so choked with the stems and leaves of water lilies that they were no good for swimming. I believe that when the place is operating normally, the guests at the hotels partake of purgative waters and talk about their insides, but by the time the First Army reached the town, in the summer of 1944, the hotels had been abandoned, and we roosted in them, doubly depressed by the lack of running water because the bathtubs reminded us of comforts we had almost forgotten.

Now only a few of the officers and enlisted men in the press-relations detachment were still around, and they were packing. In a few minutes, they informed Chitterling and me, they would be off for Paris, where they were to set up a new press headquarters in the Hôtel Scribe, near the Opéra. All my fellow-correspondents, they further related, were probably there already. What had happened, we gathered, was that the forces of the Resistance had unexpectedly risen in Paris and thrown the Germans out. They had then sent a messenger to Bradley asking him to come in fast and save them from the kind of revenge the Germans were currently visiting on Warsaw. The road to Paris was clear. The messenger had arrived in Laval after we left, and the General had revised all his thinking about Paris. I was consequently in a fair way to being scooped on the story I had been looking forward to for four years, two months, and thirteen days. As for Chitterling, my fellow-sybarite, he not only had missed the takeoff but was in Dutch with his superior officers.

I ran upstairs to the room I had shared with another correspondent, grabbed my sleeping bag off the floor, tied up all my junk in it, and came down demanding instant transportation to Paris. Chitterling would have been glad to take me, but, being in the doghouse, he had already been condemned to some menial task like checking the inventory of bales of carbon paper. There was, however, a young first lieutenant named Jack Roach, formerly a press-association reporter in Philadelphia, who controlled, on a provisional basis, a magnificent conveyance—a Chevrolet touring car built in Belgium before the war. It had been liberated from the Germans, and somehow or other Roach had got it. I can't for the life of me remember who was in command of the rear echelon of First Army Public Relations, which was rapidly dwindling as its officers, in order of seniority, provided themselves with missions to Paris. The command may have got down as far as Roach himself by that time.

At any rate, Roach and I took the Chevrolet and set out for La Ville Lumière, figuring we ought to hit it that evening if the roads ahead were as clear as had been rumored. That, I thought, would not be too late for the best of the celebration. We were intensely excited. How many times in his life does a man start out for what he is certain is going to be a phenomenally happy occasion? I don't think that Roach, who was in his middle twenties, had ever been in Paris, but that gave his anticipation a special quality. And for me, at forty, and with nearly half that many years of scattered memories of Paris behind me, it was like finding my Annabel Lee again. All the previous spring, in London, I had been reading clandestine newspapers smuggled out of France. I had cried over them. I do not regret my sentimentality; I wish I had something now that I could be as sentimental about.

When Roach and I had gone a fair piece of the way, we realized that we had brought no food along, either for ourselves or for hungry people we might meet. Living off the country was all very well in Normandy, Brittany, and Anjou—rich farming provinces unable to reach their customary markets and surcharged, like unmilked cows, with their own products. But Paris, we expected, would be short of food. We found the solution of our supply problem on the road ahead of us: a two-and-a-half-ton truck stacked high with cases of K rations, which were flat waxed-cardboard packages—thirty-six to a case—each containing the ready-to-eat components of a nourishing, harmless, and gastronomically despicable meal, calculated, I always supposed, to discourage overindulgence. (Among troops actively engaged, a K ration beat nothing to eat, but it was a photo finish.) These components were a round tin of alleged pork and egg, ground up together and worked to a consistency like the inside of a sick lobster's claw, and tasting like boardwalk cotton candy without any sugar in it; a few sourballs or other boiled sweets (I remember one particularly horrid variety that was flavored with root beer); four cigarettes; and a pinch of soluble coffee, dehydrated vegetarian bouillon, or lemonade powder. You sometimes had to open six packages to find one with coffee in it, and smokers had to open five to get the equivalent of a pack of cigarettes. The rest of a K ration so opened was then chucked away, except in Arab countries, where it could be traded for shell eggs, fowl, or little girls.

Atop the stacks of cases on the truck, at least ten feet above the road, stood a Negro soldier of the Quartermaster Corps. The crown of his helmet was a good sixteen feet above where he would land if he fell. His driver, I saw when we had overtaken the truck and were passing it, was another Q.M.C. soldier. But we did not overtake it until we had witnessed an extraordinary spectacle. There were a lot of jeeps on the road whose occupants had taken off, like us, *à l'improviste*, and as these vehicles passed the truck, the soldier up top would throw cases of K rations down into their rear seats. It was the way he did this that was remarkable. The truck was going about forty miles an hour, and a jeep would pull up on it, going about forty-five. As it did so, the soldier, standing up there, facing the rear—his feet spread wide apart to brace him on his gradually diminishing platform—would yell "How many?" and the jeep driver would hold up one, two, or three fingers, usually three. The soldier would have the first case already in the air, leading the driver, who would instinctively hunch forward over the wheel. But the case would fall harmlessly behind him every time. The second would land right on top of it. The third might land a couple of inches farther back, or even hit

the stern end of the jeep and carom in, since by now the
Q.M.C. bombardier would have to twist and throw it after the
passing vehicle. These near misses must have pained him, for
he was clearly a precisionist. He raised each successive case
high above his head before he sent it crashing down, like an
Old Black Jove hurling well-meant thunderbolts. I watched
him until we had got our share, and then I turned my head
and looked over my shoulder until we lost him from sight,
some time afterward, and I never saw him conk anybody or
throw any groceries out into the road. The driver was good,
too; he held the same even course and pace, like a well-trained
circus horse. It was, of course, a wholly unauthorized distribution of Army supplies, and maybe when that talented team
reached the end of their run, some niggling quartermaster
lieutenant chewed them out because they were a few hundred
cases short, but I would have given them the Legion of Merit.
Their gesture was so lordly that when I heard our cases crash
behind me on the floor of the Chevrolet, I momentarily
believed that they might contain fresh caviar, *écrevisses à la
nage*, and a covey of smoked partridges.

I remember no other incident between Bagnoles-de-l'Orne
and Chartres, a journey that, as the *Carte Michelin* reminds
me now, is about a hundred and sixty kilometres, or a hundred
miles. All the way to Chartres, we accepted our hot tip at its
face value and assumed that we were going straight through
into Paris that night. I recall the excitement of seeing the first
stone road markers that gave the distance not only to Alençon
and Chartres but to Paris. The excitement increased as the
number of kilometres decreased. When we reached Chartres,
we were nearly two thirds of the way from Bagnoles to Paris
and we had a couple of hours of daylight left, but there we
were held up. Army was moving divisions from north to south
and south to north, passing them through each other like a
dealer giving cards a fast shuffle—the kind of *passe-passe* that is
a good G-3's delight and that it sometimes seemed to me the
boys did just for the hell of it. To Roach and me, it was like
being caught on the wrong side of a St. Patrick's Day parade.
Then, in the mixed crowd of soldiers and civilians that was
packed around the principal *carrefour* of the city, half a dozen
blocks from the Cathedral, I noticed a small private, first class,

gesticulating and running toward us. As he approached, I saw he was Allan Morrison, a soldier-reporter for the *Stars & Stripes*, who has since become New York editor of the picture magazine *Ebony*, an ameliorated Amerafrican version of *Life*. He was the diagnostician who first divined the reason for the protracted resistance of the fort at Saint-Malo. "The C.O. is loaded," he said. "When he finishes his last bottle of sauce, they'll run up a white flag."

Morrison was hitchhiking, so I beckoned him aboard, and he climbed over the side and perched on our stack of K rations. A moment later, I recognized the lieutenant colonel who was out in the middle of the *carrefour* directing traffic, and I was able to surmise, correctly, that the shuffling of troops was not being run off in strict accordance with standard practice. The lieutenant colonel was a 1st Division fellow named Chuck Horner, and he was letting an endless column of his own people through; the only trucks that were moving were full of 1st Division soldiers. This was an old 1st Division trick. Army M.P.s were supposed to handle such matters, but those assigned to the task were usually enlisted men. If one of them showed up and tried to stop a 1st Division column to let the vehicles of some other outfit through for a while, a 1st Division lieutenant colonel, or even a higher officer in the outfit, would pull rank on him. I knew a 1st Division colonel who became a major general and got a division all his own. Once, when I was stuck for half an hour in a column halted at a road intersection, I got out of my jeep and walked up ahead to see what was happening. It was the major general personally passing his whole division through. I was glad he had not acquired a corps.

I had last seen Horner in North Africa hunting for enemy parachutists, who turned out to be soldiers of the Twelfth Air Force shooting tracers to celebrate Christmas Eve. ("It's the Air Force mentality," Horner said when he had finished his reconnaissance. He was very vexed.) I now reminded him of the occasion, and he agreed to let us through the 1st Division column. The 1st was not going into Paris, Horner told me; it would cross the Seine farther south, where there was still serious opposition. "Wouldn't you know it?" he said. "The bad divisions always get the soft jobs." The 1st pitied itself for being indispensable.

After we got on the Paris side of Chartres, traffic thinned out, and before long we were alone. "If everybody is going into Paris, I don't see why we're the only ones on the road," Roach said, with what made excellent sense. Morrison gave us the benefit of his inquiring reportorial mind by asking, "Who told you the way was clear all the way into Paris?" When we replied that everybody at Bagnoles-de-l'Orne had said so, Morrison asked, "Who told *them*? That's a long way back from here." Roach, who was not going to succumb to a climate of anxiety set up by an enlisted man, said, "Well, if the other correspondents didn't go into Paris, where are they? We haven't passed any on the road." This prompted Morrison to remark, "Maybe some prison-camp paper in Germany is going to have a hell of a staff." Twilight was coming on, and it suddenly seemed to me that my conversation with Lieutenant Colonel Horner had been a long while ago. There have been times in my life when I have missed the 1st Division more than anything else on earth.

When I was a boy member of the St. Agnes Branch of the New York Public Library, I enjoyed reading about Jeb Stuart and imagining myself in his position, but by 1944 I no longer thought of myself as a man to lead a raid behind enemy lines, and our 1937-or-so Chevrolet was no armored division. As an assimilated captain (the grade bestowed on all war correspondents), I was the senior member of the expedition. Lieutenant Roach, the ranking active soldier, had received most of his battle training in the Philadelphia Bureau of the United Press, and his combat effectiveness was not enhanced by an oversized helmet that was likely to fall over his eyes if he moved suddenly. Pfc. Morrison's attitude was that of an objective observer, exactly as it is taught in schools of journalism. He was our whole enlisted strength.

"If we keep on going, we're bound to meet someone," I said decisively.

"That is exactly what I am afraid of," Morrison said.

To turn back was unthinkable, but we continued in a mood of modified rapture. I remember getting to a spot where a road branches north toward Rambouillet. That, we later learned, was the way most of the correspondents ahead of us had gone. But we held straight on. After a while, we came upon a couple of American soldiers in a jeep, which encouraged us. They said they were members of a troop of motorized cavalry belonging to the 7th Armored Division and that their outfit was a couple of miles down a side road, preparing to spend the night there. Roach said their commanding officer ought to be able to give us some dope about what lay ahead. If the cavalry, which was made up of reconnaissance troops, was bedding down forty or fifty miles short of Paris, it hardly seemed likely that anybody had gone into the city by that route. We thought we might as well ask, though, so we turned down the side road and found the outfit, with its vehicles dispersed in a field.

"How much of our stuff is there out ahead of us, Lieutenant?" I asked the boy who was in command.

"Nothing," he replied. "Why should there be?"

I felt as mad as a man who is about to take a dip in a swimming pool and discovers that somebody has let all the water out of it. "Then why isn't there a sign on the road, or an M.P., or something?" I demanded. "After all, somebody might get captured this way."

"Ain't no Germans, either," the lieutenant replied reasonably. "We've had patrols up that road twenty miles. Can't find any."

"Well, it's a hell of a way to take Paris," I said. "Back at Bagnoles, they told us we were going right into Paris today."

"Bagnoles?" the Lieutenant said. "Where's that? I'd like to go to Paris myself someday. Always heard it well spoken of."

"It's all right to go on, then?" Roach asked.

"You'll be safe enough along the main road," the lieutenant replied. "But don't go down any of the side roads, because there might be stray krauts along them, trying to escape. And don't try to drive after dark, because the country is full of F.F.I. [Forces Françaises de l'Intérieur], and they shoot at everything."

It was nearly dark by then. We could have slept out in the field, but there didn't seem much point to that when we could probably find beds at some hotel a little farther along the highway. Besides, I wanted to be as close up as possible in order to rush into the capital the next morning. So after we got back on the highway, we pushed on as far as the first crossroads agglomeration—I think the town was called Bonnelles— where there was a building that we thought might be a hotel. It was blacked out, of course, but light leaked defiantly from around every door and window. As soon as we got inside, we could see that we were in the provinces no longer but within the Sunday-outing belt of a big city. The name of the hotel was something like Au Retour de la Chasse et Rendez-Vous des Pêcheurs à la Ligne. There was a big, bare, partly dismantled dining room that was really just a boarded-in porch— obviously designed for use only in summer, the season of *boulistes* and lovers. There was also a bar, the full length of which would be required only on Sundays during the hunting (rabbit) and fishing (carp) seasons, when the sportsmen returned to discuss their evil luck over a *pastis* before reintegrating with their socially mediocre *arrondissements*. (The huntsmen and fishermen of the better neighborhoods miss bigger game with more expensive weapons at a greater distance from the city.) Since neither ammunition nor gasoline had been available for recreational purposes during the four years of the Occupation, business had been subnormal, and the place looked it. The barnlike ground floor was overrun with young men and women wearing the tricolor armbands of the Resistance. Each of the fellows had one or two weapons; German pistols (stolen) and tommy guns (parachuted) predominated. We got a big welcome.

Part of the difficulty of trying to reconstruct the days preceding the Liberation is that one now knows too much; I have since heard and read so often about what happened in Paris between August 15, when the police went on strike, and August 25, when the German garrison surrendered, that it is hard to recall the state of ignorance in which Roach and Morrison and I approached the city. It must have been there at the crossroads hotel, on the night of Wednesday, August 23, that we first heard any of the details. There were still some organized groups of Germans in the suburbs between where we were and Paris, the F.F.I. people told us, but there was no continuous line, and some of the kids we talked with had been in and out

of the city several times during the past week, to help in the
fighting and share in the excitement. News of the battle was
on tap in the hotel twenty-four hours a day, the very shapely
sweater-girl daughter of the proprietor informed me, since the
telephone lines into Paris were still open; all you had to do was
call and ask the *téléphonistes* what was happening. The German
officers in control of the French telephone system either had
skipped or, in the confusion, had lost track of which telephone
centrals were now outside the rapidly shrinking Wehrmacht
orbit. It must have been at the hotel, too, that we first heard
how open fighting had begun in Paris on the previous Saturday, when the Germans gave the order to disarm the French
police. The latter, refusing to be disarmed, had begun the defense of their headquarters, on the Ile de la Cité. Resistance
groups had seized several other strong points, and the garrison
had besieged them. On Monday, it seemed, there had been an
abortive armistice. A distorted account of this development,
trickling through to Bagnoles, had given rise to the report that
the road was clear. But the fighting had continued, and now, as
the Germans were pulling out, leaving only a rear guard, the
Resistance, in turn, was besieging these hind-end Charlies.

"All these years, I have dreamed of seeing my first Allied soldier," the proprietor's daughter said. "This morning I saw
him. He was alone in a jeep—a scout. He stopped in front of
the door to ask directions. I rushed out, I precipitated myself
on him, I threw my arms around him, I kissed him. I broke his
glasses. He was furious."

That night, Roach, Morrison, and I slept in beds. The
young F.F.I.s stayed up, because they were too excited to
sleep, like children on the night before Christmas. They didn't
even have a collaborator to shoot as a means of passing the
time, an F.F.I. lieutenant told me shortly before I retired. "This
is such a dreary little place," he said apologetically. "We had
only a few *collabos* to start with, and now they've all skipped."

I shared the young F.F.I.s' excitement, although I realized
how irrational it was, for, no matter how delighted, I was still
capable of realizing that the liberation of Paris would not solve
all the problems of the world, or even terminate the war.
Nevertheless, before I fell asleep I saw American planes
burning on the ghostly hills above the phosphate mine at Met-

laoui, in Tunisia, and remembered the names of the pilots in them. Our side had come a long way around.

When I went downstairs next morning, a couple of jeeps bearing the emblem of the Daydaybay were parked in the garage with our Chevrolet. A French captain, a medic, was shaving painstakingly, a basin of hot water on the hood of a jeep in front of him, his field mirror hanging from a nail on a post. The captain said the Daydaybay was going to liberate Paris. When the Allied command advanced the date of the Liberation, the Daydaybay, officially attached to V Corps of the First Army, was resting after some hard fighting at the Argentan-Falaise gap, which it had helped to seal. The Daydaybay had been on the road all night long, the captain said, and by now its tanks were up ahead of us. The captain's report banished any misgivings I may still have had about those groups of Germans between us and Paris and also explained the paucity of American troops on the Paris side of Chartres. It was through the captain that I got my first hint of the Allied command's decision to have the only French division in the north rescue the capital, instead of ordering an American division straight in. It was one of the wisest decisions of the war, helping to compensate for a thousand wounding stupidities in Anglo-American relations with the French. For all practical purposes, it consituted recognition of General de Gaulle's Provisional Government as the government of France, because Leclerc was more Gaullist than his chief. The presence of the Daydaybay in Paris would preclude any last-minute State Department-Foreign Office deal with collaborationists anxious to hedge their bets, like Darlan in Africa. We had nourished angry suspicions of such a deal by declining to recognize the Provisional Government officially.

The captain was making a careful toilette for his *rentrée* into Paris, which he expected to celebrate that evening. He was a specialist in colonial medicine, he told me, and at the time Paris fell, he was in Equatorial Africa, whence he had returned by stages—Lake Chad to Fezzan, Fezzan to Tunisia, Tunisia to Morocco (where the Daydaybay was put together and given its equipment), Morocco to England, and England to Bonnelles. All these steps had been made in the train of Leclerc, who had accumulated rank and fire-power as he moved along, beginning as a thirty-eight-year-old major and winding up as a forty-one-year-old general of a division. Leclerc and the captain had left Chad in 1942 with the equivalent of one weak regiment—thirty-five hundred men in all, including three thousand Central African Negroes. Now they were on the outskirts of Paris surrounded by a magnificent division. It was a unique example of attrition in reverse. The captain's and my routes back to Paris had coincided once before. That was at Enfidaville, when the Allies were beginning their final drive to Tunis and Leclerc's troops were attached to the 4th Indian Division of the British Eighth Army. At Enfidaville, I nearly had my first encounter with Leclerc, who was sleeping in a Ford sedan out beyond his front line—"*pour être tranquille*," his aide informed me—while mortar shells burst on all sides of his improvised dormitory. The aide said that if I wished to wait around until the General awoke, the General would be glad to talk to me. I replied that I had nothing important to discuss, and went back to have tea at Division.

Leclerc had brought his officers and noncoms along with him to stiffen the cadres of his new division, but he had left his black soldiers in North Africa. Although there were thus only a few hundred Chadians in the Daydaybay, it remained, in the popular imagination, "Leclerc's Army from Chad." I had seen the division on the road above Avranches on August 8, on its way to the front. The men were exuberant, sprawling over their tanks—all span-new Shermans—like kids on a hay ride. They had painted the sides of their vehicles with the names of French towns, regions, and rivers (Tarbes, Cévennes, Moselle, La Villette, and so on), and had topped their tankers' uniforms with the forage caps of their former branches of the service— red for the artillerists, blue for the chasseurs and marines. They were all volunteers, and, on the entire western front, they were the only soldiers in either the Allied or the Axis armies who were fighting on their home territory. They were also the only ground soldiers I remember during the war who were eager to fight. Ten days after I came across the division near Avranches, I had my talk with Leclerc in the field at Fleuré. In the meanwhile, the Daydaybay had flung itself in the path of the retreating German armies, got itself surrounded, cut its way out

again, sunk its teeth in their hams, and kicked them in the ankle. It was the occasion when I asked the General about his
name. I also asked him how his fellows compared with the
blacks he had left in Africa. He replied that they fought as well
but had less discipline.

When Roach and Morrison and I got out on the road that
morning, we found ourselves in the midst of the armored infantry regiment of the Daydaybay, which was traveling in open
half-tracks. Now that the tanks of the Daydaybay had gone
through, the citizens of the populous countryside had no fear
that the Germans would return, and so they turned out en
masse to line the road as their men rode by. We were in the
truck-gardening belt that surrounds Paris, and about all the inhabitants had to offer their liberators was tomatoes. While I
know of few simple gastronomic pleasures comparable to a raw
ripe tomato, I will concede that eight or ten such vegetables,
coming at a soldier simultaneously from different directions,
soon detract from his military appearance, and this the troops
in the half-tracks, though appreciative of the generous spirit
behind the gesture, were discovering.

Above Arpajon, where the long snake of vehicles from the
west debouched into the north-south highway that connects
Paris with Orléans, we passed a middling-pretentious villa, set
back from the highway. A long-legged young woman in a
bathing suit was lounging in a deck chair by the front door,
her bare toes pointing at the oncoming column as she waved a
promise—purely symbolic, of course—of what the young men
in the half-tracks had been dreaming for four years of getting
back to. Three small children clustered about her knees, discouraging a too personal reaction. The Daydaybay crawled
by—fifteen thousand men on a moving belt of appetite.

I have read since that it rained during the night and early
morning, while the Daydaybay was moving toward Paris. But
mood and weather were in accord now, and the three of us in
the Chevrolet tried to get along to the homecoming celebration quickly. Since we were attached to none of the division
units, we were not obliged to stay in place in the line, so Roach
began to weave his way forward, at first past half-tracks and
then past tanks, scooting along the shoulders of the road when

there were any and then ducking back to travel in the wake of the armor, until another opportunity presented itself. Our appearance helped. We were Americans, and Roach's First Army shoulder patch and my correspondent's green flash gave the impression that we were on an urgent mission. I encouraged this by asking French M.P.s along the way where General Leclerc found himself. Every time I asked, they waved us forward, which didn't surprise me, remembering my near encounter with him at Enfidaville.

The solidity and nonchalance of the column, now within twenty miles of Paris, convinced me that the Germans had simply skedaddled. I surmised that as we entered the Porte d'Orléans, they would be going out the Porte de la Villette, on the other side of town. I have always preferred to enter a beleaguered city in this fashion. Violence interferes with the enjoyment of the sentiments appropriate to such an occasion; shooting, if bilateral, spoils everything. As we skittered happily along in the Chevrolet, the only question in my mind was whether Leclerc would retain enough sense of *noblesse oblige* to share with those American allies who found themselves by chance in his immediate vicinity the *vin d'honneur* that was sure to be offered him as he entered the city.

We passed the tank that was leading the procession, and Morrison, from the rear seat, asked me if I didn't think I might have received another wrong steer. For some time, as we pushed along, the welcoming throng had been thinning out, and now it had dwindled to nothing. This, of course, is always an ominous sign. No one had thrown a tomato to us for a couple of miles when, suddenly, we spotted two jeeps ahead of us, one of them flying a general's fanion. "Don't get ahead of him," I told Roach. "He might be offended." Just as we began to pull up on the jeeps, they stopped. There was the sound of an *arrivée*—incoming shell—and then a spout of dirt and smoke two hundred yards to the right of the highway; it had clearly crossed over the road between us and the jeeps. Leclerc got out of his jeep—we knew it was he because he carried a cane—and began to look about him with interest. He did not look long; within a few seconds we saw him wave his cane, like a pointer, in the direction he evidently thought the shell had come from. Then he hopped back into his jeep, and both vehi-

cles turned around and started toward us, the General undoubtedly pleased as Polichinelle at having spotted an antitank
gun before it could hurt one of his cherished armored vehicles.
He was the only divisional commander I ever saw use himself
as a decoy to draw fire. Roach asked if I thought Leclerc would
be angry if we preceded him back down the road. I replied
that in retreat the place of honor is in the rear, and we might as
well leave it to the General.

We soon reached the main body of vehicles again, and saw
that the parade had temporarily disbanded; deploying from
the Paris-Orléans highway, the tanks were taking off along
feeder roads and the half-tracks across fields, as if preparing to
pinch in on the point of resistance. Leclerc, after a brief pause
at the first tank he came to, headed down a tarred crossroad.
"Maybe he's going to try another way through," Roach said.
"Let's follow him." Not being able to read Morrison's mind, I
couldn't tell whether Roach's proposal represented the inclination of the majority, and I was ashamed to suggest putting
the matter to a vote. So we hustled along after the General.

I have no coherent recollection of the next few hours, which
we spent running up and down crossroads, hoping they would
lead us to a nice, clear, Franco-American-held path into Paris,
or else following half-tracks loaded with infantrymen along
minor lanes that ran parallel to the main highway. The men in
the half-tracks were passing wine bottles from hand to hand,
for the inhabitants of the region, having run out of tomatoes,
had levied on their cellars to produce new offerings, and there
was a festival atmosphere. Each time we attached ourselves to
a company of vehicles, one of us would say, "Maybe this outfit
will go all the way through," but each time, after a mile or
two, there would be a barrage of antitank *arrivées* and the vehicles would stop and fan out from the road.

An armored division is a superior instrument for long
sweeps across open country but ill-adapted to fighting in the
suburbs of a great city. Between Arpajon and Paris the terrain
is finely veined with roads and closely dotted with villages.
Roads converge upon each village, and every village crossroads
offers an ideal emplacement for a concealed antitank gun,
which an approaching tank, hemmed in by buildings on either
side, must face head on. In such circumstances, the safe,

cautious procedure is to stop the tanks, call up the half-tracks, and deploy infantrymen around each strong point, but there were two persuasive arguments against such strategy on that August 24. One was that there were so many antitank emplacements and so few infantrymen—since the Daydaybay, as an armored division, carried with it only one infantry regiment —that the thrust would have slowed to a crawl, and the other was Leclerc's and the whole Daydaybay's overpowering haste to get into Paris. The Germans, rightly calculating that the Allies would never again bomb them in Paris, had dismantled all their antiaircraft defenses in the zone, and the weapons taken from those installations gave them an abundance of the deadliest kind of antitank artillery. Rommel, it is now known, had wanted to bring this stuff forward months earlier and use it on the battlefield, but he had been overruled. Antiaircraft belonged to the Luftwaffe, the Luftwaffe belonged to Goering, and Goering hated Rommel.

The Daydaybay's irregularly progressing advance elements were followed by a great wheeled throng, including us, that was always just far enough back not to be shot at, which meant not quite far enough forward to see what was going on, with the result that nobody could understand why the headway being made was so intermittent; it was like a huge crowd following a pack of coon hounds by their sound, unaware that the dogs have met up with a wildcat. In the throng, in addition to the supply and ammunition trains and all the other rear elements of the division, were many vehicles whose occupants, whether military or civilian, had no connection with the Daydaybay. There were, for example, increasing numbers of American trucks carrying provisions for Paris, because Group had envisaged the possibility that the city would be found on the verge of famine, and of civilian charcoal-fueled trucks, mounting odd revolving chimneys that belched stinking smoke, and jammed with delegations of F.F.I. from behind the Allied lines. The F.F.I., who were willing enough, could have been used as infantry if the division staff had had liaison with them, but it is hard to improvise such an arrangement on a battlefield. So they mostly just followed along with the rest of us, though occasionally some of them dismounted to hunt down a German in a haystack after the tanks had cleaned out a gun position.

There were Army jeeps from all over the front, carrying officers who, like those at Bagnoles-de-l'Orne, had invented missions for themselves that would take them to Paris. And there were the correspondents, military and civilian, too. Morrison and I spotted jeeploads of our colleagues at every turning, giving me happy reassurance that I had made up the head start that so appalled me the day before.

The many tangential roads were a constant challenge, and Roach, Morrison, and I kept trying new ones, always figuring that we might still come on one that was clear all the way into Paris. But whatever road we tried led us to fighting. We could tell that the advance units were moving nearer Paris all the time, though, because at each try we got farther from our line of departure, which was where the parade had come to a halt. After we explored all the accessible roads, we went back over those on which we had first run into fighting, and here the evidence of progress was all about us, in the form of burned-out vehicles (most of them, unfortunately, bearing the Daydaybay emblem), knocked-out antitank guns, and German dead and wounded, lying by the roadside with their feet toward the pavement, waiting to be picked up, sometime, by French ambulances. They had been laid out there in orderly fashion, as if they had dressed their lines, by German prisoners, working in pairs under the orders of F.F.I. boys with tommy guns. It must have been disquieting to a member of the Führer's master race to feel, as he walked along holding a leg of a wounded man in each hand, that there was within kicking distance of his rear a seventeen-year-old with a tommy gun pointed at his kidneys and a wild desire to use it. We came across unwounded and unutilized prisoners, too, holding their hands high over their heads and doing a shoeless goose step in response to the orders of their F.F.I. guards. (Boots of real leather had become extremely scarce in France, and the F.F.I.s figured that since the collective Occupant was responsible for this state of affairs, it was fair enough to glom the individual Occupant's boots when he was taken prisoner.) The prisoners' faces had the same color as those of the dead Germans—greenish-white under the dust from the road—as if, physiologically, the processes of death had already begun, a reaction to an anticipated situation. Yet I saw only one Frenchman justify such a reaction. A wounded German was lying, quite still, by the roadside, when two armed civilians approached him. One pulled at his boots and the other pointed an automatic— German—at his head and fired. There was no excuse for it.

The Daydaybay's infantrymen, in their half-tracks, followed the tanks at a distance of a little less than a mile. The commander of each combat group—four or five tanks and as many half-tracks—committed his infantry only when he had to, since to detruck and deploy them, move them up on foot, envelop a position, and then take it by small-arms fire might require anywhere from fifteen minutes to an hour. That accounted for the heavy losses of the tankers and for the boredom of the infantry, who, in their open vehicles under a baking August sun, began to sweat wine. I remember two troglodytic types—an Arab and a Frenchman from some part of the Mediterranean littoral—locked in unfraternal combat while their *compagnons de voiture* tried unsuccessfully to pry them apart. "*Tapette!*" each of the contestants shouted in one of the other's ears as they struggled. The insult, which is French slang for "homosexual," was never used with less apparent foundation. They looked like pithecanthropi with gold teeth. (I did not see either of them at Mme la Maréchale's recent party.)

On each road we tried, we met jeeploads of correspondents and of officers attempting to maintain liaison with Division, but the jeep we met most frequently was General Leclerc's. Leaning forward as he sat, tapping on the floor with his cane, he looked as if he were riding the jeep toward an obstacle on a steeplechase course. Leclerc was forty-one, a year younger than the Ulysses S. Grant of the Wilderness Campaign, and, like Grant, he was by training and predilection a horseman. Watching him in his jeep made me realize for the first time how valuable a horse must have been in the old days as an outlet for the emotional energy of a fretting commander. The constant conflict of wills, on a level slightly below that of thought, and the horse's reflexes, impossible to ignore even during great crises, must have offered a distraction from the pressures of the moment. Leclerc, I knew, had been a cavalryman, and I have since learned that when he first saw action, as a lieutenant in Morocco in 1926, he had two horses killed under him. And now he had only a jeep to sit, and a jeep is insensitive to the eager tremolo of the legs. Still, he was riding it as best he could. To be so near Paris and not yet have it made him strain the long nose and the bristling red mustache in close pursuit of the point of the visor of his three-star-general's kepi.

I had, it is true, been talking with Leclerc only a week or so earlier, but now, as we passed and repassed each other on the road, I never found what I deemed a suitable opportunity to remind him of our acquaintance, and the same diffidence restrained me even when, just beyond a railroad culvert, his vehicle and ours stopped close together in deference to a shelling by an unanticipated battery. During a pause in the shelling, he continued on his way, but we decided to turn back and try some other route, and presently we met a jeep carrying an American brigadier general from V Corps, the unit of which the Daydaybay was theoretically a part. The general waved to us to stop, and when we did, he got out in the road and asked us if we had seen Leclerc. He was a very precise-looking brigadier general, with rimless glasses and a neatly trimmed black mustache, and he carried a well-filled map case under his right arm. We pointed in the direction in which we assumed Leclerc was still riding, if his luck had held out, and the brigadier sighed. "I've been looking for him at what is supposed to be Division Headquarters, and they told me they hadn't heard from him for hours," he said. "The division isn't where it's supposed to be, and I can't find Leclerc to tell him so. God damn it," he added, with unexpected warmth, "this isn't an advance at all! It's the march of a gypsy band." The brigadier turned, the set of his shoulders a form of professional reproof, climbed back into his vehicle, and took off after the unhorsed cavalier, who, as a matter of principle, tried to stay out of touch with Corps as much as possible. He loathed receiving orders. "He was a commander who knew how to make himself adored without making a single concession to popularity," a man who served under him said to me once. "Whenever he did a kindness, he always covered it with a hard word."

Late in the afternoon, having worked all the subsidiary roads in vain, we went back to the Paris-Orléans highway and found it clear for at least ten miles beyond where we had left it that morning. There was almost the fine free feeling of our ride to Chartres the day before as we raced up past Montlhéry and into Longjumeau, an ancient town that chiefly consists of a single endless street, walled on both sides with houses. In the coaching days, Longjumeau was the last change of horses before Paris. On its interminable street, we came upon the tail end of a long string of motionless vehicles. The Germans were making another stand up ahead, at Fresnes, where they were using a prison as an antitank fort. I acquired from a source that I believed authentic—and it turned out to be so—the information that the division would not go into Paris until the next morning. It is strange that I cannot remember now who told me, because it must have been somebody I trusted like my mother, or Roach, Morrison, and I would have waited in the street all night. The fighting at Fresnes, which we did not try to see, was savage.

Longjumeau, with its locked and tightly shuttered house fronts, offered small promise of an entertaining billet, so we turned back toward more open country and took the turnoff to the Tower of Montlhéry. A difference between the Paris suburbs and those of New York is that in the former, crabbed old medieval towns are interspersed with the latest jerry-built speculative developments. The town of Montlhéry, huddled on the slope of a hill a mile or so east of the highway, might as well be, from its appearance, in a remote corner of Burgundy as where it is, thirteen miles from the Porte d'Orléans. On the other side of the highway is the Montlhéry automobile race track, an incongruous annex to the ancient commune. We took the road that leads up through the steep, narrow streets of the town to the ancient Tower, on the top of the hill. (*Monument historique*, completed 1015 A.D., 137 metres above sea level at its base, 168 at its summit, it says in the guidebooks.)

Only the Tower remains of a castle that dominated the southern approach to Paris for six centuries, served as a fortress for insurrectionary French lords in a drawn battle against Louis XI in 1465, and was finally dismantled by Henry IV in 1591, so that it could never again be used as a center of rebellion. The four encircling walls have long since disappeared, the stones having been carted away by thrifty housebuilders. Trees have grown up over most of the site. After passing through the town, the road skirts the outline of the vanished outermost wall. In peacetime, Sunday motorists park their cars along it and walk up to where the Tower stands solitary on the wooded hilltop. To cater to these visitors, a rustic restaurant and bar, called the Auberge de la Tour, has been built near the road, with a wide concrete terrace that affords a view in the direction of Melun and Fontainebleau, and it was here that we stopped.

The interior of the Auberge de la Tour ("*Terrasse—Jeux—Panorama Splendide*"), like that of our stopping place the night before, was in a state of ecstatic ebullition. M. Bertrand, the *patron*, by whom we were made welcome, is one of those Frenchmen who wear a cap and sweater in all seasons and invariably speak in a deep baritone. His eyes bulge in a friendly but disillusioned manner, advising the world that he is not a man to be taken in. His handclasp is strong and his conversation informed and libidinous, as an innkeeper's should be. His chalet is crowded with paintings in which he descries the hands of Old Masters. M. Bertrand is the *crieur aux ventes*, or auctioneer, of the district, which is in itself an assurance that he is a glib fellow. In selling the effects of the deceased, he told me over our first glass of wine, he was occasionally able to come by some good things; he was, after all, the only connoisseur between Melun and Saint-Michel. He bought not for resale, he said, but as an investment, with a view to creating an estate for his descendants.

"That Géricault there, for example," M. Bertrand said, pointing to a dark oil painting of a lean young thoroughbred in a stall. "There aren't many *guinguettes* where you'd find a Géricault. It's unfortunate he didn't sign it, but it's the real thing. I know his style." Mme Bertrand, a stout, red-faced woman with high cheekbones and narrow eyes, produced a bottle of a dreadful sweet *apéritif* wine called Cap Corse—the only prewar *apéritif* in the house, she said—which she had saved for this great day. We all felt obliged to smack our lips over it.

An F.F.I. boy asked me if Morrison was "an American colonial." I told him no, he was an American, just like Roach and me—we came all colors. So the boy said that if Morrison was that sort of American, he must be conversant with the latest *tendances du jazz hot.* As it happened, Morrison was, and the boy went to a cupboard and fetched a clarinet. Then Roach, Morrison, and I and the boy, and about five other F.F.I. youngsters in shirt sleeves went out on to the *terrasse* with the *panorama splendide* in the late twilight and pulled up chairs around a couple of tables. The clarinetist put his feet up on his table, tilted his chair back, and announced that he was going to play "*Dans l'Ambiance*"—or, as he translated it, "Een de Mud." Then he lifted the clarinet to his lips and played "In the Mood" while Morrison encouraged him with the whole sectarian gamut of facial appreciation and a few quiet, satisfied groans. "Een de Mud" sounded better than any other music I've ever heard. The clarinet gloated over the routed Ostrogoths. The thin sound, wriggling up toward the old Tower, woke birds that had turned in for the night. M. Bertrand's son, a slight youth of eighteen, said the Germans had disapproved of jazz, regarding an interest in it as evidence of Allied sympathies, and had forbidden it to be played in public places. The *zazous*, or hepcats, however, were not discouraged by this from playing at dances but, instead, amused themselves by working out musical arrangements that began as Viennese waltzes, then switched to jazz and back again before any Germans present could call the turn. The *zazous* also affected *le genre jazz* in their clothes, the Bertrand boy said; they wore what Americans call zoot suits. There was nothing much *l'Occupant* could do about that.

In time, the clarinetist finished his recital. It was full dark by then. I could tell by his voice when he spoke that it had done him good to get that dissident music out of him, blasting it forth into the night after the hour of the Occupation curfew. He told us he was not a professional musician—as we had all suggested he must be—but a typewriter repairman. There had been no new typewriters in Paris since the Occupation, he said, and the maintenance of the old ones had become a fine art. I asked him what my banged-about portable Underwood would bring on the black market, and he said, readily, fifty-six thousand francs, which, at the going rate of fifty to the dollar, would have been eleven hundred and twenty dollars.

The jazz connoisseurs of Montlhéry had not been completely cut off from the *potins* and *nouvelles tendances* of the

American jazz world, the lads said. They had had not only the *émissions* of the London radio but reports on the situation from four American and two Canadian aviators and jazz fanciers who had lived in the village for several weeks after being shot down over France and who had departed only that afternoon, when an American detachment showed up there. The airmen had reached Montlhéry by a branch line of the underground railroad that was washed out a short while after their arrival in the village. "They were all *fanatiques du jazz*," young Bertrand said. "Unhappily, they spoke hardly any French, but by whistling, tapping with the foot, and now and then a word, we could make ourselves understood to one another."

Until D Day, Allied airmen shot down over France and retrieved by the Resistance were frequently taken to Paris and thence rerouted toward the Spanish frontier. Paris was the turntable. The Allied landings, however, had made communications between Paris and the rest of France uncertain, and from then on most of the Allied fliers who were shot down had to sit it out where they were until they were rescued. The *fanatiques du jazz* stranded in Montlhéry were in this position. All our airmen who flew over France carried photographs of themselves taken in civilian clothes and suitable for attaching to *cartes d'identité*. The Resistance supplied the *cartes*— forged, of course, and usually describing the bearer as a deaf-mute. The high incidence of deafness and mutism in Occupied territory might have astonished an Occupant with more intellectual curiosity. The airmen in Montlhéry had been dressed in French clothes and billeted with "relatives." It became easy to explain newcomers after the landings by saying they were fugitives from the war area.

"The Sunday afternoon before last, we gave a concert on the terrace here," young Bertrand said. "No jazz on the program, of course, but we had a very good crowd and had a lot of fun—all except for the best-known *collabos*. The *collabos* were feeling sick. We were very gay, because we knew by word of mouth and through the B.B.C. how fast the Americans were advancing. *Les Fritz* were furious, but they couldn't forbid innocent amusements without acknowledging that their position was becoming critical. Officially they were still saying the offensive was a local attack that would be contained. The airmen came to the concert and mingled with us young people —all pals of theirs. If a Gestapo man had asked them for their cards, he would have made the discovery that deaf men are crazy about music. Those aviators were nice boys. The town won't be the same without them. It is the only regrettable result of the Liberation."

The night was black and quiet. If there was sporadic shooting up ahead, as there must have been, the wind was wrong, for we heard none. We might have been sitting out under the trees on a New England lawn. There wasn't a uniform in the Auberge, except for Roach's, Morrison's, and mine, in which (I feel safe in speaking for my two companions) none of us had ever felt natural. We were as tired as if we had spent all day swimming, and tired in the same contented way.

I was up early next morning, and while waiting for the others to turn out, I climbed up the fifty yards or so to the Tower, traversing the remains of a causeway that crosses the remains of a moat. The top of the hill is the highest point between Montlhéry and Paris. A very informative booklet, which I did not have then but which I recently bought, for fifty francs, says that the Tower is 24.111 kilometres from the Panthéon and dominates it by 31 metres. Because of its height, the booklet adds, it was a station on the semaphore-telegraph line that linked Paris with the Spanish border in the days before the electric telegraph made the service obsolete, and in 1874 scientists used the Tower to measure the speed of light. One could hardly imagine the Germans' passing up a bet like that, and, sure enough, they had built a brick observation-and-listening post on a flat stretch beside the Tower. I was staring up at the Tower, the first ruin I had seen in months that didn't look as if it could be blamed on the Allied Air Forces, when I heard an American voice say, "Good morning!" Turning, I saw that the voice emanated from a Signal Corps lieutenant, who, I suppose, had emanated from the brick building. Neither voice (Philadelphia, perhaps) nor lieutenant (five ten, pale under a black stubble, serious mouth) was distinctive, but he was a man I won't forget.

"I've been up here since yesterday morning, sir," he said. "Recon troop brought me up here with a couple of other men, so we could look around. I haven't been of any use, but I've been having a wonderful time looking at Paris through a good glass. I've never been to Paris, but I've been reading about it all my life. I know it by heart, from the maps. Just where everything is. And there it is! God, I just can't take my eyes off it! Come over here and I'll show it to you." He handed me his binoculars, a magnificent Signal Corps pair, and led me over to the northern edge of a broken parapet. Paris was there, all right—there in the same place I had left it four years, two months, and fifteen days before.

"I got the map right here," the lieutenant said, and he unrolled it and laid it out on a flat stone. Then he straightened up and said, "But I don't need the map, because I've got all the landmarks cold. Now, over there," he went on, pointing to the dome of the Invalides, "is the Opera House. Once you get that clear, you have your orientation. And over there," he continued, pointing now to the Opéra, "is the City Hall—you know, the Chamber of Deputies. Isn't it beautiful?"

"It's beautiful," I said, and meant it.

The lieutenant got the Eiffel Tower right. "I suppose you know what that beautiful white church is up on the hill?" he next said, swiveling my elbow into line with Sacré-Coeur. I was going to name it, but something warned me not to, so I shook my head. "Why, it's Notre Dame, of course!" he said, and I was glad that I had kept my mouth shut.

"I can't wait to get down there," the lieutenant said. "It's the most beautiful city in the world."

I thanked him from the bottom of my heart. I hope he made it.

10
The Navel of the Loire

August 25; the day that began on the hill of Montlhéry, was to be one of the happiest of my life. The day is celebrated in history also as that of the Liberation of Paris. As a redundant stroke of luck, beyond mathematical probability, I was to see General von Choltitz, the German Military Governor of Paris, sign the surrender of the city and its recent jailers to Leclerc.

In Paris now there is more agreement about what went on under the Merovingians than what happened in the years between 1940 and 1944. The former Vichy people have worked so hard to deny the Resistance, and the Communists to prove there never was a liberation in which the United States had a part, that often I have found myself searching for tangible evidence of what I think I remember. I was happy, therefore, when, beside an exit from a train platform in the waiting room of the Gare Montparnasse, I came upon a plaque reading:

"Here, the 25th of August, 1944, at 17 o'clock, General Leclerc received from the German Military Governor von Choltitz the act of surrender consecrating the Liberation of the City by the People of Paris and the Allied Armies."

The Gare Montparnasse, I hear, is to be torn down soon, and then not even the plaque will remain. It was not conspicuous, and to find it I had to ask my way at the information counter. The first clerk I spoke to there, a young one, had never heard of either the surrender or the plaque, but a senior colleague said "Gate Thirty-three," and led me to it. The authorities might have given it more splash, I thought; it isn't every day a French general receives the surrender of Paris. But at least I knew now I had not suffered a hallucination.

I remembered the German staff officers—a dozen of them —in their flat, visored caps and shiny boots and the neat uniforms their batmen must have pressed for them in the beleaguered *Kommandantur* at the Hotel Meurice so that they would have something fresh to surrender in. After von

Choltitz, a worried, fat little soldier, had signed, he and his officers were ordered into command cars, in which, accompanied by officers of the Daydaybay, they were driven off to carry the news to German strong points that were still holding out.

It was by sheer chance that I got to see the ceremony. Roach, Morrison, and I entered Paris early in the afternoon, and by the time we reached the Gare, which was the temporary headquarters of the Daydaybay, the streets around it were *en fête*, and the sidewalk tables of the cafés facing it were jammed with jubilants. (There was the sound of desultory shooting fairly close—presumably spite sniping by collaborationists—but nobody paid it any heed.) After gawking about for a short while in a couple of cafés, where white wine, a rarity in Paris then, was being sold to celebrate the victory, we started down the Rue de Rennes toward the Seine. Clinging to the old Chevrolet were three or four frantic young boys of the F.F.I., who acted as guides, and they soon got us into a zone where there was nobody on the streets—a bad sign. Then we ran into shooting, so we drove back to the Gare to ask at Division if there was a safe route across the Seine. Leaving our car at the entrance to the station, we climbed the long flight of stairs to the waiting room, and there were Leclerc and the Germans.

We had seen Leclerc so often on the roads that we felt we knew him, although he never said hello. The last time, before the surrender, had been that morning in a suburb called Antony, less than five miles outside the city. The General's jeep started toward the city, and Roach, who was doing our driving, had begun to follow him, but a large, officious French captain, who looked like United States District Court Judge Thomas F. Murphy, stopped us and said we could not go on in, because we were not correspondents assigned to the division. (No American correspondents were assigned to it.) So we had had to go back six or seven miles to the headquarters of the First Army's V Corps, to which the Daydaybay was attached, and get a *laissez-passer* from the G-2 there. When we returned to Antony with this document, the officious captain was gone, and nobody wanted to see our credentials. But by then the highway leading to the Porte d'Orléans was choked with vehicles, lined up bumper to bumper, and we could advance only a few yards at a time. The German rear-guard action that had slowed the Daydaybay's advance the day before had collapsed, and there was nothing ahead to worry us but traffic. From the hill, the city looked exactly as it had when I last left it, on June 10, 1940. For four years now, however, I had been wondering what was happening to people I knew in Paris, and I wouldn't find that out until we got there. Apparently the Germans had not—as yet, at least—demolished anything, and I could see from the hill no clouds of the sort of smoke that might indicate explosions. But there was no telling what the Nazis might do at the last minute, when they saw Paris escaping them. General Hans Speidel, who was Chief of Staff of Rommel's Army Group B, has since written that von Choltitz had orders from Hitler to blow all the bridges across the Seine, and that after he surrendered the city, he was condemned, *in absentia*, by a Nazi court-martial for failing to do so. Since Leclerc sent von Choltitz a warning that he would hold him personally responsible for any damage to the city, it is possible that the German preferred the *in absentia* kind of trouble.

My anxiety increased after we left the Auberge de la Tour to continue toward our goal, and it wasn't until I saw the glum krauts in custody at the Gare Montparnasse that I was sure we and Notre Dame and the festive crowds wouldn't all go up in a cloud of black smoke. Every delay on the road, especially our reluctant rearward trip to Corps, sharpened our impatience. The endless queue of vehicles moved, but, it seemed, ever more slowly. In Longjumeau a woman rushed out of a house and presented Roach with a magnificent tricolor, big enough to drape a hearse. The flag made us look extremely impressive.

During the long crawl, I had time to think back on the events that preceded my 1940 departure from Paris, at the same jammed-road tempo. I remembered the morning when, from my window in the Hôtel Louvois, I saw the Luftwaffe make its first reconnaissance in force over the city. The Hôtel Louvois faces the Bibliothèque Nationale across the Square Louvois, a park that covers a block in front of the library and has in its center a heroic fountain ornamented with four nearly nude female figures, representing four great rivers of France. They have chests like old-fashioned contraltos. La Loire, who has faced me, off and on, for protracted periods during the last seventeen years, has a lower torso like one of the oil jars in which Ali Baba's handmaiden discovered the thieves. All four ladies hold their heads and shoulders back, in order to support the upper basin of the fountain, which is topped by a Grecian urn—a position that requires them to throw their abdomens forward, as if they were doing bumps. In summer, the water in the fountain cascades past the dryads' noses and splashes in their navels, which are as large as halves of coconut shells.

On the morning the planes came—May 10, 1940—all the inhabitants of the three more or less residential sides of the Square Louvois stood at their wide-flung windows and looked up, sensing that the *drôle de guerre* (the non-fighting one) was over even before they heard the news on their radios that the Germans had invaded the Low Countries. The planes were flying quite high, glinting like metal spinners in the sky, amid puffs of white antiaircraft smoke. One of the spectators on the Square Louvois was a woman who appeared on the narrow balcony in front of her window still wearing her nightgown. She had a figure like La Loire in flood, and she waved toward the unattainable Messerschmitts an arm like one of the statue's legs. "*Courage!*" she cried. "*On les aura!*" And now, as Roach and Morrison and I inched along toward the Square Louvois, four years and three and a half months later, her prediction had come true. I hoped the balcony lady had been patient.

When I prepared to leave Paris, just a month after the balcony scene, I was one of the last half-dozen guests at the Hôtel Louvois, which had a hundred and eighty rooms. The management had been closing floors successively, working from the top down. By the time of my departure, only the entresol and the ground floor were in use, and there remained but five or six employees; the manager, a *valet de chambre*, a *femme de chambre*, the young woman who kept the books, and the night porter, Fernand, are those I remember. Fernand was the oldest and spunkiest. The bookkeeper, Mlle Yvonne, was a good-humored girl, ash blond and plump. "*Au revoir*," I said to her as I went out the door, but I didn't think it would be soon. I headed south with a broadcaster named Waverley Root and a *Herald Tribune* man named John Elliott, who had a broken leg. I saw a great many things happen in the following four years. While I can't say that I recalled all of them there on the slow, hot road, they all jointly affected my mood.

The Square Louvois, which is again under my window as I write, is a park of modest dimensions—probably no more than a hundred and fifty feet wide or deep—with fourteen full-grown trees, as well as some bushes, and a circular path surrounding a lawn and the fountain. The park occupies one of the former sites of the Théâtre National de l'Opéra, which stood there from 1794 to 1820 and gave the neighborhood a gay Italianate flavor that Henri Beyle found congenial. The operatic flavor persists in the names of the surrounding streets—Lulli, Rameau, Cherubini. The Square has the same character as the central *place* of a provincial town. There is a school at one side, which also serves as a meeting hall and polling place, and we have a bookshop, a cobbler, and several bars. A butcher and a baker have shops in the block-long Rue Rameau, running off the Square, so, all in all, the people who live around it have little need for the rest of Paris. *Pour la vie intellectuelle*, there is the Bibliothèque.

Pigeons roost in the trees of the Square Louvois; even when the temperature is near zero, they seem none the worse for it, and no less amorous. The pigeons are collateral descendants of those I used to see there in 1940, the latter having been eaten during the Occupation. (The same people who treacherously devoured those birds now try to make it up to their successors by feeding them crumbs of *croissants* left over from breakfast.) "My God, those pigeons were tough!" says Fernand, the old night porter. "Real athletes! And with the rationing, we were hardly strong enough to chew them." Fernand has a long, downturned mustache *à la Vercingétorix* and a limp that I have always assumed is a souvenir of Verdun. (I have never asked him, for fear he might avow a less romantic etiology.) He parts his hair in the middle, wears glasses, and has one of those angular faces that anonymous sculptors used to carve over cathedral doors. He speaks with a harsh *Berrichon* accent. Back in the winter of 1939–40, whenever there was an air-raid alert and nothing happened, Fernand would take it as a personal insult. "*Ah, les salauds!*" he would fume, sounding like a band saw in need of oil. "They disturb us, but they don't come!" He believed that it was the Germans who set off the sirens, in the manner of a drunk leaning against a doorbell.

Fernand's spirit of high indignation has not diminished. Every night, when he brings a bottle of Vichy to my room, it is as if the all-clear had just sounded after a bombless alert. "*C'est la pagaille!*" he exclaims on entering, which means it's an intensified, botched-up rat race. Fernand then identifies the particular *pagaille* he is talking about, which may be local, national, or international, on a moral, governmental, or meteorological level. One evening he explained that the concierge had left word the night before for him to waken the man in No. 210 at five-thirty and take him coffee, and that when he had knocked at 210's door, 210 had "screeched like a cow." It turned out that it was 310 who had left word to be wakened, and 210 had complained to the management. "*Ah, quelle pagaille!*" Fernand wailed, stumping out, perhaps to administer a *cataplasme sinapisé*, or mustard plaster, to another guest he has known a long time; he is the unofficial house doctor. The results of the January 1956 election brought Fernand to my room crying, "*C'est la pagaille!* These elections, it's impossible! A country without a government! We'll be back at the voting urns within six months. *Ah, quelle pagaille!*" He tugged at his collar to indicate that he was choking with rage. And on the evening after Scotland beat the French Rugby team, 12–0, Fernand's reaction "A defeat without parallel in history! They marked not one point! *C'est la pagaille!*" I couldn't sleep without my nightly dose of *pagaille*. But Fernand is right: *la pagaille* is in the air. The quintessential expression of it, of course, is Poujadisme, a political movement with as much intellectual content as a scream.

I had thought of the whole war as a road back to Paris, and now that I was on the real one, I momentarily felt let down. The car barely crept; I might as well have been riding home to Manhattan on a Sunday night from a weekend in Norwalk. After we got through Longjumeau, though, we made better time, and then, as we approached the Porte d'Orléans, we began to meet cyclists coming out from the city to greet us. These cyclists (the only ones I recall, anyway) were all women, the most beautiful I have ever seen. It is an established fact that women look better at some times than at others. I once knew a chap, for instance, who claimed that a woman is never so attractive as just after a severe bout of flu, because it makes her more ethereal, and when I was a young reporter, I used to think that women looked their best in a house where a man had just died. All such previous theories of environmental cosmetology blew up, however, when I saw the Parisiennes on their bicycles. To make a woman really beautiful, liberate her. It brings her up pounds on any kind of track. She visibly exudes a generalized good will that makes you want to kiss her.

These women wore long, simple summer dresses that left their bodies very free. (Elastic for girdles had disappeared from Occupied France years earlier.) Their bare legs were more smoothly muscled than Frenchwomen's before the war, because they had been riding those bicycles or walking ever since taxis vanished from the streets of Paris, and their figures were better, because the *pâtissiers* were out of business. It was a tribute to the French frame that none of them looked scrawny or knobby. Their hair was done up high on their heads, without silly little ponytails, and they wore wooden platform shoes, because there was no leather. As they bore down upon the oncoming jeeps, I understood how those old Sag Harbor whalers must have felt when the women of the islands came swimming out to them like a school of beautiful tinker mackerel. None of ours came aboard though. They couldn't abandon their bicycles. One evening after the war, Roach and I were reminiscing about our arrival in Paris, and he told me that I cried. I have no doubt that I did, but I do not remember when.

In the Place d'Orléans, just within the city limits, we came upon a sight unique in my experience—thousands of people, tens of thousands, all demonstratively happy. In any direction we looked, there was an unending vista of cheering people. It was like an entry into Paradise, and all the sweeter because we didn't deserve it. A man goes through life feeling that he is never getting sufficient credit for what he has done, and few are ever cheered for something they haven't done. Neither Roach nor Morrison nor I had fired a single shot, but there was adulation enough for everybody. General Omar Nelson Bradley, who was not there to receive any of it, could have moved an American division into Paris twenty-four hours sooner, but instead he had sent to Normandy for the Daydaybay, because he wanted a French unit to disengage the capital. It was the most potent lift that French morale received during the war. The people crowded about the troops in the trucks and half-tracks and jeeps, sometimes making it impossible for them to move. At one point our Chevrolet was so weighted down that it came to a dead stop.

There were police lines, but the police were celebrating, too. They couldn't find it in their hearts to step on anybody's feet. Resistance organizations of Left, Center, and Right had united in the final insurrection of Paris, and the display of exuberance was therefore that rare phenomenon in France—a demonstration without a counter-demonstration. An open truck crossed the Place loaded with police, all of them carrying Sten guns. The crowd cheered madly: "*La police à l'honneur!*" The police had been the collective heroes of the uprising; they had raised the tricolor over the Préfecture of Police on August 19 and had held it against all attacks. Nobody called them *flics* or *poulets* or *la flicaille*. In a city where cop-hating is a tradition, such cordiality was without precedent. "*La police à l'honneur!*" It was like a dream.

There were considerable numbers of Moslems in the Daydaybay, but nobody was calling them *bicots*, which is the contemptuous French slang word for North Africans. It was not until a week later that I met a man, in a black-market restaurant near the Bourse, who said he thought it had been a mistake to let *indigènes*—"natives"—take part in the Liberation of Paris. It might make them uppity, he felt. I did not ask him what barricades he had stormed, for I was being friends with everybody, and so, still, was almost everybody else. But the sour note he injected into the general rejoicing was bleakly symptomatic of many things to come. Those things—some of them, at any rate—were probably inevitable. The mood of the first few days after the Liberation could not, in the nature of man, have been expected to last. It was too beatific, and the victory that we were all looking forward to did not arrive soon enough to act as a booster shot; cold weather and physical discomfort arrived first, and dampened the August enthusiasm.

Nevertheless, when I left Paris, three months after the Liberation, the romance was still on. Simply being an American predisposed Parisians in your favor.

Between late 1944 and my present visit, I returned to Paris only once—for ten days in 1948, during which I had little chance to do more than say hello to old friends. But after I came back and settled down for a while, I found it hard to believe that the girls on bicycles had ever ridden out to greet us. Although the old friends were as warm as ever, the city itself made me feel a bit like a man returning after a dozen years to a former love and finding that she is married, has four children, is worried about money, and devotes all her afternoons to the Parent-Teacher Association, the Ladies' Village Improvement Society, the Friends of Krishnamurti, and the American Red Cross. She is not hostile; she just has no time to waste on past performances. This always astonishes the man, although it shouldn't.

Such a man is likely to try to reconstruct a picture of things as they were. In a similar frame of mind during the last few months, I have occasionally felt impelled to make small expeditions in quest of the past, like Rétif de la Bretonne circumambulating the Ile Saint-Louis to read the inscriptions he had scratched on walls there on evenings when Sara was kind. (That was how I came to look up the plaque in the Gare Montparnasse.) On one of these excursions, my destination was the Boulevard Saint-Michel, in the student quarter, where I spent a good deal of time during my first visit to Paris, as a student myself, in 1926. Setting out from my hotel, I walked through the Square Louvois to the Bibliothèque and turned down the Rue de Richelieu toward the Seine, stopping, as usual, in front of the building at No. 69, where in 1830 Stendhal wrote *Le Rouge et le Noir*. It was No. 71 in his day and a hotel, like almost every other place he ever lived in. He was correcting the proofs of *Le Rouge et le Noir* when he heard the first shots of the July revolution, which substituted Louis-Philippe for Charles X on the throne. It was Stendhal's lucky year. He put on one of his light-cinnamon frock coats, for which it is highly improbable he had reimbursed his tailor, and went out to root for the mob. Two months later he had a consulate, which supported him for the rest of his life. (*Le Rouge et le Noir* was not a serious money-maker; it brought him a total of something under a thousand dollars.) A few rods farther on, I passed No. 61, where, in the eighteen-twenties, when it was No. 63, he lived in what he insisted was not sin with Mme Giuditta Pasta, the prima donna of the Théâtre-Italien.

I crossed through the Tuileries, where the 1830 shots were fired, and, when I got to the Left Bank, walked on to the Odéon, a brisk half hour's going. Leaving the Place de l'Odéon, I had a choice of several tangential streets by which to reach the Boulevard Saint-Michel. I chose the Rue Racine, and presently stopped in front of the window of a bookshop where a copy of a new collection of French cartoons was on display. The cover drawing showed a lanky, goofy-looking American soldier sitting in a swivel chair with his feet up on a desk and holding a telephone to his ear. The caption was *"Toujours occupé"*—a pun in French but not in American, since we say a country is "occupied" but a telephone line is "busy." (The English, who are foreign to both of us, say "engaged.") Pinned to the G.I.'s shoulder was a tag reading, "Go home," but he was fatuously unconscious of it. The artist had clearly been influenced by Sad Sack. It is one of the dilemmas of the young Western European anti-American that in any popular art he must express himself in an American idiom or lose his audience. Jazz, the movies, and the ten thousand pseudo-Hemingways, half of whom are European, have formed the mold. The other side has nothing to offer as an alternative. It is impossible, for instance, to imagine a young Western European cartoonist adopting the manner of the Soviet's *Krokodil*, which is that of *Punch* or *Puck* in 1905, or a Russian folk-dance ensemble taking the play away from Lionel Hampton's band at a Parisian music hall. It is our misfortune both that we have not more to offer and that the others have so much less. Everything we do is overconsidered by Europeans, like the performances of a fair three-year-old in a nothing year. An American B picture is reviewed at solemn length, as if it were a novel by an Academician, and the critic comes up at the end of two columns with the verdict that *Flaming Guns*, or whatever, is not the kind of first-rate art that one might expect from a country "with the pretension of instructing a Europe that has, after all, let us not forget, produced Corneille,

Euripides, Sartre, and Shakespeare." (Jazz alone has a consistently good press, because of the rationalization that it is the exclusive product of mutilated Negroes, who compose it on their way to the stake.)

I continued up the street to the Boulevard Saint-Michel, where thirst and curiosity prompted me to stop in at a café I had once known. Since I had last seen it, in 1944, the place had been sold and the new boss had called in a decorator to slick it up, turning the pleasant, easygoing, old-style French café into a restaurant de luxe—a cocktail lounge on Route 4 in New Jersey. The bar, too, had gone *discret*, with recorded piano music and tropical fish. The music was schmalz, and consisted of selections whose lyrics are familiar to anybody of an age that I don't like to be reminded of: "I'll see *yew* again"—things like that. The barman served cognac in a *ballon*, a burlesque gesture unless the cognac is highly distinguished, and even then it would be better off in a brandy glass of a size a man can warm in one hand. I remembered a fat French engraver named Gillet, who used to cadge drinks there back in my student days, and I couldn't imagine him at home in a bar such as this. Gillet was a fat man with a scraggly chin beard like Verlaine's, and his fingers were always blue from acid. He wore a *vie de bohème* hat—high crown and wide brim—and there were always buttons off his overcoat, because of the trouble he had in drawing it together across his belly. Gillet would have hated the music—"I'll see *yew* again." Go home, indeed! What need to, if on the Boulevard Saint-Michel they were going to change good cafés into muted mood joints?

When Roach at last succeeded in inching the Chevrolet through the crowds in the Place d'Orléans, we headed for the center of town along the Avenue d'Orléans, through more scenes of frenzied excitement, and came out on the Place Denfert-Rochereau—the first spot we reached in Paris that I distinctly remembered having been in before. It is a big *carrefour*, where six or seven boulevards and avenues converge. There are *brasseries* all around its perimeter, and in the middle of it is the bronze statue of the couchant Lion de Belfort—a memorial to the garrison of the one French fortress that held out through the war of 1870–71. The sculptor was Bartholdi, who did the Statue of Liberty, but the Lion is a better job. Bartholdi was stronger on animals than on goddesses. (If Klagmann, who did the four rolling rivers in the Square Louvois, had got the contract for Liberty, she would attract more attention.) Beneath the Place there is an old quarry full of bones removed from cemeteries that were abandoned in the eighteenth century. Although I didn't know it as we drove past, this catacomb was still serving as the headquarters of Colonel Rol, the Communist who commanded the combined forces of the Resistance during the insurrection of Paris. *Dans le civil*, he was a metal-worker in the Renault automobile plant. I met Rol a couple of weeks later, when the Era of Good Feeling was still on and the Jesuit Père Philippe was speaking from the same platforms as the communist Louis Aragon. It was the period of the Front National, which seems as distant now as Mistinguett's First Communion.

We drove down the Avenue Denfert-Rochereau, an austere thoroughfare lined with religious institutions. Most of them, housed in seventeenth- and eighteenth-century buildings behind high walls, are Catholic—an orphanage, a convent, a home for old priests, and the like. Among them, however, there used to be an American Baptist Center, with a small gymnasium and shower room at the far end of a baroque courtyard. Every Wednesday afternoon during my student days, I would walk to the gymnasium from the less bracing surroundings of the Taverne Soufflet and the d'Harcourt, in the Latin Quarter, where I spent most of my leisure. There I would have a workout and a cold shower. I did not admit these infantile regressions to anyone—not even to Angèle, my favorite companion at the Taverne Soufflet. I would as soon have had her catch me eating puffed rice with sliced bananas. But one Wednesday afternoon when I walked into my hotel, on the Rue de l'Ecole de Médecine, my right eyelid was studded with metal clamps, installed by a doctor after a Mormon missionary and I bumped heads while boxing, and I stood exposed.

The fellows I met at the Center were Americans, most of whom were living in Montparnasse and were writing or trying to learn how to paint. None of them was trying to learn how to write, because in the twenties that was supposed to come naturally, like falling off a bar stool. There were also fellows, among them the missionary, who were studying at the Sorbonne. Most of these were taking the packaged course in French culture and living with nice French families. Basketball and handball were the popular games, but I usually found somebody to box with. After a workout, several of us would walk down the Avenue Denfert-Rochereau, which at its tip merges with the Avenue de l'Observatoire, as far as the Closerie des Lilas, where we would stop in for a vermouth cassis together. Then my friends would head for the Dôme or the Sélect, on the Boulevard du Montparnasse, while I would start back for the Soufflet or the d'Harcourt, on the Boulevard Saint-Michel. I was priggishly determined not to waste my year abroad on fellow-Americans; Wednesday afternoons were simply exceptions.

The Closerie stood by itself, with gravel and trees all around it; quiet and cool, it had a touch of class. The noisy geniuses you heard at the Vikings and the Sélect and the Dôme considered it *vieux jeu* and did not frequent it. The place had a brisk, knowing barman named Dominique, a Catalan from Barcelona, who would have been a natural for a good speakeasy in the States. Sometimes, after my friends had left, I switched to hard liquor and stayed on talking to him. These interludes were part of my small weekly concession to a nostalgia I wouldn't have avowed. The most memorable customer was a Canadian painter named John Russell, who always wore a bowler hat and a Chesterfield with velvet lapels. He wasn't imitating the Edwardians; he was one. Russell was in his late forties and not yet decrepit, and this reassured me. I was twenty-two, and worried, because I associated thirty with dotage. Looking at Russell, I could see that I might still have a couple of years left to work in. Russell had white hair, which he wore rather long in back, black eyebrows, a red face, and a profile like that of an old tragedian. He was critical and imperious, and also often abusive, because he was a solvent portrait painter, producing pictures that brought high prices but that his avant-garde colleagues contemptuously referred to as "good likenesses." (They were mostly portraits of wealthy Anglo-Canadians, dressed as Masters of Foxhounds, and their

wives, to whom Russell gave a telling hint of family resemblance to Queen Mary.)

"They all sneer at Bouguereau, but I'd like to see one of
them paint a hand with five fingernails and polish on them,"
Russell used to say. "They" meant the avant-garde. Once, in
1927, I went to the Salon de Printemps to see a picture he was
showing. It was of a smart nude lying on a sofa in front of a
full-length mirror, which was so convincing that I caught myself looking into it to straighten my tie. In front of the sofa
stood a coffee table inlaid with mother-of-pearl, and on the
table was a cloisonné vase containing four flowers, all different.
It must have taken a lot of doing. *Ce vieux Russell* was often
accompanied by a tail of French painters, more advanced but
less pecunious, for whom he bought drinks. They didn't
needle him, as the young Americans did—partly, no doubt,
because they spoke no English and Russell's French was limited, but also, I suspect, because they respected his bag of
tricks, even if they didn't like them. And maybe they did like
them. Then, too, he was paying for the drinks.

In a way, I was aware of all these matters as Roach turned
the Chevrolet down the Avenue Denfert-Rochereau,
although, naturally, I said nothing about them. It would have
been hard to explain why I should recall such trivia on the day
of the Liberation of Paris, which was History with a capital
"H." But they increased my excitement. We stopped for a couple of minutes at the corner of the Avenue de l'Observatoire
and the Boulevard du Montparnasse, to consider our further
course. Before leaving Bagnoles-de-l'Orne, Roach and I had
been told that the press would set up shop in the Hôtel Scribe,
on the Boulevard des Capucines, near the Opéra. Roach
wanted to report there as soon as he could, but we had no
means of knowing whether the way was clear. I thought our
best bet would be to turn west on the Boulevard du Montparnasse, which we could see was peaceful, and then head
down toward the Seine when we were approximately opposite
where we wanted to go. During our halt, while Roach consulted a street map, I noted with satisfaction that the Closerie
was intact, although black-out blinds had been drawn behind

its plate-glass windows. Then we started up the Boulevard, past the Nègre de Toulouse, the Jockey, the Sélect, the Dôme, and the other landmarks of the prohibition emigration, all of them closed. It was a quarter I had never fancied, but I felt a certain emotion about it just the same. Any liberated place acquires a special charm, like a kitten recovered from the town dump. In the immediate neighborhood of the Gare Montparnasse, with Daydaybay vehicles parked in the adjacent streets, things were just as festive as they had been in the Place d'Orléans. And so, after turning back from our attempt to get through the Rue de Rennes with the help of the F.F.I. boys, we returned to the train shed in time for the surrender.

We were, it developed, in plenty of time, for Leclerc, ordinarily so impatient, was holding up the ceremony until General de Gaulle could get there. With the approach of the Daydaybay, one of the division's intelligence officers told me, the German garrison had given up trying to reduce Resistance strong points within the city and had been besieged in its turn, in perhaps a dozen redoubts of its own. (Von Choltitz had a rather better chance of being shot if he retreated than if he didn't, for Hitler, it was later disclosed, had directed him to fight to the last man. I think if I had known then what lay behind that troubled soup plate of a German face, I would have felt a little sorry for Von.) Leclerc had ordered an attack on the Meurice, on the Rue de Rivoli, in order to bring in von Choltitz, the only man in Paris who was qualified to sign the surrender. When the German Military Governor felt himself safely surrounded by French regulars, he had come out. All the Germans had a deadly fear of being lynched by the F.F.I.

Lieutenant General Leonard T. Gerow, of V Corps, was at the Gare. He was a tall, dry man, who might have thought that since the Daydaybay was part of his corps, *he* was the liberator of Paris, but Leclerc kept him in his place. (Paris, like practically every other town in France, has since named a street for Leclerc; it is the former Avenue d'Orléans, along which Roach drove us on the great day. The Avenue du Général Leclerc is wide but not chic, being bordered by cheap department stores and cut-rate retail markets.) Finally, de Gaulle arrived—stiff-backed, as usual, but very nearly smiling—and the surrender was signed. De Gaulle wore the expression of a poker player hauling in his first pot of the evening and trying not to show how good he feels. It was politically important, from the point of view of the Free French, that de Gaulle be on hand, because up to the last minute they were afraid that our State Department would produce somebody like Camille Chautemps or Georges Bonnet to usurp his place. They couldn't forget Darlan.

While we and von Choltitz were still waiting for de Gaulle, two more American correspondents arrived—Paul Gallico, who was writing for a monthly magazine, and Harold Denny, of *The New York Times*. They had been traveling together in a jeep, with a soldier driver, and had run into the same sort of perplexity as we had in trying to get across town. When Denny spotted the Germans, he reacted like a redbone hound to a tree full of raccoons. He saw that he had a scoop of historic dimensions, since he was the only correspondent for a daily publication present. Denny, who was one of the best reporters I have known, broke out his typewriter and went to work. The rattle of the keys, echoing under the train shed, cheered him on. He lit a cigarette, ran a hand through his hair, filled a sheet of paper, and instinctively yelled "Boy!" Only there was no boy to pick up his copy. It was then that he realized he was faced with the problem of how to get his copy from the Gare Montparnasse to a censor and a wire.

We all knew that if an American communications center had been set up in Paris, it would be at the Hôtel Scribe. The obvious person to take Denny's copy there was Roach, who, as a public-relations officer, could expedite its transmission, and who, moreover, felt obligated to get there at the earliest possible moment. I therefore agreed to give up my de luxe transportation—it was but justice—and to pig in with Gallico and Denny in their jeep. After the German surrender party had been marched away, I went downstairs and got my typewriter, sleeping bag, and musette bag out of the Chevrolet. Despite the extreme revulsion I experience at the mere thought of K rations, I took a couple of those waxed-cardboard cartons charged with soapy cheese, vegetarian bouillon powder, and similar delicacies from the supply that the lordly Negro had thrown into our car a couple of days before. Since arriving in Paris, we hadn't seen anybody who looked hungry enough to want them, and now that I figured my days in the field were about over, I was resolved never again to allow myself to get that hungry, either. Still, I thought it prudent to be prepared for the worst.

That was the end of our small Bagnoles-Chartres-Paris task force. Morrison shouldered his musette bag and went out into the streets to collect paragraphs for *Stars & Stripes*, and after Denny finished his story, Roach, with a Daydaybay soldier for a guide, left us to take it to the Scribe. There, we learned later, he found a press center installed and functioning normally—so normally that it managed to lose poor Denny's exclusive eye-witness story of the surrender. At any rate, the *Times* never received it. When the first copies of the August 26 issue of the *Times* reached Paris, flown in by the Air Transport Command, we were dismayed to see that the big story about the surrender was an Associated Press dispatch that read as if it had been assembled in London. It was the worst luck I have heard of a reporter's having. Denny died a little less than a year later. He was fifty-six—older than almost any other American correspondent in France, although he looked younger than the majority of us—and his heart failed him. I've sometimes wondered how much the lost scoop had to do with it.

Since we had no idea that the story was going to be lost, Denny and Gallico and I were in high good humor as we left the Gare. But it was getting on toward six, and they said they were tired, as I certainly was, so we decided to seek a lodging for the night. From the moment of our appearance in the station, we had been attended by a bevy of F.F.I. lads wearing tricolor brassards and strung with bandoleers and lethal weapons, mostly captured Wehrmacht machine pistols. They told us they belonged to the Service de Presse des Forces Françaises du Quatorzième Arrondissement. I asked a fellow who seemed to be their commanding officer if he could find us a billet. He replied that a hotel had been set aside for the accommodation of *La presse étrangère*—the Hôtel Néron, near the statue of the Lion de Belfort. It was an appetizingly wicked name; a good orgy would be appropriate on such a night.

Our progress to the Néron was a dashing cortege—a cross between an Arab fantasia and the reception accorded Adah Isaacs Menken by the silver miners of the Big Bonanza. Six or eight F.F.I.s, each carrying at least three firearms, hung on to the sides of our jeep, which was preceded by one captured Volkswagen and followed by another, both loaded to the Plimsoll with effervescent firepower. The Néron, despite its name, turned out to have nothing *louche* about it. Standing on a side street off the Avenue d'Orléans and a couple of hundred yards beyond the Lion, it was neither dilapidated nor elaborate. The Fourteenth Arrondissement is a neighborhood of low-salaried white-collar people, mostly civil servants, and the chief peacetime clientele of the Néron, I thought, must have consisted of old bachelor or widower postal clerks and railway conductors. Now the hotel was a combination of barracks and arsenal, with young men in berets, shirt sleeves, and pistol belts bounding up the stairs three at a time, for no apparent reason, and then dashing down again. The soldiers of the night were strutting openly at last, and enjoying it.

Two ecstatically beaming elderly women were standing in the office downstairs when we arrived at the Néron—the *patronne* and her maid, delighted to be in the midst of such excitement. The hotel, I noticed on the way to my quarters, had a bathroom, and I was soon gratified to discover that the taps worked, although they both ran cold. In all the other French cities I had been through, the Germans had succeeded in blowing the water systems before leaving. The best I had been able to manage at Bagnoles was a swim in a spinachy pond.

I had an invigorating soak, got dressed, putting on a fresh pair of socks—the only change in attire my musette-bag wardrobe permitted—and sallied out into the dusky streets, home again. It was not quite dark, and the *bistros* on either side of the Avenue d'Orléans and on the Place Denfert-Rochereau were full of men—some with F.F.I. brassards and some without —*discutant le coup*, as after a football match. I went into a bar and had one of those sticky red *apéritifs* that partly refute the notion that the French have sensitive palates. It cost a hundred francs, which was two dollars then. I was getting hungry, and looked for a place to eat, but I saw none that was open; the reports of a food shortage in Paris were evidently well founded, and I began to think grimly about my K rations. Walking along the Avenue Denfert-Rochereau, I searched for the plaque that had marked the gatepost of the American Baptist Center, and, unable to find it, presumed that the Germans had closed my old health resort during the Occupation.

By now, it was beginning to be really dark. From the direction of the Luxembourg came the sound of steady firing—small-cannon as well as machine-gun; apparently, the Germans inside hadn't listened to the officers sent out from Leclerc's headquarters. I mention this firing because it seemed part of the summer night, like thunder. There was no menace in the sound, and if it were not for plaques on the walls of houses in various parts of Paris that now commemorate the deaths of Frenchmen on that very night, I would find it difficult to believe there was real combat on the evening of my stroll. I walked on down as far as the Closerie des Lilas and crossed the Boulevard du Montparnasse to have a better look at the place. The French were never as thorough as the English were about blackouts, and I could soon see, through chinks in the curtain of a window near the side door of the café, that there was a blue light—a *veilleuse*, or night lamp—burning within. I banged on the door and shouted, in French, "It's an old customer! An old customer! An American! An American!" I thought that would interest whoever was inside, and it did, but not immediately. After I had shouted it a dozen times, the door opened a crack and a barman I had never seen looked out. I said to him, "Dominique? Where is Dominique?" I couldn't remember the boss's name. For all I knew, Dominique might have been gone seventeen years, for I hadn't visited the Closerie since 1927. In that case, the current barman might never even have heard of him. But I was in luck. Dominique had not left until 1940, when the Germans came in, and this barman had known him. "Dominique went back to Barcelona in 1940," he said. At least, I had established myself as a former customer.

I could hear another man behind the fellow at the door, talking to him, and now a new face, which I recognized as that of the *patron*, appeared at the crack. "I used to come here with Russell," I said. "*La vieux Russell*. With the *chapeau melon*. Is he still in Paris?"

The patron's face split in a grin. "*Ah, sacré Russell!*" he said. "He went to England. Come in." He opened the door.

There were no customers in the Closerie—only the *patron*,

his wife, the barman, and a waitress. Once inside, I talked to them of Russell, of the celebration at this very bar of Lindbergh's safe arrival in Paris in 1927, of the perils of D Day and the hardships of the road, and of the outstanding character of General Leclerc. It took. The four of them were preparing to dine at one of the deserted tables, and as the waitress brought in a great terrine of potato soup, the boss asked me if I had eaten. I magnanimously consented to join them, even though his wife warned that there would be nothing to follow but an omelet and a salad; the *patronne*, it was plain, had never sampled a K ration.

The firing around the Luxembourg continued. "Apparently they're still holding out," I said.

"A lot of good it will do them," the *patron* observed, with relish. "A shot of red?" He filled my glass with Bordeaux, and, as he did so, his name came back to me—M. Colin. "Do you remember how Russell used to talk about Bouguereau?" he asked. "How he was all for Bouguereau?"

"*Sacré vieux Russell!*" I said. Never had an acquaintance served me better. The omelet was as big as an eiderdown.

"The Americans will be back soon," I said. "It will be like old times here at the Closerie."

"But you are the first," M. Colin said, in a voice that had taken on a tone of significance. Up to that point, our talk had been friendly but casual, with nothing about it to suggest that we were reunited on a historic occasion. Now, however, M. Colin said, "Monsieur, at the moment of the débâcle, when the future looked blackest, I set aside two bottles against the arrival of the first American customer to return here. One is a bottle of *véritable* pernod and the other contains Black and White. Later, such bottles became impossible to find in Paris. They were beyond price. But I have never opened either. Which bottle will you drink?"

I chose the whisky, because I knew I could drink more of that, and after we had finished the wine and the omelet and the salad, M. Colin put the bottle on the table. It was the only trophy or award I won during the war, and I wouldn't have traded it for the D.S.O. We drank to Russell and Bouguereau and Lafayette and General de Gaulle, and to Angèle, upon whom I had once prevailed to accompany me as far out of the student quarter as the bar of the Closerie, where she immediately became homesick for the Taverne Soufflet, half a mile away. "She said whisky smelled of bedbugs," I recalled sentimentally. "But she admired the stimulating effect it had on me. She has been dead for seventeen years." By that time, my new honors were beginning to overwhelm me.

"A chagrin of love never forgets itself," the waitress said. "You must not make bile about it."

When we had imbibed the last of my glory, I took an effusive leave and went out into the dark street. The bars that I had passed earlier were still busy, but I had no inclination to enter. Any further drinking that night would have been a letdown. I made but one brief pause—to roar at the Lion. He wouldn't roar back, and I continued to the Hôtel Néron, which I found as easily as if I had lived there all my life.

Next morning, Denny, Gallico, and I rose early and drove across town to the Scribe. There was not even token firing now; the city was calm but exhausted, like Manhattan on a New Year's morning. I left my gear in a room at the Scribe, but I didn't bother to unpack. I knew where I was going to stay, unless something had happened to it. I went down to the street and walked by the Café de la Paix, where a few of my colleagues were already seated waiting for everybody they knew to pass. I turned down the Avenue de l'Opéra and left on the Rue Saint-Augustin, then right for one block on the Rue Sainte-Anne, and left again, and found myself staring at the navel of La Loire, who hadn't straightened her back since I last saw her. I counted the trees in the Square. There were still fourteen. The pigeons, of course, were gone, but I can't say that at that moment I really missed them.

I exchanged lubricious smiles with La Loire and then walked into the lobby of the Hôtel Louvois, for the first time in four years, two months, and sixteen days. Mlle Yvonne was sitting behind the desk, going over her accounts. "*Bonjour*, Monsieur Liebling," she said, barely looking up. It was as if I had just stepped out for a walk around the fountain.

Chronology

1904 Born Abbott Joseph Liebling on October 8 in New York City, the first child of Joseph Liebling and Anna Slone Liebling. (Father, born 1870 in Austria, immigrated to the United States in 1882. Apprenticed to a furrier on the Lower East Side of Manhattan, he later founded a successful wholesale fur business and invested in real estate. Mother, born 1878, grew up in San Francisco.) Family lives in apartment at Lexington Avenue and East 93rd Street. Both parents are Jewish, but are not religiously observant.

1907 Travels to Europe with his family and sees Kaiser Wilhelm II in Wiesbaden. Visits Paris for the first time (will later have no memory of his stay). Family moves to nine-room apartment at 307 West 79th Street, where they live with a maid and a German governess.

1909 Sister Norma born March 5.

1910 Liebling begins attending P.S. 9.

1911–12 Begins wearing glasses because of near-sightedness. Family spends four weeks at Marienbad (Mariánské Lázně) in Bohemia in the summer of 1911, then goes to Paris, where Liebling visits Napoleon's tomb (by age eight he can recite the names of Napoleon's marshals). Does well in school and becomes an avid reader of newspapers and adventure stories.

1913 Family moves to house in Far Rockaway, Queens. Liebling enters the fourth grade at P.S. 39.

1914 Family spends summer at resort on Lake Hopatcong, New Jersey. Liebling follows the outbreak of World War I and is cheered by the French victory at the Marne.

1916 Closely follows news of the battle of Verdun. Contracts typhoid fever from eating tainted shellfish from Jamaica Bay and has episode of delirium before recovering.

1917 Enters Far Rockaway High School in February.

1918–19   Publishes war stories "The Field of Glory" and "Poor
           Barrett" in the school magazine *Dolphin*.

1920   Enters Dartmouth College in September. Studies English,
           French, Latin, history, and evolution (a science course that
           includes physics and chemistry). Lives off-campus in a
           rooming house and contributes to college humor publi-
           cation *Jack O'Lantern*.

1921   Suspended from college in February for insufficient atten-
           dance at required chapel services. Takes summer school
           classes at McGill University in Montreal, then returns to
           Dartmouth in the fall.

1923   Expelled from Dartmouth in February for failing to
           attend chapel. Works as reporter for *Granite Monthly*,
           magazine published in Concord, New Hampshire, then
           returns to New York. Enters Pulitzer School of Journal-
           ism at Columbia. Signs his work "A. J. Liebling" and goes
           by name "Joe." Begins lifelong friendship with fellow stu-
           dent Hracia (Pan) Paniguian, an Armenian exile. Takes
           elective course in Old French philology.

1924   Travels with family to England, Ireland, and France during
           the summer. Learns police reporting working with Max
           Fischel of the *New York Evening World* on the Lower East
           Side.

1925   Graduates from journalism school. Begins working at *The
           New York Times* as a copyreader in late summer. Lives
           with parents in the Hotel Olcott at 27 West 72nd Street.

1926   Fired by the *Times* in March for putting fictitious names
           in sports stories. Hired as a general assignment reporter
           by the Providence (Rhode Island) *Evening Bulletin* and
           by the *Journal*, its sister morning paper. Accepts $2,000
           from his father to spend a year in Europe; spends most of
           the money before leaving the United States and during a
           week in Paris. Joins his family at Lake Como in late sum-
           mer and receives new stipend of $200 a month. Travels
           through Normandy before starting classes at the Sor-
           bonne in November. Lives at the Hotel Saint-Pierre in
           the 6th arrondissement of Paris. Works on a novel (never
           finished) about a newspaper reporter.

1927–30   Continues studies at the Sorbonne. Sails from Marseilles
           in early fall 1927 and returns to reporting job at the Prov-

idence *Journal*. Meets Ann McGinn (b. 1910), a cashier at a Providence movie theater. Sister Norma marries Harold Stonehill, who becomes a successful stockbroker. (Liebling will enjoy the company of his nephews Arthur, John, and Robert, who are born between 1931 and 1936.) Leaves the *Journal* in 1930 and becomes a free-lance contributor to the *New York World*. Ann McGinn moves to New York to be with him.

1931   After the *World* is bought by the *New York Evening Telegram*, Liebling becomes a reporter for the new *World-Telegram* at a salary of $75 a week. Begins lifelong friendship with Joseph Mitchell when Mitchell becomes a reporter for the *World-Telegram*. Enjoys discussing his favorite writers with Mitchell, including Villon, Rabelais, Defoe, Stendhal, Dickens, George Borrow, and William Cobbett.

1933   Becomes a charter member of the Newspaper Guild.

1934   *They All Sang: From Tony Pastor to Rudy Vallée*, a memoir by music publisher Edward B. Marks written by Liebling, is published by Viking. Liebling marries Ann McGinn on July 28 despite his awareness of her fragile mental health.

1935   Quits job at the *World-Telegram* after being denied a raise. (Liebling wrote more than 300 signed articles for the paper.) Works for the Hearst-owned King Features syndicate for eight weeks before being hired by Harold Ross, editor of *The New Yorker* since its founding in 1925. Begins writing unsigned "Talk of the Town" pieces for the magazine.

1936   Liebling's first signed article for *The New Yorker*, a profile of the evangelist Father Divine co-written with St. Clair McKelway, appears on June 13. Writes humorous fiction pieces for the *World-Telegram* Sunday magazine and works on novel (never finished) "The Girl with the Cauliflower Ear: A Romance." Lives in walk-up apartment at 159 East 33rd Street.

1937   Father dies. Mother goes to live with Norma and her family in Norwalk, Connecticut. Ann is hospitalized and diagnosed as suffering from schizophrenia and schizo-affective disorder.

1938   *Back Where I Came From*, a collection of pieces about New York, published by Sheridan House (some of the material had previously appeared in *The New Yorker* and the *World-Telegram*). Joseph Mitchell joins the staff of *The New Yorker*.

1939   Becomes friends with writer Philip Hamburger when Hamburger joins the magazine. France and Great Britain declare war on Germany on September 3. Ross assigns Liebling to cover the war from Paris. (Ann is hospitalized at Chestnut Lodge, a private psychiatric hospital in Rockville, Maryland.) Flies from Long Island to Lisbon on a Pan American Clipper (flying boat), then travels by train to Paris, arriving on October 12. Stays at the Hotel Louvois in the 2nd arrondissement. Begins writing "Letter from Paris" for *The New Yorker* while working on profile of General Maurice Gamelin, commander of the French army.

1940   Germany attacks France, Luxembourg, Belgium, and the Netherlands on May 10 and rapidly defeats the Allied armies. Liebling leaves Paris on June 10 and follows the fleeing French government through Orléans and Tours to Bordeaux, then takes a train to Lisbon. French sign armistice with Germany on June 22. Liebling returns to New York on June 25. Rents room in East 10th Street home of his childhood friend Fred Schwed. Sees Ann, who is now living in Providence. Writes profile of General George C. Marshall, chief of staff of the U.S. Army, for *The New Yorker*.

1941   Publishes article on propaganda in May *McCall's* and "The Jollity Building," three-part article on small-time New York promoters ("Telephone Booth Indians"), in *The New Yorker*. Flies from Canada to Britain in July onboard an RAF Liberator bomber. Stays at Fleming's Hotel on Half Moon Street in London and writes series of stories about Britain at war for *The New Yorker*. Sails for the United States on December 1 on a Norwegian tanker; learns of the Japanese attack on Pearl Harbor while at sea.

1942   Arrives in New Orleans on January 11. *The Telephone Booth Indian*, a collection of pieces for *The New Yorker*, published by Doubleday, Doran. Liebling returns to England by ship and lands in Liverpool on July 13. Stays in London at Fleming's while writing stories about American troops and aircrews in England. U.S. and British forces

invade Vichy-controlled Morocco and Algeria on November 8. Liebling sails for North Africa on November 9 and
arrives at Mers-el-Kebir, Algeria, on November 21. Visits
Oran before flying to Algiers on December 25.

1943 Stays with U.S. fighter squadrons at Youks-les-Bains, Algeria, and Thélepte, Tunisia, in early January. Travels to
Gafsa in central Tunisia and observes fighting at Sened
Station before returning to Algiers in early February to
work on stories. Accompanies U.S. 1st Infantry Division
as it reoccupies Gafsa and witnesses defeat of German attack at El Guettar on March 23. Travels to Tripoli, Libya,
in early April, then returns later in the month to the
American front in Tunisia. Campaign ends with Axis surrender on May 13. Liebling sails from Casablanca on an
American troopship and arrives in New York on May 31.
Stays at Fifth Avenue Hotel in Greenwich Village while
writing stories about the North African campaign. Returns to Liverpool by ship on November 6.

1944 *The Road Back To Paris*, an account of his war experiences
from 1939 through March 1943, published by Doubleday,
Doran. Liebling flies on a B-26 bombing mission over
France. Writes "Notes from the Kidnap House," three-
part article on the French underground press. Crosses the
Channel on D-Day, June 6, in a large landing craft carrying troops to Omaha Beach. Goes ashore on Omaha on
June 9, then sails back to England. Returns to France on
June 24 and spends the next two months with American
troops in Normandy and Brittany. Drives to Paris on August 25 and witnesses the surrender of the German garrison to the Free French. Stays in Paris for several weeks,
then goes to southeastern France to research story about
a massacre in the village of Comblanchien. Returns to
New York in late December.

1945 Stays at Fifth Avenue Hotel while working on "Quest for
Mollie," two-part article about an American soldier in the
North African campaign. Writes the first of more than 80
"Wayward Press" columns for *The New Yorker*. Works
with Columbia professor Eugene Jay Sheffer on editing
La République du silence, a collection of articles from the
French underground press.

1946 Meets Jean-Paul Sartre and Albert Camus when they visit
New York. Becomes friends with Pierre Guedenet, the

French cultural attaché in New York, and Jean Riboud, a veteran of the French resistance who had survived Buchenwald. Begins affair with Lucille Barr Spectorsky, a 35-year-old model. (Lucille is the former wife of editor A. C. Spectorsky; their daughter Susan was born in 1938.) *La République du silence*, with commentary in English by Liebling, is published by Harcourt, Brace for use in college French courses. Becomes book critic for *Esquire* in November (his reviews appear through January 1948).

1947   *The Republic of Silence*, English-language version translated by Ramon Guthrie, published by Harcourt, Brace. *The Wayward Pressman*, collection of "Wayward Press" columns prefaced by a memoir of Liebling's career as a newspaper reporter, published by Doubleday.

1948   Visits Puerto Rico, the Dominican Republic, and Haiti. Travels to Norway to meet with the crew of the tanker he had sailed on in 1941. Follows hearings on Soviet espionage held by the House Committee on Un-American Activities, including accusations made by Whittaker Chambers against former State Department official Alger Hiss (Liebling and Hiss are friendly acquaintances). Writes articles criticizing the press coverage of the hearings and shares minor background research on Chambers with one of Hiss's attorneys. Sees Camus and François Mauriac during visit to Paris.

1949   Receives $18,000 advance from *Collier's* to write series of articles on Henry Luce, publisher of Time Inc., and Robert McCormick, publisher of the *Chicago Tribune*. *Mink and Red Herring: The Wayward Pressman's Casebook* published by Doubleday. Liebling goes to Reno, Nevada, in July to obtain divorce from Ann (he will continue to send her money for the rest of his life). Marries Lucille Spectorsky in Virginia City, Nevada, on September 2, then moves with her and Susan to 1209 N. Astor Street in Chicago. Relationship with *Collier's* ends in November when the magazine rejects his Luce material for being too critical. Remains in Chicago so Susan can finish her school year there.

1950   Publishes series of "Wayward Press" columns on Robert McCormick as well as stories on gambling in Nevada, the commemoration of Abraham Lincoln in Springfield, Illinois, and the building of engines for the Indianapolis 500.

Returns with Lucille and Susan to apartment at 131 River-side Drive in New York during the summer.

1951   Continues "Wayward Press" column and begins writing about boxing for *The New Yorker*. Harold Ross dies on December 6 and is succeeded by William Shawn as the magazine's editor.

1952   Liebling takes a Caribbean cruise with Lucille, visiting Puerto Rico, St. Kitts, Antigua, St. Lucia, Barbados, St. Vincent, Grenada, and Dutch Guyana (Suriname). *Chicago: The Second City*, based on three articles for *The New Yorker*, published by Alfred A. Knopf. Liebling is made a Chevalier of the Legion of Honor. Reports on the Helsinki Summer Olympics.

1953   Buys house and 30 acres of meadowland in the Springs section of East Hampton, New York. *The Honest Rain-maker: The Life and Times of Colonel John R. Stingo*, a se-ries of pieces about New York racing columnist James A. Macdonald, published by Doubleday. Liebling is diag-nosed as suffering from advanced gout.

1954   Visits Las Vegas and Pyramid Lake, Nevada, in early win-ter. Writes stories about Nevada politics, mustang round-ups, and the Paiute Indians; continues to cover boxing.

1955   Separates from Lucille and begins extended stay in Eu-rope that will qualify him for a large tax deduction. Flies to Glasgow on April 16 and then travels to London. Writes sports stories for the London *Observer*. Suffers from worsening health problems related to his weight (at 5 foot 9 inches, he now weighs almost 250 pounds). Susan Spectorsky enters Radcliffe (Liebling pays for her college education). Liebling visits battlefields in Normandy, then returns to New York in September. Writes two-part arti-cle on Stillman's boxing gym for *Sports Illustrated*. Sails to Le Havre in November. See Camus in Paris (their last meeting).

1956   Spends two weeks at Bircher-Benner clinic in Zurich in unsuccessful attempt to lose weight, then returns to France. *The Sweet Science*, collection of boxing pieces, published by Viking. Visits Tunisia as guest of Jean Riboud and returns to Gafsa and Thélepte. Begins affair in London during the summer with the novelist and short-story writer Jean Stafford (b. 1915). Mother dies in

Norwalk on August 19. Liebling travels to Algeria to report on the ongoing insurrection against French rule. After a ceasefire ends the Suez War on November 6, Liebling goes to Italy and then accompanies U.N. peacekeeping force sent to Egypt to monitor the withdrawal of British, French, and Israeli forces. Arrives in Cairo on November 23, then goes to the U.N. base at Abu Suweir and to the Suez Canal near Ismailia. Leaves Egypt in December and goes to London.

1957   Sees Jean Stafford during two-week visit to New York in January. Returns to the Middle East, arriving in Tel Aviv on February 14. Visits Jerusalem and spends six days in the Gaza Strip shortly before the end of the Israeli occupation; writes two stories for *The New Yorker* about the Palestinian refugees in Gaza. Sails from Haifa to Greece. Applies for Lebanese visa in Athens; is initially denied one for being Jewish, but then is granted a visa after he describes himself as being "without religion." Sails in May to Alexandria and Port Said before landing in Beirut. Visits Tripoli, Baalbek, Sidon, and Tyre in Lebanon and makes a day trip to Damascus. Receives Jordanian visa after describing his religion as "humanitarian." Visits Jordanian sector of Jerusalem in early June, then goes to London, where he is joined by Jean Stafford in September. They return to New York in November and move into separate rooms at the Fifth Avenue Hotel.

1958   *Normandy Revisited* published by Simon & Schuster in the fall.

1959   Reaches divorce settlement with Lucille. Marries Jean Stafford at City Hall in New York on April 3 and moves with her into apartment at 43 Fifth Avenue. Travels to Louisiana in July to cover election campaign of Governor Earl Long, who had recently been released from a mental hospital. Sails to Europe in late August with Jean and Susan Spectorsky (Liebling will pay for her to study Arabic in Cairo for a year). Covers British general election, held on October 8, for *The Observer*, then goes to Greece and the Aegean. Returns to the United States in late November after a Mediterranean cruise. Visits Louisiana in December to cover runoff election in which Long is defeated.

1960   Saddened by death of Albert Camus in a car accident on January 4. Writes in a "Wayward Press" column on May 14: "Freedom of the press is guaranteed only to those who own one." Covers the Rome Olympics for *The New Yorker*.

1961   *The Earl of Louisiana* published by Simon and Schuster. *The Press*, a collection that includes some pieces from *The Wayward Press* and *Mink and Red Herring*, published in paperback by Ballantine Books. Moves with Jean in fall to apartment at 45 West 10th Street. Signs contract for book about the horse-drawn era in New York City.

1962   *The Jollity Building*, collection reprinting material from *The Telephone Booth Indian* and *The Honest Rainmaker*, published in paperback by Ballantine. *Between Meals: An Appetite for Paris* published by Simon and Schuster.

1963   Works on *Mollie and Other War Pieces* and revised edition of *The Press* (both are published by Ballantine in 1964). Visits Algeria for three weeks in May. Travels with Jean to Normandy, the Loire Valley, and Paris in August. Visits London before returning to New York in early September. Writes about the publication of Albert Camus' notebooks for *The New Yorker*. (Review is published on February 8, 1964, the last of Liebling's more than 500 signed and unsigned contributions to the magazine.) Hospitalized with viral pneumonia on December 21. Dies from heart and renal failure at Mount Sinai Hospital in New York City on December 28. After services at the Frank Campbell Funeral Home on the Upper East Side, Liebling is buried in Green River Cemetery in East Hampton, New York. Death by alcohol.

Note on the Texts

This volume collects writing on World War II by A. J. Liebling published between 1939 and 1964. It contains *The Road Back to Paris* (1944), which records his wartime experiences between September 1939 and March 1943; *Mollie and Other War Pieces* (1964), which collects reporting on events from January 1943 through November 1944; a section titled "Uncollected War Journalism" that includes a selection of 26 pieces that appeared in *The New Yorker* between 1939 and 1963, the preface and afterword to *The Republic of Silence* (1947), and a letter published in *The New York Times Book Review* in 1949; and *Normandy Revisited* (1958), which combines Liebling's recollections of events in 1944 with his descriptions of visiting southern England and northeastern France in the mid-1950s.

A. J. Liebling joined the staff of *The New Yorker* in 1935 and began covering World War II for the magazine in October 1939. Liebling prepared *The Road Back to Paris* for publication in the summer and fall of 1943 while he was in New York between overseas assignments. Much of the material he included in the book had previously appeared in *The New Yorker*. In Book I, "The World Knocked Down," Chapter I, "The Shape of War," incorporates part of "Gafsa II—With Dr. Freeman in Africa," which appeared in the magazine on November 13, 1943; Chapter VI, "Vire Revisited," draws on "Letter from France," December 9, 1939; Chapter VII, "Merry Christmas, Horrid New Year," incorporates material from "They Defend Themselves," February 10, 1940; Chapter IX, "Sample Supermen," incorporates material from "Prisoners of War," April 20, 1940; Chapter X, "The Knockdown: Paris Postscript," draws on "Paris Postscript," August 3 and August 10, 1940; Chapter XI, "Who Do Not Fight, but Run Away," incorporates material from "Gloomy Meadow," June 15, 1940, as well as from "Paris Postscript—II," August 10, 1940; Chapter XIII, "Once Down Is No Battle," uses material from "Letter from Lisbon," July 6, 1940. In Book II, "The World on One Knee," Chapter III, "Destination: United Kingdom," appeared under that title in different form on August 30, 1941; Chapter V, "It Showed Nice Instincts," appeared under that title in different form on January 10, 1942; a passage in Chapter IX, "They Are Not Gone" (167.4–169.33 in this volume), appeared under that title on May 23, 1942; Chapter X, "Westbound Tanker," appeared under that title in different form on March 21, March 28, and April 4, 1942. In Book

III, "The World Gets Up," Chapter III, "What Do You Think That Bugle's Blowing For?," used material from "Letter from Oran," December 19, 1942; Chapter IV, "The Hat of M. Murphy," draws on material in "Letter from Algiers," January 16, 1943; Chapter VI, "The Foamy Fields," appeared under that title in different form on March 20, April 3, April 10, and April 17, 1943; Chapter VII, "First Act at Gafsa," draws on material in "Gafsa I—The Eighth Army from Gabes," November 6, 1943, "Gafsa II—With Dr. Freeman in Africa," November 13, 1943, and "Gafsa III—The Chemounis Revisited," November 20, 1943; Chapter VIII, "Gafsa Revisited," uses material that appeared in "Find 'Em, Fix 'Em, and Fight 'Em—II" (the second part of a profile of Major General Terry Allen), May 1, 1943 and in "Gafsa III—The Chemounis Revisited," November 20, 1943; Chapter IX, "Under the Acacias," uses material from "Find 'Em, Fix 'Em, and Fight 'Em—II," May 1, 1943. *The Road Back to Paris* was published by Doubleday, Doran and Co., Inc., on January 21, 1944. This volume prints the text of the 1944 Doubleday, Doran edition, but corrects two errors that appeared in Book III, Chapter IX, where passages that had appeared in *The New Yorker* were set incorrectly. At 303.7–10, "The situation was beginning to get slightly embarrassing for General Allen, and adherents of the no-enemy theory, who had ordered the attack, were starting to speak up" is changed to "The situation was beginning to get slightly embarrassing for General Allen, who had ordered the attack, and adherents of the no-enemy theory were starting to speak up," and at 306.25–26, "The American 105 and 155 mortars" is changed to "The American 105 and 155 howitzers."

In the early 1960s Ballantine Books published two books by Liebling, *The Press* (1961) and *The Jollity Building* (1962), in mass market paperback; both titles were collections of material that had previously appeared in *The New Yorker* and, in some cases, in earlier hardcover books. Liebling then began working on a new collection of war reporting, *Mollie and Other War Pieces.* Although most of the articles he selected for publication in the new collection were written in 1944 and 1945, Liebling also chose to include some of the material from the Tunisian campaign that had appeared in *The Road Back to Paris.* In preparing the collection Liebling wrote a foreword, afterword, and linking passages, added several dedications, supplied footnotes that expanded, clarified, or commented on aspects of the original articles, and in some instances supplied details that had been withheld by wartime censorship. He also changed language that had been softened for publication in *The New Yorker*; for example, at 481.17–18, "If we hadn't fucked up" had appeared in the magazine as

"If we hadn't got bitched up." The articles included in *Mollie and Other War Pieces* appeared in *The New Yorker* as follows: "Quest for Mollie," May 26 and June 2, 1945; "The Foamy Fields," March 20, April 3, April 10, and April 17, 1943; "P.S. on Rozanoff—1954" appeared in different form as "Better as a Kick in Za Pants," May 22, 1954; "I—The Eighth Army from Gabès," November 6, 1943; "II—With Dr. Freeman in Africa," November 13, 1943; "III—The Chemounis Revisited," November 20, 1943; part of "IV—Gafsa Revisited" (425.16–429.16 in this volume) is taken from "Five-Star Schoolmaster—I" (a profile of General Omar Bradley), March 3, 1951; "Run, Run, Run, Run," September 29, 1945; "Notes from the Kidnap House," as "Notes from the Kidnap House—II," April 22, 1944 (the first and third parts of this article are included in the "Uncollected War Journalism" section of this volume at pp. 653–71); "Cross-Channel Trip," July 1, July 8, July 15, 1944; "Letter from France" (dated July 14), July 22, 1944; "Letter from France" (dated July 20), July 29, 1944; "Letter from France" (dated August 4), August 12, 1944; "My Dear Little Louise," August 19, 1944; "Letter from Paris," September 9, 1944; "Day of Victory," August 24, 1946; "The Events at Comblanchien—November 1944," as "The Events at Comblanchien," February 3 and 10, 1945. *Mollie and Other War Pieces* was registered for copyright on January 27, 1964, less than a month after Liebling's death. This volume prints the text of the 1964 Ballantine Books edition.

The 26 pieces from *The New Yorker* presented in the "Uncollected War Journalism" section of this volume appeared in the magazine between October 28, 1939, and October 19, 1963, and were not included by Liebling in either *The Road Back to Paris* or *Mollie and Other War Pieces*; of the pieces, 20 are reports based on his own wartime experiences, five are reviews of books about the war, and one relates the experiences in 1940 of a French friend of Liebling's. "Argument of this Book" and "In Lieu of Epilogue" appeared as the preface and afterword of *The Republic of Silence* (1947), a collection of writings from the French resistance press compiled and edited by Liebling. With assistance from Eugene Jay Sheffer, a professor of French at Columbia University, Liebling began making selections for the volume in the summer of 1945. The collection was first published for use in college French courses by Harcourt, Brace in 1946 as *La République du silence*, with Liebling's editorial commentary appearing in English; the English-language version, *The Republic of Silence*, with the French material translated mainly by Ramon Guthrie, was published by Harcourt, Brace in 1947. Liebling's letter to *The New York Times Book Review* of March 13, 1949, was written in response to criticism by J. Donald Adams of a negative review Liebling had published of *From the City, From the Plough*, a war novel by Alexander Baron. The texts of the pieces included in this section are presented in the order of their publication and are taken from the following sources:

Letter from Paris (dated October 22): *The New Yorker*, October 28, 1939.

Letter from Paris (dated January 12): *The New Yorker*, January 20, 1940.

Letter from France (dated February 11): *The New Yorker*, February 17, 1940.

Letter from Paris (dated March 9): *The New Yorker*, March 16, 1940.

Letter from Paris (dated April 21): *The New Yorker*, April 27, 1940.

Eight White Ships of Denmark: *The New Yorker*, January 11, 1941.

Notes on Repatriation: *The New Yorker*, February 22, 1941.

Colonel Britton and the Rhythm: *The New Yorker*, October 4, 1941.

The Lancashire Way: *The New Yorker*, November 22, 1941.

Paddy of the R.A.F.: *The New Yorker*, December 6, 1941.

Guerrilla from Erie, PA.: *The New Yorker*, February 13, 1943.

Letter from Tripoli: *The New Yorker*, May 8, 1943.

Notes from the Kidnap House I: *The New Yorker*, April 15, 1944.

Notes from the Kidnap House III: *The New Yorker*, May 6, 1944.

Letter from France (dated August 10): *The New Yorker*, August 26, 1944.

Letter from Paris (dated September 15): *The New Yorker*, September 23, 1944.

Letter from Paris (dated September 22): *The New Yorker*, September 30, 1944.

Letter from Paris (dated October 26): *The New Yorker*, November 4, 1944.

Colonel Baranoff and The Newspaper "PM": *The New Yorker*, June 23, 1945.

Colonel Grinker and Major Spiegel: *The New Yorker*, May 18, 1946.

The Conscience of Monsieur B: *The New Yorker*, September 21, 1946.

Argument of this Book: *The Republic of Silence*, compiled and edited by A. J. Liebling (New York: Harcourt, Brace and Company, 1947), pp. 3–9.

In Lieu of Epilogue: *The Republic of Silence*, compiled and edited by A. J. Liebling (New York: Harcourt, Brace and Company, 1947), pp. 519–22.

To the Editor: *The New York Times Book Review*, March 13, 1949.

France's Strange Defeat: *The New Yorker*, September 10, 1949.
Pyle Set the Style: *The New Yorker*, September 2, 1950.
The Eternally Kicked-in-the-Pants: *The New Yorker*, March 26, 1955.
Monsieur Flandin's Domaine: *The New Yorker*, September 13, 1958.
The Beginning of the End: *The New Yorker*, October 19, 1963.

In 1955 Liebling began writing "Revisited," a series of articles for *The New Yorker* describing his return visits to places he had written about as a war correspondent in 1944. These articles were published, in revised form and with additional material, as *Normandy Revisited* by Simon and Schuster in 1958. Chapter 1, "Weymouth Pier," appeared in the magazine as "Weymouth: Anniversary on a Pier," July 23, 1955; chapter 2, "The Men in the Water," appeared as "Normandy: Tickety-Boo at Last on Easy Red," September 3, 1955; chapter 3, "Tickety-Boo on Easy Red," appeared as "Normandy: Easy Red Without Matilda," September 17, 1955; chapter 4, "Madame Hamel's Cows," appeared as "Normandy: The Chatelaine of Vouilly," October 15, 1955; chapter 5, "The Communion Card," appeared as "Normandy: The Communion Card," December 10, 1955; chapter 6, "The Hounds with Sad Voices," and chapter 7, "The Farmer's Boy," appeared as "Normandy: In Quest of a Gray Granite House," November 16, 1957; chapter 9, "Days with the Daydaybay," appeared as "France: The Road Back to Paris—I," May 19, 1956; chapter 10, "The Navel of the Loire," appeared as "France: The Road Back to Paris—II," May 26, 1956. *Normandy Revisited* was registered for copyright on September 8, 1958. The text printed in this volume is taken from the 1958 Simon and Schuster edition.

This volume presents the texts of the printings chosen as sources here but does not attempt to reproduce features of their typographic design. The texts are printed without alteration except for the changes previously discussed and for the correction of typographical errors. Spelling, punctuation, and capitalization are often expressive features, and they are not altered, even when inconsistent or irregular. The following is a list of typographical errors corrected, cited by page and line number: 15.30, Orleanaise; 20.20, Gênet; 27.27, Echezeaux; 31.2, Gênet; 33.19, *General*; 33.20, Bedier's; 41.28, St-Louis; 42.35, Rightest; 71.1 them;; 163.16, pretention; 167.15, unform; 242.19, 1942; 262.15, *Parmagnac*; 298.38–39, *indigenes*; 311.9, Gabes; 343.5, went?; 346.22, as as; 356.17, Wolfe; 361.36, New Yorker; 376.36, It; 386.33, know; 417.39, man; 423.19, were; 424.34, Gabés; 444.15, thought,"; 448.37, inellectuals; 449.15, *Libértion*; 461.16, sir"; 471.7, Club*; 490.32, phychological; 497.26, Petainist; 497.32, *gelee*; 498.4, *sous-maitresse*; 508.5, titles; 509.15, St. Lô.,; 509.37, Regence; 513.9, 'clock; 520.10, outoors; 524.29–30, selfrespect; 526.10, ciy; 533.17, little-snipe; 541.11, Cote-d'Or; 564.10, Ravigneaux,; 565.13, maining; 569.16, obvious,; 642.14, [no ¶]; 667.30, Montherland; 742.31, barked; 766.2, 1943; 870.9, DUKWS; 874.24, asked; 879.23, Ça; 900.20, procelain; 906.3, *l'arretait*; 911.28, *paté*; 912.16, *paté*; 917.7, *veritable*; 921.4–5, Chateaubriand; 922.34, architypical; 924.9, Saint-Sever.; 947.12, Geneal; 960.13, d'Orleans.

Notes

In the notes below, the reference numbers denote page and line of this volume (the line count includes headings). No note is made for material included in the eleventh edition of *Merriam-Webster's Collegiate Dictionary*. Quotations from Shakespeare are keyed to *The Riverside Shakespeare*, ed. G. Blakemore Evans (Boston: Houghton Mifflin, 1974). For further biographical background, see Raymond Sokolov, *Wayward Reporter: The Life of A. J. Liebling* (New York: Harper and Row, 1980).

THE ROAD BACK TO PARIS

2.2   H. S.]   Herman Salen, "Henri" in *The Road Back to Paris*.

5.20–22   "Rolling Umpty-seventh . . . had first met]   Liebling had written a story about the unit, "The Rolling Umpty-Seventh," that appeared in *The New Yorker*, December 5 and December 12, 1942.

5.27   second day of an offensive]   The offensive began on January 31, 1943.

5.30–32   Rommel's army . . . Von Arnim]   Panzer Army Africa, commanded by Field Marshal Erwin Rommel (1891–1944), retreated across Libya following its defeat in western Egypt by the British Eighth Army at the battle of El Alamein, October 23–November 4, 1942. Colonel General Hans-Jürgen von Arnim (1889–1962) commanded the Fifth Panzer Army, which was formed in December 1942 to defend Tunisia against the Allied forces that landed in Morocco and Algeria on November 8, 1942. Both armies were placed under the newly created Army Group Africa, commanded by Rommel, in late February 1943. After Rommel left Tunisia on March 9, von Arnim commanded the army group until his surrender on May 12, 1943.

7.1   Statler people]   The Statler hotel chain.

7.14   Stukas . . . P-40's]   "Stuka," from *Sturzkampfflugzeug* ("dive bomber"), was the common name for the Junkers 87, a single-engine dive bomber with a two-man crew; the Junkers 87D used in Tunisia had a maximum speed of 255 mph, was armed with four machine guns, and could carry up to 3,500 pounds of bombs. The P-40 was a single-engine, single-seat U.S. fighter armed with six machine guns; the P-40F, used in Tunisia in early 1943, had a maximum speed of 364 mph.

7.40   Boots Norgaard]   Noland Norgaard (1905–1993).

8.37   105's]   A field artillery gun that fired a 105mm shell weighing 33 pounds, with a maximum range of almost seven miles (12,200 yards).

13.8   the Cliveden set]   A term for the social circle of politicians and journalists who gathered at Cliveden, the Buckinghamshire country estate of Lord and Lady Astor. Its members favored the appeasement of Nazi Germany.

13.26   the Munich settlement]   Hitler, Mussolini, Édouard Daladier, and Neville Chamberlain met at Munich, September 29–30, 1938, and agreed that Czechoslovakia would cede the Sudetenland to Germany. After Germany occupied the remainder of Czechoslovakia on March 15, 1939, the British and French governments committed themselves to defending Poland against German aggression.

13.33   Wolcott Gibbs]   Gibbs (1902–1958) was a staff writer and drama critic for *The New Yorker*.

15.33   Douaumont]   A key French fort near Verdun, captured by the Germans on February 25, 1916, and recaptured by the French on October 24, 1916.

15.36   *apero*]   Apertif.

16.19–20   *Les Cloches de Corneville*]   Operetta (1877) by Robert Planquette (1848–1903), with a libretto by Louis Clairville and Charles Gabet.

18.30–31   Chatterton . . . Ossian]   Thomas Chatterton (1752–1770) wrote poems that he attributed to Thomas Rowley, a fictitious 15th-century monk. James Macpherson (1736–1796) combined existing Gaelic poems with his own work to create epics he attributed to Ossian, a fictitious ancient Scottish bard.

19.27   Banse and Goebbels]   Ewald Banse, a geographer and advocate of Pan-Germanic expansionism, published *Raum und Volk im Weltkriegen* in 1932 and was appointed professor of military science at the Brunswick Technological Institute after the Nazis came to power in 1933. His book was translated as *Germany Prepares for War: A Nazi Theory of "National Defense"* in 1934 and reissued in the United States in 1941. Joseph Goebbels (1897–1945) was Minister of Public Enlightenment and Propaganda in Nazi Germany, 1933–45.

20.8   Megève]   A French Alpine ski resort.

20.13   Schiaparelli]   Elsa Schiaparelli (1896–1973), Italian-born Paris fashion designer.

20.13   Harold Ross]   Ross (1892–1951) was editor of *The New Yorker* from its founding in 1925 until his death.

20.20   Janet Flanner]   Flanner (1892–1978) began contributing her Paris letters to the magazine in 1925. She returned to Paris in late 1944 and continued writing for *The New Yorker* until 1975.

20.26   St. Clair McKelway]   McKelway (1905–1980) was managing editor
of *The New Yorker*, 1936–39, and a contributor to the magazine from 1933 to
1969. During World War II he served as a public relations officer with the
U.S. Army Air Forces.

20.29   Mollie Panter-Downes]   A novelist and short-story writer, Panter-
Downes (1906–1997) wrote the London letter for the magazine from 1939 to
1984.

20.33   Lady Mendl, Elsa Maxwell]   Elsie de Wolfe (c. 1865–1950), an
American interior decorator and society figure, was known as Lady Mendl
after her marriage in 1926. Elsa Maxwell (1883–1963) was a society hostess.

20.34–35   Mr. and Mrs. Charles Bedeaux]   Charles Bedaux (1886–1944)
was a French-American industrial engineer and efficiency expert who hosted
the wedding of the Duke and Duchess of Windsor in 1937. He was arrested
by the U.S. Army in Algiers in 1943 and was returned to the United States to
face charges of treason for his economic collaboration with Germany and
Vichy France, but he committed suicide before he could stand trial.

21.25   Joe Mitchell]   Mitchell (1908–1996) was a staff writer for *The New
Yorker* from 1938 until his death and a close friend of Liebling.

21.29   last spring]   Liebling visited the Eighth Army front in Tunisia in
April 1943.

21.30   Leclerc's]   Nom de guerre of Vicomte Jacques-Philippe de Haute-
cloque (1902–1947), a captain in the French army who escaped to England in
1940 and joined the Free French. In early 1941 Leclerc led a column from
Fort Lamy in Chad across the Sahara to Kufra, an oasis in southeastern Libya,
where he captured the Italian garrison, raised the tricolor, and led his officers
in swearing an oath that they would fight until all of France had been liberated. After conducting further operations against the Italians in southern
Libya, Leclerc and his troops joined the Eighth Army early in 1943. Leclerc
later commanded the French 2nd Armored Division in France and Germany,
1944–45.

22.8–9   Richard Harding Davis]   Davis (1864–1916) was an American
journalist who reported on the Cuban insurrection against Spain, the Greco-
Turkish War, the Spanish-American War, the Boer War, the Russo-Japanese
War, and World War I.

25.20   Pétain!]   Philippe Pétain (1856–1951) commanded the defense of
Verdun, February–April 1916, and was the commander of the French armies
on the Western Front, April 1917–November 1918.

26.13–14   *The Last Time I Saw Paris*]   Song (1941) with music by Jerome
Kern (1885–1945) and lyrics by Oscar Hammerstein II (1895–1960).

26.35–36   Rue Chabanais with its meretricious associations]   A brothel that became notorious for its elite clientele was located at 12 Rue de Cha-banais from 1878 to 1946.

27.14–16   Paul Reynaud . . . Council in March]   Reynaud (1878–1966), a member of the moderate-left Radical party, succeeded Daladier as premier (Président du Conseil des Ministres) on March 21, 1940, and served until his resignation on June 16.

27.24   John Purroy Mitchel]   Mitchel (1879–1918) was elected mayor of New York on a fusion ticket in 1913. He was defeated for reelection in 1917 and died the following year in a flying accident while in the Army Air Corps.

27.26–27   Marennes, . . . Grands Echézeaux]   Oysters, a Burgundy white wine, quail, a Burgundy red wine.

28.9   Dunn-Pattison's *Napoleon's Marshals*]   Historical work (1909) by R. P. Dunn-Pattison (1867–1916), a former British army officer and lecturer at Magdalen College, Oxford.

28.13–14   Joffre . . . "Popper."]   Joseph Joffre (1852–1931), popularly known as "Papa Joffre," commanded the French armies on the Western Front from August 1914 to December 1916, when he was replaced by General Robert Nivelle.

28.15   Gouraud]   Henri Gouraud (1867–1946), commander of the French Fourth Army, successfully led American troops during the Second Battle of the Marne in 1918.

28.39   Westbrook Pegler]   Pegler (1894–1969) was a columnist for the Chicago *Tribune*, 1925–33, the Scripps syndicate, 1933–44, and the King Features syndicate, 1944–62. He was known for his right-wing views and vehement criticism of President Roosevelt, Eleanor Roosevelt, and other public figures.

29.6   *New Yorker* profile of General Gamelin]   The profile, "Generalissimo," appeared on May 11 and May 18, 1940.

29.16   Sam Langford]   Langford (1883–1956), a black heavyweight boxer born in Nova Scotia, fought professionally from 1898 to 1926.

29.27   Weygand]   General Maxime Weygand (1867–1965) was recalled from his command in Syria on May 17, 1940, and replaced Gamelin as commander of the French army on May 20. He served as minister of defense in the Pétain government, June–September 1940, and as delegate-general to North Africa, September 1940–November 1941. Weygand was arrested and deported to Germany after the Allied landings in North Africa in November 1942.

30.17   *promotion* at St. Cyr]   Class at the French military academy.

30.18   Dreyfus case]   Captain Alfred Dreyfus (1859–1935), a Jewish artillery officer, was arrested on false charges of espionage on October 15, 1894, and convicted at a secret trial on December 22. He was fully exonerated in 1906.

30.38–39   William C. Bullitt] Bullitt (1891–1967) served as the first American ambassador to the Soviet Union, 1933–36, and as ambassador to France, 1936–40.

31.9–10   Reynaud . . . his prisons] Reynaud was imprisoned by Vichy in September 1940 and deported to a concentration camp in Germany in 1943.

31.17–19   Horace A. Fuller . . . Pacific] Fuller (1886–1966) commanded the 41st Infantry Division in New Guinea, Hollandia, and Biak, 1943–44. He resigned his command during the battle on Biak in June 1944 after being relieved as commander of the U.S. task force on the island.

33.20   Joseph Bédier's] Bédier (1864–1938) was a prominent French medievalist and literary scholar.

34.9   George] Joseph Georges (1875–1951) commanded the French armies along the frontiers with Germany, Luxembourg, and Belgium.

36.30–31   fortification . . . north of his line.] The Maginot Line of fortifications did not extend along the frontier with Belgium.

36.35–37   Allies . . . the Low Countries] British and French troops began moving into planned defensive positions in Belgium and southern Holland on May 10, 1940, in response to the German invasion of the Low Countries.

37.18   thirty-eight Communist . . . jail] The Daladier government dissolved the French Communist party on September 26, 1939, and began arresting Communist deputies in October.

39.3   André Chamson, in his journal] *Quatre mois, carnet d'un officier de liaison* (1940), by the novelist André Chamson (1900–1983).

39.22   General Robert-Georges Nivelle] Nivelle (1856–1924) succeeded Pétain as the commander of the army defending Verdun in April 1916 and replaced Joffre as commander-in-chief on the Western Front in December. He was dismissed in April 1917 and replaced by Pétain.

40.10–13   *"Hitler n'en . . . p'tit bout!"*] "Hitler doesn't have one, / At all, at all! / Hitler doesn't have one, / Not even a tiny little tip!"

40.23–24   French still held . . . Saar] The French began their advance into the Saar on September 7, halted on September 11, and withdrew to the Maginot Line on October 4.

40.33   *mousseux*] Sparkling wine.

41.22   H. R. Knickerbocker] Knickerbocker (1898–1949) joined the Chicago *Sun* in 1941. He had been expelled from Germany in 1933 for his anti-Nazi reporting and warned of the danger of Hitler in *Will War Come to Europe?* (1934).

41.32–33   Major General Terry Allen] Allen (1888–1969) commanded the 1st Infantry Division in Algeria, Tunisia, and Sicily, November 1942–August 1943. He was relieved of his command at the end of the Sicilian campaign by Omar Bradley, who believed Allen had allowed discipline in the 1st Division to become too lax. Allen returned to the United States and took charge of the training of the new 104th Infantry Division, which he then successfully led in Holland and Germany, October 1944–May 1945.

41.34–35   Clark Howell Woodward] Woodward (1877–1968), the commander of the Brooklyn Navy Yard, 1937–41, made numerous speeches urging the expansion of the U.S. Navy.

41.40   Edgar Ansel Mowrer] Mowrer (1892–1977) won the Pulitzer Prize in 1933 for his reporting from Germany, collected in *Germany Puts the Clock Back* (1933). After being expelled by the Nazis, Mowrer reported from China and then headed the Paris bureau of the *Chicago Daily News*.

42.1–2   Jean Fontenoy] Fontenoy (1899–1945) became an active member of two fascist collaborationist organizations, the Mouvement social révolutionnaire (MSR) and the Rassamblement national populaire (RNP). He committed suicide in Berlin in late April 1945 while serving with the French Waffen (Armed) SS.

42.5   Abetz] Otto Abetz (1903–1958), an associate of the German foreign minister Joachim von Ribbentrop, had worked during the 1930s to promote pro-German sentiment in France. Abetz was expelled from France in July 1939, but returned to serve as German ambassador to France, 1940–44. He was sentenced to 20 years imprisonment for war crimes by a French court in 1949 but was released in 1954.

42.13   found in the Seine with his throat cut.] A false report, circulated in 1941 by British covert propaganda organizations.

42.31–32   Maurrases and Lavals] Charles Maurras (1868–1952) was a leader of the reactionary, anti-Semitic political movement L'Action Française and an editor of its daily newspaper from 1908 to 1944. He was sentenced to life imprisonment for treason in 1945, but was released in 1952 shortly before his death. Pierre Laval (1883–1945) served as premier and foreign minister of France, January 1931–February 1932, as foreign minister, October 1934–January 1936, and as premier, June 1935–January 1936. He was the premier of the Vichy government, July–December 1940 and from April 1942 until September 1944, when he fled to Germany. Laval was convicted of treason and shot in October 1945.

42.33   *Gringoire*] A right-wing, anti-Semitic weekly magazine.

43.34   Galeries Lafayette] A Paris department store.

43.36   three Fratellinis]   The brothers Paul (1877–1940), François (1879–1951), and Albert (1886–1961) Fratellini.

43.39   liberty horses]   Riderless horses trained to perform in response to visual and spoken commands.

44.14   Vincent Sheean]   Sheean (1899–1975) was a foreign correspondent whose memoir *Personal History* (1935) became a best seller. During the war he served as an intelligence officer with the U.S. Army Air Forces.

44.32   Vercingetorix]   Gallic chieftain who led an unsuccessful rebellion against Roman rule in 52 BCE.

45.5   Larousse]   The publisher of a series of guidebooks.

45.25–26   repeal of the Neutrality Act]   The act was amended on November 4, 1939, to allow the British and French to purchase American munitions and transport them in their own shipping.

46.30   *vaux*]   Vales.

48.20   *The Man That Corrupted Hadleyburg*]   Story (1899) by Mark Twain.

48.37   Little Entente. Daladier]   The Little Entente was an alliance formed in 1920–21 by Czechoslovakia, Romania, and Yugoslavia, and joined by France during the 1920s through a series of bilateral treaties. Édouard Daladier (1884–1970), a member of the Radical party, was premier of France January–October 1930, briefly in February 1934, and April 1938–March 1940, and was minister of defense in the Reynaud government, March–June 1940.

48.39–40   Le Bourget to the Quai d'Orsay]   From Le Bourget airfield to the French foreign ministry.

49.2   *"Les cons!"*]   "The bastards!"

49.3–4   the February 1934 riots]   Amid public outrage over the Stavisky affair (see note 97.39), members of the Croix de Feu (Cross of Fire), a right-wing paramilitary league, tried to storm the Ministry of the Interior on February 5, 1934. Several right-wing groups called for demonstrations on February 6 in an attempt to bring down the newly formed Daladier government. More than 1,600 police and guards and 600 demonstrators were injured in the rioting, and 16 demonstrators were killed. Daladier resigned on February 7.

51.20   "Lieutenant Sauvageon,"]   A pseudonym for Louis Pavageau; see p. 742.11–12 in this volume.

51.35   Siegfried Line]   Fortification system built along the western German border in 1938–40, known in Germany as the West Wall.

53.31   *La Bohème*]   Opera (1896) by Giacomo Puccini (1858–1924), with a libretto by Luigi Illica and Giuseppe Giacosa.

53.36   campaign around Salonika] The French army at Salonika launched an offensive on September 15, 1918, that forced the Bulgarians to sign an armistice on September 29.

55.27   "The Stars and Stripes Forever."] March (1897) by John Philip Sousa (1854–1932).

55.37   Prince Albert coat] A double-breasted frock coat.

60.7   *divisionnaire*] Division commander.

66.8   Goering] Hermann Göring (1893–1946), a World War I fighter ace, was commander of the Luftwaffe (German air force), 1935–45. He was sentenced to death by the Nuremberg tribunal and committed suicide shortly before his scheduled execution.

66.12   "*Morgenstund,*"] Early bird.

68.18–19   Finnish Army . . . Russian troops.] The Soviet Union invaded Finland on November 30, 1939. After suffering a series of defeats, December 1939–January 1940, the Red Army began a successful offensive in February and forced the Finns to sign an armistice on March 13, 1940, ceding border territory to the U.S.S.R.

70.34–35   Spitfires . . . Curtisses] British Supermarine Spitfire I and Hawker Hurricane I fighters, and French Curtiss Hawk 75 fighters (the Hawk 75 was an export version of the American P-36).

70.35–37   I had never heard . . . through the traffic.] This chapter of *The Road Back to Paris* is based on "Prisoners of War," a story that appeared in *The New Yorker* on April 20, 1940. In the *New Yorker* version, this sentence was followed by the final paragraph of the article: "It was getting late and we had to hurry for our train. The four Germans stepped forward, one after another, and shook our hands with that effusive Teutonic cordiality which is disconcerting enough at any time and which could not have been more out of place than in this prison setting. I went away feeling sorry for those young aviators, who, probably for months and possibly for years, will live idly together in that jail, comparing the length of their beards and longing without reason to fly and fight and wear medals on their chests."

71.28–29   the Battle of Akarit] Fought in Tunisia in April 1943, the battle ended in a British victory.

72.5–7   govermental crisis . . . Churchill to power] Neville Chamberlain's conduct of the war was severely criticized during a debate in the House of Commons on the Norwegian campaign, May 7–8, 1940. Chamberlain resigned on May 10 and was succeeded by Churchill.

72.23   *Confiance!*] Confidence!

73.11   *guerre* in Norway] Norway was invaded by the Germans on April 9, 1940, and British, French, and Polish troops began landing in the country on April 14. The last Allied forces were evacuated on June 8, and the Norwegian government-in-exile ordered its forces in Norway to cease fire on June 9, 1940.

74.12   Albert Canal]   The canal runs from Liège to Antwerp in northern Belgium. It was crossed in strength by the Germans on May 11, 1940.

74.19   "They shall not pass"]   Although often attributed to Pétain, the first recorded use of the phrase is in General Robert Nivelle's order of the day to his troops at Verdun, June 23, 1916: "You will not let them pass!"

74.22–23   Alfred Duff Cooper]   Cooper (1890–1954) served as secretary of state for war, 1935–37, and as First Lord of the Admiralty, 1937–38, resigning his position in protest over the Munich agreement. He served as minister of information in the Churchill government, 1940–41, and as British ambassador to France, 1944–47.

74.25   break-through at Sedan]   The Germans crossed the Meuse River at Sedan on May 13 and broke through the French defensive positions behind the river on May 15. Their panzer (armored) divisions then rapidly advanced across northeastern France with close support from the Luftwaffe and reached the English Channel near Abbeville on May 20, completing encirclement of the British and French armies in Belgium.

78.18   Dornier]   Dornier 17, a twin-engine German light bomber.

81.22   *canaille*]   Scum.

85.40   Paul Faure]   Faure (1878–1960) was a minister in the Popular Front government, 1936–38, and secretary-general of the French Socialist party, the SFIO.

86.1   Georges Bonnet]   Bonnet (1889–1973) was foreign minister, April 1938–September 1939, and minister of justice, September 1939–40.

87.3–4   fortifying the Rhineland . . . Skoda tanks.]   Hitler reoccupied the German Rhineland, an area demilitarized under the 1919 Treaty of Versailles, in March 1936. The Germans attacked France and the Low Countries in May 1940 with 1,478 light and 961 medium tanks; 334 of the medium tanks were Czech. All four of the German tank models in use in 1940 had been introduced into service before the occupation of Czechoslovakia in 1939

88.21   "*discuter the coup.*"]   Talk about the attack.

89.30   Mandel]   Georges Mandel (1885–1944) served as a minister in several governments during the 1930s and was minister of the interior in the Reynaud government, May–June 1940. He strongly opposed seeking an armistice and went to Morocco in June 1940 in an attempt to continue the war from North Africa. Arrested by Vichy, he was imprisoned in France until 1943, when he was sent to Buchenwald. In 1944 the Germans returned Mandel to France, where he was murdered on July 7 by the Vichy militia.

89.38–39   American Volunteer Group to China] President Roosevelt signed an executive order on April 15, 1941, permitting pilots to resign from the U.S. armed forces and volunteer for combat service in China. The American Volunteer Group, later known as the "Flying Tigers," began operations in late December 1941 and became part of the U.S. Army Air Forces in summer 1942.

93.12   "New World Symphony"] Composed in 1893 by Antonín Dvořák (1841–1904).

93.22   Marin de la Meslée] Edmond Marin la Meslée (1912–1945) was credited with 16 confirmed and four probable victories in 1940. He went to Morocco at the time of the armistice and joined the Free French in 1943. Marin la Meslée returned to combat in September 1944, flying ground-attack missions over southern France in an American P-47 fighter-bomber. He was shot down and killed by anti-aircraft fire near Rustenhart in Alsace on February 4, 1945.

94.1–4   Curtisses . . . little faster] The Curtiss Hawk 75A-1 had a maximum speed of 300 mph, while the Hawk 75A-3 had a maximum speed of 311 mph; the Messerschmitt Bf 109E-3 flown by the Luftwaffe during the Battle of France had a maximum speed of 348 mph, but was less maneuverable than the Hawk 75A.

94.11   Heinkel] A twin-engine medium bomber, the Heinkel 111 had a maximum speed of 250 mph and could carry 4,400 pounds of bombs.

94.16–17   English planes . . . machine guns!] The Hurricane I had a maximum speed of 324 mph, and the Spitfire I a maximum speed of 355 mph; each was armed with eight machine guns.

95.21   *tour de main*] Knack.

97.16   defended, like Madrid] The Spanish Loyalists had successfully defended Madrid from November 1936 until the final defeat of the Republic in March 1939.

97.39   Philippe-Egalité's . . . Stavisky's] Louis-Philippe, king of France, 1830–48; Napoleon III, emperor of France, 1852–70; Serge Alexandre Stavisky (1886–1934), a Russian-born French underworld figure who engineered a series of major financial swindles involving the sale of worthless bonds. His disappearance when the fraud was discovered in December 1933 and his death, supposedly from suicide, in January 1934 were alleged to have been arranged by the police in collusion with Premier Camille Chautemps in an attempt to conceal the involvement of the police, politicians, judges, and prominent businessmen in Stavisky's crimes.

98.4   *Tant pis*] Too bad.

98.27   Waverley Root] Root (1903–1982) was a Paris correspondent for several American newspapers, magazines, and news services, 1927–40, and the author of *The Food of France* (1958).

102.18   Anthony J. Drexel Biddle, Jr.] Liebling published a profile of Biddle (1897–1961), "The Omnibus Diplomat," in *The New Yorker* in June 1942 that described his later service in London as the American diplomatic representative to the governments-in-exile of Poland, Belgium, the Netherlands, Norway, Czechoslovakia, Yugoslavia, Greece, and Luxembourg.

102.27   Hélène de Portes] Portes (1902–1940), the widow of an engineer, began an affair with Reynaud in 1938. She was killed in a car accident on June 28, 1940, while driving with Reynaud from Bordeaux to the Riviera.

106.36   Chautemps] Camille Chautemps (1885–1963) was premier of France, February–March 1930, November 1933–January 1934, and June 1937–March 1938. He briefly served in the Vichy government and was sent by Pétain in November 1940 on a diplomatic mission to the United States, where he went into exile.

107.9–10   the Goering works] In 1937 Hermann Göring used his authority as head of the Four-Year Plan for the German economy to found the Hermann Göring Reichswerke, a state-owned industrial complex designed to extract iron from low-grade German ore. The Reichswerke, which was partially funded by private investors, subsequently absorbed a series of German firms as well as companies in Austria and Czechoslovakia, and by September 1939 it had become the largest industrial enterprise in Western Europe.

107.38–39   Pétain . . . terms.] Pétain became premier on June 17 and immediately asked for an armistice, which was signed on June 22. After moving the seat of government to Vichy, Pétain was voted extraordinary powers by the National Assembly, which he used on July 11, 1940, to abolish the Third Republic and make himself Head of the French State. In April 1945 Pétain voluntarily returned to France from Germany and in August he was sentenced to death for treason. His sentence was commuted by de Gaulle, and he died in prison in 1951.

108.31–32   Huntziger] General Charles Huntziger (1880–1941) commanded an army and an army group during the Battle of France and signed the armistice with Germany. He served as the Vichy minister of national defense, September 1940–August 1941, and died in an airplane crash in November 1941 while returning from an inspection trip to North Africa.

111.16   Peninsular War] The war fought in Iberia by Britain, Portugal, and Spain against Napoleonic France between 1808 and 1814.

111.39   Sir James Barrie and Ian Hay] Barrie (1860–1937) wrote *The Admirable Crichton* (1902), *Peter Pan* (1904), *What Every Woman Knows* (1906), and several other plays; Ian Hay (John Hay Beith, 1876–1952) wrote numerous stage comedies, including *Tilly of Bloomsbury* (1919), *The Middle Watch* (1929), and *Housemaster* (1936).

112.1   Duke of Kent]   Prince George, Duke of Kent (1902–1942), a younger brother of George VI, served as an RAF officer during the war. He was killed in August 1942 when his airplane crashed in Scotland.

113.24   Charles Trenet]   A popular French singer and songwriter (1913–2001).

113.32   Jack McAuliffe]   McAuliffe (1866–1937) immigrated to the United States as a child, won the lightweight championship in 1887, and retired in 1897.

115.14–15   profile of General Marshall]   The profile, "Chief of Staff," appeared in *The New Yorker*, October 26, 1940.

115.17   Munitions Buildings]   Built in 1918, the Munitions Buildings at Constitution Avenue and 20th Street N.W. were used by the army and the War Department until the completion of the Pentagon in 1943. They were torn down in 1970.

115.24   *PM*]   A left-wing New York City tabloid newspaper, published 1940–48.

117.32–33   *New Masses*]   A weekly magazine, published 1927–48, devoted to politics, literature, and the arts, and affiliated with the Communist party of the United States.

120.13–14   Flandin . . . last winter]   Liebling met Flandin in Algeria in February 1943. He described their conversation in an article published in *The New Yorker* in 1958; see "Monsieur Flandin's Domaine," pp. 771–89 in this volume.

120.19   André Tardieu's]   Tardieu (1876–1945), a leader of the conservative Democratic Alliance, was premier November 1929–February 1930, March–December 1930, and February–May 1932. He was defeated in the 1932 elections by Édouard Herriot (1872–1957), leader of the moderate-left Radical party.

120.25–26   De la Rocque, Doriot, . . . Chiappe]   François de La Rocque (1885–1946), a retired lieutenant colonel, was the leader of the right-wing paramilitary league Croix de Feu and the founder in 1936 of the right-wing Parti Social Français. Although he initially supported the Vichy regime, La Rocque quarreled with other collaborationist leaders and began supplying information to British intelligence in 1942. He was arrested by the SS in 1943 and deported to Germany. Jacques Doriot (1898–1945), a former Communist, founded the fascist Parti Popular Français in 1936, and in 1941 helped organize the Legion des Volontaires Français contre le Bolchevisme, which fought against the Soviets on the Eastern Front. Doriot was killed in Germany by an Allied strafing attack in February 1945. Jean Chiappe (1898–1940) was the Paris prefect of police, 1927–34; his removal by Daladier in connection with the Stavisky affair helped provoke the riots of February 6, 1934. Chiappe was appointed high commissioner to Syria and Lebanon in November 1940, but was killed when his plane was accidentally shot down near Sardinia during a naval battle between the British and the Italians.

120.30–31   Front Populaire Government]   Coalition of Radicals and Socialists that held power with Communist support, June 1936–April 1938.

121.40   America First]   The Emergency Committee to Defend America First was formed in the summer of 1940 and became the leading isolationist organization in the U.S.

122.1   article . . . *McCall's Magazine*]   "Propaganda," *McCall's Magazine*, May 1941.

122.4–5   debate on the Lend-Lease Bill]   The Lend-Lease bill was introduced in Congress on January 10, 1941, and passed in its final form on March 11, 1941. It authorized the President to lease or lend war matériel to any nation "whose defense the President deems vital to the defense of the United States." The bill was bitterly opposed by isolationists.

122.9   president of America First]   Robert Wood (1879–1969), a retired brigadier general and chairman of Sears, Roebuck and Company, was acting chairman of America First.

122.11   Samuel Seabury]   Seabury (1873–1958), a former state judge, investigated corruption in New York City in the early 1930s.

122.29–30   America Firster's . . . Quaker Oats]   R. Douglas Stuart Jr., one of the founders of America First, was the son of the first vice-president of Quaker Oats.

123.8   Robert Maynard Hutchins]   Hutchins (1899–1977) was president of the University of Chicago, 1929–45.

124.25–26   big, long-range . . . Liberators]   B-24s.

124.29   Prince Bernhard of Lippe]   Bernhard (1911–2004) was the consort of Princess Juliana of the Netherlands.

128.39   *Berlin Diary*]   Best-selling book (1941) by William L. Shirer (1904–1993), an American correspondent for CBS who left Germany in December 1940.

132.29   *Non Angeli Sed Angli*]   "Not Angels, But Angles," derived from "Non Angli, sed Angeli," the remark attributed to the future Pope Gregory (540–604) after seeing children from England in the slave market at Rome.

133.25   a Waverly novel]   *Waverley* was the first in the series of historical novels by Sir Walter Scott (1771–1832) set in the Highlands.

133.27   Crrete.]   The Germans launched their airborne invasion of Crete on May 20, 1941, and the last British troops were evacuated on June 1.

134.26   second volume . . . *I, Claudius*] *Claudius the God*, published in 1934 along with *I, Claudius*, by Robert Graves (1895–1985).

135.16   *succursale*] Branch.

137.9   Lord Roberts'] Lord Roberts (1832–1914), British general famous for his service in the India mutiny (1857–58), the Second Afghan War (1878–1880), and the Boer War (1899–1902).

137.15   *en titre*] By title.

137.36   the Serpentine] A lake in Hyde Park.

139.14   Von Stroheim] The Austrian-born American actor and director Erich von Stroheim played German villains in *Five Graves to Cairo* (1942) and *The North Star* (1943).

140.13   moanin' Lizzies] Air-raid sirens.

142.32   Bovril] A brand of beef extract.

142.36   this particular field] Northolt, in northwest Greater London.

145.10   Caudron 406] The Polish fighter pilots serving with the French in 1940 flew both the Caudron C.714, with a maximum speed of 286 mph, and the Morane-Saulnier MS.406, with a maximum speed of 304 mph.

145.13   Spitfire . . . newest types] The Spitfire V, with a maximum speed of 369 mph.

145.14   cannon] An automatic 20mm cannon.

152.40   the truth-increases, the libel principle] Under English libel law a defendant could argue that an accusation was true, that it was a fair comment regarding a matter of opinion, or that the statement was protected by privilege. The burden of proving the truth of an accusation fell on the defendant, and if the defense of truth failed, the damages awarded the plaintiff would increase.

154.10   *Lettres de Mon Moulin*] Collection of stories and sketches of Provençal life (1868) by Alphonse Daudet (1840–1897).

154.27   Schutzstaffel] Literally, "Protection Detachment"; the SS. Originally founded in 1929 as Hitler's Nazi party bodyguard, by 1939 the SS controlled the German police, the secret state police (Gestapo), and the concentration camps, and had formed its own security service (the SD) and its own military force, known after 1940 as the Waffen (Armed) SS.

155.17–18   the 1941 treaty . . . Soviets] The treaty, signed in London on July 30, provided for Soviet recognition of the Polish government-in-exile, the abrogation of the 1939 German-Soviet agreement partitioning Poland, and the release of the surviving Polish prisoners of war in the Soviet Union, but did not guarantee the 1939 Polish-Soviet border.

155.25   Geneva] The site of the League of Nations.

156.3   Thomas Stow's "Survey,"] *Survey of London* (1598, revised 1603) by John Stow (1525–1605). Thomas Stow was a younger brother of John, and their quarrels are described in detail in the 1908 edition of *Survey of London*.

156.25   Sir Oswald Mosley] Mosley (1896–1980), a former member of both the Conservative and Labour parties, was the founder and leader of the British Union of Fascists, 1932–40.

156.34   Anthony Eden] Eden (1897–1977), a Conservative, served as foreign secretary in the Churchill government, December 1940–July 1945.

160.40–161.2   bases . . . destroyers in return."] In September 1940 the United States sent 50 old destroyers to Britain in return for bases in British territories in the Western Hemisphere.

162.3–4   Catroux . . . Muselier] Georges Catroux (1877–1969) was governor-general of Indochina, 1939–40, before he broke with Vichy and joined the Free French in London in September 1940. Catroux served as the Free French high commissioner in Lebanon and Syria, 1941–43, and as governor-general of Algeria, 1943–44. Muselier (1882–1965) joined de Gaulle in London in June 1940 and commanded the Free French navy, 1940–42.

162.25   Bonnet] Henri Bonnet (1888–1978), who later served as the French ambassador to the United States, 1944–54.

162.33   Darlan] Jean François Darlan (1881–1942) became commander of the French navy in 1939. He served as the premier of the Vichy government from February 1941 until April 1942, when he was replaced by Laval, although he retained his position as commander of the Vichy military. See also notes 224.24 and 228.23.

162.37   Colonel P——] Colonel Passy, nom de guerre of Major André Dewavrin (1911–1998), the founder and chief (1940–43) of the Bureau Central de Renseignments et d'Action, the Free French intelligence service. Dewavrin's enemies in London, who included André Labarthe, editor of *La France Libre*, accused him of having been a member of the Cagoule (the Hood), a secret right-wing terrorist group founded in 1937. Dewavrin denied the charge, but did recruit two former *cagoulards* as early members of the BCRA.

163.3   General Bergeret] Jean Bergeret, a former Vichy air minister.

163.38   expedition to surprise Dakar] The attempt by the British and Free French to seize Dakar from Vichy was repulsed, September 23–25, 1940.

164.22–23   *peut-être*] Perhaps.

166.20   Bofors gun] A 40mm anti-aircraft gun used on both land and sea.

169.38–39   "Give us the tools . . . job,"] From a radio speech by Winston Churchill, February 9, 1941.

170.25–30   *Regnbue* . . . "Rainbow,"] A pseudonym for the *Chr. Th. Boe*, used for security purposes. In "Reunion with a Tanker," published in *The New Yorker*, January 22, January 29, and February 5, 1949, Liebling wrote that he chose the name *Regnbue* "because she had been a lucky ship for me." The *Chr. Th. Boe* survived the war.

171.25   Petersen] A pseudonym for Jensen. Liebling wrote in 1949: ". . . I feared that if I mentioned the names of the men aboard, their families in Norway might suffer. I do not think that the Gestapo spent much time reading my articles, but at the time it did no harm to be careful." Liebling then wrote that Jensen had become the captain of the *Beduin*, a 17,500-ton Norwegian tanker.

172.9   Little Eva] A character in *Uncle Tom's Cabin*.

172.33   Harry Larsen] Pseudonym for Harry Olsen. In "Reunion with a Tanker" Liebling wrote that Olsen had later served on a Norwegian cargo ship that carried explosives to Omaha Beach in Normandy on June 15, 1944, and then had been stranded ashore with the U.S. Army after his vessel was wrecked in a storm. Olsen became the steward on a Baltic steamer after the war.

174.7–8   "The founder . . . this ship,"] The portrait was of Christian Theodore Boe, the ship's namesake.

175.13   Elder Dempster] A British shipping company engaged in the West African trade, 1868–1989.

176.24   sleepy little city in southern Norway] Arendal.

176.32   Gjertsen] Pseudonym for Terjesen. Liebling wrote in 1949 that Terjesen had become captain of the *Cleopatra*, another tanker owned by the Boe family.

177.40   Haraldsen] Pseudonym for Hermansen, who became captain of the *Chr. Th. Boe* after the war.

178.32   E-boat] Allied name for small, fast German torpedo boats.

180.10   Hotchkisses] A 47mm Hotchkiss gun that fired three-pound shells.

180.14   Lewis guns] Light machine guns, first used in World War I.

181.29–31   Hakluyt's *Principall* . . . *English Nation*] First published in 1589 by Richard Hakluyt (1552–1616), and in an expanded three-volume edition in 1598–1600.

186.5   British machine gunners] Harry Olsen, the chief steward, told Liebling that the two British gunners later deserted the ship in Capetown, South Africa.

187.19   Focke-Wulf Kuriers] Allied name for the Focke-Wulf 200 Kondor, a four-engine long-range bomber and maritime reconnaissance aircraft.

187.38   *flâneur*] Stroller.

188.3–13   The boatswain . . . French wife in Caen] Harry Olsen told Liebling that the boatswain returned to his wife in Dieppe after the war.

189.15–16   Lord Hawhaw] Popular name for William Joyce (1906–1946), a British fascist who made propaganda broadcasts from Germany, 1939–45. He was convicted of treason and hanged in 1946.

189.21   Senator Wheeler] Burton Wheeler (1882–1975), a Democratic senator from Montana, 1923–47, and a leading isolationist.

192.38   Johan Bojer] Bojer (1872–1959) was a novelist whose works included *The Great Hunger* (1916), *The Last of the Vikings* (1921), and *The Emigrants* (1925).

193.3   Kirsten Flagstad] Flagstad (1895–1962), a Wagnerian soprano, left the Metropolitan Opera in New York City in April 1941 and returned to occupied Norway.

194.16–17   John Masefield or Lincoln Colcord] Masefield (1878–1967), poet laureate of Great Britain, 1930–67, spent several years on sailing ships as a young man; Colcord (1883–1947), a short-story writer from Maine, was born and spent much of his childhood on his father's ship.

195.35   Valentine Williams] Williams (1883–1946) was a British writer of mysteries and spy stories, including *The Yellow Streak* (1922), *The Portcullis Room* (1934), and *Dead Man Manor* (1936).

197.12–13   Larsen, the chief engineer . . . Larsen the steward] In both cases Liebling used "Larsen" as a pseudonym for Olsen; the engineer Olsen retired at the end of the war.

197.14   Hendrik Willem van Loon] Van Loon (1882–1944) was a Dutch-American writer and illustrator best known for his children's book *The Story of Mankind* (1921).

197.17   Nilsen . . . ex-whaler] Pseudonym for Dahl; he returned to whaling after the war.

200.9–16   Sandor, . . . now an enemy alien] Britain declared war on Romania and Hungary on December 7, 1941, in response to their participation in the invasion of the Soviet Union. Harry Olsen told Liebling that Sandor was eventually interned by the British in Basra, Iraq.

201.26   Admiral Raeder] Erich Raeder (1876–1960), commander of the German navy from 1935 until his resignation in January 1943.

201.31–33   a battleship . . . the *Bismarck*] HMS *Ramillies*. The German battleship *Bismarck* sailed into the North Atlantic on May 22, 1941, sank the

British battlecruiser *Hood* on May 24, and was sunk by the Royal Navy on May 27; the *Ramillies* did not come into contact with the *Bismarck.*

203.20–21   Admiral Tordenskjold's]   Peter Tordenskjold (1691–1720), Norwegian naval hero who fought the Swedes during the Great Northern War.

204.39   Oxford Movement]   Moral Re-Armament, an international revivalist movement founded in 1938 by the American clergyman Frank Buchman (1878–1961) that evolved out of his earlier Oxford Group.

211.5   A.E.F.]   American Expeditionary Force.

212.25   Flying Fortress bombardment group]   The 97th Bombardment Group, which flew four-engine B-17 heavy bombers.

217.15   fight between Americans and Frenchmen]   Vichy forces in Morocco and Algeria resisted the Allied landings at Casablanca, Oran, and Algiers until a cease-fire was arranged on November 11, 1942.

219.3   Quiz Kids]   An NBC radio program, 1940–53.

222.7–8   Major General Lloyd R. Fredendall]   Fredendall (1884–1963) commanded the task force that landed at Oran on November 8, 1942. He commanded II Corps in Tunisia from January 1943 until March 6, when he was replaced by George S. Patton.

224.14–15   Légion des Anciens . . . Sturm-Abteilung]   Also known as the Légion Française des Combattants, the Légion des Anciens Combattants was the Vichy veterans organization, established in 1940 with Pétain as its honorary leader. The Sturm-Abteilung (Storm Detachment) was the Nazi party paramilitary organization, founded in 1921.

224.16   Service d'Ordre de la Légion]   A paramilitary organization founded in Nice in 1941 by Joseph Darnand (1897–1945), a former member of L'Action Française and the Croix de Feu; it became a national organization in February 1942.

224.17   Compagnons de France]   A Vichy organization for youths 15 to 20.

224.24   Darlan government]   Admiral Darlan (see note 162.33), the commander of the Vichy military, was visiting his ailing son in Algiers when the Allies landed on November 8, 1942. Darlan agreed on November 13 to abandon Vichy and was made high commissioner of French North Africa.

225.22   General Eisenhower and Robert Murphy]   Eisenhower was the Supreme Allied Commander in North Africa; Murphy (1894–1978), a career diplomat, served as the American diplomatic envoy to French North Africa, 1941–43.

228.23   Darlan's been assassinated."]   Darlan was fatally shot in his office in Algiers on December 24, 1942, by Fernand Bonnier de La Chapelle, a 20-year-old monarchist. Bonnier was tried by a military tribunal and shot on December 26.

229.10   *Pepe le Moko*] Film (1937) directed by Julien Duvivier, starring Jean Gabin.

230.15   1935 film featuring Victor Moore] *Meet the Missus* (1937), directed by Joseph Santley, with Helen Broderick.

232.9   *immeuble*] Mansion.

232.24–25   by-now famous conference] Held October 22–23, 1942, near Cherchel, about 60 miles west of Algiers.

234.17   *confiture*] Jam.

236.25   General Giraud] General Henri Giraud (1879–1949) commanded the Seventh Army during the fighting in Belgium until his capture on May 19, 1940. Giraud escaped from a German fortress in April 1942, made his way to southern France, and was brought by submarine to Gibraltar on November 7. After the Allied landings Giraud became commander of the French forces in North Africa, and on December 26, 1942, he succeeded Darlan as high commissioner. In June 1943 Giraud agreed to share the presidency of the newly formed Comité Français de la Libération Nationale with de Gaulle, but in November de Gaulle became the sole president of the committee.

238.4   Meissonier] French Classicist painter Jean-Louis-Ernest Meissonier (1815–1891).

240.35–36   Marcel Peyrouton] Peyrouton (1888–1983) served as the Vichy minister of the interior, September 1940–February 1941, and as governor-general of Algeria, January–June 1943. He was charged with treason in December 1943 but was eventually acquitted in 1948.

243.31   Coles Phillips] Phillips (1880–1927) was an American illustrator.

244.16   *The Foamy Fields*] "The Foamy Fields" originally appeared in *The New Yorker*, March 20, April 3, April 10, and April 17, 1943. When Liebling prepared it for inclusion in *Mollie and Other War Pieces* (1964), he added a series of footnotes; see pp. 346–88 in this volume for the later version.

244.20   an airfield in a valley] Youks-les-Bains, Algeria, northwest of Tebessa and close to the Tunisian border.

245.15   last night] The night of January 5, 1943.

245.26   P-38] Twin-engine, single-seat fighter with a distinctive twin-boomed airframe. The P-38F used in Tunisia in early 1943 had a maximum speed of 395 mph and was armed with a 20mm cannon and four machine guns.

245.30   B-26] A twin-engine medium bomber.

250.26   Larry Adler . . . harmonica] Adler (1914–2001) was an American harmonica virtuoso.

251.22   Junkers 52] A tri-motor transport aircraft.

251.29   belly tank] External fuel tank.

254.18   190's] Focke-Wulf 190, a single-engine, single-seat fighter that entered Luftwaffe service in 1941. The Fw 190A-3 had a maximum speed of 395 mph and was armed with four 20mm cannon and two machine guns.

256.3–4   Sam Spewack . . . Bella] Sam (1899–1971) and Bella (1899–1990) Spewack were collaborative dramatists whose Broadway plays and musicals included *Clear All Wires* (1932), *Boy Meets Girl* (1935), *Leave it to Me!* (1938), and later *Kiss Me, Kate* (1948). Both Spewacks were originally journalists.

256.16   Messerschmitts] The Bf 109G-2, used in Tunisia in early 1943, had a maximum speed of 405 mph and was armed with one 20mm cannon and two machine guns.

257.30   A-20] A twin-engine bomber that could carry 2,000 pounds of bombs.

259.5   *Journey's End*] Play (1929) by R. C. Sherriff (1896–1975) about British officers serving in the trenches in 1918; it was made into a film in 1930.

259.36   Major Philip Cochran] Liebling wrote a profile of Cochran that appeared in *The New Yorker*, February 13, 1943; see "Guerrilla from Erie, Pa.," pp. 636–47 in this volume.

260.27   Lafayette Escadrille] Named after the squadron of American pilots who flew in the French service during World War I.

260.37–38   Colonel Edson D. Raff] Raff (1907–2003) commanded the paratroop battalion that jumped into Algeria on November 8, 1942, in the first American airborne operation of the war. He later commanded the 507th Parachute Infantry Regiment in France, Belgium, and Germany, 1944–45.

261.9   Lieutenant Colonel William Momyer] Momyer (b. 1916) commanded the 33rd Fighter Group, June 1942–October 1943, and was credited with destroying eight enemy aircraft. As a general during the Vietnam War, he commanded the 7th Air Force in South Vietnam, 1966–68.

261.16   Junkers 88] Twin-engine bomber with a maximum speed of 286 mph that could carry 4,000 pounds of bombs.

262.14   *gigot*] Leg of mutton.

269.17   Flushing] Flushing, Queens, the site of the 1939 World's Fair.

272.14   General Koeltz] Louis Koeltz, the commander of the French XIX Corps in Tunisia.

278.21   that Friday] January 15, 1943.

282.24   Macchi C. 202 fighters]   Single-engine, single-seat aircraft with a
top speed of 369 mph and armed with four machine guns.

283.31   B-25 bombers]   Twin-engine medium bombers.

284.18–19   Freddie Bartholomew]   Bartholomew (1924–1992) was a child
actor who starred in films including *David Copperfield* (1935), *Little Lord
Fauntleroy* (1936), and *Captains Courageous* (1937).

285.14–26   Léon went back . . . not killed him]   The end of *The New
Yorker* version of "The Foamy Fields" reads: "Léon is now in a large Algerian city, where he has been assigned to a calmer liaison job. Cochran has been
promoted and decorated and posted to a new command. A lot of very fine
fellows are dead, and I like to think that the best possible use was made of
them." Cochran (1910–1979) became the commander of the 1st Air Commando in India, which used fighters, medium bombers, transports, gliders,
light observation planes, and a few experimental helicopters to support
ground operations behind the Japanese lines in Burma.

286.19   *Beau Geste*]   Novel (1924) by Percival Wren (1875–1941), filmed in
1926 with Ronald Colman and in 1939 with Gary Cooper.

288.9   we had abandoned Gafsa]   The Allies evacuated the town on February 14 and reoccupied it on March 17, 1943.

288.17–18   Douglas Freeman, called *Lee's Lieutenants*]   Douglas Southall
Freeman (1886–1953), *Lee's Lieutenants: A Study in Command* (3 vols., 1942–
44). Freeman was the editor of the *Richmond News Leader* (1915–53) and the
author of *R. E. Lee* (4 vols., 1934–35).

290.40–291.4   In the meanwhile . . . battalions of infantry]   The Germans began a counteroffensive in Tunisia at Sidi bou Zid on February 14,
1943, and captured the Kasserine Pass on February 20. Their advance was
halted on February 22, and Rommel withdrew his troops through the pass
the following day. The U.S. II Corps lost more than 180 tanks and 6,000
men killed, wounded, or captured during the fighting.

292.17   Brigadier General Teddy Roosevelt]   Theodore Roosevelt Jr.
(1887–1944) was the eldest son of President Theodore Roosevelt.

294.12–13   Deerfoot sausage]   A popular brand of pork sausage.

298.31   Parc Monceau]   In the 8th arrondissement of Paris.

300.8   Josef Urban]   Urban (1872–1933) was an Austrian-American architect, designer, and illustrator.

300.19–22   Ralph Ingersoll . . . *The Battle Is the Pay-off*]   Published in
1943. Ingeroll (1900–1985) also wrote *Action on All Fronts* (1942) and *Top Secret* (1946).

301.19   Dave Chasen's]   Chasen was a vaudeville performer who opened a successful restaurant in Beverly Hills in 1937.

304.18   rocket guns]   Bazookas.

304.29   The T.D. outfit]   The tank-destroyer battalion at El Guettar was equipped with half-tracks mounting 75mm guns.

306.25–26   155 howitzers]   The 155mm howitzer fired a 95-pound shell and had a range of over nine miles (16,000 yards).

306.27–28   arching trajectory . . . went to breakfast.]   The description of the battle of El Guettar in *The Road Back to Paris* incorporates material from "Find 'Em, Fix 'Em, and Fight 'Em," a profile of Major General Terry Allen that appeared in *The New Yorker* on April 24 and May 1, 1943. In *The New Yorker* version, Liebling wrote ". . . arching trajectory, but on that day they served." He then continued, in a new paragraph: "Tanks do not rush forward in a mechanized version of the flying wedge, as people at home sometimes imagine. They advance hesitatingly, like diffident fat boys coming across the floor at a party to ask for the next dance, stopping at the slightest excuse, going back, and then coming on again, and always apparently seeking the longest way around. When they have to cross a plain, they postpone the evil moment as long as possible by clinging to the lower slopes of the nearest ridge until some invisible force pushes them unhappily into the open. When they follow a road, they zigzag in a series of tangents to it, crossing it occasionally and staying on it only when there is no other way through difficult country. They are timid creatures. All day long, that day of the stadium battle . . ."

307.13–14   "*The Spartans . . . their hair*,"]   A. E. Housman (1859–1936), "The Oracles" (1922).

MOLLIE AND OTHER WAR PIECES

315.9   *Coriolanus*]   IV, v, 221–32.

315.13   *Hal Boyle*]   Boyle (1911–1974) was a war correspondent for the Associated Press in North Africa, Italy, northwest Europe, and the Pacific, 1942–45. He later reported from Korea and Vietnam and wrote a column for the A.P. until 1973.

318.9   October, 1942]   November 1942.

324.28   G-4]   Staff section for supply and maintenance.

325.8–9   Noguès, . . . Allies]   Auguste Noguès (1876–1971) served as deputy high commissioner for North Africa from December 1942 until June 1943, when the Comité Français de la Libération Nationale, led by de Gaulle and Giraud, took control of French North Africa.

325.11–12   He now commands] "Quest for Mollie" originally appeared in *The New Yorker* on May 26 and June 2, 1945.

325.30   Easter Sunday, which came late in April] On April 25 in 1943.

327.36   Lugers] German semiautomatic pistols.

328.6–8   "*Pris . . . chef*] "Took with me the American soldier Molotov, 23 April, '43, Namin, sergeant."

329.19–20   Strength through Joy] Kraft durche Freude (KdF), Nazi party organization that administered recreational activities for workers.

332.5   Astoria] A neighborhood in Queens, New York.

335.1   S-2] Intelligence officer.

342.5   Karl Warner] In a dispatch printed in the anthology *History in the Writing* (1945), correspondent Jack Belden wrote about his encounter with Company G of the 60th Infantry Regiment in Tunisia in April 1943. Belden described one soldier, "Karl Warriner of East 46th Street, New York," as a "sloppy, profane," long-haired "gremlin" who wore carnations stuck behind his ears and asked to be called "Molotov." Other soldiers from Company G told Belden that "Molotov" served as the regimental scout, did not "give a damn" about enemy fire, and had been twice recommended for the Silver Star.

342.18–344.2   When I walk . . . old-fashioned boys' book.] This passage did not appear in *The New Yorker* version.

346.5–8   tent in southern Tunisia . . . in a Tunisian valley] The airfield was at Youks-les-Bains in Algeria. The text here follows the version printed in *The New Yorker* on March 20, 1943, when the Tunisian campaign was still ongoing; the location of the airfield may have been concealed for security reasons. In the version of "The Foamy Fields" included in *The Road Back to Paris* (1944), Liebling changed the magazine text to "tent in North Africa" and "in a valley"; see p. 244.18–20 in this volume.

390.20–21   A few weeks ago . . . *Times*] The story appeared on April 4, 1954.

390.30–31   PLEVEN AND BRITISH SUPPLY CHIEF] René Pleven (1901–1993), the French defense minister, and Duncan Sandys (1908–1987), the British Minister of Supply.

392.10   Ahmed Ben Bella] Ben Bella (b. 1918) was a leader of the National Liberation Front during the war of independence, 1954–62. He was premier of Algeria, 1962–63, and its president, 1963–65, before being overthrown in a military coup.

393.36   Joseph Kessel] Kessel (1898–1979), an aviator in World War I and a war correspondent in 1939–40, joined a Resistance network in southern

France in 1941. Kessel crossed into Spain at Christmas 1942 and arrived in London in January 1943. While in England he served with the Free French air force, wrote *Army of Shadows* (1943), a novel about the Resistance, and co-wrote the words to the Resistance anthem "Chants des Partisans" (1943) with his friend Marcel Druon.

394.36 Norman Douglas] An English novelist and essayist, Douglas (1868–1952) described his visit to Gafsa in *Fountains in the Sand: Rambles Among the Oases of Tunisia* (1912).

396.1 *Gafsa*] The first three pieces collected in the "Gafsa" chapter of *Mollie and Other War Pieces*, "I—The Eighth Army from Gabès," "II—With Dr. Freeman in Africa," and "III—The Chemounis Revisited," appeared in *The New Yorker* on November 6, November 13, and November 20, 1943, and contain material that also appeared, sometimes in revised form, in *The Road Back to Paris* (1944).

396.6–8 junction . . . last April.] The junction occurred on April 7, 1943.

397.2 *tirailleurs*] Colonial infantry.

403.16 SAS, . . . Special Air Service] Founded in Egypt in July 1941 with an original strength of 66 men, the Special Air Service fought in North Africa (1941–43), Sicily and Italy (1943), and northwest Europe (1944–45); by 1944 the SAS Brigade included two British regiments, two French regiments, and a Belgian squadron.

403.25 Colonel Stirling, . . . Big Dave] Lieutenant Colonel David Stirling (1915–1990), who was six feet five inches tall, was the founder and first commander of the SAS. Stirling escaped from the German patrol in the wadi but was soon captured by Italian troops and spent the remainder of the war in a series of prison camps.

405.16 near Alamein] In western Egypt.

405.24 Long Range Desert Patrol] Long Range Desert Group, a British special forces unit that conducted reconnaissance patrols and raids behind enemy lines in North Africa, 1940–43, and in the Aegean and the Balkans, 1943–45.

407.32–33 The battle was in its second day] The offensive began on January 31, 1943.

415.11–12 General Alexander] General Harold Alexander (1891–1969), the commander of British forces in the Middle East since August 1942, assumed command of the new 18th Army Group on February 19, 1943. He later commanded the 15th Army Group in Sicily and Italy, July 1943–December 1944, and was the supreme Allied commander in the Mediterranean, December 1944–May 1945.

418.24–25 hard fight . . . El Guettar] Liebling described the battle at El Guettar on March 23, 1943, in the final chapter of *The Road Back to Paris*; see pp. 299–308 in this volume.

425.39 Green Hornet,] Nickname for George S. Patton, after the crime-fighting hero of the radio program (1936–52), movie serial (1940–41), and comic strip (1940–49).

427.10–11 Kean . . . Korea] From July 1950 to February 1951.

428.32 The Chairman] Bradley was the Chairman of the Joint Chiefs of Staff, 1949–53.

429.22 the American armored division] The 1st Armored Division, whose commander, Major General Orlando Ward, was relieved in early April 1943.

430.21 *Gasoline Alley* . . . Arthur Krock] *Gasoline Alley* was a comic strip that originally appeared in the *Chicago Tribune* and was syndicated by the Tribune company. Krock (1886–1974) was Washington bureau chief of *The New York Times*, 1932–53, and wrote a column for the paper, 1933–66.

431.6 Hotel Algonquin] Midtown New York hotel known for its literary clientele.

434.23 Robert Briffault] French novelist and social anthropologist (1876–1948) who lived in England after World War I.

434.24–25 Granville Hicks and Ouida] Hicks (1901–1982) was an American Marxist novelist and critic who left the Communist party in 1939; Ouida was the pen name of the English novelist Marie Louise de la Ramée (1839–1908).

440.8 Franchot Tone] American stage and film actor (1905–1968).

441.39 Six mediums] Six medium anti-aircraft guns. The German 37mm anti-aircraft gun could fire a shell weighing 1.4 pounds to an altitude of more than 13,500 feet.

445.39–40 ratfuck!" . . . ratfuck] In the text of "Run, Run, Run, Run" published in *The New Yorker* on September 29, 1945, this word appeared as "ratfest."

447.19 *Notes from the Kidnap House*] This is the second part of a three-part article on the French Resistance press; see pp. 653–71 in this volume for the first and third parts.

448.8–9 Pierre Cot, Vincent Auriol] Cot (1895–1977) was minister of air in several Radical governments, January 1933–February 1934, and in the Popular Front, June 1936–April 1938. He went into exile in the United States before joining the Free French in Algeria in 1943. Auriol (1884–1966) served as minister of finance and then as minister of justice in the Popular Front,

1936–38. He escaped from house arrest in October 1942 and lived underground for a year before making his way to London.

448.20–21   Léon Blum . . . Riom trial]   Léon Blum was arrested by the Vichy government in September 1940 and charged, along with several other leaders of the Third Republic, with failing to adequately prepare France for war. In October 1941 Pétain used his special powers as Head of State to declare Blum, Daladier, Reynaud, and Gamelin guilty of the charges and condemn them to life imprisonment. Despite Pétain's decree, the court began its proceedings at Riom on February 19, 1942. Blum and Daladier mounted a vigorous defense, and the trial was suspended on April 14, 1942. In the spring of 1943 Blum, Daladier, and Gamelin were deported to Germany; they were liberated in 1945.

448.22   Edouard Herriot]   Herriot (1872–1957), a Radical, served as premier in 1924–25, 1926, and 1932, and was president of the chamber of deputies, 1936–40. In September 1942 he publicly criticized Pétain and Laval for their pro-German policies and returned his Legion of Honor after the decoration was awarded to Frenchmen killed fighting with the Germans on the Eastern Front. Herriot was placed under house arrest by Vichy and later deported to Germany.

448.33   Vichy militia]   The Milice Française, founded in January 1943 by Joseph Darnand (see note 224.16), fought the Resistance and helped the SS arrest and deport Jews. Darnand was convicted of treason in October 1945 and shot.

449.7–13   *The first . . . blood*]   This passage, as well as those at 449.19–24, 449.27–29, 449.35–450.4, and 450.16–25, were not italicized in *The New Yorker* version of "Notes from a Kidnap House."

449.13   Smuts'* speech last November]   Field Marshal Jan Christian Smuts (1870–1950), prime minister of South Africa, had said that since France was no longer a great power, its only choice was to join the British Commonwealth.

449.15   Badoglio]   Pietro Badoglio (1871–1956), the former chief of staff of the Italian army, headed the coup that overthrew Mussolini on July 25, 1943, and signed an armistice with Allies on September 3. He resigned as premier of Italy on June 18, 1944, shortly after the liberation of Rome.

449.31   Ribar]   Ivan Ribar (1881–1968) presided in November 1943 over the meeting inside Yugoslavia of the Anti-Fascist Council of National Liberation that proclaimed an end to the monarchy and named Tito president of a provisional Yugoslav government. Ribar's son, Ivo-Lola Ribar (1916–1943), a leading Yugoslav Communist, Partisan leader, and close Tito associate, was killed in a German air attack shortly before the Council session.

450.26–27   Kolchak government]   Britain, France, and the United States supplied aid to Alexander Kolchak (1873–1920), "supreme ruler" of the anti-Bolshevik regime established in Omsk, Siberia, in November 1918. The Red Army captured Omsk in November 1919, and Kolchak fled to Irkutsk, where he was shot by the Bolsheviks in February 1920.

450.37   Halifax, Hoare, and Simon] Viscount Halifax (1881–1959) was foreign secretary, 1938–40, and ambassador to the United States, 1940–44. Sir Samuel Hoare (1880–1959), the home secretary, 1937–39, was ambassador to Spain, 1940–44. Sir John Simon (1873–1954), the chancellor of the exchequer, 1937–40, was Lord Chancellor, 1940–45.

451.7   AMG] Allied Military Government.

453.20   the Beveridge Plan] Proposal for establishing a comprehensive social insurance system in Britain, presented on December 1, 1942, by a committee chaired by the economist Sir William Beveridge (1879–1963). Many of its provisions, including the creation of a national health service, were implemented by the Labour government in 1945–51.

453.24–25   Stalin's decree . . . Third International] Stalin dissolved the Communist International (Comintern), also known as the Third International, on May 5, 1943.

453.26–27   Léon Jouhaux . . . du Travail] The General Confederation of Labor, founded in 1895, became the national representative of labor movements in France in 1902. Jouhaux (1879–1954), secretary-general of the CGT, 1909–47, was deported to Buchenwald in 1943.

455.20   Schutzstaffel cadet camp] The SS trained French collaborators to fight on the Eastern Front as well as against the Resistance in France.

455.21   Lorraine cross] The cross of Lorraine was adopted as the symbol of the Free French movement.

456.9   *Winterhilfe*] Winter Relief, fund administered by the Nazi party ostensibly for helping the poor.

457.4   *The Longest Day*] The film, produced by Darryl Zanuck and based on the non-fiction best seller by Cornelius Ryan, was released in 1962. Wayne played Lieutenant Colonel Benjamin Vandervoort, a paratroop battalion commander in the 82nd Airborne, and Mitchum played Brigadier General Norman Cota, assistant commander of the 29th Infantry Division.

457.12   "River Kwai March."] The "Colonel Bogey March" (1914) by Kenneth Alford (pseudonym of F. J. Ricketts, 1881–1945) is whistled by British prisoners of the Japanese in the film *The Bridge on the River Kwai* (1957).

459.19   Sheepshead Bay] In Brooklyn, New York.

462.1   Off to Buffalo] "Shuffle Off to Buffalo," by Al Dubin and Harry Warren, a dance number from the movie musical *42nd Street* (1932).

465.3   'Knight Without Armor.'] Novel (1933) about the Russian Revolution by James Hilton (1900–1954).

465.9   Pangloss]   Candide's tutor, who holds, despite the terrible misadventures that befall him and his companions, that all is for the best in the best of all possible worlds.

467.11–12   "If God . . . against us?"]   Romans 8:31.

467.16–17   General Eisenhower's message]   The message read in part: "You are about to embark upon the Great Crusade, toward which we have striven these many months. The eyes of the world are upon you. The hopes and prayers of liberty-loving people everywhere march with you."

469.19   E-boats]   Allied name for small, fast German torpedo boats.

471.7   World's . . . Club]   "Club" featured in a long-running advertising campaign for Aqua Velva aftershave; its putative members included Sir Cedric Hardwicke, Douglas Fairbanks Jr., George Biddle, Rear Admiral Yates Stirling Jr., and George Fielding Eliot.

481.18   fucked up,]   In *The New Yorker* text, "got bitched up."

482.28–29   sank a ship . . . Susan B. Anthony.]   In the text that appeared in *The New Yorker* on July 15, 1944, this read: "damaged a ship near it."

482.35–37   Susan B. put . . . got off.]   This passage did not appear in *The New Yorker*.

483.22   Higgins boats]   Name for the LCVP (Landing Craft, Vehicle and Personnel), after its designer and manufacturer, New Orleans boatbuilder Andrew J. Higgins (1886–1952).

489.35   Field Division]   An infantry division capable of undertaking mobile operations, so-called to distinguish it from lower-quality "static" divisions intended solely for manning coastal fortifications.

491.29   *Oberstleutnant*]   Lieutenant colonel.

492.16   Todt organization]   German construction organization that built major fortifications, named for Fritz Todt (1891–1942), Reich minister for armaments, 1940–42.

492.28   Duck]   Six-wheeled American amphibious truck equipped with a propeller and rudder that could carry 25 men or 5,000 pounds of cargo. Also known as the DUKW, after the code name under which it was developed.

494.24–25   Nelson's "England . . . duty."]   Sent at the Battle of Trafalgar, October 21, 1805.

494.32   V-1s]   Unmanned jet aircraft guided by a gyroscope, with a speed of 350 mph; it carried 1,870 pounds of explosive in its warhead. V-1 attacks on London began on June 13, 1944.

503.40   Défense Passive]   Civil defense.

504.30   Gouvernement Provisoire]   The Comité Français de la Libération

Nationale headed by de Gaulle declared itself to be the provisional government of the French Republic on June 3, 1944.

507.37 understanding . . . United States Government] Roosevelt announced on July 11 that the U.S. would recognize the Provisional Government as "the working authority for civil administration in the liberated areas of France." The U.S., Britain, Canada, and the Soviet Union granted full diplomatic recognition to the Provisional Government on October 23, 1944.

508.23–24 Theodore Roosevelt] Roosevelt died in his tent of a heart attack on July 12, 1944. He was posthumously awarded the Medal of Honor for his actions on D-Day, when he landed in the first wave on Utah Beach.

509.1 dilettante politican] Roosevelt had run unsuccessfully for governor of New York in 1924 against Al Smith and had served as governor of Puerto Rico (1929–32) and as governor-general of the Philippines (1932–33).

513.37–38 Many of those . . . casualties.] The short bombing on July 25, 1944, killed 111 men and wounded 490 among the attacking troops.

518.9 Year 3] September 1794–September 1795.

524.8 Forces Françaises de l'Intérieur] The FFI, created on February 1, 1944, united all of the Resistance groups within France that accepted the authority of the de Gaulle government into a single military organization.

529.18 Mark VI tank] A German Tiger heavy tank.

532.20–22 Will Irwin's . . . 'The City That Was,'"] Irwin (1873–1948) was a reporter for the *San Francisco Chronicle*, 1900–4, before joining the *New York Sun* in 1904. The story, written in New York, appeared in the *Sun* on April 21, 1906.

536.12 Lupe Velez] Mexican-American film actress (1908–1944).

541.4 David Lardner] Lardner (1919–1944), the son of Ring Lardner and brother of Ring Lardner Jr., had joined the staff of the magazine in 1939 and served as its film critic, 1942–44. He was killed on October 19, 1944.

546.4 Oberleutnant] First lieutenant.

546.22 *Feld–gendarmerie*] German military police.

546.28–29 machine pistol] Submachine gun.

547.16–17 General Koenig] Pierre Koenig (1898–1970) was the commander of the FFI.

547.29–30 French military . . . disbanded] The Germans occupied southern France in November 1942 following the Allied landings in North Africa and disbanded the small army allowed Vichy under the terms of the 1940 armistice.

547.39 Hercule Poirot] Detective character created by Agatha Christie.

551.3–4 *Volkswagen*] German military vehicle, similar to the American jeep, manufactured by the Volkswagen company.

UNCOLLECTED WAR JOURNALISM

573.25 Havas] French news agency founded in 1835. It was seized by the Germans in 1940 and became the Agence France-Presse in 1944.

573.30 Goncourt] Académie Goncourt, a French literary society founded in 1896 that has awarded the Prix Goncourt annually since 1903; its members cannot also be members of the Académie Française.

574.22 *primeurs*] Early vegetables.

576.13 Dwight Fiske] Fiske (1892–1959) was a New York nightclub pianist, singer, and raconteur.

576.32 "Entente Cordiale."] The film, directed by Marcel L'Herbier, opened in both France and the United States in 1939.

577.12 Paul Hazard] Hazard (1878–1944) taught at Columbia in 1940, then chose to return to France in January 1941, where he died in April 1944.

577.23 Jérôme Tharaud] Tharaud (1874–1953) wrote stories, essays, and novels in collaboration with his brother Jean (1877–1952).

578.14 events in Finland] See note 68.18–19.

579.16 Ambassador Biddle] Anthony J. Drexel Biddle Jr. (1897–1961) was the U.S. ambassador to Poland, 1937–39, and the ambassador to the Polish government-in-exile in France, 1939–40, and in England, 1941–43; see also note 102.18.

581.12 the day . . . Iron Guards shot] The killings on September 21, 1939, were in response to the assassination earlier in the day of Premier Armand Călinescu by members of the fascist Iron Guard organization.

581.14–15 Munich . . . beer-hall explosion] A powerful time bomb exploded in a Munich beer hall on the night of November 8, 1939, shortly after Hitler finished giving a speech to Nazi party members and left the hall. Although the Nazis accused British intelligence of involvement in the assassination attempt, the bomb was built and hidden in a pillar by Georg Elser (1903–1945), a carpenter who was arrested while trying to flee to Switzerland. Elser was shot in Dachau in April 1945.

582.3 SUMNER WELLES] Welles (1892–1961) was under secretary of state, 1937–43.

585.6–7 defeat . . . at Narvik] The Royal Navy sank ten German destroyers in Narvik fjord, April 10–13, 1940.

586.14 Copenhagen] The Germans occupied Denmark on April 9, 1940.

586.19   Lebrun]   Albert Lebrun (1871–1950) was the president of France, 1932–40.

586.25–26   Maurice Chevalier . . . Gracie Fields]   Chevalier (1888–1972) was a singer and actor; Fields (1898–1979) was a singer and music-hall comic performer.

587.6   the Westwall]   The fortifications along the western German border, also known as the Siegfried Line.

589.8–9   Danish vessels . . . United States government]   The Ship Requisition Act, signed by Roosevelt on June 6, 1941, authorized the government to seize idle foreign ships for use in national defense; its passage resulted in the requisitioning of 40 Danish vessels, all of which were renamed.

589.35–36   Sessa, . . . Marna,]   The *Sessa*, renamed *Longtaker*, was sunk by a torpedo in August 1941; *Paula*, renamed *Montana*, was sunk by a torpedo in September 1941; *Nora*, renamed *Halma*, was sunk by a mine in June 1943; *Maria*, renamed *Uranus*, survived the war; *Marna*, renamed *Azra*, was sunk in a collision with a Canadian destroyer in November 1942.

599.2   Sauvageon]   A pseudonym for Louis Pavageau; see p. 742.11–12 in this volume.

599.20   old Breughel's]   Flemish painter Pieter Brueghel the Elder (1525–1569).

599.36–37   Gauleiter Burckel's]   Josef Bürckel (1895–1944) was gauleiter of Vienna, 1939–40, and the German governor of Lorraine, 1940–44. He committed suicide in September 1944.

600.16   southern Tyrol, in Volhynia, and in Bessarabia]   In 1939–40 the Nazi regime transferred ethnic Germans into the territory of the Third Reich from the South Tyrol region of northern Italy, the Volhynia region of Soviet-occupied Poland (now part of Ukraine), and the Soviet-occupied Bessarabia region of Romania (now part of Moldova).

600.20   the Warthegau]   German name for territory in western Poland annexed in 1939.

602.20   Low's]   David Low (1891–1963), New Zealand–born political cartoonist for several British newspapers, including the *Evening Standard* (1927–50).

602.23   V for Vulgarity]   In Britain making a V sign with the palm turned inward is a rude, hostile gesture.

604.22   "Colonel Britton"]   The broadcasts were made by Douglas Ritchie (1905–1967), the assistant director of European broadcasts for the BBC. They were suspended early in 1942, in part because of concern they were creating unrealistic expectations in occupied Europe.

605.21   Ivone Kirkpatrick] Kirkpatrick (1897–1964) served as the head of chancellery at the British embassy in Berlin, 1933–38, and as director of the foreign division at the Ministry of Information before becoming controller for European services at the BBC in 1941.

605.23   Rudolf Hess] Hess (1894–1987), the deputy leader of the Nazi party, flew alone to Scotland on May 10, 1941, in a personal attempt to negotiate Britain's surrender. Hess was tried at Nuremberg and sentenced in 1946 to life imprisonment; he committed suicide in a Berlin prison in 1987.

609.23   Dorothy Thompson] Thompson (1893–1961), a well-known American reporter and newspaper columnist who had been expelled from Germany in 1934.

610.25   *facteur*] Postman.

611.4   Lord Beaverbrook] A Canadian-born British newspaper publisher, Lord Beaverbrook (1879–1964) served as minister of aircraft production, August 1940–May 1941, and minister of supply, June 1941–February 1942.

612.19   Bren gun] Standard light machine gun used by British infantry in World War II.

614.24–25   Dunkerque] The British successfully evacuated 225,000 men from Dunkirk, May 27–June 4, 1940, but almost all of their weapons and equipment were lost.

616.24   twenty-five pound shell] Used in the standard British field artillery gun.

620.5   Harold Lloyd's heyday] American comic film actor (1893–1971) who achieved his greatest success during the 1920s.

622.9   Werner Mölders] Mölders (1913–1941) was credited by the Luftwaffe with shooting down 14 aircraft during the Spanish Civil War and 101 during World War II. He was killed in airplane crash in Germany while flying as a passenger on November 22, 1941.

622.26   rigger . . . fitter] The rigger maintained the airframe and the fitter maintained the aircraft engine.

623.26–27   couple of days . . . foot.] Finucane hurt his foot on October 13, 1941.

624.12–13   American Eagle Squadron] 71 Squadron, formed in September 1940 with American volunteer pilots. The squadron was disbanded in September 1942 and its pilots were transferred to the U.S. Army Air Forces.

624.40–625.1   One Australian . . . Blue] Keith "Bluey" Truscott (1916–1943), a well-known Australian rules football player, joined 452 Squadron in May 1941 and shot down at least 11 German aircraft before being posted back to Australia in March 1942. Truscott commanded 76 Squadron, which flew

P-40 fighter-bombers in Papua, August 1942–February 1943, before being killed in a flying accident on March 27, 1943.

625.28 Messerschmitts 109 F's] The Bf 109F entered service in 1941. It had a maximum speed of 373 mph and was armed with a 15mm cannon and two machine guns.

627.9 Spit fives] See note 145.13.

627.33 "Target for Tonight"] British propaganda film (1941) about RAF Bomber Command. Directed by Harry Watt, it focused on "F for Freddie," a Wellington bomber sent to attack a German oil refinery.

628.5 Raymond Patrick] Raymond Finucane later became a Spitfire pilot and survived the war.

628.29 "Fighter Pilot,"] *Fighter Pilot: A Personal Record of the Campaign in France, September 8th, 1939, to June 13th, 1940* (1941), published anonymously by Paul Richey (1916–1989), who was credited with shooting down ten enemy aircraft while flying Hurricanes and Spitfires, 1940–41.

629.11–12 his girl friend . . . get married] Finucane and Jean Woolford, a neighbor in Richmond who worked as a secretary at the Ministry of Agriculture, became engaged in April 1942.

630.18–19 East India Squadron . . . south of England] 65 Squadron at Hornchurch, in what is now northeast Greater London.

630.28 sausage] Barrage balloon.

632.17 Bleinheims] Twin-engine British bomber with a maximum speed of 266 mph that could carry 1,000 pounds of bombs.

633.33–35 Balbo . . . late Italian aviator] Air Marshal Italo Balbo (1896–1940) was the governor of Libya, 1934–40. He was shot down by Italian anti-aircraft fire while attempting to land at Tobruk shortly after a British air raid on June 28, 1940.

633.40 Landsturm] Reservists.

634.33 new outfit . . . next spring] Finucane became the commander of 602 (City of Glasgow) Squadron in January 1942, and of the Hornchurch Wing in June, becoming the youngest wing commander in the RAF. On July 15, 1942, his Spitfire was hit by ground fire while crossing the French coast on a low-level strafing mission. Finucane turned back toward England but the damage to the radiator caused his engine to fail, and when he ditched in the Channel his plane sank immediately. At the time of his death Finucane was credited with the destruction of 28 German aircraft.

636.10 an airfield in southern Tunisia,] Thélepte.

639.17–18 "Terry and the Pirates," . . . Milton Caniff] Caniff (1907–

1988) created the strip in 1934 and produced it until 1946. He introduced the character of "Flip Corkin" in August 1942.

642.27–28   Red Grange]   Harold Grange (1903–1991) was a running back for the University of Illinois, 1923–25, and for the Chicago Bears, 1925–26 and 1929–34.

644.3   Mitchel Field]   Airfield in Uniondale, Long Island, named after John Purroy Mitchel (see note 27.24).

649.39   Italo Balbo]   See note 633.33–35.

650.3   The Eighth Army, however, arrived]   The Eighth Army entered the city on January 23, 1943.

650.20   Marshal Graziani]   Rodolfo Graziani (1882–1955) served with the Italian army in Libya, 1921–33, and was its commander, 1929–33. He later commanded the invasion of Ethiopia, 1935–36, and led the Italian army in Libya from June 1940 until February 1941, when he was relieved following the defeat of his army by the British.

653.1   *Notes from the Kidnap House*]   The first and third parts of "Notes from a Kidnap House" appear below, while the second part was included by Liebling in *Mollie and Other War Pieces*, pp. 447–56 in this volume.

653.16–17   newspaper owners Hitler and Streicher]   Eher Verlag, a publishing company owned by the Nazi party, controlled two-thirds of all German magazines and newspapers by 1939. Julius Streicher (1885–1946) published the notorious anti-Semitic newspaper *Der Stürmer* from 1923 to 1945; he was convicted at Nuremberg of incitement to mass murder and hanged.

655.30   Schmitt]   Carl Schmitt (1888–1985), professor at the University of Berlin and a prominent German legal and political theorist.

655.32   Freisler]   Roland Freisler (1893–1945) was state secretary to the minister of justice, 1934–42, and president of the People's Court, 1942–45. He presided at the trials of many opponents of the Nazi regime, including the Munich student leaders Hans and Sophie Scholl and the main conspirators in the July 1944 plot to assasinate Hitler. Freisler was killed during an air raid in Berlin.

656.5   Gabolde]   Maurice Gabolde (1891–1972) was the Vichy minister of justice, March 1943–August 1944. He lived in exile in Spain after the war.

656.18–19   Pierre Pucheu]   Pucheu (1899–1944) was Vichy minister of the interior, July 1941–April 1942. He went to Morocco in May 1943 after being offered safe passage by Giraud, but was arrested, tried for treason, and shot in March 1944.

657.9   Déat]   A former Socialist, Marcel Déat founded the fascist collaborationist organization Rassamblement national populaire (RNP) in February

1941 and became minister of labor in the Vichy government in March 1944. He escaped from Germany to Italy in 1945 and found sanctuary in a monastery, where he lived until his death.

658.11 Grasset,] Raymond Grasset was Vichy minister of health, April 1942–August 1944; he was accused of collaboration, but the charges were dismissed in 1947.

659.27 Abel Bonnard] Bonnard (1883–1968) was the Vichy minister of education, April 1942–August 1944. He escaped to Spain in 1945 and lived in exile until his death.

660.28 Ambroise Paré] Paré (c. 1510–1590) pioneered the ligation of arteries during amputations and discouraged the use of boiling oil in cauterizations.

663.26 Philippe Henriot] Henriot (1889–1944) began making collaborationist broadcasts on Radio-Paris in February 1943 and became the Vichy minister of information and propaganda in January 1944. He was assassinated by the Resistance on June 28, 1944.

664.37–38 arrested de La Rocque in Vichy] See note 120.25–26.

665.26–28 the Velodrome . . . Jewish women and children,] Acting on orders from the SS and Vichy, the Paris police rounded up more than 12,000 Jews on July 16–17, 1942. The prisoners were held in the Vel d'Hiv, an indoor stadium used for bicycle races, and then at Drancy, a French-run concentration camp near Le Bourget airport, before being deported to Auschwitz.

666.1–3 Alfred Mallet . . . I knew him,] See pp. 85.34–86.30 in this volume. Mallet later published a two-volume biography of Laval (1954–55).

666.26 Céline] Céline (1894–1961) fled to Germany in 1944 and Denmark in 1945, then returned to France in 1951 after being amnestied.

667.24 "La Madelon"] Song about a barmaid that became popular among French soldiers during World War I.

668.32–33 van Eyck's Painting "The Mystic Lamb,"] The painting was found in an Austrian salt mine by U.S. troops in 1945 and returned to Belgium.

669.2–3 Sacha Guitry . . . Cheat."] Guitry (1885–1957) wrote, directed, and starred in *Le Roman d'un Tricheur* (1936).

669.33 Ludovic Frossard] A former member of the Communist and Socialist parties, Frossard (1889–1946) served in several cabinets between 1935 and 1940.

669.36–37 Kolchak government] See note 450.26–27.

670.24–25 Cliveden set] See note 13.8.

670.38 Jacques Decour] Decour (1910–1942), a novelist who taught

German literature at the Lycée Rollin (renamed Lycée Jacques Decour after the Liberation), was arrested in February 1942.

674.19–20   Sten guns] British submachine guns.

674.33   St. Malo and Lorient] The German garrison at St. Malo surrendered on August 17, 1944, after an eight-day siege; the garrison at Lorient did not surrender until the end of the war in May 1945.

675.2   one such town] Antrain-sur-Couesnon.

682.10   Locarno,] Under the Locarno Pact of 1925 Germany agreed to maintain its postwar borders with Belgium and France, but made no commitment to its postwar borders in the east.

689.16   Ludwig Bemelmans' last book] *Now I Lay Me Down to Sleep* (1944).

690.31–32   full recognition of the Gouvernement Provisoire] See note 507.37.

691.30–31   Lafont and Bony] Henri Lafont was a petty swindler and burglar; Pierre Bony was a former member of the Sûreté. Lafont, Bony, and seven members of their gang were tried and shot in December 1944.

692.4   Lonergan affair] In 1944 Wayne Lonergan was convicted of murdering his estranged wife, Patricia Burton Lonergan, the heiress to a brewing fortune, in her Manhattan triplex.

693.18   Landru] Henri Landru (1869–1922) was arrested in 1919 for the murder of 11 people, mostly widows whose savings he stole. Landru was guillotined in 1922.

693.19–22   Doctor Petiot . . . in Germany.] Dr. Marcel Petiot (1897–1946) became a fugitive in March 1944 after the police discovered human remains in the cottage where he killed his victims. Petiot was arrested in Paris on October 31, 1944, and was guillotined after being convicted of 26 murders; no evidence of collaboration was introduced at his trial.

693.38–39   the Lublin massacres] The Majdanek concentration camp near Lublin, Poland, was liberated by the Red Army in July 1944.

695.11   Ariovistus] A Germanic chieftain who was defeated in Gaul by Julius Caesar in 58 BCE.

697.18   Alfred Jarry's "Ubu Roi."] Satiric play (1896) by Jarry (1873–1907).

699.10–11   condemnation . . . Suarez] Suarez was shot on November 9, 1944.

701.5–6   San Francisco Conference] The conference, which opened on April 25, 1945, founded the United Nations.

703.31–32   battle of Wadi el Akarit] The battle was fought in southern Tunisia, April 5–7, and ended in an Allied victory.

705.33   battle of Enfidaville] The Eighth Army began its attack on the Enfidaville position on April 19, 1943.

708.24   a Second Front.] An invasion of France.

708.29   W. L. White] White (1900–1973), a correspondent for *Reader's Digest*, described his visit to the Soviet Union in 1944 in *Report on the Russians* (1945).

715.25   P-39] A single-engine fighter that proved unsatisfactory in air-to-air combat and saw limited use as a ground-attack aircraft.

724.15–16   Rosinante] Don Quixote's horse.

734.2   *The Republic of Silence*] A collection of writing from the French Resistance press that Liebling compiled and edited.

734.5   *La Chèvre . . .* Daudet] Published in *Lettres de Mon Moulin*, a collection (1868) of stories and sketches of Provençal life by Daudet (1840–1897).

735.1–2   *The Republic of Silence*] The title of an article by Jean-Paul Sartre published in *Les Lettres Française*, September 9, 1944. Liebling included Sartre's article in his collection, and quoted its last sentence on the title page: "May this Republic about to be set up in broad daylight preserve the austere virtues of that other Republic of Silence and Night."

735.25–26   François Coppée, Edmond About] Coppée (1842–1908) was a poet and dramatist, About (1828–1885) a journalist, novelist, and story writer.

735.40   *Le Moyen De Parvenir*] A collection of satiric tales (1610) attributed to François Béroalde de Verville (1558–1612).

736.14   Vercors and Claude Roy] Vercors was the pseudonym of Henri Bruller (1902–1991), whose story *Le Silence de la mer* (1942) was one of the first literary works to be published by the clandestine French press. Roy (1915–1997) became a prolific poet, essayist, journalist, and novelist.

736.24   Some items are anonymous] One of the anonymous pieces, an account from the newspaper *Combat* of the 1944 massacre at Ascq, was written by Albert Camus.

737.12   *Wars I Have Seen*] An account of Stein's experiences in rural France during the Occupation, published in 1945.

738.16–17   Brookings Institution] A Washington research institute.

738.30–31   De Gaulle . . . stay on top.] De Gaulle resigned as premier on January 20, 1946.

738.36   Harry Butcher's . . . *Eisenhower*,] Memoir (1946) by Eisenhower's wartime naval aide.

741.4   Father Divine] African-American preacher, born George Baker (c. 1879–1965), who founded the Peace Mission Movement during the 1930s.

743.15   Brentano's] A New York City bookstore.

744.4–6   J. DONALD ADAMS . . . the Plough,"] After Liebling unfavorably reviewed *From the City, From the Plough* by Alexander Baron (pseudonym of Joseph Alexander Bernstein, 1917–1999) in the February 27, 1949, issue of the *Book Review*, Adams responded in his "Speaking of Books" column on March 6, praising Baron's novel and comparing it favorably to Norman Mailer's *The Naked and the Dead* (1948), Ira Wolfert's *An Act of Love* (1948), and Irwin Shaw's *The Young Lions* (1948), as well as Erich Maria Remarque's *All Quiet on the Western Front* (1929).

744.14   Richard Aldington and Siegfried Sassoon] In his review Liebling had cited Aldington's novel *Death of a Hero* (1930) and Sassoon's semiautobiographical *Memoirs of an Infantry Officer* (1930).

744.15   G. A. Henty] Henty (1832–1902) was a war correspondent and writer of boy's stories.

745.27   the two battles of Tobruk] In the first battle, April 11–December 10, 1941, Tobruk was successfully defended against an Axis siege by Australian, British, Polish, and Czech forces; in the second battle, June 20–21, 1942, Axis forces captured 30,000 British and South African troops.

745.31   Parson Sterne] Liebling wrote in his review that "Laurence Sterne established the two standard types of British military fiction when he created Corporal Trim and Uncle Toby" in *Tristam Shandy* (1759).

746.30–31   Georges Carpentier] Boxer (1894–1975) who held the light heavyweight championship, 1920–22.

753.16   M-1s] The semiautomatic M-1 Garand, the standard U.S. infantry rifle in World War II and Korea.

754.23   Toots Shor] A popular New York restaurant in the 1940s.

755.29–30   generals use bazookas] Major General William Dean (1899–1981), commander of the 24th Infantry Division, had personally directed bazooka teams against North Korean tanks during the fighting in Taejon on July 20, 1950.

758.12   hick character in a movie] Pyle was portrayed by Burgess Meredith in *The Story of G.I. Joe* (1945), directed by William Wellman.

759.9–10   bodies . . . Oradour] Troops of the 2nd SS Panzer Division murdered 642 people in Oradour-sur-Glane, about ten miles northwest of Limoges, on June 10, 1944. After shooting the men of the village, the SS set the church on fire and then shot at the women and children as they tried to escape. The massacre was committed in reprisal for recent attacks made by the Resistance in the region.

759.30   *Lebkuchen*]   Gingerbread.

760.1–2   unlamented Dr. Rosenberg]   Alfred Rosenberg (1893–1946) was sentenced to death by the Nuremberg tribunal and hanged.

760.23   Roehm purge]   In June 1934 Hitler ordered Ernst Röhm (1887–1934), the leader of the SA (Nazi party paramilitary force), to be shot without trial along with several of his subordinates.

762.33   *Schnitzelbank*]   Woodcarving tool.

763.12   von Seeckt]   Hans von Seeckt (1866–1936) was the commander of the Reichswehr, 1920–26.

763.32–33   commanded the Luftwaffe in the Battle of Britain]   Kesselring commanded Luftflotte 2, which was responsible for operations over London and southeast England.

764.1–2   General Adolf Galland, . . . fighter forces,]   Galland (1912–1996) held the position from November 1941 to January 1945.

764.5   Milch]   Erhard Milch (1892–1972) oversaw aircraft development and production as state secretary of the Air Ministry, 1933–44, and as inspector-general of the Luftwaffe, 1938–45. Milch received a life sentence in 1947 for using slave labor in aircraft factories, but was released in 1954.

766.17   The Remagen bridgehead fell.]   Troops from the U.S. First Army made the first Allied crossing of the Rhine when they captured the railroad bridge at Remagen on March 7, 1945.

767.21   German jet fighters, . . . fast as American Mustangs]   The Messerschmitt 262, a twin-engine, single-seat turbojet fighter had a maximum speed of 540 mph, while the North American P-51D Mustang had a maximum speed of 437 mph. Although a prototype of the Me 262 was tested successfully in 1942, the aircraft did not begin operational service as a fighter until the summer of 1944, mainly as a result of production difficulties with its engines.

768.32–33   In 1952, . . . incurable illness.]   Kesselring died in 1960 at the age of 74.

768.38   von Mackensen and Maelzer]   Eberhard von Mackensen (1889–1969), commander of the German Fourteenth Army in Italy, November 1943–June 1944, and Kurt Maelzer (1894–1952), the German military governor of Rome. Both men were convicted by a British military court in 1946 and sentenced to 21 years in prison. Maelzer died in prison; von Mackensen was released in October 1952, the same month as Kesselring.

769.11   His Lordship was the legal adviser]   Lord Russell (1895–1981) was a legal adviser to the commander of the British army in Germany, 1946–51.

769.12   Kappler]   A lieutenant colonel in the SS, Kappler (1907–1978) was given a life sentence by an Italian court. He escaped from a Rome hospital in 1977 and died in Germany.

771.3   recent day]   June 14, 1958.

771.10   youngest Premier of the Third Republic]   Flandin (1889–1958) served as premier, November 1934–May 1935, and as foreign minister, January–June 1936.

771.33   Flandin was Pétain's Foreign Minister]   Flandin succeeded Laval as Vichy foreign minister in December 1940 and was replaced by Darlan in February 1941. He was arrested in December 1943 and sentenced to five years "national degradation" in 1946, but the sentence was annulled.

773.11   *fellagha*]   Outlaw, rebel.

774.8   Anglo-Mauresque]   Anglo-Moorish.

775.8   Count of Paris]   Henri, comte de Paris (1908–1999), the Orleanist pretender to the French throne.

775.25   "Barney Google"]   The strip was created in the *Chicago Herald and Examiner* in 1919 by William De Beck (1890–1942).

777.9   Captain Randolph Churchill]   The only son of Winston Churchill, Randolph Churchill (1911–1968) was serving with General Headquarters, Middle East.

777.18–19   *grenouille* . . . toad-in-the-hole]   Frog cooked in white wine; sausages cooked in Yorkshire pudding.

782.15–16   Corsica . . . Committee of Public Safety]   A group of French officers seized power in Algiers on May 13, 1958, and demanded that de Gaulle be made premier. On May 24 the Committee sent paratroopers to seize Corsica and began preparing an operation to take control of Paris. De Gaulle became premier on May 29 and was elected as the first president of the new Fifth Republic in December 1958.

787.31   in Egypt]   In the fall of 1956 France and Britain invaded Egypt in a failed attempt to regain control of the Suez Canal.

788.18–19   Philippeville . . . horrifying massacre]   The attack killed 123 men, women, and children.

788.36–39   Mosley . . . 18-B]   Mosley was interned in May 1940 and released in November 1943.

791.7–9   Tom Treanor . . . few days earlier.]   Treanor (1908–1944), a correspondent for the *Los Angeles Times* who had covered the war in Egypt,

India, China, and Italy, was fatally injured when his jeep collided with an American tank near Chartres on August 18, 1944. He was the author of *One Damn Thing After Another: The Adventures of an Innocent Man Trapped Between Public Relations and the Axis* (1944).

791.24   General George Brinton McClellan] McClellan (1826–1885) commanded the Union Army of the Potomac from July 1861 to November 1862, when he was relieved by President Lincoln.

792.39–40   The best-seller "The Longest Day,"] Published in 1959 by Irish-American war correspondent and magazine journalist Cornelius Ryan (1920–1974).

793.26–27   *Generalleutnant* Hans Spiedel . . . write in 1949] Speidel (1897–1984) was chief of staff of Army Group B, the command responsible for defending northern France, April–September 1944, and the author of *Invasion 1944* (1949).

798.16   Prince Rupert] Prince Rupert of the Rhine (1619–1682), a nephew of Charles I, commanded the Royalist cavalry during the English Civil War, 1642–45.

799.4   Chester Wilmot] An Australian war correspondent who covered the northwest European campaign for the BBC, Wilmot (1911–1954) was the author of *The Struggle for Europe* (1952).

799.33   the 12th] The 12th SS Panzer Division.

799.36   Eberbach's *Panzerkorps*] Eberbach (1895–1992) commanded *Panzergruppe West* (renamed Fifth Panzer Army on August 5) from July 4 to August 23, 1944.

803.16   P-47s] A single-engine, single-seat fighter and fighter-bomber, the P-47 had a top speed of 429 mph and was armed with eight machine guns. When used as a fighter-bomber it could carry eight air-to-ground rockets or 2,000 pounds of bombs.

806.29   the Metropolitan or the Cosmos Club] Elite Washington social clubs.

807.4   J. Rives Childs] Childs (1893–1987) was a member of the Foreign Service from 1921 to 1951.

810.17   Leahy . . . Vichy] Admiral William Leahy (1875–1959) served as the American ambassador to Vichy from January 1941 until his recall in May 1942.

810.23   Brinon's] Fernand de Brinon (1885–1947) was the Vichy delegate to Paris, December 1940–August 1944. Brinon was convicted of treason and shot in 1947.

813.2–3   General Allen . . . a new division] See note 41.32–33.

NORMANDY REVISITED

825.19–20   Major General Clarence Huebner]   Huebner (1888–1972) replaced Terry Allen as commander of the 1st Infantry Division in August 1943 and served until December 1944, when he was made a corps commander. He was succeeded by Major General Clift Andrus, who led the division until the end of the war.

826.32–33   Sweet Alices . . . Ben Bolts]   Characters in "Ben Bolt" (1842), poem by Thomas Dunn English (1819–1902).

827.1   Dan De Quille]   Pseudonym of William Wright (1829–1898), editor of the Virginia City (Nevada) *Enterprise* and friend of Mark Twain.

827.35   John Mason Brown]   Brown (1900–1969) was a drama critic for the *New York Evening Post*, 1929–41, and a columnist for *Saturday Review*, 1944–69.

832.10   Yarmouth bloaters]   Pieces of herring.

832.36   Sam Weller]   Character in *Pickwick Papers* (1837).

833.24   "There'll Always Be an England."]   Song (1940) by Ross Parker, Harry Par-Davies, and Hugh Charles.

834.8   Home Counties]   The counties bordering London; in 1955, Kent, Surrey, Middlesex, and Essex.

836.26   the Lord Chamberlain]   Government official who until 1968 had the power to censor stage performances.

837.9–10   Rocky Marciano . . . Don Cockell]   Marciano defeated Cockell (1928–1983), a British boxer, by a ninth-round technical knockout in San Francisco, May 16, 1955.

842.28   Nansen passport]   An international travel document issued to stateless persons by the League of Nations and named after the Norwegian diplomat Fridtjof Nansen (1861–1930).

849.16–18   Regensburg, . . . Fontenoy]   Napoleon defeated the Austrians at Regensburg (Ratisbon) in Bavaria on April 23, 1809; Marshal Saxe won a victory against the British-Austrian alliance at Fontenoy in Belgium on May 11, 1745.

856.24   Rollo]   Early 10th-century Norse founder of what became the duchy of Normandy.

857.38   time of Tardieu]   See note 120.19.

861.36   "Smilin' Jack."]   "The Adventures of Smilin' Jack," aviation comic created in the *Chicago Tribune* by Zack Mosley in 1933.

862.35   Field Marshal Sir Bernard Montgomery]   Montgomery was promoted to field marshal on September 1, 1944.

866.34   Moon Mullins]   Comic strip character created by Frank Willard in 1923.

868.27   Lord Melbourne]   Viscount Melbourne (1779–1848) was prime minister, 1835–41, and a mentor to Queen Victoria.

870.9   DUKWs]   See note 492.28.

870.12   the Upper Bay]   In New York harbor.

873.21   Siegfried Sassoon]   Sassoon (1886–1967) was a British poet and novelist who wrote about his experiences as an infantry officer in World War I.

875.38   General S.L.A. Marshall]   Brigadier General Marshall (1900–1967), a U.S. Army combat historian, wrote in *Men Against Fire* (1947) that only 15–25 percent of American infantrymen ever fired their weapons during combat, and urged that army training be changed in order to increase the volume of small-arms fire.

876.27   his eviction from Burma]   In the spring of 1942.

878.28   Robert Moses]   Moses (1888–1981) was parks commissioner of New York City, 1934–60.

879.6   Denikin's army]   Anton I. Denikin commanded the White army in southern Russia and Ukraine, April 1918–April 1920.

882.1–2   jug of milk . . . Mendès-France.]   While serving as premier, June 1954–February 1955, Pierre Mendès-France (1907–1982) encouraged the French to drink more milk and less alcohol.

883.31   Vlasov Army]   Lieutenant General Andrei A. Vlasov (1900–1946) attempted to form an anti-Communist "Russian Liberation Army" after being captured by the Germans in July 1942, and he eventually led about 20,000–30,000 troops against the Soviet army in 1945. Although he had no authority over the Russians who fought with the Wehrmacht in France, Vlasov's name came to be associated with them. Vlasov was captured by the Soviets in 1945 and hanged.

886.12–13   the Air Corps . . . 30th Division]   See note 513.37–38.

887.8   Colonel John R. Stingo]   James A. Macdonald, a New York racing columnist and promoter who was the subject of Liebling's book *The Honest Rainmaker: The Life and Times of Colonel John R. Stingo* (1953).

889.20   Abbé Perreyve]   Henri Perreyve (1831–1865).

896.3–4   G-3 . . . G-4]   Division staff officers for operations (G-3) and supply (G-4).

897.3   the G-2]   Intelligence officer.

897.6–8   the Spartans . . . Thermopylae] See note 307.13–14.

900.34–35   Father Divine's chauffeur] See note 741.4.

903.20   University Place] An avenue south of Union Square in Manhattan.

904.5   Le Grand Meaulnes'] Hero and namesake of the novel (1913) by Alain-Fournier (1886–1914).

905.10   *Bel-Ami*] Novel (1885) by Guy de Maupassant.

905.40–906.4   "*M. le Vicomte . . . narine.*"] This passage appeared in English in "Normandy: In Quest of a Gray Granite House," published in *The New Yorker,* November 16, 1957: "Monsieur le Vicomte de Fives displays a magnificent bit of game. This leopard was the terror of the blacks of the Limpopo before the Norman sportsman stopped him in full fury with a well-placed bullet in each nostril."

911.28   *rillettes*] Minced pork.

914.13   *Les Grandes Manoeuvres*] Film (1955) directed by René Clair.

920.40–921.1   "There is . . . Deutschland ist,"] Cf. Rupert Brooke (1887–1915), "The Soldier" (1915): "If I should die, think only this of me: / That there's some corner of a foreign field / That is for ever England."

921.4–5   hostages executed . . . in Brittany] The Germans shot 27 hostages at Châteaubriant on October 22, 1941, in reprisal for the killing of a German lieutenant colonel in Nantes on October 20.

924.31   *Tannhäuser*] Opera (1845) by Richard Wagner.

929.6   Rommel] Erwin Rommel commanded Army Group B in northern France from January 1944 to July 17, when he was seriously wounded in a British strafing attack. He committed suicide on October 14, 1944, after being implicated in the failed attempt to assassinate Hitler on July 20.

929.36   B.E.A.] British European Airways.

930.19   General Speidel] Hans Speidel (see note 793.26–27) escaped execution for his role in the plot against Hitler, became a general in the postwar Bundeswehr (West German army), and served as commander of NATO land forces in Central Europe, 1957–63.

933.18–19   Henry Adams] Adams began his systemic study of the cathedrals of Normandy in 1895 and published *Mont Saint Michel and Chartres* in 1904.

938.28   *Cinnas* and *Athalies*] Tragedies by, respectively, Corneille (c. 1640) and Racine (1691).

948.33–34   revenge the Germans . . . Warsaw.] After the Polish Home Army began an uprising in Warsaw on August 1, 1944, the Germans used aircraft, heavy artillery, and tanks against the insurgents while sending special SS units made up of German criminals and Russian deserters into the city. More than 200,000 Poles were killed and most of Warsaw was destroyed before the fighting ended on October 2. The Soviet army, which held positions close to the city during the uprising, captured Warsaw on January 17, 1945.

949.28   Annabel Lee] Lyric poem about a lost love by Edgar Allan Poe, posthumously published in 1849.

958.27   Shermans] American medium tank that had a five-man crew, weighed 33 tons, had a maximum speed of 25 mph, and was armed with a 75mm gun.

961.2   Polichinelle] French puppet character equivalent to the English Punch.

964.29   the Wilderness Campaign] Fought in northern Virginia in May 1864.

973.30   Thomas F. Murphy] Murphy (1906–1995) successfully prosecuted Alger Hiss for perjury, 1949–50, and served as the police commissioner of New York City, 1950–51, before becoming a federal district judge in 1951.

976.31   *Vercingétorix*] See note 44.32.

977.19   the January 1956 election] The election, held on January 2, resulted in a center-left coalition led by the Socialist Guy Mollet taking office on January 31; it remained in power until June 1957.

977.29   Poujadisme] A right-wing populist movement of shopkeepers, artisans, and small businessmen that grew out of protests over taxes led by Pierre Poujade (1920–2003). Although Poujade and his followers won 53 assembly seats in the January 1956 election, the movement soon fragmented.

980.21   Rétif de la Bretonne] Novelist and memoirist (1734–1806) who published more than 200 volumes on a wide variety of subjects.

981.21   Sad Sack] Military comic strip without dialogue, created in 1942 by Sergeant George Baker (1915–1975).

981.30–31   Lionel Hampton's] Hampton (1908–2002) was an American jazz vibraphonist and bandleader.

983.3   Klagmann] Jules Klagmann (1810–1867).

983.9   Colonel Rol] Henri Rol-Tanguy (1908–2002) had fought in Spain, 1937–38, and joined the Communist Resistance movement Franc-Tireurs et Partisans in 1941.

983.16   Mistinguett's] French music hall performer (1875–1956), born Louise Bourgeois.

985.3   Bouguereau] French academic painter William Bouguereau (1825–1905).

988.39–40   Adah Isaacs Menken] American actress and poet (1835?–1868) who toured the Nevada silver fields in 1864.

989.3   Volkswagen] See note 551.3–4.

From *The Army Air Force in World War II*, vol. II (1949). Courtesy of the University of Chicago Pres

From *The Army Air Force in World War II*, vol. II (1949). Courtesy of the University of Chicago Press.

First assault wave Infantry pltn.
First assault wave Infantry landings.

CHARLIE   DOG GREEN   DOG WHITE   DOG RED   EASY GR

Vierville

Hamel-
Au-Pretre

Les Moulins

Chateau
de Vaumicel

Louvieres

Vacqueville

Diagrammatic cross-section
of
OMAHA BEACH

H.W.
L.W.

360 yds.

Shingle
few yards
wide

Shelf 200 yds.

Sand dunes or sea wall

100'-170'

From *The West Point Atlas of American Wars* (1959). Courtesy of the United States Military Academy.

OMAHA BEACHHEAD, 1944

57

V CORPS D-DAY OPERATIONS
6 JUNE 1944

0   500   1000   1500
SCALE OF YARDS

N

LEGEND

First gaps in obstacles

Main penetrations to noon

Infantry positions at close
of D-day

German strong points

Main German resistance at
close of D-day

Note: 16th, 18th and 26th Infantry
Regiments were from the 1st Division;
the 115th and 116th were from the
29th Division.

EASY RED   FOX GREEN

(4 gaps in obstacles)   (Intermingled)

Exit road
opened in afternoon

Cabourg   Le Gd.-Hameau

Colleville Sur Mer

This map is a composite of a number of charts
in the excellent publication of the Center
of Military History, Department of the Army;
Gordon A. Harrison, Cross Channel Attack.

From *The West Point Atlas of American Wars* (1959). Courtesy of the United States Military Academy.

NORMANDY, 1944
EXPANDING THE BEACHHEAD

59

Operations, 1–24 July 1944

ELEVATIONS IN METERS
100   200   OVER

SCALE OF MILES
0   5   10   15   20

From *The West Point Atlas of American Wars* (1959). Courtesy of the United States Military Academy.

NORTHWESTERN FRANCE, 1944

THE EXPLOITATION

Operations, 14-25 August 1944

Index